MICROSOFT
Word 2000
Comprehensive Concepts and Techniques

Gary B. Shelly
Thomas J. Cashman
Misty E. Vermaat

COURSE TECHNOLOGY
ONE MAIN STREET
CAMBRIDGE MA 02142

Thomson Learning™

SHELLY
CASHMAN
SERIES®

Australia • Canada • Denmark • Japan • Mexico • New Zealand • Philippines
Puerto Rico • Singapore • South Africa • Spain • United Kingdom • United States

PHOTO CREDITS: Microsoft Word 2000 *Project 2, pages WD* 2.2-3 Space photograph, Courtesy of Digital Stock; *Project 3, pages WD 3.2-3* Classified listing, pen and glasses, hand on mouse, woman in business suit, Courtesy of PhotoDisc, Inc.; Albert Einstein and signature, Courtesy of the American Institute of Physics; *Project 4, pages WD 4.2-3* Graduates, Courtesy of Image Club; Graphs and charts, Courtesy of BP Amoco; Businessman, Courtesy of Photo Disc, Inc.; *Project 5, pages WD 5.2-3* Woman reading magazine, mailbox, basketball, Courtesy of PhotoDisc, Inc.; Man and woman athletes, Courtesy of Digital Stock; Italy photos, Courtesy of Corel Corporation; *Project 6, pages WD 6.2-3* Pirate ship, Courtesy of Hector Arvizu; Horse, telephone lines, satellite dish, hand on mouse, hand on keyboard, Courtesy of PhotoDisc, Inc.; *page WD 6.5* Networked computers, globe, Courtesy of Dynamic Graphics, Inc.; *Project 7, pages WD 7.2-3* Man and woman researching, hand writing, Courtesy of PhotoDisc, Inc.; *Project 8, pages WD 8.2-3* Web site, clothing merchandise, Courtesy of Land's End; circuit board, Courtesy of PhotoDisc, Inc.; *Project 9, pages WD 9.2-3* Two dresses, shirt with tie, suit, Courtesy of EyeWire.

ISBN 0-7895-5608-1

1 2 3 4 5 6 7 8 9 10   BC   04 03 02 01 00

MICROSOFT
Word 2000
Comprehensive Concepts and Techniques

C O N T E N T S

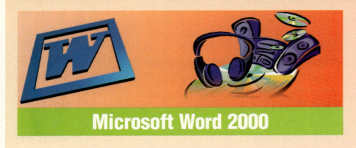

Microsoft Word 2000

Preface

The Shelly Cashman Series® offers the finest textbooks in computer education. We are proud of the fact that our *Microsoft Word 6*, *Microsoft Word 7*, and *Microsoft Word 97* textbooks have been the most widely used word processing books in education. Each edition of our Word textbooks has included innovations, many based on comments made by the instructors and students who use our books. The *Microsoft Word 2000* books continue with the innovation, quality, and reliability that you have come to expect from the Shelly Cashman Series.

In our *Microsoft Word 2000* books, you will find an educationally sound and easy-to-follow pedagogy that combines a step-by-step approach with corresponding screens. All projects and exercises in this book are designed to take full advantage of the Word 2000 enhancements. The popular Other Ways and More About features offer in-depth knowledge of Word 2000. The project openers provide a fascinating perspective of the subject covered in the project. The project material is developed carefully to ensure that students will see the importance of learning Word 2000 for future coursework.

Objectives of This Textbook

Microsoft Word 2000: Comprehensive Concepts and Techniques is intended for a three-unit course that presents Microsoft Word 2000. No experience with a computer is assumed, and no mathematics beyond the high school freshman level is required. The objectives of this book are:

- To teach the fundamentals of Microsoft Word 2000
- To expose students to practical examples of the computer as a useful tool
- To acquaint students with the proper procedures to create documents suitable for coursework, professional purposes, and personal use
- To develop an exercise-oriented approach that allows learning by example
- To encourage independent study, and help those who are working alone
- To demonstrate the Microsoft Word 2000 Expert level skill set for the Microsoft Office User Specialist Exam

Approved by Microsoft as Courseware for the Microsoft Office User Specialist Program – Expert Level

This book has been approved by Microsoft as courseware for the Microsoft Office User Specialist (MOUS) program. After completing the projects and exercises in this book, students will be prepared to take the Expert level examination for the Microsoft Office User Specialist Exam for Microsoft Word 2000. By passing the certification exam for a Microsoft software application, students demonstrate their proficiency in that application to employers. This exam is offered at participating centers, participating corporations, and participating employment agencies. See Appendix D for additional information on the MOUS program and for a table that includes the Microsoft Word 2000 MOUS skill sets for both Core level and Expert level and corresponding page numbers where a skill is discussed in the book, or visit the Web site at www.mous.net.

The Shelly Cashman Series Microsoft Office User Specialist Center Web page (Figure 1) has more than fifteen Web pages you can visit to obtain additional information on the MOUS Certification program. The Web page (www.scsite.com/off2000/cert.htm) includes links to general information on certification, choosing an application for certification, preparing for the certification exam, and taking and passing the certification exam.

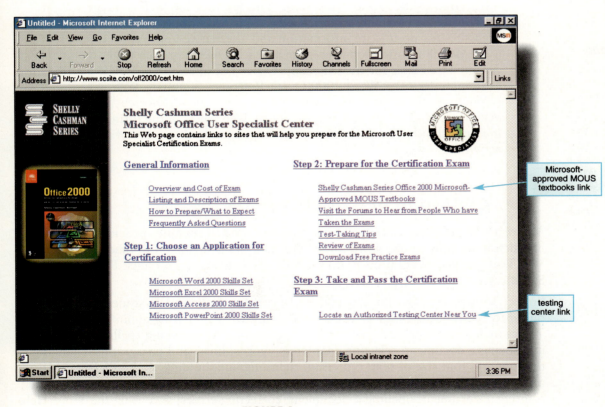

FIGURE 1

The Shelly Cashman Approach

Features of the Shelly Cashman Series *Microsoft Word 2000* books include:

- **Project Orientation:** Each project in the book presents a practical problem and complete solution in an easy-to-understand approach.

- **Step-by-Step, Screen-by-Screen Instructions:** Each of the tasks required to complete a project is shown using a step-by-step, screen-by-screen approach. The screens are shown in full color.

- **Thoroughly Tested Projects:** Every screen in the book is correct because it is produced by the author only after performing a step, resulting in unprecedented quality.

- **Other Ways Boxes and Quick Reference Summary:** Word 2000 provides a variety of ways to carry out a given task. The Other Ways boxes displayed at the end of most of the step-by-step sequences specify the other ways to do the task completed in the steps. Thus, the steps and the Other Ways box make a comprehensive reference unit. A Quick Reference Summary, available in the back of this book and on the Web, summarizes the way specific tasks can be completed.

- **More About Feature:** These marginal annotations provide background information that complements the topics covered, adding depth and perspective.

- **Integration of the World Wide Web:** The World Wide Web is integrated into the Word 2000 learning experience by (1) More Abouts that send students to Web sites for up-to-date information and alternative approaches to tasks; (2) a MOUS information Web page and a MOUS map Web page so students can prepare better for the Microsoft Office Use Specialist (MOUS) Certification examinations; (3) a Word 2000 Quick Reference Summary Web page that summarizes the ways to complete tasks (mouse, menu, shortcut menu, and keyboard); and (4) project reinforcement Web pages in the form of true/false, multiple choice, and short answer questions, and other types of student activities.

Organization of This Textbook

Microsoft Word 2000: Comprehensive Concepts and Techniques provides detailed instruction on how to use Word 2000. The material is divided into nine projects, a Web Feature, two Integration Features, four appendices, and a Quick Reference Summary.

Project 1 – Creating and Editing a Word Document In Project 1, students are introduced to Word terminology and the Word window by preparing an announcement. Topics include starting and quitting Word; entering text; checking spelling while typing; saving a document; selecting characters, words, lines, and paragraphs; changing the font and font size of text; centering, right-aligning, bolding, and italicizing text; undoing commands and actions; inserting clip art into a document; resizing a graphic; printing a document; opening a document; correcting errors; and using the Word Help system.

Project 2 – Creating a Research Paper In Project 2, students use the MLA style of documentation to create a research paper. Topics include changing margins; adjusting line spacing; using a header to number pages; entering text using Click and Type; first-line indenting paragraphs; using Word's AutoCorrect feature; adding a footnote;

Other Ways

1. Scroll through document and point to comment reference mark
2. On Select Browse Object menu click Comments
3. On File menu click Print, click Print what box arrow, click Comments, click OK button

More About 2000

Protecting Forms

If you want only authorized users to be able to unprotect a form, you should password-protect the form. To do this, click Tools on the menu bar, click Protect Document, click Forms in the Protect document for area, type the password in the Password (optional) text box, and then click the OK button. Then, reenter the password in the Confirm Password dialog box.

modifying a style; inserting a symbol; inserting a manual page break; creating a hanging indent; creating a text hyperlink; sorting paragraphs; moving text; finding a synonym; counting words in a document; and checking spelling and grammar at once.

Project 3 – Using a Wizard to Create a Resume and Creating a Cover Letter with a Table In Project 3, students create a resume using Word's Resume Wizard and then create a cover letter with a letterhead. Topics include personalizing the resume; using print preview; adding color to characters; setting and using tab stops; collecting and pasting; adding a bottom border; inserting a nonbreaking space; creating and inserting an AutoText entry; creating a bulleted list while typing; inserting a Word table; entering data into a Word table; and formatting a Word table. Finally, students prepare and print an envelope address.

Web Feature – Creating Web Pages Using Word In the Web Feature, students are introduced to creating Web pages. Topics include saving the resume created in Project 3 as a Web page; creating a Web page using the Web Page Wizard; resizing a Web page frame; editing a hyperlink; and editing a Web page from your browser.

Project 4 – Creating a Document with a Table, Chart, and Watermark In Project 4, students work with a multi-page document that has a title page. Students learn how to add an outside border with color and shading; download clip art from the Microsoft Clip Gallery Live Web page; center text vertically on a page; insert a section break; insert an existing Word document into an open document; change the starting page number in a section; create a header different from a previous header; chart a Word table; modify and format the chart; add picture bullets to a list; create a table using the Draw Table feature; change the direction of text in table cells; change the alignment of table cell text; center a table; and insert a picture as a watermark.

Project 5 – Generating Form Letters, Mailing Labels, and Envelopes In Project 5, students learn how to generate form letters, mailing labels, and envelopes from a main document and a data source. Topics include creating and editing the form letter, mailing label, and envelope main documents and their associated data source; using a template to create a letter; inserting merge fields into a main document; printing a document in landscape orientation; creating an outline numbered list; using an IF field; inserting a Fill-in field; displaying and printing field codes; merging and printing the documents; selecting data records to merge and print; sorting data records to merge and print; and inserting a bar code on the mailing labels and envelopes.

Project 6 – Creating a Professional Newsletter In Project 6, students learn how to use Word's desktop publishing features to create a newsletter. Topics include creating and formatting a WordArt drawing object; adding ruling lines; inserting the current date into a document; formatting a document into multiple columns; justifying a paragraph; formatting a character as a drop cap; inserting a column break; linking an object into a Word document; placing a vertical rule between columns; inserting and positioning a text box; changing character spacing; shading a paragraph; balancing columns; inserting a picture into a document; positioning a graphic between columns; using the Format Painter button; and highlighting text.

Integration Feature – Merging Form Letters to E-Mail Addresses Using an Access Table In the Integration Feature, students identify an existing Access database table as the data source for a main document. Then, students send the merged documents to e-mail addresses, attaching the form letter as a Word document to each e-mail message.

Project 7 – Working with a Master Document, an Index, and a Table of Contents

In Project 7, students learn how to organize and work with a long document. Topics include inserting, reviewing, and deleting comments; tracking changes; accepting and rejecting tracked changes; saving multiple versions; embedding an Excel worksheet; adding a caption; creating a cross-reference; password-protecting a document; working with a master document and subdocuments; adding an AutoShape; grouping drawing objects; creating a table of figures; marking index entries; building an index; creating a table of contents; and adding a bookmark.

Project 8 – Creating an Online Form

In Project 8, students learn how to create an online form and then use Word to fill in the form. Topics include creating a document template; highlighting text; inserting a table into a form; inserting a text box into a form;, inserting a drop-down list box into a form; inserting a check box into a form; formatting form fields; using the Format Painter button; adding Help text to form fields; drawing a rectangle; adding a texture fill effect to a drawing object; animating text; protecting a form; saving form data in a text file; and modifying the location of workgroup templates.

Project 9 – Using Visual Basic for Applications (VBA) with Word

In Project 9, students enhance an online form by modifying its appearance, adding macros, and inserting an ActiveX control. Topics include creating a new style; filling a drawing object with a bitmap picture; adding a 3-D effect to a drawing object; recording and executing a macro; assigning a macro to a toolbar button; copying, renaming, and deleting macros; viewing a macro's VBA code; adding comments and VBA code statements to a macro; attaching a macro to the exit property of a form field; inserting, formatting, and setting properties of an ActiveX control; and writing VBA code statements for an ActiveX control.

Integration Feature 2 – Linking an Excel Worksheet and Charting Its Data in Word

In the Integration Feature, students are introduced to linking Excel data to a Word document. Topics include linking an Excel worksheet to a Word document; creating a chart; linking Excel data to the chart; and editing a linked object.

Appendices

Appendix A presents a detailed step-by-step introduction to the Microsoft Word Help system. Students learn how to use the Office Assistant and the Contents, Answer Wizard, and Index sheets in the Word Help window. Appendix B describes how to publish Word Web pages to a Web server. Appendix C shows students how to reset the menus and toolbars. Appendix D introduces students to the Microsoft Office User Specialist (MOUS) Certification program and includes a MOUS map that lists a page number in the book for each of the MOUS activities for Core level and Expert level.

Quick Reference Summary

In Word, you can accomplish a task in a number of ways, such as using the mouse, menu, shortcut menu, and keyboard. The Quick Reference Summary at the back of this book provides a quick reference to the different ways to complete each task presented in this textbook. The Quick Reference Summary also is available on the Web at www.scsite.com/off2000/qr.htm.

End-of-Project Student Activities

A notable strength of the Shelly Cashman Series *Word 2000* books is the extensive student activities at the end of each project. Well-structured student activities can make the difference between students merely participating in a class and students retaining the information they learn. The activities in the Shelly Cashman Series *Microsoft Word 2000* books include the following.

- **What You Should Know** A listing of the tasks completed within a project together with the pages where the step-by-step, screen-by-screen explanations appear. This section provides a perfect study review for students.

- **Project Reinforcement on the Web** Every project has a Web page (www.scsite.com/off2000/reinforce.htm). The Web page includes true/false, multiple choice, and short answer questions, and additional project-related reinforcement activities that will help students gain confidence in their Word 2000 abilities. The Project Reinforcement exercises also are included on the Shelly Cashman Series Teaching Tools CD-ROM.

- **Apply Your Knowledge** This exercise requires students to open and manipulate a file on the Data Disk. To obtain a copy of the Data Disk, follow the instructions on the inside back cover of this book.

- **In the Lab** Three in-depth assignments per project require students to apply the knowledge gained in the project to solve problems on a computer.

- **Cases and Places** Up to seven unique case studies that require students to apply their knowledge to real-world situations.

Shelly Cashman Series Teaching Tools

A comprehensive set of Teaching Tools accompanies this textbook in the form of a CD-ROM. The CD-ROM includes an Instructor's Manual and teaching and testing aids. The CD-ROM (ISBN 0-7895-4636-1) is available through your Course Technology representative or by calling one of the following telephone numbers: Colleges and Universities, 1-800-648-7450; High Schools, 1-800-824-5179; Career Colleges, 1-800-477-3692; Canada, 1-800-268-2222; and Corporations and Government Agencies, 1-800-340-7450.

- **Instructor's Manual** The Instructor's Manual is made up of Microsoft Word files. The files include lecture notes, solutions to laboratory assignments, and a large test bank. The files allow you to modify the lecture notes or generate quizzes and exams from the test bank using your own word processing software. Where appropriate, solutions to laboratory assignments are embedded as icons in the files. When an icon appears, double-click it and the application will start and the solution will display on the screen. The Instructor's Manual includes the following for each project: project objectives; project overview; detailed lesson plans with page number references; teacher notes and activities; answers to the end-of-project exercises; test bank of 110 questions for every project (25 multiple-choice, 50 true/false, and 35 fill-in-the-blank) with page number references; and transparency references. The transparencies are available through the Figures in the Book. The test bank questions are numbered the same as in Course Test Manager. Thus, you can print a copy of the project test bank and use the printout to select your questions in Course Test Manager.

Figures in the Book Illustrations for every screen and table in the textbook are available in JPEG format. Use this ancillary to create a slide show from the illustrations for lecture or to print transparencies for use in lecture. You also may create your own PowerPoint presentations and insert these illustrations.

Course Test Manager Course Test Manager is a powerful testing and assessment package that enables instructors to create and print tests from the large test bank. Instructors with access to a networked computer lab (LAN) can administer, grade, and track tests online. Students also can take online practice tests, which generate customized study guides.

Course Syllabus Any instructor who has been assigned a course at the last minute knows how difficult it is to come up with a course syllabus. For this reason, sample syllabi are included for each of the Word 2000 products that can be customized easily to a course.

Lecture Success System Lecture Success System files are for use with the application software, a personal computer, and projection device to explain and illustrate the step-by-step, screen-by-screen development of a project in the textbook without entering large amounts of data.

Instructor's Lab Solutions Solutions and required files for all the In the Lab assignments at the end of each project are available.

Lab Tests/Test Outs Tests that parallel the In the Lab assignments are supplied for the purpose of testing students in the laboratory on the material covered in the project or testing students out of the course.

Project Reinforcement True/false, multiple choice, and short answer questions, and additional project-related reinforcement activities for each project help students gain confidence in their Word 2000 abilities.

Student Files All the files that are required by students to complete the Apply Your Knowledge exercises are included.

Interactive Labs Eighteen hands-on interactive labs that take students from ten to fifteen minutes each to step through help solidify and reinforce mouse and keyboard usage and computer concepts. Student assessment is available.

WebCT Content This ancillary includes book-related content that can be uploaded to your institution's WebCT site. The content includes a sample syllabus, practice tests, a bank of test questions, a list of book-related links, and lecture notes from the Instructor's Manual.

Acknowledgments

The Shelly Cashman Series would not be the leading computer education series without the contributions of outstanding publishing professionals. First, and foremost, among them is Becky Herrington, director of production and designer. She is the heart and soul of the Shelly Cashman Series, and it is only through her leadership, dedication, and tireless efforts that superior products are made possible. Becky created and produced the award-winning Windows series of books.

Under Becky's direction, the following individuals made significant contributions to these books: Doug Cowley, production manager; Ginny Harvey, series specialist and developmental editor; Ken Russo, senior Web designer; Mike Bodnar, associate production manager; Stephanie Nance, graphic artist and cover designer; Mark Norton, Web designer; Meena Mohtadi, production editor; Marlo Mitchem, Chris Schneider, Hector Arvizu, Kenny Tran, Kathy Mayers, and Dave Bonnewitz, graphic artists; Jeanne Black and Betty Hopkins, Quark experts; Nancy Lamm, Lyn Markowicz, Margaret Gatling, and Laurie Sullivan, copyeditors; Marilyn Martin, Kim Kosmatka, Cherilyn King, Mary Steinman, and Pat Hadden, proofreaders; Cristina Haley, indexer; Sarah Evertson of Image Quest, photo researcher; and Susan Sebok and Ginny Harvey, contributing writers.

Special thanks go to Richard Keaveny, managing editor; Jim Quasney, series consulting editor; Lora Wade, product manager; Erin Bennett, associate product manager; Francis Schurgot, Web product manager; Scott Wiseman, online developer; Rajika Gupta, marketing manager; and Erin Runyon, editorial assistant

Gary B. Shelly
Thomas J. Cashman
Misty E. Vermaat

Shelly Cashman Series – Traditionally Bound Textbooks

For more information, see your Course Technology representative, call 1-800-648-7450, or visit Shelly Cashman Online at **www.scseries.com**

COMPUTERS	
Computers	Discovering Computers 2000: Concepts for a Connected World, Web and CNN Enhanced
	Discovering Computers 2000: Concepts for a Connected World, Web and CNN Enhanced Brief Edition
	Teachers Discovering Computers: A Link to the Future, Web and CNN Enhanced
	Discovering Computers 98: A Link to the Future, World Wide Web Enhanced
	Discovering Computers 98: A Link to the Future, World Wide Web Enhanced Brief Edition
	Exploring Computers: A Record of Discovery 2e with CD-ROM
	Study Guide for Discovering Computers 2000: Concepts for a Connected World
	Essential Introduction to Computers 3e (32-page)
	Discovering Computer Certification: Planning, Prerequisites, Potential
	Discovering Internet Companies: Doing Business in the New Millennium

WINDOWS APPLICATIONS	
Microsoft Office	Microsoft Office 2000: Essential Concepts and Techniques (5 projects)
	Microsoft Office 2000: Brief Concepts and Techniques (9 projects)
	Microsoft Office 2000: Introductory Concepts and Techniques (15 projects)
	Microsoft Office 2000: Advanced Concepts and Techniques (11 projects)
	Microsoft Office 2000: Post Advanced Concepts and Techniques (11 projects)
	Microsoft Office 97: Introductory Concepts and Techniques, Brief Edition (6 projects)
	Microsoft Office 97: Introductory Concepts and Techniques, Essentials Edition (10 projects)
	Microsoft Office 97: Introductory Concepts and Techniques, Enhanced Edition (15 projects)
	Microsoft Office 97: Advanced Concepts and Techniques
Microsoft Works	Microsoft Works 4.5[1]
Windows	Microsoft Windows 98: Essential Concepts and Techniques (2 projects)
	Microsoft Windows 98: Introductory Concepts and Techniques (3 projects)
	Microsoft Windows 98: Introductory Concepts and Techniques Web Style Edition (3 projects)
	Microsoft Windows 98[2]: Complete Concepts and Techniques (6 projects)
	Microsoft Windows 98: Comprehensive Concepts and Techniques (9 projects)
	Introduction to Microsoft Windows NT Workstation 4
	Microsoft Windows 95: Introductory Concepts and Techniques (2 projects)
	Introduction to Microsoft Windows 95 (3 projects)
	Microsoft Windows 95[1]: Complete Concepts and Techniques (6 projects)
Word Processing	Microsoft Word 2000[2] • Microsoft Word 97[1] • Microsoft Word 7[1] Corel WordPerfect 8 • Corel WordPerfect 7 • WordPerfect 6.1[1]
Spreadsheets	Microsoft Excel 2000[2] • Microsoft Excel 97[1] • Microsoft Excel 7[1] • Microsoft Excel 5[1] • Lotus 1-2-3 97[1]
Database	Microsoft Access 2000[2] • Microsoft Access 97[1] • Microsoft Access 7[1]
Presentation Graphics	Microsoft PowerPoint 2000[2] • Microsoft PowerPoint 97[1] • Microsoft PowerPoint 7[1]
Desktop Publishing	Microsoft Publisher 2000[1]
Graphic Design	Microsoft PhotoDraw 2000: Essential Concepts and Techniques

PROGRAMMING	
Programming	Microsoft Visual Basic 6: Complete Concepts and Techniques[1]
	Microsoft Visual Basic 5: Complete Concepts and Techniques[1]
	QBasic • QBasic: An Introduction to Programming • Microsoft BASIC
	Structured COBOL Programming, Second Edition

INTERNET	
Browser	Microsoft Internet Explorer 5: An Introduction • Microsoft Internet Explorer 4: An Introduction Netscape Navigator 4: An Introduction
Web Page Creation	HTML: Complete Concepts and Techniques[1] • Microsoft FrontPage 2000: Complete Concepts and Techniques[1] • Microsoft FrontPage 98: Complete Concepts and Techniques[1] • Netscape Composer • JavaScript: Complete Concepts and Techniques[1]

SYSTEMS ANALYSIS/DATA COMMUNICATIONS	
Systems Analysis	Systems Analysis and Design, Third Edition
Data Communications	Business Data Communications: Introductory Concepts and Techniques, Second Edition

[1]Also available as an Introductory Edition, which is a shortened version of the complete book
[2]Also available as an Introductory Edition, which is a shortened version of the complete book and also as a Comprehensive Edition, which is an extended version of the complete book

MICROSOFT

Word 2000

The document window displays text, tables, graphics, and other items as you type or insert them into a document. Only a portion of your document, however, displays on the screen at one time. You view the portion of the document displayed on the screen

Microsoft **Word 2000**

Microsoft Word 2000

PROJECT

1

Creating and Editing a Word Document

You will have mastered the material in this project when you can:

OBJECTIVES

- Start Word
- Describe the Word window
- Zoom page width
- Change the default font size of all text
- Enter text into a document
- Check spelling as you type
- Scroll through a document
- Save a document
- Select text
- Change the font of selected text
- Change the font size of selected text
- Bold selected text
- Right-align a paragraph
- Center a paragraph
- Undo commands or actions
- Italicize selected text
- Underline selected text
- Insert clip art into a document
- Resize a graphic
- Print a document
- Open a document
- Correct errors in a document
- Use Microsoft Word Help
- Quit Word

Wobbling Words

Help for the Spelling Challenged

*" My spelling is Wobbly.
It's good spelling, but it Wobbles,
and the letters get in the wrong places. "*

Winnie-the-Pooh

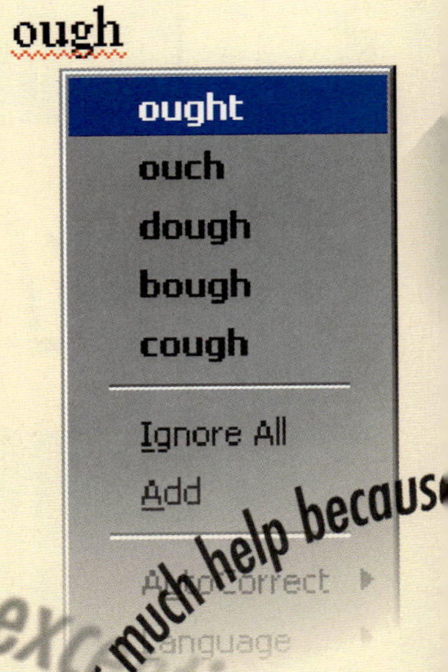

ough

ought
ouch
dough
bough
cough

Ignore All

Add

AutoCorrect

Language

No wonder Pooh has a difficult time trying to spell words correctly. If he pronounces the words bough, cough, rough, though, and through, he realizes that despite the fact they all end with the letters, ough, they all are pronounced quite differently.

If you share Pooh's spelling dilemma, you are not alone. Most people have difficulty remembering how to spell some words. One study reports 20 percent of writers do not spell well because they cannot visualize words. Even remembering the simple rules such as, i before e except after c, does not offer much assistance because of the slew of exceptions such as the words, weird science.

A spelling error in a flyer distributed on campus, a resume sent to a potential employer, or an e-mail message forwarded to an associate

gazebo

dolphin

däl-fən

homophones

bough,

cough,

rough,

ugh,

gh,

homophones

ew of exceptions, such as, weird and s

exceptions exception

could lessen your credibility, cause a reader to doubt the accuracy of your statements, and leave a negative impression. In this project, Microsoft Word will check your typing for possible spelling errors as you create an announcement for the Student Government Association's upcoming winter break ski trip at Summit Peak Resort.

If you type a word that does not appear in Word's dictionary, Word will flag the possible error with a wavy red underline. If the spelling is correct, you can instruct Word to ignore the flagged word. If it is misspelled, the spelling feature will offer a list of suggested corrections. Despite this assistance from the spelling checker, one study indicates college students repeatedly ignore or override the flagged words.

Word's spelling checker is a useful alternative to a dictionary, but you must not rely on it 100 percent. It will not flag commonly misused homophones, which are words that are pronounced alike but are spelled differently. For example, it is easy to confuse the homophones in the sentence, The Web site contains an incorrect cite to the reference materials discussing regaining sight after experiencing blindness.

Then what is a spelling-challenged writer to do? English teachers emphasize that you can learn to spell better, but not by strictly memorizing long lists or having someone mark all the errors in a paper. Instead, you need to try the following strategies to improve awareness of spelling difficulties.

First, identify error patterns. For example, do you misspell the same words repeatedly? If so, write them in a list and have a friend dictate them to you. Then write the words again. If you involve your senses, hear the words spelled correctly, and then visualize the words, you increase your awareness of the problem.

Next, always consult a dictionary when you are uncertain of a word's spelling. Note the word's etymology — its origin and history. For example, the word, science, originated from the Latin word, scientia, a form of the verb to know.

As you proofread, read from right to left. Use a pencil to point at each word as you say it aloud.

Using Microsoft Word's spelling checker and a good dictionary should enhance your spelling skills, and stop your words from *Wobbling*.

Microsoft Word 2000

Creating and Editing a Word Document

CASE PERSPECTIVE

Jackie Peterson is this year's Activities Chairperson for the Student Government Association (SGA) at Hilltop Community College. Each year, the Activities Chairperson coordinates vacation plans for the winter break and then prepares fliers announcing the exciting plans. SGA members post these announcements in locations throughout the school, print them in the school newspaper, and mail them to each student.

Because of Jackie's avid love of skiing and snowboarding, she attempts to locate a ski resort in the Midwest designed to accommodate all tastes and budgets. She succeeds! Summit Peak Resort has over 5,200 acres of groomed slopes and pristine lakes for skiing, sledding, snowboarding, ice skating, and ice fishing.

As a Marketing major, you have learned the guidelines for designing announcements. Jackie asks for your assistance with this assignment. You recommend using large, bold characters for the headline and title. To attract attention to the announcement, you suggest including a graphic of a skier sailing down the slopes. Together, you begin designing the announcement.

What Is Microsoft Word 2000?

Microsoft Word is a full-featured word processing program that allows you to create professional looking documents such as announcements, letters, resumes, and reports, and revise them easily. You can use Word's desktop publishing features to create high-quality brochures, advertisements, and newsletters. Word also provides many tools that enable you to create Web pages with ease. From within Word, you even can place these Web pages directly on a Web server.

Word has many features designed to simplify the production of documents. With Word, you easily can include borders, shading, tables, graphics, pictures, and Web addresses in your documents. You can instruct Word to create a template, which is a form you can use and customize to meet your needs. While you are typing, Word can perform tasks automatically. For example, Word can detect and correct spelling and grammar errors in a variety of languages. Word also can format text such as headings, lists, fractions, borders, and Web addresses as you type them. Word's thesaurus allows you to add variety and precision to your writing. Within Word, you can e-mail a copy of your Word document to an e-mail address.

Project One — Summit Peak Announcement

To illustrate the features of Word, this book presents a series of projects that use Word to create documents similar to those you will encounter in academic and business environments. Project 1 uses Word to produce the announcement shown in Figure 1-1.

More About
Word 2000
For more information on the features of Microsoft Word 2000, visit the Word 2000 More About Web page (www.scsite.com/wd2000/more.htm) and then click Microsoft Word 2000 Features.

FIGURE 1-1

The announcement informs students about exciting vacation packages offered by Summit Peak Resort during winter break. The announcement begins with a headline that is followed by a graphic of a skier. Below the graphic of the skier is the body title, SUMMIT PEAK RESORT, followed by the body copy that consists of a brief paragraph about the resort and another paragraph about the vacation packages. Finally, the last line of the announcement lists the resort's telephone number. The appearance of the text and graphic in the announcement is designed to catch the attention of the reader.

Starting Word

Follow these steps to start Word, or ask your instructor how to start Word for your system.

Steps To Start Word

1 Click the Start button on the taskbar and then point to New Office Document.

The programs on the Start menu display above the Start button (Figure 1-2). The New Office Document command is highlighted on the Start menu. A highlighted command displays as light text on a dark background.

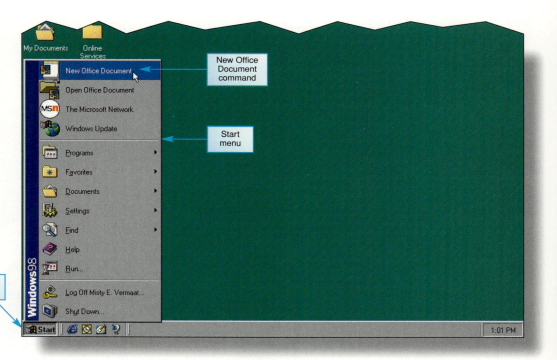

FIGURE 1-2

2 Click New Office Document. If necessary, click the General tab when the New Office Document dialog box first displays. Point to the Blank Document icon.

Office displays several icons in the General sheet in the New Office Document dialog box (Figure 1-3). The icons are large because the Large Icons button is selected. Each icon represents a different type of document you can create in Microsoft Office.

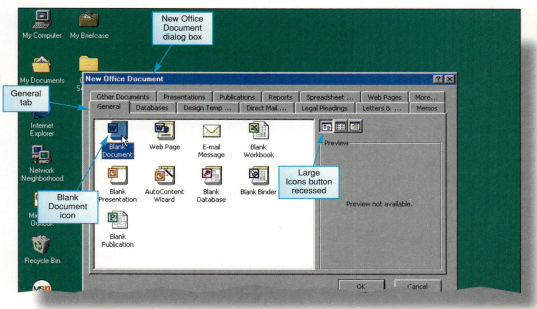

FIGURE 1-3

3 **Double-click the Blank Document icon.**

Office starts Word. While Word is starting, the mouse pointer changes to the shape of an hourglass. After a few moments, an empty document titled Document1 displays in the Word window (Figure 1-4).

4 **If the Word window is not maximized, double-click its title bar to maximize it. If the Office Assistant displays, right-click it and then click Hide on the shortcut menu. If your screen differs from Figure 1-4, click View on the menu bar and then click Normal.**

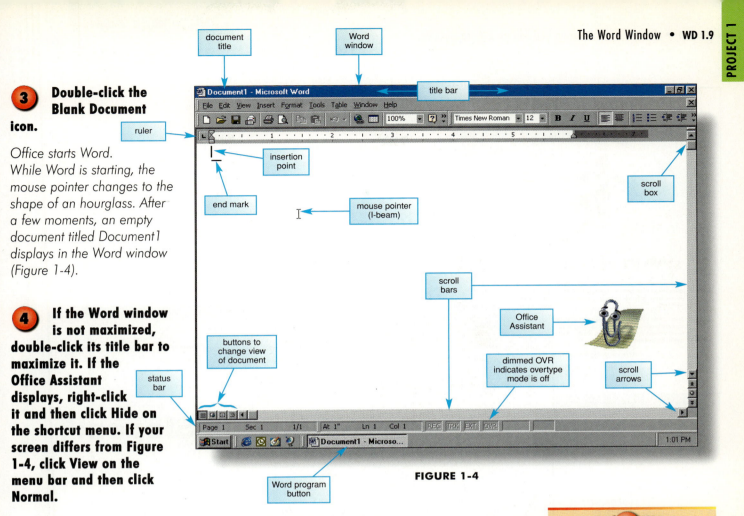

FIGURE 1-4

The Windows taskbar at the bottom of the screen displays the Word program button, indicating the Word program is open.

The Windows taskbar at the bottom of the screen displays the Word program button, indicating the Word program is open.

The Word Window

The **Word window** (Figure 1-4) consists of a variety of components to make your work more efficient and documents more professional. The following sections discuss these components.

Document Window

The document window displays text, tables, graphics, and other items as you type or insert them into a document. Only a portion of your document, however, displays on the screen at one time. You view the portion of the document displayed on the screen through the **document window** (Figure 1-5 on the next page).

Other Ways

1. Right-click Start button, click Open, double-click New Office Document, click General tab, double-click Blank Document icon

2. Click New Office Document button on Microsoft Office Shortcut Bar, click General tab, double-click Blank Document icon

3. On Start menu point to Programs, click Microsoft Word

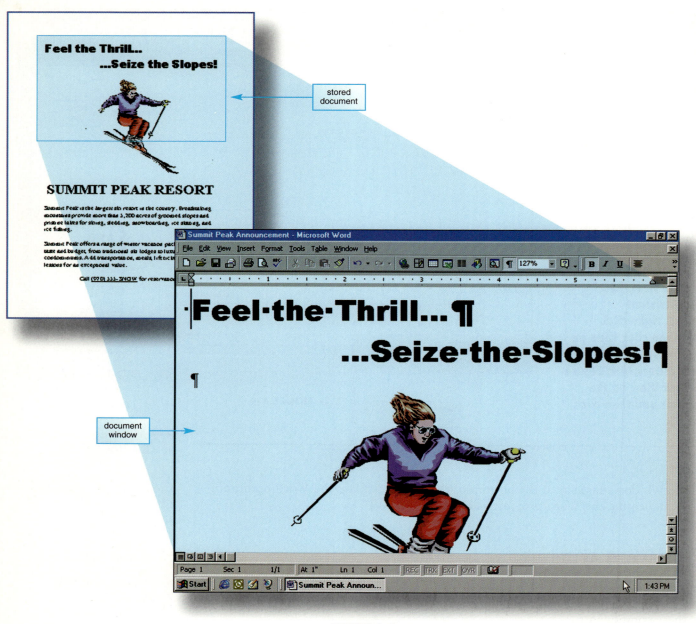

FIGURE 1-5

The document window contains several elements commonly found in other applications, as well as some elements unique to Word. The main elements of the Word document window are the insertion point, end mark, mouse pointer, rulers, scroll bars, and status bar (see Figure 1-4 on the previous page).

INSERTION POINT The **insertion point** is a blinking vertical bar that indicates where text will be inserted as you type. As you type, the insertion point moves to the right and, when you reach the end of a line, it moves downward to the next line. You also can insert graphics, tables, and other items at the location of the insertion point.

END MARK The **end mark** is a short horizontal line that indicates the end of your document. Each time you begin a new line, the end mark moves downward.

MOUSE POINTER   The **mouse pointer** becomes different shapes depending on the task you are performing in Word and the pointer's location on the screen. The mouse pointer in Figure 1-4 has the shape of an I-beam. Other mouse pointer shapes are described as they appear on the screen during this and subsequent projects.

RULERS   At the top edge of the document window is the **horizontal ruler**. You use the horizontal ruler, sometimes simply called the **ruler**, to set tab stops, indent paragraphs, adjust column widths, and change page margins.

An additional ruler, called the **vertical ruler**, sometimes displays at the left edge of the window when you perform certain tasks. The purpose of the vertical ruler is discussed as it displays on the screen in a later project. If your screen displays a vertical ruler, click View on the menu bar and then click Normal.

SCROLL BARS   You use the **scroll bars** to display different portions of your document in the document window. At the right edge of the document window is a vertical scroll bar, and at the bottom of the document window is a horizontal scroll bar. On both the vertical and horizontal scroll bars, the position of the **scroll box** reflects the location of the portion of the document displaying in the document window.

On the left edge of the horizontal scroll bar are four buttons you use to change the view of your document, and on the bottom of the vertical scroll bar are three buttons you can use to scroll through a document. These buttons are discussed as they are used in later projects.

STATUS BAR   The status bar displays at the bottom of the document window, above the Windows taskbar. The **status bar** presents information about the location of the insertion point, the progress of current tasks, as well as the status of certain commands, keys, and buttons.

From left to right, the following information displays on the status bar in Figure 1-5: the page number, the section number, the page containing the insertion point followed by the total number of pages in the document, the position of the insertion point in inches from the top of the page, the line number and column number of the insertion point, followed by several status indicators. If you perform a task that requires several seconds (such as saving a document), the status bar displays a message informing you of the progress of the task.

You use the **status indicators** to turn certain keys or modes on or off. Four of these status indicators (REC, TRK, EXT, and OVR) display darkened when on and dimmed when off. For example, the dimmed OVR indicates overtype mode is off. To turn these four status indicators on or off, double-click the status indicator. These status indicators are discussed as they are used in the projects.

The next status indicators display icons as you perform certain tasks. When you begin typing in the document window, a Spelling and Grammar Status icon displays. When Word is saving your document, a Background Save Status icon displays. When you print a document, a Background Print Status icon displays.

When you point to various areas on the status bar, Word displays a ScreenTip to help you identify it. A **ScreenTip** is a short descriptive name of a button, icon, or command associated with the item to which you are pointing.

Menu Bar and Toolbars

The menu bar displays at the top of the screen just below the title bar (Figure 1-6a on the next page). The Standard toolbar and Formatting toolbar are preset to share a single row that displays immediately below the menu bar.

More About 2000

The Horizontal Ruler

If the horizontal ruler does not display on your screen, click View on the menu bar and then click Ruler. To hide the ruler, also click View on the menu bar and then click Ruler.

More About 2000

Scroll Bars

You can use the vertical scroll bar to scroll through multi-page documents. As you drag the scroll box up or down the scroll bar, Word displays a page indicator to the left of the scroll box. If you release the mouse button, Word displays the page referenced by the page indicator in the document window.

More About 2000

Language Mode

If system support for multiple languages was installed on your computer, the status bar also displays the Language mode indicator, which shows the name of the language you are using to create the document.

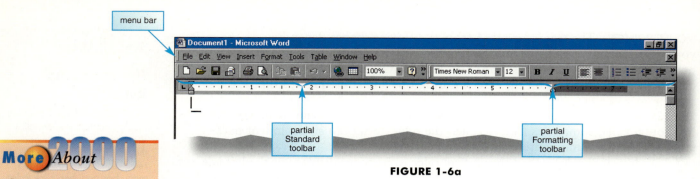

menu bar

partial Standard toolbar

partial Formatting toolbar

FIGURE 1-6a

MENU BAR   The **menu bar** displays the Word menu names. Each menu contains a list of commands you can use to perform tasks such as retrieving, storing, printing, and formatting data in your document. When you click a menu name on the menu bar, a **short menu** displays that lists your most recently used commands (Figure 1-6b). To display a menu, such as the View menu, click the menu name on the menu bar. If you point to a command on a menu with an arrow to its right, a submenu displays from which you choose a command.

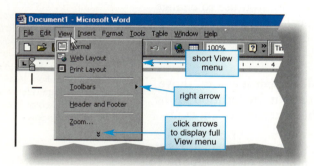

short View menu

right arrow

click arrows to display full View menu

FIGURE 1-6b

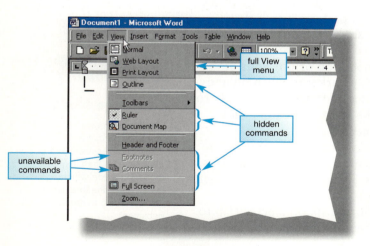

full View menu

hidden commands

unavailable commands

FIGURE 1-6c

If you wait a few seconds or click the arrows at the bottom of the short menu, it expands into a full menu. A **full menu** lists all the commands associated with a menu (Figure 1-6c). You also can display a full menu immediately by double-clicking the menu name on the menu bar. In this book, when you display a menu, always display the full menu using one of these techniques:

1. Click the menu name on the menu bar and then wait a few seconds.
2. Click the menu name and then click the arrows at the bottom of the short menu.
3. Click the menu name and then point to the arrows at the bottom of the short menu.
4. Double-click the menu name.

When a full menu displays, some of the commands are recessed into lighter gray background and some also are unavailable. A recessed command is called a **hidden command** because it does not display on a short menu. As you use Word, it automatically personalizes the short menus for you based on how often you use commands. That is, as you use hidden commands, Word *unhides* them and places them on the short menu. An **unavailable command** displays dimmed, which indicates it is not available for the current selection.

TOOLBARS   Word has many pre-defined, or built-in, toolbars. A **toolbar** contains buttons, boxes, and menus that allow you to perform tasks more quickly than using the menu bar and related menus. For example, to print a document, you click the Print button on the toolbar. Each button on a toolbar displays an image to help you remember its function. Also, when you point to a button or box on a toolbar, a ScreenTip (the item's name) displays below the mouse pointer (see Figure 1-10 on page WD 1.15).

Two built-in toolbars are the Standard toolbar and the Formatting toolbar. Figure 1-7a illustrates the Standard toolbar and identifies its buttons and boxes. Figure 1-7b illustrates the Formatting toolbar. Each button and box is explained in detail as it is used in the projects throughout the book.

The Standard toolbar and Formatting toolbar are preset to display docked on the same row immediately below the menu bar. A **docked toolbar** is one that is attached to the edge of the Word window. Because both of these toolbars cannot fit entirely on a single row, a portion or all of the Standard toolbar displays on the left of the row and a portion or all of the Formatting toolbar displays on the right (Figure 1-8a). The buttons that display on the toolbar are the more frequently used buttons.

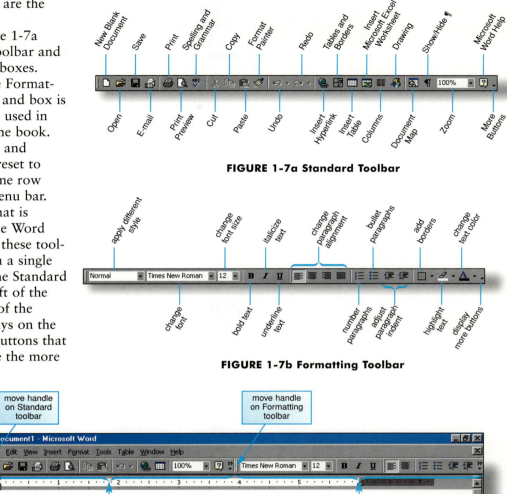

FIGURE 1-7a Standard Toolbar

FIGURE 1-7b Formatting Toolbar

FIGURE 1-8a

To display the entire Standard toolbar, double-click its **move handle**, which is the vertical bar at the left edge of a toolbar. When you display the complete Standard toolbar, only a portion of the Formatting toolbar displays (Figure 1-8b). To display the entire Formatting toolbar, double-click its move handle. When you display the complete Formatting toolbar, only a portion of the Standard toolbar displays (Figure 1-8c on the next page).

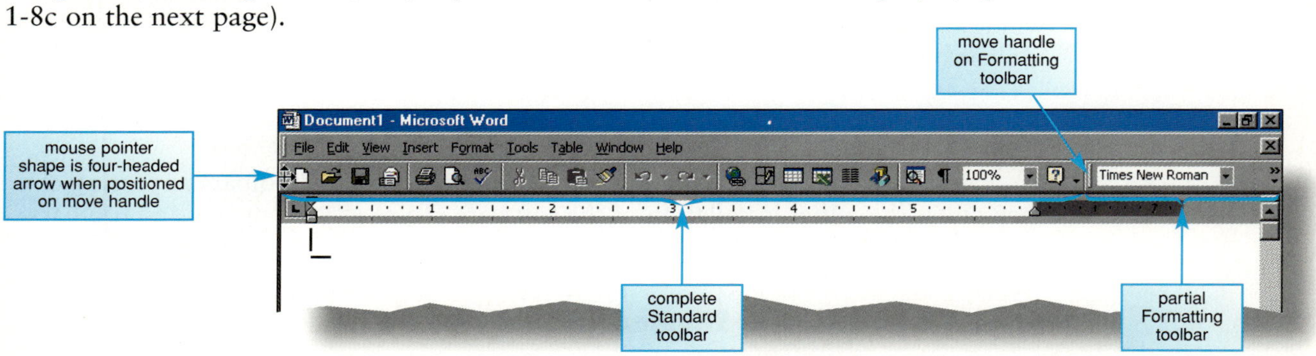

FIGURE 1-8b

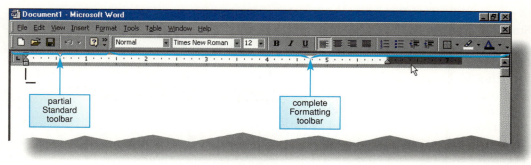

FIGURE 1-8c

An alternative to double-clicking the move handle to display an entire toolbar is to click the More Buttons button at the right edge of the toolbar. When you click a toolbar's **More Buttons** button, Word displays a **More Buttons list** that contains the toolbar's hidden buttons (Figure 1-8d).

FIGURE 1-8d

As with menus, Word personalizes toolbars. That is, once you click a hidden button in the More Buttons list, Word removes the button from the More Buttons list and places it on the toolbar. For example, if you click the Drawing button in Figure 1-8d, Word displays this button on the Standard toolbar and removes a less frequently used button to make room for the Drawing button. By adapting to the way you work, this intelligent personalization feature of Word is designed to increase your productivity.

Additional toolbars may display on the Word screen, depending on the task you are performing. These additional toolbars display either stacked below the row containing the Standard and Formatting toolbars or floating in the Word window. A **floating toolbar** is not attached to an edge of the Word window. You can rearrange the order of docked toolbars and can move floating toolbars anywhere in the Word window. Later in this book, steps are presented that show you how to float a docked toolbar or dock a floating toolbar.

Resetting Menus and Toolbars

Each project in this book begins with the menu bars and toolbars appearing as they did at the initial installation of the software. To reset your menus and toolbars so they appear exactly as shown in this book, follow the steps in Appendix C.

Displaying the Entire Standard Toolbar

Perform the following step to display the entire Standard toolbar.

To Display the Entire Standard Toolbar

1 **Double-click the move handle on the Standard toolbar.**

Word displays the entire Standard toolbar (Figure 1-9).

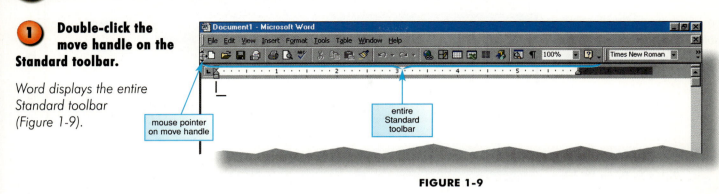

FIGURE 1-9

Zooming Page Width

Depending on your Windows and Word settings, the horizontal ruler at the top of the document window may show more inches or fewer inches than the ruler shown in Figure 1-9. The more inches of ruler that display, the smaller the text will be on the screen. The fewer inches of ruler that display, the larger the text will be on the screen. To minimize eyestrain, the projects in this book display the text as large as possible without extending the right margin beyond the right edge of the document window.

Two factors that affect how much of the ruler displays in the document window are the Windows screen resolution and the Word zoom percentage. The screens in this book use a resolution of 800 x 600. With this resolution, you can increase the preset zoom percentage beyond 100% so that the right margin extends to the edge of the document window. To increase or decrease the size of the displayed characters to a point where both the left and right margins are at the edges of the document window, use the **zoom page width** command as shown in the following steps.

To Zoom Page Width

1 **Point to the Zoom box arrow on the Standard toolbar.**

The mouse pointer shape is a left-pointing block arrow when positioned on a toolbar button or box (Figure 1-10). When you point to a toolbar button or box, Word displays a ScreenTip.

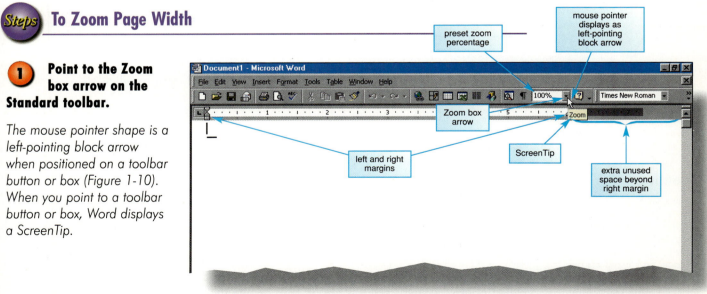

FIGURE 1-10

2 Click the Zoom box arrow.

Word displays a list of available zoom percentages and the Page Width option in the Zoom list (Figure 1-11).

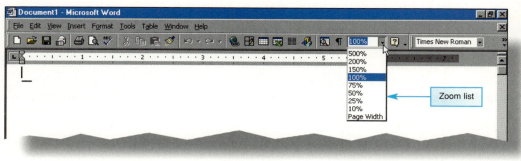

FIGURE 1-11

3 Point to Page Width in the Zoom list.

Word highlights Page Width in the Zoom list (Figure 1-12).

FIGURE 1-12

4 Click Page Width.

Word extends the right margin to the right edge of the document window (Figure 1-13).

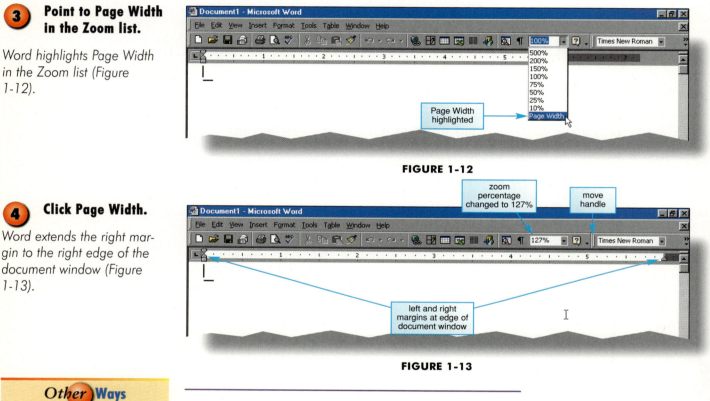

FIGURE 1-13

Zooming

If you want to zoom to a percentage not displayed in the Zoom list, you can click the Zoom box on the Standard toolbar, type the desired percentage, and then press the ENTER key; or click view on the menu bar, click Zoom, and then enter the desired zoom percentage.

If your Zoom list (Figure 1-12) displayed additional options, click View on the menu bar and then click Normal.

The Zoom box in Figure 1-13 displays 127%, which Word computes based on a variety of settings. Your percentage may be different depending on your system configuration.

Changing the Default Font Size

Characters that display on the screen are a specific shape, size, and style. The **font**, or typeface, defines the appearance and shape of the letters, numbers, and special characters. The preset, or **default**, font is Times New Roman (Figure 1-14). **Font size** specifies the size of the characters. Font size is determined by a measurement system called points. A single **point** is about 1/72 of one inch in height. Thus, a character with a font size of ten is about 10/72 of one inch in height.

If Word 2000 is installed on a new computer, then the default font size most likely is 12. If, however, you upgrade from a previous version of Word when installing Word 2000, your default font most likely is 10.

If more of the characters in your document require a larger font size than the default, you easily can change the default font size before you type. In Project 1, many of the characters in the announcement are a font size of 16. Follow these steps to increase the font size before you begin entering text.

More About

Font Size

Many people need to wear reading glasses. Thus, use a font size of at least 12 in your documents. Because an announcement usually is posted on a bulletin board, its font size should be as large as possible so that all potential readers can see the announcement easily.

Steps To Increase the Default Font Size Before Typing

1 **Double-click the move handle on the Formatting toolbar to display the entire toolbar. Click the Font Size box arrow on the Formatting toolbar and then point to 16.**

A list of available font sizes displays in the Font Size list (Figure 1-14). The available font sizes depend on the current font, which is Times New Roman.

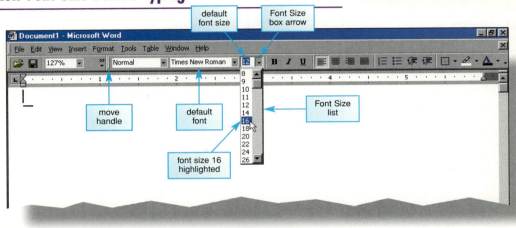

FIGURE 1-14

2 **Click 16.**

The font size for characters in this document changes to 16 (Figure 1-15). The size of the insertion point increases to reflect the new font size.

FIGURE 1-15

The new font size takes effect immediately in your document. Word uses this font size for characters you type into this announcement.

Entering Text

To create a document that contains text, you enter the text by typing on the keyboard. The example on the next page explains the steps to enter both lines of the headline of the announcement. These lines will be positioned at the left margin. Later in this project, you will format the headline so that both lines are bold and enlarged and the second line is positioned at the right margin.

Other Ways

1. Right-click above end mark, click Font on shortcut menu, click Font tab, select desired font size in Size list, click OK button

2. On Format menu click Font, click Font tab, select desired font size in Size list, click OK button

3. Press CTRL+SHIFT+P, type desired font size, press ENTER

4. Press CTRL+SHIFT+>

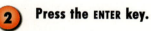

To Enter Text

1 **Type** `Feel the Thrill` **and then press the PERIOD key (.) three times. If you make an error while typing, press the BACKSPACE key until you have deleted the text in error and then retype the text correctly.**

As you type, the insertion point moves to the right (Figure 1-16).

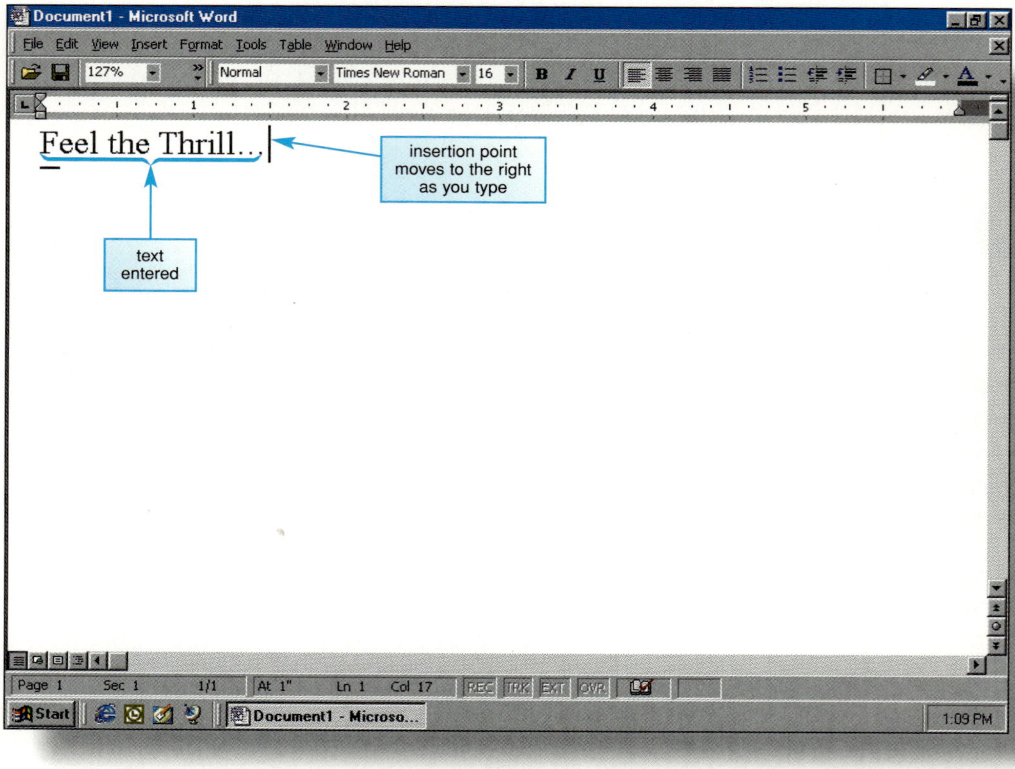

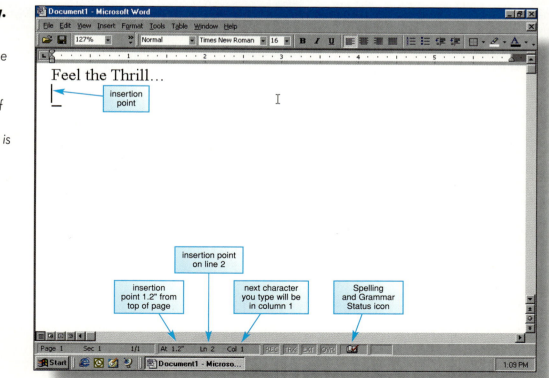

FIGURE 1-16

2 **Press the ENTER key.**

Word moves the insertion point to the beginning of the next line (Figure 1-17). Notice the status bar indicates the current position of the insertion point. That is, the insertion point currently is on line 2 column 1.

FIGURE 1-17

3 **Press the PERIOD key three times and then type** Seize the Slopes! **Press the ENTER key.**

The headline is complete (Figure 1-18). The insertion point is on line 3.

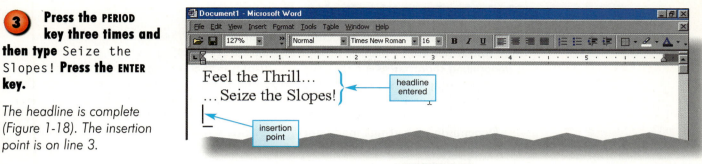

FIGURE 1-18

When you begin entering text into a document, the **Spelling and Grammar Status icon** displays at the right of the status bar (Figure 1-17). As you type, the Spelling and Grammar Status icon shows an animated pencil writing on paper, which indicates Word is checking for possible errors. When you stop typing, the pencil changes to either a red check mark or a red X. In Figure 1-17, the Spelling and Grammar Status icon displays a red check mark.

In general, if all of the words you have typed are in Word's dictionary and your grammar is correct, a red check mark displays on the Spelling and Grammar Status icon. If you type a word not in the dictionary (because it is a proper name or misspelled), a red wavy underline displays below the word. If you type text that may be grammatically incorrect, a green wavy underline displays below the text. When Word flags a possible spelling or grammar error, it also changes the red check mark on the Spelling and Grammar Status icon to a red X. As you enter text into the announcement, your Spelling and Grammar Status icon may show a red X instead of a red check mark. Later in this project, you will check the spelling of these words. At that time, the red X will return to a red check mark.

Entering Blank Lines into a Document

To enter a blank line into a document, press the ENTER key without typing any text on the line. The following example explains how to enter three blank lines below the headline.

 To Enter Blank Lines into a Document

1 **Press the ENTER key three times.**

Word inserts three blank lines into your document below the headline (Figure 1-19).

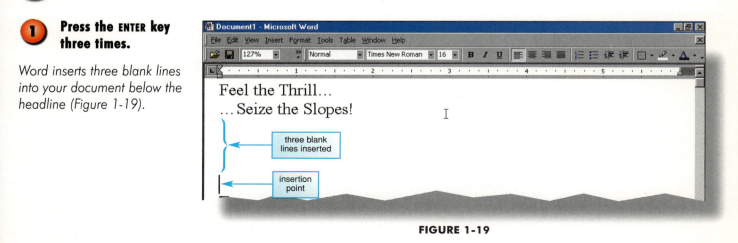

FIGURE 1-19

Displaying Formatting Marks

To indicate where in the document you press the ENTER key or SPACEBAR, you may find it helpful to display formatting marks. A **formatting mark**, sometimes called a **nonprinting character**, is a character that displays on the screen but is not visible on a printed document. For example, the paragraph mark (¶) is a formatting mark that indicates where you pressed the ENTER key. A raised dot (•) shows where you pressed the SPACEBAR. Other formatting marks are discussed as they display on the screen.

Depending on settings made during previous Word sessions, your screen may already display formatting marks (see Figure 1-21). If the formatting marks are not already displaying on your screen, perform the following steps to display them.

Steps **To Display Formatting Marks**

1 **Double-click the move handle on the Standard toolbar to display the entire toolbar. Point to the Show/Hide ¶ button on the Standard toolbar (Figure 1-20).**

2 **If it is not already recessed, click the Show/Hide ¶ button.**

Word **recesses**, or pushes in, the Show/Hide ¶ button on the Standard toolbar and displays formatting marks on the screen (Figure 1-21).

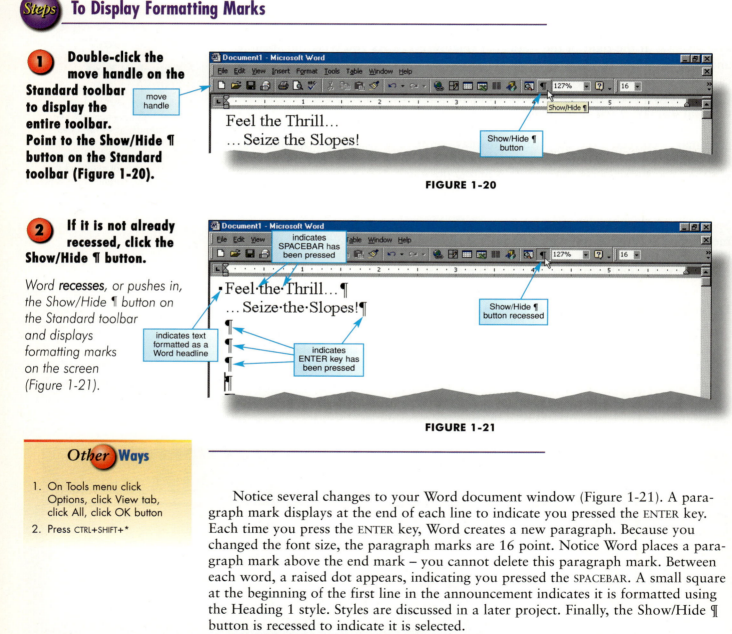

FIGURE 1-20

FIGURE 1-21

Other **Ways**

1. On Tools menu click Options, click View tab, click All, click OK button
2. Press CTRL+SHIFT+*

Notice several changes to your Word document window (Figure 1-21). A paragraph mark displays at the end of each line to indicate you pressed the ENTER key. Each time you press the ENTER key, Word creates a new paragraph. Because you changed the font size, the paragraph marks are 16 point. Notice Word places a paragraph mark above the end mark – you cannot delete this paragraph mark. Between each word, a raised dot appears, indicating you pressed the SPACEBAR. A small square at the beginning of the first line in the announcement indicates it is formatted using the Heading 1 style. Styles are discussed in a later project. Finally, the Show/Hide ¶ button is recessed to indicate it is selected.

If you feel the formatting marks clutter your screen, you can hide them by clicking the Show/Hide ¶ button again. It is recommended that you display formatting marks; therefore, the document windows presented in this book show the formatting marks.

Entering More Text

The body title (SUMMIT PEAK RESORT) in the announcement is capitalized. The next step is to enter this body title in all capital letters into the document window as explained below.

TO ENTER MORE TEXT

1 Press the CAPS LOCK key on the keyboard to turn on capital letters. Verify the CAPS LOCK indicator is lit on your keyboard.

2 Type SUMMIT PEAK RESORT and then press the CAPS LOCK key to turn off capital letters.

3 Press the ENTER key twice.

The body title displays on line 6 as shown in Figure 1-22 below.

Using Wordwrap

Wordwrap allows you to type words in a paragraph continually without pressing the ENTER key at the end of each line. When the insertion point reaches the right margin, Word positions it automatically at the beginning of the next line. As you type, if a word extends beyond the right margin, Word also positions that word automatically on the next line with the insertion point.

Thus, as you enter text using Word, do not press the ENTER key when the insertion point reaches the right margin. Because Word creates a new paragraph each time you press the ENTER key, press the ENTER key only in these circumstances:

1. To insert blank lines into a document
2. To begin a new paragraph
3. To terminate a short line of text and advance to the next line
4. In response to certain Word commands

Perform the following step to become familiar with wordwrap.

More About

Wordwrap

Your printer controls where wordwrap occurs for each line in your document. For this reason, it is possible that the same document could word-wrap on different words if printed on different printers.

Steps To Wordwrap Text as You Type

1 **Type** Summit Peak is the largest ski resort in the country. Breathtaking mountains provide **as the beginning of the body copy.**

Word wraps the word, mountains, to the beginning of line 9 because it is too long to fit on line 8 (Figure 1-22). Your document may wordwrap differently depending on the type of printer you are using.

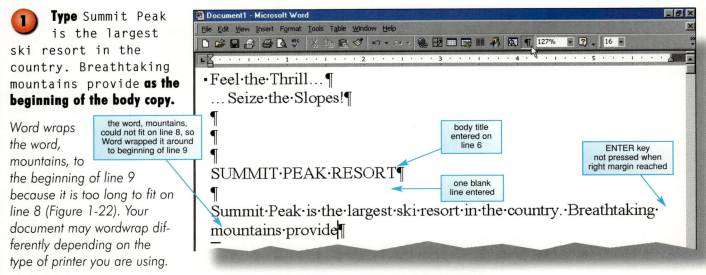

FIGURE 1-22

Checking Spelling Automatically as You Type

As you type text into the document window, Word checks your typing for possible spelling and grammar errors. If a word you type is not in the dictionary, a red wavy underline displays below it. Likewise, if text you type contains possible grammar errors, a green wavy underline displays below the text. In both cases, the Spelling and Grammar Status icon on the status bar displays a red X, instead of a check mark. Although you can check the entire document for spelling and grammar errors at once, you also can check these errors immediately.

To verify that the check spelling as you type feature is enabled, right-click the Spelling and Grammar Status icon on the status bar and then click Options on the shortcut menu. When the Spelling & Grammar dialog box displays, be sure Check spelling as you type has a check mark and Hide spelling errors in this document does not have a check mark.

When a word is flagged with a red wavy underline, it is not in Word's dictionary. A flagged word, however, is not necessarily misspelled. For example, many names, abbreviations, and specialized terms are not in Word's main dictionary. In these cases, you tell Word to ignore the flagged word. As you type, Word also detects duplicate words. For example, if your document contains the phrase, to the the store, Word places a red wavy underline below the second occurrence of the word, the. To display a list of suggested corrections for a flagged word, you right-click it.

In the following example, the word, sledding, has been misspelled intentionally as sleding to illustrate Word's check spelling as you type feature. If you are doing this project on a personal computer, your announcement may contain different misspelled words, depending on the accuracy of your typing.

Entering Sentences

Word processing documents use variable character fonts; for example, the letter w takes up more space than the letter i. With these fonts, it often is difficult to determine how many times the SPACEBAR has been pressed between sentences. Thus, the rule is to press the SPACEBAR only once after periods, colons, and other punctuation marks.

 **To Check Spelling as You Type**

1 **Press the SPACEBAR once. Type** more than 5,200 acres of groomed slopes and pristine lakes for skiing, sleding, **and then press the SPACEBAR.**

Word flags the misspelled word, sledding, by placing a red wavy underline below it (Figure 1-23). Notice the Spelling and Grammar Status icon on the status bar now displays a red X, indicating Word has detected a possible spelling or grammar error.

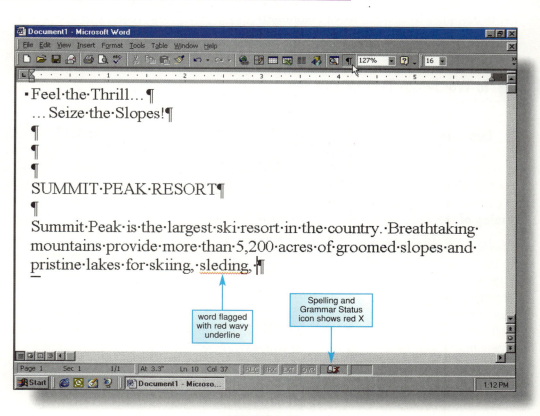

FIGURE 1-23

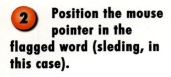

Position the mouse pointer in the flagged word (sleding, in this case).

The mouse pointer's shape is an I-beam when positioned in a word (Figure 1-24).

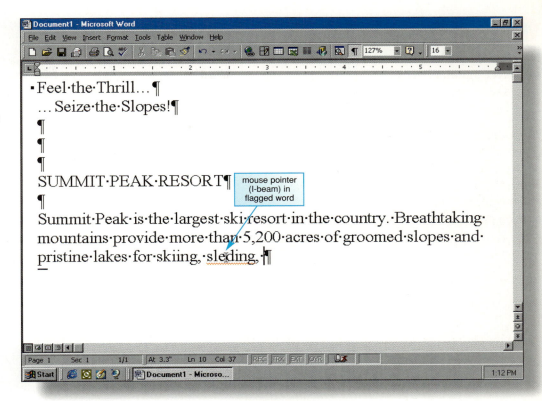

FIGURE 1-24

Right-click the flagged word, sleding. When the shortcut menu displays, point to sledding.

Word displays a shortcut menu that lists suggested spelling corrections for the flagged word (Figure 1-25).

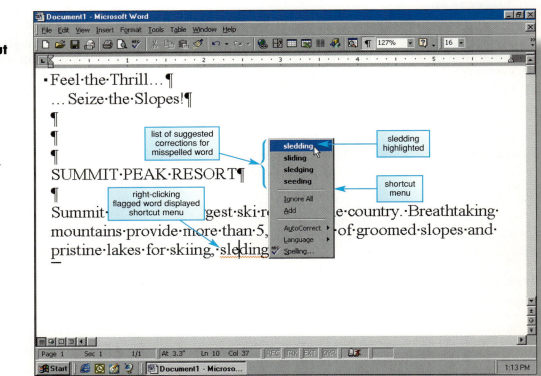

FIGURE 1-25

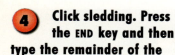
4 **Click sledding. Press the END key and then type the remainder of the sentence:** snowboarding, ice skating, and ice fishing.

Word replaces the misspelled word with the selected word on the shortcut menu (Figure 1-26). Word replaces the red X with a check mark on the Spelling and Grammar Status icon.

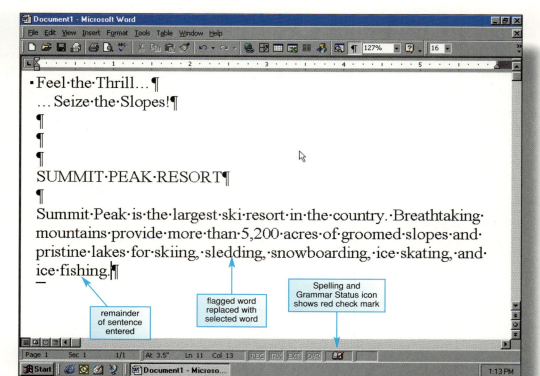

FIGURE 1-26

If the word actually is spelled correctly and, for example, is a proper name, you can right-click it and then click Ignore All on the shortcut menu (Figure 1-25 on the previous page). If, when you right-click the misspelled word, your desired correction is not in the list on the shortcut menu, you can click outside the shortcut menu to make the menu disappear and then retype the correct word, or you can click Spelling on the shortcut menu to display the Spelling dialog box. The Spelling dialog box is discussed in Project 2.

If you feel the wavy underlines clutter your document window, you can hide them temporarily until you are ready to check for spelling errors. To hide spelling errors, right-click the Spelling and Grammar Status icon on the status bar and then click Hide Spelling Errors on the shortcut menu. To hide grammar errors, right-click the Spelling and Grammar Status icon on the status bar and then click Hide Grammatical Errors on the shortcut menu.

Entering Text that Scrolls the Document Window

As you type more lines of text than Word can display in the document window, Word **scrolls** the top portion of the document upward off the screen. Although you cannot see the text once it scrolls off the screen, it remains in the document. You have learned that the document window allows you to view only a portion of your document at one time (Figure 1-5 on page WD 1.10).

Perform the following step to enter text that scrolls the document window.

More About

Scrolling

Computer users frequently switch between the keyboard and the mouse during a word processing session, which places strain on the wrist. To help prevent wrist injury, minimize switching. If your fingers are already on the keyboard, use keyboard keys to scroll; if your hand is already on the mouse, use the mouse to scroll.

Steps: To Enter Text that Scrolls the Document Window

1 **Press the ENTER key twice. Type** Summit Peak offers a range of vacation packages for every taste and budget, from traditional ski lodges to luxurious condominiums. Add transportation, meals, lift tickets, gear, and lessons for an exceptional value. **Press the ENTER key twice. Type** Call (970) 555-SNOW for reservations.

Word scrolls the headline off the top of the screen (Figure 1-27). Your screen may scroll differently depending on the type of monitor you are using.

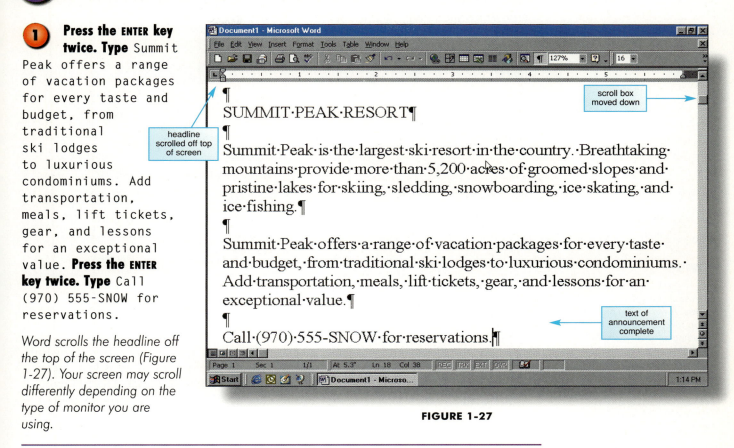

FIGURE 1-27

When Word scrolls text off the top of the screen, the scroll box on the scroll bar at the right edge of the document window moves downward (Figure 1-27). The **scroll box** indicates the current relative location of the insertion point in the document. You may use either the mouse or the keyboard to move the insertion point to a different location in a document.

With the mouse, you use the scroll arrows or the scroll box to display a different portion of the document in the document window, and then click the mouse to move the insertion point to that location. Table 1-1 explains various techniques for vertically scrolling with the mouse.

More About

Microsoft IntelliMouse®

For more information on the scrolling with the Microsoft IntelliMouse, visit the Word 2000 More About Web page (www.scsite.com/wd2000/more.htm) and then click Microsoft IntelliMouse.

Table 1-1 Techniques for Scrolling with the Mouse	
SCROLL DIRECTION	**MOUSE ACTION**
Up	Drag the scroll box upward.
Down	Drag the scroll box downward.
Up one screen	Click anywhere above the scroll box on the vertical scroll bar.
Down one screen	Click anywhere below the scroll box on the vertical scroll bar.
Up one line	Click the scroll arrow at the top of the vertical scroll bar.
Down one line	Click the scroll arrow at the bottom of the vertical scroll bar.

When you use the keyboard to scroll, the insertion point moves automatically when you press the appropriate keys. Table 1-2 outlines various techniques to scroll through a document using the keyboard.

Table 1-2	Techniques for Scrolling with the Keyboard		
SCROLL DIRECTION	**KEY(S) TO PRESS**	**SCROLL DIRECTION**	**KEY(S) TO PRESS**
Left one character	LEFT ARROW	Down one paragraph	CTRL+DOWN ARROW
Right one character	RIGHT ARROW	Up one screen	PAGE UP
Left one word	CTRL+LEFT ARROW	Down one screen	PAGE DOWN
Right one word	CTRL+RIGHT ARROW	To top of document window	ALT+CTRL+PAGE UP
Up one line	UP ARROW	To bottom of document window	ALT+CTRL+PAGE DOWN
Down one line	DOWN ARROW	Previous page	CTRL+PAGE UP
To end of a line	END	Next page	CTRL+PAGE DOWN
To beginning of a line	HOME	To the beginning of a document	CTRL+HOME
Up one paragraph	CTRL+UP ARROW	To the end of a document	CTRL+END

 More About

Saving

When you save a document, you use meaningful file names. A file name can be up to 255 characters, including spaces. The only invalid characters are back-slash (\), slash (/), colon (:), asterisk (*), question mark (?), quotation mark ("), less than symbol (<), greater than symbol (>), and vertical bar (|).

Saving a Document

As you create a document in Word, the computer stores it in memory. If you turn off the computer or if you lose electrical power, the document in memory is lost. Hence, it is mandatory to save on disk any document that you will use later. The following steps illustrate how to save a document on a floppy disk inserted in drive A using the Save button on the Standard toolbar.

Steps **To Save a New Document**

1 **Insert a formatted floppy disk into drive A. Click the Save button on the Standard toolbar.**

Word displays the Save As dialog box (Figure 1-28). The first line from the document displays high-lighted in File name text box as the default file name. With this file name selected, you can change it by immediately typing the new name.

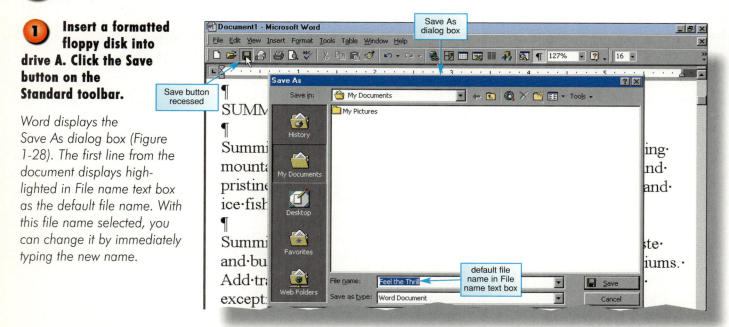

FIGURE 1-28

2 **Type** Summit Peak
Announcement **in
the File name text box. Do
not press the ENTER key
after typing the file name.**

*The file name, Summit Peak
Announcement, displays in
the File name text box (Figure
1-29). Notice that the current
save location is the My
Documents folder. A* **folder**
*is a specific location on a
disk. To change to a different
save location, you use the
Save in box.*

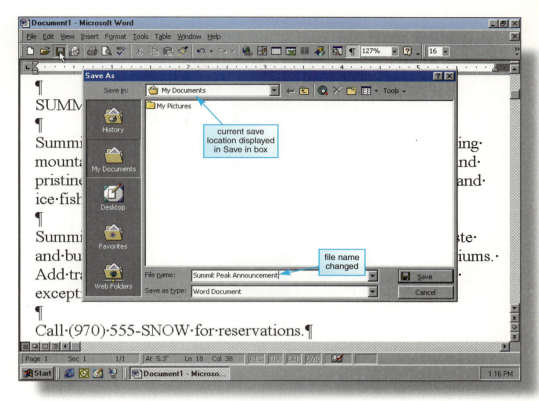

FIGURE 1-29

3 **Click the Save in
box arrow and then
point to 3½ Floppy (A:).**

*A list of the available save
locations displays (Figure
1-30). Your list may differ
depending on your system
configuration.*

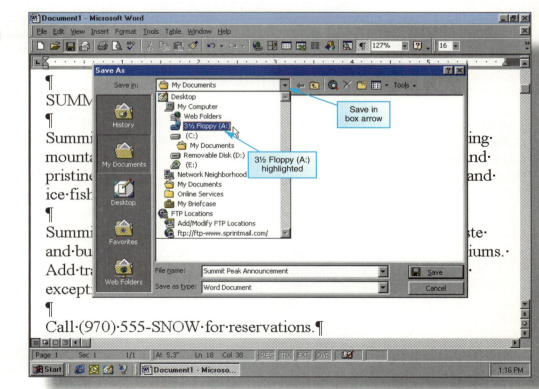

FIGURE 1-30

4 **Click 3½ Floppy (A:) and then point to the Save button in the Save As dialog box.**

The 3½ Floppy (A:) drive becomes the save location (Figure 1-31). The names of existing files stored on the floppy disk in drive A display. In Figure 1-31, no Word files currently are stored on the floppy disk in drive A.

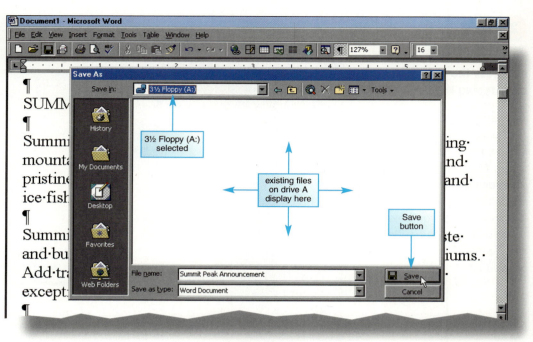

FIGURE 1-31

5 **Click the Save button in the Save As dialog box.**

Word saves the document on the floppy disk in drive A with the file name Summit Peak Announcement (Figure 1-32). Although the announcement is saved on a floppy disk, it also remains in main memory and displays on the screen.

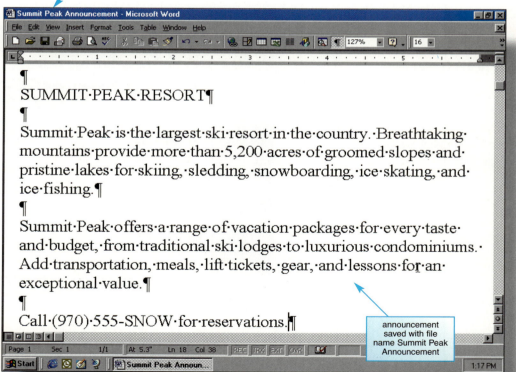

FIGURE 1-32

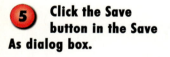

1. On File menu click Save, type file name, select location in Save in box, click Save button in dialog box
2. Press CTRL+S, type file name, select location in Save in box, click Save button in dialog box

Formatting Paragraphs and Characters in a Document

The text for Project 1 now is complete. The next step is to format the characters and paragraphs in the announcement. Paragraphs encompass the text up to and including a paragraph mark (¶). **Paragraph formatting** is the process of changing the appearance of a paragraph. For example, you can center or indent a paragraph.

Characters include letters, numbers, punctuation marks, and symbols. **Character formatting** is the process of changing the way characters appear on the screen and in print. You use character formatting to emphasize certain words and improve readability of a document.

With Word, you can format before you type or apply new formats after you type. Earlier, you changed the font size before you typed any text, and then you entered the text. In this section, you format existing text.

Figure 1-33a shows the announcement before formatting the paragraphs and characters. Figure 1-33b shows the announcement after formatting. As you can see from the two figures, a document that is formatted not only is easier to read, but it looks more professional.

More About 2000

Formatting

Character formatting includes changing the font, font style, font size; adding an underline, color, strikethrough, shadow, outline; embossing; engraving; making a superscript or subscript; and changing the case of the letters. Paragraph formatting includes alignment; indentation; and spacing above, below, and in between lines.

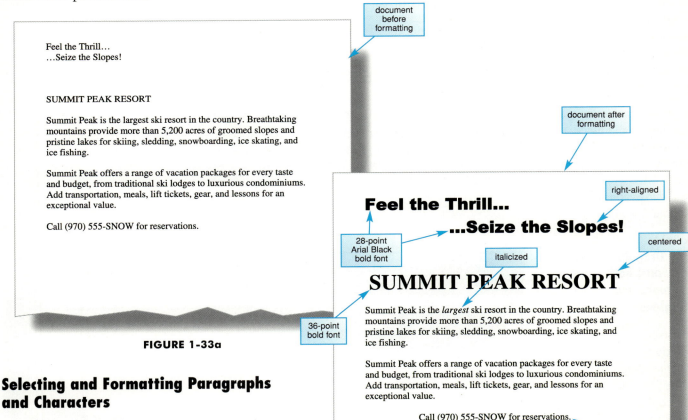

FIGURE 1-33a

FIGURE 1-33b

Selecting and Formatting Paragraphs and Characters

To format a single paragraph, move the insertion point into the paragraph and then format it. To format multiple paragraphs, however, you must first select the paragraphs you want to format and then format them. In the same manner, to format characters, a word, or words, you first must select the characters, word, or words to be formatted and then format your selection.

Selected text is highlighted. That is, if your screen normally displays dark letters on a light background, then selected text displays light letters on a dark background.

Selecting Multiple Paragraphs

The first formatting step in this project is to change the font of the characters in the headline. The headline consists of two separate lines, each ending with a paragraph mark. You have learned that each time you press the ENTER key, Word creates a new paragraph. Thus, the headline actually is two separate paragraphs.

To change the font of the characters in the headline, you must first **select**, or highlight, both paragraphs in the headline as shown in the following steps.

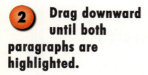

To Select Multiple Paragraphs

1 **Press CTRL + HOME; that is, press and hold the CTRL key, then press the HOME key, and then release both keys. Move the mouse pointer to the left of the first paragraph to be selected until the mouse pointer changes to a right-pointing block arrow.**

The mouse pointer changes to a right-pointing block arrow when positioned to the left of a paragraph (Figure 1-34). CTRL + HOME positions the insertion point at the top of the document.

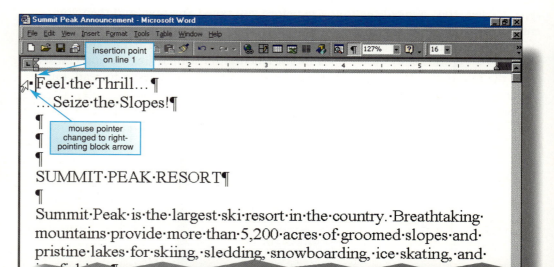

FIGURE 1-34

2 **Drag downward until both paragraphs are highlighted.**

Word selects both of the paragraphs (Figure 1-35). Recall that dragging is the process of holding down the mouse button while moving the mouse and finally releasing the mouse button.

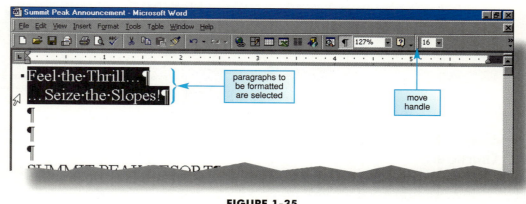

FIGURE 1-35

Other Ways

1. With insertion point at beginning of first paragraph, press CTRL+SHIFT+DOWN ARROW repeatedly

Changing the Font of Selected Text

You have learned that the default font is Times New Roman. Word, however, provides many other fonts to add variety to your documents. Thus, change the font of the headline in the announcement to Arial Black as shown in these steps.

To Change the Font of Selected Text

1 **Double-click the move handle on the Formatting toolbar to display the entire toolbar. While the text is selected, click the Font box arrow on the Formatting toolbar, scroll through the list until Arial Black displays, and then point to Arial Black.**

Word displays a list of available fonts (Figure 1-36). Your list of available fonts may differ, depending on the type of printer you are using.

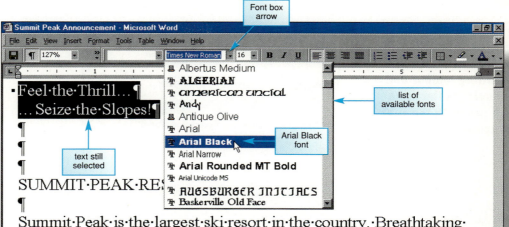

FIGURE 1-36

2 **Click Arial Black.**

Word changes the font of the selected text to Arial Black (Figure 1-37).

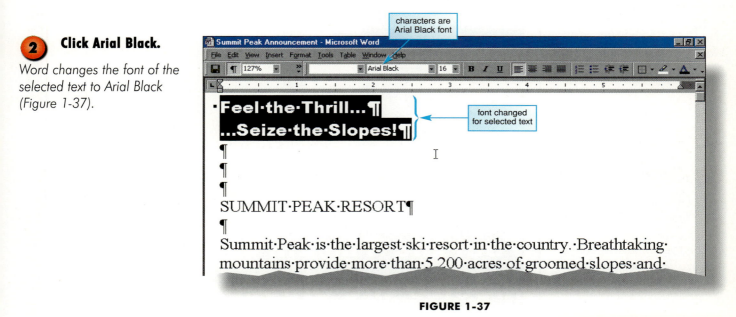

FIGURE 1-37

Changing the Font Size of Selected Text

The next step is to increase the font size of the characters in the selected headline. Recall that the font size specifies the size of the characters. Earlier in this project, you changed the font size for characters in the entire announcement to 16. To give the headline more impact, it has a font size larger than the body copy. Follow the steps on the next page to increase the font size of the headline from 16 to 28 points.

 Other Ways

1. Right-click selected text, click Font on shortcut menu, click Font tab, select desired font in Font list, click OK button

2. On Format menu click Font, click Font tab, select desired font in Font list, click OK button

3. Press CTRL+SHIFT+F, press DOWN ARROW key until desired font displays, press ENTER

To Change the Font Size of Selected Text

1 **While the text is selected, click the Font Size box arrow on the Formatting toolbar and then point to the down scroll arrow on the Font Size scroll bar.**

Word displays a list of the available font sizes (Figure 1-38). Available font sizes vary depending on the font and printer driver.

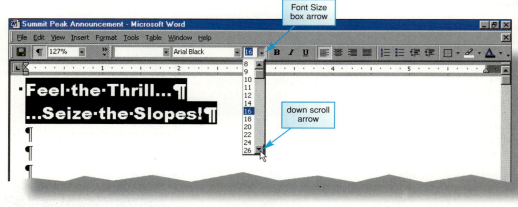

FIGURE 1-38

2 **Click the down scroll arrow on the scroll bar until 28 displays in the list and then point to 28.**

Word highlights 28 in the list (Figure 1-39).

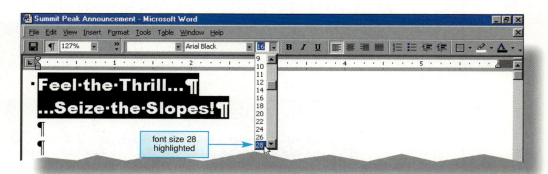

FIGURE 1-39

3 **Click 28.**

Word increases the font size of the headline from 16 to 28 (Figure 1-40). The Font Size box on the Formatting toolbar displays 28, indicating the selected text has a font size of 28.

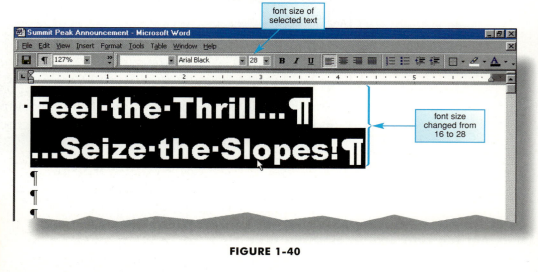

FIGURE 1-40

1. Right-click selected text, click Font on shortcut menu, click Font tab, select desired point size in Size list, click OK button

2. On Format menu click Font, click Font tab, select desired point size in Size list, click OK button

3. Press CTRL+SHIFT+P, type desired point size, press ENTER

Bold Selected Text

Bold characters display somewhat thicker than those that are not bold. To further emphasize the headline of the announcement, perform the following step to bold its characters.

Steps To Bold Selected Text

1 **While the text is selected, click the Bold button on the Formatting toolbar.**

Word formats the headline in bold (Figure 1-41). The Bold button is recessed.

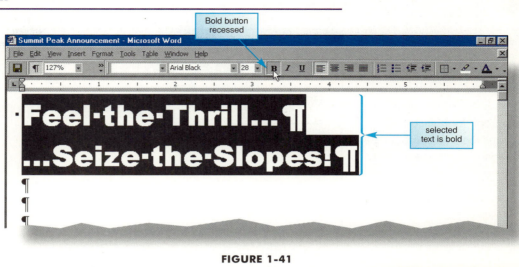

FIGURE 1-41

When the selected text is bold, the Bold button on the Formatting toolbar is recessed. If, for some reason, you wanted to remove the bold format of the selected text, you would click the Bold button a second time.

Right-Align a Paragraph

The default alignment for paragraphs is **left-aligned**; that is, flush at the left edge of the document with uneven right edges. In Figure 1-42, the Align Left button is recessed to indicate the current paragraph is left-aligned.

The second line of the headline, however, is to be **right-aligned**; that is, flush at the right edge of the document with uneven left edges. Recall that the second line of the headline is a paragraph and that paragraph formatting does not require you to select the paragraph prior to formatting. Just position the insertion point in the paragraph to be formatted and then format it accordingly.

Perform the following steps to right-align the second line of the headline.

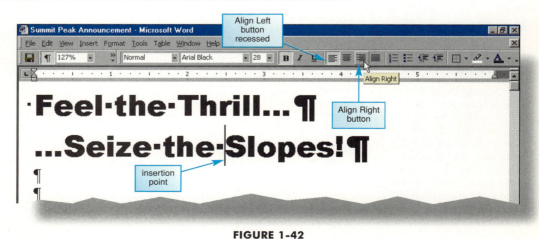

Other Ways

1. Right-click selected text, click Font on shortcut menu, click Font tab, click Bold in Font style list, click OK button
2. On Format menu click Font, click Font tab, click Bold in Font style list, click OK button
3. Press CTRL+B

Steps To Right-Align a Paragraph

1 **Click somewhere in the paragraph to be right-aligned. Point to the Align Right button on the Formatting toolbar.**

Word positions the insertion point at the location you clicked (Figure 1-42).

FIGURE 1-42

2 Click the Align Right button.

The second line of the headline is right-aligned (Figure 1-43). Notice that you did not have to select the paragraph before right-aligning it; paragraph formatting only requires the insertion point be positioned somewhere in the paragraph.

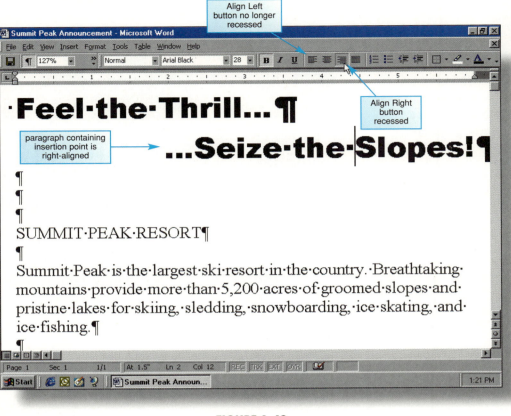

FIGURE 1-43

Other Ways

1. Right-click paragraph, click Paragraph on shortcut menu, click Indents and Spacing tab, click Alignment box arrow, click Right, click OK button
2. With insertion point in desired paragraph, on Format menu click Paragraph, click Indents and Spacing tab, click Alignment box arrow, click Right, click OK button
3. Press CTRL+R

When a paragraph is right-aligned, the Align Right button on the Formatting toolbar is recessed. If, for some reason, you wanted to return the selected paragraphs to left-aligned, you would click the Align Left button on the Formatting toolbar.

Center a Paragraph

The body title currently is left-aligned. Perform the following step to **center** it, that is, position the body title horizontally between the left and right margins on the page.

More About

Centering

The Center button on the Formatting toolbar centers text horizontally. You also can center text vertically between the top and bottom margins. To do this, click File on the menu bar, click Page Setup, click the Layout tab, click the Vertical alignment box arrow, click Center in the list, and then click the OK button.

Steps **To Center a Paragraph**

1 **Click somewhere in the paragraph to be centered. Click the Center button on the Formatting toolbar.**

Word centers the body title between the left and right margins (Figure 1-44). The Center button on the Formatting toolbar is recessed, which indicates the paragraph containing the insertion point is centered.

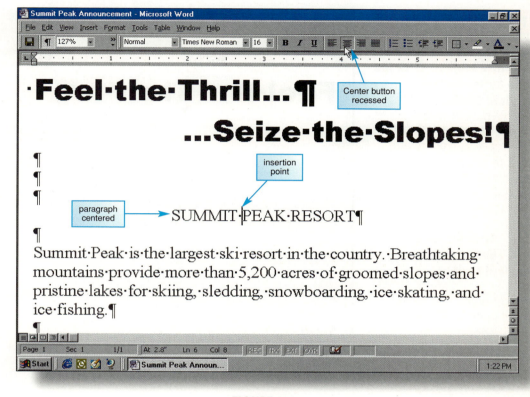

FIGURE 1-44

When a paragraph is centered, the Center button on the Formatting toolbar is recessed. If, for some reason, you wanted to return the selected paragraphs to left-aligned, you would click the Align Left button on the Formatting toolbar.

Undoing Commands or Actions

Word provides an **Undo button** on the Standard toolbar that you can use to cancel your recent command(s) or action(s). For example, if you format text incorrectly, you can *undo* the format and try it again. If, after you undo an action, you decide you did not want to perform the undo, you can use the **Redo button** to undo the undo. Some actions, such as saving or printing a document, cannot be undone or redone.

Perform the steps on the next page to *uncenter* the body title and then re-center it.

Other Ways

1. Right-click paragraph, click Paragraph on shortcut menu, click Indents and Spacing tab, click Alignment box arrow, click Centered, click OK button

2. On Format menu click Paragraph, click Indents and Spacing tab, click Alignment box arrow, click Centered, click OK button

3. Press CTRL+E

To Undo an Action

1 Double-click the move handle on the Standard toolbar to display the entire toolbar. Click the Undo button on the Standard toolbar.

Word left-aligns the body title (Figure 1-45). Word returns the body title to its formatting prior to you issuing the command to center it.

2 Click the Redo button on the Standard toolbar.

Word re-applies the center format to the body title (see Figure 1-46).

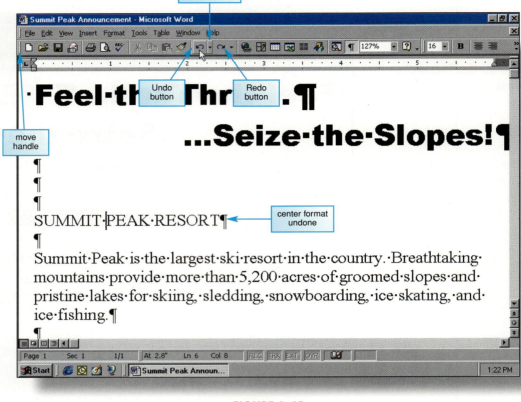

FIGURE 1-45

You also can cancel a series of prior actions by clicking the Undo button arrow (Figure 1-45) to display the undo actions list and then dragging through the actions you wish to be undone.

Whereas undo cancels an action you did not want to perform, Word also provides a **Repeat command**, which duplicates an action you wish to perform again. For example, if you format a paragraph and wish to format another paragraph the exact same way, you could click in the second paragraph to format and then click Repeat on the Edit menu.

Selecting a Line and Formatting It

The next series of steps selects the body title, SUMMIT PEAK RESORT, and formats the characters in it. First, you select the body title. To select the body title, perform the following step.

Steps ### To Select a Line

1 **Move the mouse pointer to the left of the line to be selected (SUMMIT PEAK RESORT) until it changes to a right-pointing block arrow and then click.**

The entire line to the right of the mouse pointer is highlighted (Figure 1-46).

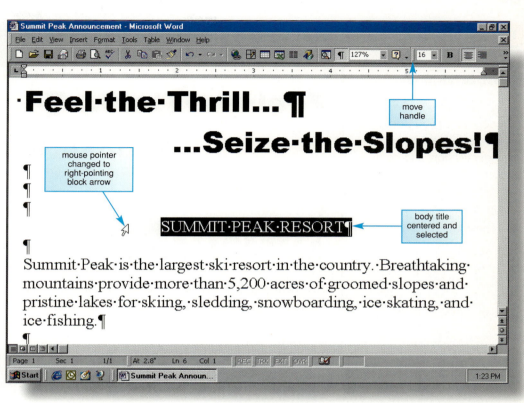

FIGURE 1-46

The next step is to increase the font size of the selected characters to 36 point and bold the selected characters, as explained in the following steps.

TO FORMAT A LINE OF TEXT

1 Double-click the move handle on the Formatting toolbar to display the entire toolbar. While the text is selected, click the Font Size box arrow on the Formatting toolbar and then scroll to 36 in the list. Click 36.

2 Click the Bold button on the Formatting toolbar.

The characters in the body title are enlarged and bold (Figure 1-47 on the next page).

Selecting a Word

To format characters in a word, you must select the entire word first. Follow the steps on the next page to select the word, largest, so you can italicize it.

Other Ways

1. Drag through the line
2. With insertion point at beginning of desired line, press SHIFT+DOWN ARROW

More About

The Formatting Toolbar

Many of the buttons on the Formatting toolbar are toggles; that is, click them once to format the selected text; and click them again to remove the format from the selected text. For example, clicking the Bold button bolds selected text; clicking the Bold button again removes the bold.

To Select a Word

1 **Position the mouse pointer somewhere in the word to be formatted (largest, in this case).**

The mouse pointer's shape is an I-beam when you position it in unselected text in the document window (Figure 1-47).

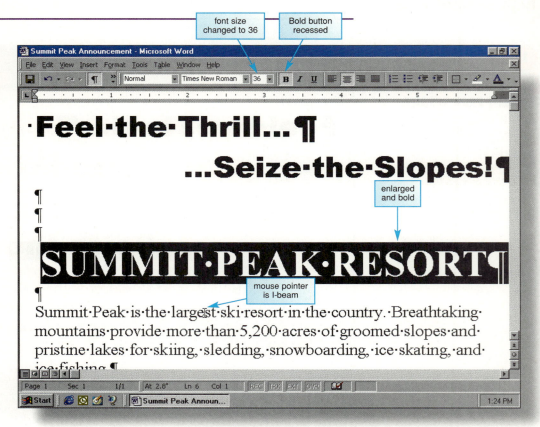

FIGURE 1-47

2 **Double-click the word to be selected.**

The word, largest, is high-lighted (Figure 1-48). Notice that when the mouse pointer is positioned in a selected word, its shape is a left-pointing block arrow.

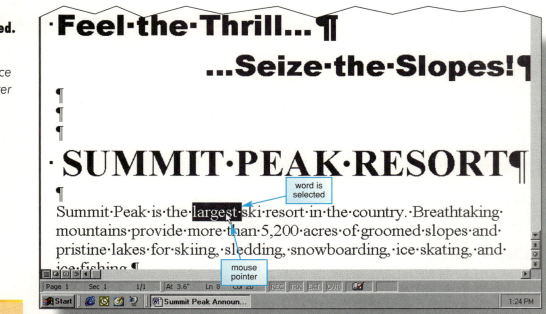

FIGURE 1-48

1. Drag through the word
2. With insertion point at beginning of desired word, press CTRL+SHIFT+RIGHT ARROW

Italicize Selected Text

To italicize the word, largest, perform the following step.

Steps **To Italicize Selected Text**

1 **With the text still selected, click the Italic button on the Formatting toolbar.**

Word italicizes the text (Figure 1-49). The Italic button on the Formatting toolbar is recessed.

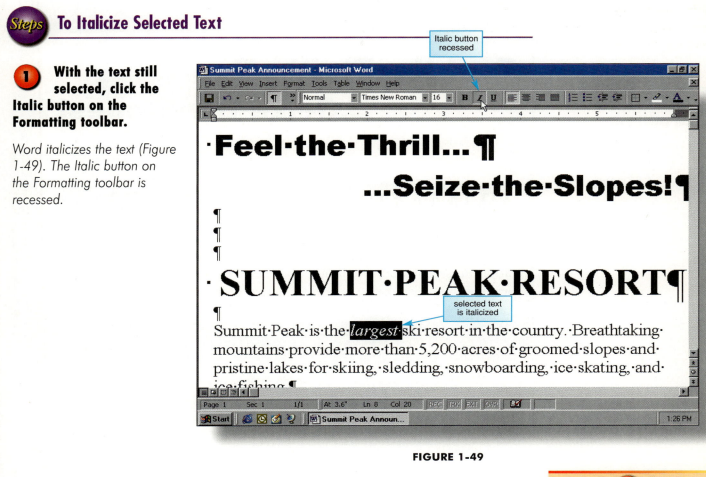

Italic button recessed

selected text is italicized

FIGURE 1-49

When the selected text is italicized, the Italic button on the Formatting toolbar is recessed. If, for some reason, you wanted to remove the italics from the selected text, you would click the Italic button a second time, or you immediately could click the Undo button on the Standard toolbar.

Scrolling

Continue formatting the document by scrolling down one screen so the bottom portion of the announcement displays in the document window. Perform the steps on the next page to display the lower portion of the document.

Other Ways

1. Right-click selected text, click Font on shortcut menu, click Font tab, click Italic in Font style list, click OK button
2. On Format menu click Font, click Font tab, click Italic in Font style list, click OK button
3. Press CTRL+I

 To Scroll Through the Document

1 Position the mouse pointer below the scroll box on the vertical scroll bar (Figure 1-50).

2 Click below the scroll box on the vertical scroll bar.

Word scrolls down one screenful in the document (see Figure 1-51). Depending on your monitor type, your screen may scroll differently.

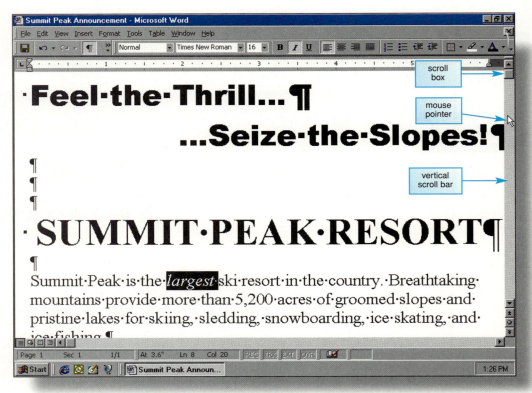

FIGURE 1-50

Other Ways

1. Drag scroll box on vertical scroll bar
2. Click scroll arrows on vertical scroll bar
3. Press PAGE DOWN or PAGE UP
4. See Tables 1-1 and 1-2 on pages WD 1.25 and WD 1.26

The next step is to center the last line of the announcement as described in the following steps.

TO CENTER A PARAGRAPH

1 Click somewhere in the paragraph to be centered.

2 Click the Center button on the Formatting toolbar.

Word centers the last line of the announcement (see Figure 1-51).

Selecting a Group of Words

The next step is to underline the telephone number in the last line of the announcement. Because the telephone number contains spaces and other punctuation, Word considers it a group of words. Thus, the telephone number is a group of words. Select the telephone number by performing the following steps.

Steps: To Select a Group of Words

1 **Position the mouse pointer immediately to the left of the first character of the text to be selected.**

The mouse pointer, an I-beam, is to the left of the parenthesis in the telephone number (Figure 1-51).

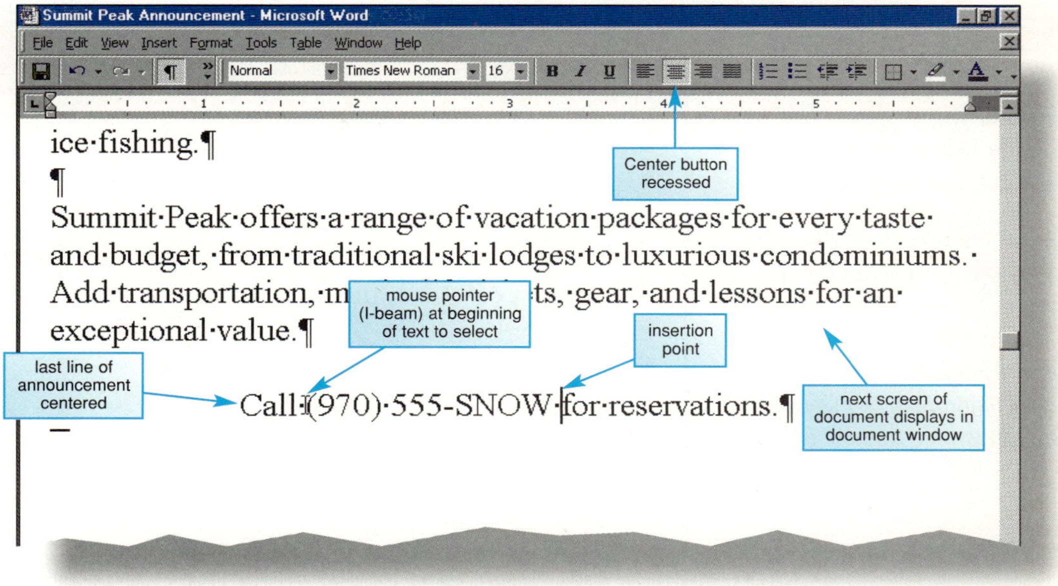

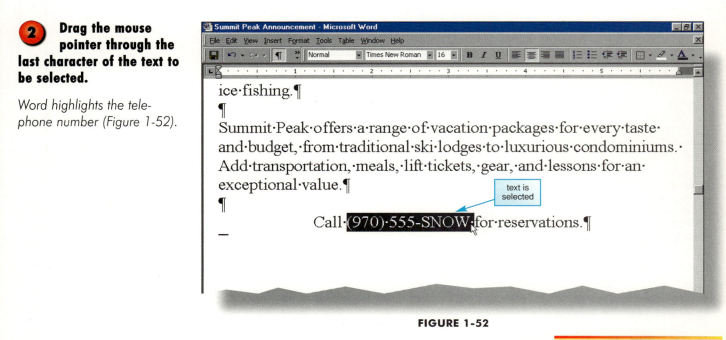

FIGURE 1-51

2 **Drag the mouse pointer through the last character of the text to be selected.**

Word highlights the telephone number (Figure 1-52).

FIGURE 1-52

Underlining Selected Text

Underlined text prints with an underscore (_) below each character. Like bold, it used to emphasize or draw attention to specific text. Follow the step on the next page to underline the selected telephone number.

Other Ways

1. With insertion point at beginning of first word in the group, press CTRL+SHIFT+RIGHT ARROW until words are selected

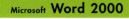

Steps To Underline Selected Text

1 With the text still selected, click the Underline button on the Formatting toolbar. Click inside the selected text to remove the highlight.

Word underlines the text and positions the insertion point inside the underlined text (Figure 1-53). When the insertion point is inside the underlined text, the Underline button is recessed.

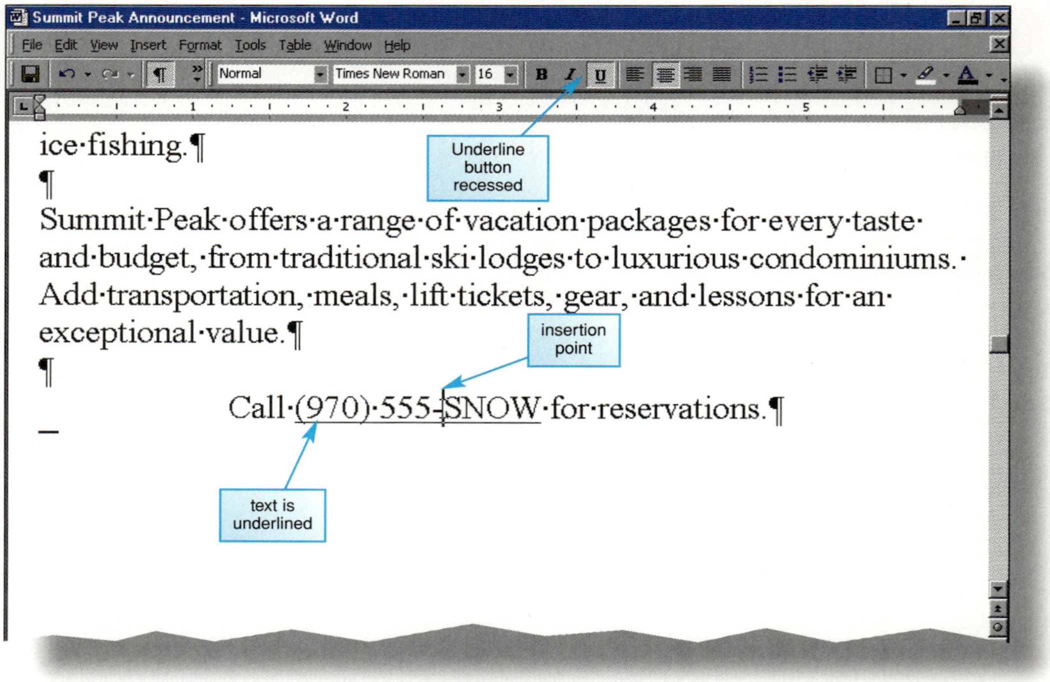

FIGURE 1-53

Other Ways

1. Right-click selected text, click Font on shortcut menu, click Font tab, click Underline style box arrow, click desired underline style, click OK button
2. On Format menu click Font, click Font tab, click Underline style box arrow, click desired underline style, click OK button
3. Press CTRL+U

To remove a highlight, click the mouse. If you click inside the highlight, the Formatting toolbar displays the formatting characteristics of the characters and paragraphs containing the insertion point.

When the selected text is underlined, the Underline button on the Formatting toolbar is recessed. If, for some reason, you wanted to remove the underline from the selected text, you would click the Underline button a second time, or you immediately could click the Undo button on the Standard toolbar.

In addition to the basic underline shown in Figure 1-53, Word has many decorative underlines that are available in the Font dialog box. For example, you can use double underlines, dotted underlines, and wavy underlines. You also can change the color of an underline and instruct Word to underline only the words and not the spaces between the words.

The formatting for the announcement is now complete. The next step is to insert a graphical image into the document and then resize the image.

More About 2000

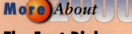

The Font Dialog Box

If a character formatting operation is not available on the Formatting toolbar, use the Font dialog box to perform the operation. To display the Font dialog box, click Format on the menu bar and then click Font.

Inserting Clip Art into a Word Document

Files containing graphical images, also called **graphics**, are available from a variety of sources. Word 2000 includes a series of predefined graphics called **clip art** that you can insert into a Word document. Clip art is located in the **Clip Gallery**, which contains a collection of **clips**, including clip art, as well as photographs, sounds, and video clips. The Clip Gallery contains its own Help system to assist you in locating clips suited to your application.

Inserting Clip Art

The next step in the project is to insert a graphic of a skier into the announcement. Perform the following steps to insert a graphic into the document.

Steps: To Insert Clip Art into a Document

1 **To position the insertion point where you want the clip art to be located, press CTRL+HOME and then press the DOWN ARROW key three times. Click Insert on the menu bar.**

The insertion point is positioned on the second paragraph mark below the headline, and the Insert menu displays (Figure 1-54). Remember that a short menu initially displays, which expands into a full menu after a few seconds.

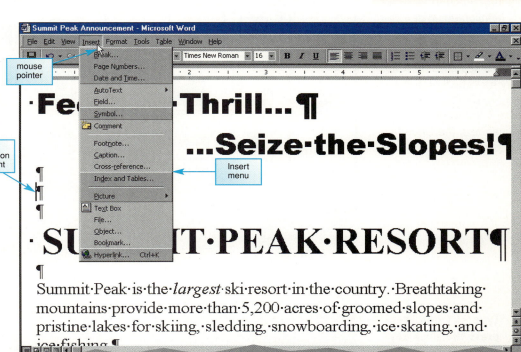

FIGURE 1-54

2 **Point to Picture and then point to Clip Art.**

The Picture submenu displays (Figure 1-55). You have learned that when you point to a command that has a small arrow to its right, Word displays a submenu associated with that command.

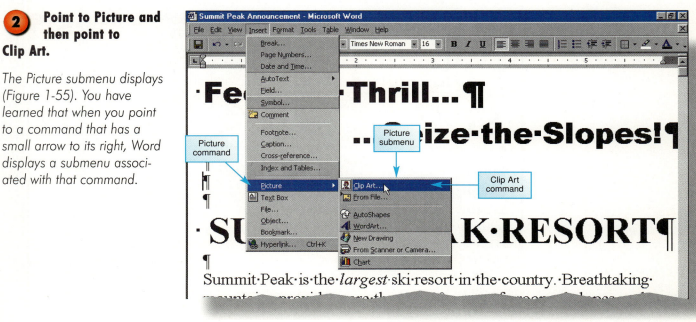

FIGURE 1-55

Microsoft **Word 2000**

3 Click Clip Art. When the Insert ClipArt window opens, click the Search for clips text box.

Word opens the Insert ClipArt window (Figure 1-56). The text in the Search for clips text box is highlighted. When you enter a description of the desired graphic in this text box, Word searches the Clip Gallery for clips that match the description.

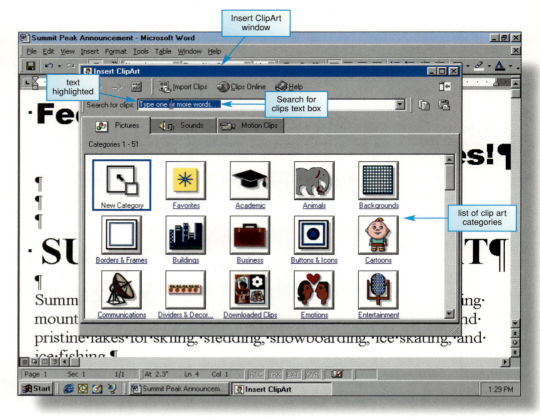

FIGURE 1-56

4 Type ski and then press the ENTER key.

A list of clips that match the description, ski, displays (Figure 1-57).

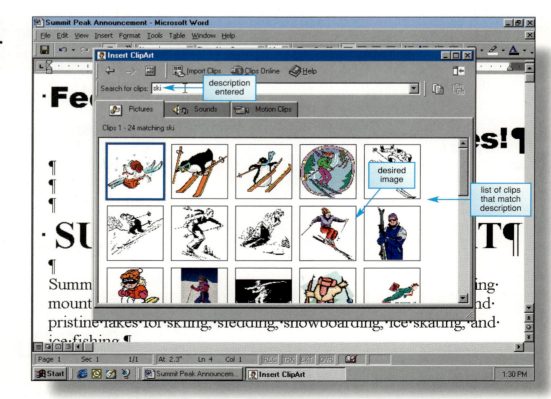

FIGURE 1-57

5 **Click the desired image and then point to the Insert clip button on the Pop-up menu.**

Word displays a Pop-up menu (Figure 1-58). The Pop-up menu contains four buttons: (1) Insert clip, (2) Preview clip, (3) Add clip to Favorites or other category, and (4) Find similar clips.

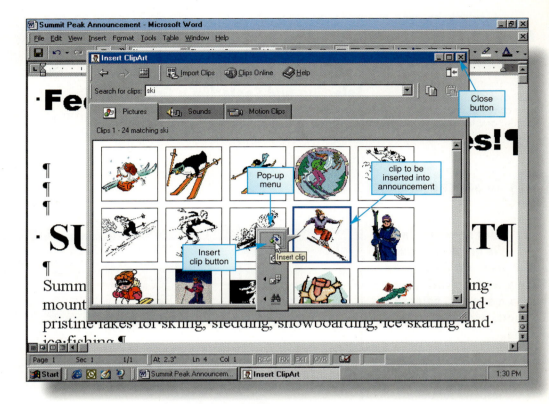

FIGURE 1-58

6 **Click the Insert clip button. Click the Close button at the right edge of the Insert ClipArt window's title bar. Press the UP ARROW key twice to display part of the headline.**

Word inserts the clip into the document at the location of the insertion point (Figure 1-59). The graphic of the skier displays below the headline in the announcement.

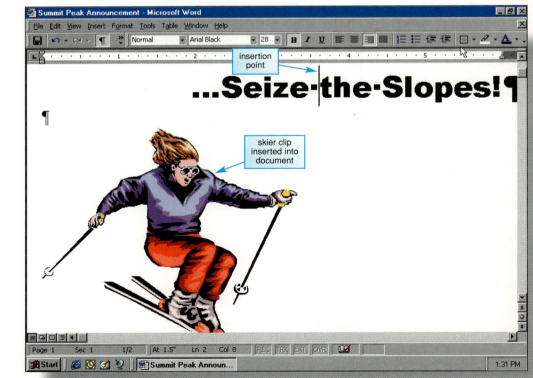

FIGURE 1-59

Obtaining Graphics

If you have a scanner or digital camera attached to your computer, Word can insert a graphic directly from these devices.

The clip art in the document is part of a paragraph. Because that paragraph is left-aligned, the clip art also is left-aligned. You can, however, use any of the paragraph alignment buttons on the Formatting toolbar to reposition the clip art.

Selecting and Centering a Graphic

To center a graphic, you first must select it. Perform the following steps to select and then center the graphic.

To Select a Graphic

1 **Click anywhere in the graphic. If your screen does not display the Picture toolbar, click View on the menu bar, point to Toolbars, and then click Picture.**

Word selects the graphic (Figure 1-60). A selected graphic displays surrounded by a selection rectangle that has small squares, called sizing handles, at each corner and middle location. You use the sizing handles to change the size of the graphic. When a graphic is selected, the Picture toolbar automatically displays on the screen.

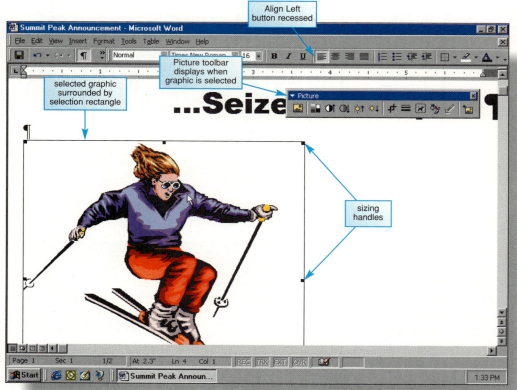

FIGURE 1-60

Graphics

Emphasize a graphic by placing it at the optical center of the page. To determine optical center, divide the page in half horizontally and vertically. The optical center is located one third of the way up the vertical line from the point of intersection of the two lines.

If the Picture toolbar covers the Standard and Formatting toolbars you can drag the title bar of the Picture toolbar to move the toolbar to a different location.

TO CENTER A SELECTED GRAPHIC

1 With the graphic still selected, click the Center button on the Formatting toolbar.

Word centers the selected graphic between the left and right margins of the document (see Figure 1-61). The Center button is recessed.

When you center the graphic, Word may scroll down so the graphic is positioned at the top of the document window. The graphic is a little too large for this announcement. The next step is to resize the graphic.

Resizing a Graphic

Once you have inserted a graphic into a document, you easily can change its size. **Resizing** includes both enlarging and reducing the size of a graphic. To resize a graphic, you first must select it. The following steps show how to resize the graphic you just inserted and selected.

More About 2000

Resizing Graphics

When you drag the sizing handles to resize a graphic, you might distort its proportions. To maintain the proportions of the graphic, press the SHIFT key while you drag a corner sizing handle.

Steps To Resize a Graphic

1 With the graphic still selected, point to the upper-left corner sizing handle.

The mouse pointer changes to a two-headed arrow when it is on a sizing handle (Figure 1-61). To resize a graphic, you drag the sizing handles until the graphic is the desired size.

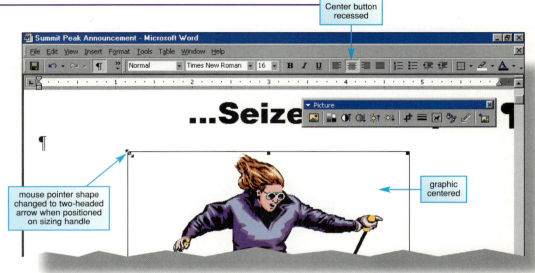

FIGURE 1-61

2 Drag the sizing handle diagonally toward the center of the graphic until the dotted selection rectangle is positioned approximately as shown in Figure 1-62.

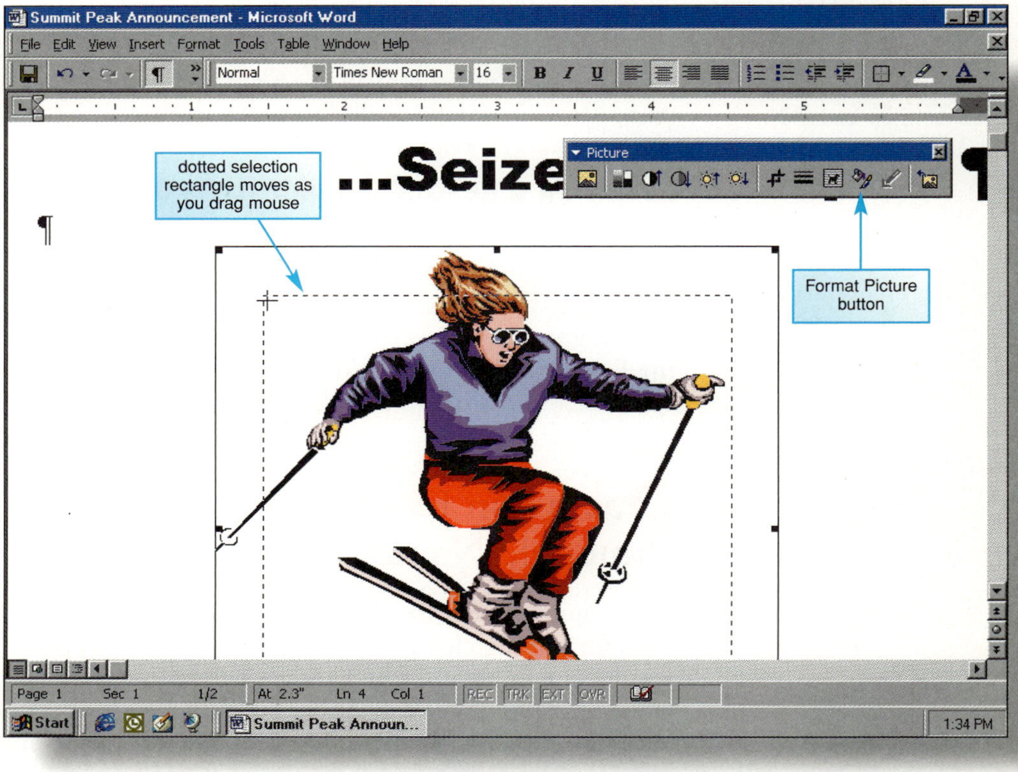

FIGURE 1-62

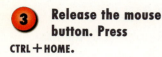

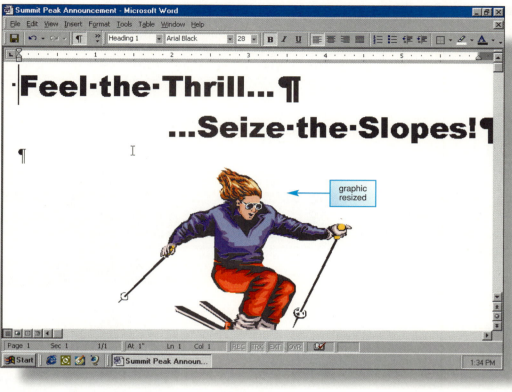

3 Release the mouse button. Press CTRL+HOME.

Word resizes the graphic (Figure 1-63). When you click outside of a graphic or press a key to scroll through a document, Word deselects the graphic. The Picture toolbar disappears from the screen when you deselect the graphic.

FIGURE 1-63

Instead of resizing a selected graphic with the mouse, you also can use the Format Picture dialog box to resize a graphic by clicking the Format Picture button (Figure 1-62 on the previous page) on the Picture toolbar and then clicking the Size tab. Using the Size sheet, you enter exact height and width measurements. If you have a precise measurement for a graphic, use the Format Picture dialog box; otherwise, drag the sizing handles to resize a graphic.

Restoring a Resized Graphic to Its Original Size

Sometimes you might resize a graphic and realize it is the wrong size. In these cases, you may want to return the graphic to its original size and start again. You could drag the sizing handle until the graphic resembles its original size. To restore a resized graphic to its exact original size, click the graphic to select it and then click the Format Picture button on the Picture toolbar to display the Format Picture dialog box. Click the Size tab and then click the Reset button. Finally, click the OK button.

Saving an Existing Document with the Same File Name

The announcement for Project 1 now is complete. To transfer the modified document with formatting changes and graphic to your floppy disk in drive A, you must save the document again. When you saved the document the first time, you assigned a file name to it (Summit Peak Announcement). If you use the following procedure, Word automatically assigns the same file name to the document each time you subsequently save it.

Steps To Save an Existing Document with the Same File Name

1 **Double-click the move handle on the Standard toolbar to display the entire toolbar. Click the Save button on the Standard toolbar.**

Word saves the document on a floppy disk inserted in drive A using the currently assigned file name, Summit Peak Announcement (Figure 1-64).

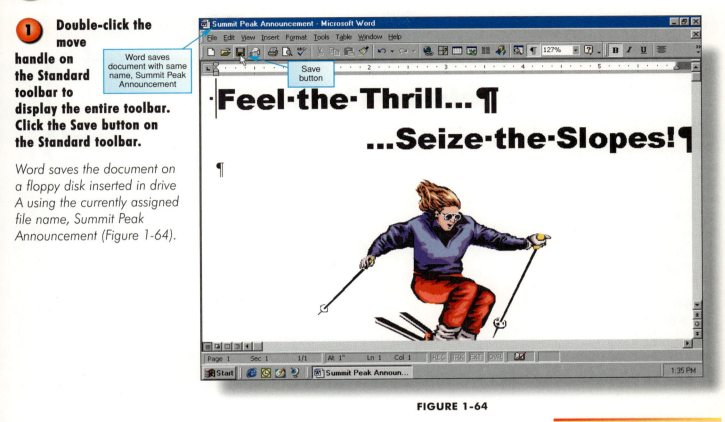

Word saves document with same name, Summit Peak Announcement

Save button

FIGURE 1-64

While Word is saving the document, the Background Save Status icon displays at the right edge of the status bar. When the save is complete, the document remains in memory and on the screen.

If, for some reason, you want to save an existing document with a different file name, click Save As on the File menu to display the Save As dialog box. Then, fill in the Save As dialog box as discussed in Steps 2 through 5 on pages WD 1.27 and WD 1.28.

Printing a Document

The next step is to print the document you created. A printed version of the document is called a **hard copy** or **printout**. Perform the steps on the next page to print the announcement created in Project 1.

Other Ways

1. On File menu click Save
2. Press CTRL+S

More About

Save As

In the Save As dialog box, you can create a new Windows folder by clicking the Create New Folder button. You also can delete or rename files by selecting the file and then clicking the Tools button arrow in the Save As dialog box. To display the Save As dialog box, click File on the menu bar and then click Save As.

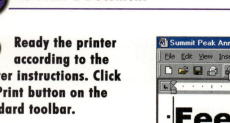

To Print a Document

1 **Ready the printer according to the printer instructions. Click the Print button on the Standard toolbar.**

The mouse pointer briefly changes to an hourglass shape as Word prepares to print the document. While the document is printing, a printer icon displays in the tray status area on the taskbar (Figure 1-65).

2 **When the printer stops, retrieve the printout (see Figure 1-1 on page WD1.7).**

FIGURE 1-65

More About 2000

Print Preview

To view a document before you print it, click the Print Preview button on the Standard toolbar. To return to the document window, click the Close Preview button on the Print Preview toolbar.

When you use the Print button to print a document, Word prints the entire document automatically. You then may distribute the hard copy or keep it as a permanent record of the document.

If you wanted to print multiple copies of the document, click File on the menu bar and then click Print to display the Print dialog box. This dialog box has several printing options, including specifying the number of copies to print.

If you wanted to cancel your job that is printing or one you have waiting to be printed, double-click the printer icon on the taskbar (Figure 1-65). In the printer window, click the job to be canceled and then click Cancel Printing on the Document menu.

Quitting Word

After you create, save, and print the announcement, Project 1 is complete. To quit Word and return control to Windows, perform the following steps.

Steps To Quit Word

1 Point to the Close button in the upper-right corner of the title bar (Figure 1-66).

2 Click the Close button.

The Word window closes.

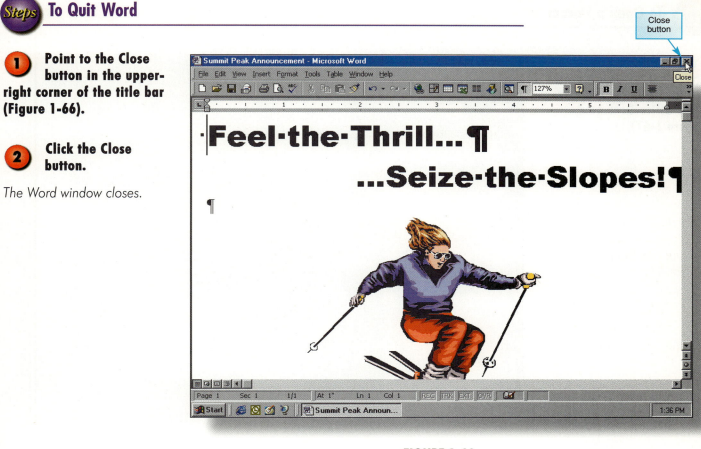

FIGURE 1-66

If you made changes to the document since the last save, Word displays dialog box asking if you want to save the changes. Clicking the Yes button saves the changes; clicking the No button ignores the changes; and clicking the Cancel button returns to the document. If you did not make any changes since you saved the document, this dialog box does not display.

You created and formatted the announcement, inserted clip art into it, printed it, and saved it. You might decide, however, to change the announcement at a later date. To do this, you must start Word and then retrieve your document from the floppy disk in drive A.

Opening a Document

Earlier, you saved the Word document created in Project 1 on a floppy disk using the file name Summit Peak Announcement. Once you have created and saved a document, you often will have reason to retrieve it from the disk. For example, you might want to revise the document or print it. The steps on the next page illustrate how to open the file Summit Peak Announcement.

Other Ways

1. On File menu click Exit
2. Press ALT+F4

More About

Opening Files

In Word, you can open a recently used file by clicking File on the menu bar and then clicking the file name on the File menu. To instruct Word to show the recently used documents on the File menu, click Tools on the menu bar, click Options, click the General tab, click Recently used file list, and then click the OK button.

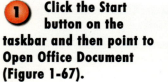 **To Open a Document**

1 **Click the Start button on the taskbar and then point to Open Office Document (Figure 1-67).**

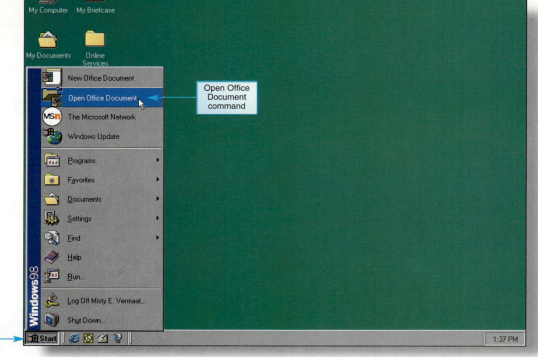

FIGURE 1-67

2 **Click Open Office Document. If necessary, click the Look in box arrow and then click 3½ Floppy (A:). If it is not selected already, click the file name Summit Peak Announcement. Point to the Open button.**

Office displays the Open Office Document dialog box (Figure 1-68). Office displays the files on the floppy disk in drive A.

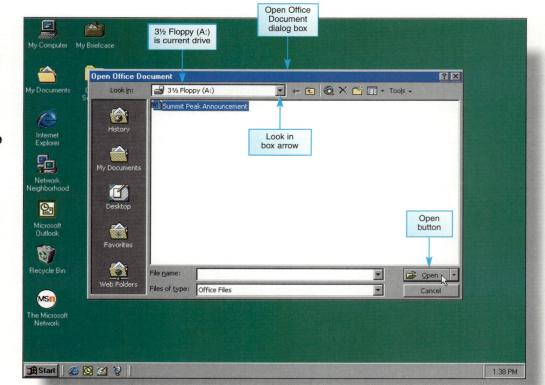

FIGURE 1-68

3 **Click the Open button.**

Office starts Word, and then Word opens the document, Summit Peak Announcement, from the floppy disk in drive A and displays the document on the screen (Figure 1-69).

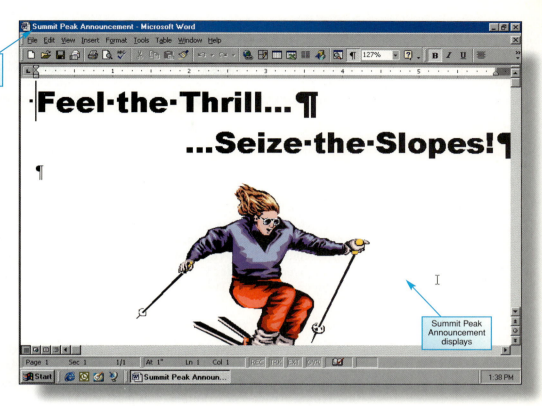

FIGURE 1-69

Correcting Errors

After creating a document, you often will find you must make changes to it. Changes can be required because the document contains an error or because of new circumstances.

Types of Changes Made to Documents

The types of changes made to documents normally fall into one of the three following categories: additions, deletions, or modifications.

ADDITIONS Additional words, sentences, or paragraphs may be required in a document. Additions occur when you omit text from a document and want to insert it later. For example, you may want to insert the word, winter, in front of vacation packages to differentiate winter packages from summer packages.

DELETIONS Sometimes, text in a document is incorrect or is no longer needed. For example, the resort might remove transportation from their package deals. In this case, you would delete the word, transportation, from the list.

MODIFICATIONS If an error is made in a document or changes take place that affect the document, you might have to revise the word(s) in the text. For example, the resort might purchase more land and have 6,500 acres of slopes and lakes; thus, you would change the number from 5,200 to 6,500.

Word provides several methods for correcting errors in a document. For each of the error correction techniques, you first must move the insertion point to the error.

Other Ways

1. In Microsoft Word, click Open button on Standard toolbar, select file name, click Open button in dialog box
2. In Microsoft Word, on File menu click Open, select file name, click Open button in dialog box
3. In Microsoft Word, press CTRL+O, select file name, press ENTER

Inserting Text into an Existing Document

If you leave a word or phrase out of a sentence, you can include it in the sentence by positioning the insertion point where you intend to insert the text. Word is preset to insert the text to the left of the insertion point. The text to the right of the insertion point moves to the right and downward to accommodate the new text.

TO INSERT TEXT INTO AN EXISTING DOCUMENT

 1 Click to left of location to insert new text.

2 Type new text.

In Word, the default typing mode is insert mode. In **insert mode**, as you type a character, Word inserts the character and moves all the characters to the right of the typed character one position to the right. You can change to overtype mode by double-clicking the **OVR status indicator** on the status bar (see Figure 1-4 on page WD 1.9). In **overtype mode**, Word replaces characters to the right of the insertion point. Double-clicking the OVR status indicator a second time returns you to insert mode.

Deleting Text from an Existing Document

It is not unusual to type incorrect characters or words in a document. You have learned that you can click the Undo button on the Standard toolbar to undo a command or action – this includes typing. Word also provides other methods of correcting typing errors. For example, you may want to delete certain letters or words.

TO DELETE AN INCORRECT CHARACTER IN A DOCUMENT

1 Click next to the incorrect character.

2 Press the BACKSPACE key to erase to the left of the insertion point; or press the DELETE key to erase to the right of the insertion point.

TO DELETE AN INCORRECT WORD OR PHRASE IN A DOCUMENT

1 Select the word or phrase you want to erase.

2 Right-click the selected word or phrase, and then click Cut on the shortcut menu; or click the Cut button on the Standard toolbar (Figure 1-7a on page WD 1.13); or press the DELETE key.

Closing the Entire Document

Sometimes, everything goes wrong. If this happens, you may want to close the document entirely and start over. You also may want to close a document when you are finished with it so you can begin your next document.

TO CLOSE THE ENTIRE DOCUMENT AND START OVER

1 Click File on the menu bar and then click Close.

2 If Word displays a dialog box, click the No button to ignore the changes since the last time you saved the document.

3 Click the New Blank Document button (see Figure 1-7a on page WD 1.13) on the Standard toolbar.

You also can close the document by clicking the Close button at the right edge of the menu bar.

Word Help System

At any time while you are using Word, you can get answers to questions by using the **Word Help system**. Used properly, this form of online assistance can increase your productivity and reduce your frustrations by minimizing the time you spend learning how to use Word.

The following section shows how to obtain answers to your questions using the Office Assistant. For additional information on using help, see Appendix A.

Using the Office Assistant

The **Office Assistant** answers your questions and suggests more efficient ways to complete a task. With the Office Assistant active, for example, you can type a question, word, or phrase in a text box and the Office Assistant provides immediate help on the subject. Also, as you create a document, the Office Assistant accumulates tips that suggest more efficient ways to do the tasks you completed while creating a document, such as formatting, printing, and saving. This tip feature is part of the **IntelliSense technology** that is built into Word, which understands what you are trying to do and suggests better ways to do it. When the light bulb displays above the Office Assistant, click it to see a tip.

The following steps show how to use the Office Assistant to obtain information on changing the size of a toolbar.

More *About* **2000**

Help

If you purchased an application program five years ago, you probably received one or more thick technical manuals explaining the software. With Microsoft Word 2000, you receive a small manual. The online Help feature of Microsoft Word 2000 replaces the reams and reams of printed pages in complicated technical manuals.

Steps To Obtain Help Using the Office Assistant

1 If the Office Assistant is not on the screen, click Help on the menu bar and then click Show the Office Assistant. With the Office Assistant on the screen, click it. Type change toolbar size in the What would you like to do? text box. Point to the Search button (Figure 1-70).

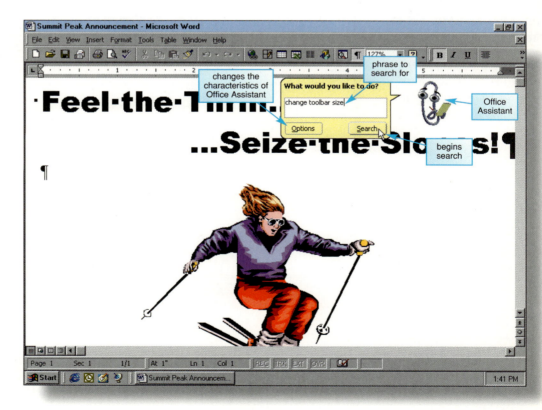

FIGURE 1-70

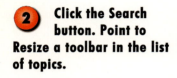

2 Click the Search button. Point to Resize a toolbar in the list of topics.

The Office Assistant displays a list of topics relating to the typed question, change toolbar size (Figure 1-71). The mouse pointer changes to a pointing hand.

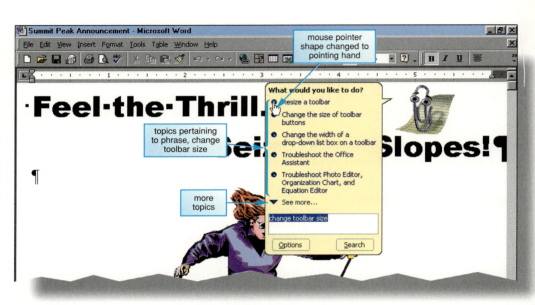

FIGURE 1-71

3 Click Resize a toolbar. When Word opens the Word Help window, click its Maximize button. If necessary, drag the Office Assistant out of the way of the Help text.

The Office Assistant opens a Word Help window that provides Help information on resizing toolbars (Figure 1-72).

4 Click the Close button on the Word Help window title bar.

The Word Help window closes and the Word document window again is active.

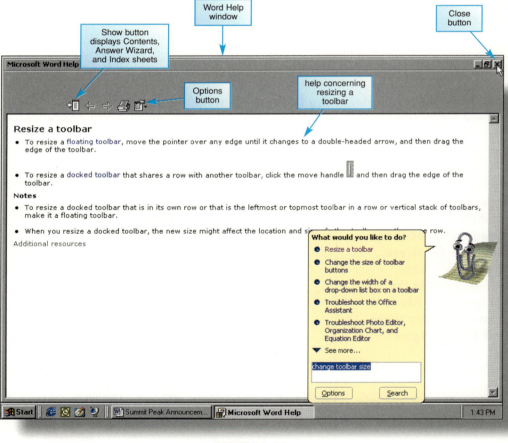

FIGURE 1-72

You can use the Office Assistant to search for Help on any topic concerning Word.

Table 1-3 summarizes the nine categories of help available to you. Because of the way the Word Help system works, please review the right-most column of Table 1-3 if you have difficulties activating the desired category of help.

Table 1-3	Word Help System		
TYPE	**DESCRIPTION**	**HOW TO ACTIVATE**	**TURNING THE OFFICE ASSISTANT ON AND OFF**
Answer Wizard	Similar to the Office Assistant in that it answers questions that you type in your own words.	Click the Microsoft Word Help button on the Standard toolbar. If necessary, maximize the Help window by double-clicking its title bar. Click the Answer Wizard tab.	If the Office Assistant displays, right-click it, click Options, click Use the Office Assistant to remove the check mark, click the OK button.
Contents sheet	Groups Help topics by general categories. Use when you know only the general category of the topic in question. Similar to a table of contents in a book.	Click the Microsoft Word Help button on the Standard toolbar. If necessary, maximize the Help window by double-clicking its title bar. Click the Contents tab.	If the Office Assistant displays, right-click it, click Options, click Use the Office Assistant to remove the check mark, click the OK button.
Detect and Repair	Automatically finds and fixes errors in the application.	Click Detect and Repair on the Help menu.	
Hardware and Software Information	Shows Product ID and allows access to system information and technical support information.	Click About Microsoft Word on the Help menu and then click the appropriate button.	
Index sheet	Similar to an index in a book; use when you know exactly what you want.	Click the Microsoft Word Help button on the Standard toolbar. If necessary, maximize the Help window by double-clicking its title bar. Click the Index tab.	If the Office Assistant displays, right-click it, click Options, click Use the Office Assistant to remove the check mark, click the OK button.
Office Assistant	Answers questions that you type in your own words, offers tips, and provides Help for a variety of Word features.	Click the Microsoft Word Help button on the Standard toolbar or double-click the Office Assistant icon. Some dialog boxes also include the Microsoft Word Help button.	If the Office Assistant does not display, click Show the Office Assistant on the Help menu.
Office on the Web	Used to access technical resources and download free product enhancements on the Web.	Click Office on the Web on the Help menu.	
Question Mark button and What's This? command	Used to identify unfamiliar items on the screen.	In a dialog box, click the Question Mark button and then click an item in the dialog box. Click What's This? on the Help menu, and then click an item on the screen.	
WordPerfect Help	Used to assist WordPerfect users who are learning Microsoft Word.	Click WordPerfect Help on the Help menu.	

The final step in this project is to quit Word.

TO QUIT WORD

1. Click the Close button in the Word window.

The Word window closes.

Quick Reference

For a table that lists how to complete the tasks covered in this book using the mouse, menu, shortcut menu, and keyboard, visit the Shelly Cashman Series Office Web page (www.scsite.com/off2000/qr.htm) and then click Microsoft Word 2000.

CASE PERSPECTIVE SUMMARY

Jackie is thrilled with the completed announcement. The characters in the headline and body title are large enough so students can read them from a distance and the graphic is quite eye-catching. She takes the announcement to the school's Promotions Department and receives approval to post it in several locations around campus, have it printed in the school newspaper, and mailed to each student's home. Members of the SGA assist Jackie with these activities.

Project Summary

Project 1 introduced you to starting Word and creating a document. Before entering any text in the document, you learned how to change the font size. You also learned how to save and print a document. You used Word's check spelling as you type feature. Once you saved the document, you learned how to format its paragraphs and characters. Then, you inserted and resized clip art. You learned how to move the insertion point so you could insert, delete, and modify text. Finally, you learned one way to use Word Help.

What You Should Know

Having completed this project, you now should be able to perform the following tasks:

- Bold Selected Text *(WD 1.33)*
- Center a Paragraph *(WD 1.35 and WD 1.40)*
- Center a Selected Graphic *(WD 1.46)*
- Change the Font of Selected Text *(WD 1.31)*
- Change the Font Size of Selected Text *(WD 1.32)*
- Check Spelling as You Type *(WD 1.22)*
- Close the Entire Document and Start Over *(WD 1.54)*
- Delete an Incorrect Character in a Document *(WD 1.54)*
- Delete an Incorrect Word or Phrase in a Document *(WD 1.54)*
- Display Formatting Marks *(WD 1.20)*
- Displays the Entire Standard Toolbar *(WD 1.15)*
- Enter Blank Lines into a Document *(WD 1.19)*

- Enter More Text *(WD 1.21)*
- Enter Text *(WD 1.18)*
- Enter Text that Scrolls the Document Window *(WD 1.25)*
- Format a Line of Text *(WD 1.37)*
- Increase the Default Font Size Before Typing *(WD 1.17)*
- Insert Clip Art into a Document *(WD 1.43)*
- Insert Text into an Existing Document *(WD 1.54)*
- Italicize Selected Text *(WD 1.39)*
- Obtain Help Using the Office Assistant *(WD 1.55)*
- Open a Document *(WD 1.52)*
- Print a Document *(WD 1.50)*
- Quit Word *(WD 1.51)*
- Resize a Graphic *(WD 1.47)*
- Right-Align a Paragraph *(WD 1.33)*
- Save a New Document *(WD 1.26)*
- Save an Existing Document with the Same File Name *(WD 1.49)*
- Scroll Through the Document *(WD 1.40)*
- Select a Graphic *(WD 1.46)*
- Select a Group of Words *(WD 1.41)*
- Select a Line *(WD 1.37)*
- Select a Word *(WD 1.38)*
- Select Multiple Paragraphs *(WD 1.30)*
- Start Word *(WD 1.8)*
- Underline Selected Text *(WD 1.42)*
- Undo an Action *(WD 1.36)*
- Wordwrap Text as You Type *(WD 1.21)*
- Zoom Page Width *(WD 1.15)*

More About 2000

Microsoft Certification

The Microsoft Office User Specialist (MOUS) Certification program provides an opportunity for you to obtain a valuable industry credential — proof that you have the Word 2000 skills required by employers. For more information, see Appendix D or visit the Shelly Cashman Series MOUS Web page at www.scsite.com/off2000/cert.htm.

Apply Your Knowledge

Project Reinforcement at www.scsite.com/off2000/reinforce.htm

1 Checking Spelling of a Document

Instructions: Start Word. Open the document, Meeting Announcement, on the Data Disk. If you did not download the Data Disk, see the inside back cover for instructions for downloading the Data Disk or see your instructor.

As shown in Figure 1-73, the document is a meeting announcement that contains many spelling and grammar errors. You are to right-click each of the errors and then click the appropriate correction on the shortcut menu.

You have learned that Word flags spelling errors with a red wavy underline. A green wavy underline indicates that Word has detected a possible grammar error. *Hint:* If your screen does not display the grammar errors, use the Word Help System to determine how to enable the check grammar feature. Perform the following tasks:

1. Position the insertion point at the beginning of the document. Right-click the flagged word, Notise. Change the incorrect word, Notise, to Notice by clicking Notice on the shortcut menu.
2. Right-click the flagged word, Januery. Change the incorrect word, Januery, to January by clicking January on the shortcut menu.
3. Right-click the flagged word, be. Click Delete Repeated Word on the shortcut menu to remove the duplicate occurrence of the word, be.

spelling and grammar errors are flagged on printout to help you identify them

Meeting Notise
All Employees

NEW HEALTH INSURANCE PLAN

Effective Januery 1, Kramer Enterprises will be be switching to a new insurance providor for major medical coverage. At that time, all employees must begin submitting claims and directing all claim-related questions to ofr new provider, Health America.

Representative's from Health America will be visiting our office on Friday, December 1, to discuss our nesw insurance plan. Please plan to attend either the morning session at 9:00 a.m. or the afternoon session at 2:00 p.m. Both session will be in the lunchroom.

insurance cards will be distributed at these meetings!

FIGURE 1-73

4. Right-click the flagged word, providor. Change the incorrect word, providor, to provider by clicking provider on the shortcut menu.
5. Right-click the flagged word, ofr. Because the shortcut menu does not display the correct word, click outside the shortcut menu to remove it from the screen. Correct the misspelled word, ofr, to the correct word, our, by removing the letter f and replacing it with the letter u.
6. Right-click the flagged word, Representative's. Change the word, Representative's, to its correct plural by clicking the word, Representatives, on the shortcut menu.
7. Right-click the incorrect word, nesw. Change the incorrect word, nesw, to new by clicking new on the shortcut menu.
8. Right-click the flagged word, session. Change the incorrect word, session, to its plural by clicking sessions on the shortcut menu.
9. Right-click the flagged word, insurance. Capitalize the word, insurance, by clicking Insurance on the shortcut menu.
10. Click File menu on the menu bar and then click Save As. Save the document using Corrected Meeting Announcement as the file name.
11. Print the revised document.

In the Lab

1 Creating an Announcement with Clip Art

Problem: The Director of the Harbor Theatre Company at your school has requested that each student in your Marketing 102 class prepare an announcement for auditions of its upcoming play. The student that creates the winning announcement will receive five complimentary tickets to the play. You prepare the announcement shown in Figure 1-74. *Hint:* Remember, if you make a mistake while formatting the announcement, you can click the Undo button on the Standard toolbar to undo your mistake.

Instructions:

1. Change the font size from 10 to 18 by clicking the Font Size box arrow on the formatting toolbar and then clicking 18.

2. If necessary, click the Show/Hide ¶ button on Standard toolbar to display formatting marks.

3. Create the announcement shown in Figure 1-74. Enter the document first without clip art and unformatted; that is without any bold, underlined, italicized, right-aligned, or centered text. If Word flags any misspelled words as you type, check the spelling of these words and correct them.

4. Save the document on a floppy disk with Grease Announcement as the file name.

Play Auditions...
... for Grease!

36-point
Broadway font

26-point
bold

HARBOR THEATRE COMPANY

The Harbor Theatre Company will be holding **acting, singing, and dancing auditions** on Friday, February 23, for roles in *Grease*. Auditions will begin at 5:00 p.m. in Alumni Hall.

<u>Only Harbor College students</u> are eligible to audition for a role in the play. Bring your student identification card.

To sign up, call 555-1929 today!

18-point

FIGURE 1-74

5. Select the two lines of the headline. Change their font to Broadway, or a similar font. Change their font size from 18 to 36.

6. Click somewhere in the second line of the headline. Right-align it.

7. Click somewhere in the body title line. Center it.

8. Select the body title line. Increase its font size from 18 to 26. Bold it.

9. In the first paragraph of the body copy, select the following phrase: acting, singing, and dancing auditions. Bold the phrase.

10. In the same paragraph, select the word, Grease. Italicize it.

11. In the second paragraph of the body copy, select the following phrase: Only Harbor College students. Underline the phrase.

12. Click somewhere in the last line of the announcement. Center it.

13. Insert the graphic of the drama masks between the headline and the body title line. Search for the text, drama, in the Clip Gallery to locate the graphic.

14. Click the graphic to select it. Center the selected graphic.

15. Save the announcement again with the same file name.

16. Print the announcement.

In the Lab

2 Creating an Announcement with Resized Clip Art

Problem: You are an assistant for the Marketing Manager at Taylor Business School. She has asked you to prepare an announcement for Fall Registration. The announcement must include clip art. You prepare the announcement shown in Figure 1-75. *Hint:* Remember, if you make a mistake while formatting the announcement, you can click the Undo button on the Standard toolbar to undo your mistake.

Instructions:

1. Change the font size from 10 to 18 by clicking the Font Size box arrow on the Formatting toolbar and then clicking 18.
2. If it is not already selected, click the Show/Hide ¶ button on the Standard toolbar to display formatting marks.
3. Create the announcement shown in Figure 1-75. Enter the document first without the clip art and unformatted; that is without any bold, underlined, italicized, right-aligned, or centered text. If Word flags any misspelled words as you type, check the spelling of these words and correct them.
4. Save the document on a floppy disk with Registration Announcement as the file name.
5. Select the two lines of the headline. Change their font to Arial, or a similar font. Change their font size from 20 to 36. Bold both lines.
6. Click somewhere in the second line of the headline. Right-align it.
7. Click somewhere in the body title line. Center it.
8. Select the body title line. Increase its font size from 18 to 28. Bold it.
9. Select the words, and much more, in the first paragraph of the body copy. Italicize the words.
10. Select the word, variety, in the second paragraph of the body copy. Underline it.
11. Click somewhere in the last line of the announcement. Center it.
12. Insert the graphic of the classroom between the headline and the body title line. Search for the text, classroom, in the Clip Gallery to locate the graphic.
13. Enlarge the graphic of the classroom. If you make the graphic too large, the announcement may flow onto two pages. If this occurs, reduce the size of the graphic so the announcement fits on a single page. *Hint:* Use Help to learn about **print preview**, which is a way to see the page before you print it. To exit print preview and return to the document window, click the Close button on the Print Preview toolbar.
14. Click the graphic to select it. Center the selected graphic.
15. Save the announcement again with the same file name.
16. Print the announcement.

FIGURE 1-75

In the Lab

3 Creating an Announcement with Resized Clip Art and a Bulleted List

Problem: You are the secretary of The Computer Club at your school. One of your responsibilities is to announce the monthly meetings. For the February meeting, you prepare the announcement shown in Figure 1-76. *Hint:* Remember, if you make a mistake while formatting the announcement, you can click the Undo button on the Standard toolbar to undo your mistake.

The Computer Club...
...for ALL Majors

28-point Arial Rounded MT Bold font

22-point Courier New bold font

MONTHLY MEETING ANNOUNCEMENT

- This month's meeting of The Computer Club is scheduled for **Monday, February 19**, from 11:30 a.m. to 2:00 p.m. in Conference Center 102. Bring a sack lunch.

bullets

- The roundtable discussion is on Internet service providers and begins at 12:00 noon.

- Anne Vance, director of office automation at our school, is our guest speaker. Anne will demonstrate how to use *Word 2000* to create a newsletter. Her presentation begins at 1:00 p.m.

Questions? Call Mark at 555-5587.

18-point

FIGURE 1-76

Instructions:

1. Change the font size from 10 to 18.
2. If they are not already showing, display formatting marks.
3. Create the announcement shown in Figure 1-76. Enter the document first without the clip art and unformatted; that is without any bulleted, bold, underlined, italicized, right-aligned, or centered text. Check spelling as you type.
4. Save the document on a floppy disk with February Announcement as the file name.
5. Format the two lines of the headline to 28-point Arial Rounded MT Bold or a similar font.
6. Right-align the second line of the headline.
7. Center the body title line. Format the body title line to 22-point Courier New bold or a similar font.
8. Add bullets to the three paragraphs of body copy. A **bullet** is a symbol positioned at the beginning of a paragraph. In Word, the default bullet symbol is a small darkened circle. A list of paragraphs with bullets is called a **bulleted list**. *Hint:* Use Help to learn how to add bullets to a list of paragraphs.
9. Bold the date, Monday, February 19, in the first paragraph of the body copy.
10. Italicize the phrase, Word 2000, in the third paragraph of the body copy.
11. Center the last line of the announcement.
12. Insert the graphic of the computer between the headline and the body title line. Search for the text, academic computer, in the Clip Gallery to locate the graphic.
13. Enlarge the graphic of the computer. If you make the graphic too large, the announcement may flow onto two pages. If this occurs, reduce the size of the graphic so the announcement fits on a single page. *Hint:* Use Help to learn about **print preview**, which is a way to see the page before you print it. To exit print preview and return to the document window, click the Close button on the Print Preview toolbar.
14. Center the graphic.
15. Save the announcement again with the same file name.
16. Print the announcement.

Cases and Places

1 ▶ You have been assigned the task of preparing an announcement for Starport Airlines. The announcement is to contain a graphic of an airplane from the Clip Gallery. Use the following text: first line of headline – Fly With Us…; second line of headline – … We Have Your Ticket; body title – Starport Airlines; first paragraph of body copy – For the month of October, we are offering flights to 25 cities nationwide for the unbelievable rate of $100 per person round trip.; second paragraph of body copy – Take advantage of these low, low rates and make your travel arrangements now for a vacation, a business trip, or a family reunion.; last line – For reservations, call 555-9898. Use the concepts and techniques presented in this project to create and format this announcement. Ask your instructor if you should bullet the list of paragraphs of the body copy.

2 ▶ You have been assigned the task of preparing an announcement for the Lake Shore Carnival. The announcement contains a graphic of a carnival from the Clip Gallery. Use the following text: first line of headline – It's Time…; second line of headline – …for Our Carnival; body title – Lake Shore Carnival; first paragraph of body copy – Join us for fun, food, entertainment, crafts, contests, and rides at the Lake Shore Carnival on the weekend of July 21 and 22.; second paragraph of body copy – Admission is $10 per adult and $5 for children under 10 years old. Gates open at 8:00 a.m. each day and close at midnight.; last line – For information, call 555-9383. Use the concepts and techniques presented in this project to create and format this announcement. Ask your instructor if you should bullet the list of paragraphs of the body copy.

3 ▶▶ Your Uncle John, a graduate of Eagle High School, will be celebrating his twenty-fifth high school reunion this year. He has asked you to prepare an announcement that can be sent to each member of the graduating class. He asks that you include a graphic of the school's mascot, an eagle. The reunion will be held at Fisher Country Club and will feature live entertainment by The Jazzicians, a local band. The reunion will be held on Saturday, October 27. The doors open at 6:00 p.m. with dinner at 7:00 p.m., followed by entertainment from 8:00 p.m. until 11:00 p.m. Cost is $50 per person. Guests will have the opportunity to reminisce about old times, catch up on current projects, and share future plans. More information can be obtained by calling Sue Nordic at 555-9808. Use the concepts and techniques presented in this project to create the announcement. Ask your instructor if you should bullet the list of paragraphs of the body copy.

Cases and Places

4 ▶▶ Your parents own a campground called Quiet Oaks. With the new season just around the corner, they have asked you to prepare an announcement for their campground. Located at the intersection of I-293 and SR-35 in southern Louisiana, Quiet Oaks is a secluded campground situated in wooded, rolling hills. It has 75 paved pull-through sites and 46 gravel sites. All have city water and electric hook-ups. Facilities include restrooms, showers, dump, security, laundry, public telephone, and a data port. Recreation includes lake fishing, swimming pool, playground, horseshoes, and a game room. The campground is open from April 1 through October 31. Rates begin at $15 per night. Call 555-9393 for more information. Use the concepts and techniques presented in this project to create the announcement. Be sure to include an appropriate graphic from the Clip Gallery. Ask your instructor if you should bullet the list of paragraphs of the body copy.

5 ▶▶ You have a part-time job as the assistant to the Marketing Director at a new office supply store called Office World. The Director has asked you to prepare an announcement for the store's grand opening. Office World stocks thousands of office products including supplies, furniture, electronics, and computer software. Office World's low price guarantee states it will refund double a customer's money if the customer finds a comparable product for a lower price within ten days of purchase. Customers can purchase at the store, via fax or telephone, or on the Web at www.officeworld.com. Fax number is 555-2982 and telephone number is 555-2983. For purchases over $45.00, delivery is free. For a catalog, customers or potential customers can call 555-2900. Use the concepts and techniques presented in this project to create the announcement. Be sure to include an appropriate graphic from the Clip Gallery. Ask your instructor if you should bullet the list of paragraphs of the body copy.

6 ▶▶▶ Schools, churches, libraries, grocery stores, and other public places have bulletin boards for announcements and other postings. Often, these bulletin boards have so many announcements that some go unnoticed. At one of the above-mentioned organizations, find a posted announcement that you think might be overlooked. Copy the text from the announcement. Using this text, together with the techniques presented in this project, create an announcement that would be more likely to catch a reader's eye. Format the announcement effectively and include a bulleted list and suitable graphic from the Clip Gallery.

7 ▶▶▶ Advertisements are a company's way of announcing products or services to the public. You can find advertisements in printed media such as newspapers and magazines. Many companies also advertise on the World Wide Web. Find a printed advertisement or one on the Web that you feel lacks luster. Copy the text from the announcement. Using this text, together with the techniques presented in this project, create an announcement that would be more likely to catch a reader's eye. Format the announcement effectively and include a bulleted list and suitable graphic from the Clip Gallery.

Microsoft **Word 2000**

Microsoft Word 2000

Creating a Research Paper

OBJECTIVES

You will have mastered the material in this project when you can:

- Describe the MLA documentation style for research papers
- Change the margin settings in a document
- Adjust line spacing in a document
- Use a header to number pages of a document
- Enter text using Click and Type
- Apply formatting using shortcut keys
- Indent paragraphs
- Use Word's AutoCorrect feature
- Add a footnote to a research paper
- Modify a style
- Insert a symbol automatically
- Insert a manual page break
- Create a hanging indent
- Create a hyperlink
- Sort selected paragraphs
- Go to a specific location in a document
- Find and replace text
- Move text
- Find a synonym for a word
- Count the words in a document
- Check spelling and grammar at once
- Display the Web site associated with a hyperlink
- E-mail a copy of a document

Elvis and Aliens Abound

Research Net Sources Carefull

The checkout line at your local grocery store is longer than the conga line at your best friend's wedding. You grab a cola and a bag of pretzels off the strategically placed displays. Then, as you shuffle to the registers, you decide to peruse the headlines of the magazines on display. You learn that two-headed aliens have abducted Elvis, that researchers are coming closer to finding a cure for the common cold, and that the Chicago Cubs are in contention for the National League pennant. Which stories do you believe? And what criteria do you use to make these decisions?

These questions are relevant not only at the grocery store but also in the computer lab. When you sit down and surf the Internet for the latest news, celebrity sightings, sports scores, and reference sources, you make decisions on which sites to visit and which sites to avoid.

Not so long ago, students relied on books and magazines in the library for the bulk of their research material. These permanent sources were professionally evaluated and edited. Not so with the Internet. The Net is chock full of everything from reliable research to fictitious opinions. No one performs quality control checks to verify accuracy and reliability. Anyone can build a Web site and fill it with any content imaginable. And this content can be updated before your eyes.

In this project, you will create a research paper on the topic of Web publishing, which is the method of developing, maintaining, and posting Web pages. You will include a hyperlink that will permit you to navigate to a specific Internet site. Your Works Cited page will list the three sources used to obtain information for the paper. Two of these sources are books; one is an article available on the Shelly Cashman Series Web site

(www.scsite.com). How can you judge the reliability of these materials, particularly the article posted on the Web? Just remember the three S's: structure, source, and style.

Structure – Does the information seem objective or biased? Are authorities used as sources? When was the site created or updated? Is a contact person listed so you can verify information? Are working hyperlinks provided that refer you to additional sources?

Source – Examine the Web address to find out the site's sponsor. Is it a nonprofit organization (.org), a school (.edu), the government (.gov), or a commercial business (.com)? Is the purpose of the site to provide information or to make a profit?

Style – Does the site look organized and professional? Can you navigate easily with a minimum of mouse clicks? Does it contain an index and the capability of searching for specific information?

William Miller, a former president of the Association of College and Research Libraries, says that on the Web, "Much of what purports to be serious information is simply junk – not current, objective, or trustworthy." And by following the three S's, you will be able to decide that neither Elvis's abduction nor the Cubs's pennant seems likely.

Microsoft Word 2000

Creating a Research Paper

C A S E   P E R S P E C T I V E

Rick Williams is a full-time college student, majoring in Communications. Mr. Claremont, the instructor in his introductory computer class, has assigned a short research paper that must have a minimum of 425 words. The paper must discuss some aspect of computers and must be written according to the MLA documentation style, which specifies guidelines for report preparation. The paper must contain one footnote and three references – one of which must be obtained from the World Wide Web.

Rick's Internet service provider recently announced that all subscribers are entitled to 6 MB of free Web space for a personal Web page. Rick plans to publish his own Web page, so he decides to write the research paper on Web publishing. Rick intends to review computer magazines at the school's library, surf the Internet, contact his Internet service provider, and interview the Webmaster at his school for information on Web publishing. He also plans to use the Internet to obtain the guidelines for the MLA style of documentation. Because you are familiar with the Internet, Rick has asked you to assist him with the Web searches.

Introduction

In both academic and business environments, you will be asked to write reports. Business reports range from proposals to cost justifications to five-year plans to research findings. Academic reports focus mostly on research findings. Whether you are writing a business report or an academic report, you should follow a standard style when preparing it.

Many different styles of documentation exist for report preparation, depending on the nature of the report. Each style requires the same basic information; the differences among styles appear in the manner of presenting the information. For example, one documentation style may use the term *bibliography*, whereas another uses *references*, and yet a third prefers *works cited*. Two popular documentation styles for research papers are the **MLA** (**Modern Language Association of America**) and **APA** (**American Psychological Association**) styles. This project uses the MLA documentation style.

Project Two – Web Publishing Research Paper

Project 2 illustrates the creation of a short research paper describing Web publishing. As shown in Figure 2-1, the paper follows the MLA documentation style. The first two pages present the research paper and the third page lists the works cited alphabetically.

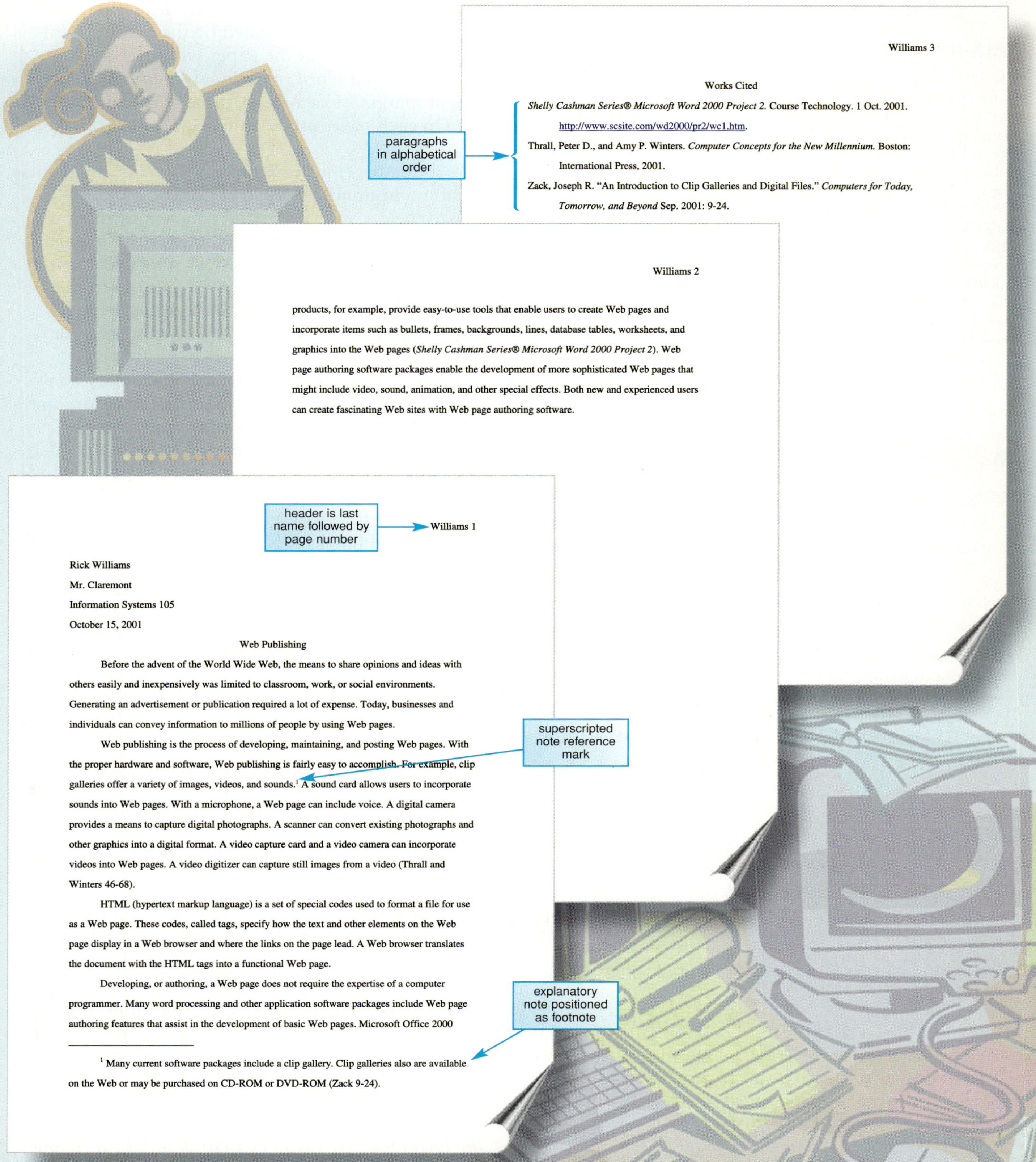

Williams 3

Works Cited

Shelly Cashman Series® Microsoft Word 2000 Project 2. Course Technology. 1 Oct. 2001.

    http://www.scsite.com/wd2000/pr2/wc1.htm.

Thrall, Peter D., and Amy P. Winters. *Computer Concepts for the New Millennium.* Boston:

    International Press, 2001.

Zack, Joseph R. "An Introduction to Clip Galleries and Digital Files." *Computers for Today,*

    Tomorrow, and Beyond Sep. 2001: 9-24.

> paragraphs in alphabetical order

Williams 2

products, for example, provide easy-to-use tools that enable users to create Web pages and incorporate items such as bullets, frames, backgrounds, lines, database tables, worksheets, and graphics into the Web pages (*Shelly Cashman Series® Microsoft Word 2000 Project 2*). Web page authoring software packages enable the development of more sophisticated Web pages that might include video, sound, animation, and other special effects. Both new and experienced users can create fascinating Web sites with Web page authoring software.

> header is last name followed by page number

Williams 1

Rick Williams

Mr. Claremont

Information Systems 105

October 15, 2001

Web Publishing

    Before the advent of the World Wide Web, the means to share opinions and ideas with others easily and inexpensively was limited to classroom, work, or social environments. Generating an advertisement or publication required a lot of expense. Today, businesses and individuals can convey information to millions of people by using Web pages.

    Web publishing is the process of developing, maintaining, and posting Web pages. With the proper hardware and software, Web publishing is fairly easy to accomplish. For example, clip galleries offer a variety of images, videos, and sounds.[1] A sound card allows users to incorporate sounds into Web pages. With a microphone, a Web page can include voice. A digital camera provides a means to capture digital photographs. A scanner can convert existing photographs and other graphics into a digital format. A video capture card and a video camera can incorporate videos into Web pages. A video digitizer can capture still images from a video (Thrall and Winters 46-68).

> superscripted note reference mark

    HTML (hypertext markup language) is a set of special codes used to format a file for use as a Web page. These codes, called tags, specify how the text and other elements on the Web page display in a Web browser and where the links on the page lead. A Web browser translates the document with the HTML tags into a functional Web page.

    Developing, or authoring, a Web page does not require the expertise of a computer programmer. Many word processing and other application software packages include Web page authoring features that assist in the development of basic Web pages. Microsoft Office 2000

> explanatory note positioned as footnote

---

[1] Many current software packages include a clip gallery. Clip galleries also are available on the Web or may be purchased on CD-ROM or DVD-ROM (Zack 9-24).

FIGURE 2-1

MLA and APA

The MLA documentation style is the standard in the humanities, and the APA style is preferred in the social sciences. For more information from the MLA about its guidelines, visit the Word 2000 More About Web page (www.scsite.com/wd2000/more.htm) and then click MLA. For more information from the APA about its guidelines, visit the Word 2000 More About Web page (www.scsite.com/wd2000/more.htm) and then click APA.

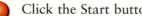

APA Style

In the APA style, double-space all pages of the paper with 1.5" top, bottom, left, and right margins. Indent the first word of each paragraph .5" from the left margin. In the upper-right margin of each page, place a running head that consists of the page number double-spaced below a summary of the paper title.

MLA Documentation Style

When writing papers, you should adhere to some style of documentation. The research paper in this project follows the guidelines presented by the MLA. To follow the MLA style, double-space text on all pages of the paper with one-inch top, bottom, left, and right margins. Indent the first word of each paragraph one-half inch from the left margin. At the right margin of each page, place a page number one-half inch from the top margin. On each page, precede the page number by your last name.

The MLA style does not require a title page; instead, place your name and course information in a block at the left margin beginning one inch from the top of the page. Center the title one double-space below your name and course information.

In the body of the paper, place author references in parentheses with the page number(s) where the referenced information is located. The MLA style uses these in-text **parenthetical citations** instead of footnoting each source at the bottom of the page or at the end of the paper. In the MLA style, footnotes are used only for explanatory notes. In the body of the paper, use **superscripts** (raised numbers) for **note reference marks**, which signal that an explanatory note exists.

According to the MLA style, explanatory notes are optional. **Explanatory notes** are used to elaborate on points discussed in the body of the paper. Explanatory notes may be placed either at the bottom of the page as footnotes or at the end of the paper as endnotes. Double-space the explanatory notes. Superscript each note reference mark, and indent it one-half inch from the left margin. Place one space following the note reference mark before beginning the note text. At the end of the note text, you may list bibliographic information for further reference.

The MLA style uses the term **works cited** for the bibliographical references. The works cited page alphabetically lists works that are referenced directly in the paper by each author's last name, or, if the author's name is not available, by the title of the work. Place the works cited on a separate numbered page. Center the title, Works Cited, one inch from the top margin. Double-space all lines. Begin the first line of each entry at the left margin; indent subsequent lines of the same entry one-half inch from the left margin.

Starting Word

Follow these steps to start Word or ask your instructor how to start Word for your system.

TO START WORD

 1 Click the Start button on the taskbar.

2 Click New Office Document on the Start menu. If necessary, click the General tab when the New Office Document dialog box first displays.

3 Double-click the Blank Document icon in the General sheet.

4 If the Word window is not maximized, double-click its title bar to maximize it. If the Office Assistant displays, right-click it and then click Hide on the shortcut menu.

Office starts Word. After a few moments, an empty document titled Document1 displays in the Word window (Figure 2-2 on page WD 2.8). If your screen differs from Figure 2-2, click View on the menu bar and then click Normal.

Resetting Menus and Toolbars

To set the menus and toolbars so they appear exactly as shown in this book, you should reset your menus and toolbars as outlined in Appendix C or follow these steps.

TO RESET MENUS AND TOOLBARS

1 Click View on the menu bar and then point to Toolbars. Click Customize on the Toolbars submenu.

2 When the Customize dialog box displays, click the Options tab, make sure the top three check boxes have check marks and then click the Reset my usage data button. When the Microsoft Word dialog box displays, click the Yes button.

3 Click the Toolbars tab. Click Standard in the Toolbars list and then click the Reset button. When the Reset Toolbar dialog box displays, click the OK button.

4 Click Formatting in the Toolbars list and then click the Reset button. When the Reset Toolbar dialog box displays, click the OK button. Click the Close button.

Word resets the menus and toolbars.

Displaying Formatting Marks

As discussed Project 1, it is helpful to display **formatting marks** that indicate where in the document you pressed the ENTER key, SPACEBAR, and other keys. Follow this step to display formatting marks.

TO DISPLAY FORMATTING MARKS

1 Double-click the move handle on the Standard toolbar to display the entire toolbar. If the Show/Hide ¶ button on the Standard toolbar is not already recessed, click it.

Word displays formatting marks in the document window, and the Show/Hide ¶ button on the Standard toolbar is recessed (Figure 2-2 on the next page).

Changing the Margins

Word is preset to use standard 8.5-by-11-inch paper, with 1.25-inch left and right margins and 1-inch top and bottom margins. These margin settings affect every page in the document. Often, you may want to change these default margin settings. You have learned that the MLA documentation style requires one-inch top, bottom, left, and right margins throughout the paper.

The steps on the next page illustrate how to change the margin settings for a document when your screen is in normal view. To verify your screen is in normal view, click View on the menu bar and then click Normal.

Writing Papers

The World Wide Web contains a host of information, tips, and suggestions on writing research papers. College professors and fellow students develop many of these Web pages. For a list of Web links to sites on writing research papers, visit the Word 2000 More About Web page (www.scsite.com/wd2000/more.htm) and then click Links to Sites on Writing Research Papers.

Changing Margins

In print layout view, you can change margins using the horizontal and vertical rulers. Current margin settings are shaded in gray. The margin boundary is located where the gray meets the white. To change a margin, drag the margin boundary. Hold down the ALT key while dragging the margin boundary to display the margin settings.

 **To Change the Margin Settings**

1 **Click File on the menu bar and then point to Page Setup (Figure 2-2).**

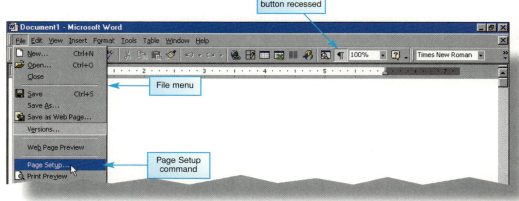

FIGURE 2-2

2 **Click Page Setup. If necessary, click the Margins tab when the Page Setup dialog box first displays.**

Word displays the Page Setup dialog box (Figure 2-3). Word lists the current margin settings in the text boxes.

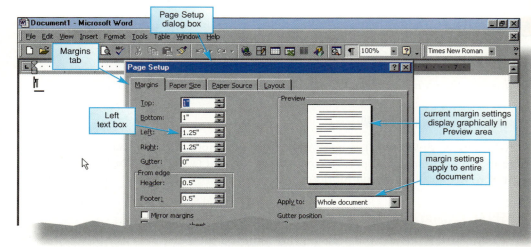

FIGURE 2-3

3 **Drag through the text in the Left text box to highlight 1.25". Type 1 and then press the TAB key. Type 1 and then point to the OK button.**

The new left and right margin settings are 1 inch (Figure 2-4).

4 **Click the OK button.**

Word changes the left and right margins.

 Other Ways

1. In print layout view, drag margin boundary(s) on ruler

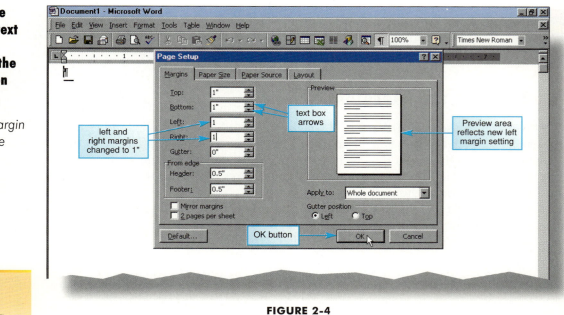

FIGURE 2-4

The new margin settings take effect in the document immediately, and Word uses these margins for the entire document.

When you change the margin settings in the text boxes in the Page Setup dialog box, the Preview area (Figure 2-4) does not adjust to reflect a changed margin setting until the insertion point leaves the respective text box. That is, you must press the TAB or ENTER key or click in another text box if you want to view the changes in the Preview area.

Zooming Page Width

As you learned in Project 1, when you **zoom page width**, Word displays text on the screen as large as possible without extending the right margin beyond the right edge of the document window. Perform the following steps to zoom page width.

TO ZOOM PAGE WIDTH

1 Click the Zoom box arrow on the Standard toolbar.

2 Click Page Width in the Zoom list.

Word extends the right margin to the right edge of the document window (Figure 2-5). Word computes the zoom percentage based on a variety of settings. Your percentage may be different depending on your system configuration.

Adjusting Line Spacing

Line spacing is the amount of vertical space between lines of text in a document. Word, by default, single-spaces between lines of text and automatically adjusts line height to accommodate various font sizes and graphics. The MLA documentation style requires that you **double-space** the entire paper; that is, one blank line should display between each line of text. Thus, you must adjust the line spacing from single to double as described in the following steps.

To Double-Space a Document

1 **Right-click the paragraph mark above the end mark in the document window. Point to Paragraph on the shortcut menu (Figure 2-5).**

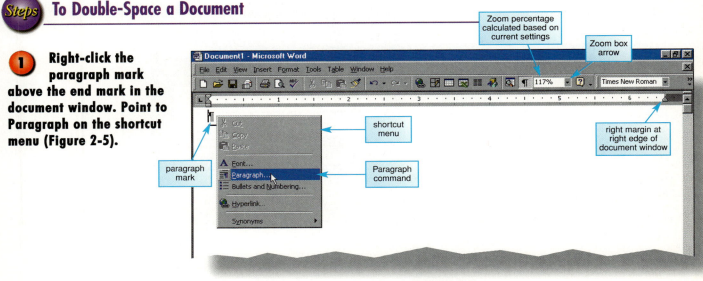

FIGURE 2-5

2 Click Paragraph. If necessary, click the Indents and Spacing tab when the Paragraph dialog box first displays. Click the Line spacing box arrow and then point to Double.

Word displays the Paragraph dialog box, which lists the current settings in the text boxes and displays them graphically in the Preview area (Figure 2-6). A list of available line spacing options displays.

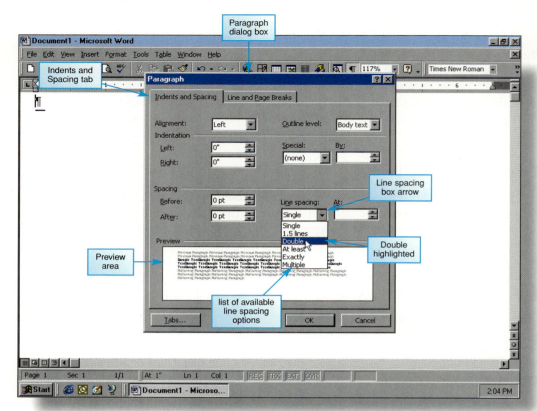

FIGURE 2-6

3 Click Double. Point to the OK button.

Word displays Double in the Line spacing box and graphically portrays the new line spacing in the Preview area (Figure 2-7).

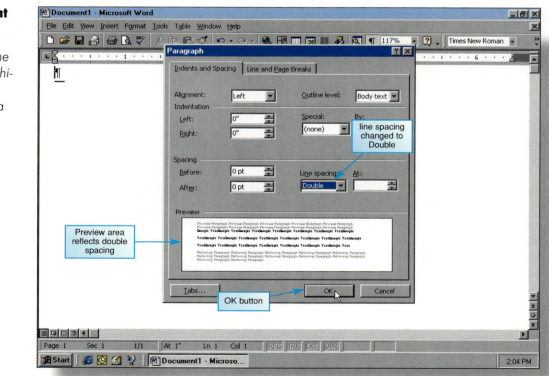

FIGURE 2-7

4 **Click the OK button.**

Word changes the line spacing to double in the current document (Figure 2-8).

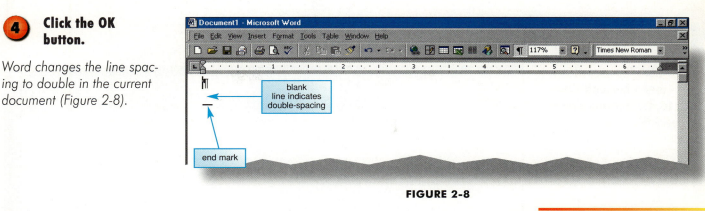

blank line indicates double-spacing

end mark

FIGURE 2-8

Notice that when line spacing is double (Figure 2-8), the end mark is positioned one blank line below the insertion point.

The Line spacing list (Figure 2-6) contains a variety of settings for the line spacing. The default, Single, and the options 1.5 lines and Double instruct Word to adjust line spacing automatically to accommodate the largest font or graphic on a line. The next two options, At least and Exactly, enable you to specify a line spacing not provided in the first three options. The difference is that the At least option instructs Word to increase the designation if necessary, whereas the Exactly option does not allow Word to increase the specification to accommodate larger fonts or graphics. With the last option, Multiple, you enter a value, which represents a percentage by which Word should increase or decrease the line spacing. For example, with the number 1 representing single-spacing, a multiple of 1.3 increases the line spacing by 30 percent and a multiple of .8 decreases the line spacing by 20 percent.

Using a Header to Number Pages

In Word, you can number pages easily by clicking Insert on the menu bar and then clicking Page Numbers. Using the Page Numbers command, you can specify the location (top or bottom of page) and alignment (right, left, or centered) of the page numbers. You cannot, however, place your name as required by the MLA style in front of the page number with the Page Numbers command. To place your name in front of the page number, you must create a header that contains the page number.

Headers and Footers

A **header** is text you want printed at the top of each page in the document. A **footer** is text you want printed at the bottom of every page. In Word, headers are printed in the top margin one-half inch from the top of every page, and footers are printed in the bottom margin one-half inch from the bottom of each page, which meets the MLA style. Headers and footers can include text and graphics, as well as the page number, total number of pages, current date, and current time.

In this project, you are to precede the page number with your last name placed one-half inch from the top of each page. Your name and the page number should print right-aligned; that is, at the right margin.

To create the header, first you display the header area in the document window and then you can enter the header text into the header area. Use the procedures on the following pages to create the header with page numbers according to the MLA documentation style.

Other **Ways**

1. On Format menu click Paragraph, click Indents and Spacing tab, click Line spacing box arrow, click Double, click OK button
2. Press CTRL+2

More *About*

Data and Statistics

When researching for a paper, you may need to access data, graphs of data, or perform statistical computations on data. For more information on statistical formulas and available data and graphs, visit the Word 2000 More About Web page (www.scsite.com/wd2000/more.htm) and then click Data and Statistics.

 To Display the Header Area

1 **Click View on the menu bar and then point to Header and Footer (Figure 2-9).**

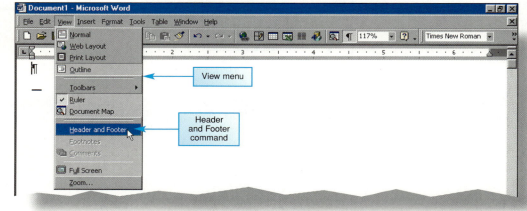

FIGURE 2-9

2 **Click Header and Footer.**

*Word switches from normal view to print layout view and displays the **Header and Footer toolbar** (Figure 2-10). You type header text in the header area.*

FIGURE 2-10

 *About*

Print Layout View

You also can switch to print layout view by clicking the Print Layout View button on the horizontal scroll bar. Print layout view shows the positioning of headers, footers, and footnotes. To move forward or backward an entire page, click the double arrows on the bottom of the vertical scroll bar.

The Header and Footer toolbar initially floats in the document window. To move a floating toolbar, drag its title bar. You can **dock**, or attach, a floating toolbar below the Standard and Formatting toolbars by double-clicking the floating toolbar's title bar. To move a docked toolbar, drag its move handle. Recall that the move handle is the vertical bar to the left of the first button on a toolbar. If you drag a floating toolbar to an edge of the window, the toolbar snaps to the edge of the window. If you drag a docked toolbar to the middle of the window, the toolbar floats in the Word window. If you double-click between two buttons or boxes on a docked toolbar, it floats in its original floating position.

The header area does not display on the screen when the document window is in normal view because it tends to clutter the screen. To display the header in the document window with the rest of the text, you must display the document in print preview, which is discussed in a later project, or switch to print layout view. When you click the Header and Footer command on the View menu, Word automatically switches to **print layout view**, which displays the document exactly as it will print.

Entering Text using Click and Type

When in print layout view, you can use **Click and Type** to format and enter text, graphics, and other items. To use Click and Type, you double-click a blank area of the document window. Word automatically formats the item you enter according to the location where you double-click. Perform the following steps to use Click and Type to right-align and then enter the last name into the header area.

> **More About**
>
> **Click and Type**
>
> Click and Type is not available in normal view, in a bulleted or numbered list, or in a document formatted into multiple columns.

Steps: To Click and Type

1 **Point to right edge of the header area so a right-align icon displays next to the I-beam.**

*As you move the **Click and Type pointer** around the window, the icon changes to represent formatting that will be applied if you double-click at that location (Figure 2-11).*

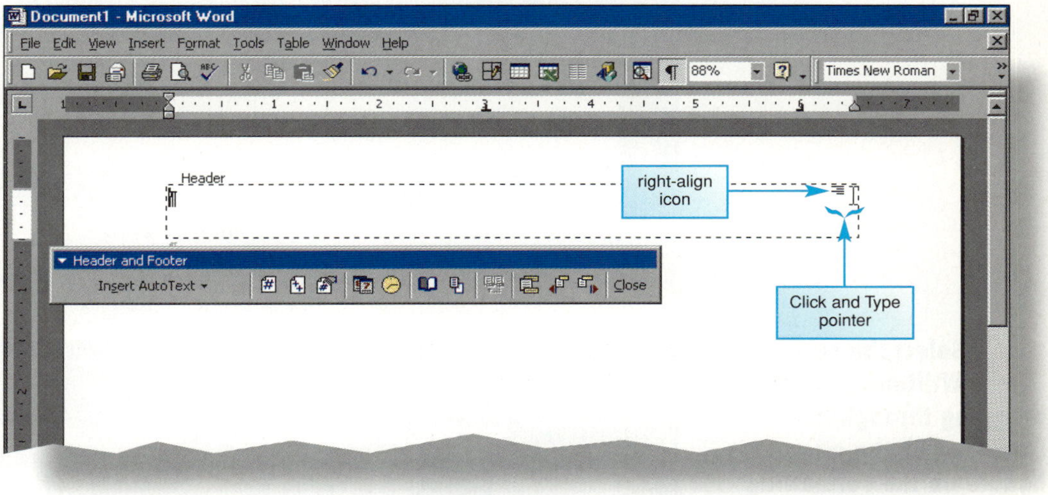

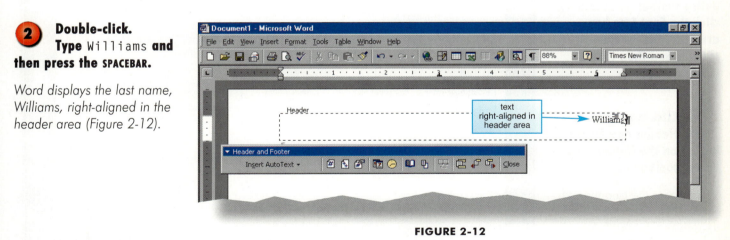

FIGURE 2-11

2 **Double-click. Type Williams and then press the SPACEBAR.**

Word displays the last name, Williams, right-aligned in the header area (Figure 2-12).

FIGURE 2-12

The next step is to enter the page number into the header area and then format it.

Entering a Page Number into the Header

Word formats the text in the header area using the current font size. Perform the steps on the next page to enter a page number into the header area and then, if necessary, format the entire line of text to 12 point.

Steps To Enter and Format a Page Number

1 **Click the Insert Page Number button on the Header and Footer toolbar.**

Word displays the page number 1 in the header area (Figure 2-13).

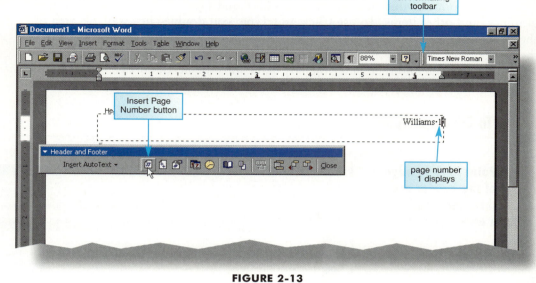

move handle on Formatting toolbar

Insert Page Number button

Williams·1

page number 1 displays

FIGURE 2-13

2 **Select the text, Williams 1, by dragging through it. Double-click the move handle on the Formatting toolbar to display the entire toolbar. If necessary, click the Font Size box arrow on the Formatting toolbar and then click 12 (Figure 2-14).**

3 **Click the Close Header and Footer button on the Header and Footer toolbar.**

Word closes the Header and Footer toolbar and returns the screen to normal view (see Figure 2-15 on page WD 2.16).

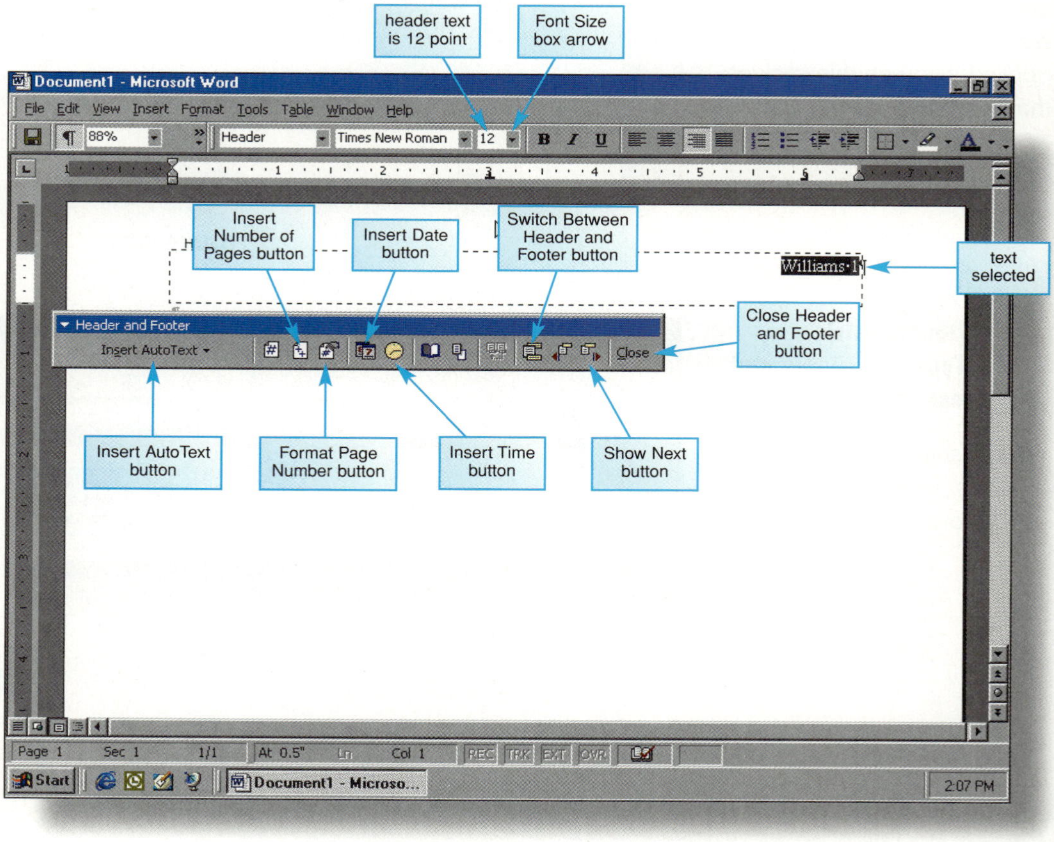

header text is 12 point

Font Size box arrow

Insert Number of Pages button

Insert Date button

Switch Between Header and Footer button

Williams·1

text selected

Close Header and Footer button

Insert AutoText button

Format Page Number button

Insert Time button

Show Next button

FIGURE 2-14

 Other Ways

1. On Insert menu click Page Numbers, click OK button

Just as the Insert Page Number button on the Header and Footer toolbar inserts the page number into the document, three other buttons on the Header and Footer toolbar (Figure 2-14) insert items into the document. The Insert Number of Pages button inserts the total number of pages in the document; the Insert Date button inserts the current date into the document; and the Insert Time button inserts the current time.

To edit an existing header, you can follow the same procedure that you use to create a new header. That is, click View on the menu bar and then click Header and Footer to display the header area; or switch to print layout view by clicking the Print Layout View button on the horizontal scroll bar and then double-click the dimmed header. If you have multiple headers, click the Show Next button on the Header and Footer toolbar (Figure 2-14) until the appropriate header displays in the header area. Edit the header as you would any Word text and then click the Close Header and Footer button on the Header and Footer toolbar.

To create a footer, click View on the menu bar, click Header and Footer, click the Switch Between Header and Footer button on the Header and Footer toolbar, and then follow the same procedure as you would to create a header.

Typing the Body of the Research Paper

The body of the research paper encompasses the first two pages in Figure 2-1 on page WD 2.5. The steps on the following pages illustrate how to enter the body of the research paper.

Changing the Default Font Size

You learned in Project 1 that depending on how Word 2000 was installed on your computer, your default font size might be either 10 or 12. A font size of 10 point is difficult for some people to read. In this project, all characters in all paragraphs should be a font size of 12. If your default font size is 10, perform the following steps to change it to 12.

TO CHANGE THE DEFAULT FONT SIZE

① If necessary, click the Font Size box arrow on the Formatting toolbar.

② Click 12.

Word changes the font size to 12 (Figure 2-15 on the next page).

Entering Name and Course Information

You have learned that the MLA style does not require a separate title page for research papers. Instead, place your name and course information in a block at the top of the page at the left margin. Thus, follow the step on the next page to begin entering the body of the research paper.

Writing Papers

When preparing to write a paper, many students take notes to keep track of information. One method is to summarize, or condense, the information. Another is to paraphrase, or rewrite the information in your own words. A third method is to quote, or record, the exact words of the original. Be sure to use quotation marks when directly quoting a source.

APA Guidelines

APA guidelines require a title page as a separate page of a research paper, instead of placing name and course information on the paper's first page. The running head (a brief summary of the title and the page number) also is on the title page, along with the page number 1.

Steps To Enter Name and Course Information

1 **Type** Rick Williams **and then press the ENTER key. Type** Mr. Claremont **and then press the ENTER key. Type** Information Systems 105 **and then press the ENTER key. Type** October 15, 2001 **and then press the ENTER key.**

The student name displays on line 1, the professor name on line 2, the course name on line 3, and the paper due date on line 4 (Figure 2-15).

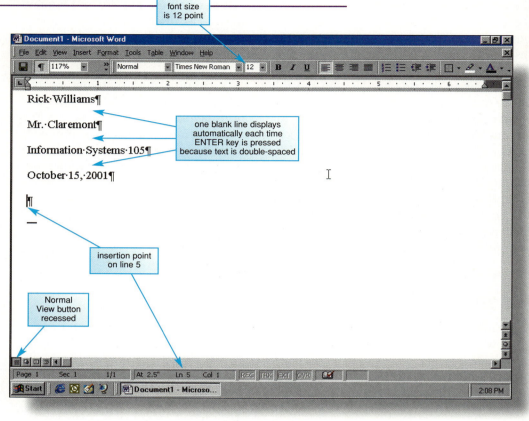

FIGURE 2-15

Notice in Figure 2-15 that the insertion point currently is on line 5. Each time you press the ENTER key, Word advances two lines on the screen, but increments the line counter on the status bar by only one because earlier you set line spacing to double.

If you watch the screen as you type, you may have noticed that as you typed the first few characters in the month, Octo, Word displayed the **AutoComplete tip**, October, above the characters. To save typing, you could press the ENTER key while the AutoComplete tip displays, which instructs Word to place the text of the AutoComplete tip at the location of your typing.

Applying Formatting Using Shortcut Keys

The next step is to enter the title of the research paper centered between the page margins. As you type text, you may want to format paragraphs and characters as you type them, instead of entering them and then formatting them later. In Project 1, you typed the characters in the document and then selected the ones to be formatted and applied the desired formatting using toolbar buttons. When your fingers are already on the keyboard, it sometimes is more efficient to use **shortcut keys**, or key z board key combinations, to format text as you type it. Perform the following steps to center a paragraph with the CTRL+E keys and then left-align a paragraph with the CTRL+L keys. (Recall from Project 1 that a notation such as CTRL+E means to press the letter E while holding the CTRL key.)

More About

Shortcut Keys

To print a complete list of shortcut keys for formatting, do the following. Click the Office Assistant, type *formatting keys* and then click the Search button. Scroll through the list and then click Format characters and paragraphs. In the Help window, click the Print button and then click the OK button.

To Use Shortcut Keys to Format Text

1 **Press the CTRL+E keys. Type** Web Publishing **and then press the ENTER key.**

Word centers the title between the left and right margins (Figure 2-16). The paragraph mark and insertion point are centered because the formatting specified in the previous paragraph is carried forward to the next paragraph.

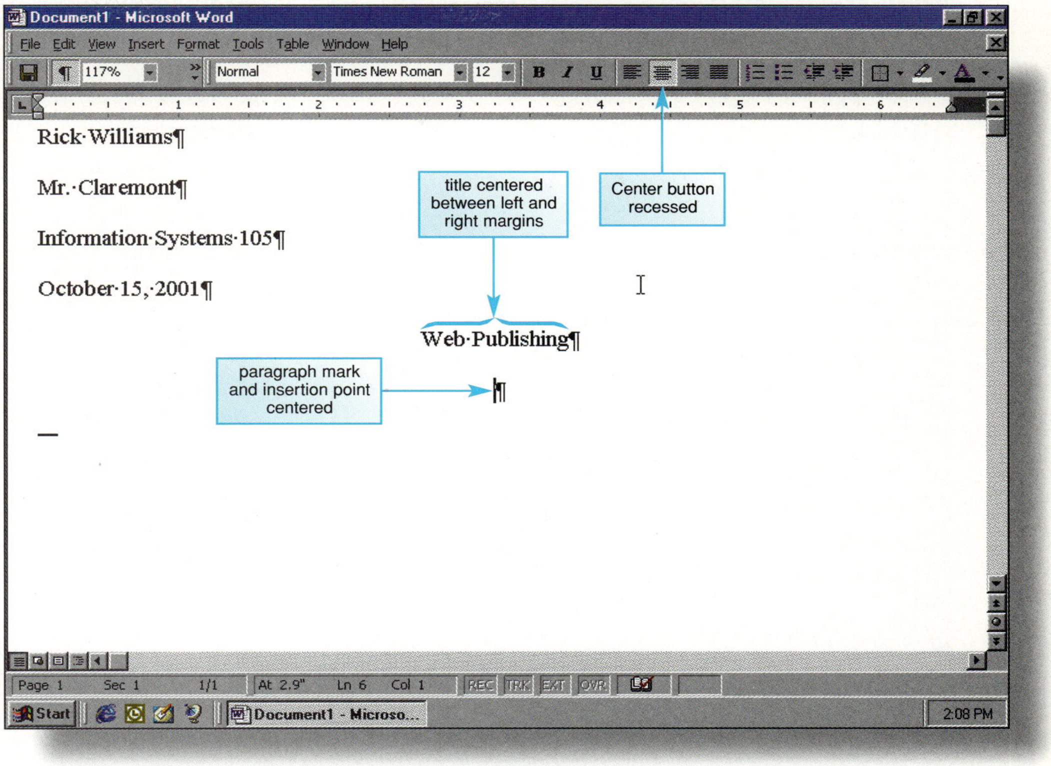

FIGURE 2-16

2 **Press the CTRL+L keys.**

Word positions the paragraph mark and the insertion point at the left margin (Figure 2-17). The next text you type will be left-aligned.

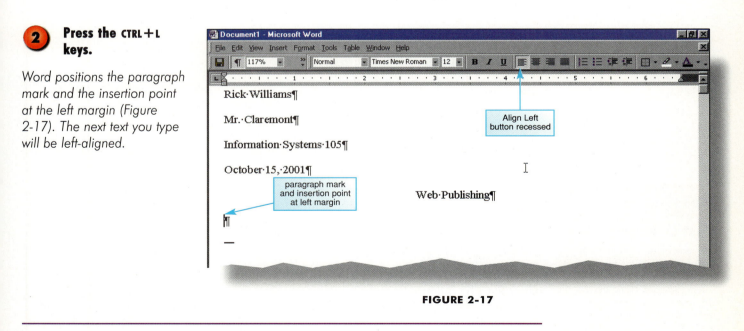

FIGURE 2-17

Word has many shortcut keys for your convenience while typing. Table 2-1 on the next page lists the common shortcut keys for formatting characters, and Table 2-2 on the next page lists common shortcut keys for formatting paragraphs.

Table 2-1 Shortcut Keys for Formatting Characters	
CHARACTER FORMATTING TASK	*SHORTCUT KEYS*
All capital letters	CTRL+SHIFT+A
Bold	CTRL+B
Case of letters	SHIFT+F3
Decrease font size	CTRL+SHIFT+<
Decrease font size 1 point	CTRL+[
Double-underline	CTRL+SHIFT+D
Increase font size	CTRL+SHIFT+>
Increase font size 1 point	CTRL+]
Italic	CTRL+I
Remove character formatting (plain text)	CTRL+SPACEBAR
Small uppercase letters	CTRL+SHIFT+K
Subscript	CTRL+=
Superscript	CTRL+SHIFT+PLUS SIGN
Underline	CTRL+U
Underline words, not spaces	CTRL+SHIFT+W

Table 2-2 Shortcut Keys for Formatting Paragraphs	
PARAGRAPH FORMATTING TASK	*SHORTCUT KEYS*
1.5 line spacing	CTRL+5
Add/remove one line above	CTRL+0
Center paragraph	CTRL+E
Decrease paragraph indent	CTRL+SHIFT+M
Double-space lines	CTRL+2
Hanging indent	CTRL+T
Increase paragraph indent	CTRL+M
Justify paragraph	CTRL+J
Left-align paragraph	CTRL+L
Remove hanging indent	CTRL+SHIFT+T
Remove paragraph formatting	CTRL+Q
Right-align paragraph	CTRL+R
Single-space lines	CTRL+1

Saving the Research Paper

You should save your research paper. For a detailed example of the procedure summarized below, refer to pages WD 1.26 through WD 1.28 in Project 1.

TO SAVE A DOCUMENT

1. Insert your floppy disk into drive A.

2. Double-click the move handle on the Standard toolbar to display the entire toolbar. Click the Save button on the Standard toolbar.

3. Type the file name Web Publishing Paper in the File name text box.

4. Click the Save in box arrow and then click 3½ Floppy (A:).

5. Click the Save button in the Save As dialog box.

Word saves your document with the name Web Publishing Paper (Figure 2-18).

Indenting Paragraphs

According to the MLA style, the first line of each paragraph in the research paper is to be indented one-half inch from the left margin. This procedure, called **first-line indent**, can be accomplished using the horizontal ruler. The **First Line Indent marker** is the top triangle at the 0" mark on the ruler (Figure 2-18). The small square at the 0" mark is the **Left Indent marker**. The Left Indent marker is used to change the entire left margin, whereas the First Line Indent marker affects only the first line of the paragraph. Perform the following steps to first-line indent the paragraphs in the research paper.

First-Line Indent

You may be tempted to use the TAB key to indent the first line of each paragraph in your research paper. Using the TAB key for this task is inefficient because you must press it each time you begin a new paragraph. First-line indent is a paragraph format; thus, it is carried forward automatically each time you press the ENTER key.

To First-Line Indent Paragraphs

1 With the insertion point on the paragraph mark in line 6, point to the First Line Indent marker on the ruler (Figure 2-18).

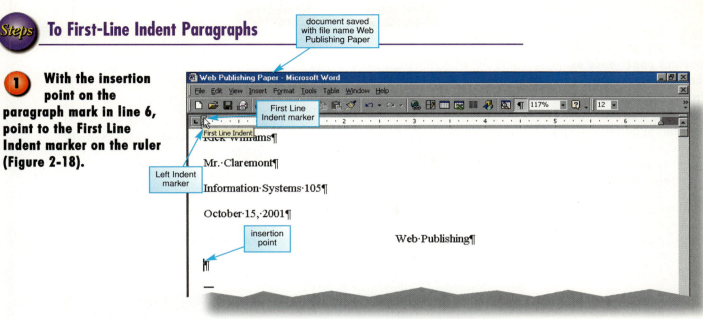

document saved with file name Web Publishing Paper

First Line Indent marker

Left Indent marker

insertion point

FIGURE 2-18

2 Drag the First Line Indent marker to the .5" mark on the ruler.

As you drag the mouse, a vertical dotted line displays in the document window, indicating the proposed location of the first line of the paragraph (Figure 2-19).

.5" mark on ruler

First Line Indent marker

vertical dotted line indicates proposed position of first line of paragraph

FIGURE 2-19

3 Release the mouse button.

The First Line Indent marker displays at the .5" mark on the ruler, or one-half inch from the left margin (Figure 2-20). The paragraph mark containing the insertion point in the document window also moves one-half inch to the right.

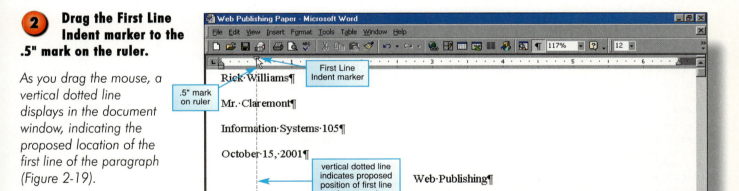

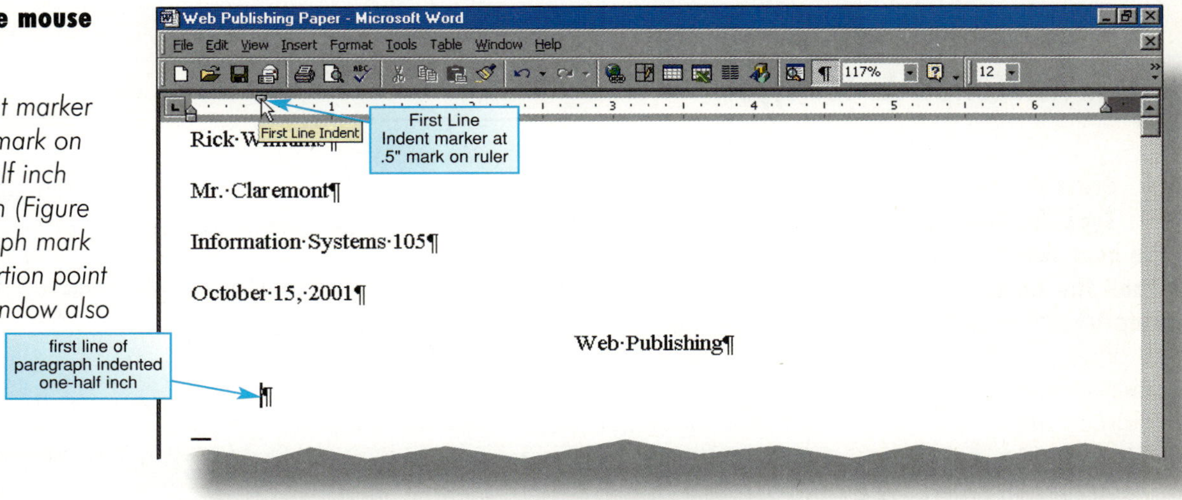

First Line Indent marker at .5" mark on ruler

first line of paragraph indented one-half inch

FIGURE 2-20

4 **Type the first paragraph of the research paper body as shown in Figure 2-21. Press the ENTER key. Type** `Web publishing is the process of developing, maintaining, and posting Web pages.`

Word automatically indents the first line of the second paragraph by one-half inch (Figure 2-21).

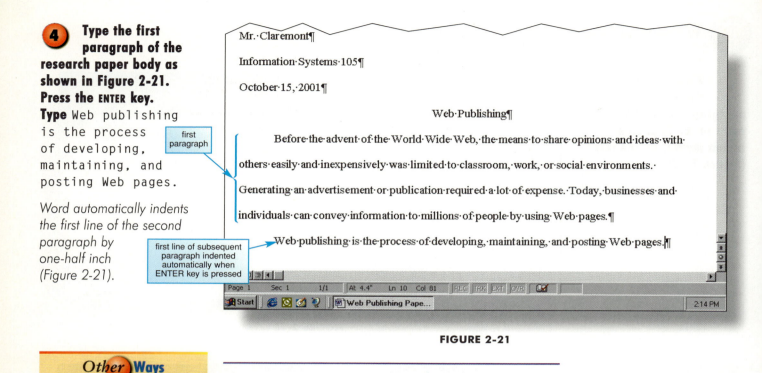

FIGURE 2-21

Other Ways

1. Right-click paragraph, click Paragraph on shortcut menu, click Indents and Spacing tab, click Special box arrow, click First line, click OK button
2. On Format menu click Paragraph, click Indents and Spacing tab, click Special box arrow, click First line, click OK button

Recall that each time you press the ENTER key, the paragraph formatting in the previous paragraph is carried forward to the next paragraph. Thus, once you set the first-line indent, its format is carried automatically to each subsequent paragraph you type.

Using Word's AutoCorrect Feature

Because you may make typing, spelling, capitalization, or grammar errors as you type, Word provides an **AutoCorrect** feature that automatically corrects these errors as you type them into the document. For example, if you type the text, ahve, Word automatically changes it to the word, have, for you when you press the SPACEBAR or a punctuation mark key. Word has predefined many commonly misspelled words, which it automatically corrects for you. Perform the following steps to use the AutoCorrect as you type feature.

Steps To AutoCorrect As You Type

1 **Press the SPACEBAR. Type the beginning of the next sentence and misspell the word, accomplish, as follows:** `With the proper hardware and software, Web publishing is fairly easy to acomplish` **as shown in Figure 2-22.**

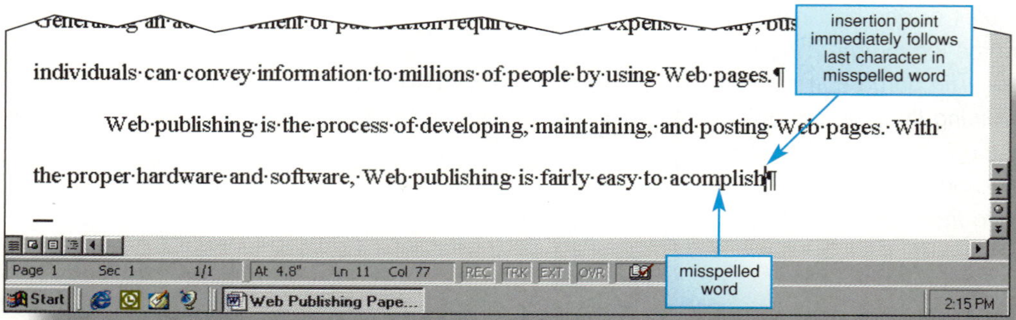

FIGURE 2-22

2 **Press the PERIOD key.**

As soon as you press the PERIOD key, Word's AutoCorrect feature detects the misspelling and corrects the misspelled word (Figure 2-23).

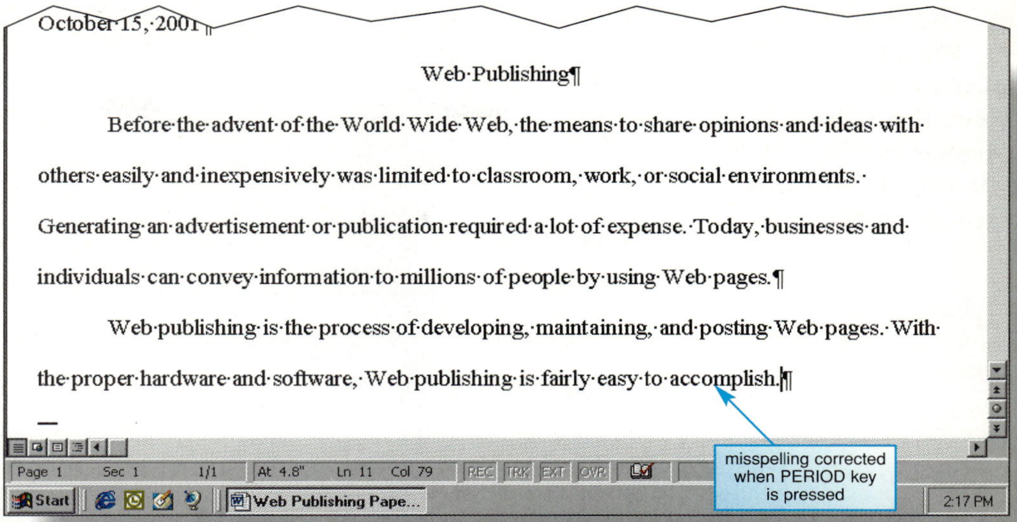

October·15,·2001¶

Web·Publishing¶

Before·the·advent·of·the·World·Wide·Web,·the·means·to·share·opinions·and·ideas·with·

others·easily·and·inexpensively·was·limited·to·classroom,·work,·or·social·environments.·

Generating·an·advertisement·or·publication·required·a·lot·of·expense.·Today,·businesses·and·

individuals·can·convey·information·to·millions·of·people·by·using·Web·pages.¶

Web·publishing·is·the·process·of·developing,·maintaining,·and·posting·Web·pages.·With·

the·proper·hardware·and·software,·Web·publishing·is·fairly·easy·to·accomplish.¶

misspelling corrected when PERIOD key is pressed

| Page 1 | Sec 1 | 1/1 | At 4.8" | Ln 11 | Col 79 | REC | TRK | EXT | OVR | |

Start | Web Publishing Pape... | 2:17 PM

FIGURE 2-23

Word has a list of predefined typing, spelling, capitalization, and grammar errors that AutoCorrect can detect and correct. In addition to the predefined list, you can create your own AutoCorrect entries to add to the list. For example, if you often misspell the word, camera, as canera, you should create an AutoCorrect entry for it as shown in these steps.

Steps **To Create an AutoCorrect Entry**

1 **Click Tools on the menu bar and then point to AutoCorrect (Figure 2-24).**

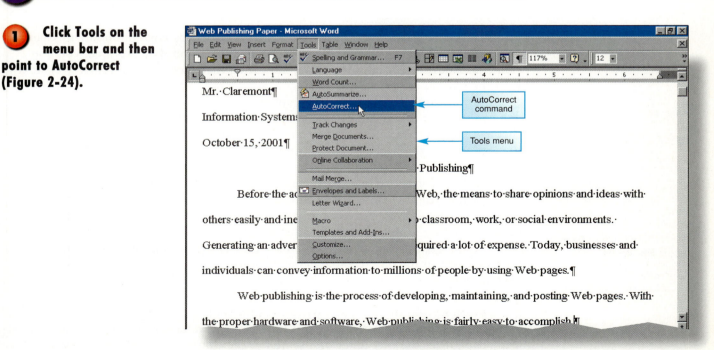

FIGURE 2-24

2 Click AutoCorrect. When the AutoCorrect dialog box displays, type camera in the Replace text box. Press the TAB key and then type camera in the With text box.

Word displays the AutoCorrect dialog box. The Replace text box contains the misspelled word, and the With text box contains its correct spelling (Figure 2-25).

3 Click the Add button. (If your dialog box displays a Replace button instead, click it and then click the Yes button in the Microsoft Word dialog box.) Click the OK button.

Word adds the entry alphabetically to the list of words to correct automatically as you type.

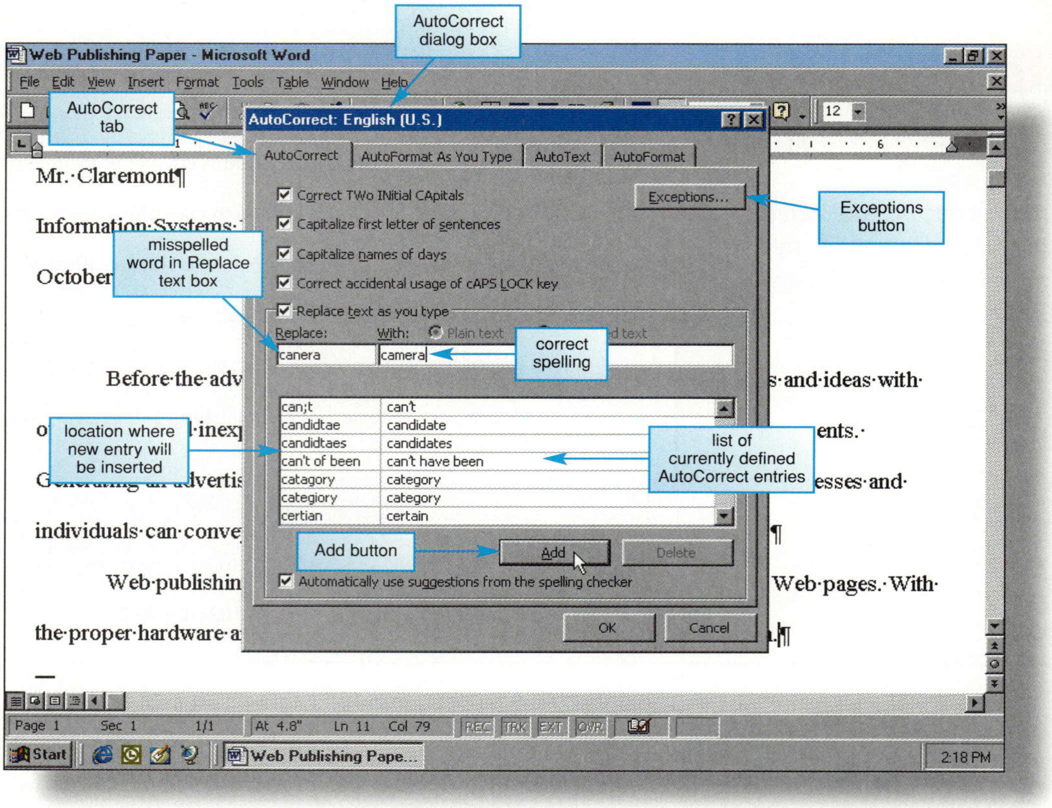

FIGURE 2-25

AutoCorrect

If you have installed the Microsoft Office 2000 Proofing Tools and have enabled editing for another language, Word automatically can detect the language you are using to create the document - as you type. These Proofing Tools provide fonts and templates, check spelling and grammar, and include AutoCorrect lists.

In addition to creating AutoCorrect entries for words you commonly misspell, you can create entries for abbreviations, codes, and so on. For example, you could create an AutoCorrect entry for asap, indicating that Word should replace this text with the phrase, as soon as possible.

If, for some reason, you do not want Word to correct automatically as you type, you can turn off the replace as you type feature by clicking Tools on the menu bar, clicking AutoCorrect, clicking the AutoCorrect tab (Figure 2-25), clicking the Replace text as you type check box to remove the check mark, and then clicking the OK button.

The AutoCorrect sheet (Figure 2-25) also contains four other check boxes that correct capitalization errors if the check boxes are selected. If you type two capital letters in a row such as TH, Word makes the second letter lowercase, Th. If you begin a sentence with a lowercase letter, Word capitalizes the first letter of the sentence. If you type the name of a day in lowercase such as tuesday, Word capitalizes the first letter of the day, Tuesday. Finally, if you leave the CAPS LOCK key on and begin a new sentence such as aFTER, Word corrects the typing, After, and turns off the CAPS LOCK key.

Sometimes you do not want Word to AutoCorrect a particular word or phrase. For example, you may use the code WD. in your documents. Because Word automatically capitalizes the first letter of a sentence, the character you enter following the period will be capitalized (in the previous sentence, it would capitalize the letter i in the word, in). To allow the code WD. to be entered into a document and still leave the AutoCorrect feature turned on, you need to set an exception. To set an exception to an AutoCorrect rule, click Tools on the menu bar, click AutoCorrect, click the AutoCorrect tab, click the Exceptions button in the AutoCorrect sheet (Figure 2-25), click the appropriate tab in the AutoCorrect Exceptions dialog box, type the exception entry in the text box, click the Add button, click the Close button in the AutoCorrect Exceptions dialog box, and then click the Close button in the AutoCorrect dialog box.

Adding Footnotes

You have learned that explanatory notes are optional in the MLA documentation style. They are used primarily to elaborate on points discussed in the body of the paper. The style specifies that a superscript (raised number) be used for a note reference mark to signal that an explanatory note exists either at the bottom of the page as a **footnote** or at the end of the document as an **endnote**.

Word, by default, places notes at the bottom of each page. In Word, **note text** can be any length and format. Word automatically numbers notes sequentially for you by placing a **note reference mark** in the body of the document and also in front of the note text. If you insert, rearrange, or remove notes, any subsequent note text and reference marks are renumbered according to their new sequence in the document. Perform the following steps to add a footnote to the research paper.

MLA and APA

Both the MLA and APA guidelines suggest the use of in-text parenthetical citations, as opposed to footnoting each source of material in a paper. These parenthetical acknowledgments guide the reader to the end of the paper for complete information on the source.

Steps To Add a Footnote

1 **Press the SPACEBAR and then type** For example, clip galleries offer a variety of images, videos, and sounds. **Click Insert on the menu bar and then point to Footnote.**

The insertion point is positioned immediately after the period following the end of the sentence (Figure 2-26).

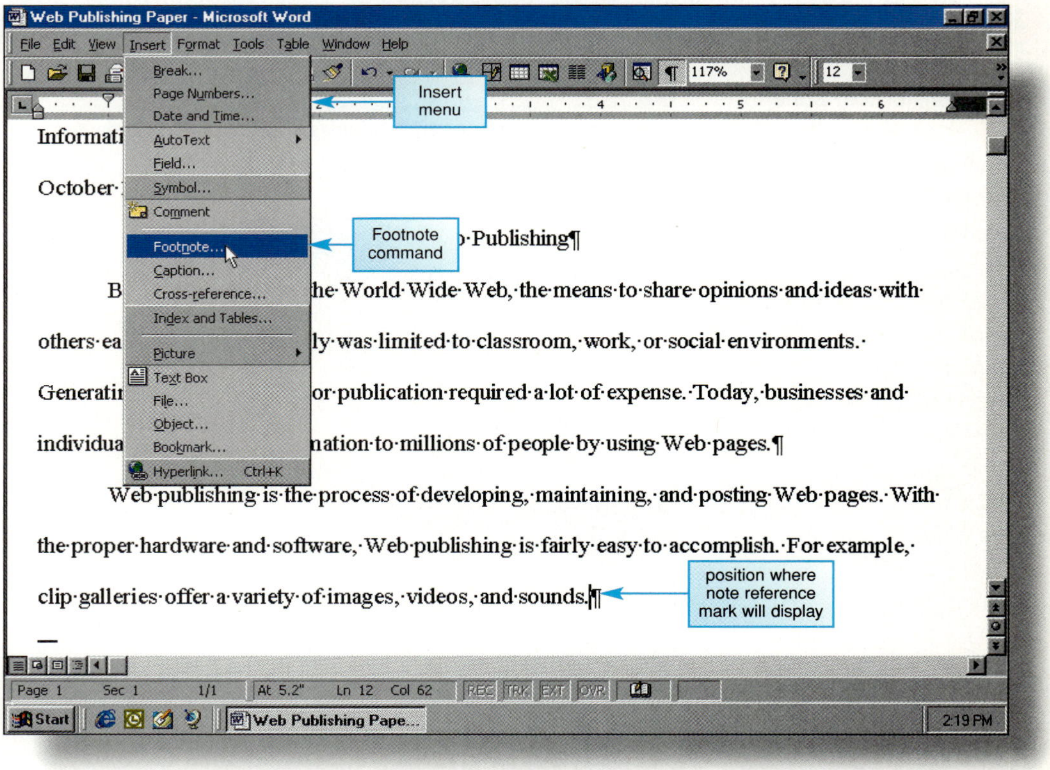

FIGURE 2-26

2 **Click Footnote. When the Footnote and Endnote dialog box displays, point to the OK button.**

Word displays the Footnote and Endnote dialog box (Figure 2-27).

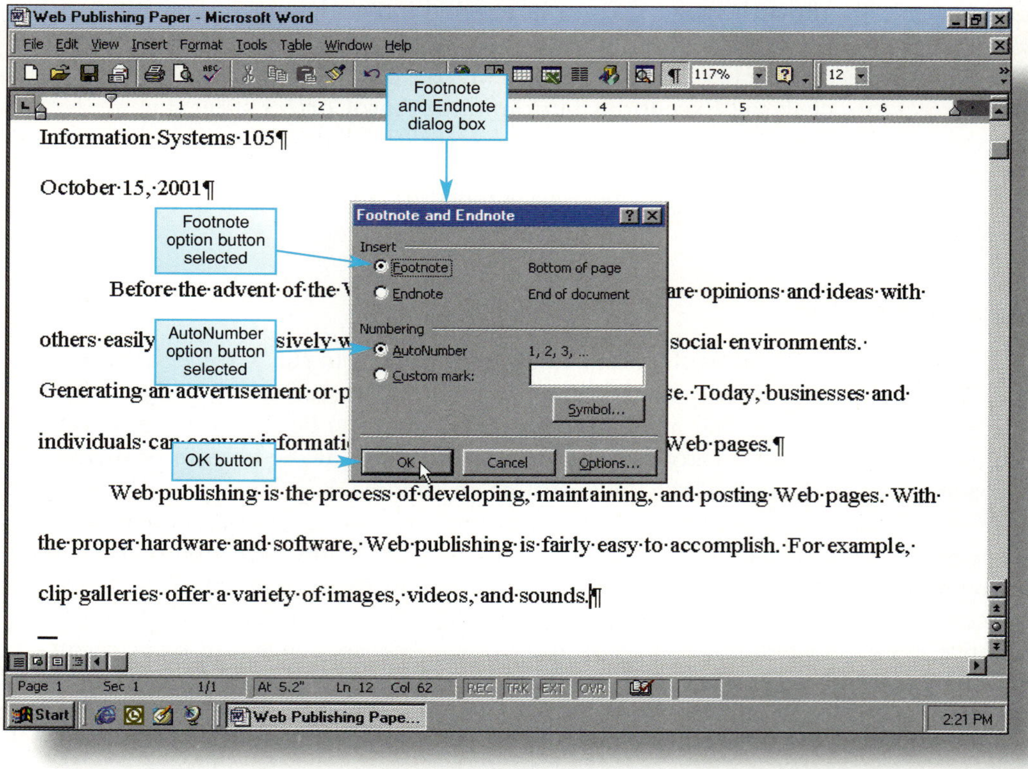

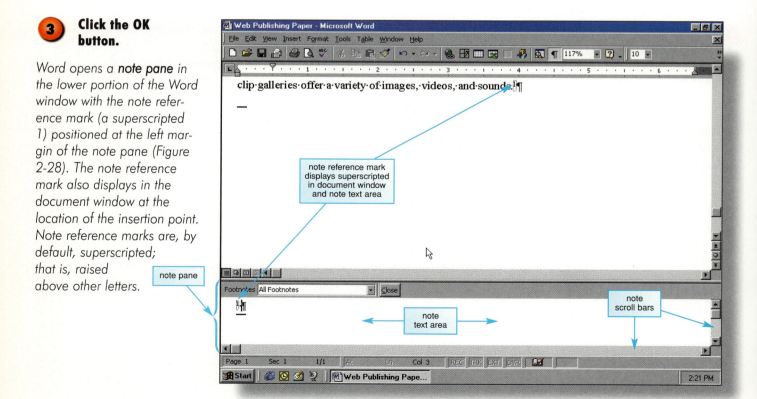

FIGURE 2-27

3 **Click the OK button.**

*Word opens a **note pane** in the lower portion of the Word window with the note reference mark (a superscripted 1) positioned at the left margin of the note pane (Figure 2-28). The note reference mark also displays in the document window at the location of the insertion point. Note reference marks are, by default, superscripted; that is, raised above other letters.*

FIGURE 2-28

4 **Type** Many
current software
packages include a
clip gallery. Clip
galleries also are
available on the Web
or may be purchased
on CD-ROM or DVD-ROM
(Zack 9-24).

*Word enters the note text in
the note pane (Figure 2-29).*

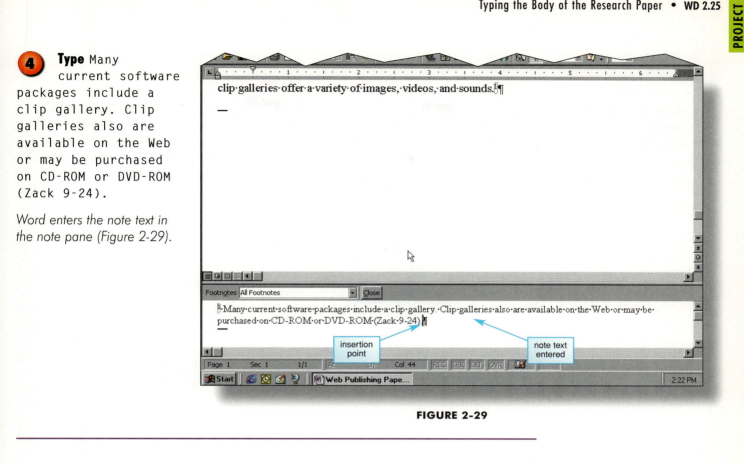

clip·galleries·offer·a·variety·of·images,·videos,·and·sounds.¶

Footnotes [All Footnotes ▼] [Close]

¹·Many·current·software·packages·include·a·clip·gallery.·Clip·galleries·also·are·available·on·the·Web·or·may·be·
purchased·on·CD-ROM·or·DVD-ROM·(Zack·9-24).¶

insertion
point

note text
entered

Page 1   Sec 1   1/1   Ac   Ln   Col 44   [REC] [TRK] [EXT] [OVR] [◻]

🏁Start 📧 🔵 📄 📝 📧Web Publishing Pape...   2:22 PM

FIGURE 2-29

The footnote is not formatted according to the MLA style. Thus, the next step is to modify the style of the footnote.

Modifying a Style

A **style** is a customized format that you can apply to text. The formats defined by a style include character formatting such as the font and font size, and paragraph formatting such as line spacing and text alignment. Word has many built-in, or predefined, styles that you may use to format text. You can modify the formatting associated with these styles, or you can define new styles.

The base style for new Word documents is called the **Normal style**, which for a new installation of Word 2000 more than likely uses 12-point Times New Roman font for characters and single-spaced, left-aligned paragraphs. Recall from Project 1 that when you upgrade to Word 2000 from a previous version of Word, the default point size more than likely is 10 instead of 12.

In Figure 2-29, the insertion point is in the note text area, which is formatted using the Footnote Text style. The Footnote Text style is based on the Normal style. Thus, the text of the footnote you entered is single-spaced and left-aligned.

You could change the paragraph formatting of the footnote text to first-line indent and double-spacing as you did for the text in the document window. If you use this technique, however, you will have to change the format of the footnote text for each footnote you enter into the document. A more efficient technique is to modify the format of the Footnote Text style so paragraphs based on this style are double-spaced with a first-line indent format. Thus, by changing the formatting associated with the Footnote Text style, every footnote you enter will use the formats defined in this style. Perform the steps on the next page to modify the Footnote Text style.

More About

Styles

The Style box on the Formatting toolbar displays the name of the style associated with the location of the insertion point. Click the Style box arrow on the Formatting toolbar to view the list of styles associated with the current document. To apply a style, select the text to format, click the Style box arrow, and then click the desired style name in the list.

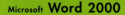

 **To Modify a Style**

1 **Click Format on the menu bar and then point to Style (Figure 2-30).**

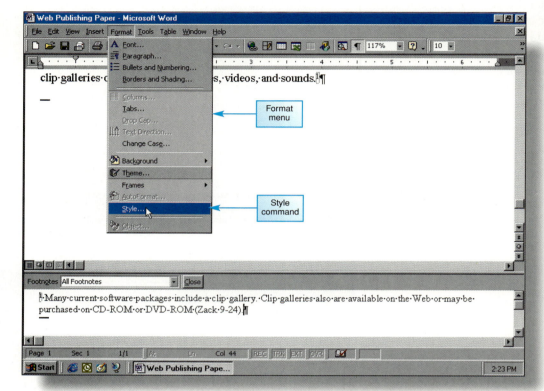

FIGURE 2-30

2 **Click Style. When the Style dialog box displays, click Footnote Text in the Styles list, if necessary, and then point to the Modify button.**

Word displays the Style dialog box (Figure 2-31). Footnote Text is highlighted in the Styles list. The Description area shows the formatting associated with the selected style.

FIGURE 2-31

3 Click the Modify button. When the Modify Style dialog box displays, click the Format button and then point to Paragraph.

Word displays the Modify Style dialog box (Figure 2-32). A list of formatting commands displays above or below the Format button.

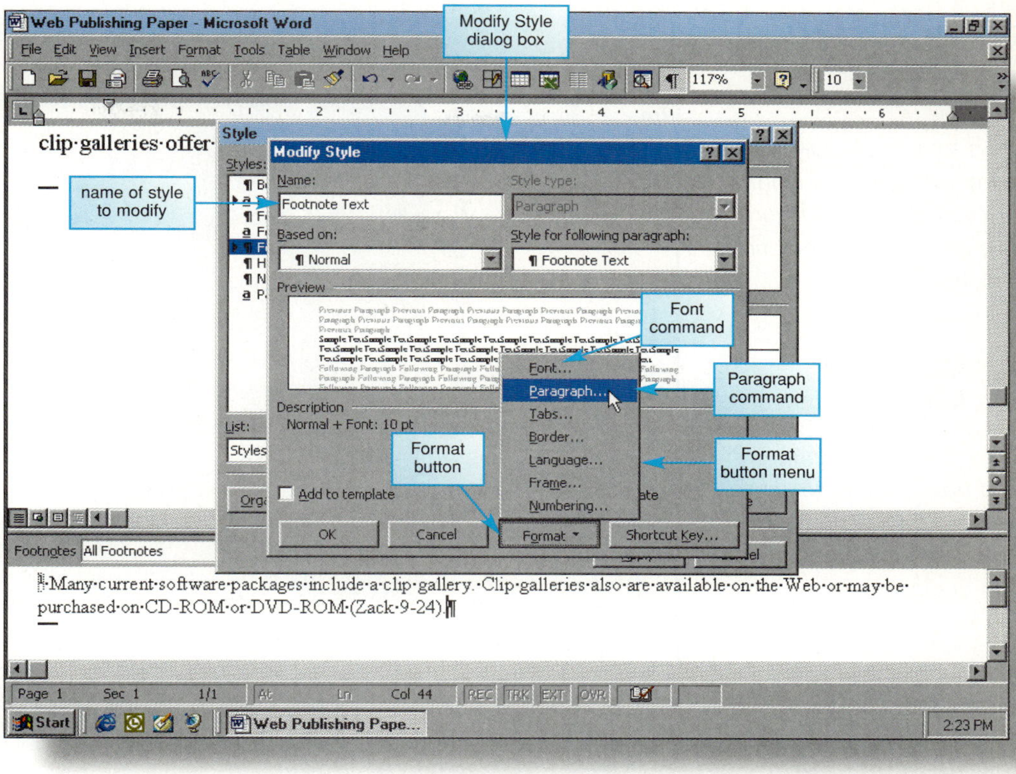

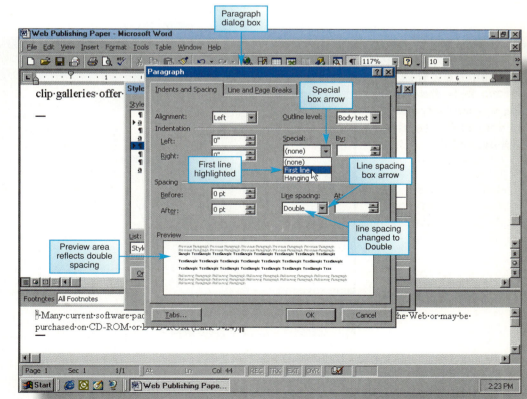

FIGURE 2-32

4 Click Paragraph. When the Paragraph dialog box displays, click the Line spacing box arrow and then click Double. Click the Special box arrow and then point to First line.

Word displays the Paragraph dialog box (Figure 2-33). The Preview area reflects the current settings in the Paragraph dialog box.

FIGURE 2-33

5 Click First line. Point to the OK button.

Word displays First line in the Special box and Double in the Line spacing box (Figure 2-34). Notice the default first-line indent is .5".

6 Click the OK button.

Word removes the Paragraph dialog box, and the Modify Style dialog box (see Figure 2-32 on the previous page) is visible again.

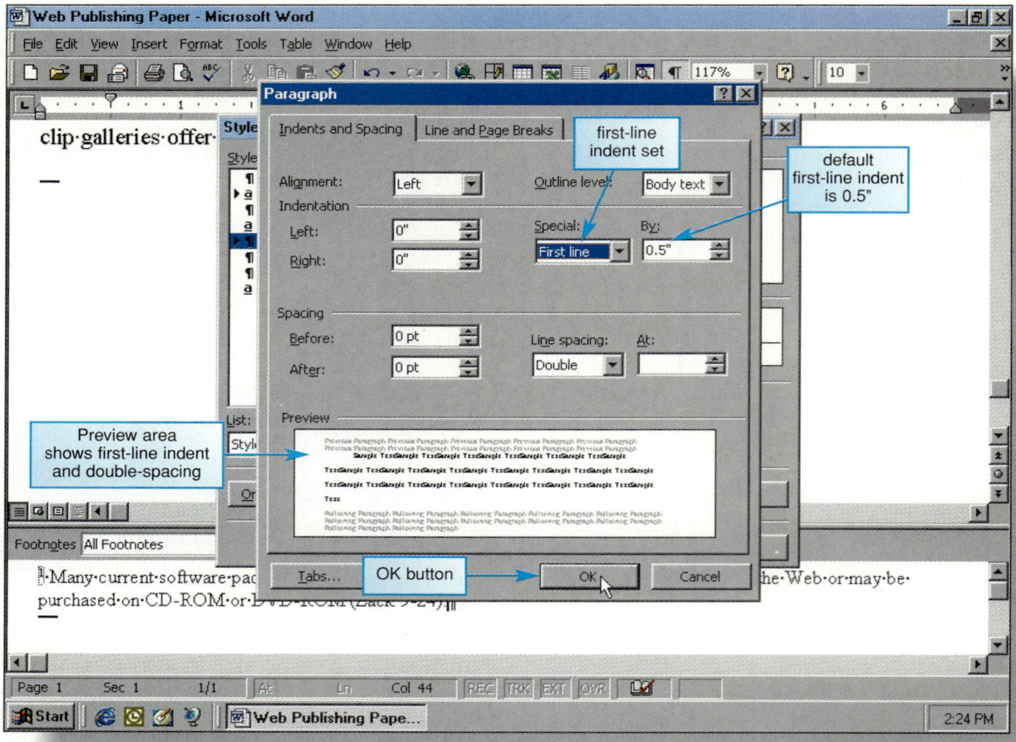

FIGURE 2-34

7 In the Modify Style dialog box, click the Format button and then click Font. When the Font dialog box displays, click 12 in the Size list. Point to the OK button.

Word displays the Font dialog box (Figure 2-35). Depending on your installation of Word 2000, the Size box already may display 12.

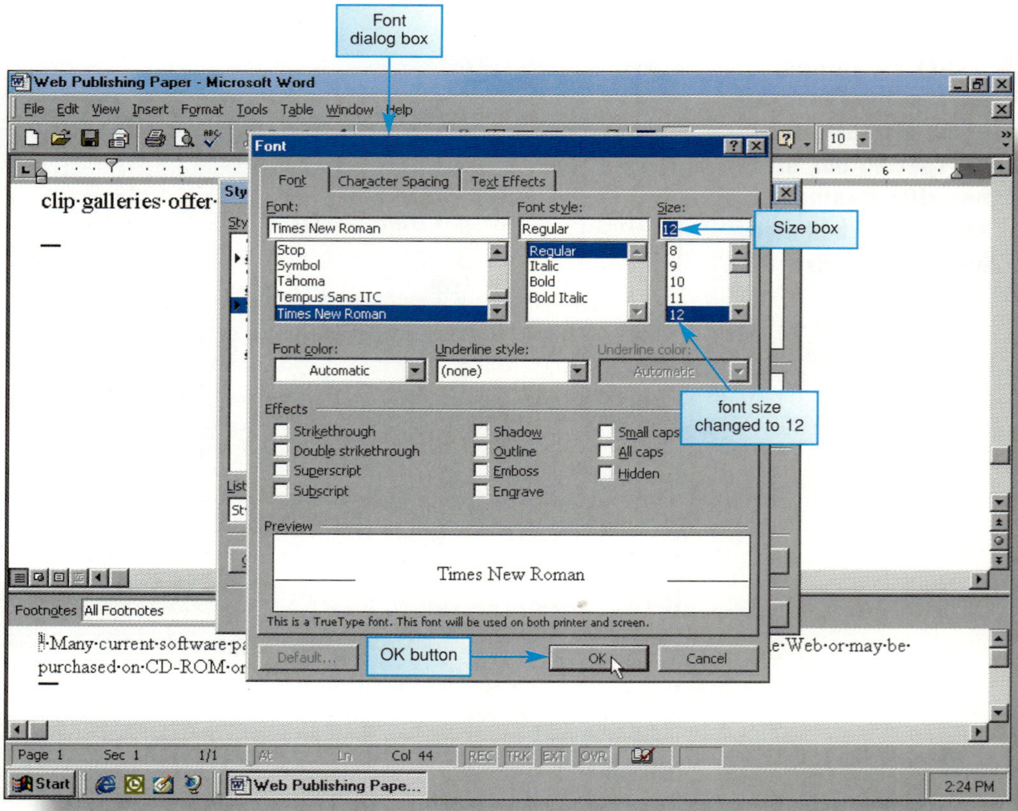

FIGURE 2-35

8 **Click the OK button. When the Modify Style dialog box is visible again, point to the OK button.**

Word removes the Font dialog box, and the Modify Style dialog box is visible again (Figure 2-36). Word modifies the Footnote Text style to a 12-point font with double-spaced and first-line indented paragraphs.

9 **Click the OK button. When the Style dialog box is visible again, click the Apply button. Click the note pane up scroll arrow to display the entire footnote.**

Word indents the first line of the note by one-half inch and sets the line spacing for the note to double (Figure 2-37 below).

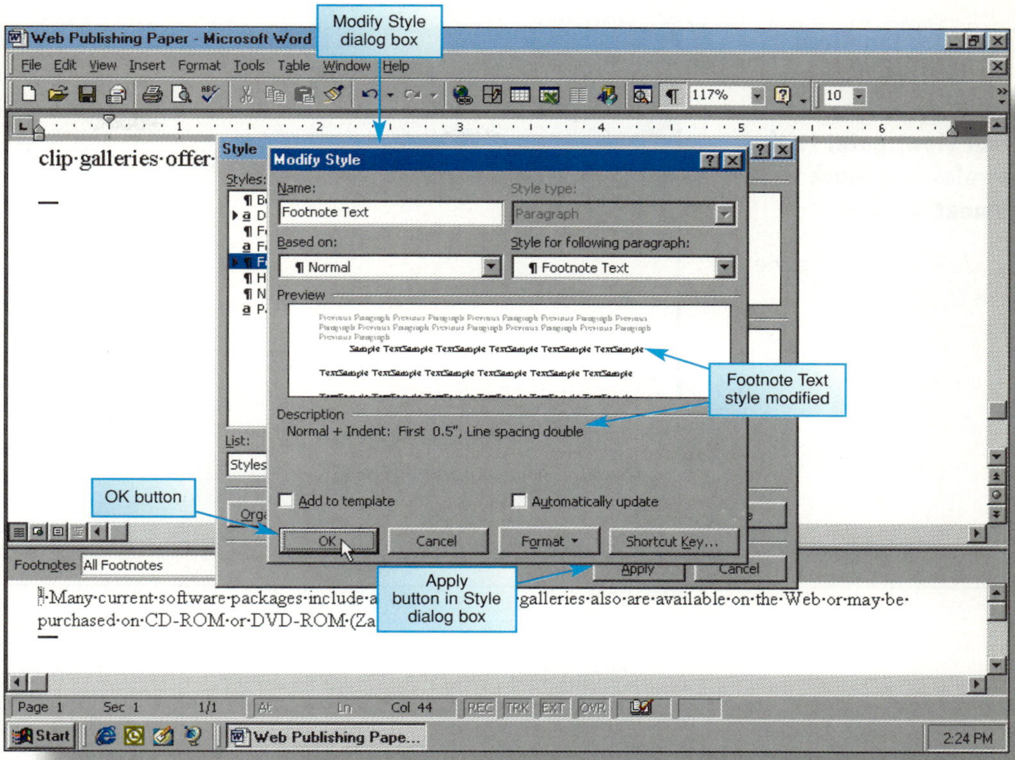

FIGURE 2-36

Any future footnotes entered into the document will use a 12-point font with first-line indented and double-spaced paragraphs. The footnote is complete. The next step is to close the note pane.

To Close the Note Pane

1 **Point to the Close button in the note pane (Figure 2-37).**

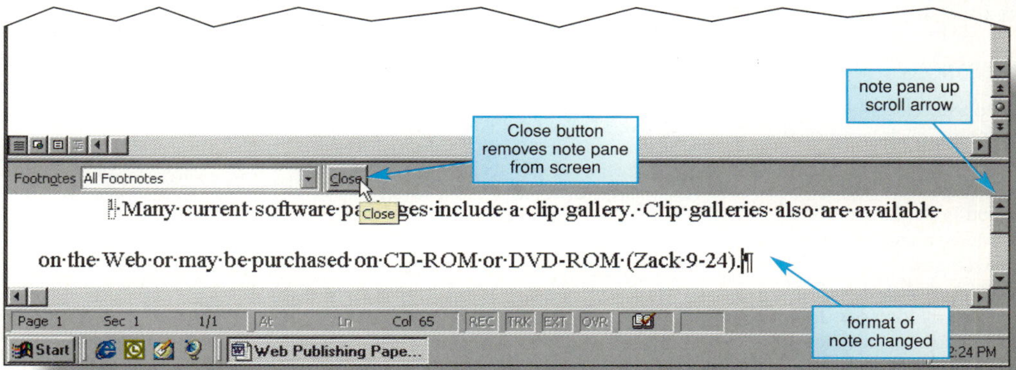

FIGURE 2-37

2 **Click the Close button. If you want to see the note text in normal view, point to the note reference mark in the document window.**

Word closes the note pane (Figure 2-38).

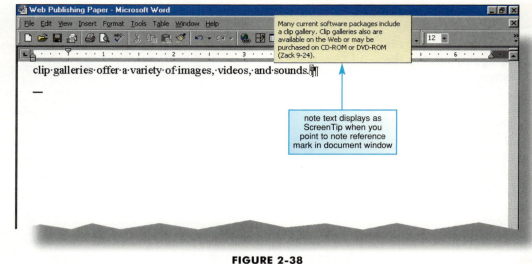

FIGURE 2-38

When Word closes the note pane and returns to the document window, the note text disappears from the screen. Although the note text still exists, it usually is not visible as a footnote in normal view. If, however, you point to the note reference mark, the note text displays above the note reference mark as a **ScreenTip** (Figure 2-38).

To delete a note, you select the note reference mark in the document window (not in the note pane) by dragging through the note reference mark and then clicking the Cut button on the Standard toolbar. Another way to delete a note is to click to the right of the note reference mark in the document window and then press BACKSPACE key twice, or click to the left of the note reference mark in the document window and then press the DELETE key twice. To move a note to a different location in a document, you select the note reference mark in the document window (not in the note pane), click the Cut button on the Standard toolbar, click the location where you want to move the note, and then click the Paste button on the Standard toolbar. When you move or delete notes, Word automatically renumbers any remaining notes in the correct sequence.

You edit note text using the note pane at the bottom of the Word window. To display the note text in a note pane, double-click the note reference mark in the document window or click View on the menu bar and then click Footnotes. Edit the note as you would any Word text and then click the Close button in the note pane. If you want to verify that the note text is positioned correctly on the page, you must switch to print layout view or display the document in print preview. These views are discussed later.

The next step is to enter more text into the body of the research paper. Follow these steps to enter more text.

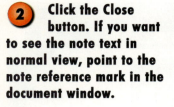

TO ENTER MORE TEXT

1 Press the SPACEBAR. Type the remainder of the second paragraph of the paper as shown in Figure 2-39.

2 Press the ENTER key. Type the third paragraph of the paper as shown in Figure 2-39.

The second and third paragraphs are entered (Figure 2-39).

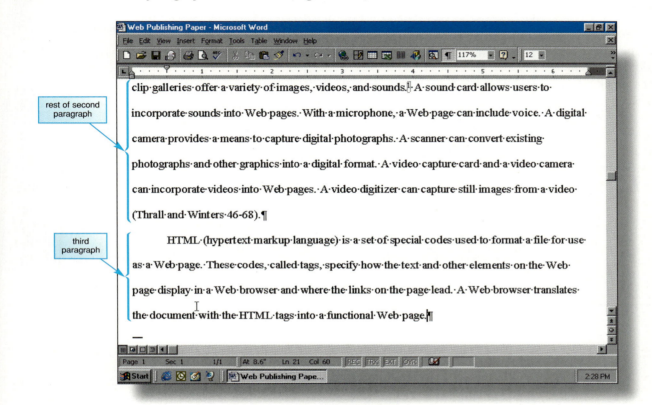

FIGURE 2-39

Automatic Page Breaks

As you type documents that exceed one page, Word automatically inserts page breaks, called **automatic page breaks** or **soft page breaks**, when it determines the text has filled one page according to paper size, margin settings, line spacing, and other settings. If you add text, delete text, or modify text on a page, Word recomputes the position of automatic page breaks and adjusts them accordingly. Word performs page recomputation between the keystrokes; that is, in between the pauses in your typing. Thus, Word refers to the automatic page break task as **background repagination**. In normal view, automatic page breaks display on the Word screen as a single dotted horizontal line. Word's automatic page break feature is illustrated in the step on the next page.

APA and MLA Documentation Styles

The World Wide Web contains a host of information on the APA and MLA documentation styles. College professors and fellow students develop many of these Web pages. For a list of Web links to sites on the APA and MLA styles, visit the Word 2000 More About Web page (www.scsite.com/wd2000/more.htm) and then click Links to Sites on the APA and MLA Styles.

To Page Break Automatically

1 Press the ENTER key and then type the first two sentences of the fourth paragraph of the paper, as shown in Figure 2-40.

As you begin typing the paragraph, Word places an automatic page break between the third and fourth paragraphs in the paper (Figure 2-40). The status bar now displays Page 2 as the current page.

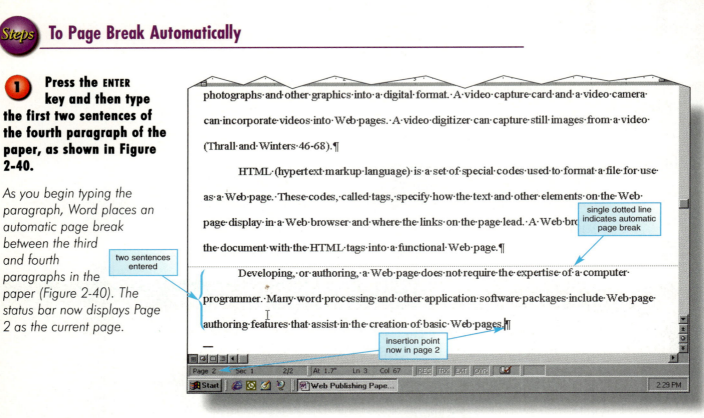

FIGURE 2-40

Your page break may occur at a different location, depending on your printer type.

The header, although not shown in normal view, contains the name Williams and the page number 2. If you wanted to view the header, click View on the menu bar and then click Header and Footer. Then, click the Close button on the Header and Footer toolbar to return to normal view.

Word, by default, prevents widows and orphans from occurring in a document. A **widow** is created when the last line of a paragraph displays by itself at the top of a page, and an **orphan** occurs when the first line of a paragraph displays by itself at the bottom of a page. You turn this setting on and off through the Paragraph dialog box. If, for some reason, you wanted to allow a widow or an orphan in a document, you would right-click the paragraph in question, click Paragraph on the shortcut menu, click the Line and Page Breaks tab in the Paragraph dialog box, click Widow/Orphan control to select or deselect the check box, and then click the OK button.

The Line and Page Breaks sheet in the Paragraph dialog box also contains two other check boxes that control how Word places automatic page breaks. If you did not want a page break to occur within a particular paragraph, you would right-click the paragraph you wanted to keep together, click Paragraph on the shortcut menu, click the Line and Page Breaks tab in the Paragraph dialog box, click Keep lines together to select the check box, and then click the OK button. If you did not want a page break to occur between two paragraphs, you would select the two paragraphs, right-click the selection, click Paragraph on the shortcut menu, click the Line and Page Breaks tab in the Paragraph dialog box, click Keep with next to select the check box, and then click the OK button.

Inserting Arrows, Faces, and Other Symbols Automatically

Earlier in this project, you learned that Word has prede-fined many commonly misspelled words, which it automati-cally corrects for you as you type. In addition to words, this built-in list of **AutoCorrect entries** also contains many com-monly used symbols. For example, to insert a smiling face into a document, you type :) and Word automatically changes it to ☺. Table 2-3 lists the characters you type to insert arrows, faces, and other symbols into a Word document.

You also can enter the first four symbols in Table 2-3 by clicking Insert on the menu bar, clicking Symbol, clicking the Special Characters tab, clicking the desired symbol in the Character list, clicking the Insert button, and then clicking the Close button in the Symbol dialog box.

If you do not like a change that Word automatically makes in a document, undo the change by clicking the Undo button on the Standard toolbar; clicking Edit on the menu bar and then clicking Undo; or pressing CTRL+Z.

The next step in the research paper is to enter a sentence that uses the registered trademark symbol. Perform the following steps to insert automatically the registered trademark symbol into the research paper.

Table 2-3 Word's Automatic Symbols		
TO DISPLAY	**DESCRIPTION**	**TYPE**
©	copyright symbol	(c)
®	registered trademark symbol	(r)
™	trademark symbol	(tm)
…	ellipsis	...
☺	smiley face	:) or :-)
☻	indifferent face	:l or :-l
☹	frowning face	:(or :-(
→	thin right arrow	-->
←	thin left arrow	<--
➜	thick right arrow	==>
←	thick left arrow	<==
⇔	double arrow	<=>

Steps To Insert a Symbol Automatically

1 **With the insertion point positioned as shown in Figure 2-40, press the SPACEBAR. Type** Microsoft Office 2000 products, for example, provide easy-to-use tools that enable users to create Web pages and include items such as bullets, frames, backgrounds, lines, database tables, worksheets, and graphics into the Web pages (**as the beginning of the sentence. Press CTRL+I to turn on italics. Type** Shelly Cashman Series(r **as shown in Figure 2-41.**

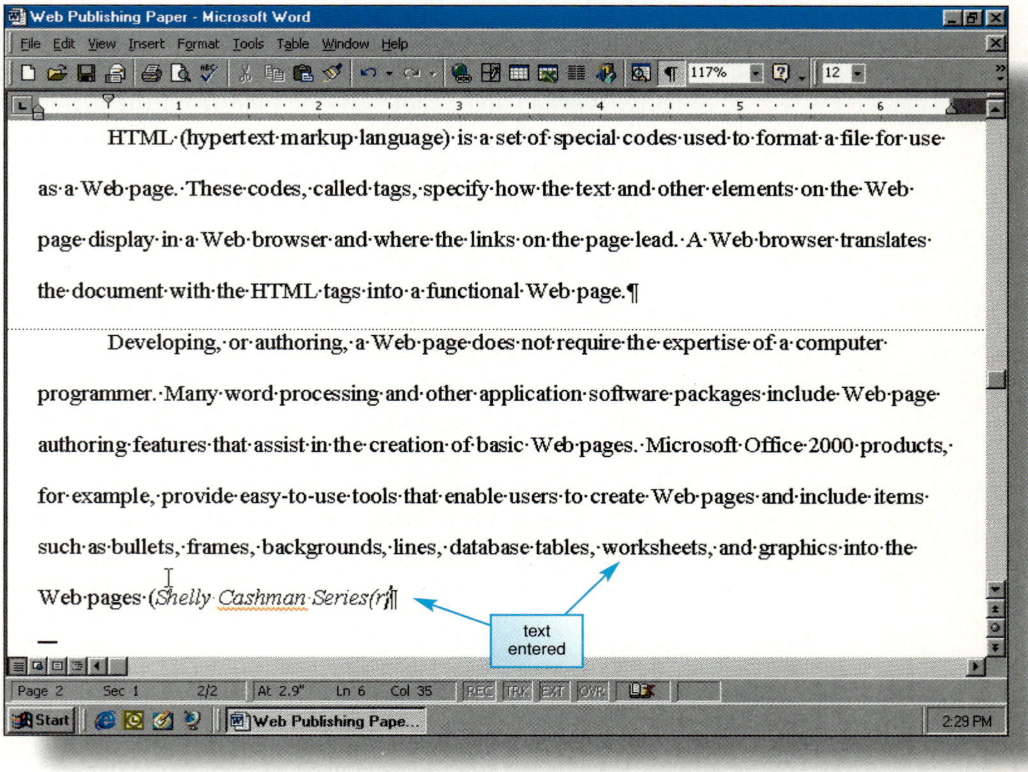

FIGURE 2-41

2 **Press the RIGHT PARENTHESIS key.**

Word automatically converts the (r) to ®, the registered trademark symbol.

3 **Press the SPACEBAR. Type** `Microsoft Word 2000 Project 2` **and then press CTRL+I to turn off italics. Press the RIGHT PARENTHESIS key and then press the PERIOD key. Press the SPACEBAR. Enter the last two sentences of the research paper as shown in Figure 2-42.**

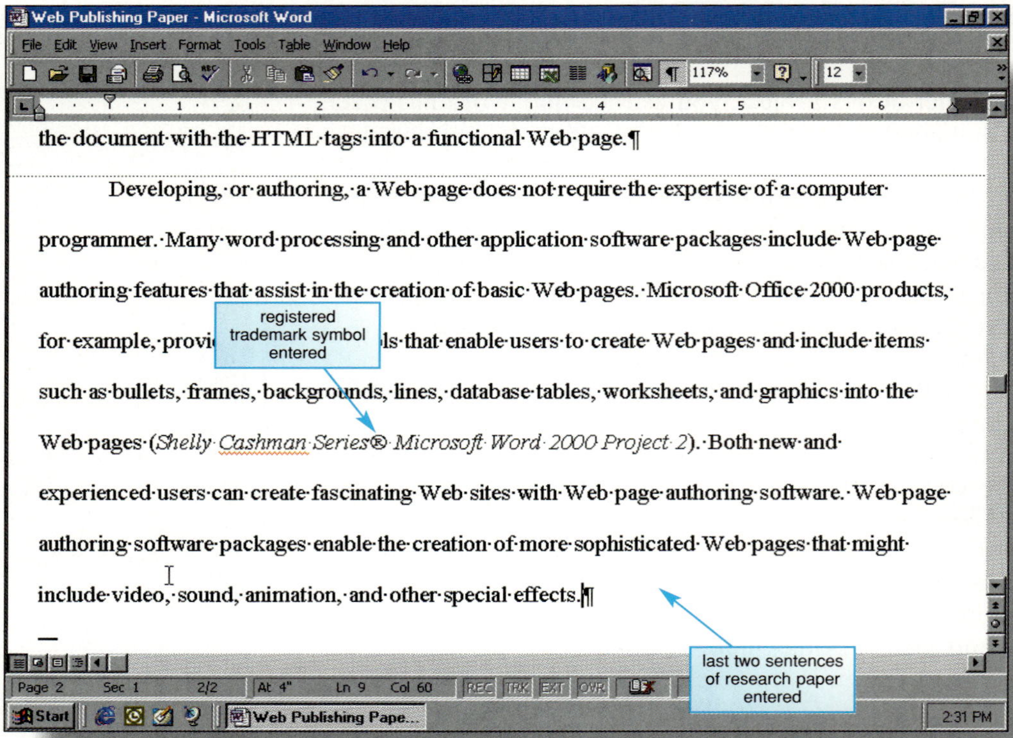
Web Publishing Paper - Microsoft Word
File Edit View Insert Format Tools Table Window Help
the document with the HTML tags into a functional Web page.¶
Developing, or authoring, a Web page does not require the expertise of a computer programmer. Many word processing and other application software packages include Web page authoring features that assist in the creation of basic Web pages. Microsoft Office 2000 products, for example, provi…ls that enable users to create Web pages and include items such as bullets, frames, backgrounds, lines, database tables, worksheets, and graphics into the Web pages (Shelly Cashman Series® Microsoft Word 2000 Project 2). Both new and experienced users can create fascinating Web sites with Web page authoring software. Web page authoring software packages enable the creation of more sophisticated Web pages that might include video, sound, animation, and other special effects.¶
registered trademark symbol entered
last two sentences of research paper entered
Page 2 Sec 1 2/2 At 4" Ln 9 Col 60
Start
Web Publishing Pape...
2:31 PM

FIGURE 2-42

Creating an Alphabetical Works Cited Page

According to the MLA style, the **works cited page** is a bibliographical list of works you reference directly in your paper. The list is placed on a separate page with the title, Works Cited, centered one inch from the top margin. The works are to be alphabetized by the author's last name or, if the work has no author, by the work's title. The first line of each entry begins at the left margin; subsequent lines of the same entry are indented one-half inch from the left margin.

The first step in creating the works cited page is to force a page break so the works cited display on a separate page.

Manual Page Breaks

Because the works cited are to display on a separate numbered page, you must insert a manual page break following the body of the research paper. A **manual page break,** or **hard page break,** is one that you force into the document at a specific location. Manual page breaks display on the screen as a horizontal dotted line, separated by the words, Page Break. Word never moves or adjusts manual page breaks; however, Word does adjust any automatic page breaks that follow a manual page break. Word inserts manual page breaks just before the location of the insertion point. Perform the following step to insert a manual page break after the body of the research paper.

Steps To Page Break Manually

1 **With the insertion point at the end of the research paper, press the ENTER key. Then, press the CTRL+ENTER keys.**

The shortcut keys, CTRL+ENTER, instruct Word to insert a manual page break immediately above the insertion point and position the insertion point immediately below the manual page break (Figure 2-43). The status bar indicates the insertion point is located on page 3.

authoring·features·that·assist·in·the·creation·of·basic·Web·pages.·Microsoft·Office·2000·products,·

for·example,·provide·easy-to-use·tools·that·enable·users·to·create·Web·pages·and·include·items·

such·as·bullets,·frames,·backgrounds,·lines,·database·tables,·worksheets,·and·graphics·into·the·

Web·pages·(*Shelly·Cashman·Series® Microsoft·Word·2000·Project·2*).·Both·new·and·

experienced·users·can·create·fascinating·Web·sites·with·Web·page·authoring·software.·Web·page·

authoring·software·packages·enable·the·creation·of·more·sophisticated·Web·pages·that·might·

include·video,·sound,·animation,·and·other·special·effects.¶

----------------------------Page Break----------------------------

insertion point on page 3

manual page break

Page 3   Sec 1   3/3   At 1"   Ln 1   Col 1   REC TRK EXT OVR

FIGURE 2-43

The manual page break displays as a horizontal dotted line with the words, Page Break, in the middle of the line. The header, although not shown in normal view, contains the name Williams and the page number 3. If you wanted to view the header, click View on the menu bar and then click Header and Footer. Then, click the Close button on the Header and Footer toolbar to return to normal view.

If, for some reason, you wanted to remove a manual page break from your document, you must first select it by double-clicking it. Then, press the DELETE key; or click the Cut button on the Standard toolbar; or right-click the selection and then click Cut on the shortcut menu.

Centering the Title of the Works Cited Page

The works cited title is to be centered between the margins. If you simply click the Center button on the Formatting toolbar, the title will not be centered properly; instead, it will be one-half inch to the right of the center point because earlier you set first-line indent at one-half inch. Thus, the first line of every paragraph is indented one-half inch. To properly center the title of the works cited page, you must move the First Line Indent marker back to the left margin before clicking the Center button as described in the steps on the next page.

More *About*

Documentation Styles

The MLA documentation style uses the title *Works Cited* for the page containing bibliographical references, whereas the APA style uses the title *References*. APA guidelines for preparing the reference list entries differ significantly from the MLA style. Refer to an APA handbook for specifics.

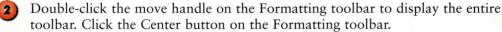

TO CENTER THE TITLE OF THE WORKS CITED PAGE

1 Drag the First Line Indent marker to the 0" mark on the ruler.

2 Double-click the move handle on the Formatting toolbar to display the entire toolbar. Click the Center button on the Formatting toolbar.

3 Type Works Cited as the title.

4 Press the ENTER key.

5 Because your fingers are on the keyboard, press the CTRL+L keys to left-align the paragraph mark.

The title displays centered properly and the insertion point is left-aligned (Figure 2-44).

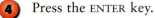

More *About*

2000

Formatting

Minimize strain on your wrist by switching between the mouse and keyboard as little as possible. If your fingers are already on the keyboard, use shortcut keys to format text; if your fingers are already on the mouse, use the mouse to format text.

FIGURE 2-44

More *About*

2000

Crediting Sources

When writing a research paper, you must acknowledge sources of information. Citing sources is a matter of ethics and honesty. Use caution when summarizing or para-phrasing a source. Be sure to avoid plagiarism, which includes using someone else's words or ideas and claiming them as your own.

Creating a Hanging Indent

On the works cited page, the first line of each entry begins at the left margin. Subsequent lines in the same paragraph are indented one-half inch from the left margin. In essence, the first line *hangs* to the left of the rest of the paragraph; thus, this type of paragraph formatting is called a **hanging indent**.

One method of creating a hanging indent is to use the horizontal ruler. The **Hanging Indent marker** is the bottom triangle at the 0" mark on the ruler (Figure 2-45). You have learned that the small square at the 0" mark is called the Left Indent marker. Perform the following steps to create a hanging indent.

Steps **To Create a Hanging Indent**

1 **With the insertion point in the paragraph to format (see Figure 2-44), point to the Hanging Indent marker on the ruler (Figure 2-45).**

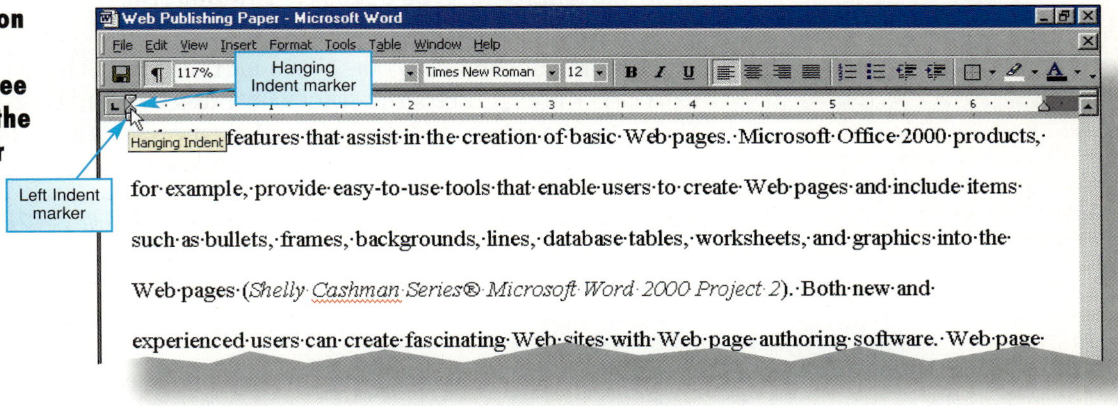

FIGURE 2-45

2 **Drag the Hanging Indent marker to the .5" mark on the ruler.**

The Hanging Indent marker and Left Indent marker display one-half inch from the left margin (Figure 2-46). When you drag the Hanging Indent marker, the Left Indent marker moves with it. The insertion point in the document window remains at the left margin because only subsequent lines in the paragraph are to be indented.

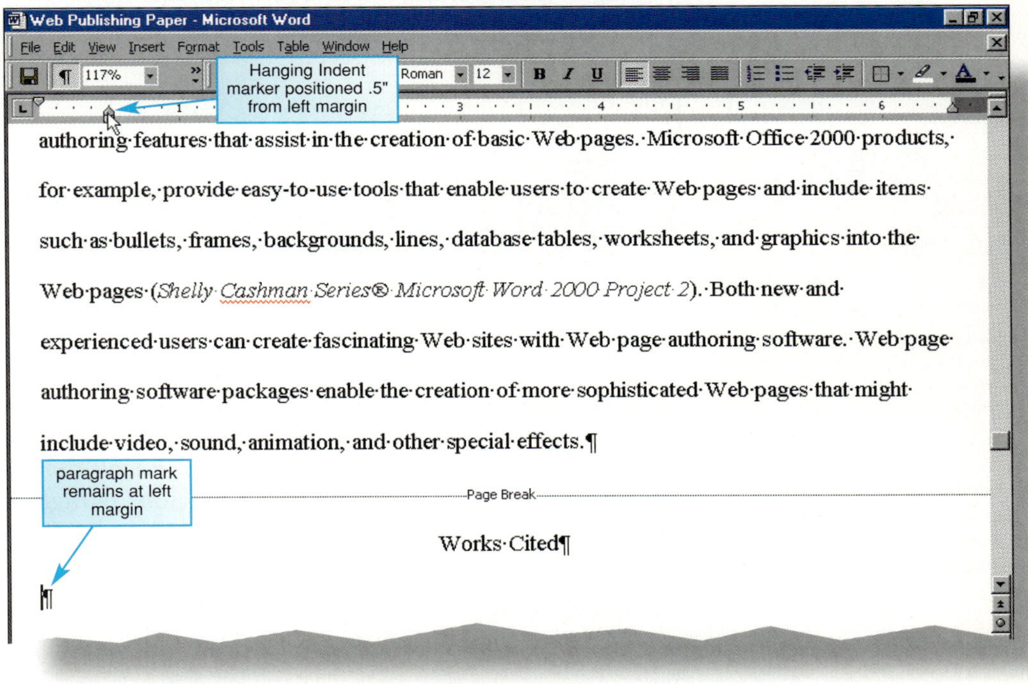

FIGURE 2-46

To drag both the First Line Indent and Hanging Indent markers at the same time, you drag the Left Indent marker on the ruler.

Enter the first two works in the works cited as explained in the steps on the next page.

Other **Ways**

1. Right-click paragraph, click Paragraph on shortcut menu, click Indents and Spacing tab, click Special box arrow, click Hanging, click OK button

2. On Format menu click Paragraph, click Indents and Spacing tab, click Special box arrow, click Hanging, click OK button

3. Press CTRL+T

More About

Citing Sources

Information that commonly is known or accessible to the audience constitutes common knowledge and does not need to be listed as a parenthetical citation or in the bibliography. If you question whether certain information is common knowledge, you should cite it – just to be safe.

TO ENTER WORK CITED PARAGRAPHS

1 Type Thrall, Peter D., and Amy P. Winters. Press the SPACEBAR. Press CTRL+I. Type Computer Concepts for the New Millennium. Press CTRL+I. Press the SPACEBAR. Type Boston: International Press, 2001. Press the ENTER key.

2 Type Zack, Joseph R. "An Introduction to Clip Galleries and Digital Files." Press the SPACEBAR. Press CTRL+I. Type Computers for Today, Tomorrow, and Beyond and then press CTRL+I. Press the SPACEBAR. Type Sep. 2001: 9-24. Press the ENTER key.

The first two works cited paragraphs are entered (Figure 2-47).

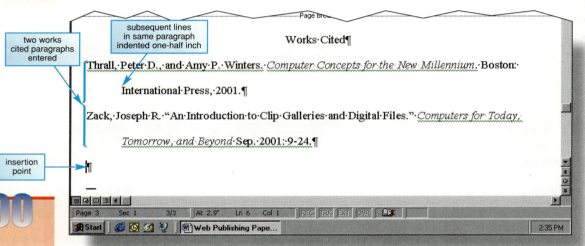

FIGURE 2-47

More About

MLA Style

Titles of books, periodicals, and Web sites typically are underlined when a research paper is submitted in printed form. Some instructors require that Web addresses be hyperlinks for online access. Word formats hyperlinks with an underline. To distinguish hyperlinks from titles, the MLA allows titles to be italicized, if approved by the instructor.

When Word wraps the text in each works cited paragraph, it automatically indents the second line of the paragraph by one-half inch. When you press the ENTER key at the end of the first paragraph of text, the insertion point returns automatically to the left margin for the next paragraph. Recall that each time you press the ENTER key, the paragraph formatting in the previous paragraph is carried forward to the next paragraph.

Creating a Hyperlink

In Word, you can create a hyperlink simply by typing the address of the file or Web page to which you want to jump and then pressing the SPACEBAR or the ENTER key. A **hyperlink** is a shortcut that allows a user to jump easily and quickly to another location in the same document or to other documents or Web pages. **Jumping** is the process of following a hyperlink to its destination. For example, by clicking a hyperlink in the document window, you jump to another document on your computer, on your network, or on the World Wide Web. When you close the hyperlink destination page or document, you return to the original location in your Word document.

More About

Hyperlinks

To verify that Word will automatically convert your Web addresses to hyperlinks, click Tools on the menu bar, click AutoCorrect, click the AutoFormat As You Type tab, verify that the Internet and network paths with hyperlinks check box contains a check mark, and then click the OK button.

In this project, one of the works cited is from a Web page on the Internet. When someone displays your research paper on the screen, you want him or her to be able to click the Web address in the work and jump to the associated Web site for more information. If you wish to create a hyperlink to a Web page from a Word document, you do not have to be connected to the Internet. Perform the following steps to create a hyperlink as you type.

Steps: To Create a Hyperlink as You Type

1 **Press CTRL+I. Type** Shelly Cashman Series(r) Microsoft Word 2000 Project 2. **Press CTRL+I. Press the SPACEBAR. Type** Course Technology. 1 Oct. 2001. http://www.scsite.com/wd2000/pr2/wc1.htm.

The insertion point immediately follows the Web address (Figure 2-48).

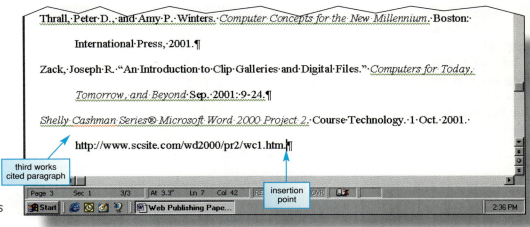

FIGURE 2-48

2 **Press the ENTER key.**

As soon as you press the ENTER key after typing the Web address, Word formats it as a hyperlink (Figure 2-49). That is, the Web address is underlined and colored blue.

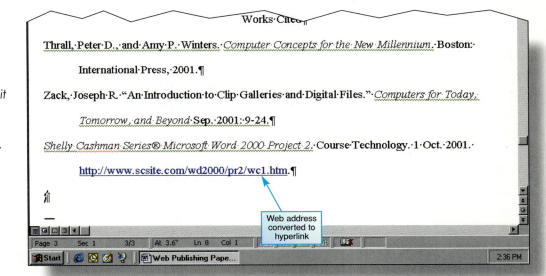

FIGURE 2-49

Later in this project, you will jump to the hyperlink destination.

Sorting Paragraphs

The MLA style requires that the works cited be listed in alphabetical order by author's last name. With Word, you can arrange paragraphs in alphabetic, numeric, or date order based on the first character in each paragraph. Ordering characters in this manner is called **sorting**. Arrange the works cited paragraphs in alphabetic order as illustrated in the steps on the next page.

Other Ways

1. Right-click text, click Hyperlink on shortcut menu, click Existing File or Web Page in the Link to list, type Web address in Type the file or Web page name text box, click OK button

2. Click text, click Insert Hyperlink button on Standard toolbar, click Existing File or Web Page in the Link to list, type Web address in Type the file or Web page name text box, click OK button

 **To Sort Paragraphs**

1 **Select all the works cited paragraphs by pointing to the left of the first paragraph and dragging down. Click Table on the menu bar and then point to Sort.**

Word displays the Table menu (Figure 2-50). All of the paragraphs to be sorted are selected.

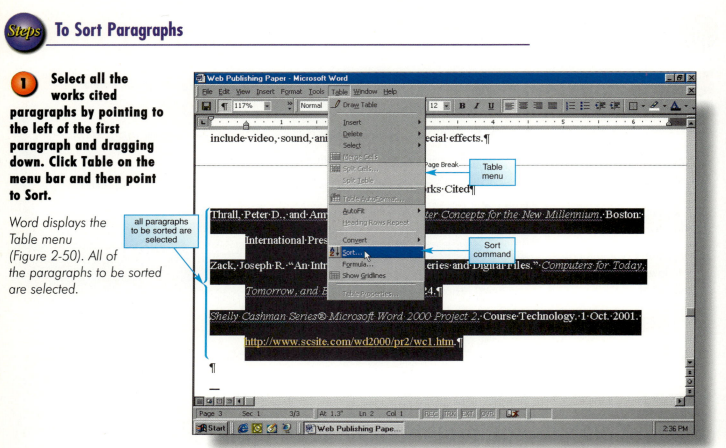

FIGURE 2-50

2 **Click Sort. Point to the OK button.**

Word displays the Sort Text dialog box (Figure 2-51). In the Sort by area, Ascending is selected. Ascending sorts in alphabetic, numeric, or earliest to latest date order.

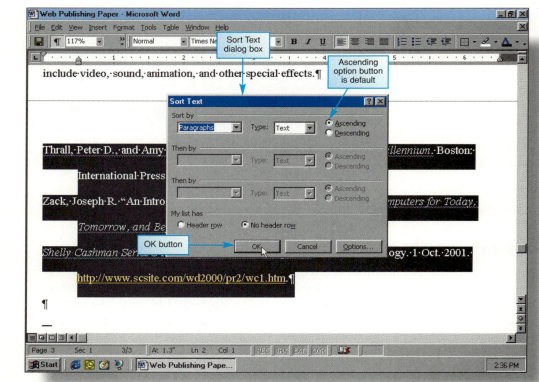

FIGURE 2-51

3 Click the OK button. Click outside of the selection to remove the highlight.

Word sorts the works cited paragraphs alphabetically (Figure 2-52).

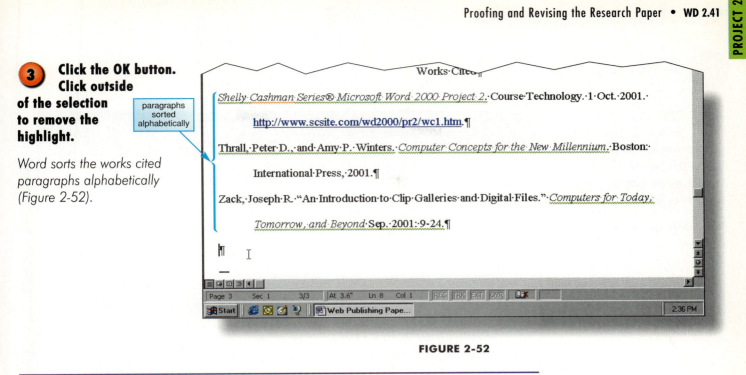

paragraphs sorted alphabetically

Works·Cited¶

Shelly·Cashman·Series®·Microsoft·Word·2000·Project·2.·Course·Technology.·1·Oct.·2001.·

http://www.scsite.com/wd2000/pr2/wc1.htm.¶

Thrall,·Peter·D.,·and·Amy·P.·Winters.·*Computer·Concepts·for·the·New·Millennium.*·Boston:·

International·Press,·2001.¶

Zack,·Joseph·R.·"An·Introduction·to·Clip·Galleries·and·Digital·Files."·*Computers·for·Today,·*

*Tomorrow,·and·Beyond·*Sep.·2001:·9-24.¶

Page 3   Sec 1   3/3   At 3.6"   Ln 8   Col 1   REC TRK EXT OVR

Start   Web Publishing Pape...   2:36 PM

FIGURE 2-52

If you accidentally sort the wrong paragraphs, you can undo a sort by clicking the Undo button on the Standard toolbar.

In the Sort Text dialog box (Figure 2-51), the default sort order is Ascending. By default, Word orders in **ascending sort order**, which means from the beginning of the alphabet to the end of the alphabet, smallest number to the largest number, or earliest date to the most recent date. For example, if the first character of each paragraph to be sorted is a letter, Word sorts the selected paragraphs alphabetically.

You also can sort in descending order by clicking Descending in the Sort Text dialog box. **Descending sort order** means sorting from the end of the alphabet to the beginning of the alphabet, the largest number to the smallest number, or the most recent date to the earliest date.

Proofing and Revising the Research Paper

As discussed in Project 1, once you complete a document, you might find it necessary to make changes to it. Before submitting a paper to be graded, you should proofread it. While **proofreading**, you look for grammatical errors and spelling errors. You want to be sure the transitions between sentences flow smoothly and sentences themselves make sense. Very often, you may count the words in a paper to meet minimum word guidelines specified by an instructor. To assist you in this proofreading effort, Word provides several tools. These tools are discussed in the following pages.

Going to a Specific Location in a Document

Often, you would like to bring a certain page, footnote, or other object into view in the document window. To accomplish this, you could scroll through the document to find the desired page, footnote, or item. Instead of scrolling through the document, Word provides an easier method of going to a specific location via the **Select Browse Object menu**. Perform the steps on the next page to go to the top of page two in the research paper.

To Browse by Page

1 **Click the Select Browse Object button on the vertical scroll bar. When the Select Browse Object menu displays, point to Browse by Page.**

Word displays the Select Browse Object menu (Figure 2-53). As you point to various commands on the Select Browse Object menu, Word displays the command name at the bottom of the menu.

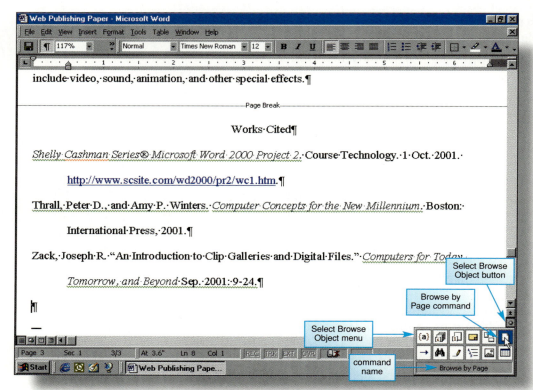

FIGURE 2-53

2 **Click Browse by Page. Point to the Previous Page button on the vertical scroll bar.**

Word closes the Select Browse Object menu and displays the top of page 3 at the top of the document window (Figure 2-54).

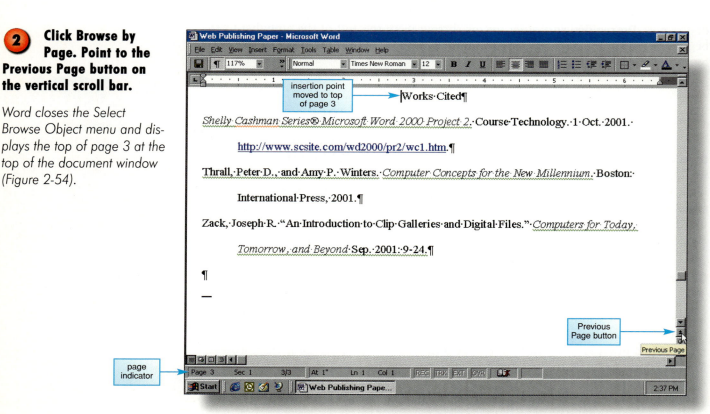

FIGURE 2-54

3 **Click the Previous Page button.**

Word places the top of page 2 (the previous page) at the top of the document window (Figure 2-55).

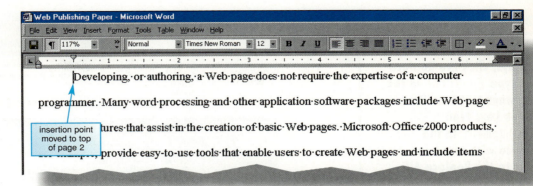

insertion point moved to top of page 2

FIGURE 2-55

Depending on the command you click in the Select Browse Object menu, the function of the buttons above and below the Select Browse Object button on the vertical scroll bar changes. When you select Browse by Page, the buttons become Previous Page and Next Page buttons; when you select Browse by Footnote, the buttons become Previous Footnote and Next Footnote buttons, and so on.

Finding and Replacing Text

While proofreading the paper, you notice that it contains the word, creation, more than once in the document (see Figure 2-56 below); and you would rather use the word, development. Therefore, you wish to change all occurrences of the word, creation, to the word, development. To do this, you can use Word's find and replace feature, which automatically locates each occurrence of a specified word or phrase and then replaces it with specified text as shown in these steps.

Other Ways

1. Double-click page indicator on status bar (Figure 2-54), click Page in Go to what list, type page number in Enter page number text box, click Go To button, click Close button

2. On Edit menu click Go To, and then proceed as described in 1 above starting with click Page in Go to what list

3. Press CTRL+G, and then proceed as described in 1 above starting with click Page in Go to what list

Steps — To Find and Replace Text

1 **Click the Select Browse Object button on the vertical scroll bar. Point to Find on the Select Browse Object menu (Figure 2-56).**

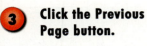

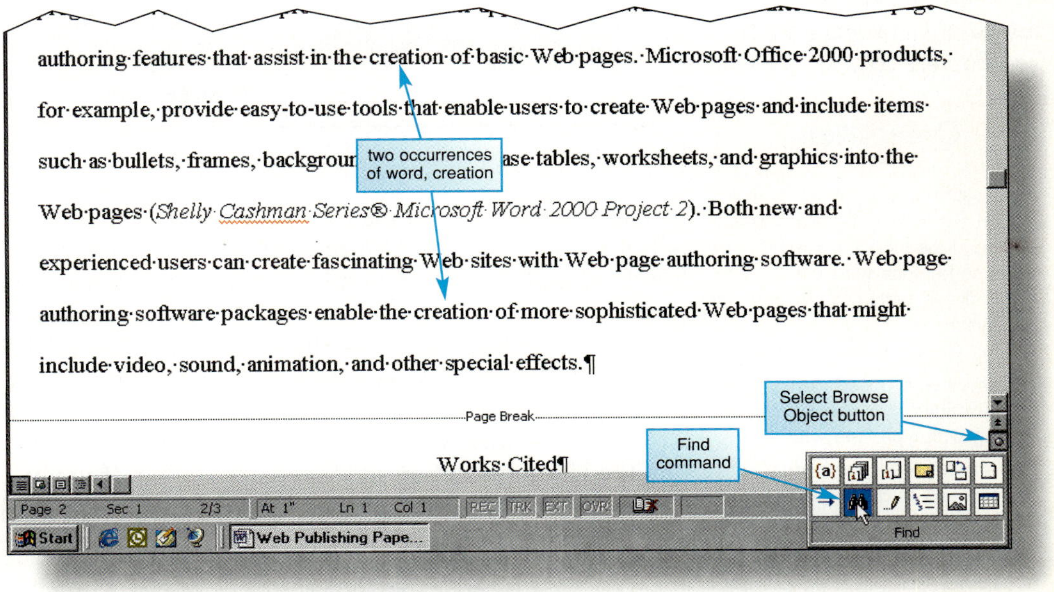

two occurrences of word, creation

Select Browse Object button

Find command

FIGURE 2-56

Click Find. When the Find and Replace dialog box displays, click the Replace tab. Type creation **in the Find what text box. Press the TAB key. Type** development **in the Replace with text box. Point to the Replace All button.**

Word displays the Find and Replace dialog box (Figure 2-57). The Replace All button replaces all occurrences of the Find what text with the Replace with text.

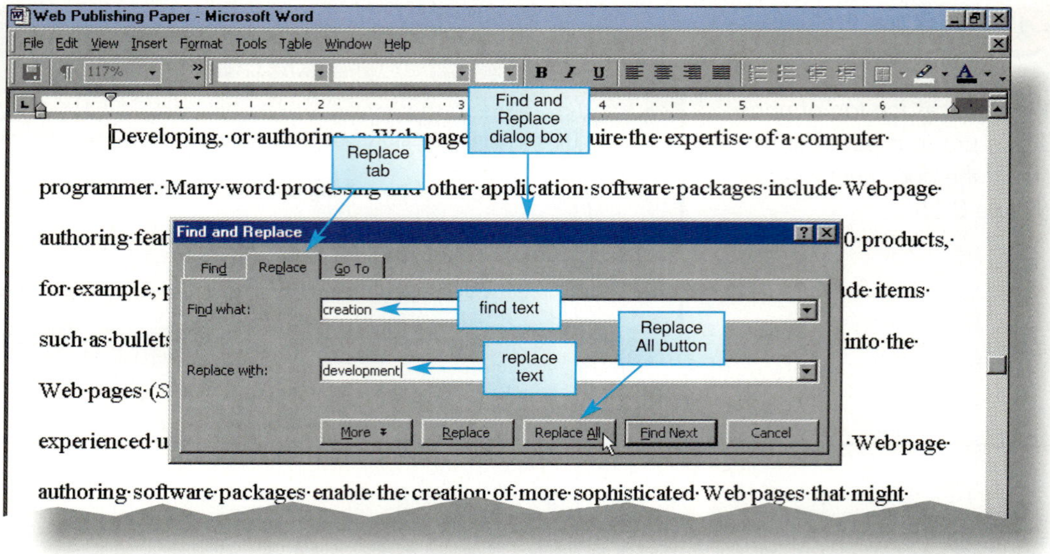

FIGURE 2-57

3 **Click the Replace All button.**

A Microsoft Word dialog box displays indicating the total number of replacements made (Figure 2-58).

4 **Click the OK button. Click the Close button in the Find and Replace dialog box.**

The word, development, displays in the document instead of the word, creation (see Figure 2-59).

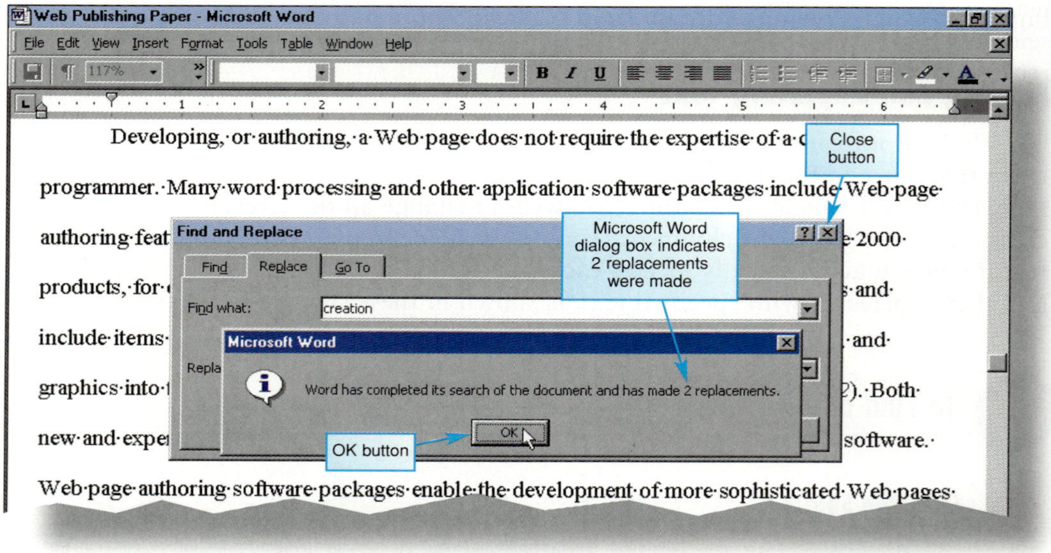

FIGURE 2-58

Other Ways

1. Double-click page indicator on status bar, click Replace tab, type Find what text, type Replace with text, click OK button, click Close button

2. On Edit menu click Replace, and then proceed as described in 1 above starting with type Find what text

3. Press CTRL+H, and then proceed as described in 1 above starting with type Find what text

In some cases, you may want to replace only certain occurrences of the text, not all of them. To instruct Word to confirm each change, click the Find Next button in the Find and Replace dialog box (Figure 2-57), instead of the Replace All button. When Word locates an occurrence of the text, it pauses and waits for you to click either the Replace button or the Find Next button. Clicking the Replace button changes the text; clicking the Find Next button instructs Word to disregard the replacement and look for the next occurrence of the Find what text.

If you accidentally replace the wrong text, you can undo a replacement by clicking the Undo button on the Standard toolbar. If you used the Replace All button, Word undoes all replacements. If you used the Replace button, Word undoes only the most recent replacement.

Finding Text

Sometimes, you may want to find only text, instead of find *and* replace text. To search for just a single occurrence of text, you would follow these steps.

TO FIND TEXT

1. Click the Select Browse Object button on the vertical scroll bar and then click Find on the Select Browse Object menu.

2. Type the text to locate in the Find what text box and then click the Find Next button. To edit the text, click the Close button in the Find and Replace dialog box; to find the next occurrence of the text, click the Find Next button.

Moving Text

While proofreading the research paper, you might realize that text in the last paragraph would flow better if the last two sentences were reversed. That is, you want to move the fourth sentence in the last paragraph to the end of the paragraph.

To move text, such as words, characters, sentences, or paragraphs, you first select the text to be moved and then use drag-and-drop editing or the cut-and-paste technique to move the selected text. With **drag-and-drop editing**, you drag the selected item to the new location and then insert, or drop, it there. **Cutting** involves removing the selected item from the document and then placing it on the **Office Clipboard**, which is a temporary storage area. **Pasting** is the process of copying an item from the Clipboard into the document at the location of the insertion point.

Use drag-and-drop editing to move an item a short distance. To drag-and-drop a sentence in the research paper, first select a sentence as shown below.

Finding

To search for formatting or special characters, click the More button in the Find dialog box. To find formatting, click the Format button, select the formats you want to search for, then click the Find button. To find a special character, click the Special button, click the special character you desire, and then click the Find button.

Cutting and Pasting

To move text a long distance (from one page to another page), the cut-and-paste technique is more efficient. When you paste text into a document, the contents of the Office Clipboard are not erased.

Steps: To Select a Sentence

1. **Position the mouse pointer (an I-beam) in the sentence to be moved. Press and hold the CTRL key. While holding the CTRL key, click the sentence. Release the CTRL key.**

Word selects the entire sentence (Figure 2-59). Notice the space after the period is included in the selection.

authoring·features·that·assist·in·the·development·of·basic·Web·pages.·Microsoft·Office·2000·

products,·for·example,·provide·easy-to-use·tools·that·enable·users·to·create·Web·pages·and·

include·items·such·as·bullets,·frames,·backgr   ·database·tables,·worksheets,·and·

graphics·into·the·Web·pages·(*Shelly·Cashman·Series ® Microsoft·Word·2000·Project·2*).·Both·

new·and·experienced·users·can·create·fascinating·Web·sites·with·Web·page·authoring·software.·

Web·page·authoring·software·packages·enable·the·development·of·more·sophisticated·Web·pages·

that·might·include·video,·sound,·animation,·and·other·special·effects.¶

—————Page Break—————

Works·Cited¶

creation changed to development

sentence selected

Page 2   Sec 1   2/3   At 2.9"   Ln 6   Col 85   REC TRK EXT OVR

Start   Web Publishing Pape...   2:39 PM

FIGURE 2-59

Other Ways

1. Drag through the sentence

Table 2-4 Techniques for Selecting Items with the Mouse

ITEM TO SELECT	MOUSE ACTION
Block of text	Click at beginning of selection, scroll to end of selection, position mouse pointer at end of selection, hold down SHIFT key and then click
Character(s)	Drag through character(s)
Document	Move mouse to left of text until mouse pointer changes to a right-pointing block arrow, then triple-click
Graphic	Click the graphic
Line	Move mouse to left of line until mouse pointer changes to a right-pointing block arrow, then click
Lines	Move mouse to left of first line until mouse pointer changes to a right-pointing block arrow, then drag up or down
Paragraph	Triple-click paragraph; or move mouse to left of paragraph until mouse pointer changes to a right-pointing block arrow, then double-click
Paragraphs	Move mouse to left of paragraph until mouse pointer changes to a right-pointing block arrow, double-click, then drag up or down
Sentence	Press and hold CTRL key, then click sentence
Word	Double-click the word
Words	Drag through words

Throughout Projects 1 and 2, you have selected text and then formatted it. Because selecting text is such a crucial function of Word, Table 2-4 summarizes the techniques used to select various items with the mouse.

With the sentence to be moved selected, you can use drag-and-drop editing to move it. You should be sure that drag-and-drop editing is enabled by clicking Tools on the menu bar, clicking Options, clicking the Edit tab, verifying a check mark is next to Drag and drop text editing, and then clicking the OK button. Follow these steps to move the selected sentence to the end of the paragraph.

Steps **To Move Text**

1 **With the mouse pointer in the selected text, press and hold the mouse button.**

*When you begin to drag the selected text, the insertion point changes to a **dotted insertion point** (Figure 2-60).*

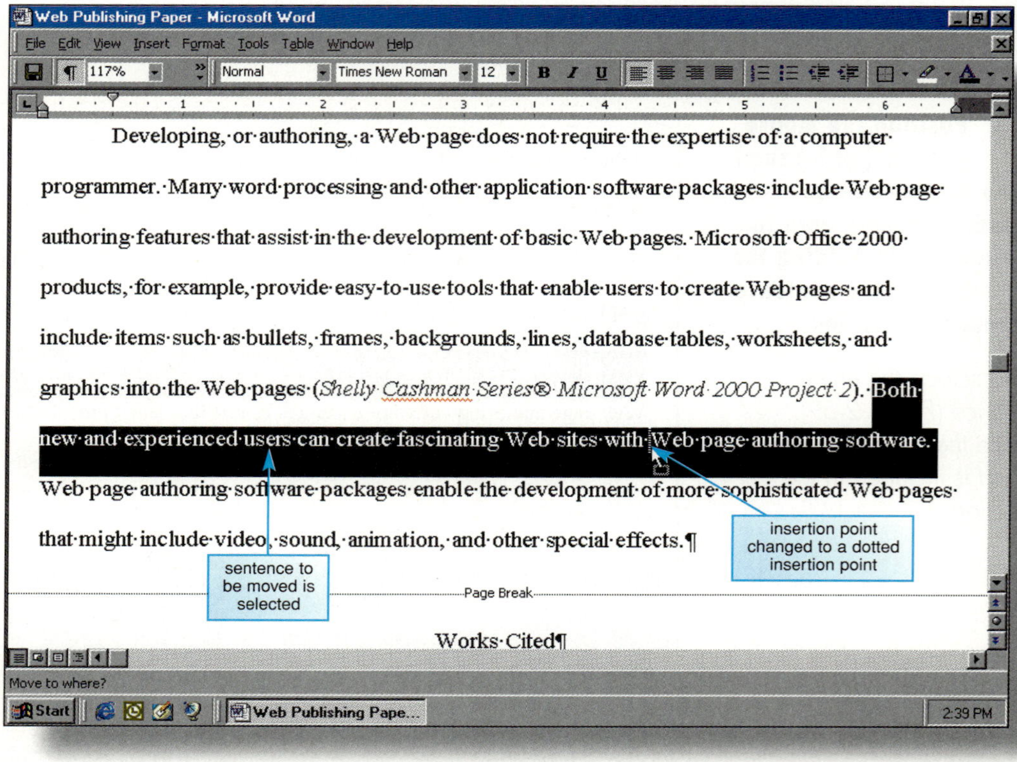

FIGURE 2-60

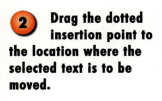

2 Drag the dotted insertion point to the location where the selected text is to be moved.

The dotted insertion point is at the end of the paragraph (Figure 2-61).

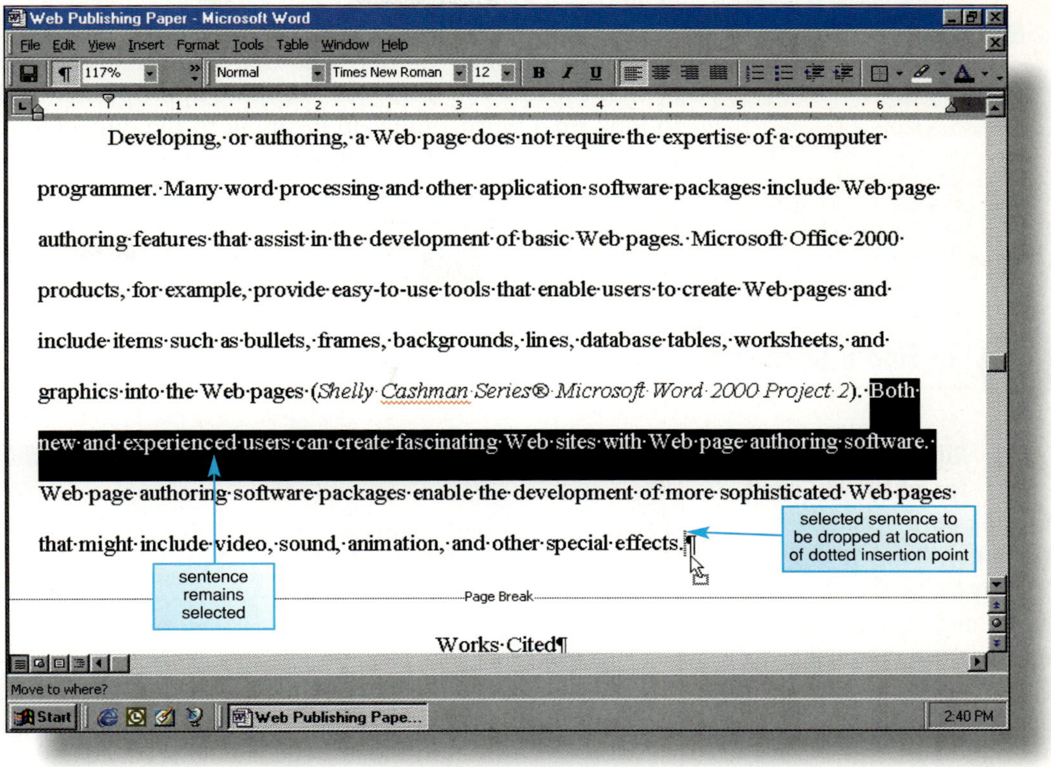

Web Publishing Paper - Microsoft Word
File Edit View Insert Format Tools Table Window Help
Developing, or authoring, a Web page does not require the expertise of a computer programmer. Many word processing and other application software packages include Web page authoring features that assist in the development of basic Web pages. Microsoft Office 2000 products, for example, provide easy-to-use tools that enable users to create Web pages and include items such as bullets, frames, backgrounds, lines, database tables, worksheets, and graphics into the Web pages (Shelly Cashman Series® Microsoft Word 2000 Project 2). Both new and experienced users can create fascinating Web sites with Web page authoring software. Web page authoring software packages enable the development of more sophisticated Web pages that might include video, sound, animation, and other special effects.
selected sentence to be dropped at location of dotted insertion point
sentence remains selected
Page Break
Works Cited
Move to where?
Start
Web Publishing Pape...
2:40 PM

FIGURE 2-61

3 Release the mouse button. Click outside selection to remove the highlight.

Word moves the selected text to the location of the dotted insertion point (Figure 2-62).

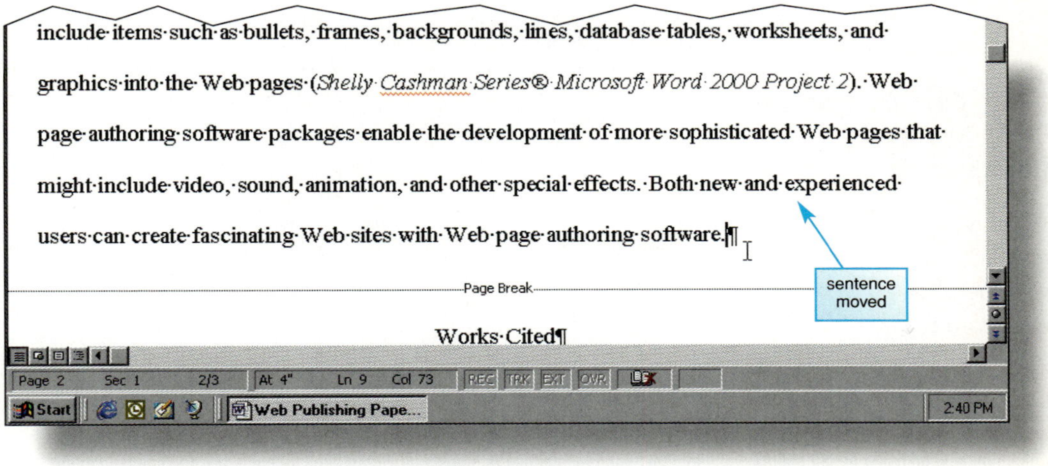

include items such as bullets, frames, backgrounds, lines, database tables, worksheets, and graphics into the Web pages (Shelly Cashman Series® Microsoft Word 2000 Project 2). Web page authoring software packages enable the development of more sophisticated Web pages that might include video, sound, animation, and other special effects. Both new and experienced users can create fascinating Web sites with Web page authoring software.
sentence moved
Page Break
Works Cited
Page 2 Sec 1 2/3 At 4" Ln 9 Col 73 REC TRK EXT OVR
Start
Web Publishing Pape...
2:40 PM

FIGURE 2-62

You can click the Undo button on the Standard toolbar if you accidentally drag text to the wrong location.

You can use drag-and-drop editing to move any selected item. That is, you can select words, sentences, phrases, and graphics and then use drag-and-drop editing to move them.

If you hold the CTRL key while dragging the selected item, Word copies the item instead of moving it.

Other Ways

1. Click Cut button on Standard toolbar, click where text is to be pasted, click Paste button on Standard toolbar
2. On Edit menu click Cut, click where text is to be pasted, on Edit menu click Paste
3. Press CTRL+X, position insertion point where text is to be pasted, press CTRL+V

Synonyms

For access to an online thesaurus, visit the Word 2000 More About Web page (www.scsite.com/wd2000/more.htm) and then click Online Thesaurus.

Finding a Synonym

When writing, you may find that you used the same word in multiple locations or that a word you used was not quite appropriate. In these instances, you will want to look up a word similar in meaning to the duplicate or inappropriate word. These similar words are called **synonyms**. A book of synonyms is referred to as a **thesaurus**. Word provides synonyms and a thesaurus for your convenience. In this project, you would like a synonym for the word, include, in the middle of the last paragraph of the research paper. Perform the following steps to find an appropriate synonym.

Steps To Find a Synonym

1 **Right-click the word for which you want to look up a synonym (include). Point to Synonyms on the shortcut menu and then point to the appropriate synonym (incorporate) on the Synonyms submenu.**

Word displays a list of synonyms for the word containing the insertion point (Figure 2-63).

2 **Click the synonym you want (incorporate).**

Word replaces the word, include, in the document with the selected word, incorporate (Figure 2-64).

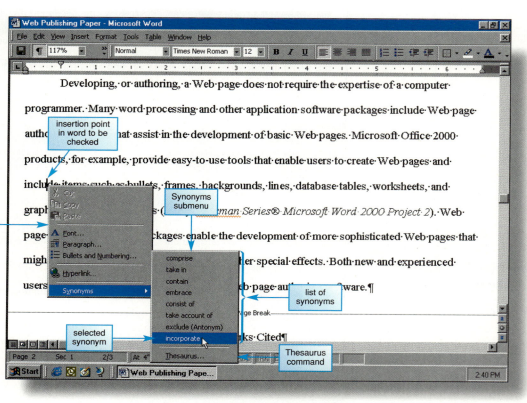

FIGURE 2-63

If the synonyms list does not display an appropriate word, you can display the Thesaurus dialog box by clicking Thesaurus on the Synonyms submenu (Figure 2-63). In the Thesaurus dialog box, you can look up synonyms for a different meaning of the word. You also can look up **antonyms**, or words with an opposite meaning.

Using Word Count

Often when you write papers, you are required to compose a paper with a minimum number of words. The requirement for the research paper in this project was a minimum of 425 words. Word provides a command that displays the number of words, as well as the number of pages, characters, paragraphs, and lines in your document. Perform the following steps to use word count.

Steps To Count Words

1 Click Tools on the menu bar and then point to Word Count (Figure 2-64).

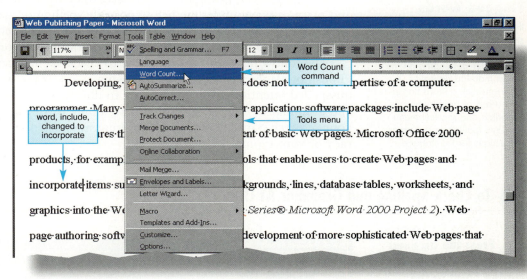

FIGURE 2-64

2 Click Word Count. When the Word Count dialog box displays, if necessary, click Include footnotes and endnotes to select the check box.

Word displays the Word Count dialog box (Figure 2-65).

3 Click the Close button in the Word Count dialog box.

Word returns you to the document.

FIGURE 2-65

Other Ways

1. On File menu click Properties, click Statistics tab, click OK button

The Word Count dialog box presents a variety of statistics about the current document, including number of pages, words, characters, paragraphs, and lines (Figure 2-65). You can choose to have note text included or not included in these statistics. If you want statistics on only a section of your document, select the section and then invoke the Word Count command.

More About

Flagged Words

If you right-click a word, a shortcut menu displays. Recall that commands in a shortcut menu differ depending on the object that you right-click. If you right-click a word flagged with a red or green wavy underline, the shortcut menu displays spelling or grammar corrections for the flagged word.

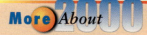

Checking Spelling and Grammar at Once

As discussed in Project 1, Word checks your spelling and grammar as you type and places a wavy underline below possible spelling or grammar errors. You learned in Project 1 how to check these flagged words immediately. You also can wait and check the entire document for spelling and grammar errors at once.

The following steps illustrate how to check spelling and grammar in the Web Publishing Paper at once. In the following example the word, maintaining, has been misspelled intentionally as maintining to illustrate the use of Word's check spelling and grammar at once feature. If you are doing this project on a personal computer, your research paper may contain different misspelled words, depending on the accuracy of your typing.

Steps To Check Spelling and Grammar At Once

1 Press the CTRL+HOME keys to move the insertion point to the beginning of the document. Double-click the move handle on the Standard toolbar to display the entire toolbar. Point to the Spelling and Grammar button on the Standard toolbar.

Word will begin the spelling and grammar check at the location of the insertion point, which is at the beginning of the document (Figure 2-66).

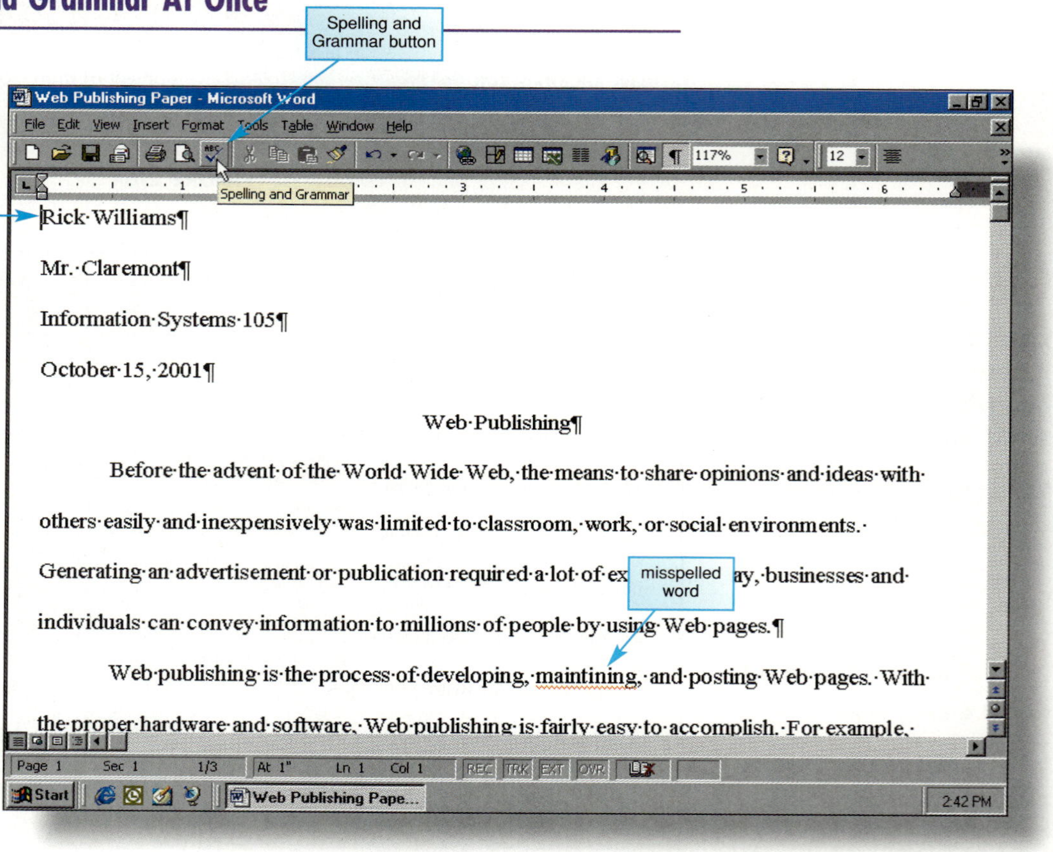

FIGURE 2-66

2 **Click the Spelling and Grammar button. When the Spelling and Grammar dialog box displays, click maintaining in the Suggestions list and then point to the Change button.**

Word displays the Spelling and Grammar dialog box (Figure 2-67). Word did not find the misspelled word, maintaining, in its dictionary. The Suggestions list displays suggested corrections for the flagged word.

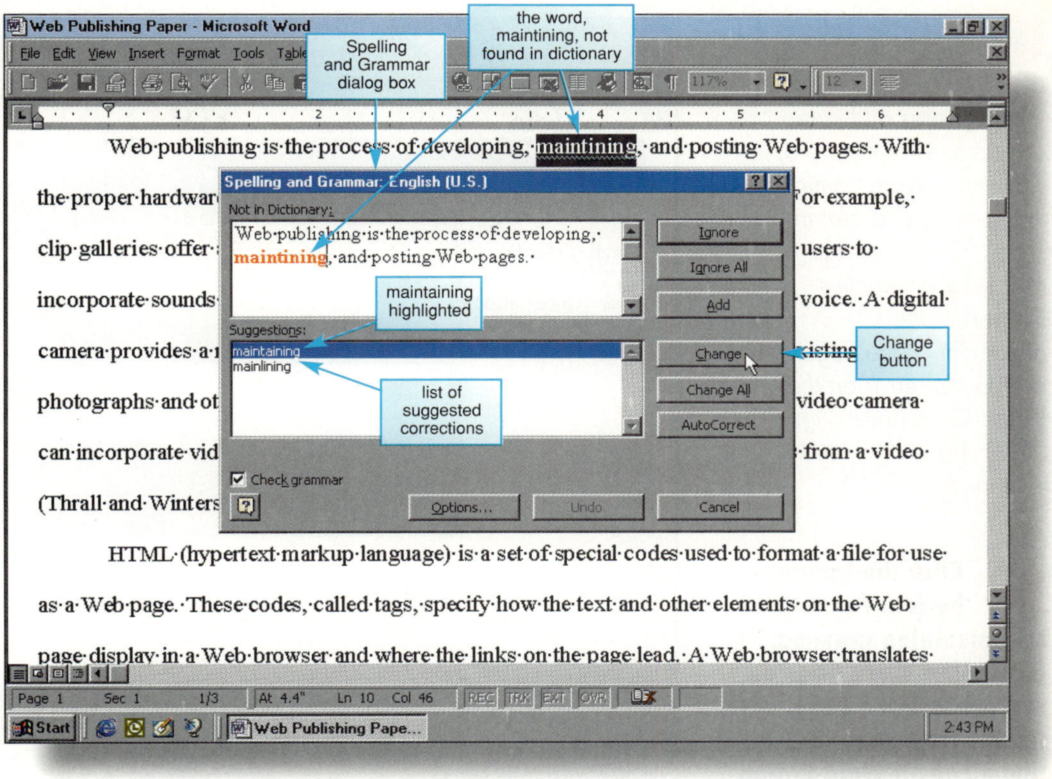

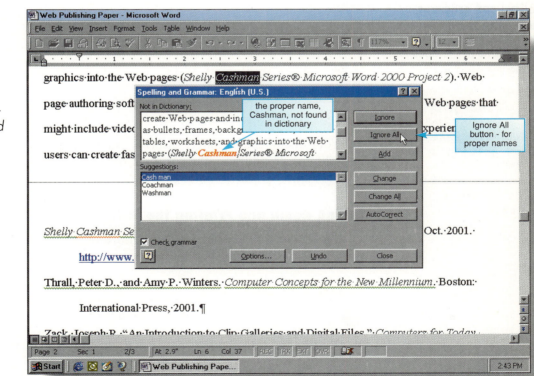

FIGURE 2-67

3 **Click the Change button.**

Word continues the spelling and grammar check until it finds the next error or reaches the end of the document (Figure 2-68). Word did not find Cashman in its dictionary because Cashman is a proper name. Cashman is spelled correctly.

FIGURE 2-68

4 **Click the Ignore All button.**

Word ignores all future occurrences of the word, Cashman. Word continues the spelling and grammar check until it finds the next error or reaches the end of the document. Word flags a grammar error on the Works Cited page (Figure 2-69). The works cited is written correctly.

5 **Click the Ignore button. For each of the remaining grammar errors that Word flags on the Works Cited page, click the Ignore button. When the Microsoft Word dialog box displays indicating Word has completed the spelling and grammar check, click the OK button.**

Word returns to the document window.

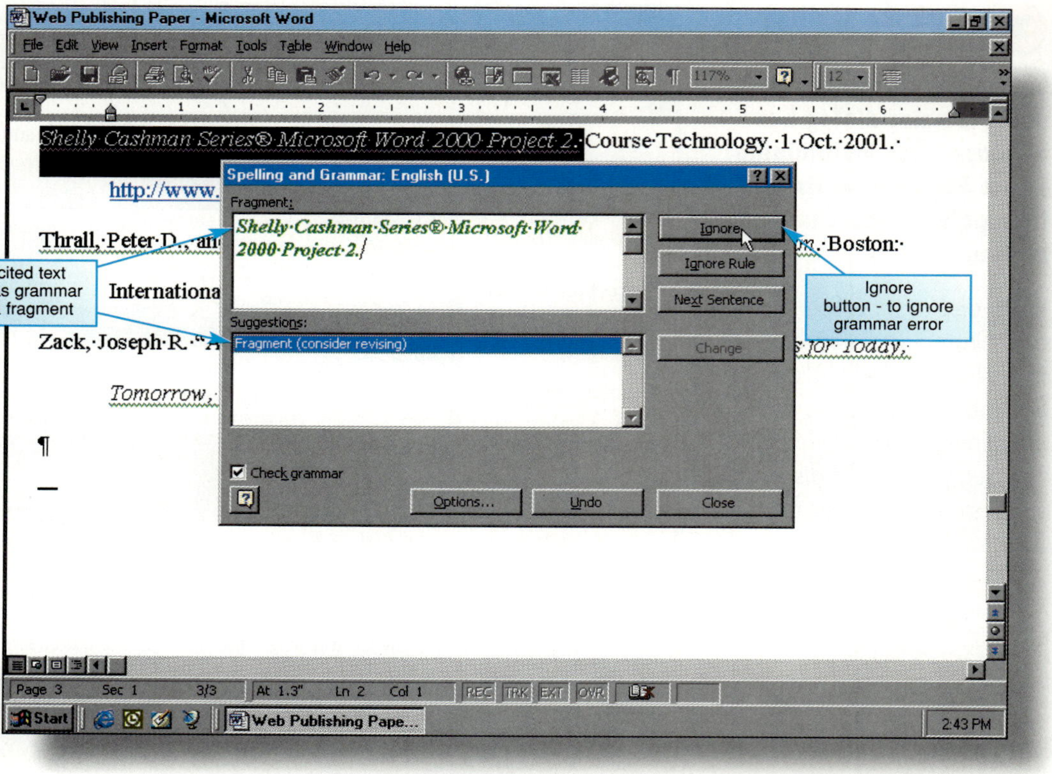

FIGURE 2-69

Other Ways

1. Right-click flagged word, click Spelling on shortcut menu
2. On Tools menu click Spelling and Grammar
3. Press F7

Your document no longer displays red and green wavy underlines below words and phrases. In addition, the red X on the Spelling and Grammar Status icon has returned to a red check mark.

Saving Again and Printing the Document

The document now is complete. You should save the research paper again and print it, as described in the following steps.

TO SAVE A DOCUMENT AGAIN

1 Click the Save button on the Standard toolbar.

Word saves the research paper with the same file name, Web Publishing Paper.

TO PRINT A DOCUMENT

1 Click the Print button on the Standard toolbar.

The completed research paper prints as shown in Figure 2-1 on page WD 2.5.

Navigating to a Hyperlink

Recall that one requirement of this research paper is that one of the works be a Web site and be formatted as a hyperlink. Perform the following steps to check your hyperlink.

To Navigate to a Hyperlink

1 **Display the third page of the research paper in the document window and then point to the hyperlink.**

When you point to a hyperlink in a Word document, the mouse pointer shape changes to a pointing hand (Figure 2-70).

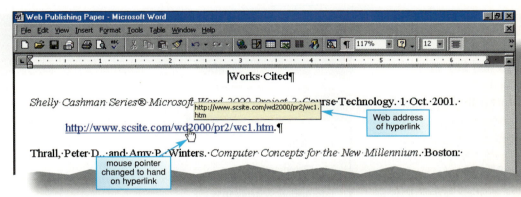

FIGURE 2-70

2 **Click the hyperlink.**

If you currently are not connected to the Web, Word connects you using your default browser. The www.scsite.com/wd2000/pr2/wc1.htm Web page displays (Figure 2-71).

3 **Close the browser window. If necessary, click the Microsoft Word program button on the taskbar to redisplay the Word window. Press CTRL+HOME.**

The first page of the research paper displays in the Word window.

FIGURE 2-71

More About 2000

E-mailing

To e-mail a document as an attachment, click File on the menu bar, point to Send To, and then click Mail Recipient (as Attachment).

E-mailing a Copy of the Research Paper

Your instructor, Mr. Claremont, has requested you e-mail him a copy of your research paper so he can verify your hyperlink. Perform the following step to e-mail the document from within Word.

Steps — To E-mail a Document

1 **Click the E-mail button on the Standard toolbar. Fill in the To text box with Mr. Claremont's e-mail address and the Subject text box (Figure 2-72) and then click the Send a Copy button.**

Word displays certain buttons and boxes from your e-mail editor inside the Word window. The document is e-mailed to the recipient named in the To text box.

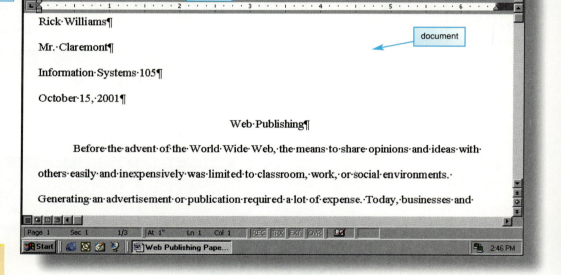

FIGURE 2-72

Other Ways

1. On File menu point to Send To, on Send To menu click Mail Recipient

More About 2000

Quick Reference

For a table that lists how to complete the tasks covered in this book using the mouse, menu, shortcut menu, and keyboard, visit the Office 2000 Web page (www.scsite.com/off2000/qr.htm) and then click Microsoft Word 2000.

If you want to cancel the e-mail operation, click the E-mail button again. The final step in this project is to quit Word, as described in the following step.

TO QUIT WORD

1 Click the Close button in the Word window.

The Word window closes.

CASE PERSPECTIVE SUMMARY

Rick accomplished his goal — learning about the basics of Web publishing while completing Mr. Claremont's research paper assignment. Now he is ready to create a personal Web page and publish it to a Web server. Rick decides to use Word's Web Page Wizard to create his Web page. He also contacts his Internet service provider to set up his free 6 MB of Web space. After receiving his personal Web site address from his Internet service provider, Rick publishes his Web page for the world to see. (For more information on publishing Web pages to a Web server, see Appendix B.) He shows Mr. Claremont the Web page, who in turn shows Rick's classmates.

Project Summary

Project 2 introduced you to creating a research paper using the MLA documentation style. You learned how to change margin settings, adjust line spacing, create headers with page numbers, and indent paragraphs. You learned how to use Word's AutoCorrect feature. Then, you added a footnote in the research paper. You alphabetized the works cited page by sorting its paragraphs and included a hyperlink to a Web page in one of the works. You learned how to browse through a Word document, find and replace text, and move text. You looked up a synonym and saw how to display statistics about your document. Finally, you navigated to a hyperlink and e-mailed a copy of a document.

What You Should Know

Having completed this project, you now should be able to perform the following tasks:

▶ Add a Footnote *(WD 2.23)*
▶ AutoCorrect As You Type *(WD 2.20)*
▶ Browse by Page *(WD 2.42)*
▶ Center the Title of the Works Cited Page *(WD 2.36)*
▶ Change the Default Font Size *(WD 2.15)*
▶ Change the Margin Settings *(WD 2.8)*
▶ Check Spelling and Grammar at Once *(WD 2.50)*
▶ Click and Type *(WD 2.13)*
▶ Close the Note Pane *(WD 2.29)*
▶ Count Words *(WD 2.49)*
▶ Create a Hanging Indent *(WD 2.37)*
▶ Create a Hyperlink as You Type *(WD 2.39)*
▶ Create an AutoCorrect Entry *(WD 2.21)*
▶ Display Formatting Marks *(WD 2.7)*
▶ Display the Header Area *(WD 2.12)*
▶ Double-Space a Document *(WD 2.9)*
▶ E-mail a Document *(WD 2.54)*
▶ Enter and Format a Page Number *(WD 2.14)*
▶ Enter More Text *(WD 2.30)*
▶ Enter Name and Course Information *(WD 2.16)*
▶ Enter Works Cited Paragraphs *(WD 2.38)*
▶ Find a Synonym *(WD 2.48)*
▶ Find and Replace Text *(WD 2.43)*
▶ Find Text *(WD 2.45)*

▶ First-Line Indent Paragraphs *(WD 2.19)*
▶ Insert a Symbol Automatically *(WD 2.33)*
▶ Modify a Style *(WD 2.26)*
▶ Move Text *(WD 2.46)*
▶ Navigate to a Hyperlink *(WD 2.53)*
▶ Page Break Automatically *(WD 2.32)*
▶ Page Break Manually *(WD 2.35)*
▶ Print a Document *(WD 2.52)*
▶ Quit Word *(WD 2.54)*
▶ Reset Menus and Toolbars *(WD 2.7)*
▶ Save a Document *(WD 2.18)*
▶ Save a Document Again *(WD 2.52)*
▶ Select a Sentence *(WD 2.45)*
▶ Sort Paragraphs *(WD 2.40)*
▶ Start Word *(WD 2.6)*
▶ Use Shortcut Keys to Format Text *(WD 2.17)*
▶ Zoom Page Width *(WD 2.9)*

More About 2000

Microsoft Certification

The Microsoft Office User Specialist (MOUS) Certification program provides an opportunity for you to obtain a valuable industry credential – proof that you have the Word 2000 skills required by employers. For more information, see Appendix D or visit the Shelly Cashman Series MOUS Web page at www.scsite.com/off2000/cert.htm.

Apply Your Knowledge

Project Reinforcement at www.scsite.com/off2000/reinforce.htm

1 Revising a Document

Instructions: Start Word. Open the document, Internet Paragraph, on the Data Disk. If you did not download the Data Disk, see the inside back cover for instructions for downloading the Data Disk or see your instructor.

The document is a paragraph of text. You are to move two sentences in the paragraph and change all occurrences of the word, Web, to the phrase, World Wide Web. The revised paragraph is shown in Figure 2-73.

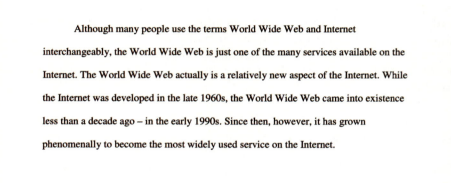

Although many people use the terms World Wide Web and Internet interchangeably, the World Wide Web is just one of the many services available on the Internet. The World Wide Web actually is a relatively new aspect of the Internet. While the Internet was developed in the late 1960s, the World Wide Web came into existence less than a decade ago – in the early 1990s. Since then, however, it has grown phenomenally to become the most widely used service on the Internet.

FIGURE 2-73

Perform the following tasks:

1. Press and hold the CTRL key. While holding the CTRL key, click in the third sentence, which begins, The Web actually is..., to select the sentence. Release the CTRL key.

2. Press and hold down the left mouse button. Drag the dotted insertion point to the left of the letter W in the second sentence beginning, While the Internet was..., and then release the mouse button to move the sentence. Click outside the selection to remove the highlight.

3. Click the Select Browse Object button on the vertical scroll bar and then click Find on the Select Browse Object menu.

4. When the Find and Replace dialog box displays, click the Replace tab. Type Web in the Find what text box, press the TAB key, and then type World Wide Web in the Replace with text box. Click the Replace All button.

5. Click the OK button in the Microsoft Word dialog box. Click the Close button in the Find and Replace dialog box.

6. Click File on the menu bar and then click Save As. Use the file name, Revised Internet Paragraph, and then save the document on your floppy disk.

7. Print the revised paragraph.

1 Preparing a Research Paper

Problem: You are a college student currently enrolled in an English composition class. Your assignment is to prepare a short research paper (400-425 words) about digital cameras. The requirements are that the paper be presented according to the MLA documentation style and have three references (Figures 2-74a through 2-74c shown below and on the next page). One of the three references must be from the Internet and formatted as a hyperlink on the Works Cited page.

Thornton 1

Anne Thornton

Ms. Baxter

English 105

March 12, 2001

Digital Cameras

Digital cameras allow computer users to take pictures and store the photographed images digitally instead of on traditional film. With some digital cameras, a user downloads the stored pictures from the digital camera to a computer using special software included with the camera. With others, the camera stores the pictures directly on a floppy disk or on a PC Card. A user then copies the pictures to a computer by inserting the floppy disk into a disk drive or the PC Card into a PC Card slot (Chambers and Norton 134). Once stored on a computer, the pictures can be edited with photo-editing software, printed, faxed, sent via electronic mail, included in another document, or posted to a Web site for everyone to see.

Three basic types of digital cameras are studio cameras, field cameras, and point-and-shoot cameras (*Shelly Cashman Series® Microsoft Word 2000 Project 2*). The most expensive and highest quality of the three, a studio camera, is a stationary camera used for professional studio work. Photojournalists frequently use field cameras because they are portable and have a variety of lenses and other attachments. As with the studio camera, a field camera can be quite expensive.

Reliable and lightweight, the point-and-shoot camera provides acceptable quality photographic images for the home or small business user. A point-and-shoot camera enables these users to add pictures to personalized greeting cards, a computerized photo album, a family

FIGURE 2-74a

(*continued*)

In the Lab

Preparing a Research Paper *(continued)*

Thornton 2

newsletter, certificates, awards, or a personal Web site. Because of its functionality, it is an ideal

camera for mobile users such as real estate agents, insurance agents, and general contractors.

The image quality produced by a digital camera is measured by the number of bits it

stores in a dot and the resolution, or number of dots per inch. The higher each number, the better

the quality, but the more expensive the camera. Most of today's point-and-shoot digital cameras

are at least 24-bit with a resolution ranging from 640 x 480 to 1024 x 960 (Walker 57-89). Home

and small business users can find an affordable camera with a resolution in this range that

delivers excellent detail for less than $400.

FIGURE 2-74b

Thornton 3

Works Cited

Chambers, John Q., and Theresa R. Norton. *Understanding Computers in the New Century*.

Chicago: Midwest Press, 2001.

Shelly Cashman Series® Word 2000 Project 2. Course Technology. 5 Mar. 2001.

http://www.scsite.com/wd2000/pr2/wc2.htm.

Walker, Marianne L. "Understanding the Resolutions of Digital Cameras and Imaging Devices."

Computing for the Home Feb. 2001: 57-89.

FIGURE 2-74c

Instructions:

1. If necessary, click the Show/Hide ¶ button on the Standard toolbar. Change all margins to one inch. Adjust line spacing to double. Create a header to number pages. If necessary, change the font size of all characters to 12 point. Type the name and course information at the left margin. Center and type the title. First-line indent all paragraphs in the paper.
2. Type the body of the paper as shown in Figure 2-74a on the previous page and Figure 2-74b. At the end of the body of the research paper, press the ENTER key and insert a manual page break.
3. Create the works cited page (Figure 2-74c).
4. Check the spelling of the paper at once.
5. Save the document on a floppy disk with Digital Camera Paper as the file name.
6. If you have access to the Web, test your hyperlink by clicking it.
7. Print the research paper. Above the title of your printed research paper, handwrite the number of words in the research paper.

In the Lab

2 **Preparing a Research Report with Footnotes**

Problem: You are a college student currently enrolled in an English composition class. Your assignment is to prepare a short research paper in any area of interest to you. The requirements are that the paper be presented according to the MLA documentation style and have three references. One of the three references must be from the Internet and formatted as a hyperlink on the works cited page. You decide to prepare a paper on virtual reality (Figures 2-75 below and on the next page).

Jameson 1

Casey Jameson

Mr. Brookfield

English 105

September 14, 2001

Virtual Reality

Virtual reality (VR) is the use of a computer to create an artificial environment that appears and feels like a real environment and allows users to explore a space and manipulate the environment. In its simplest form, a VR application displays what appears to be a three-dimensional view of a place or object, such as a landscape, building, molecule, or red blood cell, which users can explore. For example, architects can use VR software to show clients how a building will look after a construction or remodeling project.

In more advanced forms, VR software requires that users wear specialized headgear, body suits, and gloves to enhance the experience of the artificial environment (Vance and Reed 34-58). The headgear displays the artificial environment in front of a user's eyes.[1] The body suit and the gloves sense motion and direction, allowing a user to move through, pick up, or hold items displayed in the virtual environment. Experts predict that eventually the body suits will provide tactile feedback so users can experience the touch and feel of the virtual world.

Many games, such as flight simulators, use virtual reality. In these games, special visors allow users to see the computer-generated environment. As the user walks around the game's electronic landscape, sensors in the surrounding game machine record movements and change the view of the landscape accordingly.

---

[1] According to Vance and Reed, patients in one dental office wear VR headsets to relax them during their visit with the dentist.

FIGURE 2-75a

(continued)

In the Lab

Preparing a Research Report with Footnotes *(continued)*

Jameson 2

Companies increasingly are using VR for more practical commercial applications, as well. Automobile dealers, for example, use virtual showrooms in which customers can view the exterior and interior of available vehicles. Airplane manufacturers use virtual prototypes to test new models and shorten product design time. Many firms use personal computer-based VR applications for employee training (*Shelly Cashman Series® Microsoft Word 2000 Project 2*). As computing power and the use of the Web increase, practical applications of VR continue to emerge in education, business, and entertainment.[2]

---

[2] Henry Davidson, a developer of VR applications, predicts that in the future, moviegoers will be able to pretend they are one of a movie's characters. In this environment, the VR technology will link the moviegoer's sensory system (sight, smell, hearing, taste, and touch) to the character's sensory system (Holloway 46-52).

FIGURE 2-75b

In the Lab

Part 1 Instructions: Perform the following tasks to create the research paper:

1. If necessary, click the Show/Hide ¶ button on the Standard toolbar. Change all margin settings to one inch. Adjust line spacing to double. Create a header to number pages. If necessary, change the font size of all characters to 12 point. Type the name and course information at the left margin. Center and type the title. First-line indent all paragraphs in the paper.

2. Type the body of the paper as shown in Figure 2-75a on page WD 2.59 and Figure 2-75b. At the end of the body of the research paper, press the ENTER key once and insert a manual page break.

3. Create the works cited page. Enter the works cited shown below as separate paragraphs and then sort the paragraphs.

   (a) *Shelly Cashman Series® Microsoft Word 2000 Project 2*. Course Technology. 3 Sep. 2001. http://www.scsite.com/wd2000/pr2/wc3.htm.

   (b) Holloway, April I. "The Future of Virtual Reality Applications." *Computers for Today, Tomorrow, and Beyond* Sep. 2001: 46-52.

   (c) Vance, Dale W., and Karen P. Reed. *The Complete Book of Virtual Reality*. Dallas: Worldwide Press, 2001.

4. Check the spelling of the paper.

5. Save the document on a floppy disk with Virtual Reality Paper as the file name.

6. If you have access to the Web, test your hyperlink by clicking it.

7. Print the research paper. Above the title of your printed research paper, handwrite the number of words, including the footnotes, in the research paper.

Part 2 Instructions: Perform the following tasks to modify the research paper:

1. Use Word to find a synonym of your choice for the word, eventually, in the second paragraph.

2. Change all occurrences of the word, artificial, to the word, simulated.

3. In the second footnote, change the word, link, to the word, connect.

4. Convert the footnotes to endnotes. You have learned that endnotes appear at the end of a document. *Hint:* Use Help to learn about converting footnotes to endnotes.

5. Modify the Endnote text style to 12-point font, double-spaced text with a first-line indent. Insert a page break so the endnotes are placed on a separate numbered page. Center the title, Endnotes, double-spaced above the notes.

6. Change the format of the note reference marks from Arabic numbers (1., 2., etc.) to capital letters (A., B., etc.). *Hint*: Use Help to learn about changing the number format of note reference marks.

7. Save the document on a floppy disk with Revised Virtual Reality Paper as the file name.

8. Print the revised research paper.

In the Lab

3 Composing a Research Paper from Notes

Problem: You have drafted the notes shown in Figure 2-76. Your assignment is to prepare a short research paper from these notes. Review the notes and then rearrange and reword them. Embellish the paper as you deem necessary. Add a footnote elaborating on a personal experience you have had. Present the paper according to the MLA documentation style.

Instructions: Perform the following tasks:

1. Change all margin settings to one inch. Adjust line spacing to double. Create a header to number pages. If necessary, change the font size of all characters to 12 point. Type the name and course information at the left margin. Center and type the title. First-line indent all paragraphs in the paper.

Productivity software makes people more efficient and effective in their daily activities. Three popular applications are (1) word processing, (2) spreadsheet, and (3) database.

Word Processing: Widely used application for creating, editing, and formatting text-based documents such as letters, memos, reports, fax cover sheet, mailing labels, and newsletters. Formatting features include changing font and font size, changing color of characters, organizing text into newspaper-style columns. Other features include adding clip art, changing margins, finding and replacing text, checking spelling and grammar, inserting headers and footers, providing a thesaurus, developing Web pages, and inserting tables. Source: "Evaluating Word Processing and Spreadsheet Software," an article in Computers Weekly, January 12, 2001 issue, pages 45-78, author Kimberly G. Rothman.

Spreadsheet: Used to organize data in rows and columns in a worksheet. Data is stored in cells, the intersection of rows and columns. Worksheets have more than 16 millions cells that can hold data. Cells can hold numbers, formulas, or functions. Formulas and functions perform calculations. When data in cells changes, the formulas and functions automatically recalculate formulas and display new values. Many spreadsheet packages allow you to create macros, which hold a series of keystrokes and instructions – a real timesaver. Most also include the ability to create charts, e.g. line charts, column charts, and pie charts, from the data. Source: same as for word processing software.

Database: Used to collect data and allow access, retrieval, and use of that data. Data stored in tables, which consists of rows (records) and columns (fields). Data can contain text, numbers, dates, or hyperlinks. When data is entered, it can be validated (compared to a set of stored rules or values to determine if the entered data is correct). Once the data is stored, you can sort it, query it, and generate reports from it. Sometimes called a database management system (DBMS). Source: Understanding Databases, a book published by Harbor Press in Detroit, Michigan, 2001, pages 35-56, authors Mark A. Greene and Andrea K. Peterson.

Microsoft Word 2000 is word processing software; Microsoft Excel 2000 is an example of spreadsheet software; and Microsoft Access 2000 is a database software package. Source: a Web site titled Shelly Cashman Series® Microsoft Word 2000 Project 2 sponsored by Course Technology; site visited on March 12, 2001; Web address is http://www.scsite.com/wd2000/pr2/wc4.htm.

FIGURE 2-76

2. Compose the body of the paper from the notes in Figure 2-76. Be sure to include a footnote as specified. At the end of the body of the research paper, press the ENTER key once and insert a manual page break. Create the works cited page from the listed sources. Be sure to sort the works.

3. Check the spelling and grammar of the paper. Save the document on a floppy disk with Software Research Paper as the file name. Print the research paper. Above the title of the printed research paper, handwrite the number of words, including the footnote, in the research paper.

Cases and Places

The difficulty of these case studies varies:
▶ are the least difficult; ▶▶ are more difficult; and ▶▶▶ are the most difficult.

1 ▶ Project 1 of this book discussed the components of the Word document window. These components include the menu bar, toolbars, rulers, scroll bars, and status bar. In your own words, write a short research paper (400-450 words) that describes the purpose and functionality of one or more of these components. Use your textbook, Word Help, and any other resources available. Include at least two references and one explanatory note. Use the concepts and techniques presented in this project to format the paper.

2 ▶ Having completed two projects using Word 2000, you should be comfortable with some of its features. To reinforce your knowledge of Word's features, write a short research paper (400-450 words) that discusses a few of the features that you have learned. Features might include items such as checking spelling, inserting clip art, adding text using Click and Type, sorting paragraphs, and so on. Use your textbook, Word Help, and any other resources available. Include at least two references and one explanatory note. Use the concepts and techniques presented in this project to format the paper.

3 ▶▶ A pointing device is an input device that allows a user to control a pointer on a computer screen. Common pointing devices include the mouse, trackball, touchpad, pointing stick, joystick, touch screen, light pen, and graphics tablet. Using the school library, other textbooks, magazines, the Internet, or other resources, research two or more of these pointing devices. Then, prepare a brief research paper (400-450 words) that discusses the pointing devices. Include at least one explanatory note and two references, one of which must be a Web site on the Internet. Use the concepts and techniques presented in this project to format the paper.

4 ▶▶ A utility program, also called a utility, is a type of software that performs a specific task, usually related to managing a computer, its devices, or its programs. Popular utility programs are file viewers, file compression utilities, diagnostic utilities, disk scanners, disk defragmenters, uninstallers, backup utilities, antivirus programs, and screensavers. Using the school library, other textbooks, the Internet, magazines, or other resources, research two or more of these utility programs. Then, prepare a brief research paper (400-450 words) that discusses the utilities. Include at least one explanatory note and two references, one of which must be a Web site on the Internet. Use the concepts and techniques presented in this project to format the paper.

Cases and Places

5 ▶▶ Communications technologies have changed the way individuals interact, by allowing for instant and accurate information transfer, 24 hours a day. Today, uses of communications technology are all around and include e-mail, voice mail, fax, telecommuting, videoconferencing, groupware, global positioning systems (GPSs), bulletin board systems (BBSs), the Internet, the World Wide Web, e-commerce, and telephony. Using the school library, other textbooks, the Internet, magazines, or other resources, research two or more of these communications technologies. Then, prepare a brief research paper (400-450 words) that discusses the communications technologies. Include at least one explanatory note and two references, one of which must be a Web site on the Internet. Use the concepts and techniques presented in this project to format the paper.

6 ▶▶▶ In today's technology-rich world, a great demand for computer and information systems professionals exists and continues to grow. Career opportunities are available in many different areas including an information systems department, education and training, sales, service and repair, and consulting. Select an area of interest and research it. Obtain information about job titles, job functions, educational requirements, experience requirements, and salary ranges. Look through the classified section of a newspaper for job listings. Visit the career development and placement office at your school. Search the Web for employment opportunities at major companies. Then, prepare a brief research paper (400-450 words) on the career opportunities available. Indicate which ones you would pursue. Include at least two explanatory notes and three references, one of which must be a Web site on the Internet. Use the concepts and techniques presented in this project to format the paper.

7 ▶▶▶ The decision to purchase a personal computer is an important one – and finding and purchasing the right computer requires an investment of both time and money. In general, personal computers fall into three types: desktop computers, laptop computers, and handheld computers. Select one of these types of computers and shop for the best package deal. Many retailers offer software or additional hardware as part of a package deal. Visit or call a computer store. Search the Web for an online store. Look through newspapers or magazines for retailers, and obtain prices for their latest computer package deals. Then, prepare a brief research paper (400-450 words) on the various computer deals and recommend the one you feel is the best buy for the price. Include at least two explanatory notes and three references, one of which must be a Web site on the Internet. Use the concepts and techniques presented in this project to format the paper.

Microsoft Word 2000

P R O J E C T

3

Using a Wizard to Create a Resume and Creating a Cover Letter with a Table

O B J E C T I V E S

You will have mastered the material in this project when you can:

- Create a resume using Word s Resume Wizard
- Identify the Word screen in print layout view
- Zoom text width
- Identify styles in a document
- Replace selected text with new text
- Insert a line break
- Use print preview to view, reduce the size of, and print a document
- Open a new document window
- Add color to characters
- Set and use tab stops
- Switch from one open Word document to another
- Collect and paste
- Insert a symbol
- Add a bottom border to a paragraph
- Identify the components of a business letter
- Create an AutoText entry
- Insert a nonbreaking space
- Insert an AutoText entry
- Create a bulleted list as you type
- Insert a Word table
- Enter data into a Word table
- Format a Word table
- Prepare and print an envelope address
- Close all open Word documents

Personalized Letters and Résumés

Get You the Job!

"Young physicist seeks teaching position at the university level. Ph.D. thesis submitted, awaiting acceptance. Works include papers on particle theory, quantum theory, and special theory of relativity. Family man, enjoys playing the violin and sailing. Contact A. Einstein.**"**

Yes, *that* A. Einstein, who, in 1905, wrote by hand literally dozens of letters seeking employment as a teacher while he labored in relative obscurity at the Swiss patent office. The same year, he published three studies that set the world of science on its ear. Fame eventually helped, but persistence in his search paid off when he finally landed a teaching appointment at the University of Zurich after years as a patent clerk.

No one can tell whether Einstein might have met his goals more quickly if he would have had the benefit of modern word processing software, but certainly Microsoft Word would have made his life easier.

As you embark on your professional life, you have the advantage of using Word to prepare a resume and a personalized cover letter. In this project, you will learn these skills. Because employers review many resumes, the content of your resume is very important and its design and detail should represent you as the best candidate for the job. Providing a personalized cover letter with each resume enables you to elaborate on positive points in your resume and gives you an opportunity to show a potential employer your written communications skills.

Using the Résumé Wizard creates a resume that is tailored to your preferences. The Wizard provides the style, formats the resume with appropriate headings and spacing, and makes it easy for you to present your best qualities.

> "Be studious in your profession, and you will be learned.
> Be industrious and frugal, and you will be rich.
> Be sober and temperate, and you will be healthy.
> Be in general virtuous, and you will be happy.
> At least you will, by such conduct, stand the best
> chance for such consequences."
>
> Benjamin Franklin

If good guidelines exist for doing something, then why not use them? This same practicality is built into the Résumé Wizard. Word provides the tools that eliminate the need to start from scratch every time, while you provide responses and supply the substance.

To understand the importance of using these guidelines, consider the meaning of the word represent: to bring clearly before the mind. When creating letters and résumés, which are two elements of business life that are fundamental to success, it is critical to bring a favorable image to mind. These documents must be crisp, to the point, and good-looking, because usually they are the first glimpse a prospective employer gets of a job-seeker.

Even if an individual's personal trip through the universe does not include physics or violins, a good résumé and cover letter may be the launch vehicles that start the journey.

Microsoft **Word 2000**

Microsoft Word 2000

Using a Wizard to Create a Resume and Creating a Cover Letter with a Table

PROJECT

3

C A S E   P E R S P E C T I V E

Paulette Rose Brandon recently graduated from Illinois State College with a B.S. in Management, specializing in Marketing. She also has an A.S. in Business and an A.S. in Computer Technology. Ready to embark on a full-time career in computer sales management, Paulette knows she needs a resume and an accompanying cover letter to send to prospective employers. Because you work as an intern in the school's Office of Career Development, she has asked you to help her create a professional resume and cover letter.

While reading through the classified section of the *Chicago Times*, Paulette locates a computer sales management trainee position at Deluxe Computers that sounds perfect for her.

Paulette will use Word's Resume Wizard to create a resume. She will compose the cover letter to Mr. Carl Reed, personnel director at Deluxe Computers, being certain to include all essential business letter components. With her strong business sense and your resume writing expertise, you create an effective package that should ensure Paulette's success in obtaining the position.

Introduction

At some time in your professional life, you will prepare a resume along with a personalized cover letter to send to a prospective employer(s). In addition to some personal information, a **resume** usually contains the applicant's educational background and job experience. Because employers review many resumes for each vacant position, you should design your resume carefully so it presents you as the best candidate for the job. You also should attach a personalized cover letter to each resume you send. A **cover letter** enables you to elaborate on positive points in your resume; it also provides you with an opportunity to show a potential employer your written communication skills. Thus, it is important that your cover letter is written well and follows proper business letter rules.

Because composing documents from scratch is a difficult process for many people, Word provides templates and wizards to assist you in preparing documents. A **template** is similar to a form with prewritten text; that is, Word prepares the requested document with text and/or formatting common to all documents of this nature. By asking you several basic questions, a **wizard** prepares and formats a document for you based on your responses. Once Word creates a document from either a template or a wizard, you then fill in the blanks or replace prewritten words in the document.

Project Three — Resume and Cover Letter

Paulette Rose Brandon, a recent college graduate, is seeking a full-time position as a computer sales manager. Project 3 uses Word to produce her resume shown in Figure 3-1 and a personalized cover letter and envelope shown in Figure 3-2 on page WD 3.6.

WD 3.4

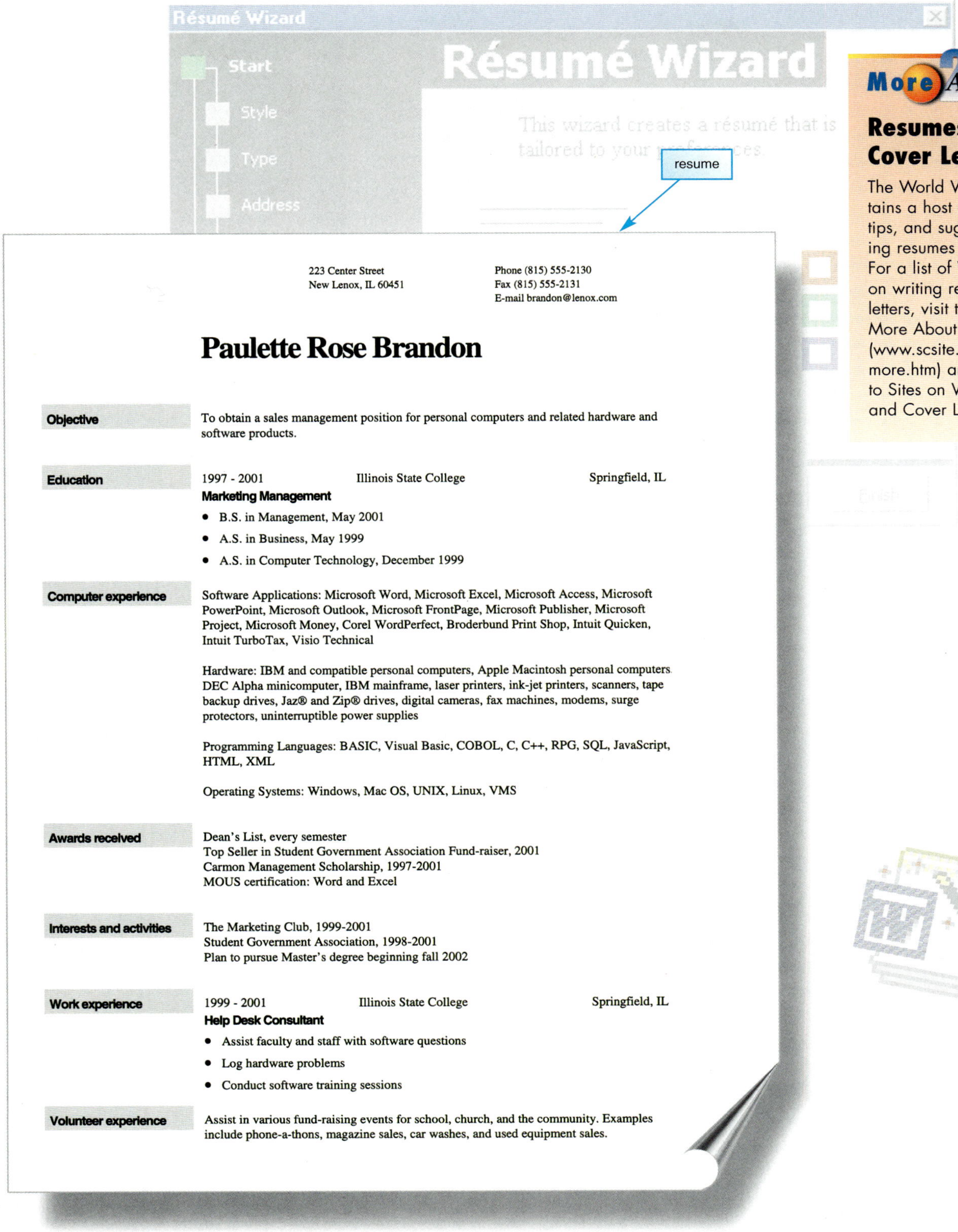

Résumé Wizard

Résumé Wizard

This wizard creates a résumé that is
tailored to your preferences.

- Start
- Style
- Type
- Address

resume

223 Center Street
New Lenox, IL 60451

Phone (815) 555-2130
Fax (815) 555-2131
E-mail brandon@lenox.com

Paulette Rose Brandon

Objective

To obtain a sales management position for personal computers and related hardware and software products.

Education

1997 - 2001   Illinois State College   Springfield, IL
Marketing Management
- B.S. in Management, May 2001
- A.S. in Business, May 1999
- A.S. in Computer Technology, December 1999

Computer experience

Software Applications: Microsoft Word, Microsoft Excel, Microsoft Access, Microsoft PowerPoint, Microsoft Outlook, Microsoft FrontPage, Microsoft Publisher, Microsoft Project, Microsoft Money, Corel WordPerfect, Broderbund Print Shop, Intuit Quicken, Intuit TurboTax, Visio Technical

Hardware: IBM and compatible personal computers, Apple Macintosh personal computers, DEC Alpha minicomputer, IBM mainframe, laser printers, ink-jet printers, scanners, tape backup drives, Jaz® and Zip® drives, digital cameras, fax machines, modems, surge protectors, uninterruptible power supplies

Programming Languages: BASIC, Visual Basic, COBOL, C, C++, RPG, SQL, JavaScript, HTML, XML

Operating Systems: Windows, Mac OS, UNIX, Linux, VMS

Awards received

Dean's List, every semester
Top Seller in Student Government Association Fund-raiser, 2001
Carmon Management Scholarship, 1997-2001
MOUS certification: Word and Excel

Interests and activities

The Marketing Club, 1999-2001
Student Government Association, 1998-2001
Plan to pursue Master's degree beginning fall 2002

Work experience

1999 - 2001   Illinois State College   Springfield, IL
Help Desk Consultant
- Assist faculty and staff with software questions
- Log hardware problems
- Conduct software training sessions

Volunteer experience

Assist in various fund-raising events for school, church, and the community. Examples include phone-a-thons, magazine sales, car washes, and used equipment sales.

FIGURE 3-1

More About 2000

Resumes and Cover Letters

The World Wide Web contains a host of information, tips, and suggestions on writing resumes and cover letters. For a list of Web links to sites on writing resumes and cover letters, visit the Word 2000 More About Web page (www.scsite.com/wd2000/more.htm) and then click Links to Sites on Writing Resumes and Cover Letters.

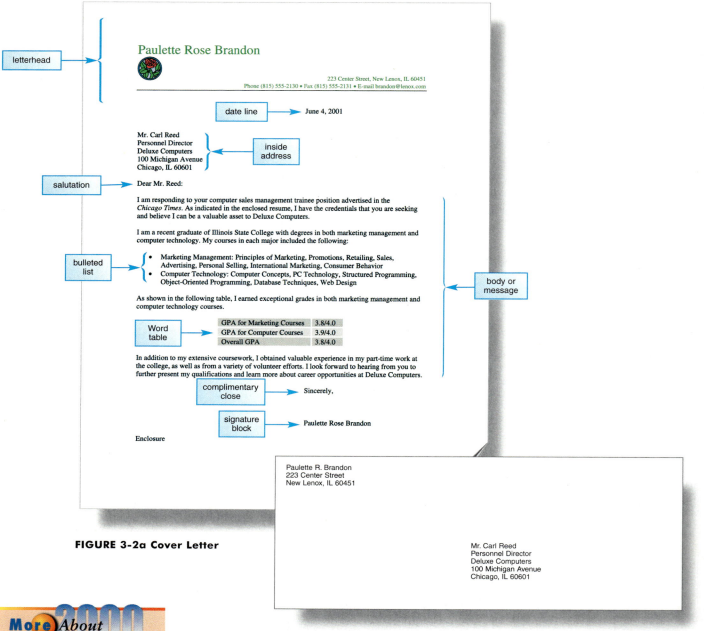

FIGURE 3-2a Cover Letter

FIGURE 3-2b Envelope

More *About* **2000**

Business Letters

A finished business letter should look like a symmetrically framed picture with even margins, all balanced below an attractive letterhead. In addition, the contents of the letter should contain proper grammar, correct spelling, logically constructed sentences, flowing paragraphs, and sound ideas.

Using Word's Resume Wizard to Create a Resume

You can type a resume from scratch into a blank document window, or you can use the **Resume Wizard** and let Word format the resume with appropriate headings and spacing. Then, you can customize the resulting resume by filling in the blanks or selecting and replacing text.

When you use a wizard, Word displays a dialog box with the wizard's name in its title bar. A wizard's dialog box displays a list of **panel names** along its left side with the currently selected panel displaying on the right side of the dialog box (see Figure 3-4). Each panel presents a different set of options, in which you select preferences or enter text. You click the Next button to move from one panel to the next within the wizard's dialog box.

Perform the following steps to create a resume using the Resume Wizard. Because a wizard retains the settings selected by the last person that used the wizard, your selections initially may display differently. Be sure to verify that your settings match the screens shown in the following steps.

Steps **To Create a Resume Using Word's Resume Wizard**

1 **Click the Start button on the taskbar and then click New Office Document. If necessary, click the Other Documents tab when the New Office Document dialog box displays. Click the Resume Wizard icon.**

Office displays several wizard and template icons in the Other Documents sheet in the New Office Document dialog box (Figure 3-3). Icons without the word, wizard, are templates. If you click an icon, a sample of the resulting document displays in the Preview area.

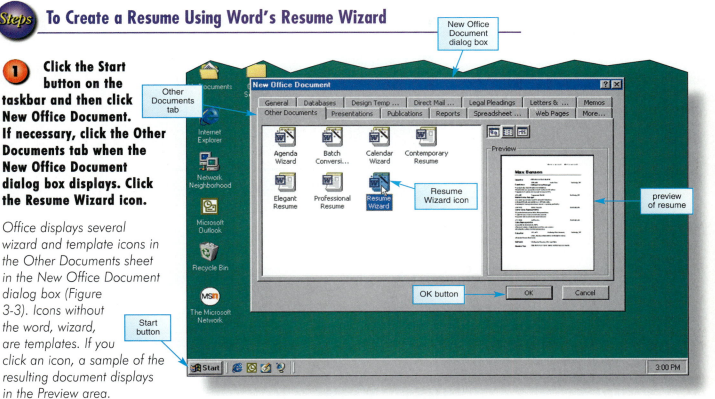

FIGURE 3-3

2 **Click the OK button. When the Resume Wizard dialog box displays, point to the Next button.**

After a few seconds, Word displays the Start panel of the Resume Wizard dialog box, informing you the Resume Wizard has started (Figure 3-4). Notice this dialog box has a Microsoft Word Help button you can click to obtain help while using this wizard. Depending on your system, the Word window may or may not be maximized behind the Resume Wizard dialog box.

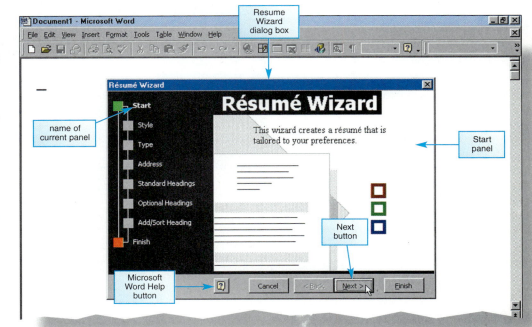

FIGURE 3-4

3 Click the Next button. When the Style panel displays, click Contemporary, if necessary, and then point to the Next button.

Word displays the *Style panel* in the Resume Wizard dialog box, requesting the style of your resume (Figure 3-5). Word provides three styles of wizards and templates: Professional, Contemporary, and Elegant. A sample of each resume style displays in this panel.

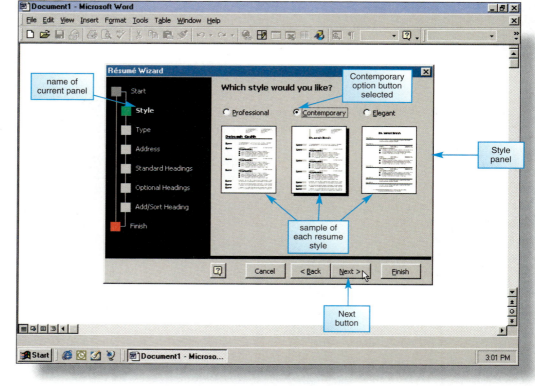

FIGURE 3-5

4 Click the Next button. When the Type panel displays, click Entry-level resume, if necessary, and then point to the Next button.

Word displays the *Type panel* in the Resume Wizard dialog box, asking for the type of resume that you want to create (Figure 3-6).

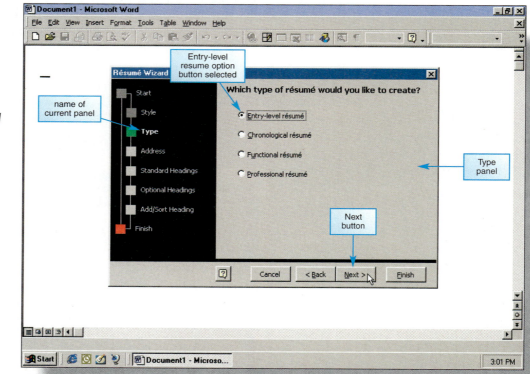

FIGURE 3-6

5 **Click the Next button.**

*Word displays the **Address panel** in the Resume Wizard dialog box, with the current name selected (Figure 3-7). The name displayed and selected in your Name text box will be different, depending on the name of the last person using the Resume Wizard.*

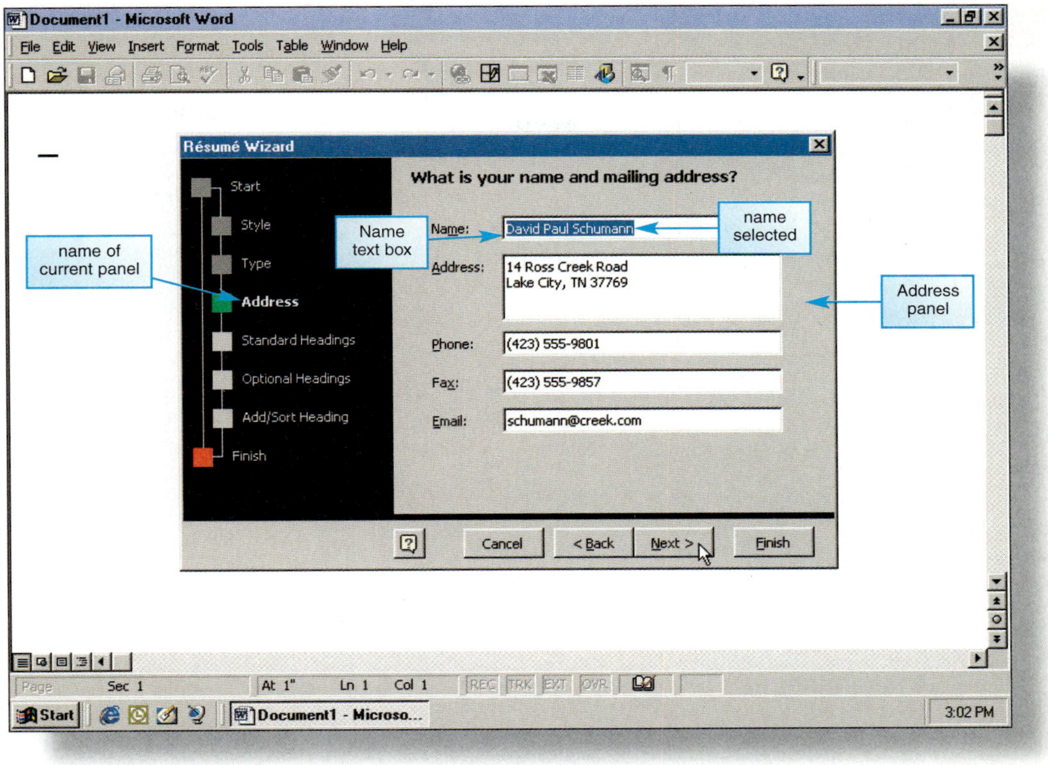

FIGURE 3-7

6 **With the name in the Name text box selected, type** Paulette Rose Brandon **and then press the TAB key. Type** 223 Center Street **and then press the ENTER key. Type** New Lenox, IL 60451 **and then press the TAB key. Type** (815) 555-2130 **and then press the TAB key. Type** (815) 555-2131 **and then press the TAB key. Type** brandon@lenox.com **and then point to the Next button.**

As you type the new text, it automatically replaces the selected text (Figure 3-8).

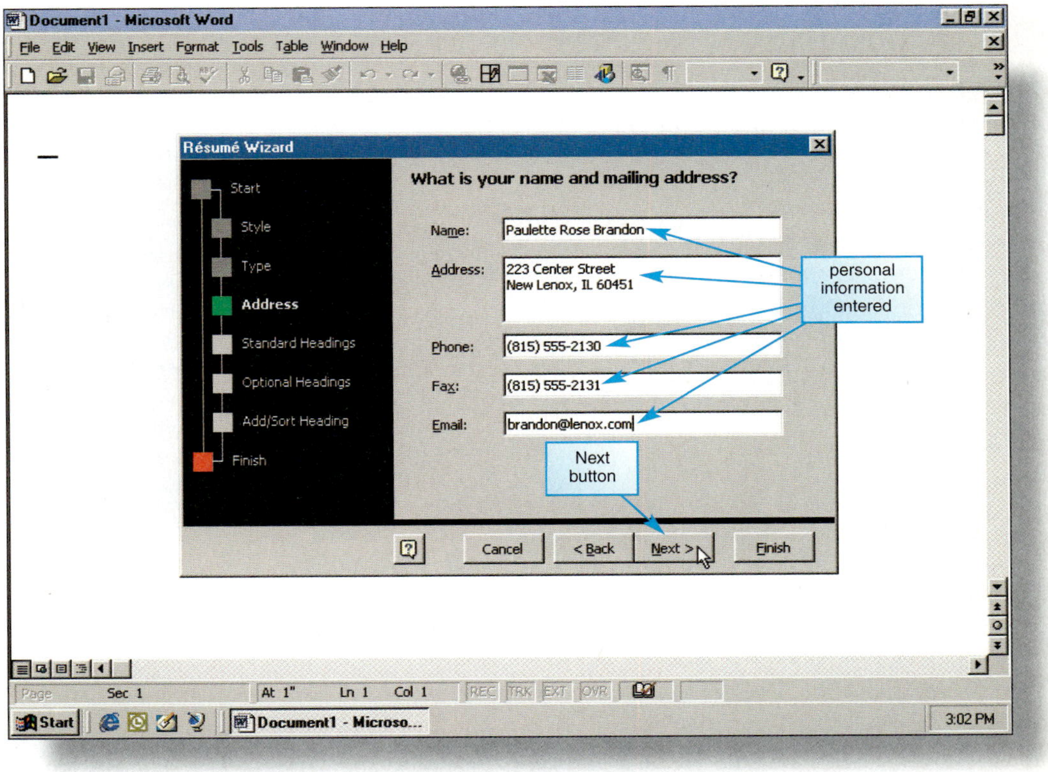

FIGURE 3-8

7 Click the Next button. When the Standard Headings panel displays, if necessary, click Languages, Hobbies, and References to remove the check marks. All other check boxes should have check marks. Point to the Next button.

Word displays the Standard Headings panel in the Resume Wizard dialog box, which requests the headings you want on your resume (Figure 3-9). You want all headings, except for these three: Languages, Hobbies, and References.

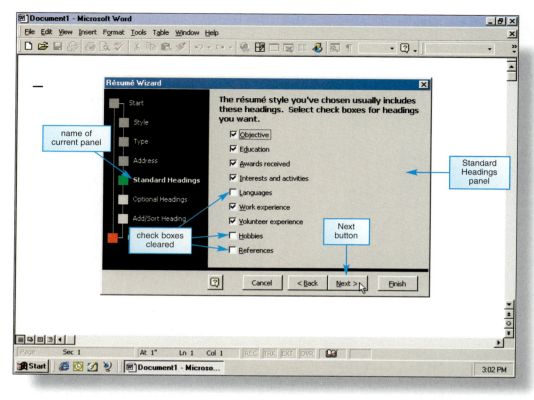

FIGURE 3-9

8 Click the Next button. Point to the Next button in the Optional Headings panel.

Word displays the Optional Headings panel in the Resume Wizard dialog box, which allows you to choose additional headings for your resume (Figure 3-10). All of these check boxes should be empty because none of these headings is required on your resume.

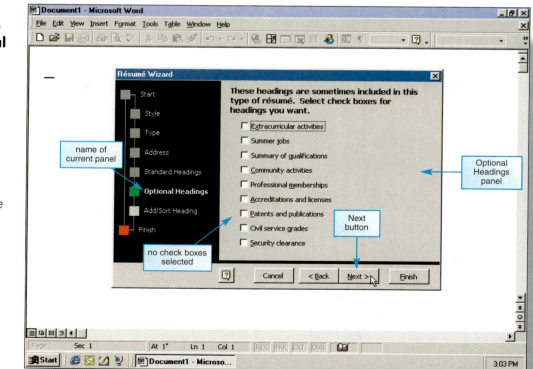

FIGURE 3-10

9 **Click the Next button. When the Add/Sort Heading panel displays, type** Computer experience **in the additional headings text box. Point to the Add button.**

*Word displays the **Add/Sort Heading panel** in the Resume Wizard dialog box, which allows you to enter any additional headings you want on your resume (Figure 3-11).*

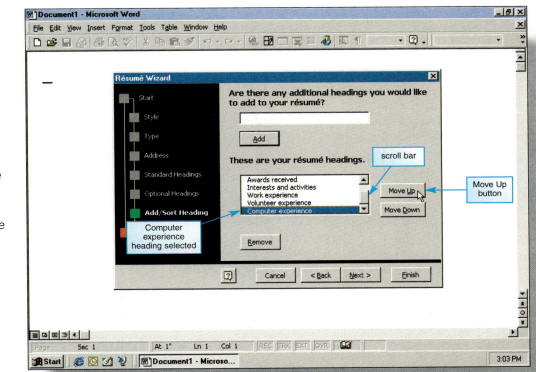

FIGURE 3-11

10 **Click the Add button. Scroll to the bottom of the list of resume headings and then click Computer experience. Point to the Move Up button.**

The Computer experience heading is selected (Figure 3-12). You can rearrange the order of the headings on your resume by selecting a heading and then clicking the appropriate button (Move Up button or Move Down button).

FIGURE 3-12

11 **Click the Move Up button four times.**

Word moves the heading, Computer experience, above the Awards received heading (Figure 3-13).

12 **If the last person using the Resume Wizard included additional headings, you may have some unwanted headings. Your heading list should be as follows: Objective, Education, Computer experience, Awards received, Interests and activities, Work experience, and Volunteer experience. If you have an additional heading(s), click the unwanted heading and then click the Remove button.**

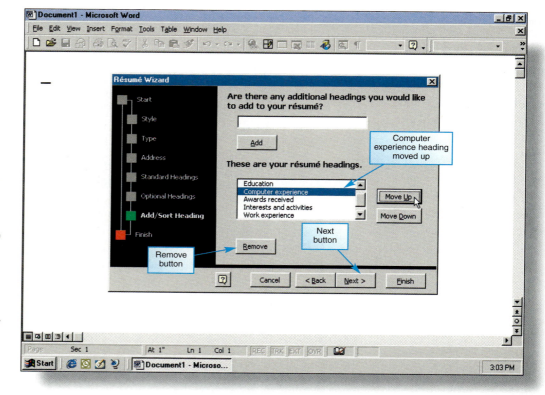

FIGURE 3-13

13 **Click the Next button. When the Finish panel displays, point to the Finish button.**

Word displays the Finish panel in the Resume Wizard dialog box, which indicates the wizard is ready to create your document (Figure 3-14).

FIGURE 3-14

14 Click the Finish button. If the Word window is not maximized, click its Maximize button. If the Office Assistant displays, click its Cancel button. To close the Office Assistant, if necessary, right-click it and then click Hide on the shortcut menu.

Word creates an entry-level contemporary style resume layout (Figure 3-15). You are to personalize the resume as indicated.

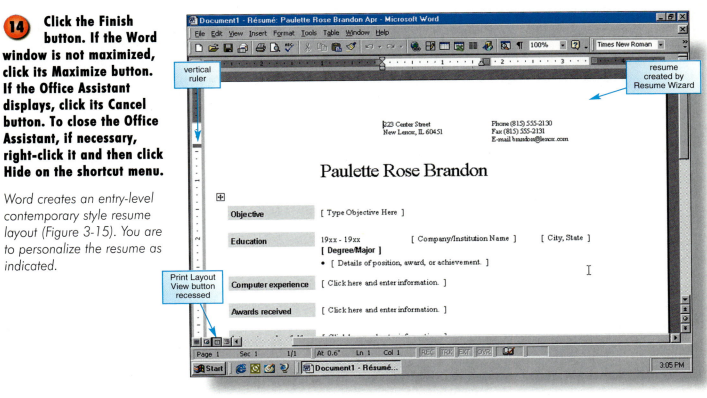

FIGURE 3-15

When you create a resume using the Resume Wizard (see Figure 3-14), you can click the Back button in any panel of the Resume Wizard dialog box to change any of the previous options you selected. To exit from the Resume Wizard and return to the document window without creating the resume, click the Cancel button in any panel of the Resume Wizard dialog box.

In addition to the Resume Wizard, Word provides many other wizards to assist you in creating documents: agenda for a meeting, calendar, envelope, fax cover sheet, legal pleading, letter, mailing label, memorandum, and Web page.

Word displays the resume in the document window in print layout view. You can tell you are in print layout view by looking at the Word window (Figure 3-15). Notice that in print layout view, the **Print Layout View button** on the horizontal scroll bar is recessed. Also, notice that a **vertical ruler** displays at the left edge of the document window, in addition to the horizontal ruler at the top of the window.

Your screen was in normal view when you created documents in Project 1 and for most of Project 2. In Project 2, when you created the header, you were in print layout view. In both normal view and print layout view, you can type and edit text. The difference is that **print layout view** shows you exactly how the printed page will print. That is, in print layout view, Word places the entire piece of paper in the document window, showing precisely the positioning of the text, margins, headers, footers, and footnotes on the printed page.

Resetting Menus and Toolbars

To set the menus and toolbars so they appear exactly as shown in this book, you should reset your menus and toolbars as outlined in Appendix C or follow the steps on the next page.

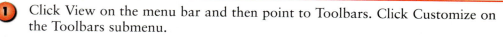

TO RESET MENUS AND TOOLBARS

1 Click View on the menu bar and then point to Toolbars. Click Customize on the Toolbars submenu.

2 When the Customize dialog box displays, click the Options tab, make sure the top three check boxes have check marks and then click the Reset my usage data button. When the Microsoft Word dialog box displays, click the Yes button.

3 Click the Toolbars tab. Click Standard in the Toolbars list and then click the Reset button. When the Reset Toolbar dialog box displays, click the OK button.

4 Click Formatting in the Toolbars list and then click the Reset button. When the Reset Toolbar dialog box displays, click the OK button. Click the Close button.

Word resets the menus and toolbars.

To see the entire resume created by the Resume Wizard, you should print the resume.

TO PRINT THE RESUME CREATED BY THE RESUME WIZARD

1 Double-click the move handle on the Standard toolbar to display the entire toolbar. Ready the printer and then click the Print button on the Standard toolbar.

2 When the printer stops, retrieve the hard copy resume from the printer.

The printed resume is shown in Figure 3-16.

More About

Resume Contents

Omit the following items from a resume: social security number, marital status, age, height, weight, gender, physical appearance, health, citizenship, references, previous pay rates, reasons for leaving a prior job, current date, and high school information (if you are a college graduate).

resume generated by Resume Wizard

223 Center Street
New Lenox, IL 60451

Phone (815) 555-2130
Fax (815) 555-2131
E-mail brandon@lenox.com

Paulette Rose Brandon

Objective	[Type Objective Here]		
Education	19xx - 19xx	[Company/Institution Name]	[City, State]
	[Degree/Major]		
	• [Details of position, award, or achievement.]		
Computer experience	[Click here and enter information.]		
Awards received	[Click here and enter information.]		
Interests and activities	[Click here and enter information.]		
Work experience	19xx - 19xx	[Company/Institution Name]	[City, State]
	[Job Title]		
	• [Details of position, award, or achievement.]		
Volunteer experience	[Click here and enter information.]		

first column of table

second column of table

FIGURE 3-16

Personalizing the Resume

The next step is to personalize the resume. Where Word has indicated, you type the objective, education, computer experience, awards received, interests and activities, work experience, and volunteer experience next to the respective headings. In the education and work experience sections, you select and replace text to customize these sections. The following pages show how to personalize the resume generated by the Resume Wizard.

Displaying Formatting Marks

As you have learned, it is helpful to display **formatting marks** that indicate where in the document you pressed the ENTER key, SPACEBAR, and other keys. If formatting marks do not display already on your screen, follow this step to display them.

TO DISPLAY FORMATTING MARKS

1 If the Show/Hide ¶ button on the Standard toolbar is not already recessed, click it.

Word displays formatting marks in the document window, and the Show/Hide ¶ button on the Standard toolbar is recessed (see Figure 3-17 on the next page).

Tables

When the Resume Wizard prepares a resume, it arranges the body of the resume as a table. A Word **table** is a collection of rows and columns. As shown in Figure 3-16, the section headings (Objective, Education, Computer experience, Awards received, Interests and activities, Work experience, and Volunteer experience) are placed in the first column of the table; the details for each of these sections are placed in the second column of the table. Thus, this table contains two columns (see Figure 3-17 on the next page). It also contains seven rows – one row for each section of the resume.

The intersection of a row and a column is called a **cell**, and cells are filled with text. Each cell has an **end-of-cell mark**, which is a formatting mark, that you use to select and format cells. You have learned that formatting marks do not print on a hard copy.

To see clearly the rows, columns, and cells in a Word table, some users prefer to show gridlines. As illustrated in Figure 3-17, **gridlines** help identify the rows and columns in a table. If you want to display gridlines in a table, position the insertion point somewhere in the table, click Table on the menu bar, and then click **Show Gridlines**. If you want to hide the gridlines, click somewhere in the table, click Table on the menu bar, and then click **Hide Gridlines**.

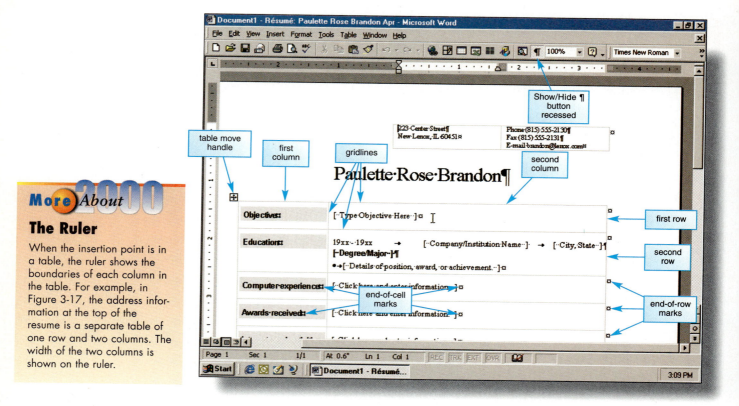

FIGURE 3-17

The upper-left corner of the table displays the **table move handle**, which you drag to move the table to a new location. You also can resize a table, add or delete rows or columns in a table, and format a table. These and other features of tables are discussed in more depth when you create the cover letter later in this project.

Zooming Text Width

In Projects 1 and 2, your screen was in normal view and you used the zoom page width command to display text on the screen as large as possible without extending the right margin beyond the right edge of the document window. When you are in print layout view, the zoom page width command extends the edges of the paper to the margins —making the text smaller on the screen. To make the text as large as possible on the screen in print layout view, you should **zoom text width** as shown in the following steps.

To Zoom Text Width

1 **Click the Zoom box arrow on the Standard toolbar and then point to Text Width in the Zoom list (Figure 3-18).**

2 **Click Text Width.**

Word extends the text to the right edge of the document window (see Figure 3-19 on the next page).

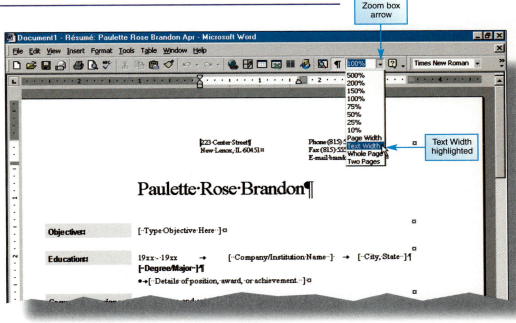

FIGURE 3-18

Other Ways

1. On View menu click Zoom, select Text Width, click OK button

Word computes a zoom percentage based on a variety of settings. The percentage that displays in your Zoom box may be different, depending on your system configuration. Notice in Figure 3-18 that the Zoom list contains more options when the Word window is in print layout view than in normal view.

The next step is to bold the name, Paulette Rose Brandon, in the resume as described in the following steps.

TO BOLD TEXT

1 Drag through the name, Paulette Rose Brandon, to select it.

2 Double-click the move handle on the Formatting toolbar to display the entire toolbar. Click the Bold button on the Formatting toolbar.

Word bolds the name, Paulette Rose Brandon (see Figure 3-19 on the next page).

Styles

When you use a wizard to create a document, Word formats the document using styles. You learned in Project 2 that a **style** is a customized format that you can apply to text. Recall that the formats defined by a style include character formatting, such as the font and font size, and paragraph formatting, such as line spacing and text alignment.

The Style box on the Formatting toolbar displays the name of the style associated with the location of the insertion point. You can identify many of the characteristics assigned to a style by looking at the Formatting toolbar. For example, in Figure 3-19 on the next page, the insertion point is in a paragraph formatted with the Objective style, which uses the 10-point Times New Roman font for the characters.

Styles

To apply a different style to a paragraph, click in the paragraph, click the Style box arrow on the Formatting toolbar, and then click the desired paragraph style. To apply a different style to characters, select the characters, click the Style box arrow on the Formatting toolbar, and then click the desired character style.

If you click the Style box arrow on the Formatting toolbar, the list of styles associated with the current document displays. Paragraph styles affect an entire paragraph, whereas character styles affect only selected characters. In the Style list, **paragraph style** names are followed by a proofreader's paragraph mark (¶), and **character style** names are followed by an underlined letter a (**a**).

In Project 2, you changed the formats assigned to a style by changing the Footnote Text style. You also may select the appropriate style from the Style list before entering the text so that the text you type will be formatted according to the selected style.

Selecting and Replacing Text

The next step in personalizing the resume is to select text that the Resume Wizard inserted into the resume and replace it with personal information. The first heading on the resume is the objective. You enter the objective where the Resume Wizard inserted the words, Type Objective Here, which is called **placeholder text**.

To replace text in Word, select the text to be removed and then type the desired text. To select the placeholder text, Type Objective Here, you click it. Then, you type the objective. As soon as you begin typing, the selected placeholder text is deleted; thus, you do not have to delete the selection before you begin typing. Perform the following steps to enter the objective into the resume.

 **To Select and Replace Placeholder Text**

1 **Click the placeholder text, Type Objective Here.**

Word highlights the placeholder text in the resume (Figure 3-19). Notice the style is Objective in the Style box on the Formatting toolbar.

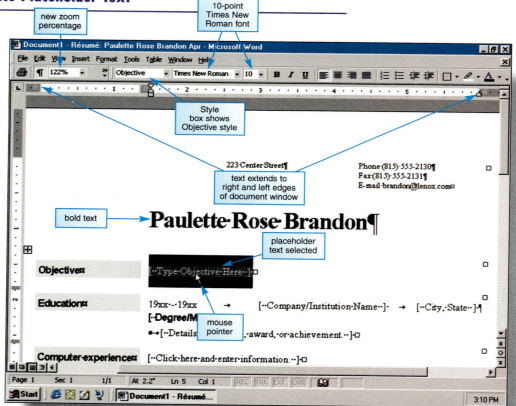

FIGURE 3-19

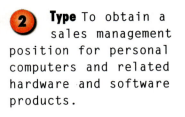

2 **Type** To obtain a sales management position for personal computers and related hardware and software products.

Word replaces the high-lighted placeholder text, Type Objective Here, with the objective you type (Figure 3-20). Your document may wordwrap on a different word depending on the type of printer you are using.

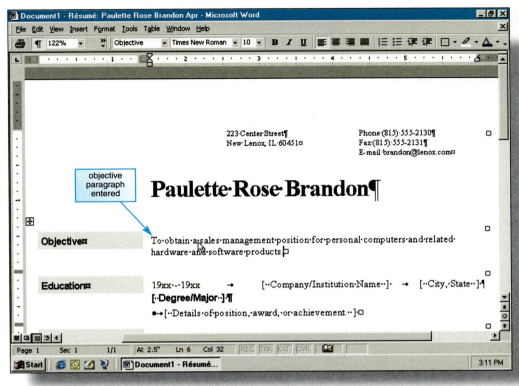

FIGURE 3-20

The next step in personalizing the resume is to replace the wizard's words and phrases in the education section of the resume with your own words and phrases as shown in the following steps.

Steps **To Select and Replace Resume Wizard Supplied Text**

1 **If necessary, scroll down to display the entire education section of the resume. Drag through the xx in the first 19xx of the education section.**

Word selects the xx in the first year (Figure 3-21).

FIGURE 3-21

2 Type **97** and then drag through the **19xx** in the second year of the education section. Type **2001** and then click the placeholder text, **Company/Institution Name.**

Word highlights the place-holder text, Company/Institution Name (Figure 3-22). The years now display as 1997 - 2001 in the educa-tion section.

FIGURE 3-22

3 Type **Illinois State College** and then click the placeholder text, **City, State.** Type **Springfield, IL** and then click the placeholder text, **Degree/Major.** Type **Marketing Management** and then click the placeholder text, **Details of position, award, or achievement.** Type **B.S. in Management, May 2001** and then press the **ENTER** key. Type **A.S. in Business, May 1999** and then press the **ENTER** key. Type **A.S. in Computer Technology, December 1999** as the last item in the list (Figure 3-23).

FIGURE 3-23

A **bullet** is a symbol positioned at the beginning of a paragraph. A list of para-graphs with bullets is called a **bulleted list.** The list of degrees in the education section of the resume, for example, is a bulleted list. When the insertion point is in a para-graph containing a bullet, the Bullets button on the Formatting toolbar is recessed. In a bulleted list, each time you press the ENTER key, a bullet displays at the beginning of the new paragraph.

The next step is to enter the computer experience section of the resume as described in the following steps.

TO ENTER PLACEHOLDER TEXT

1 If necessary, scroll down to display the computer experience section of the resume. Click the placeholder text, Click here and enter information, to select it.

2 Type the first paragraph of computer experience (software applications) as shown in Figure 3-24.

3 Press the ENTER key. Type the second paragraph of computer experience (hardware) as shown in Figure 3-24.

4 Press the ENTER key. Type the third paragraph of computer experience (programming languages) as shown in Figure 3-24.

5 Press the ENTER key. Type the fourth paragraph of computer experience (operating systems) as shown in Figure 3-24. Do not press the ENTER key at the end of this line.

The computer experience section of the resume is entered (Figure 3-24).

The Registered Trademark Symbol

To automatically enter the registered trademark symbol, type (r). Or, press ALT+CTRL+R. Or, click Insert on the menu bar, click Symbol, click the Special Characters tab, click Registered in the Character list, click the Insert button, and then click the Close button.

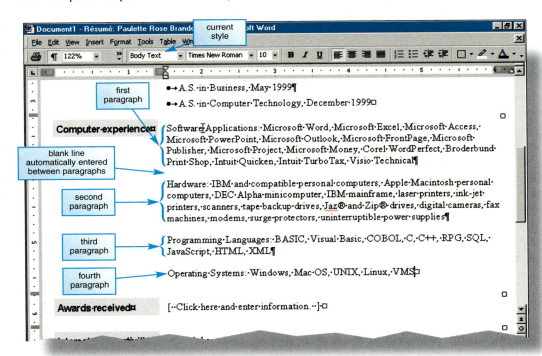

FIGURE 3-24

Entering a Line Break

The next step in personalizing the resume is to enter the awards received section. The style used for the characters in the awards received section of the resume is the Objective style. A paragraph formatting characteristic of the Objective style is that when you press the ENTER key, the insertion point advances downward at least 11 points, which leaves nearly an entire blank line between each paragraph. For example, each time you pressed the ENTER key in the computer experience section, Word placed a blank line between each paragraph (Figure 3-24).

You want the lines within the awards received section to be close to each other (see Figure 3-1 on page WD 3.5). Thus, you will not press the ENTER key between each award received. Instead, you will create a **line break**, which advances the insertion point to the beginning of the next physical line– ignoring any paragraph formatting instructions. Perform the following steps to enter the awards received section using a line break, instead of a paragraph break, between each line.

Steps To Enter a Line Break

1 If necessary, scroll down to display the awards received section of the resume. In the awards received section, click the placeholder text, Click here and enter information. **Type** Dean's List, every semester **and then press the SHIFT + ENTER keys.**

Word inserts a line break character, which is a formatting mark, after the named award and moves the insertion point to the beginning of the next physical line (Figure 3-25).

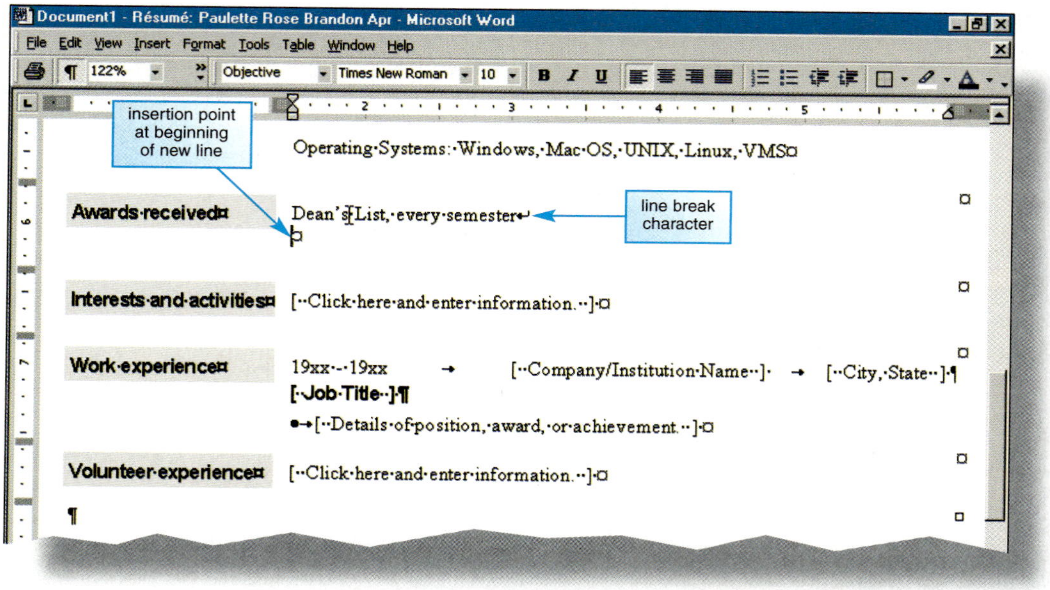

FIGURE 3-25

2 **Type** Top Seller in Student Government Association Fund-raiser, 2001 **and then press the SHIFT + ENTER keys.** **Type** Carmon Management Scholarship, 1997-2001 **and then press the SHIFT + ENTER keys. Type** MOUS certification: Word and Excel **as the last award. Do not press the SHIFT + ENTER keys at the end of this line.**

The awards received section is entered (Figure 3-26).

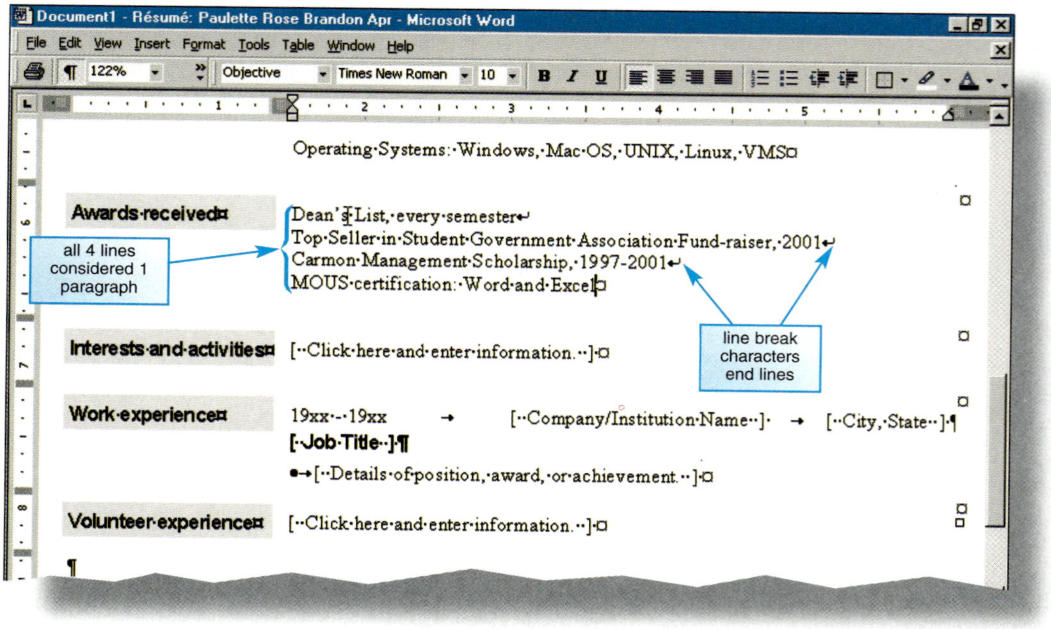

FIGURE 3-26

Enter the remaining text for the resume as described in the following steps.

TO ENTER THE REMAINING SECTIONS OF THE RESUME

1 If necessary, scroll down to display the interests and activities section of the resume. Click the placeholder text, Click here and enter information. Type The Marketing Club, 1999-2001 and then press the SHIFT+ENTER keys.

2 Type Student Government Association, 1998-2001 and then press the SHIFT+ENTER keys.

3 Type Plan to pursue Master's degree beginning fall 2002 as the last activity. Do not press the SHIFT+ENTER keys at the end of this line.

4 If necessary, scroll down to display the work experience section of the resume. Drag through the xx in the first 19xx, type 99 and then drag through the 19xx in the second year. Type 2001 as the year.

5 Click the placeholder text, Company/Institution Name. Type Illinois State College as the new text. Click the placeholder text, City, State. Type Springfield, IL as the city and state.

6 Click the placeholder text, **Job Title**. Type Help Desk Consultant as the title.

7 Click the placeholder text, Details of position, award, or achievement. Type Assist faculty and staff with software questions and then press the ENTER key. Type Log hardware problems and then press the ENTER key. Type Conduct software training sessions as the last item in the list.

8 If necessary, scroll down to display the volunteer experience section of the resume. Click the placeholder text, Click here and enter information. Type Assist in various fund-raising events for school, church, and the community. Examples include phone-a-thons, magazine sales, car washes, and used equipment sales. Do not press the ENTER key at the end of this line.

The interests and activities, work experience, and volunteer experience sections of the resume are complete (Figure 3-27).

More About 2000

References

Do not state "References Available Upon Request" on your resume; nor should references be listed on the resume. Employers assume you will give references, if asked, and this information simply clutters a resume. Often you are asked to list references on your application. Be sure to give your references a copy of your resume.

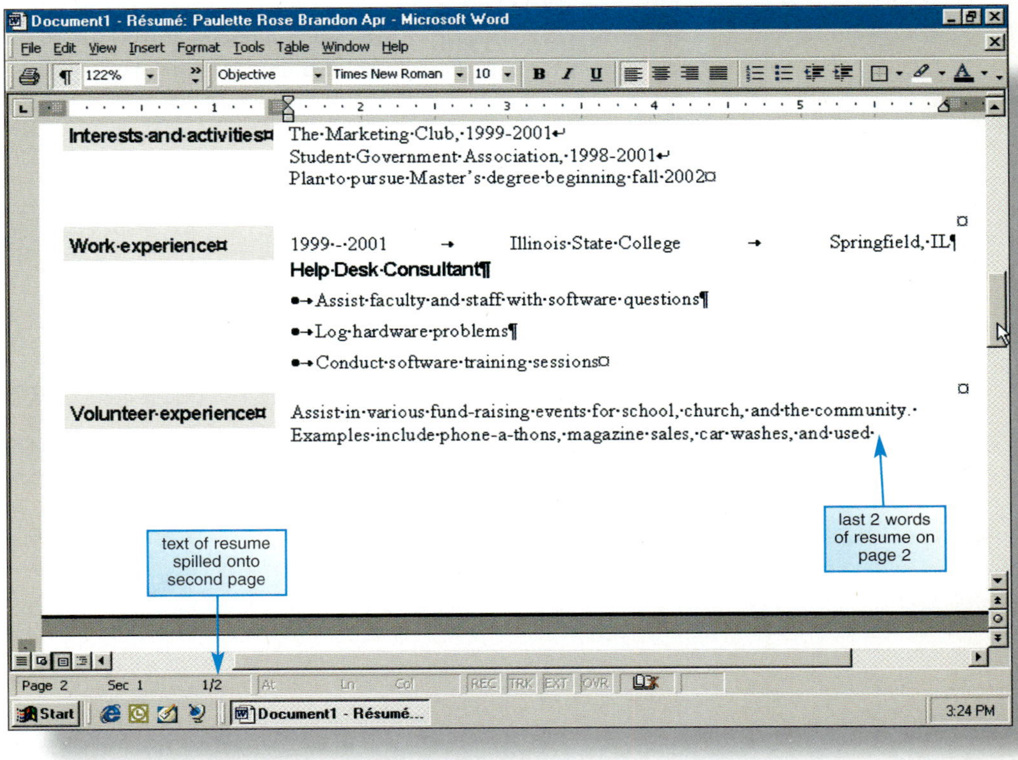

FIGURE 3-27

More About

Print Preview

To magnify a page in print preview, be sure the Magnifier button is recessed on the Print Preview toolbar and then click in the document to zoom in or out. Magnifying a page has no effect on the printed document. To edit a document in print preview, be sure the Magnifier button is not recessed and then edit the text.

Notice in Figure 3-27 on the previous page that the last two words of the resume spilled onto a second page. The next section illustrates how to shrink the resume so it fits on a single page.

Viewing and Printing the Resume in Print Preview

To see exactly how a document will look when you print it, you should display it in **print preview**. Print preview displays the entire document in reduced size on the Word screen. In print preview, you can edit and format text, adjust margins, view multiple pages, reduce the document to fit on a single page, and print the document.

If a document *spills* onto a second page by just a line or two, you can try to shrink the document so it fits onto a single page using the **Shrink to Fit button** in print preview. In the previous steps, the last two words of the resume spilled onto a second page. Perform the following steps to view the resume, display both pages of the resume, shrink the resume, and finally print the resume in print preview.

Steps **To Print Preview a Document**

1. **Double-click the move handle on the Standard toolbar to display the entire toolbar. Point to the Print Preview button on the Standard toolbar (Figure 3-28).**

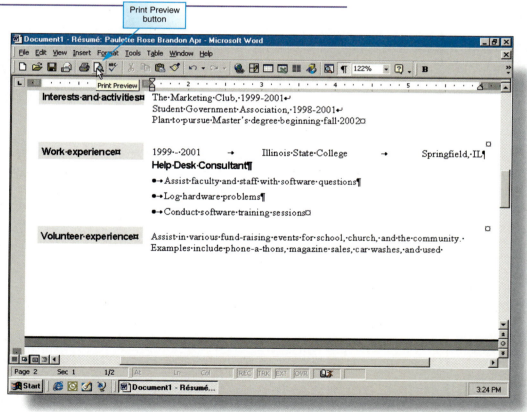

FIGURE 3-28

2 Click the Print Preview button.

Word displays the document in print preview. The **Print Preview toolbar** *displays below the menu bar; the Standard and Formatting toolbars disappear from the screen. Depending on your settings, your screen may display one or two pages in the Preview window.*

3 Click the Multiple Pages button on the Print Preview toolbar. Point to the icon in the first row and second column of the grid.

Word displays a **grid** *so you can select the number of pages to display (Figure 3-29). With the current selection, Word will display one row of two pages (1 x 2) – or two pages side by side.*

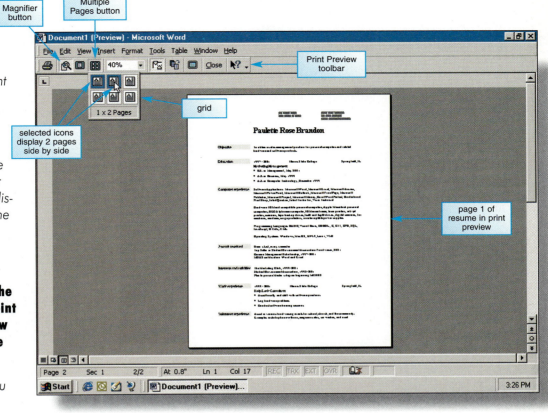

FIGURE 3-29

4 Click the icon in the first row and second column of the grid. Point to the Shrink to Fit button on the Print Preview toolbar.

Word displays the two pages of the resume side by side (Figure 3-30).

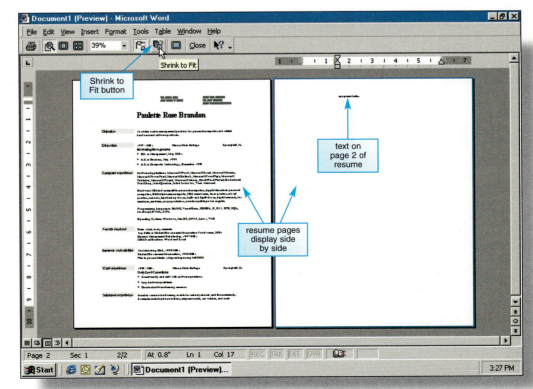

FIGURE 3-30

5 **Click the Shrink to Fit button.**

Word shrinks the resume to a single page by reducing font sizes (Figure 3-31).

6 **Click the Print button on the Print Preview toolbar. When the printer stops, retrieve the printout.**

Word prints the resume on the printer (see Figure 3-1 on page WD 3.5).

7 **Click the Close Preview button on the Print Preview toolbar.**

Word returns to the document window, displaying the resume.

Other Ways

1. On File menu click Print Preview
2. Press CTRL+F2

Printing

If you want to save ink, print faster, or decrease printer overrun errors, lower the printer resolution. Click File on the menu bar, click Print, click the Properties button in the Print dialog box, click the Graphics tab, click the Resolution box arrow, click a lower resolution than displayed currently, click the Apply button, click the OK button, and then click the Close button.

Close Preview button

Shrink to Fit button

Print button

resume fits on a single page

FIGURE 3-31

Saving the Resume

Because the resume now is complete, you should save it. For a detailed example of the procedure summarized below, refer to pages WD 1.26 through WD 1.28 in Project 1.

TO SAVE A DOCUMENT

1 Insert your floppy disk into drive A.

2 Click the Save button on the Standard toolbar.

3 Type Brandon Resume in the File name text box. Do not press the ENTER key.

4 Click the Save in box arrow and then click 3½ Floppy (A:).

5 Click the Save button in the Save As dialog box.

Word saves the document on a floppy disk in drive A with the file name, Brandon Resume.

The resume now is complete. The next step in Project 3 is to create a cover letter to send with the resume to a potential employer. Do not close the Brandon Resume. You will use it again later in this project to copy the address, telephone, fax, and e-mail information.

Creating a Letterhead

You have created a resume to send to prospective employers. Along with the resume, you will attach a personalized cover letter. You would like the cover letter to have a professional looking letterhead (see Figure 3-2a on page WD 3.6). The following pages describe how to use Word to create a letterhead.

In many businesses, letterhead is preprinted on stationery that is used by everyone throughout the corporation. For personal letters, the expense of preprinted letterhead can be costly. Thus, you can create your own letterhead and save it in a file. When you want to create a letter with the letterhead, you simply open the letterhead file and then save the file with a new name, preserving the original letterhead file.

The steps on the following pages illustrate how to create a personal letterhead file.

Letterhead Design

Letterhead designs vary. Some are centered at the top of the page, while others have text or graphics aligned with the left and right margins. Another style places the company's name and logo at the top of the page with the address and other information at the bottom. Well-designed letterheads add professionalism to correspondence.

Opening a New Document Window

The resume currently displays in the document window. You want to leave the resume open because you intend to use it again during this Word session. Thus, you want to work with two documents at the same time: the resume and the letterhead. Each of these documents will display in a separate document window. Perform the following steps to open a new document window for the letterhead file.

Steps To Open a New Document Window

1 **Point to the New Blank Document button on the Standard toolbar (Figure 3-32).**

2 **Click the New Blank Document button.**

Word opens a new document window (see Figure 3-33 on the next page).

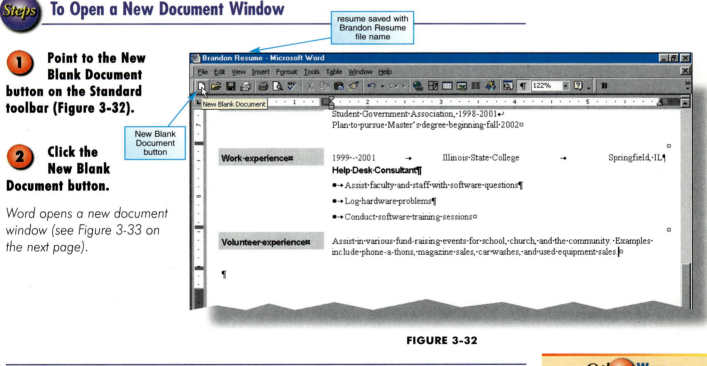

FIGURE 3-32

The Brandon Resume document still is open. The program buttons on the taskbar display the names of the open Word document windows. In Figure 3-33 on the next page, the Brandon Resume is open and Document2 is open. The Document2 button on the taskbar is recessed, indicating that it is the active document displayed in the document window.

The name in the letterhead is to be a font size of 20. Perform the following steps to change the font size.

TO CHANGE THE FONT SIZE

1 Double-click the move handle on the Formatting toolbar to display the entire toolbar. Click the Font Size box arrow on the Formatting toolbar.

2 Scroll to and then click 20 in the Font Size list.

Word changes the displayed font size to 20 (Figure 3-33).

Adding Color to Characters

The characters in the letterhead are to be green. Perform the following steps to change the color of the characters before you enter them.

Steps **To Color Characters**

1 **Point to the Font Color button arrow on the Formatting toolbar (Figure 3-33).**

The color that displays below the letter A on the Font Color button is the most recently used color for characters; thus, the color on your button may differ from this figure.

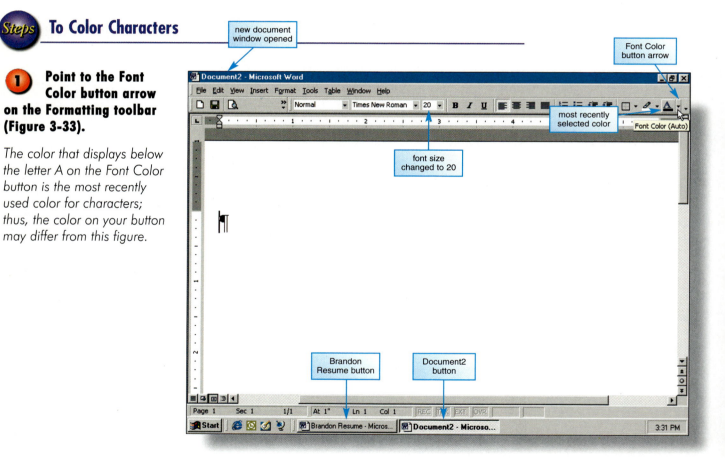

FIGURE 3-33

2 **Click the Font Color button arrow. Point to Green on the color palette.**

Word displays a list of available colors on the color palette (Figure 3-34). Automatic is the default color, which usually is black.

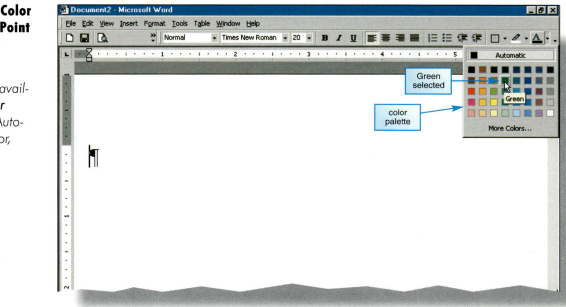

FIGURE 3-34

3 **Click Green. Type** Paulette Rose Brandon **and then press the ENTER key.**

Word displays the first line of the letterhead in green (Figure 3-35).

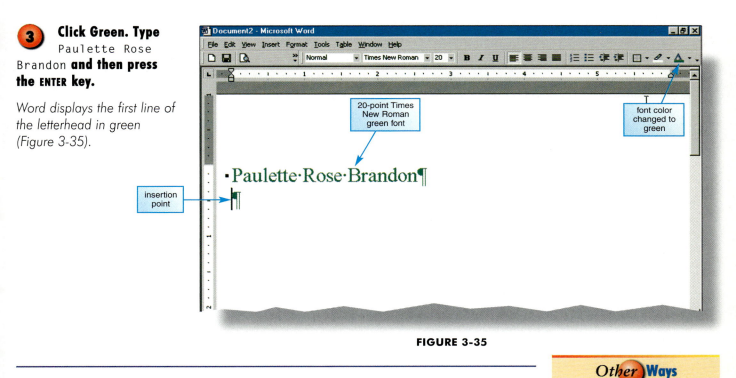

FIGURE 3-35

Notice the paragraph mark on line 2 is green. Recall that each time you press the ENTER key, formatting is carried forward to the next paragraph. If, for some reason, you wanted to change the text back to black at this point, you would click the Font Color button arrow on the Formatting toolbar and then click Automatic.

Other Ways

1. Right-click paragraph mark or selected text, click Font on shortcut menu, click Font tab, click Font Color box arrow, click desired color, click OK button

2. On Format menu click Font, click Font tab, click Font Color box arrow, click desired color, click OK button

The next step is to insert a graphic of a rose and resize it as described in the following steps.

TO ENTER AND RESIZE A GRAPHIC

1 If necessary, scroll up so that the name, Paulette Rose Brandon, is positioned at the top of the document window. With the insertion point below the name, click Insert on the menu bar, point to Picture, and then click Clip Art.

2 When the Insert ClipArt window opens, click the Search for clips text box. Type rose and then press the ENTER key.

3 Click the clip of the rose that matches the one shown in Figure 3-36. Click the Insert clip button on the Pop-up menu. Click the Close button on the Insert ClipArt window's title bar.

4 Click the graphic to select it. Drag the upper-right corner sizing handle diagonally toward the center of the graphic until the selection rectangle is positioned approximately as shown in Figure 3-36.

5 Click the paragraph mark to the right of the graphic to position the insertion point to the right of the graphic.

Word inserts the clip art and resizes it to approximately one-fourth of its original size (Figure 3-36).

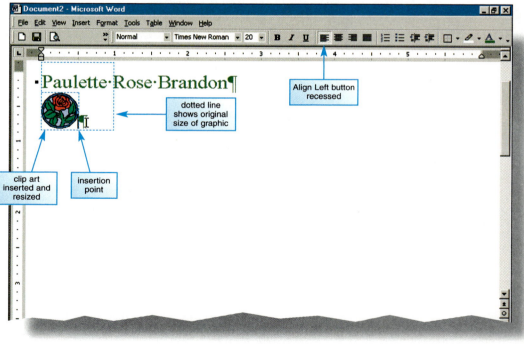

FIGURE 3-36

Setting Tab Stops Using the Tabs Dialog Box

The graphic of the rose is left-aligned (Figure 3-36). The address is to be positioned at the right margin of the same line. If you click the Align Right button, the graphic will be right-aligned. In Word, a paragraph cannot be both left-aligned and right-aligned. To place text at the right margin of a left-aligned paragraph, you set a tab stop at the right margin.

Word, by default, places **tab stops** at every .5" mark on the ruler (see Figure 3-38). These default tabs are indicated on the horizontal ruler by small **tick marks**. You also can set your own custom tab stops. When you set a **custom tab stop**, Word clears all default tab stops to the left of the custom tab stop. You also can specify how the text will align at a tab stop: left, centered, right, or decimal. Word stores tab settings in the paragraph mark at the end of each paragraph. Thus, each time you press the ENTER key, any custom tab stops are carried forward to the next paragraph.

In this letterhead, you want the tab stop to be right-aligned with the right margin; that is, at the 6" mark on the ruler. One method of setting custom tab stops is to click on the ruler at the desired location of the tab stop. You cannot, however, click at the right margin location. Thus, use the Tabs dialog box to set this custom tab stop as shown in the following steps.

More About

The Tabs Dialog Box

You can use the Tabs dialog box to change an existing tab stop's alignment or position. You also can place leader characters in the empty space occupied by the tab. Leader characters, such as a series of dots, often are used in a table of contents to precede the page number. Simply click the desired leader in the Leader area of the Tabs dialog box.

 To Set Custom Tab Stops Using the Tabs Dialog Box

1 **With the insertion point positioned between the paragraph mark and the graphic, click Format on the menu bar and then point to Tabs (Figure 3-37).**

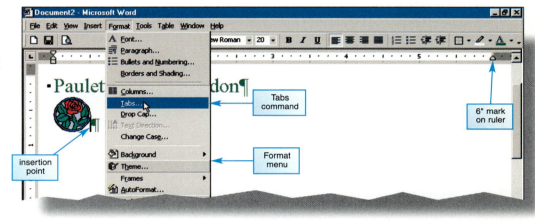

FIGURE 3-37

2 **Click Tabs. When the Tabs dialog box displays, type 6 in the Tab stop position text box and then click Right in the Alignment area. Point to the Set button.**

Word displays the Tabs dialog box (Figure 3-38).

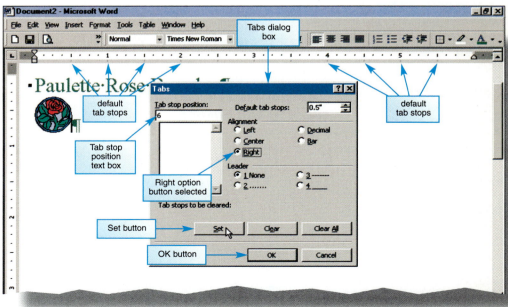

FIGURE 3-38

3 **Click the Set button and then click the OK button.**

Word places a *tab marker* at the 6" mark on the ruler and removes all default tab stops to the left of the tab marker (Figure 3-39).

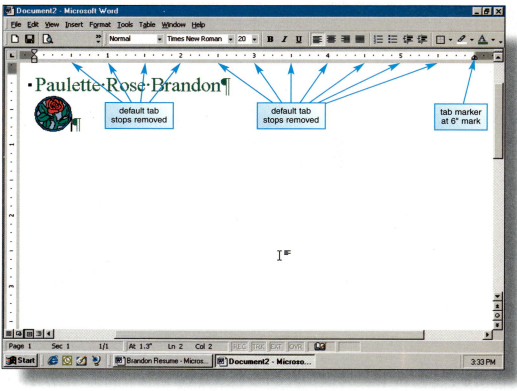

FIGURE 3-39

More *About*

Tab Stop Alignment

If you have a series of numbers that you want aligned on the decimal point, such as dollar amounts, use a decimal-aligned tab stop for the data.

More *About*

Clipboards

The Windows Clipboard holds only one item at a time. When you collect multiple items on the Office Clipboard, the last copied item also is copied to the Windows Clipboard. When you clear the Office Clipboard, the Windows Clipboard also is cleared.

When you set a custom tab stop, the tab marker on the ruler reflects the tab stop alignment. A capital letter L indicates a left-aligned tab stop; a mirror image of a capital letter L indicates a right-aligned tab stop; an upside down T indicates a centered tab stop; and an upside down T with a dot next to it indicates a decimal-aligned tab stop. The tab markers are discussed as they are presented in these projects. The tab marker on the ruler in Figure 3-39 indicates text entered at that tab stop will be right-aligned.

To move from one tab stop to another, you press the TAB key. When you press the TAB key, a formatting mark, called a **tab character**, displays in the empty space between tab stops.

Collecting and Pasting

The next step in creating the letterhead is to copy the address, telephone, fax, and e-mail information from the resume to the letterhead. When you want to copy multiple items from one location to another, you use the Office Clipboard to copy these items, or **collect** them, and then paste them in a new location. You have learned that **pasting** is the process of copying an item from the Office Clipboard into the document at the location of the insertion point. When you paste text into a document, the contents of the Office Clipboard are not erased.

To copy the address, telephone, fax, and e-mail information from the resume to the letterhead, you first switch to the resume, copy the items to the Office Clipboard, switch back to the letterhead, and then paste the information into the letterhead. The following pages illustrate this process.

Follow these steps to switch from the letterhead to the resume.

Steps To Switch from One Open Document to Another

1 Point to the **Brandon Resume - Microsoft Word button** on the taskbar (Figure 3-40).

2 Click the **Brandon Resume - Microsoft Word button**.

Word switches from the cover letter to the resume (see Figure 3-41 below).

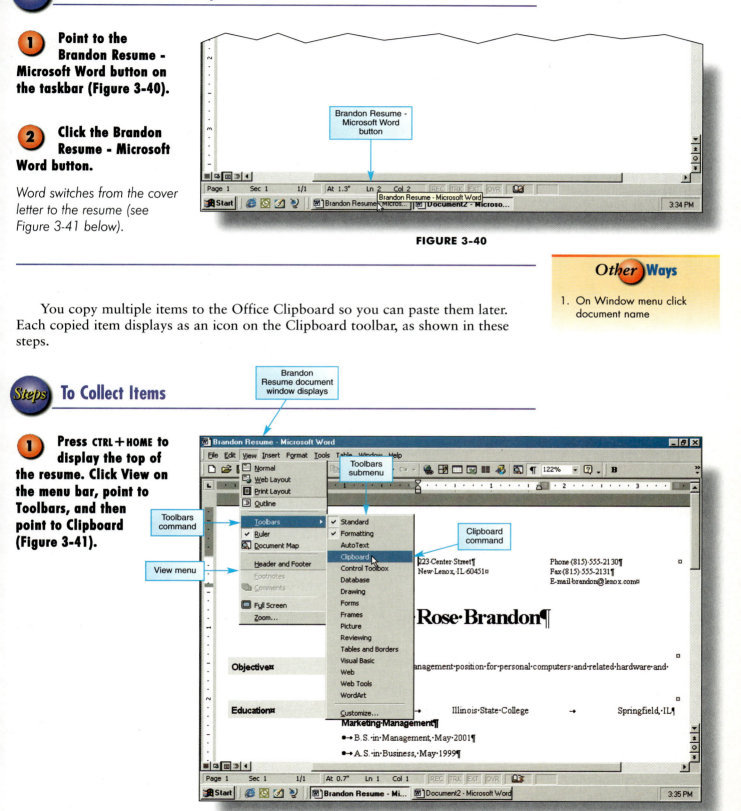

FIGURE 3-40

You copy multiple items to the Office Clipboard so you can paste them later. Each copied item displays as an icon on the Clipboard toolbar, as shown in these steps.

Other Ways

1. On Window menu click document name

Steps To Collect Items

1 Press CTRL+HOME to display the top of the resume. Click **View** on the menu bar, point to **Toolbars**, and then point to **Clipboard** (Figure 3-41).

FIGURE 3-41

2 Click Clipboard. If it is not dimmed, click the Clear Clipboard button on the Clipboard toolbar. If necessary, drag the Clipboard toolbar's title bar so the toolbar does not cover the address information in the resume. Drag through the street address, 223 Center Street (do not select the paragraph mark after the address). Point to the Copy button on the Clipboard toolbar.

The Clipboard toolbar displays in the document window (Figure 3-42). The street address is selected.

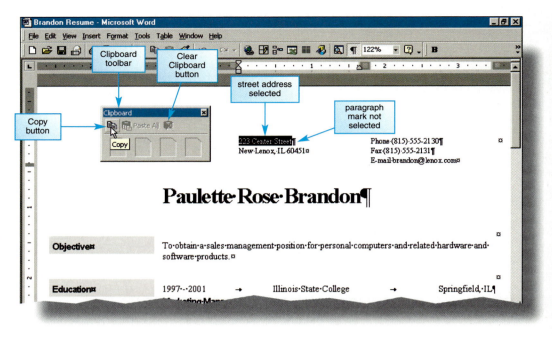

FIGURE 3-42

3 Click the Copy button on the Clipboard toolbar.

Word places a copy of the street address on the Office Clipboard and displays an icon that represents the copied item on the Clipboard toolbar.

4 Drag through the city, state, and postal code information and then click the Copy button on the Clipboard toolbar. Drag through the telephone information and then click the Copy button on the Clipboard toolbar. Drag through the fax information and then click the Copy button on the Clipboard toolbar. Drag through the e-mail information and then click the Copy button on the Clipboard toolbar (Figure 3-43).

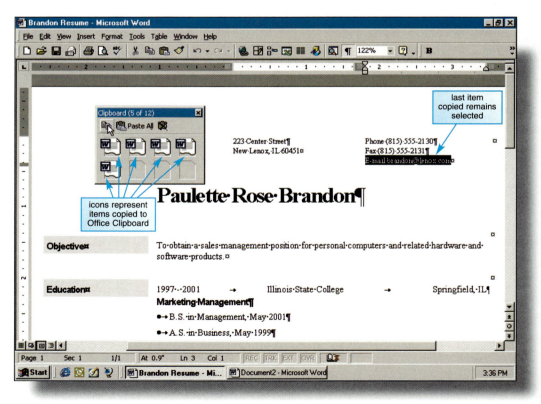

FIGURE 3-43

Other Ways

1. Click the Copy button on the Standard toolbar two consecutive times

The Office Clipboard can store up to 12 items at one time. When you copy a thirteenth item, Word deletes the first item to make room for the new item. When you point to the icons on the Clipboard toolbar, the first 50 characters of text in the item display as a ScreenTip.

Perform the following steps to paste the items from the Office Clipboard into the letterhead.

Steps To Paste from the Office Clipboard

1 Click the Document2 - Microsoft Word button on the taskbar to display the letterhead document window.

2 With the insertion point between the paragraph mark and the rose graphic, press the TAB key.

Word displays the letterhead with the Clipboard toolbar in the middle of the Word window (Figure 3-44). The insertion point is positioned at the 6" mark on the ruler, which is the location of the right-aligned tab stop. The right-pointing arrow is a tab character that displays each time you press the TAB key.

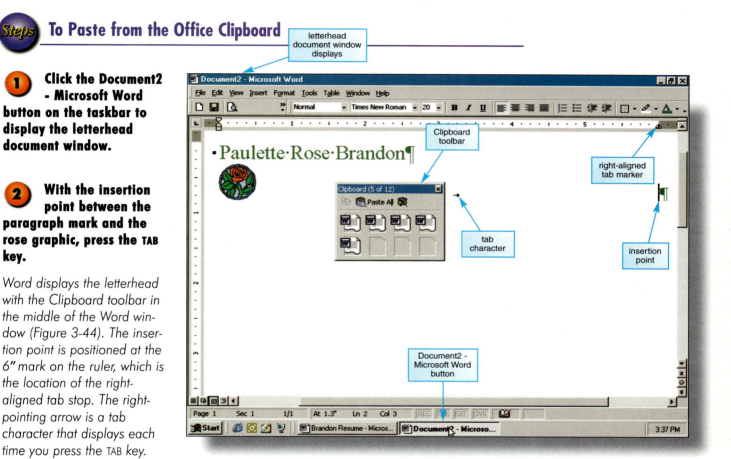

FIGURE 3-44

3 Click the first icon on the Clipboard toolbar.

Word pastes the contents of the clicked item at the location of the insertion point (Figure 3-45). Notice the text is aligned with the right margin because of the right-aligned tab stop.

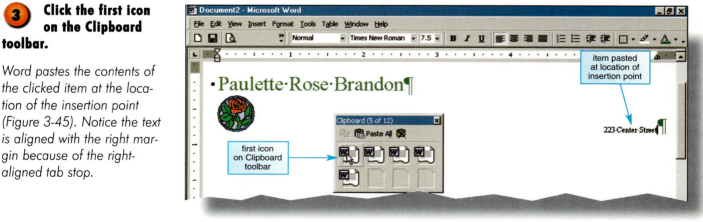

FIGURE 3-45

4 Press the COMMA key and then the SPACEBAR. Click the second icon on the Clipboard toolbar and the press the ENTER key. Press the TAB key. Click the third icon on the Clipboard toolbar and then press the SPACEBAR twice. Click the fourth icon on the Clipboard toolbar and then press the SPACEBAR twice. Click the fifth icon on the Clipboard toolbar. If the Clipboard toolbar covers the pasted text, drag the toolbar to a new location.

Word pastes all items from the Office Clipboard into the letterhead (Figure 3-46).

5 Click the Close button on the Clipboard toolbar.

Word removes the Clipboard toolbar from the window.

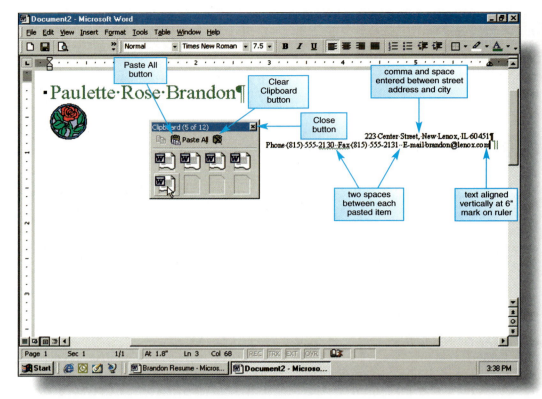

FIGURE 3-46

If you wanted to paste all items in a row without any characters or formatting in between them, you would click the Paste All button on the Clipboard toolbar. If, for some reason, you wanted to erase all items on the Office Clipboard, click the Clear Clipboard button on the Clipboard toolbar (Figure 3-46).

The next step is to change the font size to 9 and the color of the characters to green in the address, telephone, fax, and e-mail information in the letterhead. Recall that the Font Color button displays the most recently used color, which is green, in this case. When the color you want to use displays on the Font Color button, you simply click the button as shown in the following steps.

To Color More Characters the Same Color

1 **Drag through the address, telephone, fax, and e-mail information in the letterhead, including both paragraph marks at the end of the lines. Click the Font Size box arrow on the Formatting toolbar and then click 9 in the Font Size list. Point to the Font Color button on the Formatting toolbar (Figure 3-47).**

2 **Click the Font Color button. Click inside the selected text to remove the highlight.**

Word changes the color of the selected characters to green (see Figure 3-48).

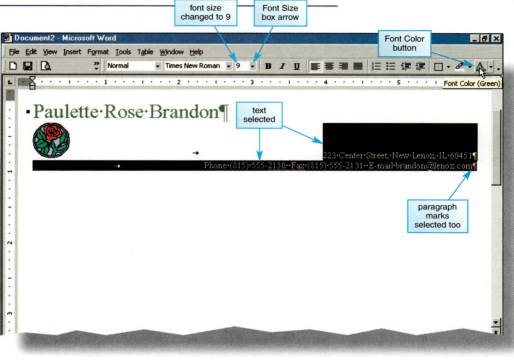

FIGURE 3-47

Inserting Symbols into a Document

To visually separate the telephone and fax information in the letterhead, you want a small round dot to display between them. Likewise, you want a small round dot to display between the fax and e-mail information. To insert symbols, such as dots, letters in the Greek alphabet, and mathematical characters, you can use the Symbol dialog box, as shown in the following steps.

To Insert a Symbol into Text

1 **Click where you want to insert the symbol, in this case, the space between the telephone and fax information. Click Insert on the menu bar and then point to Symbol (Figure 3-48).**

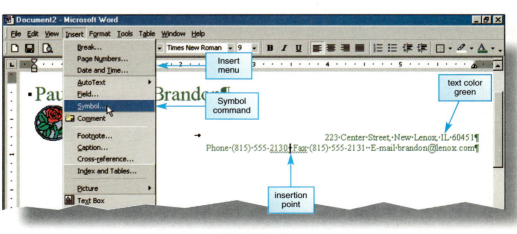

FIGURE 3-48

2 Click Symbol. If necessary, click the Symbols tab when the Symbol dialog box first displays. If necessary, click the Font box arrow, scroll through the list of fonts, and then click Symbol. If it is not selected already, click the dot symbol. Click the Insert button.

Word displays the Symbol dialog box (Figure 3-49). When you click a symbol, it becomes enlarged. The dot symbol displays in the document at the location of the insertion point.

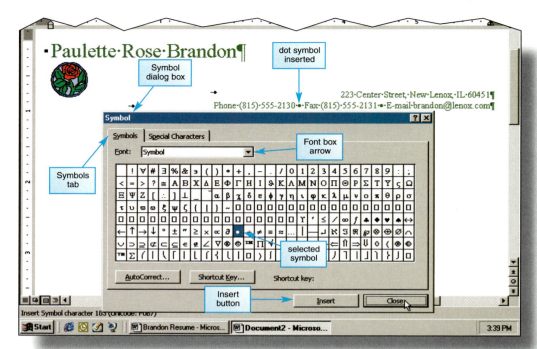

FIGURE 3-49

3 Click where you want to insert the next symbol, in this case, the space between the fax and e-mail information in the document window. With the dot symbol still selected in the dialog box, click the Insert button. Point to the Close button in the Symbol dialog box.

Word inserts the selected symbol at the location of the insertion point (Figure 3-50).

4 Click the Close button in the Symbol dialog box.

Word closes the Symbol dialog box.

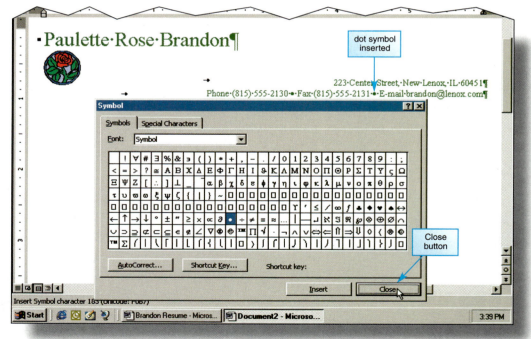

FIGURE 3-50

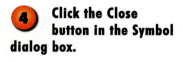

1. Type ALT+0 (zero) followed by ANSI character code for symbol using numeric keypad

You also can insert ANSI (American National Standards Institute) characters into a document by entering the ANSI code directly into the document. The **ANSI characters** are a predefined set of characters, including both characters on the keyboard and special characters, such as the dot symbol. To enter the ANSI code, make sure the NUM LOCK key is on. Press and hold the ALT key and then type the numeral zero followed by the ANSI code for the characters. You *must* use the numeric keypad when entering the ANSI code. For a complete list of ANSI codes, see your Microsoft Windows documentation.

Adding a Bottom Border to a Paragraph

To add professionalism to the letterhead, you would like to draw a horizontal line from the left margin to the right margin immediately below the telephone, fax, and e-mail information. In Word, you can draw a solid line, called a **border**, at any edge of a paragraph. That is, borders may be added above or below a paragraph, to the left or right of a paragraph, or any combination of these sides.

When adding a border to a paragraph, it is important that you have an extra paragraph mark below the paragraph you intend to border. Otherwise, each time you press the ENTER key, the border will be carried forward to each subsequent paragraph. If you forget to do this after you have added a border, simply click the Undo button on the Standard toolbar and begin again.

Perform the following steps to add a bottom border to the paragraph containing telephone, fax, and e-mail information.

Special Characters

In addition to symbols, you can insert special characters including a variety of dashes, hyphens, spaces, apostrophes, and quotation marks through the Symbol dialog box. Click Insert on the menu bar, click Symbol, click the Special Characters tab, click the desired character in the Character list, click the Insert button, and then click the Close button.

Steps To Add a Bottom Border to a Paragraph

1 Press the END key to move the insertion point to the end of the line and then press the ENTER key to create a paragraph mark below the line you want to border. Press CTRL+Z to undo the AutoFormat of the e-mail address. Press the UP ARROW key to reposition the insertion point in the paragraph that will contain the border. Point to the Border button arrow on the Formatting toolbar.

The name of this button changes depending on the last border type added. In this figure, it is the Outside Border button (Figure 3-51).

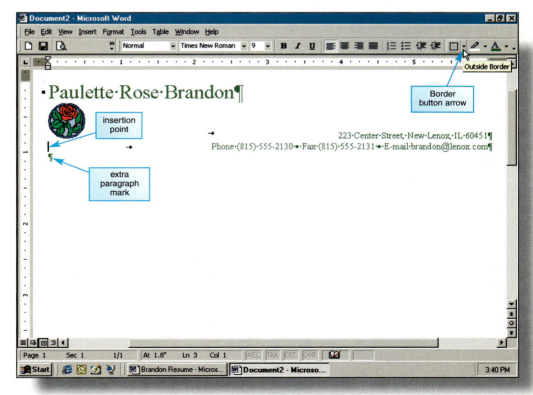

FIGURE 3-51

2 **Click the Border button arrow and then point to the Bottom Border button.**

*Word displays the border palette (Figure 3-52). Using the **border palette**, you can add a border to any edge of a paragraph.*

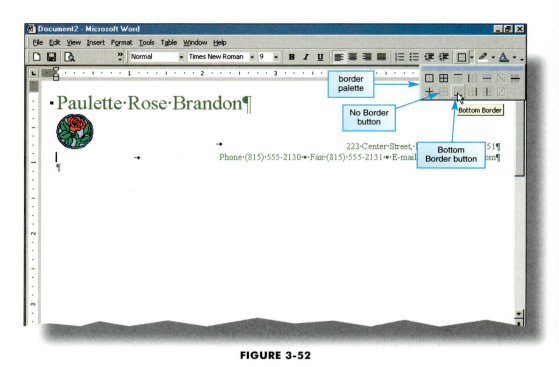

FIGURE 3-52

3 **Click the Bottom Border button.**

Word places a bottom border below the paragraph containing the insertion point (Figure 3-53). The Border button on the Formatting toolbar now displays the icon for a bottom border.

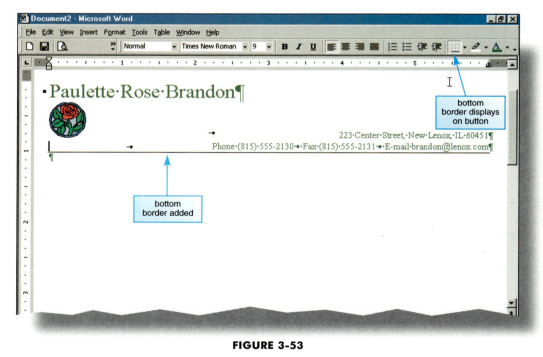

FIGURE 3-53

If, for some reason, you wanted to remove a border from a paragraph, you would position the insertion point in the paragraph, click the Border button arrow on the Formatting toolbar, and then click the No Border button (Figure 3-52) on the border palette.

Perform the following step to change the color of the text below the border back to Automatic (black).

TO CHANGE COLOR OF TEXT

1 Press the DOWN ARROW key.

2 Click the Font Color button arrow and then click Automatic.

Word changes the color of the paragraph mark below the border to black (see Figure 3-54 on page WD 3.43).

Now that you have created your letterhead, you should save it in a file.

TO SAVE THE LETTERHEAD

1 Insert your floppy disk into drive A.

2 Double-click the move handle on the Standard toolbar to display the entire toolbar. Click the Save button on the Standard toolbar.

3 Type the file name Brandon Letterhead in the File name text box.

4 If necessary, click the Save in box arrow and then click 3½ Floppy (A:).

5 Click the Save button in the Save As dialog box.

Word saves the document on a floppy disk in drive A with the file name, Brandon Letterhead.

Each time you wish to create a letter, you would open your letterhead file (Brandon Letterhead) and then immediately save it with a new file name. By doing this, your letterhead file will remain unchanged for future use.

Creating a Cover Letter

You have created a letterhead for your cover letter. The next step is to compose the cover letter. The following pages outline how to use Word to compose a cover letter with a bulleted list and a table.

Components of a Business Letter

During your professional career, you will create many business letters. A **cover letter** is one type of business letter. All business letters contain the same basic components. When preparing business letters, you should include all essential elements. **Essential business letter elements** include the date line, inside address, message, and signature block (see Figure 3-2a on the page WD 3.6). The **date line**, which consists of the month, day, and year, is positioned two to six lines below the letterhead. The **inside address**, placed three to eight lines below the date line, usually contains the addressee's courtesy title plus full name, business affiliation, and full geographical address. The **salutation**, if present, begins two lines below the last line of the inside address. The body of the letter, the **message**, begins two lines below the salutation. Within the message, paragraphs are single-spaced with double-spacing between paragraphs. Two lines below the last line of the message, the **complimentary close** displays. Capitalize only the first word in a complimentary close. Type the **signature block** at least four lines below the complimentary close, allowing room for the author to sign his or her name.

Table 3-1	Common Business Letter Styles	
LETTER STYLES	**FEATURES**	
Block	All components of the letter begin flush with the left margin.	
Modified Block	The date, complimentary close, and signature block are centered, positioned approximately ½" to the right of center, or at the right margin. All other components of the letter begin flush with the left margin.	
Modified Semi-Block	The date, complimentary close, and signature block are centered, positioned approximately ½" to the right of center, or at the right margin. The first line of each paragraph in the body of the letter is indented ½" to 1" fom the left margin. All other components of the letter begin flush with the left margin.	

You can follow many different styles when you create business letters. The cover letter in this project follows the **modified block style**. Table 3-1 outlines the differences between three common styles of business letters.

Saving the Cover Letter with a New File Name

The document in the document window currently has the name Brandon Letterhead, the name of the personal letterhead. Because you want the letterhead to remain unchanged, save the document with a new file name as described in these steps.

Templates

As an alternative to saving the letterhead as a Word document, you could save it as a template by clicking the Save as type box arrow in the Save As dialog box and then clicking Document Template. To use the template, click File on the menu bar, click New, click the General tab, and then click the template icon or name.

TO SAVE THE DOCUMENT WITH A NEW FILE NAME

1. If necessary, insert your floppy disk into drive A.

2. Click File on the menu bar and then click Save As.

3. Type the file name Brandon Cover Letter in the File name text box.

4. If necessary, click the Save in box arrow and then click 3½ Floppy (A:).

5. Click the Save button in the Save As dialog box.

Word saves the document on a floppy disk in drive A with the file name, Brandon Cover Letter (see Figure 3-54).

The font size of characters in the resume is 10. You want the size of the characters in the cover letter to be slightly larger, yet close to the size of those in the resume. Perform the following steps to increase the font size of characters in the cover letter to 11.

TO INCREASE THE FONT SIZE

1. If necessary, click the paragraph mark below the border to position the insertion point below the border.

2. Double-click the move handle on the Formatting toolbar to display the entire toolbar. Click the Font Size box arrow on the Formatting toolbar and then click 11 in the Font Size list.

The font size of characters in the cover letter is 11 (see Figure 3-54).

Bar Tabs

To insert a vertical line at a tab stop, set a bar tab. To do this, click the button at the left edge of the horizontal ruler until its icon changes to a Bar Tab icon (a vertical bar) and then click the location on the ruler. Or, click Bar in the Alignment area of the Tabs dialog box.

Setting Tab Stops Using the Ruler

The first required element of the cover letter is the date line, which is positioned three lines below the letterhead. The month, day, and year in the date line begins 3.5 inches from the left margin, which is one-half inch to the right of center. Thus, you should set a custom tab stop at the 3.5" mark on the ruler.

Earlier you used the Tabs dialog box to set a tab stop because you could not use the ruler to set a tab stop at the right margin. In the following steps, you set a left-aligned tab stop using the ruler.

To Set Custom Tab Stops Using the Ruler

1 **Press the ENTER key twice. If necessary, click the button at the left edge of the horizontal ruler until it displays the left tab icon. Point to the 3.5" mark on the ruler.**

Each time you click the button at the left of the horizontal ruler, its icon changes (Figure 3-54). The left tab icon looks like a capital letter L.

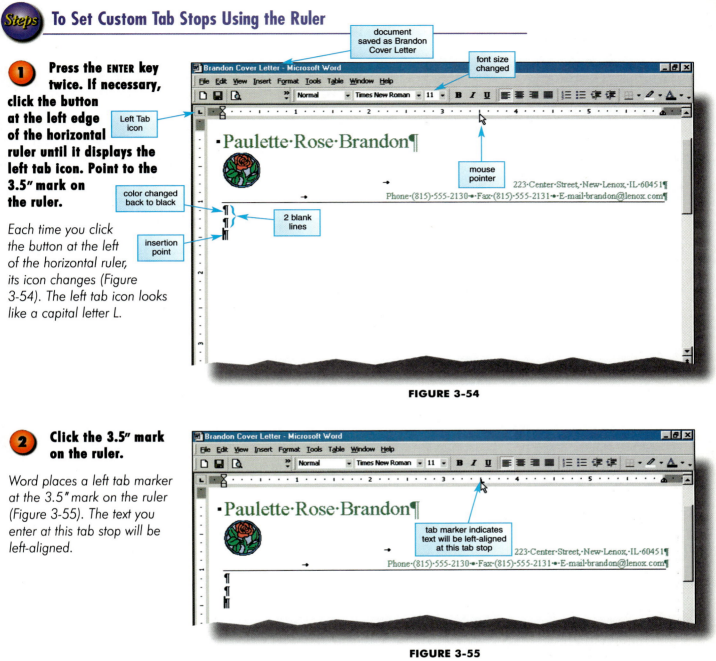

FIGURE 3-54

2 **Click the 3.5" mark on the ruler.**

Word places a left tab marker at the 3.5" mark on the ruler (Figure 3-55). The text you enter at this tab stop will be left-aligned.

FIGURE 3-55

Other Ways

1. On Format menu click Tabs, enter tab stop position, click appropriate alignment, click OK button

If, for some reason, you wanted to move a custom tab stop, you would drag the tab marker to the desired location on the ruler. If you wanted to change the alignment of a custom tab stop, you could remove the existing tab stop and then insert a new one as described in the steps above. To remove a custom tab stop, point to the tab marker on the ruler and then drag the tab marker down and out of the ruler. You also could use the Tabs dialog box to change an existing tab stop's alignment or position. You have learned that you click Format on the menu bar and then click Tabs to display the Tabs dialog box.

The next step is to enter the date, inside address, and salutation in the cover letter as described in the following steps.

TO ENTER THE DATE, INSIDE ADDRESS, AND SALUTATION

1 Press the TAB key. Type June 4, 2001 and press the ENTER key three times.

2 Type Mr. Carl Reed and then press the ENTER key. Type Personnel Director and then press the ENTER key. Type Deluxe Computers and then press the ENTER key. Type 100 Michigan Avenue and then press the ENTER key. Type Chicago, IL 60601 and then press the ENTER key twice.

3 Type Dear Mr. Reed and then press the COLON key (:).

The date, inside address, and salutation are entered (Figure 3-56).

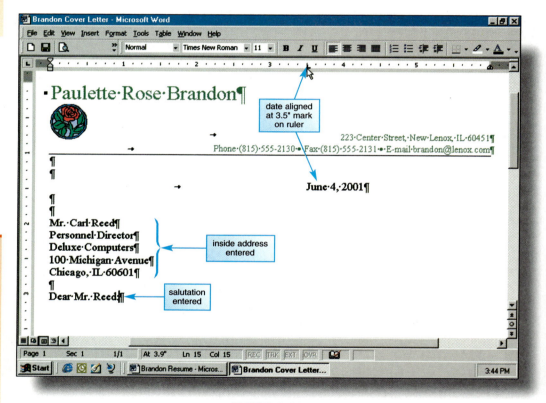

FIGURE 3-56

Creating an AutoText Entry

If you use the same text frequently, you can store the text in an **AutoText entry** and then use the stored entry throughout this document, as well as future documents. That is, you type the entry only once, and for all future occurrences of the text, you access the stored entry as you need it. In this way, you avoid entering the text inconsistently or incorrectly in different locations throughout the same document. Follow these steps to create an AutoText entry for the prospective employer's company name.

Steps **To Create an AutoText Entry**

1 Drag through the text to be stored, in this case, Deluxe Computers. Be sure not to select the paragraph mark at the end of the text. Click Insert on the menu bar and then point to AutoText. Point to New on the AutoText submenu.

Word highlights the company name, Deluxe Computers, in the inside address (Figure 3-57). Notice the paragraph mark is not part of the selection.

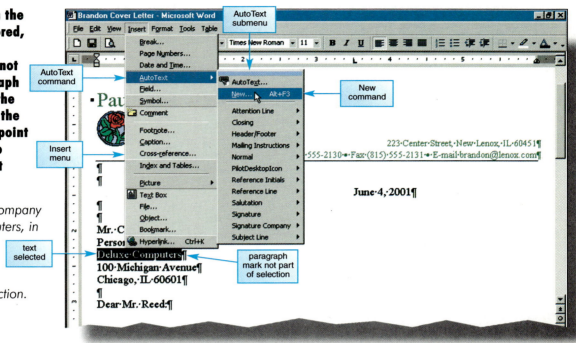

FIGURE 3-57

2 Click New on the AutoText submenu. When the Create AutoText dialog box displays, type dc and then point to the OK button.

Word displays the Create AutoText dialog box (Figure 3-58). In this dialog box, Word proposes a name for the AutoText entry, which usually is the first word(s) of the selection. You change it to a shorter name, dc.

3 Click the OK button. If Word displays a dialog box, click the Yes button.

Word stores the AutoText entry and closes the AutoText dialog box.

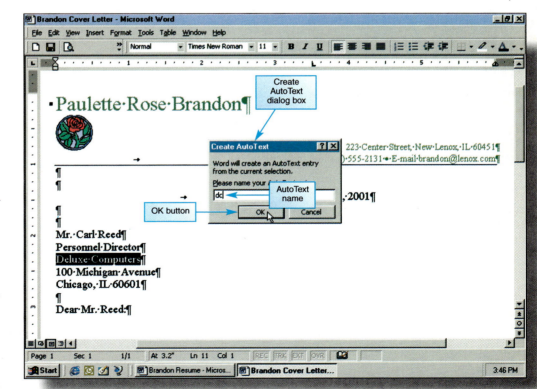

FIGURE 3-58

The name, dc, has been stored as an AutoText entry. Later in the project, you will use the AutoText entry, dc, instead of typing the company name, Deluxe Computers.

Entering a Nonbreaking Space

Some compound words, such as proper names, dates, units of time and measure, abbreviations, and geographic destinations, should not be divided at the end of a line. These words either should fit as a unit at the end of a line or be wrapped together to the next line.

Word provides two special characters to assist with this task: nonbreaking space and nonbreaking hyphen. You press CTRL+SHIFT+SPACEBAR to enter a **nonbreaking space**, which is a special space character that prevents two words from splitting if the first word falls at the end of a line. Likewise, you press CTRL+SHIFT+HYPHEN to enter a **nonbreaking hyphen**, which is a special type of hyphen that prevents two words separated by a hyphen from splitting at the end of a line. When you enter these characters into a document, a special formatting mark displays on the screen.

Perform the following steps to enter a nonbreaking space between the words in the newspaper name.

Steps ## To Insert a Nonbreaking Space

1 **Scroll the salutation to the top of the document window. Click after the colon in the salutation and then press the ENTER key twice. If the Office Assistant displays, click its Cancel button. Type** I am responding to your computer sales management trainee position advertised in the **and then press the SPACEBAR. Press CTRL+I to turn on italics. Type** Chicago **and then press CTRL + SHIFT + SPACEBAR.**

Word enters a nonbreaking space after the word, Chicago (Figure 3-59).

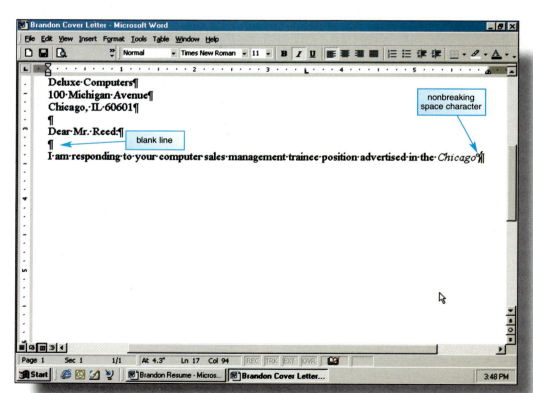

FIGURE 3-59

2 **Type** Times **and then press** CTRL+I **to turn off italics. Press the** PERIOD **key.**

Word wraps the two words in the newspaper title, Chicago Times, to the next line (Figure 3-60).

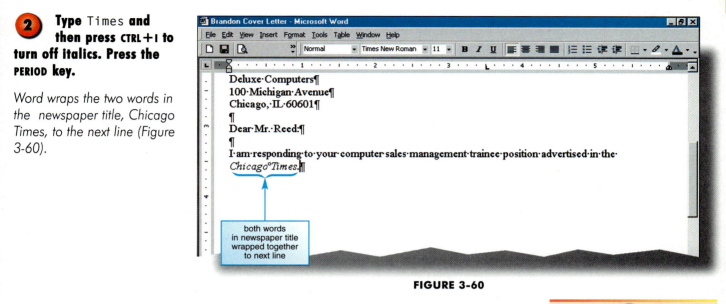

FIGURE 3-60

Inserting an AutoText Entry

At the end of the next sentence in the body of the cover letter, you want to put the company name, Deluxe Computers. Recall that earlier in this project, you stored an AutoText entry name of dc for Deluxe Computers. Thus, you will type the AutoText entry's name and then instruct Word to replace the AutoText entry's name with the stored entry of Deluxe Computers. Perform the following steps to insert an AutoText entry.

Other **Ways**

1. On Insert menu click Symbol, click Special Characters tab, click Nonbreaking Space in Character list, click Insert button, click Close button

To Insert an AutoText Entry

1 **Press the** SPACEBAR. **Type** As indicated in the enclosed resume, I have the credentials that you are seeking and believe I can be a valuable asset to dc **as shown in Figure 3-61.**

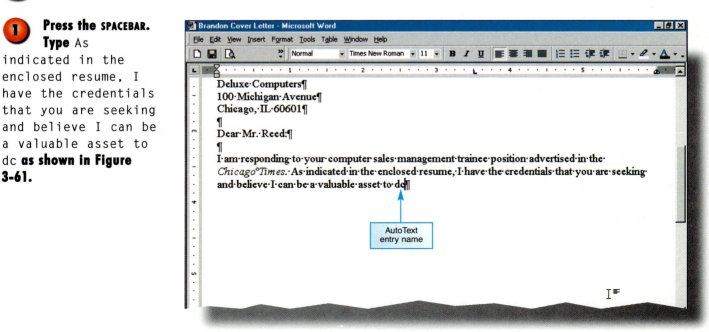

FIGURE 3-61

2 **Press F3. Press the PERIOD key.**

Word replaces the characters, dc, with the stored AutoText entry, Deluxe Computers (Figure 3-62).

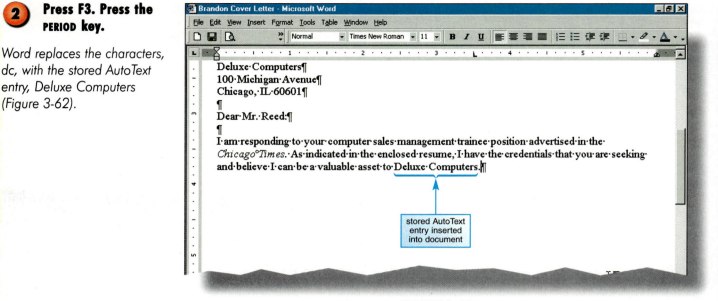

FIGURE 3-62

Pressing F3 instructs Word to replace the AutoText entry name with the stored AutoText entry. In Project 2, you learned how to use the AutoCorrect feature, which enables you to insert and also create AutoCorrect entries (just as you did for this AutoText entry). The difference between an AutoCorrect entry and an AutoText entry is that the AutoCorrect feature makes corrections for you automatically as soon as you press the SPACEBAR or a punctuation mark key, whereas you must press F3 or click the AutoText command to instruct Word to make an AutoText correction.

If you watch the screen as you type, you may discover that AutoComplete tips display on the screen. As you type, Word searches the list of AutoText entry names and if one matches your typing, Word displays its complete name above your typing as an **AutoComplete tip**. In addition to AutoText entries, Word proposes AutoComplete tips for the current date, a day of the week, a month, and so on. If your screen does not display AutoComplete tips, click Tools on the menu bar, click AutoCorrect, click the AutoText tab, click Show AutoComplete tip for AutoText and dates to select it, and then click the OK button. To view the complete list of entries, click Tools on the menu bar, click AutoCorrect, click the AutoText tab, and then scroll through the list of entries. To ignore an AutoComplete tip proposed by Word, simply continue typing to remove the AutoComplete tip from the screen.

Perform the following steps to enter the next paragraph into the cover letter.

TO ENTER A PARAGRAPH

1 Press the ENTER key twice.

2 Type I am a recent graduate of Illinois State College with degrees in both marketing management and computer technology. My courses in each major included the following and then press the COLON key.

3 Press the ENTER key twice.

The paragraph is entered (Figure 3-63 on page WD 3.50).

AutoFormat As You Type

As you type text into a document, Word automatically formats it for you. Table 3-2 outlines commonly used AutoFormat As You Type options and their results.

Table 3-2 Commonly Used AutoFormat As You Type Options		
TYPED TEXT	**AUTOFORMAT FEATURE**	**EXAMPLE**
Quotation marks or apostrophes	Changes straight quotation marks or apostrophes to curly ones	"the" becomes "the"
Text, a space, one hyphen, one or no spaces, text, space	Changes the hyphen to an en dash	ages 20 - 45 becomes ages 20 — 45
Text, two hyphens, text, space	Changes the two hyphens to em dash	Two types--yellow and red becomes Two types—yellow and red
Web address followed by space or ENTER key	Formats address as a hyperlink	www.scsite.com becomes www.scsite.com
Three hyphens, underscores, equal signs, asterisks, tildes, or number signs and then ENTER key	Places a border above a paragraph	--- Hyphens converted to line becomes _____ Hyphens converted to line
Number followed by a period, hyphen, right parenthesis, or greater than sign and then a space or tab followed by text	Creates a numbered list when you press the ENTER key	1. Word 2. Excel becomes 1. Word 2. Excel
Asterisk, hyphen, greater than sign and then a space or tab followed by text	Creates a bulleted list when you press the ENTER key	* Standard toolbar * Formatting toolbar becomes • Standard toolbar • Formatting toolbar
Fraction and then a space or hyphen	Converts the entry to a fraction-like notation	1/2 becomes $\frac{1}{2}$
Ordinal and then a space or hyphen	Makes the original a superscript	3rd becomes 3rd

You can type a list and then place the bullets on the paragraphs at a later time, or you can use Word's AutoFormat As You Type feature to bullet the paragraphs as you type them. Because your fingers are on the keyboard already, perform the steps on the next page to add bullets automatically to a list as you type.

More About

AutoFormat

For an AutoFormat option to work as expected, it must be turned on. To check if an AutoFormat option is enabled, click Tools on the menu bar, click AutoCorrect, click the AutoFormat As You Type tab, select the appropriate check boxes, and then click the OK button. For example, Format beginning of list item like the one before it and Automatic bulleted lists should both contain check marks for automatic bullets.

Steps: To Bullet a List as You Type

1 **Press the ASTERISK key (*) and then press the SPACEBAR.** **Type** Marketing Management: Principles of Marketing, Promotions, Retailing, Sales, Advertising, Personal Selling, International Marketing, Consumer Behavior **as the first list item (Figure 3-63).**

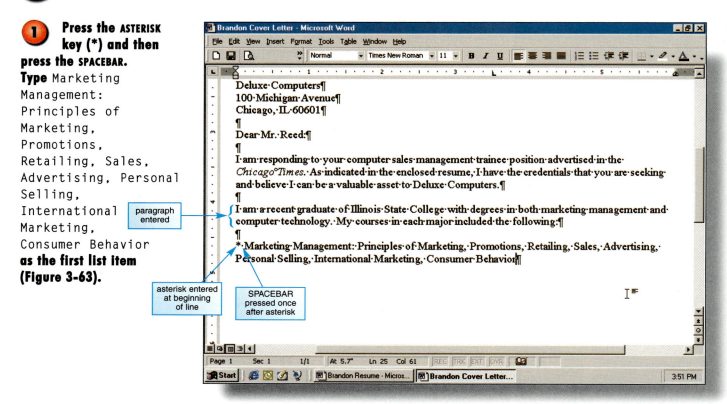

FIGURE 3-63

2 **Press the ENTER key.**

Word converts the asterisk to a bullet character, places another bullet on the second list item, and indents the two bulleted paragraphs.

3 **Type** Computer Technology: Computer Concepts, PC Technology, Structured Programming, Object-Oriented Programming, Database Techniques, Web Design **and then press the ENTER key.**

Word places a bullet on the next line (Figure 3-64).

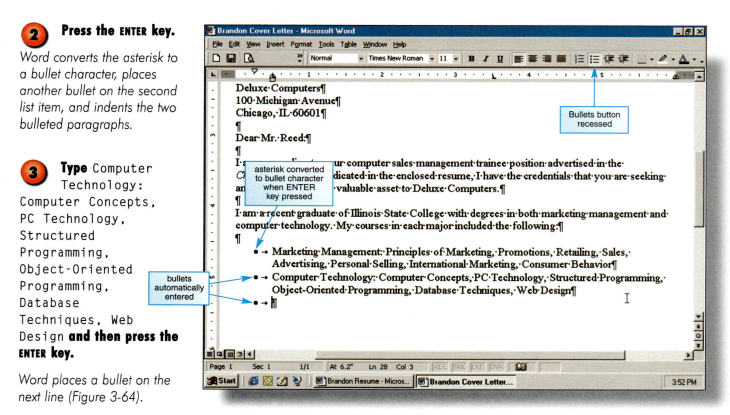

FIGURE 3-64

4 **Press the ENTER key.**

Word removes the lone bullet because you pressed the ENTER key twice (Figure 3-65). The Bullets button no longer is recessed.

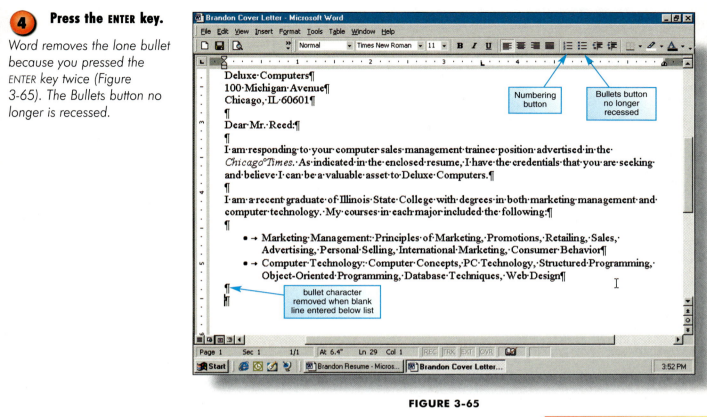

FIGURE 3-65

When the insertion point is in a bulleted list, the Bullets button on the Formatting toolbar is recessed. To instruct Word to stop bulleting paragraphs, you press the ENTER key twice or click the Bullets button.

If you know before you type a list that it is to be numbered, you can add numbers as you type, just as you can add bullets as you type. To number a list, type the number one followed by a period and then a space (1.) at the beginning of the first item and then type your text. When you press the ENTER key, Word places the number two (2.) at the beginning of the next line automatically. As with bullets, press the ENTER key twice at the end of the list or click the Numbering button on the Formatting toolbar to stop numbering (Figure 3-66).

Perform the following steps to enter the next paragraph into the cover letter.

TO ENTER A PARAGRAPH

1 Scroll up and then type As shown in the following table, I earned exceptional grades in both marketing management and computer technology courses.

2 Press the ENTER key twice.

The paragraph is entered (see Figure 3-66 on the next page).

More *About* **2000**

Outline Numbered Lists

To create an outline numbered list, click Format on the menu bar, click Bullets and Numbering, click the Outline Numbered tab, and then click a style that does not contain the word 'Heading.' To promote or demote a list item to the next or previous levels, click the Increase Indent and Decrease Indent buttons on the Formatting toolbar.

More About

Word Tables

Although you can use the TAB key to create a table, many Word users prefer to use its table feature. With a Word table, you can arrange numbers in columns. For emphasis, tables can be shaded and have borders. Word tables can be sorted, and you can have Word add the contents of an entire row or column.

Creating a Table with the Insert Table Button

The next step in composing the cover letter is to place a table listing your GPAs (Figure 3-2a on page WD 3.6). You create this table using Word's table feature. As discussed earlier in this project, a Word table is a collection of rows and columns, and the intersection of a row and a column is called a cell.

Within a Word table, you easily can rearrange rows and columns, change column widths, sort rows and columns, and sum the contents of rows and columns. You can use the Table AutoFormat dialog box to make the table display in a professional manner. You also can chart table data.

The first step in creating a table is to insert an empty table into the document. When inserting a table, you must specify the total number of rows and columns required, which is called the **dimension** of the table. The table in this project has two columns. Because you often do not know the total number of rows in a table, many Word users create one row initially and then add rows as they need them. The first number in a dimension is the number of rows, and the second is the number of columns. Perform the following steps to insert a 1 x 2 table; that is, a table with one row and two columns.

Steps To Insert an Empty Table

1 Double-click the move handle on the Standard toolbar. Click the Insert Table button on the Standard toolbar. Point to the cell in the first row and second column of the grid to highlight the first two cells in the first row of the grid.

Word displays a grid to define the dimension of the desired table (Figure 3-66). Word will insert the table immediately above the insertion point.

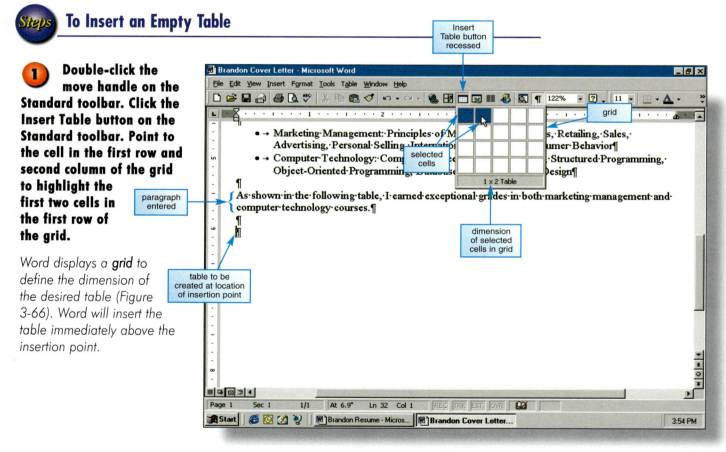

FIGURE 3-66

② Click the cell in the first row and second column of the grid.

Word inserts an empty 1 × 2 table into the document (Figure 3-67). The insertion point is in the first cell (row 1 and column 1) of the table.

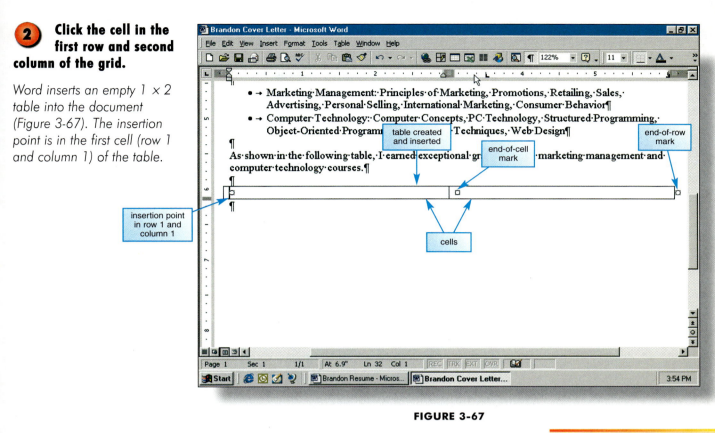

FIGURE 3-67

As you learned earlier in this project, each row of a table has an end-of-row mark, which you use to add columns to the right of a table. Each cell has an end-of-cell mark, which you use to select a cell. The end-of-cell mark currently is left-aligned; thus it is positioned at the left edge of each cell. You can use any of the paragraph formatting buttons on the Formatting toolbar to change the alignment of the text within the cells. For example, if you click the Align Right button on the Formatting toolbar, the end-of-cell mark and any entered text will display at the right edge of the cell.

For simple tables, such as the one just created, Word users click the Insert Table button to create a table. For more complex tables, such as one with a varying number of columns per row, Word has a Draw Table feature that allows you to use a pencil pointer to draw a table on the screen. Project 4 discusses the Draw Table feature.

Entering Data into a Word Table

The next step is to enter data into the empty table. Cells are filled with data. The data you enter within a cell wordwraps just as text does between the margins of a document. To place data into a cell, you click the cell and then type. To advance rightward from one cell to the next, press the TAB key. When you are at the rightmost cell in a row, also press the TAB key to move to the first cell in the next row; do not press the ENTER key. The ENTER key is used to begin a new paragraph within a cell.

To add new rows to a table, press the TAB key with the insertion point positioned in the bottom right corner cell of the table. Perform the steps on the next page to enter data into the table.

1. On Table menu point to Insert, click Table, enter number of columns, enter number of rows, click OK button

Draw Table

To use Draw Table, click the Tables and Borders button on the Standard toolbar to change the mouse pointer to a pencil. Use the pencil to draw from one corner to the opposite diagonal corner to define the perimeter of the table. Then, draw the column and row lines inside the perimeter. To remove a line, use the Eraser button on the Tables and Borders toolbar.

Steps **To Enter Data into a Table**

1 **With the insertion point in the left cell of the table, type** GPA for Marketing Courses **and then press the TAB key. Type** 3.8/4.0 **and then press the TAB key.**

Word enters the table data into the first row of the table and adds a second row to the table (Figure 3-68). The insertion point is positioned in the first cell of the second row.

Brandon Cover Letter - Microsoft Word

File Edit View Insert Format Tools Table Window Help

• → Marketing·Management:·Principles·of·Marketing,·Promotions,·Retailing,·Sales,· Advertising,·Personal·Selling,·International·Marketing,·Consumer·Behavior¶
• → Computer·Technology:·Computer·Concepts,·PC·Technology,·Structured·Programming,· Object-Oriented·Programming,·Da [row 1 data entered] niques,·Web·Design¶

As·shown·in·the·following·table,·I·earned·exceptional·grades·in·both·marketing·management·and· computer·technology·courses.¶

| GPA·for·Marketing·Courses□ | 3.8/4.0□ |
| □ | □ |

[blank row 2 added]

[insertion point]

FIGURE 3-68

2 **Type** GPA for Computer Courses **and then press the TAB key. Type** 3.9/4.0 **and then press the TAB key. Type** Overall GPA **and then press the TAB key. Type** 3.8/4.0 **as shown in Figure 3-69.**

Brandon Cover Letter - Microsoft Word

File Edit View Insert Format Tools Table Window Help

• → Marketing·Management:·Principles·of·Marketing,·Promotions,·Retailing,·Sales,· Advertising,·Personal·Selling,·International·Marketing,·Consumer·Behavior¶
• → Computer·Technology:·Computer·Concepts,·PC·Technology,·Structured·Programming,· Object-Oriented·Programming,·Database·Techniques,·Web·Design¶

As·shown·in·the·following·table,·I·earned·exceptional·grades·in·both·marketing·management·and· computer·technology·courses.¶

[table data entered]

GPA·for·Marketing·Courses□	3.8/4.0□
GPA·for·Computer·Courses□	3.9/4.0□
Overall·GPA□	3.8/4.0□

FIGURE 3-69

You modify the contents of cells just as you modify text in a document. To delete the contents of a cell, select the cell contents by pointing to the left edge of a cell, clicking when the mouse pointer changes direction, and then pressing the DELETE key. To modify text in a cell, click in the cell and then correct the entry. You can double-click the OVR indicator on the status bar to toggle between insert and overtype modes. You also may drag and drop or cut and paste the contents of cells.

Formatting a Table

Although you can format each row, column, and cell of a table individually, Word provides a Table AutoFormat feature that contains predefined formats for tables. Perform the following steps to format the entire table using Table AutoFormat.

More About

Table Commands

If a Table command is dimmed on the Table menu, it is likely that the insertion point is not in the table.

Steps **To AutoFormat a Table**

1 With the insertion point in the table, click Table on the menu bar and then point to Table AutoFormat (Figure 3-70).

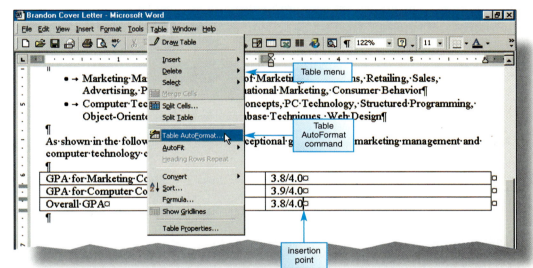

FIGURE 3-70

2 Click Table AutoFormat. When the Table AutoFormat dialog box displays, scroll through the Formats list and then click Contemporary. If necessary, click Heading rows in the Apply special formats to area to remove the check mark. Be sure the remaining check boxes match Figure 3-71.

Word displays the Table AutoFormat dialog box (Figure 3-71). This table does not have a heading row.

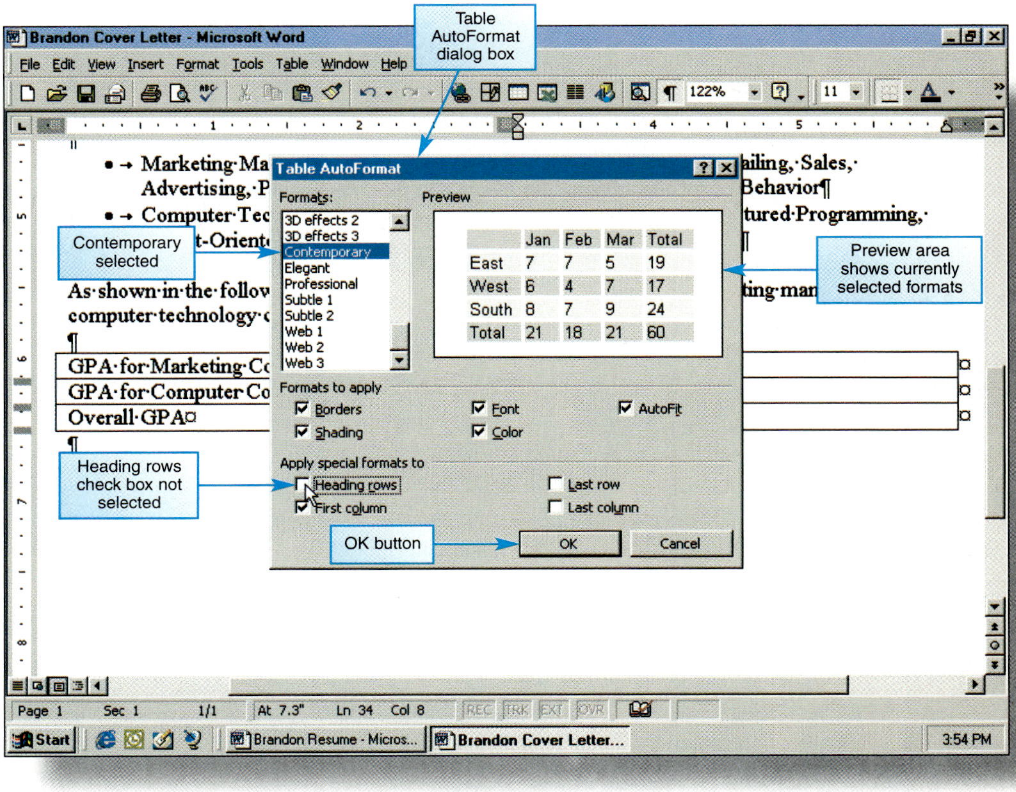

FIGURE 3-71

3 **Click the OK button.**

Word formats the table according to the Contemporary format (Figure 3-72).

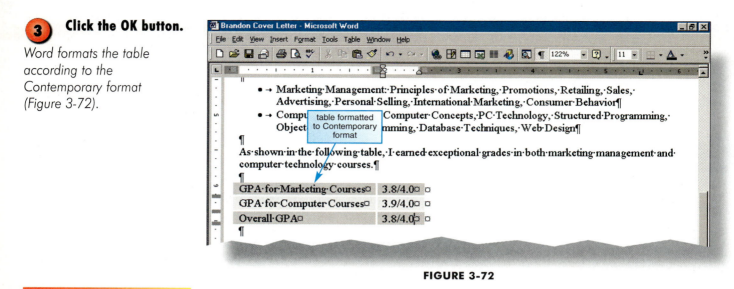

FIGURE 3-72

Because AutoFit was selected in the Table AutoFormat dialog box (see Figure 3-71 on the previous page), Word automatically adjusted the widths of the columns based on the amount of text in the table. In this case, Word reduced the size of the column widths.

Changing the Table Alignment

When you first create a table, it is left-aligned; that is, flush with the left margin. This table should be centered. To center a table, you first must select the entire table and then center it using the Center button on the Formatting toolbar, as shown in the following steps.

Steps

To Select a Table

1 **With the insertion point in the table, click Table on the menu bar, point to Select, and then point to Table (Figure 3-73).**

FIGURE 3-73

Center button recessed

2 **Click Table.**

Word highlights the contents of the entire table.

3 **Double-click the move handle on the Formatting toolbar. Click the Center button on the Formatting toolbar.**

Word centers the table between the left and right margins (Figure 3-74).

Brandon Cover Letter - Microsoft Word

File Edit View Insert Format Tools Table Window Help

Normal | Times New Roman | 11 | **B** *I* U

- → Marketing·Management:·Principles·of·Marketing,·Promotions,·Retailing,·Sales,· Advertising,·Personal·Selling,·International·Marketing,·Consumer·Behavior¶
- → Computer·Technology:·Computer·Concepts,·PC·Technology,·Structured·Programming,· Object-Oriented·Programming, ~~niques,·Web·Design¶~~

table selected and centered

¶

As·shown·in·the·following·table,·I·earned·exceptional·grades·in·both·marketing·management·and· computer·technology·courses.¶

¶

GPA·for·Marketing·Courses□	3.8/4.0□
GPA·for·Computer·Courses□	3.9/4.0□
Overall·GPA□	3.8/4.0□

FIGURE 3-74

Perform the following steps to enter the remainder of the cover letter.

TO ENTER THE REMAINDER OF THE COVER LETTER

1 Click the paragraph mark below the table. Press the ENTER key. Type the paragraph shown in Figure 3-75, making certain you use the AutoText entry, dc, to insert the company name.

2 Press the ENTER key twice. Press the TAB key. Type Sincerely and then press the COMMA key.

3 Press the ENTER key four times. Press the TAB key. Type Paulette Rose Brandon and then press the ENTER key twice.

4 Type Enclosure as the final text.

The cover letter text is complete (Figure 3-75).

GPA·for·Marketing·Courses□	3.8/4.0□	□
GPA·for·Computer·Courses□	3.9/4.0□	□
Overall·GPA□	3.8/4.0□	□

paragraph mark below table

¶

In·addition·to·my·extensive·coursework,·I·obtained·valuable·experience·in·my·part-time·work·at· the·college,·as·well·as·from·a·variety·of·volunteer·efforts.·I·look·forward·to·hearing·from·you·to· further·present·my·qualifications·and·learn·more·about·career·opportunities·at·Deluxe·Computers.¶

¶

→ **Sincerely,**¶

¶
¶
¶

→ **Paulette·Rose·Brandon**¶

¶

Enclosure¶

completed cover letter

Page 1 Sec 1 1/1 At 9.4" Ln 46 Col 10 REC TRK EXT OVR

Start Brandon Resume - Micros... **Brandon Cover Letter...** 3:57 PM

FIGURE 3-75

Other Ways

1. With insertion point in table, press ALT+5 (using the 5 on the numeric keypad with NUM LOCK off)

More About

Selecting Tables

If you use the keyboard shortcut to select a table, ALT+NUM5, you must be careful to press the 5 on the numeric keypad. You cannot use the 5 on the keyboard area. Also, be sure that NUM LOCK is off; otherwise, the keyboard shortcut will not work.

More About

Proofreading

You should be absolutely certain that your resume and accompanying cover letter are error free. Check spelling and grammar using Word. Proofread for grammatical errors. Set the resume and cover letter aside for a couple of days, and then proofread them again. Ask others, such as a friend or teacher, to proofread them also.

Saving Again and Printing the Cover Letter

The cover letter for the resume now is complete. You should save the cover letter again and then print it as described in the following steps.

TO SAVE A DOCUMENT AGAIN

1. Double-click the move handle on the Standard toolbar. Click the Save button on the Standard toolbar.

Word saves the cover letter with the same file name, Brandon Cover Letter.

TO PRINT A DOCUMENT

1. Click the Print button on the Standard toolbar.

The completed cover letter prints as shown in Figure 3-2a on page WD 3.6.

Preparing and Printing an Envelope Address

The final step in this project is to prepare and print an envelope address, as shown in the following steps.

More About 2000

Printing

Use a laser printer to print the resume and cover letter on standard letter-size white or ivory paper. Be sure to print a copy for yourself. And read it - especially before the interview. Most likely, the interviewer will have copies in hand, ready to ask you questions about the contents of both the resume and cover letter.

Steps: To Prepare and Print an Envelope Address

1. **Scroll through the cover letter to display the inside address in the document window. Drag through the inside address to select it. Click Tools on the menu bar and then point to Envelopes and Labels (Figure 3-76).**

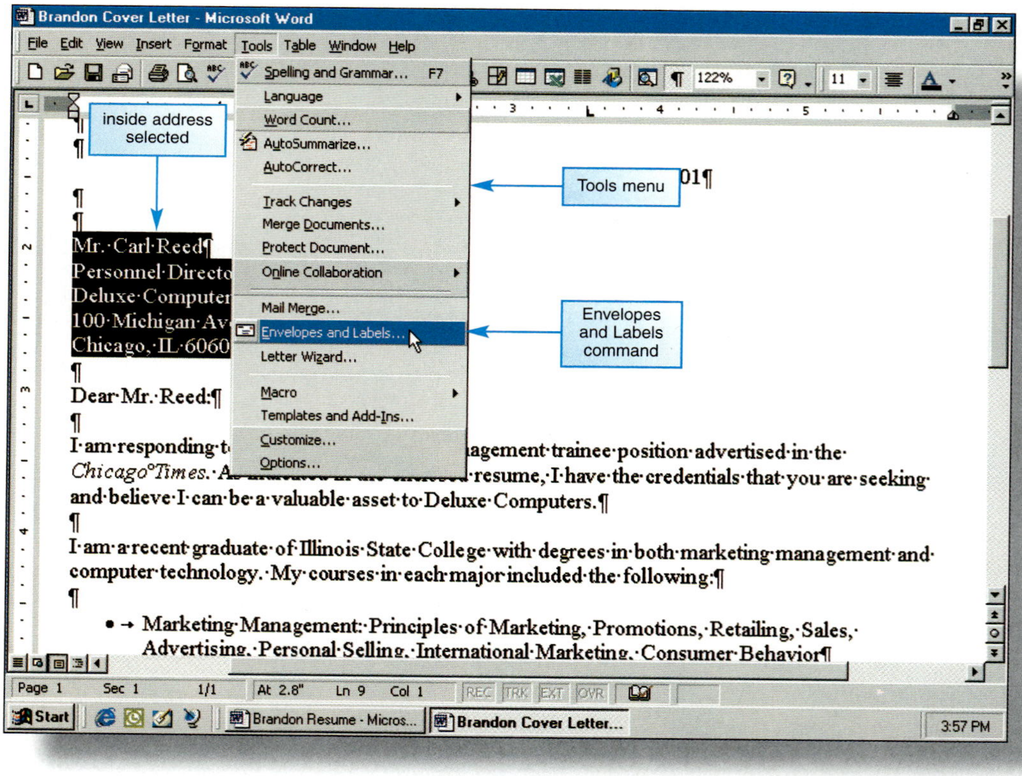

FIGURE 3-76

2 **Click Envelopes and Labels. When the Envelopes and Labels dialog box displays, if necessary, click the Envelopes tab. Click the Return address text box. Type** Paulette R. Brandon **and then press the ENTER key. Type** 223 Center Street **and then press the ENTER key. Type** New Lenox, IL 60451 **and then point to the Print button in the Envelopes and Labels dialog box.**

Word displays the Envelopes and Labels dialog box (Figure 3-77). The selected inside address displays in the Delivery address text box.

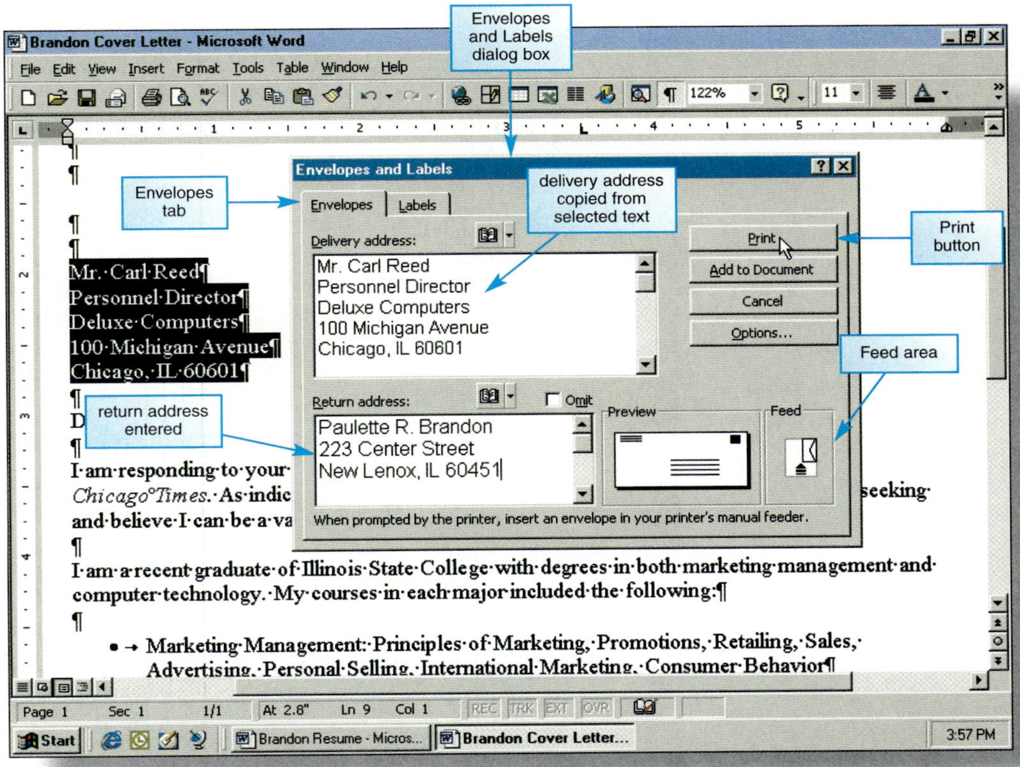

FIGURE 3-77

3 **Insert an envelope into your printer as shown in the Feed area of the Envelopes and Labels dialog box and then click the Print button in the dialog box. If a Microsoft Word dialog box displays, click the No button.**

Word prints the envelope (Figure 3-78).

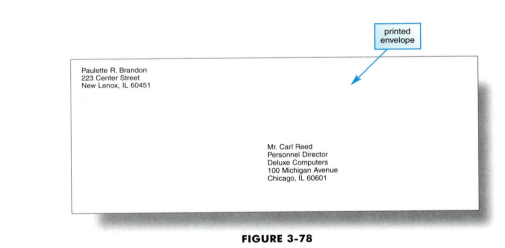

FIGURE 3-78

Instead of printing an envelope, you can print a mailing label. To do this, click the Labels tab in the Envelopes and Labels dialog box.

Currently, you have two documents open: the resume and cover letter. When you are finished with both documents, you may wish to close them. Instead of closing each one individually, you can close all open files at once as shown in the steps on the next page.

More About 2000

Office Supplies

For more information on where to obtain supplies for printing documents, visit the Word 2000 More About Web page (www.scsite.com/wd2000/more.htm) and then click Online Office Supplies.

Steps To Close All Open Word Documents

1 Press and hold the SHIFT key and then click File on the menu bar. Release the SHIFT key. Point to Close All on the File menu.

Word displays a Close All command, instead of a Close command, on the File menu because you pressed the SHIFT key when clicking the menu name (Figure 3-79).

2 Click Close All.

Word closes all open documents and displays a blank document window. If at this point you wanted to begin a new document, you would click the New Blank Document button on the Standard toolbar.

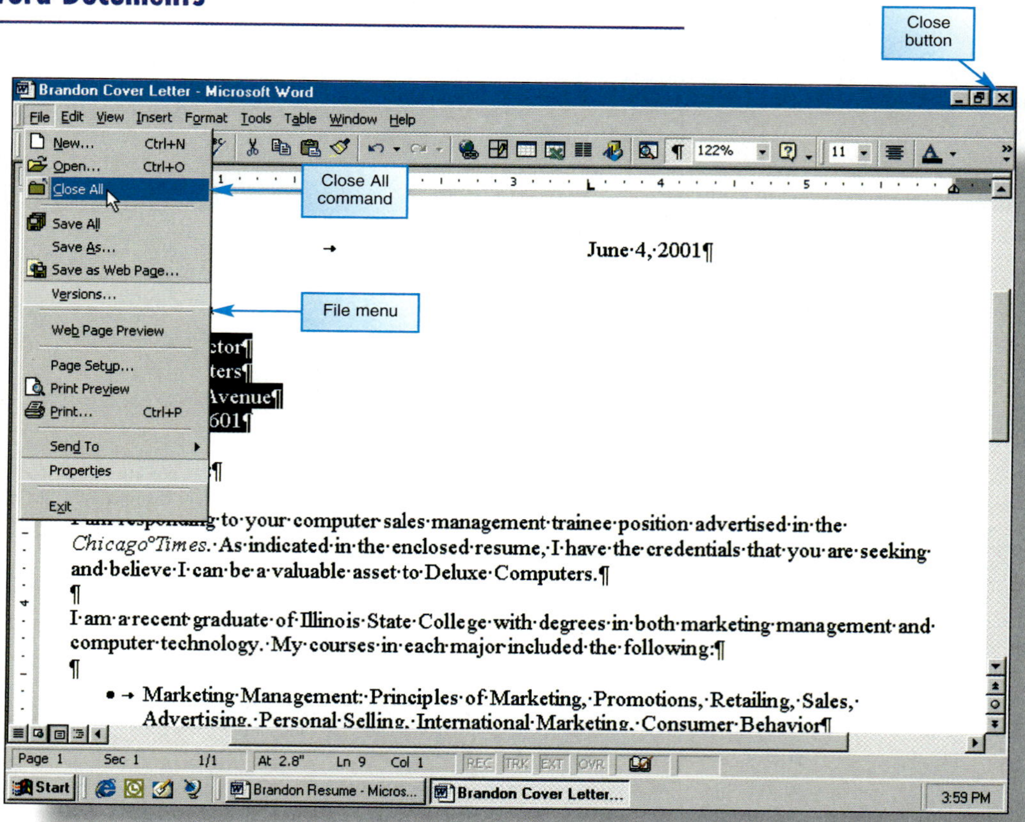

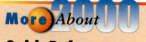

FIGURE 3-79

More About 2000

Quick Reference

For a table that lists how to complete the tasks covered in this book using the mouse, menu, shortcut menu, and keyboard, visit the Shelly Cashman Series Office Web page (www.scsite.com/off2000/qr.htm) and then click Microsoft Word 2000.

The final step in this project is to quit Word as described in the step below.

TO QUIT WORD

1 Click the Close button in the Word window.

The Word window closes.

CASE PERSPECTIVE SUMMARY

With your resume writing expertise and Paulette's business sense, you have created an effective resume and cover letter. Paulette immediately staples the two documents together, places them in the envelope, adds necessary postage, and delivers the envelope to the post office. As she places her cover letter and resume in the mail, Paulette dreams about a career at Deluxe Computers. She plans to wait one week to hear from Mr. Reed, the personnel director at Deluxe Computers. If he has not contacted her in that time, Paulette plans to follow up with a telephone call to him.

Project Summary

Project 3 introduced you to creating a resume using a wizard and creating a cover letter with a letterhead, a bulleted list, and a table. You used the Resume Wizard to create a resume, and then used several formatting techniques to personalize the resume. You viewed, reduced the size of, and printed the resume in print preview. You created a letterhead and then created the cover letter. While creating the letterhead, you learned how to add color to characters, set custom tab stops, collect and paste between documents, add a symbol to a document, and add a border to a paragraph. You created an AutoText entry, which you used when you personalized the cover letter. Finally, you prepared and printed an envelope.

What You Should Know

Having completed this project, you now should be able to perform the following tasks:

▶ Add a Bottom Border to a Paragraph (WD 3.39)
▶ AutoFormat a Table (WD 3.55)
▶ Bold Text (WD 3.17)
▶ Bullet a List as You Type (WD 3.50)
▶ Change Color of Text (WD 3.41)
▶ Change the Font Size (WD 3.28)
▶ Close All Open Word Documents (WD 3.60)
▶ Collect Items (WD 3.33)
▶ Color Characters (WD 3.28)
▶ Color More Characters the Same Color (WD 3.37)
▶ Create a Resume Using Word's Resume Wizard (WD 3.7)
▶ Create an AutoText Entry (WD 3.45)
▶ Display Formatting Marks (WD 3.15)
▶ Enter a Line Break (WD 3.22)
▶ Enter a Paragraph (WD 3.48, WD 3.51)
▶ Enter and Resize a Graphic (WD 3.30)
▶ Enter Data into a Table (WD 3.54)
▶ Enter Placeholder Text (WD 3.21)
▶ Enter the Date, Inside Address, and Salutation (WD 3.44)
▶ Enter the Remainder of the Cover Letter (WD 3.57)
▶ Enter the Remaining Sections of the Resume (WD 3.23)
▶ Increase the Font Size (WD 3.42)
▶ Insert a Nonbreaking Space (WD 3.46)
▶ Insert a Symbol into Text (WD 3.37)
▶ Insert an AutoText Entry (WD 3.47)
▶ Insert an Empty Table (WD 3.52)
▶ Open a New Document Window (WD 3.27)
▶ Paste from the Office Clipboard (WD 3.35)
▶ Prepare and Print an Envelope Address (WD 3.58)
▶ Print a Document (WD 3.58)
▶ Print Preview a Document (WD 3.24)

▶ Print the Resume Created by the Resume Wizard (WD 3.14)
▶ Quit Word (WD 3.60)
▶ Reset Menus and Toolbars (WD 3.14)
▶ Save a Document (WD 3.26)
▶ Save a Document Again (WD 3.58)
▶ Save the Document with a New File Name (WD 3.42)
▶ Save the Letterhead (WD 3.41)
▶ Select a Table (WD 3.56)
▶ Select and Replace Placeholder Text (WD 3.18)
▶ Select and Replace Resume Wizard Supplied Text (WD 3.19)
▶ Set Custom Tab Stops Using the Ruler (WD 3.43)
▶ Set Custom Tab Stops Using the Tabs Dialog Box (WD 3.31)
▶ Switch From One Open Document to Another (WD 3.33)
▶ Zoom Text Width (WD 3.17)

More About 2000

Microsoft Certification

The Microsoft Office User Specialist (MOUS) Certification program provides an opportunity for you to obtain a valuable industry credential - proof that you have the Word 2000 skills required by employers. For more information, see Appendix D or visit the Shelly Cashman Series MOUS Web page at www.scsite.com/off2000/cert.htm.

Apply Your Knowledge

⊕ **Project Reinforcement at www.scsite.com/off2000/reinforce.htm**

1 Working with a Table

Instructions: Start Word. Open the document, Expenses Table, on the Data Disk. If you did not download the Data Disk, see the inside back cover for instructions for downloading the Data Disk or see your instructor.

The document is a Word table that you are to edit and format. The revised table is shown in Figure 3-80.

Monthly Home Expenses

	Electric	Gas	Refuse	Insurance	Total
January	148.77	166.89	15.00	55.00	**385.66**
February	137.67	99.44	15.00	55.00	**307.11**
March	135.34	92.55	15.00	55.00	**297.89**
April	125.20	60.89	15.00	55.00	**256.09**
May	158.13	12.06	15.00	55.00	**240.19**
June	210.88	14.55	15.00	58.50	**298.93**

FIGURE 3-80

Perform the following tasks:

1. With the insertion point in the table, click Table on the menu bar and then click Table AutoFormat. In the Table AutoFormat dialog box, scroll to and then click Grid 8 in the Formats list. All check boxes should have check marks except for these two: Last row and Last column. Click the OK button.

2. Select the Phone column by pointing to the top of the column until the mouse pointer changes to a downward pointing arrow and then clicking. Right-click in the selected column and then click Delete Columns on the shortcut menu to delete the Phone column.

3. Add a new row to the table for June as follows: Electric– 210.88; Gas– 14.55; Refuse– 15.00; Insurance – 58.50.

4. With the insertion point in the table, click Table on the menu bar, point to Select, and then click Table. Double-click the move handle on the Formatting toolbar. Click the Center button on the Formatting toolbar to center the table.

5. Click in the rightmost column, Insurance. Click Table on the menu bar, point to Insert, and then click Columns to the Right. Type Total as the new column's heading.

6. Position the insertion point in the January Total cell (second row, sixth column). Click Table on the menu bar and then click Formula. When the Formula dialog box displays, be sure the formula is =SUM(LEFT) and then click the OK button to place the Total expenses for January in the cell. Repeat for each month s total expense. For these expenses, you will need to edit the formula so it reads =SUM(LEFT) instead of =SUM(ABOVE).

7. Select the cells containing the total expense values and then click the Bold button on the Formatting toolbar.

8. Click File on the menu bar and then click Save As. Use the file name, Revised Expenses, to save the document on your floppy disk.

9. Print the revised table.

1 Using Word's Resume Wizard to Create a Resume

Problem: You are a student at University of Tennessee expecting to receive your Bachelor of Science degree in Restaurant/Hotel Management this May. As the semester end is approaching quickly, you are beginning a search for full-time employment upon graduation. You prepare the resume shown in Figure 3-81 using Word's Resume Wizard.

Instructions:

1. Use the Resume Wizard to create a resume. Select the Contemporary style for the resume. Use the name and address information in Figure 3-81 when the Resume Wizard requests it.

2. Personalize the resume as shown in Figure 3-81. When entering multiple lines in the Awards received, Memberships, Languages, and Hobbies sections, be sure to enter a line break at the end of each line, instead of a paragraph break.

3. Check the spelling of the resume.

4. Save the resume on a floppy disk with Schumann Resume as the file name.

5. View the resume from within print preview. If the resume exceeds one page, use print preview to shrink it to a page. Print the resume.

9-point font

14 Ross Creek Road
Lake City, TN 37769

Phone (423) 555-9801
Fax (423) 555-9857
E-mail schumann@creek.com

David Paul Schumann   ← **24-point font**

Objective	To obtain a restaurant management position for a restaurant specializing in French cuisine.
Education	1997 - 2001 University of Tennessee Knoxville, TN **Restaurant/Hotel Management** • B.S. in Restaurant/Hotel Management, May 2001 • A.S. in Food Service, May 1999
Awards received	Dean's List, six semesters Liberal Arts Honor Society, every semester Taller Nutrition Award, October 1999 Food Preparation Competition, 1st Place, May 1999 Marge Rae Scholarship, 1998-1999
Memberships	Nutrition Services of America National Restaurant Management Association Alpha Beta Lambda Fraternity, Vice President Student Government Association Restaurant/Hotel Club
Languages	English (fluent) French (fluent) Spanish (working knowledge)
Work experience	1998 - 2001 Regis Food Service Knoxville, TN **Assistant Cafeteria Director** • Supervise kitchen staff • Organize work schedules • Cater meetings and ceremonies • Plan meals for staff and students on campus • Prepare food • Serve dining patrons
Hobbies	Camping Soccer Classic Cars Boy Scouts of America, Leader

FIGURE 3-81

In the Lab

2 Creating a Cover Letter with a Table

Problem: You have just prepared the resume shown in Figure 3-81 on the previous page and now are ready to create a cover letter to send to a prospective employer. In yesterday's edition of the *West Coast Tribune*, you noticed an advertisement for a restaurant manager at Worldwide Hotels and Suites. You prepare the cover letter shown in Figure 3-82 to send with your resume.

Instructions:

1. Create the letterhead shown at the top of Figure 3-82. Save the letterhead with the file name, Schumann Letterhead.

2. Create the letter shown in Figure 3-82 using the modified block style. Set a tab stop at the 3.5" mark on the ruler for the date line, complimentary close, and signature block. After entering the inside address, create an AutoText entry for Worldwide Hotels and Suites,

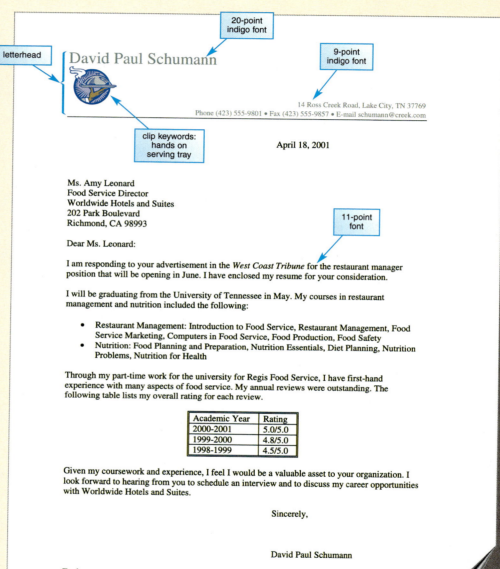

FIGURE 3-82

and use the AutoText entry whenever you have to enter the company name, Worldwide Hotels and Suites. Center the table and format it using the Elegant format in the Table AutoFormat dialog box.

3. Save the letter on a floppy disk with Schumann Cover Letter as the file name.

4. Check the spelling of the cover letter. Save the cover letter again with the same file name.

In the Lab

5. View the cover letter from within print preview. If the cover letter exceeds one page, use print preview to shrink it to a single page. Print the cover letter.

6. Prepare and print an envelope address and mailing label using the inside address and return address in the cover letter.

3 Using Wizards to Compose a Personal Cover Letter and Resume

Problem: You are currently in the market for a new job and are ready to prepare a resume and cover letter.

Instructions: Obtain a copy of last Sunday's newspaper. Look through the classified section and cut out a want ad in an area of interest. Assume you are in the market for the position being advertised. Use the Resume Wizard to create a resume. Use the Letter Wizard to create the cover letter. Display the Letter Wizard by clicking Tools on the menu bar and then clicking Letter Wizard. *Hint:* Use Help for assistance in using the Letter Wizard. Use the want ad for the inside address and your personal information for the return address. Try to be as accurate as possible when personalizing the resume and cover letter. Submit the want ad with your cover letter and resume.

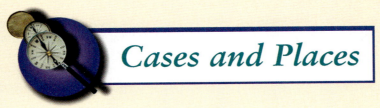

Cases and Places

The difficulty of these case studies varies:
▶ are the least difficult; ▶▶ are more difficult; and ▶▶▶ are the most difficult.

1 ▶ Your boss has asked you to create a calendar for October so he can post it on the office bulletin board. Use the Calendar Wizard in the Other Documents sheet of the New Office Document dialog box. Use the following settings in the wizard: boxes & borders style, landscape print direction, leave room for a picture, October 2001 for both the start and end date. With the calendar on the screen, click the current graphic and delete it. Insert a clip art image of a haunted house or a similar seasonal graphic and then resize the image so it fits in the entire space for the graphic.

2 ▶ You have been asked to prepare the agenda for the next monthly department meeting. Use the Agenda Wizard in the Other Documents sheet of the New Office Document dialog box. Use the following settings in the wizard: style– modern; meeting date– 4/18/2001; meeting time– 2:00 p.m.; title– Monthly Meeting; meeting location– Conference Room B; headings– Please read and Please bring; names on agenda – Meeting called by, Note taker, and Attendees; Topics, People, and Minutes– Approve March Minutes, C. Dolby, 5; Department News, E. Jones, 10; Budget Status, J. Peterson, 15; Annual Kick-Off Dinner, T. Greeson, 15; New Business, Floor, 15; add a form for recording the minutes. On the agenda created by the wizard, add the following names in the appropriate spaces: C. Dolby called the meeting; R. Wilson will be the note taker; all people listed in this assignment will be attending – including you. Also, attendees should bring the 2001 Budget Report and read the March Minutes.

Cases and Places

3 ▶ You notice that Word has a Letter Wizard, which you can begin by clicking Tools on the menu bar and then clicking Letter Wizard. To assist you with letter preparation, you decide to prepare the letter shown in Figure 3-82 on page WD 3.64 using the Letter Wizard. How does the document prepared using the Letter Wizard differ from the one created from scratch? Do you prefer using a wizard or composing a letter from scratch?

4 ▶▶ A potential employer has asked you to fax your cover letter and resume so she may review it immediately. Use the Fax Wizard and the following settings: create the fax cover sheet with a note and print the fax so you can send it on a separate fax machine. It must be faxed to K. J. Buchham at Jade Enterprises (One Main Street, Cambridge, MA 02142; telephone 617-555-0098; fax 617-555-0099). Each is one page in length. Fax a copy to T. R. Green at the same number. In the fax, write a message informing K. J. Buchham that your cover letter and resume are attached and if she has any questions, she can contact you. Use your own name, address, and telephone information in the fax.

5 ▶▶ As chairperson of the Annual Company Picnic, you look for volunteers to assist with various activities. You have compiled a list of jobs for the picnic: prepare fliers, distribute fliers, plan meal and order food, plan and organize games, plan children's activities, reserve park pavilion, setup on day of picnic, and cleanup on day of picnic. You prepare a memorandum asking fellow employees for their assistance. A copy of the memo should be sent to Howard Bender. Use the Memo Wizard, together with the concepts and techniques presented in this project, to create and format the interoffice memorandum.

6 ▶▶▶ You have been asked to locate a speaker for this year's commencement address at your school. Locate the address of someone you feel would be a highly respected and enthusiastic speaker for the commencement address. Using Word's Letter Wizard, write the individual a letter inviting him or her to speak at the commencement. In the letter, present a background of your school, the student body, the staff, and any other aspects of your school that would make this speaker want to attend your commencement. Be sure to list the date, time, and location of the commencement in the letter. Apply the concepts and techniques presented in this project to personalize the letter.

7 ▶▶▶ Many individuals place their resumes on the World Wide Web for potential employers to see. Find a resume on the Web that you believe could be improved if it were designed differently. Print the resume. Using the text on the resume, Word's Resume Wizard, and the techniques presented in this project, create a new resume that would be more likely to catch a potential employer's attention. Turn in both the resume from the Web and your newly designed version of the resume.

Microsoft Word 2000

Creating Web Pages Using Word

CASE PERSPECTIVE

In Project 3, Paulette Rose Brandon created her resume (Figure 3-1 on page WD 3.5). Paulette graduated with you from Illinois State College. She was proficient in business, and you excelled at Internet skills. Recently, Paulette has been surfing the Internet on her own and has discovered that many people have their own personal Web pages with links to other Web sites and Web pages such as resumes and schedules. These personal Web pages are very impressive. To make herself more attractive to a potential employer, Paulette has asked you to help her create a personal Web page that contains a hyperlink to her resume. To do this, she must save her resume as a Web page. Paulette also wants her Web page to contain two more hyperlinks: one to her favorite Web site (www.scsite.com) and another to her e-mail address. This way, potential employers easily can send her a message.

To complete this Web Feature, you will need the resume created in Project 3 so you can save it as a Web page and then use the resulting Web page as a hyperlink destination. (If you did not create the resume, see your instructor for a copy.)

Introduction

Word provides two techniques for creating Web pages. If you have an existing Word document, you can save it as a Web page. If you do not have an existing Word document, you can create a new Web page by using a Web page template or the Web Page Wizard, which provides customized templates you can modify easily. In addition to these Web tools, Word has many other **Web page authoring** features. For example, you can include frames, hyperlinks, sounds, videos, pictures, scrolling text, bullets, horizontal lines, check boxes, option buttons, list boxes, text boxes, and scripts on Web pages.

In this Web Feature, you save the resume created in Project 3 as a Web page. You then use Word's Web Page Wizard to create another Web page that contains two frames (Figure 1a on the next page). A **frame** is a rectangular section of a Web page that can display another separate Web page. Thus, a Web page that contains multiple frames can display multiple Web pages simultaneously. Word stores all frames associated with a Web page in a single file called the **frames page**. The frames page is not visible on the screen; it simply is a container for all frames associated with a Web page. When you open the frames page in Word or a Web browser, all frames associated with the Web page display on the screen.

In this Web Feature, the file name of the frames page is Brandon Personal Web Page. When you initially open this frames page, the left frame contains the title Paulette Rose Brandon and two hyperlinks – My Resume and My Favorite Site; the right frame displays Paulette's resume (Figure 1a). You have learned that a hyperlink is a shortcut that allows a user to jump easily and quickly to another location in the same document or to other documents or Web pages. The My Resume hyperlink is a connection to the resume, and the My Favorite Site hyperlink is a connection to www.scsite.com.

When you click the My Favorite Site hyperlink, the www.scsite.com Web site displays in the right frame (Figure 1b). When you click the My Resume hyperlink, the resume displays in the right frame. The resume itself contains a hyperlink to an e-mail address. When you click the e-mail address, Word opens your e-mail program automatically with the recipient's address (brandon@lenox.com) already filled in (Figure 1c). You simply type a message and then click the Send button, which places the message in the Outbox or sends it if you are connected to an e-mail server.

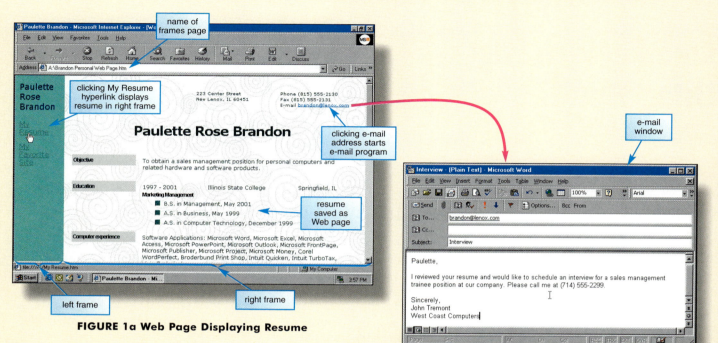

FIGURE 1a Web Page Displaying Resume

FIGURE 1c E-mail Program

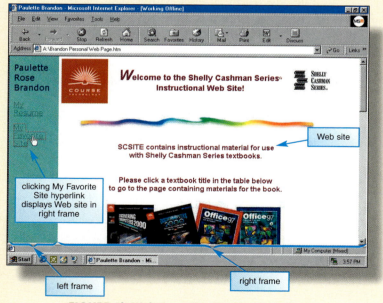

FIGURE 1b Web Page Displaying Web Site

Once you have created Web pages, you can publish them. **Publishing** is the process of making Web pages available to others, for example on the World Wide Web or on a company's intranet. In Word, you can publish Web pages by saving them to a Web folder or to an FTP location. The procedures for publishing Web pages in Microsoft Office are discussed in Appendix B.

Because this Web Feature is for instructional purposes, you create and save your frames page and associated Web pages on a floppy disk rather than to the Web. Saving these pages to the floppy disk may be a slow process – please be patient.

Saving a Word Document as a Web Page

Once you have created a Word document, you can save it as a Web page so that it can be published and then viewed by a Web browser, such as Internet Explorer. Perform the following steps to save the resume created in Project 3 as a Web page.

Steps To Save a Word Document as a Web Page

1 **Start Word and then open the Brandon Resume created in Project 3. Reset your toolbars as described in Appendix C. Click File on the menu bar and then point to Save as Web Page (Figure 2).**

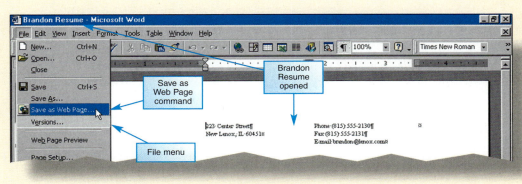

FIGURE 2

2 **Click Save as Web Page. When the Save As dialog box displays, type** Brandon Resume Web Page **in the File name text box and then, if necessary, change the Save in location to 3½ Floppy (A:) as shown in Figure 3.**

3 **Click the Save button in the Save As dialog box.**

Word displays the Brandon Resume Web Page in the Word window (see Figure 4 on the next page).

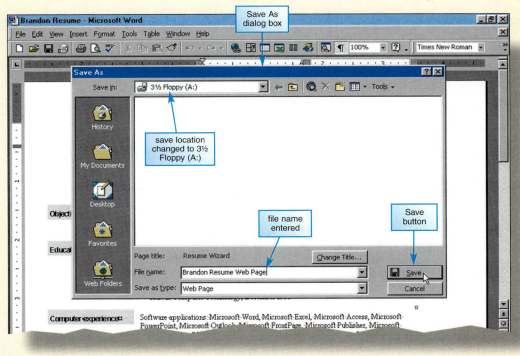

FIGURE 3

Word switches to Web layout view and also changes some of the toolbar buttons and menu commands to provide Web page authoring features. For example, the Standard toolbar now displays a New Web Page button (Figure 4 on the next page). The Web Layout View button on the horizontal scroll bar is recessed.

The resume displays on the Word screen similar to how it will display in a Web browser. Some of Word's formatting features are not supported by Web pages; thus, your Web page may display slightly different from the original Word document.

Formatting the E-mail Address as a Hyperlink

You want the e-mail address in your resume to be formatted as a hyperlink so that when someone clicks the e-mail address on your Web page, his or her e-mail program opens automatically with your e-mail address already filled in.

You have learned that when you press the SPACEBAR or ENTER key after a Web or e-mail address, Word automatically formats it as a hyperlink. Perform the following steps to format the e-mail address as a hyperlink.

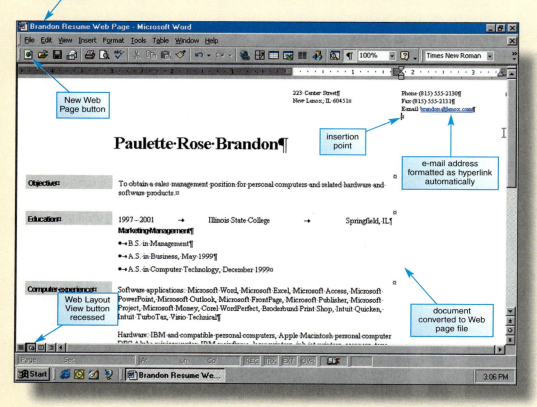

FIGURE 4

TO FORMAT A HYPERLINK AUTOMATICALLY

1 Position the insertion point immediately after the e-mail address; that is, after the m in com.

2 Press the ENTER key.

Word automatically formats the e-mail address as a hyperlink; that is, it is colored blue and underlined (Figure 4).

You are now finished modifying the Brandon Resume Web Page file. Thus, perform the following steps to save the file again and then close it.

TO SAVE AND CLOSE A WEB PAGE

1 Click the Save button on the Standard toolbar.

2 Click File on the menu bar and then click Close.

Word saves the file and closes it. The Word window is empty.

Web Page Design

For more information on guidelines for designing Web pages, visit the Word 2000 More About Web page (www.scsite.com/wd2000/more.htm) and then click Web Page Design.

Using Word's Web Page Wizard to Create a Web Page

In the previous section, you saved an existing Word document as a Web page. Next, you want to create a brand new Web page. You can create a Web page from scratch using a Web page template or you can use the **Web Page Wizard**. Because this is your first experience creating a new Web page with frames, you should use the Web Page Wizard as shown in the following steps.

Steps To Create a Web Page Using the Web Page Wizard

1 **Click File on the menu bar and then click New. If necessary, click the Web Pages tab when the New dialog box first displays. Point to the Web Page Wizard icon.**

Word displays several Web page template icons and the Web Page Wizard in the Web Pages sheet (Figure 5).

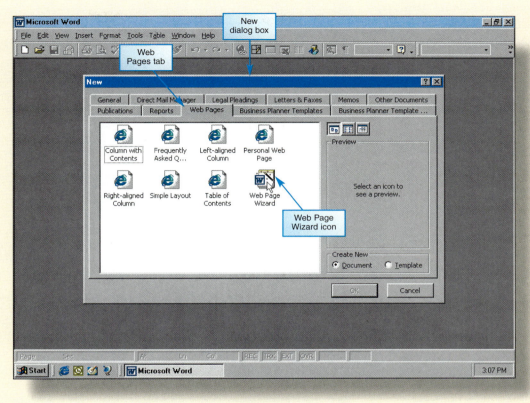

FIGURE 5

2 **Double-click the Web Page Wizard icon. When the Start panel displays in the Web Page Wizard dialog box, click the Next button. When the Title and Location panel displays, type** Paulette Brandon **in the Web site title text box. Press the TAB key and then type** a: **in the Web site location text box.**

Word displays the Title and Location panel in the Web Page Wizard dialog box (Figure 6). In this dialog box, the title you enter displays in the Web browser's title bar.

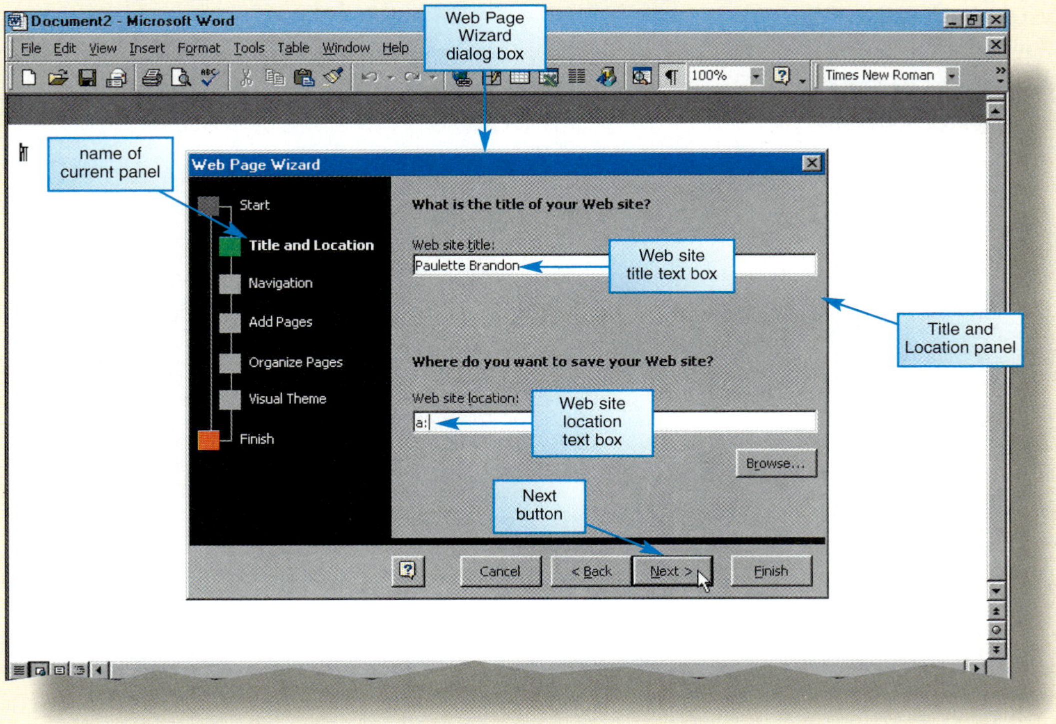

FIGURE 6

3 **Click the Next button. When the Navigation panel displays, click Vertical frame, if necessary, and then point to the Next button.**

*Word displays the **Navigation panel** in the Web Page Wizard dialog box (Figure 7). In this dialog box, you select the placement of hyperlinks on your Web page(s).*

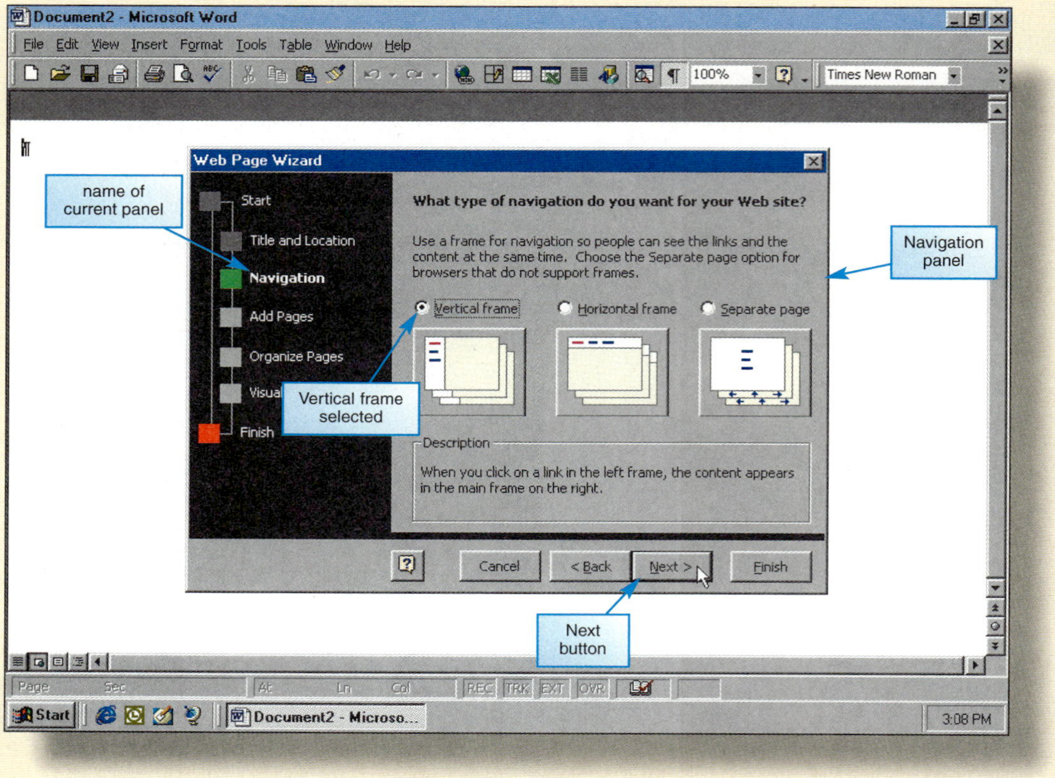

FIGURE 7

4 **Click the Next button. When the Add Pages panel displays, click the Remove Page button three times and then point to the Add Existing File button.**

*Word displays the **Add Pages panel** that initially lists three Web page names: Personal Web Page, Blank Page 1, and Blank Page 2. You do not want any of these Web page names on your Web page; thus, you remove them (Figure 8). You will click the Add Existing File button to add Brandon Resume Web Page to the list.*

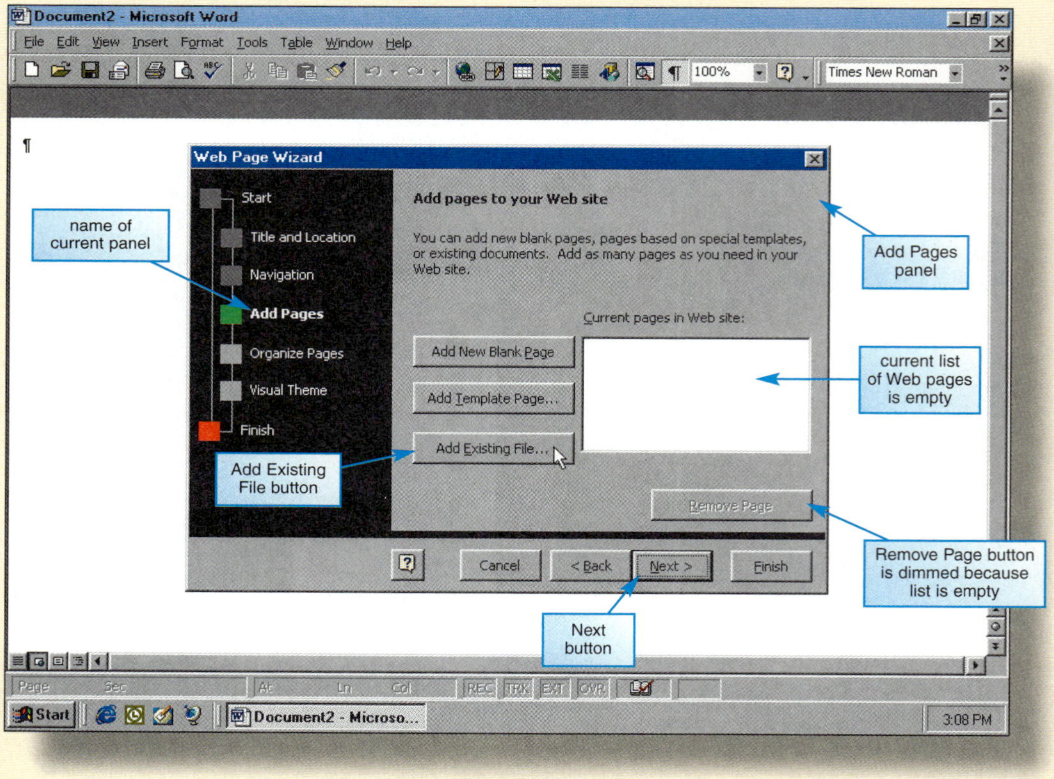

FIGURE 8

5 **Click the Add Existing File button** to display the Open dialog box. If necessary, change the Look in location to 3½ Floppy (A:). Click Brandon Resume Web Page and then point to the Open button in the Open dialog box (Figure 9).

6 **Click the Open button in the Open dialog box.**

The wizard adds Brandon Resume Web Page to the list in the Add Pages panel.

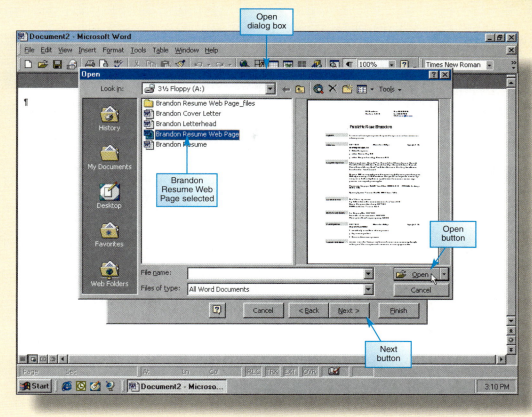

FIGURE 9

7 **Click the Next button in the Add Pages panel. When the Organize Pages panel displays, click the Rename button. When the Rename Hyperlink dialog box displays, type** My Resume **in the text box. Point to the OK button.**

In the Organize Pages panel in the Web Page Wizard, you specify the sequence and names of the hyperlinks to be in the left frame of the Web page (Figure 10).

8 **Click the OK button.**

Word renames the hyperlink to My Resume.

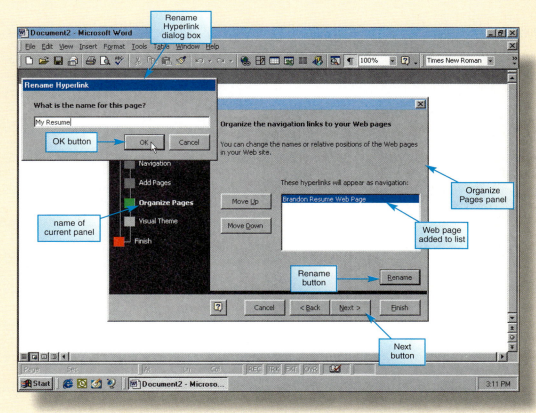

FIGURE 10

9 **Click the Next button. If the displayed theme in the Visual Theme panel is not Spiral, click the Browse Themes button. When the Theme dialog box displays, scroll to and then click Spiral in the Choose a Theme list. Click the OK button.**

Word displays the Visual Theme panel in the Web Page Wizard dialog box (Figure 11). A theme is a collection of defined design elements and color schemes.

10 **Click the Next button. When the Finish panel displays, click the Finish button. If the Office Assistant displays a message about navigation features, click the Yes button. If a Frames toolbar displays in your document window, click its Close button to remove it from the screen.**

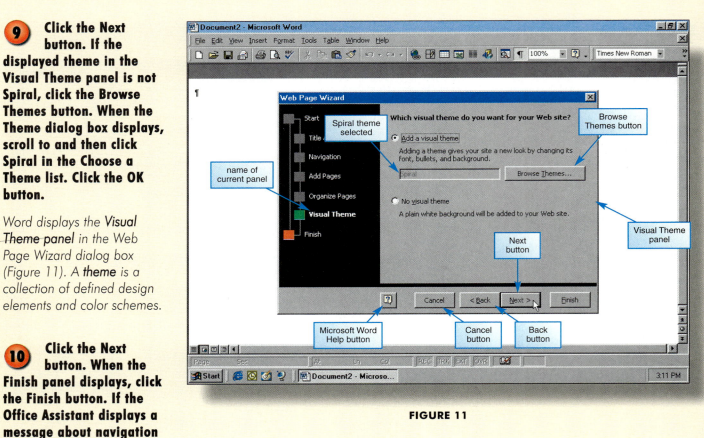

FIGURE 11

After about a minute, Word displays a layout of the Web pages (see Figure 12). The My Resume hyperlink displays in a frame on the left and the resume displays in a frame on the right.

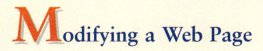

Other Ways

1. On Start menu click New Office Document, click Web Pages tab, double-click Web Page Wizard icon

2. Click New Office Document button on Microsoft Office Shortcut Bar, click Web Pages tab, double-click Web Page Wizard icon

When creating a Web page using the Web Page Wizard, you can click the Back button (Figure 11) in any panel of the Web Page Wizard dialog box to change any previously entered information. For help with entering information into the Web Page Wizard, click the Microsoft Word Help button in the appropriate panel. To exit from the Web Page Wizard and return to the document window without creating the Web page, click the Cancel button in any of the Web Page Wizard dialog boxes.

Modifying a Web Page

The next step is to modify the Web pages. First, you make the left frame smaller and then you add the My Favorite Site hyperlink.

The Web page is divided into two frames, one on the left and one on the right. A **frame border** separates the frames. When you point to the frame border, the mouse pointer shape changes to a double-headed arrow.

You want to make the left frame narrower. To do this, you drag the frame border as illustrated in the following steps.

Steps **To Resize a Web Page Frame**

1 Point to the frame border.

The mouse pointer shape changes to a double-headed arrow and Word displays the ScreenTip, Resize (Figure 12).

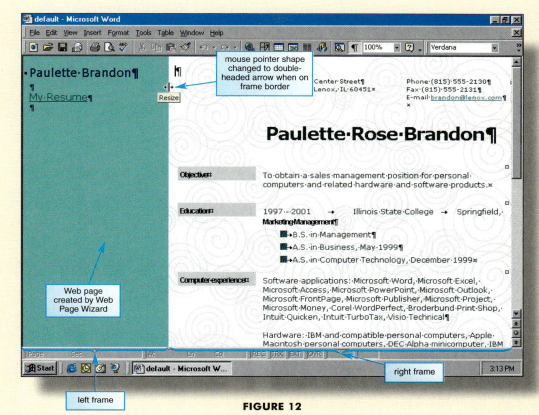

FIGURE 12

2 Drag the frame border to the left until it is positioned under the r in Brandon (Figure 13).

Word narrows the left frame and widens the right frame (see Figure 14 on the next page).

FIGURE 13

In the left frame, you want to add a My Favorite Site hyperlink. You used the Web Page Wizard to link the My Resume hyperlink to the Web page file called Brandon Resume Web Page, which means when you click the My Resume link in the left frame, the Brandon Resume Web Page file displays in the right frame. Similarly, when you click the My Favorite Site hyperlink, you want a Web site to display in the right frame.

The first step is to enter the hyperlink text into the left frame as described in the steps on the next page.

More *About* **2000**

Highlighting

To add color to an online document or e-mail communication, highlight the text. Highlighting alerts the reader to the text's importance, much like a highlight marker does in a textbook. To highlight text, select it, click the Highlight button arrow on the Formatting toolbar, and then click the desired highlight color.

TO ENTER AND FORMAT TEXT

1 Click in the left frame of the Web page. Click the paragraph mark below the My Resume hyperlink and then press the ENTER key.

2 Double-click the move handle on the Formatting toolbar to display the entire toolbar. Click the Font Size box arrow and then click 12.

3 Type My Favorite Site as the text.

Word enters the text, My Favorite Site, in the left frame using a font size of 12.

Perform the following steps to link the My Favorite Site text to a Web site.

 Steps **To Add a Hyperlink**

1 **Drag through the My Favorite Site text. Double-click the move handle on the Standard toolbar to display the entire toolbar. Click the Insert Hyperlink button on the Standard toolbar. When the Insert Hyperlink dialog box displays, if necessary, click Existing File or Web Page in the Link to list. Type** http://www.scsite.com **in the Type the file or Web page name text box (Figure 14).**

2 **Click the OK button.**

Word formats the My Favorite Site text as a hyperlink that when clicked displays the associated Web site in the right frame (see Figure 1b on page WDW 1.2).

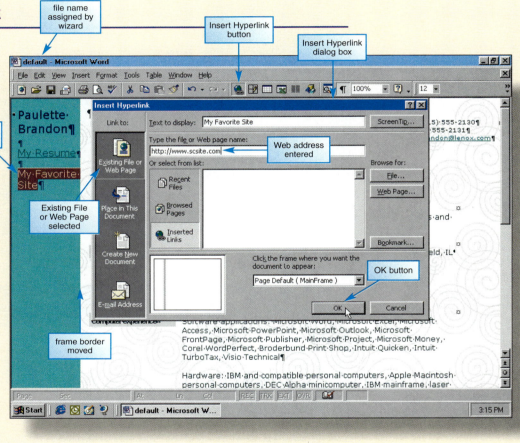

FIGURE 14

 Other **Ways**

1. Right-click selected text, point to Hyperlink on shortcut menu, click Edit hyperlink on Hyperlink submenu

If you wanted to edit an existing hyperlink, you would drag through the hyperlink text and then click the Insert Hyperlink button on the Standard toolbar. Word will display the Edit Hyperlink dialog box instead of the Insert Hyperlink dialog box. Other than the title bar, these two dialog boxes are the same.

The Resume Wizard assigned the file name, default, to this frames page (Figure 14). Save the frames page with a new name as described in the following steps.

TO SAVE THE FRAMES PAGE WITH A NEW FILE NAME

1 Insert your floppy disk into drive A.

2 Click File on the menu bar and then click Save As.

3 Type the file name Brandon Personal Web Page in the File name text box. Do not press the ENTER key.

4 If necessary, click the Save in box arrow and then click 3½ Floppy (A:).

5 Click the Save button in the Save As dialog box.

Word saves the frames page and associated frames on a floppy disk in drive A with the file name Brandon Personal Web Page.

Viewing the Web Page in Your Default Browser

To see how the Web page looks in your default browser without actually connecting to the Internet, you use the **Web Page Preview command**. That is, if you click File on the menu bar and then click Web Page Preview, Word opens your Web browser in a separate window and displays the open Web page file in the browser window.

From the browser window, you can test your hyperlinks to be sure they work – before you publish them to the Web. For example, in the left frame, click the My Favorite Site link to display the Web site www.scsite.com in the right frame. (If you are not connected to the Internet, your browser will connect you and then display the Web site.) Click the My Resume link to display the Brandon Resume Web Page in the right frame. Click the e-mail address to open your e-mail program with the address, brandon@lenox.com, entered in the recipient's address box. When finished, close the browser window.

The next step is to quit Word.

TO QUIT WORD

1 Click the Close button at the right edge of Word's title bar.

The Word window closes.

Editing a Web Page from Your Browser

One of the powerful features of Office 2000 is the ability to edit a Web page directly from Internet Explorer. The steps on the next page illustrate how to open your Web page in Internet Explorer and then edit it from Internet Explorer.

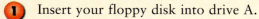

More About

Web Pages

Use horizontal lines to separate sections of a Web page. To add a horizontal line at the location of the insertion point, click Format on the menu bar, click Borders and Shading, click the Horizontal Line button, click the desired line type in the Horizontal Line dialog box, and then click the Insert Clip button on the Pop-up menu.

More About

HTML

If you wish to view the HTML source code associated with the Web page you have created, click View on the menu bar and then click HTML Source, which starts the HTML Source Editor. To close the HTML Source Editor, click File on the menu bar and then click Exit.

More About

Microsoft Certification

The Microsoft Office User Specialist (MOUS) Certification program provides an opportunity for you to obtain a valuable industry credential - proof that you have the Word 2000 skills required by employers. For more information, see Appendix D or visit the Shelly Cashman Series MOUS Web page at www.scsite.com/off2000/cert.htm.

Steps **To Edit a Web Page from Your Browser**

1 **Click the Start button on the taskbar, point to Programs, and then click Internet Explorer. When the Internet Explorer window displays, type** a:Brandon Personal Web Page.htm **in the Address Bar and then press the** ENTER **key. Point to the Edit with Microsoft Word for Windows button on the toolbar.**

Internet Explorer opens the Brandon Personal Web Page and displays it in the browser window (Figure 15). Internet Explorer determines the Office program you used to create the Web page and associates that program with the Edit button.

2 **Click the Edit with Microsoft Word for Windows button.**

Internet Explorer starts Microsoft Word and displays the Brandon Personal Web Page in the Word window.

3 **In the left frame, click immediately to the left of the B in Brandon. Type** Rose **and then press the** SPACEBAR**.**

Paulette's middle name displays in the left frame of the Web page (Figure 16).

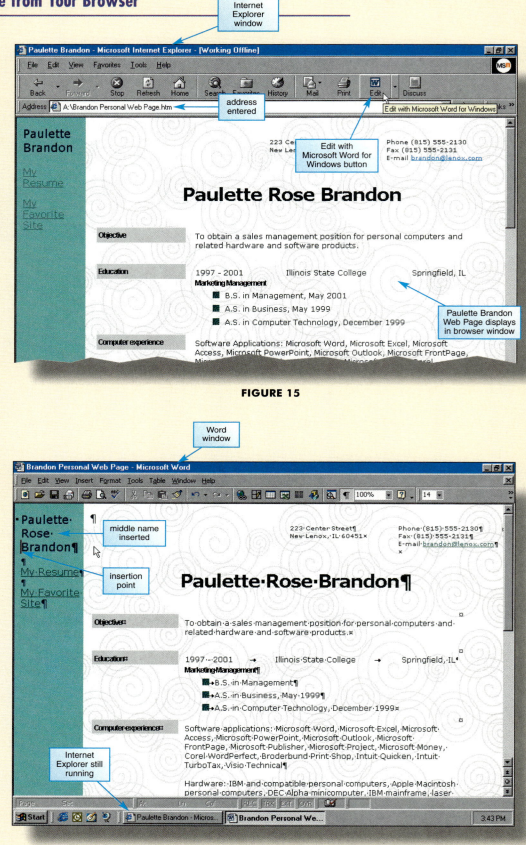

FIGURE 15

FIGURE 16

4 Click the Save button on the Standard toolbar. Click the Close button at the right edge of Word's title bar.

Word saves the revised Web page and, after about a minute, the Word window closes.

5 When the Internet Explorer window redisplays, click the Refresh button on the toolbar.

Internet Explorer displays the revised Web page (Figure 17).

6 Click the Close button at the right edge of the Internet Explorer window.

The Internet Explorer window closes.

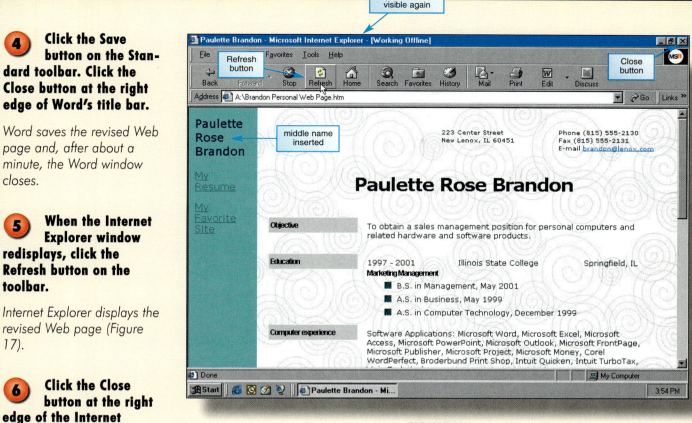

FIGURE 17

If the right edge of the resume wraps when you display it in the browser, you can follow the steps above to edit it in Word and drag the right border of the resume table to the right.

The final step is to make your Web pages and associated files available to others on your network, on an intranet, or on the World Wide Web. See Appendix B and then talk to your instructor about how you should do this for your system.

Quick Reference

For a table that lists how to complete the tasks covered in this book using the mouse, menu, shortcut menu, and keyboard, visit the Shelly Cashman Series Office Web page (www.scsite.com/off2000/qr.htm) and then click Microsoft Word 2000.

CASE PERSPECTIVE SUMMARY

Paulette is thrilled with her personal Web pages. They look so professional! Paulette now is ready to publish the Web pages and associated files to the World Wide Web. After talking with her ISP's technical support staff, she learns she can use Word to save a copy of her Web page files directly on her ISP's Web server. You are familiar with this feature of Word and assist Paulette with this task. Next, she connects to the Web and displays her personal Web pages from her browser. Paulette is quite impressed with herself!

Web Feature Summary

This Web Feature introduced you to creating a Web page by saving an existing Word document as a Web Page file. You also created a new Web page with frames using the Web Page Wizard and then modified this Web page. You created a hyperlink to an e-mail address, one to a Web page file, and another to a Web site.

In the Lab

1 Saving a Word Document as a Web Page

Problem: You created the research paper shown in Figure 2-74 on pages WD 2.57 and WD 2.58 in Project 2. You decide to save this research paper as a Web page.

Instructions:

1. Open the Digital Camera Paper shown in Figure 2-74. (If you did not create the research paper, see your instructor for a copy.) Then, save the paper as a Web page using the file name Digital Camera Web Page.
2. Print the Web page. Click File on the menu bar and then click Web Page Preview to view the Web page in your browser. Close the browser window. Quit Word.

2 Creating a Web Page with a Hyperlink to a Web Site

Problem: You created the resume shown in Figure 3-81 on page WD 3.63 in Project 3. You decide to create a personal Web page with a link to this resume. Thus, you also must save the resume as a Web page.

Instructions:

1. Open the Schumann Resume shown in Figure 3-81. (If you did not create the resume, see your instructor for a copy.) Then, save the resume as a Web page using the file name Schumann Resume Web Page. Convert the e-mail address to a Web page by clicking immediately to the right of the address and pressing the ENTER key. Save the Web page again.
2. Create a personal Web page with frames using the Web Page Wizard. Use the following settings as the wizard requests them: apply vertical frame navigation; create a hyperlink to the Schumann Resume Web Page; change the name of the hyperlink to My Resume; select a visual theme you like best.
3. Insert a hyperlink called My Favorite Site and link it to your favorite Web address.
4. Save the Web page. Test your Web page links. Print the Web page. Click File on the menu bar and then click Web Page Preview to view the Web page in your browser. Close the browser window. Quit Word.

3 Creating a Personal Web Page

Problem: You have decided to create your own personal Web page using the Personal Home Page template in the Web Page Wizard.

Instructions:

1. Create your own personal Web page using the Web Page Wizard. Use Horizontal frame as your navigation method. When the Add Pages panel displays, keep the Personal Web Page, and delete Blank Page 1 and Blank Page 2. Select a theme you like best.
2. Personalize the Personal Web Page as indicated on the template. For each bullet in the Favorite Links section, enter a URL of a site on the Web that interests you.
3. Save the Web page. Test your Web page links.
4. Ask your instructor for instructions on how to publish your Web page so that others may have access to it.

Microsoft Word 2000

PROJECT

4

Creating a Document with a Table, Chart, and Watermark

OBJECTIVES

You will have mastered the material in this project when you can:

- Add an outside border with color and shading to a paragraph
- Download clip art from the Microsoft Clip Gallery Live Web page
- Add a shadow to characters
- Center text vertically on a page
- Return formatting to the Normal style
- Insert a section break
- Insert an existing Word document into an open document
- Save an active document with a new file name
- Create a header different from a previous header
- Change the starting page number in a section
- Create a chart from a Word table
- Modify a chart in Microsoft Graph
- Format a chart in Word
- Add picture bullets to a list
- Use the Draw Table feature to create a table
- Change the direction of text in table cells
- Change alignment of text in table cells
- Insert a picture as a watermark
- Format a watermark

The Successful Job Search

A Look at Prospective Companies

As you near completion of your formal education, your activities begin to focus on the pursuit of employment and securing your future. Part of a successful job search involves researching a prospective company. Its financial situation, hiring plans, and growth strategies are important factors to consider in deciding whether to apply. In an interview, recruiters determine an applicant's familiarity with the corporation by asking such questions as, What do you know about the corporation?

An easy way to locate such relevant information is through the corporation's annual report. This document contains narratives explaining the corporation's mission, vision for expansion, and significant developments. These features are enhanced and supplemented by the plethora of charts and graphs reflecting the company's activities during the year compared to previous years.

An annual report is similar to the sales proposal you will create in Project 4. Both documents are tailored to specific audiences. Each publication contains an attractive title page, tables, charts, and a variety of design elements. The sales proposal in this project contains a graphic watermark that

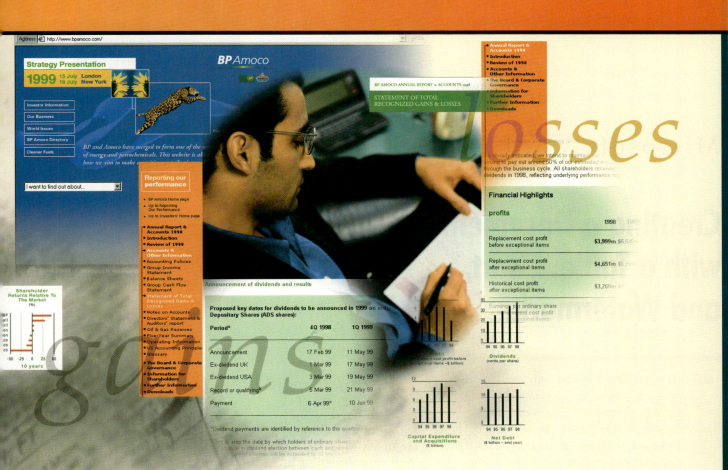

displays behind the first and second pages of the proposal. Companies sometimes use their logos or other graphics as watermarks on documents to add visual appeal.

Say you are an engineering major looking for a career with an international corporation known for research and development. At your college's placement office, you locate the annual report for BP Amoco, a large integrated petroleum and chemical company.

Turning to the inside cover, you glance at the table containing BP Amoco's financial and operating highlights. From your perusal of the report, you find that BP and Amoco have merged to form BP Amoco, one of the world's leading providers of energy and petrochemicals. You find information about the proposal to merge the two companies, its combined markets, financial highlights, brands, and the board of directors. You determine reported revenues and shareholders' cash dividends. Graphs and charts distributed throughout the report depict the tracked data.

In addition to the charts and graphs comprising the annual report, the document contains features on environmental and social issues and highlights the company's worldwide exploration. You conclude that this is a successful company.

Although the report is distributed to share-holders once a year, production takes nearly six months and requires a team approach involving personnel throughout the corporation. For example, while managers are writing their reports about activities in their departments, photographers are capturing images of oil fields and personnel throughout the world, accountants are gathering financial data, and design team members are planning the document's organization. As press time nears, personnel review manuscripts for accuracy and legality, produce charts and graphs, scan photos, and design pages. Computers allow last-minute changes to be made so the document is as accurate as possible.

Certainly a document such as this company's annual report, complete with charts, tables, and graphs, provides the opportunity for job seekers to analyze their prospects with any prospective employer.

Microsoft Word 2000

Creating a Document with a Table, Chart, and Watermark

P R O J E C T

4

Introduction

In all probability, sometime during your professional life, you will find yourself placed in a sales role. You might be selling a tangible product, such as vehicles or books, or a service, such as Web page design or interior decorating. Within an organization, you might be selling an idea, such as a benefits package to company employees or a budget plan to upper management. To sell an item, whether tangible or intangible, you often will find yourself writing a proposal. Proposals vary in length, style, and formality, but all are designed to elicit acceptance from the reader.

A proposal may be one of three types: planning, research, or sales. A **planning proposal** offers solutions to a problem or improvement to a situation. A **research proposal** usually requests funding for a research project. A **sales proposal** offers a product or service to existing or potential customers.

Project Four — Sales Proposal

Project 4 uses Word to produce the sales proposal shown in Figures 4-1a, 4-1b, and 4-1c. The sales proposal is designed to persuade the reader to hire Super Sounds, a disc jockey service, for his or her next special event. The proposal has a colorful title page to attract the reader's attention. To add impact, the body of the sales proposal has a watermark behind the text and uses tables and a chart to summarize data.

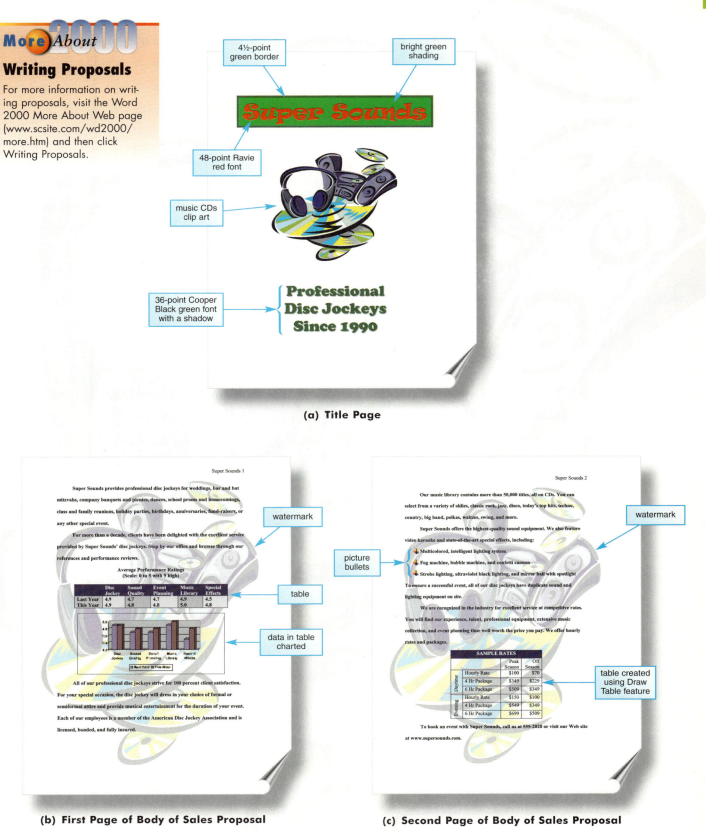

(a) **Title Page**

(b) **First Page of Body of Sales Proposal**

(c) **Second Page of Body of Sales Proposal**

FIGURE 4-1

Sales Proposals

A sales proposal may be solicited or unsolicited. If someone else requests that you develop the proposal, it is solicited, whereas if you write the proposal because you recognize a need, the proposal is unsolicited. A sales proposal is successful if it addresses how its product or service meets the reader's needs better than the competition does.

Starting Word

Follow these steps to start Word or ask your instructor how to start Word for your system.

TO START WORD

1. Click the Start button on the taskbar.

2. Click New Office Document on the Start menu. If necessary, click the General tab when the New Office Document dialog box displays.

3. Double-click the Blank Document icon in the General sheet.

4. If the Word window is not maximized, double-click its title bar to maximize it. Click View on the menu bar and then click Print Layout. If the Office Assistant displays, right-click it and then click Hide on the shortcut menu.

Office starts Word. After a few moments, an empty document titled Document1 displays in the Word window. Because this project contains tables, you will use print layout view; thus, the Print Layout View button on the horizontal scroll bar is recessed.

Resetting Menus and Toolbars

To set the menus and toolbars so they appear exactly as shown in this book, reset your menus and toolbars as outlined in Appendix C or follow these steps.

TO RESET MENUS AND TOOLBARS

1. Click View on the menu bar and then point to Toolbars. Click Customize on the Toolbars submenu.

2. When the Customize dialog box displays, click the Options tab, make sure the top three check boxes have check marks and then click the Reset my usage data button. When the Microsoft Word dialog box displays, click the Yes button.

3. Click the Toolbars tab. Click Standard in the Toolbars list and then click the Reset button. When the Reset Toolbar dialog box displays, click the OK button.

4. Click Formatting in the Toolbars list and then click the Reset button. When the Reset Toolbar dialog box displays, click the OK button. Click the Close button.

Zooming Text Width

As you have learned, when you **zoom text width**, Word displays text on the screen as large as possible in print layout view without extending the right margin beyond the right edge of the document window. Perform these steps to zoom text width.

TO ZOOM TEXT WIDTH

1. Double-click the move handle on the Standard toolbar so the entire toolbar displays. Click the Zoom box arrow on the Standard toolbar.

2 Click Text Width in the Zoom list.

Word computes the zoom percentage based on a variety of settings (see Figure 4-2 on the next page). Your percentage may be different depending on your system configuration.

Displaying Formatting Marks

You have learned that it is helpful to display formatting marks that indicate where in the document you pressed the ENTER key, SPACEBAR, and other keys. Follow this step to display formatting marks.

TO DISPLAY FORMATTING MARKS

1 If the Show/Hide ¶ button on the Standard toolbar is not already recessed, click it.

Word displays formatting marks on the screen (Figure 4-2).

Creating a Title Page

A **title page** should be designed to attract the reader's attention. The title page of the sales proposal in Project 4 (Figure 4-1a on page WD 4.5) contains color, shading, an outside border, shadowed text, clip art, and a variety of fonts and font sizes. The steps on the following pages discuss how to create this title page.

Formatting and Entering Characters

The first step in creating the title page is to enter the company name, centered using 48-point Ravie red font as described below.

TO FORMAT CHARACTERS

1 Double-click the move handle on the Formatting toolbar to display the entire toolbar. Click the Center button on the Formatting toolbar.

2 Click the Font box arrow on the Formatting toolbar. Scroll to and then click Ravie (or a similar font) in the list of available fonts.

3 Click the Font Size box arrow on the Formatting toolbar. Scroll to and then click 48.

4 Click the Font Color button arrow on the Formatting toolbar. Click Red on the color palette.

5 Type Super Sounds and then press the ENTER key.

Word enters the company name, Super Sounds, in 48-point Ravie red font (Figure 4-2).

Adding an Outside Border in Color with Shading

The next step is to surround the company name with a border. You want a 4½-point green outside border with shading in light green. One method of specifying the point size, color, shading, and placement of a border is to use the **Tables and Borders toolbar**. To display the Tables and Borders toolbar, you click the **Tables and Borders button** on the Standard toolbar. When you click the Tables and Borders button, the

Title Pages

Formal proposals often require a specific format for the title page. Beginning about 3-4" from the top margin, the following components are each centered and on separate lines: title; the word, for; reader's name, position, organization, and address; the word, by; your name, position, and organization; and the date the proposal was written.

Borders

You can add a border to any edge of a paragraph. That is, borders may be added above or below a paragraph, to the left or right of a paragraph, or any combination of these sides. To add the most recently defined border, click the Border button on the Formatting toolbar. To change border specifications, use the Tables and Borders toolbar.

Microsoft **Word 2000**

Tables and Borders toolbar displays in the Word window and the Tables and Borders button on the Standard toolbar is recessed. Also, if your screen is not already in print layout view, Word switches to print layout view.

Perform the following steps to add a 4½-point green outside border around the company name.

Steps **To Border a Paragraph**

1 **Click somewhere in line 1 to position the insertion point in the company name. Double-click the move handle on the Standard toolbar to display the entire toolbar. Point to the Tables and Borders button on the Standard toolbar (Figure 4-2).**

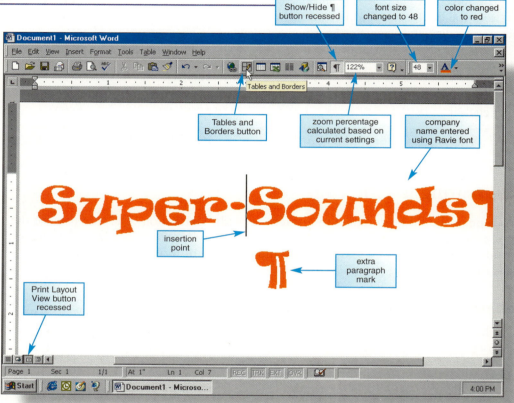

FIGURE 4-2

2 **Click the Tables and Borders button. If the Tables and Borders toolbar is floating in the Word window, point to its title bar.**

The Tables and Borders toolbar displays (Figure 4-3). Depending on the last position of this toolbar, it may be floating or it may be docked.

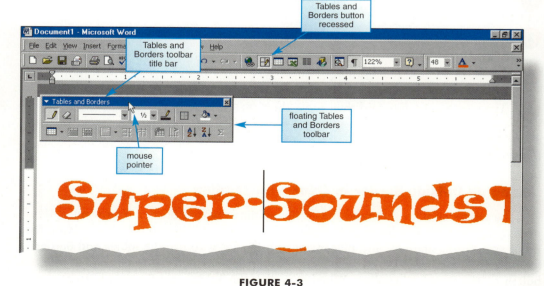

FIGURE 4-3

3 If the Tables and Borders toolbar is floating in the Word window, double-click the title bar of the Tables and Borders toolbar.

Word docks the Tables and Borders toolbar below the Standard and Formatting toolbars.

4 Click the Line Weight box arrow on the Tables and Borders toolbar and then point to 4 ½ pt.

Word displays a list of available line weights (Figure 4-4).

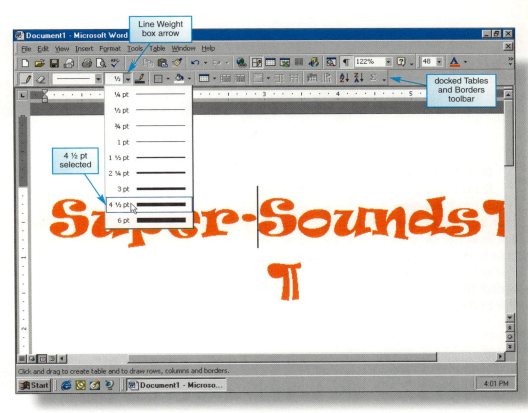

FIGURE 4-4

5 Click 4 ½ pt.

Word changes the line weight to 4 ½ point.

6 Click the Border Color button on the Tables and Borders toolbar. Point to Green on the color palette.

Word displays a color palette for border colors (Figure 4-5).

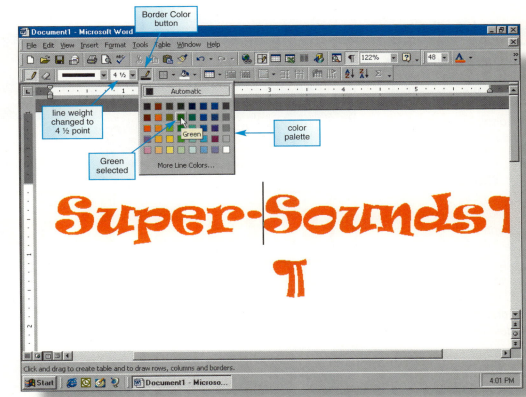

FIGURE 4-5

7 **Click Green.**

Word changes the color of the border to green, as shown in the Line Style box and on the Border Color button.

8 **Click the Outside Border button on the Tables and Borders toolbar. (If your Border button does not show an outside border, click the Border button arrow and then click the Outside Border button.)**

Word places a 4½-point green outside border around the company name (Figure 4-6). The Outside Border button on the Tables and Borders toolbar is recessed.

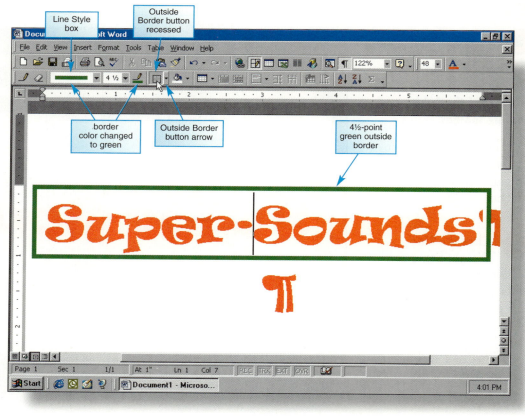

FIGURE 4-6

 9 **Click the Shading Color button arrow on the Tables and Borders toolbar. Point to Bright Green on the color palette.**

Word displays a color palette for shading (Figure 4-7).

10 **Click Bright Green.**

Word shades the current paragraph bright green. To ensure that the next border you draw is not 4½-point green with shading, you should reset the line weight, color, and shading settings to their defaults.

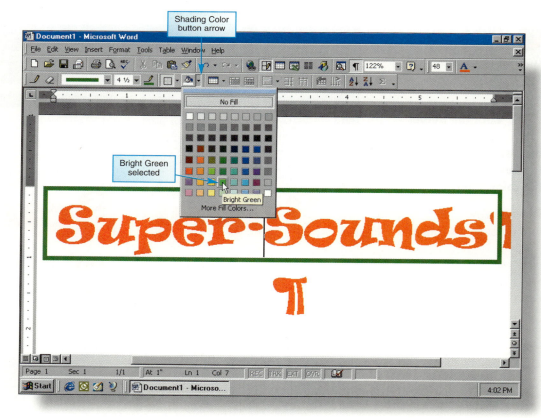

FIGURE 4-7

11 Position the insertion point on the paragraph mark on line 2. Click the Line Weight box arrow on the Tables and Borders toolbar and then click ½ pt. Click the Border Color button on the Tables and Borders toolbar and then click Automatic. Click the Shading Color button arrow and then click No Fill. Point to the Tables and Borders button on the Standard toolbar (Figure 4-8).

12 Click the Tables and Borders button.

The Tables and Borders toolbar no longer displays on the Word screen, and the Tables and Borders button no longer is recessed.

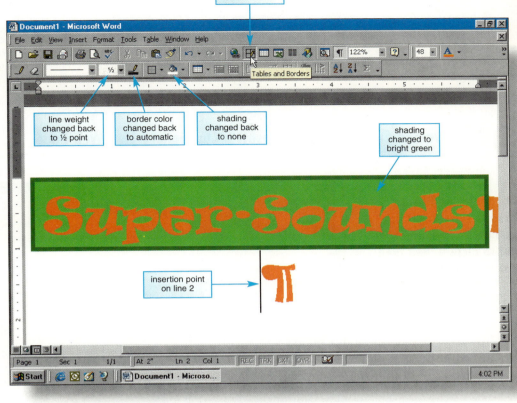

FIGURE 4-8

In an earlier project, you learned the Formatting toolbar also contains a Border button. Word provides two Border buttons. If you want to place a border using the same settings as the most recently defined border, then you simply click the Border button on the Formatting toolbar. If you want to change the size, color, shading, or other settings of the border, then you must use the Tables and Borders toolbar or the Borders and Shading dialog box.

Inserting Clip Art from the Web into a Word Document

You may recall that Word 2000 includes a series of predefined graphics called **clip art** that you can insert into a Word document. This clip art is located in the Clip Gallery, which contains a collection of **clips**, including clip art, photographs, sounds, and video clips.

If you cannot locate an appropriate clip art image in Word's Clip Gallery and have access to the Web, Microsoft provides a special Web page with additional clips, called the **Clip Gallery Live**. Navigating the Clip Gallery Live Web page is similar to using Word's Clip Gallery; that is, you can search for clips based on keywords you enter or you can display categories of clips. If you locate a clip you like, you can download it from the Clip Gallery Live Web page into Word's Clip Gallery.

The next series of steps illustrate how to download a music CDs clip art image from Microsoft's Clip Gallery Live Web page and then insert the clip art image into the Word document.

Other Ways

1. On Format menu click Borders and Shading, click Borders tab, click Box in Setting list, click desired style, color, and width, click Shading tab, click desired shading color, click OK button

More About 2000

The Normal Style

If you forget to leave an extra paragraph mark below a border, the border will carry forward each time you press the ENTER key. To remove a border from the current paragraph, you can click the Style box arrow on the Formatting toolbar and then click Normal. This applies the Normal style to the current paragraph.

Note: The following steps assume you are using Microsoft Internet Explorer as your browser and that you have access to the Web. If you are not using Internet Explorer, you may need to perform a different set of steps. Your browser's handling of pictures on the Web will be discovered in Step 6 on page WD 4.14. If necessary, you may be directed to follow the steps on page WD 4.15 to import the clip art image from the Data Disk. If you do not have access to the Web, go directly to the steps on page WD 4.15.

Steps To Download Clip Art from Microsoft's Clip Gallery Live Web Page

1 **With the insertion point on line 2, press the ENTER key. Click Insert on the menu bar, point to Picture, and then point to Clip Art.**

The insertion point is on line 3 in the document (Figure 4-9).

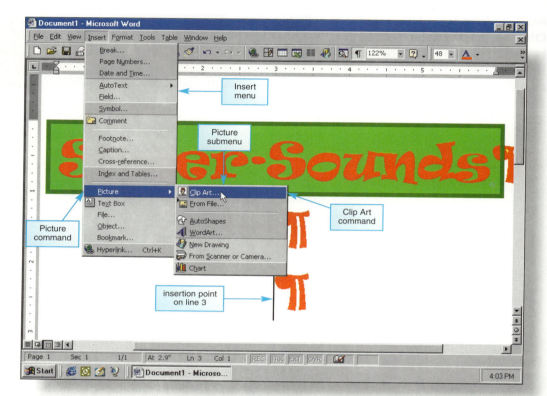

FIGURE 4-9

2 **Click Clip Art. If necessary, click the Pictures tab when the Insert ClipArt window opens. Point to the Clips Online button.**

Word opens the Insert ClipArt window (Figure 4-10).

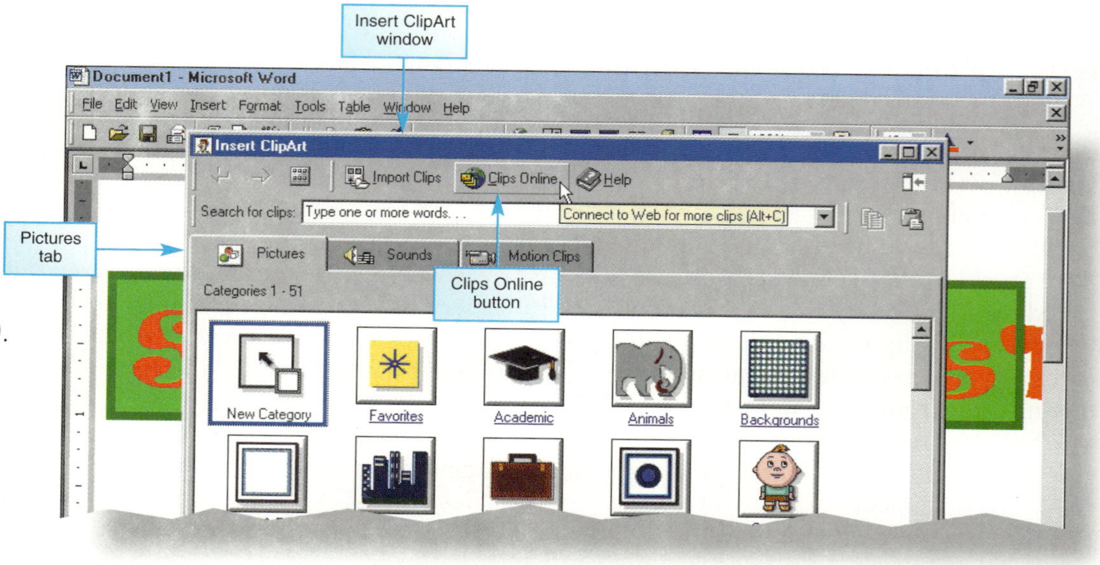

FIGURE 4-10

Click the Clips Online button. If a Connect to Web for More Clip Art, Photos, Sounds dialog box displays, click its OK button. If necessary, maximize your browser window. If Microsoft displays an End-User License Agreement (EULA) in the Clip Gallery Live window, read the EULA and then click the Accept button.

If you currently are not connected to the Web, Word connects you using your default browser. Microsoft Clip Gallery Live displays in a new window.

Click the SEARCH by keyword text box. Type music CDs **and then point to the go button (Figure 4-11).**

Click the go button. Point to the Download This Clip Now icon below the clip you want to download.

Clip Gallery Live displays the clip art associated with key-words you entered (Figure 4-12). The size of each clip art file displays below its image. To download a file into the Clip Gallery, you click the Download This Clip Now icon that displays below the clip.

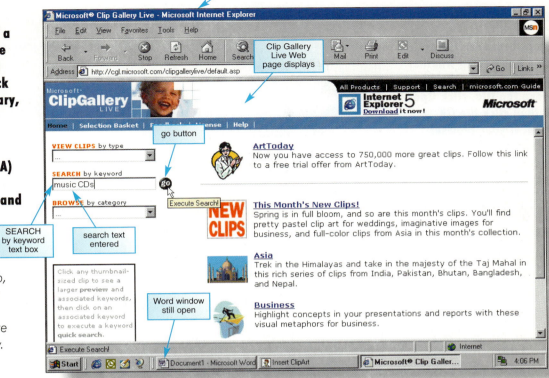

FIGURE 4-11

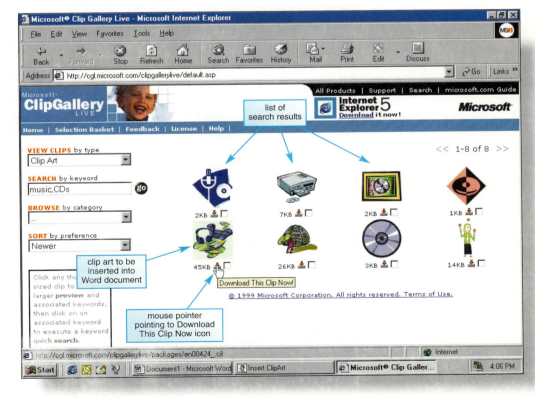

FIGURE 4-12

6 Click the Download This Clip Now icon. (If your browser displays a dialog box asking whether you want to open the file or save the file, click Open and then click the OK button. If your browser displays a dialog box and Open is not an option, close your browser window, and then go to Step 3 on page WD 4.15)

Your browser downloads the file into the Downloaded Clips category of Word's Clip Gallery.

7 When the Insert ClipArt window redisplays, click the downloaded music CDs image and then point to the Insert clip button on the Pop-up menu (Figure 4-13).

8 Click the Insert clip button. Close the Insert ClipArt window. Close your browser window.

Word inserts the clip into your document at the location of the insertion point (Figure 4-14).

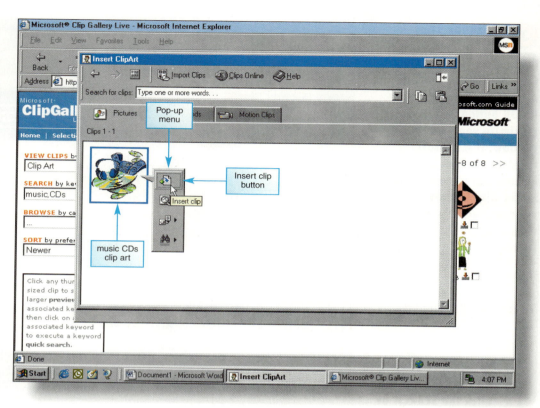

FIGURE 4-13

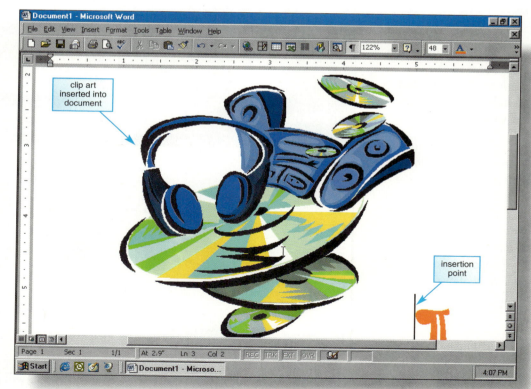

FIGURE 4-14

If you do not have access to the Web, you can import the clip art file into Word's Clip Gallery from the Data Disk as described in the following steps. If you did not download the Data Disk, see the inside back cover for instructions for downloading the Data Disk or see your instructor.

TO IMPORT CLIP ART FROM THE DATA DISK

1 With the insertion point on line 2, press the ENTER key.

2 Click Insert on the menu bar, point to Picture, and then click Clip Art. If necessary, click the Picture tab when the Insert ClipArt window opens.

3 Insert the Data Disk into drive A. Click the Import Clips button in the Insert ClipArt window.

4 When the Add clip to Clip Gallery dialog box displays, click the Look in box arrow and then click 3½ Floppy (A:). Click the file name EN00424_ and then click the Import button. When the Clip Properties dialog box displays, type music CDs, and then click the OK button.

5 When the Insert ClipArt window redisplays, click the music CDs image and then click the Insert clip button on the Pop-up menu. Close the Insert ClipArt window.

Word inserts the clip into your document at the location of the insertion point (see Figure 4-14).

Entering and Formatting the Company Slogan

The next step is to enter the company slogan below the graphic on the title page. The slogan is 36-point Cooper Black green font. The characters also are formatted with a shadow. A **shadow** is a light gray duplicate image that displays on the lower-right edge of a character or object.

Because you display the Font dialog box to add a shadow to characters, you can change the font, font size, and font color all at once using the Font dialog box, instead of using the Formatting toolbar. Perform the following steps to format the slogan using the Font dialog box.

Steps To Format and Enter the Company Slogan

1 With the insertion point positioned as shown in Figure 4-14, press the ENTER key twice. Right-click the paragraph mark at the end of the document and then point to Font on the shortcut menu.

Word displays a shortcut menu (Figure 4-15). The insertion point is immediately in front of the last paragraph mark in the document (line 5).

FIGURE 4-15

Removing Borders

If you wanted to remove a border from a paragraph, you would position the insertion point somewhere in the paragraph containing the border, click the Border button arrow on either the Formatting toolbar or on the Tables and Borders toolbar, and then click No Border on the border palette.

Graphics

In addition to clip art, you can insert drawing objects such as shapes, lines, curves, arrows, flowchart symbols, and stars into Word documents. To do this, display the Drawing toolbar by clicking the Drawing button on the Standard toolbar. Then, click the appropriate button on the Drawing toolbar and use the mouse to draw the object on the screen.

Clip Art

For more information on clip art, visit the Word 2000 More About Web page (www.scsite.com/wd2000/more.htm) and then click Clip Art.

2 **Click Font. If necessary, click the Font tab when the Font dialog box displays. Scroll through the Font list and then click Cooper Black (or a similar font). Scroll through the Size list and then click 36. Click the Font color box arrow and then click Green. Click Shadow in the Effects area. Point to the OK button.**

The Preview area reflects the current selections (Figure 4-16).

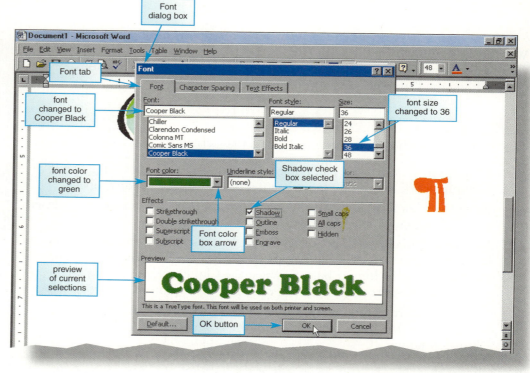

FIGURE 4-16

3 **Click the OK button. Type** Professional **and then press the ENTER key. Type** Disc Jockeys **and then press the ENTER key. Type** Since 1990 **to complete the slogan.**

Word displays the company slogan formatted to 36-point Cooper Black green font with a shadow (Figure 4-17).

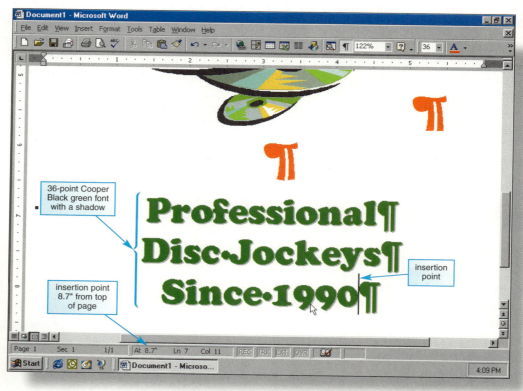

FIGURE 4-17

In addition to a shadow, the Font dialog box (Figure 4-16) contains many other effects you can add to characters in a document. Table 4-1 illustrates the result of each of these effects.

Centering the Title Page Text Vertically on the Page

For visual appeal, you would like to center the text on the title page vertically; that is, between the top and bottom margins. You have learned that the default top margin in Word is one inch, which includes a one-half inch header. Notice in Figure 4-17 that the insertion point, which is at the end of the title page text, is 8.7" from the top of the page. Thus, the space at the bottom of the page currently is approximately two and one-third inches.

Perform the following steps to center text vertically on a page.

Table 4-1	Character Effects Available in Font Dialog Box	
TYPE OF EFFECT	**PLAIN TEXT**	**FORMATTED TEXT**
Strikethrough	Super Sounds	~~Super Sounds~~
Double strikethrough	Professional	~~Professional~~
Superscript	102	10^2
Subscript	H20	H_2O
Shadow	Disc Jockey	**Disc Jockey**
Outline	Disc Jockey	Disc Jockey
Emboss	Disc Jockey	Disc Jockey
Engrave	Disc Jockey	Disc Jockey
Small caps	Disc Jockey	DISC JOCKEY
All caps	Disc Jockey	DISC JOCKEY
Hidden	Disc Jockey	

To Center Text Vertically

1 Click File on the menu bar and then point to Page Setup (Figure 4-18).

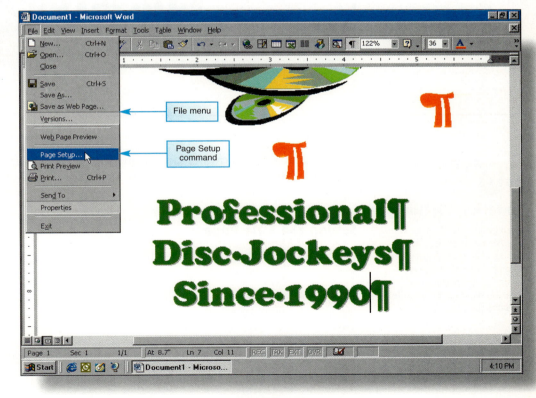

FIGURE 4-18

2 Click Page Setup. If necessary, click the Layout tab when the Page Setup dialog box displays. Click the Vertical alignment box arrow and then click Center. Point to the OK button.

Word displays the Page Setup dialog box (Figure 4-19). The vertical alignment is changed to Center.

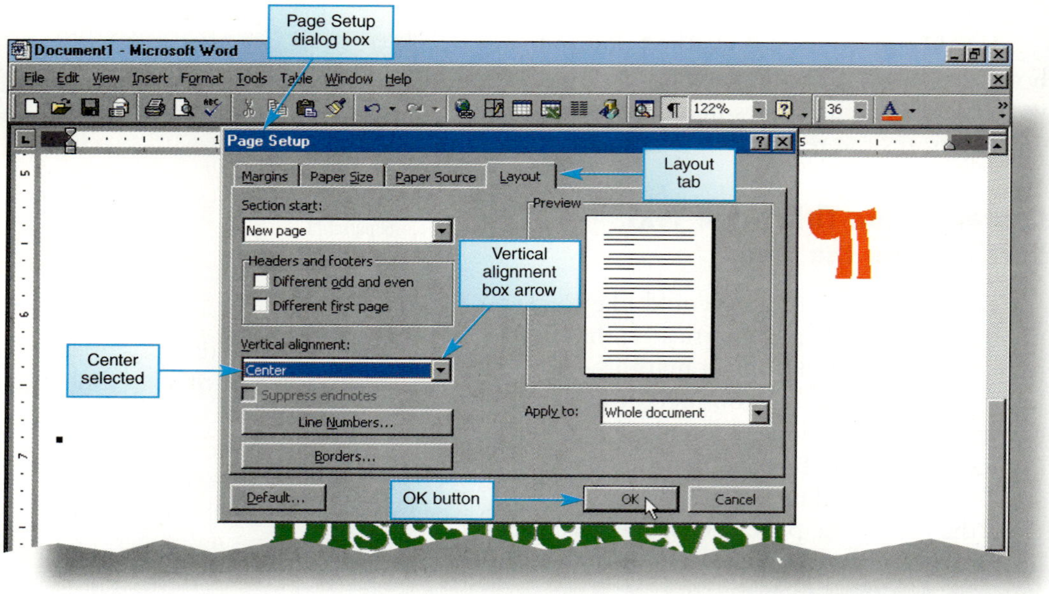

FIGURE 4-19

3 Click the OK button.

Word centers the text on the title page vertically (Figure 4-20).

FIGURE 4-20

Centering Vertically

When you center a page vertically, Word does not change the size of the top and bottom margins. Instead, it changes the size of the header and footer areas to accommodate the extra spacing.

The status bar shows the insertion point now is 9" from the top of the document (Figure 4-20), which means the empty space above and below the text totals approximately two inches.

Saving the Title Page

Save the title page by performing the following steps.

TO SAVE A DOCUMENT

1 Insert a floppy disk into drive A. Click the Save button on the Standard toolbar.

2 Type Super Sounds Title Page in the File name text box.

3 Click the Save in box arrow and then click 3½ Floppy (A:).

4 Click the Save button in the Save As dialog box.

Word saves the document on a floppy disk in drive A with the file name Super Sounds Title Page (Figure 4-21).

The title page for the sales proposal is complete. The next step is to insert a draft of the proposal after the title page.

Inserting an Existing Document into an Open Document

Assume you already have prepared a draft of the body of the proposal and saved it with the file name Super Sounds Draft. You would like the draft to display on a separate page below the title page. Once the two documents display on the screen together as one document, you would like to save this active document with a new name so each of the original documents remains intact.

You want the inserted pages of the sales proposal to use the Times New Roman font and be left-aligned. That is, you want to return to the Normal style. Because the text to be entered at the insertion point currently is formatted for paragraphs to be centered using 36-point Cooper Black green font with a shadow, you should apply the Normal style as shown in the steps below.

More About

Drafting a Proposal

All proposals should have an introduction, body, and conclusion. The introduction could contain the subject, purpose, statement of problem, need, background, or scope. The body may include available or required facilities, cost, feasibility, methods, timetable, materials, or equipment. The conclusion summarizes key points or requests some action.

Steps To Apply the Normal Style

1 **Be sure the insertion point is on the paragraph mark on line 7 and then press the ENTER key. Double-click the move handle on the Formatting toolbar to display the entire toolbar. Click the Style box arrow on the Formatting toolbar and then point to Normal.**

Word displays the list of available styles (Figure 4-21). Notice the paragraph mark on line 8 is formatted the same as the slogan because when you press the ENTER key, formatting is carried forward to the next paragraph.

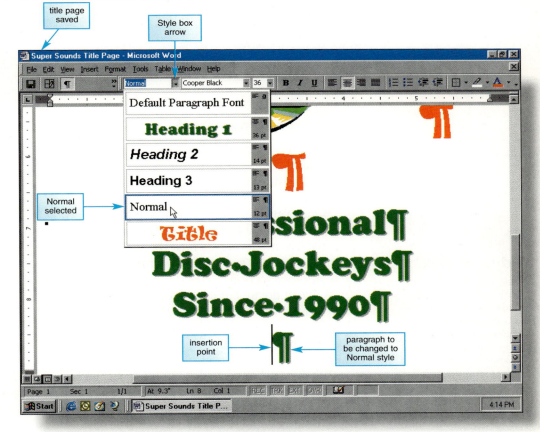

FIGURE 4-21

2 **Click Normal.**

Word returns the paragraph mark at the location of the insertion point to the Normal style (Figure 4-22). That is, the paragraph mark is left-aligned and the text to be entered is 12-point Times New Roman. Depending on your installation of Word, the Normal style might be a different font or font size.

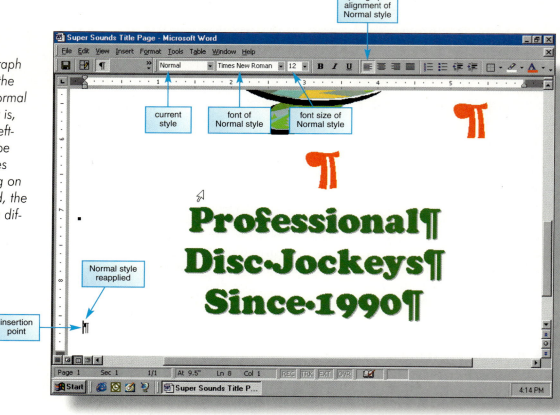

FIGURE 4-22

Inserting a Section Break

The body of the sales proposal requires different page formatting than the title page. Recall that you vertically centered the text on the title page. The body of the proposal should have top alignment; that is, it should begin one inch from the top of the page.

Whenever you want to change page formatting for a portion of a document, you must create a new **section** in the document. Each section then may be formatted differently than the others. Thus, the title page formatted with vertical alignment must be in one section, and the body of the proposal formatted with top alignment must be in another section.

A Word document can be divided into any number of sections. All documents have at least one section. If during the course of creating a document, you need to change the top margin, bottom margin, page alignment, paper size, page orientation, page number position, or contents or position of headers, footers, or footnotes, you must create a new section.

When you create a new section, a **section break** displays on the screen as a double dotted line separated by the words, Section Break. Section breaks do not print. When you create a section break, you specify whether or not the new section should begin on a new page.

The body of the sales proposal is to be on a separate page after the title page. Perform the following steps to insert a section break that begins the new section on the next page of the document.

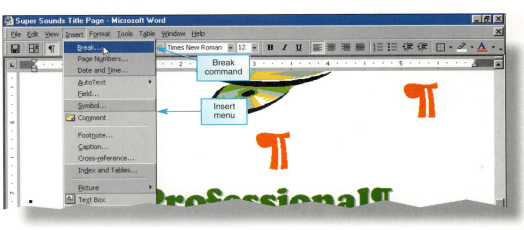

Steps: To Insert a Next Page Section Break

1 Be sure the insertion point is positioned on the paragraph mark on line 8 (see Figure 4-22). Click Insert on the menu bar and then point to Break (Figure 4-23).

FIGURE 4-23

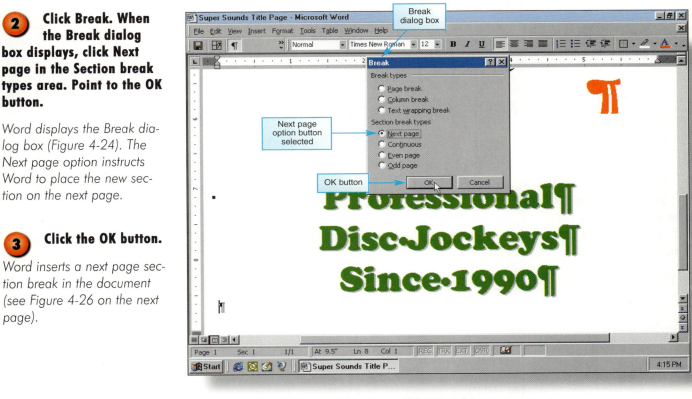

2 Click Break. When the Break dialog box displays, click Next page in the Section break types area. Point to the OK button.

Word displays the Break dialog box (Figure 4-24). The Next page option instructs Word to place the new section on the next page.

3 Click the OK button.

Word inserts a next page section break in the document (see Figure 4-26 on the next page).

FIGURE 4-24

The insertion point and paragraph mark are placed in the new section, which Word places on a new page. Notice in Figure 4-25 on the next page that the status bar indicates the insertion point is on page 2 in section 2. Also, the insertion point is set at 5.4" because earlier you changed the page formatting to vertical alignment. You want the body of the proposal to have top alignment. Thus, follow the steps on the next page to change the alignment of section 2 from center to top.

To Align Text with Top of Page

1 **Be sure the insertion point is in section 2. Click File on the menu bar and then click Page Setup. If necessary, click the Layout tab when the Page Setup dialog box displays. Click the Vertical alignment box arrow and then click Top. Point to the OK button.**

Word displays the Page Setup dialog box (Figure 4-25).

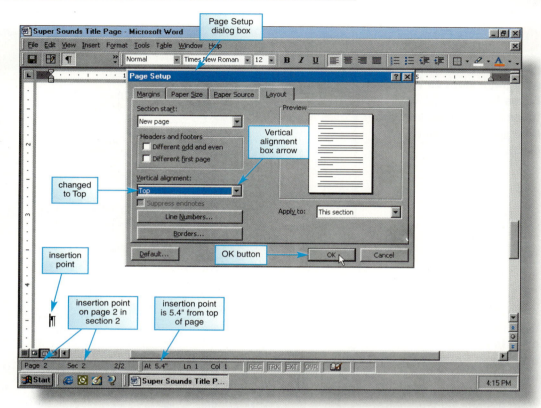

FIGURE 4-25

2 **Click the OK button. Scroll up so the bottom of page 1 and the top of page 2 display in the document window.**

Word changes the vertical alignment to top (Figure 4-26). Notice the status bar indicates the insertion point now is positioned 1" from the top of the page, which is the top margin setting.

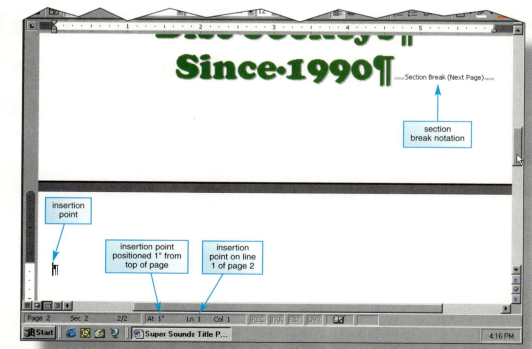

FIGURE 4-26

Word stores all section formatting in the section break. Notice in Figure 4-26 that the section break notation displays on the screen as the words, Section Break (Next Page). You can delete a section break and all associated section formatting by selecting the section break notation, right-clicking the selection, and then clicking Cut on the shortcut menu. To select a section break, point to its left until the mouse pointer changes direction and then click. If you accidentally delete a section break, you can bring it back by clicking the Undo button on the Standard toolbar.

Inserting a Word Document into an Open Document

The next step is to insert the draft of the sales proposal after the section break. The draft is located on the Data Disk. If you did not download the Data Disk, see the inside back cover for instructions for downloading the Data Disk or see your instructor.

If you created a Word file at an earlier time, you may have forgotten its name. For this reason, Word provides a means to display the contents of, or **preview**, any file before you insert it. Perform the following steps to preview and then insert the draft of the proposal into the open document.

Files

In the Insert and Open File dialog boxes, click the Views button arrow to change how the files display in the dialog box. Click the Tools button arrow and then click Delete to delete the selected file. Click the Tools button arrow and then click Properties to display a variety of information about the selected file.

Steps **To Insert a Word Document into an Open Document**

1 **If necessary, insert the Data Disk into drive A. Be sure the insertion point is positioned on the paragraph mark immediately below the section break. Click Insert on the menu bar and then point to File (Figure 4-27).**

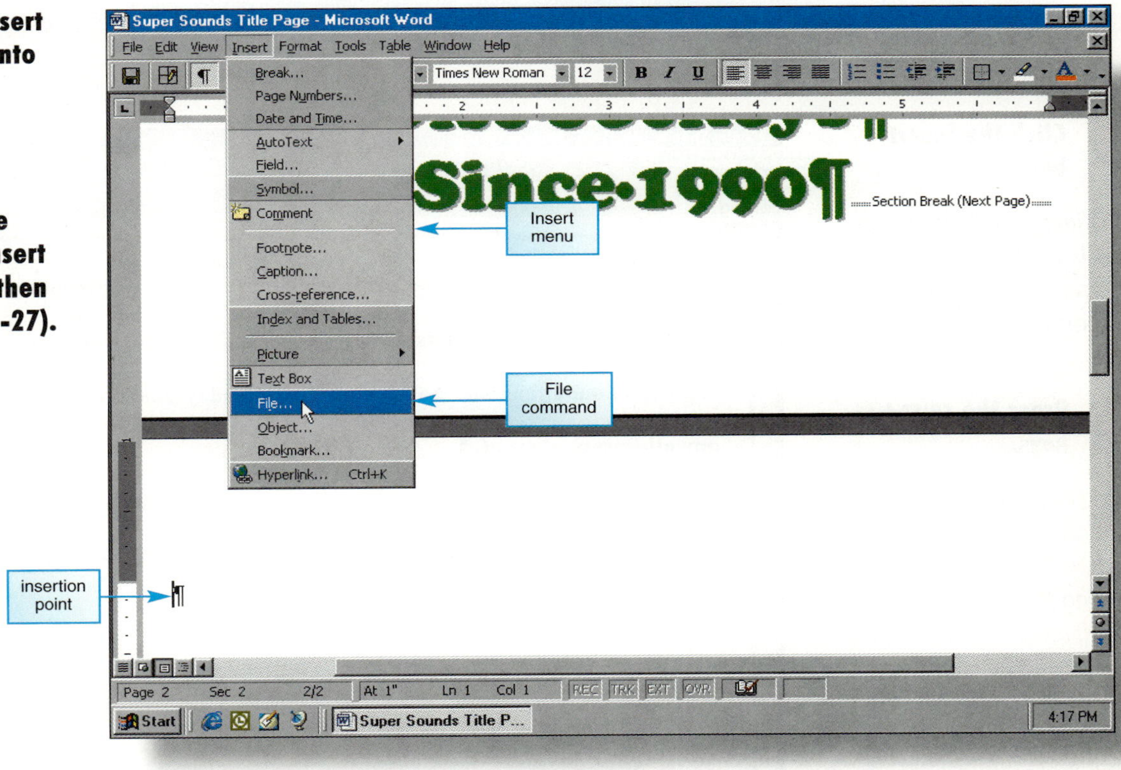

FIGURE 4-27

2 **Click File. When the Insert File dialog box displays, click the Look in box arrow and then click 3½ Floppy (A:). Click the Views button arrow and then click Preview. Click Super Sounds Draft and then point to the Insert button.**

Word displays the Insert File dialog box (Figure 4-28). A list of Word documents on the Data Disk displays. The contents of the selected file (Super Sounds Draft) display on the right side of the dialog box.

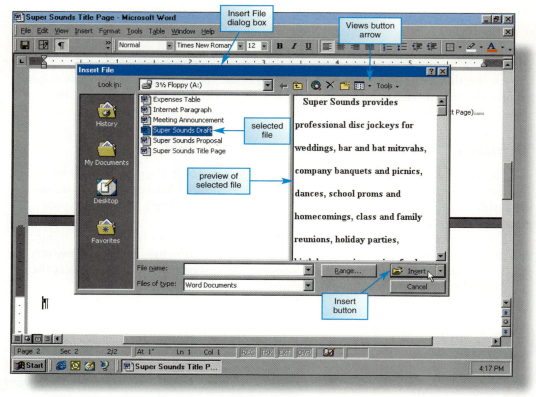

FIGURE 4-28

3 **Click the Insert button.**

Word inserts the file, Super Sounds Draft, into the open document at the location of insertion point.

4 **Press the SHIFT+F5 keys.**

Word positions the insertion point on line 1 of page 2, which was its location prior to inserting the new Word document (Figure 4-29). Pressing the SHIFT+F5 keys instructs Word to return the insertion point to your last editing location.

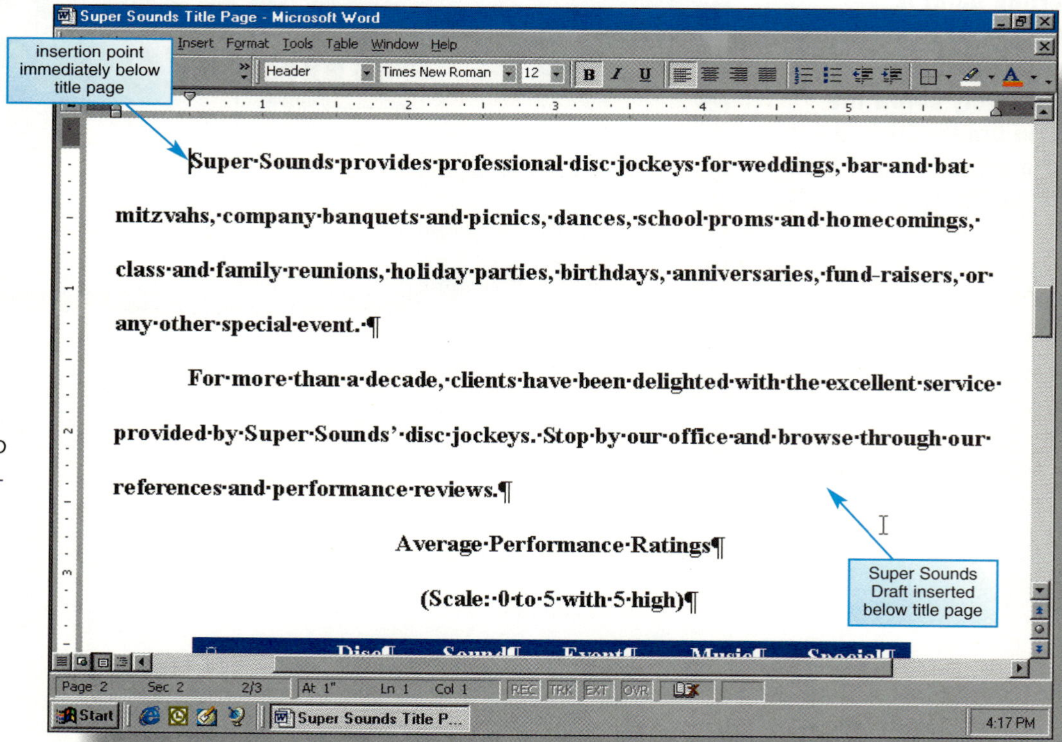

FIGURE 4-29

Word inserts the entire document at the location of the insertion point. If the insertion point, therefore, is positioned in the middle of the open document when you insert another Word document, the open document continues after the last character of the inserted document.

As illustrated in Figure 4-28, previewing files before opening them is very useful if you have forgotten the name of a particular file. For this reason, you can preview files by clicking the Views button arrow in both the Open and Insert File dialog boxes.

Saving the Active Document with a New File Name

The current file name on the title bar is Super Sounds Title Page, yet the active document contains both the title page and the draft of the sales proposal. Because you might want to keep the title page as a separate document called Super Sounds Title Page, you should save the active document with a new file name. If you save the active document by clicking the Save button on the Standard toolbar, Word will assign it the current file name. You want the active document to have a new file name. Thus, use the following steps to save the active document with a new file name.

TO SAVE AN ACTIVE DOCUMENT WITH A NEW FILE NAME

① If necessary, insert the floppy disk containing your title page into drive A.

② Click File on the menu bar and then click Save As.

③ Type Super Sounds Proposal in the File name text box. Do not press the ENTER key.

④ If necessary, click the Save in box arrow and then click 3½ Floppy (A:).

⑤ Click the Save button in the Save As dialog box.

Word saves the document on a floppy disk in drive A with the file name Super Sounds Proposal (see Figure 4-31 on page WD 4.28).

Printing Certain Pages in a Document

The title page is the first page of the proposal. The body of the proposal is the second and third pages. To see a hard copy of the body of the proposal, perform the following steps.

TO PRINT A DOCUMENT

① Ready the printer.

② Click File on the menu bar and then click Print.

③ When the Print dialog box displays, click Pages in the Page range area. Type 2-3 and then click the OK button.

Word prints the draft of the sales proposal (Figure 4-30a on the next page).

SHIFT+F5

Word remembers your last three editing or typing locations. Thus, you can press the SHIFT+F5 keys up to three times to move the insertion point to previous editing locations in your document. This feature works even after you save and then re-open a document.

File Save As

You can press F12 to display the Save As dialog box when you want to assign a new file name to an existing file.

Printing Colors

If you have a black-and-white printer and print a document with colors, the colors other than black or white will print in shades of gray.

header to contain company name and page number

bullet style to change

- **Multicolored, intelligent lighting system**
- **Fog machine, bubble machine, and confetti cannon**
- **Strobe lighting, ultraviolet black lighting, and mirror ball with spotlight**

To ensure a successful event, all of our disc jockeys have duplicate sound and lighting equipment on site.

We are recognized in the industry for excellent service at competitive rates. You will find our experience, talent, professional equipment, extensive music collection, and event planning time well worth the price you pay. We offer hourly rates and packages.

location for table to be created with Draw Table feature

To book an event with Super Sounds, call us at 555-2020 or visit our Web site at www.supersounds.com.

header to contain company name and page number

Super Sounds provides professional disc jockeys for weddings, bar and bat mitzvahs, company banquets and picnics, dances, school proms and homecomings, class and family reunions, holiday parties, birthdays, anniversaries, fund-raisers, or any other special event.

For more than a decade, clients have been delighted with the excellent service provided by Super Sounds' disc jockeys. Stop by our office and browse through our references and performance reviews.

Average Performance Ratings

(Scale: 0 to 5 with 5 high)

Word table created with Insert Table button

	Disc Jockey	Sound Quality	Event Planning	Music Library	Special Effects
Last Year	4.9	4.7	4.7	4.9	4.5
This Year	4.9	4.8	4.8	5.0	4.8

location for chart of Word table

All of our professional disc jockeys strive for 100 percent client satisfaction. For your special occasion, the disc jockey will dress in your choice of formal or semiformal attire and provide musical entertainment for the duration of your event. Each of our employees is a member of the American Disc Jockey Association and is licensed, bonded, and fully insured.

Our music library contains more than 50,000 titles, all on CDs. You can select from a variety of oldies, classic rock, jazz, disco, today's top hits, techno, country, big band, polkas, waltzes, swing, and more.

Super Sounds offers the highest-quality sound equipment. We also feature video karaoke and state-of-the-art special effects, including:

More About 2000

Proposal Wording

Be specific with descriptions in the sales proposal. Avoid vague, general, or abstract words, which could be misinterpreted by the reader. For example, the sentence, "the house is large," is too general. The sentence, "the house has 4,500 square feet with 5 bedrooms and 3 bathrooms," is more descriptive.

FIGURE 4-30a Super Sounds Draft

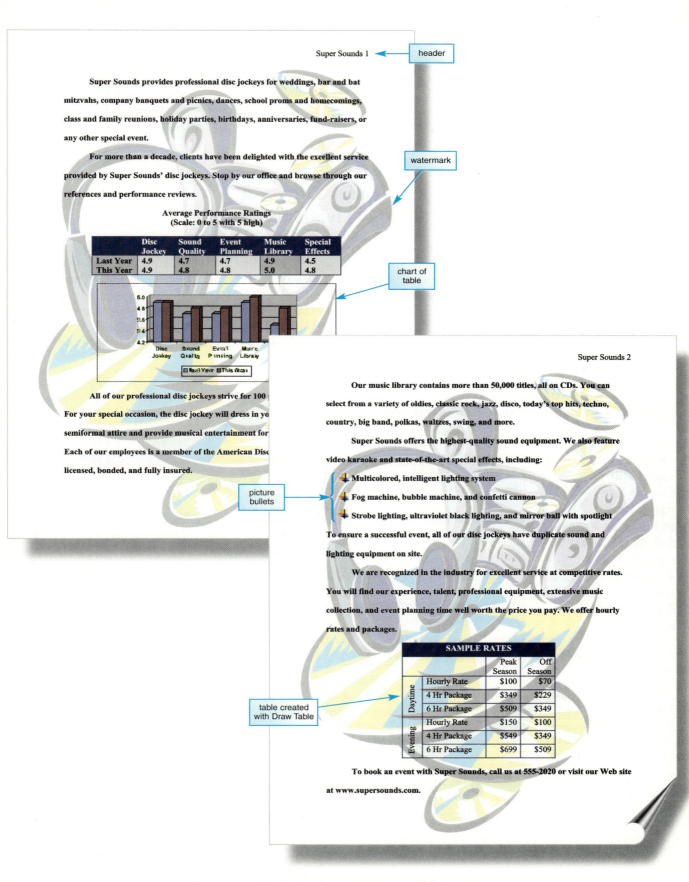

FIGURE 4-30b Body of Sales Proposal with Enhancements

When you remove the document from the printer, review it carefully. Depending on the printer driver you are using, wordwrap may occur in different locations from those shown in Figure 4-30a on the previous page.

By adding a header, charting the table, changing the bullets to picture bullets, and inserting another table into the document, you can make the body of the proposal more pleasing to the eye. These enhancements to the body of the sales proposal are shown in Figure 4-30b on the previous page and are discussed in the following pages.

Creating a Header Different from the Previous Header

You want the company name and page number to display on the body of the sales proposal; however, you do not want this header on the title page. Recall that the title page and the body of the sales proposal are in separate sections. You do not want a header in section 1, but you do want a header in section 2. When you initially create a header, Word assumes you want it in all sections. Thus, when you create the header in section 2, you must instruct Word to not place it in section 1.

Perform the following steps to add a header to the pages in the body of the sales proposal.

Steps: To Add a Header Different from a Previous Header

1 **With the insertion point still positioned on line 1 of page 2, click View on the menu bar and then click Header and Footer. Point to the Same as Previous button on the Header and Footer toolbar.**

Word displays the Header and Footer toolbar (Figure 4-31). Notice the Same as Previous button is recessed, which, when recessed, instructs Word to place the header in the previous section also.

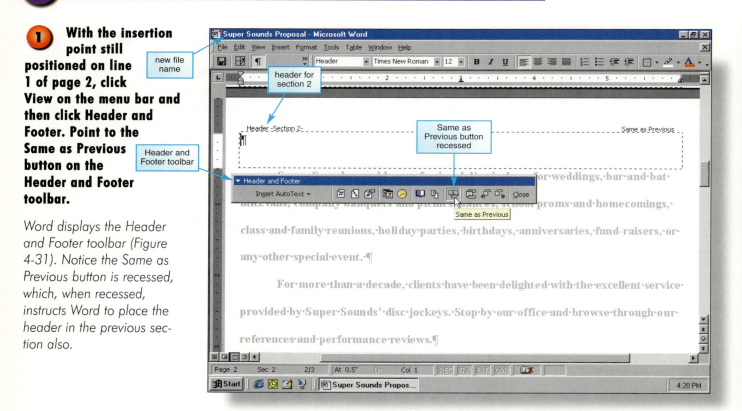

FIGURE 4-31

2 **Click the Same as Previous button.**
Point to the right edge of the header area and then double-click when a right-align icon displays next to the I-beam. Type Super Sounds **and then press the SPACEBAR. Click the Insert Page Number button on the Header and Footer toolbar.**

Word displays the header for section 2 (Figure 4-32). The Same as Previous button no longer is recessed.

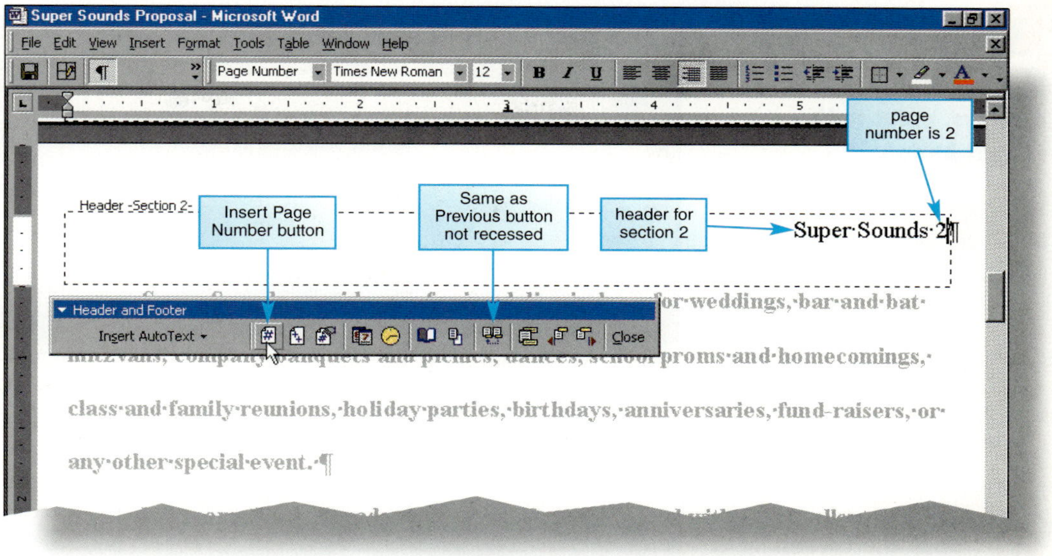

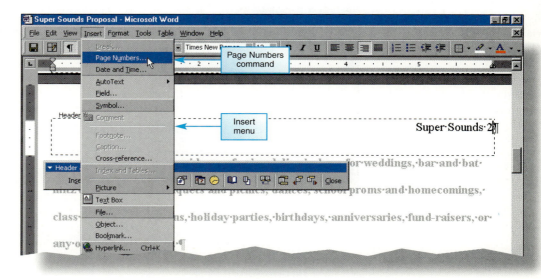

FIGURE 4-32

The next step is to change the starting page number in a section. Leave the header displaying on the screen for the next series of steps.

Changing the Starting Page Number in a Section

In Figure 4-32, the page number is a 2 because Word begins numbering pages from the beginning of the document. You want to begin numbering the body of the sales proposal with a number 1. Thus, you need to instruct Word to begin numbering the pages in section 2 with the number 1.

Perform the following steps to page number differently in a section.

 To Page Number Differently in a Section

1 **With the header displayed on the screen, click Insert on the menu bar and then point to Page Numbers (Figure 4-33).**

FIGURE 4-33

2 **Click Page Numbers. When the Page Numbers dialog box displays, point to the Format button.**

Word displays the Page Numbers dialog box (Figure 4-34).

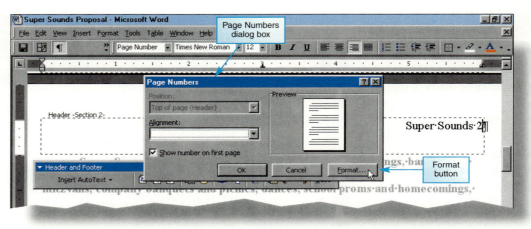

FIGURE 4-34

3 **Click the Format button. When the Page Number Format dialog box displays, click Start at in the Page numbering area and then point to the OK button.**

Word displays the Page Number Format dialog box (Figure 4-35). By default, the number 1 displays in the Start at box.

FIGURE 4-35

4 **Click the OK button. When the Page Numbers dialog box is visible again, click its Close button.**

Word changes the starting page number for section 2 to the number 1 (Figure 4-36).

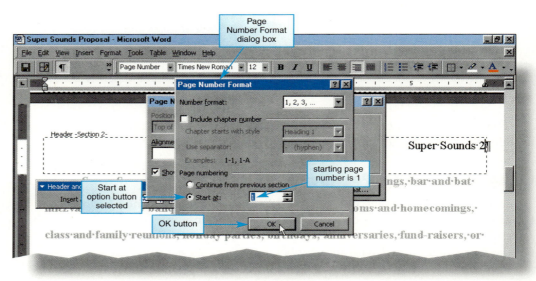

FIGURE 4-36

The next step is to close the header area as described in the following step.

TO CLOSE THE HEADER AREA

1 Click the Close Header and Footer button on the Header and Footer toolbar.

Word removes the Header and Footer toolbar from the screen.

Charting a Table

The sales proposal draft contains a Word table (see Figure 4-30a on page WD 4.26) that was created using the Insert Table button on the Standard toolbar. This table contains three rows and six columns. The first row identifies the performance category; the second and third rows show the average performance ratings for last year and this year, respectively. The first column identifies the year, and the remaining columns show the average performance rating for each performance category.

You would like to create a chart of this table (see Figure 4-30b on page WD 4.27) to show graphically the average performance ratings for Super Sounds. The following pages explain how to modify the table, chart its contents, modify the chart, and then format the chart.

Changing Line Spacing

You would like to modify the paragraph containing the table title so that it is single-spaced, instead of double-spaced. Perform the following steps to single-space this paragraph.

TO SINGLE-SPACE A PARAGRAPH

1 Scroll down to display the table title. Click in the table title, Average Performance Ratings.

2 Press CTRL+1 (the numeral one).

Word removes the blank line between the first and second lines of the table title (Figure 4-37).

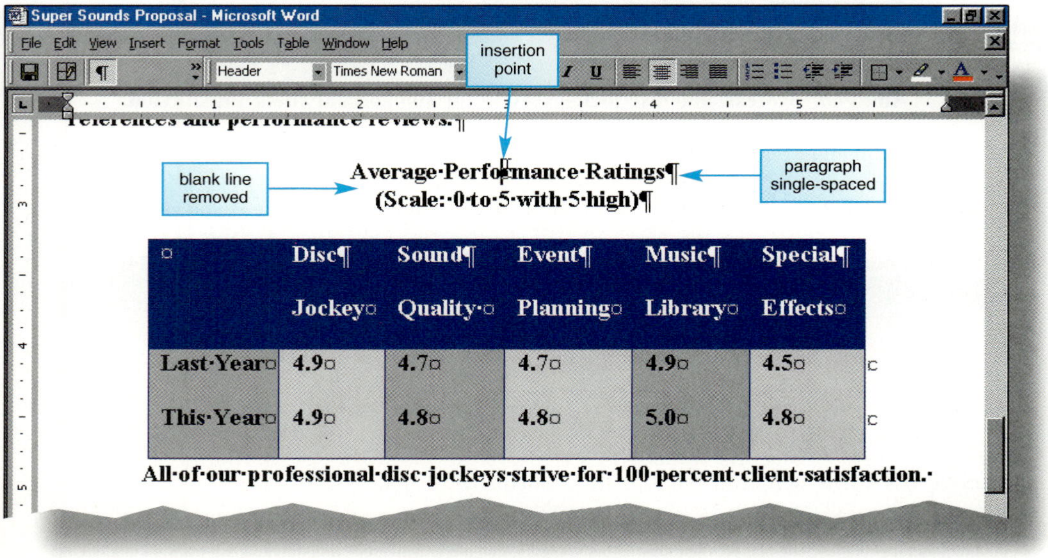

Word 2000 Features

For more information on features and capabilities of Word 2000, visit the Word 2000 More About Web page (www.scsite.com/wd2000/more.htm) and then click Features and Capabilities of Word 2000.

FIGURE 4-37

You also would like the contents of the table to be single-spaced, instead of double-spaced. To accomplish this, you first select the entire table and then change the line spacing to single, as shown in the following steps.

Steps **To Change Line Spacing in a Table**

1 **Position the insertion point somewhere in the table. Click Table on the menu bar, point to Select, and then point to Table (Figure 4-38).**

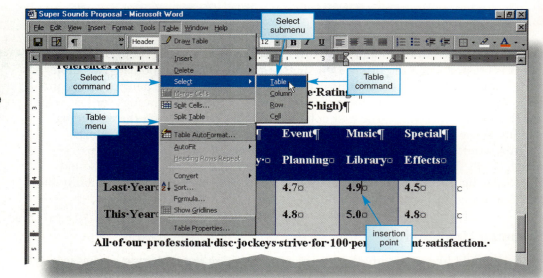

FIGURE 4-38

2 **Click Table to select the entire table. Press CTRL+1 (the numeral one).**

Word single-spaces the contents of the table (Figure 4-39).

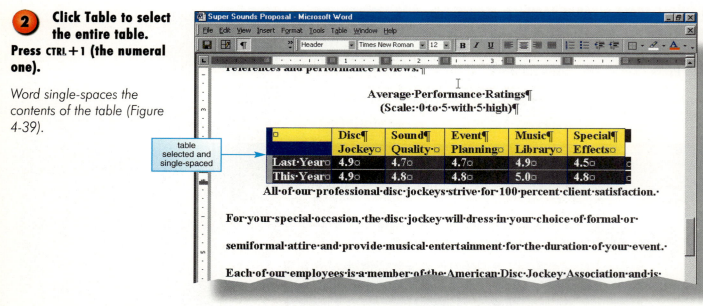

FIGURE 4-39

Other **Ways**

1. On Format menu click Paragraph, click Indents and Spacing tab, click Line spacing box arrow, click Single, click OK button

Leave the table selected for the next series of steps.

Creating a Chart from a Word Table

When you create a Word table, you easily can chart the data using an embedded charting application called **Microsoft Graph 2000**. Because Graph is an embedded application, it has its own menus and commands. With these commands, you can modify the appearance of the chart.

To create a chart from a Word table, the top row and left column of the table must contain text labels, and the other cells in the table must contain numbers. The table in the Super Sounds Draft meets these criteria.

To chart a Word table, you first select it and then chart it. The table in this document still is selected from the previous steps. Thus, perform the following steps to chart a selected table.

Steps: To Chart a Table

1 With the table selected as shown in Figure 4-39, click Insert on the menu bar, point to Picture, and then point to Chart (Figure 4-40).

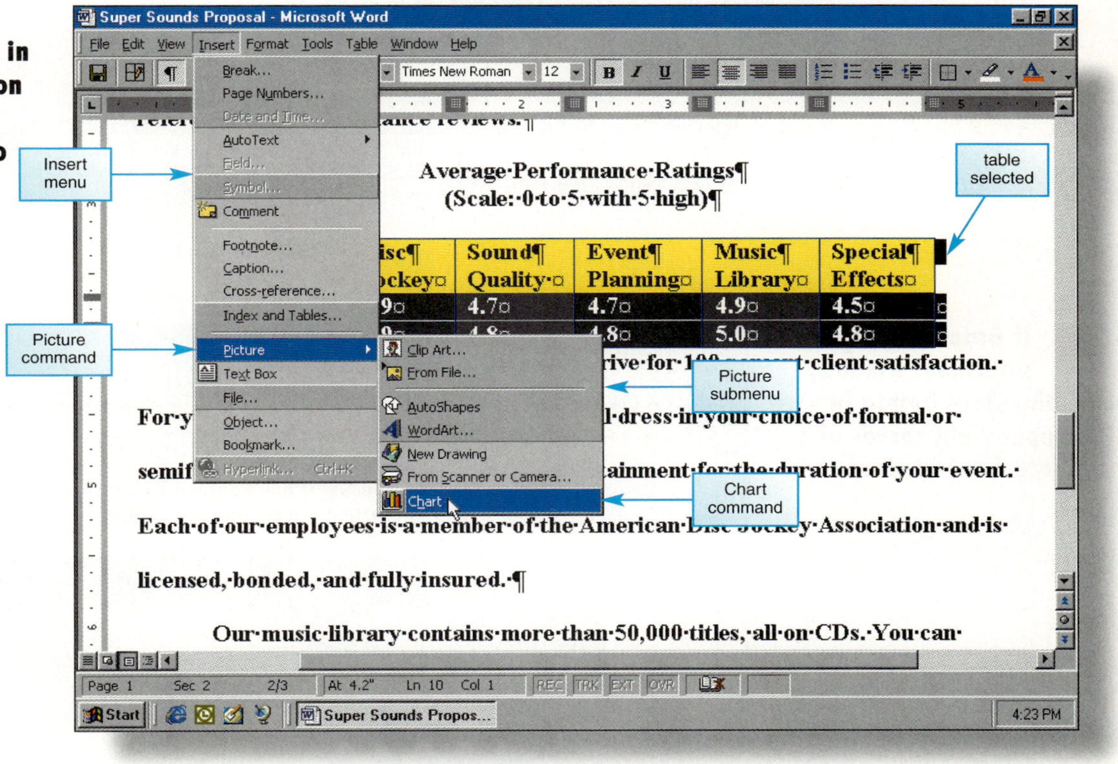

FIGURE 4-40

2 **Click Chart.**

Word starts the Microsoft Graph 2000 application (Figure 4-41). Graph creates a chart of the selected table.

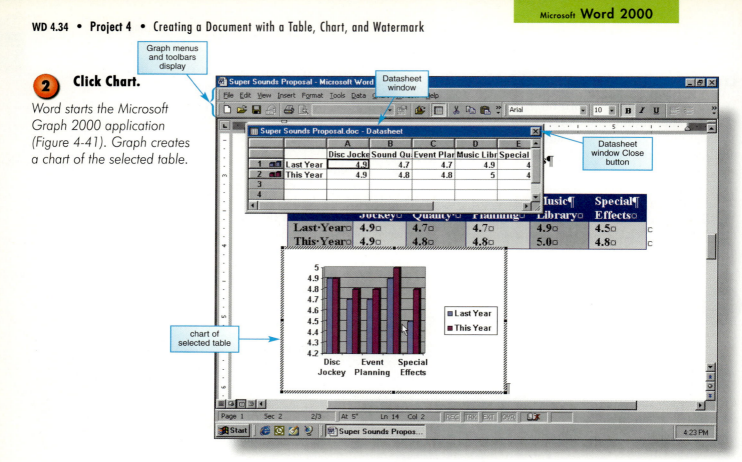

FIGURE 4-41

3 **If Graph displays a Datasheet window, click the Close button in the upper-right corner of the Datasheet window.**

Word closes the Datasheet window (Figure 4-42).

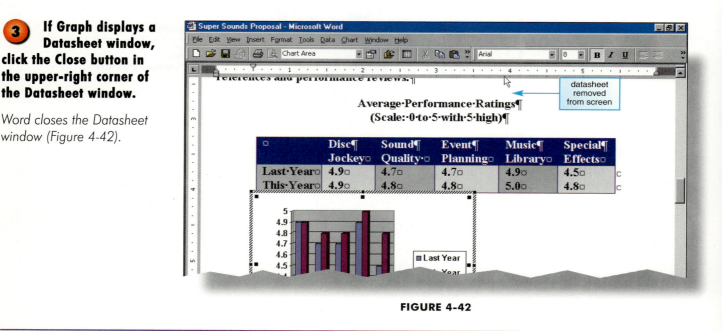

FIGURE 4-42

The menus on the menu bar and buttons on the toolbars change to Graph menus and toolbars. The Graph program is running inside your Word program.

Graph places the contents of the table into a **Datasheet window**, also called a **datasheet** (see Figure 4-41). Graph then charts the contents of the datasheet. Although you can modify the contents of the datasheet, it is not necessary in this project; thus, you close the Datasheet window.

Changing the Chart in Graph

You would like to change the format of the numbers on the value axis, move the legend so it displays below the chart, and resize the chart.

The **value axis** is a vertical axis along the left edge of the chart. Most numbers along the value axis display with one position after the decimal point; however, the top number displays as a whole number with no positions after the decimal point.

Perform the following steps so that all the numbers on the value axis display with one position after the decimal point.

Steps **To Format Numbers on the Value Axis of a Chart**

1 **Point to the value axis.**

Graph displays the ScreenTip, Value Axis (Figure 4-43).

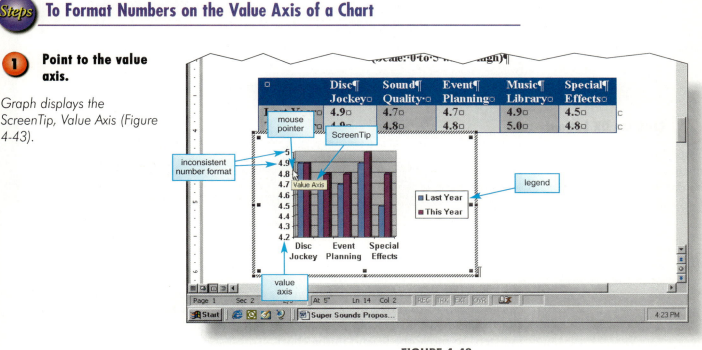

FIGURE 4-43

2 **Right-click the value axis. Point to Format Axis on the shortcut menu.**

Graph displays a shortcut menu (Figure 4-44).

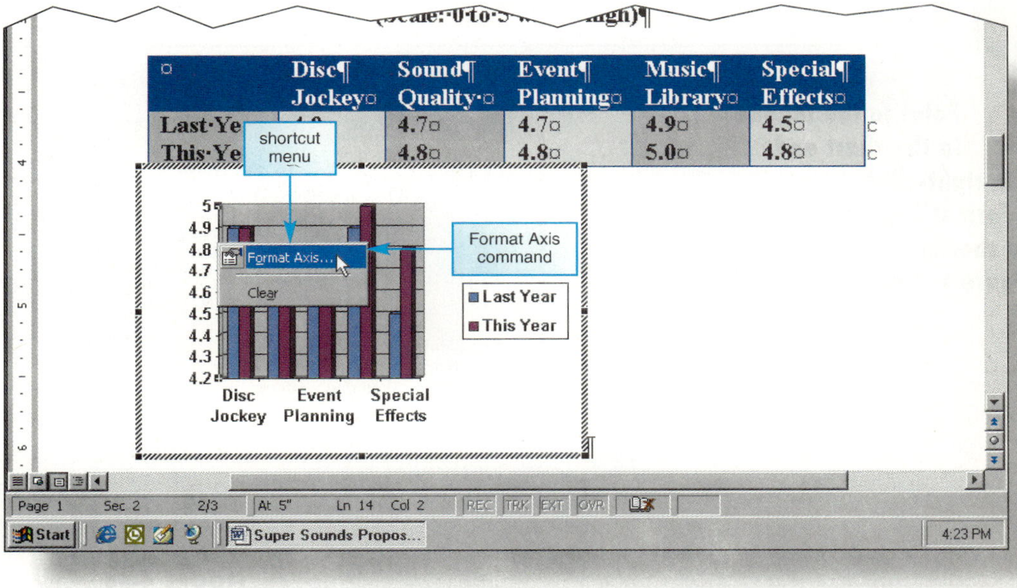

FIGURE 4-44

3 **Click Format Axis. If necessary, click the Number tab when the Format Axis dialog box displays. Click Number in the Category list and then click the Decimal places down arrow once. Point to the OK button.**

Graph displays the Format Axis dialog box (Figure 4-45). The Sample area displays a sample number formatted using the current selections.

4 **Click the OK button.**

Graph formats the value axis labels to one position after the decimal point (see Figure 4-46 below).

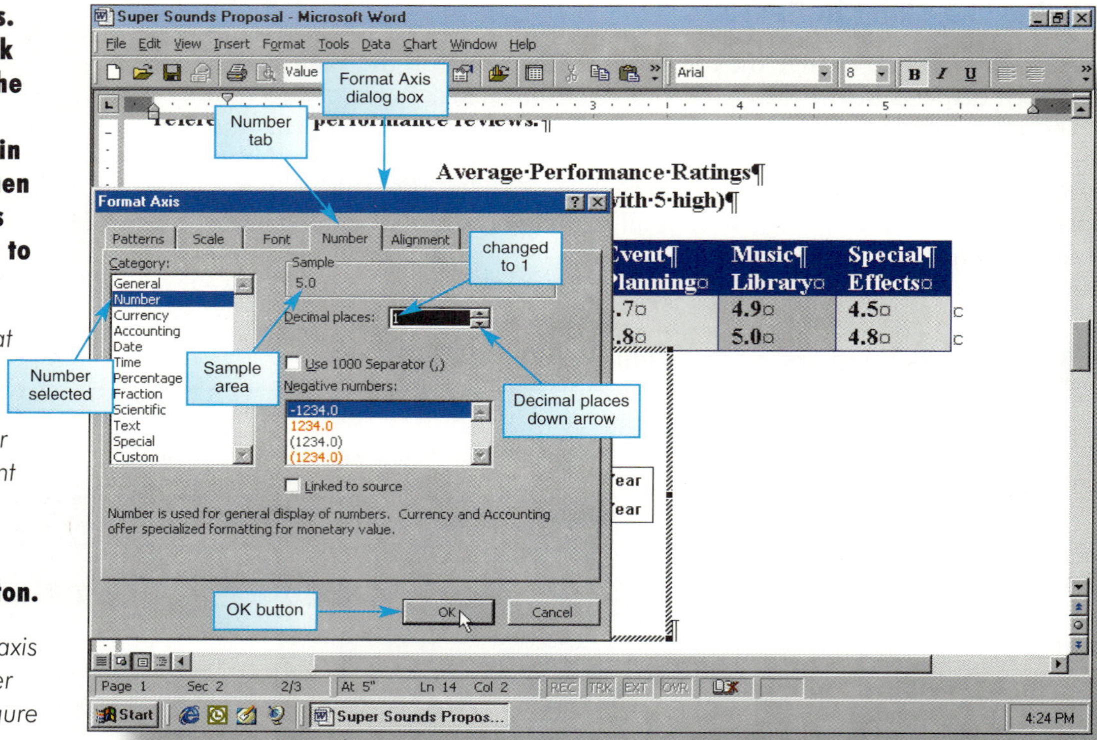

FIGURE 4-45

The next step in changing the chart is to move the legend so it displays below the chart instead of to the right of the chart. The **legend** is a box on the right side of the chart that identifies the colors assigned to categories in the chart. Perform the following steps to move the legend in the chart.

Steps **To Move Legend Placement in a Chart**

1 **Point to the legend in the chart and then right-click. Point to Format Legend on the shortcut menu (Figure 4-46).**

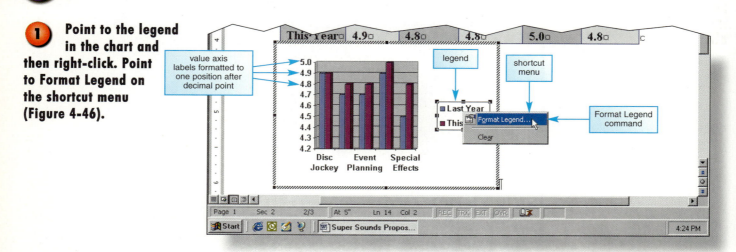

FIGURE 4-46

2 Click Format Legend. If necessary, click the Placement tab when the Format Legend dialog box displays. Click Bottom in the Placement area and then point to the OK button.

Graph displays the Format Legend dialog box (Figure 4-47).

3 Click the OK button.

Graph places the legend below the chart (see Figure 4-48 below).

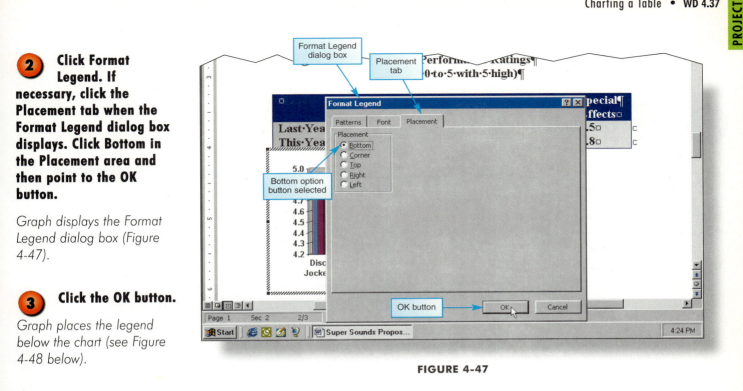

FIGURE 4-47

Notice that the Sound Quality and Music Library labels currently do not show on the category axis (the horizontal axis) because the chart is too narrow. Thus, the next step is to resize the chart so it is wider.

You resize a chart the same way you do any other graphical object. That is, you drag the chart's sizing handles as shown in the following steps.

 To Resize a Chart

1 Point to the right-middle sizing handle and drag to the right as shown in Figure 4-48.

2 Release the mouse button.

Graph resizes the chart (see Figure 4-49 on the next page).

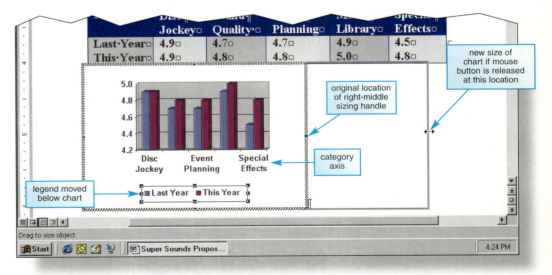

FIGURE 4-48

You are finished modifying the chart. The next step is to exit Graph and return to Word.

Steps: To Exit Graph and Return to Word

1 **Click somewhere outside the chart.**

Word closes the Graph application (Figure 4-49). Word's menus and toolbars redisplay below the title bar.

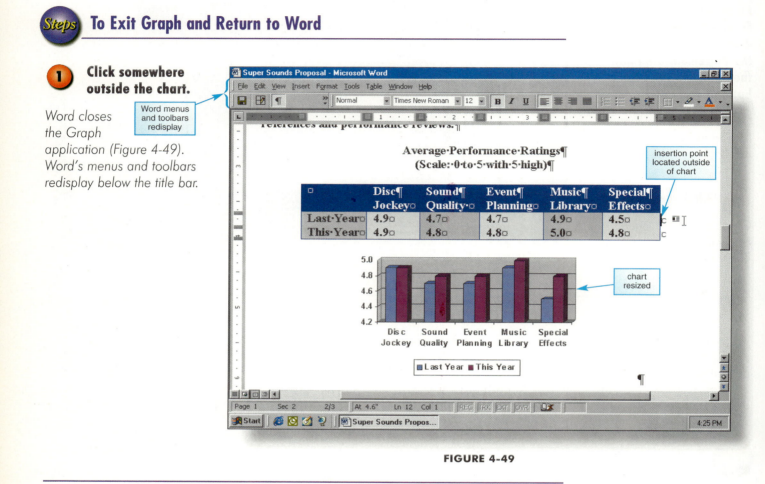

FIGURE 4-49

If, for some reason, you wanted to modify an existing chart in a document, you would double-click the chart to reopen the Microsoft Graph 2000 application. Then, you can make any necessary changes to the chart. When you are finished making changes to the chart, click anywhere outside the chart to return to Word.

Formatting the Chart in Word

The chart now is part of the paragraph below the table. Thus, you can apply any paragraph alignment settings to the chart. The chart should be centered. If you select the chart and then click the Center button on the Formatting toolbar, the chart will not be centered properly. Instead, it will be one-half inch to the right of the center point because first-line indent is set at one-half inch (see Figure 4-50).

You also want to add an outside border to the chart and add a blank line between the chart and the table. Because the chart is part of the paragraph, you will add a blank line above the paragraph by pressing the **CTRL+0** keys.

Perform the following steps to center, outline, and add a blank line above the chart.

Steps **To Format a Chart**

1 Click anywhere in the chart.

Word selects the chart (Figure 4-50). A selected chart displays surrounded by a selection rectangle that has sizing handles at each corner and middle location.

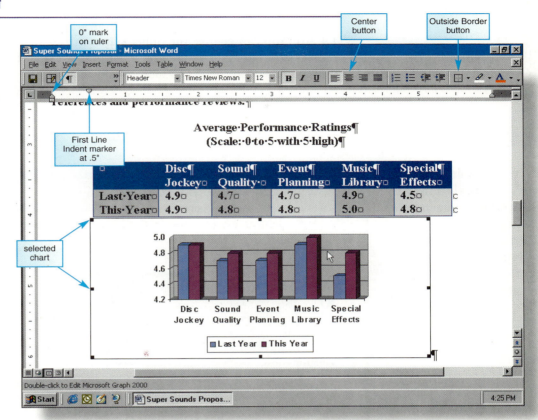

FIGURE 4-50

2 Drag the First Line Indent marker to the 0" mark on the ruler. Click the Center button on the Formatting toolbar. Click the Outside Border button on the Formatting toolbar. Press CTRL+0 (the numeral zero) to insert a blank line above the paragraph containing the chart. Click outside the chart to deselect it.

Word centers the chart between the left and right margins, places an outside border around the chart, and inserts a blank line above the chart (Figure 4-51).

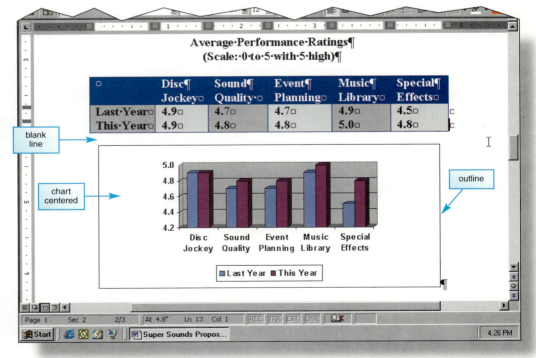

FIGURE 4-51

Customizing Bullets in a List

The draft of the sales proposal contains a bulleted list (see Figure 4-30a on page WD 4.26). You can change the bullet symbol from a small, solid circle to a graphical object as shown in Figure 4-30b on page WD 4.27. Perform the following steps to change the bullets in the list to picture bullets.

Steps To Add Picture Bullets to a List

1 **Scroll down and then select the paragraphs in the bulleted list. Right-click the selection. Point to Bullets and Numbering on the shortcut menu (Figure 4-52).**

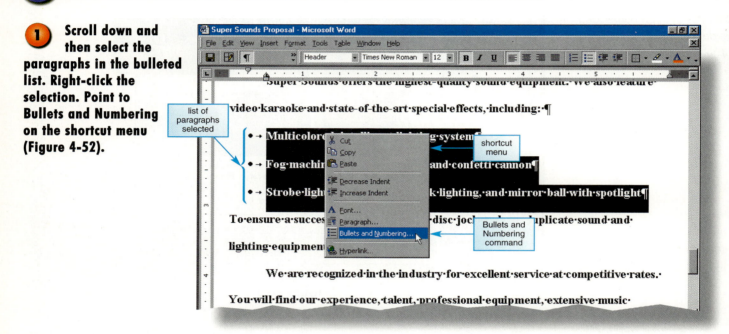

FIGURE 4-52

2 **Click Bullets and Numbering. If necessary, click the Bulleted tab when the Bullets and Numbering dialog box displays. Point to the Picture button.**

Word displays the Bullets and Numbering dialog box (Figure 4-53).

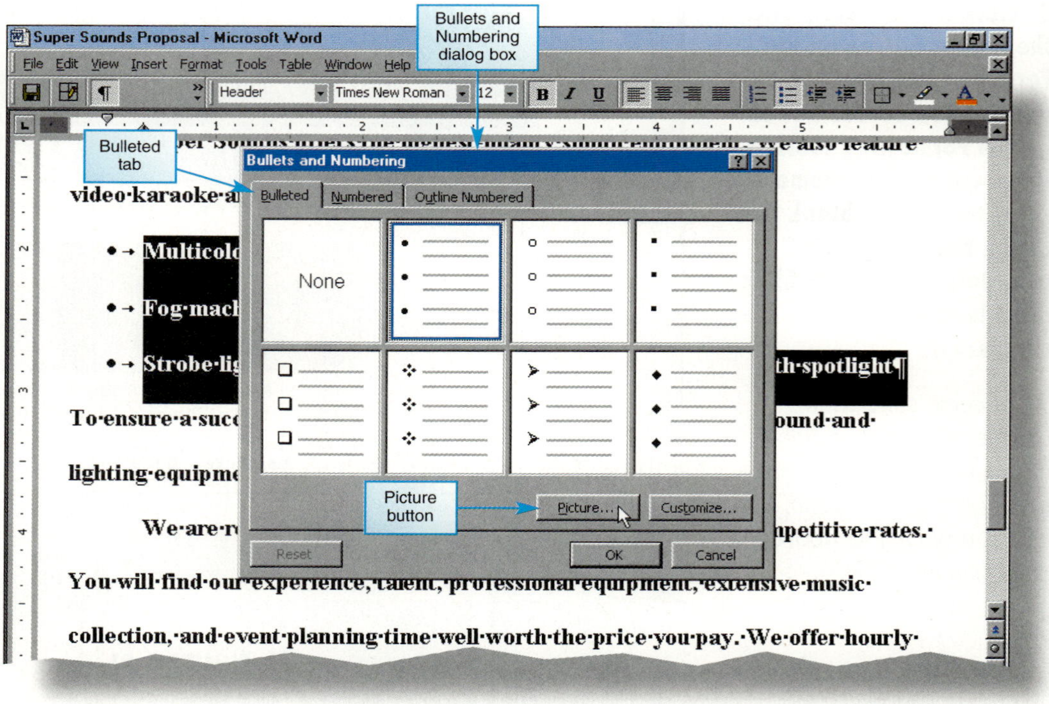

FIGURE 4-53

3 Click the Picture button. If necessary, click the Pictures tab when the Picture Bullet dialog box displays. Click the desired picture bullet and then point to the Insert clip button on the Pop-up menu.

Word displays the Picture Bullet dialog box (Figure 4-54). The selected picture bullet has a box around it, indicating it is selected.

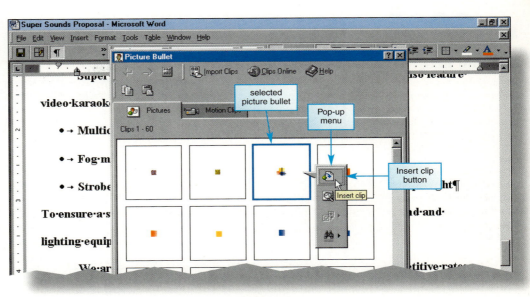

FIGURE 4-54

4 Click the Insert clip button. When the Word window is visible again, click outside the selection to remove the highlight.

Word changes the default bullets to picture bullets on the paragraphs (Figure 4-55).

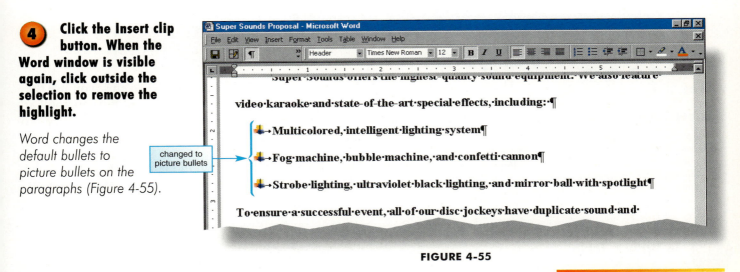

FIGURE 4-55

In addition to picture bullets, the Bullets and Numbering dialog box (Figure 4-53) provides a number of other bullet styles. To use one of these styles, simply click the desired style in the dialog box and then click the OK button.

Creating a Table Using the Draw Table Feature

Before the last paragraph of the sales proposal draft, you are to insert a table (Figure 4-30b on page WD 4.27). You have learned that a Word table is a collection of rows and columns and that the intersection of a row and a column is called a cell. Cells are filled with data.

When you want to create a simple table, one with the same number of rows and columns, use the Insert Table button on the Standard toolbar to create the table. This table, however, is more complex (Figure 4-56 on the next page). It contains a varying number of columns per row. To create a complex table, use Word's **Draw Table feature**.

Other Ways

1. Select the list, on Format menu click Bullets and Numbering, click Bullets tab, click Picture button, click desired bullet style, click OK button

More About 2000

Bullet Symbols

For more bullet symbols, click Bullets and Numbering on the Format menu, click the Bulleted tab, click the Customize button, click the Bullets button, select desired bullet symbol, and click the OK button.

More About

Aligning Text

You may be tempted to vertically-align text by pressing the SPACEBAR. The problem is that word processing software uses variable character fonts; that is, the letter w takes up more space than the letter l. Thus, when you use the SPACEBAR to vertically-align text, the column has a wavy look because each character does not begin at the same location.

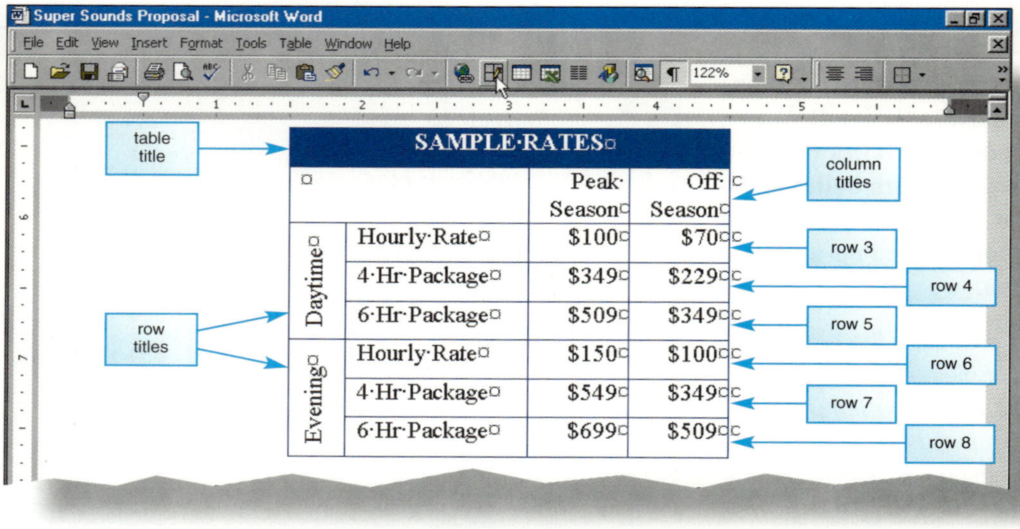

FIGURE 4-56

The following pages discuss how to create a complex table using Word's Draw Table feature.

Drawing a Table

The first step is to draw an empty table in the document. To do this, you use the **Draw Table button** on the Tables and Borders toolbar. The Tables and Borders toolbar contains a **Draw Table button** that, when recessed, changes the mouse pointer shape to a pencil. To draw the boundary, rows, and columns of the table, you drag the pencil pointer on the screen.

Perform the following steps to draw the table shown in Figure 4-56. If you make a mistake while drawing the table, remember that you can click the Undo button on the Standard toolbar to undo your most recent action.

More About

Draw Table

If you make a mistake while drawing a table, remember you always can click the Undo button to undo your most recent action.

Steps | To Draw a Table

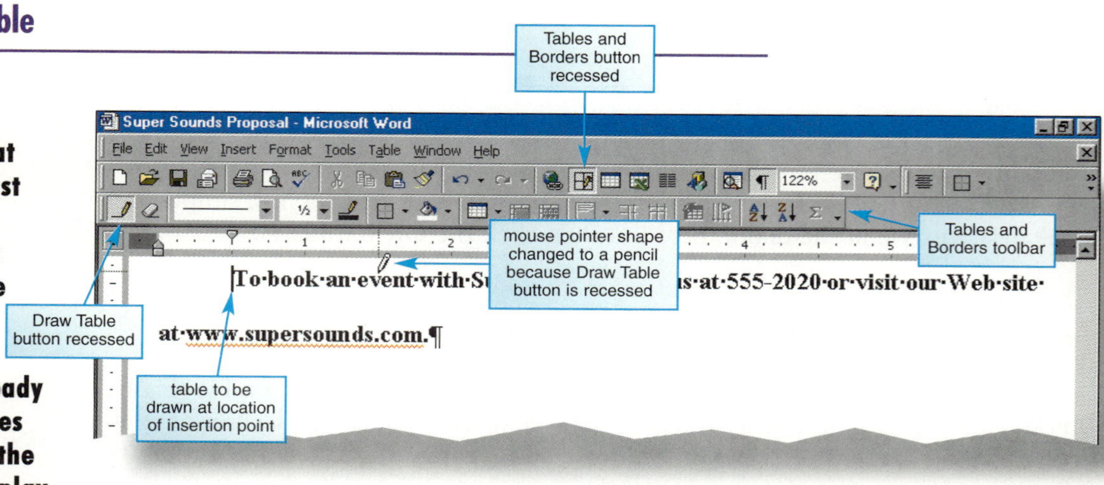

1 **Position the insertion point at the beginning of the last paragraph (before the word, To). Double-click the move handle on the Standard toolbar to display the entire toolbar. If it is not already recessed, click the Tables and Borders button on the Standard toolbar to display the Tables and Borders toolbar. If it is not already recessed, click the Draw Table button on the Tables and Borders toolbar. Move the mouse pointer, which is the shape of a pencil, into the document window to the location shown in Figure 4-57.**

FIGURE 4-57

2 Drag the pencil pointer downward and to the right until the dotted rectangle is positioned similarly to the one shown in Figure 4-58.

Word displays a dotted rectangle that indicates the table's size (Figure 4-58).

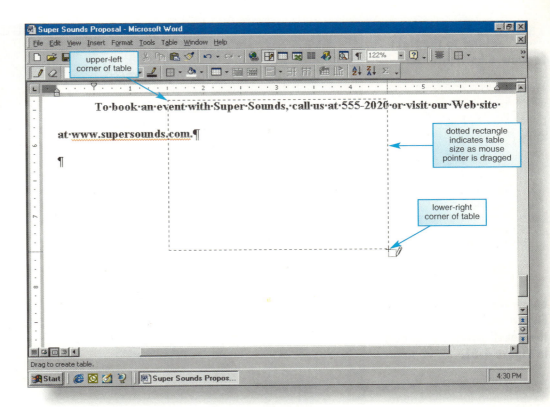

FIGURE 4-58

3 Release the mouse button. If necessary, scroll to display the entire table in the document window. If Word wraps the text around the table, click Edit on the menu bar, click Undo, and then begin these steps again - moving the pencil pointer closer to the word, event.

Word draws the table border. The Outside Border button on the Tables and Borders toolbar is recessed.

4 Position the pencil pointer as shown in Figure 4-59.

FIGURE 4-59

5 **Drag the pencil pointer to the right to draw a horizontal line.**

Word draws a horizontal line, which forms the bottom border of the first row in the table (Figure 4-60).

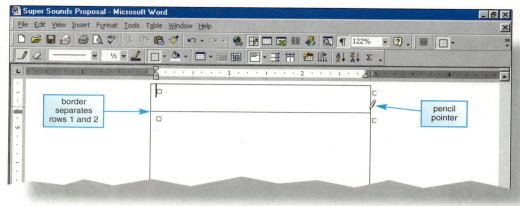

FIGURE 4-60

6 **Draw another horizontal line below the first as shown in Figure 4-61. Then, position the pencil pointer as shown in Figure 4-61.**

Word draws a second horizontal line to form the bottom border of the second row in the table (Figure 4-61). The pencil pointer is positioned to draw the first column.

FIGURE 4-61

7 **Draw three vertical lines to form the column borders similar to those shown in Figure 4-62.**

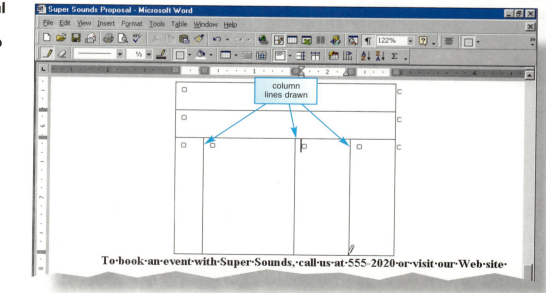

FIGURE 4-62

8 Draw five horizontal lines to form the row borders similar to those shown in Figure 4-63.

The empty table displays as shown in Figure 4-63.

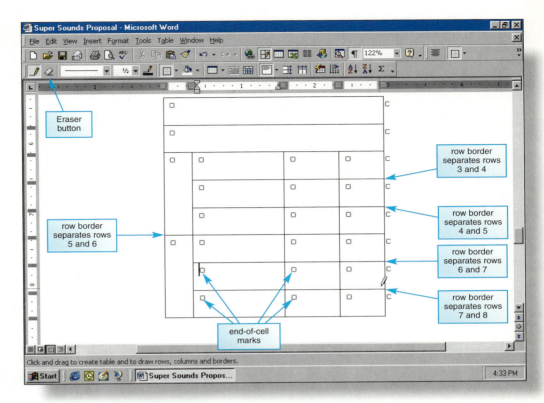

FIGURE 4-63

If, after drawing rows and columns in the table, you want to remove and redraw a line, click the **Eraser button** on the Tables and Borders toolbar (Figure 4-63) and then drag the mouse pointer (an eraser shape) through the line to erase. Click the Eraser button again to turn the eraser pointer off.

All Word tables that you draw have a .5-point border. To change this border, you can use the Tables and Borders toolbar as described earlier in this project.

You have learned that each row has an **end-of-row mark** (see Figure 4-59 on page WD 4.43), which is used to add columns to the right of a table, and each cell has an **end-of-cell mark**, which is used to select a cell. Notice the end-of-cell marks currently are left-aligned in each cell (Figure 4-63), which indicates the data will be left-aligned in the cells.

To format a table or data in a table, first you must select the cell(s) and then apply the appropriate formats. Because selecting table text is such a crucial function of Word tables, techniques to select these items are described in Table 4-2.

Table 4-2 Techniques for Selecting Items in a Table	
ITEM TO SELECT	ACTION
Cell	Click the left edge of the cell.
Row	Click to the left of the row.
Column	Click the column's top gridline or border.
Cells, rows, or columns	Drag through the cells, rows, or columns.
Text in next cell	Press the TAB key.
Text in previous cell	Press the SHIFT+TAB keys.
Entire table	Click the table, click Table on the menu bar, point to Select, and then click Table.

Table Wrapping

When you draw a table, Word may wrap the text of the document around the table. To remove the text wrapping, right-click the table, click Table Properties, click the Table tab, click None in Text wrapping area, and then click the OK button. To have Word automatically wrap text around the table, hold down the CTRL key while you draw the table.

Because the text of the draft of the sales proposal is double-spaced and bold, the table also is formatted to double-spaced and bold. You want the table to be single-spaced and not bold. Thus, perform the following steps to change the line spacing of the table from double to single and remove the bold format from the cells in the table.

TO CHANGE TABLE FORMATS

1. Be sure the insertion point is somewhere in the table.
2. Click Table on the menu bar, point to Select, and then click Table.
3. Press CTRL+1 (the numeral one) to single-space the rows in the table.
4. Press CTRL+B to remove the bold format from the cells in the table.

Word changes the table line spacing to single and removes the bold format (Figure 4-64).

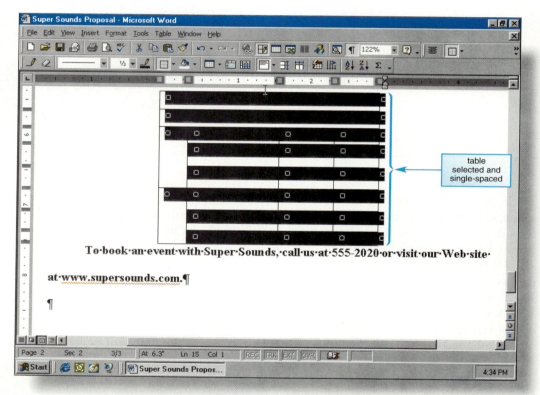

FIGURE 4-64

Because you drew the table borders with the mouse, some of the rows may be varying heights. Perform the following step to make the row spacing in the table even.

Table Line Spacing

If you have distributed rows evenly and then want to change line spacing, you first must do the following: select the table, right-click the selection, click Table Properties on the shortcut menu, click the Row tab, remove the check mark from the Specify height check box, and then click the OK button.

Steps To Distribute Rows Evenly

1 **With the table still selected, click the Distribute Rows Evenly button on the Tables and Borders toolbar.**

Word makes the height of the selected rows uniform (Figure 4-65).

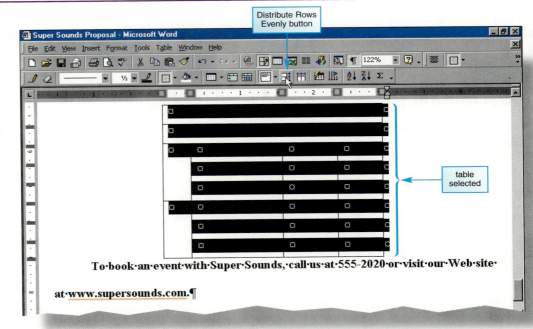

FIGURE 4-65

Other Ways

1. Select cells, on Table menu point to AutoFit, on AutoFit menu click Distribute Rows Evenly
2. Drag row boundaries (borders) on table
3. Drag Adjust Table Row markers on vertical ruler
4. On Table menu click Table Properties, click Row tab, enter desired height, click OK button

Two additional lines for column headings are required in the table. Perform the following steps to continue drawing the table.

Steps To Draw More Table Lines

1 **Click inside the table to remove the highlight. Click the Draw Table button on the Tables and Borders toolbar. Position the pencil pointer as shown in Figure 4-66.**

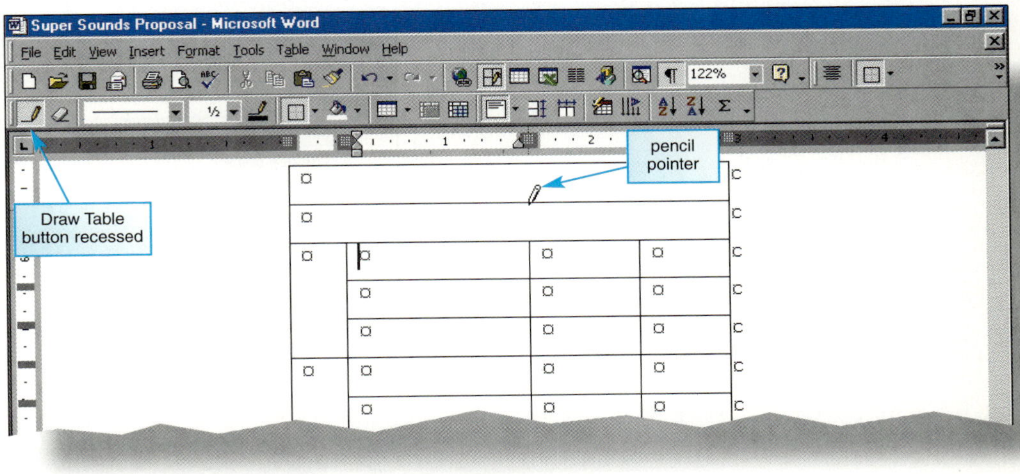

FIGURE 4-66

2 Draw a line downward until you reach the existing column border. Draw a second line as shown in Figure 4-67. Click the Draw Table button on the Tables and Borders toolbar to deselect it.

The table is drawn completely (Figure 4-67).

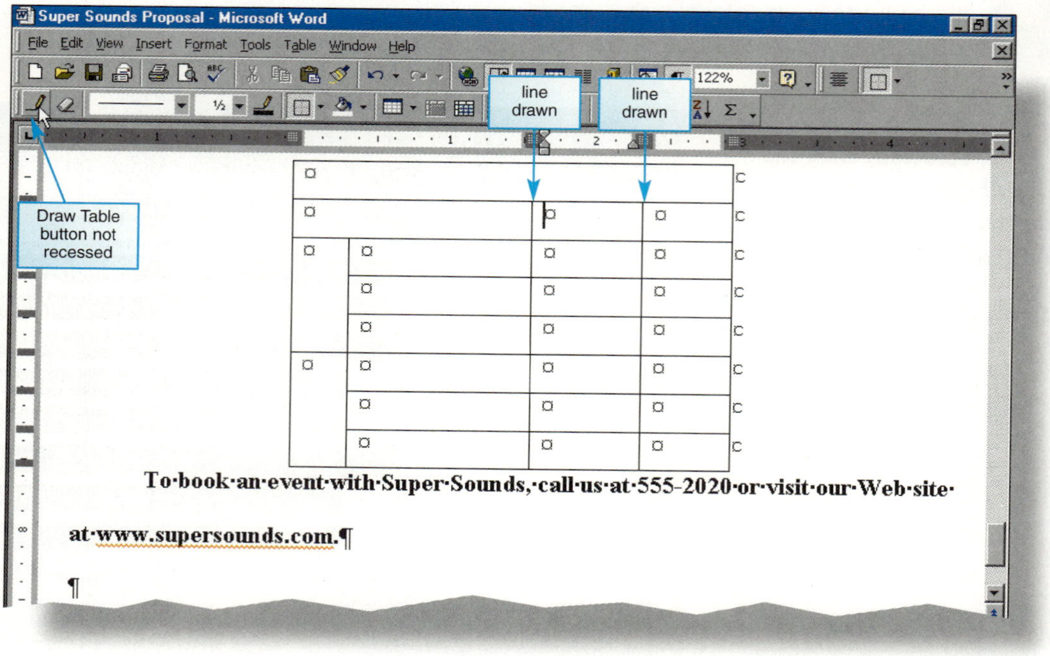

FIGURE 4-67

The last two columns in the table must be the same width. Because you drew the borders of these columns, they may be varying widths. Perform the following steps to evenly size these columns.

 Steps **To Distribute Columns Evenly**

1 Point to the left of the cell shown in Figure 4-68 until the mouse pointer changes to a right-pointing solid arrow.

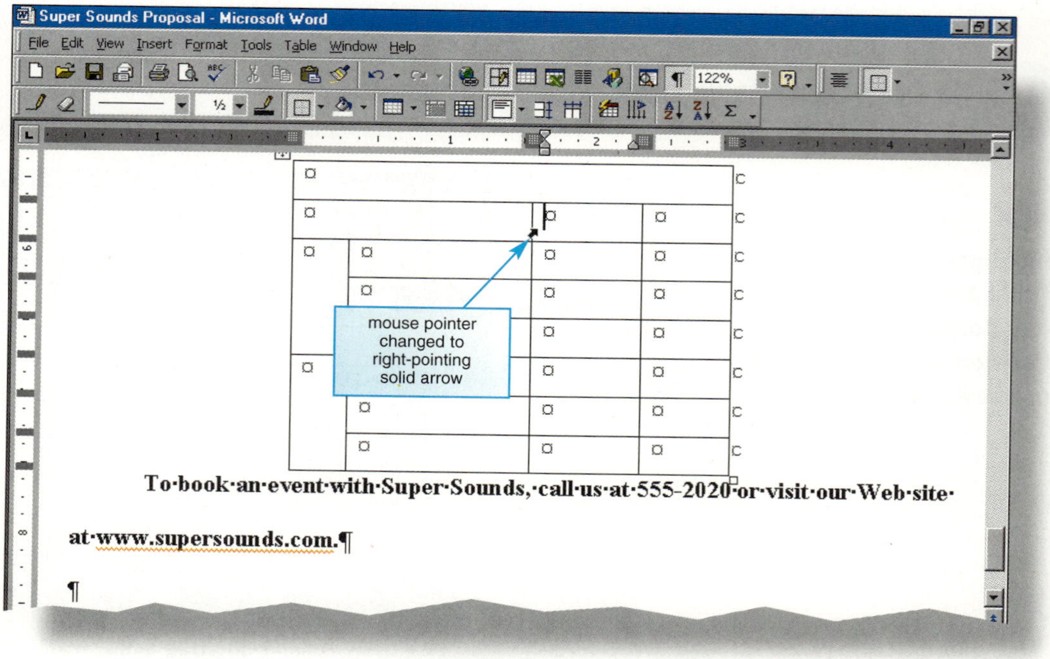

FIGURE 4-68

2 Drag through the 14 cells shown in Figure 4-69 and then click the Distribute Columns Evenly button on the Tables and Borders toolbar.

Word applies uniform widths to the selected columns (Figure 4-69).

3 Click outside the selection to remove the highlight.

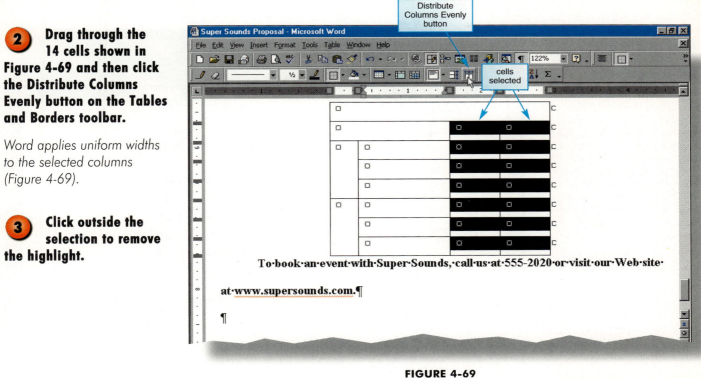

FIGURE 4-69

Entering Data into the Table

The next step is to enter the data into the table. To advance from one column to the next, press the TAB key. To advance from one row to the next, also press the TAB key; do not press the ENTER key. The ENTER key is used to begin new paragraphs within a cell. Perform the following steps to enter the data into the table.

TO ENTER DATA INTO A TABLE

1 Click in the first cell of the table. Double-click the move handle on the Formatting toolbar to display the entire toolbar. Click the Center button on the Formatting toolbar. Type SAMPLE RATES and then press the TAB key twice.

2 Type Peak Season and then press the TAB key. Type Off Season and then press the TAB key.

3 Type Daytime and then press the TAB key. Type Hourly Rate and then press the TAB key. Type $100 and then press the TAB key. Type $70 and then press the TAB key twice. Type 4 Hr Package and then press the TAB key. Type $349 and then press the TAB key. Type $229 and then press the TAB key twice. Type 6 Hr Package and then press the TAB key. Type $509 and then press the TAB key. Type $349 and then press the TAB key.

4 Type Evening and then press the TAB key. Type Hourly Rate and then press the TAB key. Type $150 and then press the TAB key. Type $100 and then press the TAB key twice. Type 4 Hr Package and then press the TAB key. Type $549 and then press the TAB key. Type $349 and then press the TAB key twice. Type 6 Hr Package and then press the TAB key. Type $699 and then press the TAB key. Type $509 as the last entry.

The table data is entered (Figure 4-70 on the next page).

Other Ways

1. Select cells, on Table menu point to AutoFit, on AutoFit menu click Distribute Columns Evenly
2. Drag column boundaries (borders) on table
3. Drag Move Table Column markers on horizontal ruler
4. On Table menu click Table Properties, click Column tab, enter desired width, click OK button

More About 2000

Table Columns

When the insertion point is in a table, the ruler displays column markers that indicate the beginning and ending of columns. A column boundary is the vertical gridline immediately to the right of a column in the table itself. To resize a column width, drag the column boundary in the table or the column marker on the ruler. Holding down the ALT key while dragging markers displays column width measurements.

Microsoft **Word 2000**

Table Contents

You can sum a column or row of numbers in a table. First, click the cell where you want the sum to appear. Then, click Formula on the Table menu. If you agree with the formula Word proposes in the Formula dialog box, click the OK button; otherwise, delete the formula and then build your own formula using the Paste Function list box.

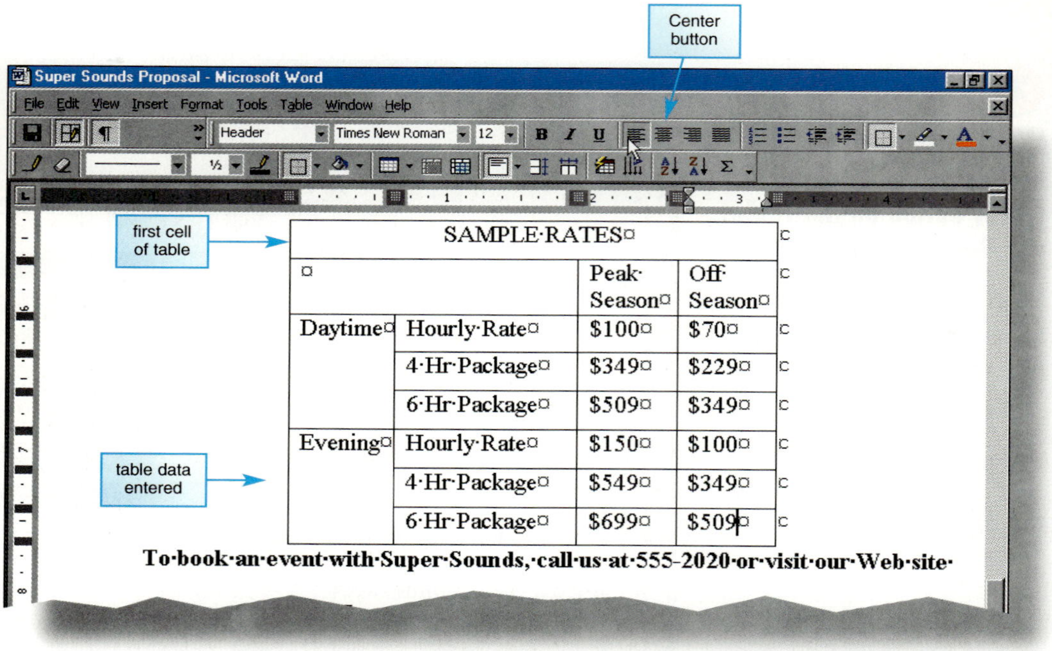

FIGURE 4-70

The next step is to rotate the row heading text, Daytime and Evening, so it displays vertically instead of horizontally.

Formatting the Table

The data you enter in cells displays horizontally. You can change the text so it displays vertically. Changing the direction of text adds variety to your tables. Perform the following steps to display the row heading text vertically.

Steps To Vertically Display Text in a Cell

1 **Select the row heading text cells containing the words, Daytime and Evening. Point to the Change Text Direction button on the Tables and Borders toolbar.**

The cells to be formatted are selected (Figure 4-71).

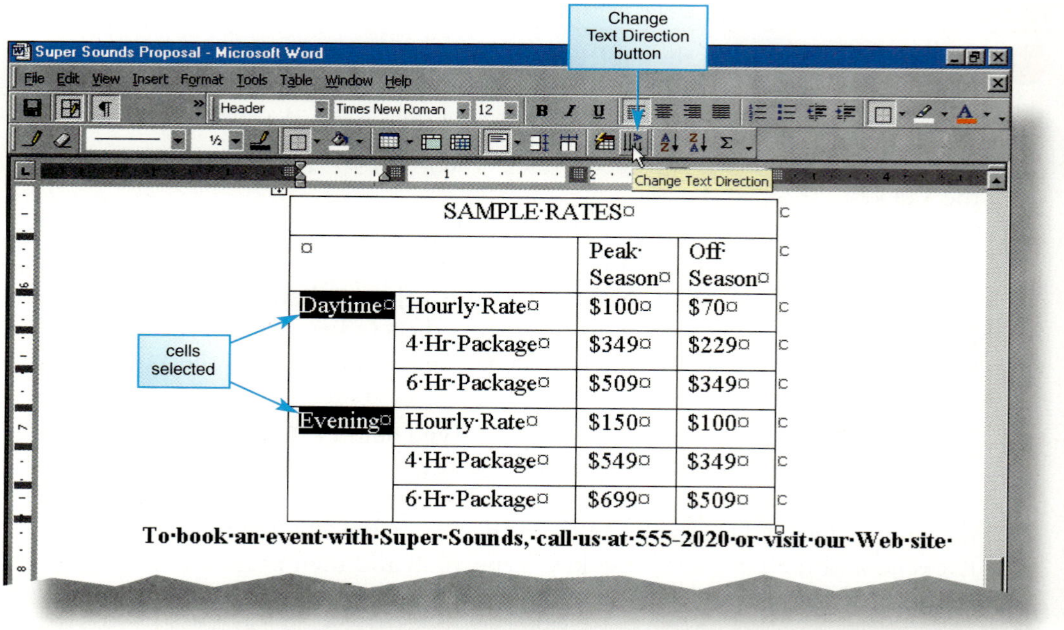

FIGURE 4-71

2 **Click the Change Text Direction button twice.**

Word displays the text vertically so you read it from bottom to top (Figure 4-72).

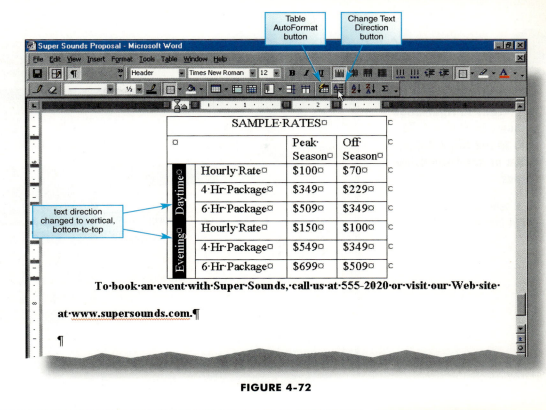

FIGURE 4-72

The first time you click the Change Text Direction button, Word displays the text vertically so you read it from top to bottom. The second time you click the Change Text Direction button, Word displays the text vertically so you read it from bottom to top (Figure 4-72). If you click the button a third time, the text would display horizontally again.

Perform the following steps to format the table using the Table AutoFormat command.

TO AUTOFORMAT A TABLE

1 Click somewhere in the table. Click the Table AutoFormat button on the Tables and Borders toolbar (see Figure 4-72).

2 When the Table AutoFormat dialog box displays, scroll through the Formats list and then click Grid 8. Be sure these check boxes contain check marks: Borders, Shading, Font, Color, Heading rows, and First column. All other check boxes should be cleared.

3 Click the OK button.

Word formats the table using the Grid 8 format (Figure 4-73 on the next page).

Just as with paragraphs, you can left-align, center, or right-align the end-of-cell marks in a table. The data you enter into the cells is left-aligned, by default. You can change the alignment just as you would for a paragraph. Before changing the alignment, you must select the cell(s). Perform the steps on the next page to right-align the end-of-cell marks for cells containing dollar amounts.

Other Ways

1. Select cells, click Text Direction on shortcut menu, click desired orientation, click OK button
2. Select cells, on Format menu click Text Direction, click desired orientation, click OK button

Shading

You can shade paragraphs or the cells in a table. To do this, click the cell(s) or paragraph(s) to shade, click the Shading Color button arrow on the Tables and Borders toolbar, and then click the desired shade color on the shade palette. To remove shading, click No Fill on the shade palette.

Steps **To Right-Align Cell Contents**

1 **Drag through the cells to right-align as shown in Figure 4-73. Point to the Align Right button on the Formatting toolbar.**

Word selects the cells to format (Figure 4-73).

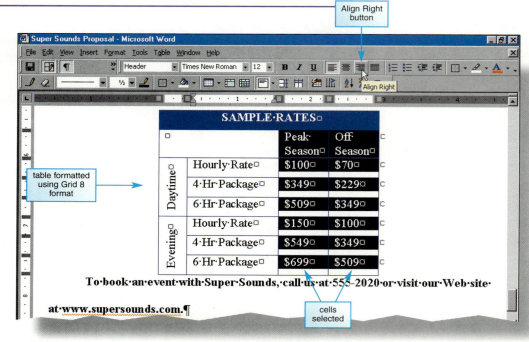

FIGURE 4-73

2 **Click the Align Right button.**

Word right-aligns the data and end-of-cell marks in the selected area (Figure 4-74).

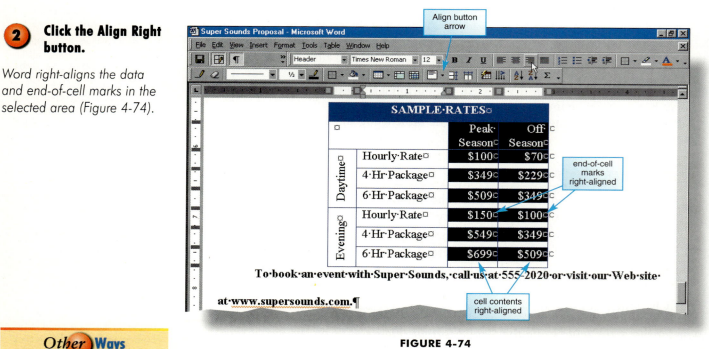

FIGURE 4-74

Other **Ways**

1. Select cells, point to Cell Alignment on shortcut menu, click Align Top Right icon
2. Select cells, on Format menu click Paragraph, click Indents and Spacing tab, click Alignment box arrow, click Right, click OK button
3. Select cells, press CTRL+R

In addition to aligning text horizontally in a cell (left, centered, or right), you can center it vertically using the Align button arrow on the Tables and Borders toolbar. If you wanted to center text vertically, or both vertically and horizontally, you could click the Align button arrow and then click the appropriate button. Table 4-3 illustrates the various alignment options.

Table 4-3 Cell Alignment Options

Align Top Left	Hourly Rate		
Align Top Center		Hourly Rate	
Align Top Right			Hourly Rate
Align Center Left	Hourly Rate		
Align Center		Hourly Rate	
Align Center Right			Hourly Rate
Align Bottom Left	Hourly Rate		
Align Bottom Center		Hourly Rate	
Align Bottom Right			Hourly Rate

Cell Alignment

Cell alignment options also are available on the Table menu. Right-click the cell(s) to align, point to Cell Alignment on the shortcut menu, and then click the desired cell alignment icon.

Working with Tables

At times you might want to insert additional rows or columns in a table. To add a row to the end of a table, position the insertion point in the bottom-right corner cell and then press the TAB key.

Depending on the task you want to perform in a table, the function of the Table button on the Standard toolbar changes, and the commands on the Table menu and associated shortcut menu change. To **add rows** in the middle of a table, select the row below where the new row is to be inserted, then click the Insert Rows button (the same button you clicked to insert a table); or click Insert Rows on the shortcut menu; or click Table on the menu bar, point to Insert, and then click Rows Above. To **add a column** in the middle of a table, select the column to the right of where the new columns is to be inserted and then click the Insert Columns button (the same button you clicked to insert a table); click Insert Columns on the shortcut menu; or click Table on the menu bar, point to Insert, and then click Columns to the Left. To add a column to the right of a table, select the end-of-row marks at the right edge of the table, then click the Insert Columns button; click Insert Columns on the shortcut menu; or click Table on the menu bar, point to Insert, and then click Columns to the Right.

If you want to **delete row(s)** or **delete column(s)** from a table, select the row(s) or column(s) to delete and then click **Delete Rows** or **Delete Columns** on shortcut menu, or click Table on the menu bar, click Delete, and then click the appropriate item to delete.

The final step in formatting the table is to add a blank line between the table and the paragraph below it, as described in the following step.

TO ADD A BLANK LINE ABOVE A PARAGRAPH

1. Position the insertion point in the last paragraph of the proposal and then press CTRL+0 (the numeral zero). Double-click the move handle on the Standard toolbar to display the entire toolbar. Click the Tables and Borders button on the Standard toolbar.

Word adds a blank line above the paragraph (Figure 4-75 on the next page). Word removes the Tables and Borders toolbar from the window.

Moving Tables

To move a table to a new location, point to the upper-left corner of the table until the table move handle displays (a small box containing a four-headed arrow). Point to the table move handle and then drag the table to its new location.

Resizing Tables

If you wanted to resize a table, you would click the Draw Table button on the Tables and Borders toolbar to turn off the Draw Table feature and then drag the table or column boundaries to their new locations.

More About

Proofreading

Ask yourself these questions when proofreading the proposal: Is the subject original and specific? Is its purpose clear? Does the proposal provide specifics, rather than generalizations? Is the product or service beneficial? Is the length appropriate for the subject? Is the wording appropriate for the reader's background?

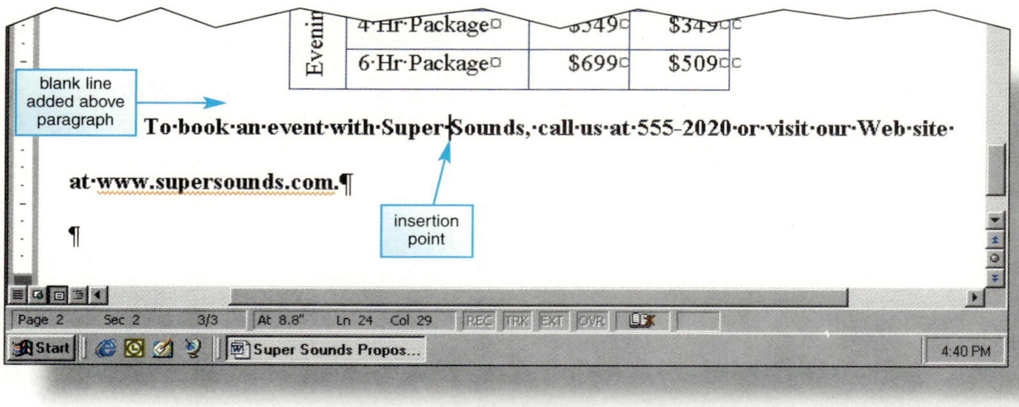

FIGURE 4-75

Creating a Watermark

More About

Watermarks

To create a watermark of text, you insert a text box into the header or footer. To insert a text box, first display the Drawing toolbar by clicking the Drawing button on the Standard toolbar. Then click the Text Box button on the Drawing toolbar and drag the mouse pointer to form a box that will contain the text.

A **watermark** is text or a graphic that displays on top of or behind the text in a document. For example, a catalog may print the words, Not Available, on top of sold-out items. A product manager may want the word, Draft, to print behind his or her first draft of a five-year plan. Some companies use their logos or other graphics as watermarks on documents to add visual appeal to the document.

To create a watermark in a document, you add the text or graphic to the header in the section you want the watermark. Then, you resize and position the watermark where you want it to display. You can move the watermark anywhere on the page; its location is not restricted to the area at the top or bottom of the page.

In this project, the owners of Super Sounds would like the music CDs graphic to display on the pages of the body of the proposal. Perform the following steps to create this watermark.

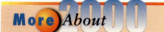

Steps To Create a Watermark of a Graphic

1 Click View on the menu bar and then click Header and Footer. When the header area displays on the screen, press the END key, press the ENTER key twice, and then press CTRL+E to center the insertion point and paragraph mark. Click Insert on the menu bar, point to Picture, and then point to Clip Art.

Word centers the insertion point on line 3 of the header (Figure 4-76).

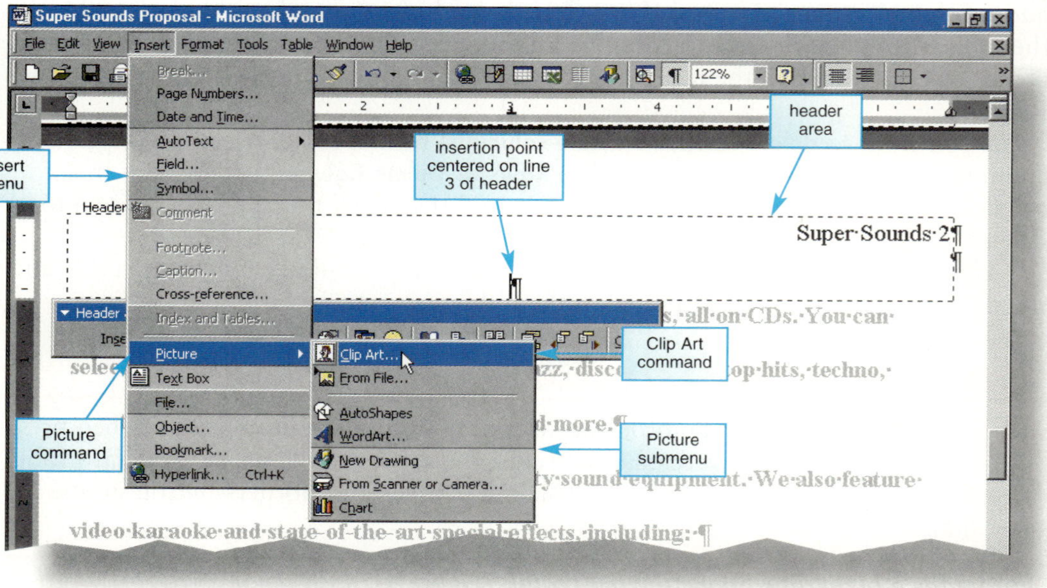

FIGURE 4-76

2 Click Clip Art. In the Insert ClipArt window, click the Downloaded Clips category, click the music CDs graphic, click the Insert clip button on the Pop-up menu, and then close the Insert ClipArt window. When the graphic displays in the header of the document, click it to select it. (If the Picture toolbar does not display, click View on the menu bar, point to Toolbars, and then click Picture.) Point to the Format Picture button on the Picture toolbar (Figure 4-77).

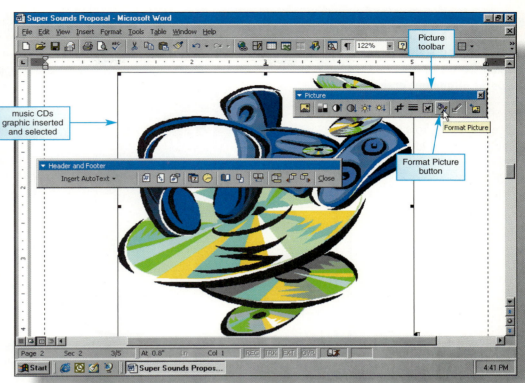

FIGURE 4-77

3 Click the Format Picture button. When the Format Picture dialog box displays, if necessary, click the Picture tab. Click the Color box arrow and then click Watermark.

Word displays the Format Picture dialog box (Figure 4-78). The Watermark setting adjusts the brightness and contrast so the graphic displays faded.

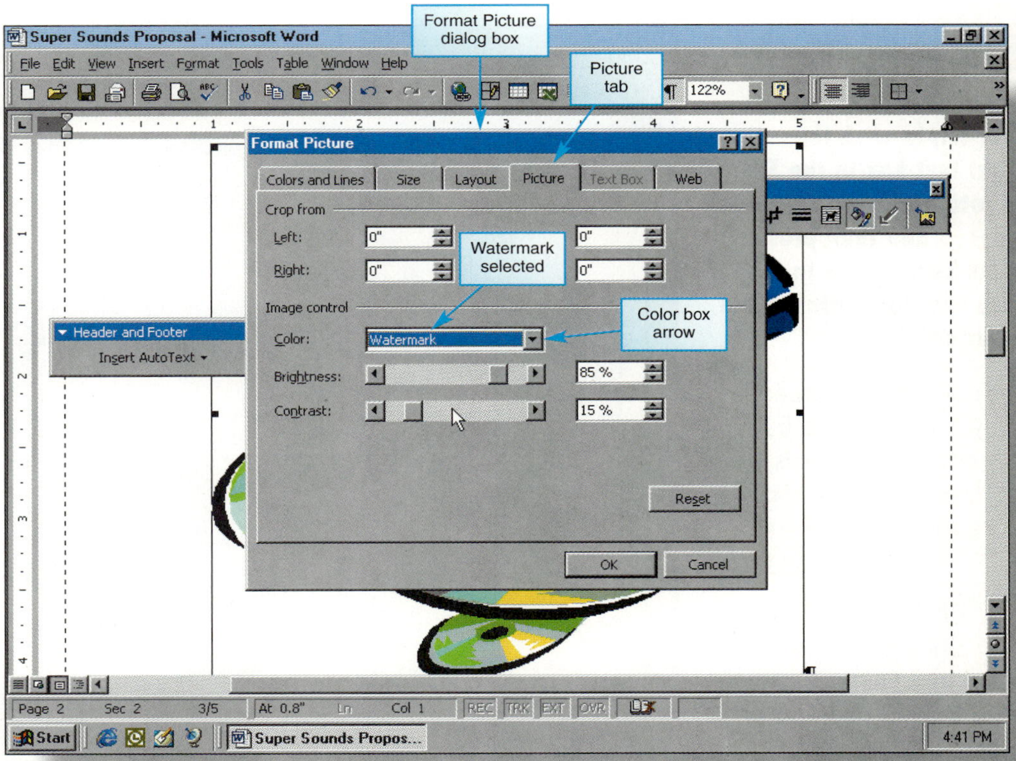

FIGURE 4-78

4 Click the Layout tab. Click Behind text in the Wrapping style area and Center in the Horizontal alignment area.

These settings instruct Word to place the text in front of the image, which is to be centered horizontally on the page (Figure 4-79).

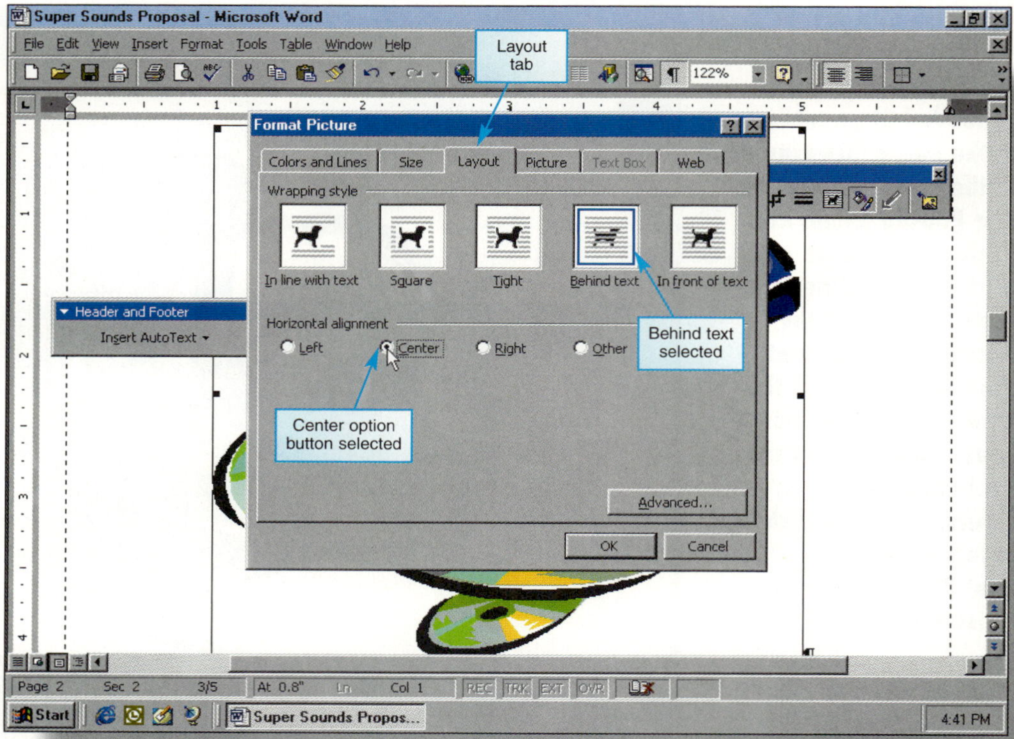

FIGURE 4-79

5 Click the Size tab. Click Lock aspect ratio to remove the check mark. Triple-click the Height text box in the Size and rotate area to select it. Type 9.5 and then press the TAB key. Type 7 in the Width text box. Point to the OK button.

By deselecting Lock aspect ratio, you can vary the height and width measurements from their original proportions (Figure 4-80).

6 Click the OK button. Click the Close Header and Footer button on the Header and Footer toolbar.

The watermark displays faded behind the body proposal.

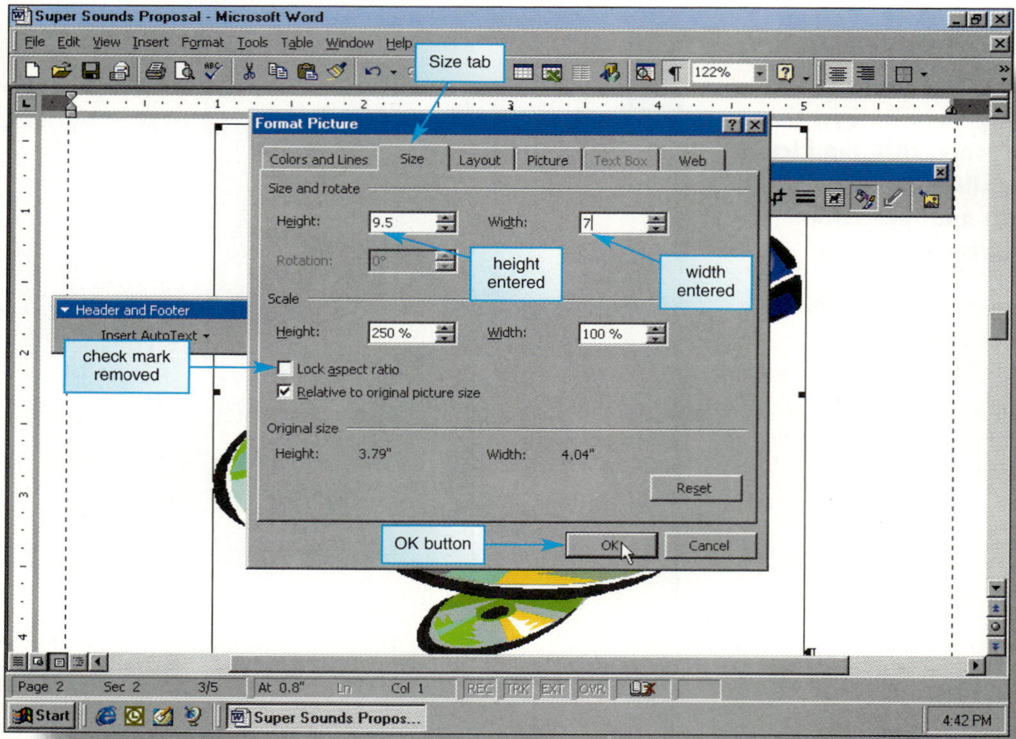

FIGURE 4-80

If you want to remove a watermark, you would delete it from the header or footer.

To see how the watermark looks in the entire document, view the document in print preview as described in the following steps.

TO PRINT PREVIEW A DOCUMENT

 Click the Print Preview button on the Standard toolbar. If necessary, click the Multiple Pages button on the Print Preview toolbar and then click the third icon in the first row of the grid (1 × 3 Pages) to display all three pages of the proposal as shown in Figure 4-81.

 When finished viewing the document, click the Close Preview button on the Print Preview toolbar.

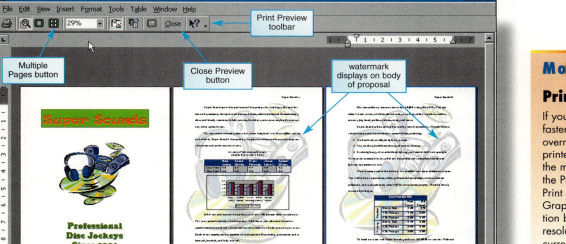

FIGURE 4-81

Checking Spelling, Saving Again, and Printing the Sales Proposal

Check the spelling of the document by clicking the Spelling and Grammar button on the Standard toolbar. Save the document one final time by clicking the Save button on the Standard toolbar, then print the sales proposal by clicking the Print button. The printed document displays as shown in Figure 4-1 on page 4.5.

Project 4 now is complete. Follow this step to quit Word.

TO QUIT WORD

 Click the Close button in the Word window.

The Word window closes.

CASE PERSPECTIVE SUMMARY

As promised, you finish the sales proposal for Super Sounds within a week and set up an appointment to meet with Juan and Nora Garcia. Juan and Nora are quite impressed with the proposal. They mention that your creativity with colors and graphics makes this proposal much more appealing than any other they have seen. In fact, they would like to incorporate your work into their Web site. You point out that you have experience developing Web pages and would be willing to update theirs, if they would like. Without hesitation, they offer you the job.

Project Summary

Project 4 introduced you to creating a proposal with a title page, table, chart, and a watermark. First, you created a title page that contained a graphic you downloaded from the Web. You learned how to insert an existing Word document into the active document. You inserted a header for the body of the proposal that was different from the title page header. Next, you charted an existing Word table. You added picture bullets to a list. Then, you used the Draw Table feature to create a complex table.

What You Should Know

Having completed this project, you now should be able to perform the following tasks:

- Add a Blank Line Above a Paragraph *(WD 4.53)*
- Add a Header Different from a Previous Header *(WD 4.28)*
- Add Picture Bullets to a List *(WD 4.40)*
- Align Text with Top of Page *(WD 4.22)*
- Apply the Normal Style *(WD 4.19)*
- AutoFormat a Table *(WD 4.51)*
- Border a Paragraph *(WD 4.8)*
- Center Text Vertically *(WD 4.17)*
- Change Line Spacing in a Table *(WD 4.32)*
- Change Table Formats *(WD 4.46)*
- Chart a Table *(WD 4.33)*
- Close the Header Area *(WD 4.31)*
- Create a Watermark of a Graphic *(WD 4.54)*
- Display Formatting Marks *(WD 4.7)*
- Distribute Columns Evenly *(WD 4.48)*
- Distribute Rows Evenly *(WD 4.47)*
- Download Clip Art from Microsoft's Clip Gallery Live Web Page *(WD 4.12)*
- Draw a Table *(WD 4.42)*
- Draw More Table Lines *(WD 4.47)*
- Enter Data into a Table *(WD 4.49)*
- Exit Graph and Return to Word *(WD 4.38)*
- Format a Chart *(WD 4.39)*
- Format and Enter the Company Slogan *(WD 4.15)*
- Format Characters *(WD 4.7)*
- Format Numbers on the Value Axis of a Chart *(WD 4.35)*
- Import Clip Art from the Data Disk *(WD 4.15)*
- Insert a Next Page Section Break *(WD 4.21)*
- Insert a Word Document into an Open Document *(WD 4.23)*
- Move Legend Placement in a Chart *(WD 4.36)*
- Page Number Differently in a Section *(WD 4.29)*
- Print a Document *(WD 4.25)*
- Print Preview a Document *(WD 4.57)*
- Quit Word *(WD 4.57)*
- Reset Menus and Toolbars *(WD 4.6)*
- Resize a Chart *(WD 4.37)*
- Right-align Cell Contents *(WD 4.52)*
- Save a Document *(WD 4.18)*
- Save an Active Document with a New File Name *(WD 4.25)*
- Single-space a Paragraph *(WD 4.31)*
- Start Word *(WD 4.6)*
- Vertically Display Text in a Cell *(WD 4.50)*
- Zoom Text Width *(WD 4.6)*

Apply Your Knowledge

➕ Project Reinforcement at www.scsite.com/off2000/reinforce.htm

1 Working with Tables

Instructions: Start Word. Open the document, Weekly Sales Report, on the Data Disk. If you did not download the Data Disk, see the inside back cover for instructions for downloading the Data Disk or see your instructor.

The document contains a table created with the Draw Table feature. You are to modify the table so it looks like Figure 4-82.

Perform the following tasks.

1. Select the cell containing the title, Shoe World. Center it, bold it, and change its font size to 28. If necessary, click the Tables and Borders button on the Standard toolbar to display the Tables and Borders toolbar. Click the Shading Color button arrow on the Tables and Borders toolbar and then click Plum. Click the Font Color button arrow on the Formatting toolbar and then click White.

Shoe World						
Weekly Sales Report						
		Monday	Tuesday	Wednesday	Thursday	Friday	Total
Zone 1	Chicago	45,443	34,221	41,202	40,112	38,556	199,534
	Dallas	67,203	52,202	39,668	45,203	43,223	247,499
	San Francisco	68,778	60,980	49,127	57,009	31,101	266,995
Zone 2	Boston	79,985	68,993	45,024	54,897	71,992	320,891
	Detroit	45,494	41,220	22,101	29,445	34,003	172,263
	Miami	57,925	56,898	49,056	51,119	54,395	269,393
Total Weekly Sales		364,828	314,514	246,178	277,785	273,270	1,476,575

FIGURE 4-82

2. Select the row containing the subtitle, Weekly Sales Report. Center and bold the subtitle. Click the Font Color button arrow on the Formatting toolbar and then click Teal.

3. Select the cells containing the row headings, Zone 1 and Zone 2. Click the Change Text Direction button on the Tables and Borders toolbar twice.

4. Select the cells containing the column headings, Monday, Tuesday, Wednesday, Thursday, and Friday. Click Table on the menu bar, point to AutoFit, and then click AutoFit to Contents. These columns now are as wide as the column headings.

5. Select the cell containing the label, Total Weekly Sales, and the cell immediately to its right. Click the Merge Cells button on the Table and Borders toolbar.

6. Click the cell in the last row to contain the total weekly cells for Monday and then click the AutoSum button on the Tables and Borders toolbar. Repeat this process for each cell in the bottom row of the table. If the totals do not fit in the existing column widths, drag the column borders to the right to increase the width of the affected columns.

7. Click the cell to contain the Total Sales for Miami. Click the AutoSum button on the Tables and Borders toolbar. Repeat this process for each cell in the rightmost column of the table – working your way up the table. If your totals are incorrect, click Table on the menu bar, click Formula, be sure the formula is =SUM(LEFT), and then click the OK button.

8. Center the cells containing the column headings, e.g, Monday, Tuesday, etc.

9. Right-align the cells containing numbers.

10. Select the rows below the subtitle, Weekly Sales Report, and then click the Distribute Rows Evenly button on the Tables and Borders toolbar.

11. Bold the cells in the last row and also in the rightmost column.

12. Click File on the menu bar and then click Save As. Use the file name Revised Weekly Sales Report.

13. Print the revised document.

In the Lab

1 Creating a Proposal Using the Draw Table Feature

Problem: The owner of The Computer Doctor has hired you to prepare a sales proposal describing his services (Figures 4-83a and 4-83b), which will be mailed to all community residents.

Instructions:

1. Create the title page as shown in Figure 4-83a. The computer is located in the Cartoons category of the Clip Gallery or search for the keywords, sick computer, to locate the image of the computer. Resize the graphic to 175% of the original size (approximately 3.5" wide and 3" high). *Hint*: Click the Format Picture button on the Picture toolbar and then click the Size tab.

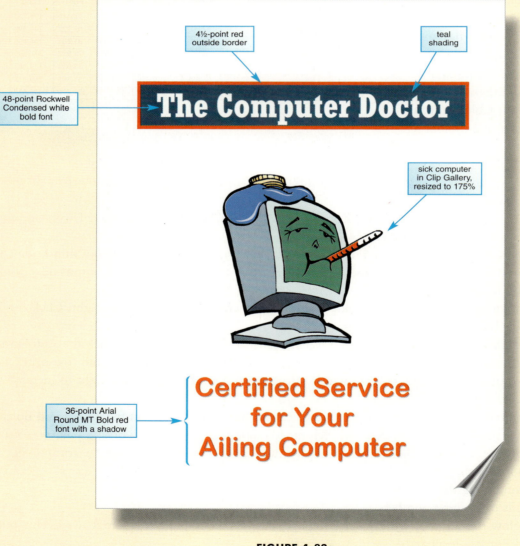

FIGURE 4-83a

In the Lab

2. Center the title page vertically. Insert a section break. Return to the Normal style. Change the vertical alignment for the second section to top. Adjust line spacing to double. If necessary, change the font size to 12 for the body of the proposal.

3. Enter the body of the proposal as shown in Figure 4-83b. The body of the proposal has a list with red picture bullets and a table created with the Draw Table feature. Single-space the table. Change the alignment of the row titles, Software and Hardware, to Align Center Left. *Hint:* Use the Align button arrow on the Tables and Borders toolbar. Select the table and shade it Light Turquoise using the Shading Color button arrow on the Tables and Borders toolbar.

4. Check the spelling. Save the document with Computer Doctor Proposal as the file name. View and print the document in print preview.

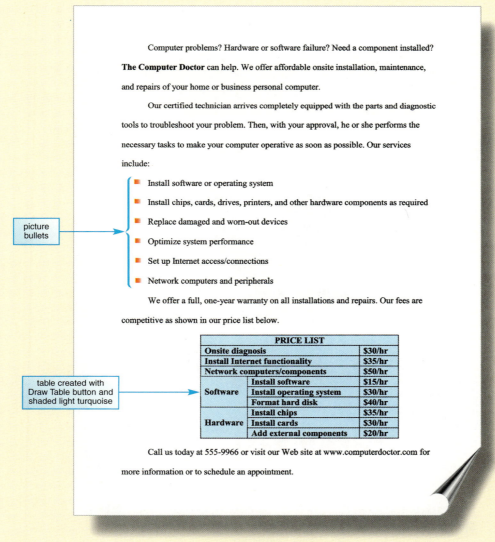

FIGURE 4-83b

2 Creating a Proposal Using Downloaded Clip Art and a Chart

Problem: Your neighbor owns Entertainment Enterprises and has hired you to create a sales proposal for Sunshine the Clown. You develop the proposal shown in Figures 4-84a and 4-84b.

Instructions:

1. Create the title page as shown in Figure 4-84a. Download the clip art from Microsoft's Clip Gallery Live Web page. To reach this file, type `clown` in the SEARCH by keyword text box. If you do not have access to the Web, you can import the file (file name PE03690_) from the Data Disk. If you did not download the Data Disk, see the inside back cover for instructions for downloading the Data Disk or see your instructor.

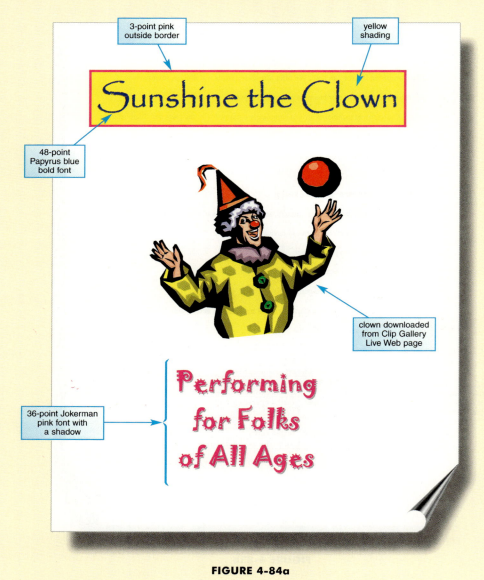

FIGURE 4-84a

In the Lab

2. Center the title page vertically. Insert a section break. Return to the Normal style. Change the Vertical alignment for the second section to top. Adjust line spacing to double. If necessary, change the font size to 12 for the body of the proposal.

3. Create the body of the proposal as shown in Figure 4-84b. The body of the proposal has picture bullets and a table created with the Insert Table button. The table contains five columns and two rows and is formatted using the Grid 3 AutoFormat option. Center the table between the page margins. Chart the table. Change the chart type to Pie with a 3-D visual effect. *Hint*: Right-click when the ScreenTip is Chart Area and then click Chart Type on the shortcut menu.

4. In the second section of the document, create a watermark of the clown graphic.

5. Check the spelling. Save the document with Sunshine Proposal as the file name. View and print the document in print preview.

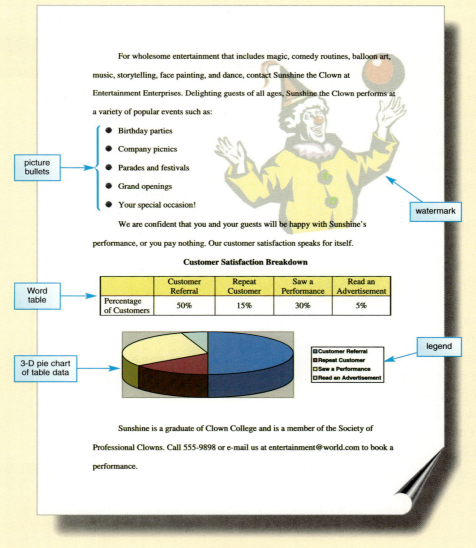

FIGURE 4-84b

In the Lab

3 Enhancing a Draft of a Proposal

Problem: You work for the marketing director at Antique Autos. You create a title page (Figure 4-85a) for an informal sales proposal that your boss has drafted (Figures 4-85b and 4-85c) to be sent to prospective customers around the country. You decide to add picture bullets, another table, a chart, and a watermark to the body of the proposal.

This lab uses the Data Disk. If you did not download the Data Disk, see the inside back cover for instructions for downloading the Data Disk or see your instructor.

Instructions:

1. Create the title page as shown in Figure 4-85a. *Hint:* Use the Format dialog box to apply the wave double underline and the outline format to the text. The antique car clip art is located at Microsoft's Clip Gallery Live Web page. To reach this file, type `antique car` in the SEARCH by keyword text box. If you do not have access to the Web, you can import the file (file name TN00288_) from the Data Disk.

2. Center the title page vertically. Insert a section break. Return to the Normal style. Insert the draft of the body of the proposal below the title page using the File command on the Insert menu. The draft is called Antique Autos Draft on the Data Disk. The draft of the body of the proposal is shown in Figures 4-85b and 4-85c. Be sure change the alignment to Top for section 2.

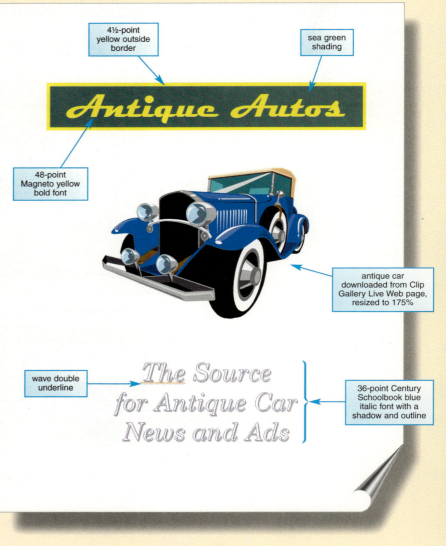

4½-point yellow outside border

sea green shading

48-point Magneto yellow bold font

antique car downloaded from Clip Gallery Live Web page, resized to 175%

wave double underline

36-point Century Schoolbook blue italic font with a shadow and outline

FIGURE 4-85a

In the Lab

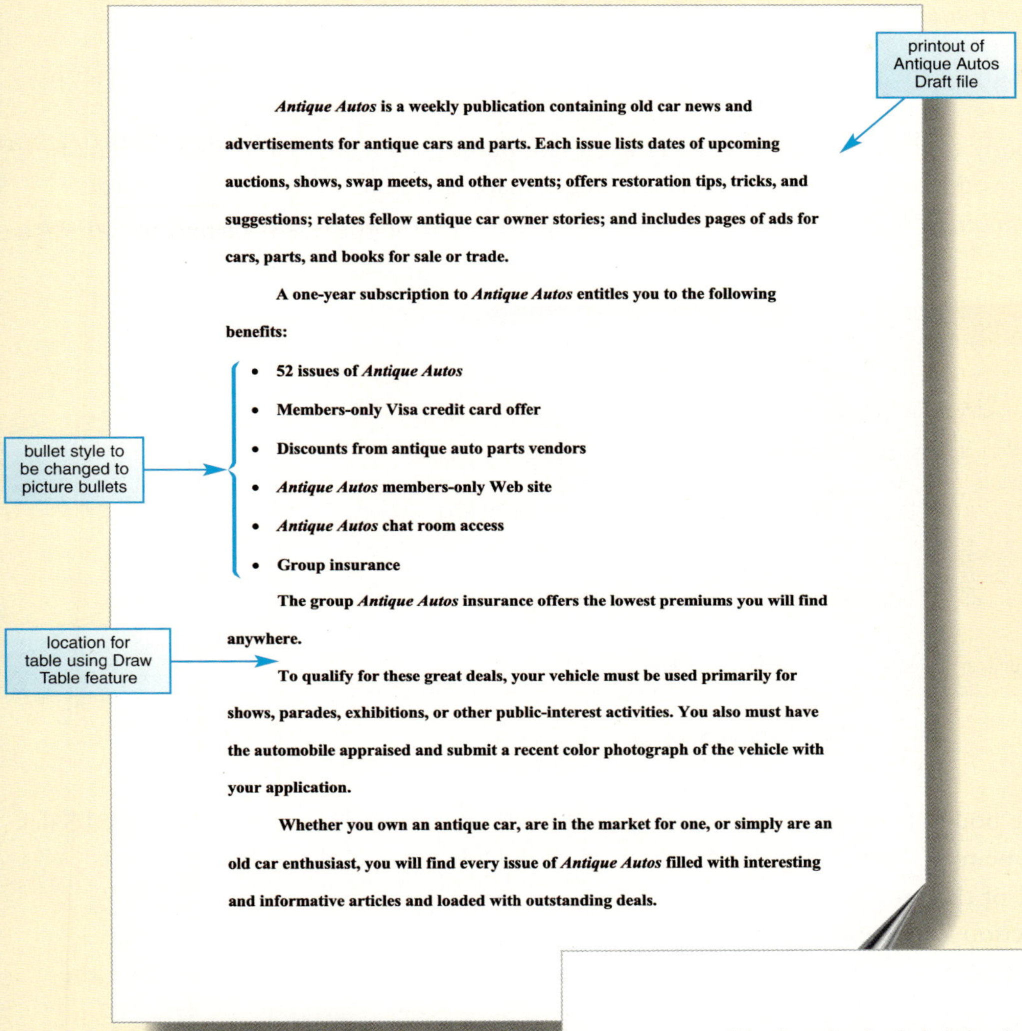

printout of
Antique Autos
Draft file

Antique Autos is a weekly publication containing old car news and advertisements for antique cars and parts. Each issue lists dates of upcoming auctions, shows, swap meets, and other events; offers restoration tips, tricks, and suggestions; relates fellow antique car owner stories; and includes pages of ads for cars, parts, and books for sale or trade.

A one-year subscription to *Antique Autos* entitles you to the following benefits:

bullet style to be changed to picture bullets

- 52 issues of *Antique Autos*
- Members-only Visa credit card offer
- Discounts from antique auto parts vendors
- *Antique Autos* members-only Web site
- *Antique Autos* chat room access
- Group insurance

The group *Antique Autos* insurance offers the lowest premiums you will find anywhere.

location for table using Draw Table feature

To qualify for these great deals, your vehicle must be used primarily for shows, parades, exhibitions, or other public-interest activities. You also must have the automobile appraised and submit a recent color photograph of the vehicle with your application.

Whether you own an antique car, are in the market for one, or simply are an old car enthusiast, you will find every issue of *Antique Autos* filled with interesting and informative articles and loaded with outstanding deals.

FIGURE 4-85b

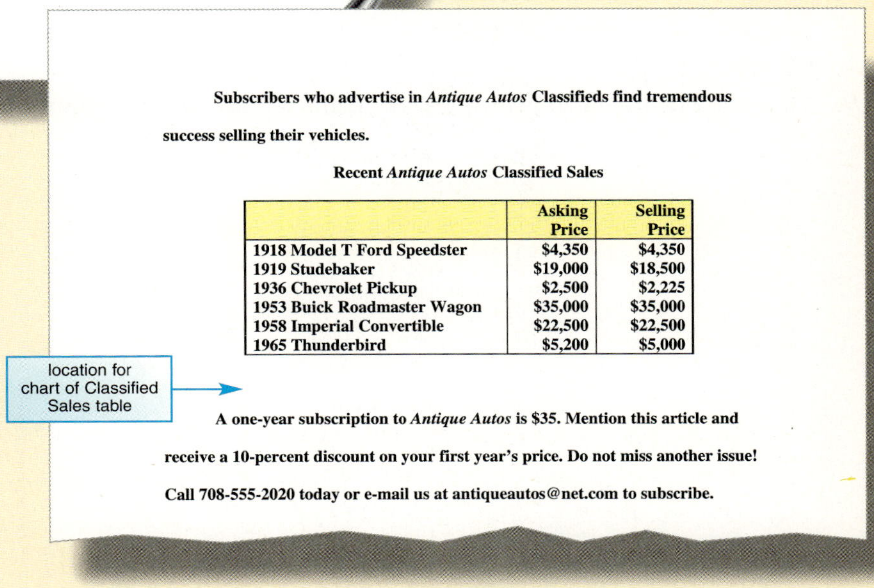

Subscribers who advertise in *Antique Autos* Classifieds find tremendous success selling their vehicles.

Recent *Antique Autos* Classified Sales

	Asking Price	Selling Price
1918 Model T Ford Speedster	$4,350	$4,350
1919 Studebaker	$19,000	$18,500
1936 Chevrolet Pickup	$2,500	$2,225
1953 Buick Roadmaster Wagon	$35,000	$35,000
1958 Imperial Convertible	$22,500	$22,500
1965 Thunderbird	$5,200	$5,000

location for chart of Classified Sales table

A one-year subscription to *Antique Autos* is $35. Mention this article and receive a 10-percent discount on your first year's price. Do not miss another issue!

Call 708-555-2020 today or e-mail us at antiqueautos@net.com to subscribe.

FIGURE 4-85c

(continued)

In the Lab

Enhancing a Draft of a Proposal *(continued)*

3. On the first page of the body of the proposal, change the style of the bullet characters in the list to picture bullets.

4. On the first page of the body of the proposal, use the Draw Table button to create a table that is similar to Figure 4-86 below the third paragraph in the proposal. Single-space the table, adjusting table borders to fit all text as necessary. *Hint*: Use Help to learn about resizing tables. Format the table using the Grid 8 AutoFormat option.

Sample Antique Auto Insurance Premiums		1st Car	2nd Car	3rd Car
Liability ($300,000 single limit)		$15.00	$10.00	$5.00
Medical Payments ($1,000 limit)		$3.00	$2.00	$1.00
Physical Damage	Comprehensive	$0.35 per $100 of appraisal value		
	Collision	$0.40 per $100 of appraisal value		
Uninsured/Underinsured Motorist	determined by state			

FIGURE 4-86

5. On the second page of the body of the proposal, create a chart of the Recent Antique Autos Classified Sales table. Change the chart type to Cylinder. Enlarge the chart so all the labels are visible.

6. Add a header to section 2 of the proposal.

7. Create a watermark in section 2 of the proposal using the antique auto graphic.

8. Save the active document with the file name Antique Autos Proposal using the Save As command on the File menu.

9. View the document in print preview. Print the document from within print preview.

Cases and Places

The difficulty of these case studies varies:
◗ are the least difficult; ◗◗ are more difficult; and ◗◗◗ are the most difficult.

1 ◗ As assistant to the promotions director, you have been assigned the task of preparing a sales proposal that recruits new members to the Camper Club. The title page is to contain the name, Camper Club, followed by an appropriate camping graphic, and then the slogan, Experiencing Outdoor Adventures with Friends. The body of the proposal should contain the following: first paragraph – Looking for adventures in the great outdoors? Want to meet new friends? Do you like to camp? The Camper Club is looking for new members. As a member you are entitled to a variety of benefits.; list with picture bullets – Monthly Issue of Camper Club, Reduced rates at campgrounds across the country, Discounts on Camp America orders, Low-rate recreational vehicle insurance protection, Listings of Camper Club Chapter members in your area, Participation in Camper Club Chapter outings; next paragraph – The Camper Club currently has more than 50,000 members nationwide. Upon membership, you will be sent a current catalog of all members across the nation; the data for the table is shown in Figure 4-87; last paragraph - A membership costs just $25 per year. Mention this article when you join and receive a 20 percent discount on your first year's membership. Call 708-555-1818, e-mail us at camperclub@hill.com, or visit our Web site at www.camperclub.com to join today!

Sample Chapter Breakdowns		Male	Female
Southern Indiana	Adult	75	79
	Teen	23	27
	Child	35	32
Northern Texas	Adult	101	98
	Teen	33	40
	Child	56	43

FIGURE 4-87

2 ◗◗ Assume you are running for an office in your school's Student Government Association. You plan to design a sales proposal to post around campus that sells *you*; that is, it explains why you are the best candidate for the job. Create a proposal that outlines your interests, summarizes your activities, and highlights your accomplishments. It also may present your background, education, and other pertinent experiences. Use whatever personal information you believe is relevant to the office being sought. Place your name, an appropriate graphic, and a slogan on the title page. Be sure the body of the proposal includes the following items: a list with picture bullets, a table, a chart, and a watermark.

Cases and Places

3 ▶▶ During the course of a semester, you utilize several facilities on campus. These may include registration, advising, cafeteria, day care, computer facilities, career development, fitness center, library, bookstore, student government, and/or the tutoring center. Select an item from this list, or one of your own, that you feel needs improvement at your school. Visit the library or surf the Internet for guidelines on preparing a planning proposal. Develop a planning proposal you could submit to the Dean of Students that recommends some action the school could take to improve the situation. Design an appropriate title page. Be sure the body of the proposal includes the following items: a list with picture bullets, a table, a chart, and a watermark.

4 ▶▶ Assume your school is creating or modifying a core curriculum, which is a list of courses that every enrolled student must complete prior to graduation – regardless of major. Much discussion/controversy centers on the list of *essential* courses. As an active member of the Student Government Association, you have been asked for your recommendations on which classes you feel should be in the core curriculum and why. Visit the library or surf the Internet for guidelines on preparing a planning proposal. Develop a planning proposal that recommends a core curriculum to your school's Curriculum Committee. Design an appropriate title page. Be sure the body of the proposal includes the following items: a list with picture bullets, a table, a chart, and a watermark.

5 ▶▶▶ You have been assigned the task of writing a proposal to request funds to landscape or enhance the landscape on the grounds at your school. The proposal should describe the current condition of the grounds, as well as the proposed landscaping designs (e.g, trees, grass, sod, flowers, shrubs, etc.). Provide a minimum of two alternative cost quotations, with sources of the quotations cited. Visit the library or surf the Internet for guidelines on preparing a research proposal. Draft a research proposal that presents your findings, suggests two alternatives, and then recommends your suggested design to your school's decision-making body. Design an appropriate title page. Be sure the body of the proposal includes the following items: a list with picture bullets, a table, a chart, a header with a page number, and a watermark.

6 ▶▶▶ Your school has a budget for student trips. You have been assigned the task of writing a proposal to request funds for your entire class to attend an out-of-town conference. Locate a conference that appeals to you. The proposal should describe the conference, its relevance, and all associated costs (e.g., travel, conference, meals, lodging, supplies, etc.). For travel and lodging, provide a minimum of two alternative cost quotations, with sources of the quotations cited. Visit the library or surf the Internet for guidelines on preparing a research proposal. Draft a research proposal that presents your findings, suggests the cost alternatives, and then recommends the best package to your school's decision-making body. Design an appropriate title page. Be sure the body of the proposal includes the following items: a list with picture bullets, a table, a chart, a header with a page number, and a watermark.

Microsoft **Word 2000**

Microsoft Word 2000

Generating Form Letters, Mailing Labels, and Envelopes

You will have mastered the material in this project when you can:

- Explain the merge process
- Explain the terms, data field and data record
- Use a template to create a letter
- Create a data source
- Print a document in landscape orientation
- Switch from a data source to the main document
- Insert merge fields into the main document
- Create an outline numbered list
- Use an IF field in the main document
- Insert a Fill-in field in the main document
- Merge and print form letters
- Selectively merge and print form letters
- Sort a data source
- Address mailing labels
- Address envelopes

True to Form

Personalization Yields a Definite Response

S orting your mail is a lingering task in this age of personalized junk mail. At times, it is hard to determine which letters have merit. You dare not discard them all for fear of tossing an important notice or missing an official date. In the stack of correspondence are credit card applications, clothing catalogs, free vacations to interesting places, announcements of sales and grand openings, free subscriptions, sweepstakes forms, and other envelopes, all with your name on them.

The U.S. Postal Service calls these unsolicited offers "bulk business mail," and they are big business. As much as we complain about this mail, Americans are responding to these pitches in record numbers.

Part of the reason for this success is the sellers' ability to send form letters and offers tailored to individuals' specific interests and buying habits. The personalized Eagle Run Golf Club form letters and corresponding mailing labels and envelopes you will

Title	FirstName	LastName	Address1	Address2	City	State	PostalCode	Student
Ms.	Akilah	Green	15 Park Boulevard		Brea	CA	92821	N
Mr.	James	Wheeler	113 Fourth Street	Apt. 3C	Placentia	CA	82870	Y
Dr.	Vidya	Garlapati	P.O. Box 1015	15 Central Avenue	Los Alamitos	CA	90720	N
Prof.	David	Raminski	1145 Sunset Street		Anaheim	CA	90205	N
Mrs.	May	Li	189 Eastern Avenue		Fullerton	CA	92805	Y

Mr. James Wheeler
113 Fourth Street
Apt. 3C
Placentia, CA 82870

Dr. Vidya Garlapati
P.O. Box 1015
15 Central Avenue
Los Alamitos, CA 90720

Prof. David Raminski
1145 Sunset Street
Anaheim, CA 92905

Ms. Akilah Green
15 Park Boulevard
Brea, CA 92821

Mrs. May Li
189 Eastern Avenue
Fullerton, CA 92831

WELLCOME TO
ITALY TRAVEL GROUP

The best your vacation

ITALY

Your Vacation

FREE PAY PER VIEW MOVIE

Take the family to the movies on us!

Order any Pay Per View movie of your choice:

Then fill out the coupon on the

back and return it with your bill.

Your accou...

So...

GRAND OPENING
SPORTS STORE

50% off
on every items

FRIDAY & SATURDAY
JULY - 12 &13

12692 DELEMEAN AVE.
GRANDWOOD, CA 00001
(745) 555-0001

Certificate
of Birth

NEILL
last
Hospital: Foutain Valley
1968
State: Texas

create in Project 5 are an example of this capability. Individuals and business executives are more likely to open and read a personalized letter than a standard bulk mail letter.

Where do these marketers get your name? How do they know you just bought a house, had a baby, or like to golf? Whether you like it or not, specific details of all phases of your life are fields in highly specialized databases used to churn out four million tons of personalized letters every year.

Much of the data in these databases comes from public records in local governmental offices: birth certificates, business licenses, and marriage certificates. Real estate records contain the owner, price, and date sold of every parcel of land. State and federal tax lien information, civil lawsuits, and bankruptcy filings are easily obtainable. Records are generated each time you use or apply for a credit card. Consumers volunteer information when they describe their family size, income, and hobbies on product warranty cards. Telephone

books and U.S. Postal Service address change forms also are major sources of profitable data.

Companies research, compile, and rent this data to marketers at the rate of $50 to $150 per 1,000 names. List makers boast they have more than 10,000 customized lists for rent, including those containing the names and addresses of 35 million college students, 750,000 professors, 7 million credit card holders, and 5 million pet owners.

Companies can rent several lists and search for the same names appearing on each one. For example, a financial institution marketing credit cards to affluent homeowners with good credit histories can merge lists with Census Bureau records of people living in specific areas, the buying habits of people in these neighborhoods, and credit reports showing good credit risks. Some companies may use up to 100 lists to fine-tune the names in an attempt to find appropriate mail prospects.

These targeted mailings are an efficient way for direct marketers to find nearly 100 times as many consumers as they would by running a television ad. With this success, be prepared to receive even more personalized solicitations.

Microsoft Word 2000

Generating Form Letters, Mailing Labels, and Envelopes

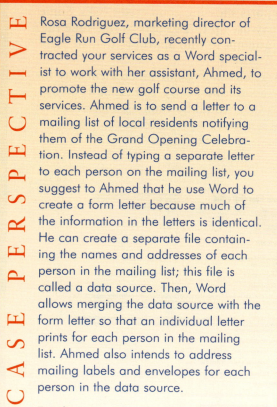

Rosa Rodriguez, marketing director of Eagle Run Golf Club, recently contracted your services as a Word specialist to work with her assistant, Ahmed, to promote the new golf course and its services. Ahmed is to send a letter to a mailing list of local residents notifying them of the Grand Opening Celebration. Instead of typing a separate letter to each person on the mailing list, you suggest to Ahmed that he use Word to create a form letter because much of the information in the letters is identical. He can create a separate file containing the names and addresses of each person in the mailing list; this file is called a data source. Then, Word allows merging the data source with the form letter so that an individual letter prints for each person in the mailing list. Ahmed also intends to address mailing labels and envelopes for each person in the data source.

For those people who become a member during the Grand Opening Celebration, Rosa wants two separate discount rates, with the lower rate being offered to students. That is, students receive a 75 percent discount and all other people receive a 25 percent discount.

Introduction

An individual or business executive is more likely to open and read a personalized letter than a standard Dear Sir or Dear Madam letter. Because typing individual letters to many people is a time-consuming task, you can generate personalized letters in Word by creating a form letter. Form letters are used regularly in both business and personal correspondence. The basic content of a group of **form letters** is similar; however, items such as name, address, city, state, and postal code change from one letter to the next. Thus, form letters are personalized to the addressee.

Form letters usually are sent to a group of people. **Business form letters** include announcements of sales to customers or notices of benefits to employees. **Personal form letters** include letters of application for a job or invitations to participate in a sweepstakes giveaway. With Word, you easily can address envelopes or mailing labels for the form letters.

Project Five — Form Letters, Mailing Labels, and Envelopes

Project 5 illustrates how to create a business form letter and address corresponding mailing labels and envelopes. The form letter is sent to local residents, informing them of Eagle Run Golf Club's upcoming Grand Opening Celebration. For those people who become a member during the Grand Opening Celebration, a varying discount rate applies, depending on whether or not the new member is a student.

The process of generating form letters involves creating a main document for the form letter and a data source, and then merging, or *blending*, the two together into a series of individual letters as shown in Figure 5-1.

(a) Main Document for the Form Letter

Eagle Run Golf Club

14500 Windy Creek Road, Anaheim, CA 92805
Telephone: (714) 555-0056 Fax: (714) 555-0057
Web: www.eaglerun.com
E-mail: eaglerun@link.com

Fill-in field

{ FILLIN "What date will you be mailing these letters?" \o }

{ MERGEFIELD Title } { MERGEFIELD FirstName } { MERGEFIELD LastName }
{ MERGEFIELD Address1 }
{ MERGEFIELD Address2 }
{ MERGEFIELD City }, { MERGEFIELD State } { MERGEFIELD PostalCode }

Dear { MERGEFIELD Title } { MERGEFIELD LastName }:

Eagle Run Golf Club invites you to attend its Grand Opening Celebration on Saturday, August 25. Our 36-hole golf course is challenging and enjoyable for golfers of all skills. Tour our 25,000 square-foot facility with clubhouse, pro shop, formal dining/banquet room, and our casual Eagle Run Grille.

For those interested in joining Eagle Run, our members receive a 15 percent discount on all pro shop services and merchandise and on meals served in both restaurants. A membership also entitles you to these additional benefits:

❖ Tee Time Reservations and Fees

➢ Tee time reservations instantly from the Web

➢ Seven-day advance preferred tee times

➢ No green or cart fees, with member guest discount on green fees

❖ Golf Events

➢ Monthly couples and singles tournaments

➢ Active men's and ladies' leagues

➢ Individual lessons and group clinics

outline numbered list

To receive a { IF { MERGEFIELD Student } = "Y" "75" "25" } percent discount on the initiation fee, become a member during our Grand Opening Celebration.

{ AUTOTEXTLIST }

IF field

Rosa Rodriguez
Marketing Director

(b) Data Source

Title	FirstName	LastName	Address1	Address2	City	State	PostalCode	Student
Ms.	Akilah	Green	15 Park Boulevard		Brea	CA	92821	N
Mr.	James	Wheeler	113 Fourth Street	Apt. 3C	Placentia	CA	82870	Y
Dr.	Vidya	Garlapati	P.O. Box 1015	15 Central Avenue	Los Alamitos	CA	90720	N
Prof.	David	Raminski	1145 Sunset Street		Anaheim	CA	92805	N
Mrs.	May	Li	189 Eastern Avenue		Fullerton	CA	92831	Y

MERGE

(c) Form Letters

form letter 1

Eagle Run Golf Club

14500 Windy Creek Road, Anaheim, CA 92805
Telephone: (714) 555-0056 Fax: (714) 555-0057
Web: www.eaglerun.com
E-mail: eaglerun@link.com

August 6, 2001

resident name and address from first data record

Ms. Akilah Green
15 Park Boulevard
Brea, CA 92821

title and last name from first data record

Dear Ms. Green:

Eagle Run Golf Club invites you to attend its Grand Opening Celebration on Saturday, August 25. Our 36-hole golf course is challenging and enjoyable for golfers of all skills. Tour our 25,000 square-foot facility with clubhouse, pro shop, formal dining/banquet room, and our casual Eagle Run Grille.

For those interested in joining Eagle Run, our members receive a 15 percent discount on all pro shop services and merchandise and on meals served in both restaurants. A membership also entitles you to these additional benefits:

❖ Tee Time Reservations and Fees

➢ Tee time reservations instantly from the Web

➢ Seven-day advance preferred tee times

➢ No green or cart fees, with member guest discount on green fees

❖ Golf Events

➢ Monthly couples and singles tournaments

➢ Active men's and ladies' leagues

➢ Individual lessons and group clinics

To receive a 25 percent discount on the initiation fee, become a member during our Grand Opening Celebration.

Sincerely,

Rosa Rodriguez
Marketing Director

25% discount because first data record is not a student

form letter 2

August 6, 2001

Mr. James Wheeler
113 Fourth Street
Apt. 3C
Placentia, CA 82870

resident name and address from second data record

Dear Mr. Wheeler:

title and last name from second data record

Eagle Run Golf Club invites you to attend its Grand Opening Ce... 36-hole golf course is challenging and enjoyable for golfers of a... facility with clubhouse, pro shop, formal dining/banquet room, a...

For those interested in joining Eagle Run, our members receive services and merchandise and on meals served in both restaur... these additional benefits:

❖ Tee Time Reservations and Fees

➢ Tee time reservations instantly from the Web

➢ Seven-day advance preferred tee times

➢ No green or cart fees, with member guest discount on...

❖ Golf Events

➢ Monthly couples and singles tournaments

➢ Active men's and ladies' leagues

➢ Individual lessons and group clinics

To receive a 75 percent discount on the initiation fee, become a... Celebration.

Sincerely,

Rosa Rodriguez
Marketing Director

75% discount because second data record is a student

FIGURE 5-1

form letter 3

form letter 4

form letter 5

Merging is the process of combining the contents of a data source with a main document. A **main document** contains the constant, or unchanging, text, punctuation, spaces, and graphics. In Figure 5-1a on the previous page, the main document represents the portion of the form letter that repeats from one merged letter to the next. Conversely, the **data source** contains the variable, or changing, values for each letter. In Figure 5-1b, the data source contains five different people. Thus, one form letter is generated for each person listed in the data source.

Using a Template to Create a Letter

You can type a letter from scratch into a blank document window, as you did with the cover letter in Project 2; or you can use the letter wizard and let Word format the letter based on your responses to the wizard; or you can use a letter template. You have learned that a **template** is similar to a form with prewritten text. In the case of the letter template, Word prepares a letter with text and/or formatting common to all letters. Then, you can customize the resulting letter by selecting and replacing prewritten text.

Word provides three styles of wizards and templates: Professional, Contemporary, and Elegant. Perform the following steps to use the Professional Letter template to create a letter.

Steps To Create a Letter Using a Word Template

1 **Click the Start button on the taskbar and then click New Office Document. If necessary, click the Letters & Faxes tab when the New Office Document dialog box displays. Click the Professional Letter icon.**

Office displays several wizard and template icons in the Letters & Faxes sheet in the New Office Document dialog box (Figure 5-2). You have learned that icons without the word, Wizard, below them are templates. A sample of the Professional Letter template displays in the Preview area.

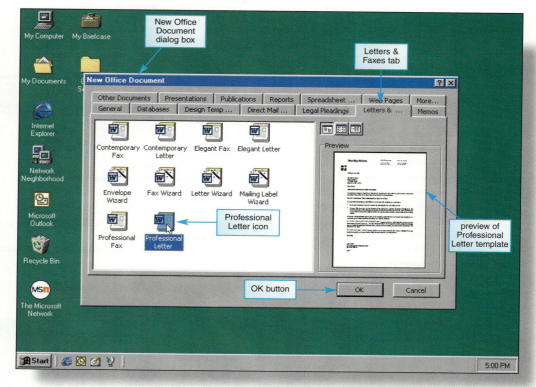

FIGURE 5-2

2 **Click the OK button.**

Office starts Word, which in turn creates a professional style letter by using the Professional Letter template and displays the letter in a document window in print layout view (Figure 5-3). Because the letter template instructs Word to display the current date in the letter, your date line more than likely will display a different date.

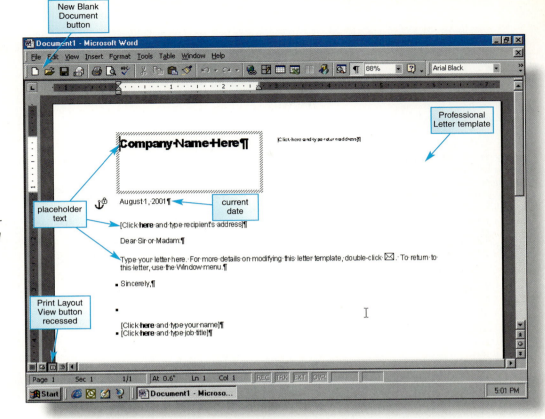

FIGURE 5-3

You have learned that a template displays prewritten text, called **placeholder text,** that you select and replace to personalize the document. Figure 5-3 identifies some of the placeholder text created by the Professional Letter template.

You learned in Project 3 that with Word on the screen, you can create a new document using the New Blank Document button (Figure 5-3) on the Standard toolbar. When you click this button, Word uses the Blank Document template located in the General sheet in the New dialog box. If you want to use a different template or a wizard, you cannot use the New Blank Document button; instead, you must display the New dialog box by clicking File on the menu bar and then clicking New.

The Professional Letter template is based on a **block style** letter; that is, all components below the company name in the letter begin flush with the left margin. In Project 3, you learned that all business letters have common elements such as a date line, inside address, message, and signature block.

In creating the template, Word uses different styles to represent various elements of the letter. You have learned that a style is a customized format that Word applies to characters or paragraphs. Figure 5-4 on the next page identifies the styles used in the Professional Letter template. The Style box on the Formatting toolbar displays the name of the style associated with the location of the insertion point (see Figure 5-6 on page WD 5.10). When you modify the cover letter, the style associated with the location of the insertion point will be applied to the text you type.

Other Ways

1. In Microsoft Word, on File menu click New, click Letters & Faxes tab, double-click Professional Letter template

More About

New Documents

When you click File on the menu bar and then click New, Word displays the New dialog box. When you click the Start button and then click New Office Document, Office displays the New Office Document dialog box. The New Office Document dialog box contains all the tabbed sheets in Word's New dialog box, in addition to those sheets associated with other Office applications.

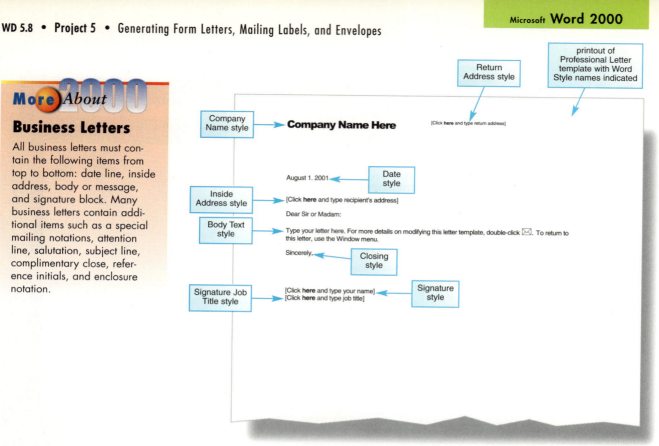

FIGURE 5-4

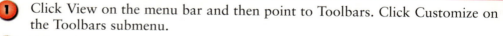

Resetting Menus and Toolbars

To set the menus and toolbars so they appear exactly as shown in this book, you should reset your menus and toolbars as outlined in Appendix C or follow these steps.

TO RESET MENUS AND TOOLBARS

1 Click View on the menu bar and then point to Toolbars. Click Customize on the Toolbars submenu.

2 When the Customize dialog box displays, click the Options tab, make sure the top three check boxes have check marks and then click the Reset my usage data button. When the Microsoft Word dialog box displays, click the Yes button.

3 Click the Toolbars tab. Click Standard in the Toolbars list and then click the Reset button. When the Reset Toolbar dialog box displays, click the OK button.

4 Click Formatting in the Toolbars list and then click the Reset button. When the Reset Toolbar dialog box displays, click the OK button. Click the Close button.

Word resets the menus and toolbars.

Zooming Text Width

As you have learned, when you **zoom text width**, Word displays text on the screen as large as possible in print layout view without extending the right margin beyond the right edge of the document window. Perform the following steps to zoom text width.

TO ZOOM TEXT WIDTH

1. Double-click the move handle on the Standard toolbar to display the entire toolbar. Click the Zoom box arrow on the Standard toolbar.

2. Click Text Width in the Zoom list.

Word computes the zoom percentage based on a variety of settings (see Figure 5-5). Your percentage may be different depending on your system configuration.

Displaying Formatting Marks

You have learned that it is helpful to display formatting marks that indicate where in the document you pressed the ENTER key, SPACEBAR, and other keys. Follow this step to display formatting marks.

TO DISPLAY FORMATTING MARKS

1. If the Show/Hide ¶ button on the Standard toolbar is not already recessed, click it.

Word displays formatting marks in the document window, and the Show/Hide ¶ button on the Standard toolbar is recessed (see Figure 5-5).

Selecting and Replacing Template Placeholder Text

The first step in personalizing the letter is to create the company letterhead. As this is the golf club's grand opening, they do not yet have any preprinted letterhead. Thus, you create a letterhead by filling in the placeholder text as indicated in the letter template. Select, format, and then replace the text as shown in the following steps.

To Select and Replace Placeholder Text

1. **Drag through the placeholder text, Company Name Here.**

The placeholder text displays surrounded by a frame (Figure 5-5). Word frames the company name to provide flexibility in its location. Frames are discussed in more depth in the next project.

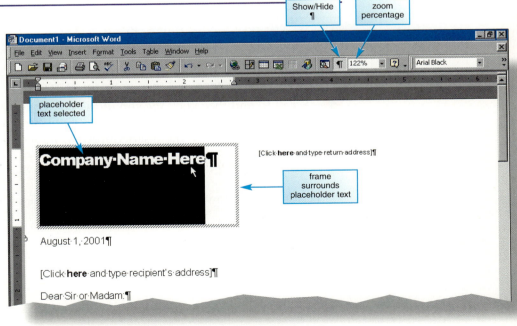

FIGURE 5-5

2 **Double-click the move handle on the Formatting toolbar to display the entire toolbar. Click the Font box arrow. Scroll to and then click Script MT Bold, or a similar font, in the Font list. Click the Font Size box arrow and then click 24. Click the Font Color button arrow and then click Green. Type** `Eagle Run Golf Club` **and then press the ENTER key.**

Word displays the company name in 24-point Script MT Bold green font (Figure 5-6).

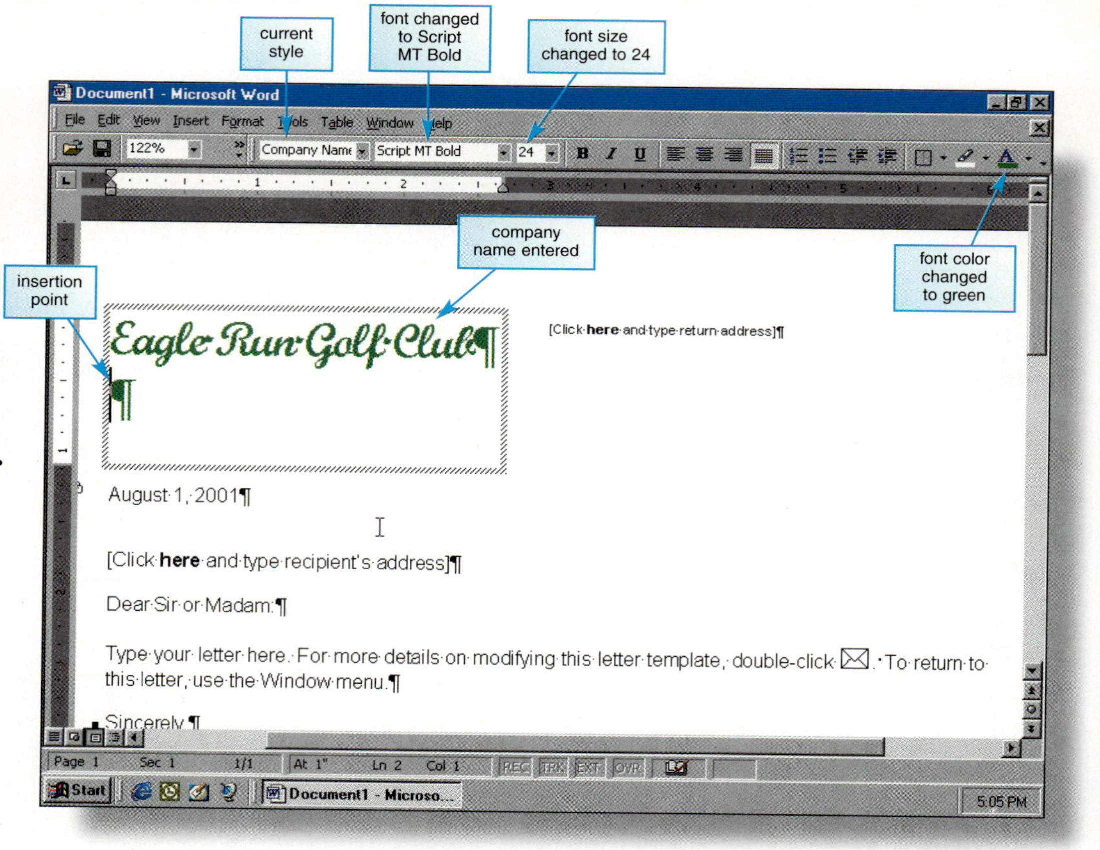

current style

font changed to Script MT Bold

font size changed to 24

company name entered

insertion point

font color changed to green

FIGURE 5-6

The next step is to insert a graphic of a golf course from the Clip Gallery below the company name, and then reduce the size of the graphic to 25 percent of its original size. Perform the following steps to insert the golf course graphic.

TO INSERT CLIP ART

1 With the insertion point on line 2 as shown in Figure 5-6, click Insert on the menu bar, point to Picture, and then click Clip Art.

2 When the Insert ClipArt window opens, click the Search for clips text box. Type `golf course` and then press the ENTER key.

3 Scroll to and then click the clip of the golf course that matches the one shown in Figure 5-7. Click the Insert clip button on the Pop-up menu. Click the Close button on the Insert ClipArt window's title bar.

Word inserts the golf course image into the document.

Perform the following steps to resize the graphic to 25 percent of its original size.

Steps To Resize a Graphic

1 **Click the graphic to select it. If the Picture toolbar does not display on the screen, right-click the graphic and then click Show Picture Toolbar on the shortcut menu. Point to the Format Picture button on the Picture toolbar (Figure 5-7).**

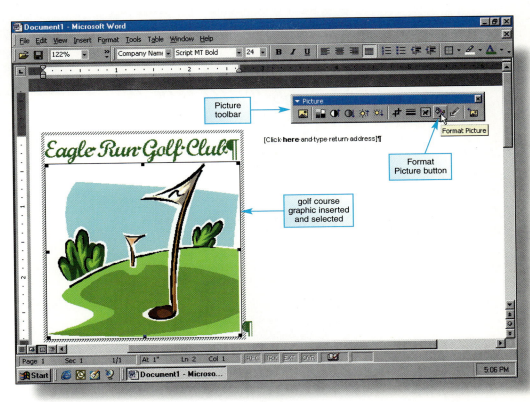

FIGURE 5-7

2 **Click the Format Picture button. When the Format Picture dialog box displays, click the Size tab. In the Scale area, drag through the text in the Height box. Type** 25 **and then press the TAB key. If necessary, type** 25 **in the Width box. Point to the OK button.**

Word displays the Format Picture dialog box (Figure 5-8).

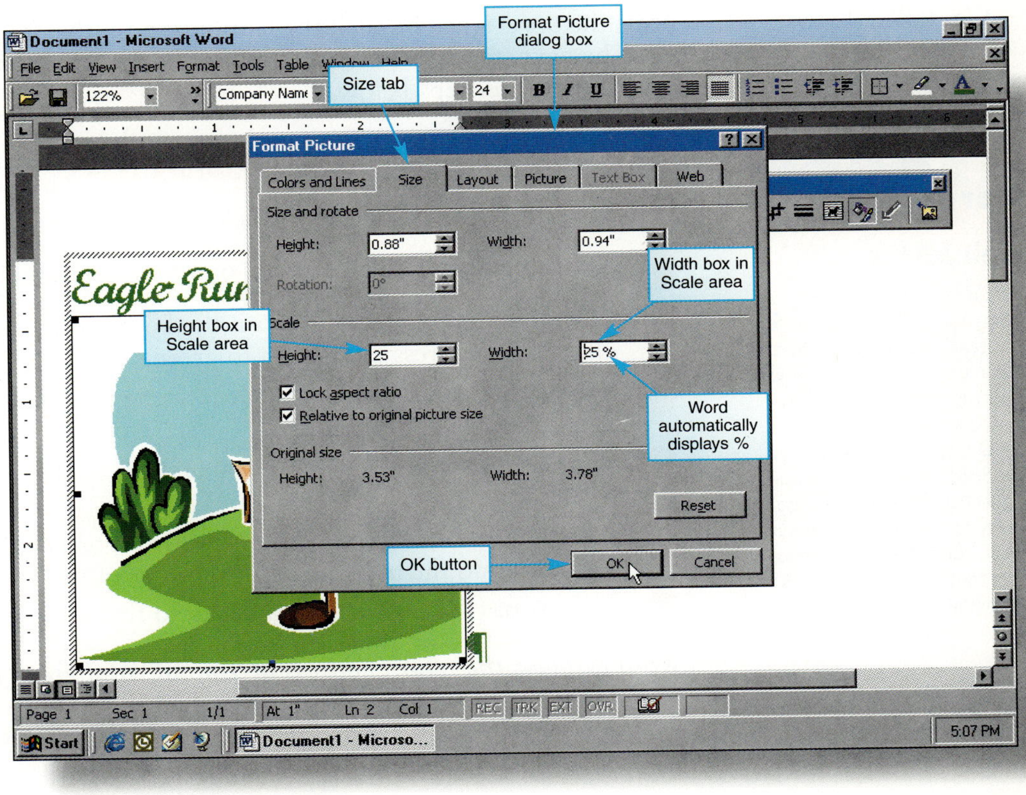

FIGURE 5-8

3 **Click the OK button.**

Word resizes the graphic to 25 percent of its original size (Figure 5-9).

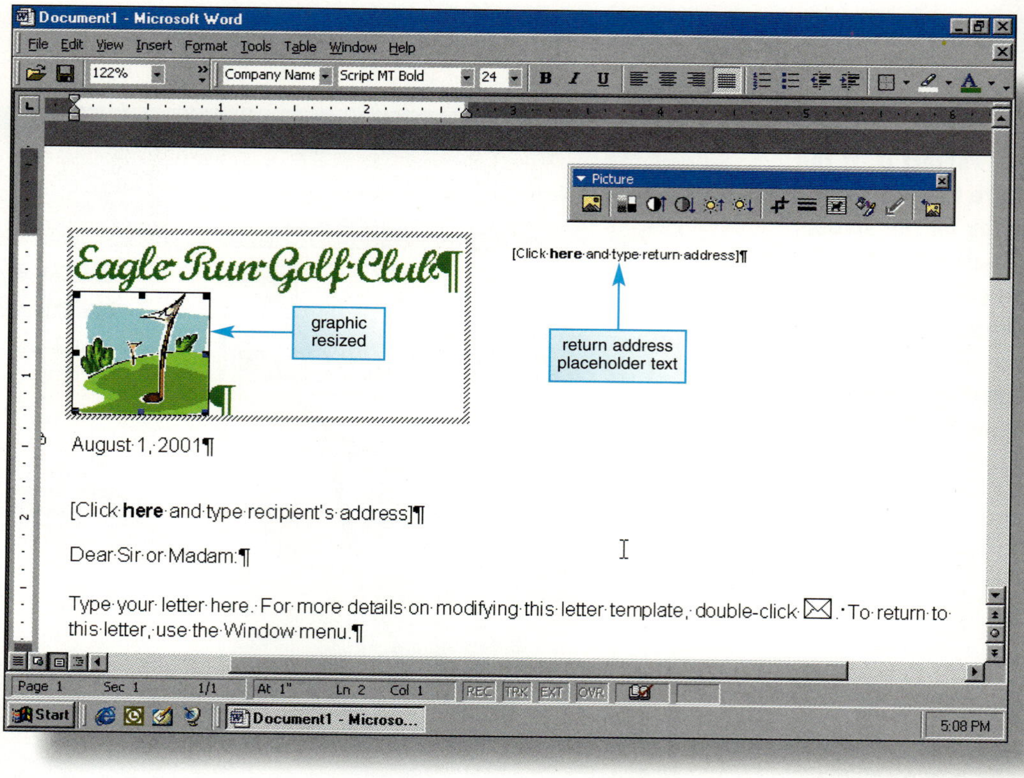

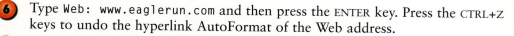

FIGURE 5-9

If, for some reason, you wanted to delete a graphic, you would select it and then press the DELETE key or click the Cut button on the Standard toolbar.

The next step is to enter the return address in 9-point Arial green font as described in the steps below.

TO SELECT AND REPLACE MORE PLACEHOLDER TEXT

1 Click the placeholder text, Click **here** and type return address (see Figure 5-9).

2 Click the Font Size box arrow on the Formatting toolbar and then click 9.

3 Click the Font Color button on the Formatting toolbar to change the color of the return address paragraph to green.

4 Type 14500 Windy Creek Road, Anaheim, CA 92805 and then press the ENTER key.

5 Type Telephone: (714) 555-0056 Fax: (714) 555-0057 and then press the ENTER key.

6 Type Web: www.eaglerun.com and then press the ENTER key. Press the CTRL+Z keys to undo the hyperlink AutoFormat of the Web address.

7 Type E-mail: eaglerun@link.com to finish the return address.

Word displays the return address in 9-point Arial green font (Figure 5-10).

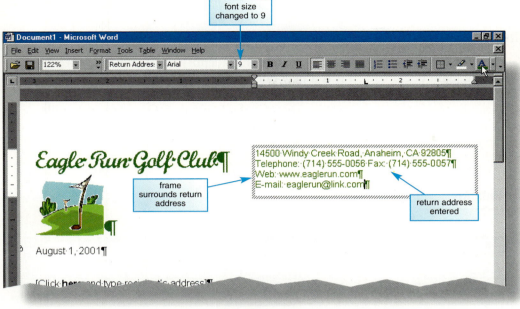

FIGURE 5-10

Because you have performed several tasks, you should save the document as described in the following steps.

TO SAVE THE LETTER

1 Insert your floppy disk into drive A.

2 Double-click the move handle on the Standard toolbar to display the entire toolbar. Click the Save button on the Standard toolbar.

3 Type Eagle Run Grand Opening in the File name text box. Do not press the ENTER key after typing the file name.

4 If necessary, click the Save in box arrow and then click 3½ Floppy (A:).

5 Click the Save button in the Save As dialog box.

Word saves the document on a floppy disk on drive A with the file name, Eagle Run Grand Opening (see Figure 5-11 on the next page).

You are ready to begin typing the body of the form letter. To do this, you work with two documents: the form letter, which contains constant text, and the data source, which contains varying data. The next series of steps illustrate how to link these two documents together so that you can work between them.

Identifying the Main Document and Creating the Data Source

Creating form letters requires merging a main document with a data source. To create form letters using Word's mail merge, you perform these tasks: (1) identify the main document, (2) create or specify the data source, (3) enter the main document for the form letter, and (4) merge the data source with the main document to generate and print the form letters. The following pages illustrate these tasks.

Identifying the Main Document

The first step in the mail merge process is to identify the document you will use as the main document. If it is a new document, you can click the New Blank Document button on the Standard toolbar to open a new document window. Because the main document in this project is the Eagle Run Grand Opening file, you should leave the current document open. With the main document file open, you must identify it as such to Word's mail merge, as shown in these steps.

Steps **To Identify the Main Document**

1 **Click Tools on the menu bar and then point to Mail Merge (Figure 5-11).**

FIGURE 5-11

2 **Click Mail Merge. When the Mail Merge Helper dialog box displays, point to the Create button.**

Word displays the Mail Merge Helper dialog box (Figure 5-12). Using this dialog box, you identify the main document and can create the data source. Notice the instructions at the top of this dialog box.

FIGURE 5-12

3 Click the Create button. Point to Form Letters.

Word displays a list of main document types (Figure 5-13).

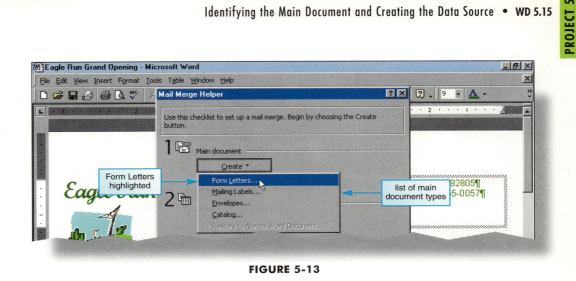

FIGURE 5-13

4 Click Form Letters.

Word displays a Microsoft Word dialog box asking if you want to use the active document window for the form letters (Figure 5-14). The Active Window button will use the current open document, Eagle Run Grand Opening, for the main document, whereas the New Main Document button opens a new document window for the main document — a procedure similar to clicking the New Blank Document button on the Standard toolbar.

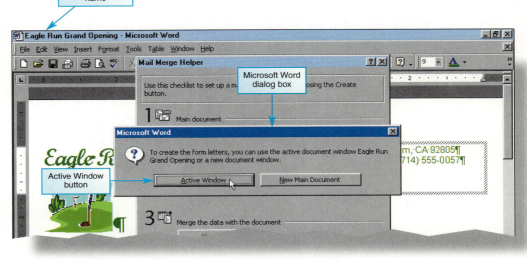

FIGURE 5-14

5 Click the Active Window button.

Word returns to the Mail Merge Helper dialog box (Figure 5-15). The merge type is identified as Form Letters and the main document is A:\Eagle Run Grand Opening.doc. An Edit button now displays in the Mail Merge Helper dialog box so you can modify the contents of the main document.

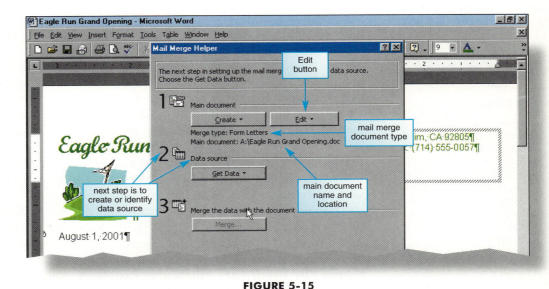

FIGURE 5-15

At this point, you will not enter the main document text; you simply identify it. As indicated in the Mail Merge Helper dialog box, the next step is to create or identify the data source. After you create the data source, you will enter the main document text.

Creating a Data Source

A data source can be a Word table (Figure 5-16). You have learned that a **Word table** is a series of rows and columns. The first row of a data source is called the **header row.** Each row below the header row is called a **data record**. Data records contain the text that varies from one merged document to the next. The data source for this project contains five data records. In this project, each data record identifies a different person. Thus, five form letters will be generated from this data source.

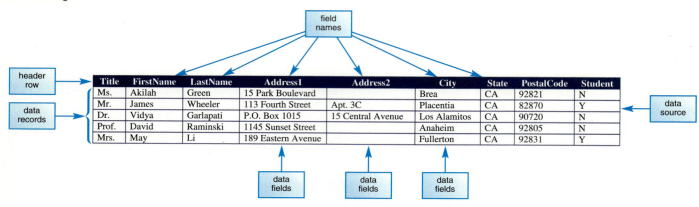

FIGURE 5-16

Each column in the data source is called a **data field**. A data field represents a group of similar data. In this project, the data source contains nine data fields: Title, FirstName, LastName, Address1, Address2, City, State, PostalCode, and Student.

In a data source, each data field must be identified uniquely with a name, called a **field name**. For example, FirstName is the name of the field (column) containing the first names. Field names are placed in the header row of the data source to identify the name of each column.

The first step in creating a data source is to decide which fields it will contain. That is, you must identify the information that will vary from one merged document to the next. In this project, each record contains up to nine different fields for each person: a courtesy title (e.g., Mrs.), first name, last name, first line of street address, second line of street address (optional), city, state, postal code, and student. The student field contains the value, Y (for Yes), or the value, N (for No), depending on whether the recipient is a student. The discount percent on the membership initiation fee is determined based on the value of the student field.

For each field, you must decide on a field name. Field names must be unique; that is, no two field names may be the same. Field names may be up to 40 characters in length, can contain only letters, numbers, and the underscore (_), and must begin with a letter. Field names cannot contain spaces.

Because data sources often contain the same fields, Word provides you with a list of 13 commonly used field names. To improve the readability of field names, Word uses a mixture of uppercase and lowercase letters to separate words within the field name (remember spaces are not allowed). You will use eight of the 13 field names supplied by Word: Title, FirstName, LastName, Address1, Address2, City, State, and PostalCode. You will delete the other five field names from the list supplied by Word. That is, you will delete JobTitle, Company, Country, HomePhone, and

WorkPhone. In this project, the only field that Word does not supply is the Student field. Thus, you will add a field name called Student.

Fields and related field names may be listed in any order in the data source. The order of fields has no effect on the order in which they will print in the main document.

Perform the following steps to create a new data source.

More About

Mail Merge Helper

If the Mail Merge Helper is not on the screen, click Tools on the menu bar and then click Mail Merge.

Steps To Create a Data Source in Word

1 **In the Mail Merge Helper dialog box, click the Get Data button and then point to Create Data Source.**

Word displays a list of data source options (Figure 5-17). You can create your own data source in Word; use a data source already created in Word; or use a file from another program such as Access, Excel, or Outlook as a data source.

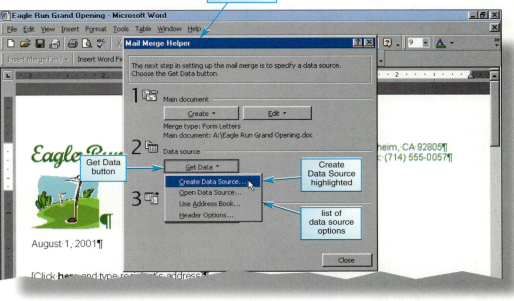

FIGURE 5-17

2 **Click Create Data Source. When the Create Data Source dialog box displays, click JobTitle in the Field names in header row list. Point to the Remove Field Name button.**

Word displays the Create Data Source dialog box (Figure 5-18). In the Field names in header row list, Word displays a list of commonly used field names. You can remove a field name from this list if you do not want it in the header row of your data source. JobTitle is highlighted for removal.

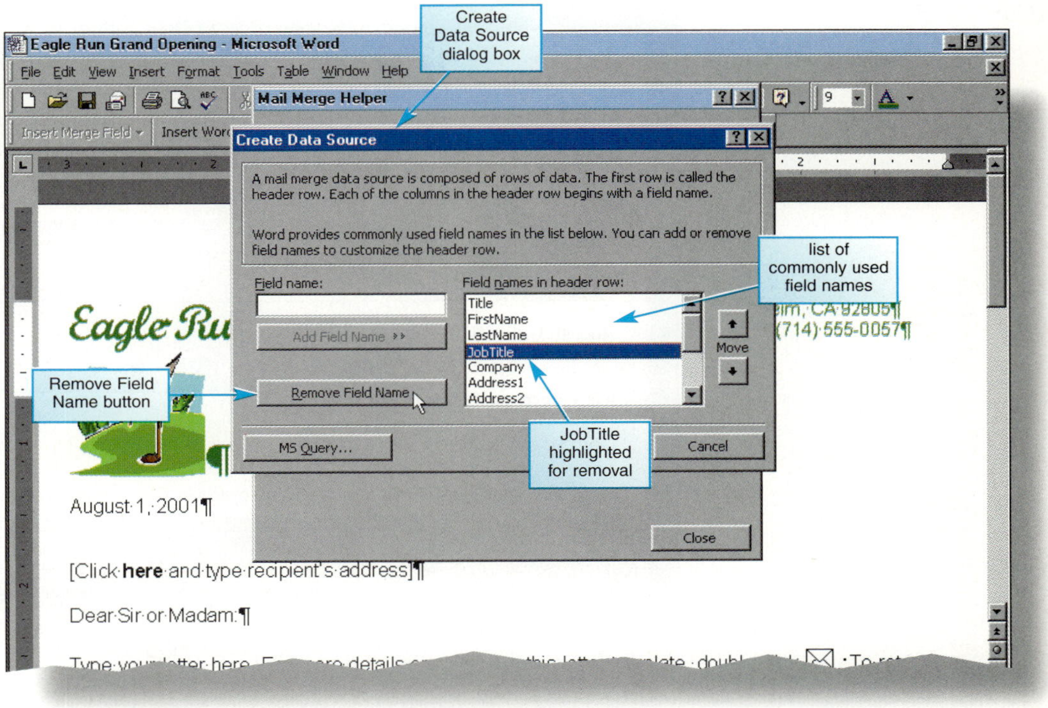

FIGURE 5-18

3 Click the Remove Field Name button to remove the JobTitle field. Click the Remove Field Name button again to remove the Company field. Scroll to the bottom of the list and then click Country. Click the Remove Field Name button three times to remove the Country, HomePhone, and WorkPhone field names.

Word removes five field names from the list (Figure 5-19). The last field name removed, WorkPhone, displays in the Field name text box. The next step is to add the Student field name to the list.

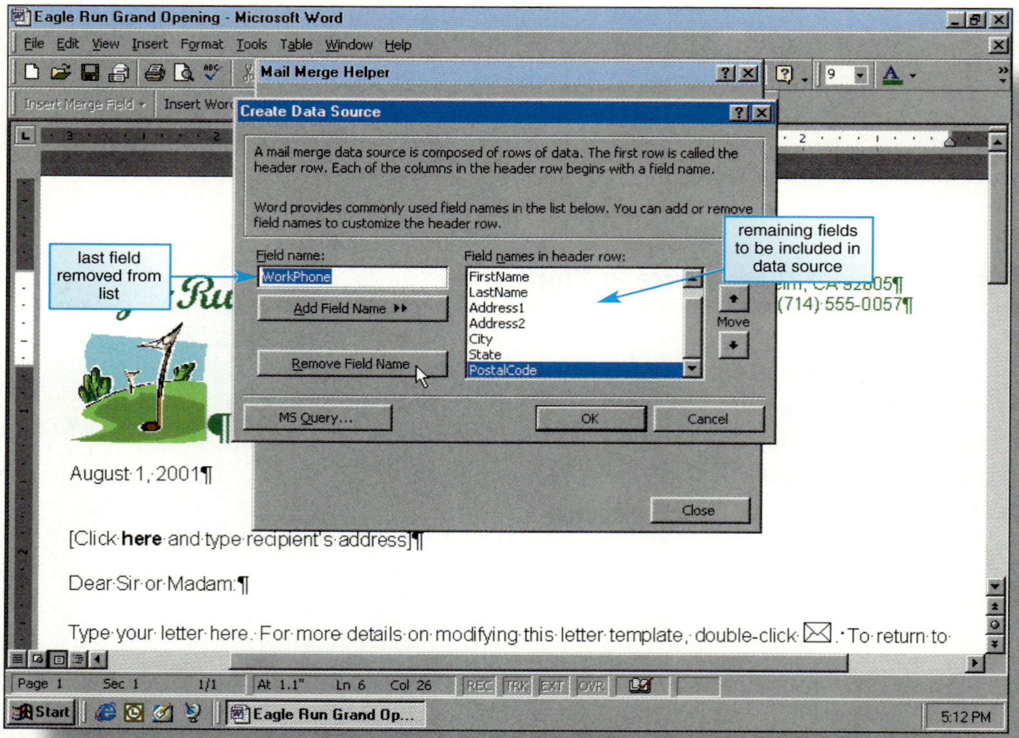

FIGURE 5-19

4 Type Student in the Field name text box and then point to the Add Field Name button (Figure 5-20).

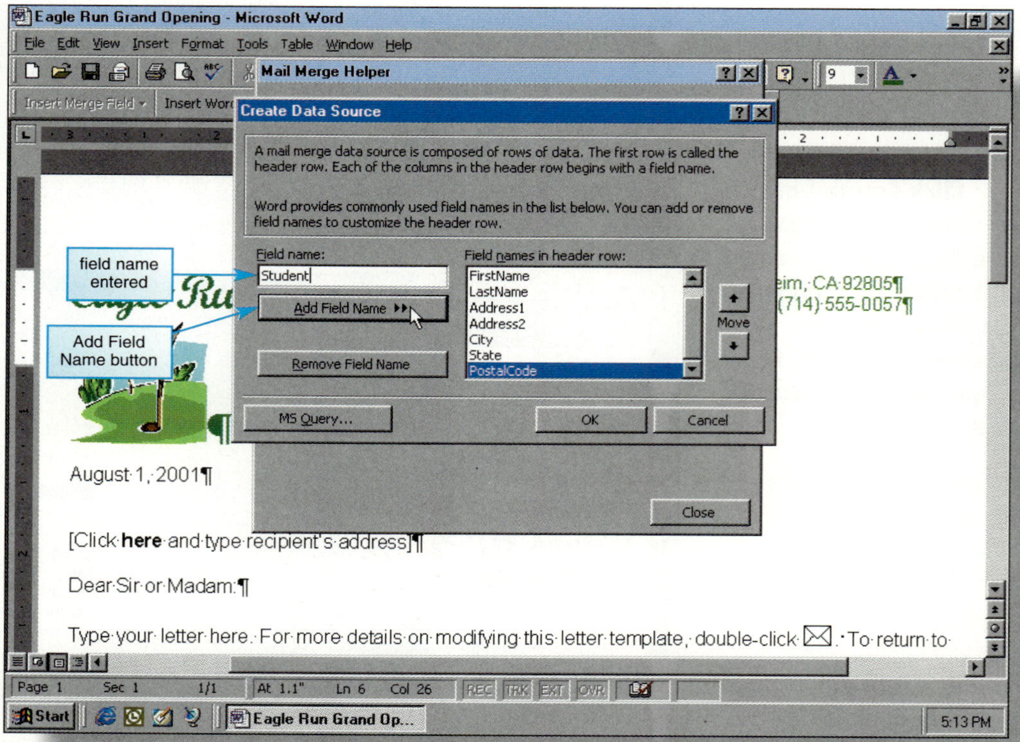

FIGURE 5-20

5 **Click the Add Field Name button. Point to the OK button.**

Word adds the Student field name to the bottom of the Field names in header row list (Figure 5-21).

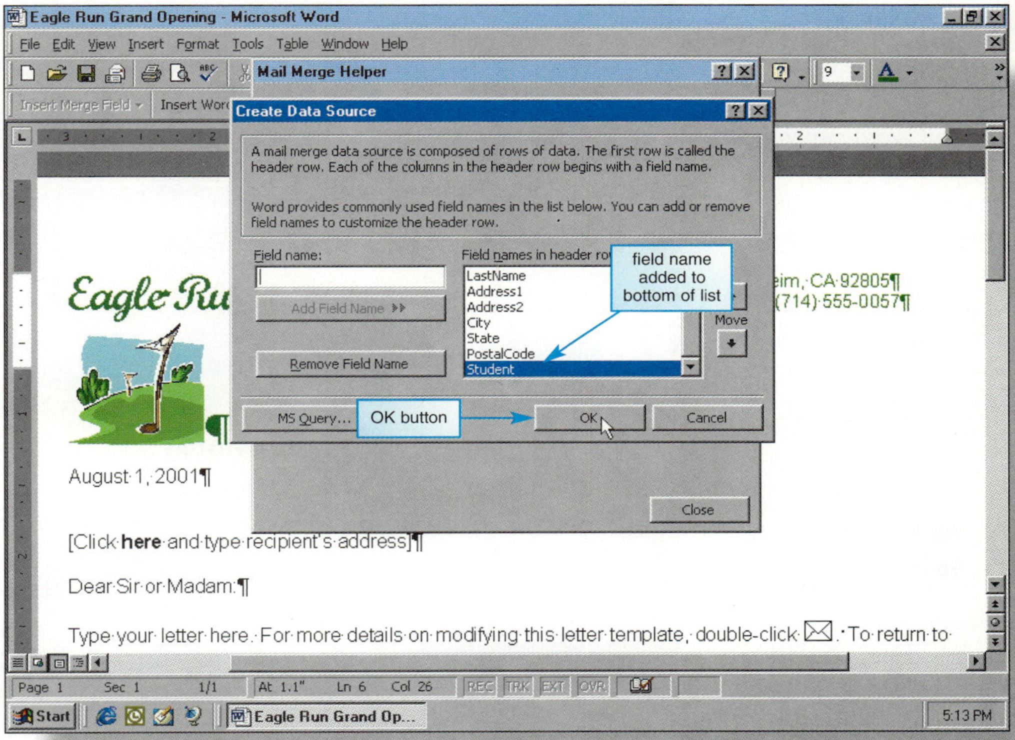

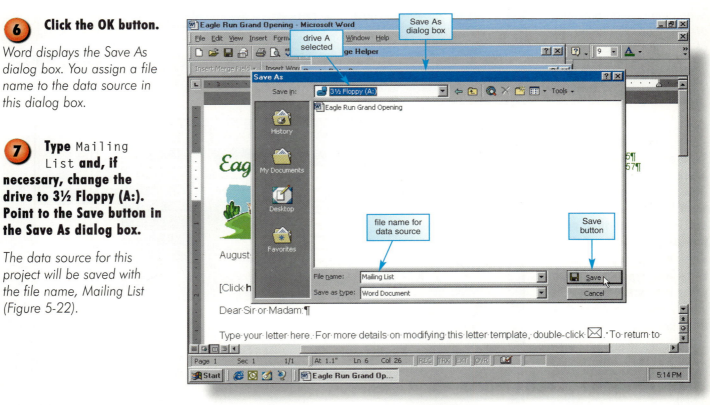

FIGURE 5-21

6 **Click the OK button.**

Word displays the Save As dialog box. You assign a file name to the data source in this dialog box.

7 **Type** Mailing List **and, if necessary, change the drive to 3½ Floppy (A:). Point to the Save button in the Save As dialog box.**

The data source for this project will be saved with the file name, Mailing List (Figure 5-22).

FIGURE 5-22

8 **Click the Save button in the Save As dialog box.**

A Microsoft Word dialog box displays asking if you would like to edit the data source or edit the main document at this point (Figure 5-23). Because you want to add data records to the data source, you will edit the data source now.

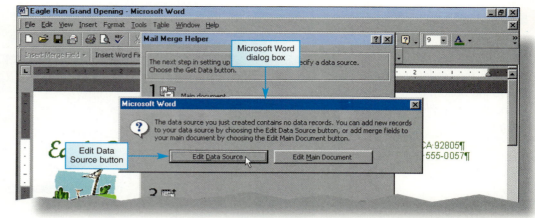

FIGURE 5-23

9 **Click the Edit Data Source button.**

Word displays a Data Form dialog box (Figure 5-24). You can use this dialog box to enter the data records into the data source. Notice the field names from the header row display along the left edge of the dialog box with an empty text box to the right of each field name. The insertion point is in the first text box.

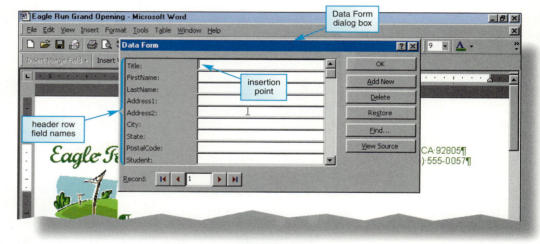

FIGURE 5-24

10 **Type** Ms. **and then press the ENTER key. Type** Akilah **and then press the ENTER key. Type** Green **and then press the ENTER key. Type** 15 Park Boulevard **and then press the ENTER key twice. Type** Brea **and then press the ENTER key. Type** CA **and then press the ENTER key. Type** 92821 **and then press the ENTER key. Type** N **(Figure 5-25).**

If you notice an error in a text box, click the text box and then correct the error as you would in the document window.

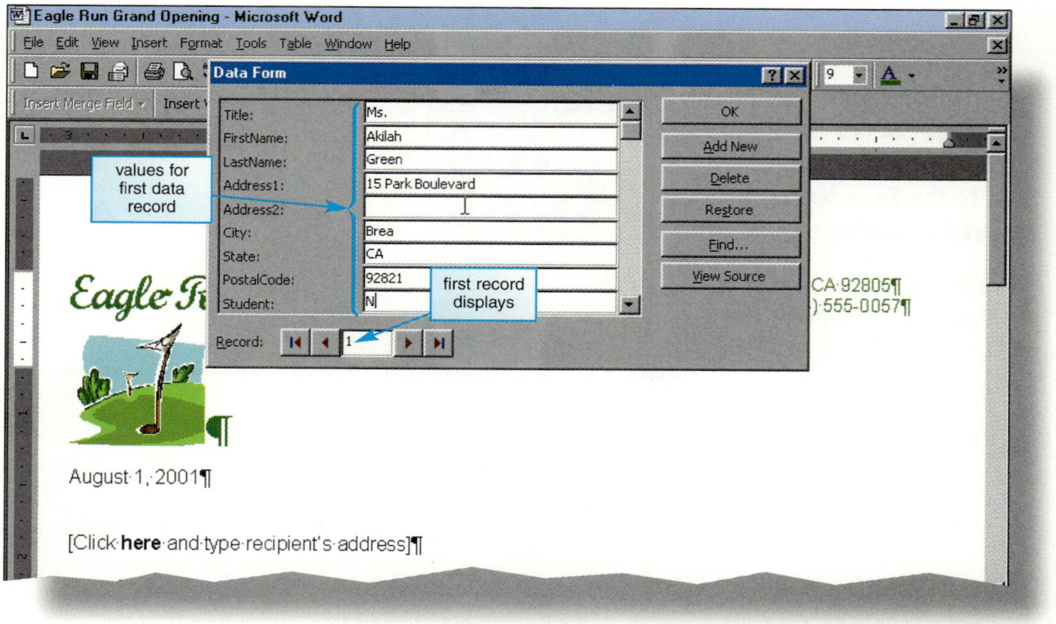

FIGURE 5-25

11 Press the ENTER key to display a blank data form for the second data record. Type Mr. and then press the ENTER key. James and then press the ENTER key. Type Wheeler and then press the ENTER key. Type 113 Fourth Street and then press the ENTER key. Type Apt. 3C and then press the ENTER key. Type Placentia and then press the ENTER key. Type CA and press the ENTER key. Type 82870 and then press the ENTER key. Type Y (Figure 5-26).

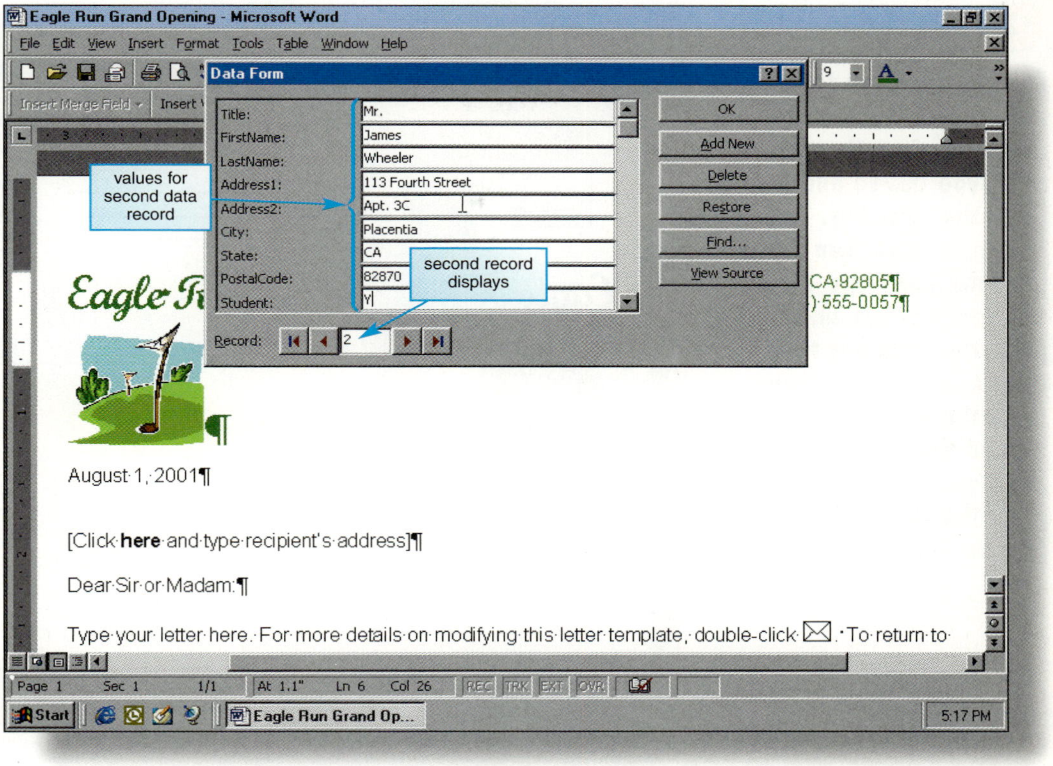

FIGURE 5-26

12 Press the ENTER key to display a blank data form for the third data record. Type Dr. and then press the ENTER key. Type Vidya and then press the ENTER key. Type Garlapati and then press the ENTER key. Type P.O. Box 1015 and then press the ENTER key. Type 15 Central Avenue and then press the ENTER key. Type Los Alamitos and then press the ENTER key. Type CA and press the ENTER key. Type 90720 and then press the ENTER key. Type N (Figure 5-27).

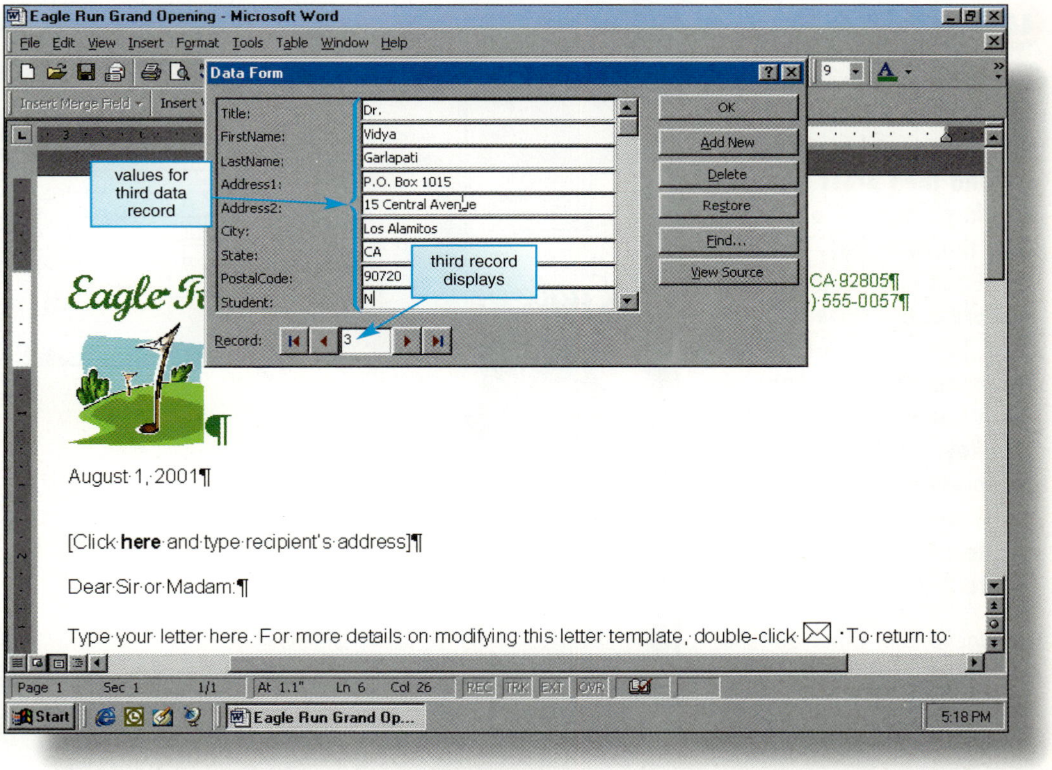

FIGURE 5-27

Microsoft **Word 2000**

13 Press the ENTER key to display a blank data form for the fourth data record. Type Prof. and then press the ENTER key. Type David and then press the ENTER key. Type Raminski and then press the ENTER key. Type 1145 Sunset Street and then press the ENTER key twice. Type Anaheim and then press the ENTER key. Type CA and then press the ENTER key. Type 92805 and then press the ENTER key. Type N (Figure 5-28).

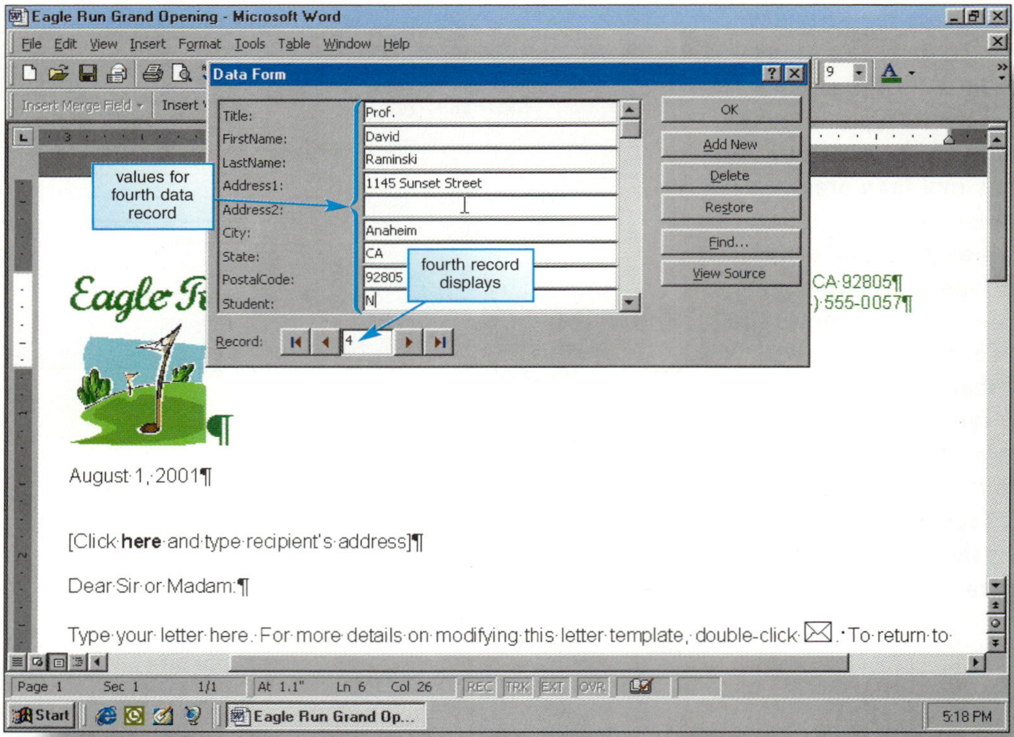

FIGURE 5-28

14 Press the ENTER key to display a blank data form for the fifth data record. Type Mrs. and then press the ENTER key. Type May and then press the ENTER key. Type Li and then press the ENTER key. Type 189 Eastern Avenue and then press the ENTER key twice. Type Fullerton and then press the ENTER key. Type CA and then press the ENTER key. Type 92831 and then press the ENTER key. Type Y and then point to the View Source button (Figure 5-29).

The functions of other buttons in this dialog box are discussed in the next section.

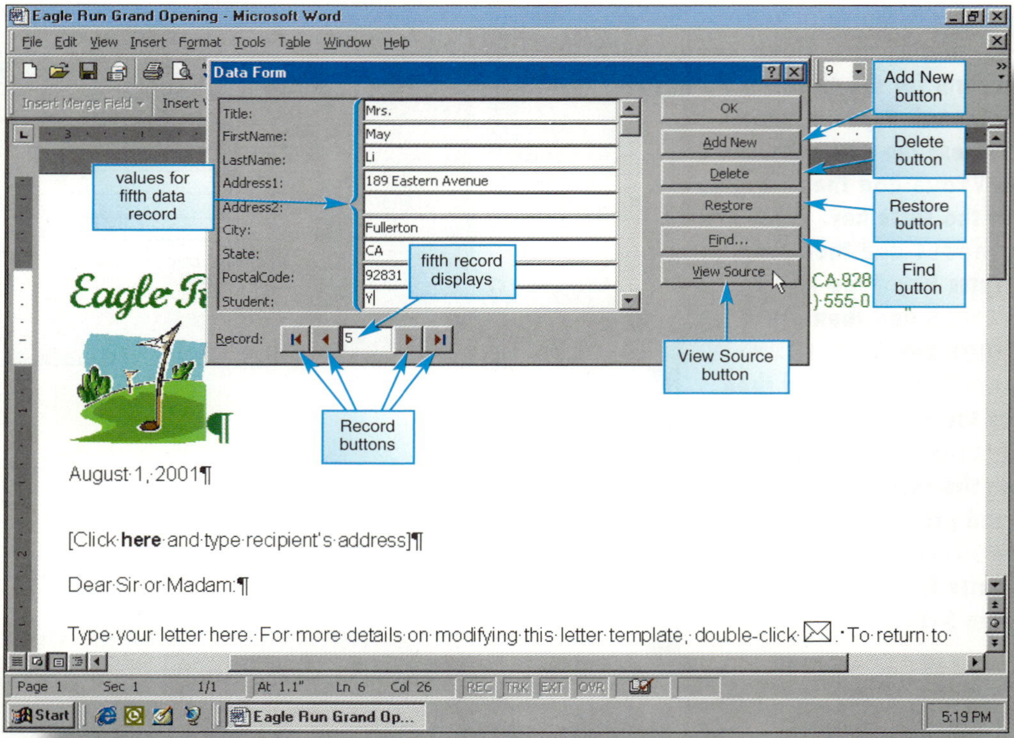

FIGURE 5-29

15 **Click the View Source button. If necessary, scroll up to view all the records. Click the Save button on the Standard toolbar.**

Word displays the data records as a Word table (Figure 5-30). Because the data records are not saved in the data source file when you fill in the Data Form dialog box, you must save them now. The Database toolbar displays below the Standard and Formatting toolbars. The next section discusses the function of several buttons on the Database toolbar.

Manage Fields button

Delete Record button

Sort Ascending button

Sort Descending button

Data Form button

Add New Record button

header row

Find Record button

data records

Database toolbar

Title	FirstName	LastName	Address1	Address2	City	State	PostalCode	S
Ms.	Akilah	Green	15 Park Boulevard		Brea	CA	92821	N
Mr.	James	Wheeler	113 Fourth Street	Apt. 3C	Placentia	CA	82870	Y
Dr.	Vidya	Garlapati	P.O. Box 1015	15 Central Avenue	Los Alamitos	CA	90720	N
Prof.	David	Raminski	1145 Sunset Street		Anaheim	CA	92805	N
Mrs.	May	Li	189 Eastern Avenue		Fullerton	CA	92831	Y

FIGURE 5-30

Your data source table may display **gridlines** that separate the rows and columns. You have learned that gridlines do not print. Some users display gridlines to help identify rows and columns in a table. If you want to hide the gridlines, click somewhere in the table, click table on the menu bar, and then click Hide Gridlines.

All of the data records have been entered into the data source and saved with the file name, Mailing List. If, when you are entering your data records into the Data Form dialog box, you accidentally click the OK button, Word returns you to the main document. To redisplay the Data Form dialog box and continue adding data records, click the Edit Data Source button on the Mail Merge toolbar shown in Figure 5-34 on page WD 5.26.

Editing Records in the Data Source

If the data source displays as a Word table and you would like to redisplay the Data Form dialog box, click the Data Form button (Figure 5-30) on the Database toolbar. In the Data Form dialog box, you can add, change, or delete data records. To **add a new record**, press the ENTER key with the insertion point in the last field on the form as shown in the previous steps or click the Add New button (Figure 5-29). To **change an existing record**, display it in the Data Form dialog box by clicking the appropriate Record button(s) or using the Find button to locate a particular data item. For example, to find David Raminski, you could click the Find button, enter `Prof.` in the Find What box and then click the OK button. Once you have changed an existing record's data, click the OK button in the Data Form dialog box. To **delete a record**, display it in the Data Form dialog box, and then click the Delete button. If you accidentally delete a data record, click the Restore button to bring it back.

Organizing Data

Organize the information in a data source so it is reusable. For example, you may want to print a person's title, first, middle, and last name (e.g., Mr. Roger A. Bannerman) in the inside address but only the title and last name in the salutation (Dear Mr. Bannerman). Thus, you should break the name into separate fields: title, first name, middle initial, and last name.

Modifying Fields

You can add a field name to a data source, change an existing field name, or remove a field by using the Manage Fields dialog box. To display the Manage Fields dialog box, click the Manage Fields button (Figure 5-30) on the Database toolbar.

You also can add, change, and delete data records when you are viewing the source as a Word table as shown in Figure 5-30 on the previous page. Click the Add New Record button on the Database toolbar to add a blank row to the bottom of the table and then fill in the field values. To delete a row, click somewhere in the row and then click the Delete Record button on the Database toolbar. Because the data source is a Word table, you can also add and delete records the same way you add and delete rows in a Word table, which was discussed in Projects 3 and 4. You can edit the data as you would in any other Word table.

The data source now is complete. You have learned in earlier projects that you can use the Table AutoFormat command to format a table. The data source is a table. Thus, perform the following steps to format the data source using the Table AutoFormat command.

TO AUTOFORMAT A TABLE

1 With the insertion point somewhere in the table, click Table on the menu bar and then click Table AutoFormat.

2 When the Table AutoFormat dialog box displays, scroll through the Formats list and then click Grid 8. Be sure these check boxes contain check marks: Borders, Shading, Font, Color, AutoFit, and Heading rows. All other check boxes should be cleared.

3 Click the OK button.

Word formats the table using the Grid 8 format (see Figure 5-16 on page WD 5.16).

Printing a Document in Landscape Orientation

The mailing list table is too wide to fit on a piece of paper in **portrait orientation**; that is, with the short edge of the paper at the top. You can instruct Word to print a document in **landscape orientation** so the long edge of the paper is at the top. Perform the following steps to change the orientation of the Mailing List from portrait to landscape.

More About

Page Orientation

You can change the page orientation for part of a document by selecting the pages to be changed prior to displaying the Page Setup dialog box. With the pages selected, click the Apply to box arrow and then click Selected text in the Paper Size sheet of the Page Setup dialog box. Word inserts a section break before and after the selected pages.

Steps To Change Page Orientation

1 Click File on the menu bar and then point to Page Setup (Figure 5-31).

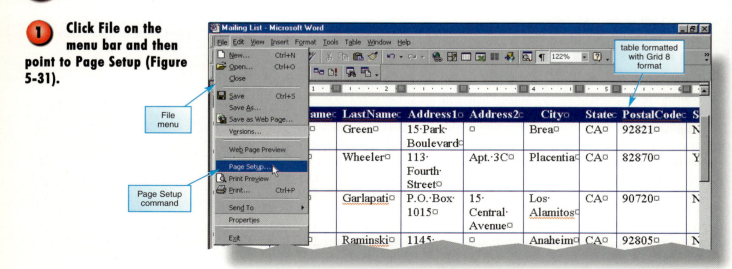

FIGURE 5-31

2 **Click Page Setup. When the Page Setup dialog box displays, click the Paper Size tab. Click Landscape in the Orientation area and then point to the OK button.**

Word displays the Page Setup dialog box (Figure 5-32).

3 **Click the OK button.**

Word changes the print orientation to landscape.

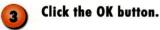

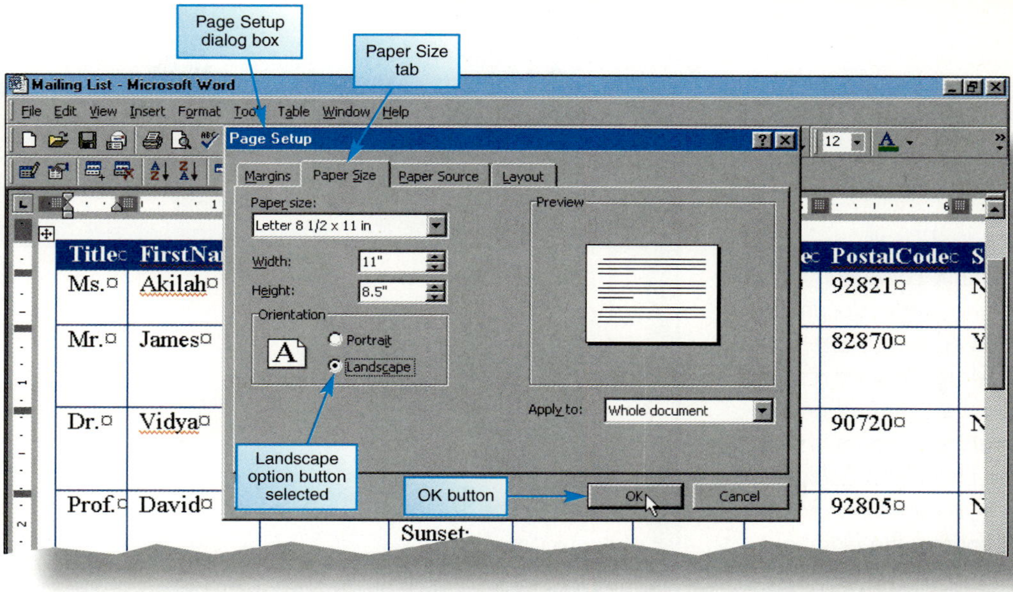

FIGURE 5-32

Other Ways

1. On File menu click Print, click Properties button, click Paper tab, click Landscape, click OK button

To print the document, perform the following step.

TO PRINT A DOCUMENT

1 Click the Print button on the Standard toolbar.

Word prints the document in landscape orientation (see Figure 5-16 on page WD 5.16).

Switching from the Data Source to the Main Document

The next step is to switch from the data source to the main document so that you can enter the contents of the form letter into the main document. Perform the following steps to switch from the data source to the main document for the form letter.

Steps To Switch from the Data Source to the Main Document

1 **Point to the Mail Merge Main Document button on the Database toolbar (Figure 5-33).**

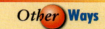

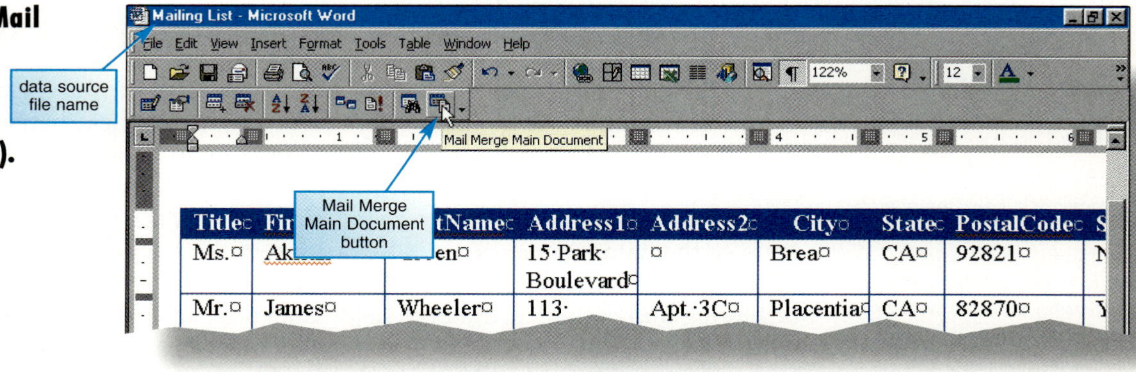

FIGURE 5-33

2 Click the Mail Merge Main Document button.

Word displays the main document, Eagle Run Grand Opening, in the document window (Figure 5-34). The Mail Merge toolbar displays below the Standard and Formatting toolbars in place of the Database toolbar. When you are viewing the data source, the Database toolbar displays; when you are viewing the main document, the Mail Merge toolbar displays.

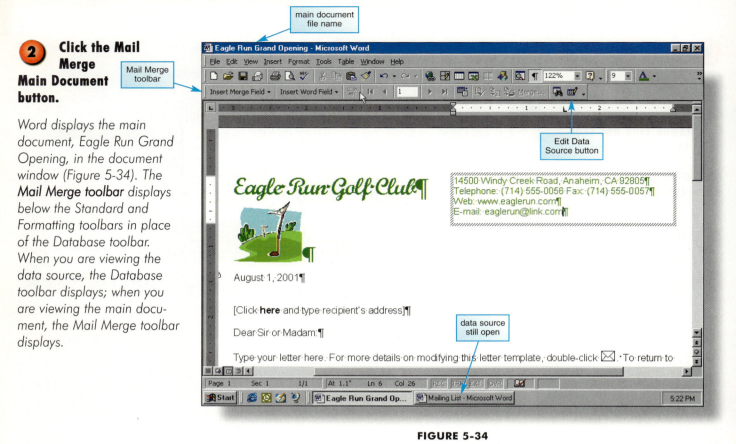

FIGURE 5-34

If, for some reason, you wanted to edit the data source, you would click the Edit Data Source button on the Mail Merge toolbar (Figure 5-34).

Entering the Main Document for the Form Letter

The next step is to create the **main document**, which in this case is the form letter (see Figure 5-1a on page WD 5.5). The steps on the following pages illustrate how to create the main document for the form letter.

The first item to be entered in the main document is the inside address on the letter. The contents of the inside address are located in the data source. Thus, you insert fields from the data source into the main document.

Inserting Merge Fields into the Main Document

In the previous steps, you created the data source for the form letter. The first record in the data source, the header row, contains the field names of each field in the data source. To link the data source to the main document, you must insert these field names into the main document. In the main document, these field names are called **merge fields** because they merge, or combine, the main document with the contents of the data source. When a field is inserted into the main document from the data source, Word surrounds the field name with chevrons. These **chevrons** mark the beginning and ending of a merge field. Chevrons are not on the keyboard; therefore, you cannot type them directly into the document. They display as a result of inserting a merge field with the **Insert Merge Field button** on the Mail Merge toolbar.

Perform the following steps to insert a merge field from the data source.

More About

Fields

When you position the insertion point in a field, the entire field is shaded gray. The shading displays on the screen only to help you identify fields; the shading does not print on a hard copy. Thus, the merge fields appear shaded when you click them. To select an entire field, double-click it.

Steps ## To Insert a Merge Field into the Main Document

1 If necessary, scroll down and click the placeholder text, Click here and type recipient's address. Click the Insert Merge Field button on the Mail Merge toolbar. In the list of fields, point to Title.

Word displays a list of fields from the data source (Figure 5-35). The field you select will replace the selected placeholder text in the main document.

FIGURE 5-35

2 Click Title. When the list of fields disappears from the screen, press the SPACEBAR.

Word displays the field name, Title, surrounded with chevrons in the main document (Figure 5-36). When you merge the data source with the main document, the customer's title (e.g., Mr. or Ms.) will print at the location of the merge field, Title. One space follows the ending chevron after the Title merge field.

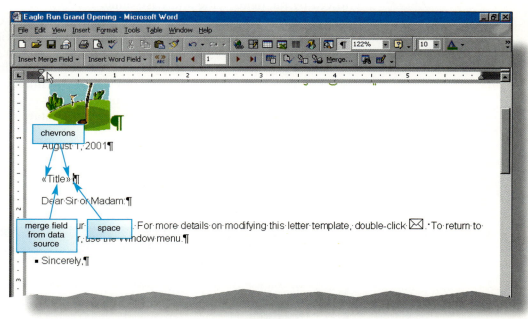

FIGURE 5-36

Perform the following steps to enter the remaining merge fields for the recipient's address.

TO ENTER MORE MERGE FIELDS

1 Click the Insert Merge Field button on the Mail Merge toolbar and then click FirstName. Press the SPACEBAR.

2 Click the Insert Merge Field button on the Mail Merge toolbar and then click LastName. Press the ENTER key.

More About

Field Codes

If, when you insert fields into a document, the fields display surrounded by braces instead of chevrons and extra instructions appear between the braces, then field codes have been turned on. To turn off field codes, press the ALT+F9 keys.

3 Click the Insert Merge Field button on the Mail Merge toolbar and then click Address1. Press the ENTER key.

4 Click the Insert Merge Field button on the Mail Merge toolbar and then click Address2. Press the ENTER key.

5 Click the Insert Merge Field button on the Mail Merge toolbar and then click City. Press the COMMA key and then press the SPACEBAR.

6 Click the Insert Merge Field button on the Mail Merge toolbar and then click State. Press the SPACEBAR.

7 Click the Insert Merge Field button on the Mail Merge toolbar and then click PostalCode.

The inside address is complete (see Figure 5-37).

Unlinking a Field

The salutation is currently a Word field. When you point to it, a ScreenTip displays and when you right-click it, a list of salutations displays from which you may select one. The salutation currently reads, Dear Sir or Madam (see Figure 5-37). You want the salutation to be personalized to the recipient; that is, the word, Dear, followed by the fields, Title and LastName.

To change the salutation, you must remove the field designation, or **unlink the field**. To do this, you position the insertion point in the field and then press CTRL+SHIFT+F9. When you position the insertion point in a Word field, the entire field is shaded gray. The shading displays on the screen to help you identify fields; the shading does not print on a hard copy. Once you unlink the field, Word removes the gray shading because the text is no longer a field.

Perform the following steps to unlink the salutation field and enter a personalized salutation.

Steps To Unlink a Field

1 Click in the salutation field.

The field displays shaded in gray (Figure 5-37).

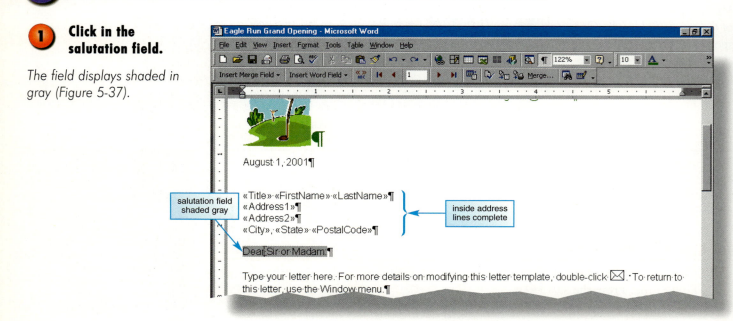

FIGURE 5-37

2 Press CTRL+SHIFT+F9. Click anywhere to remove the highlight.

Word removes the field designation from the salutation.

3 Drag through the text, Sir or Madam, in the salutation. Click the Insert Merge Field button on the Mail Merge toolbar. Point to Title in the list (Figure 5-38).

4 Click Title. Press the SPACEBAR. Click the Insert Merge Field button on the Mail Merge toolbar and then click LastName.

The salutation is complete (see Figure 5-39).

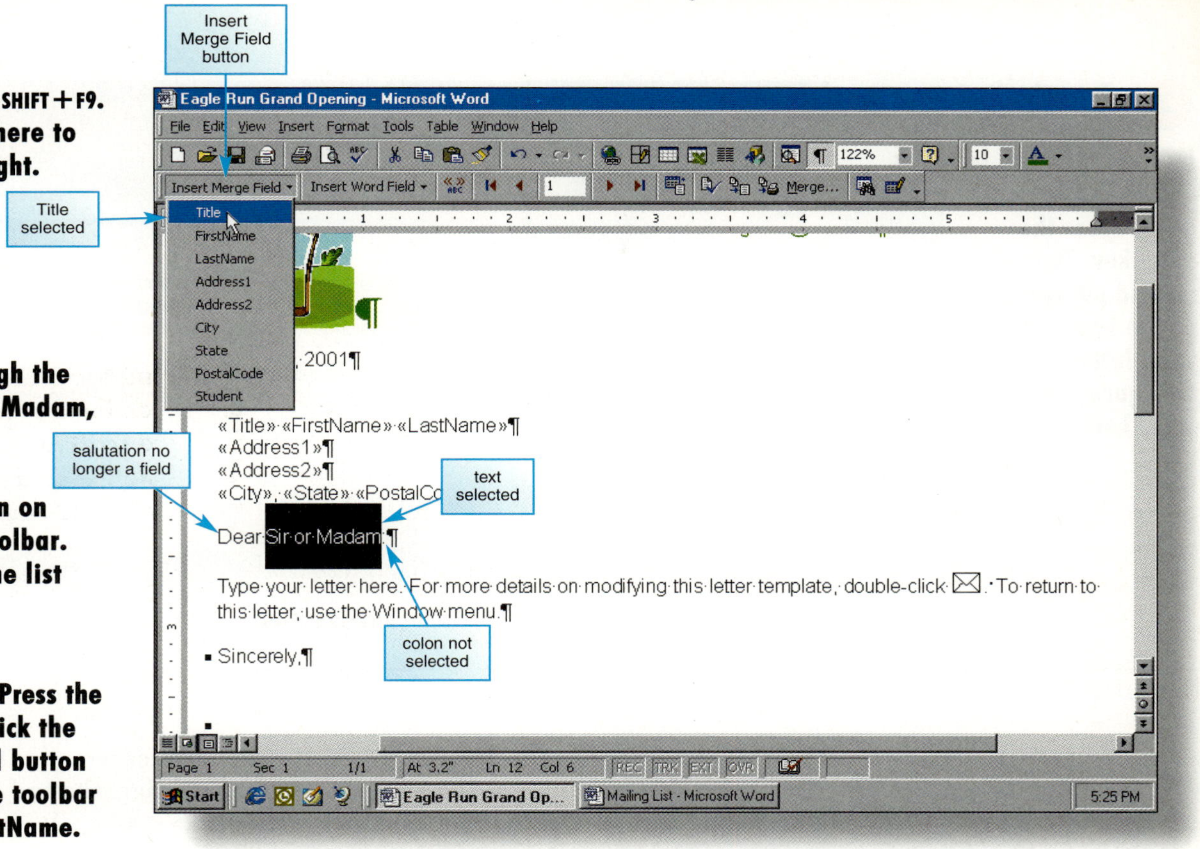

FIGURE 5-38

Entering the Body of a Letter Template

The next step is to enter the first two paragraphs in the body of the form letter. These paragraphs contain constant, or unchanging, text to be printed in each form letter. Perform the following steps to select the placeholder text in the letter template and enter the first two paragraphs of the form letter.

Steps To Enter the Body of the Letter

1 Scroll down and then triple-click the placeholder text that begins with Type your letter here.

Word selects the entire paragraph in the body of the letter (Figure 5-39).

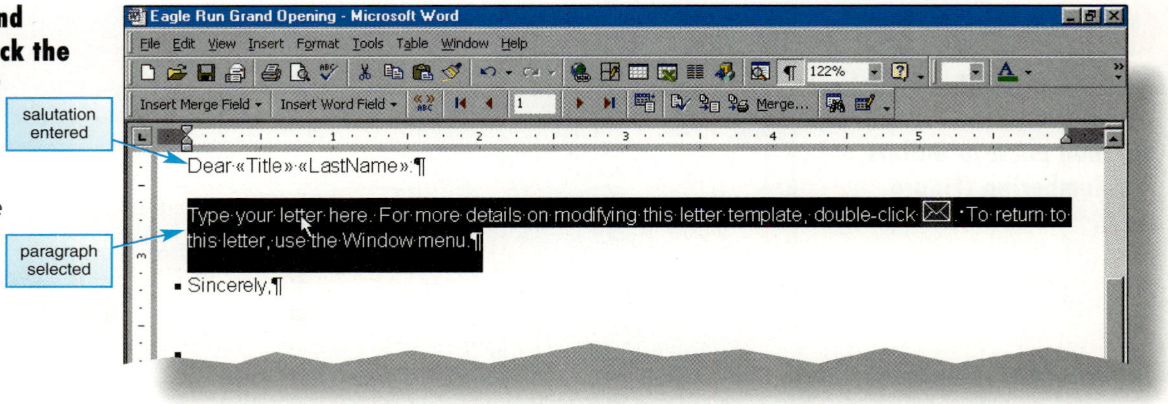

FIGURE 5-39

2 Type the first paragraph of the body of the form letter as shown in Figure 5-40. Press the ENTER key. Type the second paragraph of the body of the form letter as shown in Figure 5-40. Press the ENTER key.

Depending on your printer driver, your wordwrap may occur in different locations (Figure 5-40).

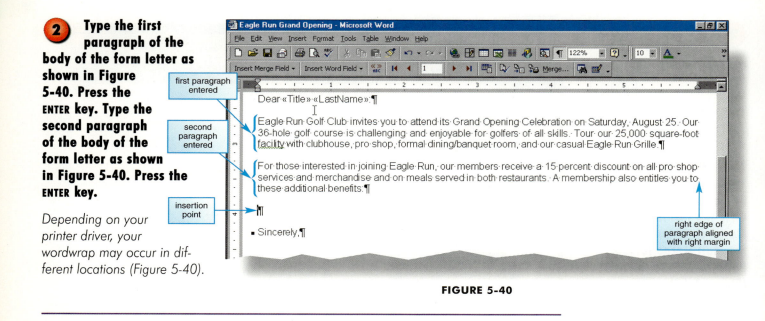

FIGURE 5-40

The paragraphs of the body of the Professional Letter template use the Body Text style. This style specifies single-spacing within paragraphs and double-spacing between paragraphs. Thus, each time you press the ENTER key, Word places a blank line between paragraphs.

The Body Text style also specifies to **justify** paragraphs, which means the left and right edges of the paragraphs are aligned with the left and right margins, respectively, like the edges of newspaper columns.

Creating an Outline Numbered List

The next step is to enter an outline numbered list in the form letter (see Figure 5-1 on page 5.5). An **outline numbered list** is a list that contains several levels of items, with each level displaying a different numeric, alphabetic, or bullet symbol. Perform the following steps to create an outline numbered list that uses bullet symbols.

To Create an Outline Numbered List

1 With the insertion point positioned as shown in Figure 5-40, click Format on the menu bar and then point to Bullets and Numbering (Figure 5-41).

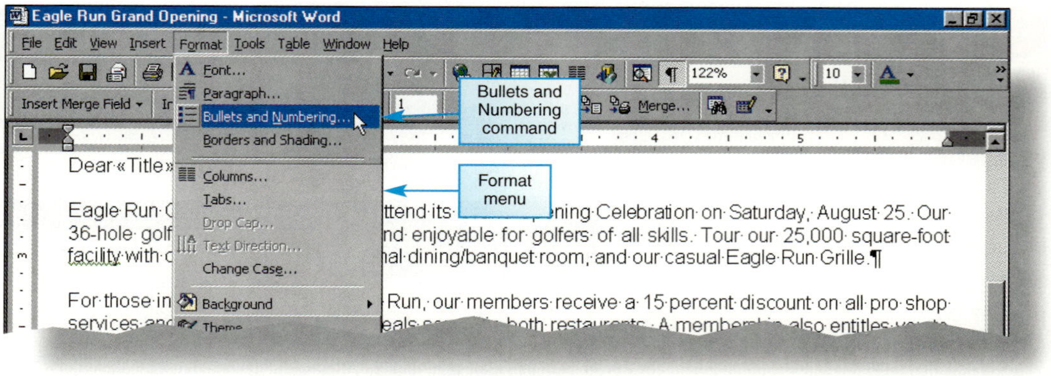

FIGURE 5-41

2 Click Bullets and Numbering. When the Bullets and Numbering dialog box displays, if necessary, click the Outline Numbered tab. Click the desired number or bullet style in the list and then point to the OK button.

Word displays the Bullets and Numbering dialog box (Figure 5-42).

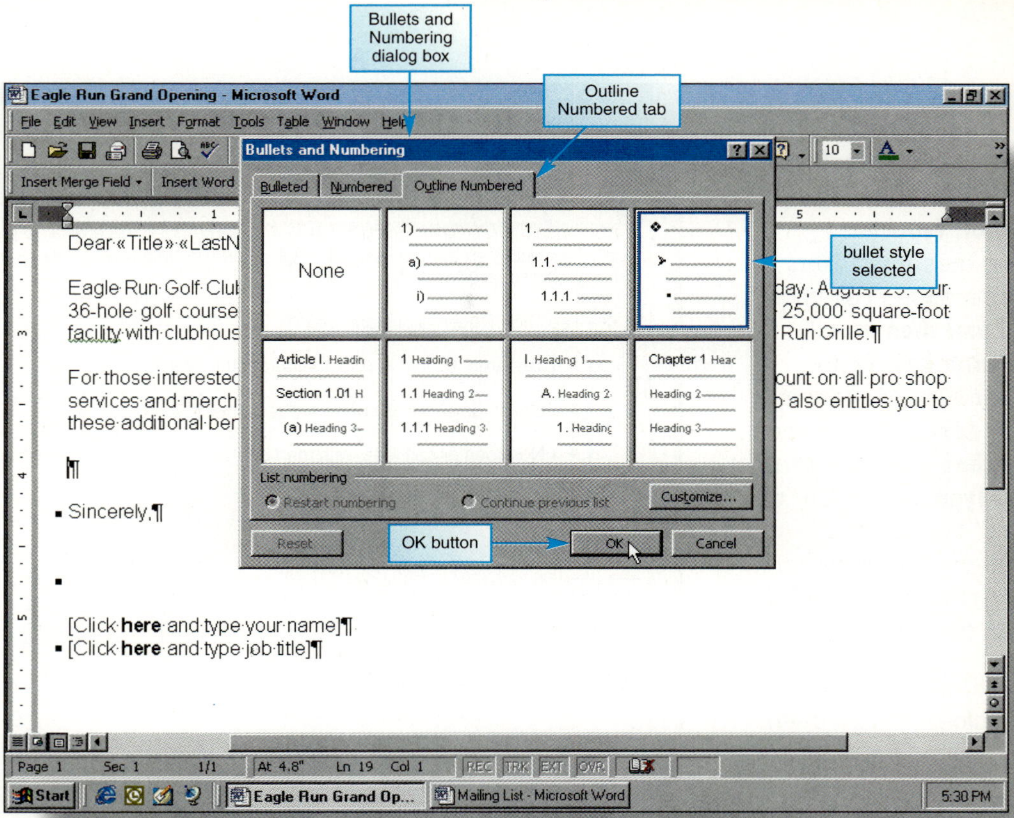

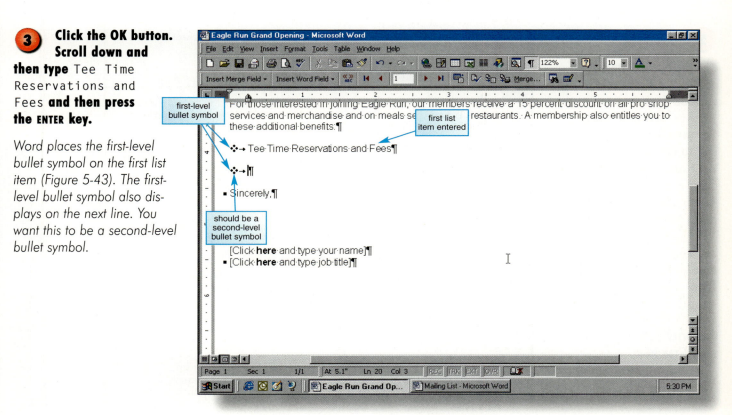

FIGURE 5-42

3 Click the OK button. Scroll down and then type Tee Time Reservations and Fees and then press the ENTER key.

Word places the first-level bullet symbol on the first list item (Figure 5-43). The first-level bullet symbol also displays on the next line. You want this to be a second-level bullet symbol.

FIGURE 5-43

4 Press the TAB key to demote the current list item so it displays a second-level bullet symbol. Type Tee time reservations instantly from the Web **and then press the ENTER key. Type** Seven-day advance preferred tee times **and then press the ENTER key. Type** No green or cart fees, with member guest discount on green fees **and then press the ENTER key.**

The second level list items are entered (Figure 5-44).

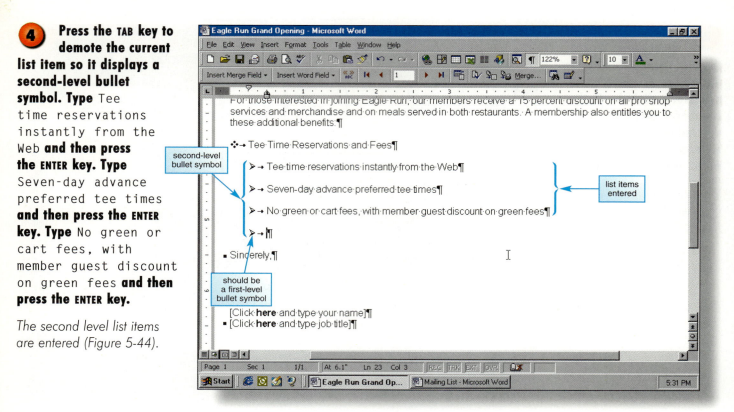

FIGURE 5-44

5 Press the SHIFT+TAB keys to promote the current list item so it displays a first-level bullet symbol. Type Golf Events **and then press the ENTER key. Press the TAB key to demote the current list item. Type** Monthly couples and singles tournaments **and then press the ENTER key. Type** Active men's and ladies' leagues **and then press the ENTER key. Type** Individual lessons and group clinics **and then press the ENTER key. Press the SHIFT+TAB keys.**

The items in the list are entered (Figure 5-45).

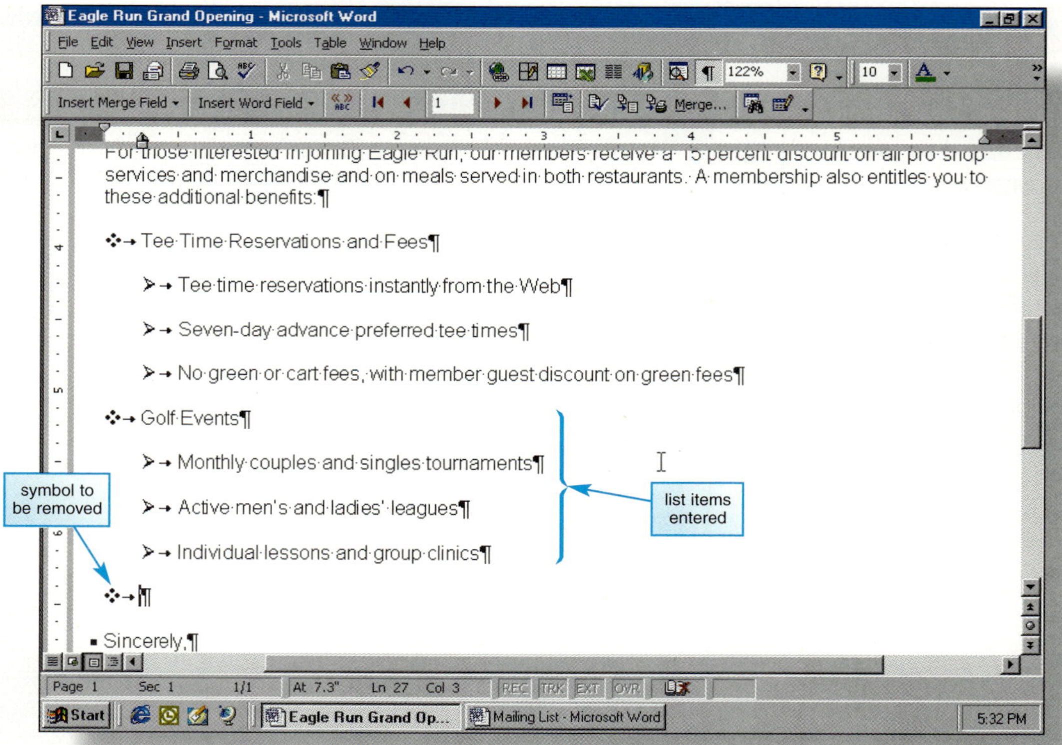

FIGURE 5-45

6 **Double-click the move handle on the Formatting toolbar to display the entire toolbar. Click the Numbering button on the Formatting toolbar.**

Word removes the numbered list bullet symbol from the current paragraph (Figure 5-46).

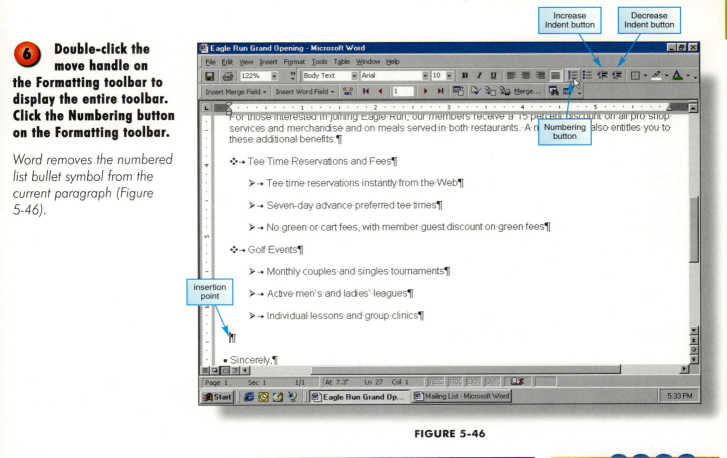

FIGURE 5-46

You also can click the Increase Indent button on the Formatting toolbar to demote a list item in an outline numbered list. Likewise, you can click the Decrease Indent button on the Formatting toolbar to promote a list item.

Using an IF Field to Conditionally Print Text in a Form Letter

In addition to merge fields, you can insert other types of fields in your main document. One type of field is called an **IF field**. One form of the IF field is: If a condition is true, then perform an action. For example, If Mary owns a house, then send her information on homeowner's insurance. This type of IF field is called **If...Then**. Another form of the IF field is: If a condition is true, then perform an action; else perform a different action. For example, If John has an e-mail address, then send him an e-mail message; else send him the note via the postal service. This type of IF field is called **If...Then...Else**.

In this project, the form letter checks whether the person on the mailing list is a student. If he or she is a student, then the discount is 75 percent. If he or she is not a student, then the discount is 25 percent. For Word to determine which discount percent to use, you must enter an If...Then...Else: If Student is equal to Y (for Yes), then print 75 percent as the discount, else print 25 percent as the discount.

The phrase that appears after the word If is called a condition. A **condition** is composed of an expression, followed by a comparison operator, followed by a final expression.

EXPRESSIONS The **expression** in a condition can be a merge field, a number, a series of characters, or a mathematical formula. Word surrounds a series of characters with quotation marks ("). To indicate an empty, or **null**, expression, you place two quotation marks together ("").

More About 2000

Word Fields

In addition to the IF field, Word provides other fields that may be used in form letters. For example, the ASK and FILLIN fields prompt the user to enter data for each record in the data source. The SKIP RECORD IF field instructs the mail merge to not generate a form letter for a data record if a specific condition is met.

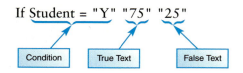

IF Fields

The term, IF field, originates from computer programming. Don't be intimidated by the terminology. An IF field simply specifies a decision. Some programmers refer to it as an IF statement. An IF field can be quite simple or complex. Complex IF fields include nested IF fields, which is a second IF field inside true or false text of the first IF field.

COMPARISON OPERATORS   The **comparison operator** in a condition must be one of six characters: = (equal to or matches the text), <> (not equal to or does not match text), < (less than), <= (less than or equal to), > (greater than), >= (greater than or equal to).

If the result of a condition is true, then the **true text** is evaluated; otherwise, if the result of a condition is false, the **false text** is evaluated. In this project, the first expression in the condition is a merge field (Student); the comparison operator is an equal sign (=); and the second expression is the text "Y". The true text is "75" and the false text is "25". That is, the complete IF field is as follows:

If Student = "Y" "75" "25"

Condition   True Text   False Text

Perform the following steps to insert the IF field into the form letter.

To Insert an IF Field into the Main Document

1   Scroll down and then type To receive a **and then press the SPACEBAR. Click the Insert Word Field button on the Mail Merge toolbar. When the list of Word fields displays, point to If...Then...Else.**

A list of Word fields that may be inserted into the main document displays (Figure 5-47).

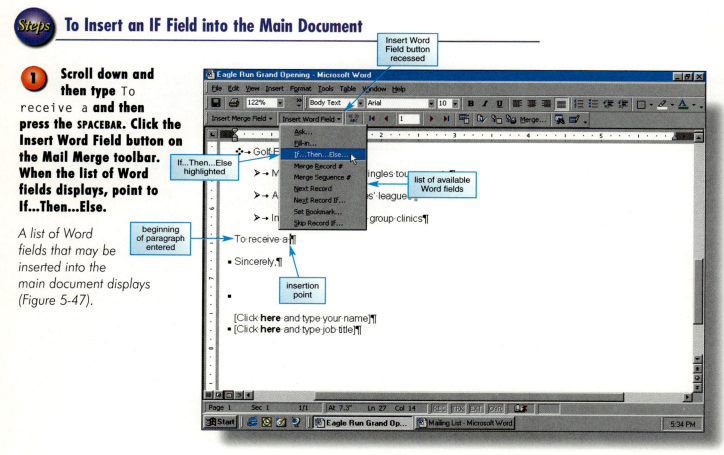

FIGURE 5-47

2 Click If...Then...Else. When the Insert Word Field: IF dialog box displays, point to the Field name box arrow.

Word displays the Insert Word Field: IF dialog box (Figure 5-48). You can specify the condition in the IF area of this dialog box.

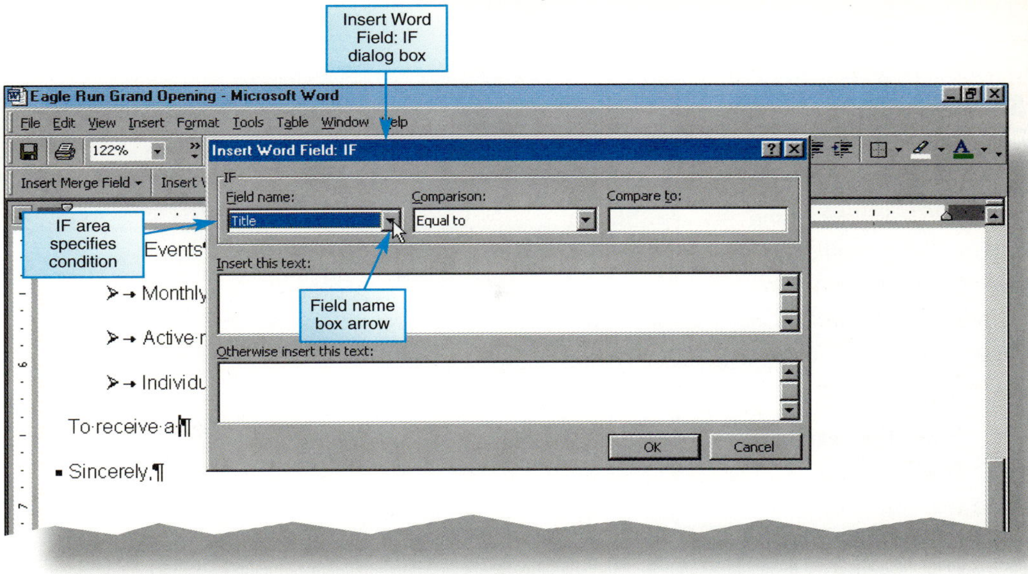

FIGURE 5-48

3 Click the Field name box arrow. Scroll through the list of fields and then point to Student.

Word displays a list of fields from the data source (Figure 5-49).

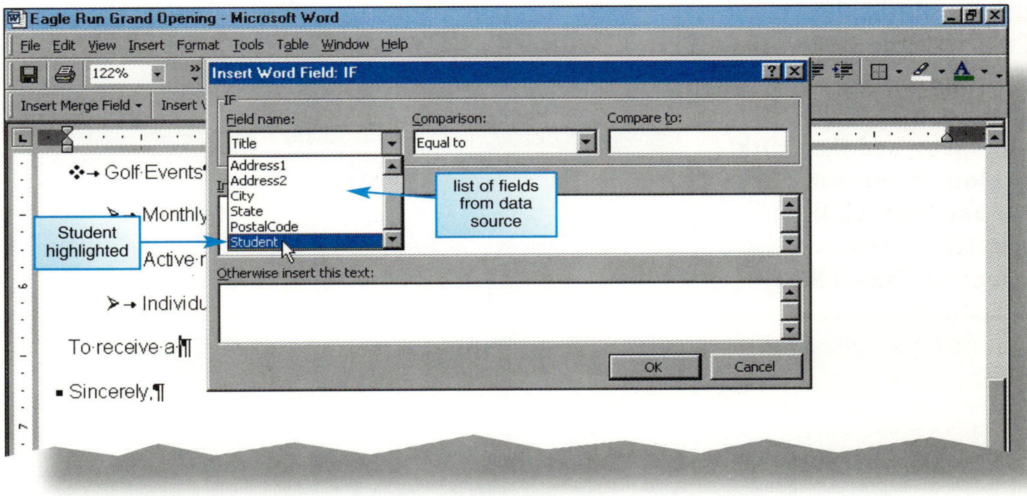

FIGURE 5-49

4 Click Student. Click the Compare to text box. Type Y and then press the TAB key. Type 75 and then press the TAB key. Type 25 and then point to the OK button.

The entries in the Insert Word Field: IF dialog box are complete (Figure 5-50).

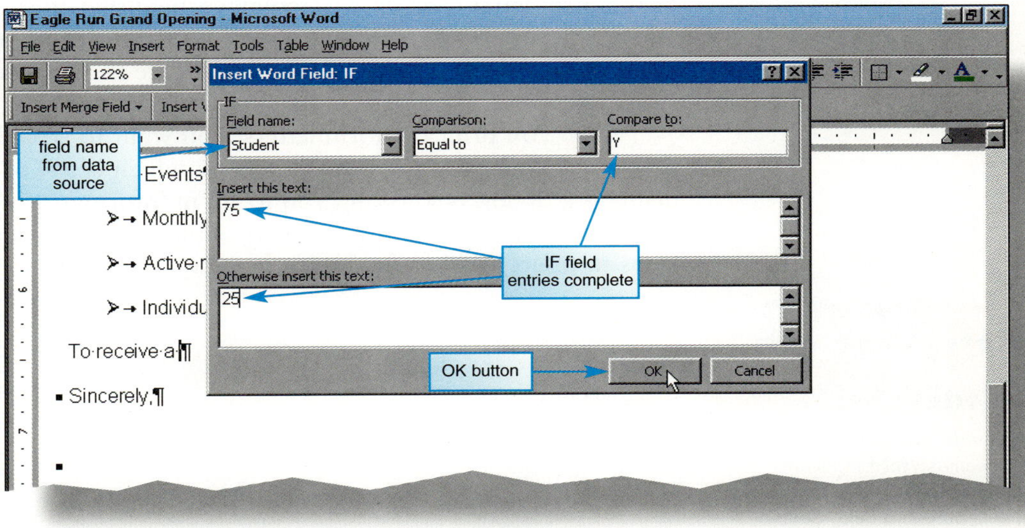

FIGURE 5-50

⑤ Click the OK button.

Word returns you to the document. The discount percent, 25, displays at the location of the insertion point because the first record in the data source is not a student.

⑥ Press the SPACEBAR. Type percent discount on the initiation fee, become a member during our Grand Opening Celebration. **Click the placeholder text in the signature block, Click here and type your name. Type** Rosa Rodriguez **and then click the placeholder text, Click here and type job title. Type** Marketing Director **(Figure 5-51).**

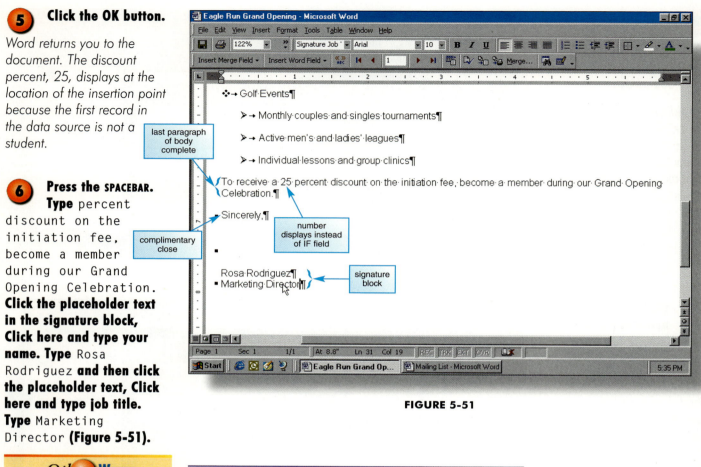

FIGURE 5-51

The next step is to enter a Fill-in field for the mailing date of the letters.

Inserting a Fill-in Field

The Professional Letter template currently displays the date as a field at the top of the form letter. The date is actually a field that Word updates to the current date when it prints the document. You do not, however, want the computer's system date to print on the form letters. Instead, the date that prints at the top of the form letters should be the date the letters are placed in the mail.

When you print the form letters, you want to be able to enter the mailing date at that time. Thus, you insert a **Fill-in field**, which is a Word field that when executed displays a dialog box asking you to fill in information. In this case, when you merge the form letters, the dialog box will ask for the mailing date. Perform the following steps to insert a Fill-in field into the form letter.

Steps To Insert a Fill-in Field

1 Scroll up to display the date in the form letter. Double-click the month or the year to select the entire date field. Click the Insert Word Field button on the Mail Merge toolbar and then point to Fill-in (Figure 5-52).

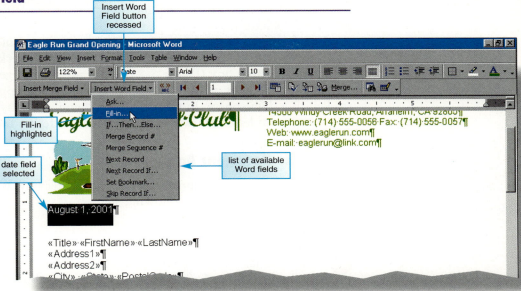

FIGURE 5-52

2 Click Fill-in. When the Insert Word Field: Fill-in dialog box displays, type What date will you be mailing these letters? in the Prompt text box. Click Ask once to select the check box.

Word displays the Insert Word Field: Fill-in dialog box (Figure 5-53). By selecting the Ask once check box, Word will ask the question when you begin the mail merge process – instead of repeatedly for each letter.

3 Click the OK button. When Word displays a sample dialog box showing the prompt question, click the OK button.

Word leaves the date line of the form letter blank (see Figure 5-55 on page WD 5.40).

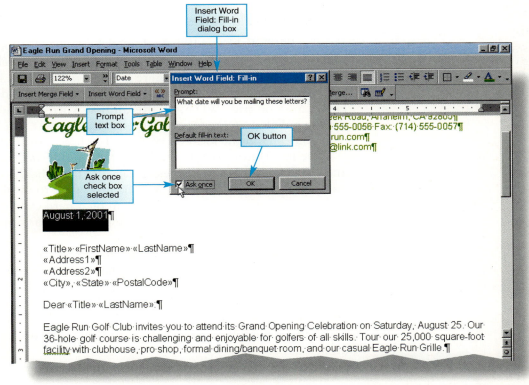

FIGURE 5-53

Other Ways

1. On Insert menu click Field, click Mail Merge in Fields list, click Fill-in in Field names list, enter expression in text box, click OK button

When you merge the form letters, the Fill-in field instructs Word to display the dialog box that requests the mailing date of the form letters so that the correct date prints on the letters.

If you wanted to enter varying responses to a particular question for each record in a data source, you would not check the Ask once check box in the Insert Word Field: Fill-in dialog box (Figure 5-53 on the previous page). For example, a school's advising office might want to enter a specific advising appointment time for each student in a data source. In this case, Word would display the dialog box for each individual form letter, allowing you to enter a different time for each letter.

Saving the Document Again

Because the main document for the form letter now is complete, you should save it again, as described in the following step.

TO SAVE A DOCUMENT AGAIN

1 Double-click the move handle on the Standard toolbar to display the entire toolbar. Click the Save button on the Standard toolbar.

Word saves the main document for the form letter with the same name, Eagle Run Grand Opening.

Displaying Field Codes

The Fill-in field and IF field do not display in the document window. At the location of the IF field, the value of the IF field, called the **field results,** displays. That is, the number 25 displays (see Figure 5-51 on page WD 5.36) because the first data record is not a student. At the location of the Fill-in field, nothing displays (see Figure 5-55 on page WD 5.40). Recall that when you merge the letters, Word will display a dialog box requesting you enter a date. At that time, Word will place the date you enter at the location of the Fill-in field – the date line.

The instructions within the Fill-in field and IF field are referred to as **field codes,** and the default for Word is field codes off. Thus, field codes do not print or display unless you turn them on. You use one procedure to display field codes on the screen and a different procedure to print them on a hard copy. To display field codes on the screen, you press the ALT+F9 keys. The procedure for printing field codes is discussed in the next section.

Whether field codes are on or off on your screen has no effect on the print merge process. The following steps illustrate how to turn on field codes so you may see them on the screen. Most Word users only turn on field codes to verify their accuracy. Because field codes tend to clutter the screen, you may want to turn them off after checking their accuracy.

Perform the following steps to turn field codes on for display and then turn them off again.

Locking Fields

If you wanted to lock a field so that its field results cannot be changed, click the field and then press CTRL+F11. To subsequently unlock a field so that it may be updated, click the field and then press CTRL+SHIFT+F11.

To Turn Field Codes On and Off for Display

1 **Press the ALT + F9 keys.**

Word displays the main document with field codes on (Figure 5-54). With field codes on, the term, MERGEFIELD, displays before each field from the data source. The instructions in the Fill-in and IF fields also display. With field codes on, braces surround the fields instead of chevrons.

2 **Press the ALT + F9 keys again.**

Word turns field codes off in the main document.

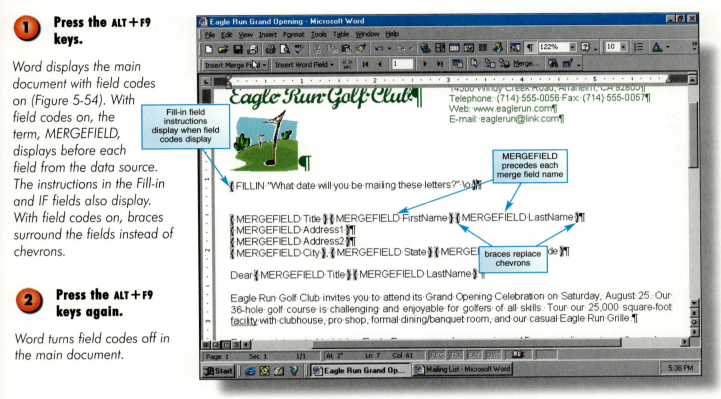

FIGURE 5-54

Printing Field Codes

You also may want to print the field codes version of the form letter so that you have a hard copy of the fields for future reference (see Figure 5-1a on page WD 5.5). When you print field codes, you must remember to turn off the field codes option so that future documents print field results instead of field codes. For example, with field codes on, merged form letters will display field codes instead of data. Perform the steps on the next page to print the field codes in the main document and then turn off the field codes print option for future printing.

1. On Tools menu click Options, click View tab, click Field Codes, click OK button

Printing

If you want to save ink, print faster, or decrease printer overrun errors, lower the printer resolution. Click File on the menu bar, click Print, click the Properties button in the Print dialog box, click the Graphics tab, click the Resolution box arrow, click a lower resolution than that displayed, click the Apply button, click the OK button, and then click the Close button.

Steps **To Print Field Codes in the Main Document**

1 **Click Tools on the menu bar and then point to Options (Figure 5-55).**

2 **Click Options. When the Options dialog box displays, click the Print tab. Click Field codes in the Include with document area. Point to the OK button.**

Word displays the Options dialog box (Figure 5-56). The Field codes check box is selected.

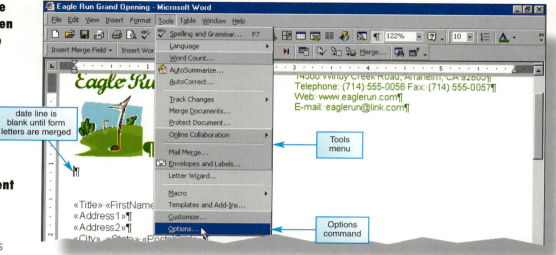

FIGURE 5-55

3 **Click the OK button. Click the Print button on the Standard toolbar.**

Word prints the main document with field codes (see Figure 5-1a on page WD 5.5). Notice the Fill-in and IF field instructions display on the printout.

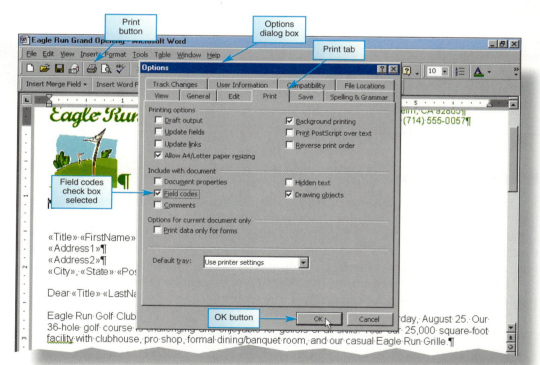

FIGURE 5-56

Other Ways

1. On File menu click Print, click Options button, click Field codes, click OK button, click OK button

2. Press CTRL+P, click Options button, click Field codes, click OK button, click OK button

You should turn off printed field codes so that future documents do not print field codes. Perform the following steps to turn off field codes for printing.

More About

Main Documents

When you open a main document, Word attempts to open the associated data source file, too. If the data source is not in exactly the same location (i.e., drive and folder) as when it was saved originally, Word displays a dialog box indicating that it could not find the data source. When this occurs, click the Find Data Source button to display the Open Data Source dialog box.

TO TURN FIELD CODES OFF FOR PRINTING

1. Click Tools on menu bar and then click Options.
2. When the Options dialog box displays, if necessary, click the Print tab. Click Field codes in the Include with document area to remove the check mark.
3. Click the OK button.

Word turns off field codes for printed documents.

Merging the Documents and Printing the Letters

The data source and main document for the form letter are complete. The next step is to merge them together to generate the individual form letters as shown in the following steps.

Steps To Merge the Documents and Print the Form Letters

1. **Point to the Merge to Printer button on the Mail Merge toolbar (Figure 5-57).**

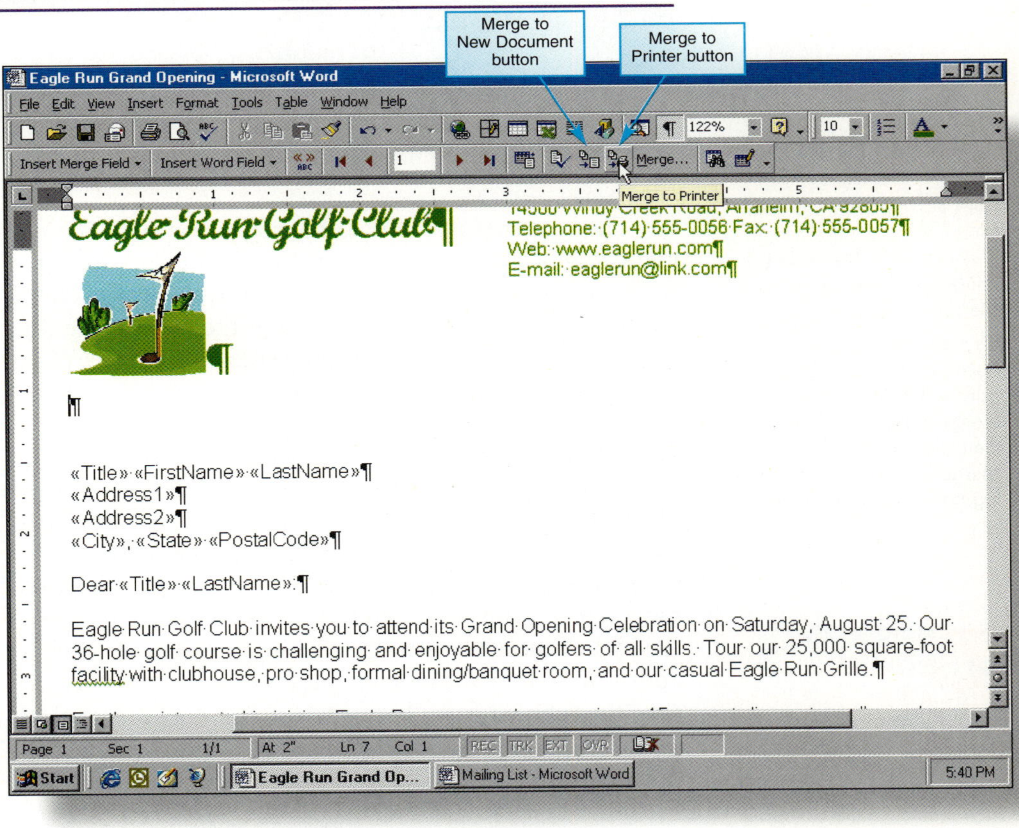

FIGURE 5-57

2 **Click the Merge to Printer button. When the Print dialog box displays, click the OK button. When the Microsoft Word dialog box displays, type** August 6, 2001 **and then point to the OK button.**

The Fill-in field instructs Word to display the dialog box requesting the mailing date of the form letters (Figure 5-58).

3 **Click the OK button.**

Word prints five separate letters, one for each person in the data source (see Figure 5-1c on page WD 5.5).

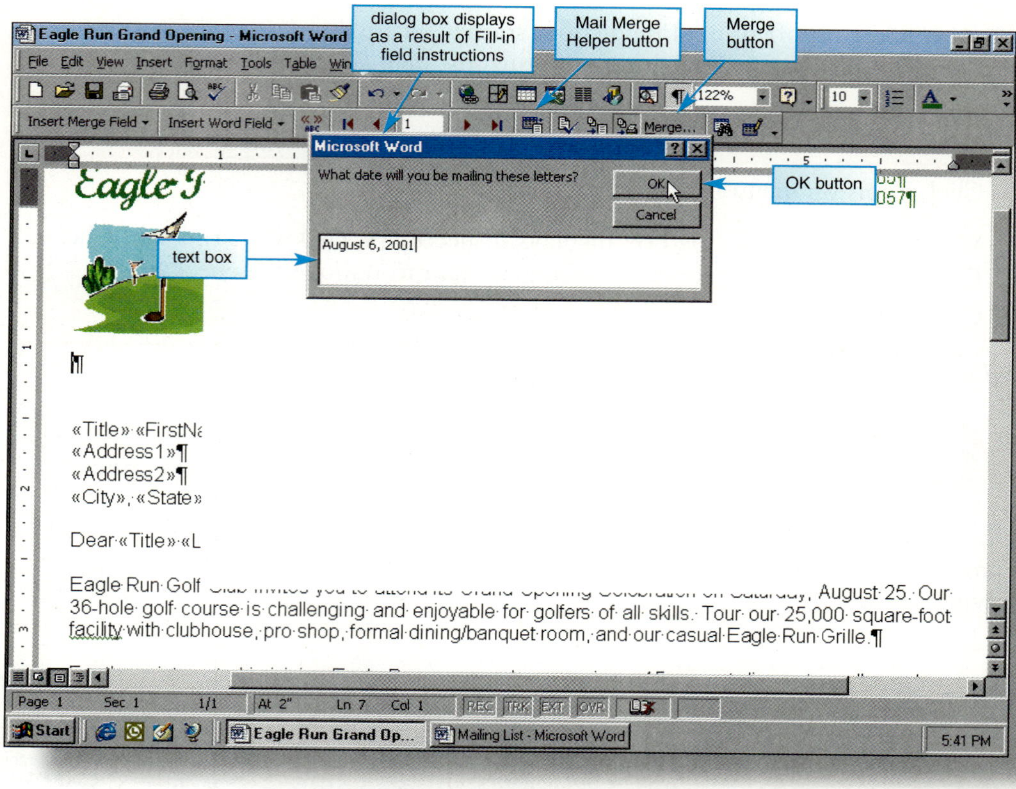

FIGURE 5-58

Conditions

The merge condition is case sensitive, which means the criteria you enter in the Compare to text box (Figure 5-60) must be the same case as the text in the data source. That is, if the data in the data source is in upper case, then the criteria entered in the Filter Records sheet also must be in upper case.

The contents of the data source merge with the merge fields in the main document to generate the form letters. Word prints five form letters because the data source contains five records. The address lines *suppress* blanks. That is, customers without a second address line begin the city on the line immediately below the first address line. Also, the discount percent changes from one letter to the next based on whether or not the person in the mailing list is a student.

If you notice errors in your form letters, you can edit the main document the same way you edit any other document. Then, save your changes and merge again.

Instead of printing the merged form letters, you could send them into a new document window by clicking the Merge to New Document button on the Mail Merge toolbar (see Figure 5-57 on the previous page). With this button, you view the merged form letters in a new document window on the screen to verify their accuracy before printing the letters. When you are finished viewing the merged form letters, you can print them by clicking the Print button on the Standard toolbar. In addition, you also can save these merged form letters in a file. If you do not want to save the merged form letters, close the document window by clicking the Close button at the right edge of the menu bar and then click the No button to not save the document.

Selecting Data Records to Merge and Print

Instead of merging and printing all of the records in the data source, you can choose which records will merge, based on a condition you specify. For example, to merge and print only those people in the mailing list who are students, perform the following steps.

To Selectively Merge and Print Records

1 **Click the Merge button on the Mail Merge toolbar. When Word displays the Merge dialog box, point to the Query Options button.**

Word displays the Merge dialog box (Figure 5-59).

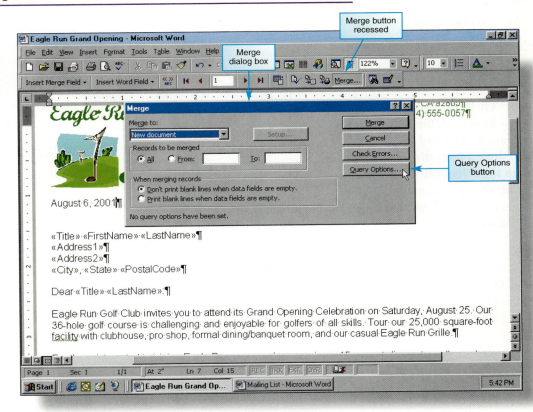

FIGURE 5-59

2 **Click the Query Options button. When the Query Options dialog box displays, if necessary, click the Filter Records tab. Click the Field box arrow to display a list of fields from the data source. Scroll to the bottom of the list and then click Student. In the Compare to text box, type Y and then point to the OK button.**

Word displays the Query Options dialog box (Figure 5-60). Student displays in the Field box, Equal to displays in the Comparison box, and Y displays in the Compare to box.

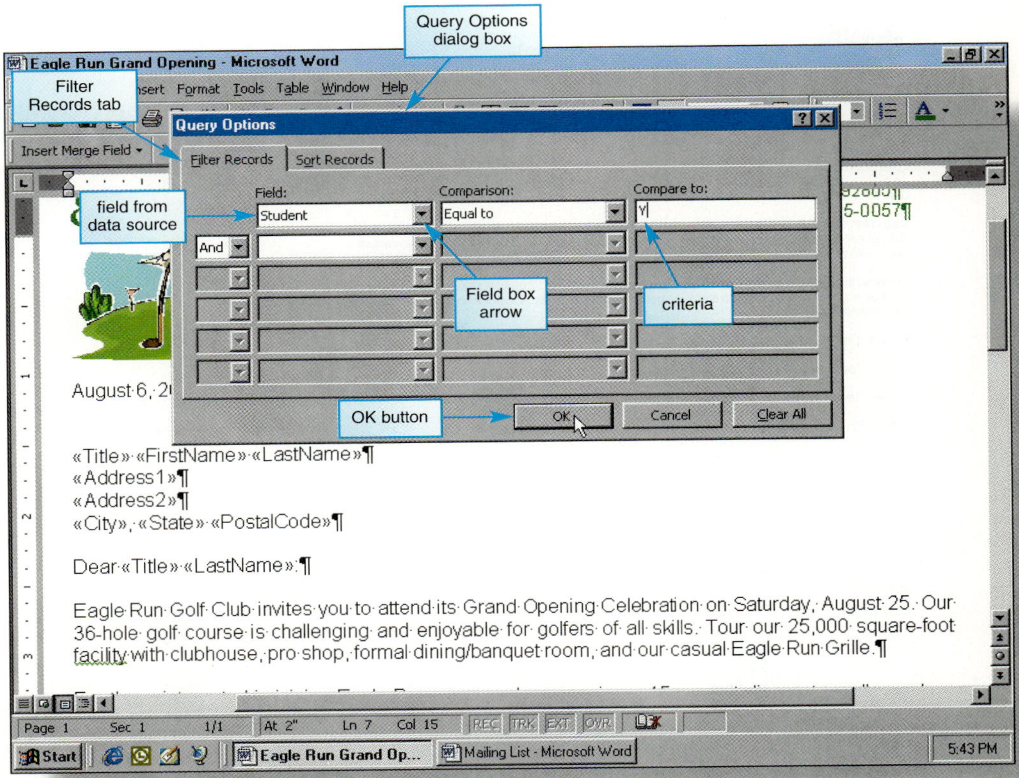

FIGURE 5-60

3 **Click the OK button. When the Merge dialog box redisplays, click its Close button.**

Word returns to the Merge dialog box. You close this dialog box.

4 **Click the Merge to Printer button on the Mail Merge toolbar. When Word displays the Print dialog box, click the OK button. When the Microsoft Word dialog box displays, if necessary, type** `August 6, 2001` **and then click the OK button.**

Word prints the form letters that match the specified condition: Student is Equal to Y (Figure 5-61). Two form letters print because two people in the mailing list are students.

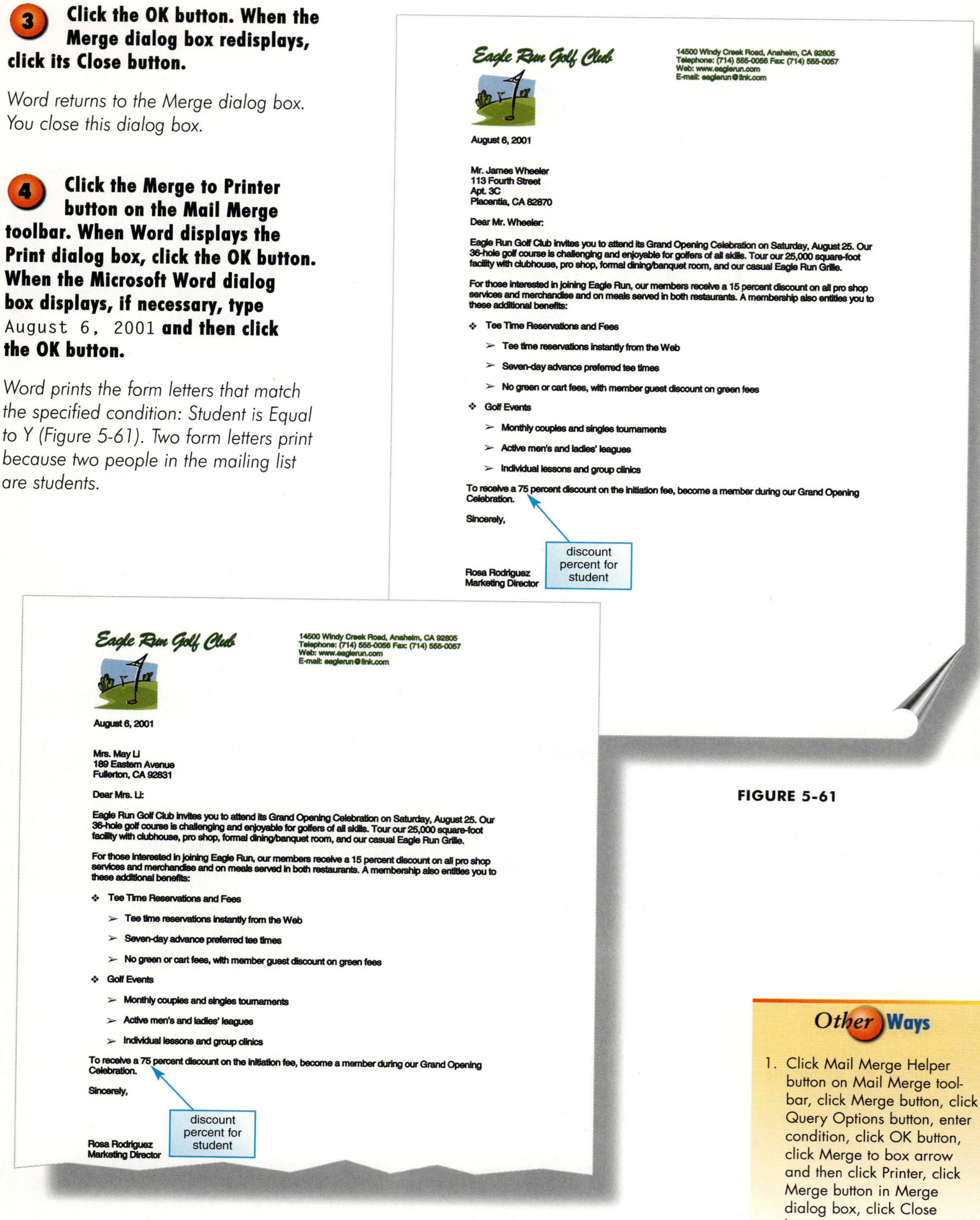

Eagle Run Golf Club

14500 Windy Creek Road, Anaheim, CA 92805
Telephone: (714) 555-0056 Fax: (714) 555-0057
Web: www.eaglerun.com
E-mail: eaglerun@link.com

August 6, 2001

Mr. James Wheeler
113 Fourth Street
Apt. 3C
Placentia, CA 82870

Dear Mr. Wheeler:

Eagle Run Golf Club invites you to attend its Grand Opening Celebration on Saturday, August 25. Our 36-hole golf course is challenging and enjoyable for golfers of all skills. Tour our 25,000 square-foot facility with clubhouse, pro shop, formal dining/banquet room, and our casual Eagle Run Grille.

For those interested in joining Eagle Run, our members receive a 15 percent discount on all pro shop services and merchandise and on meals served in both restaurants. A membership also entitles you to these additional benefits:

- Tee Time Reservations and Fees
  - Tee time reservations instantly from the Web
  - Seven-day advance preferred tee times
  - No green or cart fees, with member guest discount on green fees
- Golf Events
  - Monthly couples and singles tournaments
  - Active men's and ladies' leagues
  - Individual lessons and group clinics

To receive a 75 percent discount on the initiation fee, become a member during our Grand Opening Celebration.

Sincerely,

Rosa Rodriguez
Marketing Director

Eagle Run Golf Club

14500 Windy Creek Road, Anaheim, CA 92805
Telephone: (714) 555-0056 Fax: (714) 555-0057
Web: www.eaglerun.com
E-mail: eaglerun@link.com

August 6, 2001

Mrs. May Li
189 Eastern Avenue
Fullerton, CA 92831

Dear Mrs. Li:

Eagle Run Golf Club invites you to attend its Grand Opening Celebration on Saturday, August 25. Our 36-hole golf course is challenging and enjoyable for golfers of all skills. Tour our 25,000 square-foot facility with clubhouse, pro shop, formal dining/banquet room, and our casual Eagle Run Grille.

For those interested in joining Eagle Run, our members receive a 15 percent discount on all pro shop services and merchandise and on meals served in both restaurants. A membership also entitles you to these additional benefits:

- Tee Time Reservations and Fees
  - Tee time reservations instantly from the Web
  - Seven-day advance preferred tee times
  - No green or cart fees, with member guest discount on green fees
- Golf Events
  - Monthly couples and singles tournaments
  - Active men's and ladies' leagues
  - Individual lessons and group clinics

To receive a 75 percent discount on the initiation fee, become a member during our Grand Opening Celebration.

Sincerely,

Rosa Rodriguez
Marketing Director

FIGURE 5-61

Other Ways

1. Click Mail Merge Helper button on Mail Merge toolbar, click Merge button, click Query Options button, enter condition, click OK button, click Merge to box arrow and then click Printer, click Merge button in Merge dialog box, click Close button

You should remove the merge condition so that future merges will not be restricted to Student is Equal to Y.

TO REMOVE A MERGE CONDITION

① Click the Merge button on the Mail Merge toolbar.

② Click the Query Options button in the Merge dialog box.

③ Click the Clear All button. Click the OK button.

④ Click the Close button in the Merge dialog box.

Word removes the specified condition.

Sorting Data Records to Merge and Print

If you mail your form letters using the U.S. Postal Service's bulk rate mailing service, the post office requires you to sort and group the form letters by zip code. Thus, follow these steps to sort the data records by zip code.

More *About*

Electronic Signatures

For more information on electronic signatures, visit the Word 2000 More About Web page (www.scsite.com/wd2000/more.htm) and then click Electronic Signatures.

Steps To Sort the Data Records

① **Click the Merge button on the Mail Merge toolbar. When Word displays the Merge dialog box, click the Query Options button (see Figure 5-59 on page WD 5.43). If necessary, click the Sort Records tab when the Query Options dialog box displays. Point to the Sort by box arrow.**

Word displays the Query Options dialog box (Figure 5-62). You can order the data source records by any field.

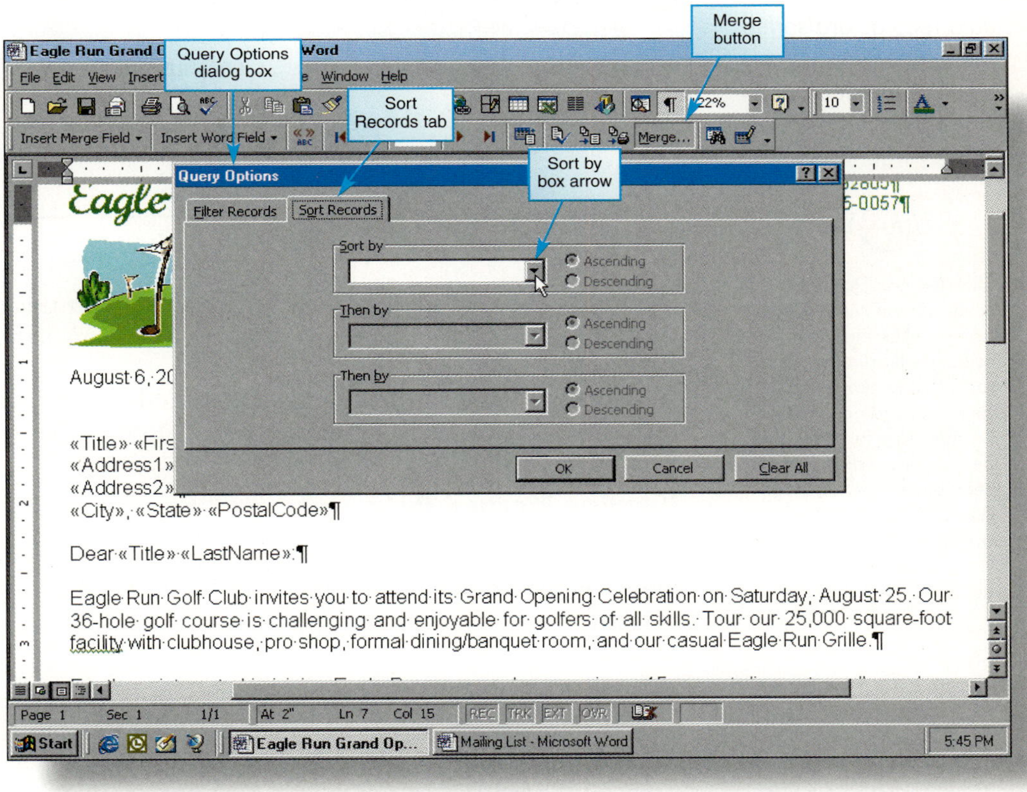

FIGURE 5-62

2 Click the Sort by box arrow to display a list of fields from the data source. Scroll to the bottom of the list and then click PostalCode.

Word displays PostalCode in the Sort by box (Figure 5-63). The Ascending option button is selected. Thus, the smallest postal code (those beginning with zero) will be listed first in the data source and the largest postal code will be last.

3 Click the OK button. When the Merge dialog box redisplays, click its Close button.

The data records are sorted in ascending order by postal code. Future merged documents will print in postal code order.

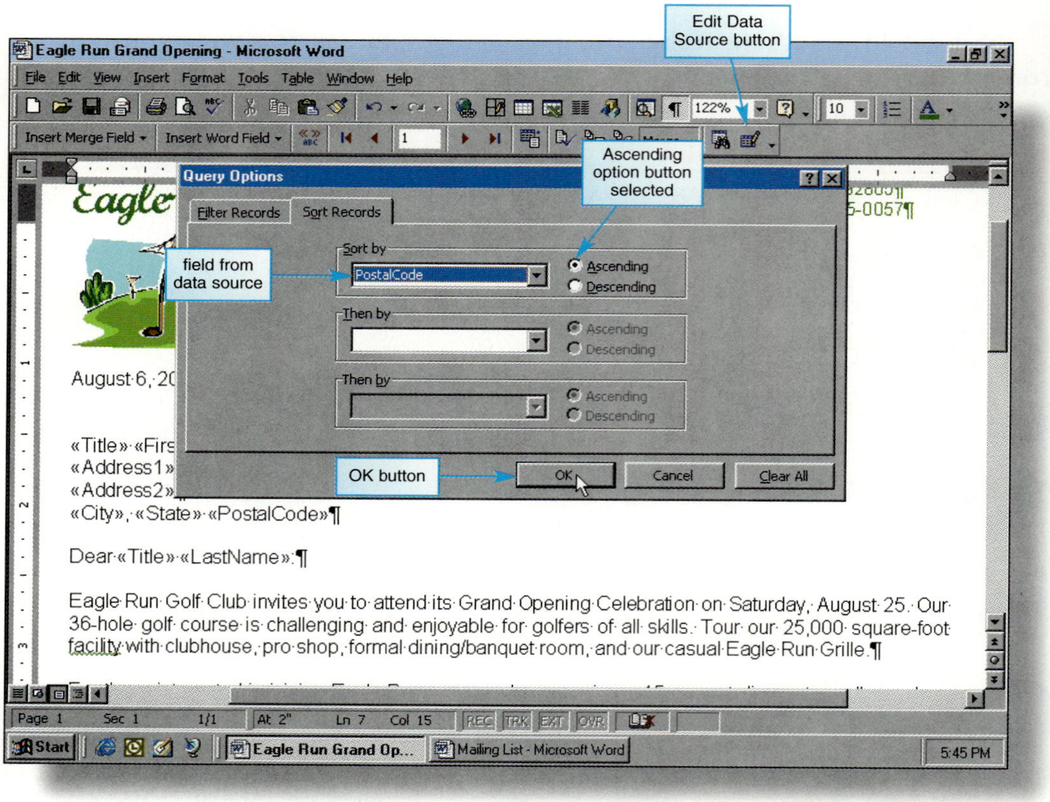

FIGURE 5-63

Other Ways

1. Click the Edit Data Source button on the Mail Merge toolbar, click the View Source button in the Data Form dialog box, click in the PostalCode column of the data source table, click the Sort Ascending button (see Figure 5-30 on page WD 5.23) on the Database toolbar, click the Mail Merge Main Document button on the Database toolbar

If you chose to merge the form letters again at this point, Word would print them in postal code order; that is, James Wheeler's letter would print first and May Li's letter would print last.

Because you want the mailing labels and envelopes to print in order of zip code, leave the sort condition set in the Query Options dialog box.

Viewing Merged Data

You can verify the order of the data records without printing them by using the **View Merged Data button** on the Mail Merge toolbar as shown in the following steps.

To View Merged Data in the Main Document

1 **Click the View Merged Data button on the Mail Merge toolbar.**

Word displays the contents of the first data record in the main document, instead of the merge fields (Figure 5-64). The View Merged Data button is recessed.

2 **Click the View Merged Data button on the Mail Merge toolbar again.**

Word displays the merge fields in the main document, instead of the field values.

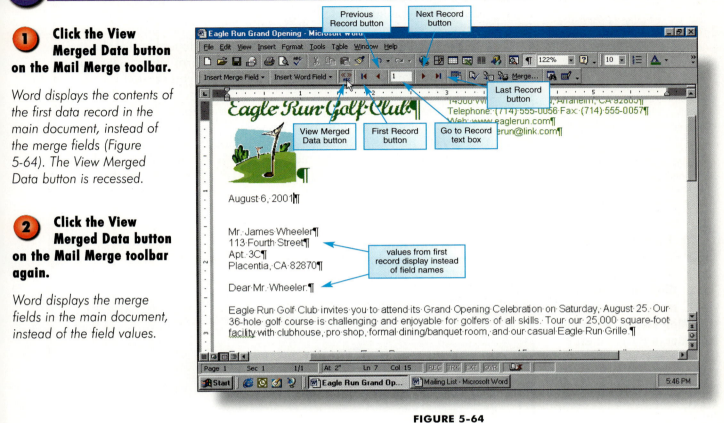

FIGURE 5-64

When you are viewing merged data in the main document (the View Merged Data button is recessed), you can click the **Last Record button** (see Figure 5-64) on the Mail Merge toolbar to display the values from the last record of the data source, the **Next Record button** to display the values from the next consecutive record number, the **Previous Record button** to display the values from the previous record number, or the **First Record button** to display the values from record one. You also can display a particular record by clicking the **Go to Record text box**, typing the record number you would like to display in the main document, and then pressing the ENTER key.

Addressing Mailing Labels

Now that you have merged and printed the form letters, the next step is to print addresses on **mailing labels** to be adhered to envelopes for the form letters. The mailing labels will use the same data source as the form letter, Mailing List. The format and content of the mailing labels will be exactly the same as the inside address in the main document for the form letter. That is, the first line will contain the resident's title, followed by the first name, followed by the last name. The second line will contain his or her street address, and so on.

More About

Mailing Labels

Instead of addressing mailing labels from a data source, you can print a label(s) for a single address. Click Tools on the menu bar, click Envelopes and Labels, click the Labels tab, type the name and address in the Address text box, click the Options button and select the label type, click the OK button, and then click the Print button in the Envelopes and Labels dialog box.

If your printer can print graphics, you can add a **POSTNET (POSTal Numeric Encoding Technique) delivery-point bar code,** usually referred to simply as a **bar code,** above the address on each mailing label. Using a bar code speeds up delivery by the U.S. Postal Service. A bar code represents the addressee's zip code and first street address.

You follow the same basic steps to create the main document for the mailing labels as you did to create the main document for the form letters. The major difference is that the data source already exists because you created it earlier in this project.

To address mailing labels, you need to specify the type of labels you intend to use. Word will request the manufacturer's name, as well as a product number and name. You can obtain this information from the box of labels. For illustration purposes in addressing these labels, the manufacturer is Avery, and the product name is address labels, which has a product number of 5160. The following pages illustrate how to address these mailing labels from an existing data source.

Steps: To Address Mailing Labels from an Existing Data Source

1 Click Tools on the menu bar and then click Mail Merge. When the Mail Merge Helper dialog box displays, click the Create button. Point to Mailing Labels (Figure 5-65).

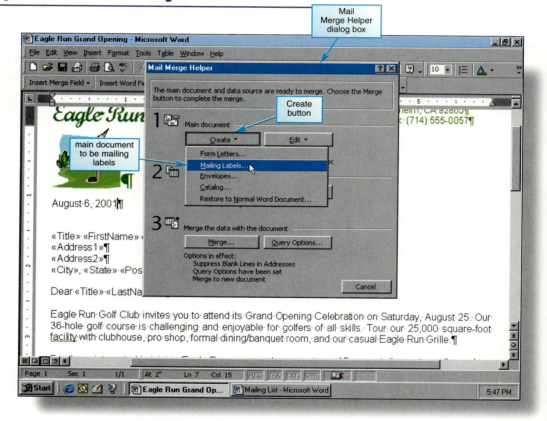

FIGURE 5-65

2 **Click Mailing Labels. Point to the New Main Document button in the Microsoft Word dialog box.**

A Microsoft Word dialog box displays asking if you want to change the active window main document to mailing labels or if you want to open a new window for the mailing labels (Figure 5-66). You want to open a new document window for the mailing labels.

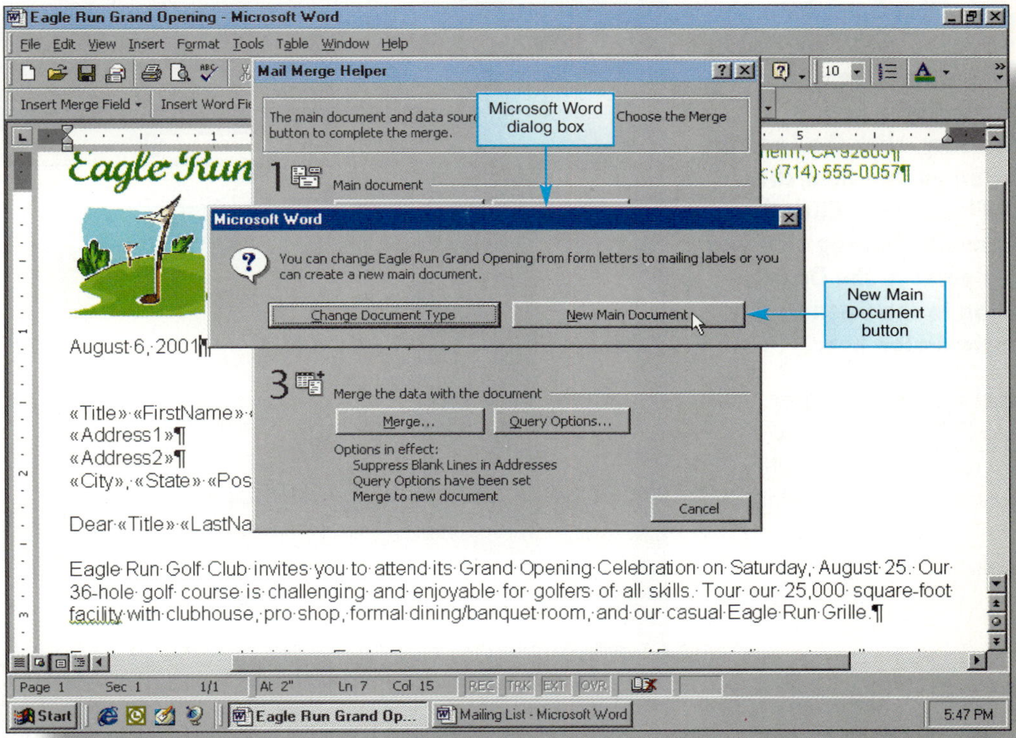

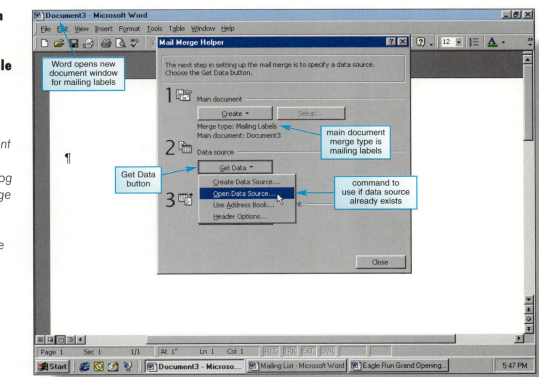

FIGURE 5-66

3 **Click the New Main Document button. When the Mail Merge Helper dialog box is visible again, click the Get Data button and then point to Open Data Source.**

Word opens a new document window and returns you to the Mail Merge Helper dialog box (Figure 5-67). The merge type is identified as mailing labels for the main document. You will open and use the same data source you created for the form letters.

FIGURE 5-67

4 Click Open Data Source. When Word displays the Open Data Source dialog box, if necessary, click the Look in box arrow and then click 3½ Floppy (A:). Click the file name, Mailing List, and then point to the Open button in the Open Data Source dialog box.

Word displays the Open Data Source dialog box (Figure 5-68). You use the existing data source, Mailing List, to address the mailing labels.

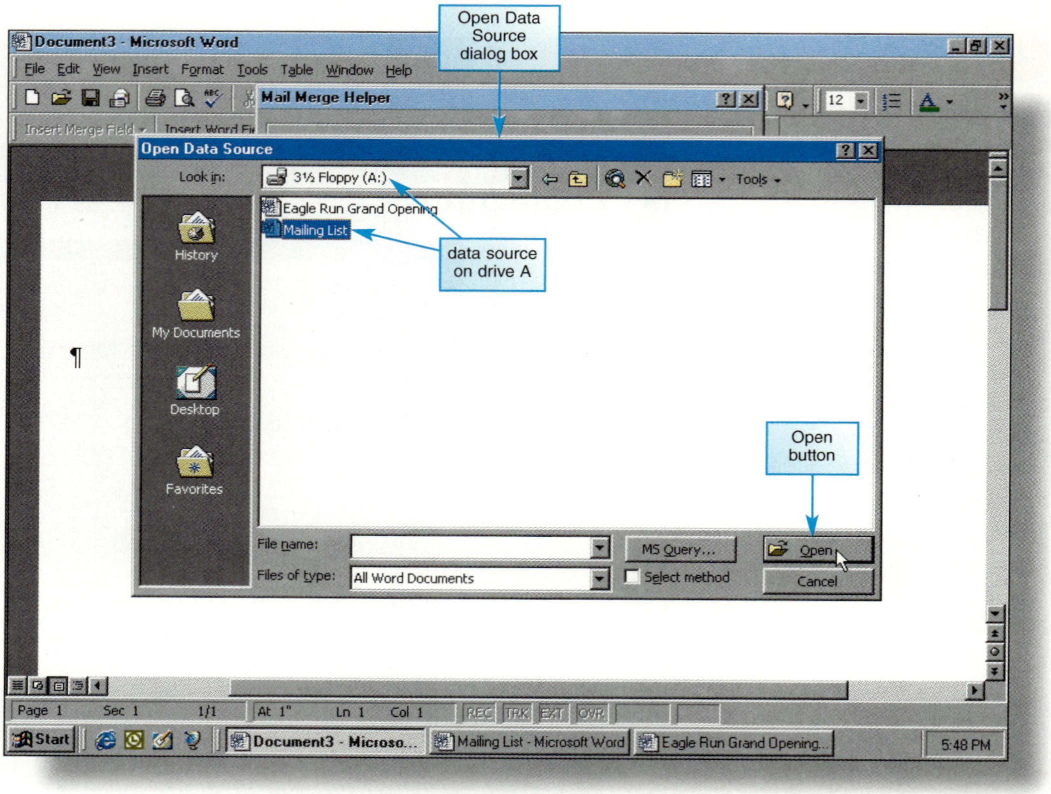

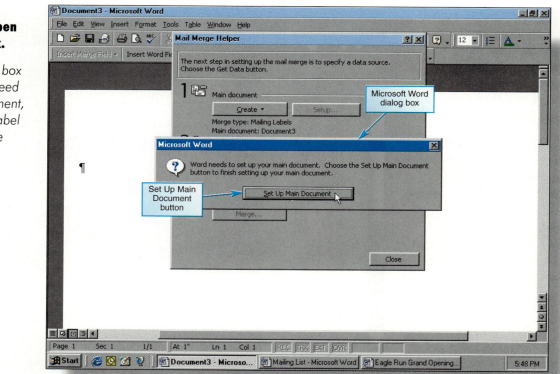

FIGURE 5-68

5 Click the Open button in the Open Data Source dialog box.

A Microsoft Word dialog box displays indicating you need to set up the main document, which will be a mailing label layout in this case (Figure 5-69).

FIGURE 5-69

6 **Click the Set Up Main Document button. When the Label Options dialog box displays, click the desired Avery product number in the Product number list. Point to the OK button.**

Word displays the Label Options dialog box (Figure 5-70). If you have a dot matrix printer, your printer information will differ from this figure. The Product number list displays the product numbers for all possible Avery mailing label sheets compatible with your printer.

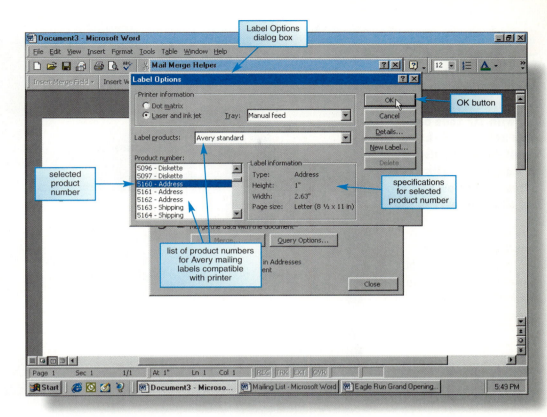

FIGURE 5-70

7 **Click the OK button.**

Word displays the Create Labels dialog box. You insert merge fields into the Sample label area of this dialog box using a technique similar to how you inserted merge fields into the main document for the form letter.

8 **Using the Insert Merge Field button in the Create Labels dialog box, follow Steps 1 and 2 on page WD 5.27 and then Steps 1 through 7 on pages WD 5.27 and WD 5.28 to address the mailing label. Point to the Insert Postal Bar Code button (Figure 5-71).**

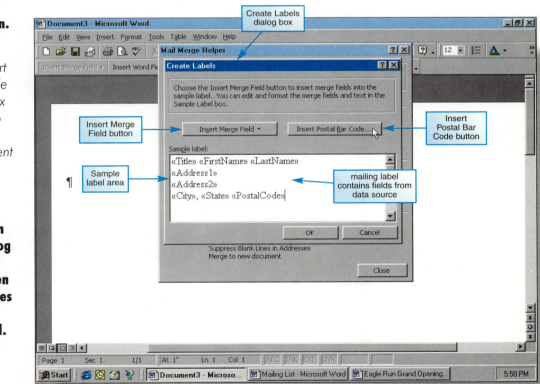

FIGURE 5-71

9 Click the Insert Postal Bar Code button. When the Insert Postal Bar Code dialog box displays, click the Merge field with ZIP code box arrow and then click PostalCode in the list. Click the Merge field with street address box arrow and then click Address1 in the list.

Word displays the Insert Postal Bar Code dialog box (Figure 5-72). A bar code contains the zip code and the first address line.

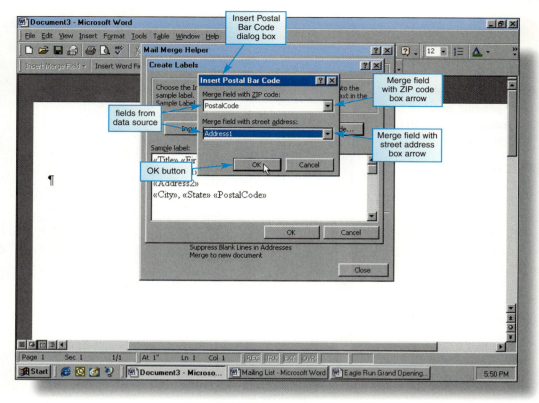

FIGURE 5-72

10 Click the OK button in the Insert Postal Bar Code dialog box.

Word returns to the Create Labels dialog box, which indicates where the bar code will print on each mailing label (Figure 5-73).

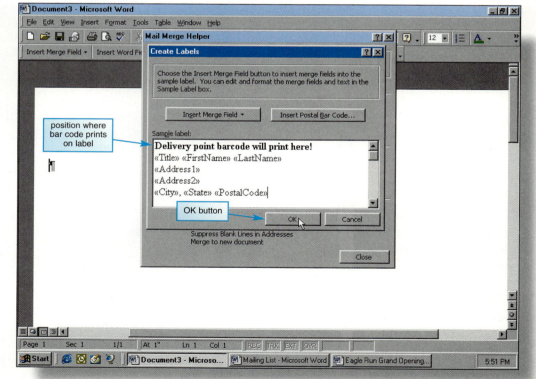

FIGURE 5-73

11 Click the OK button in the Create Labels dialog box. Click the Close button in the Mail Merge Helper dialog box. When the main document displays in the document window, click the Merge to Printer button on the Mail Merge toolbar. When the Print dialog box displays, click the OK button.

Word returns to the document window with the mailing label layout as the main document (Figure 5-74). The bar codes will print correctly even if your screen displays an error message or if the merge fields appear misaligned.

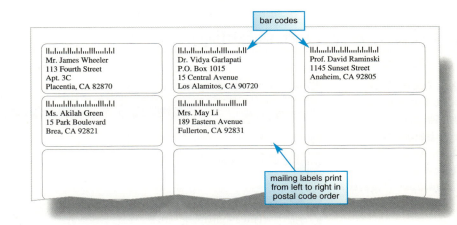

FIGURE 5-74

12 Retrieve the mailing labels from the printer.

The mailing labels print as shown in Figure 5-75. The mailing labels print in zip code order because earlier in this project you sorted the data source by zip code.

Mr. James Wheeler
113 Fourth Street
Apt. 3C
Placentia, CA 82870

Dr. Vidya Garlapati
P.O. Box 1015
15 Central Avenue
Los Alamitos, CA 90720

Prof. David Raminski
1145 Sunset Street
Anaheim, CA 92805

Ms. Akilah Green
15 Park Boulevard
Brea, CA 92821

Mrs. May Li
189 Eastern Avenue
Fullerton, CA 92831

bar codes

mailing labels print from left to right in postal code order

FIGURE 5-75

Other Ways

1. Click Mail Merge Helper button on Mail Merge toolbar

More About 2000

Bar Codes

If the bar code option is not available, the mailing label size you selected might not be wide enough to accommodate a bar code.

Saving the Mailing Labels

Perform the following steps to save the mailing labels.

TO SAVE THE MAILING LABELS

1 Insert your floppy disk into drive A.

2 Click the Save button on the Standard toolbar.

3 Type the file name `Eagle Run Labels` in the File name text box. Do not press the ENTER key after typing the file name.

4 If necessary, click the Save in box arrow and then click 3½ Floppy (A:).

5 Click the Save button in the Save As dialog box.

Word saves the document on a floppy disk on drive A with the file name, Eagle Run Labels.

Addressing Envelopes

Instead of addressing mailing labels to affix to envelopes, your printer may have the capability of printing directly onto envelopes. To print the label information directly on envelopes, follow the same basic steps as you did to address the mailing labels. Perform the following steps to address envelopes using an existing data source.

More About 2000

Mail Merge Helper Button

If the Mail Merge toolbar displays in the Word window, you can click the Mail Merge Helper button on the Mail Merge toolbar to display the Mail Merge Helper dialog box. If the Mail Merge toolbar does not display, click Tools on the menu bar and then click Mail Merge to display the Mail Merge Helper dialog box.

Steps: To Address Envelopes from an Existing Data Source

1 **Click Tools on the menu bar and then click Mail Merge. When the Mail Merge Helper dialog box displays, click the Create button and then point to Envelopes (Figure 5-76).**

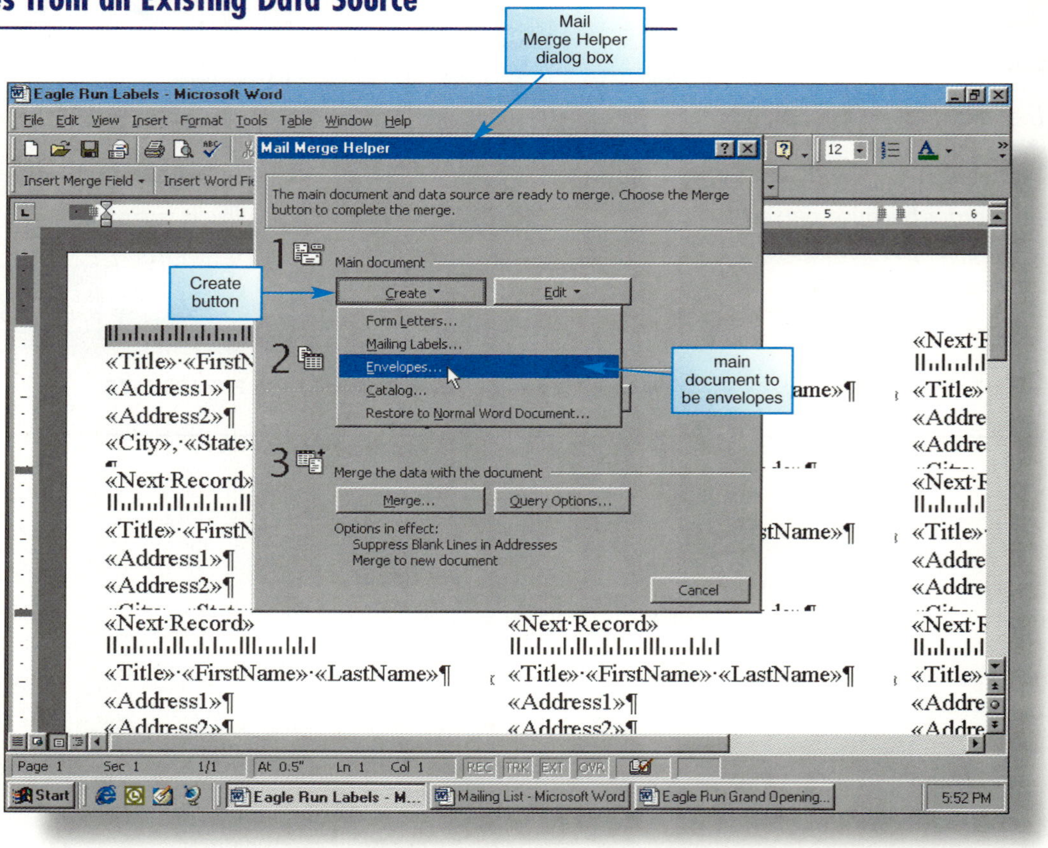

FIGURE 5-76

2 **Click Envelopes. Click the New Main Document button. Click the Get Data button and then click Open Data Source. When the Open Data Source dialog box displays, if necessary, change the Look in location to drive A. Click the file name, Mailing List, and then click the Open button in the Open Data Source dialog box. Click the Set Up Main Document button. If necessary, click the Envelope Options tab when the Envelope Options dialog box displays.**

Word displays the Envelope Options dialog box (Figure 5-77). Depending on your printer, your Envelope Options sheet may differ from this figure.

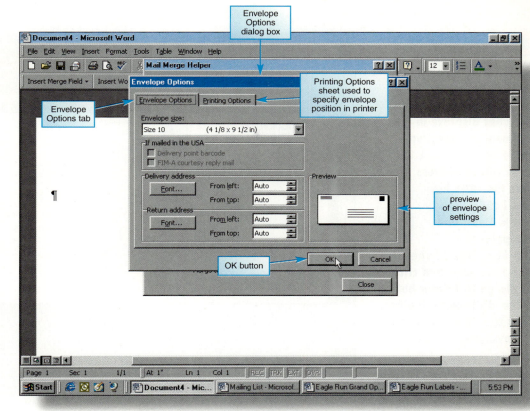

FIGURE 5-77

3 **Click the OK button.**

Word displays the Envelope address dialog box. You insert merge fields into the Sample envelope address area of this dialog box the same way you inserted merge fields into the main document for the mailing labels and the main document for the form letter.

4 **Follow Steps 8 through 11 on pages WD 5.51 through WD 5.53 to address the envelopes with a bar code.**

Word displays the completed envelope layout (Figure 5-78).

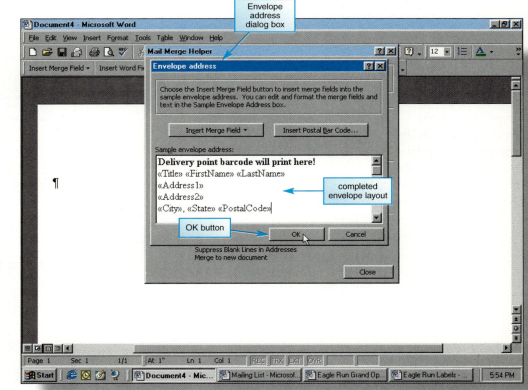

FIGURE 5-78

5 Click the OK button. When the Mail Merge Helper dialog box displays, click the Close button. When the main document displays in the document window, type `Eagle Run Golf Club` in the return address area. Press the ENTER key. Type `14500 Windy Creek Road` and then press the ENTER key. Type `Anaheim, CA 92805` and then click the Merge to Printer button on the Mail Merge toolbar. When the Print dialog box displays, click the OK button.

Word returns to the document window with the envelope layout as the main document (Figure 5-79). The bar codes will print correctly even if your screen displays an error message.

6 Retrieve the envelopes from the printer.

The envelopes print as shown in Figure 5-80. The envelopes print in postal code order because earlier in this project you sorted the data source by postal code.

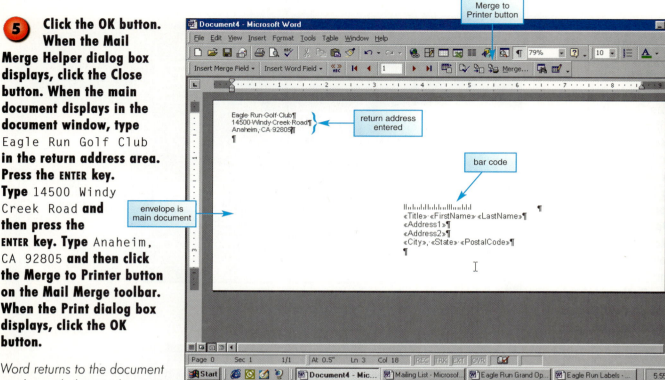

FIGURE 5-79

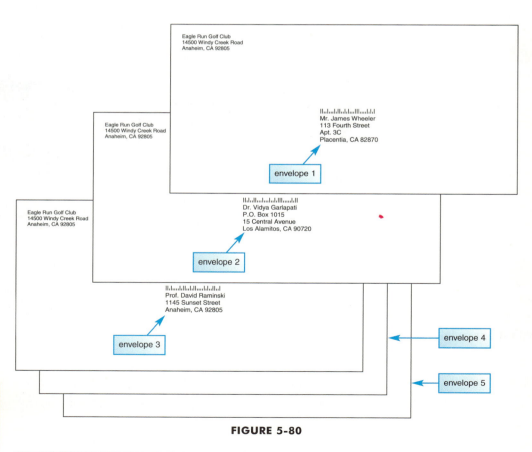

FIGURE 5-80

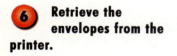

1. Click Mail Merge Helper button on Mail Merge toolbar

Saving the Envelopes

Perform the following steps to save the envelopes.

TO SAVE THE ENVELOPES

1 Insert your floppy disk into drive A.

2 Click the Save button on the Standard toolbar.

3 Type the file name Eagle Run Envelopes in the File name text box. Do not press the ENTER key after typing the file name.

4 If necessary, click the Save in box arrow and then click 3½ Floppy (A:).

5 Click the Save button in the Save As dialog box.

Word saves the document on a floppy disk on drive A with the file name, Eagle Run Envelopes.

Closing All Open Files and Quitting Word

You currently have four files open: Mailing List, Eagle Run Golf Opening, Eagle Run Mailing Labels, and Eagle Run Envelopes. Close all open files at once as described in these steps.

TO CLOSE ALL OPEN DOCUMENTS

1 Press and hold the SHIFT key. While holding the SHIFT key, click File on the menu bar. Release the SHIFT key.

2 Click Close All.

3 If a Microsoft Word dialog box displays, click the Yes button to save any changes made to the individual documents. If you do not want the data records to be saved in sorted order (by postal code), you would click the No button when Word asks if you want to save changes to Mailing List.

Word closes all open documents and displays a blank document window.

Project 5 now is complete. Follow this step to quit Word.

TO QUIT WORD

1 Click the Close button in the Word window.

The Word window closes.

Quick Reference

For a table that lists how to complete the tasks covered in this book using the mouse, menu, shortcut menu, and keyboard, visit the Shelly Cashman Series Office Web page (www.scsite.com/off2000/qr.htm) and then click Microsoft Word 2000.

Closing Form Letters

Word always asks if you want to save changes when you close a main document, even if you just saved the document. If you are sure that no additional changes were made to the document, click the No button; otherwise, click the Yes button - just to be safe.

CASE PERSPECTIVE SUMMARY

Ahmed inserts the form letters into the preaddressed envelopes, seals them, and applies necessary postage. He takes the stack of envelopes to the post office to expedite the delivery of the letters. Rosa and her staff prepare diligently for the upcoming celebration.

The Grand Opening Celebration is a smashing success. The weather is quite accommodating – sunny, 85 degrees, and a gentle breeze. More than 1,000 people visit Eagle Run on August 25, touring the club, taking advantage of the pro shop sale, and enjoying fabulous food. Best of all, 257 of the visitors become members during the celebration.

Project Summary

Project 5 introduced you to creating and printing form letters and addressing corresponding mailing labels and envelopes. First, you used a letter template to begin creating the letter, then identified the letter as the main document and created a data source. Next, you entered the main document for the form letter. The form letter included merge fields, an IF field, a Fill-in field, and an outline numbered list. In this project, you learned how to merge and print all the records in the data source, as well as only records that meet a certain criterion. You also learned how to sort the data source records. Finally, you addressed mailing labels and envelopes to accompany the form letters.

What You Should Know

Having completed this project, you should now be able to perform the following tasks:

- Address Envelopes from an Existing Data Source (WD 5.54)
- Address Mailing Labels from an Existing Data Source (WD 5.48)
- AutoFormat a Table (WD 5.24)
- Change Page Orientation (WD 5.24)
- Close All Open Documents (WD 5.57)
- Create a Data Source in Word (WD 5.17)
- Create a Letter Using a Word Template (WD 5.6)
- Create an Outline Numbered List (WD 5.30)
- Display Formatting Marks (WD 5.9)
- Enter More Merge Fields (WD 5.27)
- Enter the Body of the Letter (WD 5.29)
- Identify the Main Document (WD 5.14)
- Insert a Fill-in Field (WD 5.37)
- Insert a Merge Field into the Main Document (WD 5.27)

- Insert an IF Field into the Main Document (WD 5.34)
- Insert Clip Art (WD 5.10)
- Merge the Documents and Print the Form Letters (WD 5.41)
- Print a Document (WD 5.25)
- Print Field Codes in the Main Document (WD 5.40)
- Quit Word (WD 5.57)
- Remove a Merge Condition (WD 5.45)
- Reset Menus and Toolbars (WD 5.8)
- Resize a Graphic (WD 5.11)
- Save a Document Again (WD 5.38)
- Save the Envelopes (WD 5.57)
- Save the Letter (WD 5.13)
- Save the Mailing Labels (WD 5.54)
- Select and Replace More Placeholder Text (WD 5.12)
- Select and Replace Placeholder Text (WD 5.9)
- Selectively Merge and Print Records (WD 5.43)
- Sort the Data Records (WD 5.45)
- Switch from the Data Source to the Main Document (WD 5.25)
- Turn Field Codes Off for Printing (WD 5.41)
- Turn Field Codes On or Off for Display (WD 5.39)
- Unlink a Field (WD 5.28)
- View Merged Data in the Main Document (WD 5.47)
- Zoom Text Width (WD 5.9)

More About

Microsoft Certification

The Microsoft Office User Specialist (MOUS) Certification program provides an opportunity for you to obtain a valuable industry credential - proof that you have the Word 2000 skills required by employers. For more information, see Appendix D or visit the Shelly Cashman Series MOUS Web page at www.scsite.com/off2000/cert.htm.

Project Reinforcement at www.scsite.com/off2000/reinforce.htm

1 Working with a Form Letter

Instructions: Start Word. Open the document, Orland Flowers Holiday Special, on the Data Disk. If you did not download the Data Disk, see the inside back cover for instructions for downloading the Data Disk or see your instructor.

The document is a main document for Orland Flowers and Gifts. You are to print field codes in the main document (Figure 5-81), edit and print a formatted data source in landscape orientation, and then merge the form letters to a file and the printer.

Orland Flowers and Gifts

15220 Oak Avenue, Orland Park, IL 60462
Telephone: (708) 555-0045
Web: www.orlandflowers.com

{ FILLIN "What date will you be mailing these letters?" \o }

{ MERGEFIELD Title } { MERGEFIELD FirstName } { MERGEFIELD LastName }
{ MERGEFIELD Address1 }
{ MERGEFIELD Address2 }
{ MERGEFIELD City }, { MERGEFIELD State } { MERGEFIELD PostalCode }

Dear { MERGEFIELD Title } { MERGEFIELD LastName }:

With the holiday season quickly approaching, now is the time to take advantage of our great prices on flower arrangements and customized gift baskets. We will deliver your order locally or package and send it anywhere in the country.

As a valued customer, we want to thank you for choosing Orland Flowers and Gifts. Simply bring in this letter to receive a { IF { MERGEFIELD PreferredCard } = "Y" "20" "10" } percent discount on any purchase until the end of the year.

{ AUTOTEXTLIST }

Marianne Pulaski
Owner

FIGURE 5-81

Apply Your Knowledge

✚ Project Reinforcement at www.scsite.com/off2000/reinforce.htm

Working with a Form Letter *(continued)*

Perform the following tasks:

1. Click the Print button on the Standard toolbar.
2. Click Tools on the menu bar and then click Options. When the Options dialog box displays, if necessary, click the Print tab. Click Field codes to select the check box and then click the OK button. Click the Print button on the Standard toolbar.
3. Click Tools on the menu bar and then click Options. When the Options dialog box displays, if necessary, click the Print tab. Click Field codes to turn off the check box and then click the OK button.
4. Click the Edit Data Source button on the Mail Merge toolbar and then click the View Source button in the Data Form dialog box to display the data source, Orland Flowers Customer List, as a Word table.
5. Click Table on the menu bar and then click Table AutoFormat. When the Table AutoFormat dialog box displays, scroll through the list of formats, and then click Grid 8. Click the OK button.
6. Click the Add New Record button on the Database toolbar. Add a record containing your personal information; enter Y in the PreferredCard field.
7. Click in the LastName column of the data source. Click the Sort Ascending button on the Database toolbar.
8. Click File on the menu bar and then click Save As. Use the file name Revised Orland Flowers Customer List.
9. Click File on the menu bar and then click Page Setup. When the Page Setup dialog box displays, click the Paper Size tab. Click Landscape in the Orientation area and then click the OK button. Click the Print button on the Standard toolbar.
10. Click the Mail Merge Main Document button on the Database toolbar.
11. Click the Merge to New Document button on the Mail Merge toolbar. Type December 3, 2001 in the text box and then click the OK button. Click the Print button on the Standard toolbar. Click File on the menu bar and then click the Close button. Click the No button in the Microsoft Word dialog box.
12. Click the Merge to Printer button on the Mail Merge toolbar. Click the OK button in the Print dialog box. If necessary, type December 3, 2001 in the text box and then click the OK button.
13. Hold down the SHIFT key while clicking File on the menu bar. Click Close All.

In the Lab

1 Creating a Data Source, Form Letter, and Mailing Labels

Problem: Martin Popovich, the director of admissions at Taxton Community College, has asked you to send an orientation announcement letter to all incoming freshman. You decide to use a form letter (Figure 5-82).

Instructions:

1. Use the Professional Letter template to create a letter. Enter the letterhead shown at the top of Figure 5-82 into the appropriate areas of the template.

In the Lab

2. Begin the mail merge process by clicking Tools on the menu bar and then clicking Mail Merge. Specify the current document window as the main document.

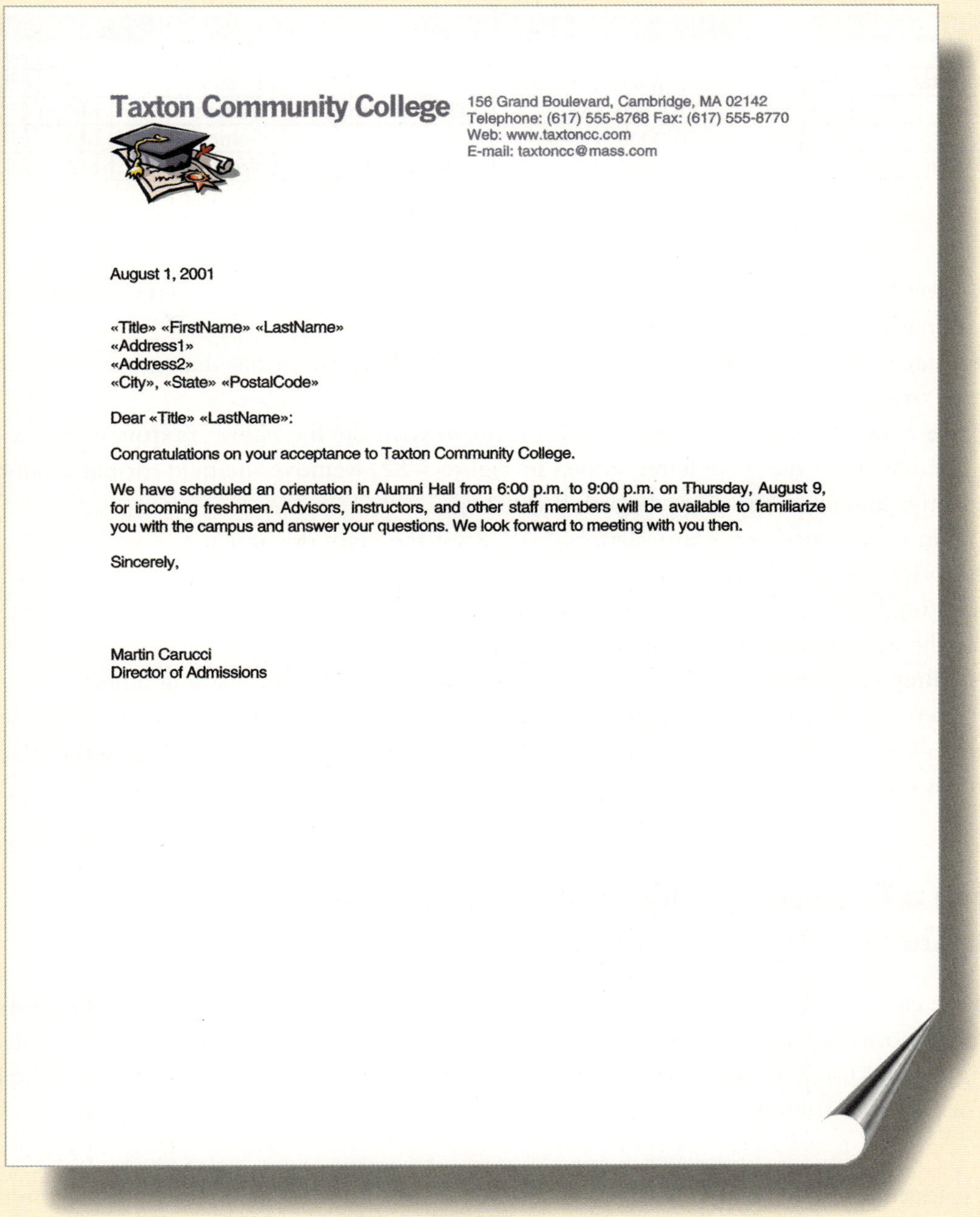

Taxton Community College

156 Grand Boulevard, Cambridge, MA 02142
Telephone: (617) 555-8768 Fax: (617) 555-8770
Web: www.taxtoncc.com
E-mail: taxtoncc@mass.com

August 1, 2001

«Title» «FirstName» «LastName»
«Address1»
«Address2»
«City», «State» «PostalCode»

Dear «Title» «LastName»:

Congratulations on your acceptance to Taxton Community College.

We have scheduled an orientation in Alumni Hall from 6:00 p.m. to 9:00 p.m. on Thursday, August 9, for incoming freshmen. Advisors, instructors, and other staff members will be available to familiarize you with the campus and answer your questions. We look forward to meeting with you then.

Sincerely,

Martin Carucci
Director of Admissions

FIGURE 5-82

(continued)

In the Lab

Creating a Data Source, Form Letter, and Mailing Labels *(continued)*

3. Create the data source shown in Figure 5-83.

Title	FirstName	LastName	Address1	Address2	City	State	PostalCode
Mr.	Raul	Ramos	145 Sunset Road	Apt. 4D	Cambridge	MA	02142
Ms.	Crystal	Weaver	13 Western Avenue		Boston	MA	02102
Mr.	Fred	VanWijk	P.O. Box 889	143 Third Street	Boston	MA	02125
Mr.	Ed	Spelbring	103 Oak Avenue		Somerville	MA	01245
Ms.	Dawn	Nitz	P.O. Box 113	15 Center Street	West Medford	MA	02156

FIGURE 5-83

4. Click the View Data Source button in the Data Form dialog box to view the data source in table form. Save the data source with the file name Taxton New Students.

5. Format the data source using the Grid 8 format in the Table AutoFormat dialog box. Print the data source in landscape orientation.

6. Switch to the main document. Save the main document with the file name, Taxton Welcome Letter. Create the main document for the form letter shown in Figure 5-82. Remove the field format from the date at the top of the letter and enter the date, August 1, 2001.

7. Save the main document for the form letter again. Print the main document.

8. Merge and print the form letters.

9. Address mailing labels using the same data source you used for the form letters. Specify a new document window as the main document. Put bar codes on the mailing labels.

10. Save the mailing labels with the name Taxton Mailing Labels. Print the mailing labels.

11. If your printer allows, address envelopes using the same data source you used for the form letters. Specify a new document window as the main document. Put bar codes on the envelopes. Save the envelopes with the name Taxton Envelopes. Print the envelopes.

2 Creating a Form Letter with an IF Field, a Fill-in Field, and an Outline Numbered List

Problem: As the computer specialist at Williams Landscaping, the owner has asked you to send a letter to all former customers, notifying them that the nursery will be moving to a new location. You have decided to use a form letter (Figure 5-84). For business customers, you print the word, business, at the end of the last paragraph of the letter; for home customers, you print the word, home, at the end of the last paragraph of the letter.

Instructions:

1. Use the Professional Letter template to create a letter. Enter the letterhead shown at the top of Figure 5-84 on the previous page into the appropriate areas of the template.

In the Lab

2. Begin the mail merge process by clicking Tools on the menu bar and then clicking Mail Merge. Specify the current document window as the main document.

Williams Landscaping

135 Stafford Drive, Hobart, IN 46342
Telephone: (219) 555-5757 Fax (219) 555-5777
E-mail: williams@earth.com
Web: www.williams.com

Fill-in field → { FILLIN "What date will you be mailing these letters?" \o }

{ MERGEFIELD Title } { MERGEFIELD FirstName } { MERGEFIELD LastName }
{ MERGEFIELD JobTitle }
{ MERGEFIELD Company }
{ MERGEFIELD Address1 }
{ MERGEFIELD Address2 }
{ MERGEFIELD City }, { MERGEFIELD State } { MERGEFIELD PostalCode }

Dear { MERGEFIELD Title } { MERGEFIELD LastName }:

Williams Landscaping is moving. Effective October 1, stop by our new, larger location at 14 River Road in Hobart. Our telephone, fax, e-mail address, and Web address remain unchanged.

Our expanded nursery now supplies all of your landscaping needs, including the following:

outline numbered list

❖ Trees

   ➢ Evergreens – arborvitae, fir, hemlock, pine, spruce

   ➢ Shade trees – ash, birch, elm, hackberry, linden, maple, oak, poplar, walnut, willow

   ➢ Ornamental trees – cherry, crabapple, hawthorn, magnolia, pear, plum, serviceberry

❖ Shrubs and Vines

   ➢ Shrubs – barberry, hydrangea, lilac, rose, spirea, sumac

   ➢ Vines – bittersweet, clematis, creeper, honeysuckle, ivy

To enhance the natural beauty of your { IF { MERGEFIELD CustomerType } = "Home" "home" "business" }, allow our specialists at Williams Landscaping to assist you with selecting and planting a variety of trees, shrubs, vines, hedges, plants, and flowers. We look forward to seeing you soon.

IF field

{ AUTOTEXTLIST }

Robert Beatty
Owner

FIGURE 5-84

(continued)

In the Lab

Creating a Form Letter with an IF Field, a Fill-in Field, and an Outline Numbered List *(continued)*

3. Create the data source shown in Figure 5-85.

Title	FirstName	LastName	JobTitle	Company	Address1	Address2	City	State	PostalCode	CustomerType
Mr.	Joel	Puntillo	Grounds Manager	Wilson Plastics	P.O. Box 145		Merrillville	IN	46410	Business
Ms.	Shauna	Gupta			14 Duluth Street		Highland	IN	46322	Home
Dr.	Maria	Lopez			P.O. Box 56	156 Grand Street	Munster	IN	46321	Business
Mrs.	Lisa	Pavlowski	Owner	Hobart Flowers	15 Lincoln Highway		Hobart	IN	46342	Business
Mr.	Arnie	Kristoff			P.O. Box 72	147 Highway Avenue	Griffith	IN	46319	Home

FIGURE 5-85

4. Click the View Data Source button in the Data Form dialog box to view the data source in table form. Save the data source with the file name Williams Landscaping Customers.
5. Format the data source using the Grid 8 format in the Table AutoFormat dialog box. Print the data source in landscape orientation.
6. Switch to the main document. Save the main document with the file name, Williams Landscaping Form Letter. Create the main document for the form letter shown in Figure 5-84. The IF field tests if CustomerType is equal to Home; if it is, then print the word, home; otherwise print the word, business. Use a Fill-in field with the following text for the date: What date will you be mailing these letters?
7. Save the main document for the form letter again.
8. Print the main document with field codes on. Do not forget to turn the field codes off.
9. Merge and print the form letters.

3 Designing a Data Source, Form Letter, and Mailing Labels from Sample Memos

Problem: The benefits coordinator at Geo Consulting, Inc., would like to schedule a benefits enrollment session for all employees. Two separate session times will be scheduled: one for salaried employees and one for hourly employees. Sample drafted memos are shown in Figure 5-86.

Instructions:

1. Use the Professional Memo template to create an interoffice memorandum. Enter the company name as shown at the top of Figure 5-86 on the previous page into the appropriate area of the template.
2. Begin the mail merge process by clicking Tools on the menu bar and then clicking Mail Merge. Specify the current document window as the main document.
3. Decide on field names to use in the data source. Create a data source with five sample employees. Two of the sample employees may be the ones shown in Figure 5-86.

In the Lab

4. Format the data source. Print the data source in landscape orientation.
5. Switch to the main document. Save the main document with the file name, Geo Benefits Memo. Create the main document for the form letter shown in Figure 5-86. The current date should print at the top of the form letter. The IF field tests the EmployeeType: if EmployeeType is Salaried, then the meeting is from 10:00 – 11:00 A.M.; otherwise the meeting is from 2:00 – 3:00 P.M.

Geo Consulting, Inc.

Memo

To: Mr. Jason Carter
       Accountant
       Office: A-224

From: Huang Chin
       Benefits Coordinator

Date: October 1, 2001

Re: 2002 Health Benefits Enrollment

Geo Consulting, Inc. health benefits enrollment takes place from October 8 through October 26, 2001. You will receive the benefits enrollment package within the next few days. During open enrollment, you will have the opportunity to review your plan choices and make changes. If you have any questions, please call our office at x272.

Your enrollment session has been scheduled for Monday, October 21, from 10:00 a.m. to 11:00 a.m. If you are unable to attend this general session, please call Gina at x277 to schedule a personal session.

Thank you.

{ PAGE }

FIGURE 5-86a

(continued)

In the Lab

Designing a Data Source, Form Letter, and Mailing Labels from Sample Memos *(continued)*

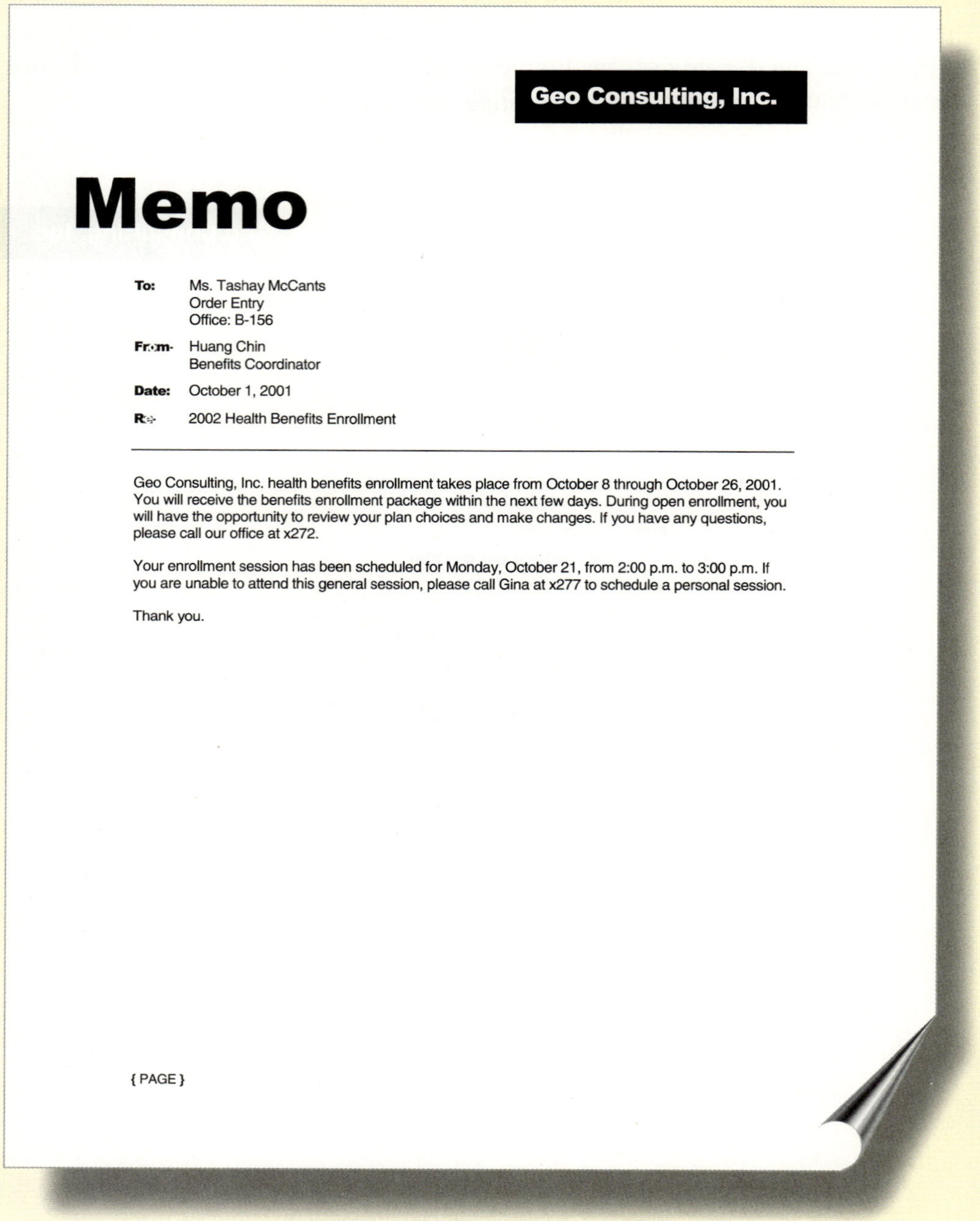

Geo Consulting, Inc.

Memo

To:	Ms. Tashay McCants Order Entry Office: B-156
From:	Huang Chin Benefits Coordinator
Date:	October 1, 2001
Re:	2002 Health Benefits Enrollment

Geo Consulting, Inc. health benefits enrollment takes place from October 8 through October 26, 2001. You will receive the benefits enrollment package within the next few days. During open enrollment, you will have the opportunity to review your plan choices and make changes. If you have any questions, please call our office at x272.

Your enrollment session has been scheduled for Monday, October 21, from 2:00 p.m. to 3:00 p.m. If you are unable to attend this general session, please call Gina at x277 to schedule a personal session.

Thank you.

{ PAGE }

FIGURE 5-86b

---

6. Save the main document for the form letter again.
7. Print the main document with field codes. Do not forget to turn off the field codes after printing them.
8. Merge and print the form letters.
9. Address mailing labels using the same data source you used for the form letters. Specify a new document window as the main document.
10. Save the mailing labels with the name Geo Mailing Labels. Print the mailing labels.

Cases and Places

The difficulty of these case studies varies:
◗ are the least difficult; ◗◗ are more difficult; and ◗◗◗ are the most difficult.

1 ◗ You are activities chairperson for the Summer Day Camp at your church. Letters must be sent to all parents informing them of the rules for the event. Create a form letter using the following information: Company Name: First United Church; Address: 15 Park Avenue, Oviedo, FL 32765; Telephone: (407) 555-2828; Fax: (407) 555-2929. Create the data source shown in Figure 5-87. Use merge fields to create the inside address and salutation. All recipients live in Oviedo Florida 32765. First paragraph: <u>Summer Day Camp is scheduled from June 25 through June 29 at the church campgrounds. Camp will be from 9:00 A.M. until 3:00 P.M. each day. Your {MERGEFIELD ChildGender} should bring the following items in a backpack to camp.</u> Create an outline numbered list using the bullet character for the following list items: Extra clothes – socks, tennis shoes, sweatshirt, raincoat; Sundries – water bottle, insect repellent, mess kit, sit-upon. Last paragraph – <u>If you have any questions, please contact Geri at 555-2828</u>. Use your name in the signature block. Then, create and address accompanying labels or envelopes for the form letters.

Title	FirstName	LastName	Address1	Address2	ChildGender
Mrs.	Effie	Maniotes	1567 Cedar Boulevard		son
Ms.	Juanita	Espinoza	15 Carroll Street		daughter
Dr.	John	Parker	P.O. Box 1128	1128 Eastern Avenue	daughter
Mrs.	Kimberly	Johnson	998 Sycamore Road		son
Mr.	Mohammed	Ashved	P.O. Box 7786	14 Franklin Road	daughter

FIGURE 5-87

2 ◗◗ You are organizing a block party for Saturday, August 18. The party will begin at 9:00 A.M. and end at 11:00 P.M. Each family is to bring a side dish or dessert that will feed at least 15 people. You need volunteers for setup, games, cooks, and refreshments. Anyone with questions should contact you. Create a form letter announcing the block party and requesting volunteers. Use the text, First Annual Block Party, at the top of the letter with an appropriate clip art image. Obtain the names and addresses of five of your family members and use them as records in the data source. Then, address accompanying labels or envelopes for the form letters.

3 ◗◗ The bookstore at your school will be holding its annual Book Buy Back on May 10 and May 11 from 8:00 A.M. to 5:00 P.M. each day. The books will be bought at 50 percent of their original purchase price. Only books that are being used in the fall semester may be returned. Books must be in a usable condition. Create a form letter announcing the Book Buy Back. Be sure the top of the form letter contains the school name, address, and an appropriate clip art image. Obtain the names and addresses of five of your classmates and use them as records in the data source. Then, address accompanying labels or envelopes for the form letters.

Cases and Places

4 ▶▶ You currently are seeking an employment position in your field of study. You already have prepared a resume and would like to send it to a group of potential employers. You decide to design a cover letter to send along with the resume. Obtain a recent newspaper and cut out three classified advertisements pertaining to your field of study. Locate two job advertisements on the Internet. Create the cover letter for your resume as a form letter. Be sure the top of the cover letter contains your name, address and telephone number, as well as an appropriate clip art image. Use the information in the classified ads from newspapers and the Internet for the data source. The data source should contain potential employers' names, addresses, and position being sought. Then, address accompanying labels or envelopes for the cover letters. Turn in the want ads with your printouts.

5 ▶▶▶ As assistant to the sales manager at your company, you are responsible for providing each salesperson with a company car. This year, you need ten new cars. Obtain the names and addresses of five new car dealerships in your area. Research the types of vehicles that would be best suited as company cars and then create a form letter requesting quotations on these cars. Be sure the letter has an attractive letterhead with an appropriate clip art image. Use dealership names and addresses as records in your data source. Then, address accompanying labels or envelopes for the cover letters.

6 ▶▶▶ If Microsoft Access is installed on your system, you can use it to create a table and then use that table as the data source in a mail merge document. Start Access and then create the table in Project 5 (Figure 5-16 on page WD 5.16) as an Access database table. You may need to use Help in Access to assist you in the procedure for creating and saving a database that contains a table. Exit Access. Start Word. Begin the mail merge process as discussed in Project 5. When specifying the data source, click Open Data Source. In the Open Data Source dialog box, change the file type to MS Access Databases and then click the database name of the file you created in Access. Create the form letter in Project 5 so it uses the fields in the Access database table. Then, address accompanying labels or envelopes for the cover letters.

7 ▶▶▶ If Microsoft Access is installed on your system, you can use it to create a table and then use that table as the data source in a mail merge document. Start Access and then create the table for the In the Lab 2 exercise as an Access table (Figure 5-85 on page WD 5.62). You may need to use Help in Access to assist you in the procedure for creating and saving a database that contains a table. Exit Access. Start Word. Begin the mail merge process as discussed in Project 5. When specifying the data source, click Open Data Source. In the Open Data Source dialog box, change the file type to MS Access Databases and then click the database name of the file you created in Access. Create the form letter in Figure 5-84 on page WD 5.61 so it uses the fields in the Access database table. Then, address accompanying labels or envelopes for the cover letters.

Microsoft **Word 2000**

Microsoft Word 2000

Creating a Professional Newsletter

OBJECTIVES

You will have mastered the material in this project when you can:

- Define desktop publishing terminology
- Create a WordArt drawing object
- Format a WordArt drawing object
- Add ruling lines above and below paragraphs
- Insert the current date into a document
- Format a document into multiple columns
- Justify a paragraph
- Format a character as a dropped capital letter
- Insert a column break
- Link an object to a Word document
- Place a vertical rule between columns
- Insert a text box
- Change character spacing
- Shade a paragraph
- Position a text box
- Balance columns
- Insert a picture into a document
- Position a graphic between columns
- Use the Format Painter button
- Place a border on a page
- Highlight text

From the Earliest Times

Simple Systems for Sending Messages

In 1501, a Portuguese ship captain set sail for destinations unknown. Aware that he would be at sea for many years and wishing to send news of himself and his crew to those back home, he went ashore at the Cape of Good Hope on the southern tip of Africa and deposited a letter wrapped in pitch-covered canvas under a stone. On the stone, he inscribed a request to whoever found his message that they forward it to his homeland. This launched the tradition of the **post office stone**. Sea captains on their way to Europe — even bitter enemies of the writers — would pick up the letters and deliver them. This may have been the first example of global newsletter messenger service.

Humankind always has thirsted for information about news and events. Native Americans used **smoke signals** to convey news. **Africans used drums**. Some say Australian aborigines developed telepathic powers. The Spanish Conquistadores scratched their news onto **Inscription Rock** in New Mexico. Armies of old relied on mirrors and semaphores. Then, as technology progressed, the means of delivery grew more sophisticated, evolving from **Pony Express** and **telegraph** to modern **fiber-optic cables**, **microwaves**, and **satellite relays**.

Newsletters likewise have evolved into highly specialized vehicles that number in the thousands, addressing everything from astrology to investments to medicine to zoology. No matter what the association, cause, or subject, a newsletter for it is likely to exist. Besides the blizzard of hardcopy newsletters delivered by mail every day, e-mail and Web sites reach millions more.

A good reason for the explosive growth of newsletters is they get results. To unite people, organize an activity, persuade, or simply to pour out one's feelings, an attractive, well-written newsletter can boost sales, promote morale, raise money, or send your personal news to friends during the holiday season.

Snappy content, however, is not good enough. To reach out and seize someone's attention, newsletters must be more than merely attractive. Your newsletter must make a statement, provide appeal, and elicit interest.

In Word 2000, you have the ideal partner for creating eye-catching, dynamic newsletters. Word lets you produce crisp banner headlines; create WordArt drawing objects; manipulate columns, fonts, and blocks of copy at will; insert pictures into documents; link another document to the newsletter, then spice the whole thing with graphics and borders. Once you have the newsletter just right, Word also provides the capability of merging names and addresses from a separate database, such as a student organization, your clients, or your family and friends. You can also e-mail the newsletter to others for approval before making many copies for distribution.

Unlike that sixteenth century ship captain who had to rely on chance that someone would find the mail he deposited under the post office stone, once you finish creating that professional looking newsletter using Word's desktop publishing features, you can whisk it on its way via the Internet or the corner mailbox — without getting pitch on your hands.

Microsoft Word 2000

Creating a Professional Newsletter

P R O J E C T

6

C A S E   P E R S P E C T I V E

You are vice president of The Web Club at your school. Because you are majoring in Office Information Systems, you prepare the club's monthly newsletter. Each month, the newsletter contains a feature article and announcements. You decide that this month's feature article will cover communications and modems. You plan to create the article as a Word document, discussing items such as signal conversion; definition of a modem; modem speed; and internal, external, PC Card, fax, and cable modems. The announcements will remind readers about the upcoming field trip, notify them of new club discounts, and inform them of the club's new Web site.

After you create the article, Jamie Navaro, president of The Web Club, will review it. Then, you will insert the Word document into your newsletter in the appropriate column. Your task now is to design the newsletter so the feature article spans the first two columns of page 1 and then continues on page 2. The announcements should be located in the third column of page 1 of The Web Club newsletter.

Introduction

Professional looking documents, such as newsletters and brochures, often are created using desktop publishing software. With **desktop publishing software**, you can divide a document into multiple columns, wrap text around pictures and other objects, change fonts and font sizes, add color and lines, and so on to create an attention-grabbing document. A traditionally held opinion of desktop publishing software, such as Adobe PageMaker or QuarkXpress, is that it enables you to open an existing word processing document and enhance it through formatting not provided in your word processing software. Word, however, provides you with many of the formatting features that you would find in a desktop publishing package. Thus, you can create eye-catching newsletters and brochures directly within Word.

Project Six – Newsletter

Project 6 uses Word to produce the monthly newsletter shown in Figure 6-1. The newsletter is a monthly publication for members of The Web Club. Notice that it incorporates the desktop publishing features of Word. The body of each page of the newsletter is divided into three columns. A variety of fonts, font sizes, and colors add visual appeal to the document. The first page has text wrapped around a pull-quote and the second page has text wrapped around a picture. Horizontal and vertical lines separate distinct areas of the newsletter, including a page border around the perimeter of each page.

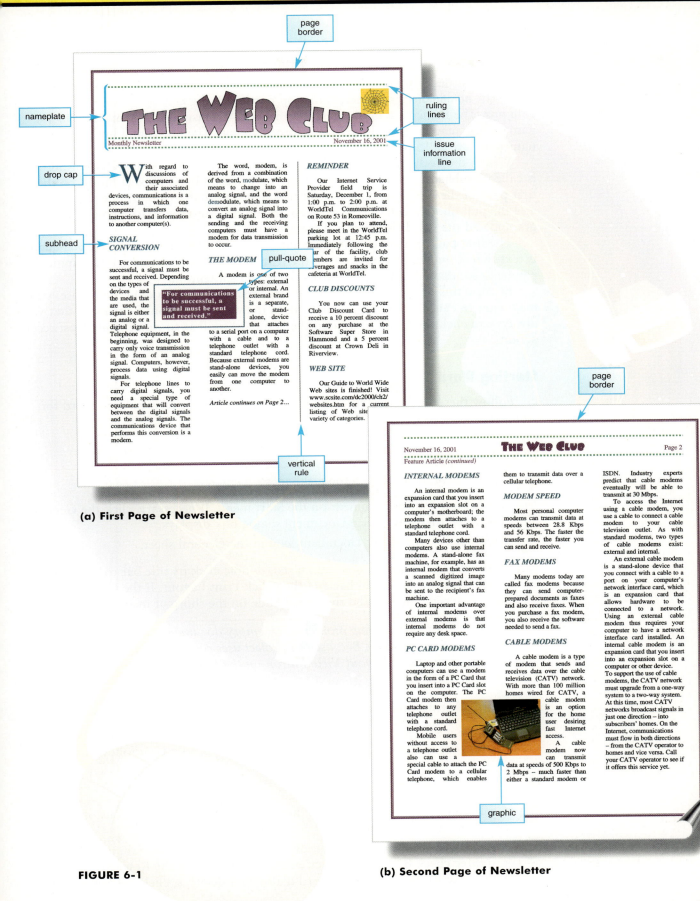

page border

nameplate

ruling lines

issue information line

drop cap

subhead

pull-quote

vertical rule

page border

graphic

(a) First Page of Newsletter

(b) Second Page of Newsletter

FIGURE 6-1

Desktop Publishing Terminology

As you create professional looking newsletters and brochures, you should understand several desktop publishing terms. In Project 6 (Figure 6-1 on the previous page), the **nameplate**, or **banner**, is the top portion of the newsletter above the three columns. The nameplate on the first page is more extensive because it contains the name of the newsletter and the **issue information line**. The horizontal lines in the nameplate are called **rules**, or **ruling lines**.

Within the body of the newsletter, a heading, such as SIGNAL CONVERSION, is called a **subhead**. The vertical line dividing the second and third columns on the first page of the newsletter is a **vertical rule**. The text that wraps around the picture and the pull-quote is referred to as **wrap-around text**, and the space between the graphic and the words is called the **run-around**.

The first page of the newsletter contains a pull-quote (Figure 6-1a). A **pull-quote** is text that is *pulled*, or copied, from the text of the document and given graphical emphasis so it stands apart and grasps the reader's attention.

Because this project involves several steps requiring you to drag the mouse, you may want to cancel an action if you drag to the wrong location. Remember that you always can click the Undo button on the Standard toolbar to cancel your most recent action.

Starting Word

Follow these steps to start Word or ask your instructor how to start Word for your system.

TO START WORD

1 Click the Start button on the taskbar.

2 Click New Office Document on the Start menu. If necessary, click the General tab when the New Office Document dialog box displays.

3 Double-click the Blank Document icon in the General sheet.

4 If the Word window is not maximized, double-click its title bar to maximize it. Click View on the menu bar and then click Print Layout. If the Office Assistant displays, right-click it and then click Hide on the shortcut menu.

Office starts Word. After a few moments, an empty document titled Document1 displays in the Word window. Because this project uses columns, you will use print layout view; thus, the Print Layout View button on the horizontal scroll bar is recessed.

Resetting Menus and Toolbars

To set the menus and toolbars so they appear exactly as shown in this book, you should reset your menus and toolbars as outlined in Appendix C or follow these steps.

TO RESET MENUS AND TOOLBARS

1 Click View on the menu bar and then point to Toolbars. Click Customize on the Toolbars submenu.

2 When the Customize dialog box displays, click the Options tab, make sure the top three check boxes have check marks and then click the Reset my usage data button. When the Microsoft Word dialog box displays, click the Yes button.

3 Click the Toolbars tab. Click Standard in the Toolbars list and then click the Reset button. When the Reset Toolbar dialog box displays, click the OK button.

4 Click Formatting in the Toolbars list and then click the Reset button. When the Reset Toolbar dialog box displays, click the OK button. Click the Close button.

Word resets the menus and toolbars.

Displaying Formatting Marks

You have learned that it is helpful to display formatting marks that indicate where in the document you pressed the ENTER key, SPACEBAR, and other keys. Follow this step to display formatting marks.

TO DISPLAY FORMATTING MARKS

1 If the Show/Hide ¶ button on the Standard toolbar is not already recessed, click it.

Word displays formatting marks in the document window, and the Show/Hide ¶ button on the Standard toolbar is recessed.

Changing All Margin Settings

You have learned that Word is preset to use standard 8.5-by-11-inch paper, with 1.25-inch left and right margins and 1-inch top and bottom margins. For the newsletter in this project, you want all margins (left, right, top, and bottom) to be .75 inch. Perform the following steps to change these margin settings.

TO CHANGE ALL MARGIN SETTINGS

1 Click File on the menu bar and then click Page Setup.

2 When the Page Setup dialog box displays, if necessary, click the Margins tab. Type .75 in the Top text box and then press the TAB key.

3 Type .75 in the Bottom text box and then press the TAB key.

4 Type .75 in the Left text box and then press the TAB key.

5 Type .75 in the Right text box and then point to the OK button (Figure 6-2 on the next page).

6 Click the OK button to change the margin settings for this document.

Depending on the printer you are using, you may need to set the margins differently for this project.

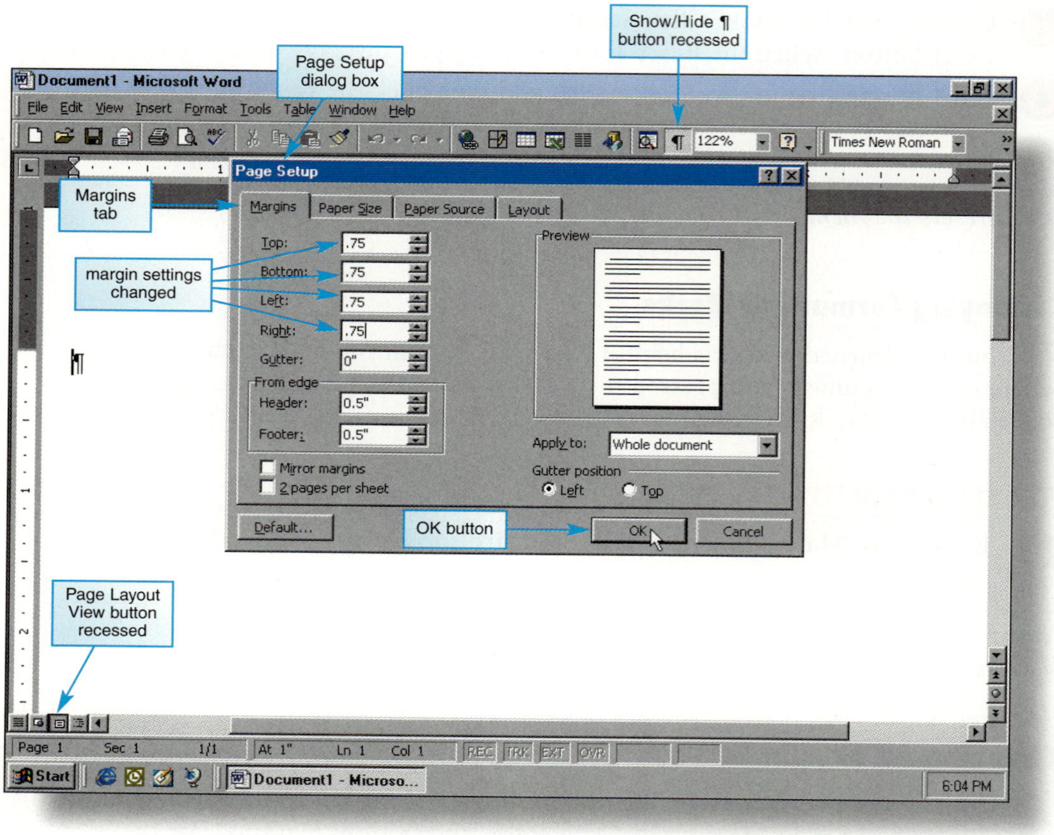

FIGURE 6-2

Zooming Text Width

As you have learned, when you zoom text width, Word displays text on the screen as large as possible in print layout view without extending the right margin beyond the right edge of the document window. Perform the following steps to zoom text width.

TO ZOOM TEXT WIDTH

1 Double-click the move handle on the Standard toolbar so that the entire toolbar displays. Click the Zoom box arrow on the Standard toolbar.

2 Click Text Width in the Zoom list.

Word places the right margin at the right edge of the document window (see Figure 6-3). Word computes the zoom percentage based on a variety of settings. Your percentage may be different depending on your system configuration.

Creating the Nameplate

The nameplate on the first page of this newsletter consists of the information above the multiple columns (see Figure 6-1a on page WD 6.5). The nameplate is composed of the newsletter title, THE WEB CLUB, and the issue information line. The steps on the following pages illustrate how to create the nameplate for the first page of the newsletter in this project.

Nameplates

The nameplate should contain, at a minimum, the title and date of the newsletter. The title should be displayed in as large a font size as possible. You also may include a logo in the nameplate. Many nameplates include a headline outlining the function of the newsletter. Some nameplates also include a short table of contents.

Creating a WordArt Drawing Object

You can insert two types of graphics into a Word document: a picture and a drawing object. A **picture** is a graphic that was created in another program. Examples of pictures are scanned images, photographs, and clip art. In earlier projects, you inserted clip art from the Clip Gallery. Later in this project, you insert a scanned photograph into the newsletter.

A **drawing object** is a graphic you create using Word. You can modify or enhance drawing objects using the Drawing toolbar. You display the Drawing toolbar by clicking the Drawing button on the Standard toolbar (see Figure 6-3).

Examples of drawing objects include shapes, curves, lines, and WordArt objects. With **WordArt**, you can create special effects such as shadowed, rotated, stretched, skewed, and wavy text. This project uses a WordArt drawing object in the nameplate on the first page of the newsletter. Perform the following steps to insert a WordArt drawing object.

More About

WordArt Drawing Objects

Keep in mind that WordArt drawing objects are not treated as Word text. Thus, if you misspell the contents of a WordArt drawing object and then spell check the document, Word will not flag a misspelled word(s) in the WordArt drawing object.

Steps To Insert a WordArt Drawing Object

1 If the Drawing toolbar does not display in the Word window, click the Drawing button on the Standard toolbar. Point to the Insert WordArt button on the Drawing toolbar (Figure 6-3).

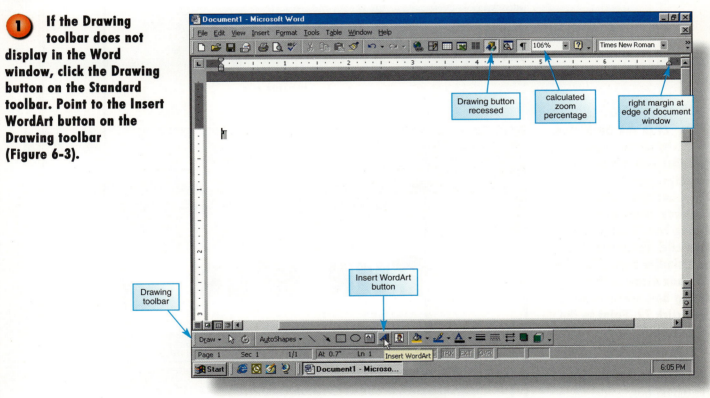

FIGURE 6-3

2 **Click the Insert WordArt button. When the WordArt Gallery dialog box displays, if necessary, click the style in the upper-left corner and then point to the OK button.**

The WordArt Gallery dialog box displays (Figure 6-4). Because you will add your own special text effects, the style in the upper-left corner is selected.

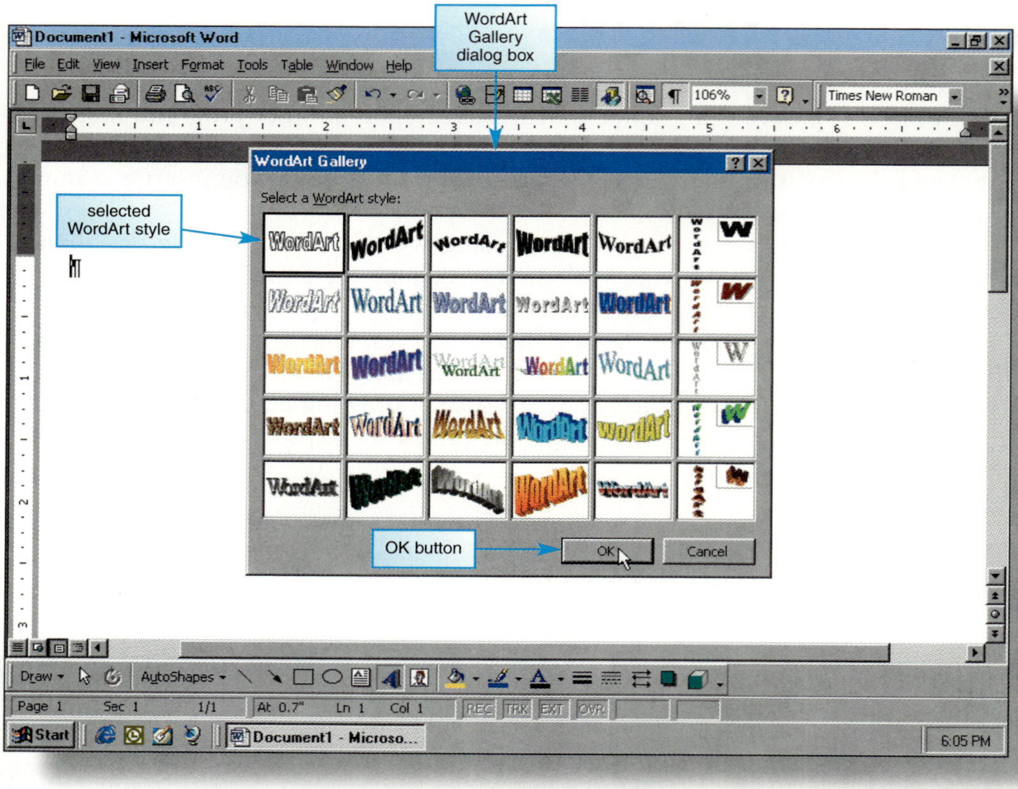

FIGURE 6-4

3 **Click the OK button. When the Edit WordArt Text dialog box displays, type** The Web Club **and then click the Font box arrow in the dialog box. Scroll to and then click Beesknees ITC, or a similar font. Click the Size box arrow in the dialog box, scroll to and then click 72. Point to the OK button.**

The Edit WordArt Text dialog box displays (Figure 6-5). In this dialog box, you enter the WordArt text and change its font, font size, and font style.

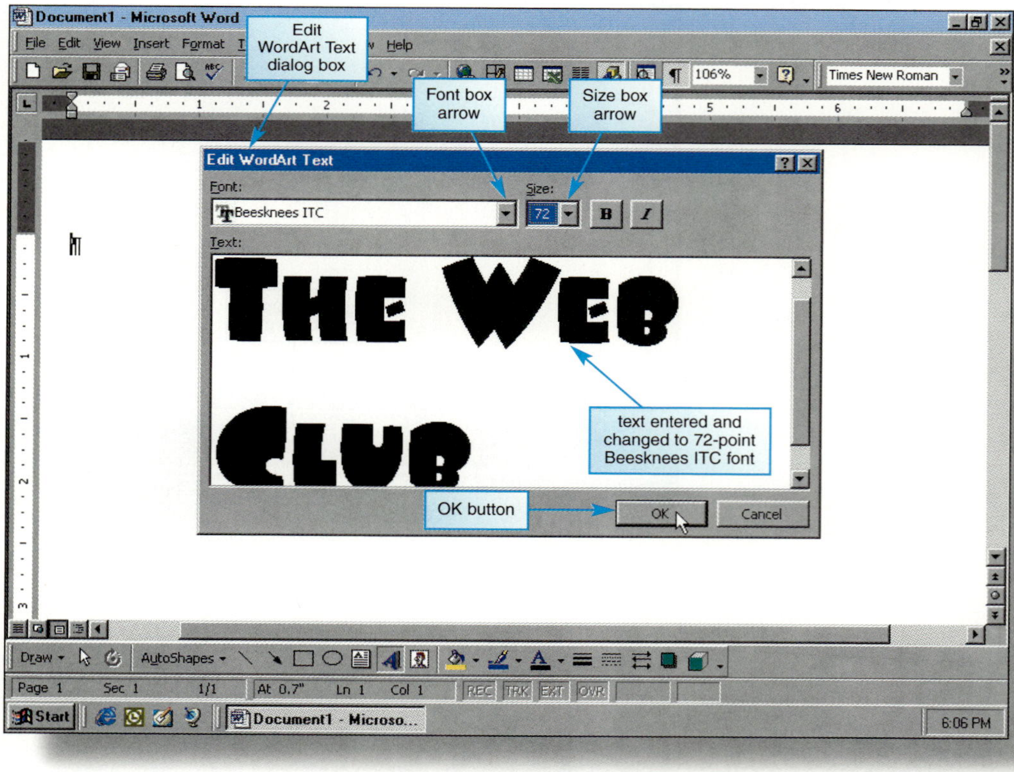

FIGURE 6-5

4 Click the OK button. If the WordArt toolbar does not display on your screen, right-click the WordArt drawing object and then click Show WordArt Toolbar.

A WordArt drawing object displays selected in the document window (Figure 6-6). When a WordArt drawing object is selected, the WordArt toolbar displays in the Word window.

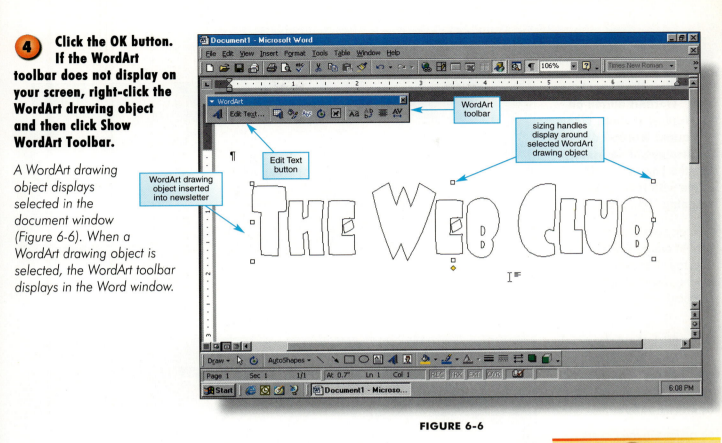

FIGURE 6-6

If a WordArt drawing object is too wide, you can decrease its point size (if it contains text) or you can reduce its width. To change the size (width and height) of a WordArt drawing object, you drag its sizing handles, just as you resize any other graphic. If, for some reason, you wanted to delete the WordArt drawing object, you could right-click it and then click Cut on the shortcut menu, or you could click it and then press the DELETE key.

To change the WordArt text, its font, its font size, or its font style, you would display the Edit WordArt Text dialog box (Figure 6-5) by clicking the Edit Text button on the WordArt toolbar.

Formatting a WordArt Drawing Object

Currently, the WordArt drawing object is a **floating object**, which is one positioned at a specific location in a document or in a layer over or behind text in a document. You can position a floating object anywhere on the page. You do not want the WordArt drawing object to be a floating object; instead, you want it to be an **inline object** that is positioned as part of a paragraph in the Word document at the location of the insertion point.

You change a WordArt drawing object from inline to floating and vice-versa by changing its wrapping style in the Format WordArt dialog box. In this dialog box, you also can change the color of the WordArt drawing object. Perform the steps on the next page to change the wrapping style of the WordArt drawing object and use a gradient (blended) color of violet into lavender.

Other Ways

1. Point to Picture on Insert menu, click WordArt on Picture submenu

More About 2000

Fonts

For more information on fonts, visit the Word 2000 More About Web page (www.scsite.com/wd2000/more.htm) and then click Fonts.

Steps **To Format a WordArt Drawing Object**

1 **Click the Format WordArt button on the WordArt toolbar. When the Format WordArt dialog box displays, if necessary, click the Layout tab. Click In line with text in the Wrapping style area.**

Word displays the Format WordArt dialog box (Figure 6-7). You change a WordArt drawing object to inline in the Wrapping style area.

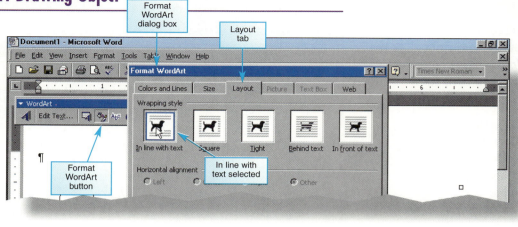

FIGURE 6-7

2 **Click the Colors and Lines tab. Click the Color box arrow in the Fill area and then point to the Fill Effects button.**

The options in the Colors and Lines sheet display (Figure 6-8). You can add a gradient color using the Fill Effects command.

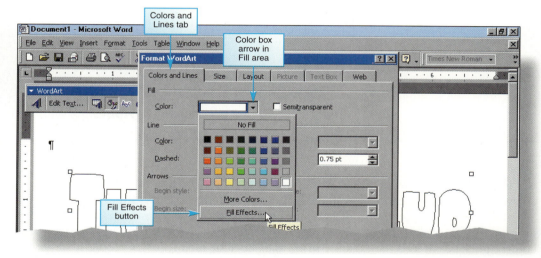

FIGURE 6-8

3 **Click the Fill Effects button. When the Fill Effects dialog box displays, if necessary, click the Gradient tab. Click Two colors in the Colors area and then point to the Color 1 box arrow.**

Word displays the Fill Effects dialog box (Figure 6-9). When you use two colors for a drawing object, color 1 displays at the top of the drawing object and blends down into color 2.

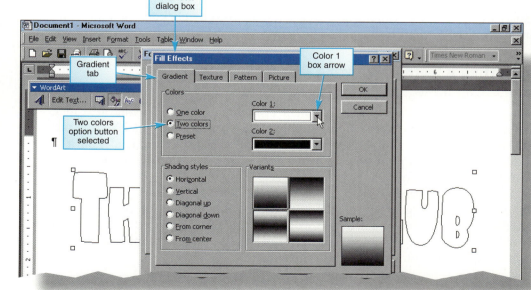

FIGURE 6-9

4 Click the Color 1 box arrow and then click Violet. Click the Color 2 box arrow and then click Lavender. Point to the OK button.

The selected gradient colors for the WordArt object display in the Sample box (Figure 6-10).

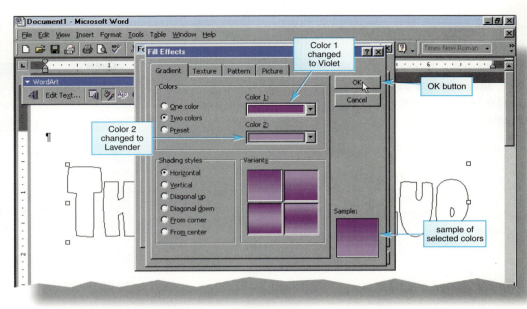

FIGURE 6-10

5 Click the OK button. Click the OK button in the Format WordArt dialog box.

Word formats the WordArt object as inline and changes its colors (Figure 6-11).

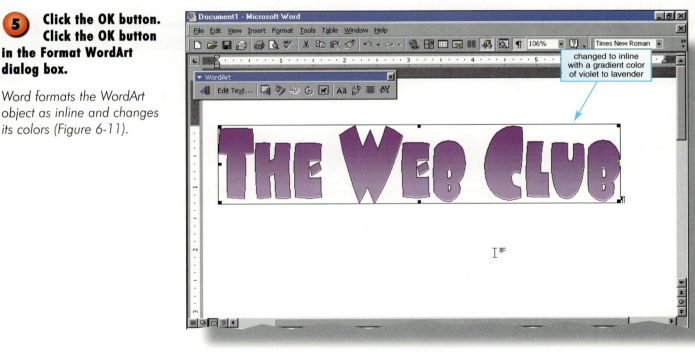

FIGURE 6-11

Changing the WordArt Shape

Word provides a variety of shapes to make your WordArt drawing object more interesting. Perform the steps on the next page to change the WordArt drawing object to a triangular shape.

Other Ways

1. Right-click WordArt object, click Format WordArt on shortcut menu, change desired options, click OK button

2. On Format menu click WordArt, change desired options, click OK button

Steps To Change the Shape of a WordArt Drawing Object

1 **Click the WordArt Shape button on the WordArt toolbar. Point to Triangle Up.**

Word displays a graphical list of available shapes (Figure 6-12). The WordArt drawing object forms itself into the selected shape when you click the shape.

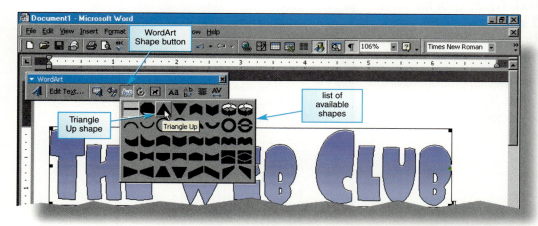

FIGURE 6-12

2 **Click Triangle Up. Click the paragraph mark to the right of the WordArt text.**

The newsletter title displays in a triangular shape (Figure 6-13). The WordArt toolbar no longer displays in the Word window.

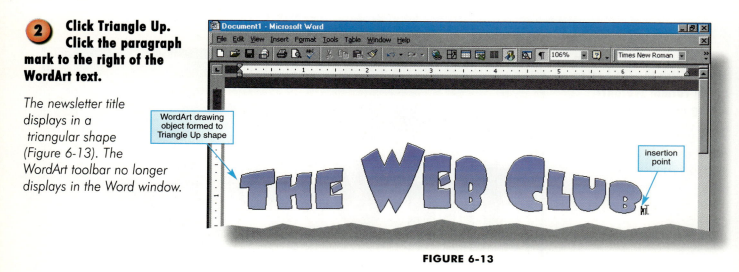

FIGURE 6-13

You will use the Drawing toolbar again later in this project. Thus, leave it displaying in the Word window.

Because you changed the WordArt drawing object from a floating object to an inline object, it is part of the current paragraph. Thus, you can use any of the paragraph alignment buttons on the Formatting toolbar to reposition the object. Perform the following step to center the WordArt drawing object.

TO CENTER AN INLINE OBJECT

1 Double-click the move handle on the Formatting toolbar to display the entire toolbar. Click the Center button on the Formatting toolbar.

Word centers the WordArt drawing object between the left and right margins (see Figure 6-14).

The next step is to add a rule, or ruling line, above the newsletter title.

Adding Ruling Lines

In Word, you use borders to create **ruling lines**. You have learned that borders can be placed on any edge of a paragraph(s), that is, the top, bottom, left, or right edges. Perform the following steps to place a ruling line above the newsletter title.

TO USE BORDERS TO ADD A RULING LINE

1 Double-click the move handle on the Standard toolbar to display the entire toolbar. If necessary, click the Tables and Borders button on the Standard toolbar to display the Tables and Borders toolbar.

2 Click the Line Style box arrow on the Tables and Borders toolbar and then click the first dotted line in the list.

3 Click the Line Weight box arrow on the Tables and Borders toolbar and then click 3 pt.

4 Click the Border Color button on the Tables and Borders toolbar and then click Teal.

5 Click the Border button arrow on the Tables and Borders toolbar and then click Top Border.

The newsletter title and Tables and Borders toolbar display as shown in Figure 6-14.

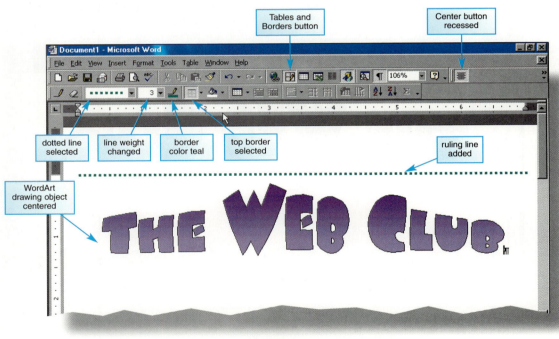

FIGURE 6-14

Because you will use the Tables and Borders toolbar again in the next steps, leave it displaying in the Word window.

The next step is to enter the issue information line. Thus, you will press the ENTER key at the end of the newsletter title so that you can enter the issue information line. You have learned that when you press the ENTER key, Word carries paragraph formatting to the next paragraph. You do not want the issue information line to be formatted the same as the newsletter title line. Instead, you want to apply the Normal style to the paragraph below the newsletter title line. Perform the steps on the next page to apply the Normal style to a paragraph.

To Apply the Normal Style

1 If necessary, scroll down. With the insertion point on the paragraph mark in line 1, press the ENTER key. Double-click the move handle on the Formatting toolbar to display the entire toolbar. Click the Style box arrow and then point to Normal (Figure 6-15).

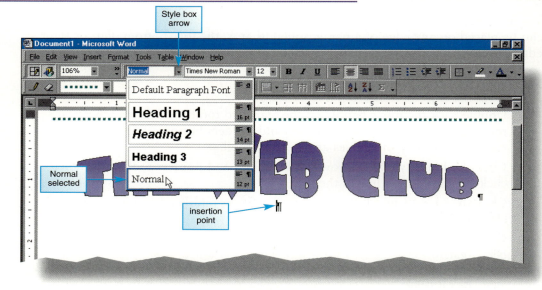

FIGURE 6-15

2 Click Normal.

Word applies the Normal style to the current paragraph (Figure 6-16). The paragraph is left-aligned.

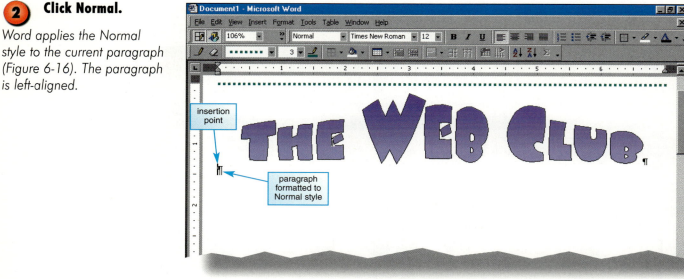

FIGURE 6-16

1. On Format menu click Style, click Normal in Styles list, click Apply button
2. Press CTRL+SHIFT+N

The next step is to enter the issue information line in the nameplate of the newsletter.

Inserting the Current Date into a Document

The issue information line is to contain the text, Monthly Newsletter, at the left margin and the current date at the right margin. You have learned that a paragraph cannot be formatted as both left-aligned and right-aligned. To place text at the right margin of a left-aligned paragraph, you set a tab stop at the right margin.

Perform the following steps to enter text at the left margin and then set a right-aligned tab stop at the right margin.

TO SET A RIGHT-ALIGNED TAB STOP

1 Click the Font Color button arrow on the Formatting toolbar and then click Violet. Type `Monthly Newsletter` on line 2 of the newsletter.

2 Click Format on the menu bar and then click Tabs. When the Tabs dialog box displays, type 7 in the Tab stop position text box, and then click Right in the Alignment area. Click the Set button (Figure 6-17).

3 Click the OK button.

After clicking the OK button, Word places a right-aligned tab stop at the right margin.

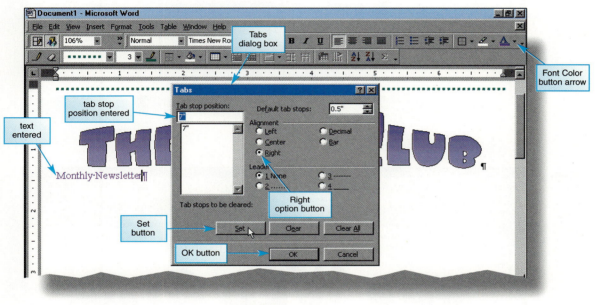

FIGURE 6-17

The next step is to enter the current date at the right margin of the issue information line. Word provides a method of inserting the computer's system date into a document. Perform the following steps to insert the current date into a document.

To Insert the Current Date into a Document

1 Press the TAB key. Click Insert on the menu bar and then point to Date and Time (Figure 6-18).

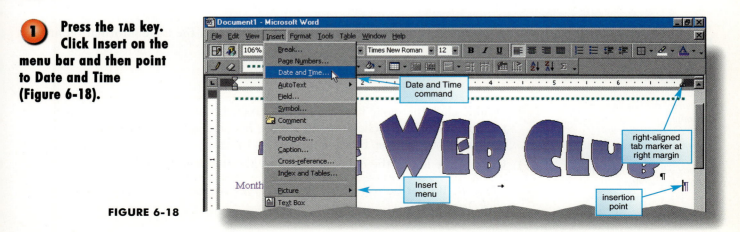

FIGURE 6-18

2 **Click Date and Time. When the Date and Time dialog box displays, click the desired format (in this case, November 16, 2001).**

Word displays the Date and Time dialog box (Figure 6-19). A list of available formats for dates and times displays. Your screen will not show November 16, 2001; instead, it will display the current system date stored in your computer.

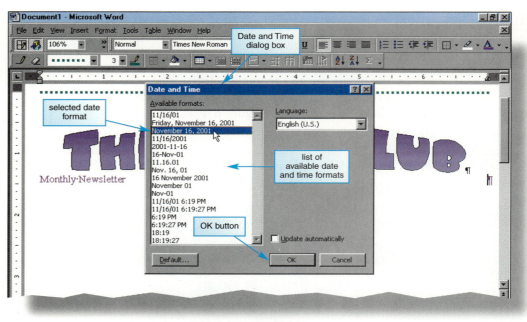

FIGURE 6-19

3 **Click the OK button.**

Word displays the current date in the newsletter at the right margin (Figure 6-20).

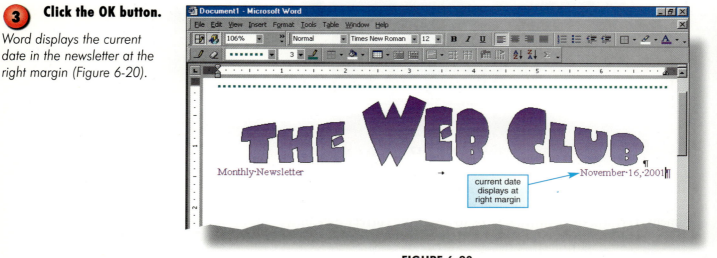

FIGURE 6-20

Dates

If you want Word to display the current date or time when you print a document, make it a field. That is, click the Update automatically check box in the Date and Time dialog box when you insert the current date or time.

The next step is to place top and bottom borders on the issue information line as described in the following steps.

TO ADD MORE RULING LINES

 Double-click the move handle on the Standard toolbar to display the entire toolbar. If necessary, click the Tables and Borders button on the Standard toolbar to display the Tables and Borders toolbar.

2 Click to the left of the issue information line to select it.

3 Click the Border button arrow on the Tables and Borders toolbar and then click Top Border.

4 Click the Border button arrow on the Tables and Borders toolbar and then click Bottom Border.

5 Click the Tables and Borders button on the Standard toolbar to remove the Tables and Borders toolbar from the Word window.

6 Click in the issue information line to remove the highlight.

Word places a 3-point dotted teal top and bottom border on the issue information line (Figure 6-21).

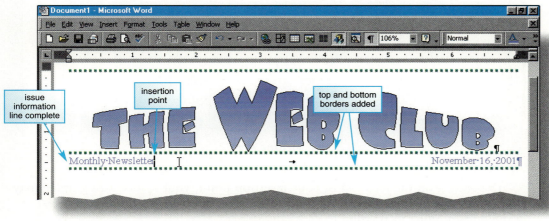

FIGURE 6-21

The next step is to insert a spider web clip art image into the nameplate.

Inserting a Floating Graphic

When you insert a clip art image into a document, Word inserts the picture as part of the current paragraph. You have learned that this is called an inline object. With this format, you change the location of the graphic by setting paragraph options, such as centered, right-aligned, and so on.

In many cases, you want more flexibility in positioning graphics. That is, you want to position a graphic at a specific location in a document; this is called a floating object. In this project, for example, you want the spider web graphic to be positioned in the upper-right corner of the first page of the newsletter. Perform the following steps to insert a clip art image and then change it from an inline to a floating object.

TO INSERT CLIP ART

1 Click Insert on the menu bar, point to Picture, and then click Clip Art.

2 When the Insert ClipArt window opens, click the Search for clips text box. Type spider web and then press the ENTER key.

3 Click the clip that matches the one shown in Figure 6-22 on the next page.

4 Click the Insert clip button on the Pop-up menu.

5 Click the Close button on the Insert ClipArt window's title bar.

Word inserts the spider web graphic at the location of the insertion point as an inline object (Figure 6-22).

More *About* **2000**

Designing Newsletters

For more information on designing newsletters, visit the Word 2000 More About Web page (www.scsite.com/wd2000/more.htm) and then click Designing Newsletters.

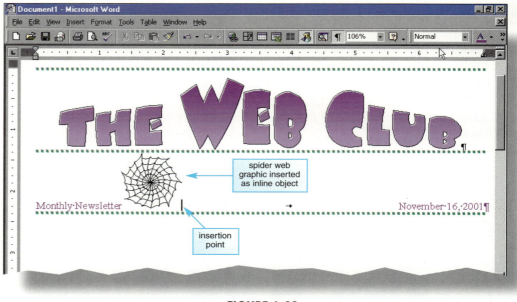

FIGURE 6-22

Depending on the location of your insertion point, your spider web graphic may be in a different position. Perform the following steps to change the spider web graphic from inline to floating.

Steps To Format a Graphic as Floating

1 In the document window, click the graphic to select it. If the Picture toolbar does not display, right-click the graphic and then click **Show Picture Toolbar**. Click the Text Wrapping button on the Picture toolbar and then point to In Front of Text (Figure 6-23).

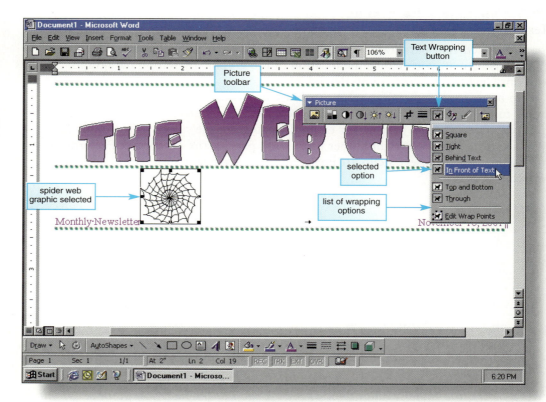

FIGURE 6-23

**2** **Click In Front of Text.**

Word changes the format of the graphic from inline to floating. You can position a floating object anywhere in the document.

3 **If necessary, scroll up. Point to the middle of the graphic and drag it to the position shown in Figure 6-24. Resize the graphic by dragging its lower-left sizing handle toward the middle of the graphic.**

The graphic is resized and positioned in the upper-right corner of the document (Figure 6-24).

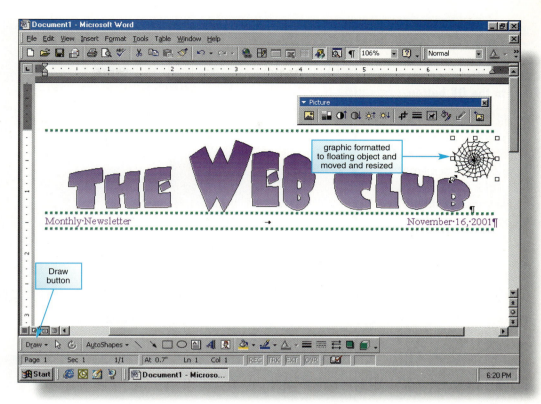

FIGURE 6-24

To place an object behind text, instead of in front of text, you select the Behind Text wrapping style (Figure 6-23). You can change the order of text and graphical objects by clicking the Draw button (Figure 6-24) on the Drawing toolbar, pointing to Order, and then clicking the desired location for the currently selected object.

The next step is to shade the graphic, as shown in the following steps.

To Shade a Graphic

1 **With the graphic still selected, click the Format Picture button on the Picture toolbar. When the Format Picture dialog box displays, if necessary, click the Colors and Lines tab. Point to the Color box arrow in the Fill area.**

Word displays the Format Picture dialog box (Figure 6-25).

FIGURE 6-25

2 **Click the Color box arrow in the Fill area and then click Gold. Click Semitransparent. Point to the OK button.**

The fill color is gold and a check mark displays in the Semitransparent check box (Figure 6-26). A semitransparent color is one that is partially transparent; that is, not opaque.

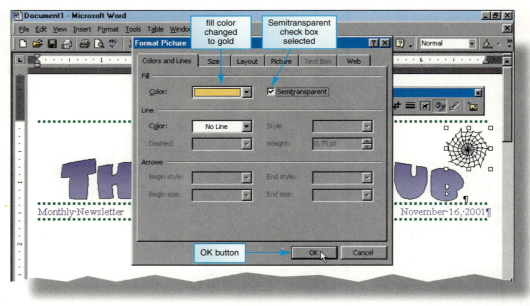

FIGURE 6-26

3 **Click the OK button.**

Word shades the graphic in a partially transparent gold color (Figure 6-27).

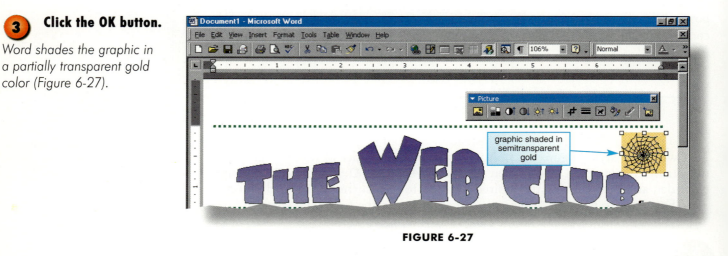

FIGURE 6-27

When you press the ENTER key in a bordered paragraph, such as at the end of the issue information line, Word carries the border forward to the next paragraph. Thus, apply the Normal style to the new paragraph to remove the border and other formatting, as described in the following steps.

TO APPLY THE NORMAL STYLE

1 If necessary, scroll down. Position the insertion point at the end of the issue information line. Press the ENTER key.

2 Double-click the move handle on the Formatting toolbar to display the entire toolbar. Click the Style box arrow and then click Normal.

Word applies the Normal style to the current paragraph (Figure 6-28). The paragraph no longer contains any borders and is left-aligned.

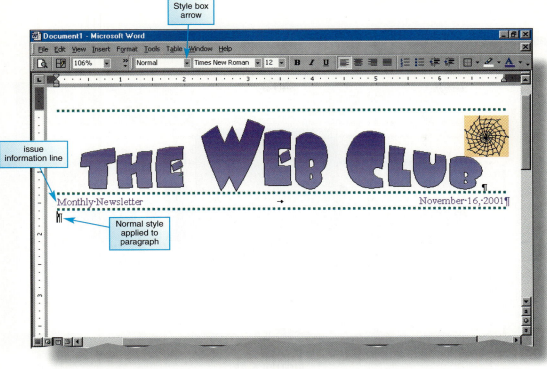

Style box arrow

issue information line

Normal style applied to paragraph

FIGURE 6-28

Formatting the First Page of the Body of the Newsletter

The body of the newsletter in this project is divided into three columns (see Figure 6-1a on page WD 6.5). The characters in the paragraphs are aligned on both the right and left edges – similar to newspaper columns. The first letter in the first paragraph is much larger than the rest of the characters in the paragraph. A vertical rule separates the second and third columns. The steps on the following pages illustrate how to format the first page of the body of the newsletter using these desktop publishing features.

Formatting a Document into Multiple Columns

The text in **snaking columns,** or newspaper-style columns, flows from the bottom of one column to the top of the next. The body of the newsletter in Project 6 uses snaking columns.

When you begin a document in Word, it has one column. You can divide a portion of a document or the entire document into multiple columns. Within each column, you can type, modify, or format text.

To divide a portion of a document into multiple columns, you use section breaks. That is, Word requires that a new section be created each time you alter the number of columns in a document. Thus, if a document has a nameplate (one column) followed by an article of three columns followed by an article of two columns, then the document would be divided into a total of three sections.

In this project, the nameplate is one column and the body of the newsletter is three columns. Thus, you must insert a continuous section break below the nameplate. *Continuous* means you want the new section on the same page as the previous section. Perform the steps on the next page to divide the body of the newsletter into three columns.

Newspaper-Style Columns

Narrow columns generally are easier to read than wide ones. Columns, however, can be too narrow; try to have between five and fifteen words per line. To do this, you may need to adjust the column width, the font size, or the leading. Leading is the line spacing, which can be adjusted through the Paragraph dialog box in Word.

Steps To Insert a Continuous Section Break

1 **With the insertion point on line 3, press the ENTER key twice. Click Insert on the menu bar and then click Break. When the Break dialog box displays, click Continuous in the Section break types area. Point to the OK button.**

Word displays the Break dialog box (Figure 6-29). Continuous means you want the new section on the same page as the previous section.

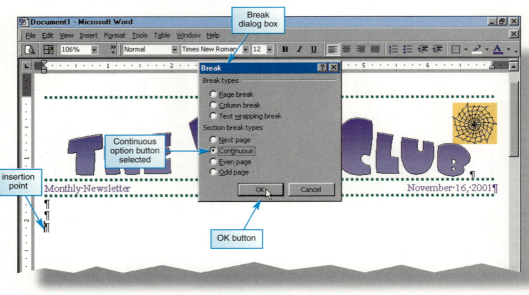

FIGURE 6-29

2 **Click the OK button.**

Word inserts a section break above the insertion point (Figure 6-30). The insertion point now is located in section 2.

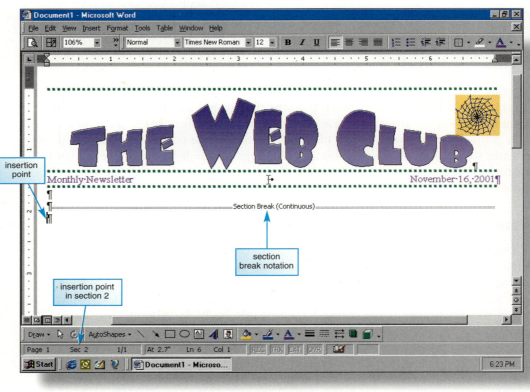

FIGURE 6-30

The next step is to format the second section to three columns, as shown in the following steps.

Steps **To Format Columns**

1 If necessary, scroll down. Be sure the insertion point is in section 2. Double-click the move handle on the Standard toolbar to display the entire toolbar. Point to the Columns button on the Standard toolbar (Figure 6-31).

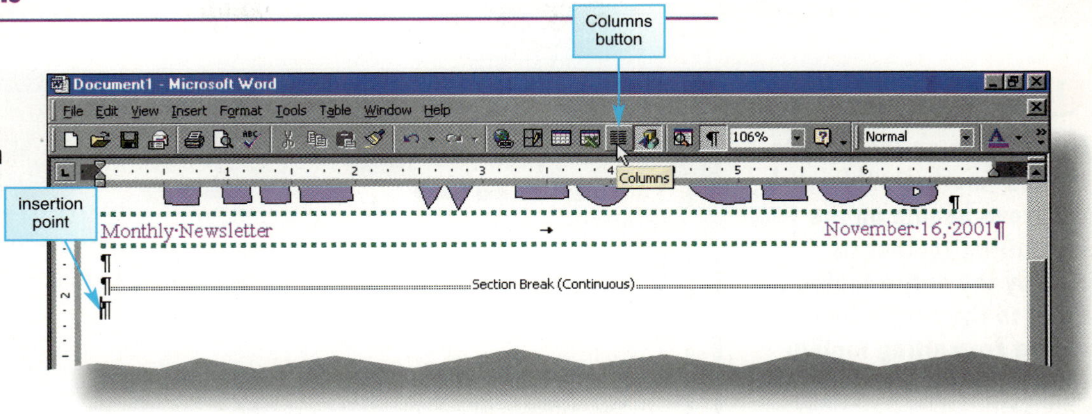

FIGURE 6-31

2 Click the Columns button. Point to the third column in the columns list graphic.

Word displays a columns list graphic below the Columns button (Figure 6-32).

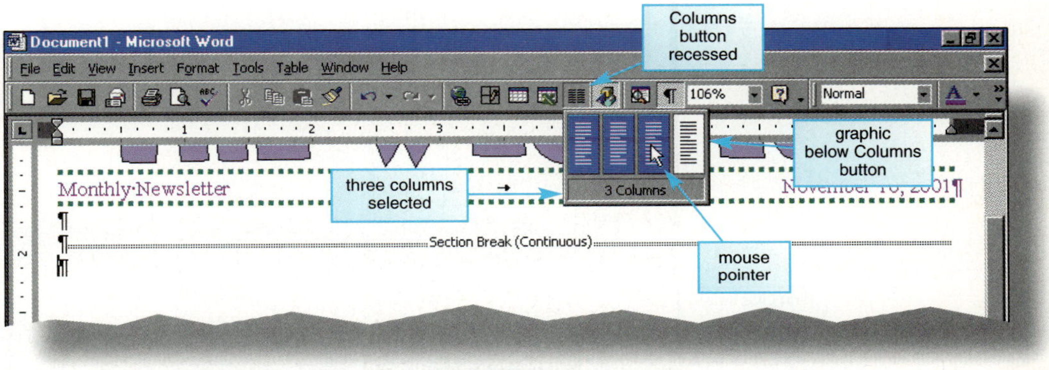

FIGURE 6-32

3 Click the third column.

Word divides the section containing the insertion point into three evenly sized and spaced columns (Figure 6-33). Notice that the ruler indicates the width of each column.

FIGURE 6-33

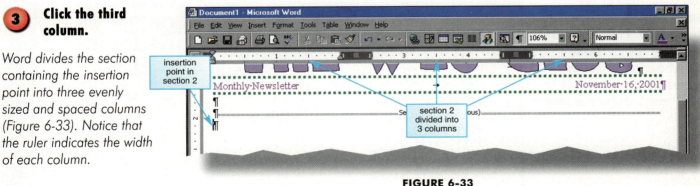

When you use the Columns button to create columns, Word creates columns of equal width. You can create columns of unequal width by clicking the Columns command on the Format menu.

Other Ways

1. On Format menu click Columns, click desired columns in Presets area, click OK button

Justifying a Paragraph

The text in the paragraphs of the body of the newsletter is **justified**, which means that the left and right margins are aligned, like the edges of newspaper columns. The first line of each paragraph is indented .25-inch. Perform the steps on the next page to enter the first paragraph of the feature article using justified alignment.

Steps To Justify a Paragraph

1 **Drag the First Line Indent marker in the first column on the ruler to the .25" mark. Double-click the move handle on the Formatting toolbar to display the entire toolbar. Point to the Justify button on the Formatting toolbar (Figure 6-34).**

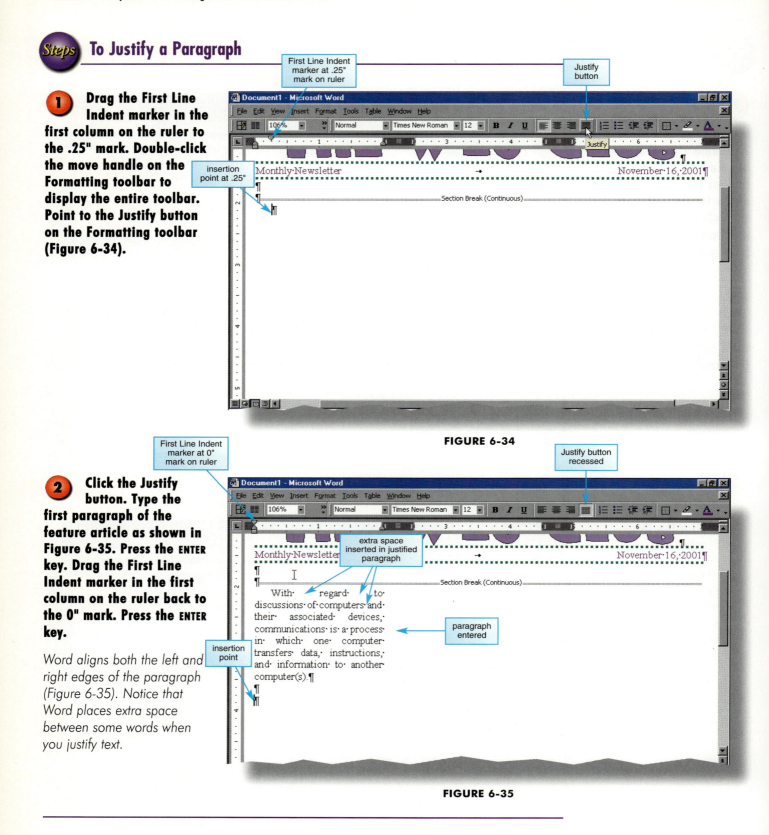

FIGURE 6-34

2 **Click the Justify button. Type the first paragraph of the feature article as shown in Figure 6-35. Press the ENTER key. Drag the First Line Indent marker in the first column on the ruler back to the 0" mark. Press the ENTER key.**

Word aligns both the left and right edges of the paragraph (Figure 6-35). Notice that Word places extra space between some words when you justify text.

FIGURE 6-35

Saving the Newsletter

Because you have performed several steps, you should save the newsletter as described in the following steps.

TO SAVE THE NEWSLETTER

 1 Insert a floppy disk into drive A.

2 Double-click the move handle on the Standard toolbar to display the entire toolbar. Click the Save button on the Standard toolbar.

3 Type `Web Club Newsletter` in the File name text box. Do not press the ENTER key.

4 Click the Save in box arrow and then click 3½ Floppy (A:).

5 Click the Save button in the Save As dialog box.

Word saves the document on a floppy disk in drive A with the file name Web Club Newsletter.

More *About* 2000

Justification

The paragraphs within the columns of a newsletter very often are justified; that is, flush at both left and right margins. This alignment often causes rivers, which are large gaps between words. One solution is to rearrange the words or add additional words to minimize the rivers. Another solution, not quite as common, is to use left-aligned text.

Inserting the Remainder of the Feature Article

Instead of entering the rest of the feature article into the newsletter for this project, you insert the file named Communications Article into the newsletter. This file contains the remainder of the feature article.

The Communications Article file is located on the Data Disk. If you did not download the Data Disk, see the inside back cover for instructions for downloading the Data Disk or see your instructor. Perform the following steps to insert the Communications Article into the newsletter.

Steps To Insert a File into the Newsletter

1 If necessary, insert the Data Disk into drive A. Click Insert on the menu bar and then click File. If necessary, click the Look in box arrow and then click 3½ Floppy (A:). Click Communications Article and then point to the Insert button.

Word displays the Insert File dialog box (Figure 6-36). The file will be inserted at the location of the insertion point in the document.

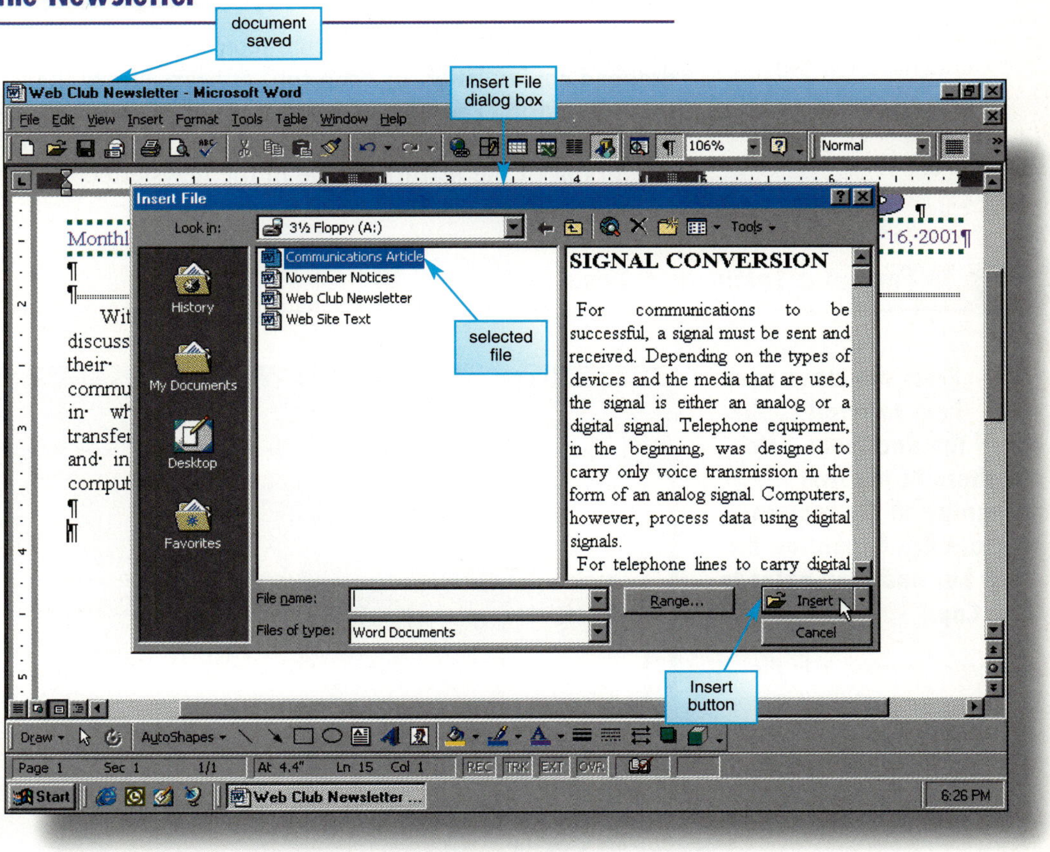

FIGURE 6-36

2 **Click the Insert button.**

Word inserts the file, Communications Article, into the file Web Club Newsletter at the location of the insertion point (Figure 6-37). The text automatically is formatted into columns.

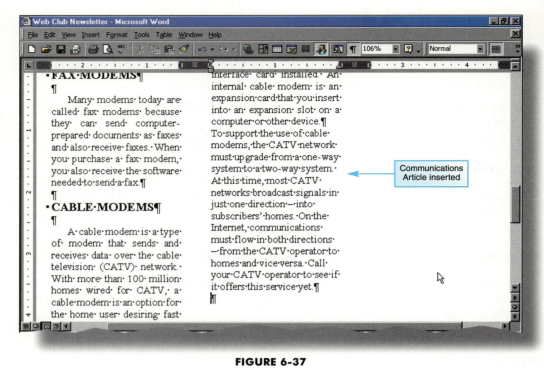

FIGURE 6-37

Formatting a Letter as a Dropped Capital

You can format the first character or word in a paragraph to be dropped. A **dropped capital letter,** or **drop cap,** appears larger than the rest of the characters in the paragraph. The text in the paragraph then wraps around the dropped capital letter. Perform the following steps to create a dropped capital letter in the first paragraph of the feature article in the newsletter.

Steps **To Format a Letter as a Drop Cap**

1 **Press the CTRL+HOME keys to scroll to the top of the document. Click anywhere in the first paragraph of the feature article. Click Format on the menu bar and then point to Drop Cap.**

The insertion point is in the first paragraph of the feature article (Figure 6-38).

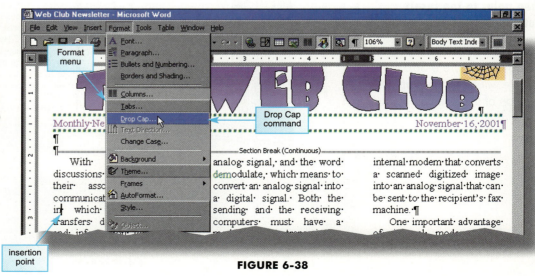

FIGURE 6-38

2 Click Drop Cap. When the Drop Cap dialog box displays, click Dropped in the Position area. Point to the OK button.

Word displays the Drop Cap dialog box (Figure 6-39).

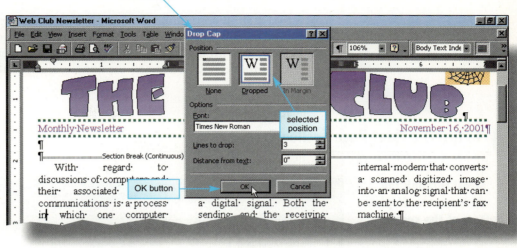

FIGURE 6-39

3 Click the OK button.

Word drops the letter W in the word, With, and wraps subsequent text around the dropped capital W (Figure 6-40).

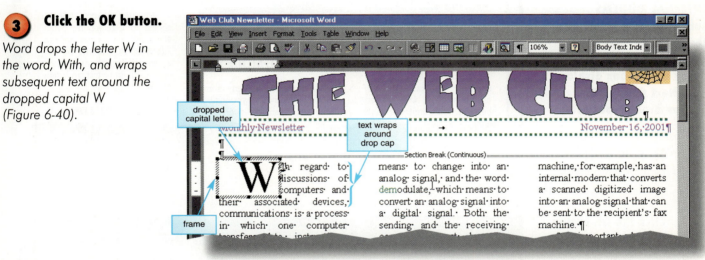

FIGURE 6-40

When you drop cap a letter, Word places a text frame around it. A **text frame** is a container for text that allows you to position the text anywhere on the page. As illustrated in the previous steps, Word can format the frame so that text wraps around it.

To remove the frame from displaying in the document window, you simply click outside the frame to display the insertion point elsewhere in the document.

The next step is to insert a column break before the subhead, INTERNAL MODEMS.

Inserting a Column Break

Notice in Figure 6-1a on page WD 6.5 that the third column is not a continuation of the feature article. The third column contains several club announcements. The feature article continues on the second page of the newsletter (Figure 6-1b). In order for the club announcements to display in the third column, you must force a **column break** at the bottom of the second column. Word inserts column breaks at the location of the insertion point.

More About

Drop Caps

A drop cap often is used to mark the beginning of an article. To format the first word as a drop cap, select the word. An alternative to a drop cap is a stick-up cap, which extends into the left margin, instead of sinking into the first few lines of the text. To insert a stick-up cap, click In Margin in the Drop Cap dialog box.

The first step in continuing the feature article on the second page and placing club announcements into the third column is to force the feature article to continue on the next page with a **next page section break**, and then insert a column break at the bottom of the second column so the announcements always display in the third column.

Steps To Insert a Next Page Section Break

1 Scroll through the document to display the bottom of the second column of the first page in the document window. Click before the I in the **INTERNAL MODEMS** subhead. Click Insert on the menu bar and then click Break. When the Break dialog box displays, click Next page in the Section break types area.

The insertion point is at the beginning of the INTERNAL MODEMS subhead (Figure 6-41).

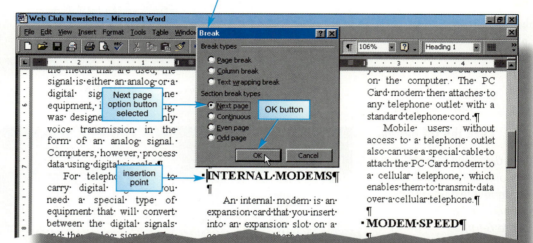

FIGURE 6-41

2 Click the OK button.

Word inserts a section break at the location of the insertion point (Figure 6-42). The rest of the article displays on page 2 of the document because a next page section break includes a page break. On page 1, the bottom of the second column and the entire third column are empty.

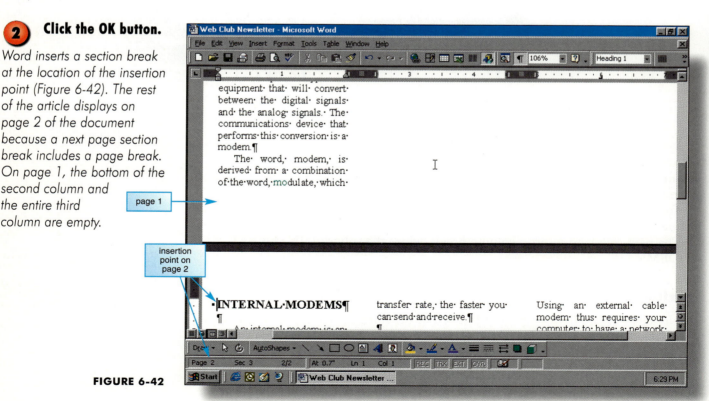

FIGURE 6-42

Because you want the club announcements to begin at the top of the third column, the next step is to insert a column break at the end of the text in the second column as shown in these steps.

 Steps ## To Insert a Column Break

1 **Position the insertion point at the end of the second column on the first page of the newsletter. Press the ENTER key. Drag the First Line Indent marker on the ruler in column 2 to the 0" mark. Press the CTRL+I keys to turn on italics. Type** Article continues on Page 2... **and then press the CTRL+I keys again. Press the ENTER key. Click Insert on the menu bar and then click Break. Click Column break in the Break dialog box (Figure 6-43).**

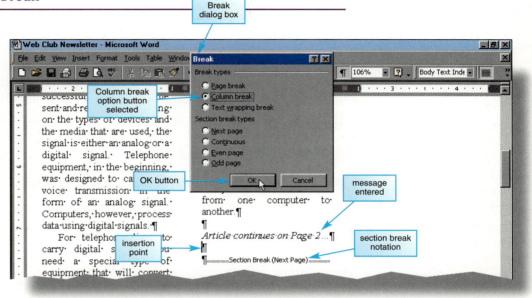

FIGURE 6-43

2 **Click the OK button.**

Word inserts a column break at the bottom of the second column and places the insertion point at the top of the third column (Figure 6-44).

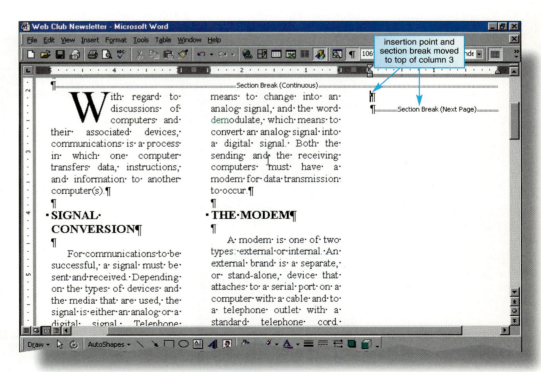

FIGURE 6-44

Other Ways

1. Press CTRL+SHIFT+ENTER

To eliminate having to enter the entire column of announcements into the newsletter, you insert the file named November Notices into the third column of the newsletter. This file contains the first two announcements (REMINDER and CLUB DISCOUNTS) for this November issue of the newsletter.

The November Notices file is located on the Data Disk. If you did not download the Data Disk, see the inside back cover for instructions for downloading the Data Disk or see your instructor. Perform the following steps to insert the November Notices file into the newsletter.

TO INSERT A FILE INTO A COLUMN OF THE NEWSLETTER

1 If necessary, insert the Data Disk into drive A. With the insertion point at the top of the third column, click Insert on the menu bar and then click File.

2 When the Insert File dialog box displays, if necessary, click the Look in box arrow and then click 3½ Floppy (A:). Click November Notices.

3 Click the Insert button.

Word inserts the file November Notices into the third column of the newsletter.

Perform the following step to display the entire page in the document window so that you can see the layout of the first page of the newsletter thus far.

TO ZOOM WHOLE PAGE

1 Click the Zoom box arrow and then click Whole Page in the list.

Word displays the first page of the newsletter in reduced form so that the entire page displays in the document window (Figure 6-45).

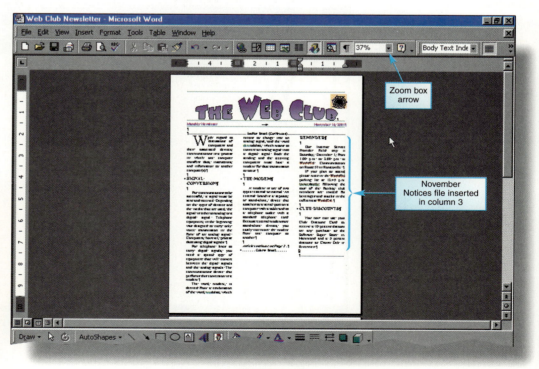

FIGURE 6-45

Perform the following step to return the display to zoom text width.

TO ZOOM TEXT WIDTH

(1) Click the Zoom box arrow and then click Text Width.

Word extends the right margin to the right edge of the document window.

The next step is to enter the subhead for the last announcement in the third column of the first page of the newsletter.

Applying a Style

The subheads, such as REMINDER and CLUB DISCOUNTS, are formatted using the Heading 1 style, which in this case uses 14-point Times New Roman bold font. Instead of changing the font size and font style individually for the new WEB SITE subhead, apply the Heading 1 style as shown in the following steps.

Steps **To Apply the Heading 1 Style**

(1) **With the insertion point at the end of the third column, press the ENTER key. Double-click the move handle on the Formatting toolbar to display the entire toolbar. Click the Style box arrow on the Formatting toolbar and then point to Heading 1.**

Word displays a list of available styles for this document (Figure 6-46).

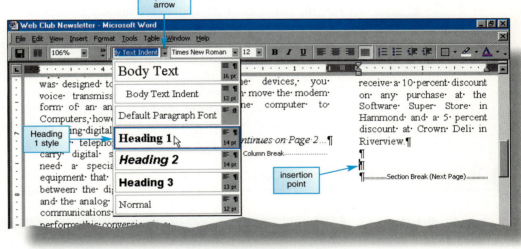

FIGURE 6-46

(2) **Click Heading 1. Type WEB SITE and then press the RIGHT ARROW key. Press the ENTER key.**

Word enters the subhead, WEB SITE, and formats it according to the Heading 1 style (Figure 6-47).

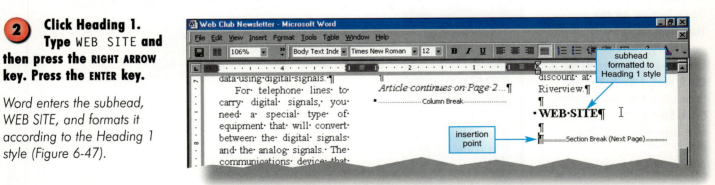

FIGURE 6-47

Many different styles are associated with a document. To view a complete list of available styles for a document, click Format on the menu bar and then click Styles. As you click each style name in the Styles list of the Styles dialog box, a preview of the selected style displays on the right side of the dialog box. To save time while composing a document, use styles to format characters and paragraphs.

The next step is to insert the last announcement in the third column of the first page of the newsletter.

Linking an Object into a Word Document

The last announcement in the third column of the newsletter notifies club members of the new Guide to World Wide Web sites. The text for this announcement is in a file named Web Site Text. Because the contents of this file might change between now and when the newsletter is printed, you want to be sure to use the most updated version of the Web Site Text file. To do this, you will link the Web Site Text file to the Web Club Newsletter.

In this case, the file named Web Site Text is called the **source file**. The file named Web Club Newsletter is called the **destination file**. When you **link** an object, such as a file, the contents of the source file display in the destination file, but the contents of the link actually are stored in the source file. That is, the destination file stores only the location of the source file. When the source file (Web Site Text) is updated, the destination file also can be updated.

One method of linking documents is to copy the text of the source document and then use the Paste Special command to insert it as a linked object into the destination document. Perform the following steps to link the Word document, Web Site Text, that is located on the Data Disk, into the newsletter.

Steps **To Link an Object**

1 **Double-click the move handle on the Standard toolbar to display the entire toolbar. Click the Open button on the Standard toolbar. If necessary, change the Look in location to drive A. Click Web Site Text and then click the Open button. Click Edit on the menu bar and then point to Select All.**

Word opens the Web Site Text document (Figure 6-48). You want to copy the entire document.

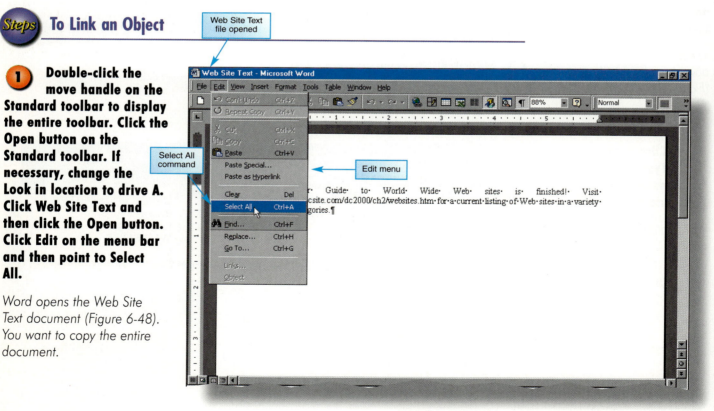

FIGURE 6-48

2 Click Select All. Click the Copy button on the Standard toolbar. Point to the Web Club Newsletter program button on the taskbar.

Word highlights the entire document (Figure 6-49). The selection is copied to the Office Clipboard.

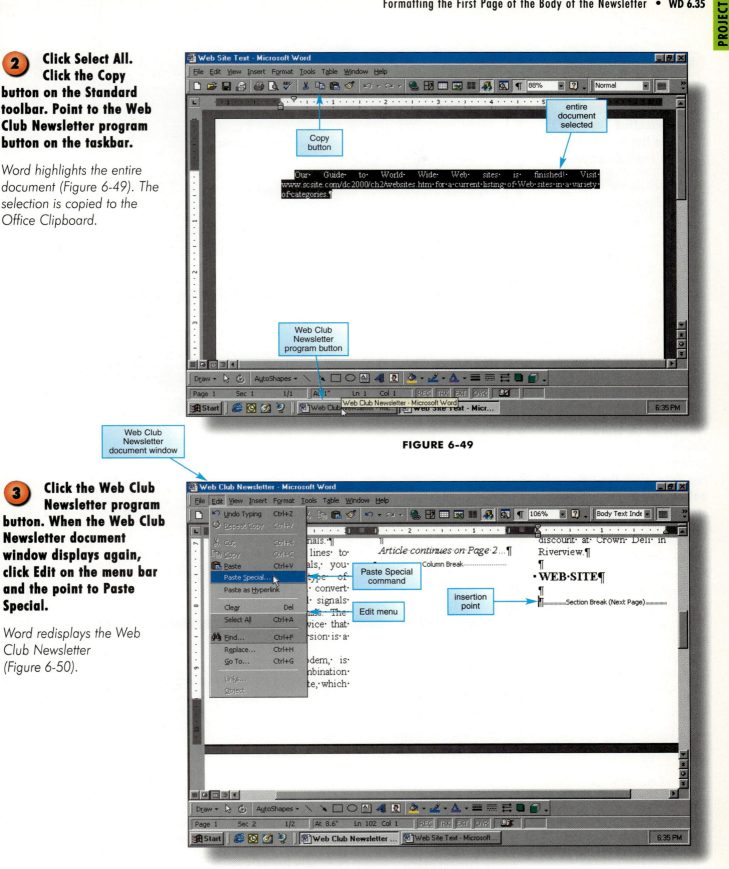

FIGURE 6-49

3 Click the Web Club Newsletter program button. When the Web Club Newsletter document window displays again, click Edit on the menu bar and the point to Paste Special.

Word redisplays the Web Club Newsletter (Figure 6-50).

FIGURE 6-50

 **Click Paste Special. When the Paste Special dialog box displays, click Paste link. Click Formatted Text (RTF) in the As list and then point to the OK button.**

Word displays the Paste Special dialog box (Figure 6-51).

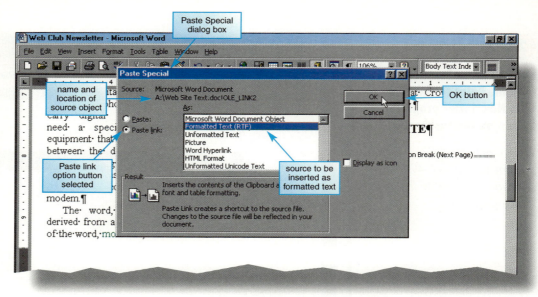

FIGURE 6-51

 **Click the OK button. Drag the First Line Indent marker in the third column of the ruler to the .25" mark. (If Word displays a dialog box indicating it cannot obtain the data, click the OK button and perform these steps again.)**

Word links the source into the destination at the location of the insertion point (Figure 6-52).

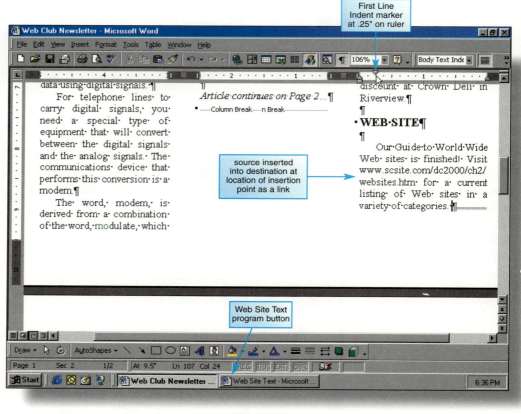

FIGURE 6-52

Other Ways

1. On Insert menu click Object, click Create from File tab, enter file name, click Link to file, click OK button

The contents of the source file display in the third column of the newsletter as a link. Word automatically updates links if the source file changes while the destination file is open. If the destination file is closed, Word updates the links the next time you open or print the destination file. If a link, for some reason, is not updated automatically, click the link and then press F9 to update it manually.

You are finished with the source file. Perform the following steps to close it.

TO CLOSE A FILE

① Click the Web Site Text program button on the taskbar.

② When the Web Site Text document window displays, click File on the menu bar and then click Close.

③ If Word displays a dialog box, click the No button.

Word closes the Web Site Text document window and redisplays the Web Club Newsletter document window.

The next step is to place a vertical rule between the second and third columns of the newsletter.

Adding a Vertical Rule Between Columns

In newsletters, you often see a vertical rule separating columns. With Word, you can place a vertical rule between *all* columns by clicking the Columns command on the Format menu and then clicking the Line between check box.

In this project, you want a vertical rule between *only* the second and third columns. To do this, you place a left border spaced several points from the text. You have learned that a point is approximately 1/72 of an inch. Perform the following steps to place a vertical rule between the second and third columns of the newsletter.

More About

Links

If you wanted to modify the location of the source file in a link or remove a link while leaving the source text in the destination document, click the link, click Edit on the menu bar and then click Links to display the Links dialog box.

More About

Vertical Rules

A vertical rule is used to guide the reader through the newsletter. If a multi-column newsletter contains a single article, place a vertical rule between every column. If different columns present different articles, place a vertical rule between each article.

Steps **To Place a Vertical Rule between Columns**

① **Drag the mouse from the top of the third column down to the bottom of the third column. Click Format on the menu bar and then point to Borders and Shading.**

Word highlights the entire third column of page 1 in the newsletter (Figure 6-53).

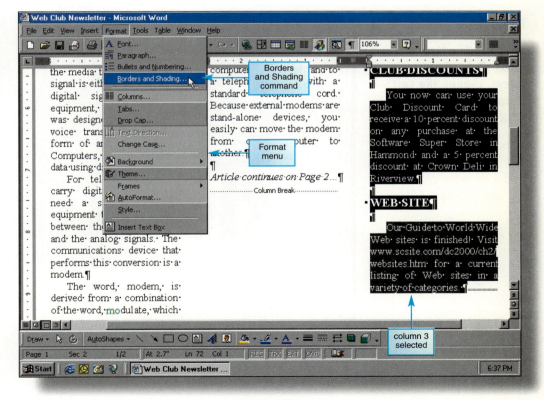

FIGURE 6-53

2 **Click Borders and Shading. When the Borders and Shading dialog box displays, if necessary, click the Borders tab. Click the Left Border button in the Preview area. Point to the Options button.**

Word displays the Borders and Shading dialog box (Figure 6-54). The border diagram graphically shows the selected borders.

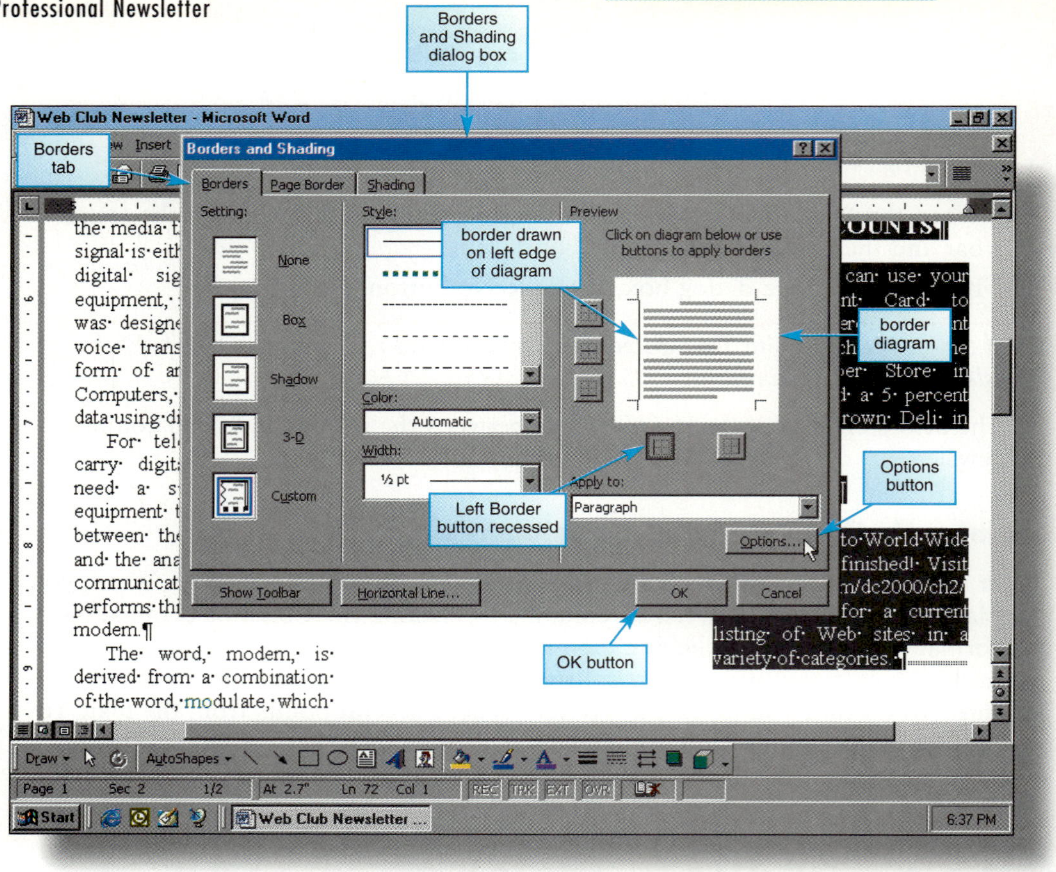

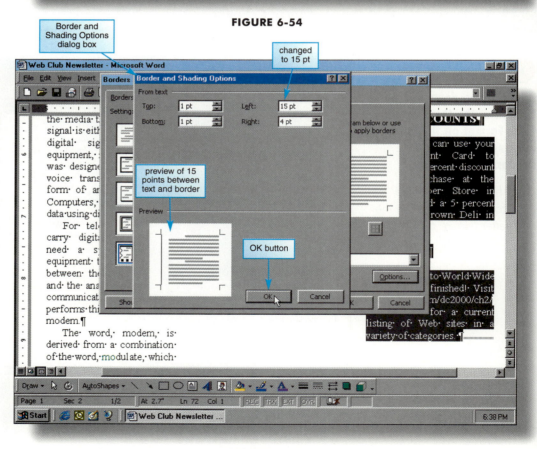

FIGURE 6-54

3 **Click the Options button. When the Border and Shading Options dialog box displays, change the Left text box to 15 pt. Point to the OK button.**

The Preview area shows the border positioned 15 points from the left edge of the paragraph (Figure 6-55).

FIGURE 6-55

4 Click the OK button. When the Borders and Shading dialog box is visible again, click its OK button. Click in the second column to remove the selection from the third column.

Word draws a border positioned 15 points from the left edge of the text in the third column (Figure 6-56). The border displays as a vertical rule between the second and third columns of the newsletter.

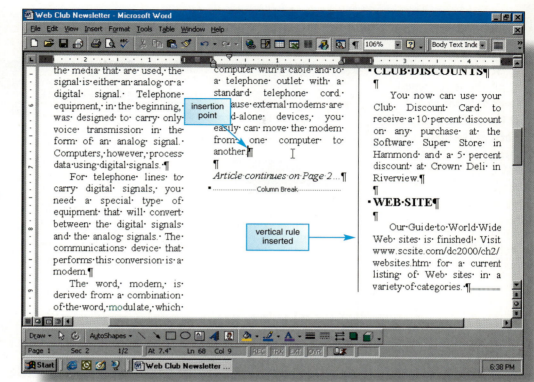

FIGURE 6-56

Creating a Pull-Quote

You have learned that a pull-quote is text *pulled*, or copied, from the text of the document and given graphical emphasis so it stands apart and grasps the reader's attention. The newsletter in this project has a pull-quote on the first page between the first and second columns (see Figure 6-1a on page WD 6.5).

To create a pull-quote, you copy the text in the existing document to the Office Clipboard and then paste it into a column of the newsletter. To position it between columns, you place a text box around it. A **text box**, like a text frame, is a container for text that allows you to position the text anywhere on the page. The difference between a text box and a frame is that a text box has more graphical formatting options than does a frame.

The steps on the following pages discuss how to create the pull-quote shown in Figure 6-1a on page WD 6.5.

Inserting a Text Box

The first step in creating the pull-quote is to copy the sentence to be used in the pull-quote and then insert a text box around it as shown in the steps on the next page.

More *About* 2000

Pull-Quotes

Because of their bold emphasis, pull-quotes should be used sparingly in a newsletter. Pull-quotes are useful for breaking the monotony of long columns of text. Quotation marks are not required around a pull-quote; however, if you use them, use curly (or smart) quotes instead of straight quotes.

Steps **To Insert a Text Box**

1 Scroll to the middle of the first column of the newsletter and select the entire first sentence of the first paragraph below the SIGNAL CONVERSION subhead. Click the Copy button on the Standard toolbar.

The text for the pull-quote is highlighted (Figure 6-57).

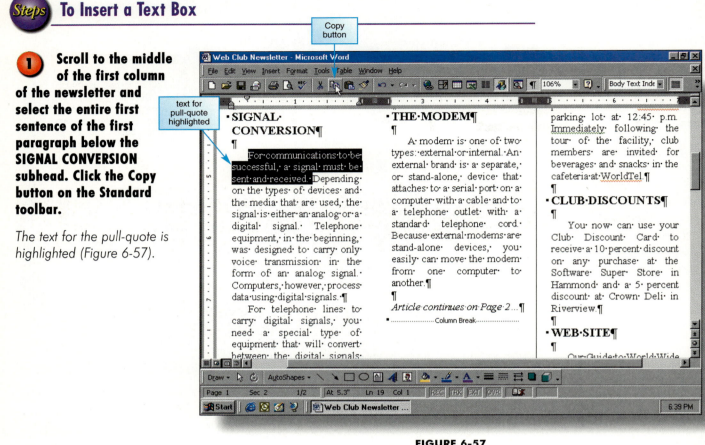

FIGURE 6-57

2 Click the paragraph mark below the SIGNAL CONVERSION subhead. Click the Paste button on the Standard toolbar. Type a quotation mark (") at the end of the pull-quote, and then type a quotation mark (") at the beginning of the pull-quote. Select the entire pull-quote (do not select the paragraph mark). If necessary, click the Drawing button on the Standard toolbar to display the Drawing toolbar. Point to the Text Box button on the Drawing toolbar (Figure 6-58).

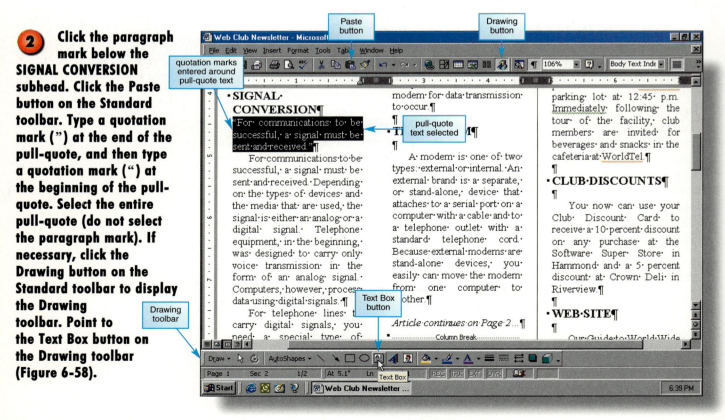

FIGURE 6-58

Click the Text Box button.

Word places a text box around the pull-quote (Figure 6-59). The pull-quote now may be positioned anywhere on the page.

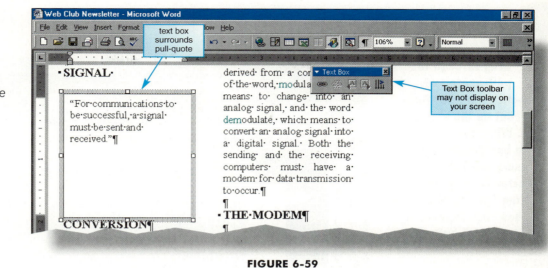

FIGURE 6-59

Other Ways

1. On Insert menu click Text Box

The next step in formatting the pull-quote is to change the color and increase the weight of the text box as described in the following steps.

Steps **To Format a Text Box**

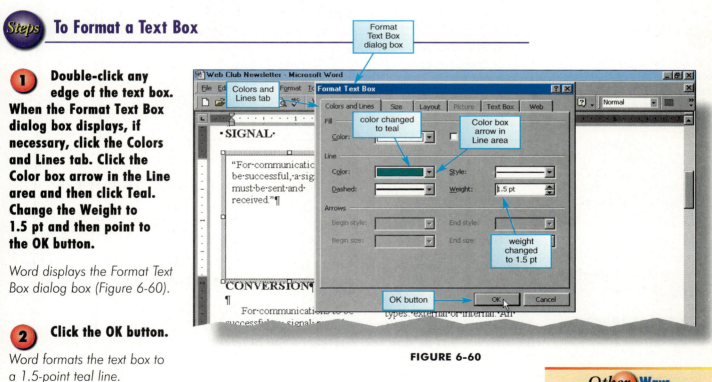

FIGURE 6-60

1 **Double-click any edge of the text box. When the Format Text Box dialog box displays, if necessary, click the Colors and Lines tab. Click the Color box arrow in the Line area and then click Teal. Change the Weight to 1.5 pt and then point to the OK button.**

Word displays the Format Text Box dialog box (Figure 6-60).

2 **Click the OK button.**

Word formats the text box to a 1.5-point teal line.

Other Ways

1. Right-click text box, click Format Text Box on shortcut menu, change settings, click OK button

2. On Format menu click Format Text Box, change settings, click OK button

The next step in formatting the pull-quote is to increase the spacing between the characters, in order to enhance the readability of the text. Perform the steps on the next page to expand the character spacing.

To Increase Character Spacing

1 **Drag through the pull-quote text. Right-click the selection. Click Font on the shortcut menu. When the Font dialog box displays, if necessary, click the Character Spacing tab. Click the Spacing box arrow and then click Expanded. Point to the OK button.**

The Preview area shows the selected text with one point placed between each character (Figure 6-61). Depending on your printer, the characters displayed in the Preview area may differ.

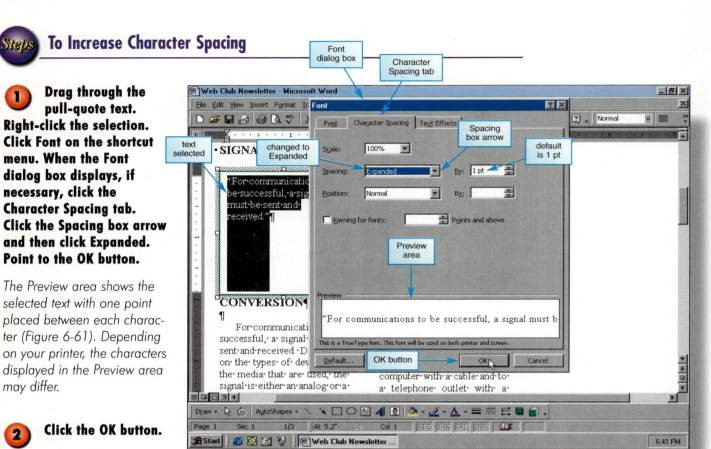

FIGURE 6-61

2 **Click the OK button.**

Word increases the spacing between each character in the pull-quote by one point (see Figure 6-62).

More About 2000

Character Spacing

In addition to increasing the spacing between characters, you also can decrease the spacing between characters in the Character Spacing sheet. To make spacing in a word more proportional, select the word and then click the Kerning for fonts check box in the Character Spacing sheet.

The next step is to bold the characters in the pull-quote as described in the following step.

TO BOLD TEXT

1 Double-click the move handle on the Formatting toolbar to display the entire toolbar. With the pull-quote text still selected, click the Bold button on the Formatting toolbar.

Word bolds the characters in the pull-quote (Figure 6-62). Depending on your printer, the text in your text box may wrap differently than shown in this figure.

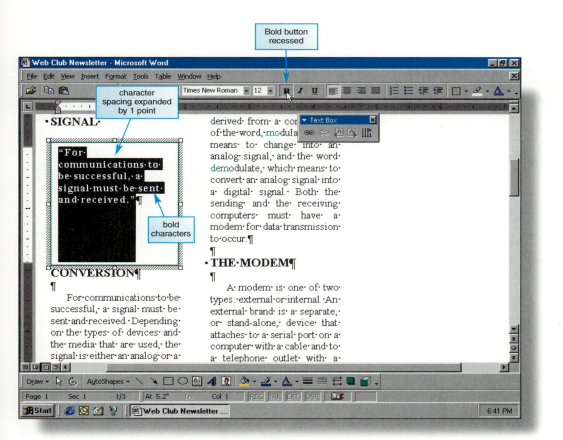

FIGURE 6-62

Notice in Figure 6-62 that the text is positioned closely to the text box on the top and left sides of the text box. You want more space between the pull-quote in the text box and the text box itself. Perform the following steps to increase the left and right indentation and the spacing above and below the paragraph in the text box.

TO CHANGE PARAGRAPH INDENTATION AND SPACING

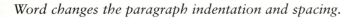

1 Position the insertion point in the pull-quote text. Click Format on the menu bar and then click Paragraph. If necessary, click the Indents and Spacing tab when the Paragraph dialog box displays.

2 In the Indentation area, change Left to 0.1" and Right to 0.1" to increase the amount of space between the left and right edges of the pull-quote and the text box.

3 In the Spacing area, change Before to 6 pt and After to 12 pt to increase the amount of space above and below the pull-quote (Figure 6-63 on the next page).

4 Click the OK button.

Word changes the paragraph indentation and spacing.

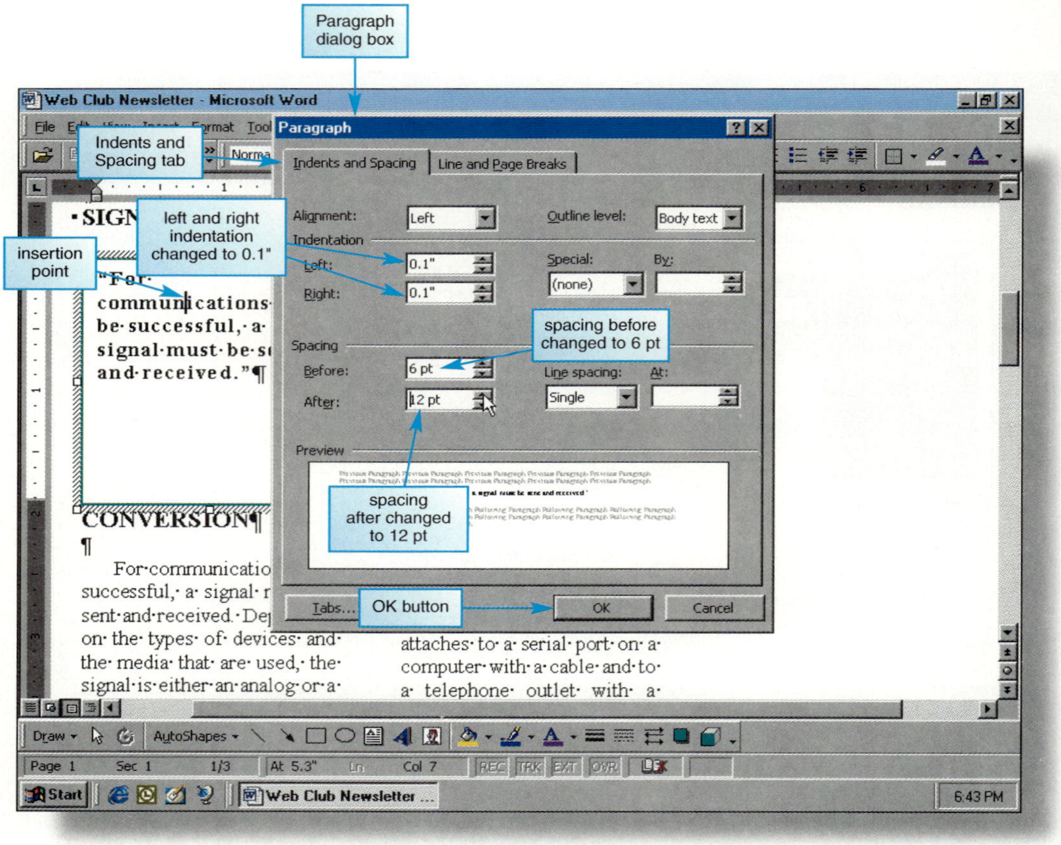

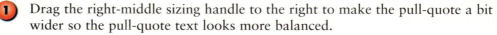

FIGURE 6-63

The next step in formatting the pull-quote is to resize it as described in the following steps.

TO RESIZE A TEXT BOX

1. Drag the right-middle sizing handle to the right to make the pull-quote a bit wider so the pull-quote text looks more balanced.

2. Drag the bottom-middle sizing handle up so the text box looks similar to that shown in Figure 6-65.

Word resizes the text box.

The next step in formatting the pull-quote is to shade the pull-quote paragraph violet as shown in the following steps.

Text Boxes

You learned in Project 4 how to create a graphic watermark. You also can create text watermarks by inserting a text box into the header or footer of the document. To lighten the text so it does not interfere with the document text, change its font color to a lighter shade.

Steps **To Shade a Paragraph**

1 **Select the pull-quote paragraph in the text box, including the paragraph mark. Click Format on the menu bar and then click Borders and Shading. When the Borders and Shading dialog box displays, if necessary, click the Shading tab. Click Violet. Point to the OK button.**

Word displays the Borders and Shading dialog box (Figure 6-64).

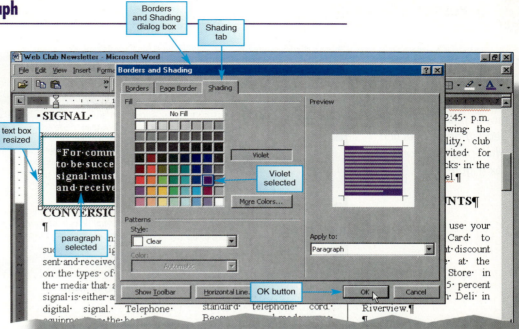

FIGURE 6-64

2 **Click the OK button.**

Word shades the paragraph violet. The characters in the paragraph currently are black, which is difficult to read on a violet background. Thus, change the color of the characters to white.

3 **Click the Font Color button arrow on the Formatting toolbar and then click White. Click outside the selection to remove the highlight.**

Word changes the color of the characters in the pull-quote to white (Figure 6-65).

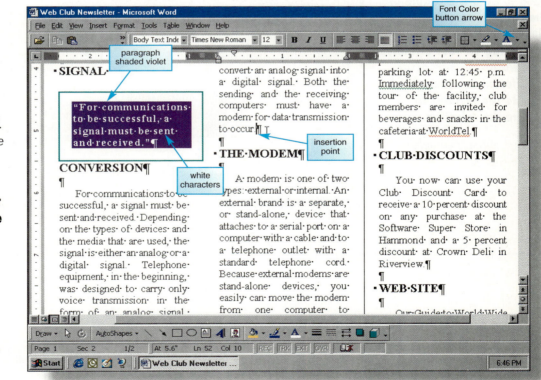

FIGURE 6-65

The final step is to position the pull-quote between the first and second columns of the newsletter as shown in the steps on the next page.

Other Ways

1. Click Shadow Color button on Tables and Borders toolbar

Steps **To Position a Text Box**

1 **Click the text box to select it. Point to the text box.**

The mouse pointer has a four-headed arrow attached to it when positioned on a text box (Figure 6-66).

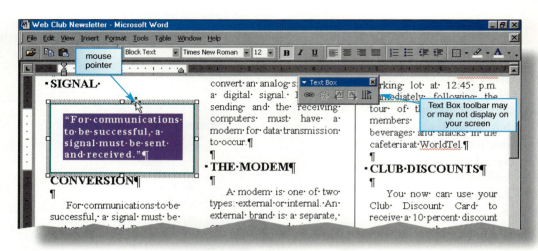

FIGURE 6-66

2 **Drag the text box to its new position (Figure 6-67). You may need to drag it a couple of times to position it similarly to this figure. Depending on your printer, your wordwrap may occur in different locations. Click outside the text box to remove the selection.**

The pull-quote is complete (Figure 6-67).

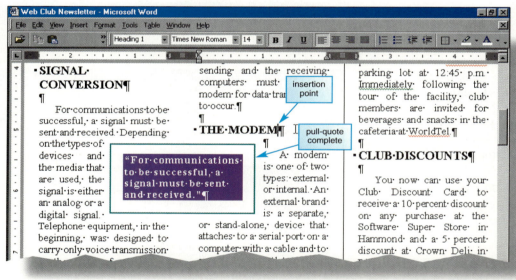

FIGURE 6-67

Perform the following steps to save the document again.

TO SAVE A DOCUMENT

1 Double-click the move handle on the Standard toolbar to display the entire toolbar. With your disk containing the newsletter file in drive A, click the Save button on the Standard toolbar.

Word saves the document again.

The first page of the newsletter is finished, with the exception of the page border, which will be added later in this project. Perform the following steps to print the first page of the newsletter.

TO PRINT A PAGE

1. Click File on the menu bar and then click Print.

2. When the Print dialog box displays, click Current page in the Page range area.

3. Click the OK button.

Word prints the first page of the newsletter (Figure 6-68).

FIGURE 6-68

Formatting the Second Page of the Newsletter

The second page of the newsletter (see Figure 6-1b on page WD 6.5) continues the feature article that began in the first two columns of the first page. The nameplate on the second page is much more concise than the one on the first page of the newsletter. In addition to the text in the feature article, page two contains a picture. The following pages illustrate how to format the second page of the newsletter in this project.

More *About*

Printing

If you want to save ink, print faster, or minimize printer overrun errors, lower the printer resolution. Click File on the menu bar, click Print, click the Properties button in the Print dialog box, click the Graphics tab, click the Resolution box arrow, click a lower resolution than that displayed currently, click the Apply button, click the OK button, and then click the Close button.

More *About*

Jump Lines

An article that spans multiple pages should contain a jump or jump line, which informs the reader where to look for the rest of the article or story. The message on the first page is called a jump-to line, and a jump-from line marks the beginning of the continuation. The alignment of the jump-to and jump-from lines should be the same.

Creating the Nameplate on the Second Page

Because the document currently is formatted into three columns and the name-plate is a single column, the next step is to change the number of columns to one at the top of the second page. You have learned that Word requires a new section each time you change the number of columns in a document. Thus, you will insert a section break and then format the section to one column so you can enter the nameplate. Perform the following steps to format and enter the nameplate on the second page of the newsletter.

Steps · To Change Column Formatting

1 Scroll through the document and position the mouse pointer at the upper-left corner of the second page of the newsletter. Click Insert on the menu bar and then click Break. When the Break dialog box displays, click Continuous in the Section break types area.

Word displays the Break dialog box (Figure 6-69). This section break will place the nameplate on the same physical page as the three columns of the continued feature article.

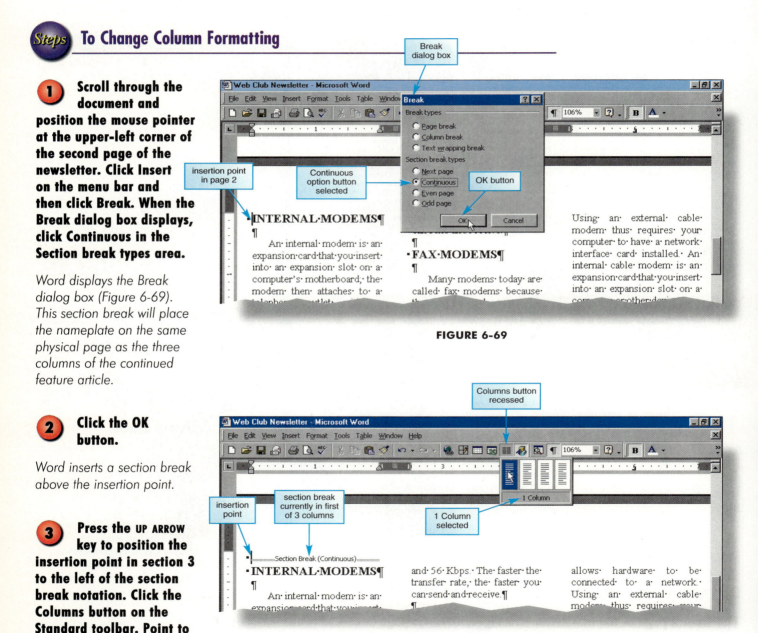

FIGURE 6-69

2 Click the OK button.

Word inserts a section break above the insertion point.

3 Press the UP ARROW key to position the insertion point in section 3 to the left of the section break notation. Click the Columns button on the Standard toolbar. Point to the first column of the columns list graphic.

FIGURE 6-70

Word highlights the left column in the columns list graphic and displays 1 Column below the graphic (Figure 6-70). The current section, for the nameplate, will be formatted to one column.

4 **Click the first column in the columns list graphic.**

Word formats the current section to one column (Figure 6-71).

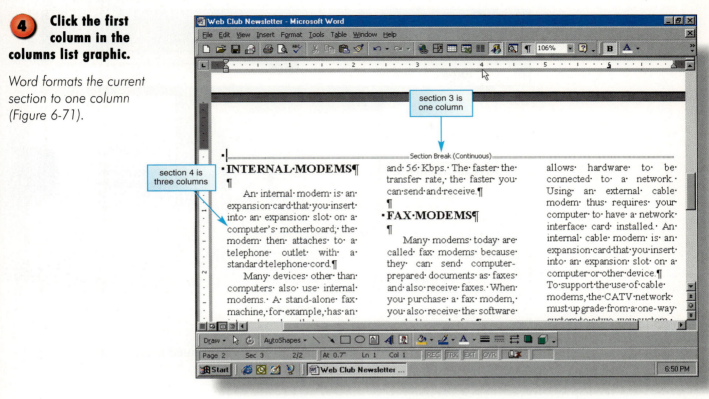

FIGURE 6-71

In the nameplate on the second page, the date is to display at the left margin; the newsletter title, The Web Club, is to be centered; and the page number is to display at the right margin. Thus, you set a centered and right-aligned tab stop for the nameplate as described in the following steps.

TO SET TAB STOPS

1 Be sure the insertion point is in section 3. Double-click the move handle on the Formatting toolbar to display the entire toolbar. Click the Style box arrow on the Formatting toolbar and then click Normal.

2 Press the ENTER key twice and then press the UP ARROW key. Click Format on the menu bar and then click Tabs.

3 When the Tabs dialog box displays, type 3.5 and then click Center in the Alignment area. Click the Set button.

4 Type 7 in the Tab stop position text box and then click Right in the Alignment area (Figure 6-72 on the next page). Click the Set button.

5 Click the OK button.

Word places a centered tab marker at the 3.5" mark on the ruler and a right-aligned tab marker at the right margin.

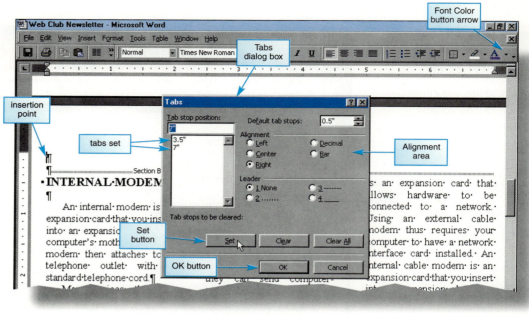

FIGURE 6-72

The next step is to enter the nameplate and a continued message at the top of the first column in the second page of the newsletter.

TO ENTER THE NAMEPLATE AND CONTINUED MESSAGE ON THE SECOND PAGE

1 Click the Font Color button arrow on the Formatting toolbar and then click Violet. Click Insert on the menu bar, click Date and Time, click the date format of month, day, year (November 16, 2001), and then click the OK button.

2 Press the TAB key. Change the font to Beesknees ITC, or a similar font. Change the font size to 24. Type The Web Club and then change the font size back to 12. Change the font back to Times New Roman.

3 Press the TAB key. Type Page 2 and then press the ENTER key.

4 Click somewhere in the line typed in Steps 1 through 3. Double-click the move handle on the Standard toolbar to display the entire toolbar. If necessary, click the Tables and Borders button on the Standard toolbar to display the Tables and Borders toolbar.

5 Click the Line Style box arrow on the Tables and Borders toolbar and then click the first dotted line in the list.

6 Click the Border button arrow on the Tables and Borders toolbar and then click Top Border. Click the Border button arrow on the Tables and Borders toolbar and then click Bottom Border. Click the Tables and Borders button on the Standard toolbar to remove the Tables and Borders toolbar from the Word window.

7 Click the paragraph mark in line 2 (below the dotted line border). Type Feature Article and then press the SPACEBAR. Press the CTRL+I keys to turn on italics. Type (continued) and then press the CTRL+I keys to turn off italics. Double-click the move handle on the Formatting toolbar to display the entire toolbar. Change the font color back to Automatic.

The nameplate and article continued message for page two are complete (Figure 6-73).

Inner Page Nameplates

The top of the inner pages of the newsletter may or may not have a nameplate. If you choose to create one for your inner pages, it should not be the same as, or compete with, the one on the first page. Inner page nameplates usually contain only a portion of the nameplate from the first page of a newsletter.

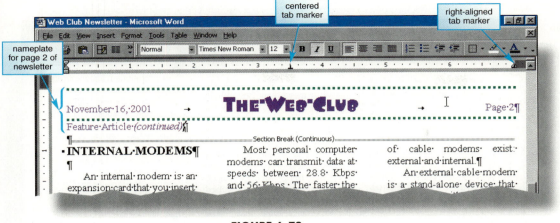

FIGURE 6-73

The next step is to balance the columns on the second page of the newsletter.

Balancing Columns

Currently, the text on the second page of the newsletter fills up the first and second columns completely and spills into a portion of the third column. You would like the text in the three columns to consume the same amount of vertical space; that is, they should be balanced. To balance columns, you insert a continuous section break at the end of the text as shown in the following steps.

Steps To Balance Columns

1 **Scroll to the bottom of the text in the third column on the second page of the newsletter and then click the paragraph mark below the text. Click Insert on the menu bar and then click Break. When the Break dialog box displays, click Continuous in the Section break types area. Point to the OK button.**

Word displays the Break dialog box (Figure 6-74).

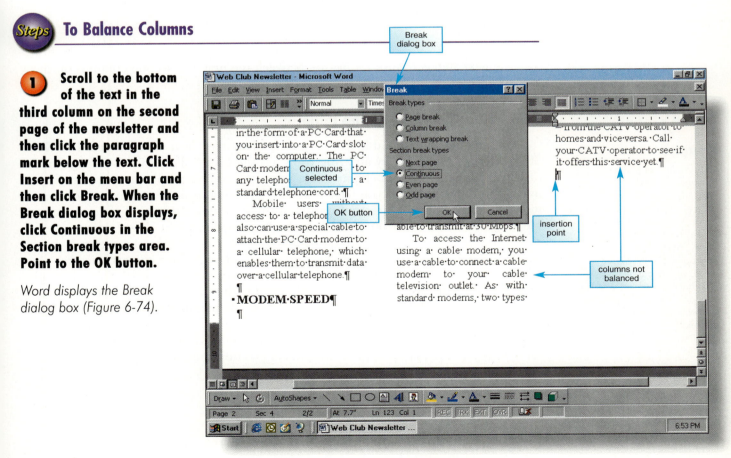

FIGURE 6-74

Click the OK button.

Word inserts a continuous section break, which balances the columns on the second page of the newsletter (Figure 6-75).

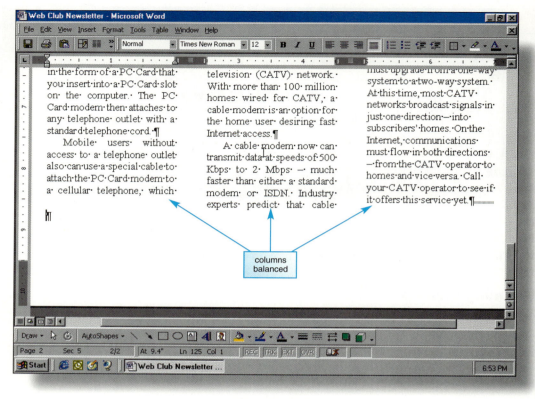

FIGURE 6-75

The next step is to insert a picture between the first and second columns on the second page of the newsletter.

Positioning Graphics on the Page

Graphics

The use of real photographs in a newsletter adds professionalism to the document. You can insert them yourself if you have a scanner; otherwise, you can work with a print shop. When using photographs, you may need to crop, or trim out, the edges. If you have a scanner, you usually can crop the images using software provided with the scanner.

Graphic files are available from a variety of sources. You have learned that Word 2000 includes a clip gallery and Microsoft has the Clip Gallery Live Web page, both of which provide a host of clip art files. You also can insert a picture or photograph into a Word document. If you have a scanner attached to your computer, Word can insert a scanned picture directly from the scanner; or you can scan the picture into a file and then insert the scanned file into the Word document at a later time.

In this project, you insert a scanned file into the newsletter and position it between the first and second columns on the second page. Like clip art, pictures are inserted as inline. You want the text in the first two columns to wrap around the picture. An inline picture can be moved only from within one column to another; that is, not between columns. Thus, you must change the picture from inline to floating so you can position it between the columns.

The picture is named PC Card and is located on the Data Disk. Perform the following steps to insert the picture and then position it between columns in the newsletter.

To Insert a Picture

1 Scroll through the document and position the insertion point on the paragraph mark immediately below the PC CARD MODEMS subhead in the first column on the second page of the newsletter. Click Insert on the menu bar, point to Picture, and then point to From File (Figure 6-76).

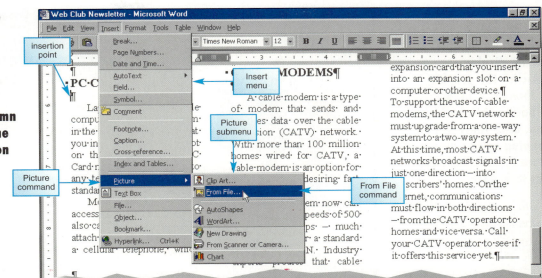

FIGURE 6-76

2 If necessary, insert the Data Disk into drive A. Click From File. When the Insert Picture dialog box displays, if necessary, change the Look in location to drive A. Click PC Card. Point to the Insert button.

Word displays the Insert Picture dialog box (Figure 6-77).

3 Click the Insert button.

Word inserts the picture into your document as an inline object (see Figure 6-78 on the next page).

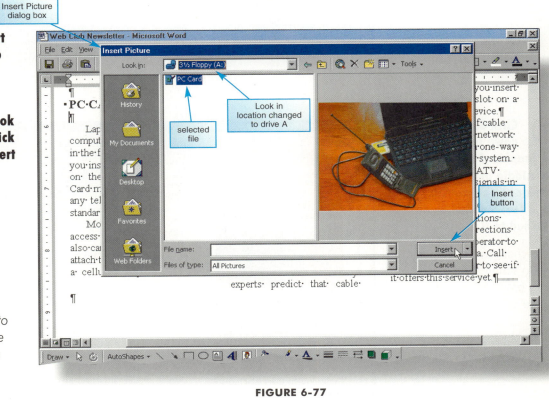

FIGURE 6-77

The next step is to change the graphic from inline to floating and then position it between the first and second columns on the second page of the newsletter.

To Wrap Text Around a Graphic

1 **Click the picture graphic to select it. If the Picture toolbar does not display, right-click the graphic and then click Show Picture Toolbar on the shortcut menu. Click the Text Wrapping button on the Picture toolbar and then point to Square.**

The wrapping styles specify how the text in the document displays with or around the graphic (Figure 6-78).

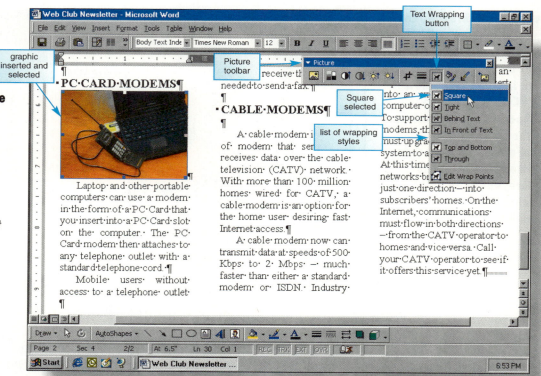

FIGURE 6-78

2 **Click Square. Scroll down to display the graphic. Point to the middle of the graphic so the mouse has a four-headed arrow attached to it.**

Word changes the wrapping style to square so that the text wraps around the graphic (Figure 6-79).

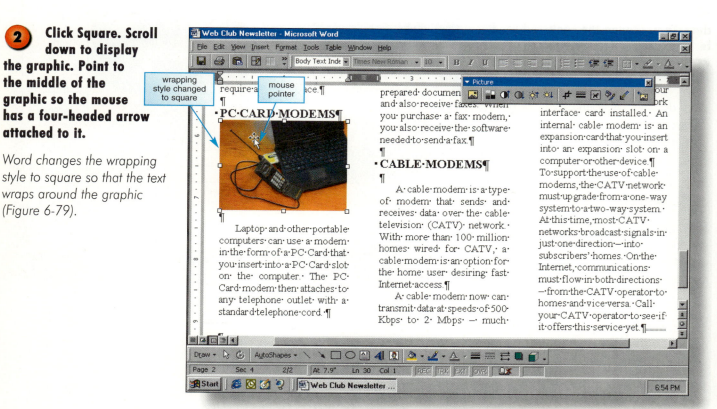

FIGURE 6-79

3 Drag the graphic to the desired location. You may have to drag the graphic a couple of times to position it similarly to Figure 6-80. Click outside the graphic to remove the selection.

As the graphic moves, a dotted border indicates its new location if you release the mouse button at that moment (Figure 6-80). Depending on the printer you are using, your wordwrap may occur in different locations.

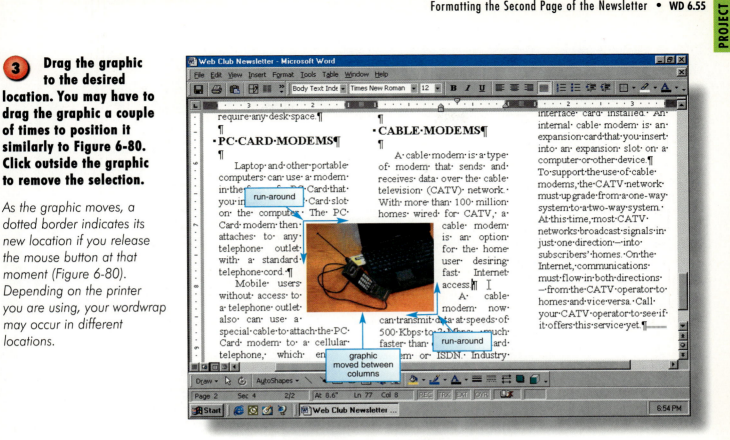

FIGURE 6-80

Notice in Figure 6-80 that the text in columns one and two wraps around the picture. Thus, it is called wrap-around text. The wrap-around forms a square because of the wrapping style set in Step 3. The space between the picture and the wrap-around text is called the run-around.

The second page of the newsletter is complete, with the exception of the page border. Perform the following steps to print the second page of the newsletter.

TO PRINT A PAGE

1 Click File on the menu bar and then click Print.

2 When the Print dialog box displays, click Current page in the Page range area.

3 Click the OK button.

Word prints the second page of the newsletter (Figure 6-81 on the next page).

Run-Around

The run-around should be at least 1/8" and should be the same for all graphics in the newsletter. Adjust the run-around of a selected graphic by clicking the Format Picture button on the Picture toolbar, clicking the Layout tab, clicking the Advanced button, adjusting the Distance from text boxes, and then clicking the OK button.

November 16, 2001 THE WEB CLUB Page 2
Feature Article *(continued)*

INTERNAL MODEMS

An internal modem is an expansion card that you insert into an expansion slot on a computer's motherboard; the modem then attaches to a telephone outlet with a standard telephone cord.

Many devices other than computers also use internal modems. A stand-alone fax machine, for example, has an internal modem that converts a scanned digitized image into an analog signal that can be sent to the recipient's fax machine.

One important advantage of internal modems over external modems is that internal modems do not require any desk space.

PC CARD MODEMS

Laptop and other portable computers can use a modem in the form of a PC Card that you insert into a PC Card slot on the computer. The PC Card modem then attaches to any telephone outlet with a standard telephone cord.

Mobile users without access to a telephone outlet also can use a special cable to attach the PC Card modem to a cellular telephone, which enables them to transmit data over a cellular telephone.

MODEM SPEED

Most personal computer modems can transmit data at speeds between 28.8 Kbps and 56 Kbps. The faster the transfer rate, the faster you can send and receive.

FAX MODEMS

Many modems today are called fax modems because they can send computer-prepared documents as faxes and also receive faxes. When you purchase a fax modem, you also receive the software needed to send a fax.

CABLE MODEMS

A cable modem is a type of modem that sends and receives data over the cable television (CATV) network. With more than 100 million homes wired for CATV, a cable modem is an option for the home user desiring fast Internet access.

A cable modem now can transmit data at speeds of 500 Kbps to 2 Mbps – much faster than either a standard modem or

ISDN. Industry experts predict that cable modems eventually will be able to transmit at 30 Mbps.

To access the Internet using a cable modem, you use a cable to connect a cable modem to your cable television outlet. As with standard modems, two types of cable modems exist: external and internal.

An external cable modem is a stand-alone device that you connect with a cable to a port on your computer's network interface card, which is an expansion card that allows hardware to be connected to a network. Using an external cable modem thus requires your computer to have a network interface card installed. An internal cable modem is an expansion card that you insert into an expansion slot on a computer or other device. To support the use of cable modems, the CATV network must upgrade from a one-way system to a two-way system. At this time, most CATV networks broadcast signals in just one direction – into subscribers' homes. On the Internet, communications must flow in both directions – from the CATV operator to homes and vice versa. Call your CATV operator to see if it offers this service yet.

FIGURE 6-81

Enhancing the Newsletter with Color and a Page Border

You already have added color to many of the characters and lines in the newsletter in this project. You also want to color all of the subheads and add a border around each page of the newsletter. The following pages illustrate these tasks.

The first step is to color the dropped capital letter.

TO COLOR THE DROP CAP

1 Scroll to the top of the newsletter and then select the drop cap by clicking to its left.

2 Click the Font Color button arrow on the Formatting toolbar and then click Teal.

Word changes the color of the dropped capital letter to teal (see Figure 6-82).

Using the Format Painter Button

You have learned that subheads are internal headings placed throughout the body of the newsletter, such as SIGNAL CONVERSION and THE MODEM. Thus far, the subheads are bold and have a font size of 14. You also want all of the sub-heads italicized and colored teal.

Instead of selecting each subhead one at a time and then formatting it to italics and changing its color, you can format the first subhead and then copy its formatting to another location. To copy formatting, use the **Format Painter button** on the Standard toolbar as shown in the following steps.

To Use the Format Painter Button

1 **Select the characters in the subhead, SIGNAL CONVERSION. Click the Italic button on the Formatting toolbar. Click the Font Color button on the Formatting toolbar. Click somewhere in the SIGNAL CONVERSION subhead. Double-click the move handle on the Standard toolbar to display the entire toolbar. Click the Format Painter button on the Standard toolbar. Move the mouse pointer into the document window.**

Word attaches a paintbrush to the mouse pointer when the Format Painter button is recessed (Figure 6-82). The 14-point Times New Roman teal, bold italic font has been copied by the format painter.

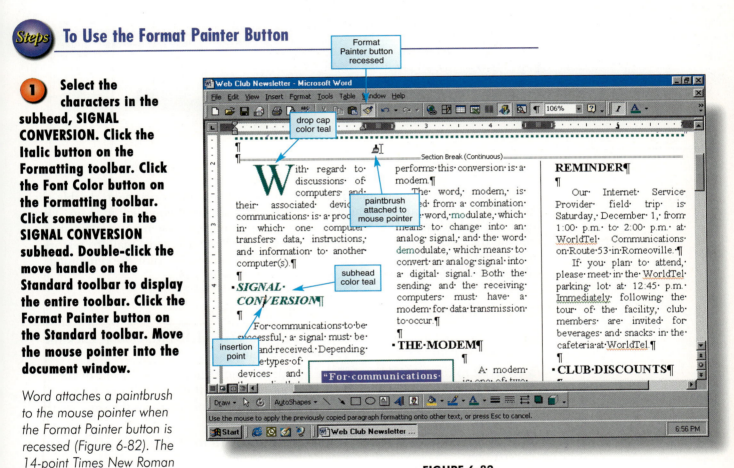

FIGURE 6-82

2 Scroll through the newsletter to the next subhead, THE MODEM. Select the subhead by clicking to its left. Click outside the selection to remove the highlight.

Word copies the 14-point Times New Roman teal, bold italic font to the subhead THE MODEM (Figure 6-83). The Format Painter button on the Standard toolbar no longer is recessed.

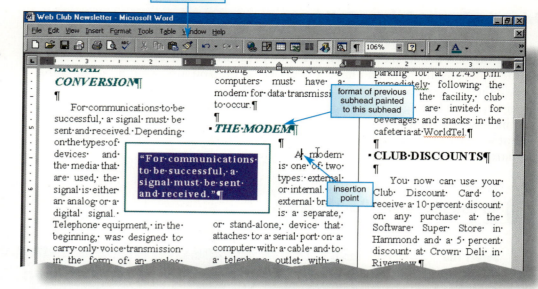

FIGURE 6-83

If you want to copy formatting to multiple locations in a document, double-click the Format Painter button, which will remain recessed until you click it again. Then highlight each location where you want the format copied. When you are finished copying the character formatting, click the Format Painter button again to restore the normal I-beam pointer. Use the Format Painter button to color the remaining subheads in the newsletter as described in the following steps.

TO COLOR THE REMAINING SUBHEADS IN THE NEWSLETTER

1 Position the insertion point in the subhead THE MODEM. Double-click the Format Painter button on the Standard toolbar.

2 Scroll to the second page of the newsletter and then click to the left of the INTERNAL MODEMS, PC CARD MODEMS, MODEM SPEED, FAX MODEMS, and CABLE MODEMS subheads to format them the same as the subhead THE MODEM.

3 Click the Format Painter button on the Standard toolbar to turn off the format painter.

4 Scroll to the top of the third column in the first page of the newsletter. Selec the REMINDER subhead. Double-click the move handle on the Formatting toolbar to display the entire toolbar. Click the Italic button on the Formatting toolbar. Click the Font Color button on the Formatting toolbar.

5 Double-click the move handle on the Standard toolbar to display the entire toolbar. Double-click the Format Painter button on the Standard toolbar.

6 Scroll to and then click to the left of the CLUB DISCOUNTS and WEB SITE subheads.

7 Click the Format Painter button on the Standard toolbar to turn off the format painter.

The subheads in the newsletter are formatted (see Figure 6-1 on page WD 6.5).

The next step in enhancing the newsletter is to add a border around each page.

Adding a Page Border

You have added borders to the edges of a paragraph(s). In Word, you also can add a border around the perimeter of an entire page. Page borders add professionalism to your documents. Perform the following steps to add a violet page border to the pages of the newsletter.

Steps **To Add a Page Border**

1 **Click Format on the menu bar and then click Borders and Shading. When the Borders and Shading dialog box displays, if necessary, click the Page Border tab. Click Box in the Setting area. Scroll through the Style list and click the style shown in Figure 6-84. Click the Color box arrow and then click Violet. Point to the OK button.**

Word displays the Borders and Shading dialog box (Figure 6-84). The page border is set to a 3-point violet box.

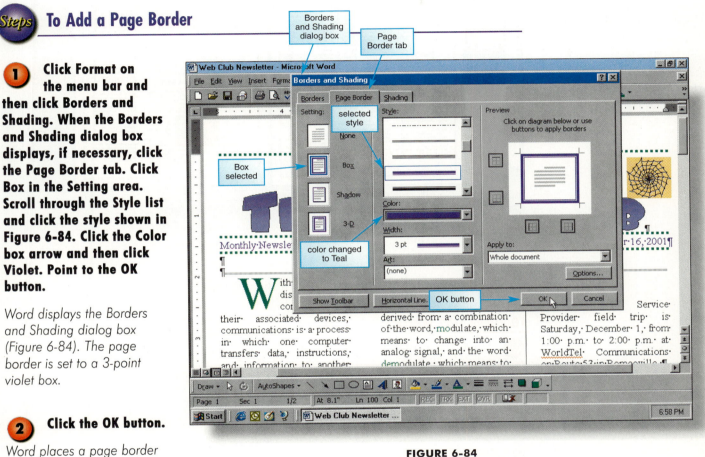

FIGURE 6-84

2 **Click the OK button.**

Word places a page border on each page of the newsletter (see Figure 6-85 on the next page).

To see the borders on the newsletter, display both pages in the document window as described in the following step.

TO ZOOM TWO PAGES

1 Click the Zoom box arrow and then click Two Pages in the list.

Word displays the pages of the newsletter in reduced form so both pages display in the document window (Figure 6-85 on the next page).

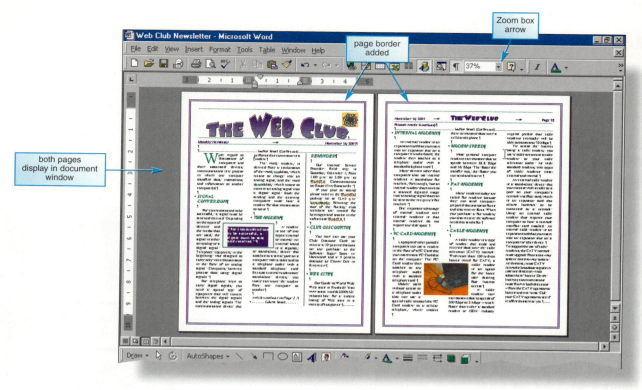

FIGURE 6-85

Perform the following step to return the display to zoom text width.

TO ZOOM TEXT WIDTH

1 Click the Zoom box arrow and then click Text Width.

Word extends the right margin to the right edge of the document window.

The newsletter now is complete. You should save the document again and print it as described in the following series of steps.

TO SAVE A DOCUMENT

1 With the disk containing the newsletter file in drive A, click the Save button on the Standard toolbar.

Word saves the document again with the name, Web Club Newsletter.

TO PRINT A DOCUMENT

1 Click the Print button on the Standard toolbar.

The printed newsletter is shown in Figure 6-1 on page WD 6.5.

Highlighting Text

If you send this document via e-mail so recipients can view it on line, you may wish to highlight text. **Highlighting** alerts the reader to the text's importance, much like a highlight marker does in a textbook. The following steps illustrate how to highlight text yellow.

Quick Reference

For a table that lists how to complete the tasks covered in this book using the mouse, menu, shortcut menu, and keyboard, visit the Shelly Cashman Series Office Web page (www.scsite.com/off2000/qr.htm) and then click Microsoft Word 2000.

Steps **To Highlight Text**

1 **Press CTRL+HOME. Double-click the move handle on the Formatting toolbar to display the entire toolbar. Click the Highlight button arrow on the Formatting toolbar and then point to Yellow.**

Word displays a variety of highlight color options (Figure 6-86).

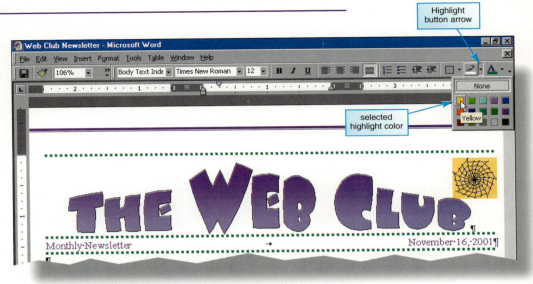

FIGURE 6-86

2 **Click Yellow. Drag through the REMINDER subhead in the document.**

Word highlights the selection yellow (Figure 6-87).

3 **Click the Highlight button to turn highlighting off.**

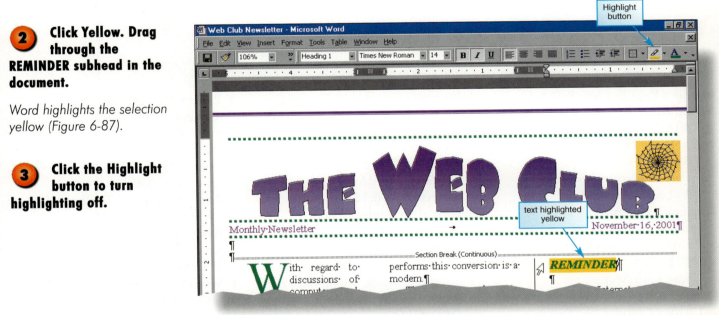

FIGURE 6-87

When the Highlight button is recessed, you can continue selecting text to be highlighted. Notice in Figure 6-86 that Word provides a variety of colors for highlighting text.

TO QUIT WORD

1 Click the Close button in the Word window.

The Word window closes.

Microsoft Certification

The Microsoft Office User Specialist (MOUS) Certification program provides an opportunity for you to obtain a valuable industry credential - proof that you have the Word 2000 skills required by employers. For more information, see Appendix D or visit the Shelly Cashman Series MOUS Web page at www.scsite.com/off2000/cert.htm.

C A S E   P E R S P E C T I V E   S U M M A R Y

Upon completion, you e-mail the newsletter to Jamie Navaro, president of The Web Club, for his review. He thinks it looks great and gives you approval to distribute.

You print the newsletter on a color printer and send the color printout to the Duplicating Center to have 1,000 copies made. While the copies are being made, you submit the newsletter to the school's Public Relations department for their approval to post it around campus. Then, you recruit a couple of friends to assist you in posting the newsletter around campus and distributing it to club members.

Project Summary

Project 6 introduced you to creating a professional looking newsletter using Word's desktop publishing features. You created a nameplate using a WordArt drawing object and the current computer date. You formatted the body of the newsletter into three columns and added a vertical rule between the second and third columns. You linked another document to the newsletter. You created a pull-quote, inserted a picture, and learned how to move these graphical objects between columns. Finally, you used the Format Painter button and added a page border to the newsletter.

What You Should Know

Having completed this project, you should now be able to perform the following tasks:

- Add a Page Border *(WD 6.59)*
- Add More Ruling Lines *(WD 6.18)*
- Apply the Heading 1 Style *(WD 6.33)*
- Apply the Normal Style *(WD 6.16, WD 6.22)*
- Balance Columns *(WD 6.51)*
- Bold Text *(WD 6.42)*
- Center an Inline Object *(WD 6.14)*
- Change All Margin Settings *(WD 6.7)*
- Change Column Formatting *(WD 6.48)*
- Change Paragraph Indentation and Spacing *(WD 6.43)*
- Change the Shape of a WordArt Drawing Object *(WD 6.14)*
- Close a File *(WD 6.37)*
- Color the Drop Cap *(WD 6.56)*
- Color the Remaining Subheads in the Newsletter *(WD 6.58)*
- Display Formatting Marks *(WD 6.7)*
- Enter the Nameplate and Continued Message on the Second Page *(WD 6.50)*
- Format a Graphic as Floating *(WD 6.20)*
- Format a Letter as a Drop Cap *(WD 6.28)*
- Format a Text Box *(WD 6.41)*
- Format a WordArt Drawing Object *(WD 6.12)*
- Format Columns *(WD 6.25)*
- Highlight Text *(WD 6.61)*
- Increase Character Spacing *(WD 6.42)*
- Insert a Column Break *(WD 6.31)*
- Insert a Continuous Section Break *(WD 6.24)*
- Insert a File into a Column of the Newsletter *(WD 6.32)*
- Insert a File into the Newsletter *(WD 6.27)*
- Insert a Next Page Section Break *(WD 6.30)*
- Insert a Picture *(WD 6.53)*
- Insert a Text Box *(WD 6.40)*
- Insert a WordArt Drawing Object *(WD 6.9)*
- Insert Clip Art *(WD 6.19)*
- Insert the Current Date into a Document *(WD 6.17)*
- Justify a Paragraph *(WD 6.26)*
- Link an Object *(WD 6.34)*
- Place a Vertical Rule Between Columns *(WD 6.37)*
- Position a Text Box *(WD 6.46)*
- Print a Document *(WD 6.60)*
- Print a Page *(WD 6.47, WD 6.55)*
- Quit Word *(WD 6.61)*
- Reset Menus and Toolbars *(WD 6.6)*
- Resize a Text Box *(WD 6.44)*
- Save a Document *(WD 6.46, WD 6.60)*
- Save the Newsletter *(WD 6.27)*
- Set a Right-Aligned Tab Stop *(WD 6.17)*
- Set Tab Stops *(WD 6.49)*
- Shade a Graphic *(WD 6.21)*
- Shade a Paragraph *(WD 6.45)*
- Start Word *(WD 6.6)*
- Use Borders to Add a Ruling Line *(WD 6.15)*
- Use the Format Painter Button *(WD 6.57)*
- Wrap Text around a Graphic *(WD 6.54)*
- Zoom Text Width *(WD 6.8, WD 6.33, WD 6.60)*
- Zoom Two Pages *(WD 6.59)*
- Zoom Whole Page *(WD 6.32)*

Apply Your Knowledge

➕ Project Reinforcement at www.scsite.com/off2000/reinforce.htm

1 Linking and Editing an Object

Instruction: Start Word. Open the documents, Play-Dough and Thank You Note, on the Data Disk. If you did not download the Data Disk, see the inside back cover for instructions for downloading the Data Disk or see your instructor.

Performing the steps below, you are to link the Play-Dough document into the Thank You Note document and then modify the source document (Play-Dough). The revised destination document (Thank You Note) is shown in Figure 6-88.

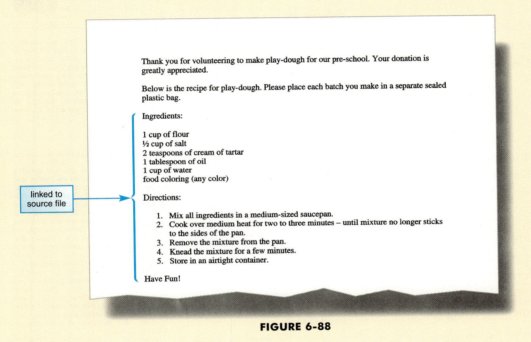

Thank you for volunteering to make play-dough for our pre-school. Your donation is greatly appreciated.

Below is the recipe for play-dough. Please place each batch you make in a separate sealed plastic bag.

Ingredients:

1 cup of flour
½ cup of salt
2 teaspoons of cream of tartar
1 tablespoon of oil
1 cup of water
food coloring (any color)

linked to source file →

Directions:

1. Mix all ingredients in a medium-sized saucepan.
2. Cook over medium heat for two to three minutes -- until mixture no longer sticks to the sides of the pan.
3. Remove the mixture from the pan.
4. Knead the mixture for a few minutes.
5. Store in an airtight container.

Have Fun!

FIGURE 6-88

Perform the following tasks:

1. Click the Play-Dough program button on the taskbar. When the Play-Dough document window displays, click Edit on the menu bar and then click Select All. Click the Copy button on the Standard toolbar.
2. Click the Thank You Note program button on the taskbar. When the Thank You Note document window displays, position the insertion point on line 7. Click Edit on the menu bar and then click Paste Special. When the Paste Special dialog box displays, click Paste link, click Formatted Text (RTF) in the list, and then click the OK button.
3. Click the Play-Dough program button on the taskbar. When the Play-Dough document window displays, click anywhere to remove the selection. Highlight the text between the words, Directions and Have Fun. Click the Numbering button on the Formatting toolbar to number the list of directions.
4. Click the Save button on the Standard toolbar to save the revised Play-Dough file. Close the Play-Dough document window.
5. When the Thank You Note document window redisplays, click somewhere in the directions and then press F9.
6. Save the destination document with the name Revised Thank You Note.
7. Print the revised destination document.

In the Lab

1 Creating a Newsletter with a Picture and an Article on File

Problem: You are an editor of the *Home Photography* newsletter. The December 6th edition is due out next Thursday. The feature article will present options for electronic photographs (Figure 6-89). The newsletter also includes a scanned picture. The feature article and the picture are on the Data Disk. If you did not download the Data Disk, see the inside back cover for instructions for downloading the Data Disk or see your instructor.

Instructions:

1. Change all margins to .75 inch. Depending on your printer, you may need different margin settings.
2. Create the nameplate using the formats identified in Figure 6-89. Create a continuous section break below the nameplate. Format section 2 to two columns.
3. Insert the Electronic Photo Article on the Data Disk into section 2 below the nameplate.
4. Format the newsletter according to Figure 6-89. Use the Format Painter button to automate some of your formatting tasks. Insert the picture named, filmbag, from the Data Disk. Format the picture to square wrapping.
5. Save the document with Home Photography Newsletter as the file name. Print the newsletter.

Figure callouts:

- teal page border
- 60-point Bauhaus 93 WordArt font with gradient color (turquoise to black) and Cascade Up shape
- ½-point red double ruling lines
- 12-point Times New Roman dark teal font
- clip art keyword: camera
- 14-point Times New Roman dark teal, bold font for subheads
- picture named, filmbag, on Data Disk

Home Photography

Monthly Newsletter   December 6, 2001

Home photographers have a variety of options for making electronic photo albums. Three of these are color scanners, digital cameras, and PhotoCDs. The images on each of these devices can be printed, faxed, sent via electronic mail, included in another document, or posted to a Web site for everyone to see.

Color Scanner

A color scanner is a light-sensing device that reads printed text and graphics and then translates the results into a form the computer can use. A scanner is similar to a copy machine, except it creates a file of the document instead of a paper copy.

When a picture is scanned, the results are stored in rows and columns of dots. The more dots, the better the detail and clarity of the resulting image. Today, most of the reasonably priced color desktop scanners for the home or small business user range from 300 to 2,000 dots per inch, with the latter being a higher quality, but more expensive.

Digital Camera

Another easy and effective way to obtain color photographs is by using a digital camera. Digital cameras work similarly to regular cameras, except they store digital photographs.

With some digital cameras, you transfer a copy of the stored pictures to your computer by connecting a cable between the digital camera and your computer and using special software included with the camera. With other digital cameras, the pictures are stored directly on a floppy disk or on a PC Card. You then copy the pictures to your computer by inserting the floppy disk into a disk drive or the PC Card into a PC Card slot.

PhotoCD

A CD-ROM is a compact disc that uses the same laser technology as audio CDs for recording music. Unlike an audio CD, though, a CD-ROM can contain text, graphics, video, and sound.

A variation of the standard CD-ROM is the PhotoCD. Based on a file format that was developed by Eastman Kodak, a PhotoCD is a compact disc that contains only digital photographic images saved in the PhotoCD format.

You can buy PhotoCDs that include pictures, or you can have your own photographs or negatives recorded onto PhotoCDs, allowing you to archive digital versions of your favorite photos. Many film developers offer this service when you drop off film to be developed.

Practically any computer with a CD-ROM or DVD-ROM drive can read photographs stored on a PhotoCD.

FIGURE 6-89

In the Lab

2 Creating a Newsletter with a Text Box and an Article on File

Problem: You are responsible for the monthly preparation of *Remodeling*, a newsletter for club members. The next edition is due out in two weeks, which is to discuss the layout, setting, and cutting of tiles for ceramic tile installation (Figure 6-90). This article already has been prepared and is on the Data Disk. If you did not download the Data Disk, see the inside back cover for instructions for downloading the Data Disk or see your instructor. You need to create the text box.

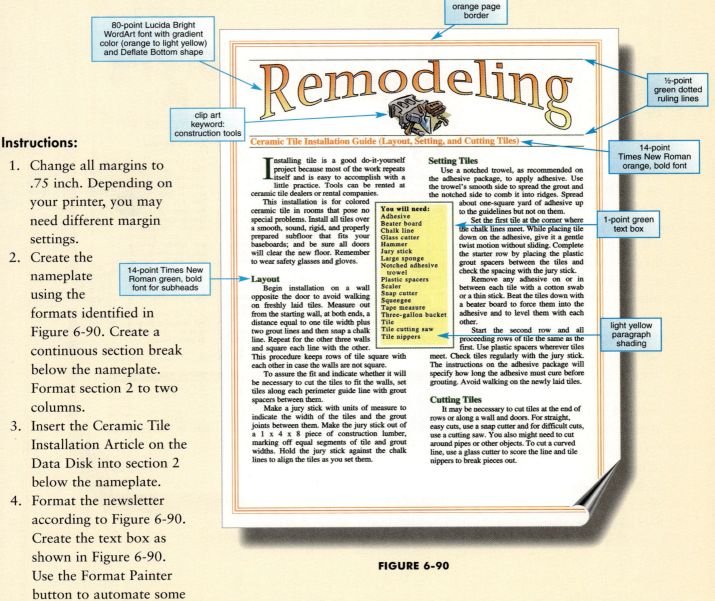

FIGURE 6-90

Instructions:

1. Change all margins to .75 inch. Depending on your printer, you may need different margin settings.
2. Create the nameplate using the formats identified in Figure 6-90. Create a continuous section break below the nameplate. Format section 2 to two columns.
3. Insert the Ceramic Tile Installation Article on the Data Disk into section 2 below the nameplate.
4. Format the newsletter according to Figure 6-90. Create the text box as shown in Figure 6-90. Use the Format Painter button to automate some of your formatting tasks.
5. Save the document with Remodeling Newsletter as the file name. Print the newsletter.

In the Lab

3 Creating a Newsletter from Scratch

Problem: You are a leader of *Young Explorers*, which publishes a newsletter for parents of children in your unit. You prepare a newsletter for distribution at each meeting (Figure 6-91).

Instructions:

1. Change all margins to .75 inch. Depending on your printer, you may need different margin settings.

2. Create the nameplate using the formats identified in Figure 6-91. *Hint*: Use the Shadow button on the Drawing toolbar to apply the shadow effect. Create a continuous section break below the nameplate. Format section 2 to three columns.

3. Enter announcements into section 2 below the nameplate.

4. Insert a continuous section break at the end of the announcements. Format section 3 to one column. Create the table as shown at the bottom of the newsletter.

5. Format the newsletter according to Figure 6-91. Place a vertical rule between all columns in section 2. Use the Line between check box in the Columns dialog box (Format menu) to do this. Use the Format Painter button to automate some of your formatting tasks.

6. Save the document with Young Explorers Newsletter as the file name. Print the newsletter.

Figure callouts:

rose page border

shadow

clip art keyword: owl

66-point Comic Sans MS WordArt font with gradient color (dark red to rose) and Wave 2 shape

2¼-point blue-gray dotted ruling lines

14-point Times New Roman blue-gray, bold font

clip art keyword: fall leaves

clip art keyword: bowling pin; fill color gold

14-point Times New Roman dark red, bold font for subheads

white font; dark red shading

Young Explorers

Unit #135 News   September 10, 2001

Outing

The Nature Exploration outing is Saturday, September 22, from 10:00 a.m. to 3:00 p.m. at Camp Ottawa.

The following explorers signed up for this event:
1. Helen
2. Leila
3. Jackie
4. Whitney
5. Rachel
6. Willow

Please drop off your daughter by 8:30 a.m. at the Coal City Groceland parking lot.

We will return between 4:00 p.m. and 4:15 p.m. Please arrive promptly at 4:00 p.m. at the same parking lot to pick up your daughter. Thanks!

Fund-raiser

Our unit will have a craft booth at the Fall Harvest Festival at Camp Ottawa on Saturday, October 20. Profits from all sales will go directly to our unit.

If you would like to donate a craft or staff the booth, call Mary at 555-0909.

Thank You!

We would like to thank each of you for donating to the World Young Explorer Foundation.

Your donation helps Young Explorers around the world.

Family Bowling

Registrations for Family Bowling are due at our next meeting. The event is from 6:00 p.m. to 8:00 p.m. at Lemont Lanes on Friday, December 14.

The fee is $7 per person and includes bowling and family-style buffet. Bumper lanes will be available for children ages seven-years-old and under.

Next Meeting

At our next meeting, we will be making sit-upons – to sit on at outdoor events when the ground is damp.

Current Schedule

Date	Time and Place	Activity
September 22 (Saturday)	10:00 a.m. to 3:00 p.m. at Camp Ottawa	Nature Exploration
September 24 (Monday)	4:30 p.m. to 6:00 p.m. at Mary's house	September Meeting
October 8 (Monday)	4:30 p.m. to 6:00 p.m. at Rita's house	October Meeting
October 20 (Saturday)	9:00 a.m. to 4:00 p.m. at Camp Ottawa	Fall Harvest Festival
October 22 (Monday)	4:30 p.m. to 6:00 p.m. at Mary's house	October Meeting
October 24 (Saturday)	10:00 a.m. at Peace Church	Picture Day

FIGURE 6-91

Cases and Places

The difficulty of these case studies varies:
▶ are the least difficult; ▶▶ are more difficult; and ▶▶▶ are the most difficult.

1 ▶ As your final project in CIS 144, you have been assigned the task of creating page WD 4.58 in this textbook. The page contains many desktop publishing elements: shading in the header and CASE PERSPECTIVE SUMMARY sections, extra space between characters in the CASE PERSPECTIVE SUMMARY, drop caps in the Project Summary and What You Should Know subheads, a variety of font sizes and font color, a paragraph border around the CASE PERSPECTIVE SUMMARY, and balanced columns in the What You Should Know section. You may need to resize and move the drop cap frame so it aligns properly with the subheads. To display the half moon bullets, click on the Customize button in the Bullets and Numbering dialog box. Click the Bullet button in the dialog box to locate the half moon bullet, and click the Font button in the dialog box to change the bullet color.

2 ▶▶ You are an editor of *Home Photography*, a one-page newsletter for amateur photographers. Last week's edition is shown in Figure 6-89 on page WD 6.64. The January 3rd edition is due out next Thursday. Your assignment is to decide on a feature article for the next edition of the *Home Photography* newsletter. Use your personal experiences as the basis for your feature article. Your article could address an item such as these: taking pictures, types of cameras, camera features, making photo albums, and so on. The newsletter should contain an appropriate photograph or clip art, a text box, or a pull-quote for the feature article. Enhance the newsletter with WordArt, color, ruling lines, and a page border using colors different from those used in Figure 6-89.

3 ▶▶ You are responsible for the monthly preparation of *Remodeling*, a one-page newsletter for club members. Last month's edition is shown in Figure 6-90 on page WD 6.65. The next edition is due out in two weeks. Your assignment is to decide on a feature article for the next edition of the newsletter. The feature article should address some aspect of remodeling. For example, your feature article could discuss remodeling tools, remodeling projects, remodeling tips, or any other remodeling topic that interests you. Visit a home improvement store for information for your article. The newsletter should contain an appropriate photograph or clip art, a text box, or a pull-quote for the feature article. Enhance the newsletter with WordArt, color, ruling lines, and a page border using colors different from those used in Figure 6-90.

4 ▶▶ You are the editor of *Young Explorers*, a one-page monthly newsletter for the parents of unit members. Last meeting's newsletter is shown in Figure 6-91. The next meeting is on September 24. Your assignment is to develop some announcements for the next meeting of the *Young Explorers*. Your announcements could address items such as these: upcoming events and activities, meeting plans, notices, and so on. The newsletter should contain an appropriate photograph or clip art, a text box, or a pull-quote for the feature article. Enhance the newsletter with WordArt, color, ruling lines, and a page border using colors different from those used in Figure 6-91.

Cases and Places

5 ▶▶▶ You are a member of your child's parent-teacher organization (PTO). The PTO has decided to publish a two-page monthly newsletter to be sent home with all children in the district. You must decide on a title for the newsletter. Your assignment is to design the newsletter and develop the first issue. The newsletter could include a feature article, announcements, information, notices, or other items of interest to parents. Visit a school in your district to obtain information about schools in the district. Use the Internet, school newsletters, PTO meeting minutes, school board meeting minutes, teacher interviews, and parent interviews for information on your article. Enhance the newsletter with WordArt, color, shading, ruling lines, and a page border. Use an appropriate graphic and a pull-quote in the newsletter.

6 ▶▶▶ You are a member of a restaurant and food review club. Because you have a background in desktop publishing, you prepare the monthly two-page newsletter for club members. Your assignment is to design the newsletter and develop the next issue. The newsletter should have a feature article and some announcements for club members. Your feature article could discuss/review a restaurant, a deli, an online or in town grocery store, a recipe, or any other aspect of food or food service. Use the Internet, visit a restaurant, interview restaurant or grocery store patrons, prepare a dish using a new recipe, and so on, to obtain information for the feature article. The feature article should span both pages of the newsletter and club announcements should be on the first page of the newsletter. Enhance the newsletter with WordArt, color, shading, ruling lines, and a page border. Use an appropriate graphic and a pull-quote in the newsletter.

Microsoft **Word 2000**

Microsoft Word 2000

Merging Form Letters to E-Mail Addresses Using an Access Table

In Project 5, Rosa Rodriguez contracted your services to create form letters notifying local residents of Eagle Run Golf Club's upcoming Grand Opening Celebration (see Figure 5-1 on page WD 5.5). Having completed these letters, you mention to Rosa that the form letters also can be e-mailed using Word – as long as you have e-mail addresses. Rosa asks Ahmed, her assistant, to locate a mailing list that contains e-mail addresses, as well as the name and address information for the form letters. Ahmed finds a Microsoft Access database containing the necessary information.

Word can use an Access database as a data source, providing the fields are set up to match the form letter fields. Because the database is missing the Student field, you explain to Ahmed how to add a new field to a database table and how to enter data into the field. Then, with your assistance, Ahmed sends the form letters to e-mail addresses using the Access database table.

To complete this Integration Feature, you will need the main document for the form letters created in Project 5. (If you did not create the form letters, see your instructor for a copy.)

Introduction

You learned in Project 5 that the basic content of a group of **form letters** is similar; however, items such as name, address, city, state, and postal code change from one letter to the next. Thus, form letters are personalized to the addressee.

The process of generating form letters involves creating a main document for the form letters and a data source, and then merging the two together into a series of individual letters. In Project 5, you set up a Word table as a data source. In addition to Word tables, you can use a Microsoft Outlook contact list, a Microsoft Excel worksheet, a Microsoft Access database table, or a text file as the data source for form letters.

In this Integration Feature, you open the Eagle Run Grand Opening main document file (Figure 1a on the next page). Then, you specify that you will use an Access database table (Figure 1b on the next page) as the data source. The database table, which contains an Email field, is located on the Data Disk. Next, you merge data from the Access database table into the main document, Eagle Run Grand Opening.

In Project 5, you learned that you can send merged documents to the printer or to a new document window. In this Integration Feature, you send the merged documents to e-mail addresses – attaching the form letter as a Word document to each e-mail message. This merge process creates a separate e-mail message for each person in the database table. Figure 1c on the next page shows the five e-mail messages created by this merge. Each message contains an icon that when opened, displays the merged document in a Word window.

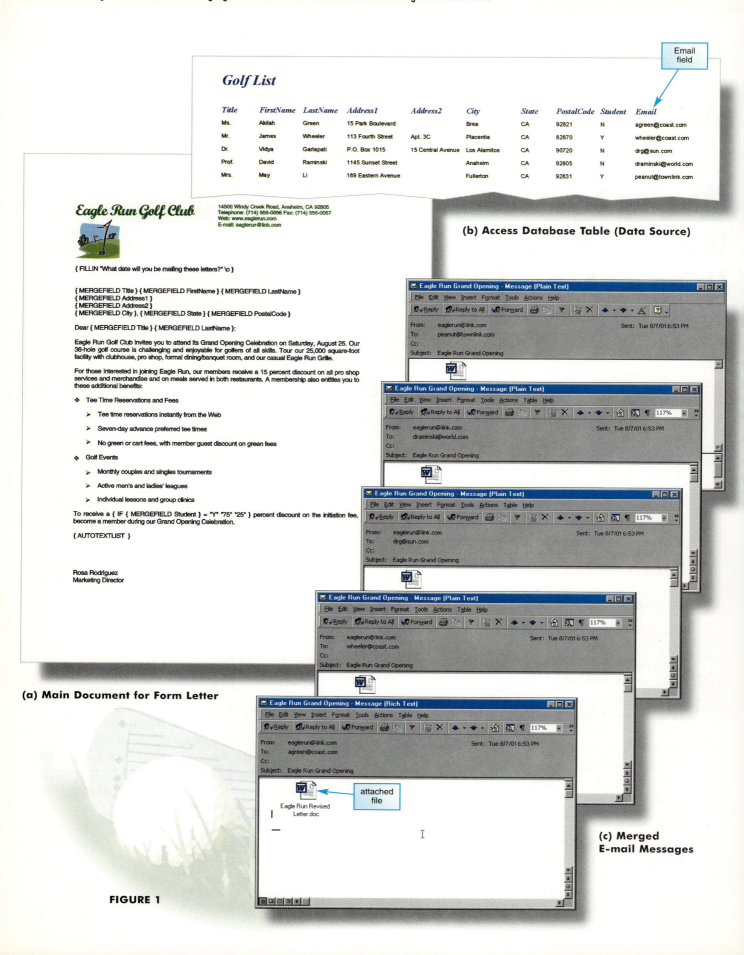

(a) Main Document for Form Letter

(b) Access Database Table (Data Source)

(c) Merged E-mail Messages

FIGURE 1

Unlinking a Field

The date line in the main document for the form letter currently is a Fill-in field. When you merge the letters, the Fill-in field instructs Word to display a dialog box requesting that you enter the date these letters will be mailed. In Project 5, you indicated that the question should display only once – at the beginning of the merge process. When you merge to e-mail addresses, Word asks the question for each record; thus, you should remove this field designation, or **unlink the field**, so that it displays as regular text.

Perform the following steps to unlink the Fill-in field.

TO UNLINK A FIELD

1 Start Word and then open the Eagle Run Grand Opening file created in Project 5. Reset your toolbars as described in Appendix C.

2 Click in the date field.

3 Press CTRL+SHIFT+F9. Click anywhere in the date field to remove the highlight.

Word removes the field designation from the date (Figure 2).

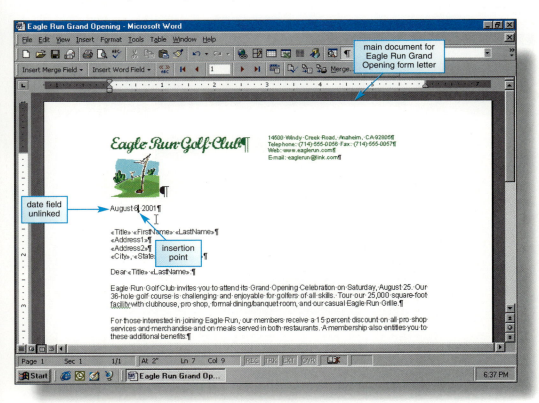

FIGURE 2

Changing the Data Source in a Form Letter

Currently, the data source for the Eagle Run Grand Opening form letter is a Word table that you saved in a file named Mailing List. The data source in this Integration Feature should be an Access database table.

Mailing Lists

For more information on mailing lists available for purchase or download, visit the Word 2000 More About Web page (www.scsite.com/wd2000/more.htm) and then click Mailing Lists.

A **database** is a collection of data organized in a manner that allows access, retrieval, and use of that data. **Database software**, also called a **database management system** (**DBMS**), allows you to create a computerized database; add, change, and delete data; sort and retrieve data from the database; and create forms and reports using the data.

Microsoft Access is database software included with Microsoft Office. In Access, a database consists of a collection of tables, organized in rows and columns. You have learned that a row in a table also is called a **record**; and a column in a table also is called a **field**.

The Access database you will use for this Integration Feature is called Golf Prospects and is located on the Data Disk. The table in the database that you will link to the form letters is called Golf List. If you did not download the Data Disk, see the inside back cover for instructions for downloading the Data Disk or see your instructor.

Perform the following steps to change the data source designation to an Access database table.

Steps To Change a Data Source Designation

① **Click the Mail Merge Helper button on the Mail Merge toolbar. Click the Get Data button and then point to Open Data Source (Figure 3).**

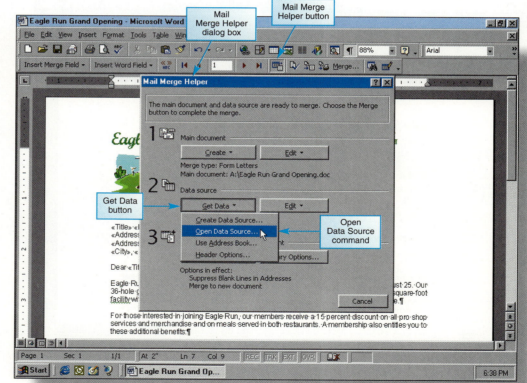

FIGURE 3

2 If necessary, insert the Data Disk into drive A. Click Open Data Source. If necessary, when the Open Data Source dialog box displays, change the Look in location to 3½ Floppy (A:). Click the Files of type box arrow and then click MS Access Databases. Click Golf Prospects in the Look in list and then point to the Open button in the Open Data Source dialog box.

Word displays the Open Data Source dialog box (Figure 4). The Access database you will use is named Golf Prospects.

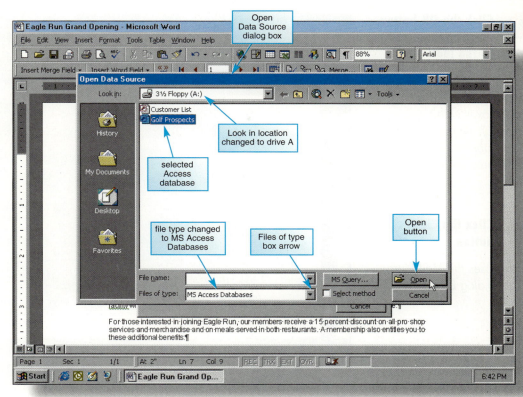

FIGURE 4

3 Click the Open button in the Open Data Source dialog box. If necessary, when the Microsoft Access dialog box displays, click the Tables tab. Click Golf List in the Tables in Golf Prospects list and then point to the OK button.

Word closes the Open Data Source dialog box and starts Microsoft Access; a Microsoft Access dialog box displays, listing the tables in the Golf Prospects database (Figure 5). You select the table to be linked to the form letter.

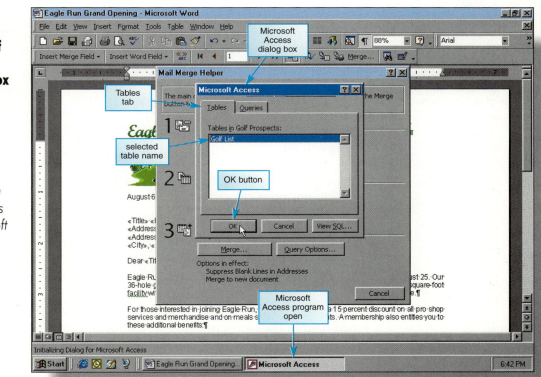

FIGURE 5

4 **Click the OK button. Point to the Close button in the Mail Merge Helper dialog box.**

The Mail Merge Helper dialog box is visible again (Figure 6). Word lists the Access table name as the data source for the form letters.

5 **Click the Close button.**

Word closes the Mail Merge Helper dialog box.

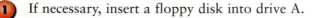

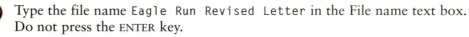

FIGURE 6

Other Ways

1. On Tools menu click Mail Merge, click Get Data button, click Open Data Source, select file type and file name, click Open button, click table name, click OK button, click Close button.

The Access table now is the data source for the form letter. To maintain the original form letter with the Word table as the data source, save this form letter with a new file name as described in the following steps.

TO SAVE THE FORM LETTER WITH A NEW FILE NAME

1 If necessary, insert a floppy disk into drive A.

2 Click File on the menu bar and then click Save As.

3 Type the file name `Eagle Run Revised Letter` in the File name text box. Do not press the ENTER key.

4 If necessary, click the Save in box arrow and then click 3½ Floppy (A:).

5 Click the Save button in the Save As dialog box.

Word saves the form letter on a floppy disk in drive A with the file name Eagle Run Revised Letter.

The next step is to merge the documents to the e-mail addresses specified in the Email field of the Golf List table.

Merging to E-Mail Addresses

When you merge to e-mail addresses, you can instruct Word to insert the merged document into the body of the e-mail message or to include the merged document as a separate Word document that is attached to each e-mail message. By sending the merged document as an attachment, you preserve all Word formatting. Thus, perform the following steps to merge the form letters to e-mail addresses, sending each merged document as an attachment to each e-mail message.

Steps **To Merge to E-Mail Addresses**

1 **Click the Merge button on the Mail Merge toolbar. When the Merge dialog box displays, point to the Merge to box arrow.**

Word displays the Merge dialog box (Figure 7).

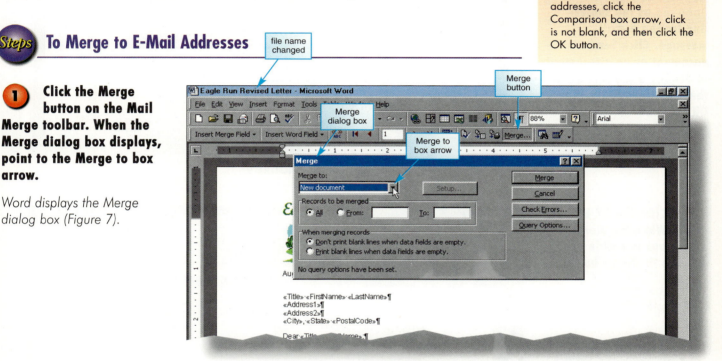

FIGURE 7

2 **Click the Merge to box arrow and then click Electronic mail. Point to the Setup button (Figure 8).**

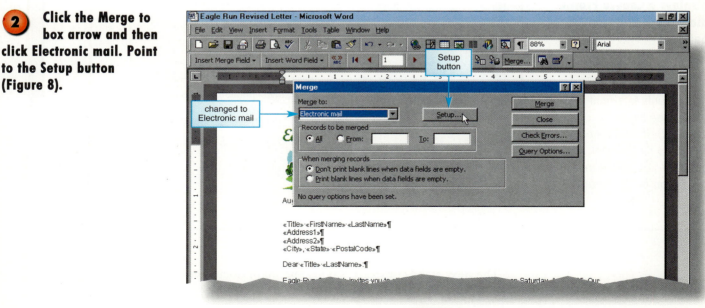

FIGURE 8

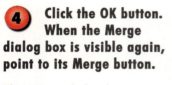 **Click the Setup button. When Word displays the Merge To Setup dialog box, click the Data field with Mail/Fax address box arrow. Scroll to and then click Email. Press the TAB key and then type** Eagle Run Grand Opening **as the subject line for the e-mail message. Click Send document as an attachment to display a check mark in the check box. Point to the OK button.**

Word displays the Merge To Setup dialog box (Figure 9).

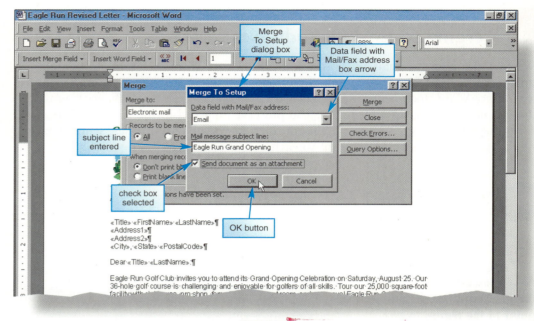

FIGURE 9

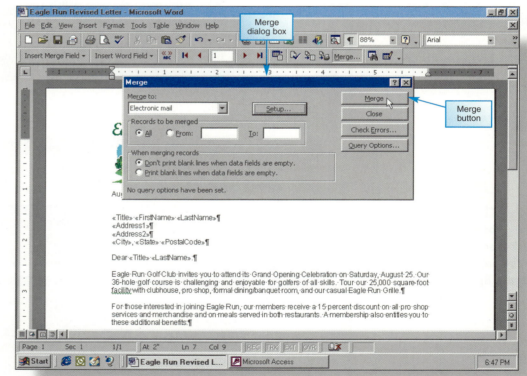

Click the OK button. When the Merge dialog box is visible again, point to its Merge button.

The Merge dialog box is visible again (Figure 10).

Click the Merge button in the Merge dialog box. If Word displays a Choose Profile dialog box, click the OK button.

Word merges the form letters and distributes them as attachments to e-mail messages (see Figure 1c on page WDI 1.2). If you are not connected to the Internet, Word connects you so the messages can be delivered.

FIGURE 10

The next steps consist of saving the main document again and then quitting Word.

TO SAVE THE MAIN DOCUMENT AGAIN

1 Click the Save button on the Standard toolbar.

Word saves the form letters with the name Eagle Run Revised Letter on a disk in drive A.

TO QUIT WORD

1 Click the Close button at the right edge of Word's title bar.

The Word window closes.

More About 2000

Quick Reference

For a table that lists how to complete the tasks covered in this book using the mouse, menu, shortcut menu, and keyboard, visit the Shelly Cashman Series Office Web page (www.scsite.com/off2000/qr.htm) and then click Microsoft Word 2000.

CASE PERSPECTIVE SUMMARY

To verify that the merge worked correctly, Ahmed added his own personal information as a record in the Access database table — which means he should have an e-mail message with the subject of Eagle Run Grand Opening in his Inbox. Ahmed starts Outlook and checks his messages. The announcement of the grand opening is there!

Ahmed is amazed at how easy it is to distribute form letters to e-mail addresses. He shows Rosa the e-mail message he sent himself. He informs Rosa that the announcement also has been e-mailed to all the people listed in the Golf List database table. She is impressed.

Integration Feature Summary

This Integration Feature introduced you to specifying an existing Access database as a data source. You also learned how to merge documents and distribute them to e-mail addresses as attachments to the e-mail messages.

More About 2000

Microsoft Certification

The Microsoft Office User Specialist (MOUS) Certification program provides an opportunity for you to obtain a valuable industry credential - proof that you have the Word 2000 skills required by employers. For more information, see Appendix D or visit the Shelly Cashman Series MOUS Web page at www.scsite.com/off2000/cert.htm.

In the Lab

1 Using an Access Database Table for a Merge

Problem: Marianne Pulaski, owner of Orland Flowers and Gifts, has an Access database table that she would like you to merge with the form letter shown in Figure 5-81 on page WD 5.59 in Project 5.

Instructions:

1. Open the document, Orland Flowers Holiday Special, on the Data Disk. If you did not download the Data Disk, see the inside back cover for instructions for downloading the Data Disk or see your instructor.
2. Using the Get Data button in the Mail Merge Helper dialog box, specify the data source as the database file called Customer List on the Data Disk. The table name is Customers.
3. Save the main document using Orland Flowers Revised Letter as the file name.
4. Merge the documents to the printer.

2 Distributing Form Letters to E-Mail Addresses

Problem: You created the form letter shown in Figure 5-82 on page WD 5.60 in Project 5. You decide to modify the Word data source to include e-mail addresses and then distribute the letter to the e-mail addresses.

Instructions:

1. Open the Taxton Welcome Letter shown in Figure 5-82. (If you did not create the form letter, see your instructor for a copy.)
2. Switch to the data source so that it displays as a Word table on the screen. Add a field called, Email, to the data source. Enter the following e-mail addresses: ramos@ocean.com, cw@eastern.com, van@worldwide.com, spelbring@somer.com, dawn@ocean.com. Add a row to the table containing your personal information. Save the revised data source with the file name Taxton New Students Revised.
3. Switch to the main document. Merge the form letters to the e-mail addresses, sending the letter as an attachment to the e-mail messages. Print the e-mail message that is delivered to your Inbox.
4. Save the main document using Taxton Revised Letter as the file name.

In the Lab

3 Creating an Access Table for a Merge to E-Mail Addresses

Problem: Robert Beatty, owner of Williams Landscaping, would like you to create an Access database table that he could merge with the form letter shown in Figure 5-84 on page WD 5.61 in Project 5.

Instructions:

1. Start Access. Create a database called Landscaping that contains a table called Landscaping Customers. The data for the table is shown in Figure 5-85 on page WD 5.62 in Project 5. Add an Email field with suitable e-mail adresses. Add a record to the table containing your personal information. You may need to use Help in Access to assist you in the procedure for creating and saving a database that contains a table. Save the table and then quit Access.
2. Start Word. Open the document, Williams Landscaping Form Letter, from your floppy disk. (If you did not create the form letter, see your instructor for a copy.)
3. Using the Get Data button in the Mail Merge Helper dialog box, specify the data source as the database file you created in Step 1.
4. Merge the form letters to the e-mail addresses, sending the letter as an attachment to the e-mail messages. Print the e-mail message that is delivered to your Inbox.
5. Save the main document using Williams Landscaping Revised Letter as the file name.

Microsoft **Word 2000**

Microsoft Word 2000

Microsoft Word 2000

P R O J E C T

7

Working with a Master Document, an Index, and a Table of Contents

O B J E C T I V E S

You will have mastered the material in this project when you can:

- Insert, modify, review, and delete comments
- Track changes in a document
- Save multiple versions of a document
- Accept and reject tracked changes
- Embed an Excel worksheet into a Word document
- Add and modify a caption
- Create a cross-reference
- Mark index entries
- Keep paragraphs together
- Password-protect a document
- Work with a master document and subdocuments
- Create and modify an outline
- Add an AutoShape
- Group drawing objects
- Create a table of figures
- Build and modify an index
- Create and modify a table of contents
- Add a bookmark
- Create alternating headers
- Set a gutter margin
- Use the Document Map

Hot Topics

So Many Papers, So Many Styles

Assistive Technology for Special Education. History and Myth. Journalism Ethics. Healthcare Reform. Internet Issues. All of these topics and many more may be the subject of one of your next papers. Depending on your course of study, you are likely to encounter a variety of styles from a number of established documentation sources that will direct you in the composition of research papers, reports, and reference documents. In Project 7, you will use Word 2000 to produce a reference document titled Computer Security containing multiple pages, a table of contents, a table of figures, and an index.

After selecting a topic, the work begins: researching your subject, finding reference materials, taking notes, and outlining. Then you write a series of drafts, check language and style, and rewrite the final paper, and maybe more than once! To ensure that the reader of your paper can navigate easily, you need a table of contents and an index. It is a good habit to verify your references and make certain that all your sources are given the appropriate credit. The citation procedure may seem tedious, but it is the way your readers know how to find additional information on the subjects and the way you

ultiple pages

le of contents

ble of figures

index

reference documents

ethically give credit to the individuals who have researched these topics before you.

Finally, you must consider the type of binding. You do not want your hard work misplaced or lost. Although folders or other kinds of binders are a nice final addition, some instructors have certain preferences for handing in your completed work, and you always should be aware of their requirements.

In academia, three major style systems for writers of research and scientific papers generally are recognized. Scholars in the humanities fields use The Modern Language Association (MLA). The MLA style is organized in the *MLA Handbook for Writers of Research Papers*. Researchers in the social sciences use another popular style developed by the American Psychological Association (APA). The APA style is documented in the *Publication Manual of the American Psychological Association*. The third style is the number system used by the Council of Biology Editors (CBE). The CBE manual, *Scientific Style and Format*, describes the citation-sequence system

and the name-year system used by writers in the applied sciences.

Writers also consult other style handbooks such as *The Chicago Manual of Style*, the *American Chemical Society Handbook for Authors*, the *Microsoft Manual of Style for Technical Writers*, and others.

Teams of instructors and scholars develop the style guidelines in each of these major publications. The *MLA Handbook*, for example, originated in 1951 for MLA members, and later was expanded to become a guide for undergraduates. Subsequent revisions are published on a regular basis. The MLA makes the guide available on the Internet, which includes up-to-date conventions for documenting sources on the World Wide Web. You can visit MLA online (www.mla.org).

Keeping up with the latest revisions can be a challenge for both the developers of the guides and the individuals who need to access them for their academic, professional, or personal use. With the vast amount of information available on the Web, however, it is easy to find a host of tips and suggestions that can provide documentation, resource directories, topics, ideas, assistance, and more. For additional information, visit the Word 2000 More About Web page (www.scsite.com/wd2000/more.htm).

Microsoft Word 2000

Working with a Master Document, an Index, and a Table of Contents

P R O J E C T

7

C A S E   P E R S P E C T I V E

Textbooks Press is an international company that publishes college textbooks. Personnel director, Marge Bauer, strongly believes that a company's success depends on solid communications with and among employees. To this end, Marge has implemented a variety of strategies aimed at improving employee relations. One of these, a multipage reference document, called the Employee Information and Guidelines (EIG), is distributed to all employees. Employees at Textbooks Press find the EIG documents extremely valuable, ranging from topics covering employee behavior to ethical activities to technical skills. Suggestions, however, have been made that the EIG documents be more organized including items such as a table of contents and index.

Employees in the personnel department assemble these documents, often with assistance from employees in other departments. In coordinating all the comments and edits of these documents, Marge has noticed a lot of inefficiencies. As a part-time computer specialist at Textbooks Press, you have been assigned the task of redesigning the production of the EIG documents.

Introduction

During the course of your academic studies and professional endeavors, you may find it necessary to compose a document that is many pages in length or even one that is hundreds of pages. When composing a long document, you must ensure that the document is organized so that a reader easily can locate material within the document. Sometimes a document of this nature is called a **reference document**.

By placing a table of contents at the beginning of the document and an index at the end, you help a reader navigate through a long document. If a document contains several illustrations, each illustration should have a caption. Also, the illustrations could be listed in a table, called a table of figures, that identifies the location of each figure in the document. For long documents that will be viewed online, you should incorporate hyperlinks so that a user can click the link to jump from one portion of the document to another.

Project Seven — Master Document, Index, and Table of Contents

Project 7 uses Word to produce the reference document shown in Figure 7-1. The document, called the Employee Information and Guidelines (EIG) #22, is distributed to all employees at Textbooks Press. Notice that the inner margin between facing pages has extra space to allow duplicated copies of the documents to be bound – without the binding covering the words.

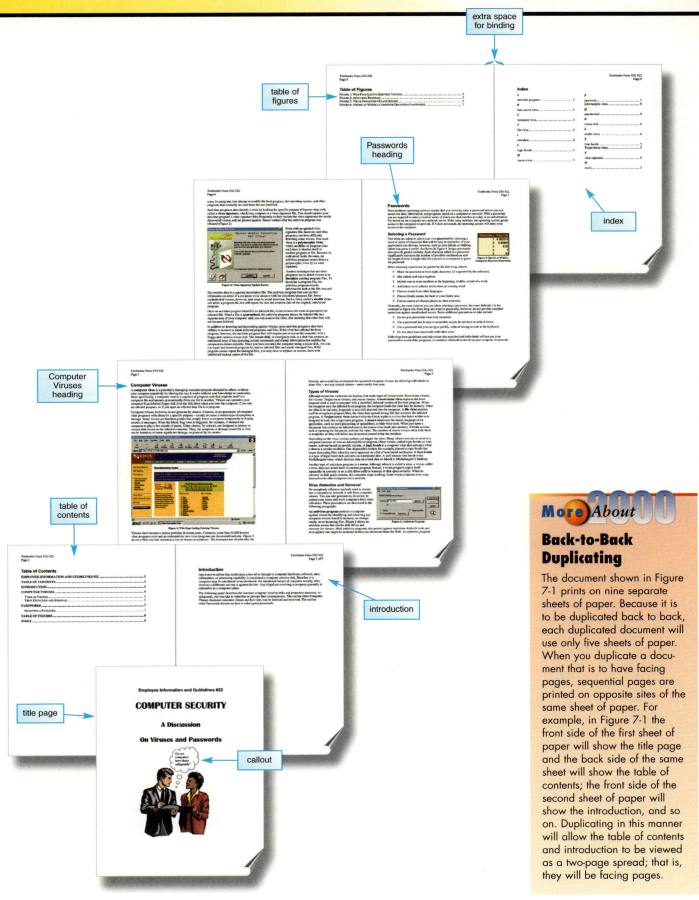

FIGURE 7-1

extra space for binding

table of figures

Passwords heading

index

Computer Viruses heading

table of contents

introduction

title page

callout

Back-to-Back Duplicating

The document shown in Figure 7-1 prints on nine separate sheets of paper. Because it is to be duplicated back to back, each duplicated document will use only five sheets of paper. When you duplicate a document that is to have facing pages, sequential pages are printed on opposite sites of the same sheet of paper. For example, in Figure 7-1 the front side of the first sheet of paper will show the title page and the back side of the same sheet will show the table of contents; the front side of the second sheet of paper will show the introduction, and so on. Duplicating in this manner will allow the table of contents and introduction to be viewed as a two-page spread; that is, they will be facing pages.

More About 2000

Reference Documents

For a sample reference document on the Web that contains elements commonly found in long documents, visit the Word 2000 More About Web page (www.scsite.com/wd2000/more.htm) and then click Sample Reference Document.

The EIG #22 document begins with a title page. The callout on the title page is designed to entice the receiver to open the document and read it. Next is the table of contents, followed by an introduction. The document then discusses two issues: computer viruses and passwords. At the end of the document is a table of figures and an index to assist a reader in locating information. A miniature version of the EIG #22 document is shown in Figure 7-1; for a more readable view, visit www.scsite.com/wd2000/project7.htm.

The personnel department has asked employees in the information systems department to write the content for the computer viruses and passwords sections of the document and then e-mail the files for inclusion in EIG #22. Jean, a systems analyst in the information systems department, has e-mailed the completed Computer Viruses file to the personnel department. Jeff, an IS auditor, has written a first draft of the passwords section and e-mailed it to his boss, Carlos, for review. After Jeff receives it back from Carlos, he will make any necessary adjustments to the document and then e-mail it to the personnel department.

The personnel department will incorporate the two completed files, Computer Viruses and Passwords, into a single file. They will create a title page, table of contents, introduction, table of figures, and index so the document is organized.

The following pages explain how Carlos reviews the document, how Jeff modifies it, and how the personnel department assembles the final document. For purposes of this project, certain files that are e-mailed to various people or departments are included on the Data Disk. If you did not download the Data Disk, see the inside back cover for instructions for downloading the Data Disk or see your instructor.

Starting Word

Follow these steps to start Word or ask your instructor how to start Word for your system.

TO START WORD

1 Click the Start button on the taskbar.

2 Click New Office Document on the Start menu. If necessary, click the General tab when the New Office Document dialog box displays.

3 Double-click the Blank Document icon in the General sheet.

4 If the Word window is not maximized, double-click its title bar to maximize it. Click View on the menu bar and then click Print Layout. If the Office Assistant displays, right-click it and then click Hide on the shortcut menu.

Office starts Word. After a few moments, an empty document titled Document1 displays in the Word window. Because this project uses floating graphics, you will use print layout view; thus, the Print Layout View button on the horizontal scroll bar is recessed.

Resetting Menus and Toolbars

To set the menus and toolbars so they appear exactly as shown in this book, you should reset your menus and toolbars as outlined in Appendix C or follow these steps.

TO RESET MENUS AND TOOLBARS

1 Click View on the menu bar and then point to Toolbars. Click Customize on the Toolbars submenu.

2 When the Customize dialog box displays, click the Options tab, make sure the top three check boxes have check marks and then click the Reset my usage data button. When the Microsoft Word dialog box displays, click the Yes button.

3 Click the Toolbars tab. Click Standard in the Toolbars list and then click the Reset button. When the Reset Toolbar dialog box displays, click the OK button.

4 Click Formatting in the Toolbars list and then click the Reset button. When the Reset Toolbar dialog box displays, click the OK button. Click the Close button.

Word resets the menus and toolbars.

Displaying Formatting Marks

It is helpful to display formatting marks that indicate where in the document you pressed the ENTER key, SPACEBAR, and other keys. Follow this step to display formatting marks.

TO DISPLAY FORMATTING MARKS

1 Double-click the move handle on the left side of the Standard toolbar to display the entire toolbar. If the Show/Hide ¶ button on the Standard toolbar is not recessed already, click it.

Word displays formatting marks in the document window, and the Show/Hide ¶ button on the Standard toolbar is recessed.

Reviewing a Document

Jeff, the IS auditor in the Information Systems department at Textbooks Press, has written a first draft of the section of the EIG #22 document that is to discuss passwords. He has e-mailed this draft to his supervisor, Carlos, for review. After reading through the Passwords Draft file, Carlos has some suggested changes.

Carlos could print a copy of the document and write his suggested changes using proofreader's revision marks as shown in Figure 7-2a on the next page. Instead of writing his suggestions on the printed draft copy, however, Carlos plans to use Word's **change-tracking feature** and enter his suggested changes directly into the document. Then, Jeff can choose to accept or reject each of the changes online. As a comparison, Figure 7-2b on the next page shows the final copy of the Passwords file, after Jeff reviews the changes suggested by Carlos and modifies the document accordingly. When comparing Figures 7-2a and 7-2b, you will notice that Jeff makes most of the changes suggested by Carlos.

The following pages illustrate the change-tracking feature of Word.

More About

Proofreading Marks

For more information on marks and abbreviations used by proofreaders, visit the Word 2000 More About Web page (www.scsite.com/wd2000/more.htm) and then click Proofreading Marks.

Passwords

Most multiuser operating systems require that you correctly enter a password before you can access the data, information, and programs stored on a computer or network. With a password, you are required to enter a word or series of characters that matches an entry in an authorization file stored on the computer or a network server. If the entry matches, the operating system grants access to the computer or network. If it does not match, the operating system will deny your access to the computer.

Selecting a Password

You often are asked to select your own **password** by choosing a word or series of characters that will be easy to remember. If your password is too obvious, however, such as your initials or birthday, others can guess it easily. As shown in Figure 1, longer passwords also provide greater security. Each character added to a password significantly increases the number of possible combinations and the length of time it might take for a person or a computer to guess the password.

Characters	Seconds
1	0.000018
2	0.00065
3	0.02
4	1
5	30

Figure 1: Speeds at Which a Computer Discovers Passwords

When choosing a password, be guided by the following criteria:

- Make the password at least eight characters (if supported by the software).
- Mix initials and dates together.
- Include one or more numbers at the beginning, middle, or end of a word.
- Add letters to or subtract letters from an existing word.
- Choose words from other languages.
- Choose family names far back in your family tree.
- Choose names of obscure places in other countries.

Generally, the more creative you are when selecting a password, the more difficult it is for someone to figure out. Even long and creative passwords, however, do not provide complete ~~protection against unauthorized~~ access. Some additional precautions to take include:

- ~~Do not post passwords~~ near your computer.
- ~~Use a password that is~~ easy to remember so you do not have to write it down.
- ~~Use a password that~~ you can type quickly, without having to look at the keyboard.
- ~~Do not share your pass~~words with other users.

~~Following these guidelines ca~~n help ensure that unauthorized individuals will not use your ~~password to access data, prog~~rams, or sensitive information stored on your computer or network.

(b) Final Version of Passwords File

Passwords

Most multiuser operating systems require that you correctly enter a password before you can access the data, information, and programs stored on a computer or network. With a password, you are required to enter a word or series of characters that matches an entry in an authorization file stored on the computer or a network server. If the entry matches, the operating system grants access to the computer or network. If it does not match, the operating system will deny your access to the computer.

Selecting a Password

remember

insert chart here

You often are asked to select your own password by choosing a word or series of characters that will be easy to ~~learn by heart.~~ If your password is too obvious, however, such as your initials or birthday, others can guess it easily. Longer passwords also provide greater security. Each character added to a password significantly increases the number of possible combinations and the length of time it might take for a person or a computer to guess the password.

When choosing a password, be guided by the following criteria: *or more*

- Make the password at least eight characters (if supported by the software).
- Mix initials and dates together.
- Include one or more numbers at the beginning, middle, or end of a word.
- Add letters to or subtract letters from an existing word.
- Choose words from other languages.
- Choose family names far back in your family tree.
- Choose names of obscure places in other countries.

Generally, the more creative you are when selecting a password, the more difficult it is for someone to figure out. Even long and creative passwords, however, do not provide complete protection against unauthorized access. Some additional precautions to take include:

- Do not post passwords near your computer.
- Use a password that is easy to remember so you do not have to write it down.
- Use a password that you can type quickly, without having to look at the keyboard.
- Do not share your passwords with other users.

Following these guidelines can help ensure that unauthorized individuals will not use your password to access data, programs, or sensitive information stored on your computer or network.

FIGURE 7-2

(a) Draft of Passwords File with Suggested Changes

Opening a Document

The first step in reviewing a document is to open it. Carlos is to review the Passwords Draft file that Jeff has completed. For purposes of this book, the Passwords Draft file that Carlos is to review is located on the Data Disk. If you did not download the Data Disk, see the inside back cover for instructions for downloading the Data Disk or see your instructor.

Open the Passwords Draft file as described in the steps below.

TO OPEN A DOCUMENT

1 If necessary, insert the Data Disk into drive A. Click the Open button on the Standard toolbar.

2 When the Open dialog box displays, if necessary, click the Look in box arrow and then click 3½ Floppy (A:). Click Passwords Draft.

3 Click the Open button in the Open dialog box.

Word opens the Passwords Draft file and displays it in the Word window.

Saving the Document with a New Name

To preserve the contents of the original Passwords Draft file, save a copy of it with a new name as described in the following steps.

TO SAVE A DOCUMENT WITH A NEW FILE NAME

1 With a floppy disk in drive A, click File on the menu bar and then click Save As.

2 Type Passwords in the File name text box. Do not press the ENTER key.

3 If necessary, click the Save in box arrow and then click 3½ Floppy (A:).

4 Click the Save button in the Save As dialog box.

Word saves the document on a floppy disk in drive A with the file name Passwords (see Figure 7-3 on the next page).

Zooming Text Width

When you zoom text width, Word displays text on the screen as large as possible in print layout view without extending the right margin beyond the right edge of the document window. Perform the following steps to zoom text width.

TO ZOOM TEXT WIDTH

1 Click the Zoom box arrow on the Standard toolbar.

2 Click Text Width in the Zoom list.

Word places the right margin at the right edge of the document window. Word computes the zoom percentage based on a variety of settings. Your percentage may be different.

Microsoft **Word 2000**

More About 2000

Comments

If you have a pen-equipped computer, you can insert pen comments that become drawing objects in the document. Likewise, if your computer has a microphone and sound card, you can record voice comments that are attached to the document as recordings.

Inserting Comments

A **comment**, or annotation, is a note inserted into a document that does not affect the text of the document. Reviewers often use comments to communicate suggestions, tips, and other messages to the author of a document. For example, Carlos believes that the last sentence in the first paragraph below the Selecting a Password heading would have more impact if it referenced a table. Perform the following steps to insert a comment of this nature into the document.

Steps To Insert a Comment

1 Select the text on which you wish to comment (in this case, the last sentence of the first paragraph below the Selecting a Password heading). Click Insert on the menu bar and then point to Comment (Figure 7-3).

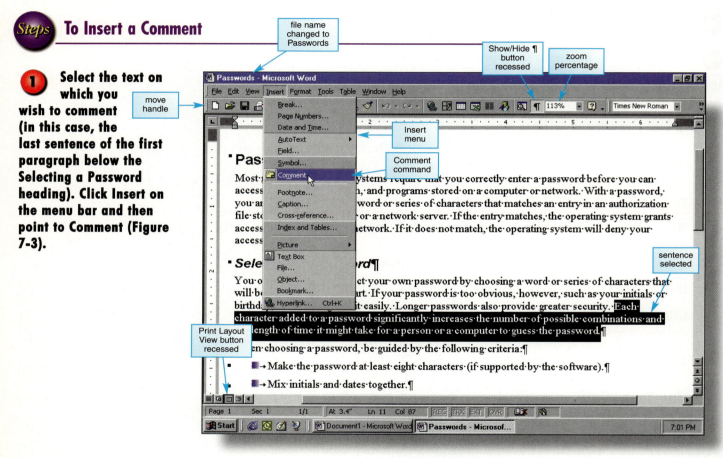

FIGURE 7-3

2 **Click Comment.**

Word opens a comment pane in the lower portion of the Word window and highlights in yellow the selected text in the document window (Figure 7-4). The insertion point is positioned in the comment pane to the right of the comment reference mark, which contains the reviewer's initials followed by the comment number. The comment reference mark also displays in the document window to the right of the selected text. Your reviewer initials will differ from this figure.

Passwords - Microsoft Word

File Edit View Insert Format Tools Table Window Help

Times New Roman   100%

Most multiuser operating systems require that you correctly enter a password before you can access the data, information, and programs stored on a computer or network. With a password, you are required to enter a word or series of characters that matches an entry in an authorization file stored on the computer or a network server. If the entry matches, the operating system grants access to the computer or network. If it does not match, the operating system will deny your access to the computer. ¶

■ *Selecting a Password*¶

You often are asked to select your own password by choosing a word or series of characters that will be easy to learn by heart. If your password is too obvious, however, such as your initials or birthday, others can guess it easily. Longer passwords also provide greater security. Each character added to a password significantly increases the number of possible combinations and the length of time it might take for a person or a computer to guess the password.[CDG1]¶

When choosing a password, be guided by the following criteria:¶

selected text highlighted in light yellow

insertion point

comment pane

Comments From: All Reviewers   Close

[CDG1]¶

comment reference mark displays in document window and comment pane

Page   Sec 1   At   Ln   OVR

Start   Document1 - Micros...   Microsof...   7:01 PM

FIGURE 7-4

3 **Press the SPACEBAR. Type** I suggest you insert a table here to emphasize the importance of this sentence. **Point to the Close button in the comment pane (Figure 7-5).**

4 **Click the Close button.**

Word closes the comment pane.

Most multiuser operating systems require that you correctly enter a password before you can access the data, information, and programs stored on a computer or network. With a password, you are required to enter a word or series of characters that matches an entry in an authorization file stored on the computer or a network server. If the entry matches, the operating system grants access to the computer or network. If it does not match, the operating system will deny your access to the computer. ¶

■ *Selecting a Password*¶

You often are asked to select your own password by choosing a word or series of characters that will be easy to learn by heart. If your password is too obvious, however, such as your initials or birthday, others can guess it easily. Longer passwords also provide greater security. Each character added to a password significantly increases the number of possible combinations and the length of time it might take for a person or a computer to guess the password.[CDG1]¶

When choosing a password, be guided by the following criteria:¶

Comments From: All Reviewers   Close

[CDG1] I suggest you insert a table here to emphasize the importance of this sentence.¶

Close button removes comment pane from screen

comment pane scroll arrows

comment entered

Page   Sec 1   At   Ln   Col 82   REC TRK EXT OVR

Start   Document1 - Microsoft Word   Passwords - Microsof...   7:02 PM

FIGURE 7-5

Other Ways

1. Click Insert Comment button on Reviewing toolbar

When Word closes the comment pane and returns to the document window, the comment disappears from the screen. If, when you close the comment pane, the comment reference mark does not display in the document window, click the Show/Hide ¶ button on the Standard toolbar. As with footnotes, if you point to the comment reference mark, Word displays the comment and the name of the comment's author above the comment reference mark as a ScreenTip.

Word uses predefined settings for the reviewer initials that display in the comment pane and the document window. If the initials that display are not correct, you can change them by clicking Tools on the menu bar, clicking Options, clicking the User Information tab, entering correct initials in the Initials text box, and then clicking the OK button.

Instead of selecting text on which you wish to comment (as shown in Step 1 on page WD 7.10), you simply can click at the location where you want to insert the comment. In this case, only the word next to the insertion point is highlighted.

Word sequentially numbers each additional comment you insert into a document. Notice that the comment reference mark contains the reviewer's initials. Thus, you can determine the writer of a comment when multiple reviewers insert comments into the same document. Also, each reviewer's comments are highlighted in a different color to visually help you differentiate reviewer's comments.

You modify comments using the comment pane at the bottom of the Word window. To display the comments in the comment pane, double-click the comment reference mark in the document window, or click View on the menu bar and then click Comments, or click the Edit Comment button on the Reviewing toolbar. Edit the comment as you would any Word text and then click the Close button in the comment pane.

When you print a document, comments normally do not print. If you want them to print along with the document, click File on the menu bar, click Print, click the Options button, place a check mark in the Comments check box, and then click the OK button twice. If you want to print the comments only (without printing the document), click File on the menu bar, click Print, click the Print what box arrow, click Comments, and then click the OK button.

The next step is to track changes while editing the document.

Tracking Changes

Carlos has two suggested changes for the Passwords document: (1) change the phrase, learn by heart, to the word, remember, and (2) insert the words, or more, between the words, eight characters. To track changes in a document, you turn on the change-tracking feature by double-clicking the TRK status indicator on the status bar. When you edit a document that has the change-tracking feature enabled, Word marks all text or graphics that you insert, delete, or modify. Thus, an author can identify the changes a reviewer has made by looking at the revision marks in the document. The author also has the ability to accept or reject any change that a reviewer has made to a document.

The following pages illustrate how a reviewer tracks changes to a document and then how the author reviews the tracked changes made to the document.

The Reviewing Toolbar

To display the Reviewing toolbar, click View on the menu bar, point to Toolbars, and then click Reviewing. The Reviewing toolbar contains buttons that enable you to work with comments, tracked changes, highlighting, and document versions.

Color of Tracked Changes

If multiple reviewers track changes to a document, the changes of each reviewer are marked in a different color. To change the color or other aspects of reviewer marks, right-click the TRK status indicator on the status bar, click Options on the shortcut menu, adjust settings in the Track Changes dialog box, and then click the OK button.

To Track Changes

1 **Double-click the TRK status indicator on the status bar.**

Word darkens the characters in the TRK status indicator on the status bar (Figure 7-6).

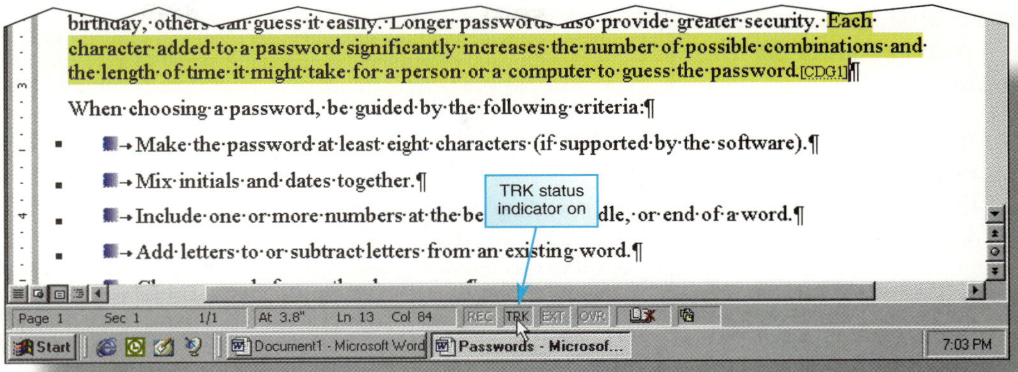

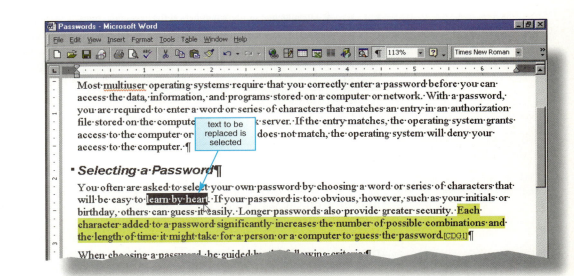

FIGURE 7-6

2 **Select the text, learn by heart (Figure 7-7).**

FIGURE 7-7

3 **With the text still selected, type** remember **as the replacement text.**

Word marks the selection, learn by heart, as deleted, and marks the word, remember, as inserted (Figure 7-8). Deleted text displays in color with a horizontal line through it, called a **strikethrough**, *and inserted text displays in color and underlined.*

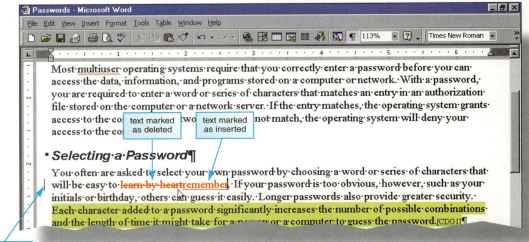

FIGURE 7-8

4   **Click to the left of the first letter c in the word, characters, in the first bulleted item. Type** or more **and then press the SPACEBAR.**

Word marks the inserted text, or more, as inserted (Figure 7-9). That is, it displays in color and underlined.

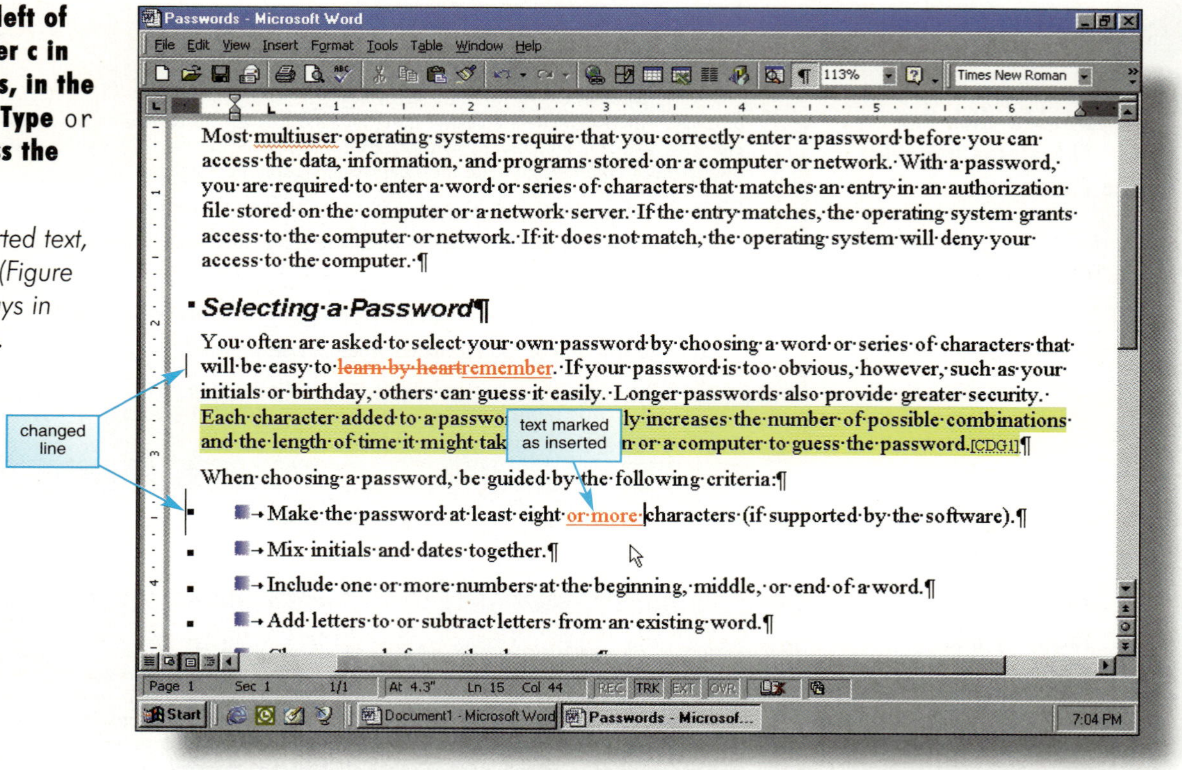

changed line

text marked as inserted

FIGURE 7-9

If the tracked changes do not display on your screen, right-click the TRK status indicator on the status bar, click Highlight Changes, place a check mark in the Highlight changes on screen check box, and then click the OK button.

Notice in Figure 7-9 that Word places a **changed line** at the left edge of each line that contains a tracked change. These changed lines, along with the strikethrough for deleted text and the underline for inserted text, are called **revision marks**.

As with comments, if you point to a tracked change, Word displays a ScreenTip that identifies the reviewer's name and the type of change made by that reviewer.

The next step is to turn off the change-tracking feature, as described in the following step.

TO STOP TRACKING CHANGES

1   Double-click the TRK status indicator on the status bar.

Word dims the characters in the TRK indicator on the status bar (see Figure 7-10).

Comparing Documents

If a reviewer does not remember to use the change-tracking feature while editing a document, you can have Word compare the reviewer's document to your original document. In doing so, Word uses revision marks to mark all differences between the two documents – which you can accept or reject later. To compare two documents, open the reviewer's document, click Tools on the menu bar, point to Track Changes, click Compare Documents, and then open your original document.

More *About* **2000**

Tracked Changes

To display or print a document with tracked changes showing, right-click the TRK status indicator on the status bar, click Highlight Changes on the shortcut menu, place a check mark in the appropriate check box, and then click the OK button. If you remove the check marks from the check boxes, Word displays and prints the document as if all changes were accepted.

Saving Multiple Versions of a Document

When Jeff receives the reviewed document from Carlos via e-mail, he wants to preserve a copy of the document that contains the tracked changes. Instead of saving it with a new file name, he opts to save a separate version of the document. Using the version feature saves disk space because Word only saves changes among versions – as opposed to a complete copy of the file. The downside is that you cannot modify a version; you only can open and print versions.

When you save a version of a document, you insert a description of the version so you can identify it at a later time. The version represents the current state, or snapshot, of the document.

For purposes of this project, you will save a version of the Passwords document that is on your disk. Perform the following steps to save a version of a document.

More About

Versions

To automatically save a version of a document when you close the document, click File on the menu bar, click Versions, place a check mark in the Automatically save a version on close check box, and then click the Close button.

Steps **To Save a Version of a Document**

1 **Click File on the menu bar and then point to Versions (Figure 7-10).**

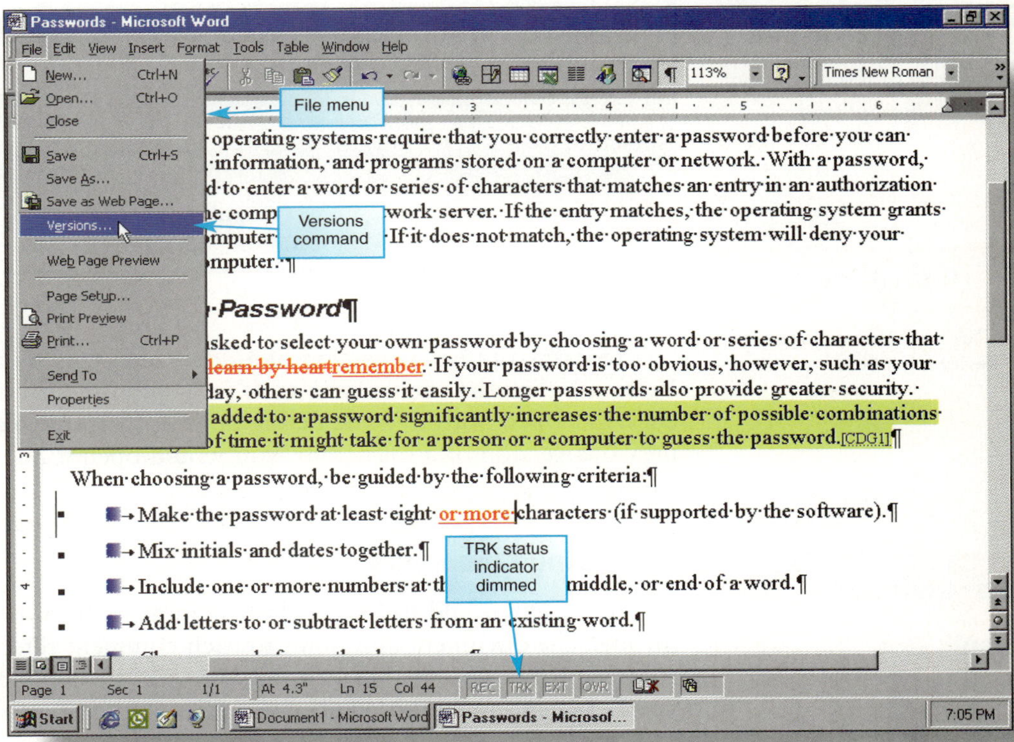

FIGURE 7-10

2 Click Versions. When the Versions in Passwords dialog box displays, click the Save Now button. When Word displays the Save Version dialog box, type Contains comments and tracked changes from Carlos. Point to the OK button.

Word displays the Versions in Passwords dialog box, followed by the Save Version dialog box (Figure 7-11).

3 Click the OK button.

Word saves the current state of the document along with the entered comment.

FIGURE 7-11

To open a previous version of a document, click File on the menu bar, click Versions, click the version you wish to open in the Existing versions list, and then click the Open button in the dialog box. If, for some reason, you wanted to edit a previous version of a document, you would open it and then save it with a new file name.

Reviewing Comments

Next, Jeff would like to read the comments from Carlos. You could scroll through the document and point to each comment reference mark to read the comments, but you might overlook one or more comments using this technique. A more efficient method is to use the Reviewing toolbar as shown in the following steps.

More About

Displaying Comments

If a comment's text does not display in a ScreenTip when you point to the comment reference mark or if the comment is not highlighted in yellow, click Tools on the menu bar, click Options, click the View tab, place a check mark in the ScreenTips check box, and then click the OK button.

Steps: To Review Comments

1 If the Reviewing toolbar does not display on your screen, click **View** on the menu bar, point to **Toolbars**, and then click **Reviewing**. Press **CTRL+HOME** to position the insertion point at the top of the document. Point to the Next Comment button on the Reviewing toolbar.

With the insertion point at the top of the document, the review of comments will begin at the top of the document (Figure 7-12).

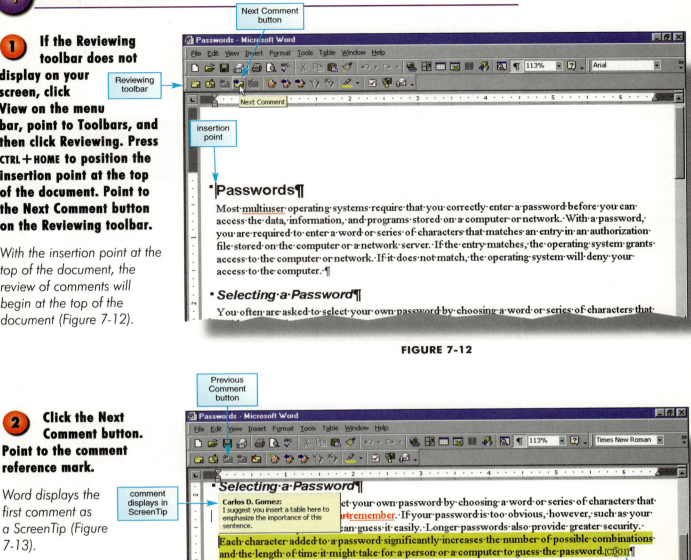

Next Comment button

Reviewing toolbar

Next Comment

insertion point

Passwords¶

Most multiuser operating systems require that you correctly enter a password before you can access the data, information, and programs stored on a computer or network. With a password, you are required to enter a word or series of characters that matches an entry in an authorization file stored on the computer or a network server. If the entry matches, the operating system grants access to the computer or network. If it does not match, the operating system will deny your access to the computer. ¶

Selecting a Password¶

You often are asked to select your own password by choosing a word or series of characters that

FIGURE 7-12

2 Click the Next Comment button. Point to the comment reference mark.

Word displays the first comment as a ScreenTip (Figure 7-13).

Previous Comment button

comment displays in ScreenTip

Selecting a Password¶

ct your own password by choosing a word or series of characters that

Carlos D. Gomez:
I suggest you insert a table here to emphasize the importance of this sentence.

remember. If your password is too obvious, however, such as your can guess it easily. Longer passwords also provide greater security.

Each character added to a password significantly increases the number of possible combinations and the length of time it might take for a person or a computer to guess the password.[CDG1]¶

When choosing a password, be guided by the following criteria:¶

■→ Make the password at least eight or more characters (if supported by the softw

comment reference mark

FIGURE 7-13

If the document contains multiple comments, you would click the Next Comment button on the Reviewing toolbar to display each subsequent comment. You also can click the Previous Comment button to display a comment earlier in the document.

Deleting Comments

After you have finished reviewing a comment, you can remove it from the document. When you delete a comment, Word automatically renumbers all remaining comments.

Other Ways

1. Scroll through document and point to comment reference mark
2. On Select Browse Object menu, click Comments
3. On File menu click Print, click Print what box arrow, click Comments, click OK button

You delete comments from the document window, not from the comment pane. To delete a comment, you first move the insertion point to it. Then, perform the following step to delete the comment.

Steps **To Delete a Comment**

1 With the insertion point at the beginning of the yellow highlight of the comment to delete, click the Delete Comment button on the Reviewing toolbar.

Word removes the comment from the document (Figure 7-14).

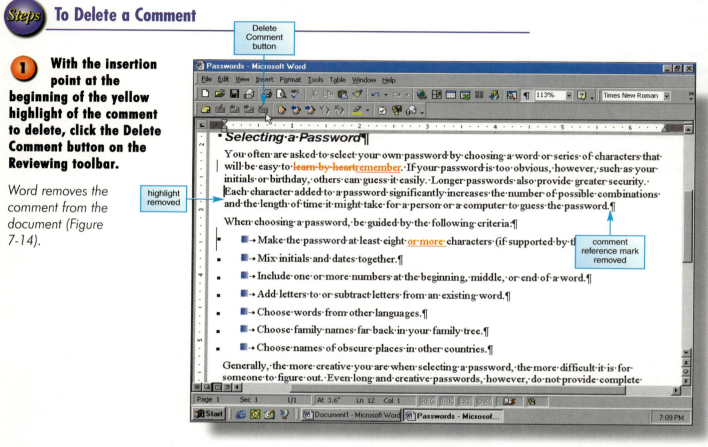

FIGURE 7-14

Other Ways

1. Right-click the comment reference mark, click Delete Comment on shortcut menu

If, when you attempt to delete a comment, the Delete Comment button is dimmed, you need to go to the comment by clicking the Next Comment or Previous Comment button on the Reviewing toolbar.

Reviewing Tracked Changes

The next step for Jeff is to review the changes made by Carlos and decide if he wants to accept or reject them. To do this, be sure the revision marks display on the screen. If they do not, right-click the TRK status indicator on the status bar, click Highlight Changes on the shortcut menu, be sure the Highlight changes on screen check box contains a check mark, and then click the OK button. With the revision marks displaying on the screen, perform the following steps to review the tracked changes.

To Review Tracked Changes

1 **Press CTRL + HOME. Right-click the TRK status indicator on the status bar. Point to Accept or Reject Changes.**

Word displays a tracking changes shortcut menu (Figure 7-15).

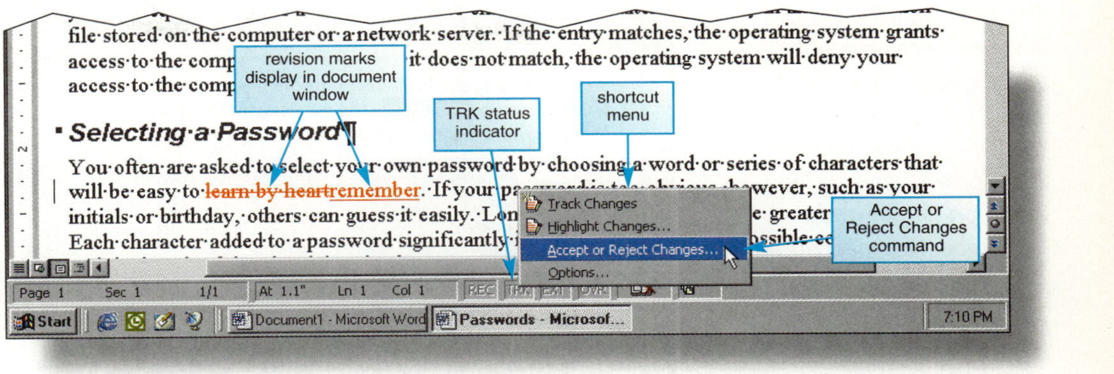

FIGURE 7-15

2 **Click Accept or Reject Changes. When the Accept or Reject Changes dialog box displays, be sure Changes with highlighting is selected in the View area and then point to the Find Next button.**

Word displays the Accept or Reject Changes dialog box (Figure 7-16). The Changes with highlighting option ensures that tracked changes display on the screen for your review.

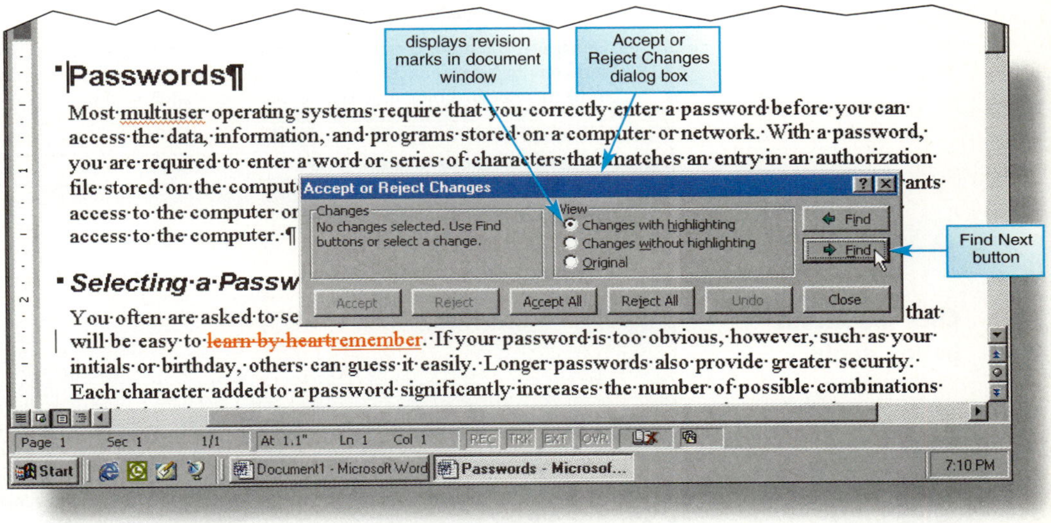

FIGURE 7-16

3 **Click the Find Next button. Point to the Accept button.**

Word highlights the first change in the document, which is the deletion of the phrase, learn by heart (Figure 7-17). If you look to the right of this change, you see the insertion of the word, remember. Thus, the reviewer suggests you replace the phrase, learn by heart, with the word, remember. You agree with this change and, therefore, wish to accept it.

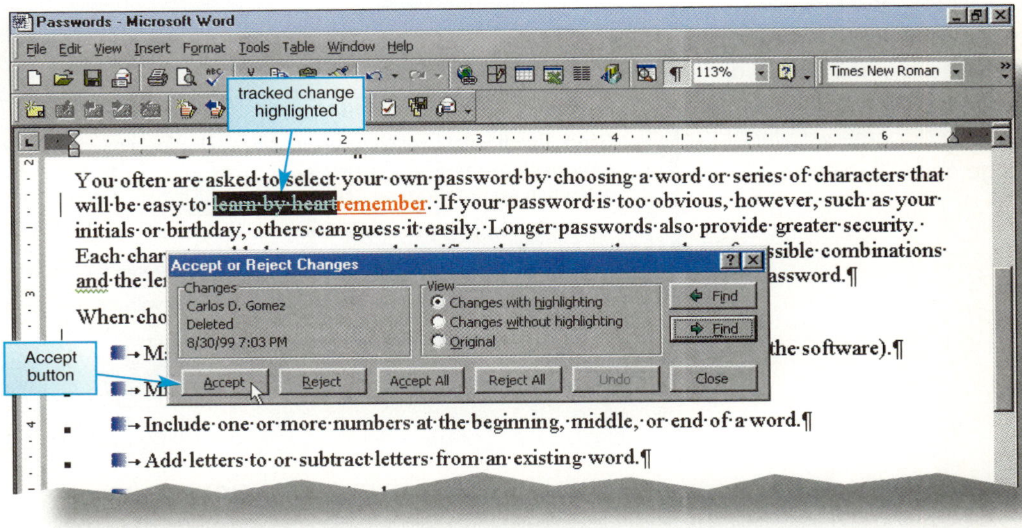

FIGURE 7-17

4 **Click the Accept button.**

Word accepts the tracked change by removing the phrase, learn by heart, from the document (Figure 7-18). The next tracked change is highlighted, which is the insertion of the word, remember. You also agree with this change.

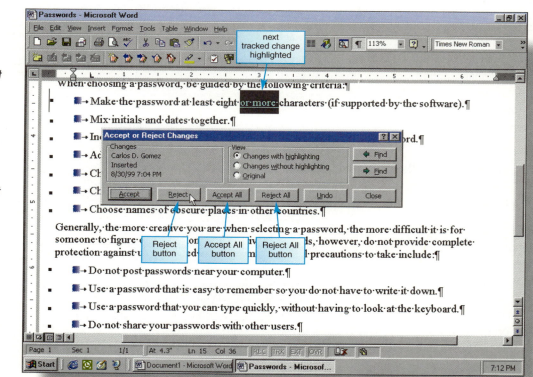

FIGURE 7-18

5 **Click the Accept button again.**

Word inserts the word, remember, into the document and removes its revision marks (Figure 7-19). The next tracked change is highlighted, which is the insertion of the words, or more. You feel this change is not necessary because of the words, at least, in the same sentence. Thus, you disagree with this change and will reject it.

FIGURE 7-19

6 Click the Reject button. If Word displays a dialog box asking if you wish to search from the beginning of the document, click the OK button.

Word rejects the tracked change and does not insert the words, or more, into the document (Figure 7-20). Because this is the last tracked change in the document, Word displays a dialog box indicating no tracked changes remain.

7 Click the OK button. Click the Close button in the Accept or Reject Changes dialog box. Click View on the menu bar, point to Toolbars, and then click Reviewing.

Word removes the Accept or Reject Changes dialog box and the Reviewing toolbar from the screen.

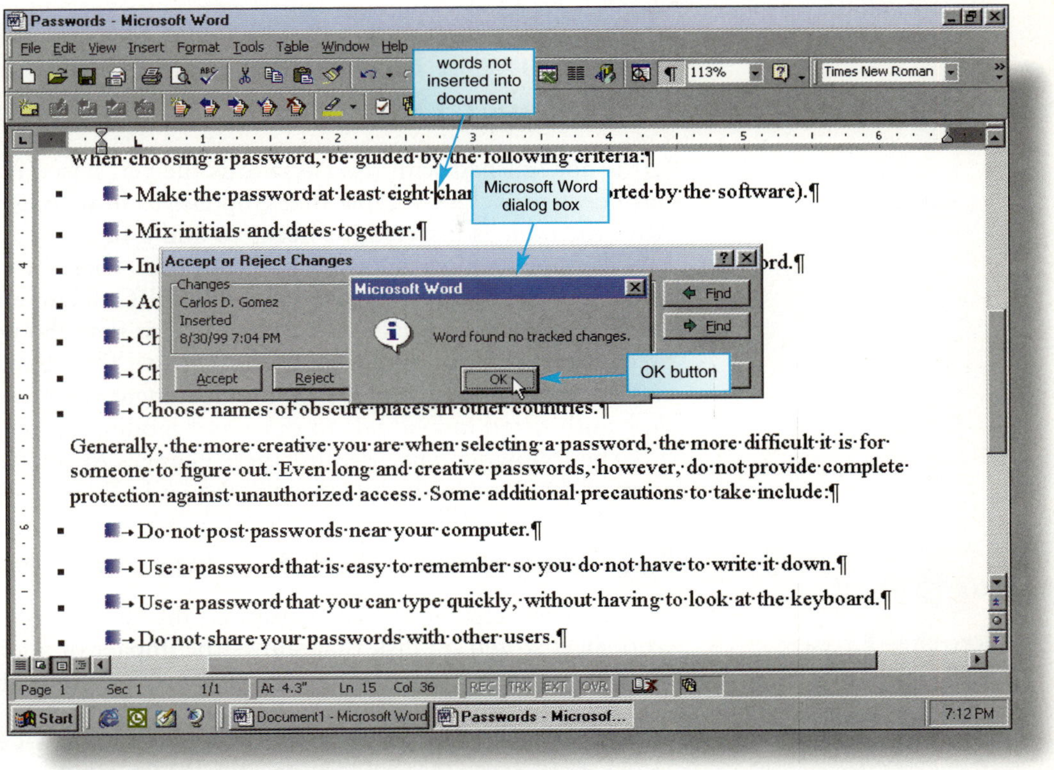

FIGURE 7-20

If you are certain you plan to accept all changes in a document containing tracked changes, you can accept all the changes at once by clicking the Accept All button in the Accept or Reject Changes dialog box (see Figure 7-19). Likewise, you can click the Reject All button in the Accept or Reject Changes dialog box to reject all the changes at once. If you click either of these buttons by mistake, you can click the Undo button on the Standard toolbar to undo the action.

You can see how a document will look if you accept all the changes, without actually accepting them, by right-clicking the TRK status indicator on the status bar, clicking Highlight Changes, removing the check mark from the Highlight changes on screen check box, and then clicking the OK button. If you want a hard copy that shows how the document will look if you accept all the changes, right-click the TRK status indicator on the status bar, click Highlight Changes, remove the check mark from the Highlight changes in printed document check box and then print the document.

Other Ways

1. Click Next Change button on Reviewing toolbar, click Accept Change button on Reviewing toolbar to accept change or click Reject Change button on Reviewing toolbar to reject change

Preparing a Document to be Included in a Longer Document

Jeff is not finished with the Passwords file yet. Based on the comment from Carlos, Jeff needs to include a table that emphasizes how longer passwords are more secure. After the table is inserted, he needs to add a figure caption to the table – because the EIG documents always have figure captions. Then, he will modify the text so that it references the figure. The last page of the EIG documents is an index, so Jeff will mark any words in the Passwords document that should appear in the index. As a precaution, Jeff will ensure that the items within the bulleted lists do not split across two pages. Finally, Jeff will save the document with a password, which will allow only authorized individuals to open and modify the file in the future.

The following pages outline these changes to the Passwords document. The final copy of the Passwords document is shown in Figure 7-2b on page WD 7.8.

Embedding an Excel Worksheet into a Word Document

The first step for Jeff is to insert a table as suggested by Carlos. Jeff has an Excel worksheet stored on disk that shows the impact of adding more characters to a password (see Figure 7-2b). Jeff will embed the Excel worksheet on disk into the Word document.

When you **embed** an object, such as an Excel worksheet, the object becomes part of the destination file, which is the Passwords document in this case. That is, if the contents of the object (the Excel worksheet) change, the change will not be reflected in the embedded object. If you want to change the contents of the object, you double-click it to open the application in which the object was created (Excel, in this case). Any changes you make to the source file (the Excel worksheet) in the source application (Excel) will be reflected in the destination document (the Passwords file).

By contrast, when you **link** an object and the contents of this object changes, the change is reflected automatically in the destination file. With a linked object, the destination file stores a link, or connection, to the location of the source file. Because you want to send only a single file to the personnel department for inclusion in the EIG #22 document, you will embed the Excel worksheet instead of link it.

For purposes of this project, the Excel worksheet named Passwords Table is located on the Data Disk. If you did not download the Data Disk, see the inside back cover for instructions for downloading the Data Disk or see your instructor.

Perform the following steps to embed the Passwords Table (source file) into the Passwords file (destination file).

Steps: To Embed an Object

1 **Position the insertion point at the end of the last sentence in the first paragraph below the Selecting a Password heading. Click Insert on the menu bar and then point to Object (Figure 7-21).**

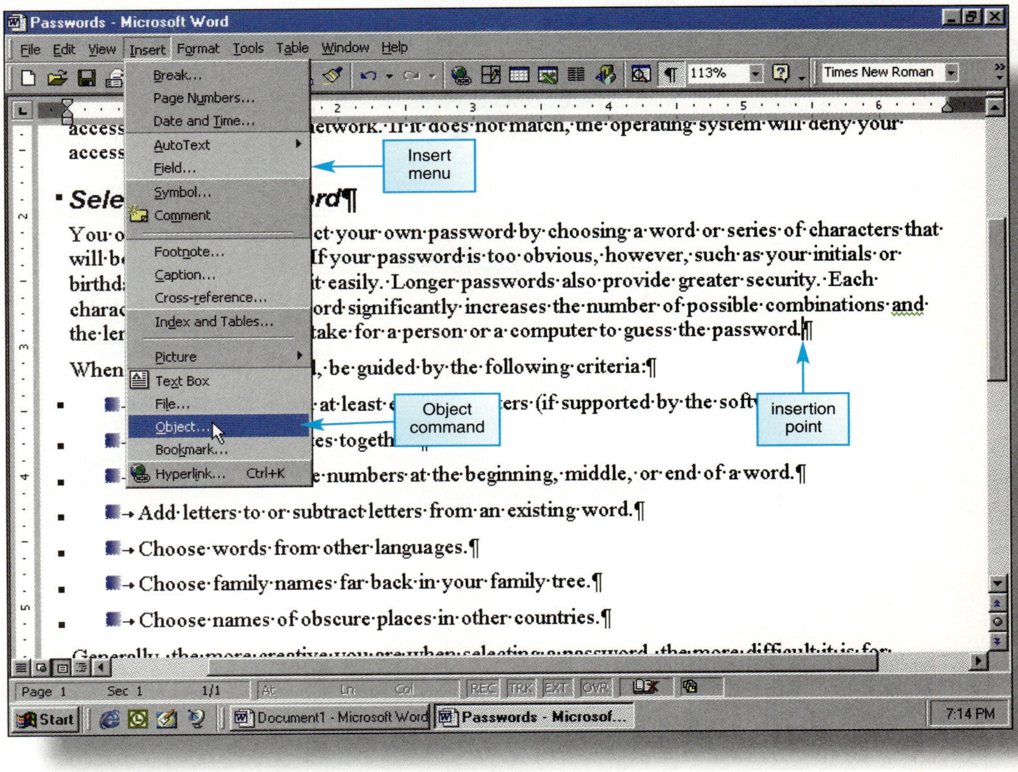

FIGURE 7-21

2 **Click Object. When the Object dialog box displays, if necessary, click the Create from File tab. With the Data Disk in drive A, click the Browse button. When the Browse dialog box displays, locate the Passwords Table file on the Data Disk. Click Passwords Table in the list and then click the Insert button in the Browse dialog box. When the Object dialog box is visible again, point to the OK button.**

Word displays the Object dialog box (Figure 7-22). The xls following the file name, Passwords Table, identifies the file as an Excel worksheet.

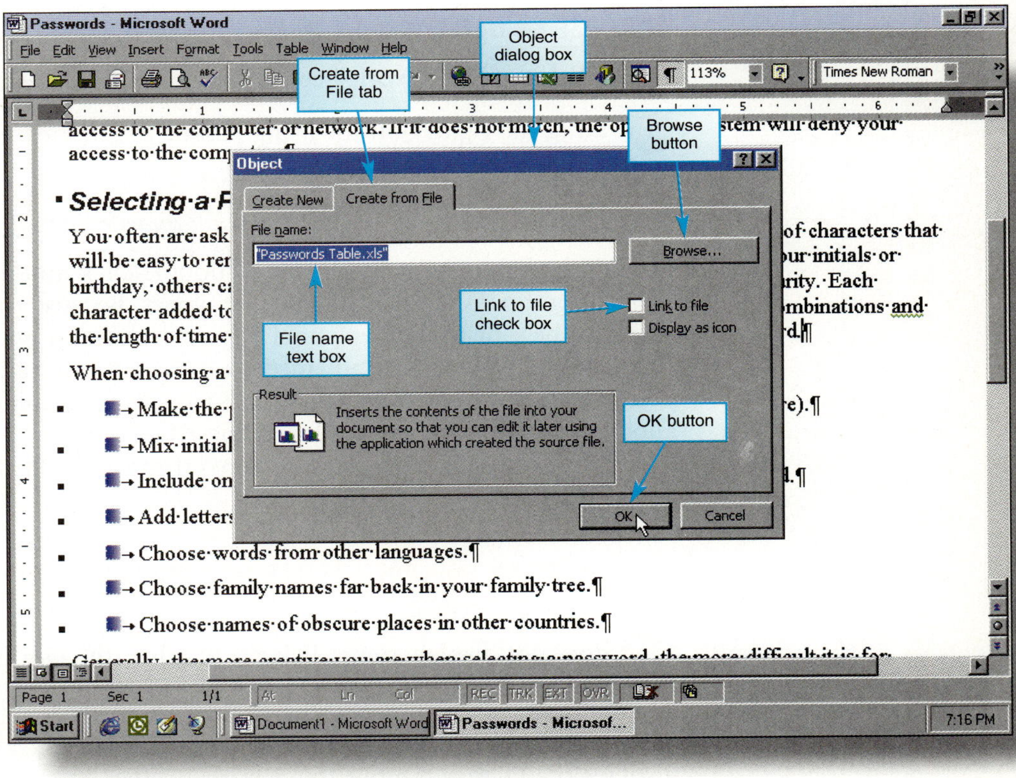

FIGURE 7-22

3 **Click the OK button.**

Word inserts the Excel work-sheet as an embedded object (Figure 7-23).

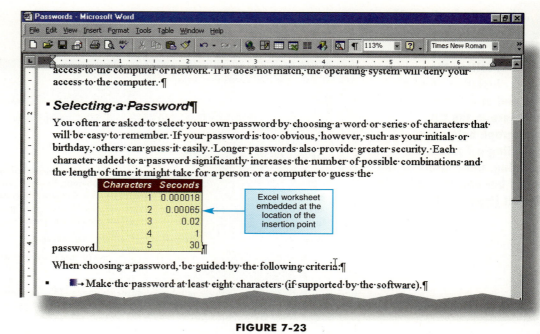

FIGURE 7-23

Other Ways

1. Copy object in source appli-cation to Office Clipboard; in destination application, on Edit menu click Paste Special, click Paste, click Formatted Text (RTF), click OK button

If you wanted to link the Excel worksheet instead of embed it, you would place a check mark in the Link to file check box in the Object dialog box (see Figure 7-22 on the previous page).

You want the Excel worksheet to be slightly larger in the document. Thus, perform the following steps to resize the object.

TO RESIZE AN OBJECT

1 Click the Excel worksheet to select the embedded object.

2 Drag the right, bottom sizing handle approximately one-quarter inch outward to enlarge the object.

Word enlarges the worksheet about one-quarter inch (see Figure 7-24).

You have learned that when you double-click an embedded object, the source application opens so you can edit the object. Because this document (the Passwords file) is to be sent to the personnel department and users in this department have not worked with some of the advanced features of Word and are unfamiliar with Excel, you will convert the embedded object to a Word graphic. Doing so will prevent another user from accidentally starting Excel while in Word.

Perform the following step to convert the embedded object (the Excel worksheet) to a Word graphic.

TO CONVERT AN EMBEDDED OBJECT TO A WORD GRAPHIC

1 With the embedded object selected, press CTRL+SHIFT+F9. If the Picture toolbar does not display, right-click the graphic (the worksheet) and then click Show Picture Toolbar.

Word converts the Excel worksheet from an embedded object to a Word graphic and displays the Picture toolbar (see Figure 7-24).

The worksheet no longer is an embedded object – it is a Word graphic. Thus, you cannot double-click it to edit it in Excel.

Notice in Figure 7-23 that the worksheet is inline; that is, the worksheet is part of the current paragraph. You want to position the worksheet to the right of the paragraph and have the text wrap to the left of the worksheet. Thus, the graphic needs to be a floating graphic instead of an inline graphic. To do this, you change the graphic's wrapping style to Square as shown in the following steps.

To Change an Inline Graphic to a Floating Graphic

1 **With the graphic still selected, click the Text Wrapping button on the Picture toolbar and then point to Square (Figure 7-24).**

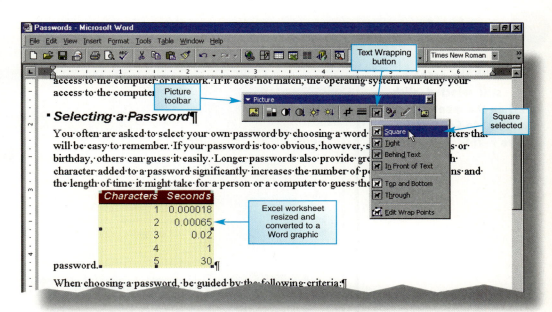

FIGURE 7-24

2 **Click Square. If necessary, scroll down to display the graphic and then drag the graphic to the right of the paragraph as shown in Figure 7-25.**

Word converts the graphic from inline to floating so you can position it anywhere on the page.

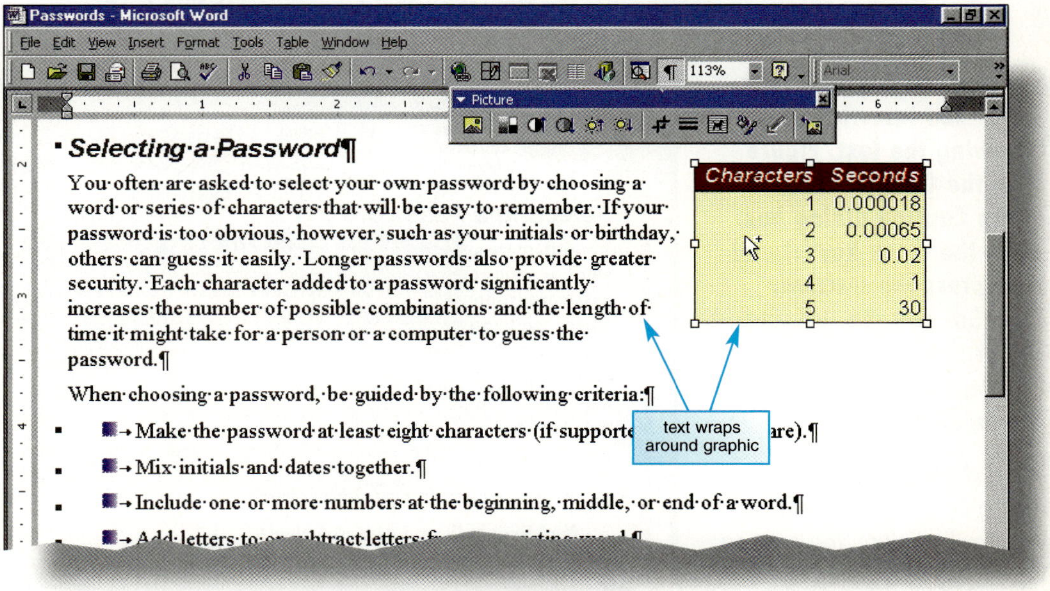

FIGURE 7-25

The next step is to add a caption to the graphic.

Adding a Caption

At the end of the EIG documents is a table of figures, which lists all figures and their corresponding page numbers. Word generates this table of figures from the captions in the document. A **caption** is a label with a number that you can add to a graphic, table, or other object. If you move, delete, or add captions in a document, Word renumbers remaining captions in the document automatically.

Perform the following steps to add a caption to the graphic.

To Add a Caption

1 With the graphic still selected, click **Insert** on the menu bar and then point to **Caption** (Figure 7-26).

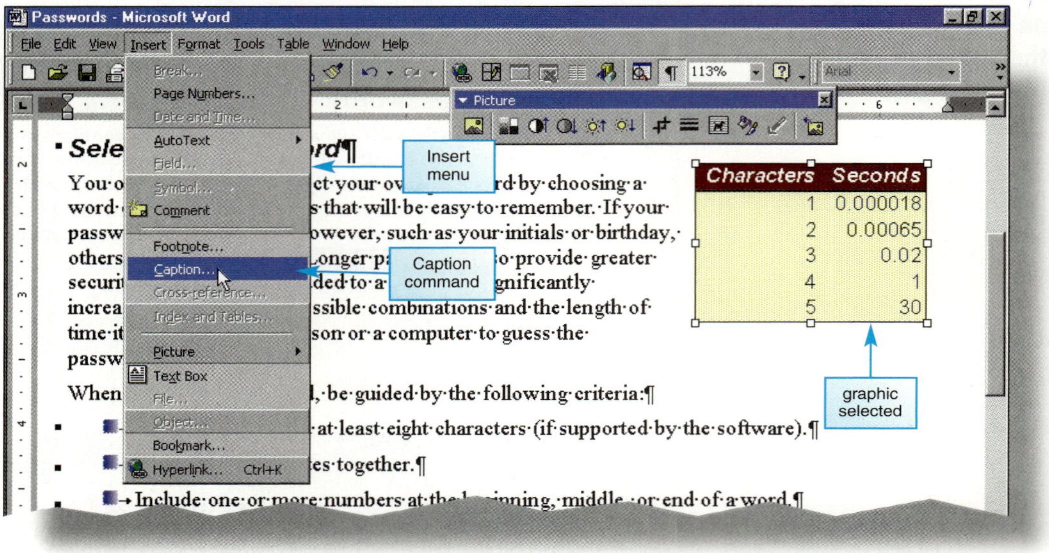

FIGURE 7-26

2 Click Caption. With the insertion point following the text, Figure 1, in the Caption text box of the Caption dialog box, press the COLON key (:) and then press the SPACEBAR. Type Speeds at Which a Computer Discovers Passwords and then point to the OK button.

Word displays the Caption dialog box (Figure 7-27). Word will position the caption for this figure below the graphic.

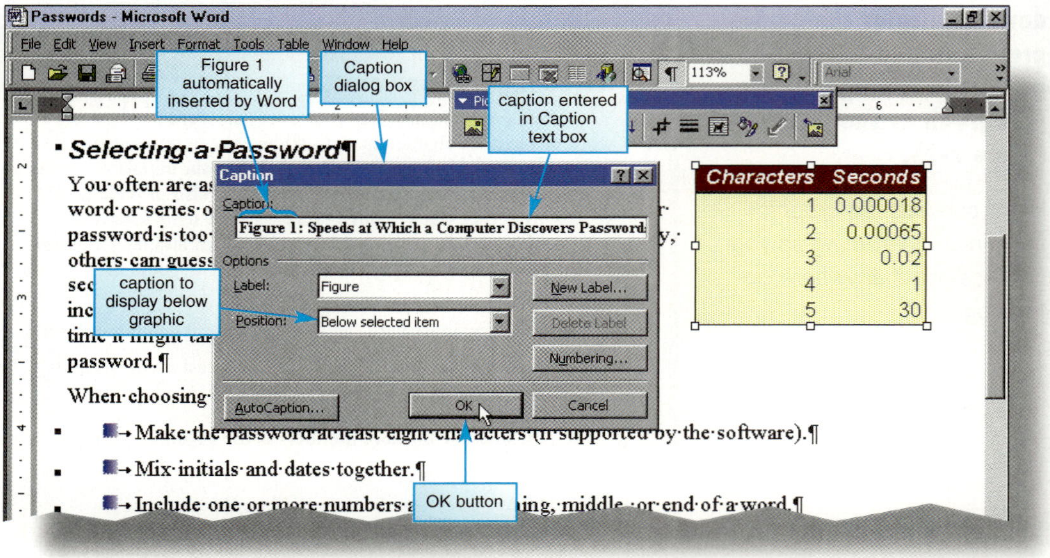

FIGURE 7-27

3 Click the OK button.

Word inserts the caption in a text box below the selected graphic (Figure 7-28). In a later step, you will resize the caption so that all of its text displays on two lines.

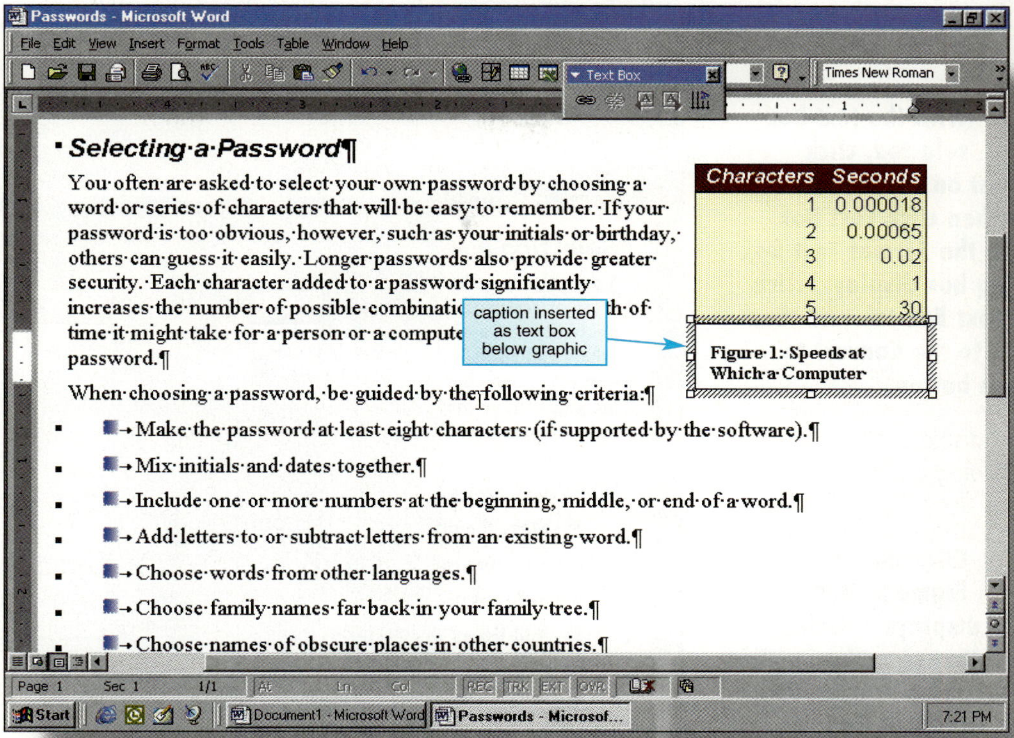

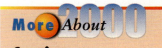

FIGURE 7-28

If, at a later time, you insert a new item with a caption or move or delete items containing captions, Word automatically updates caption numbers throughout the document. For example, this caption currently has a figure number of 1. When you insert this document into the EIG #22 document, it actually will be figure number 4. Word automatically will renumber it after you insert this document into the EIG #22 document.

A caption contains a field. In Word, a **field** is a placeholder for data that you expect might change in a document. Examples of fields you have used in previous projects are page numbers, merge fields, IF fields, Fill-in fields, and the current date.

Because the caption number is a field, you update it using the same technique used to update a field. That is, to update all caption numbers, select the entire document and then press F9 or right-click the selection and then click Update Field. When you print a document, Word updates the caption numbers automatically, whether or not the document window displays the updated caption numbers.

When you add a caption to an inline graphic, the caption is not inserted in a text box. As just illustrated, however, the caption for a floating graphic is inserted in a text box. If you plan to generate a table of figures for a document, a caption cannot be in a text box. Instead, it has to be in a frame. Perform the steps on the next page to convert the text box to a frame.

More About 2000

Captions

If your caption displays with extra characters inside curly braces {}, then Word is displaying field codes instead of field results. Press ALT+F9 to display the caption correctly as field results. If your caption prints field codes, click Tools on the menu bar, click Options, click the Print tab, remove the check mark from the Field codes check box, click the OK button, and then print the document again.

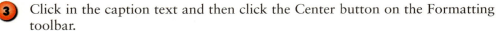

Microsoft **Word 2000**

Steps **To Convert a Text Box to a Frame**

1 **With the text box selected, click Format on the menu bar, and then click Text Box. When the Format Text Box dialog box displays, click the Text Box tab and then point to the Convert to Frame button.**

Word displays the Format Text Box dialog box (Figure 7-29).

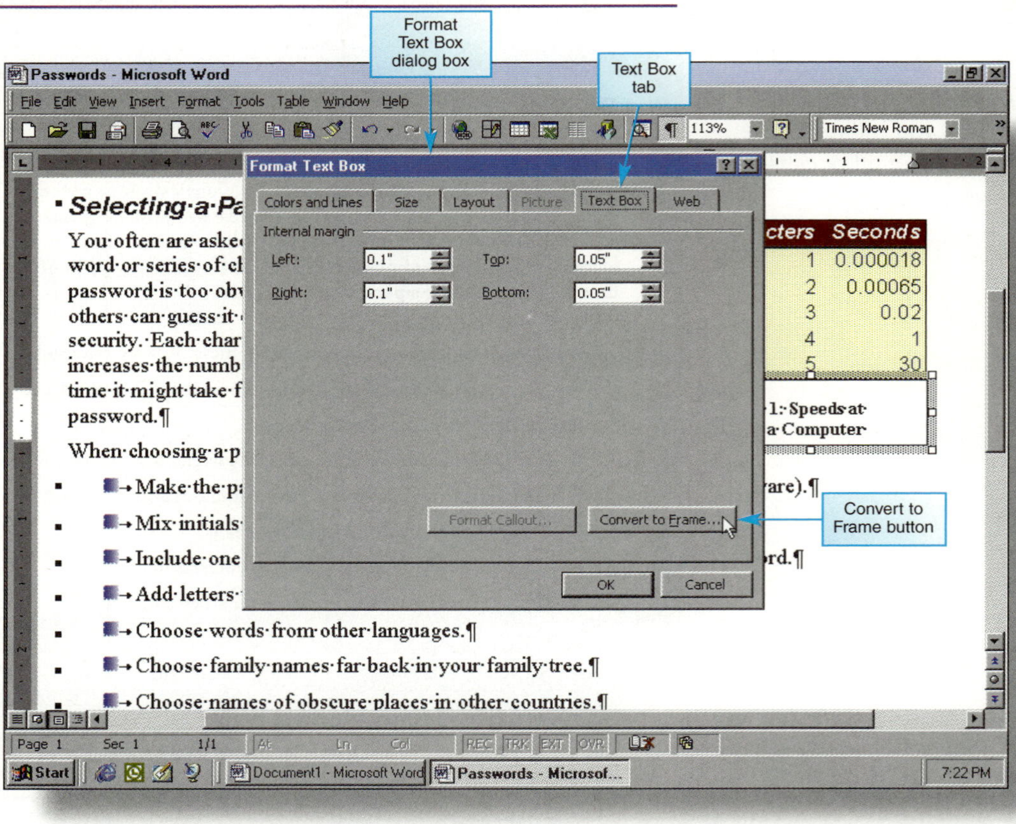

2 **Click the Convert to Frame button. When Word displays a dialog box indicating some formatting of the frame may be lost, click the OK button. If Word displays a dialog box asking if you want a Frame command on the Insert menu, click the Cancel button.**

Word converts the text box to a frame. You did not format the text box; thus, you will not lose any formatting in the conversion from a text box to the frame.

FIGURE 7-29

Notice in Figure 7-28 on the previous page that the caption has a border around it. This is because Word automatically placed a border around the caption when it was a text box. You do not want the border around the caption. You also want to center and resize the caption. Perform the following steps to modify the caption.

TO MODIFY THE CAPTION

1 Double-click the move handle on the Formatting toolbar to display the entire toolbar. With the caption frame selected, click the Border button arrow and then click No Border.

2 If necessary, drag the middle, right sizing handle until the text of the caption displays in the frame as two lines.

3 Click in the caption text and then click the Center button on the Formatting toolbar.

4 If necessary, drag the text box to center the caption below the graphic. Do not drag in the middle of the text box; you must drag the text box rectangle to move the text box.

The caption displays as shown in Figure 7-30.

The next step is to refer to the new figure in the document text.

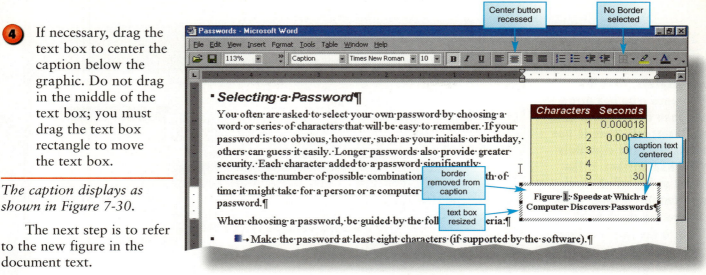

FIGURE 7-30

Creating a Cross-Reference

In the EIG documents, the text always makes reference to any figure and explains the contents of the figure. Thus, you want to enter a phrase into the document that refers to the figure. Recall that the Passwords file will be inserted into a larger file. You do not know what the figure number of the graphic will be in the new document. In Word, you can create a **cross-reference**, which is a link to an item such as a heading, caption, or footnote in a document. By creating a cross-reference to the caption, the text that mentions the figure will update whenever the caption to the figure updates.

Perform the following steps to create a cross-reference.

Steps To Create a Cross-Reference

1 Position the insertion point in front of the sentence beginning with the text, **Longer passwords also provide. Type** As shown in **and then press the SPACEBAR. Click Insert on the menu bar and then point to Cross-reference (Figure 7-31).**

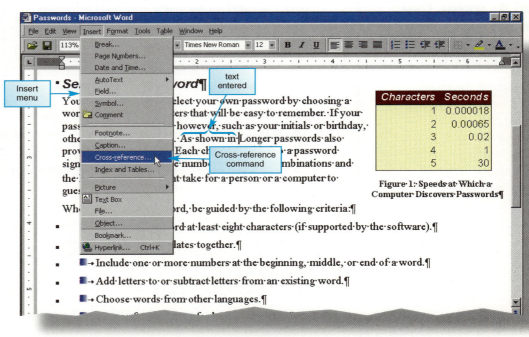

FIGURE 7-31

Microsoft **Word 2000**

2 **Click Cross-reference. When the Cross-reference dialog box displays, click the Reference type box arrow and then click Figure. Click the Insert reference to box arrow and then click Only label and number. If the Insert as hyperlink check box contains a check mark, remove the check mark. Point to the Insert button.**

Word displays the Cross-reference dialog box (Figure 7-32). You want the text to display only the label (the word, Figure) and the label number (the figure number).

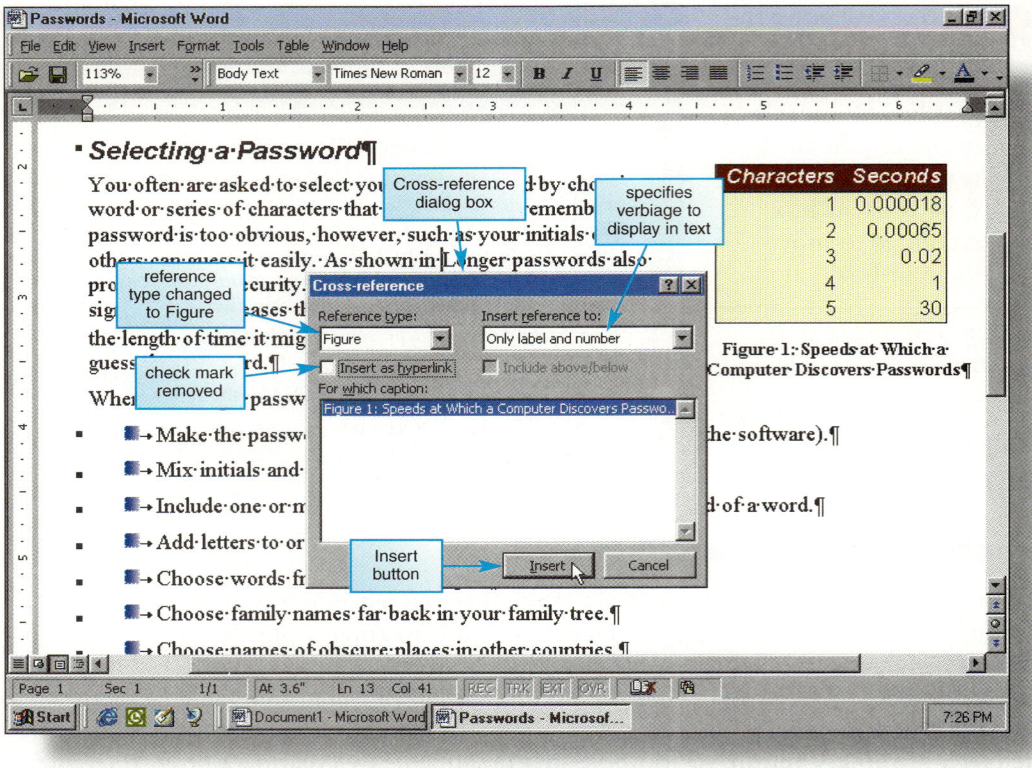

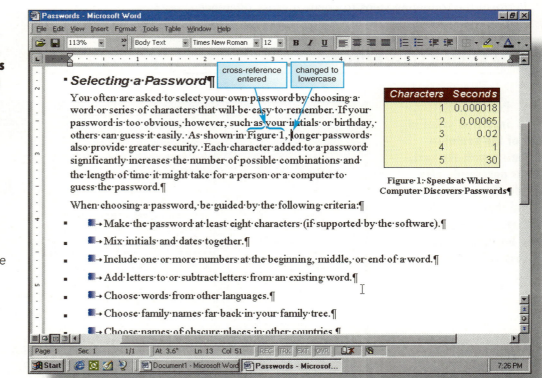

FIGURE 7-32

3 **Click the Insert button. Click the Close button in the Cross-reference dialog box. Press the COMMA key (,) and then press the SPACEBAR. Press the SHIFT+F3 keys twice to change the entire word, longer, to lowercase.**

Word inserts the cross-reference to the figure into the text (Figure 7-33). Because the word, longer, has moved to the middle of the sentence, it should not be capitalized.

FIGURE 7-33

Each time you press the SHIFT+F3 keys, Word changes the case of the selected text or of the word containing the insertion point. That is, it cycles from initial caps (capitalizing the first letter of each word) to all uppercase to all lowercase.

Like caption numbers, a cross-reference is a field. In many cases, Word automatically updates cross-references in a document if the item it refers to changes. To manually update a cross-reference, select the cross-reference and then press F9, or right-click the selection and then click Update Field.

The next step is to mark any index entries in this document.

Marking Index Entries

At the end of the EIG documents is an index, which lists important terms discussed in the document along with each term's corresponding page number. For Word to generate the index, you first must mark any item you wish to appear in the index. When you mark an index entry, Word creates a field that is used to build the index. The fields are hidden and display on the screen only when you are displaying formatting marks; that is, when the Show/Hide ¶ button on the Standard toolbar is recessed.

In this document, you want the word, password, in the first sentence below the Selecting a Password heading to be marked as an index entry. To alert the reader that this term is in the index, you also bold it in the document. Perform the following steps to mark this index entry.

More About

Cross-References

If your cross-reference displays odd characters inside curly braces {}, then Word is displaying field codes instead of field results. Press ALT+F9 to display the cross-reference correctly. If your cross-reference prints field codes, click Tools on the menu bar, click Options, click the Print tab, remove the check mark from the Field codes check box, click the OK button, and then print the document again.

 To Mark an Index Entry

1 Select the text you wish to appear in the index (the word, password, in this case). Press ALT+SHIFT+X.

Word displays the Mark Index Entry dialog box (Figure 7-34).

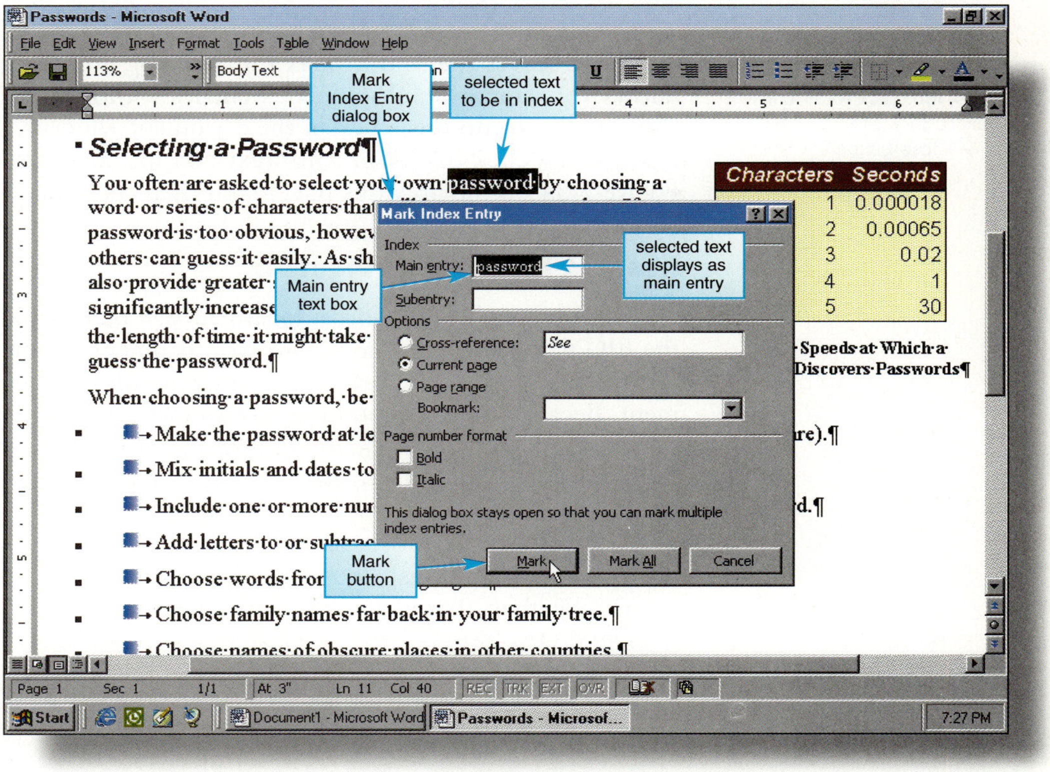

FIGURE 7-34

2 **Click the Mark button. Click the Close button in the Mark Index Entry dialog box. Select the word, password, in front of the left brace and then bold it.**

Word inserts an index entry field into the document (Figure 7-35). These fields display on the screen only when the Show/Hide ¶ button on the Standard toolbar is recessed.

FIGURE 7-35

Other Ways

1. Select text, on Insert menu click Index and Tables, click Index tab, click Mark Entry button, click Mark button, click Close button

Word leaves the Mark Index Entry dialog box open until you close it, which allows you to mark multiple index entries without having to reopen the dialog box continually. To do this, click in the document window, scroll to and select the next index entry, click the Main entry text box in the Mark Index Entry dialog box (see Figure 7-34 on the previous page), and then click the Mark button.

Keeping Paragraphs Together

Recall that the Passwords document will be incorporated into a larger document, the EIG #22. Although the Passwords document fits on a single page now, Jeff is unsure as to how the Passwords document will be inserted into the EIG #22 document. Because it is not good practice to print part of a bulleted list at the bottom of one page and print the remaining portion of the same bulleted list at the top of the following page, Jeff will ensure that the items within the bulleted lists do not split across two pages.

The paragraph before the bulleted list and the items within the bulleted list are all separate paragraphs. Thus, you must instruct Word to print all of these paragraphs together; that is, on the same page, as shown in the following steps.

To Keep Paragraphs Together

1 Select the paragraphs to keep together (the paragraph before the bulleted list and the bulleted list). Right-click the selection and then click Paragraph on the shortcut menu. When the Paragraph dialog box displays, click the Line and Page Breaks tab and then make sure the Keep lines together check box contains a check mark. Point to the OK button.

Word displays the Paragraph dialog box (Figure 7-36). A check mark displays in the Keep lines together check box.

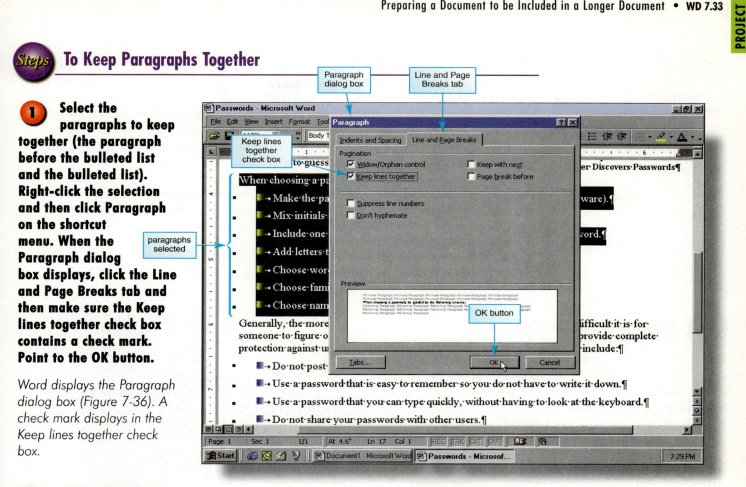

FIGURE 7-36

2 Click the OK button.

Word keeps the eight paragraphs that comprise the bulleted list and the paragraph preceding the list together so that they print on the same page.

3 Repeat Steps 1 and 2 for the second bulleted list in the Passwords document. Click outside the selection to remove the highlight.

The options in the Line and Page Breaks tab of the Paragraph dialog box (Figure 7-36) are designed to provide you with options in how paragraphs print. The Keep lines together check box that was illustrated in the previous steps also can be used to ensure that a page break does not occur within a single paragraph, by positioning the insertion point in the appropriate paragraph and then selecting the check box. If you do not want a page break to occur between two paragraphs, you would click in the appropriate paragraph and then place a check mark in the Keep with next check box. Similarly, if you want a page break to occur immediately before a paragraph, you would place a check mark in the Page break before check box.

A **widow** is created when the last line of a paragraph displays by itself at the top of a page, and an **orphan** occurs when the first line of a paragraph displays by itself at the bottom of a page. Word, by default, prevents widows and orphans from occurring in a document. If, for some reason, you wanted to allow a widow or an orphan in a document, you would position the insertion point in the appropriate paragraph, display the Line and Page Breaks sheet in the Paragraph dialog box, and then remove the check mark from the Widow/Orphan control check box.

More *About* **2000**

Selecting Passwords

For more information on selecting good passwords, visit the Word 2000 More About Web page (www.scsite.com/wd2000/more.htm) and then click Selecting Passwords.

Password-Protecting a File

Jeff is finished with the Passwords file and is ready to send it to you for inclusion in the EIG #22 document. You have specified that all incoming documents be password-protected, which requires a user to enter a password if he or she wishes to open or modify the document. This procedure helps to ensure that the document inserted into the EIG #22 document is correct and has been modified by only authorized individuals.

In Word, a password may be up to 15 characters in length and can include letters, numbers, spaces, and symbols. Passwords are **case-sensitive**, which means that the password always must be entered in the same case in which it was saved. That is, if you enter a password in all capital letters, it must be entered in capital letters when the file is opened or modified.

You instruct Jeff to use the password, sunshine (in lowercase), for the file. Perform the following steps to password-protect the file.

Steps To Password-Protect a File

1 **Click File on the menu bar and then click Save As. When the Save As dialog box displays, if necessary, change the Save in location to drive A. Click the Tools button arrow and then point to General Options.**

Word displays the Save As dialog box (Figure 7-37).

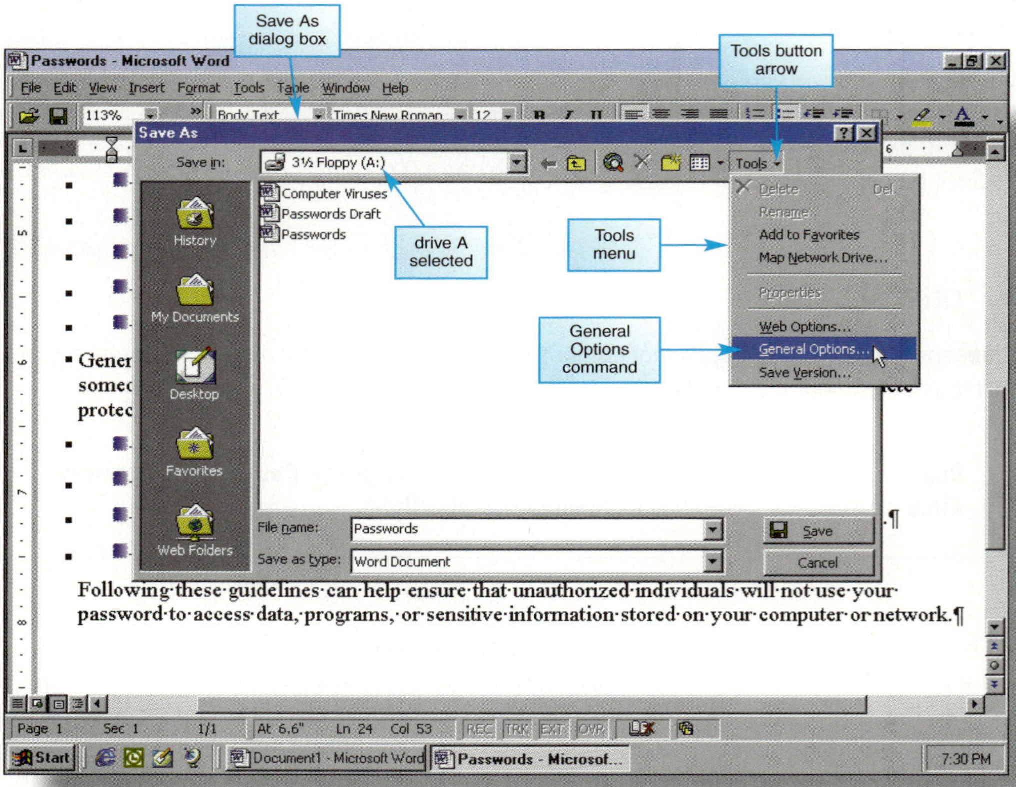

FIGURE 7-37

2 **Click General Options. When the Save dialog box displays, type** sunshine **in the Password to open text box. Point to the OK button.**

Word displays the Save dialog box (Figure 7-38). When you enter the password, sunshine, Word displays a series of asterisks (*) instead of the actual characters you type.

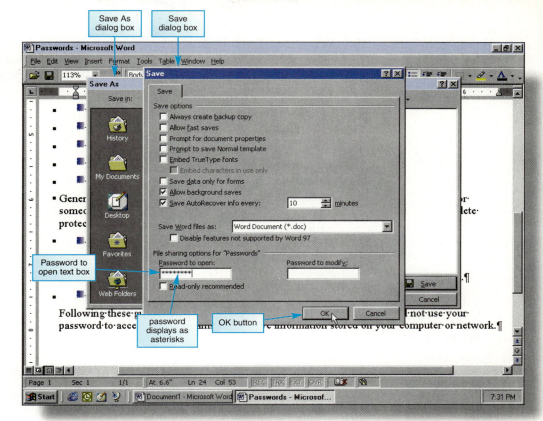

FIGURE 7-38

3 **Click the OK button. When Word displays the Confirm Password dialog box, type** sunshine **in the text box. Point to the OK button in the Confirm Password dialog box.**

Word displays the Confirm Password dialog box (Figure 7-39). Again, the password displays as a series of asterisks (*) instead of the actual characters you type.

4 **Click the OK button. When the Save As dialog box is visible again, click its Save button.**

Word saves the document with the password, sunshine.

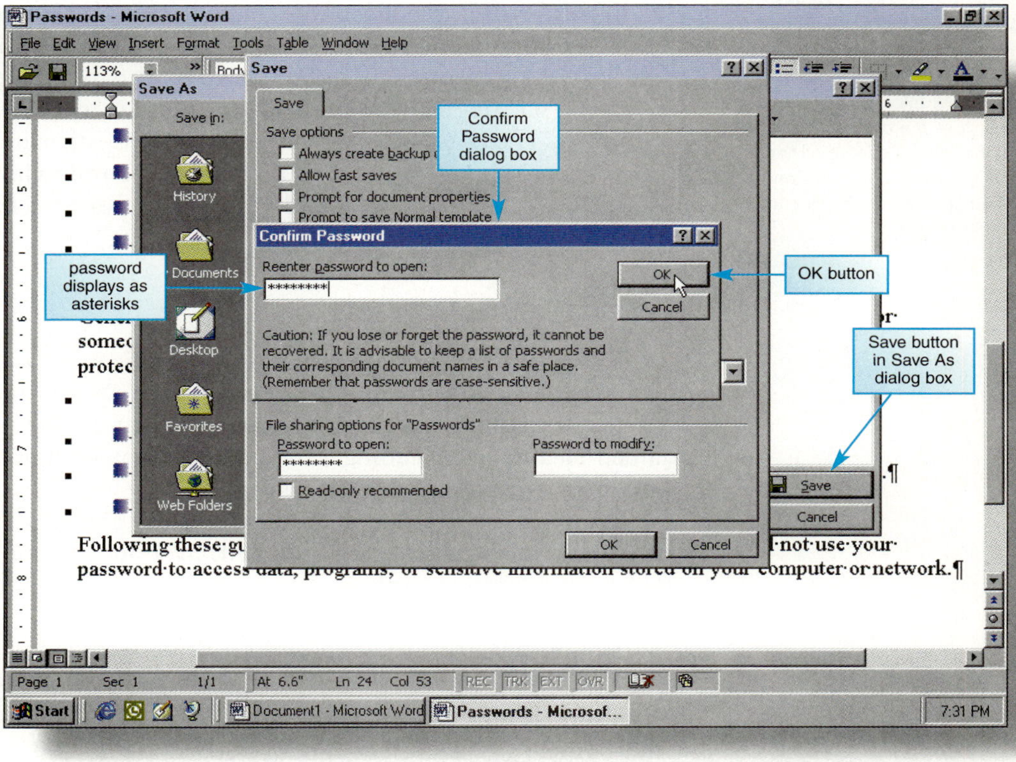

FIGURE 7-39

When someone attempts to open the document in the future, he or she will be prompted to enter the password. Recall that the password must be entered in the same case in which it was saved. The Passwords file is complete. Perform the following steps to close the file.

TO CLOSE THE DOCUMENT

1 Click File on the menu bar and then click Close.

2 If necessary, click the Document1 program button on the taskbar to display the blank document in the document window. If you do not have a Document1 button on the taskbar, click the New Blank Document button on the Standard toolbar.

Word closes the Passwords file and displays a blank document in the document window.

Jeff e-mails the Passwords document to you for inclusion in the EIG #22 document. For purposes of this book, the document is on your disk.

More *About* 2000

Master Documents

Master documents can be used when multiple people prepare different sections of a document or when a document contains separate elements such as the chapters in a book. If multiple people in a network need to work on the same document, divide the document into subdocuments and store the master document on the network server. Then, multiple users can work on different sections of the document simultaneously.

Working with a Master Document

When you are creating a document from a series of other documents, you may want to create a master document to organize all the documents. A **master document** is simply a document that contains other documents, which are called the **subdocuments**. In addition to subdocuments, a master document can contain its own text and graphics.

In this project, the master document is EIG #22, which contains three subdocuments: an Introduction file, the Computer Viruses file, and the Passwords file. The first has yet to be written, and the latter two (Computer Viruses and Passwords) have been written by other individuals and e-mailed for inclusion in the EIG #22 document. The master document also contains other items: a title page, a table of contents, a table of figures, and an index. The following pages illustrate how to create this master document and insert the necessary elements into the document to create the EIG #22 document.

Creating an Outline

To create a master document, you must be in outline view. You then enter the headings of the document as an outline using Word's built-in heading styles. A **style** is a customized format that you can apply to text. Word has nine heading styles named Heading 1, Heading 2, and so on. Each contains different formatting that you can apply to headings in a document.

In an outline, the major heading displays at the left margin with each subordinate, or lower-level, heading indented. In Word, the built-in Heading 1 style displays at the left margin in outline view. Heading 2 style is indented, Heading 3 style is indented more, and so on.

You do not want to use a built-in heading style for the paragraphs of text within the document because when you create a table of contents, Word places all lines formatted using the built-in heading styles in the table of contents. Thus, the text below each heading is formatted using the Body Text style. By using styles for the document, all pages will be formatted similarly – even though various people create them.

The EIG #22 document contains the following seven major headings: Employee Information and Guidelines #22, Table of Contents, Introduction, Computer Viruses, Passwords, Table of Figures, and Index (see Figure 7-1 on page WD 7.5). Two of these headings (Computer Viruses and Passwords) are not entered in the outline; instead they are part of the subdocuments that you insert into the master document in the next section. You want each heading to print at the top of a new page. Because you might want to format the pages within a heading differently from those pages in other headings, you will insert next page section breaks between each heading as shown in the following steps.

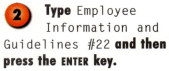
To Create an Outline

1 **Click the Outline View button on the** horizontal scroll bar. **If your screen does not display the Outlining toolbar, click View on the menu bar, point to Toolbars, and then click Outlining. If the three buttons identified on the Outlining toolbar in this figure are not recessed on your screen, click the button(s).**

Word switches to outline view (Figure 7-40). An **outline symbol** *displays to the left of each paragraph. You use outline symbols to rearrange text or display and hide text.*

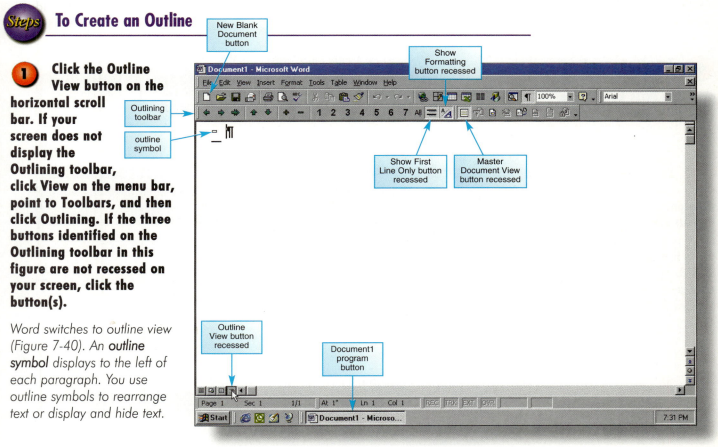

FIGURE 7-40

2 **Type** Employee Information and Guidelines #22 **and then press the ENTER key.**

Word enters the first heading using the built-in Heading 1 style (Figure 7-41).

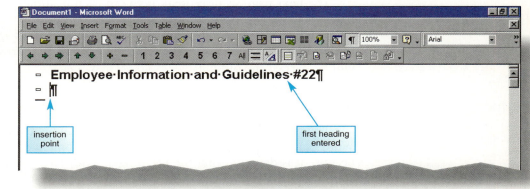

FIGURE 7-41

3 Click Insert on the menu bar and then click Break. When the Break dialog box displays, click Next page in the Section break types area and then click the OK button.

Word inserts a next page section break below the first heading.

4 **Type** Table of Contents **and then press the ENTER key (Figure 7-42).**

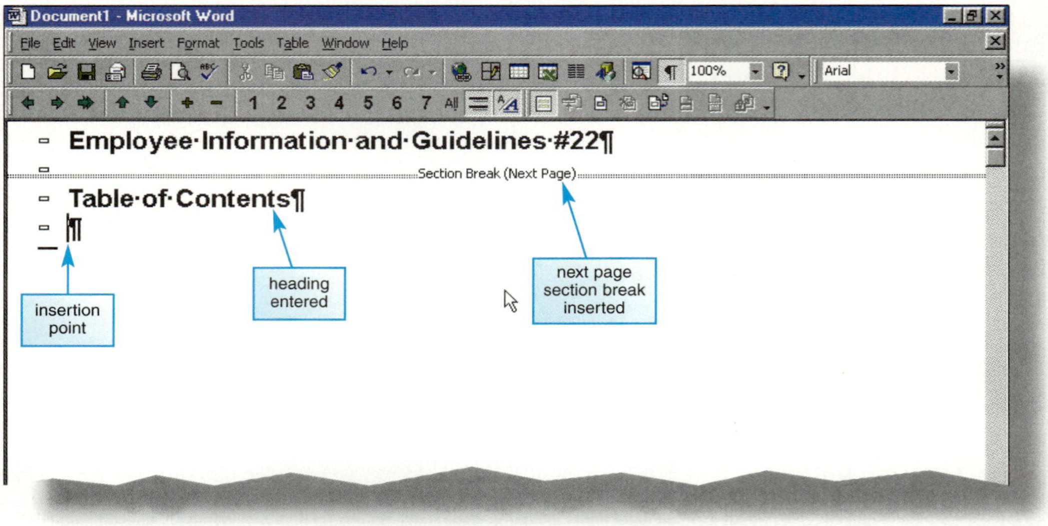

FIGURE 7-42

5 **Repeat Step 3. Type** Introduction **and then press the ENTER key. Repeat Step 3. Type** Table of Figures **and then press the ENTER key. Repeat Step 3. Type** Index **and then press the ENTER key (Figure 7-43).**

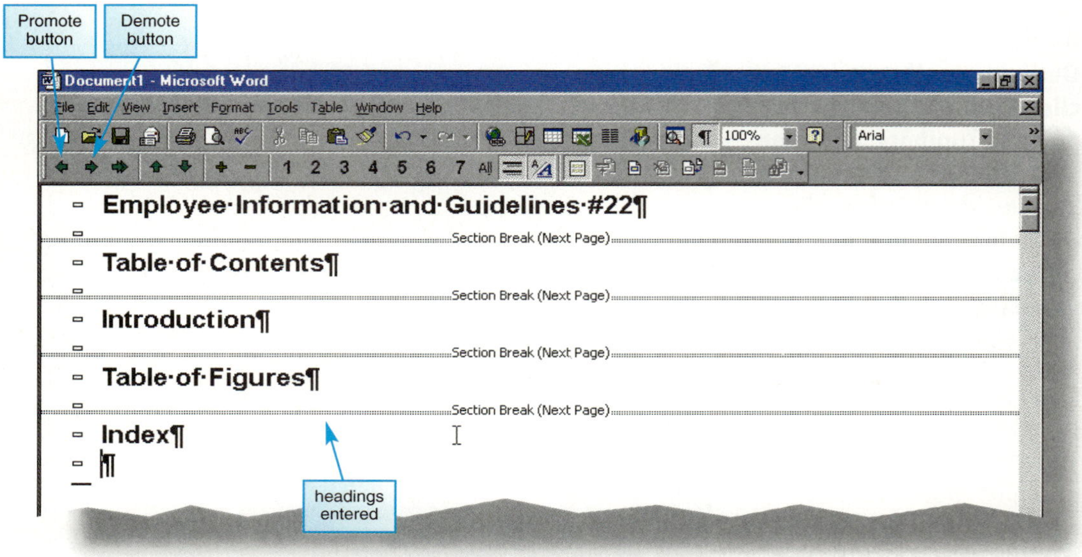

FIGURE 7-43

Other Ways

1. On View menu click Outline

More About 2000

Outlines

If you wanted to rearrange the headings in an outline, for example move one up, you would drag its outline symbol in the direction you wanted to move it.

The next page section break between each heading will cause each heading to begin at the top of a new page.

The two missing major headings (Computer Viruses and Passwords) are in the files on the Data Disk. When you insert these files as subdocuments, the headings will be part of the outline.

Inserting a Subdocument in a Master Document

The next step is to insert one of the subdocuments into the master document. Word places the first line of text in the subdocument at the first heading level because it is defined using the Heading 1 style. The remaining two headings in the subdocument use the Heading 2 style, and thus are subordinate to the first heading. Nonheading text uses the Body Text style. Figure 7-44 shows the Computer Viruses subdocument and identifies the styles used in the document.

Body Text style

Antivirus programs also identify a virus by looking for specific patterns of known virus code, called a **virus signature**, which they compare to a virus signature file. You should update your antivirus program's virus signature files frequently so they include the virus signatures for newly discovered viruses and can protect against viruses written after the antivirus program was released (Figure 3).

Figure 3

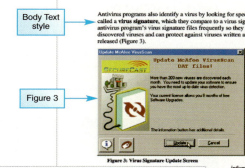
Figure 3: Virus Signature Update Screen

Even with an updated virus signature file, however, antivirus programs can have difficulty detecting some viruses. One such virus is a **polymorphic virus**, which modifies its program code each time it attaches itself to another program or file. Because its code never looks the same, an antivirus program cannot detect a polymorphic virus by its virus signature.

Another technique that antivirus programs use to detect viruses is to **inoculate** existing program files. To inoculate a program file, the antivirus program records information such as the file size and file
The antivirus program then can use this information
the inoculated program file. Some sophisticated
on. Such a virus, called a **stealth virus**, can infect a
ation date of the original, uninfected program.

ected file, it can remove the virus or quarantine the
he antivirus program places the infected file in a
remove the virus, thus insuring that other files will

inst viruses, most antivirus programs also have
ns and files. If the virus has infected the boot
ost will require you to restart the computer with a
disk, or emergency disk, is a disk that contains an
mmands and startup information that enables the
e restarted the computer using a rescue disk, you can
infected files and repair damaged files. If the
u may have to replace, or restore, them with

Heading 2 style

Internet, and e-mail has accelerated the spread of computer viruses, by allowing individuals to share files – and any related viruses – more easily than ever.

Types of Viruses

Although numerous variations are known, four main types of viruses exist: boot sector viruses, file viruses, Trojan horse viruses, and macro viruses. A **boot sector virus** replaces the boot program used to start a computer with a modified, infected version of the boot program. When the computer runs the infected boot program, the computer loads the virus into its memory. Once the virus is in memory, it spreads to any disk inserted into the computer. A **file virus** attaches itself to or replaces program files; the virus then spreads to any file that accesses the infected program. A **Trojan horse virus** (named after the Greek myth) is a virus that hides within or is designed to look like a legitimate program. A **macro virus** uses the macro language of an application, such as word processing or spreadsheet, to hide virus code. When you open a document that contains an infected macro, the macro virus loads into memory. Certain actions, such as opening the document, activate the virus. The creators of macro viruses often hide them in templates so they will infect any document created using the template.

Body Text style

Depending on the virus, certain actions can trigger the virus. Many viruses activate as soon as a computer accesses or runs an infected file or program. Other viruses, called logic bombs or time bombs, activate based on specific criteria. A **logic bomb** is a computer virus that activates when it detects a certain condition. One disgruntled worker, for example, planted a logic bomb that began destroying files when his name appeared on a list of terminated employees. A **time bomb** is a type of logic bomb that activates on a particular date. A well-known time bomb is the Michelangelo virus, which destroys data on a hard disk on March 6, Michelangelo's birthday.

Another type of malicious program is a **worm**. Although often it is called a virus, a worm, unlike a virus, does not attach itself to another program. Instead, a worm program copies itself repeatedly in memory or on a disk drive until no memory or disk space remains. When no memory or disk space remains, the computer stops working. Some worm programs even copy themselves to other computers on a network.

Virus Detection and Removal

No completely effective methods exist to ensure

Heading 1 style

Figure 2

Figure 2: Antivirus Program

Computer Viruses

A **computer virus** is a potentially damaging computer program designed to affect, or infect, your computer negatively by altering the way it works without your knowledge or permission. More specifically, a computer virus is a segment of program code that implants itself in a computer file and spreads systematically from one file to another. Viruses can spread to your computer if an infected floppy disk is in the disk drive when you boot the computer, if you run an infected program, or if you open an infected data file in a program.

Computer viruses, however, do not generate by chance. Creators, or programmers, of computer virus programs write them for a specific purpose – usually to cause a certain type of symptom or damage. Some viruses are harmless pranks that simply freeze a computer temporarily or display sounds or messages. When the Music Bug virus is triggered, for example, it instructs the computer to play a few chords of music. Other viruses, by contrast, are designed to destroy or corrupt data stored on the infected computer. Thus, the symptom or damage caused by a virus can be harmless or cause significant damage, as planned by its creator.

Body Text style

rams also protect against malicious ActiveX code and
es you download from the Web. An antivirus program
y the boot program, the operating system, and other
t not modified.

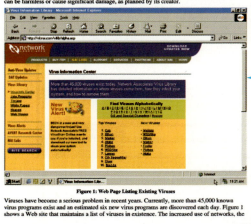
Figure 1: Web Page Listing Existing Viruses

Figure 1

Viruses have become a serious problem in recent years. Currently, more than 45,000 known virus programs exist and an estimated six new virus programs are discovered each day. Figure 1 shows a Web site that maintains a list of viruses in existence. The increased use of networks, the

FIGURE 7-44

The subdocument to be inserted is named Computer Viruses and is located on the Data Disk. If you did not download the Data Disk, see the inside back cover for instructions for downloading the Data Disk or see your instructor. Perform the following steps to insert a subdocument.

Steps **To Insert a Subdocument**

1 **Position the insertion point where you want to insert the subdocument (on the section break between the Introduction and Table of Figures headings). Point to the Insert Subdocument button on the Outlining toolbar (Figure 7-45).**

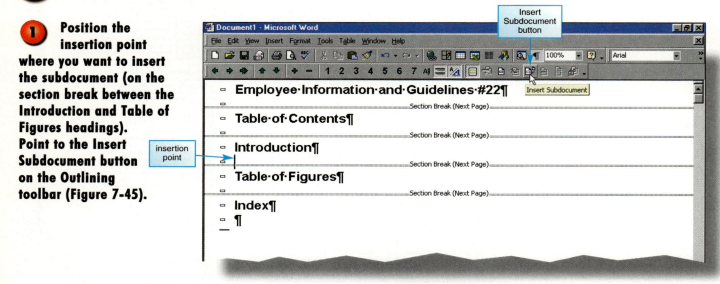

FIGURE 7-45

2 **With the Data Disk in drive A, click the Insert Subdocument button. When the Insert Subdocument dialog box displays, if necessary, change the Look in location to drive A. Click Computer Viruses and then point to the Open button in the dialog box.**

Word displays the Insert Subdocument dialog box (Figure 7-46). The document will be inserted at the location of the insertion point in the outline.

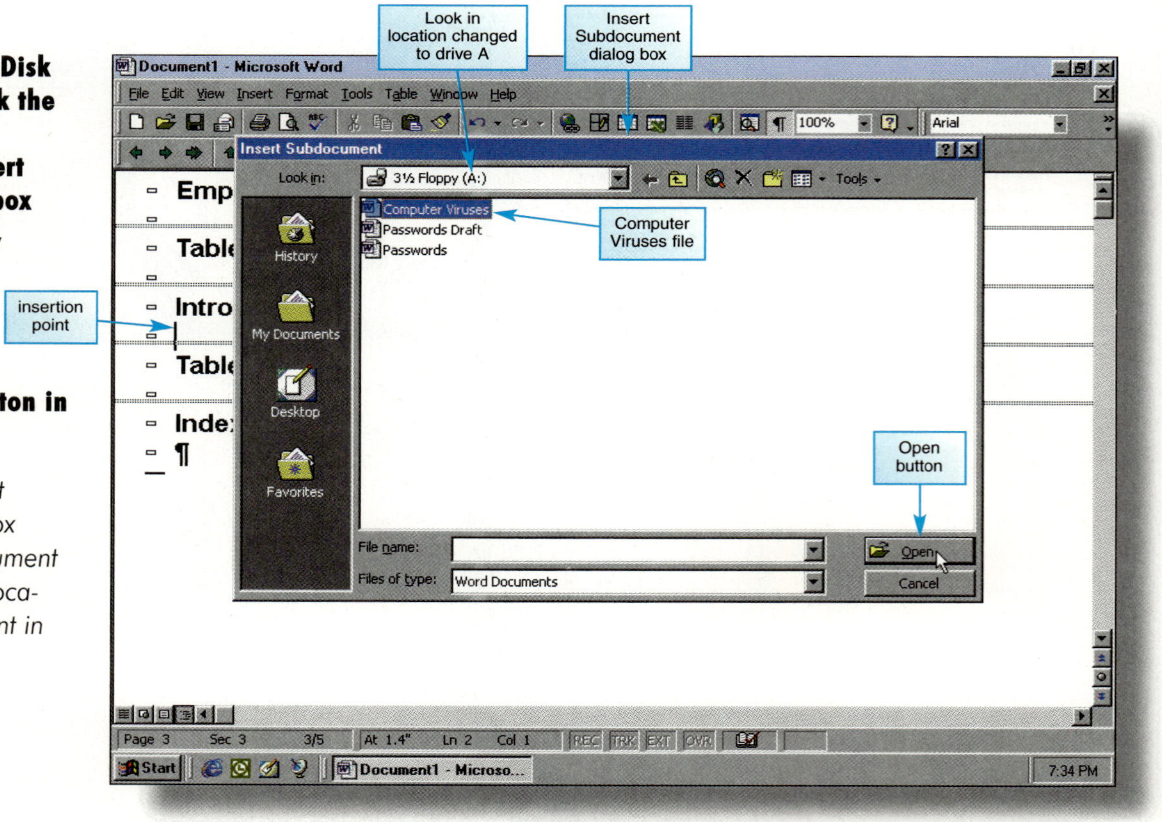

FIGURE 7-46

3 Click the Open button in the Insert Subdocument dialog box. Scroll up to display the top of the inserted subdocument.

Word inserts the Computer Viruses file into the outline (Figure 7-47). Notice the document contains marked index entries. Only the first line of each paragraph displays because the Show First Line Only button on the Outlining toolbar is recessed.

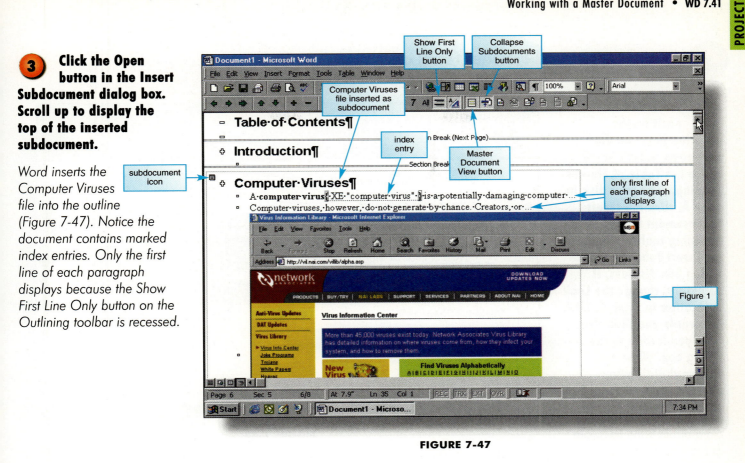

FIGURE 7-47

The inserted file shown in Figure 7-47 is the same document shown in Figure 7-44 on page WD 7.39. Notice that in Figure 7-47 only the first line of each paragraph displays. This is because the Show First Line Only button on the Outlining toolbar is recessed. If you wanted to display all lines in all paragraphs, you would click the Show First Line Only button so it is not recessed.

The master document shown in Figure 7-47 is expanded. When in outline view, an **expanded** document is one that displays the contents of its subdocuments. A **collapsed** document, by contrast, displays subdocuments as hyperlinks; that is, instead of displaying the contents of the subdocuments, Word displays the name of the subdocuments in blue and underlined. Later in this project, you work with a collapsed document.

To collapse an expanded document and display subdocuments as hyperlinks, click the Collapse Subdocuments button on the Outlining toolbar. To expand subdocuments, click the Expand Subdocuments button on the Outlining toolbar.

You can open a subdocument in a separate document window and modify it. To open a collapsed subdocument, click the hyperlink. To open an expanded subdocument, double-click the subdocument icon (see Figure 7-47) to the left of the document heading. If the subdocument icon does not display on the screen, click the Master Document View button on the Outlining toolbar. When you are finished working on a subdocument, close it and return to the master document by clicking File on the menu bar and then clicking Close.

The next step is to insert another subdocument below the Computer Viruses subdocument. The subdocument to be inserted is the Passwords file that you modified earlier in this project. Recall that you saved the document with the password, sunshine. Thus, you will enter that password when prompted by Word as shown in the steps on the next page.

More About

The Lock Icon

If a lock icon displays next to a subdocument's name, either the master document is collapsed or the subdocument is locked. If the master document is collapsed, simply click the Expand Subdocuments button on the Outlining toolbar. If the subdocument is locked, you will be able to open the subdocument but will not be able to modify it.

To Insert a Password-Protected File as a Subdocument

1 **Scroll down and position the insertion point on the next page section break above the Table of Figures heading. With your disk in drive A, click the Insert Subdocument button on the Outlining toolbar. When the Insert Subdocument dialog box displays, if necessary, change the Look in location to drive A. Click Passwords and then click the Open button in the dialog box. When the Password dialog box displays, type** sunshine **as the password.**

Word displays the Password dialog box, which requests your password for the Passwords file (Figure 7-48). Asterisks display instead of the actual password.

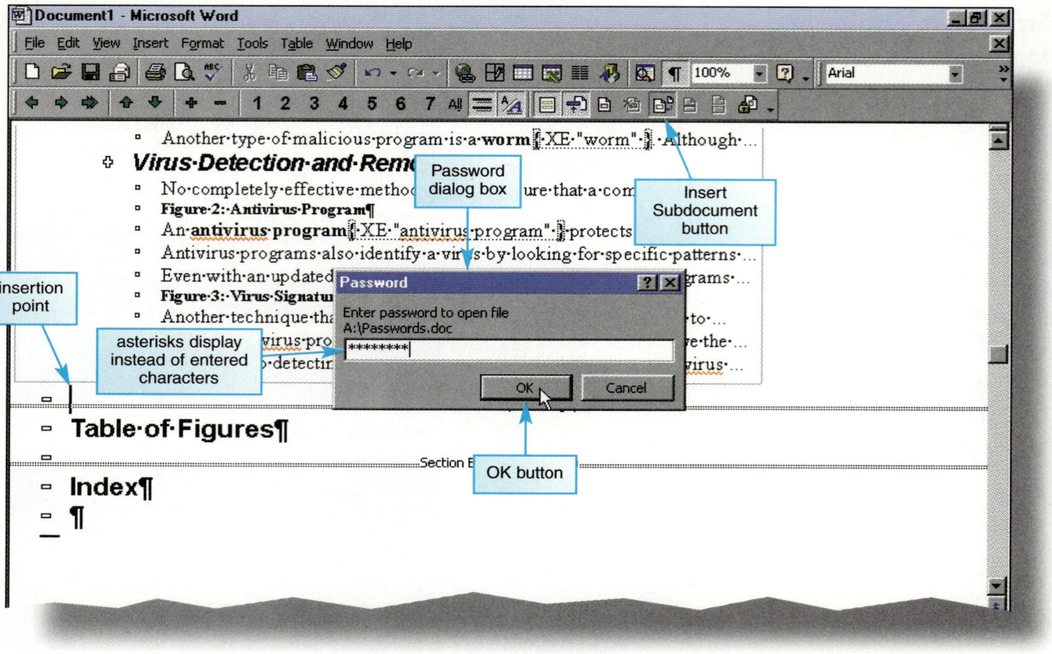

2 **Click the OK button.**

Word inserts the Passwords file into the document (Figure 7-49). The document shown in this figure is the same one shown in Figure 7-2b on page WD 7.8.

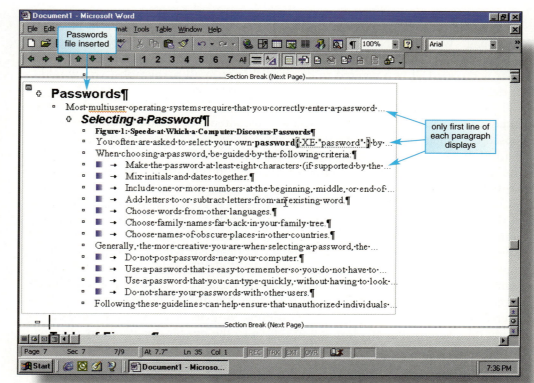

FIGURE 7-48

FIGURE 7-49

Because you have performed several tasks, you should save the document as described in the following steps.

TO SAVE A DOCUMENT

1. With your floppy disk in drive A, click the Save button on the Standard toolbar.

2. Type EIG #22 in the File name text box. Do not press the ENTER key after typing the file name.

3. If necessary, change the Save in location to drive A. Click the Save button in the Save As dialog box.

Word saves the document on a floppy disk in drive A with the file name, EIG #22 (see Figure 7-50).

When you save a master document, Word also saves the subdocument files on the disk. Thus, the EIG #22 file, the Computer Viruses file, and the Passwords file all are saved when you save the EIG #22 file.

Creating a Subdocument from a Master Document

The next step is to create a subdocument for the Introduction section of the EIG #22 document. Perform the following steps to create a subdocument.

More About

Creating Subdocuments

If the Create Subdocument button is dimmed, you need to expand subdocuments by clicking the Expand Subdocuments button on the Outlining toolbar. Then, the Create Subdocument button should be available.

Steps: To Create a Subdocument

1. **Press CTRL+HOME and then double-click the heading, Introduction, to select it. Point to the Create Subdocument button on the Outlining toolbar (Figure 7-50).**

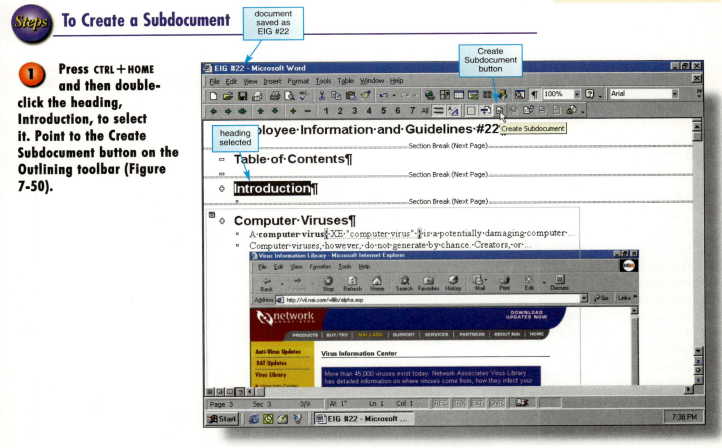

FIGURE 7-50

2 **Click the Create Subdocument button.**

Word creates a subdocument for the Introduction heading (Figure 7-51). Word places a continuous section break above the subdocument; do not remove this section break.

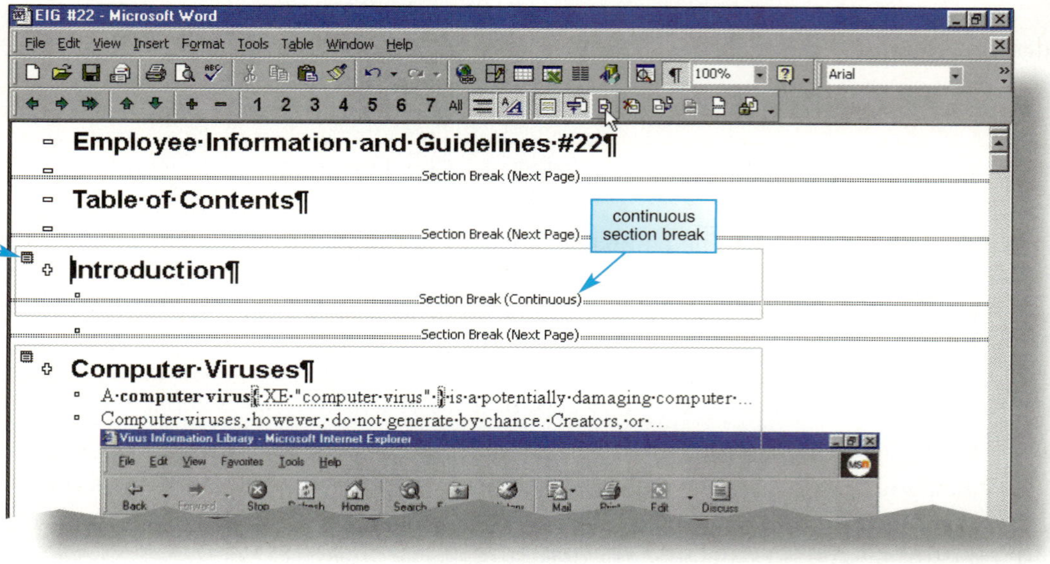

FIGURE 7-51

The next time you save the EIG #22 document, Word will create another document called Introduction on your disk.

Modifying an Outline

You would like to enter the text for the Introduction section of the document. The paragraphs of text in the Introduction should not use a built-in heading style; instead, they should be formatted using the Body Text style. You can enter the text in outline view as shown in the following steps.

Steps To Modify an Outline

1 **Position the insertion point immediately after the last n in the heading, Introduction. Press the ENTER key twice and then press the UP ARROW key to position the insertion point on the blank line below the Introduction heading. Point to the Demote to Body Text button on the Outlining toolbar (Figure 7-52).**

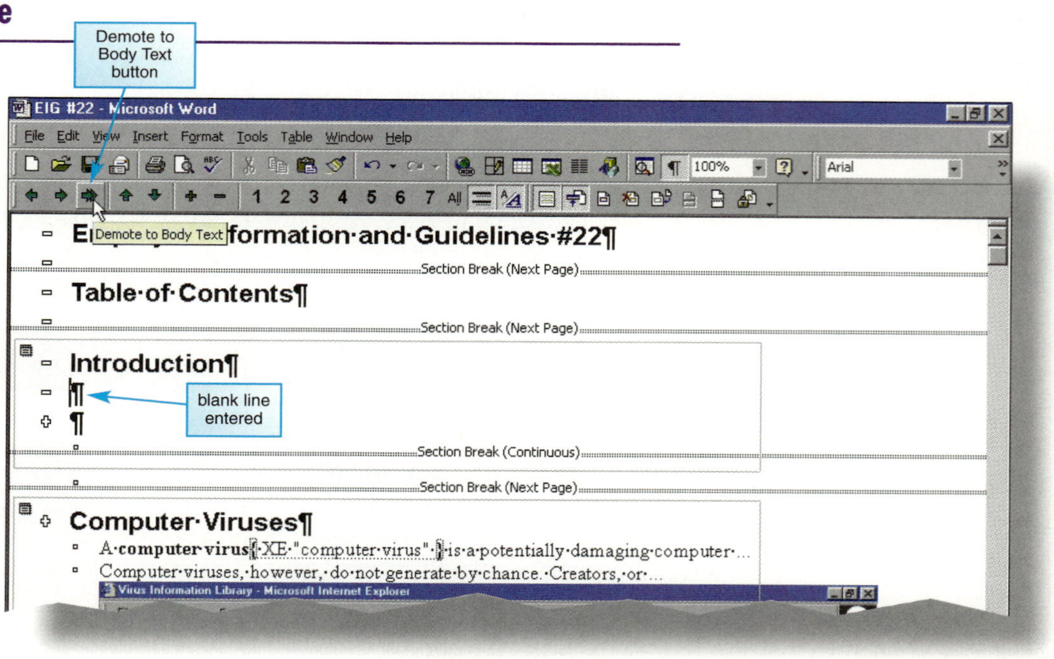

FIGURE 7-52

2 **Click the Demote to Body Text button.**

Word changes the style of the current line from Heading 1 to Body Text (Figure 7-53).

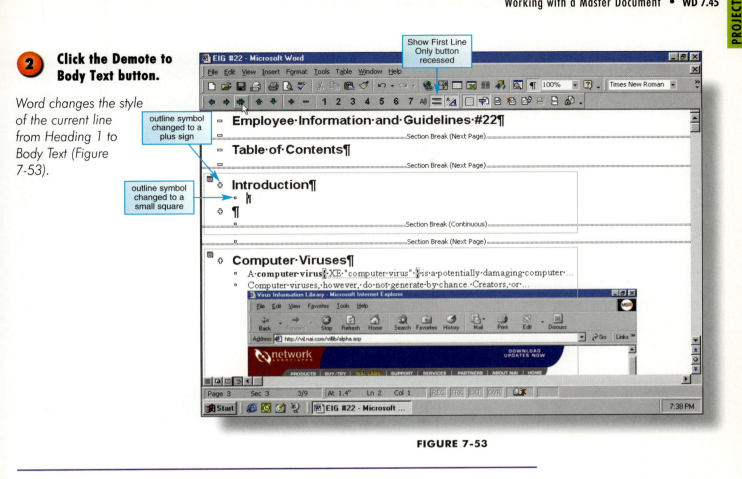

FIGURE 7-53

Notice in Figure 7-53 that the outline symbols changed. The outline symbol to the left of the Introduction heading changed from a minus sign to a plus sign, indicating the heading has subordinate text displaying on the screen. The outline symbol below the Introduction heading changed from a minus sign to a small square, indicating it is formatted using the Body Text style.

If you wanted to change a heading to a lower-level, or subordinate, heading style instead of to the Body Text style, such as for a subheading, you would press the TAB key or click the Demote button on the Outlining toolbar or drag the outline symbol to the right. Likewise, to change a heading to a higher-level heading, you would press the SHIFT+TAB keys or click the Promote button on the Outlining toolbar or drag the outline symbol to the left.

The next step is to enter the text of the introduction as described in the following steps.

TO ENTER BODY TEXT INTO AN OUTLINE

1 If the Show First Line Only button on the Outlining toolbar is recessed, click it.

2 With the insertion point on the line below the Introduction heading, type the first paragraph shown in Figure 7-54 on the next page. Press the ENTER key.

3 Type the second paragraph shown in Figure 7-54.

The Introduction section is complete (Figure 7-54).

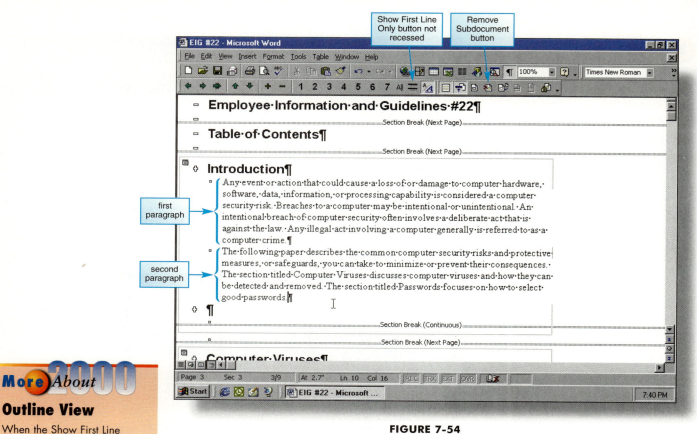

FIGURE 7-54

In outline view, text does not display formatted. Instead, each subheading is intended below the previous heading. Text formatted using the Body Text style, such as that shown in Figure 7-54, also displays indented. To display text properly formatted, switch to print layout view.

If, for some reason, you wanted to remove a subdocument from a master document, you would expand the subdocuments, click the subdocument icon to the left of the subdocument's first heading, and then press the DELETE key. Although Word removes the subdocument from the master document, the subdocument file remains on disk.

You may, for some reason, want to convert a subdocument to part of the master document – breaking the connection between the text in the master document and the subdocument. To do this, expand the subdocuments, click the subdocument icon, and then click the Remove Subdocument button on the Outlining toolbar.

Entering Text and Graphics as Part of the Master Document

The next step is to create the title page for the EIG #22 document. The completed title page is shown in Figure 7-55. You decide not to create a subdocument for the title page; instead you will enter the text as part of the master document. Because the title page contains graphics, however, you will work in print layout view as opposed to outline view.

On the title page, you want only the first line of text (Employee Information and Guidelines #22) to show up in the table of contents. Thus, only the first line should be the Heading 1 style. The remaining lines will be formatted using the Body Text style. To be sure that all text below the Heading 1 style is formatted to the Body Text style, demote the blank line below the heading to body text as described in the following steps.

FIGURE 7-55

TO DEMOTE A LINE TO BODY TEXT

1 In outline view, position the insertion point on the section break below the Employee Information and Guidelines #22 heading.

2 Click the Demote to Body Text button on the Outlining toolbar.

Word changes the current line from Heading 1 style to Body Text style (Figure 7-56).

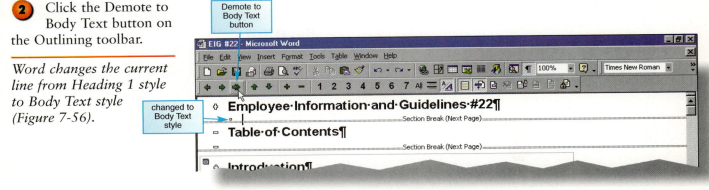

FIGURE 7-55

Enter the text for the title page as described in the following steps.

TO ENTER AND FORMAT TITLE PAGE TEXT

1 Click the Print Layout View button on the horizontal scroll bar to switch to print layout view. Click the Zoom box arrow and then click Page Width.

2 With the insertion point at the end of the first line on the title page, press the ENTER key twice. Press the UP ARROW key to position the insertion point on the blank line.

3 Press CTRL+2 to change line spacing to double. Press the ENTER key.

4 Type COMPUTER SECURITY and then press the ENTER key. Type A Discussion and then press the ENTER key. Type On Viruses and Passwords and then press the ENTER key two times.

5 Center all lines on the title page, including the blank lines.

6 Change the COMPUTER SECURITY line to 36-point Britannic Bold font.

7 Change the lines, A Discussion and On Viruses and Passwords, to 26-point Britannic Bold font.

The title page displays as shown in Figure 7-57.

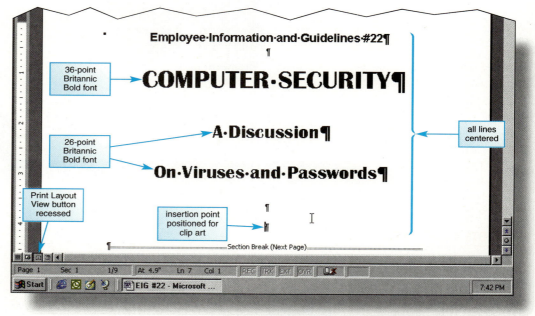

FIGURE 7-57

The next step is to insert the clip art image of a man and woman talking as described in the following steps.

TO INSERT CLIP ART

1 Click the second paragraph mark below the last line of text on the title page (see Figure 7-57). Click Insert on the menu bar, point to Picture, and then click Clip Art.

2 When the Insert ClipArt window opens, click the Search for clips text box. Type man woman talking and then press the ENTER key.

③ Click the clip that matches the one shown in Figure 7-58. Click the Insert clip button on the Pop-up menu.

④ Click the Close button on the Insert ClipArt window's title bar.

Word inserts the graphic of the man and woman talking at the location of the insertion point as an inline object (see Figure 7-58).

The next step is to add a callout to the title page.

Adding an AutoShape

You can insert two types of graphics into a Word document: a picture and a drawing object. A **picture** is a graphic that was created in another program. Examples of pictures are scanned images, photographs, and clip art. A **drawing object** is a graphic that you create using Word. You can modify or enhance drawing objects using the Drawing toolbar. Examples of drawing objects include AutoShapes, curves, lines, and WordArt drawing objects.

In a previous project, you created special text effects using WordArt. In this project, you add an **AutoShape**, which is a predefined shape in Word. Examples of AutoShapes include rectangles, circles, triangles, arrows, flowcharting symbols, stars, banners, and callouts. You can add text to most AutoShapes simply by clicking the shape and typing the text.

Perform the following steps to add a callout AutoShape that contains text.

More About

AutoShapes

To fill an AutoShape with color, change the color of its borders, rotate the AutoShape, or add shadow or 3-D effects to an AutoShape, select the drawing object and then click the appropriate button on the Drawing toolbar.

Steps **To Add an AutoShape**

① **Double-click the move handle on the Standard toolbar to display the entire toolbar. If the Drawing toolbar is not displaying on your screen, click the Drawing button on the Standard toolbar. Click the AutoShapes button on the Drawing toolbar, point to Callouts, and then point to the Cloud Callout (Figure 7-58).**

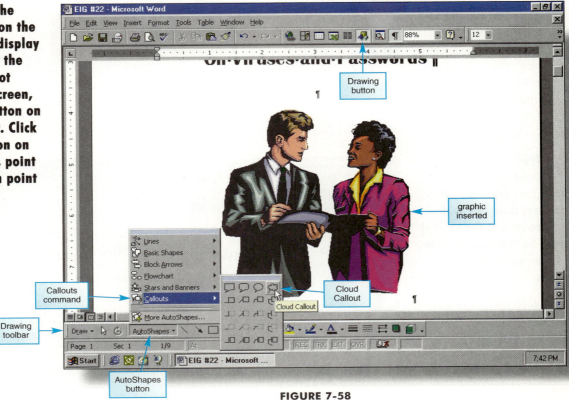

FIGURE 7-58

2 **Click the Cloud Callout. Position the mouse pointer as shown in Figure 7-59.**

Word displays the crosshair mouse pointer in the document window (Figure 7-59). You drag the crosshair mouse pointer to form the AutoShape.

FIGURE 7-59

3 **Drag the mouse upward and rightward to form a cloud callout similar to the one shown in Figure 7-60. If, once the callout is drawn, you need to resize it, simply drag the sizing handles.**

Word displays the cloud callout in the document (Figure 7-60). The insertion point blinks inside the callout. The callout may cover a portion of the graphic; if this occurs, you will move it in the next step.

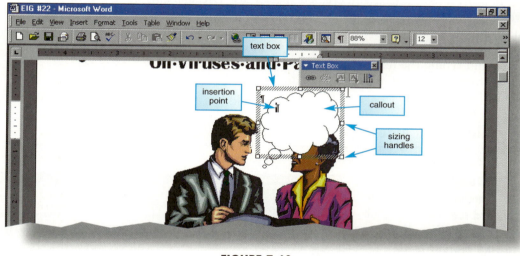

FIGURE 7-60

4 **Type** Do our computers have these safeguards? **If necessary, drag the text box surrounding the callout upward so the callout does not cover any part of the graphic.**

Word enters the callout text and displays the callout in its new location (Figure 7-61).

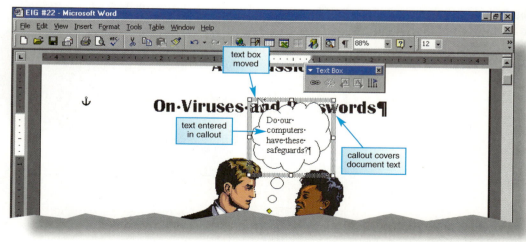

FIGURE 7-61

Even though the text displays in the callout on the screen and more than likely displays properly in print preview, some printers will not print the text in the callout unless the callout is a certain width. The width requirement varies from printer to printer. You should print the title page now to determine if your callout text prints properly. If it does not, make the callout wider and try printing the title page again. Repeat this process until the text in the callout prints properly.

If, when you create an AutoShape, the insertion point is not in the shape, you can add text to an AutoShape by right-clicking the AutoShape and then clicking Add Text on the shortcut menu. To edit existing text, click in the existing text or right-click the existing text and then click Edit Text on the shortcut menu.

Grouping Drawing Objects

Notice in Figure 7-61 that the callout now covers a portion of the title page text. Thus, the next step is to move the callout and the graphic. If you move the callout, it moves independent of the graphic; likewise, if you move the graphic, it moves independent of the callout. You would like both objects (the callout and the graphic) to move together as a single unit. Thus, you must group the objects together.

The objects you wish to group must be floating. Recall that the graphic of the man and woman talking is inline. Perform the following steps to change the inline graphic to a floating graphic.

TO CHANGE AN INLINE GRAPHIC TO FLOATING GRAPHIC

1. Click the graphic of the man and woman talking.

2. If the Picture toolbar does not display, right-click the graphic and then click Show Picture toolbar on the shortcut menu. Click the Text Wrapping button on the Picture toolbar and then point to Square (Figure 7-62).

3. Click Square on the Picture toolbar.

Word changes the graphic from inline to floating.

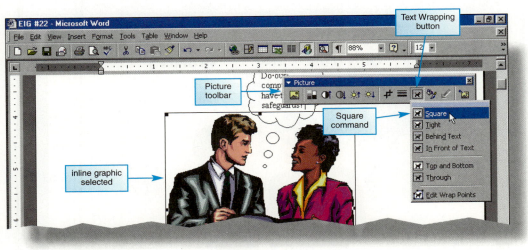

FIGURE 7-62

The next step is to group the two floating objects together so they can be moved as a single unit. Perform the steps on the next page to group objects.

More About

Rotating an Object

To rotate a drawing object or flip a drawing object 90 degrees, select the object, click the Draw button on the Drawing toolbar, point to Rotate or Flip, and then select the desired command. You also can rotate a selected object to any degree by clicking the Free Rotate button on the Drawing toolbar and then dragging a round handle on a corner of the object. When the object is in the desired position, click outside the object.

 **To Group Objects**

1 If necessary, scroll down to display both graphics. With the graphic of the man and woman talking still selected, hold down the SHIFT key while clicking the cloud callout. Click the Draw button on the Drawing toolbar and then point to Group.

Word selects both objects, the graphic of the man and woman talking and the cloud callout (Figure 7-63).

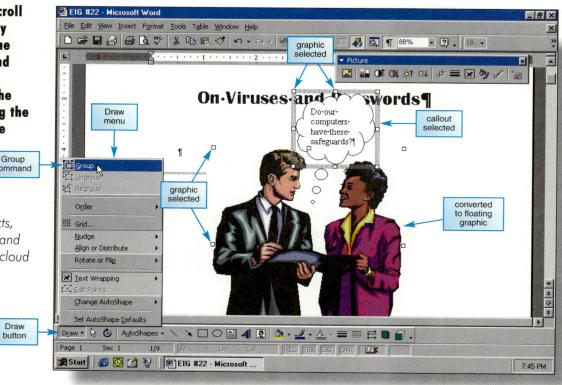

FIGURE 7-63

2 Click Group.

Word groups the two objects together into a single object (Figure 7-64). Notice the sizing handles now display surrounding both objects together.

FIGURE 7-64

If, for some reason, you wanted the objects to be separated again, you could **ungroup** them by selecting the grouped object, clicking the Draw button on the Drawing toolbar and then clicking Ungroup. If the Ungroup command is dimmed, you are attempting to ungroup an image that Word cannot ungroup.

The next step is to move the grouped object down so it does not cover the text of the title page. Because the graphic is so large and you want to see the entire graphic on the page as you move it, you display the entire page in the document window before moving the graphic, as described in the following steps.

TO MOVE A GRAPHIC

1 Click the Zoom box arrow on the Standard toolbar and then click Whole Page.

2 Point to the middle of the graphic and drag the graphic to its new location; in this case, drag it down so it does not cover any words on the title page (Figure 7-65).

3 Click the Zoom box arrow on the Standard toolbar and then click Page Width.

4 Click the Drawing button on the Drawing toolbar to remove the Drawing toolbar from the screen.

5 Click the Save button on the Standard toolbar to save the document.

Word moves both objects together as a single unit.

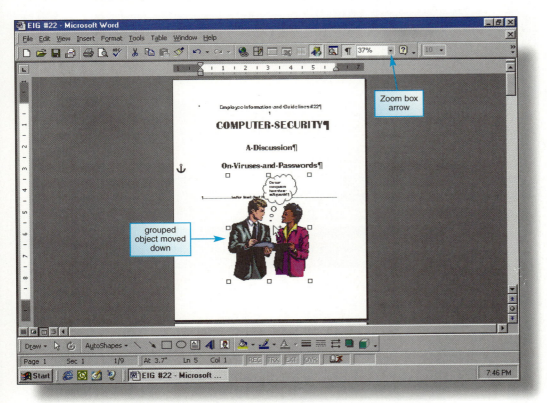

FIGURE 7-65

The title page is complete. The next step is to create the table of figures for the EIG #22 document.

Creating a Table of Figures

All EIG #22 documents have a table of figures following the text of the document. A **table of figures** is a list of all illustrations such as graphics, pictures, and tables in a document. Word creates the table of figures from the captions in the document. Perform the following steps to create a table of figures.

Steps To Create a Table of Figures

1 Scroll down to display the Table of Figures heading. Position the insertion point at the end of the heading. Press the ENTER key. Click Insert on the menu bar and then point to Index and Tables (Figure 7-66).

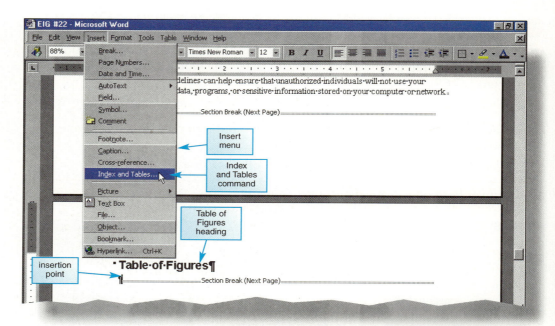

FIGURE 7-66

2 Click Index and Tables. When the Index and Tables dialog box displays, if necessary, click the Table of Figures tab. Be sure that the three check boxes in your dialog box contain check marks. Point to the OK button.

Word displays the Table of Figures sheet in the Index and Tables dialog box (Figure 7-67).

FIGURE 7-67

3 Click the OK button.

Word creates a table of figures at the location of the insertion point (Figure 7-68).

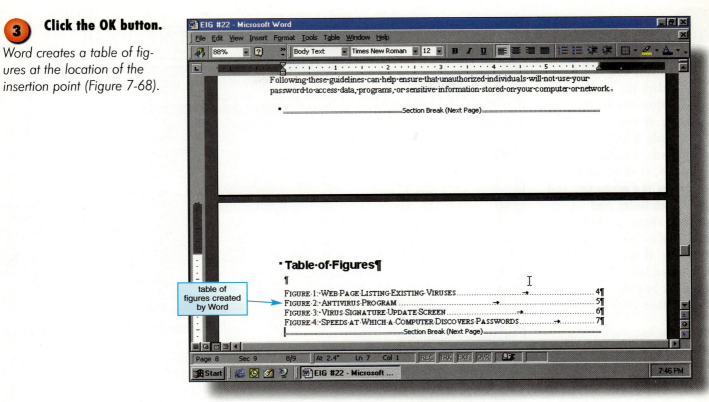

FIGURE 7-68

When you modify captions in a document or move illustrations to a different location in the document, you will have to update the table of figures. To do this, click to the left of the table and then press F9.

If you did not use captions to create labels for your illustrations in a document and would like Word to generate a table of figures, you can instruct Word to create the table using the built-in style you used for the captions. To do this, click the Options button in the Table of Figures sheet to display the Table of Figures Options dialog box.

The next step is to build an index for the document.

Building an Index

As mentioned earlier in this project, the EIG documents end with an **index**, which lists important terms discussed in the document along with each term's corresponding page number. For Word to generate the index, you first must mark any item you wish to appear in the index. Earlier in this project, you marked an entry in the Passwords file. The Computer Viruses file also already has index entries marked.

When you have marked all index entries, you can have Word build the index from the index entry fields in the document. The index entry fields display on the screen when the Show/Hide ¶ button on the Standard toolbar is recessed; that is, when you display formatting marks. Because these index entry field codes may alter the document pagination, you should hide field codes before building an index. Perform the tasks on the next page to build an index.

Steps **To Build an Index**

1 Scroll down and click the paragraph mark below the Index heading. If the Show/Hide ¶ button on the Standard toolbar is recessed, click it. Click Insert on the menu bar and then click Index and Tables. When the Index and Tables dialog box displays, if necessary, click the Index tab. Click the Formats box arrow. Scroll to and then click Formal.

Word displays the Index sheet in the Index and Tables dialog box (Figure 7-69). The Formats box contains a variety of available index styles.

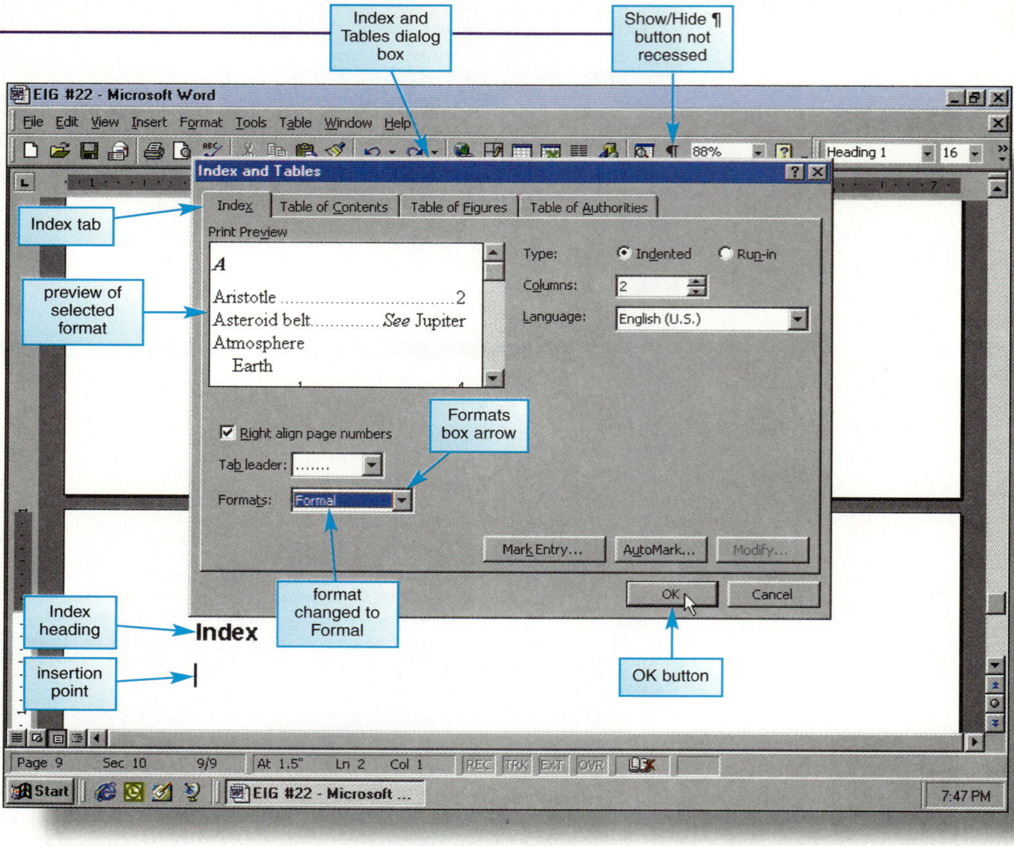

FIGURE 7-69

2 Click the OK button. If necessary, click outside the index to remove the selection.

Word creates a formal index at the location of the insertion point (Figure 7-70).

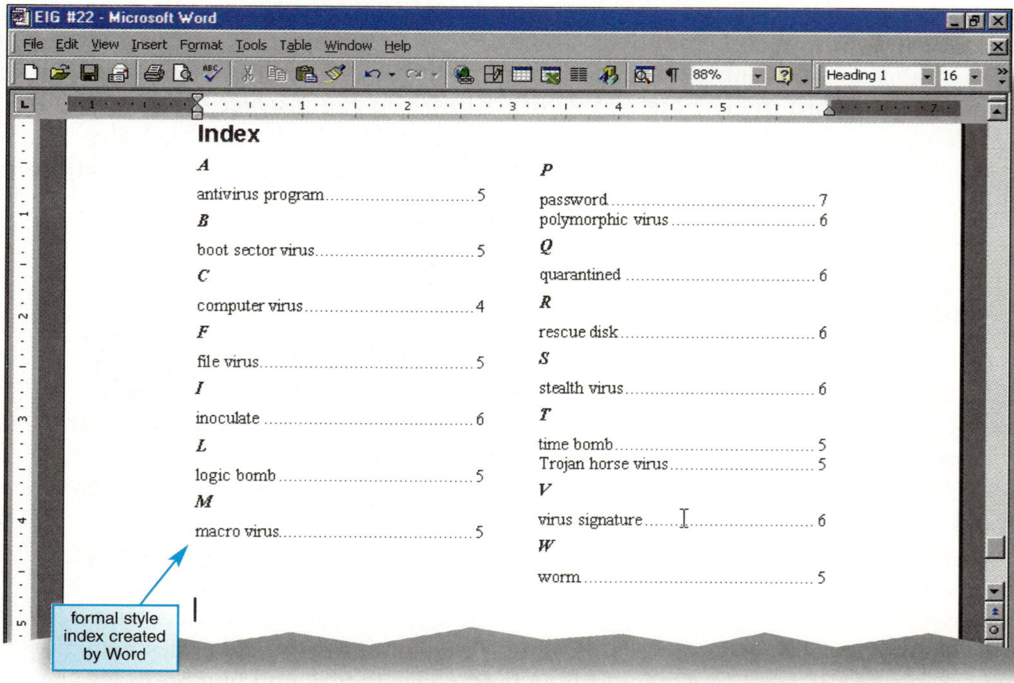

FIGURE 7-70

To update an index, click to the left of the index and then press F9. To delete an index, click to the left of the index and then press SHIFT+F9 to display field codes. Drag through the entire field code, including the braces, and then press the DELETE key.

The next step is to create the table of contents for the EIG #22 document.

Creating a Table of Contents

A **table of contents** is a list of all headings in a document and their associated page numbers. When you use Word's built-in heading styles (e.g., Heading 1), you can instruct Word to create a table of contents from these headings. In the EIG #22 document, the heading of each section used the Heading 1 style and subheadings used the Heading 2 style. Thus, perform the following steps to create a table of contents from heading styles.

More About 2000

Indexes and Tables

If your index, table of contents, or table of figures displays odd characters inside curly braces {}, then Word is displaying field codes instead of field results. Press ALT+F9 to display the index or table correctly. If your index or table prints field codes, click Tools on the menu bar, click Options, click the Print tab, remove the check mark from the Field codes check box, click the OK button, and then print the document again.

Steps: To Create a Table of Contents

1 **Scroll up and click to the right of the Table of Contents heading. Press the ENTER key. Click Insert on the menu bar and then click Index and Tables. When the Index and Tables dialog box displays, if necessary, click the Table of Contents tab. Click the Formats box arrow and then click Formal.**

Word displays the Table of Contents sheet in the Index and Tables dialog box (Figure 7-71). The Formats list contains a variety of available table of contents styles.

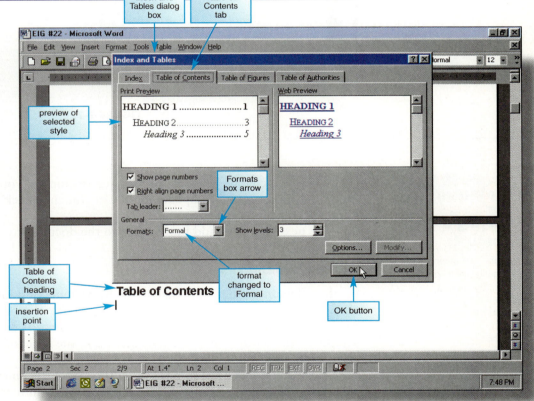

FIGURE 7-71

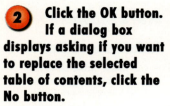

Microsoft **Word 2000**

2 **Click the OK button. If a dialog box displays asking if you want to replace the selected table of contents, click the No button.**

Word creates a formal table of contents at the location of the insertion point (Figure 7-72).

table of contents created by Word →

FIGURE 7-72

More *About* **2000**

Modifying a Table of Contents

If the table of contents that Word generates contains a heading that you do not want, change the style applied to the heading from a built-in heading to a non-heading style. Then, update the table of contents.

More *About* **2000**

Bookmarks

To show bookmarks in a document, click Tools on the menu bar, click Options, click the View tab, place a check mark in the Bookmarks check box, and then click the OK button. If your bookmark displays an error message, select the entire document and then press F9 to update the fields in the document.

When you change headings or text in a document, you should update its associated table of contents. To update a table of contents, click to the left of the table of contents and then press F9.

The next step is to add bookmarks to the document.

Adding Bookmarks

In a document that contains a table of contents or a table of figures, you can use these tables to navigate through a document. That is, you can click any of the entries in either table and Word displays the associated text or graphics in the document window. For example, if you click Figure 2 in the table of figures, Word displays the page containing Figure 2.

To further assist users in navigating through a document, you can add bookmarks. A **bookmark** is an item in a document that you name for future reference. For example, you could bookmark the two headings, Computer Viruses and Passwords, so that users easily could jump to these two areas of the document. Perform the following steps to add these bookmarks.

 **To Add a Bookmark**

1 Scroll to the Computer Viruses heading in the document. Drag through the heading Computer Viruses. Click Insert on the menu bar and then point to Bookmark (Figure 7-73).

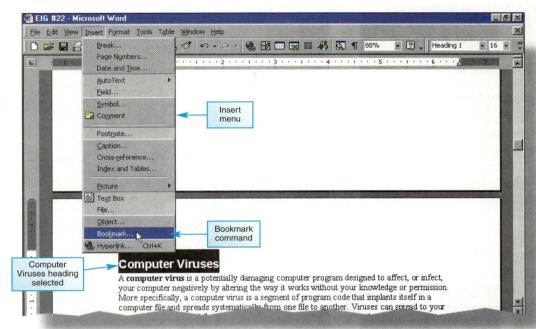

FIGURE 7-73

2 Click Bookmark. When the Bookmark dialog box displays, type ComputerViruses in the Bookmark name text box and then point to the Add button.

Word displays the Bookmark dialog box (Figure 7-74). Bookmark names can contain only letters, numbers, and the underscore character (_). Also, they must begin with a letter and contain no spaces.

3 Click the Add button.

Word adds the bookmark name to the list of existing bookmarks for the document.

4 Repeat Steps 1 through 3 for the Passwords heading in the document.

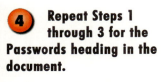

FIGURE 7-74

Once you have added bookmarks, you can jump to a bookmark by displaying the Bookmark dialog box, clicking the bookmark name in the list, and then clicking the Go To button; or by displaying the Go To dialog box, clicking bookmark in the list, selecting the bookmark name, and then clicking the Go To button.

The text of the document now is complete. The next step is to place a header on all pages except the title page.

Creating Alternating Headers and Footers

The EIG documents are designed so that they can be duplicated back to back. That is, the document prints on nine separate pages. When you duplicate it, however, pages one and two are printed on opposite sides of the same sheet of paper. Thus, the nine page document when printed back-to-back only uses five sheets of paper.

In many books and documents that have facing pages, the page number is on the outside edges of the pages. In Word, you accomplish this task by specifying one type of header for even-numbered pages and another type of header for odd-numbered pages. Perform the following steps to create alternating headers beginning with the second page of the document.

Steps **To Create Alternating Headers**

1 **Position the insertion point in the Table of Contents heading (section 2 of the document), click View on the menu bar and then click Header and Footer. Click the Page Setup button on the Header and Footer toolbar. When the Page Setup dialog box displays, if necessary, click the Layout tab. Click Different odd and even. Click the Apply to box arrow and then click This point forward.**

Word displays the Page Setup dialog box (Figure 7-75).

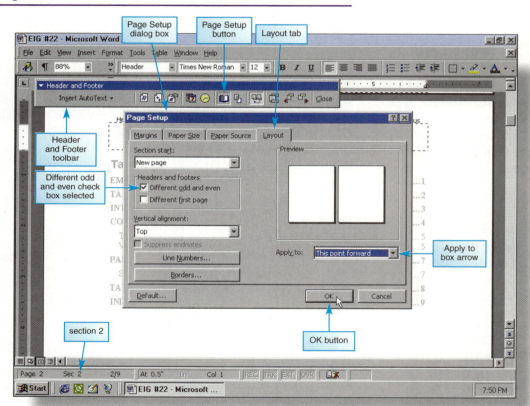

FIGURE 7-75

2 **Click the OK button. If the Same as Previous button on the Header and Footer toolbar is recessed, click it. Type** Textbooks Press EIG #22 **and then press the ENTER key. Type** Page **and then press the SPACEBAR. Click the Insert Page Number button on the Header and Footer toolbar. Press the ENTER key. Point to the Show Next button on the Header and Footer toolbar.**

Word displays the Even Page Header area (Figure 7-76). You want text on even page numbers to be left-aligned and text on odd page numbers to be right-aligned. The Show Next button will display the Odd Page Header area.

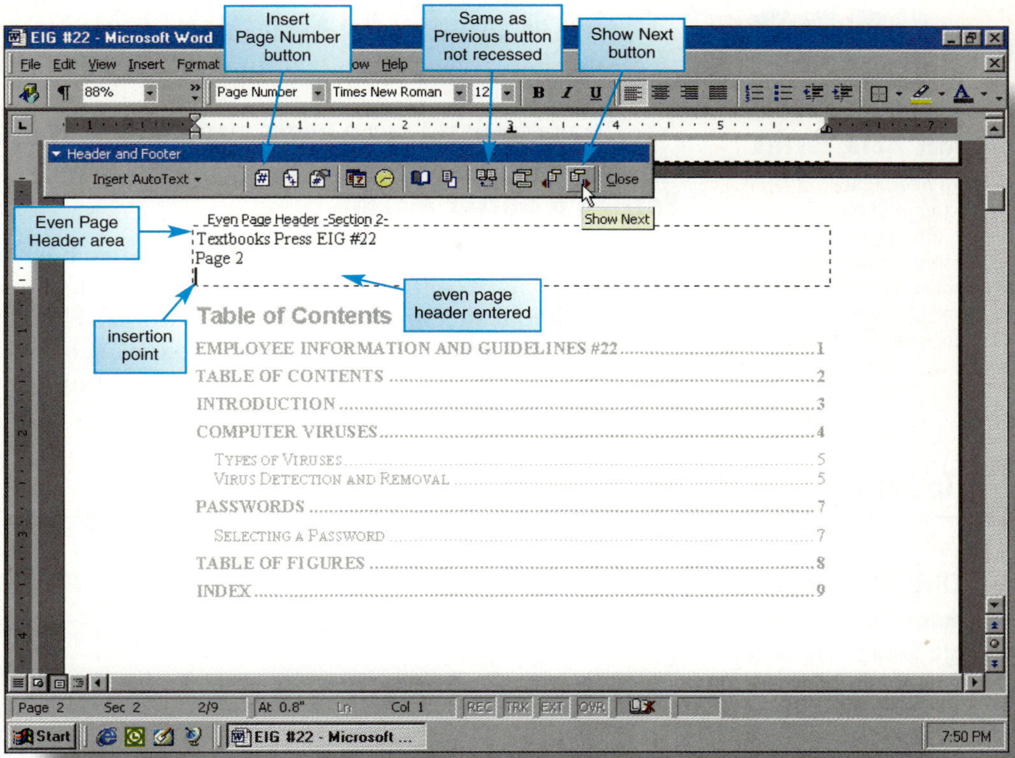

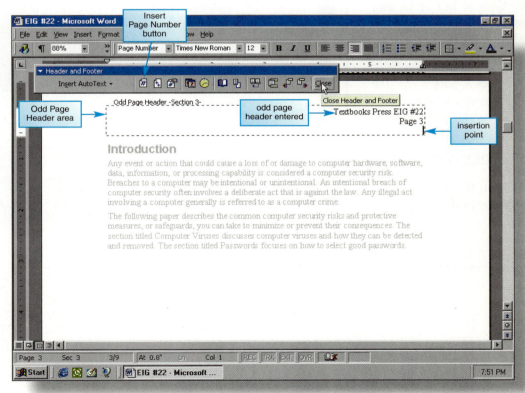

FIGURE 7-76

3 **Click the Show Next button. If the Same as Previous button on the Header and Footer toolbar is recessed, click it. Point to the right edge of the Odd Page Header area so a right-align icon displays next to the mouse pointer and then double-click. Type** Textbooks Press EIG #22 **and then press the ENTER key. Type** Page **and then press the SPACEBAR. Click the Insert Page Number button on the Header and Footer toolbar. Press the ENTER key.**

The odd page header is complete (Figure 7-77).

4 **Click the Close button on the Header and Footer toolbar.**

FIGURE 7-77

More *About*

Publishing and Graphic Arts Terms

For more information on terms used in publishing and graphic arts, visit the Word 2000 More About Web page (www.scsite.com/wd2000/more.htm) and then click Publishing and Graphic Arts Terms.

To create alternating footers, you follow the same basic procedure as you would to create alternating headers, except you enter text in the footer area instead of the header area.

The next step is to set a gutter margin for the document.

Setting a Gutter Margin

The EIG documents are designed so that the inner margin between facing pages has extra space to allow printed versions of the documents to be bound (such as stapled) – without the binding covering the words. This extra space in the inner margin is called the **gutter margin**. Perform the following steps to set a three-quarter inch left and right margin and a one-half inch gutter margin.

Steps **To Set a Gutter Margin**

1 **Click File on the menu bar and then click Page Setup. When the Page Setup dialog box displays, if necessary, click the Margins tab. Type** .75 **in the Left text box,** .75 **in the Right text box, and** .5 **in the Gutter text box. Click the Apply to box arrow and then click Whole document. Point to the OK button.**

Word displays the Page Setup dialog box (Figure 7-78). The Preview area illustrates the position of the gutter margin.

2 **Click the OK button.**

Word sets the gutter margin for the entire document.

FIGURE 7-78

Because you have changed the margins, it is possible the page numbers of the headings, figures, and index entries may have changed. Whenever you modify pages in a document, you should update the page numbers in the table of contents, table of figures, and index as shown in the following steps.

Steps **To Update the Table of Contents, Table of Figures, and Index**

1 **Be sure the Show/ Hide ¶ button on the Standard toolbar is not recessed. Click Edit on the menu bar and then click Select All. Press F9. When the Update Table of Contents dialog box displays, if necessary, click Update page numbers only to select it. Point to the OK button.**

Word displays the Update Table of Contents dialog box (Figure 7-79). The entire document is selected.

2 **Click the OK button. When the Update Table of Figures dialog box displays, click the OK button. Click to remove the selection.**

Word updates the page numbers in the table of figures, table of contents, and index.

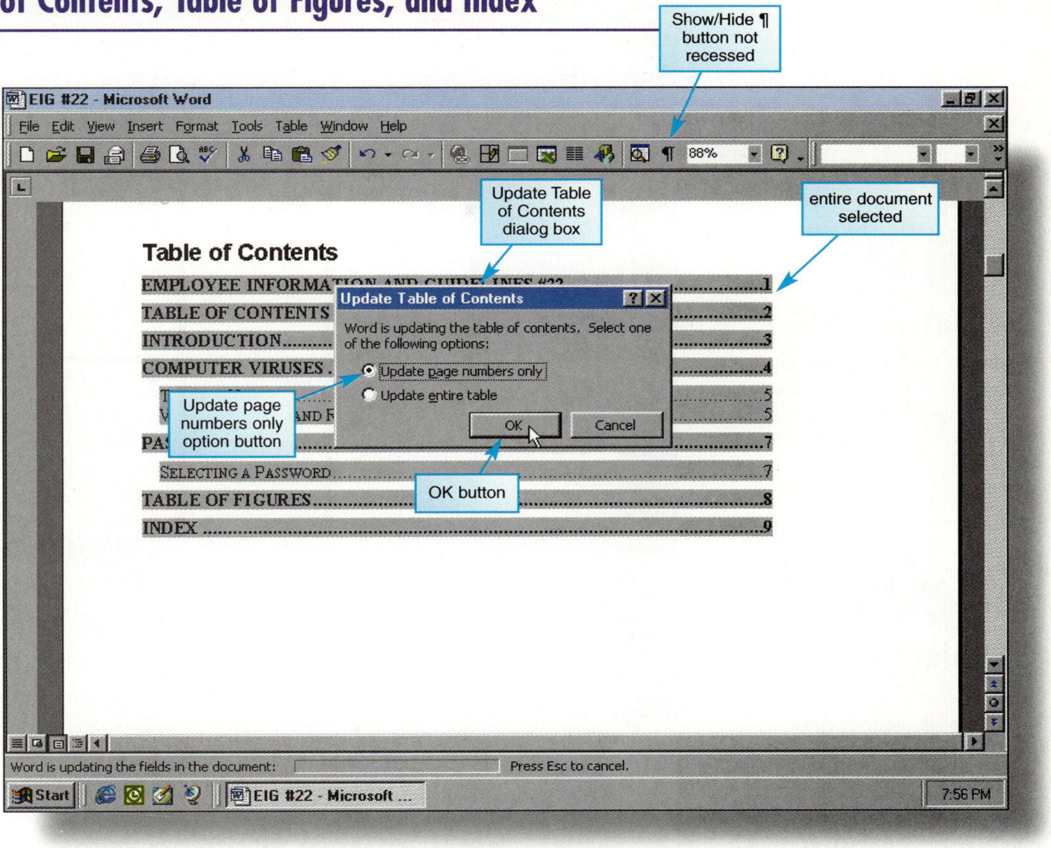

FIGURE 7-79

To visually see the layout of all of the pages in the document, display all the pages in print preview as described in the following steps.

TO DISPLAY SEVERAL PAGES IN PRINT PREVIEW

1 Double-click the move handle on the Standard toolbar to display the entire toolbar. Click the Print Preview button on the Standard toolbar.

2 Click the Multiple Pages button on the Print Preview toolbar. Click the right-bottom icon in the grid (when the description reads 2 x 6 pages) to display the pages in the EIG document as shown in Figure 7-80 on the next page.

3 Click the Close button on the Print Preview toolbar.

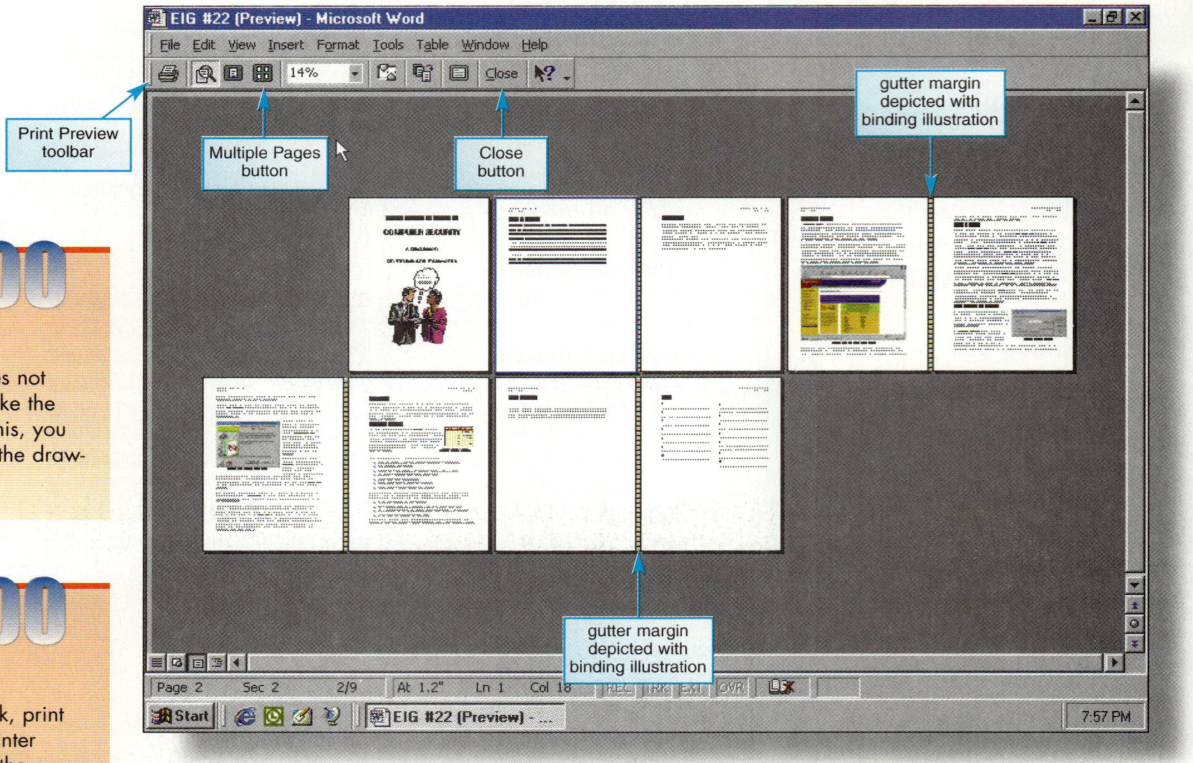

Callouts

If text in a callout does not print, you need to make the callout wider. To do this, you will need to ungroup the drawing object first.

Printing

If you want to save ink, print faster, or minimize printer overrun errors, lower the printer resolution. Click File on the menu bar, click Print, click the Properties button in the Print dialog box, click the Graphics tab, click the Resolution box arrow, click a lower resolution than that displayed currently, click the Apply button, click the OK button, and then click the Close button.

Subdocuments

If you want to change the name of a subdocument, you cannot use Windows Explorer. Instead, display the document in outline view, click the Collapse Subdocuments button on the Outlining toolbar, and then click the hyperlink of the document to be renamed. When the subdocument displays in its own Word window, click File on the menu bar, click Save As, change the document name, and then click the Save button in the dialog box. Then, return to the master document by clicking File on the menu bar and then clicking Close.

FIGURE 7-80

The reference document for this project now is complete. Perform the following steps to save it again, print it, and then close the document.

TO SAVE THE DOCUMENT AGAIN

1 Click the Save button on the Standard toolbar.

Word saves the reference document with the same file name, EIG #22.

TO PRINT THE DOCUMENT

1 Click the Print button on the Standard toolbar.

The completed reference document prints each page shown in Figure 7-1 on page WD 7.5 on a separate piece of paper.

TO CLOSE THE DOCUMENT

1 Click File on the menu bar and then click Close.

Opening a Master Document

You may wish to open a master document at a later date to edit or print its contents. When you open the master document, the subdocuments are collapsed; that is, the subdocuments display as hyperlinks. Thus, switch to outline view and expand the subdocuments as shown in the following steps.

Steps   **To Open a Master Document**

1 **Open the EIG #22 document. Click the Outline View button on the horizontal scroll bar. Be sure the Show All Headings button on the Outlining toolbar is recessed and the Show First Line Only button is not recessed. Scroll down to display the hyperlinks. Point to the Expand Subdocuments button on the Outlining toolbar.**

Word displays the EIG #22 document in outline view (Figure 7-81).

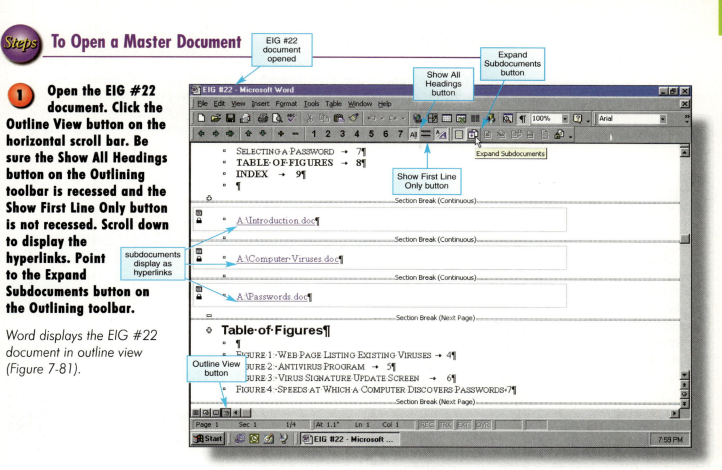

FIGURE 7-81

2 **Click the Expand Subdocuments button. When the Passwords dialog box displays, type** sunshine **and then click the OK button.**

Word displays the contents of the subdocuments in the master document (Figure 7-82).

3 **Click the Print Layout View button.**

The master document is ready to be printed or modified.

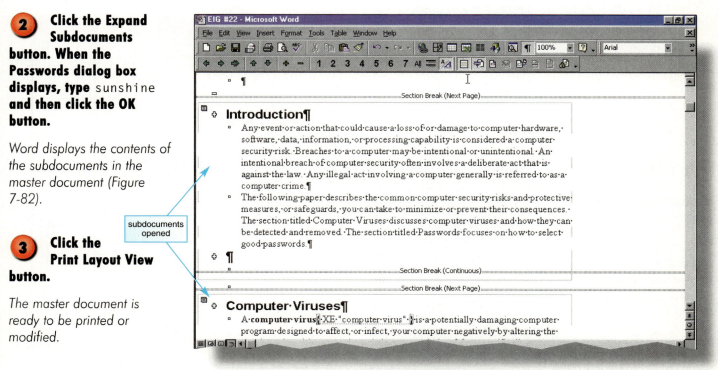

FIGURE 7-82

Using the Document Map

When you use Word's built-in heading styles in a document, you can use the Document Map to quickly navigate through the document. The **Document Map** is a separate area at the left edge of the Word window that displays these headings in an outline format. When you click a heading in the Document Map, Word scrolls to and displays that heading in the document window. Perform the following steps to use the Document Map.

Steps To Use the Document Map

1   Click the Document Map button on the Standard toolbar. Right-click the Document Map and then click All on the shortcut menu to ensure that all headings display.

Word displays the Document Map in a separate pane at the left edge of the Word window (Figure 7-83). The Document Map lists all headings that are formatted using Word's built-in heading styles.

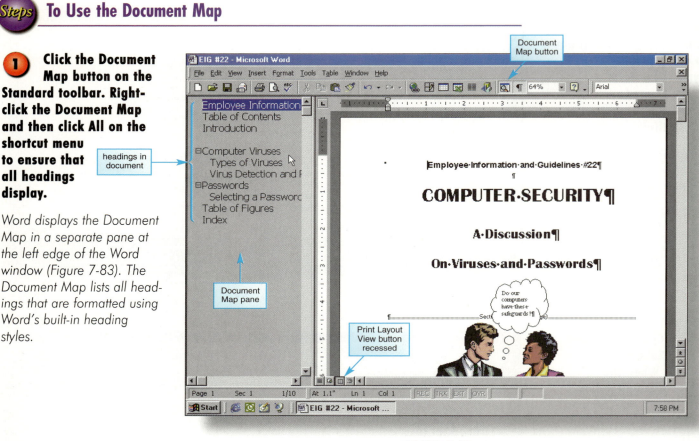

FIGURE 7-83

2   Click Table of Contents in the Document Map pane.

Word scrolls to and displays the Table of Contents heading at the top of the document window (Figure 7-84).

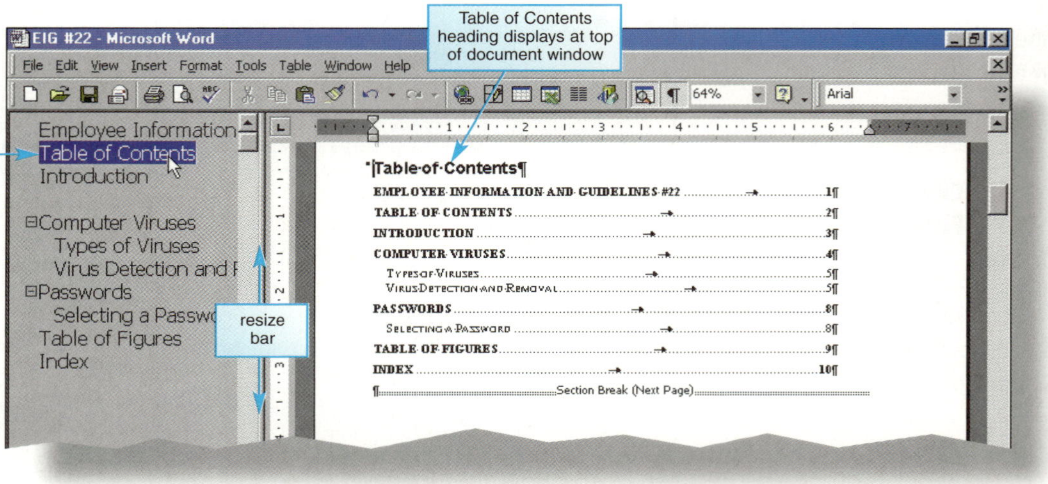

FIGURE 7-84

To display any subheadings below a heading, click the plus sign (+) to the left of the heading. Likewise, to hide any subheadings below a heading, click the minus sign (-) to the left of the heading.

If a heading is too wide for the Document Map pane, you do not need to make the Document Map pane wider – simply point to the heading to display a ScreenTip that shows the complete heading. You can, however, change the width of the Document Map pane by dragging the resize bar to the left or right.

Modifying the Table of Contents and Index

Assume you wanted to change the title of the Table of Contents to just the word, Contents. Assume also that you want to change the index entry for computer virus to just the word, virus. After making these changes to the document, you must update the table of contents and the index as shown in the following steps.

Quick Reference

For a table that lists how to complete the tasks covered in this book using the mouse, menu, shortcut menu, and keyboard, see the Word Quick Reference Summary at the back of this book or visit the Shelly Cashman Series Office Web page (www.scsite.com/off2000/qr.htm) and then click Microsoft Word 2000.

Steps: To Modify a Table of Contents and Index

1 Drag through the words, Table of, in the Table of Contents heading and then press the DELETE key. If the Show/Hide ¶ button on the Standard toolbar is not recessed, click it. Click the Computer Viruses heading in the Document Map pane. Double-click the move handle on the Formatting toolbar to display the entire toolbar. Double-click the bold word, computer, to select it and then click the Bold button to remove the bold. Double-click the word, computer, inside the braces and then press the DELETE key.

The document is modified (Figure 7-85). You display formatting marks to change the index entry fields.

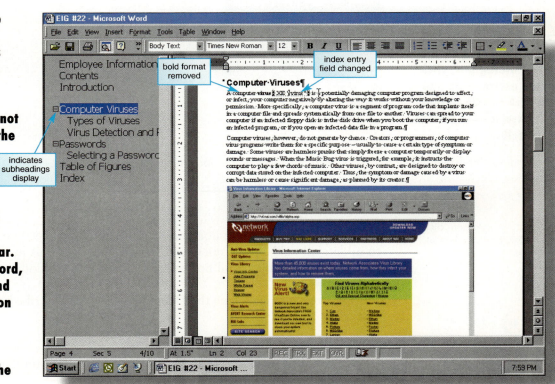

FIGURE 7-85

2 **Double-click the Standard toolbar to display the entire toolbar. Click the Show/Hide ¶ button on the Standard toolbar. Click Edit on the menu bar and then click Select All. Press F9. When the Update Table of Contents dialog box displays, click Update entire table and then point to the OK button.**

Word displays the Update Table of Contents dialog box (Figure 7-86).

3 **Click the OK button. When Word displays the Update Table of Figures dialog box, click Update entire table and then click the OK button. Click anywhere to remove the selection.**

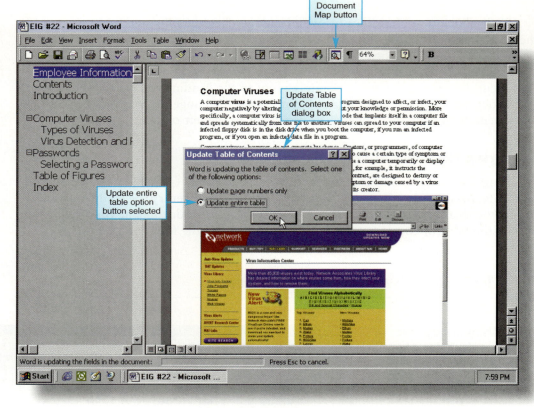

FIGURE 7-86

Word updates the Table of Figures, along with any fields in the document, including the index.

1. Right-click selection, click Update Field on shortcut menu

By selecting the entire document and then pressing F9, you are instructing Word to update all fields in the document, which includes fields in the table of contents, table of figures, index, and bookmarks. If you want to update a single field, select it and then press F9.

The next step is to hide the Document Map, as described in the following step.

TO HIDE THE DOCUMENT MAP

1 Click the Document Map button on the Standard toolbar.

Word removes the Document Map pane from the Word window.

You also can hide the Document Map by double-clicking the resize bar to its right. You are finished modifying the document. Perform the following step to quit Word.

TO QUIT WORD

1 Click the Close button in the Word window. When Word displays a dialog box asking if you wish to save changes, click the No button.

The Word window closes.

Microsoft Certification

The Microsoft Office User Specialist (MOUS) Certification program provides an opportunity for you to obtain a valuable industry credential - proof that you have the Word 2000 skills required by employers. For more information, see Appendix D or visit the Shelly Cashman Series MOUS Web page at www.scsite.com/off2000/cert.htm.

C A S E   P E R S P E C T I V E   S U M M A R Y

You send the redesigned EIG #22 document to Marge for her approval. She is thrilled with the new design. The table of contents, table of figures, and index really organize the document for a reader. She gives you approval to duplicate and distribute the document.

Marge would like you to conduct training classes for company employees on the change-tracking features of Word. You send an e-mail announcing the schedule and topic of the training classes. Next, you write a set of instructions to distribute to each attendee at the training classes. Your first class is tomorrow — it sure will be nice to be on the other side of the podium!

Project Summary

Project 7 introduced you to creating a long document with a table of contents, a table of figures, and an index. You inserted, modified, reviewed, and deleted comments. You also tracked changes and accepted and rejected the tracked changes. You learned how to save multiple versions of a document, embed an Excel worksheet, add and modify a caption, create a cross-reference, mark index entries, add a bookmark, keep paragraphs together, password-protect a document, create alternating headers, set a gutter margin, add an AutoShape, and group drawing objects. You also worked with master documents and subdocuments. Finally, you used the Document Map to navigate through the document.

What You Should Know

Having completed this project, you should now be able to perform the following tasks:

- Add a Bookmark *(WD 7.59)*
- Add a Caption *(WD 7.26)*
- Add an AutoShape *(WD 7.49)*
- Build an Index *(WD 7.56)*
- Change an Inline Graphic to a Floating Graphic *(WD 7.25, WD 7.51)*
- Close the Document *(WD 7.36, WD 7.64)*
- Convert a Text Box to a Frame *(WD 7.28)*
- Convert an Embedded Object to a Word Graphic *(WD 7.24)*
- Create a Cross-Reference *(WD 7.29)*
- Create a Subdocument *(WD 7.43)*
- Create a Table of Contents *(WD 7.57)*
- Create a Table of Figures *(WD 7.54)*
- Create Alternating Headers *(WD 7.60)*
- Create an Outline *(WD 7.37)*
- Delete a Comment *(WD 7.18)*
- Demote a Line to Body Text *(WD 7.47)*
- Display Formatting Marks *(WD 7.7)*
- Display Several Pages in Print Preview *(WD 7.63)*
- Embed an Object *(WD 7.23)*
- Enter and Format Title Page Text *(WD 7.48)*
- Enter Body Text into an Outline *(WD 7.45)*
- Group Objects *(WD 7.52)*
- Hide the Document Map *(WD 7.68)*
- Insert a Comment *(WD 7.10)*
- Insert a Password-Protected File as a Subdocument *(WD 7.42)*
- Insert a Subdocument *(WD 7.40)*
- Insert Clip Art *(WD 7.48)*
- Keep Paragraphs Together *(WD 7.33)*
- Mark an Index Entry *(WD 7.31)*
- Modify a Table of Contents and Index *(WD 7.67)*
- Modify an Outline *(WD 7.44)*
- Modify the Caption *(WD 7.28)*
- Move a Graphic *(WD 7.53)*
- Open a Document *(WD 7.9)*
- Open a Master Document *(WD 7.65)*
- Password-Protect a File *(WD 7.34)*
- Print the Document *(WD 7.64)*
- Quit Word *(WD 7.68)*
- Reset Menus and Toolbars *(WD 7.7)*
- Resize an Object *(WD 7.24)*
- Review Comments *(WD 7.17)*
- Review Tracked Changes *(WD 7.19)*
- Save a Document *(WD 7.43)*
- Save a Document with a New File Name *(WD 7.9)*
- Save a Version of a Document *(WD 7.15)*
- Save the Document Again *(WD 7.64)*
- Set a Gutter Margin *(WD 7.62)*
- Start Word *(WD 7.6)*
- Stop Tracking Changes *(WD 7.14)*
- Track Changes *(WD 7.13)*
- Update the Table of Contents, Table of Figures, and Index *(WD 7.63)*
- Use the Document Map *(WD 7.66)*
- Zoom Text Width *(WD 7.9)*

Apply Your Knowledge

➕ **Project Reinforcement at www.scsite.com/off2000/reinforce.htm**

1 Using Word's Change-Tracking Feature

Instructions: Start Word. Open the document, Faxes Draft, on the Data Disk. If you did not download the Data Disk, see the inside back cover for instructions for downloading the Data Disk or see your instructor.

As shown in Figure 7-87, the document contains reviewer's comments and tracked changes. You are to review and delete the comments and then accept or reject each of the tracked changes.

A facsimile (fax) machine [CDG1] is a device that transmits and receives documents over telephone lines. The documents can contain text, drawings, or photographs, or can be handwritten. When sent or received via a fax machine, these documents are known as faxes. A stand-alone fax machine reads scans the original document, converts the image into digitized data, and transmits the digitized image. A fax machine at the other receiving end reads the incoming data, converts the digitized data into an image, and prints or stores a copy of the original image. ¶

Fax capability also can be added to your computer using a fax modem. A fax modem is a communications device that allows you to send (and sometimes receive) electronic documents as faxes. A fax modem transmits computer-prepared documents [CDG2] such as a word processing letter, or documents that have been digitized with a scanner or digital camera. A fax modem is like a regular modem except that it is designed to transmit documents to a fax machine or to another fax modem. ¶

When a computer (instead of a fax machine) receives a fax document, you can view the document on the screen or print it using special fax software. The quality of the viewed or printed fax is less than that of a word processing document because the fax actually is a large image. If you have optical character recognition (OCR) software, you also can edit the document. ¶

A fax modem can be an external peripheral that plugs into a port on the back of the system unit or an internal card that is inserted into an expansion slot on the motherboard. In addition, most fax modems function as regular modems. ¶

Close Full Screen

FIGURE 7-87

Perform the following tasks:

1. Right-click the TRK status indicator on the status bar and then click Highlight Changes on the shortcut menu. Verify the bottom two check boxes in the Highlight Changes dialog box contain check marks and then click the OK button. Print the document to see how it looks with tracked changes.
2. Click File on the menu bar, click Print, click the Options button, place a check mark in the Comments check box, click the OK button, and then click the OK button to print the document with comments. Click File on the menu bar, click Print, click the Options button, remove the check mark from the Comments check box, click the OK button, and then click the Close button to prevent comments from printing.
3. Click File on the menu bar, click Print, click the Print what box arrow, click Comments, and then click the OK button to print just the comments.
4. Right-click the TRK status indicator on the status bar and then click Highlight Changes on the shortcut menu. Remove the check mark from the Highlight changes in printed document check box and then click the OK button. Print the document to see how it looks with all marked changes made.

Apply Your Knowledge

Project Reinforcement at www.scsite.com/off2000/reinforce.htm

5. Press CTRL+HOME. Display the Reviewing toolbar. Be sure the TRK status indicator on the status bar is turned off. If it is not, double-click it to dim it. Click the Next Comment button on the Reviewing toolbar. Read the comment. Click the Delete Comment button on the Reviewing toolbar to delete the comment.

6. Click the Next Comment button on the Reviewing toolbar. Read the comment. Click the Delete Comment button on the Reviewing toolbar.

7. Press CTRL+HOME. Right-click the TRK status indicator on the status bar and then click Accept or Reject Changes on the shortcut menu. Click the Find Next button.

8. Click the Accept button to accept the insertion of the phrase, (fax).

9. Click the Accept button twice to accept the replacement of the word, reads, with the word, scans.

10. Click the Accept button twice to accept the replacement of the word, other, with the word, receiving.

11. Click the Accept button to accept the insertion of the example.

12. Click the Reject button to reject the insertion of the word, document.

13. Click the Accept button to accept the insertion of the phrase, a port on.

14. Click the Accept button to accept the insertion of the phrase, an expansion slot on.

15. Click the Reject button to reject the deletion of the word, regular. Click the Yes or OK button in each dialog box that displays. Click the Close button in the Accept or Reject Changes dialog box.

16. At the end of the document, insert the following comment: <u>Tracked changes accepted and rejected.</u>

17. Save the reviewed document with the name Faxes Revised. Print the document with comments.

In the Lab

1 Working with an Embedded Worksheet and Index

Problem: You work part-time for the computing services department at your school. Your supervisor has asked you to prepare a Personal Computer Buyer's Guide for students at the school. The Buyer's Guide will be available in the computer laboratory, campus library, and information booth. It will also be published on the school's intranet. A miniature version of the Personal Computer Buyer's Guide is shown in Figure 7-88 on the next page; for a more readable view, visit www.scsite.com/wd2000/project7.htm.

The Personal Computer Buyer's Guide uses an Excel worksheet, which is located on the Data Disk. If you did not download the Data Disk, see the inside back cover for instructions for downloading the Data Disk or see your instructor.

Instructions:

1. Open the document Personal Computer Buyer's Guide Draft from the Data Disk. Save the document with a new name, Personal Computer Buyer's Guide.

2. Change all margins to 1" with a gutter margin of .5". Note: Because you do not have alternating headers in this document, the gutter automatically will be at the left margin for binding at the left edge of each page.

(continued)

In the Lab

Working with an Embedded Worksheet and Index *(continued)*

3. Insert right-aligned page numbers as a header on every page after the first.

4. Below the paragraph in item number six (Use a worksheet to compare computers, services, and other considerations), embed the Excel worksheet named Computer System Cost Comparison, which is located on the Data Disk. Resize the chart so it fits on the page (approximately 70 percent of its original size).

5. Switch to Print Layout View. Add the following captions to the figures:
Figure 1: Some mail-order companies, such as Dell Computer Corporation, sell computers online.
Figure 2: A worksheet is an effective tool for summarizing and comparing the prices and components of different computer vendors.

6. Indent the left margin of each caption by .25" so that they align with the left edge of the figures. (*Hint:* Click in the caption and then drag the Left Indent Marker on the ruler to the .25" mark.)

embedded worksheet

7. At the end of the paragraph above Figure 1, add the following sentence: <u>Figure 1 shows a Web page for a popular mail-order company.</u> The text, Figure 1, in the sentence should be a cross-reference.

8. In the Item #6 paragraph (above Figure 2), add the following phrase to the end of the second sentence: <u>such as the one shown in Figure 2.</u> The text, Figure 2, in the phrase should be a cross-reference.

9. Add a bookmark, named BuyerWorksheet, to the figure caption for Figure 2.

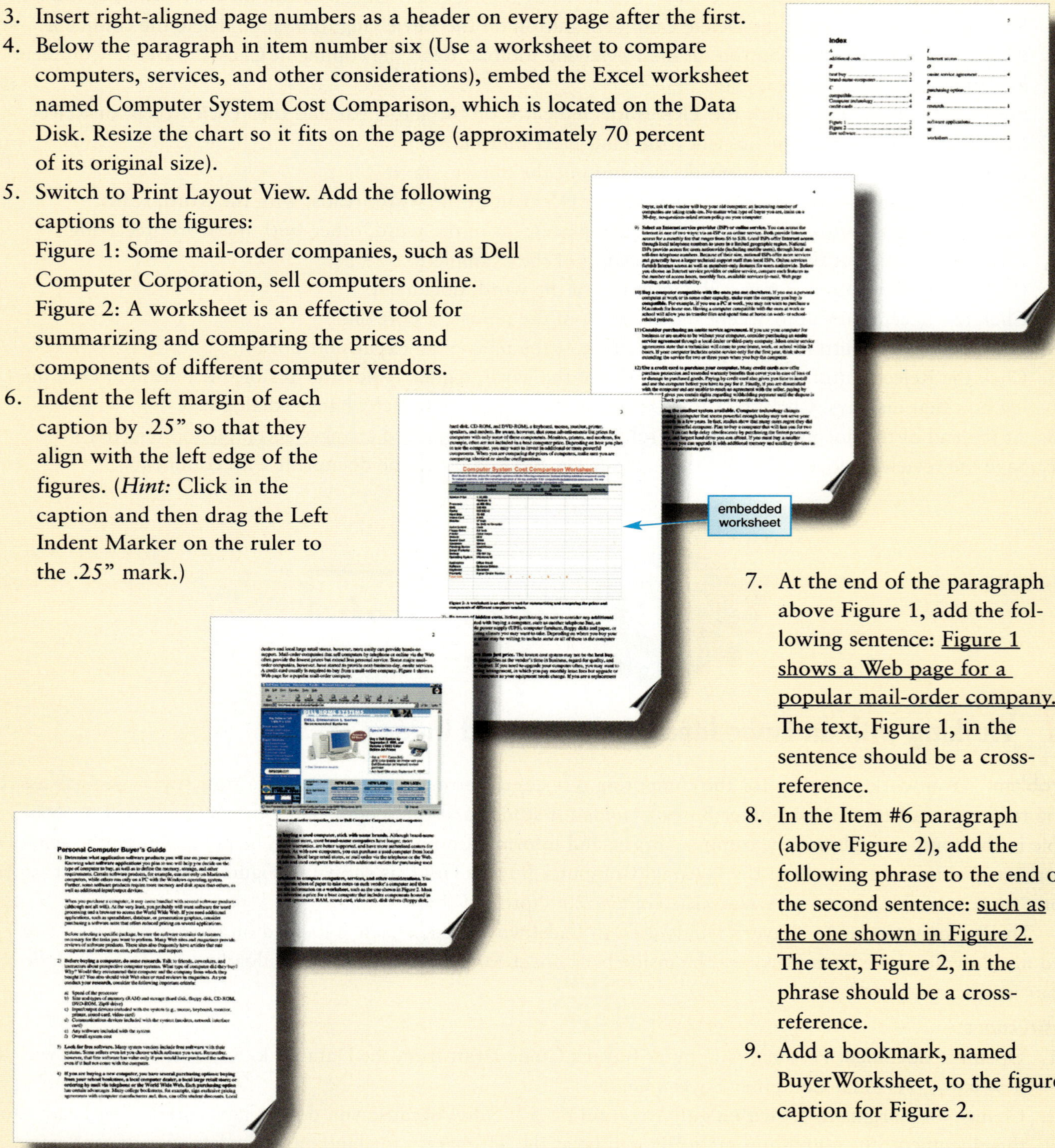

FIGURE 7-88

In the Lab

10. Mark the following text as index entries: software applications, research, free software, purchasing option, brand-name computers, worksheet, additional costs, best buy, Internet access, compatible, onsite service agreement, credit cards, and Computer technology. You will find each of the index entry phrases in the first paragraph of each bulleted item. After marking the entries, bold them in the text.

11. Insert a page break at the end of the document. Change the style of the first line on the new page from List Number to Heading 1. On the new page, type the heading Index using the Heading 1 style. Below the heading, build an index for the document. Use the formal format for the index. Remember to hide formatting marks prior to building the index.

12. Modify the document as follows: mark the two figure captions as index entries.

13. Update the index. Remember to hide formatting marks prior to re-building the index.

14. Go to the bookmark using the Go To dialog box.

15. Save the document again. Print the document. Staple the document along the gutter margin.

2 Working with a Master Document, Table of Contents, and Index

Problem: You are an editor for Textbooks Press, an international company that publishes college textbooks. You are to begin assembling Chapter 6 of a word processing textbook. You design chapters of the books as master documents and insert subdocuments as you receive chapter text from authors. You are responsible for inserting figure captions, creating the table of contents and index, and formatting the chapter. A miniature version of the Chapter 6 document is shown in Figure 7-89 on the next page; for a more readable view, visit www.scsite.com/wd2000/project7.htm.

You just received the first subdocument for Chapter 6. Thus, you lay out the master document for the chapter. The subdocument used in this lab is on the Data Disk. If you did not download the Data Disk, see the inside back cover for instructions for downloading the Data Disk or see your instructor.

Instructions:

1. Open the document Chapter 6 Introductory Material Draft from the Data Disk. Save the document with a new name, Chapter 6 Introductory Material.

2. If necessary, switch to print layout view. Add the following caption to the figure: The Web Club Newsletter. After it is inserted, italicize the text, The Web Club, in the caption.

3. Below the heading, Chapter Six – Newsletter, the first sentence should end with the phrase, as shown in Figure 1, with the text Figure 1 being a cross-reference. Modify the sentence accordingly.

4. Mark the phrase, desktop publishing software, in the Introduction as an index entry. Bold the phrase in the text. In the Desktop Publishing Terminology section, mark these words as index entries: nameplate, banner, issue information line, rules, ruling lines, subhead, vertical rule, wrap-around text, run-around, and pull-quote. Bold each of these words in the text.

5. Save the Chapter 6 Introductory Material file again and then close the file.

(continued)

In the Lab

Working with a Master Document, Table of Contents, and Index *(continued)*

6. Start a new Word document. Switch to outline view. Enter the following Heading 1 headings on separate lines of the outline: Chapter 6 – Creating a Professional Newsletter, Table of Contents, and Index. Insert a next page section break between the headings.

7. Save the master document with the file name, Newsletter Chapter. Between the Table of Contents and Index headings, insert the Chapter 6 Introductory Material file as a subdocument.

8. If necessary, switch to print layout view. On page 1 (the title page) below the Chapter 6 – Creating a Professional Newsletter heading, enter this line double-spaced in 20-point Times New Roman: Confidential Work in Progress. Below that text, insert a clip art image of a book growing. Use the keywords, nurturing a book, to locate the

graphic. Below the graphic, enter these lines double-spaced in 20-point Times New Roman: Authors: J. Riggins and H. Stein; Editor: B. Baccaro; Proofreader: L. Lopez; Date to Film: 10/22/2001; and Bound Book Date: 11/19/2001. Center all text and graphics on the title page.

9. Build an index for the document. In the Index sheet, use the formal format for the index and place a check mark in the Right align page numbers check box. Remember to hide formatting marks prior to building the index.

10. Create a table of contents for the document. Use the Formal format.

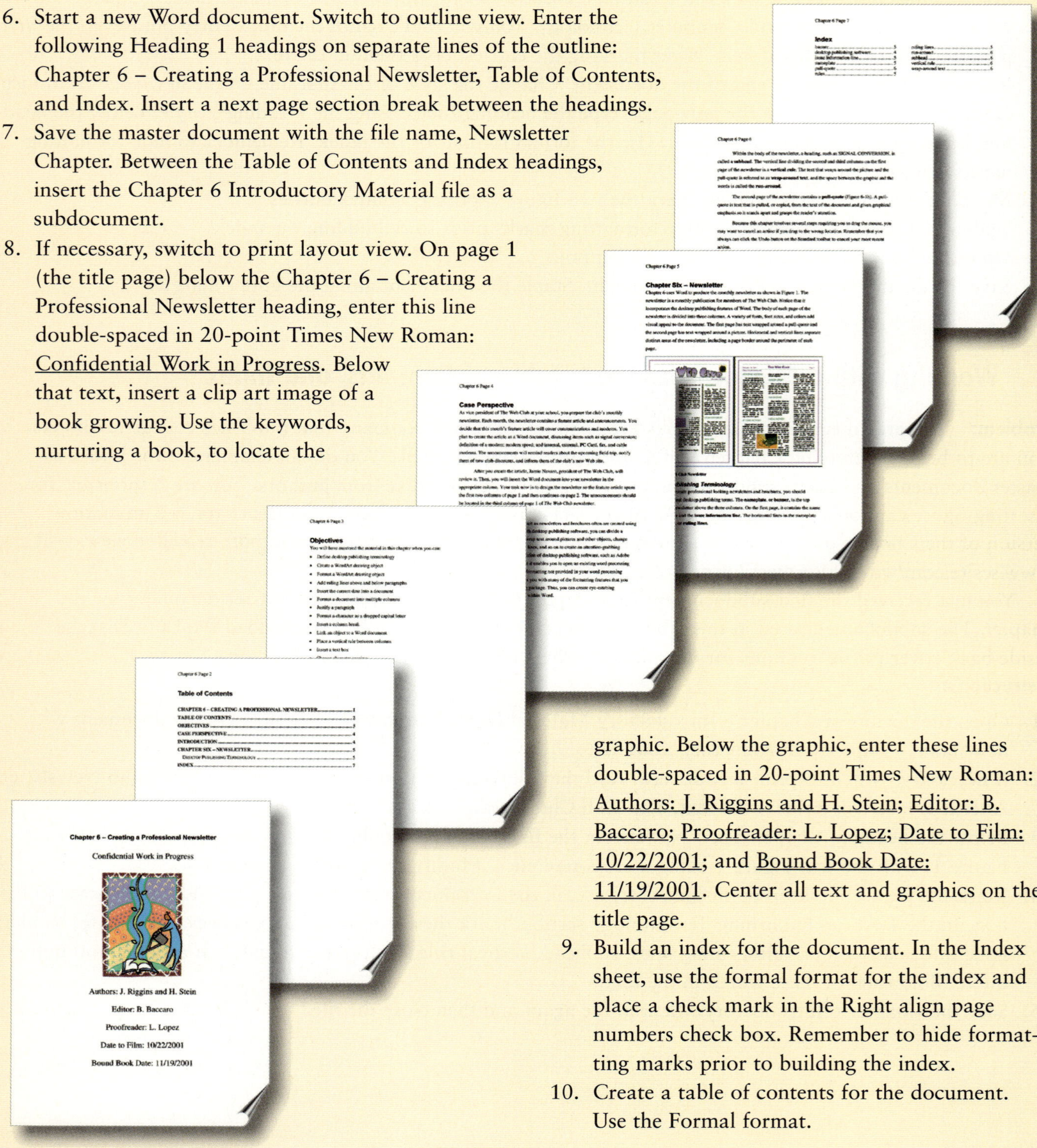

FIGURE 7-89

In the Lab

11. Beginning on the second page (the table of contents), create a header as follows: print the words, Chapter 6 Page, followed by the page number at the left margin. The title page does not have a header. Note: Because you do not want facing pages in this document, you do not create alternating headers.

12. Change all margins to 1" with a gutter margin of .5". Be sure to change the Apply to box to Whole document. Note: Because you do not have alternating headers in this document, the gutter automatically will be at the left margin for binding at the left edge of each page.

13. Verify that the following headings begin on a new page: Table of Contents, Objectives, Case Perspective, Chapter Six – Newsletter, and Index. If any do not, insert a next page section break.

14. Because you modified the margins, update the table of contents and index.

15. Save the document again. Print the document. Staple the document along the gutter margin.

3 Working with a Master Document, Index, Tables of Figures and Contents, and Callouts

Problem: You are the computer specialist at Triton Library. The head librarian mentions to you that the librarians constantly are receiving questions about using the computer. Thus, she has asked you to create a series of instructional booklets, similar to mini-user manuals, for library patrons that explain various aspects of computers. The first one you create is titled How to Use Windows Explorer. A miniature version of this document is shown in Figure 7-90 on the next page; for a more readable view, visit www.scsite.com/wd2000/project7.htm.

You design the instructional booklet as a master document. You create one subdocument and insert an existing document as the other. The existing subdocument is on the Data Disk. If you did not download the Data Disk, see the inside back cover for instructions for downloading the Data Disk or see your instructor.

Instructions:

1. Open the document How to Use Windows Explorer Draft from the Data Disk. Save the document with a new name, How to Use Windows Explorer.

2. Switch to Print Layout View. Add the following captions to the figures:
   Figure 1: Step 1 in Starting Windows Explorer
   Figure 2: Step 2 in Starting Windows Explorer
   Figure 3: Step 1 in Displaying the Contents of a Folder
   Figure 4: Step 2 in Displaying the Contents of a Folder
   Figure 5: Step 1 in Expanding a Folder
   Figure 6: Step 2 in Expanding a Folder
   Figure 7: Step 1 in Collapsing a Folder
   Figure 8: Step 2 in Collapsing a Folder
   Figure 9: Step 1 in Quitting Windows Explorer

3. Add a callout to each figure, except Figure 2, that identifies the mouse pointer in each figure. Use the Line Callout 3 style of callout with each callout containing the text, mouse pointer.

4. Insert a cross-reference for each figure. Insert the cross-reference in the parenthesis that ends each sentence immediately above each figure. Insert only the word, Figure, and the figure number as the cross-reference. For cross-references in an italicized sentence, italicize the cross-reference (after inserting the cross-reference, select it and then italicize it).

(continued)

In the Lab

Working with a Master Document, Index, Tables of Figures and Contents, and Callouts *(continued)*

5. In the section titled The Exploring – My Computer Window, mark these words/phrases as index entries: menu bar, hierarchy, contents, folder, minus sign, subfolders, collapsing the folder, plus sign, expanding the folder, and status bar. Also, bold each of these words/phrases in the text. Mark each of the STEPS headings as index entries.

6. Save the How to Use Windows Explorer file again and then close the file.

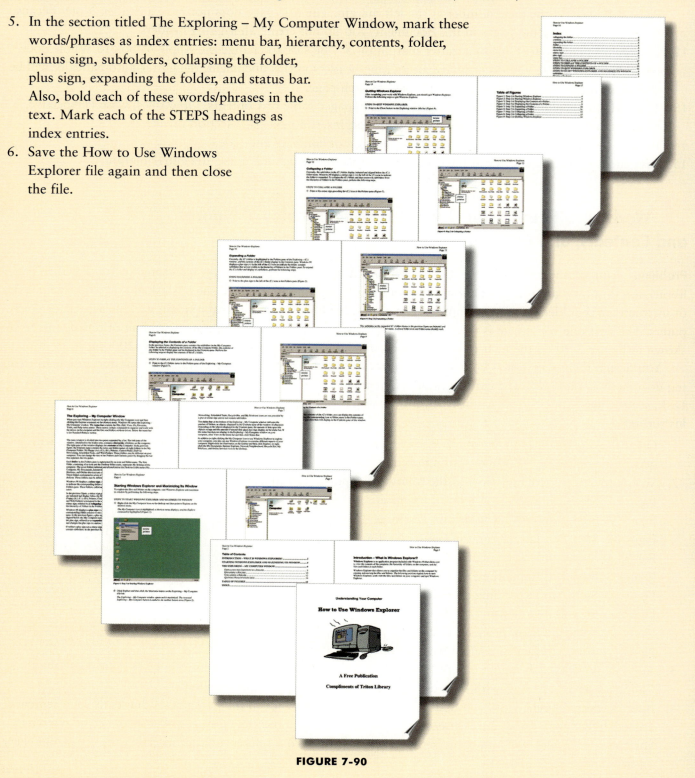

FIGURE 7-90

In the Lab

7. Start a new Word document. Switch to outline view. Enter the following Heading 1 headings on separate lines of the outline: Understanding Your Computer, Table of Contents, Introduction – What Is Windows Explorer?, Table of Figures, and Index. Insert a next page section break between each heading.

8. Save the master document with the file name, Understanding Your Computer. Between the Introduction and Table of Figures headings, insert the How to Use Windows Explorer file as a subdocument.

9. Create a subdocument using the Introduction – What Is Windows Explorer? heading. Using the Body Text style, enter the text for the two paragraphs shown in Figure 7-91 for the Introduction – What is Windows Explorer? section. In the Introduction, mark the phrase, Windows Explorer, as an index entry. Also, bold the phrase.

Windows Explorer is an application program included with Windows 98 that allows you to view the contents of the computer, the hierarchy of folders on the computer, and the files and folders in each folder.

Windows Explorer also allows you to organize the files and folders on the computer by copying and moving the files and folders. The following sections explain how to start Windows Explorer; work with the files and folders on your computer; and quit Windows Explorer.

FIGURE 7-91

10. On page 1 (the title page), double-spaced below the Understanding Your Computer heading, enter the following text in 28-point Rockwell bold font: How to Use Windows Explorer. Then, insert a clip art image of a computer. Use the keywords, computer cartoon, to locate the graphic. Enlarge the graphic. Below the graphic, enter these lines double-spaced in 24-point Times New Roman: A Free Publication, Compliments of the Triton Library. Center all text and graphics on the title page.

11. Build an index for the document that does not include the headings on the title page or the table of contents page. In the Index sheet, use the From template format for the index, place a check mark in the Right align page numbers check box, and change the number of columns to 1. Remember to hide formatting marks prior to building the index. *Hint:* To not include certain headings in the index, change the style of the heading to a style other than a heading style.

(continued)

In the Lab

Working with a Master Document, Index, Tables of Figures and Contents, and Callouts *(continued)*

12. Create a table of figures for the document. Use the From template format.

13. Create a table of contents for the document. Use the Formal format.

14. Beginning on the second page (the table of contents), create alternating headings as follows: even-numbered pages should print at the left margin the words, How to Use Windows Explorer, on the first line and Page, followed by the page number on the second line. Odd-numbered pages should print the same text at the right margin. The title page does not have a header.

15. For the entire document, set the left and right margins to 1" and set a gutter margin of .5".

16. Verify that the following headings begin on a new page: Table of Contents, Introduction – What is Windows Explorer?, Starting Windows Explorer and Maximizing Its Window, The Exploring – My Computer Window, Table of Figures, and Index. If any do not, insert a next page section break.

17. Because margins have changed, update the fields, table of contents, and index. (Select the entire document and then press F9.)

18. Save the document again. Print the document. If you have access to a copy machine, duplicate the document back-to-back.

Cases and Places

The difficulty of these case studies varies:
◗ are the least difficult; ◗◗ are more difficult; and ◗◗◗ are the most difficult.

1 ◗ As editor for the school newspaper, you review all articles before they are published. One section of the newspaper spotlights a local business or organization. For the next issue, the author has prepared an article about a local hospital and sent it to you for review. The article, named Northwestern Memorial Hospital Article, is located on the Data Disk. If you did not download the Data Disk, see the inside back cover for instructions for downloading the Data Disk or see your instructor. When you review the article, you find several areas where you wish to make changes and offer suggestions. You are to use Word's change-tracking feature to insert, delete, and replace text in the article. Make at least ten changes to the article and add at least three comments. Print the article with tracked changes showing and without tracked changes showing. Also, print comments. Save the article containing the tracked changes as a version. Assume you are the author of the article and have received it back from the editor. Delete the comments and accept all the changes in the document.

2 ◗ You are an editor for Textbooks Press, an international company that publishes college textbooks. The chapter you are working on is called Project 7. You design the chapters as master documents and insert subdocuments as you receive chapter text from authors. You are responsible for creating the table of contents and index and formatting the chapter. You just received the first subdocument for Project 7. The article, named Reviewing a Document, is located on the Data Disk. If you did not download the Data Disk, see the inside back cover for instructions for downloading the Data Disk or see your instructor. Set up a master document that contains the following: title page, table of contents, reviewing a document file as a subdocument, table of figures, and index. Use the concepts and techniques presented in this project to format the document.

3 ◗◗ As your final project in CIS 210, your instructor has asked you to prepare a master document that has at least one subdocument, a title page, a table of contents, a table of figures, and an index. The subdocument is to contain the text and figures on pages 7.22 through 7.25 in this project. To capture a screen shot, display the screen on your computer and then press the PRINT SCREEN key. Then, to include the screen shot in your Word document, click the Paste button on the Standard toolbar in the Word window. Use the concepts and techniques presented in this project to format the document.

Cases and Places

4 ▶▶ You are the computer specialist at Triton Library. The head librarian has asked you to create a series of instructional booklets, similar to mini-user manuals, for library patrons that explain the various aspects of computers. The first instructional booklet you prepared is shown in Figure 7-90 on page WD 7.76. Your assignment is to prepare the next instructional booklet for the library. Write the instructional booklet on a software application with which you are familiar and to which you have access. Use the software application's Help system, textbooks, and other instructional books for reference. The booklet is to be a how-to type of document that includes screen shots. To capture a screen shot, display the screen on your computer and then press the PRINT SCREEN key. Then, to include the screen shot in your Word document, click the Paste button on the Standard toolbar in the Word window. The figures should contain captions. The document should contain the following sections: title page, table of contents, how-to discussion, table of figures, and index. Use the concepts and techniques presented in this project to format the document.

5 ▶▶▶ You are vice president of your school's computer club. At the last meeting, several members were inquiring about MOUS (Microsoft Office User Specialist) certification. Because you also are interested in the MOUS certification, you decide to prepare a document outlining information about the exam (cost, description, how to prepare, where to take the exam, etc.). You obtain most of your information through links at the Shelly Cashman Series MOUS Web page at http://www.scsite.com/off2000/cert.htm. Because the document will be quite lengthy with many headings and subheadings, you organize it as a master document. In addition to information about MOUS, the document also contains the following: title page, table of contents, and index. Include at least one screen shot as a figure. To capture a screen shot, display the screen on your computer and then press the PRINT SCREEN key. Then, to include the screen shot in your Word document, click the Paste button on the Standard toolbar in the Word window. All figures should contain captions. Use the concepts and techniques presented in this project to format the document.

6 ▶▶▶ Your instructor in CIS 215 has distributed a worksheet that can be used to compare computers, services, and other considerations. The worksheet is an Excel document, named Computer System Cost Comparison, which is located on the Data Disk. If you did not download the Data Disk, see the inside back cover for instructions for downloading the Data Disk or see your instructor. Your assignment is to prepare a Word document that explains the type of computer you are seeking and identifies criteria important to you in purchasing a computer. The Word document should also contain the Excel worksheet as an embedded object. Edit the Excel object by double-clicking the object. Then, modify the Desired System column so that it is tailored to your specific needs. You are to obtain prices for your desired system from two local dealers and two online dealers. Again, edit the Excel worksheet from Word as you receive pricing information. When the worksheet is complete, write a paragraph below the worksheet that recommends the dealer from which you would purchase the computer along with a justification of why you selected that dealer. Use the concepts and techniques presented in this project to format the document.

Microsoft **Word 2000**

Microsoft Word 2000

8

Creating an Online Form

You will have mastered the material in this project when you can:

Online Reality

Form, Fit, and Function

Whether searching the Net, investing or shopping online, sending e-mail, taking distance-learning courses, or simply browsing the Web, today's virtual individuals spend many hours a day online in some form of communication, research, commerce, or education.

No other facet of the Internet has garnered more interest than e-commerce. With hunderds of e-consumers attracted to the vast numbers of sales channels from e-retail to e-financial, sales are in the billions of dollars. Buying online is a bit more complicated, however, when it comes to purchasing clothing. Without the ability to try on the selected garments, how can you be sure of the fit?

This logistical problem can be frustrating to shoppers who are expected to spend $13 billion online for apparel by 2003.

Lands' End has come up with a solution to these virtual shopping woes. This Wisconsin-based direct merchant of traditional, casual clothes has developed Your Personal Model, a personalized 3-D representation of female customers that selects the most flattering clothes for their figures, suggests specific outfits for various occasions, and provides an online dressing room to try on the garments.

Shoppers begin their Your Personal Model shopping adventure by answering several questions regarding their physical features, such as specific skin tones, face shapes, hairstyles, and hair colors. They save their profiles for future shopping sprees, and proceed to the Welcome Page.

At this point, their models appear along with custom outfits designed for their bodies and for their lifestyles. The site may make suggestions for specific occasions such as gray Chinos and a beige sweater set for a casual workplace and a simple black knit dress for an informal weekend party.

The next step is to take these garments to The Dressing Room. There, the shoppers can view the particular clothes on their models. The site gives advice on choosing the proper size and then places the items in the customers' virtual shopping carts.

Ordering is easy. If they use Your Personal Model, the contents of their shopping carts display automatically in an order form.

Gary C. Comer, an avid sailor and advertising copywriter, founded Lands' End in 1961 in Chicago to sell sailing equipment and hardware via a catalog. In the 1970s, the company's focus switched to clothing. Today, Lands' End is the second largest apparel mail-order company with sales of more than $1.37 billion to its 6.1 million customers. The Lands' End Web site (www. landsend.com) was unveiled in 1995 and receives 15 million visitors yearly.

As widespread as Internet shopping is, likewise, the emergence of the distance education environment has created a new focus for the use of forms and online communication. In Project 8, you will develop a form by creating a template in Word 2000. The form is a questionnaire for students attending distant-learning classes on the Web through Raven Community College. The form makes it possible for the college to minimize the requests about the distant-learning courses by requesting information from the students who have completed the curriculum via the online form. Students supply information about the type of equipment used in the course. This information then is provided to other students interested in the class through the school's schedule of courses.

Using Word's automated tools, the process of creating an online form is a simple task; one that will make it possible for an online reality in many aspects of your course work, professional endeavors, and personal use.

Microsoft Word 2000

Creating an Online Form

P R O J E C T

8

C A S E   P E R S P E C T I V E

For the past three years, the computer information systems (CIS) department at Raven Community College has offered distance-learning (DL) courses. These classes, which are conducted completely on the Web, are extremely popular among the student body because they allow students to attend class from home or at any time that fits their schedules. Consequently, students are requesting that other departments also offer courses in a DL format. In a response to student needs, the administration has requested that each academic department at the college offer one DL section of each introductory class – beginning next semester. The scheduling department has recommended that a typical computer configuration for DL courses be included as a list in the upcoming *Schedule of Courses*.

As a part-time assistant in the CIS department, you have been assigned the task of compiling this list. You decide to send an online questionnaire to all students who have completed a DL course this past semester. The questionnaire will ask for the student name, browser used, method used to connect to the Internet, type and speed of computer, and any special equipment used in the course.

Introduction

During your personal and professional life, you undoubtedly have filled out countless forms. Whether a federal tax form, a timecard, an application, an order, a deposit slip, or a questionnaire, a **form** is designed to collect information. In the past, forms were printed; that is, you received the form on a piece of paper, filled it in with a pen or pencil, and then returned it manually.

Today, people are concerned with using resources efficiently. To minimize waste of paper, save the world's trees, improve office efficiency, and improve access to data, many businesses attempt to become a paperless office. Thus, the online form has emerged. With an **online form**, you access the form using your computer, fill it out using the computer, and then return it via the computer. You may access the form at a Web site, on your company's intranet, or from your inbox if you receive it via e-mail.

Not only does an online form reduce the need for paper, it saves the time spent duplicating a form and distributing it. With more and more people owning a home computer, online forms have become a popular means of collecting personal information, as well. In Word, you easily can create an online form for distribution electronically, which then can be filled in using Word.

Project Eight — Online Form

Project 8 uses Word to create the online form shown in Figure 8-1. The form is a questionnaire e-mailed to all students that completed a distance-learning course at Raven Community College during the past semester. Upon receipt of the form, students fill it in, save it, and then e-mail it back to the college. Figure 8-1a shows how the form displays on a student's screen initially (as a blank form); Figure 8-1b shows the form partially filled in by one student; and Figure 8-1c shows how one student filled in the form.

(a) Blank Form

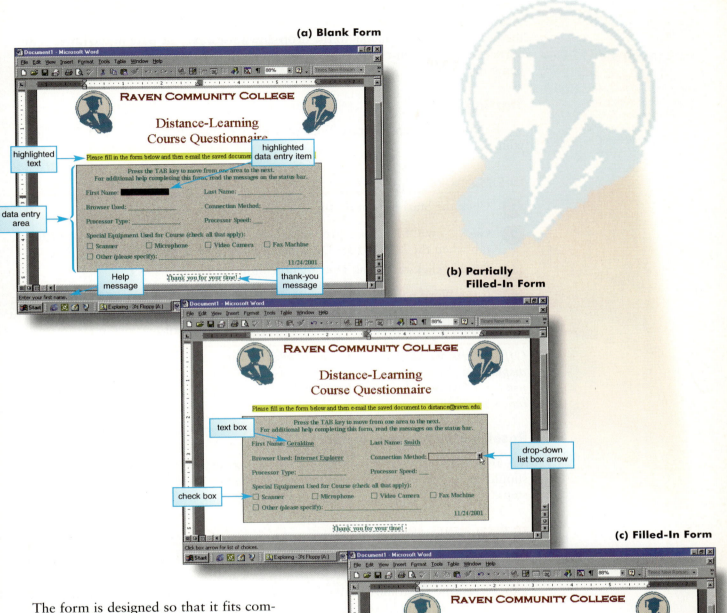

(b) Partially Filled-In Form

(c) Filled-In Form

The form is designed so that it fits completely within the Word window – without a user having to scroll while filling in the form. The **data entry area** of the form is enclosed by a rectangle that is shaded in beige. The line above the data entry area is highlighted in yellow to draw the user's attention to the message. The thank-you message below the data entry area is surrounded by a moving rectangle.

The data entry area of the form contains four text boxes (First Name, Last Name, Processor Speed, and Other), three drop-down list boxes (Browser Used, Connection Method, and Processor Type), and five check boxes (Scanner, Microphone, Video Camera, Fax Machine, and Other). As a user presses the TAB key to move the highlight from one data entry

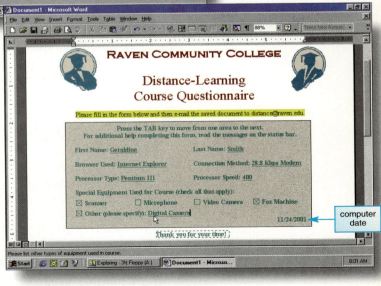

FIGURE 8-1

Online Forms

For a sample online form on the Web, visit the Word 2000 More About Web page (www.scsite.com/wd2000/more.htm) and then click Sample Online Form.

item to the next, the status bar displays a brief Help message that is related to the location of the highlight. Note that in Word the drop-down list boxes do not display the box arrow until you TAB to the drop-down list box. The date in the lower-right corner of the data entry area is the date from the computer on which the form is being displayed.

Starting Word

Follow these steps to start Word or ask your instructor how to start Word for your system.

TO START WORD

1 Click the Start button on the taskbar.

2 Click New Office Document on the Start menu. If necessary, click the General tab when the New Office Document dialog box displays.

3 Double-click the Blank Document icon in the General sheet.

4 If the Word window is not maximized, double-click its title bar to maximize it. Click View on the menu bar and then click Print Layout. If the Office Assistant displays, right-click it and then click Hide on the shortcut menu.

Office starts Word. After a few moments, an empty document titled Document1 displays in the Word window. Because this project uses floating graphics, you will use print layout view; thus, the Print Layout View button on the horizontal scroll bar is recessed.

Resetting Menus and Toolbars

To set the menus and toolbars so they appear exactly as shown in this book, you should reset your menus and toolbars as outlined in Appendix C or follow these steps.

TO RESET MENUS AND TOOLBARS

1 Click View on the menu bar and then point to Toolbars. Click Customize on the Toolbars submenu.

2 When the Customize dialog box displays, click the Options tab, make sure the top three check boxes have check marks and then click the Reset my usage data button. When the Microsoft Word dialog box displays, click the Yes button.

3 Click the Toolbars tab. Click Standard in the Toolbars list and then click the Reset button. When the Reset Toolbar dialog box displays, click the OK button.

4 Click Formatting in the Toolbars list and then click the Reset button. When the Reset Toolbar dialog box displays, click the OK button. Click the Close button.

Word resets the menus and toolbars.

Displaying Formatting Marks

It is helpful to display formatting marks that indicate where in the document you pressed the ENTER key, SPACEBAR, and other keys. Follow this step to display formatting marks.

TO DISPLAY FORMATTING MARKS

1 Double-click the move handle on the left side of the Standard toolbar to display the entire toolbar. If the Show/Hide ¶ button on the Standard toolbar is not already recessed, click it.

Word displays formatting marks in the document window, and the Show/Hide ¶ button on the Standard toolbar is recessed.

Zooming Page Width

When you zoom page width, Word displays the page on the screen as large as possible in print layout view. Perform the following steps to zoom page width.

TO ZOOM PAGE WIDTH

1 Click the Zoom box arrow on the Standard toolbar.

2 Click Page Width in the Zoom list.

Word displays an entire piece of paper as large as possible in the document window. Word computes the zoom percentage based on a variety of settings. Your percentage may be different.

More About 2000

Fields

For more information about fields, visit the Word 2000 More About Web page (www.scsite.com/wd2000/more.htm) and then click Fields.

Designing an Online Form

To minimize the time spent creating a form on the computer, you should sketch it out on a piece of paper first. A design for the online form in this project is shown in Figure 8-2.

During the **form design**, you should create a well-thought-out draft of the form that attempts to include all essential form elements. These elements include the form's title, placement of text and graphics, instructions for users of the form, and field specifications. A **field** is a placeholder for data. A **field specification** defines characteristics of a field such as the field's type, length, format, and a list of possible values that may be entered into the field. Many users place Xs in fields where a user will be allowed to enter any type of character and 9s in fields where a user will be allowed to enter numbers only. For example, in Figure 8-2, a user can enter up to 15 of any type of character in the First Name text box and can enter up to 3 numbers in the Processor Speed text box.

With this draft of the form in hand, the next step is to create the form in Word.

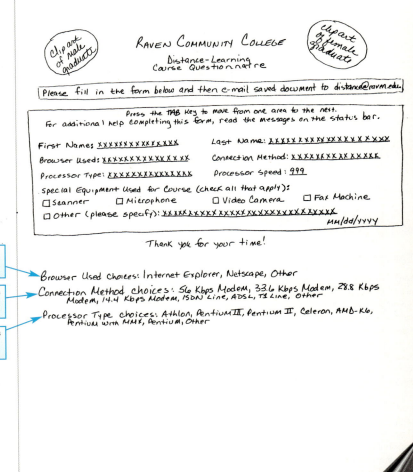

FIGURE 8-2

Creating an Online Form

The process of creating an online form begins with creating a template. Next, you insert and format any text, graphics, and fields where data is to be entered on the form. Finally, before you save the form for electronic distribution, you protect it. With a protected form, users can enter data only where you have placed form fields; that is, they will not be able to modify any other items on the form. Many menu commands and toolbar buttons are dimmed, and thus unavailable, in a protected form. The steps on the following pages illustrate how to create an online form.

Creating a Template

A **template** is a file that contains the definition of the appearance of a Word document, including items such as default font, font size, margin settings, and line spacing; available styles; and even placement of text. Every Word document you create is based on a template. When you select the Blank Document icon in the New dialog box or when you click the New Blank Document button on the Standard toolbar, Word creates a document based on the Normal template. Word also provides other templates for more specific types of documents such as memos, letters, and fax cover sheets. Creating a document based on these templates can improve your productivity because Word has defined much of the document's appearance for you.

If you create and save an online form as a Word document that is based on the Normal template, users will be required to open that Word document to display the form on the screen. Next, they will fill in the form. Then, to preserve the content of the original form, they will have to save the form with a new name. If they accidentally click the Save button on the Standard toolbar, the original blank form will be replaced with a filled-in form.

If you, instead, create and save the online form as a **document template**, users will open a new document window that is based on that template. This displays the form on the screen as a brand new Word document; that is, the document does not have a file name. Thus, the user fills in the form and then simply saves it. By using a template for the form, the original form remains intact when the user clicks the Save button.

Perform the following steps to create a document template to be used for the online form and then save the template with the name Distance-Learning Questionnaire.

To Create a Document Template

1 **Click File on the menu bar and then click New. When the New dialog box displays, if necessary, click the General tab. Click the Blank Document icon and then click Template in the Create New area. Point to the OK button.**

Word displays the New dialog box (Figure 8-3). The Template option button instructs Word to create a new template, instead of a new Word document.

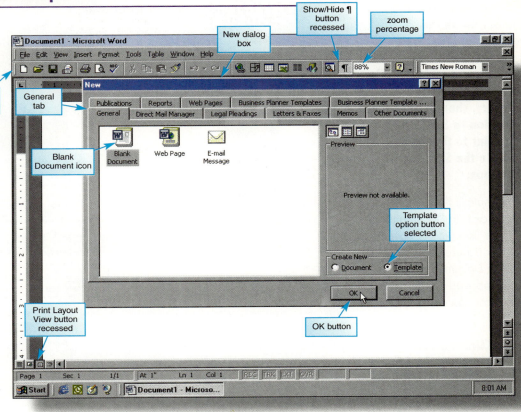

FIGURE 8-3

2 **Click the OK button.**

Word displays a blank template titled Template1 in the Word window (Figure 8-4).

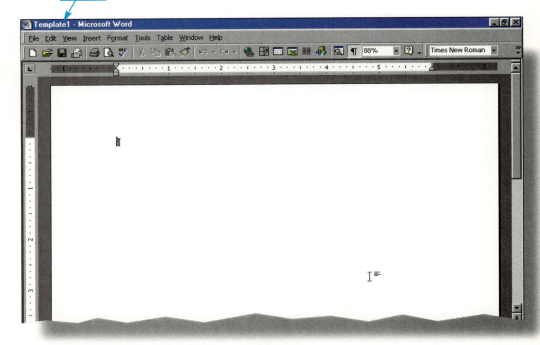

FIGURE 8-4

3 With a disk in drive A, click the Save button on the Standard toolbar. Type `Distance-Learning Questionnaire` in the File name text box. If necessary, change the Save in location to 3½ Floppy (A:). Point to the Save button in the Save As dialog box.

Word displays the Save As dialog box with Document Template listed in the Save as type box (Figure 8-5). Because Document Template is dimmed, you cannot change the document type.

4 Click the Save button in the Save As dialog box.

Word saves the template on the floppy disk in drive A with the file name Distance-Learning Questionnaire (see Figure 8-6).

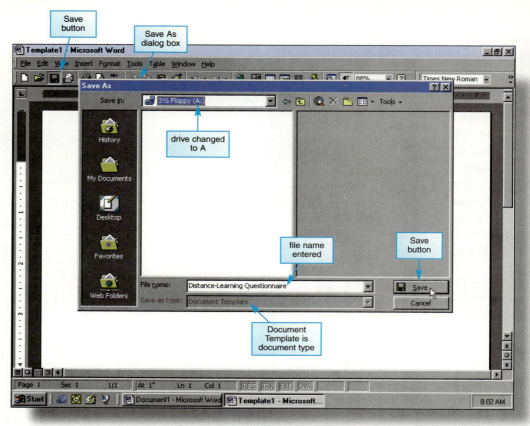

FIGURE 8-5

The next step in creating the online form is to enter the text, graphics, and fields into the template.

Perform the following steps to format and enter the college name and questionnaire title.

TO ENTER AND FORMAT TEXT

1 Double-click the move handle on the Formatting toolbar to display the entire toolbar. Click the Font box arrow on the Formatting toolbar, scroll to and then click Copperplate Gothic Bold. Click the Font Size box arrow on the Formatting toolbar and then click 22. Click the Font Color button arrow on the Formatting toolbar and then click Brown. Click the Center button on the Formatting toolbar. Type `Raven Community College` and then press the ENTER key twice.

2 Click the Font box arrow on the Formatting toolbar and then click Times New Roman. Click the Font Size box arrow on the Formatting toolbar and then click 26. Type `Distance-Learning` and then press then ENTER key. Type `Course Questionnaire` and then press the ENTER key.

The school name and questionnaire title display as shown in Figure 8-6.

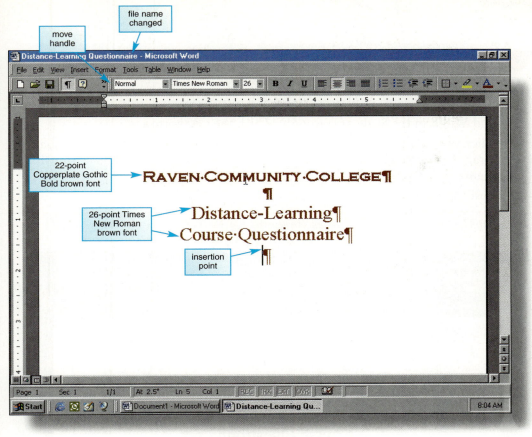

FIGURE 8-6

The next step is to insert the clip art of the male and female graduates. Word inserts clip art as inline graphics; that is, part of the current paragraph. You want to position the image of the male graduate to the left of the college name and the image of the female graduate to the right of the college name (see Figure 8-1 on page WD 8.5). Thus, the graphics need to be floating graphics instead of inline graphics. Also, the graphics are too large for this form. Thus, after you insert the graphics you will reduce their size and change their wrapping styles to Square as described in the following steps.

TO INSERT AND FORMAT CLIP ART

1. With the insertion point on line 5, click Insert on the menu bar, point to Picture, and then click Clip Art. When the Insert ClipArt window opens, click the Search for clips text box. Type degrees caps and then press the ENTER key.

2. Click the clip of the male graduate that matches the one shown in Figure 8-7 on the next page. Click the Insert clip button on the Pop-up menu. Click the clip of the female graduate that matches the one shown in Figure 8-7. Click the Insert clip button on the Pop-up menu. Click the Close button on the Insert ClipArt window's title bar.

3. Click the male graduate graphic to select it. If the Picture toolbar does not display, click View on the menu bar, point to Toolbars, and then click Picture. Click the Format Picture button on the Picture toolbar. When the Format Picture dialog box displays, if necessary, click the Size tab. Change the Height and Width in the Scale area to 65%. Click the OK button.

4. Click the Text Wrapping button on the Picture toolbar and then click Square. Drag the male graduate graphic to the left of the college name as shown in Figure 8-7.

5 Click the female graduate graphic to select it. If the Picture toolbar does not display, click View on the menu bar, point to Toolbars, and then click Picture. Click the Format Picture button on the Picture toolbar. When the Format Picture dialog box displays, if necessary, click the Size tab. Change the Height and Width in the Scale area to 65%. Click the OK button.

6 Click the Text Wrapping button on the Picture toolbar and then click Square. Drag the female graduate graphic to the right of the college name as shown in Figure 8-7.

7 Position the insertion point on the paragraph mark on line 5.

The graphics display on the form as shown in Figure 8-7.

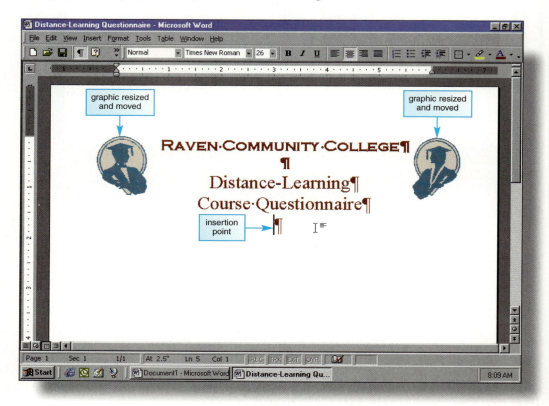

FIGURE 8-7

The next step is to enter the instructions highlighted in yellow.

Highlighting Text

You **highlight** text in an online document to alert the reader to the text's importance, much like a highlight marker does in a textbook. Because you want to draw attention to the instructions that specify where to mail the completed form, you highlight this line.

Perform the following steps to highlight text in a document.

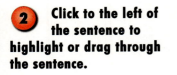

To Highlight Text

1 **Click the Font Size box arrow on the Formatting toolbar and then click 12. Click the Font Color button arrow on the Formatting toolbar and then click Automatic. Press the ENTER key. Type** Please fill in the form below and then e-mail the saved document to distance@raven.edu. **Press the ENTER key. Press CTRL+Z to undo the hyperlink format of the e-mail address. If the Highlight button on the Formatting toolbar displays yellow on its face, click the button; otherwise, click the Highlight button arrow and then click Yellow. Position the mouse pointer in the document window.**

The Highlight button is recessed and displays yellow on its face (Figure 8-8). The mouse pointer displays as an I-beam with a highlighter attached to it.

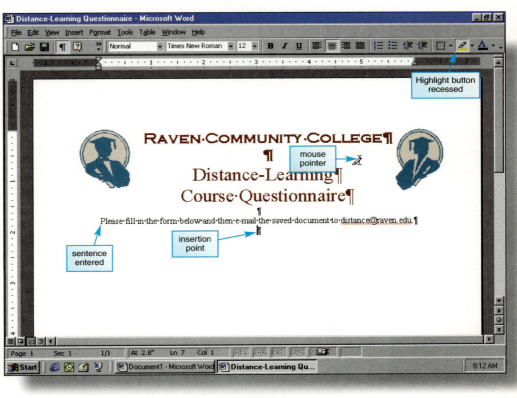

FIGURE 8-8

2 **Click to the left of the sentence to highlight or drag through the sentence.**

Word highlights the selected text in yellow (Figure 8-9). The Highlight button remains recessed.

3 **Click the Highlight button on the Formatting toolbar to turn highlighting off.**

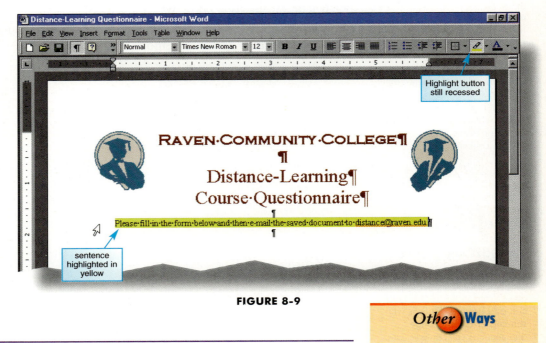

FIGURE 8-9

Other Ways

1. Click Highlight button on Reviewing toolbar

When the Highlight button is recessed, you can continue to select text to be highlighted. The highlighter remains active until you click the Highlight button or press the ESC key to turn it off.

Word provides a variety of highlighter colors. To change the color, click the Highlight button arrow and then click the desired color.

The next step is to enter the instructions for filling in the form as described in the following steps.

TO ENTER TEXT

1 Position the insertion point on the paragraph mark below the highlighted text and then press the ENTER key.

2 Click the Font Color box arrow and then click Teal. Click the Bold button. Type `Press the TAB key to move from one area to the next.` Press the ENTER key.

3 Type `For additional help completing this form, read the messages on the status bar.` Press the ENTER key twice.

4 Press CTRL+L to left-align the current paragraph.

The form instructions are entered.

The next step is to enter the fields into the data entry area of the form.

Inserting a Table into a Form

The first line of data entry in the form consists of the First Name text box, which begins at the left margin, and the Last Name text box, which begins at the center point. Although you could set tab stops to align the data in a form, it is easier to insert a table. For example, the first line could be a 1 x 2 table; that is, a table with one row and two columns. By inserting a 1 x 2 table, Word automatically positions the second column at the center point. Using tables in forms also keeps the data entered within the same region of the form, in case the user enters data that wraps to the next line of the screen.

When you insert a table, Word automatically surrounds it with a border. You do not want borders on tables in forms. Perform the following steps to enter a 1 x 2 table into the form and then remove its border.

Using Tables in Forms

At first glance, it might seem easier to set a tab stop wherever you would like a form field to display. Actually, it can become a complex task. Consider a row with three form fields. To space them evenly, you must calculate where each tab stop should begin. If you insert a 1 x 3 table instead, Word automatically calculates the size of three evenly spaced columns.

Formatting Tables

You can format a table in a form just as you format any other Word table. That is, you can add borders, fill cells with shading or color, change alignment of cell contents, and so on.

To Insert a Borderless Table into a Form

1 If the Forms toolbar does not display on the screen, click View on the menu bar, point to Toolbars, and then click Forms. If necessary, scroll up so that the college name is positioned at the top of the document window. With the insertion point in line 11, click the Insert Table button on the Forms toolbar. Point to the cell in the first row and second column of the grid to highlight the first two cells in the first row of the grid.

*Word displays a **grid** to define the dimension of the desired table (Figure 8-10). Word will insert the table immediately above the insertion point.*

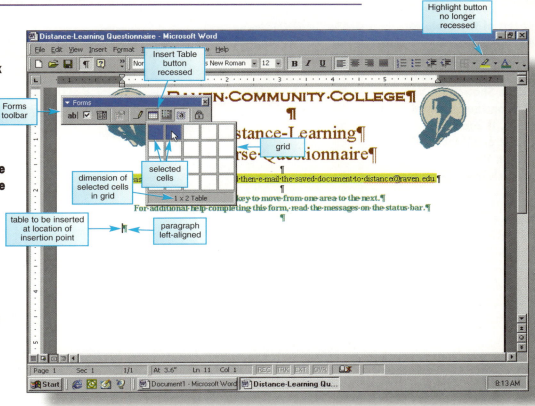

FIGURE 8-10

2 Click the cell in the first row and second column of the grid.

Word inserts an empty 1 x 2 table into the form. The insertion point is in the first cell (row 1 and column 1) of the table.

3 Click Table on the menu bar, point to Select, and then click Table to select the table. Click the Border button arrow on the Formatting toolbar and then point to the No Border button.

Word displays a list of border types (Figure 8-11). The table is selected in the document.

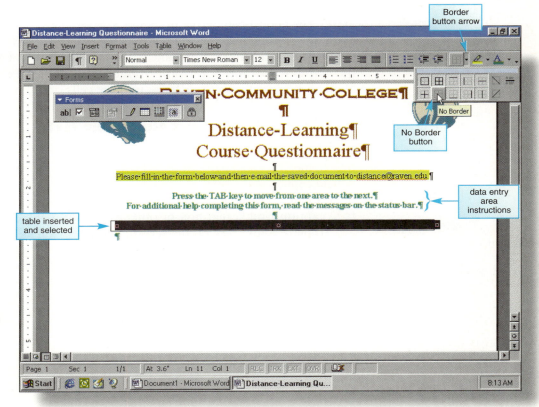

FIGURE 8-11

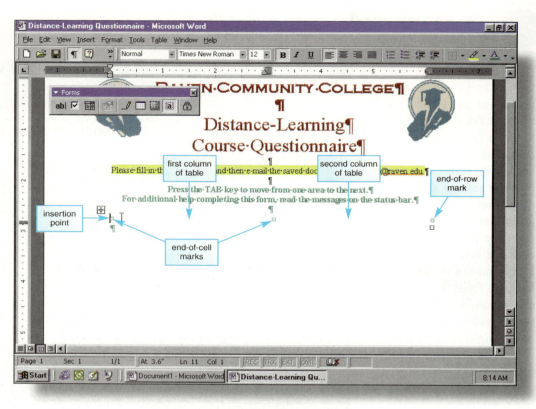

4   **Click the No Border button. Click in the first cell of the table to remove the highlight. If your screen does not display end-of-cell marks, click the Show/Hide ¶ button on the Standard toolbar. If your table displays gridlines, click Table on the menu bar and then click Hide Gridlines.**

Word removes the border from the cells in the table (Figure 8-12). Only the end-of-row and end-of-cell marks display in the document window to identify cells in the table.

FIGURE 8-12

Each row of a table has an end-of-row mark, and each cell has an end-of-cell mark. The end-of-cell marks in Figure 8-12 are left-aligned because the cells are formatted as left-aligned. The data you enter within a cell wordwraps just as text does between the margins of a document. To place data into a cell, you click the cell and then type. To advance rightward from one cell to the next, press the TAB key.

The next step is to enter fields into the cells of the table.

Inserting a Text Box that Accepts Any Text

The first item users enter on the Distance-Learning Course Questionnaire is their first name. The field caption text, First Name, is to display to the left of a text box. A **field caption** is the text on the screen that informs the user what to enter into the field. Often a colon or some other character follows a field caption to separate the field caption from a text box or other data entry field.

To place a text box on the screen, you insert a text form field. A **text form field** allows users to enter letters, numbers, and other characters into the field. Perform the following steps to enter the field caption and the text form field into the first cell of the table.

Steps To Insert a Text Form Field

1 **With the insertion point in the first cell of the table (see Figure 8-12), type** First Name **and then press the COLON key (:). Press the SPACEBAR. Point to the Text Form Field button on the Forms toolbar.**

Word places the field caption into the first cell of the table (Figure 8-13).

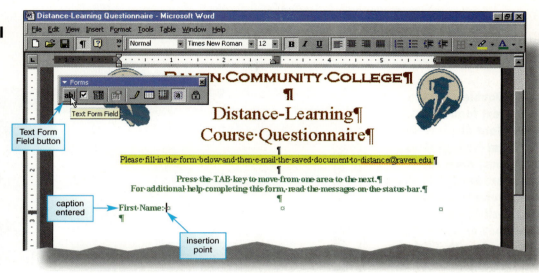

FIGURE 8-13

2 **Click the Text Form Field button. If the form field does not display shaded in gray, click the Form Field Shading button on the Forms toolbar.**

Word inserts a text form field at the location of the insertion point (Figure 8-14). The form field displays shaded in gray.

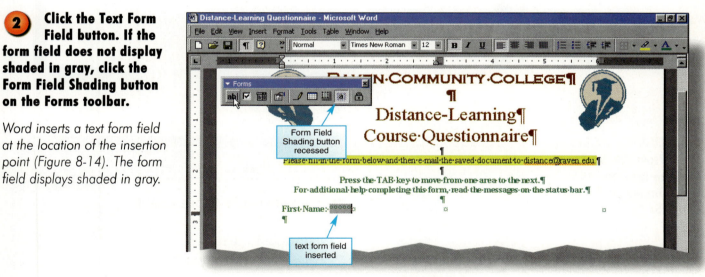

FIGURE 8-14

The text form field inserted by Word is five characters wide. You change its width, along with other characteristics of the form field, through the Text Form Field Options dialog box. You display this dialog box by double-clicking the text form field.

When this form displays on the screen initially (as a blank form), you want the text boxes and drop-down list boxes to display an underline that signifies the data entry area. The text displayed initially in a field is called the **default text**. Thus, the default text for these text boxes and drop-down list boxes on the Distance-Learning Course Questionnaire is an underline.

Because you want to limit a user's entry for the first name to 15 characters, the underline should consume 15 spaces. You also want the first letter of each word that a user enters into the First Name text box to be capitalized.

Perform the following steps to set the text form field for the first name so it displays 15 underscores as default text, limits the user's entry to 15 characters, and capitalizes the first letter of each word the user enters.

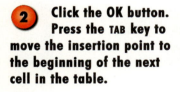
To Specify Text Form Field Options

1 **Double-click the text form field. When Word displays the Text Form Field Options dialog box, press the UNDERSCORE key (_) 15 times in the Default text text box. Double-click the Maximum length box and then type 15 as the length. Click the Text format box arrow and then click First capital. Point to the OK button.**

Word displays the Text Form Field Options dialog box (Figure 8-15).

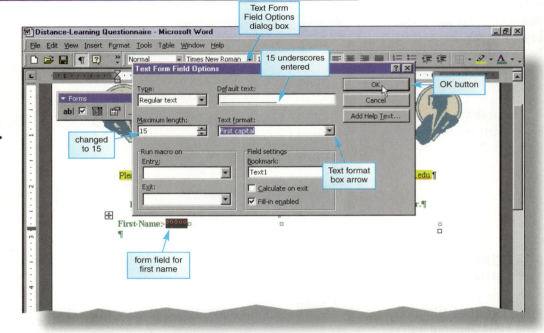

FIGURE 8-15

2 **Click the OK button. Press the TAB key to move the insertion point to the beginning of the next cell in the table.**

The text form field options are set (Figure 8-16).

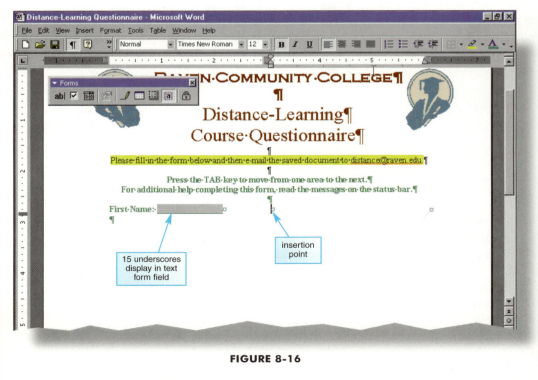

FIGURE 8-16

Other Ways

1. Click Form Field Options button on Forms toolbar
2. Right-click form field, click Properties on shortcut menu

When you click the Text format box arrow in the Text Form Field Options dialog box (see Figure 8-15), you have four choices: Uppercase, Lowercase, First capital, and Title case. If you select one of these options, Word displays a user's entry according to your selection – after the user presses the TAB key to advance out of the form field. Table 8-1 illustrates how each option displays text that a user enters into the form field.

The next form field to enter into the Distance-Learning Course Questionnaire is the last name. The only difference between the options for the form fields for the last name and first name is the last name allows up to 20 characters, instead of 15. Perform the following steps to insert and specify options for another text form field.

Table 8-1	Text Formats for Text Form Fields
TEXT FORMAT	**EXAMPLE**
Uppercase	ALL LETTERS IN ALL WORDS ARE CAPITALIZED.
Lowercase	all letters in all words display as lowercase letters.
First capital	The first letter of the first word is capitalized.
Title case	The First Letter Of Every Word Is Capitalized.

TO INSERT AND SPECIFY OPTIONS FOR A TEXT FORM FIELD

1 With the insertion point at the beginning of the second cell of the table, type Last Name and then press the COLON key. Press the SPACEBAR.

2 Click the Text Form Field button on the Forms toolbar.

3 Double-click the text form field for the last name. When Word displays the Text Form Field Options dialog box, press the UNDERSCORE key 20 times in the Default text text box. Double-click the Maximum length box and then type 20 as the length. Click the Text format box arrow and then click First capital (Figure 8-17).

4 Click the OK button.

Word displays the form field for the last name according to the settings in the Text Form Field Options dialog box.

The next step in creating the Distance-Learning Course Questionnaire is to insert a drop-down list box.

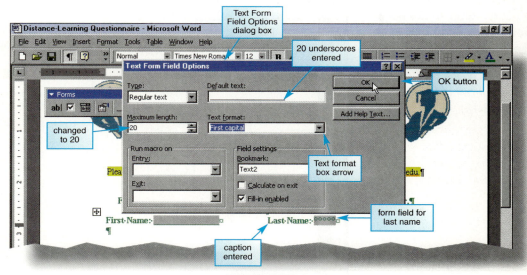

FIGURE 8-17

Inserting a Drop-Down List Box

You use a **drop-down form field** when you want to present a set of choices to a user in the form of a drop-down list box. To view the set of choices, the user clicks a box arrow that displays at the right edge of the list box (see Figure 8-1b on page WD 8.5). In this online form, the type of browser used is the first drop-down form field to be inserted. The valid choices to be presented to the user are Internet Explorer, Netscape, and Other.

Just as the first name and last name were inserted into a 1 x 2 table, the next two form fields will be inserted into a 1 x 2 table. The steps on the following pages explain how to insert the table, insert the drop-down form field, and then define the valid choices for the drop-down list.

TO INSERT A BORDERLESS TABLE INTO A FORM

1 Position the insertion point on the paragraph mark below the table containing the form field for the first name and last name. Press the ENTER key.

2 Click the Insert Table button on the Forms toolbar and then click the cell in the first row and second column of the grid.

3 Click Table on the menu bar, point to Select, and then click Table. Click the No Border button on the Formatting toolbar. Click in the first cell of the table.

Word inserts a 1 x 2 table at the location of the insertion point (see Figure 8-18). One blank line separates the two tables in the form.

Perform the following steps to insert a drop-down form field into the first cell of the table.

 Steps

To Insert a Drop-Down Form Field

1 **With the insertion point in the first cell of the table, type** Browser Used **and then press the** COLON **key. Press the** SPACEBAR. **Point to the Drop-Down Form Field button on the Forms toolbar.**

Word places the field caption in the first cell of the table (Figure 8-18).

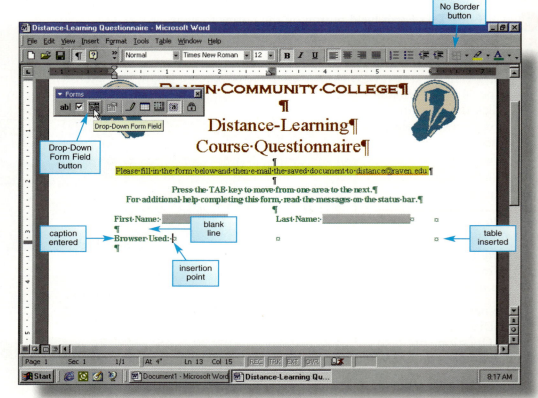

FIGURE 8-18

2 **Click the Drop-Down Form Field button.**

Word inserts a drop-down form field at the location of the insertion point (Figure 8-19). The form field displays shaded in gray.

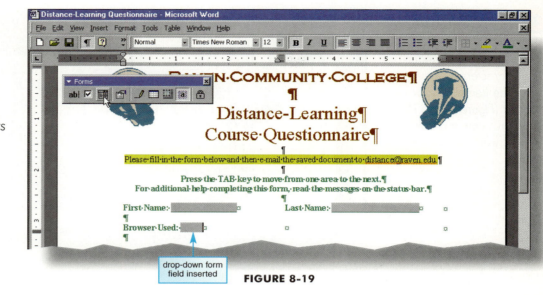

drop-down form field inserted

FIGURE 8-19

Recall that when the form displays on the screen initially (as a blank form), you want underscore characters to display where the text boxes and drop-down list boxes are located. This will help the user identify the data entry areas. In the text form field, you entered underscore characters as the default text. With a drop-down form field, Word displays the first item in the list on a blank form. Thus, you will enter 15 underscores as the first list item.

The drop-down form field initially is five characters wide. As you enter items into the drop-down list, Word increases the width of the form field to accommodate the item with the most number of characters. Perform the following steps to enter the items in the drop-down list, with the first item being 15 underscores.

Steps **To Specify Drop-Down Form Field Options**

1 **Double-click the drop-down form field. When Word displays the Drop-Down Form Field Options dialog box, press the UNDERSCORE key 15 times in the Drop-down item text box and then point to the Add button.**

Word displays the Drop-Down Form Field Options dialog box (Figure 8-20).

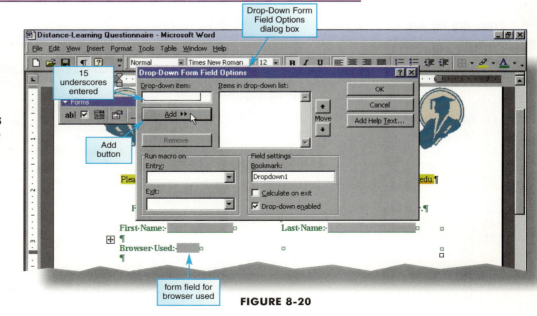

Drop-Down Form Field Options dialog box

15 underscores entered

Add button

form field for browser used

FIGURE 8-20

2 Click the Add button.

Word places the 15 underscore characters as the first item in the Items in drop-down list (Figure 8-21). The Drop-down item text box now is empty, waiting for your next entry.

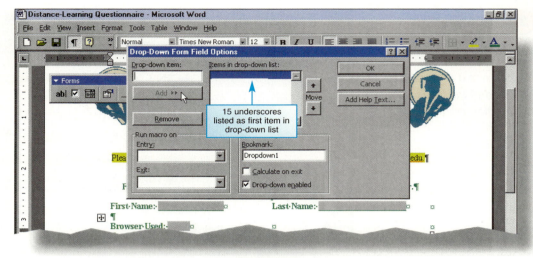

FIGURE 8-21

3 Type Internet Explorer and then click the Add button. Type Netscape and then click the Add button. Type Other and then click the Add button. Point to the OK button.

The items in the drop-down list are entered (Figure 8-22).

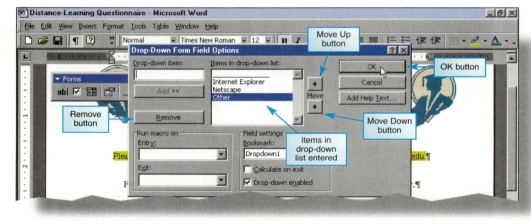

FIGURE 8-22

4 Click the OK button. Press the TAB key to move the insertion point to the beginning of the next cell in the table.

The list for the drop-down form field is defined (Figure 8-23).

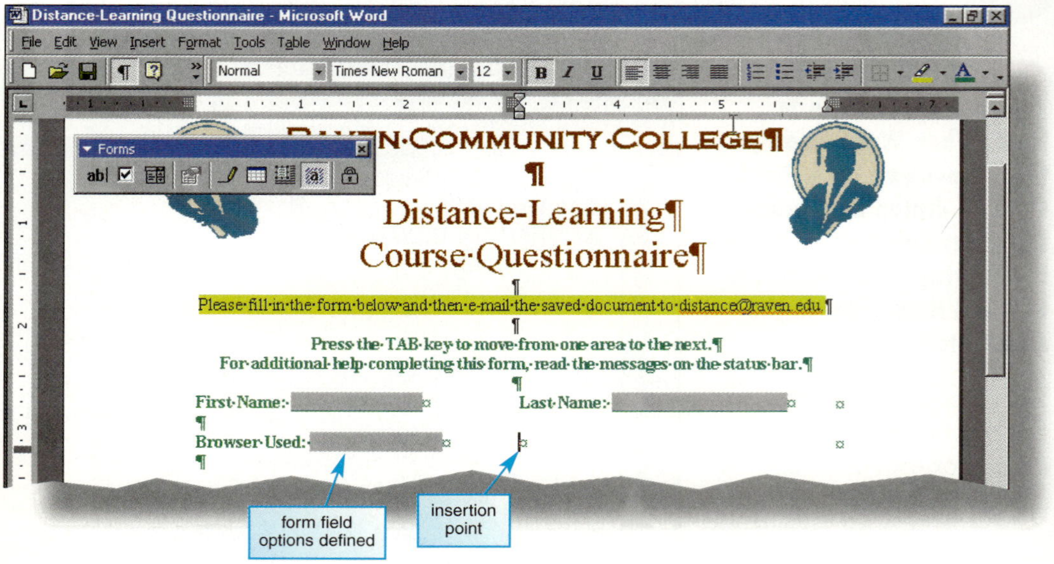

Other Ways

1. Click Form Field Options button on Forms toolbar
2. Right-click form field, click Properties on shortcut menu

FIGURE 8-23

Instead of clicking the Add button (Figure 8-22) to move items from the Drop-down item text box to the Items in drop-down list, you can press the ENTER key. This alternative method will be used later in this project.

Notice in Figure 8-23 that the 15 underscores do not display on the screen yet. Word displays the first item in the drop-down list on the screen when you protect the form, which you will do later in this project.

If, after you enter items in a list box, you want to modify their order or add or delete one or more items, you would display the Drop-Down Form Field Options dialog box (Figure 8-22) by double-clicking the drop-down form field. To add more items, you simply enter the text into the Drop-down item text box and then click the OK button. To remove an item, click it in the Items in drop-down list and then click the Remove button. To reorder the list, click an item in the Items in drop-down list and then click the Move Up button or Move Down button to move the item up or down one position each time you click the appropriate button.

The Distance-Learning Course Questionnaire has two more drop-down list boxes. One requests the user's connection method and the other requests the processor type. The list for connection method is to contain these eight items: 56 Kbps Modem, 33.6 Kbps Modem, 28.8 Kbps Modem, 14.4 Kbps Modem, ISDN Line, ADSL, T1 Line, and Other. Recall that when the form displays on the screen initially (as a blank form), you want underscore characters to display where the form fields are located. To do this, you will enter 15 underscores as the first list item.

Perform the following steps to insert another drop-down form field.

TO INSERT AND SPECIFY OPTIONS FOR A DROP-DOWN FORM FIELD

1 With the insertion point in the second cell of the table, type Connection Method and then press the COLON key. Press the SPACEBAR.

2 Click the Drop-Down Form Field button on the Forms toolbar.

3 Double-click the drop-down form field just entered. When Word displays the Drop-Down Form Field Options dialog box, press the UNDERSCORE key 15 times in the Drop-down item text box and then press the ENTER key.

4 Type 56 Kbps Modem and then press the ENTER key. Type 33.6 Kbps Modem and then press the ENTER key. Type 28.8 Kbps Modem and then press the ENTER key. Type 14.4 Kbps Modem and then press the ENTER key. Type ISDN Line and then press the ENTER key. Type ADSL and then press the ENTER key. Type T1 Line and then press the ENTER key. Type Other and then press the ENTER key. Point to the OK button (Figure 8-24 on the next page).

5 Click the OK button.

Word defines the drop-down form field as specified in the Drop-Down Form Field Options dialog box.

More *About*

Drop-Down Form Fields

Instead of clicking the Add button in the Drop-Down Form Field Options dialog box (see Figure 8-20 on page WD 8.21) to move an item from the Drop-down item text box to the Items in drop-down list, you can press the ENTER key.

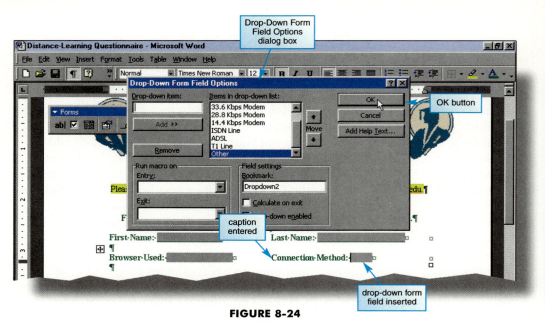

FIGURE 8-24

Just as the First Name and Last Name text boxes were inserted into a 1 x 2 table and the Browser Used and Connection Method drop-down list boxes were inserted into a 1 x 2 table, the next two form fields also will be inserted into a 1 x 2 table. Perform the following steps to insert the next 1 x 2 table.

TO INSERT A BORDERLESS TABLE INTO A FORM

1. Position the insertion point on the paragraph mark below the table containing the Browser Used and Connection Method drop-down list boxes. Press the ENTER key.

2. Click the Insert Table button on the Forms toolbar and then click the cell in the first row and second column of the grid.

3. Click Table on the menu bar, point to Select, and then click Table. Click the No Border button on the Formatting toolbar. Click in the first cell of the table.

Word inserts a 1 x 2 table two lines below the current 1 x 2 table (see Figure 8-25).

The first cell of the newly inserted table is to contain a drop-down list box that requests the processor type. The valid processor types to be in the list are Athlon, Pentium III, Pentium II, Celeron, AMD-K6, Pentium with MMX, Pentium, and Other. You also will enter 15 underscore characters as the first list item. Perform the following steps to insert another drop-down form field.

TO INSERT AND SPECIFY OPTIONS FOR A DROP-DOWN FORM FIELD

1. With the insertion point in the first cell of the table, type Processor Type and then press the COLON key. Press the SPACEBAR.

2. Click the Drop-Down Form Field button on the Forms toolbar.

3. Double-click the drop-down form field just inserted. When Word displays the Drop-Down Form Field Options dialog box, press the UNDERSCORE key 15 times in the Drop-down item text box and then press the ENTER key.

4 Type `Athlon` and then press the ENTER key. Type `Pentium III` and then press the ENTER key. Type `Pentium II` and then press the ENTER key. Type `Celeron` and then press the ENTER key. Type `AMD-K6` and then press the ENTER key. Type `Pentium with MMX` and then press the ENTER key. Type `Pentium` and then press the ENTER key. Type `Other` and then press the ENTER key. Point to the OK button (Figure 8-25).

5 Click the OK button. Press the TAB key to move the insertion point to the beginning of the next cell in the table.

Word defines the drop-down form field as specified in the Drop-Down Form Field Options dialog box.

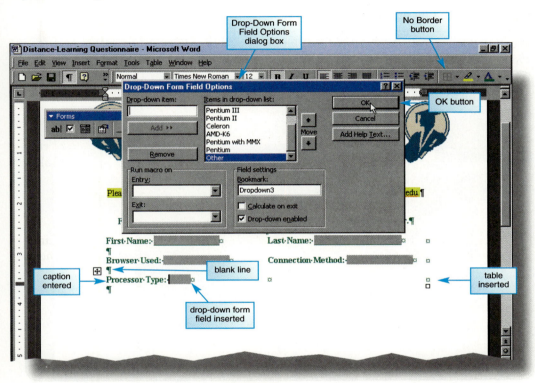

FIGURE 8-25

The next step is to insert a text form field that requires a number.

Inserting a Text Box that Requires a Number

The next form field to be entered into the Distance-Learning Course Questionnaire is for the processor speed. Processor speeds for microcomputers generally are three numbers in length such as 333, 400, or 450. You, therefore, will instruct Word to display three underscore characters when the form initially displays on the screen (as a blank form).

Valid speeds entered will vary greatly, but all speeds entered should be numeric. If you ultimately will be analyzing the data entered in a form with another type of software package such as a database, you do not want non-numeric data in fields that require numeric entries. Thus, Word can convert a non-numeric entry such as ABC to a zero.

Perform the steps on the next page to insert and format this text form field.

More About 2000

Text Form Field Types

When you click the Type box arrow in the Text Form Field Options dialog box (see Figure 8-26), you have six options: Regular text, Number, Date, Current date, Current time, and Calculation. Regular text accepts any keyboard character. Number requires a numeric entry. Date requires a valid date. The last three options display the date, time, or result of a calculation and do not allow a user to change this displayed value.

TO INSERT AND SPECIFY OPTIONS FOR A TEXT FORM FIELD

1 With the insertion point at the beginning of the second cell of the table, type `Processor Speed` and then press the COLON key. Press the SPACEBAR.

2 Click the Text Form Field button on the Forms toolbar.

3 Double-click the text form field for the processor speed. When Word displays the Text Form Field Options dialog box, click the Type box arrow and then click Number. Press the TAB key to position the insertion point in the Maximum length box and then type 3 as the length. Press the TAB key to position the insertion point in the Default number text box and then press the UNDERSCORE key three times. Point to the OK button (Figure 8-26).

4 Click the OK button.

Word displays the text form field for the processor speed according to the settings in the Text Form Field Options dialog box.

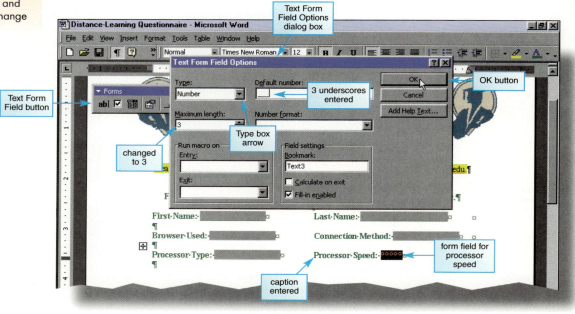

FIGURE 8-26

By changing the Type box to Number (Figure 8-26), Word will convert any non-numeric entry in this form field to a zero. Other valid text form field types are discussed later in this project.

The next step is to enter the check boxes into the Distance-Learning Course Questionnaire.

Inserting a Check Box

The bottom of the data entry area of the Distance-Learning Course Questionnaire contains five check boxes, one each for scanner, microphone, video camera, fax machine, and other. The latter (other) also has a text box to its right to allow a user to explain further. Above the check boxes is a line of instructions pertaining to the check boxes. The following pages explain how to enter this section of the form.

The first step is to enter the line of text containing instructions for the check boxes. Perform the following steps to enter this line of text.

TO ENTER TEXT

 1 Position the insertion point on the paragraph mark below the table containing the fields for processor type and processor speed. Press the ENTER key.

2 Type Special Equipment Used for Course (check all that apply) and then press the COLON key.

3 Press CTRL+5 to change the line spacing for this and subsequent paragraphs to 1.5 lines. Press the ENTER key.

The instructions for the check boxes display as shown in Figure 8-27.

You want four check boxes to display horizontally below the check box instructions. To do this and align the check boxes evenly across the line, you insert a 1 x 4 table; that is, a table with one row and four columns. Perform the following steps to insert a 1 x 4 table into the form.

TO INSERT A BORDERLESS TABLE INTO A FORM

1 With the insertion point on the paragraph mark below the check box instructions, click the Insert Table button on the Forms toolbar and then point to the cell in the first row and fourth column of the grid (Figure 8-27).

2 Click the cell in the first row and fourth column of the grid.

3 Click Table on the menu bar, point to Select, and then click Table. Click the No Border button on the Formatting toolbar.

4 Click in the first cell of the table.

Word inserts a 1 x 4 table at the location of the insertion point (see Figure 8-28 on the next page).

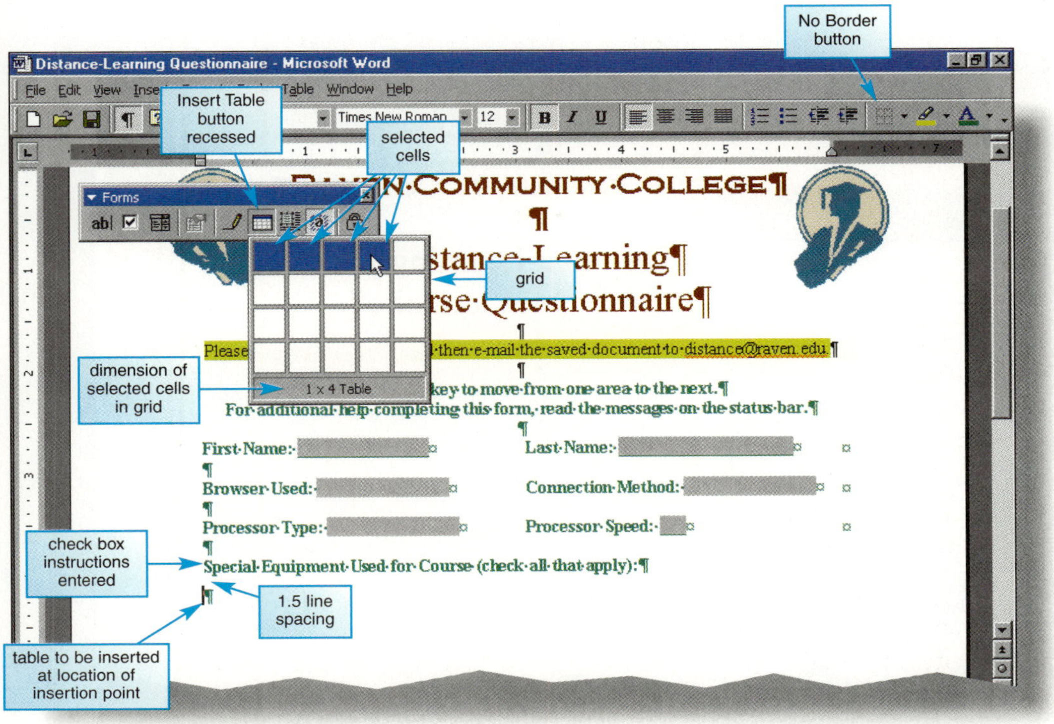

FIGURE 8-27

The next step is to insert the first check box into the first cell of the table as shown in the following steps.

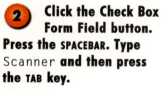

To Insert a Check Box

1 **With the insertion point in the first cell of the table, point to the Check Box Form Field button on the Forms toolbar (Figure 8-28).**

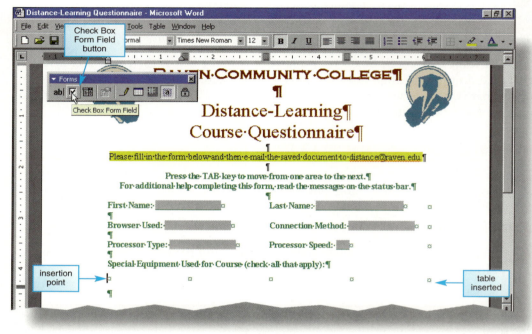

FIGURE 8-28

2 **Click the Check Box Form Field button. Press the SPACEBAR. Type** Scanner **and then press the TAB key.**

Word inserts a check box form field at the location of the insertion point (Figure 8-29).

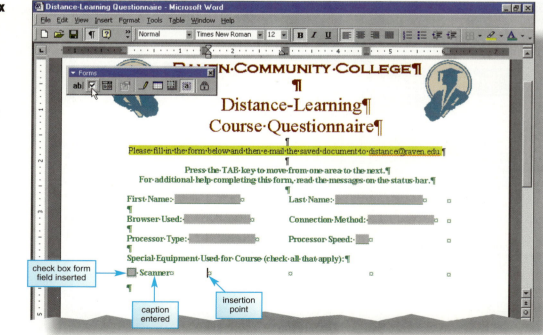

FIGURE 8-29

The next step is to enter the remaining check box fields into the form as described in the following steps.

TO ENTER ADDITIONAL CHECK BOX FORM FIELDS

 1 With the insertion point in the second cell of the table, click the Check Box Form Field button on the Forms toolbar. Press the SPACEBAR. Type Microphone and then press the TAB key.

2 With the insertion point in the third cell of the table, click the Check Box Form Field button on the Forms toolbar. Press the SPACEBAR. Type Video Camera and then press the TAB key.

3 With the insertion point in the fourth cell of the table, click the Check Box Form Field button on the Forms toolbar. Press the SPACEBAR. Type Fax Machine and then click the paragraph mark below the 1 x 4 table.

4 With the insertion point below the 1 x 4 table, click the Check Box Form Field button on the Forms toolbar. Press the SPACEBAR. Type Other (please specify) and then press the COLON key. Press the SPACEBAR.

The check box form fields are inserted (Figure 8-30).

Check Boxes

If you want an X to display in a check box when the form initially displays on the screen (as a blank form), you would double-click the check box form field, click Checked in the Default value area of the Check Box Form Field Options dialog box, and then click the OK button.

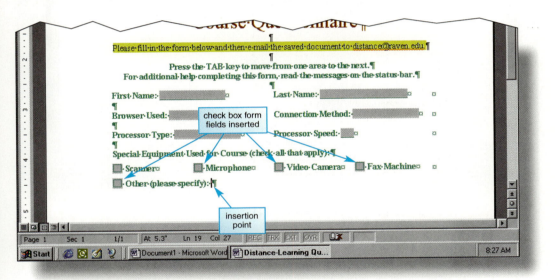

FIGURE 8-30

If users select the check box with the Other caption, you want them to explain the other type of equipment they used in the distance-learning course. To allow this, you insert a text form field as described in the following steps.

TO INSERT AND SPECIFY OPTIONS FOR A TEXT FORM FIELD

 1 Click the Text Form Field button on the Forms toolbar.

2 Double-click the text form field for other (please specify). When Word displays the Text Form Field Options dialog box, press the UNDERSCORE key 30 times in the Default text text box. Point to the OK button (Figure 8-31 on the next page).

3 Click the OK button.

4 Press CTRL+1 (the numeral one) to change the line spacing to single for this paragraph.

Word displays the text form field for the other types of equipment according to the settings in the Text Form Field Options dialog box. You change line spacing back to single so that the highlight on the text box consumes only one line instead of one and one-half lines.

FIGURE 8-31

The next step is to display the current date on the form.

Inserting a Text Box that Displays the Current Date

The next form field to be entered into the Distance-Learning Course Questionnaire is the current date. You do not want the user to enter the date; instead, you simply want the current date to display on the form. When a user fills in and e-mails the completed form, the date the user completed the form will display.

You could insert the current date as a field by clicking Insert on the menu bar and then clicking Date and Time. If, however, you plan to analyze the data at a later time using a database or some other software and you want the current date to be part of the data saved with the form, then you must insert a text box that displays the current date. Perform the following steps to insert and specify options for this text form field as the current date.

Steps ## To Insert and Specify Options for a Text Form Field as the Current Date

1 Click at the end of the last text form field entered and then press the ENTER key. Press CTRL+R to right-align the paragraph. Click the Text Form Field button on the Forms toolbar. Double-click the text form field for the current date. When Word displays the Text Form Field Options dialog box, click the Type box arrow and then click Current date. Click the Date format box arrow and then click M/d/yyyy. Point to the OK button (Figure 8-32).

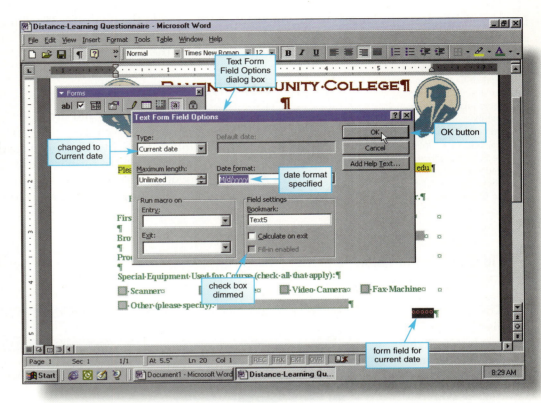

FIGURE 8-32

2 Click the OK button. Click outside the field to remove the highlight.

Word displays the current date in the form field (Figure 8-33). Your date displayed will be different.

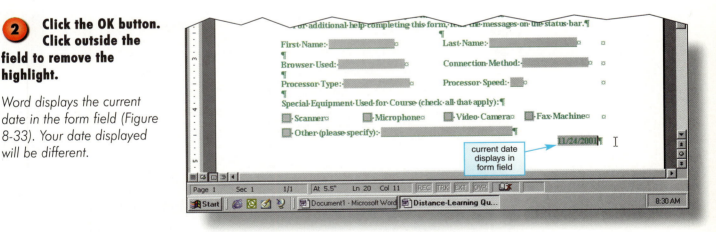

FIGURE 8-33

Notice in Figure 8-32 that the Fill-in enabled check box is dimmed in the Text Form Field Options dialog box. Word automatically dims this check box when you select Current date as the text type. When this check box is dimmed, a user is not allowed to modify the contents of the field when it displays on the screen. If you want a user to enter a date, you would select Date in the Type list instead of Current date.

Date and Time

If a text form field type has been changed to Current date (see Figure 8-32 on the previous page) or Current time and you intend to print the form, you should ensure that the date and time are current in the hard copy. Click Tools on the menu bar, click Options, click the Print tab, place a check mark in the Update fields check box, and then click the OK button.

Two other options in the Type list that also dim the Fill-in enabled check box are Current time and Calculation. That is, if you select Current time as the text type, Word displays the current time on the screen – so a user cannot change the time displayed. If you select Calculation as the text type, Word displays the result of a formula you enter.

The next step is to format the data entry fields.

Formatting Form Fields

As users enter data into the text boxes and drop-down list boxes on the form, you want the characters they type to be underlined in teal. Word prevents users from formatting data they enter into form fields. Thus, you specify any desired field formatting to fields on the form template. To format a field, you select the field and then format it as you do any other text. In this case, you use the Font dialog box to specify an underline color. Perform the following steps to underline the field for the first name in teal.

Steps **To Underline in Color**

1 **Click the text form field for the first name to select it. Right-click the selection and then point to Font on the shortcut menu (Figure 8-34).**

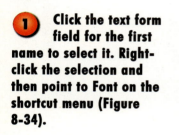

FIGURE 8-34

2 Click Font. When the Font dialog box displays, if necessary, click the Font tab. Click the Underline style box arrow and then click the first underline in the list. Click the Underline color box arrow and then click Teal. Point to the OK button.

Word displays the Font dialog box (Figure 8-35).

3 Click the OK button.

Word formats the data entry for the field to 12-point Times New Roman underlined bold teal font.

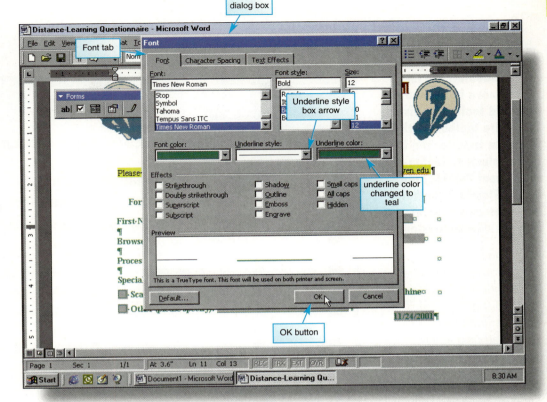

FIGURE 8-35

Other Ways

1. On Format menu click Font, click Font tab, select desired underline style, select desired underline color, click OK button

Because earlier you set the text form fields to display an underline when the form displays initially on the screen (as a blank form), you will not notice a change to the First Name text box after formatting it. The formatting options will take effect when you enter data into the form.

The next step is to copy this formatting to the other data entry fields on the screen.

Using the Format Painter Button

Instead of selecting each form field one at a time and then formatting it with the teal underline, you will copy the format assigned to the form field for the first name to the other text form fields and the drop-down form fields.

To copy formats from one form field to another, you select the form field from which you wish to copy formatting, click the Format Painter button to copy the selected form field's formatting specifications, and then select the form field to which you wish to copy the formatting. To select a text form field, you simply click it or drag through it. To select a drop-down form field, you drag through it.

In this project, you want to copy formats from one form field to multiple form fields. Thus, you double-click the Format Painter button so that the format painter remains active until you turn it off as shown in the steps on the next page.

More About

Copying Formatting

If you want to copy paragraph formatting, such as alignment and line spacing, select the paragraph mark at the end of the paragraph prior to clicking the Format Painter button. If you want to copy just character formatting, such as fonts and font sizes, do not select the paragraph mark.

Steps **To Use the Format Painter Button**

1 **Double-click the move handle on the Standard toolbar to display the entire toolbar. With the text form field for the first name selected, double-click the Format Painter button on the Standard toolbar. Move the mouse pointer into the document window.**

Word attaches a paintbrush to the mouse pointer when the Format Painter button is recessed (Figure 8-36). The 12-point Times New Roman underlined bold teal font has been copied by the format painter.

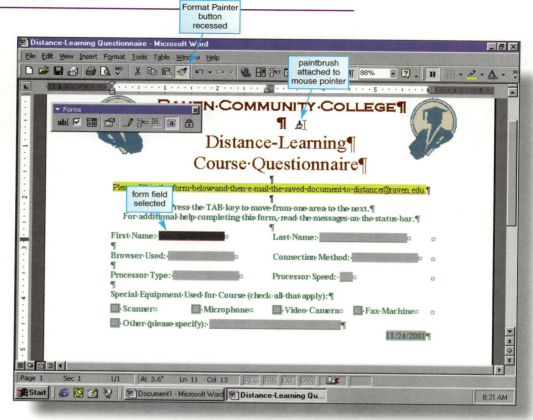

FIGURE 8-36

2 **Click the text form field for the last name.**

Word copies the 12-point Times New Roman underlined bold teal font to the text form field for the last name (Figure 8-37). The last name field is highlighted, and the format painter remains active, allowing you to select more fields to which you wish to copy the format.

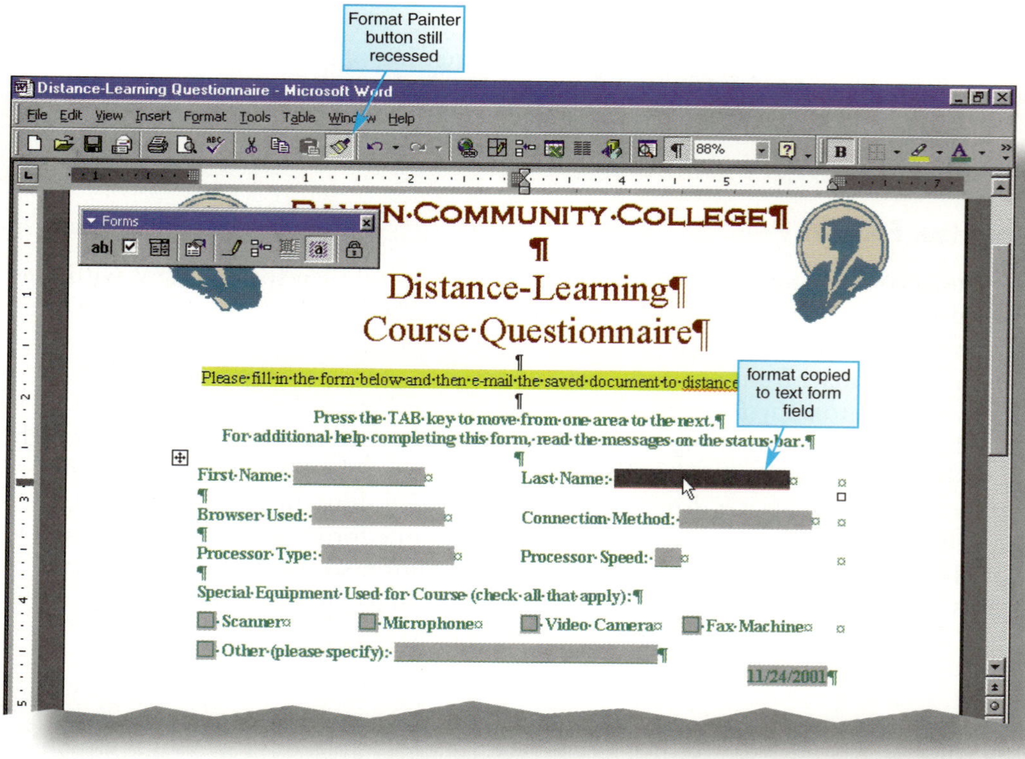

FIGURE 8-37

3 **Drag through the drop-down form field for the browser used. Drag through the drop-down form field for the connection method. Drag through the drop-down form field for the processor type. Click the text form field for processor speed. Click the text form field for other (please specify). Click the Format Painter button on the Standard toolbar.**

The format in the text form field for the first name is copied to all other text form fields and to the drop-down form fields, and the Format Painter button no longer is recessed (Figure 8-38).

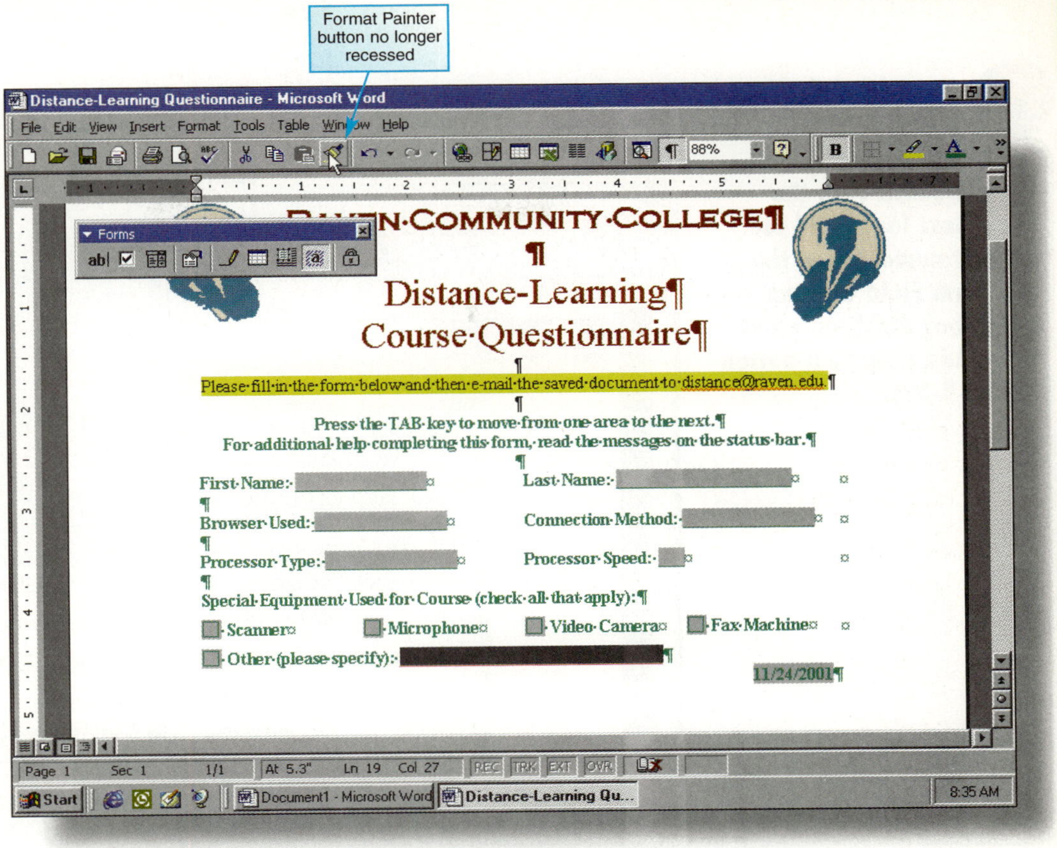

Format Painter button no longer recessed

FIGURE 8-38

The next step is to add help for users to the form.

Adding Help Text to Form Fields

As users enter data into form fields, they may have a question about the purpose or function of a particular field. Thus, Word provides two Help mechanisms by which you can assist users during their data entry process. You can display a Help message on the status bar that relates to the current data entry field and/or you can display a Help dialog box when a user presses F1. In this project, you want to display brief Help messages on the status bar as a user moves from form field to form field. Perform the steps on the next page to display a Help message on the status bar when the user is entering the first name.

More *About*

Help Text

When you enter Help text to display on the status bar, you are limited to 138 characters. You can create longer Help text, up to 255 characters, for those that display in a dialog box when the user presses F1. A good practice is to provide users as much help as possible; thus, you may wish to create both status bar Help text and dialog box Help text.

Steps **To Add Help Text to a Form**

1 **Double-click the text form field for the first name. When the Text Form Field Options dialog box displays, point to the Add Help Text button (Figure 8-39).**

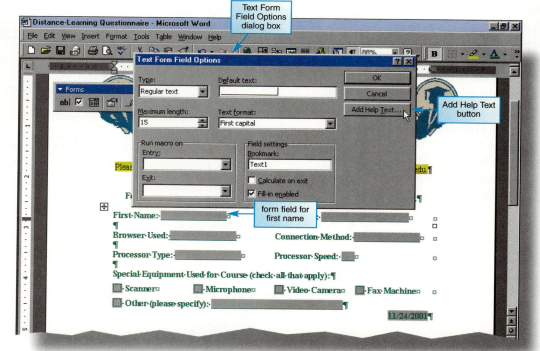

FIGURE 8-39

2 **Click the Add Help Text button. When the Form Field Help Text dialog box displays, if necessary, click the Status Bar tab. Click Type your own. Type** Enter your first name. **Point to the OK button.**

Word displays the Form Field Help Text dialog box (Figure 8-40).

3 **Click the OK button. Click the OK button in the Text Form Field Options dialog box.**

The Help text is entered for the text form field for the first name.

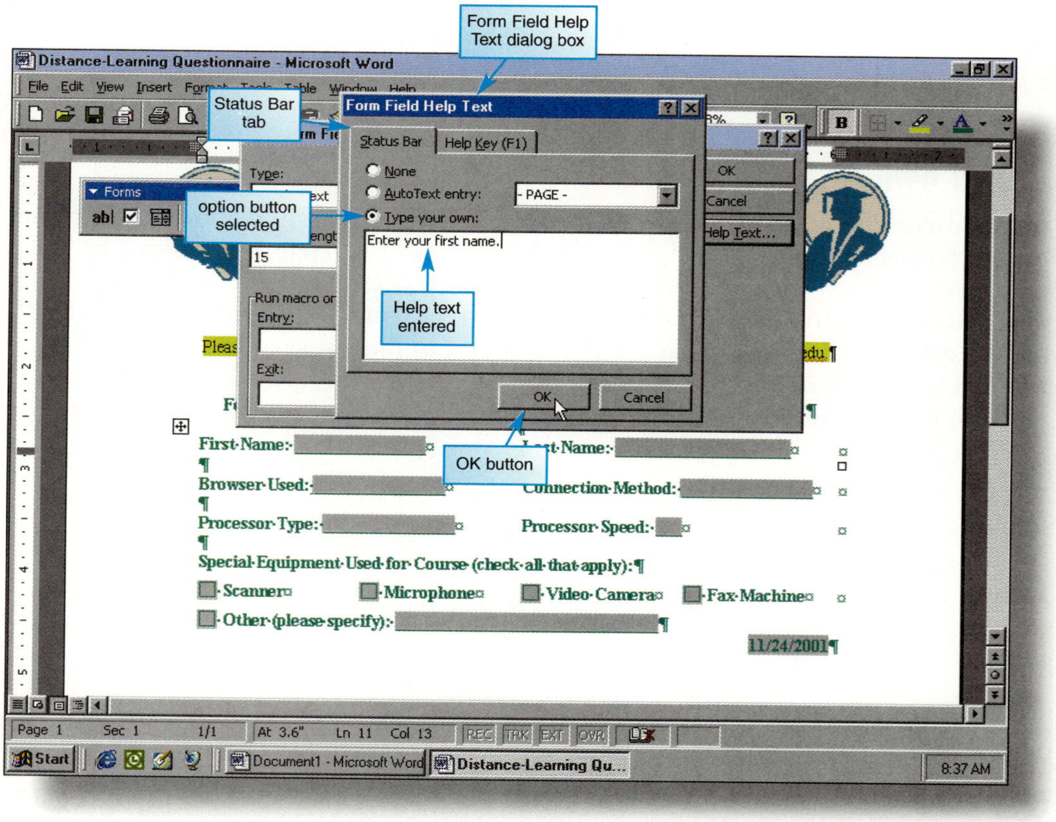

FIGURE 8-40

The Help text does not display on the status bar until you protect the form, which you will do later in this project. At that time, you will enter data into the form and see the Help text display on the status bar.

The next step is to enter the Help text for the remaining form fields in the form. You repeat the procedure in the previous steps for each data entry field on the form. The Help text for each field on the Distance-Learning Course Questionnaire is shown in Table 8-2.

More *About*

F1

If you want to enter Help text in a dialog box that displays when a user presses F1, click the Help Key (F1) tab in the Form Field Help Text dialog box (see Figure 8-40). You enter Help text in the Help Key (F1) sheet in the same manner as the Status Bar sheet.

Table 8-2	Help Text for Fields on the Form	
FIELD CAPTION	**FIELD TYPE**	**HELP TEXT TO DISPLAY ON STATUS BAR**
First Name	Text Form Field	Enter your first name.
Last Name	Text Form Field	Enter your last name.
Browser Used	Drop-Down Form Field	Click box arrow for list of choices.
Connection Method	Drop-Down Form Field	Click box arrow for list of choices.
Processor Type	Drop-Down Form Field	Click box arrow for list of choices.
Processor Speed	Text Form Field	Enter MHz in numbers.
Scanner	Check Box Form Field	Click check box to select or deselect.
Microphone	Check Box Form Field	Click check box to select or deselect.
Video Camera	Check Box Form Field	Click check box to select or deselect.
Fax Machine	Check Box Form Field	Click check box to select or deselect.
Other	Check Box Form Field	Click check box to select or deselect.
Other	Text Form Field	Please list other types of equipment used in course.

The following steps describe how to add the Help text shown in Table 8-2.

TO ADD MORE HELP TEXT

1. Double-click the text form field for the last name. Click the Add Help Text button in the Text Form Field Options dialog box. When the Form Field Help Text dialog box displays, if necessary, click the Status Bar tab. Click Type your own. Type Enter your last name. Click the OK button. Click the OK button in the Text Form Field Options dialog box.

2. Double-click the drop-down form field for the browser used.

3. Click the Add Help Text button in the Drop-Down Form Field Options dialog box. When the Form Field Help Text dialog box displays, if necessary, click the Status Bar tab. Click Type your own. Type Click box arrow for list of choices. Click the OK button. Click the OK button in the Text Form Field Options dialog box.

4. Double-click the drop-down form field for the connection method. Repeat Step 3.

5. Double-click the drop-down form field for the processor type. Repeat Step 3.

6. Double-click the text form field for the processor speed. Click the Add Help Text button in the Text Form Field Options dialog box. When the Form Field Help Text dialog box displays, if necessary, click the Status Bar tab. Click Type your own. Type Enter MHz in numbers. Click the OK button. Click the OK button in the Text Form Field Options dialog box.

7 Double-click the check box form field for scanner.

8 Click the Add Help Text button in the Check Box Form Field Options dialog box. When the Form Field Help Text dialog box displays, if necessary, click the Status Bar tab. Click Type your own. Type Click check box to select or deselect. Click the OK button. Click the OK button in the Text Form Field Options dialog box.

9 Double-click the check box form field for microphone. Repeat Step 8.

10 Double-click the check box form field for video camera. Repeat Step 8.

11 Double-click the check box form field for fax machine. Repeat Step 8.

12 Double-click the check box form field for other (please specify). Repeat Step 8.

13 Double-click the text form field for other (please specify). Click the Add Help Text button in the Text Form Field Options dialog box. When the Form Field Help Text dialog box displays, if necessary, click the Status Bar tab. Click Type your own. Type Please list other types of equipment used in course. Click the OK button. Click the OK button in the Text Form Field Options dialog box. Click outside the selection to remove the highlight.

Help text is entered for all data entry fields according to Table 8-2 on the previous page.

If you would like to change the Help text for any of the form fields, simply double-click the form field and then click the Add Help Text button in the dialog box. When the Form Field Help Text dialog box displays, if necessary, click the Status Bar tab. Make any necessary changes to the existing Help text and then click the OK button in the dialog boxes.

The next step is to remove the form field shading.

Removing Form Field Shading

The fields on the form currently are shaded (see Figure 8-41). During the design of a form, it is helpful to display field shading so that you easily can identify the fields. You, however, do not want the fields to be shaded when a user is entering data into a form. Thus, perform the following steps to remove form field shading.

More *About*

Form Field Shading

If you print a form that displays form field shading, the shading will not print. To add shading to a field on a printed form, you must select the form field, click the Shading Color button arrow on the Tables and Borders toolbar, and then click the desired shading color. Likewise, if you want a border surrounding a field, select the form field, click the Border button arrow on the Tables and Borders toolbar, and then click the Outside Border button.

To Remove Form Field Shading

1 **Point to the Form Field Shading button on the Forms toolbar (Figure 8-41).**

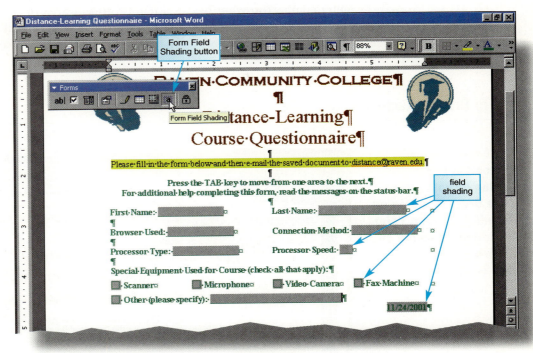

FIGURE 8-41

2 **Click the Form Field Shading button.**

Word removes the shading from the form fields (Figure 8-42).

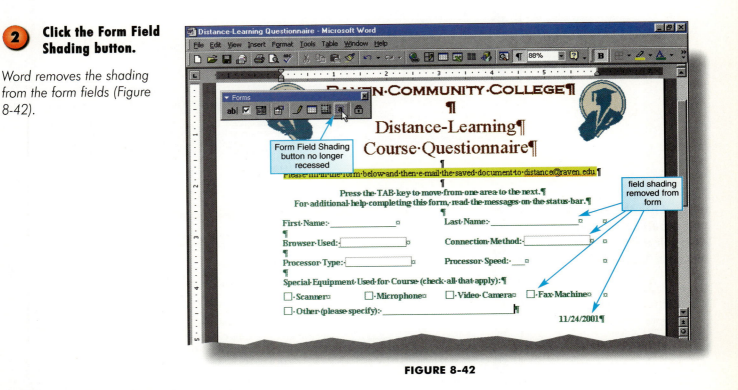

FIGURE 8-42

The next step is to emphasize the data entry area of the form.

Drawing and Formatting a Rectangle

The data entry area of the form includes all the form fields into which a user enters data. You want to call attention to this area of the form. Thus, you decide to place a rectangle around the data entry area and then fill the rectangle with a texture. To draw a rectangle, you use the Drawing toolbar as shown in the following steps.

Steps **To Draw a Rectangle**

1 **If the Drawing toolbar is not displaying on your screen, click the Drawing button on the Standard toolbar. Point to the Rectangle button on the Drawing toolbar (Figure 8-43).**

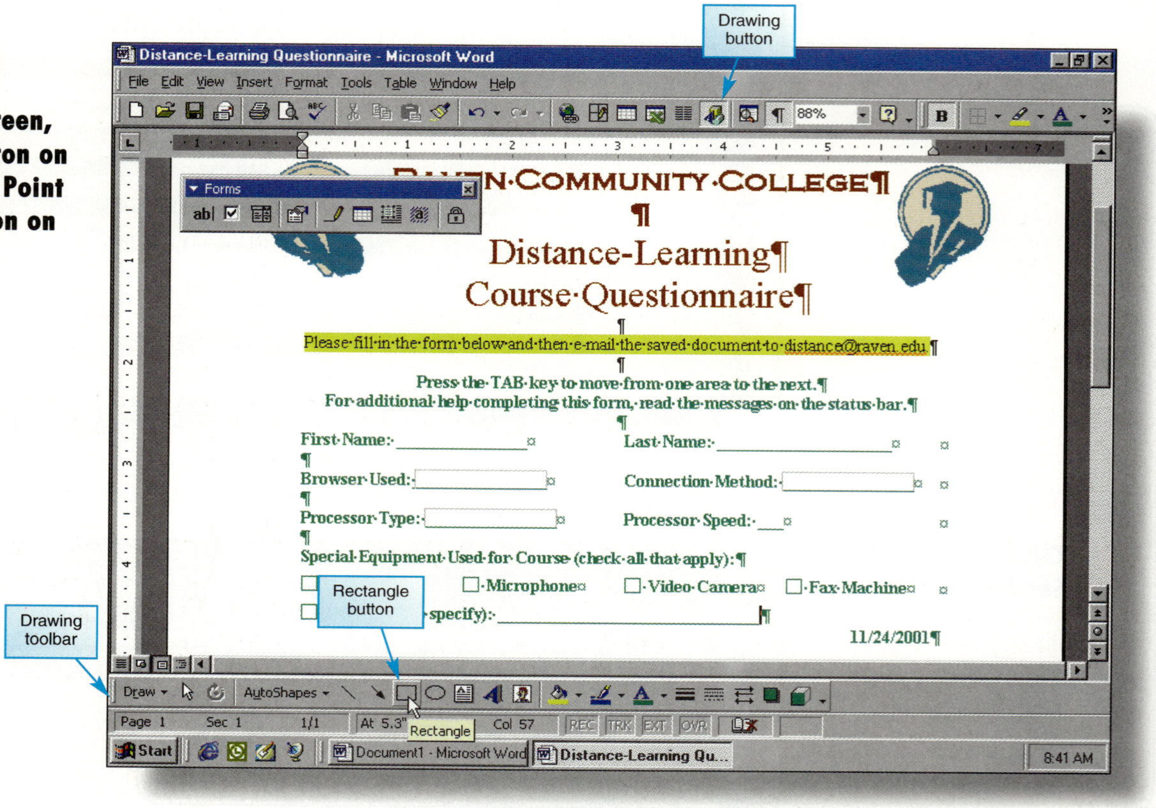

FIGURE 8-43

2 **Click the Rectangle button. Position the crosshair mouse pointer as shown in Figure 8-44.**

Word displays the mouse pointer as a crosshair, which you drag to form the size of the rectangle.

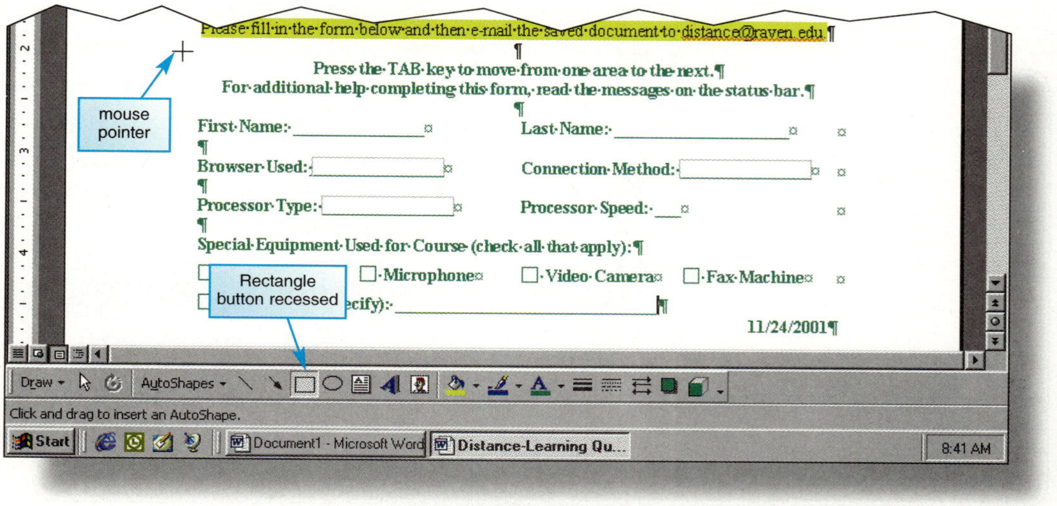

FIGURE 8-44

3 Drag the mouse pointer downward and rightward to form a rectangle similar to the one shown in Figure 8-45.

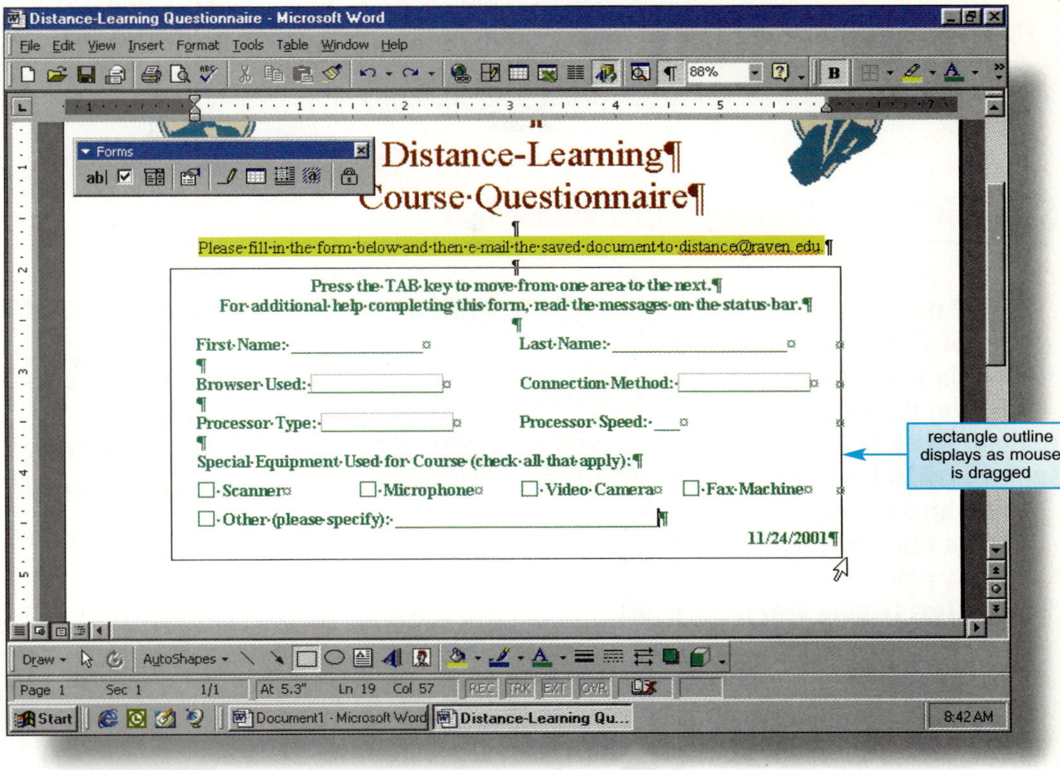

FIGURE 8-45

4 Release the mouse button. If Word positions the text below the rectangle, click Format on the menu bar, click AutoShape, click the Layout tab, click In front of text, and then click the OK button. If, once the rectangle is drawn, you need to resize it, simply drag the sizing handles.

When you release the mouse button, Word positions the rectangle on top of the text behind it, thus hiding the data entry area from view (Figure 8-46).

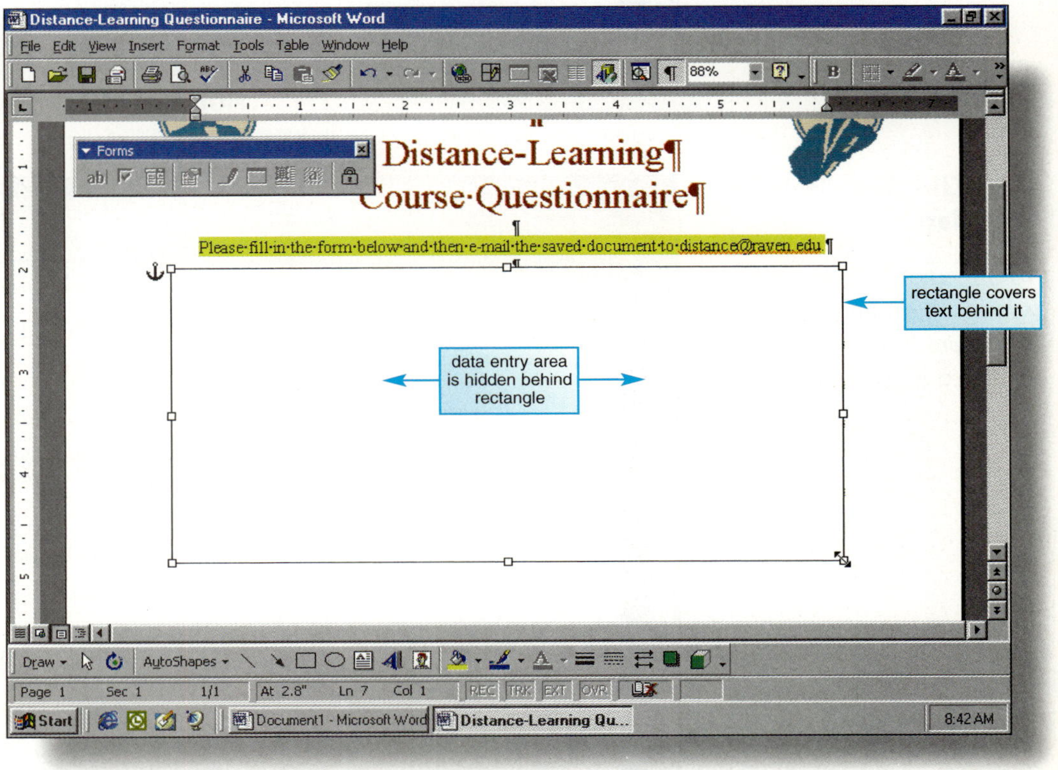

FIGURE 8-46

A rectangle is a type of drawing object. When you add a drawing object to a document, Word initially places it in front of, or on top of, any text behind it. You can change the stacking order of the drawing object so that it displays behind the text as shown in the following steps.

Steps **To Send a Drawing Object Behind Text**

1 **Point to the edge of the drawing object (in this case, the rectangle) until the mouse pointer has a four-headed arrow attached to it and then right-click. Point to Order on the shortcut menu and then point to Send Behind Text (Figure 8-47).**

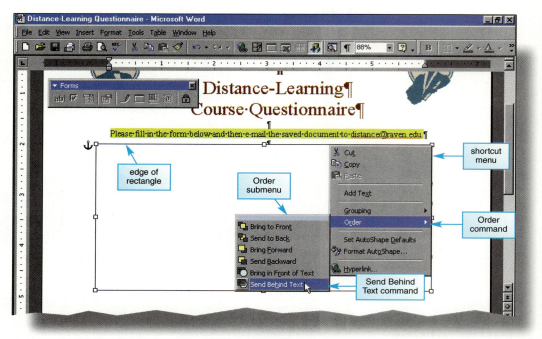

FIGURE 8-47

2 **Click Send Behind Text.**

Word positions the rectangle drawing object behind the text (Figure 8-48). The data entry area is visible again.

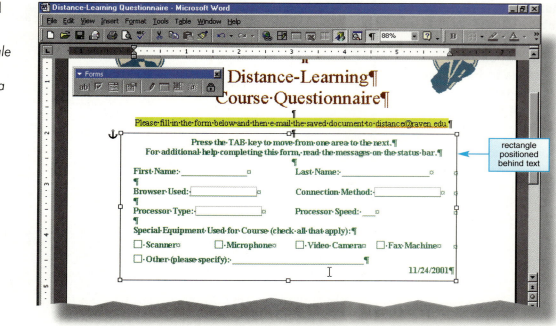

FIGURE 8-48

If you wanted to bring the drawing object on top of the text again, you would right-click one of its edges, point to Order on the shortcut menu, and then click Bring in Front of Text.

If you have multiple graphics displaying on the screen and would like them to overlap, you can change their stacking order by right-clicking the graphic to reorder, pointing to Order on the shortcut menu, and then clicking one of the first four commands on the Order submenu (see Figure 8-47). The Bring to Front command displays the selected object at the top of the stack and the Send to Back command displays the selected object at the bottom of the stack. The Bring Forward and Send Backward commands each move the drawing object forward or backward one layer in a stack.

The next step is to fill the inside of the rectangle. In Word, you can **fill**, or paint, the inside of a drawing object with a color or with an effect. **Fill effects** include gradient (two-toned) colors, textures, patterns, and pictures. Perform the following steps to format the rectangle using a texture fill effect.

More About

Drawing Objects

To change the color of a drawing object, click the Line Color button arrow on the Drawing toolbar and then click the desired color. To add a shadow to a drawing object, click the Shadow button arrow on the Drawing toolbar and then click the desired shadow. To add a 3-D effect to a drawing object, click the 3-D button arrow on the Drawing toolbar and then click the desired effect.

Steps To Fill a Drawing Object with a Texture

1 **With the drawing object selected, click the Fill Color button arrow on the Drawing toolbar and then point to the Fill Effects button.**

The available predefined fill colors display, as well as the More Colors and Fill Effects buttons (Figure 8-49).

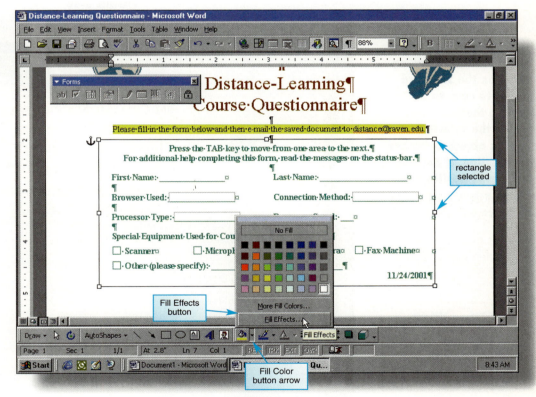

FIGURE 8-49

2 **Click the Fill Effects button. When the Fill Effects dialog box displays, if necessary, click the Texture tab. Click the Recycled Paper texture in the list of textures and then point to the OK button.**

Word displays the Fill Effects dialog box (Figure 8-50).

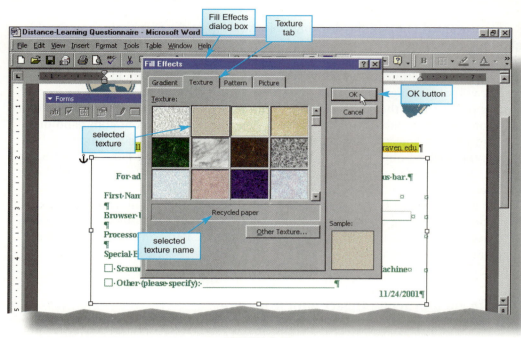

FIGURE 8-50

3 **Click the OK button. Click the Drawing button on the Standard toolbar to remove the Drawing toolbar. Click outside the selected drawing object to remove the selection. If necessary, scroll up to position the college name at the top of the document window.**

Word fills the rectangle with the recycled paper texture (Figure 8-51).

Other Ways

1. Right-click edge of drawing object, click Format AutoShape on shortcut menu, click Colors and Lines tab, click Fill Color button arrow, click Fill Effects button, click Texture tab, click desired texture, click OK button twice

2. Select drawing object, click AutoShape on Format menu, click Colors and Lines tab, click Fill Color button arrow, click Fill Effects button, click Texture tab, click desired texture, click OK button twice

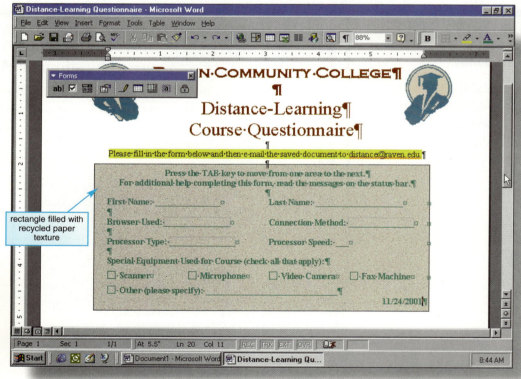

FIGURE 8-51

The next step is to enter and format the thank-you message below the data entry area.

Animating Text

In an online document, you can animate text to which you wish to draw the reader's attention. When you **animate text**, it has the appearance of motion. To animate text in Word, you select it and then apply one of the predefined text effects in the Font dialog box.

For this form, you want the thank-you message below the data entry area to have a moving black rectangle around it, which is called the Marching Black Ants animation in the Font dialog box. Perform the following steps to animate the thank-you message on the online form.

Steps To Animate Text

1 **Position the insertion point at the end of the current date in the data entry area and then press the ENTER key twice. Press CTRL + E to center the paragraph and then type** Thank you for your time!

The thank-you message is entered below the data entry area (Figure 8-52).

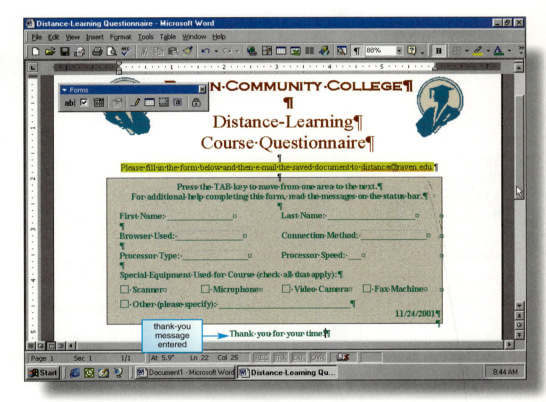

FIGURE 8-52

2 **Select the sentence just entered. Right-click the selection and then click Font on the shortcut menu. When the Font dialog box displays, if necessary, click the Text Effects tab. Click Marching Black Ants in the Animations list. Point to the OK button.**

Word displays the Font dialog box (Figure 8-53). The Preview area shows a sample of the selected animation.

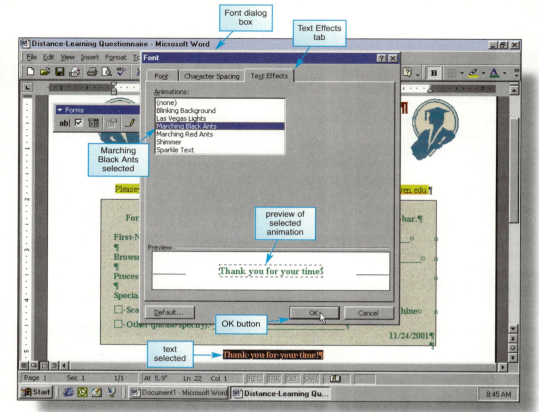

FIGURE 8-53

3 **Click the OK button. Click outside the selection to remove the highlight.**

Word applies the animation to the selected text (Figure 8-54).

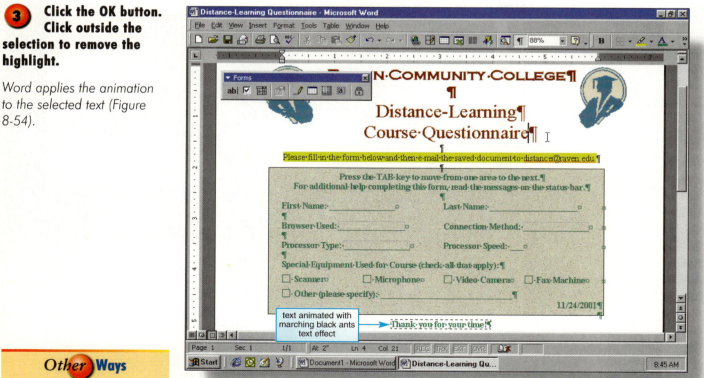

FIGURE 8-54

Other Ways

1. Select text, click Font on Format menu, click Text Effects tab, click desired animation, click OK button

If you wanted to remove an animation from text, you would select the text, right-click the selection, click Font on the shortcut menu, click the Text Effects tab, click (none) in the Animations list, and then click the OK button.

If you print a document that contains animated text, the animations do not show on the hard copy; instead, the text prints as regular text. Thus, animations are designed specifically for documents that will be viewed online.

The next step in this project is to protect the Distance-Learning Course Questionnaire.

Protecting a Form

Before you allow users to work with a form you have created, you should protect it. When you **protect a form**, you are allowing users only to enter data in designated areas – specifically, the form fields that are enabled. Thus, it is crucial that you protect a form before making it available to users. Perform the following steps to protect the Distance-Learning Course Questionnaire.

More About 2000

Protecting Forms

If you want only authorized users to be able to unprotect a form, you should password-protect the form. To do this, click Tools on the menu bar, click Protect Document, click Forms in the Protect document for area, type the password in the Password (optional) text box, and then click the OK button. Then, reenter the password in the Confirm Password dialog box.

Steps **To Protect a Form**

1 **Point to the Protect Form button on the Forms toolbar (Figure 8-55).**

2 **Click the Protect Form button. Remove the Forms toolbar from the screen by clicking its Close button.**

Word protects the form. Word highlights the first form field on the form (see Figure 8-56 on the next page).

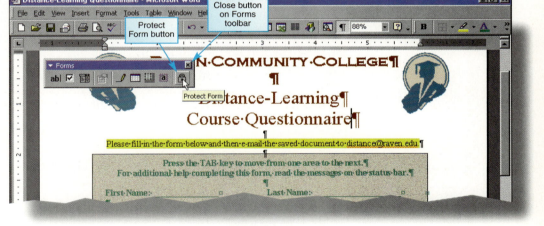

FIGURE 8-55

Other Ways

1. On Tools menu click Protect Document, click Forms, click the OK button

When the form is protected, a highlight displays in the first form field. To advance to the next form field, press the TAB key. To move to a previous form field, press the SHIFT+TAB keys. You will enter data into this form later in the project.

The next step is to turn off the display of formatting marks. You do not want them on the form when a user opens it. Perform the following steps to hide formatting marks.

TO HIDE FORMATTING MARKS

1 If the Show/Hide ¶ button on the Standard toolbar is recessed, click it.

Word hides the formatting marks (Figure 8-56 on the next page).

More About 2000

Docked Toolbars

To hide a docked toolbar, click View on the menu bar, click Toolbars, and then click the toolbar name.

More About

Borders

If a form filled an entire page and you wanted to add a border around the perimeter of the page, you would click Format on the menu bar; click Borders and Shading; click the Page Border tab; click the desired border setting, style, color, and width; and then click the OK button. You modify the border in the same manner; that is, through the Page Border sheet in the Borders and Shading dialog box.

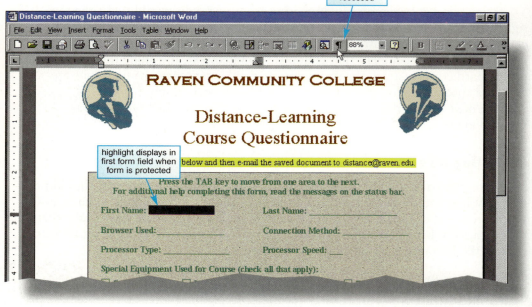

FIGURE 8-56

The online form template for this project now is complete. Perform the following steps to save it again and then quit Word.

TO SAVE THE DOCUMENT AGAIN

1. Click the Save button on the Standard toolbar.

Word saves the template with the same file name, Distance-Learning Questionnaire.

TO QUIT WORD

1. Click File on the menu bar and then click Exit.

The Word window closes.

Working with an Online Form

Once you have created a template, you then can make it available to users. Users do not open templates with the Open button on the Standard toolbar in Word. A developer of a template uses the Open button to open the template so it can be modified.

A user, by contrast, starts a new Word document that is based on the template. That is, when a user accesses a template, the title bar displays the default file name, Document1 (or a similar name). Instead of the Word window being blank, however, it contains text and formatting associated with the template that the user accesses. For example, Word provides a variety of templates such as those for memos, letters, fax cover sheets, and resumes. If a user accesses a memo template, Word displays the contents of a basic memo in a new document window.

When you save the template to a disk in drive A, as instructed earlier in this project, a user can access your template through the My Computer window or Windows Explorer. Perform the following steps to display a new Word document window that is based on the Distance-Learning Questionnaire template.

Steps **To Access a Template through Windows Explorer**

① **Right-click the My Computer icon on the Windows desktop and then click Explore on the shortcut menu. When the Exploring window displays, click the Address text box to select it. Type** a: **and then press the ENTER key.**

The Exploring - 3½ Floppy (A:) window displays (Figure 8-57). Notice the icon for the Distance-Learning Questionnaire template has a small yellow bar at its top.

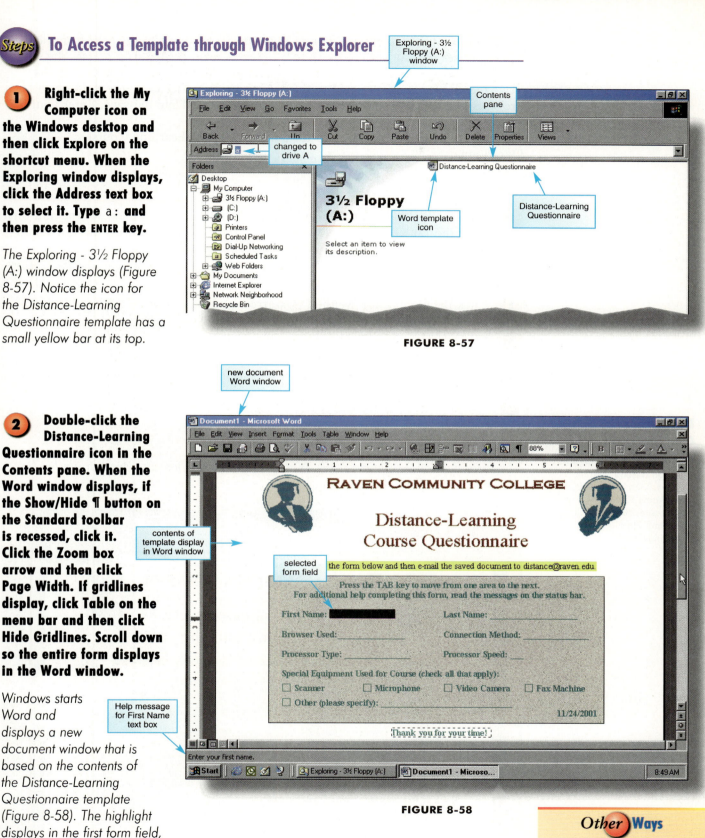

FIGURE 8-57

② **Double-click the Distance-Learning Questionnaire icon in the Contents pane. When the Word window displays, if the Show/Hide ¶ button on the Standard toolbar is recessed, click it. Click the Zoom box arrow and then click Page Width. If gridlines display, click Table on the menu bar and then click Hide Gridlines. Scroll down so the entire form displays in the Word window.**

Windows starts Word and displays a new document window that is based on the contents of the Distance-Learning Questionnaire template (Figure 8-58). The highlight displays in the first form field, ready for a user's data entry.

FIGURE 8-58

Other Ways

1. If the template was saved in the User Templates folder, click New on File menu, click appropriate tab, and then click icon attached to template

The next step is to enter data into the form. To advance to the next form field, a user presses the TAB key. To move to a previous form field, a user presses the SHIFT+TAB keys. As a user tabs from one form field to the next, the status bar displays the Help messages related to the current field. Notice in Figure 8-58 on the previous page that the status bar currently displays the Help message, Enter your first name.

Perform the following steps to fill out the Distance-Learning Course Questionnaire.

TO FILL OUT A FORM

1 With the highlight in the form field for the first name, type Geraldine and then press the TAB key. Type Smith in the Last Name text box. Press the TAB key to highlight the Browser Used drop-down list box and display its box arrow.

2 Click the Browser Used box arrow and then click Internet Explorer. Press the TAB key.

3 Click the Connection Method box arrow and then click 28.8 Kbps Modem. Press the TAB key.

4 Click the Processor Type box arrow and then click Pentium III. Press the TAB key.

5 Type 400 in the Processor Speed text box. Press the TAB key.

6 Click the following check boxes: Scanner, Fax Machine, and Other. Press the TAB key.

7 Type Digital Camera in the Other text box.

The form is filled in (Figure 8-59). Notice that the text box and drop-down list box entries are underlined in teal.

More About 2000

Designing Questionnaires

For more information on how to design a good questionnaire, visit the Word 2000 More About Web page (www.scsite.com/wd2000/more.htm) and then click Designing Questionnaires.

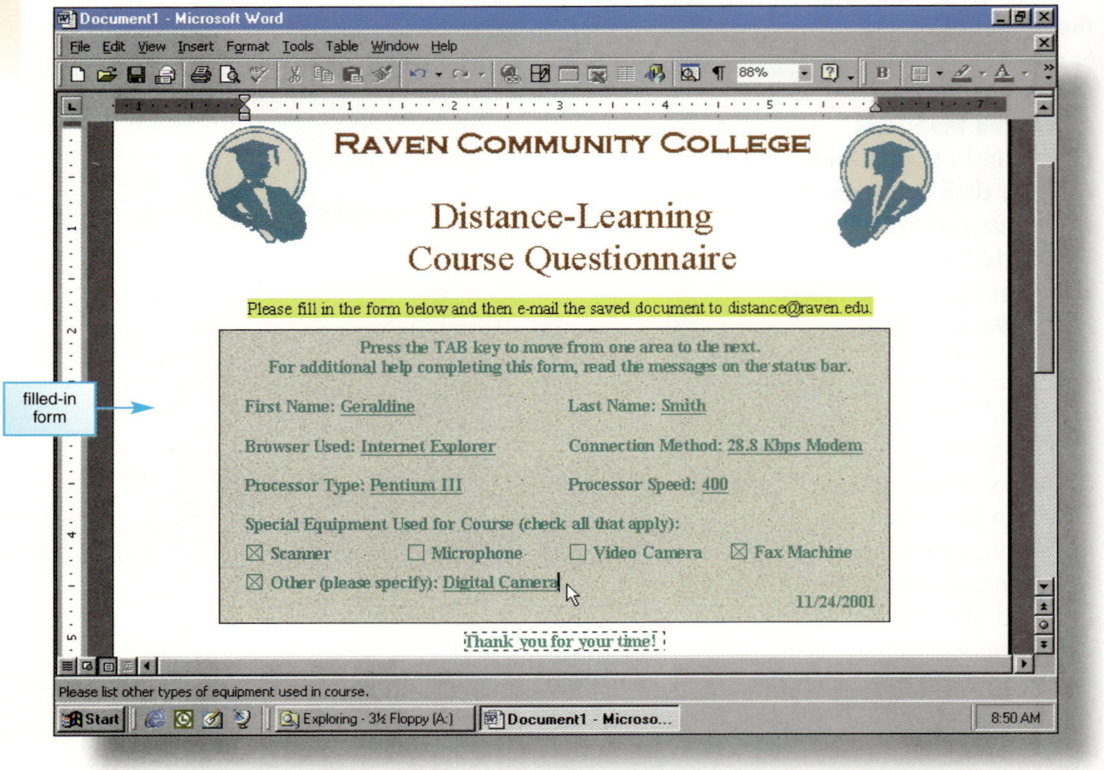

FIGURE 8-59

With the form filled in, a user can save it by clicking the Save button on the Standard toolbar. By basing the new document on a template, the blank Distance-Learning Course Questionnaire remains unchanged because users are saving a new document instead of saving a modification to the questionnaire. Perform the following steps to save the document that contains your responses.

TO SAVE A DOCUMENT

1 With a floppy disk in drive A, click the Save button on the Standard toolbar.

2 Type Smith Form in the File name text box.

3 If necessary, click the Save in box arrow and then click 3½ Floppy (A:).

4 Click the Save button in the Save As dialog box.

Word saves the document with the file name Smith Form on a disk in drive A (see Figure 8-61 on the next page).

You can print the document as you print any other document. Keep in mind, though, that the colors used were designed for viewing online. Thus, different color schemes would have been selected if the form had been designed for a printout. Perform the following step to print the filled-in form.

TO PRINT A FORM

1 Click the Print button on the Standard toolbar.

Word prints the form (Figure 8-60). Notice the animation on the thank-you message does not print.

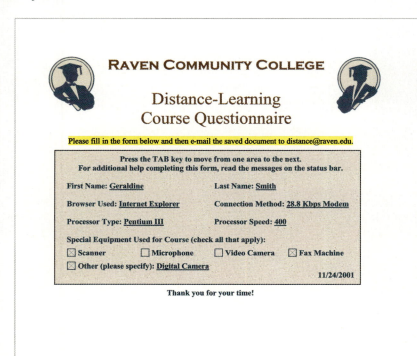

FIGURE 8-60

Printing

If you want to save ink, print faster, or minimize printer overrun errors, lower the printer resolution. Click File on the menu bar, click Print, click the Properties button in the Print dialog box, click the Graphics tab, click the Resolution box arrow, click a lower resolution than that displayed currently, click the Apply button, click the OK button, and then click the Close button.

Printing Data Only

If you wanted to print only data instead of the entire form, click File on the menu bar, click Print, click the Options button, place a check mark in Print data only for forms check box, click the OK button, and then click the OK button. Then, remove the check mark from the Print data only for forms check box so that future prints will print the entire form.

Microsoft Access 2000

For more information on features of Access, visit the Word 2000 More About Web page (www.scsite.com/wd2000/more.htm) and then click Microsoft Access 2000.

Saving Data on the Form

You may wish to gather the responses from the filled in questionnaires and analyze them. Depending on the number of forms completed, tabulating the data manually could be a time-consuming and monumental task. One alternative is to use database software, such as Access, to assist you in analyzing the responses. To do this, you must save the data on each questionnaire in a manner that will be recognized by the database software.

Word provides a means through the Save As dialog box to save the data in a comma-delimited text file so that it can be recognized by database software packages. A **comma-delimited text file** is a file that separates each data item with a comma and places quotation marks around text data items. See Figure 8-65 on page WD 8.55 for an example of a comma-delimited text file.

Perform the following steps to save the data from the form into a text file.

To Save Form Data in a Text File

1 Click File on the menu bar and then click Save As. When the Save As dialog box displays, click the Tools button arrow and then point to General Options.

Word displays the Save As dialog box (Figure 8-61).

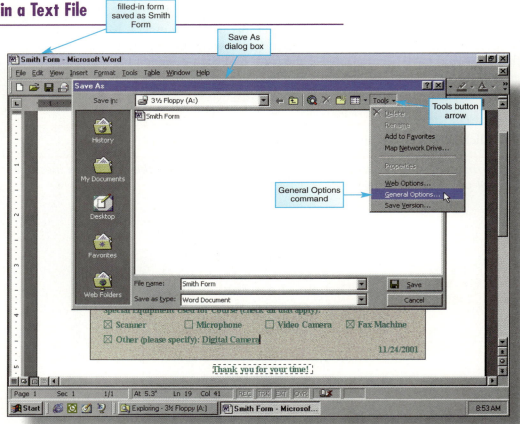

FIGURE 8-61

2 Click General Options. When the Save dialog box displays, place a check mark in the Save data only for forms check box and then point to the OK button.

Word displays the Save dialog box (Figure 8-62).

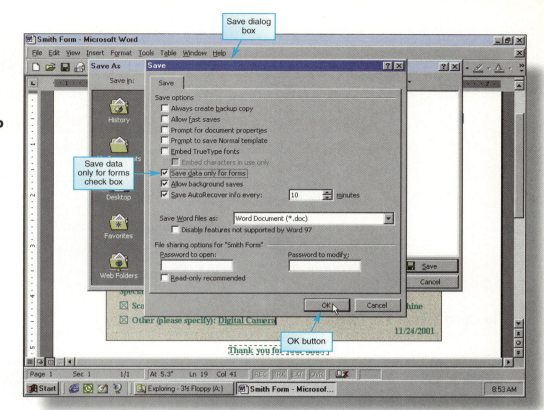

FIGURE 8-62

3 Click the OK button. When the Save As dialog box is visible again, point to its Save button.

Word changes the document type in the Save as type text box to Text Only (Figure 8-63).

4 Click the Save button in the Save As dialog box. If Word displays a dialog box indicating that some formatting may be lost, click the Yes button to continue the save because text files should not have formatting.

Word saves the data on the form in a text file called Smith Form.

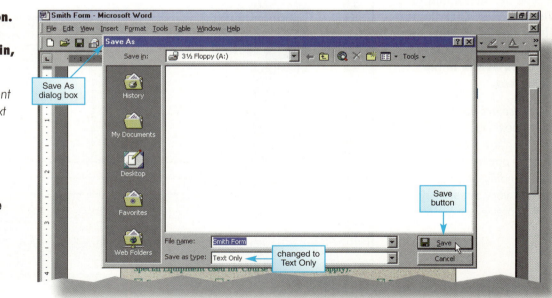

FIGURE 8-63

1. On Tools menu click Options, click Save tab, place a check mark in Save data only for forms check box, click OK button, on File menu click Save Copy As, click Save button in Save Copy As dialog box

Microsoft **Word 2000**

After you save the data to a text file, you should remove the check mark from the Save data only for forms check box so that Word will save the entire form the next time you save the document. Perform the following steps to uncheck the Save data only for forms check box.

TO UNCHECK THE SAVE DATA ONLY FOR FORMS CHECK BOX

1 Click Tools on the menu bar and then click Options. When the Options dialog box displays, click the Save tab.

2 Click the Save data only for forms check box to remove the check mark. Click the OK button.

Future saves of the document will save the entire form.

If you wanted to view the contents of the text file, you could open it in Word by performing the following steps.

Steps To Open a Text File in Word

1 **Click the Open button on the Standard toolbar. When the Open dialog box displays, if necessary, click the Files of type box arrow and then click All Files. Click the text file called Smith Form in the list and then point to the Open button in the dialog box.**

Word displays the Open dialog box (Figure 8-64). The icon for a text file looks like a piece of paper with writing on it. Depending on previous settings, your screen may not show a preview of the file.

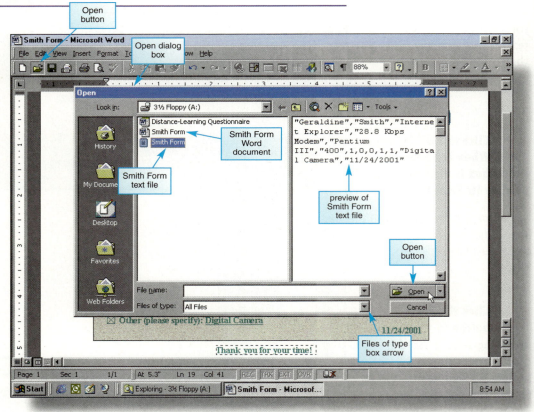

FIGURE 8-64

 **Click the Open button in the Open dialog box.**

The text file displays in the Word window (Figure 8-65).

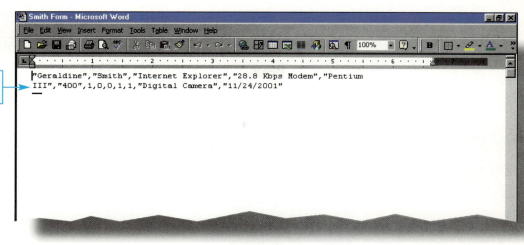

text file opened in Word window

FIGURE 8-65

You also can display a text file in a text editor such as Notepad. If you wanted to print the text file, you would click the Print button on the Standard toolbar.

Notice that the text file lists all data from the form fields, separating each form field with a comma. All text box and drop-down list box entries are surrounded with quotation marks. Table 8-3 shows the form field and the corresponding entry in the text file.

For the check boxes, a value of 1 (one) indicates that the user selected the check box, and a value of 0 (zero) indicates that a user did not select the check box. The text file is ready to be imported into a database table.

Perform the following steps to close the window displaying the text file.

Table 8-3 Mapping of Form Fields to Contents of Text File		
FORM FIELD CAPTION	**FORM FIELD TYPE**	**TEXT FILE ENTRY**
First Name	Text Box	"Geraldine"
Last Name	Text Box	"Smith"
Browser Used	Drop-Down List Box	"Internet Explorer"
Connection Method	Drop-Down List Box	"28.8 Kbps Modem"
Processor Type	Drop-Down List Box	"Pentium III"
Processor Speed	Text Box	"400"
Scanner	Check Box	1
Microphone	Check Box	0
Video Camera	Check Box	0
Fax Machine	Check Box	1
Other	Check Box	1
Other	Text Box	"Digital Camera"
Date		"11/24/2001"

TO CLOSE A WINDOW

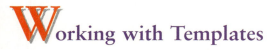 Click File on the menu bar and then click Close.

Word closes the window displaying the text file.

Working with Templates

If you want to modify the template, you open it by clicking the Open button on the Standard toolbar, clicking the template name, and then clicking the Open button in the dialog box. Then, you must unprotect the form by clicking the Protect Form document on the Forms toolbar or by clicking Tools on the menu bar and then clicking Unprotect Document.

When you created the template in this project, you saved it to a floppy disk in drive A. In environments other than an academic setting, you would not save the template to a floppy disk. Instead, you would save it to the Templates folder, which is the folder Word initially displays in the Save As dialog box for a file type of document template. When you save a template in the Templates folder, Word places an icon for the template in the General sheet of the New dialog box. Thus, to open a new Word document that is based on a template that has been saved in the Templates folder, you click File on the menu bar, click New, click the General tab, and then double-click the template icon. Figure 8-66 shows the template icon for the Distance-Learning Questionnaire in the General Sheet of the New dialog box.

More *About* **2000**

Templates Folder

If you want a template to display in a tabbed sheet other than the General sheet, you would save the template in the appropriate subfolder of the Templates folder. If you wish to create a custom tabbed sheet, you must create a new subfolder in the Templates folder. The subfolder name will be the name of the tabbed sheet.

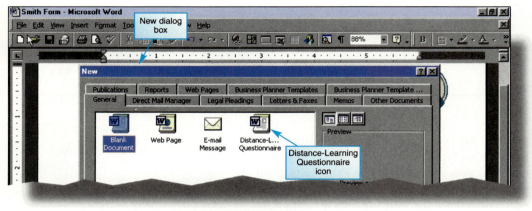

FIGURE 8-66

You also can make templates available on a network so others can share them. These templates, called **workgroup templates**, typically are stored on the network server by the network administrator as read-only files, which prevents users from inadvertently modifying them. You can change the location of workgroup templates in the Options dialog box (Figure 8-67) by clicking Tools on the menu bar, clicking Options, clicking the File Locations tab, clicking Workgroup templates in the File types list, and then clicking the Modify button. Locate the folder assigned to workgroup templates (as specified by the network administrator), and then click the OK button. With the workgroup template location specified, these templates also display in the General tab sheet in the New dialog box.

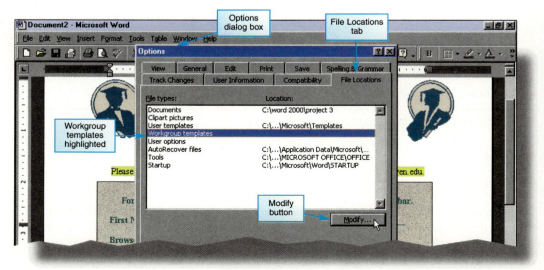

FIGURE 8-67

Notice that the Options dialog box also lists locations of other files accessed by Word. Although you can change any of these locations through the Modify button, use caution when doing so because Word may not be able to access these types of files if you move their location.

Perform the following steps to quit Word and close Windows Explorer.

TO QUIT WORD

1 Click File on the menu bar and then click Exit.

The Word window closes.

TO CLOSE WINDOWS EXPLORER

1 Click the Close button on the Exploring – 3½ Floppy (A:) window's title bar.

Windows Explorer closes.

C A S E   P E R S P E C T I V E   S U M M A R Y

You e-mail the Distance-Learning Course Questionnaire to the 120 students that completed a distance-learning course last semester. Of the 120, you receive 77 completed forms. You decide to use Access to analyze the student responses. Thus, you save each completed form as a text file.

You create an Access database that contains a table named Distance-Learning Questionnaire Results. The table contains one field for each form field on the questionnaire. After you import the data from each text file into the table, you create a report that lists the total number of students that selected each option on the form. From this report, you create a typical computer configuration list for distance-learning courses so that it can be included in the upcoming *Schedule of Courses*.

Project Summary

Project 8 introduced you to creating an online form. You created a document template as the basis for the form. Then, you added text boxes, drop-down list boxes, and check boxes to the form. You added Help text to each of these form fields. On the form, you also highlighted text, animated text, and added a rectangle around the data entry area. After you protected the form, you opened a new document based on the template and filled out the form. You also learned how to save the data on a form in a text file and how to modify the location of workgroup templates.

Quick Reference

For a table that lists how to complete the tasks covered in this book using the mouse, menu, shortcut menu, and keyboard, see the Word Quick Reference Summary at the back of this book or visit the Shelly Cashman Series Office Web page (www.scsite.com/off2000/qr.htm) and then click Microsoft Word 2000.

What You Should Know

Having completed this project, you should now be able to perform the following tasks:

▶ Access a Template through Windows Explorer *(WD 8.49)*

▶ Add Help Text to a Form *(WD 8.36)*

▶ Add More Help Text *(WD 8.37)*

▶ Animate Text *(WD 8.45)*

▶ Close a Window *(WD 8.55)*

▶ Close Windows Explorer *(WD 8.57)*

▶ Create a Document Template *(WD 8.9)*

▶ Display Formatting Marks *(WD 8.7)*

▶ Draw a Rectangle *(WD 8.40)*

▶ Enter Additional Check Box Form Fields *(WD 8.29)*

▶ Enter and Format Text *(WD 8.10)*

▶ Enter Text *(WD 8.14, WD 8.27)*

▶ Fill a Drawing Object with a Texture *(WD 8.43)*

▶ Fill Out a Form *(WD 8.50)*

▶ Hide Formatting Marks *(WD 8.47)*

▶ Highlight Text *(WD 8.13)*

▶ Insert a Borderless Table into a Form *(WD 8.15, WD 8.20, WD 8.24, WD 8.27)*

▶ Insert a Check Box *(WD 8.28)*

▶ Insert a Drop-Down Form Field *(WD 8.20)*

▶ Insert a Text Form Field *(WD 8.17)*

▶ Insert and Format Clip Art *(WD 8.11)*

▶ Insert and Specify Options for a Drop-Down Form Field *(WD 8.23, WD 8.24)*

▶ Insert and Specify Options for a Text Form Field *(WD 8.19, WD 8.26, WD 8.29)*

▶ Insert and Specify Options for a Text Form Field as the Current Date *(WD 8.31)*

▶ Open a Text File in Word *(WD 8.54)*

▶ Print a Form *(WD 8.51)*

▶ Protect a Form *(WD 8.47)*

▶ Quit Word *(WD 8.48, WD 8.57)*

▶ Remove Form Field Shading *(WD 8.39)*

▶ Reset Menus and Toolbars *(WD 8.6)*

▶ Save a Document *(WD 8.51)*

▶ Save Form Data in a Text File *(WD 8.52)*

▶ Save the Document Again *(WD 8.48)*

▶ Send a Drawing Object Behind Text *(WD 8.42)*

▶ Specify Drop-Down Form Field Options *(WD 8.21)*

▶ Specify Text Form Field Options *(WD 8.18)*

▶ Start Word *(WD 8.6)*

▶ Uncheck the Save Data Only for Forms Check Box *(WD 8.54)*

▶ Underline in Color *(WD 8.32)*

▶ Use the Format Painter Button *(WD 8.34)*

▶ Zoom Page Width *(WD 8.7)*

More About 2000

Microsoft Certification

The Microsoft Office User Specialist (MOUS) Certification program provides an opportunity for you to obtain a valuable industry credential - proof that you have the Word 2000 skills required by employers. For more information, see Appendix D or visit the Shelly Cashman Series MOUS Web page at www.scsite.com/off2000/cert.htm.

Apply Your Knowledge

✚ Project Reinforcement at www.scsite.com/off2000/reinforce.htm

1 Filling Out a Form

Instructions: In this assignment, you access a template through Windows Explorer. As shown in Figure 8-68, the template contains an online form. You are to fill in the form, save it, and print it. The template is located on the Data Disk. If you did not download the Data Disk, see the inside back cover for instructions for downloading the Data Disk or see your instructor. Perform the following tasks:

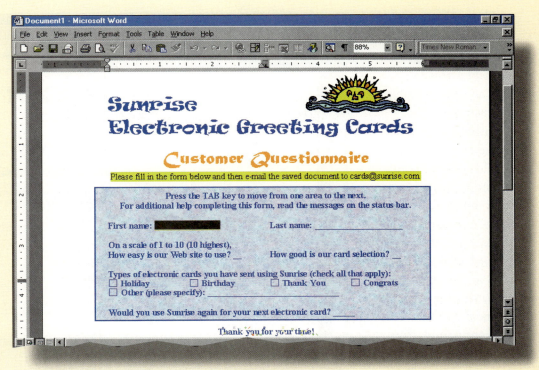

FIGURE 8-68

1. Right-click the My Computer icon on the Windows desktop and then click Explore on the shortcut menu. When the Exploring window displays, click the Address text box to select it. With the Data Disk in drive A, type a: and then press the ENTER key. Double-click the Sunrise Questionnaire icon in the Contents pane.

2. When Word displays a new document based on the Sunrise Questionnaire template, scroll down so the entire form fits in the Word window. If the Show/Hide ¶ button on the Standard toolbar is recessed, click it.

3. With the highlight in the First name text box, type Julianne and then press the TAB key.

4. With the highlight in the Last name text box, type Robledo and then press the TAB key.

5. Type 9 in response to How easy is our Web site to use and then press the TAB key.

6. Type 10 in response to How good is our card selection and then press the TAB key.

7. Place an X in the Birthday, Thank You, and Other check boxes by clicking them. Press the TAB key to highlight the Other (please specify) text box.

8. Type Get Well, Good Luck in the Other (please specify) text box and then press the TAB key.

9. With the highlight in the drop-down list box at the bottom of the form, click the box arrow and then click Yes.

10. Save the file with the name Robledo Form. Print the form.

11. Click File on the menu bar and then click Save As. When the Save As dialog box displays, click the Tools button arrow and then click General Options. When the Save dialog box displays, place a check mark in the Save data only for forms check box and then click the OK button. Click the Save button in the Save As dialog box. If Word displays a dialog box indicating that some formatting may be lost, click the Yes button.

12. Click Tools on the menu bar and then click Options. When the Options dialog box displays, click the Save tab. Click the Save data only for forms check box to remove the check mark. Click the OK button.

13. Click the Open button on the Standard toolbar. When the Open dialog box displays, click the Files of type box arrow and then click All Files. Click the text file called Robledo Form in the list and then click the Open button in the dialog box. Print the text file.

In the Lab

1 Creating an Online Form with a Texture Fill Effect

Problem: You work part-time for The Web Grocer. Your supervisor has asked you to prepare an online survey for customers that recently have shopped online. The survey should obtain the following information from the customer: first name, last name, time of day usually shopped, average time it takes to shop in minutes, shopping methods used, and payment method most frequently used. You prepare the online form shown in Figure 8-69.

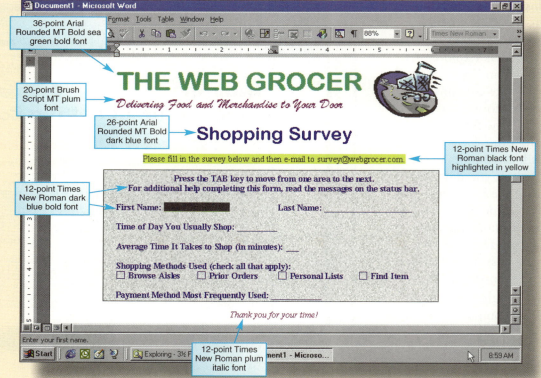

FIGURE 8-69

Instructions:

1. Create a template called Web Grocer Survey for the online form.

2. Enter and format the company name, slogan, clip art, and form title as shown in Figure 8-69.

3. Enter the form instructions and highlight them in yellow.

4. Enter the instructions in the data entry area, form field captions, and form fields as shown in Figure 8-69. First Name and Last Name are text boxes. Time of Day You Usually Shop is a drop-down list box with these choices: Morning, Afternoon, Evening, Late Night, Times Vary. The four Shopping Methods Used are check boxes. Payment Method Most Frequently Used is a drop-down list box with these choices: Personal Check, Credit Card. When the form initially displays on the screen as a blank form, the text boxes and drop-down list boxes should display underlines.

5. Enter the thank-you message as shown in Figure 8-69.

6. Draw a rectangle around the data entry area. Fill the rectangle with the newsprint texture.

7. Add Help text to all the form fields.

8. Check the spelling of the form. Protect the form. Save the form again. Print the blank form.

9. Access the template through Windows Explorer. Fill out the form. Save the filled-out form. Print the filled-out form.

In the Lab

2 Creating an Online Form with a Gradient Fill Effect

Problem: You work part-time for Lincoln State Bank. Your supervisor has asked you to prepare an online survey for bank customers. The survey should obtain the following information from the customer: first name, last name, method customers use to balance their bank statements, banking methods customers use, bank services customers use, and a bank service rating. You prepare the online form shown in Figure 8-70.

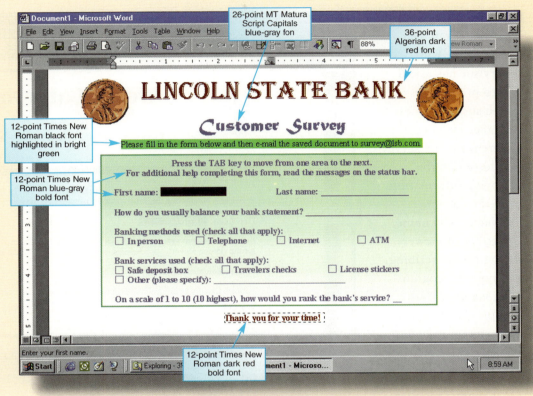

FIGURE 8-70

Instructions:

1. Create a template called Lincoln Bank Survey for the online form.
2. Enter and format the company name, clip art, and form title as shown in Figure 8-70.
3. Enter the form instructions and highlight them in bright green.
4. Enter the instructions in the data entry area, form field captions, and form fields as shown in Figure 8-70. First name and Last name are text boxes. How do you usually balance your bank statement? is a drop-down list box with these choices: Check book register, Computer software, My accountant, Other. The choices below Bank methods used and Bank services used are check boxes. The Other check box also has a text box to its right for further explanation. The bank's service rating is a text box that requires a numeric entry. When the form initially displays on the screen as a blank form, the text boxes and drop-down list boxes should display underlines.
5. Enter the thank-you message with the marching black ants animation as shown in Figure 8-70.
6. Draw a rectangle around the data entry area. Change the rectangle line color to sea green (select the rectangle and then click the Line Color box arrow on the Drawing toolbar). Fill the rectangle with a two-color gradient of light green to white (*Hint:* Click the Gradient tab in the Fill Effects dialog box).
7. Add Help text to all the form fields.
8. Check the spelling of the form. Protect the form. Save the form again. Print the blank form.
9. Access the template through Windows Explorer. Fill out the form. Save the filled-out form. Print the filled-out form.

In the Lab

3 Creating an Online Form with a Pattern Fill Effect

Problem: You work part-time for World Cablevision. Your supervisor has asked you to prepare an online survey requesting customer viewing preferences. The survey should obtain the following information from the customer: first name, last name, age group of viewers, reason for subscribing, and type of programming watched daily. You prepare the online form shown in Figure 8-71.

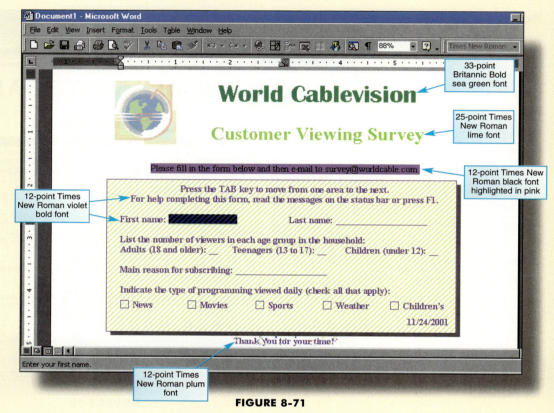

FIGURE 8-71

Instructions:

1. Create a template called World Cablevision Survey for the online form.

2. Enter and format the company name, clip art, and form title as shown in Figure 8-71.

3. Enter the form instructions and highlight them in pink.

4. Enter the instructions in the data entry area, form field captions, and form fields as shown in Figure 8-71. First name and Last name are text boxes. Number of viewers in household are text boxes each requiring numeric entries. Main reason for subscribing is a drop-down list box with these choices: Better Reception, Larger Variety of Movies, Sporting Events, More Channels, Other. The five choices in the type of programming viewed daily are check boxes. The current date is a form field. When the form initially displays on the screen as a blank form, the text boxes and drop-down list boxes should display underlines.

5. Enter the thank-you message as shown in Figure 8-71.

6. Draw a rectangle around the data entry area. Change the rectangle line color to violet (select the rectangle and then click the Line Color box arrow on the Drawing toolbar). Fill the rectangle with a Wide upward diagonal pattern that has a foreground color of yellow. (*Hint*: Click the Gradient tab in the Fill Effects dialog box). Add a shadow to the rectangle (*Hint*: Use the Shadow button on the Drawing toolbar.)

7. Add Help text to all the form fields. The Help should display on the status bar, as well as when the user presses F1.

8. Check the spelling of the form. Protect the form. Save the form again. Print the blank form.

9. Access the template through Windows Explorer. Fill out the form. Save the filled-out form. Print the filled-out form.

Cases and Places

The difficulty of these case studies varies:
◗ are the least difficult; ◗◗ are more difficult; and ◗◗◗ are the most difficult.

1 ◗ As a part-time assistant for Worldwide Travel, your supervisor has asked you to prepare and send an online customer preference survey to users of the online reservation system. The top of the survey should list the travel agency name, Worldwide Travel, along with the title of the survey, Customer Preference Survey. Insert an appropriate graphic of an airplane from the Clip Gallery. Immediately above the data entry area, the following sentence should be highlighted: Please fill in the form below and then e-mail the saved document to survey@wt.com. The data entry area contains the following two sentences of instructions: Press the TAB key to move from one area to the next. For help completing this form, read the messages on the status bar or press F1. The data entry area should request the customer's first name, last name, preferred ticket type (coach class, business class, first class), preferred seat type (aisle, window, no preference), number of adult passengers that usually travels with the customer, number of child passengers that usually travels with the customer, and the ticket selection criteria (lowest cost, nonstop flights, airline name, airplane type, other). If the customer selects other for the ticket selection criteria, he or she should be asked to explain further. The form should contain the current date as a form field. The data entry area should be surrounded by a rectangle filled in with an appropriate fill effect. Below the form, place an animated thank-you message. All data entry fields should have Help text that displays on the status bar, as well as when the user presses F1. Use the concepts and techniques presented in this project to create and format this online form.

2 ◗◗ As a vice president of the Student Government Association at your school, you have been asked to send a questionnaire to all students requesting feedback on the class schedules. Because each student on campus has an e-mail account, you decide to send an online form. The form should ask for student opinions and preferences on the most recent schedule of classes. Areas of interest might include satisfaction or preferences of days and times classes are offered, frequency of class meetings, class fees, and class formats (on campus, distance-learning, labs, etc.). The form should contain the current date as a form field. Include at least one text box, one drop-down list box, and three check boxes on the form. Use the concepts and techniques presented in this project to create and format the online form. Be sure to include an appropriate graphic from the Clip Gallery.

3 ◗◗ As a part-time assistant for your school's fitness center, you have been asked to send a questionnaire to all students requesting their opinion of the fitness center. Because each student on campus has an e-mail account, you decide to send an online form. The form should ask for student opinions and preferences on various aspects of the fitness center. Areas of interest might include satisfaction or preferences of hours of operation, type and availability of fitness equipment, training, fees, and facility appearance. The form should contain the current date as a form field. Include at least one text box, one drop-down list box, and three check boxes on the form. Use the concepts and techniques presented in this project to create and format the online form. Be sure to include an appropriate graphic(s) from the Clip Gallery.

Cases and Places

4 ▶▶   As a laboratory assistant for the computing center at your school, you have been asked to send a questionnaire to all students requesting feedback on the computer laboratory. Because each student on campus has an e-mail account, you decide to send an online form. The form should ask for student opinions and preferences on the computer lab facility. Areas of interest might include satisfaction or preferences of days and times the lab is open, quality and availability of personal help in the lab room, and availability and currency of equipment. The form should contain the current date as a form field. Include at least one text box, one drop-down list box, and three check boxes on the form. Use the concepts and techniques presented in this project to create and format the online form. Be sure to include an appropriate graphic from the Clip Gallery.

5 ▶▶▶ If Microsoft Access is installed on your computer, you can use it to create a database table and then use that table to analyze the data from Word forms. Your supervisor at Raven Community College would like to analyze the results of the questionnaires sent using Microsoft Access. To generate data for the database table, fill out the Project 5 Word form (Figure 8-1a on page WD 8.5) five times (acting as five separate students) and save the form data for each filled-in form in a separate text file. Start Access and then click File on the menu bar, point to Get External Data, and then click Import. When the Import dialog box displays, change the file type to Text File, locate the text file that contains one of the form's data, and then click the Import button. Use the Import Text Wizard to create a table for the form in Figure 8-1. Data in the text file is comma delimited. Use field names that match the field captions on the form. Each form field, including the current date, should have a field name. Then, import each of the remaining four text files into the existing table. After the table contains the five records, generate a report in Access that lists all the data collected from the forms.

6 ▶▶▶ If Microsoft Access is installed on your computer, you can use it to create a database table and then use that table to analyze the data from Word forms. Your supervisor at Sunrise Electronic Greeting Cards would like to analyze the results of the questionnaires sent using Microsoft Access. To generate data for the database table, fill out the Apply Your Knowledge Exercise form (Figure 8-68 on page WD 8.59) five times (acting as five separate customers) and save the form data for each filled-in form in a separate text file. Start Access and then click File on the menu bar, point to Get External Data, click Import. When the Import dialog box displays, change the file type to Text File, locate the text file that contains one of the form's data, and then click the Import button. Use the Import Text Wizard to create a table for the form in Figure 8-68. Data in the text file is comma delimited. Use field names that define the field captions on the form. Each form field should have a field name. Then, import each of the remaining four text files into the existing table. After the table contains the five records, generate a report in Access that lists all the data collected from the forms.

Microsoft **Word 2000**

Microsoft Word 2000

P R O J E C T

9

Using Visual Basic for Applications (VBA) with Word

You will have mastered the material in this project when you can:

- Set a security level in Word
- Unprotect a document
- Format a character as an in margin drop cap
- Create a new style
- Fill a drawing object with a bitmap picture
- Add a 3-D effect to a drawing object
- Record and execute a macro
- Assign a macro to a toolbar button
- Record an automatic macro
- View a macro's VBA code
- Add comments to a macro's VBA code
- Modify a macro's VBA code
- Add code statements to a macro's VBA code
- Insert a VBA procedure
- Plan a VBA procedure
- Enter code statements in a VBA procedure
- Run a macro when a user exits a form field
- Insert an ActiveX control
- Format and set properties for an ActiveX control
- Write a VBA procedure for an ActiveX control

WINTER DANCE PARTY

BUDDY HOLLY

JP RICHARDSON

RITCHIE VALENS

Chantilly Lace Makes Me Spend My Money

On a snowy night, Buddy Holly, Ritchie Valens, and J.P. Richardson climbed aboard a chartered plane to travel from Iowa to their next gig in North Dakota. These vocalists were part of the Winter Dance Party, a whirlwind tour of top recording artists performing nightly throughout the Midwest. That day, February 3, 1959, is what Don McLean calls, the day the music died, in his hit record, "American Pie," as the plane crashed five miles from the airport. No one aboard survived.

Chantilly Lace
J.P. Richardson

45 RPM   **side 2**

These performers were at the peak of their careers. J.P. Richardson, better known as the Big Bopper, had broken into Billboard's Top 100 with "Chantilly Lace." He had written that song and many others while taking breaks at his disc jockey job at a small Texas radio station.

He used "Chantilly Lace" on the flip side of a record featuring "The Purple People Eater Meets the Witch Doctor," his mix of two successful songs, "The Purple People Eater" and "Witch Doctor." Most radio stations, however, preferred to play "Chantilly Lace," and when the Big Bopper performed it on "The Dick Clark Saturday Night Beech-Nut Show," he was an overnight sensation. "Chantilly Lace" was the third most played record in 1958.

In the song, Chantilly Lace is the name of the woman with a pretty face and a ponytail hangin' down. She is named after the city in northern France famous for producing delicate lace. No doubt this big-eyed girl with a giggle in her talk would like the finer things in life, including elegant apparel and designer sportswear.

This clothing is the mainstay of The Warnaco Group, a New York-based manufacturer of women's and men's apparel and accessories. This merchandise is sold under such brand names as Warner's, Calvin Klein, and Chaps by Ralph Lauren in more than 16,000 stores throughout North America and Europe.

Warnaco CEO Linda Wachner keeps close tabs on manufacturing costs and inventory. Although she pleasantly refers to herself as Miss Linda to her business associates, her hard-hitting management style has helped name her as one of Fortune's 50 Most Powerful Women in American Business. She also is CEO of California-based Authentic Fitness, the manufacturer of Speedo® swimsuits, so she knows how consumers spend their money.

Warnaco produces approximately eight million garments per year. To keep track of the fabrics and trimmings needed to produce these garments, the company has developed a database application similar to the one you will produce in this Word 2000 project.

The database consists of thousands of records containing details about each item in the company's warehouse, such as a specific button shape, a bow size, and a lace color. The program allows employees to access, retrieve, and use this data efficiently. In only a few minutes, an employee can gather all the materials needed to fill an order.

And whether that order calls for 1,000 zippers or 5,000 yards of lace, you can bet Miss Linda says this database helps make her corporation, in the Big Bopper's words, a-what I like.

Microsoft Word 2000

Using Visual Basic for Applications (VBA) with Word

P R O J E C T

9

CASE PERSPECTIVE

As a part-time assistant in the CIS department, you were asked to design an online questionnaire for students who recently completed a distance-learning course. Your supervisor has several suggestions for improving the form. First, you are to change the color scheme and the graphics on the form. Second, the form should display without formatting marks showing and be positioned properly in the Word window without the user having to scroll. Third, if a user enters a letter or other nonnumeric value into the Processor Speed text box, the form should display an error message. Fourth, if a user enters text into the Other text box, the form automatically should place an X in the Other check box. Finally, you are to add a button to the Standard toolbar that instructs Word to save the data only when you save the form. Then, instead of setting options in a dialog box for each form you receive, you simply click this button, saving you many extra steps in the process of analyzing the student responses.

To complete this project, you will need the online form template created in Project 8. (If you did not create the template, see your instructor for a copy.)

Introduction

When you issue an instruction to Word by clicking a button or a command, Word must have a step-by-step description of the task to be accomplished. For example, when you click the Print button on the Standard toolbar, Word follows a precise set of steps to print your document. In Word, this precise step-by-step series of instructions is called a **procedure**. A procedure also is referred to as a **program** or **code**.

The process of writing a procedure is called **computer programming**. Every Word command on a menu and button on a toolbar has a corresponding procedure that executes when you click the command or button. **Execute** means that the computer carries out the step-by-step instructions. In a Windows environment, an event causes the instructions associated with a task to be executed. An **event** is an action such as clicking a button, clicking a command, dragging a scroll box, or right-clicking selected text.

Although Word has many toolbar buttons and menu commands, it does not include a command or button for every possible task. Thus, Microsoft has included with Word a powerful programming language called Visual Basic for Applications. The **Visual Basic for Applications (VBA)** programming language allows you to customize and extend the capabilities of Word.

Project Nine — Visual Basic for Applications (VBA)

In this project, you improve upon the online form created in Project 8 (see Figure 8-1 on page WD 8.5). Figure 9-1a shows the revised blank form, in which the fonts, font sizes, graphics, highlight color, and fill effect in the drawing object are changed. Figure 9-1b shows an error message that displays if a user makes

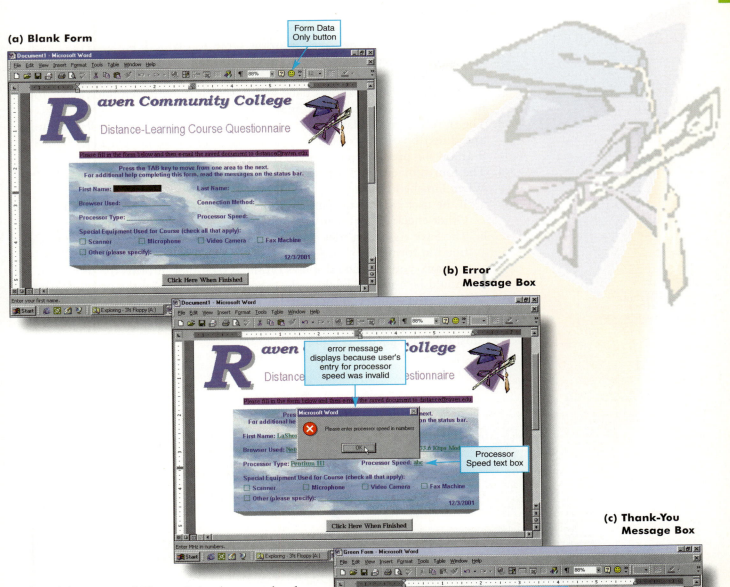

(a) Blank Form

Form Data
Only button

**(b) Error
Message Box**

error message
displays because user's
entry for processor
speed was invalid

Processor
Speed text box

**(c) Thank-You
Message Box**

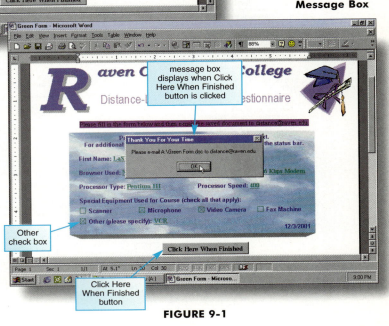

message box
displays when Click
Here When Finished
button is clicked

Other
check box

Click Here
When Finished
button

FIGURE 9-1

an invalid entry, and Figure 9-1c shows a thank-you message that displays when the user clicks the button at the bottom of the form.

Four macros are saved with the template file so that they can be used while the template or a document based on the template displays in the Word window. A **macro** is a procedure made up of VBA code. The four macros are designed to make the form more efficient:

1. The first macro places a check mark in the Save data only for forms check box in the Save tab of the Options dialog box. With this check box selected, the next time you click the Save button, Word will save the form data in a comma-delimited text file. Additionally, the Standard toolbar contains a new button called the Form Data Only button.

When you click the Form Data Only button or press ALT+D (the shortcut key assigned to the button), Word places a check mark in the Save data only for forms check box in the Save tab of the Options dialog box.

2. The second macro controls how the form initially displays on the screen (as a blank form). When a user starts a new Word document that is based on the form template, Word zooms page width, scrolls down seven lines, hides formatting marks, and hides gridlines.

3. The third macro displays an error message if the user leaves the Processor Speed text box blank or enters a nonnumeric entry in the text box. Figure 9-1b on the previous page shows the error message.

4. The fourth macro performs three actions when the user clicks the Click Here When Finished button:

   a. If the user entered text in the Other text box, then Word places an X in the Other check box (just in case the user left it blank).

   b. The Save As dialog box displays so the user can assign a file name to the filled-in form.

   c. A thank-you message displays on the screen that informs the user what file should be e-mailed back to the school. Figure 9-1c on the previous page shows the thank-you message for a filled-in form.

Figure 9-2 shows the VBA code for these macros. You have learned that code, such as this, often is called a computer program.

macro that executes when Form Data Only button is clicked

macro that executes when form initially displays on screen (as a blank form)

macro that executes when user TABs out of Processor Speed text box

macro that executes when Click Here When Finished button is clicked

```
Sub FormDataOnly()
'
' FormDataOnly Macro
' Places a check mark in the Save data only for forms check box.
'
    Application.DisplayStatusBar = True
    With ActiveWindow
        .DisplayHorizontalScrollBar = True
        .DisplayVerticalScrollBar = True
        .DisplayLeftScrollBar = False
        .StyleAreaWidth = InchesToPoints(0)
        .DisplayVerticalRuler = True
        .DisplayRightRuler = False
        .DisplayScreenTips = True
        With .View
            .ShowAnimation = True
            .Draft = False
            .WrapToWindow = False
            .ShowPicturePlaceHolders = False
            .ShowFieldCodes = False
            .ShowBookmarks = False
            .FieldShading = wdFieldShadingWhenSelected
            .ShowTabs = False
            .ShowSpaces = False
            .ShowParagraphs = False
            .ShowHyphens = False
            .ShowHiddenText = False
            .ShowAll = True
            .ShowDrawings = True
            .ShowObjectAnchors = False
            .ShowTextBoundaries = False
            .ShowHighlight = True
        End With
    End With
    With Options
        .AllowFastSave = False
        .BackgroundSave = True
        .CreateBackup = False
        .SavePropertiesPrompt = False
        .SaveInterval = 10
        .SaveNormalPrompt = False
        .OptimizeForWord97byDefault = False
    End With
    With ActiveDocument
        .ReadOnlyRecommended = False
        .EmbedTrueTypeFonts = False
        .SaveFormsData = True
        .SaveSubsetFonts = False
        .Password = ""
        .WritePassword = ""
        .OptimizeForWord97 = False
    End With
    Application.DefaultSaveFormat = ""
End Sub
```

```
Sub AutoNew()
'
' AutoNew Macro
' Specifies how the form initially displays (as a blank form).
'
    ' Sets screen to page width zoom
    ActiveWindow.ActivePane.View.Zoom.PageFit = wdPageFitBestFit
    ' Scrolls down from top of page so entire form fits in window
    ActiveWindow.ActivePane.VerticalPercentScrolled = 0
    ActiveWindow.ActivePane.SmallScroll Down:=7
    ' Turns off table gridlines
    ActiveDocument.ActiveWindow.View.TableGridlines = False
    ' Turns off formatting marks
    ActiveDocument.ActiveWindow.View.ShowAll = False
End Sub

Public Sub ProcessorSpeed()
'
' ProcessorSpeed Macro
' Displays error message if entered processor speed is not numeric.
'
    ' Test if entry in EnteredSpeed text form field is numeric
    If IsNumeric(ActiveDocument.FormFields("EnteredSpeed").Result) = False Then
        ' Display error message
        MsgBox "Please enter processor speed in numbers", vbOKOnly + vbCritical
        ' Redisplay underscores in text form field
        ActiveDocument.FormFields("EnteredSpeed").Result = "___"
        ' Reposition highlight in text form field
        ActiveDocument.FormFields("EnteredType").Select
        SendKeys "{TAB}"
    End If
End Sub

Private Sub CommandButton1_Click()
'
' CommandButton1_Click Macro
' Executes when user clicks button called Click Here When Finished.
'
    ' If user entered text in Other text box, put X in Other check box
    If Left(ActiveDocument.FormFields("OtherText").Result, 1) <> "_" Then
        ActiveDocument.FormFields("OtherCheck").CheckBox.Value = True
    End If
    ' Display Save As dialog box
    Dialogs(wdDialogFileSaveAs).Show
    ' Display thank-you message
    TitleBarText = "Thank You For Your Time"
    MessageText = "Please e-mail " & ActiveDocument.FullName & " to distance@raven.edu."
    MsgBox MessageText, , TitleBarText

End Sub
```

FIGURE 9-2

Starting Word and Opening an Office Document

The first step in this project is to open the template for the online form that was created in Project 8 so that you can modify it. (If you did not create the template, see your instructor for a copy.) Perform the following steps to start Word and open the Distance-Learning Questionnaire file.

TO START WORD AND OPEN AN OFFICE DOCUMENT

1 With the disk containing the Distance-Learning Questionnaire file in drive A, click the Start button on the taskbar and then click Open Office Document.

2 When the Open Office Document dialog box displays, if necessary, click the Look in box arrow and then click 3½ Floppy (A:). Click the Files of type box arrow and then click All Files.

3 Double-click the file named Distance-Learning Questionnaire.

4 If the Word window is not maximized, double-click its title bar to maximize it. Click View on the menu bar and then click Print Layout. If the Office Assistant displays, right-click it and then click Hide on the shortcut menu.

5 Scroll down so the entire form displays in the Word window.

Office starts Word. After a few moments, an empty document titled Document1 displays in the Word window. Because this project uses floating graphics, you will use print layout view; thus, the Print Layout View button on the horizontal scroll bar is recessed.

Saving the Document with a New File Name

To preserve the contents of the Distance-Learning Questionnaire file created in Project 8, save a copy of it with a new file name as described in the following steps.

TO SAVE THE DOCUMENT WITH A NEW FILE NAME

1 With a floppy disk in drive A, click File on the menu bar and then click Save As.

2 Type DL Course Questionnaire in the File name text box. Do not press the ENTER key.

3 If necessary, click the Save in box arrow and then click 3½ Floppy (A:).

4 Click the Save button in the Save As dialog box.

Word saves the document on a floppy disk in drive A with a new file name of DL Course Questionnaire.

Unprotecting a Document

The template for the Distance-Learning Course Questionnaire online form is protected. When a document is **protected**, users cannot modify it in any manner – except for entering values into form fields placed on the form. Thus, before you can modify the online form, you must unprotect the form as shown in the steps on the next page.

More About 2000

Unprotecting Documents

If Word requests a password when you attempt to unprotect a document, you must enter a password in order to unprotect and then change the document. If you do not know the password, you cannot change the look of the form but you can enter data into its form fields.

Steps: To Unprotect a Document

1 **Click Tools on the menu bar and then point to Unprotect Document (Figure 9-3).**

2 **Click Unprotect Document.**

Word unprotects the DL Course Questionnaire template.

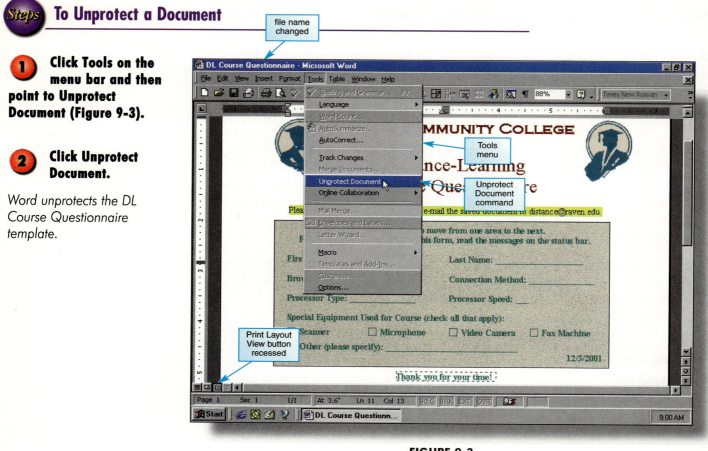

FIGURE 9-3

With the template unprotected, you can change its contents. Later in this project, after you have completed the modifications, you will protect the document again.

Resetting Menus and Toolbars

To set the menus and toolbars so they appear exactly as shown in this book, you should reset your menus and toolbars as outlined in Appendix C or follow these steps.

TO RESET MENUS AND TOOLBARS

1 Click View on the menu bar and then point to Toolbars. Click Customize on the Toolbars submenu.

2 When the Customize dialog box displays, click the Options tab, make sure the top three check boxes have check marks and then click the Reset my usage data button. When the Microsoft Word dialog box displays, click the Yes button.

3 Click the Toolbars tab. Click Standard in the Toolbars list and then click the Reset button. When the Reset Toolbar dialog box displays, click the OK button.

4 Click Formatting in the Toolbars list and then click the Reset button. When the Reset Toolbar dialog box displays, click the OK button. Click the Close button.

Word resets the menus and toolbars.

Displaying Formatting Marks

It is helpful to display formatting marks that indicate where in the document you pressed the ENTER key, SPACEBAR, and other keys. Follow this step to display formatting marks.

TO DISPLAY FORMATTING MARKS

1 Double-click the move handle on the left side of the Standard toolbar to display the entire toolbar. If the Show/Hide ¶ button on the Standard toolbar is not already recessed, click it.

Word displays formatting marks in the document window, and the Show/Hide ¶ button on the Standard toolbar is recessed.

Zooming Page Width

When you zoom page width, Word displays the page on the screen as large as possible in print layout view. Perform the following steps to zoom page width.

TO ZOOM PAGE WIDTH

1 Click the Zoom box arrow on the Standard toolbar.

2 Click Page Width in the Zoom list.

Word displays the left and right edges of a piece of paper as large as possible in the document window. Word computes the zoom percentage based on a variety of settings. Your percentage may be different.

Setting a Security Level in Word

A **computer virus** is a potentially damaging computer program designed to affect, or infect, your computer negatively by altering the way it works without your knowledge or permission. Currently, more than 45,000 known computer viruses exist and an estimated six new viruses are discovered each day. The increased use of the networks, the Internet, and e-mail has accelerated the spread of computer viruses.

To combat this evil, most computer users run antivirus programs that search for viruses and destroy them before they ever have a chance to infect the computer. Macros are a known carrier of viruses, because of the ease with which a person can write code for a macro. For this reason, you can reduce the chance your computer will be infected with a macro virus by setting a **security level** in Word. These security levels allow you to enable or disable macros. An **enabled macro** is a macro that Word will execute, and a **disabled macro** is a macro that is unavailable to Word. Table 9-1 on the next page summarizes the three available security levels in Word.

Viruses

For more information about viruses, visit the Word 2000 More About Web page (www.scsite.com/wd2000/more.htm) and then click Viruses.

Digital Signatures

A digital signature is a digital identification code that you can attach to a macro so that a user can verify the macro's legitimacy. To attach a digital signature, you must have a digital certificate installed on your computer. For more information on digital signatures, search for help using the phrase, protecting documents from viruses.

Table 9-1	Word Security Levels
SECURITY LEVEL	**CONDITION**
High	Word will execute only macros that are digitally signed. All other macros are disabled when the document is opened.
Medium	Upon opening a document that contains macros from an unknown source, Word displays a dialog box asking if you wish to enable the macros.
Low	Word turns off macro virus protection. The document is opened with all macros enabled, including those from unknown sources.

If Word security is set to high and you attach a macro to a document, Word will disable that macro when you open the document. Because you will be creating macros in this project, you should ensure that your security level is set to medium. Thus, each time you open this Word document or any other document that contains a macro from an unknown source, Word displays a dialog box warning that a macro is attached and allows you to enable or disable the macros. If you are confident of the source (author) of the document and macros, you should click the Enable Macros button in the dialog box. If you are uncertain about the reliability of the source of the document and macros, then you should click the Disable Macros button.

Perform the following steps to set Word's security level to medium.

To Set a Security Level in Word

1 Click Tools on the menu bar, point to Macro, and then point to Security (Figure 9-4).

FIGURE 9-4

2 Click Security. When the Security dialog box displays, if necessary, click the Security Level tab. Click Medium and then point to the OK button.

Word displays the Security dialog box (Figure 9-5). The Medium option button is selected.

3 Click the OK button.

Word sets its security level to medium.

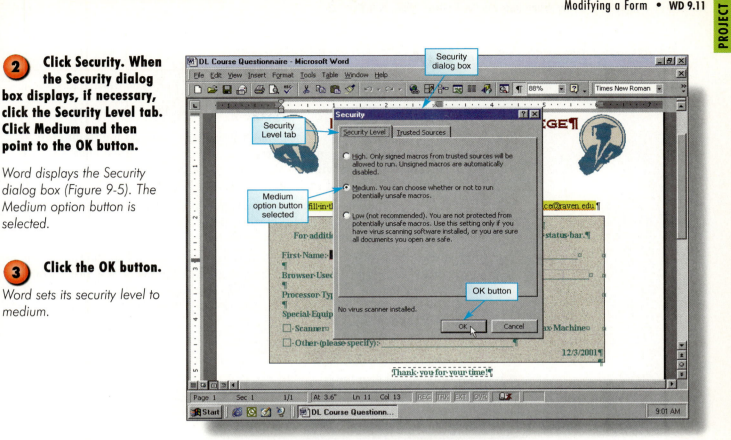

FIGURE 9-5

The next time you open a document that contains a macro from an unauthorized source, Word will ask if you wish to enable or disable them.

Modifying a Form

As requested by your supervisor, you will change the look of the Distance-Learning Course Questionnaire. You will change the graphics, the fonts, the font sizes, the highlight color, and the fill inside the rectangle drawing object. The following pages discuss how you modify the online form.

Modifying Graphics, Fonts, and Font Sizes

The first step in modifying the online form is to remove the existing graphics of the male and female graduates and insert a new graphic of a graduation cap and diploma. The new clip art image is too large for the form; thus, you will reduce it to 40 percent of its original size. Because Word inserts the clip art image as inline, you will change it to floating by clicking the Square command on the Text Wrapping menu. Then, you will move the graphic to the right of the college name and form name. Perform the steps on the next page to change the graphics on the form.

TO CHANGE GRAPHICS

1 Click the graphic of the male graduate to select it. Press the DELETE key.

2 Click the graphic of the female graduate to select it. Press the DELETE key.

3 Position the insertion point on the blank line above the text highlighted in yellow. Click Insert on the menu bar, point to Picture, and then click Clip Art. When the Insert ClipArt window opens, click the Search for clips text box. Type graduation cap and then press the ENTER key.

4 Click the clip of the diploma and graduation cap that matches the one shown in Figure 9-6. Click the Insert clip button on the Pop-up menu. Click the Close button on the Insert ClipArt window's title bar.

5 Click the graphic to select it. If the Picture toolbar does not display, click View on the menu bar, point to Toolbars, and then click Picture. Click the Format Picture button on the Picture toolbar. When the Format Picture dialog box displays, if necessary, click the Size tab. Change the Height and Width in the Scale area to 40%. Click the OK button.

6 Click the Text Wrapping button on the Picture toolbar and then click Square. Drag the graphic to the right of the college name as shown in Figure 9-6.

7 Click outside the graphic to deselect it.

The graphic is resized and positioned as shown in Figure 9-6.

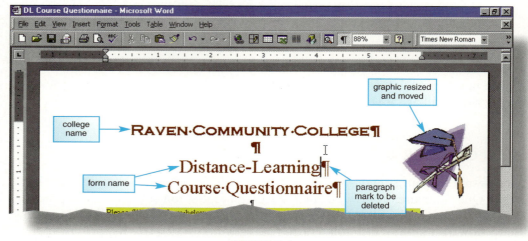

FIGURE 9-6

The next step in modifying the Distance-Learning Course Questionnaire is to change the alignment, font, font style, font size, and color of the college name and form name as described in the following steps.

TO MODIFY TEXT

1 Select the line containing the college name, Raven Community College. Right-click the selection and then click Font on the shortcut menu. When the Font dialog box displays, if necessary, click the Font tab. Scroll to and then click Bookman Old Style in the Font list. Click Bold Italic in the Font style list. Scroll to and then click 28 in the Size list. Click the Font color box arrow and then click Light Blue. Click Shadow in the Effects area. Click the OK button.

2 Double-click the move handle on the Formatting toolbar to display the entire toolbar. Click the Align Left button on the Formatting toolbar.

3 Click the paragraph mark following the word, Learning, in the form name, Distance-Learning (see Figure 9-6). Press the DELETE key to remove the paragraph mark.

4 Press the SPACEBAR. Select the two lines containing the form name, Distance-Learning Course Questionnaire. Right-click the selection and then click Font on the shortcut menu. When the Font dialog box displays, if necessary, click the Font tab. Scroll to and then click Arial Narrow in the Font list. If necessary, click Regular in the Font style list. Click 24 in the Size list. Click the Font color box arrow and then click Lavender. Click the OK button.

5 Click the paragraph mark below the selected form name. Press the ENTER key to insert another blank line between the form name and the yellow highlighted text.

The college name and form name display as shown in Figure 9-7.

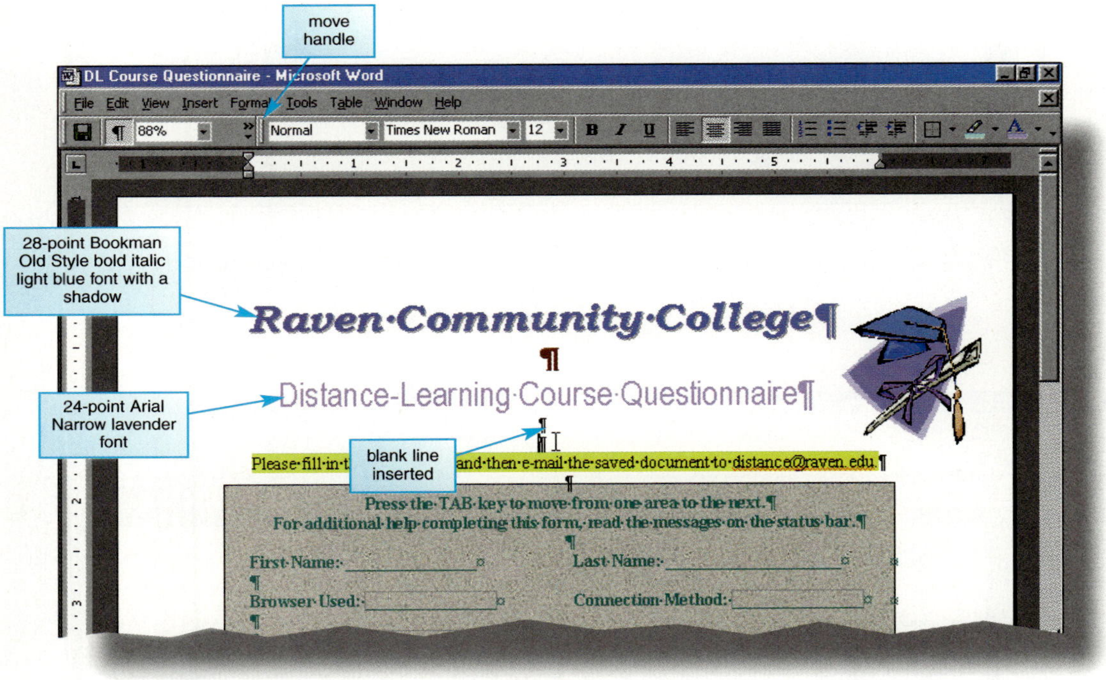

FIGURE 9-7

The next step is to format the first character of the college name as a drop cap.

Formatting a Character as an In Margin Drop Cap

You can format the first character or word to be dropped in a paragraph. A **dropped capital letter**, or **drop cap**, appears larger than the rest of the characters in the paragraph. In Word, text in the paragraph can wrap around the dropped character or the drop cap can display in the margin to the left of the paragraph text. Word refers to the latter as an in margin drop cap. Perform the steps on the next page to format a character as an in margin drop cap.

More *About*

Drop Caps

In the desktop publishing field, an in margin drop cap sometimes is referred to as a stick-up cap. If you wanted text to wrap around a drop cap instead of extending it into the margin, you would click Dropped in the Drop Cap dialog box.

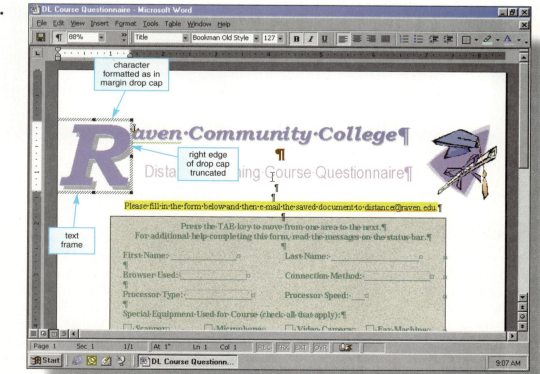

To Format a Character as an In Margin Drop Cap

1 **Position the insertion point in the paragraph to contain the drop cap, in this case, the college name. Click Format on the menu bar and then click Drop Cap. When the Drop Cap dialog box displays, click In Margin and then point to the OK button.**

Word displays the Drop Cap dialog box (Figure 9-8).

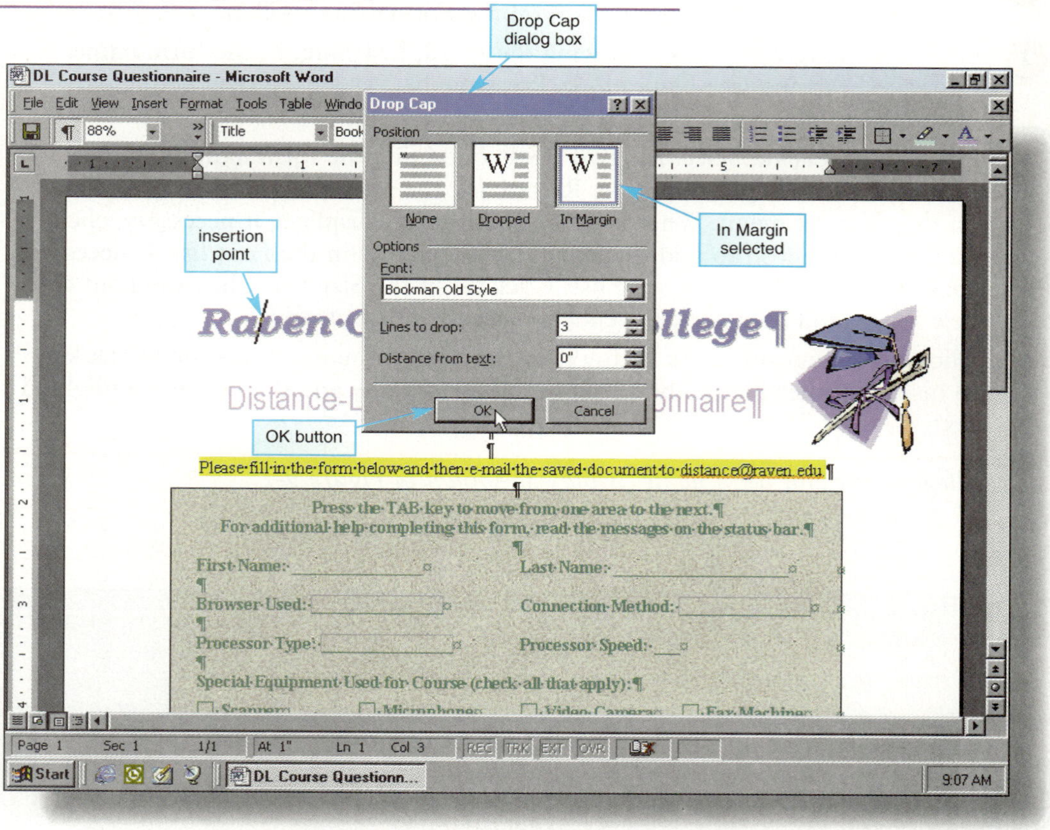

FIGURE 9-8

2 **Click the OK button.**

Word drops the letter R into the margin of the document and places a text frame around the drop cap (Figure 9-9). Notice that the right edge of the letter R is truncated, or chopped off.

FIGURE 9-9

3 Drag the right-middle sizing handle on the text frame rightward until the entire drop cap displays. With the text frame selected, click the Font Size box on the Formatting toolbar, type 121 as the new font size, and then press the ENTER key. Point to an edge of the text frame until the mouse pointer displays a four-headed arrow and then drag the drop cap rightward and align it with the college name as shown in Figure 9-10. If necessary, drag the graphic of the diploma and cap to the left so the top of the form is centered.

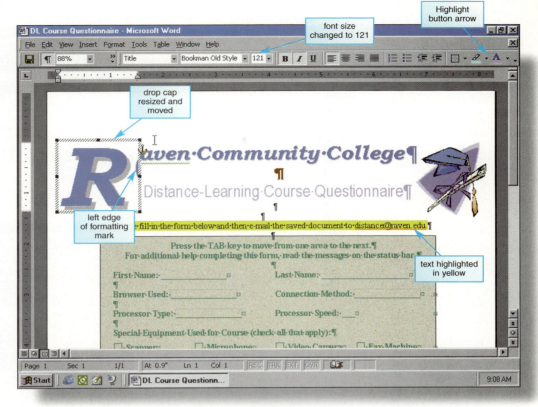

FIGURE 9-10

As shown in Figure 9-9, Word places a text frame around a drop cap. A **text frame** is a container for text that allows you to position the text anywhere on the page. The text inside the text frame is a separate paragraph and, thus, ends with a proofreaders paragraph mark. In Figure 9-10, notice that only the left edge of the paragraph mark displays. Depending on your settings, a portion of this paragraph mark may or may not display on your screen. This formatting mark will not print. Also, if you click the Show/Hide ¶ button on the Standard toolbar, the paragraph mark will disappear from the screen.

As illustrated in the previous steps, you also can resize a text frame. To remove the frame from displaying in the document window, simply click outside the frame to display the insertion point elsewhere in the document.

The next step is to change the highlight color of the format instructions from yellow to pink as described in the following steps.

TO CHANGE A HIGHLIGHT COLOR

1 Select the form instructions that currently are highlighted in yellow.

2 Click the Highlight button arrow on the Formatting toolbar and then click Pink.

Word changes the highlight on the form instructions from yellow to pink (Figure 9-11 on the next page).

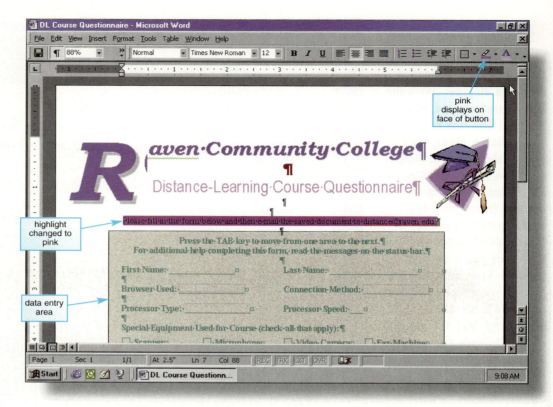

FIGURE 9-11

The next step is to change the format of the text in the data entry area.

Creating a New Style

All text in the data entry area should be formatted to 11-point Arial bold indigo font. You could select each text item in the data entry area, one at a time, and change its font to Arial, its font size to 11, its font style to bold, and its font color to indigo.

A timesaving alternative is to use a style. A **style** is a customized format that you can apply to text. Although Word has many built-in styles, none of them is an 11-point Arial bold indigo font. Thus, you can create your own new style and then apply this style to the text in the data entry area of the form.

Word has two types of styles: character and paragraph. A **character style** defines attributes for selected text such as font, font size, and font style. A **paragraph style** defines formatting for a paragraph such as line spacing, text alignment, and borders. Paragraph styles also can include a character style definition. In the data entry area of this form, you want to change text to 11-point Arial bold indigo font. Thus, you will create a character style.

Perform the following steps to create a new character style, called DataEntryArea, that formats selected text to 11-point Arial bold indigo font.

Styles

To create a character style, click the Style type box arrow in the New Style dialog box and then click Character. To create a paragraph style, click the Style type box arrow in the New Style dialog box and then click Paragraph. If you accidentally create a paragraph style for a character style, all current paragraph formatting will be applied to the selected text. In this case, for example, a paragraph style would include the centered format.

To Create a Style that has a Shortcut Key

1 **Click Format on the menu bar and then click Style. When the Style dialog box displays, point to the New button.**

Word displays the Style dialog box (Figure 9-12). Your list of styles may be different.

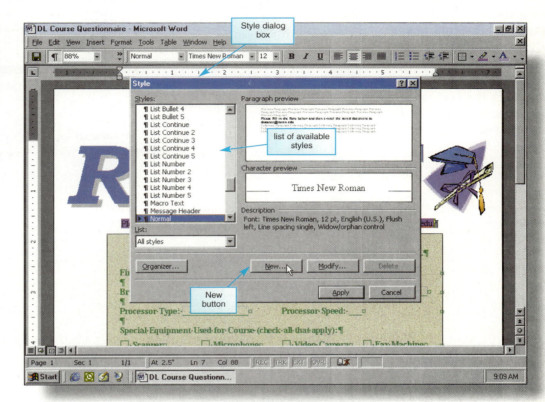

FIGURE 9-12

2 **Click the New button. When the New Style dialog box displays, type** `DataEntryArea` **in the Name text box. Click the Style type box arrow and then click Character. Click the Format button and then point to Font.**

Word displays the New Style dialog box (Figure 9-13). A list of available formatting commands displays above or below the Format button. Some commands are dimmed because they relate to paragraph styles.

FIGURE 9-13

3 Click Font. When the Font dialog box displays, if necessary, click the Font tab. Scroll to and click Arial in the Font list. Click Bold in the Font style list. Click 11 in the Size list. Click the Font color button arrow and then click Indigo. Point to the OK button.

Word displays the Font dialog box (Figure 9-14). The Preview area reflects the current settings in the dialog box.

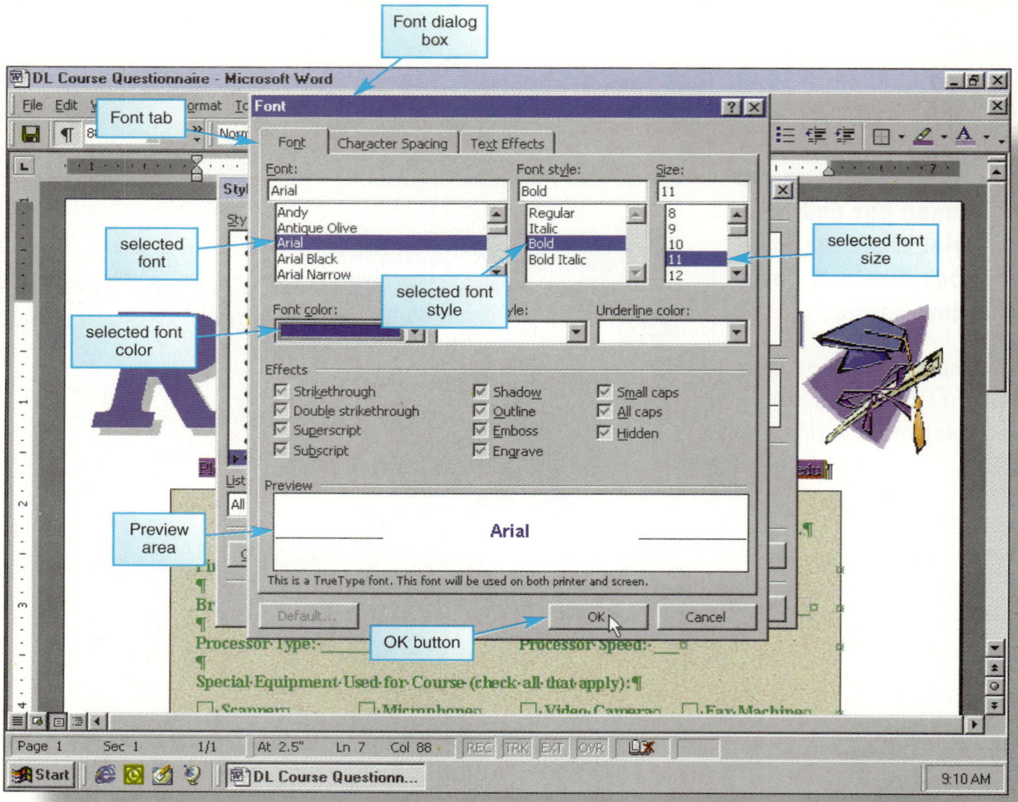

FIGURE 9-14

4 Click the OK button. Point to the Shortcut Key button in the New Style dialog box.

Word closes the Font dialog box and the entire New Style dialog box is visible again (Figure 9-15). The Description area lists the formatting assigned to the DataEntryArea style.

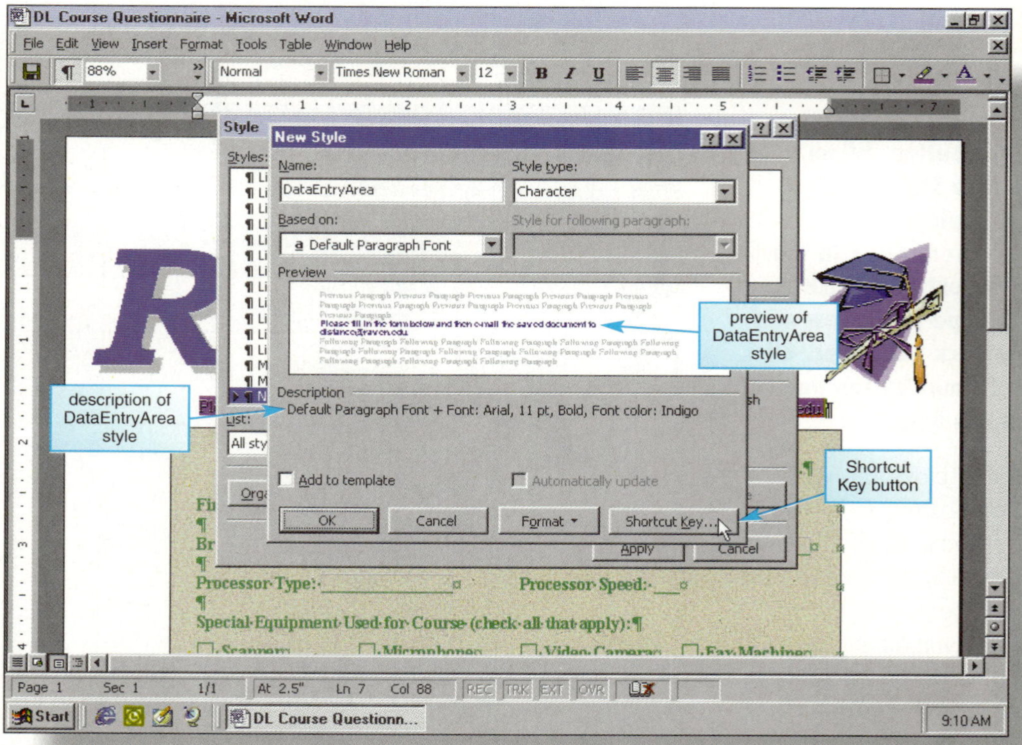

FIGURE 9-15

5 **Click the Shortcut Key button. When the Customize Keyboard dialog box displays, press the ALT+C keys. Point to the Assign button.**

Word displays the Customize Keyboard dialog box (Figure 9-16). The characters you pressed, ALT+C, display in the Press new shortcut key text box.

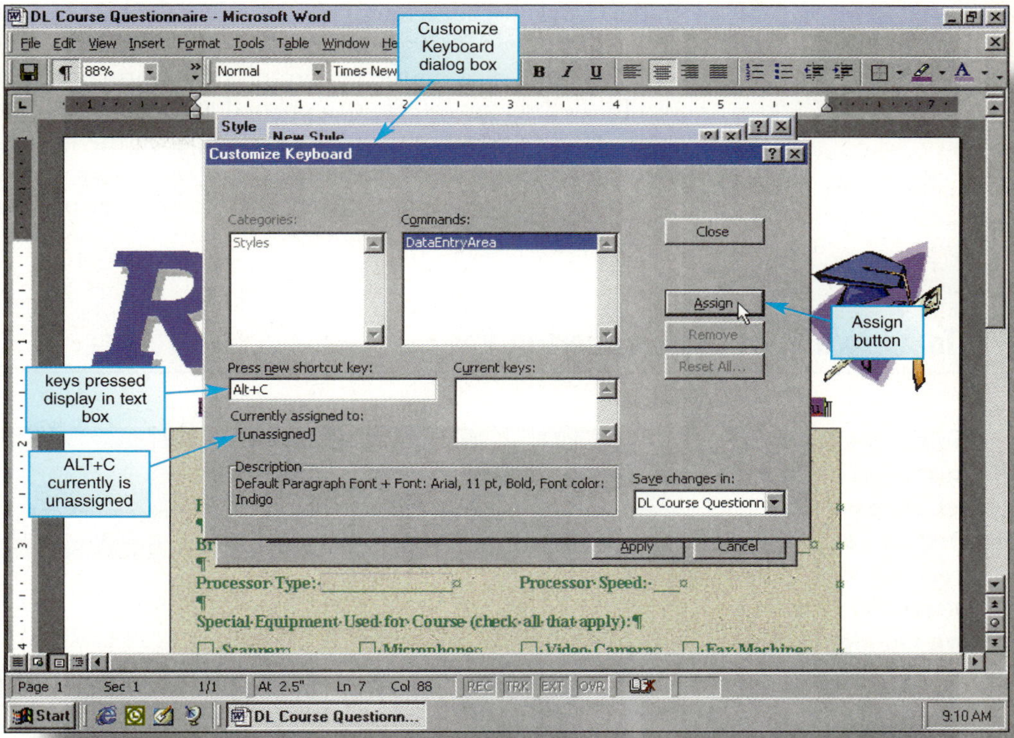

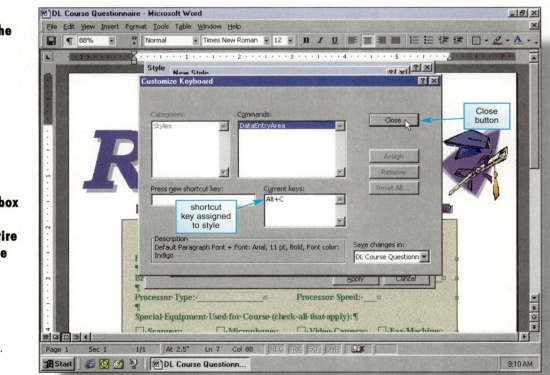

FIGURE 9-16

6 **Click the Assign button. Point to the Close button.**

Word assigns the shortcut key, ALT+C, to the style named DataEntryArea (Figure 9-17).

7 **Click the Close button. When the entire New Style dialog box is visible again, click its OK button. When the entire Style dialog box is visible again, click its Close button.**

Word creates the DataEntryArea style along with its shortcut key, ALT+C.

FIGURE 9-17

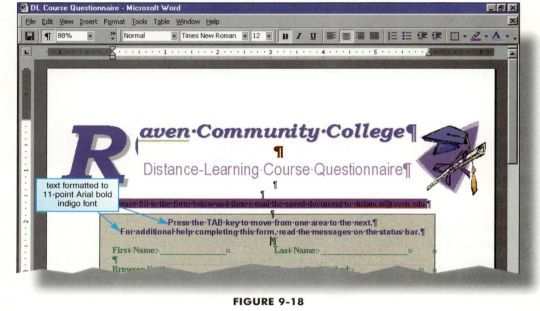
To apply a character style, you select the text to be formatted and then apply the style. To apply a paragraph style, you do not need to select text before applying the style – simply click in the paragraph to be formatted and then apply the style.

In the previous steps, you created a shortcut key of ALT+C for the DataEntryArea style. Thus, instead of using the Style box on the Formatting toolbar to apply the DataEntryArea style to text in the data entry area of the Distance-Learning Course Questionnaire, you will use the shortcut key. Perform the following step to apply a style using a shortcut key.

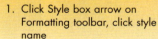

To Apply a Style Using a Shortcut Key

1 **Select the first two sentences of data entry instructions in the data entry area of the form. Press the ALT+C keys. Click outside the selection to remove the highlight.**

Word formats the selected text to 11-point Arial bold indigo font (Figure 9-18).

FIGURE 9-18

Perform the following steps to format the remaining text in the data entry area of the Distance-Learning Course Questionnaire to the DataEntryArea style using the ALT+C keys.

TO APPLY A STYLE USING A SHORTCUT KEY

1 Select the text, First Name:, and then press the ALT+C keys.

2 Select the text, Last Name:, and then press the ALT+C keys.

3 Select the text, Browser Used:, and then press the ALT+C keys.

4 Select the text, Connection Method:, and then press the ALT+C keys.

5 Select the text, Processor Type:, and then press the ALT+C keys.

6 Select the text, Processor Speed:, and then press the ALT+C keys.

7 Select the text, Special Equipment Used for Course (check all that apply):, and then press the ALT+C keys.

8. Select the text, Scanner, and then press the ALT+C keys.

9. Select the text, Microphone, and then press the ALT+C keys.

10. Select the text, Video Camera, and then press the ALT+C keys.

11. Select the text, Fax Machine, and then press the ALT+C keys.

12. Select the text, Other (please specify):, and then press the ALT+C keys.

13. Select the date in the lower-right corner of the data entry area and then press the ALT+C keys. Click outside the selection to remove the highlight.

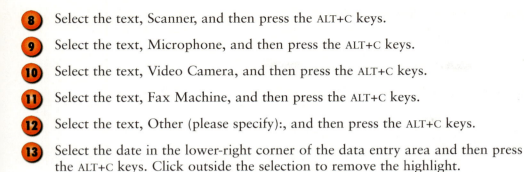

The text in the data entry area is formatted to 11-point Arial bold indigo font (Figure 9-19).

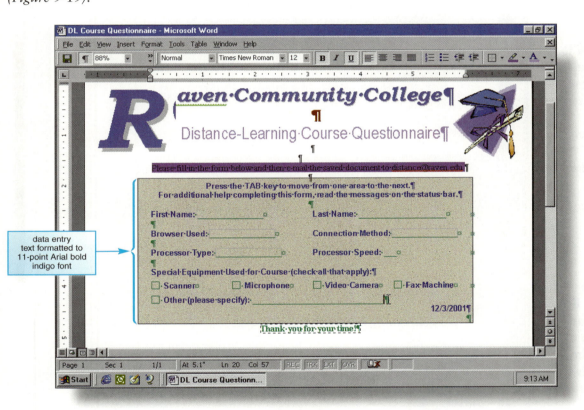

data entry text formatted to 11-point Arial bold indigo font

FIGURE 9-19

Filling a Drawing Object with a Bitmap Picture

The data entry area in the form is surrounded with a rectangle drawing object, which currently is filled with the recycled paper texture. Other available fill effects include gradient (two-toned) colors, patterns, and pictures. In this project, you want a bitmap picture in the rectangle drawing object. A **bitmap** is a graphic composed of rows and columns of dots that form a picture.

Windows includes several bitmap files that it uses for wallpaper. These bitmap files often are stored in the Windows folder on the hard drive or server. You will use the one called Clouds as fill in the rectangle drawing object. If you cannot locate the Clouds bitmap file, it also is on the Data Disk. If you did not download the Data Disk, see the inside back cover for instructions for downloading the Data Disk.

Perform the steps on the next page to fill the rectangle with the Clouds bitmap file.

Steps: **To Fill a Drawing Object with a Bitmap Picture**

1 **Point to an edge of the rectangle and then click when the mouse pointer has a four-headed arrow attached to it. Double-click the move handle on the Standard toolbar to display the entire toolbar. If the Drawing toolbar is not on the screen, click the Drawing button on the Standard toolbar. Click the Fill Color button arrow on the Drawing toolbar and then click the Fill Effects button. When the Fill Effects dialog box displays, if necessary, click the Picture tab. Point to the Select Picture button.**

Word displays the Fill Effects dialog box (Figure 9-20). The rectangle is selected.

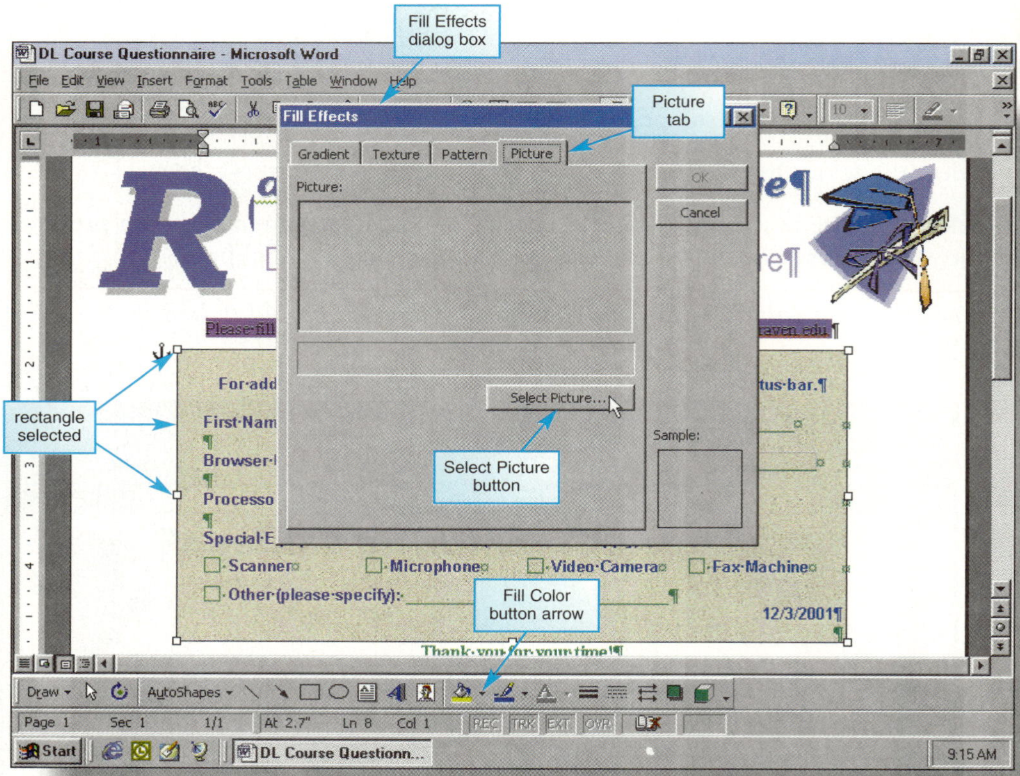

FIGURE 9-20

2 **Click the Select Picture button. Use the Look in box to locate the Clouds bitmap file on your computer or on the Data Disk. Click Clouds in the list and then point to the Insert button.**

Word displays the Select Picture dialog box (Figure 9-21). Depending on your computer settings, a sample of the Clouds bitmap file may or may not display as a preview.

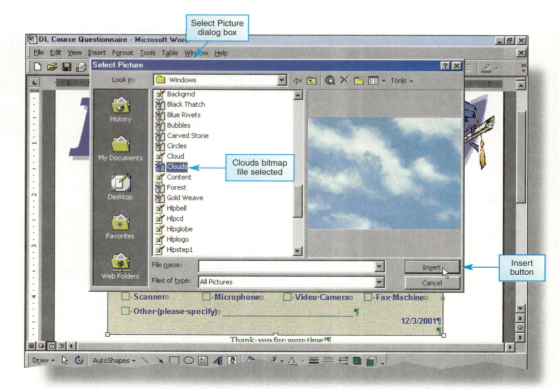

FIGURE 9-21

③ **Click the Insert button. When the entire Fill Effects dialog box is visible again, point to its OK button.**

Word displays the selected picture in the Picture area of the Fill Effects dialog box (Figure 9-22).

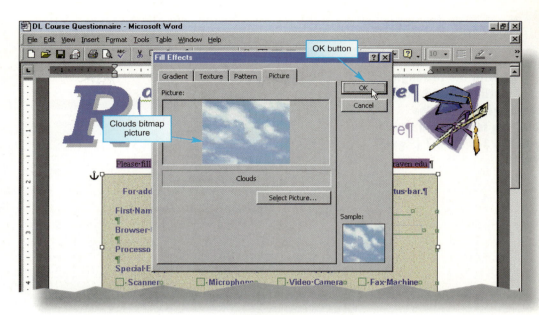

FIGURE 9-22

④ **Click the OK button.**

Word fills the rectangle with the Clouds bitmap picture (Figure 9-23).

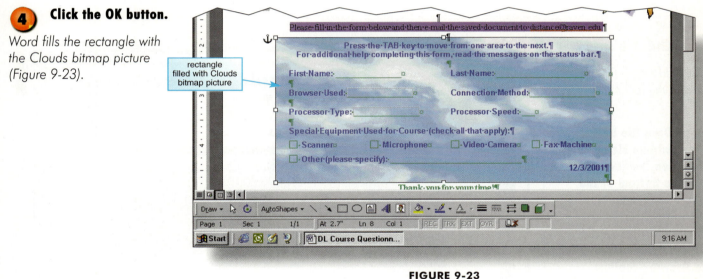

FIGURE 9-23

Notice in Figure 9-23 that Word stretches the picture so that it fills the entire drawing object.

The next step is to add a 3-D effect to the rectangle.

Adding a 3-D Effect to a Drawing Object

You can add a shadow or a 3-D effect to a drawing object by using the Shadow button and 3-D buttons on the Drawing toolbar, respectively. Perform the steps on the next page to add a 3-D effect to the rectangle surrounding the data entry area of the Distance-Learning Course Questionnare.

Other Ways

1. Right-click edge of drawing object, click Format AutoShape on shortcut menu, click Colors and Lines tab, click Fill Color button arrow, click Fill Effects button, click Picture tab

2. Select drawing object, click Format AutoShape on Format menu, click Colors and Lines tab, click Fill Color button arrow, click Fill Effects button, click Picture tab

Steps **To Add a 3-D Effect**

1 **With the rectangle still selected, click the 3-D button on the Drawing toolbar and then point to 3-D Style 7 (Figure 9-24).**

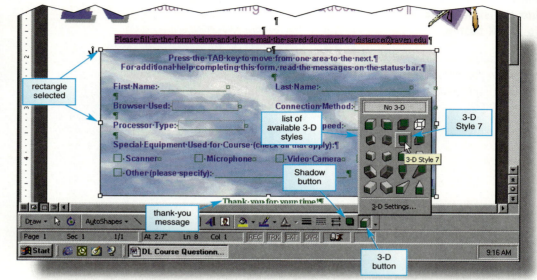

FIGURE 9-24

2 **Click 3-D Style 7.**

Word adds the 3-D Style 7 effect to the rectangle.

3 **Drag the bottom-middle sizing handle on the rectangle up until the bottom of the rectangle is immediately below the date. Click the Drawing button on the Standard toolbar to remove the Drawing toolbar. Delete the line below the data entry area that contains the thank-you message.**

The online form displays as shown in Figure 9-25.

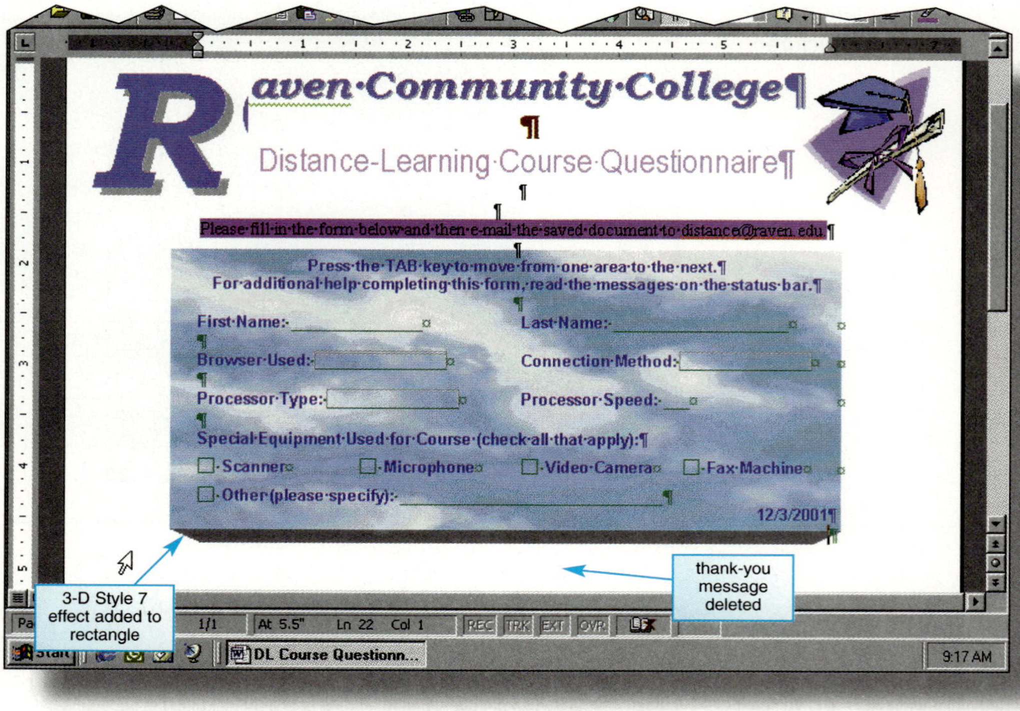

FIGURE 9-25

If you wanted to add a shadow instead of a 3-D effect, you would click the Shadow button on the Drawing toolbar (see Figure 9-24).

Because you have performed many formatting tasks thus far, perform the following step to save the form again.

TO SAVE A DOCUMENT

1 Click the Save button on the Standard toolbar.

Word saves the DL Course Questionnaire on a floppy disk in drive A.

Using a Macro to Automate a Task

As previously discussed, a macro consists of a series of Word commands or instructions that are grouped together as a single command. This single command is a convenient way to automate a difficult or lengthy task. Macros often are used for formatting or editing activities, to combine multiple commands into a single command, or to select an option in a dialog box with a single keystroke.

To create a macro, you can use the macro recorder or the Visual Basic Editor. The following pages discuss how to use the macro recorder to create a macro. Later in this project, you use the Visual Basic Editor to create a macro.

Recording and Executing a Macro

When you receive filled-in forms from users, your next step will be to analyze the data on the forms. Often, you want to use database software, such as Access, to assist you in analyzing the responses on the forms. You have learned that you must save the data on each questionnaire in a comma-delimited text file so that Access can use the data. To do this, you must place a check mark in the Save data only for forms check box in the Save sheet in the Options dialog box – prior to clicking the Save button on the Standard toolbar.

If you receive 70 completed forms, then you will be performing the following steps 70 times: click Tools on the menu bar, click Options, click the Save tab, place a check mark in the Save data only for forms check box, and then click the OK button. A timesaving alternative is to create a macro that places the check mark in the check box. Then, you simply execute the macro and click the Save button. Thus, the purpose of the first macro you create in this project is to select an option in a dialog box.

Word has a **macro recorder** that creates a macro automatically based on a series of actions you perform while it is recording. The macro recorder is similar to a video camera in that it records all actions you perform on a document over a period of time. Once you turn on the macro recorder, it records your activities; when you are finished recording activities, you turn off the macro recorder to stop the recording. After you have recorded a macro, you can **execute the macro**, or play it back, any time you want to perform that same set of actions.

To create the macro that will place a check mark in the Save data only for forms check box, you will follow this sequence of steps:

1. Start the macro recorder and specify options about the macro.
2. Place a check mark in the Save data only for forms check box in the Save sheet in the Options dialog box.
3. Stop the macro recorder.

The impressive feature of the macro recorder is that you actually step through the task as you create the macro – allowing you to see exactly what the macro will do before you use it.

When you first create the macro, you have to name it. The name for this macro is FormDataOnly. **Macro names** can be up to 255 characters long; they can contain numbers, letters, and underscores; they cannot contain spaces and other punctuation.

More About

3-D Effects

You can change the color, rotation, depth, lighting, or texture of a 3-D effect by using the 3-D Settings toolbar. To display this toolbar, click the 3-D button on the Drawing toolbar and then click the 3-D Settings button in the list.

Earlier in this project, you assigned a shortcut key to a style. Likewise, you can assign a shortcut key to a macro, which allows you to run the macro by using its name or by pressing the shortcut key. Perform the following steps to record the macro and assign ALT+D as its shortcut key.

Steps To Record a Macro

1 **Double-click the REC status indicator** on the status bar. When the Record Macro dialog box displays, type `FormDataOnly` in the Macro name text box. Click the Store macro in box arrow and then click **Documents Based On DL Course Questionnaire.** Select the text in the Description box and then type `Places a check mark in the Save data only for forms check box.` **Point to the Keyboard button.**

Word displays the Record Macro dialog box (Figure 9-26).

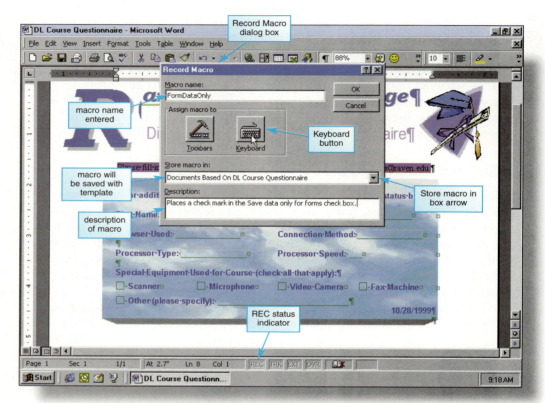

FIGURE 9-26

2 **Click the Keyboard button. When the Customize Keyboard dialog box displays, press the ALT+D keys. Point to the Assign button.**

Word displays the Customize Keyboard dialog box (Figure 9-27). The characters you pressed, ALT+D, display in the Press new shortcut key text box.

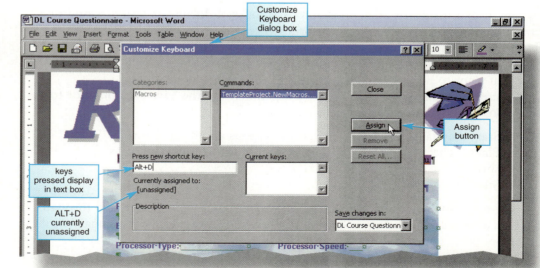

FIGURE 9-27

3 Click the Assign button. Click the Close button in the Customize Keyboard dialog box.

Word assigns the shortcut key, ALT+D, to the FormDataOnly macro, closes the Customize Keyboard and Record Macro dialog boxes, darkens the REC characters on the status bar, and then displays the Stop Recording toolbar in the document window (Figure 9-28). Any task you do will be part of the macro. When you are finished recording the macro, you will click the Stop Recording button on the Stop Recording toolbar.

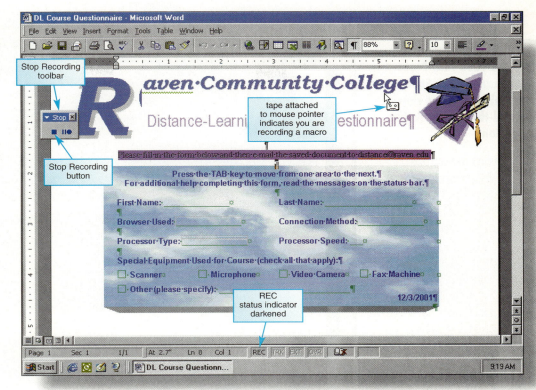

FIGURE 9-28

4 Click Tools on the menu bar and then point to Options.

When you are recording a macro and the mouse pointer is in a menu or pointing to a command button, the tape does not display next to the pointer (Figure 9-29).

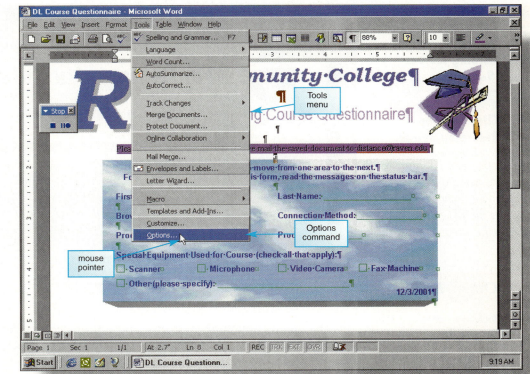

FIGURE 9-29

5 **Click Options. When the Options dialog box displays, if necessary, click the Save tab. Place a check mark in the Save data only for forms check box and then point to the OK button.**

The Options dialog box displays as shown in Figure 9-30.

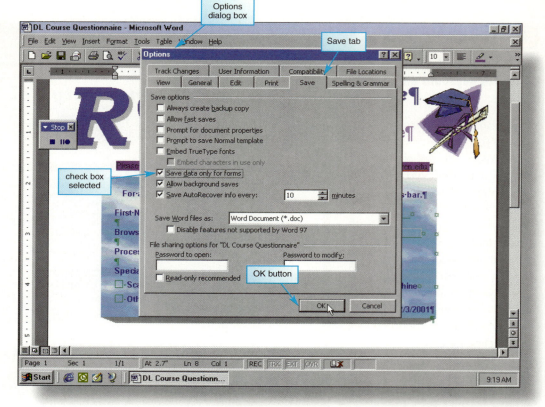

FIGURE 9-30

6 **Click the OK button. Point to the Stop Recording button on the Stop Recording toolbar (Figure 9-31).**

7 **Click the Stop Recording button.**

Word stops recording the document activities, closes the Stop Recording toolbar, and dims the REC status indicator on the status bar.

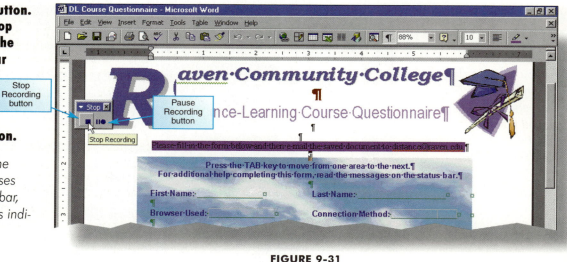

FIGURE 9-31

Other Ways

1. On Tools menu point to Macro, click Record New Macro, enter macro name, click Keyboard button, press shortcut keys, click Assign button, click Close button, record macro, click Stop Recording button on Stop Recording toolbar

The menu commands, buttons, and options you clicked while the macro recorder was running are stored in the macro. If you recorded the wrong actions, delete the macro and record it again. You delete a macro by clicking Tools on the menu bar, pointing to Macro on the Tools menu, and then clicking Macros on the Macro submenu. When the Macro dialog box displays, click the name of the macro (FormDataOnly), click the Delete button, and then click the Yes button. Finally, record the macro again.

If, while recording a macro, you want to perform some actions that should not be part of the macro, click the Pause Recording button on the Stop Recording toolbar (see Figure 9-31) to suspend the macro recorder. The Pause Recording button changes to a Resume Recorder button that you click when you want to continue recording.

In the Record Macro dialog box (Figure 9-26 on page WD 9.26), you select the location to store the macro in the Store macro in box. If you wanted a macro to be available to all documents you create that are based on the normal template, you would select All Documents (Normal.dot) in the Store macro in list. Most macros created with the macro recorder, however, are document specific, and thus are stored in the current template or document.

The next step is to execute, or run, the macro to ensure that it works. Recall that you assigned the shortcut key, ALT+D, to this macro. Perform the following steps to run the macro.

The Macro Recorder

While recording a macro, you must use the keyboard to record your actions because the macro recorder does not record mouse movements. For example, to move the insertion point to the top of the document, you would press the CTRL+HOME keys instead of dragging the scroll box to the top of the scroll bar. Likewise, you would use keyboard keys to move the insertion point or to select, copy, or move items.

 To Run a Macro

1 **Click Tools on the menu bar and then click Options. When the Options dialog box displays, if necessary, click the Save tab. Remove the check mark from the Save data only for forms check box and then click the OK button. Press the ALT+D keys.**

Word performs the instructions stored in the FormDataOnly macro. Verify that the macro worked properly by displaying the Options dialog box.

2 **Click Tools on the menu bar and then click Options. When the Options dialog box displays, if necessary, click the Save tab. Point to the OK button.**

A check mark displays in the Save data only for forms check box, indicating that the macro executed properly (Figure 9-32).

3 **Click the OK button.**

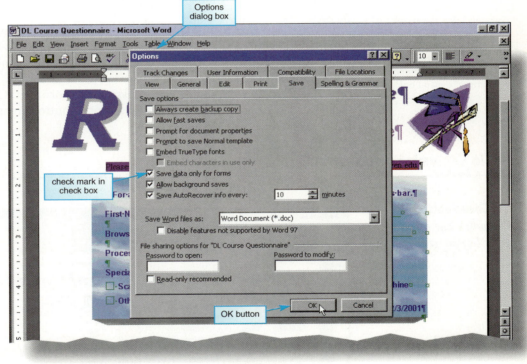

FIGURE 9-32

Other Ways

1. On Tools menu point to Macro, click Macros, click macro name in Macro name list box, click Run button
2. Press ALT+F8, click macro name in macro name list box, click Run button
3. Click Run Macro button on Standard toolbar in Visual Basic Editor

You should remove the check mark from the Save data only for forms check box so that future saves will save the entire form.

TO UNCHECK THE SAVE DATA ONLY FOR FORMS CHECK BOX

1 Click Tools on the menu bar and then click Options. When the Options dialog box displays, if necessary, click the Save tab.

2 Remove the check mark from the Save data only for forms check box. Click the OK button.

Word removes the check mark from the Save data only for forms check box.

Assigning a Macro to a Toolbar Button

You can customize toolbars by adding buttons, deleting buttons, and changing the function or appearance of buttons. You also can assign a macro to a button. In this project, you want to create a toolbar button for the FormDataOnly macro so that instead of pressing the shortcut keys, you can click the button to place a check mark in the Save data only for forms check box in the Save sheet in the Options dialog box.

You customize a toolbar through the Customize command on the Tools menu. The key to understanding how to customize a toolbar is to recognize that when you have the Customize dialog box open, Word's toolbars and menus are in Edit mode. **Edit mode** allows you to modify the toolbars and menus.

Perform the following steps to assign the FormDataOnly macro to a new button on the Standard toolbar and then change the button image.

More *About* **2000**

Customizing Word

In addition to customizing toolbars and their buttons, you can customize menus using the Customize dialog box. To add a command to a menu, for example, you click Commands in the Categories list in the Commands sheet and then drag the desired command to the appropriate menu name.

Steps **To Customize a Toolbar**

1 Click Tools on the menu bar and then point to Customize (Figure 9-33).

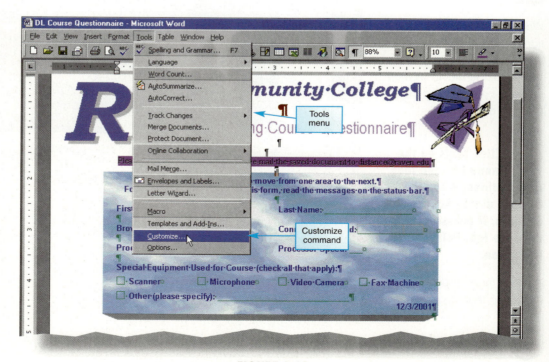

FIGURE 9-33

2 **Click Customize. When the Customize dialog box displays, if necessary, click the Commands tab. Scroll to and then click Macros in the Categories list. Click Template.Project. NewMacros.FormDataOnly in the Commands list.**

The Customize dialog box displays (Figure 9-34).

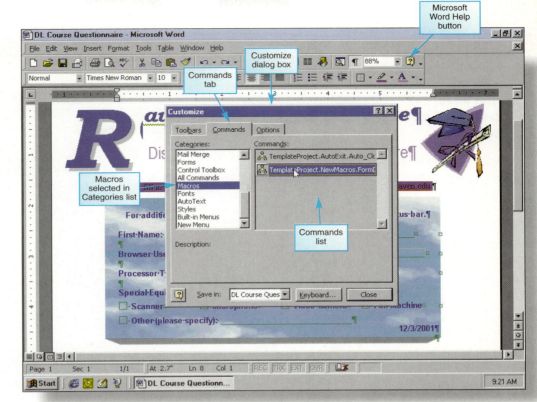

FIGURE 9-34

3 **Drag the selected command in the Commands list to the right of the Microsoft Word Help button on the Standard toolbar.**

A button containing the text, TemplateProject. NewMacros.FormDataOnly, displays next to the Microsoft Word Help button on the Standard toolbar (Figure 9-35). Because the button is so long, the toolbar may wrap to two lines. A thick border surrounds the new button indicating Word is in Edit mode.

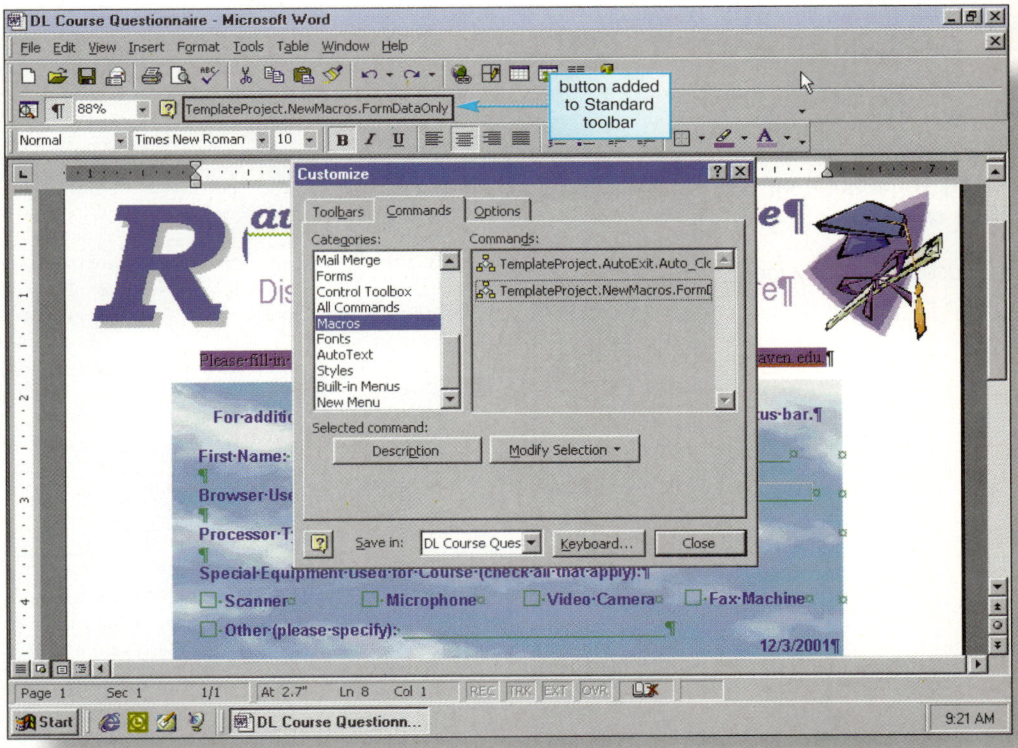

FIGURE 9-35

4 **Right-click the button just added to the Standard toolbar, point to Change Button Image on the shortcut menu, and then point to the happy face image.**

Word displays a palette of button images from which you can select (Figure 9-36).

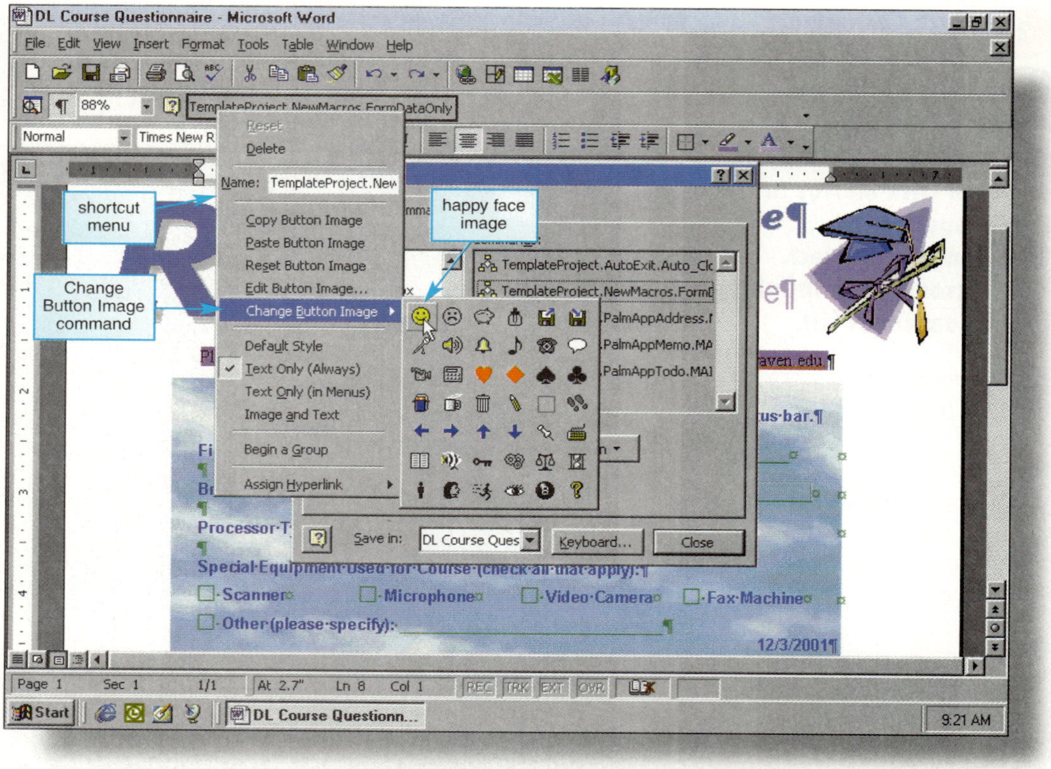

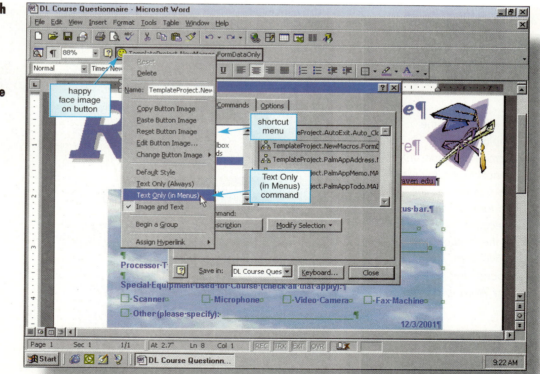

FIGURE 9-36

5 **Click the button with the happy face image. Right-click the button just added to the Standard toolbar. Point to Text Only (in Menus) on the shortcut menu.**

Word places the happy face image on the button (Figure 9-37).

FIGURE 9-37

6 Click Text Only (in Menus). Point to the Close button in the Customize dialog box.

The text, TemplateProject. NewMacros.FormDataOnly, no longer displays on the button (Figure 9-38). If you add the macro to a menu at a later time, the text will display in the menu.

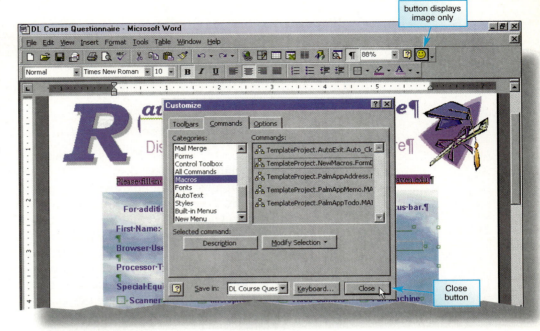

FIGURE 9-38

7 Click the Close button in the Customize dialog box. Point to the Form Data Only button on the Standard toolbar.

Word quits Edit mode. The Form Data Only button displays on the Standard toolbar with the ScreenTip, Form Data Only (Figure 9-39).

8 Click the Form Data Only button on the Standard toolbar.

Word places a check mark in the Save data only for forms check box in the Save sheet in the Options dialog box.

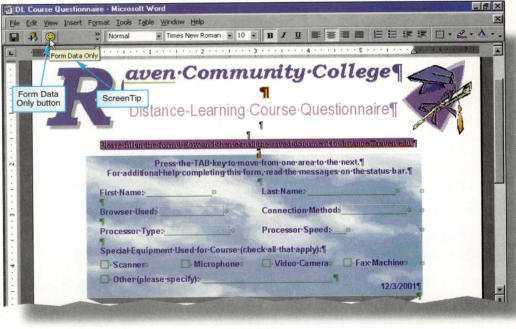

FIGURE 9-39

You can verify that the Form Data Only button worked by clicking Tools on the menu bar, clicking Options, clicking the Save tab, and then confirming that a check mark displays in the Save data only for forms check box. Because you do not want the check mark in the check box now, remove it as described in the steps on the next page.

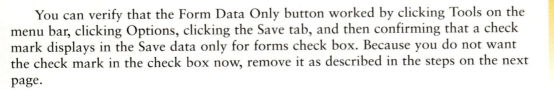

Other Ways

1. Right-click toolbar, click Customize on the shortcut menu, click Commands tab
2. Click View, click Toolbars, click Customize, click Commands tab

TO UNCHECK THE SAVE DATA ONLY FOR FORMS CHECK BOX

 1 Click Tools on the menu bar and then click Options. When the Options dialog box displays, if necessary, click the Save tab.

2 Remove the check mark from the Save data only for forms check box. Click the OK button.

Word removes the check mark from the Save data only for forms check box.

If you wanted to assign a Web address to a button so that when the user clicks the button the associated Web page displays on the screen, you would right-click the button with the Customize dialog box displaying as shown in Figure 9-37 on page WD 9.32, point to the Assign Hyperlink command, click Open, enter the Web address in the Assign Hyperlink dialog box, and then click the OK button.

You can add as many buttons as you want to a toolbar. You also can change the image on any button or change an existing button's function. For example, when in Edit mode (the Customize dialog box is active), you can right-click the Save button on the Standard toolbar and assign it a macro or a hyperlink. The next time you click the Save button, Word would execute the macro or start the application associated with the hyperlink, instead of saving a document.

As you add buttons, other buttons on the toolbar will be demoted to the More Buttons list. You also can create new toolbars. To create a new toolbar, click the Toolbars tab in the Customize dialog box and then click the New button.

To remove a button from a toolbar, while in Edit mode, right-click the button and then click Delete on the shortcut menu.

You reset the toolbars to their installation default by clicking the Toolbars tab in the Customize dialog box, selecting the toolbar name in the Toolbars list, and then clicking the Reset button. Because it is so easy to change the buttons on a toolbar, each project in this book begins by resetting the toolbars.

Recording an Automatic Macro

In the previous section, you created a macro, assigned it a unique name (FormDataOnly), and then created a toolbar button that executed the macro. Word also has five prenamed macros, called **automatic macros**, that execute automatically when a certain event occurs. Table 9-2 lists the name and function of these automatic macros.

Automatic Macros

A document can contain only one AutoClose, AutoNew, and AutoOpen macro. The AutoExec and AutoExit macros, however, are not stored with the document; instead, they must be stored in the Normal template. Thus, one AutoExec and only one AutoExit macro can exist for all Word documents.

Table 9-2	Automatic Macros
MACRO NAME	**RUNS**
AutoClose	When you close a document containing the macro
AutoExec	When you start Word
AutoExit	When you quit Word
AutoNew	When you create a new document based on a template containing the macro
AutoOpen	When you open a document containing the macro

The name you use for an automatic macro depends on when you want certain actions to occur. In this project, when a user creates a new Word document that is based on the DL Course Questionnaire template, you want the online form to display properly in the Word window. Thus, you will create an AutoNew macro using the macro recorder.

Because the form displays properly when zoom is set to page width, you will record the steps to change the zoom to page widt. Also, you want the entire form to display in the Word window so that the user does not have to scroll to position the form. When you display the form in the Word window, the top of the form displays. Thus, you will go to the top of the page by dragging the scroll box to the top of the vertical scroll bar and then click the scroll arrow at the bottom of the vertical scroll bar several times to position the form properly.

Perform the following steps to create an AutoNew macro.

Steps: To Create an Automatic Macro

1 **Double-click the REC status indicator on the status bar. When the Record Macro dialog box displays, type** AutoNew **in the Macro name text box. Click the Store macro in box arrow and then click Documents Based On DL Course Questionnaire. In the Description text box, type** Specifies how the form initially displays (as a blank form). **Point to the OK button.**

Word displays the Record Macro dialog box (Figure 9-40).

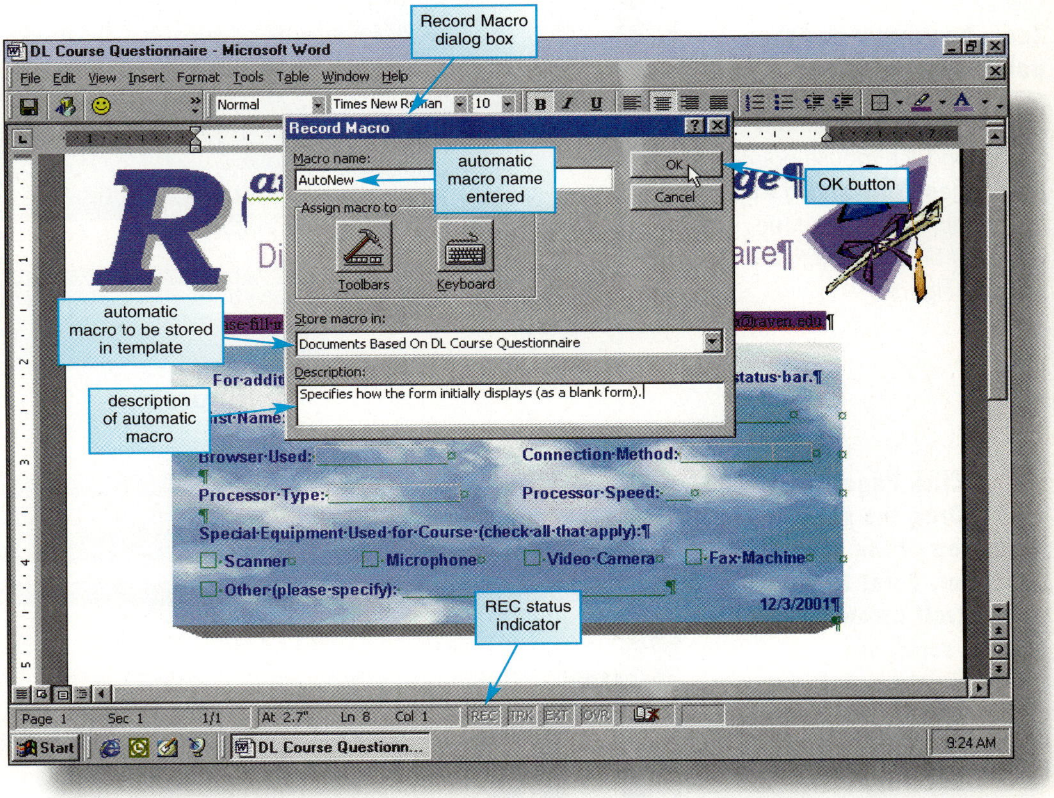

FIGURE 9-40

2 **Click the OK button.**

Word closes the Record Macro dialog box and then displays the Stop Recording toolbar in the document window.

3 **Double-click the move handle on the Standard toolbar to display the entire toolbar. Click the Zoom box arrow and then point to Page Width.**

When you are recording a macro and the mouse pointer is in a menu or pointing to a command button, the tape does not display next to the pointer (Figure 9-41).

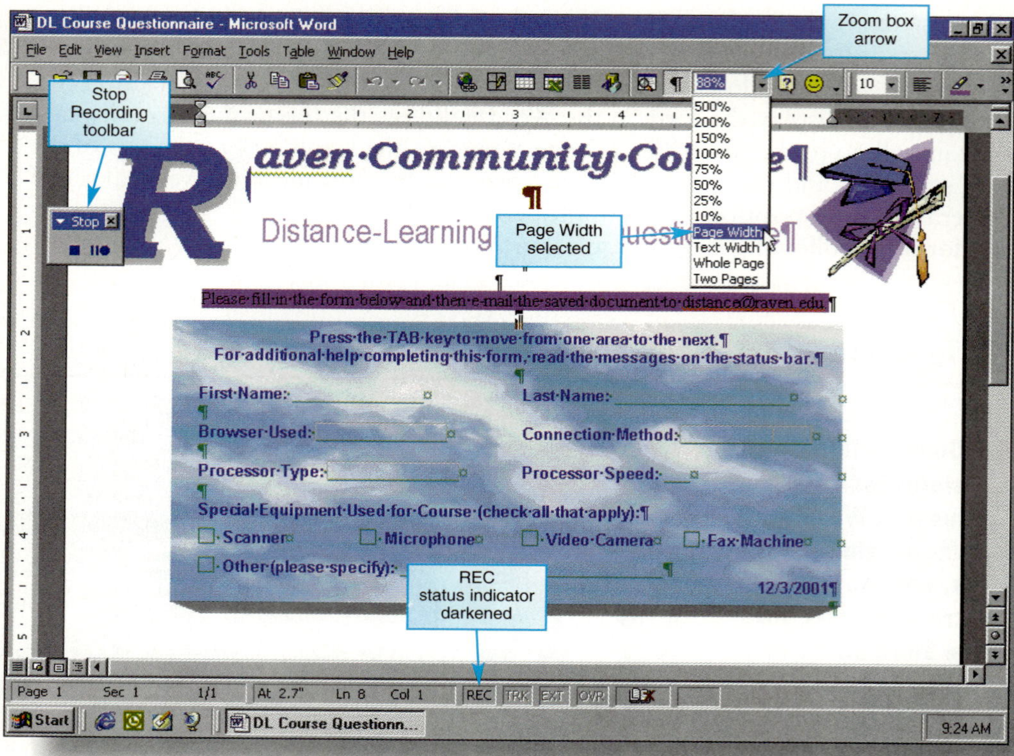

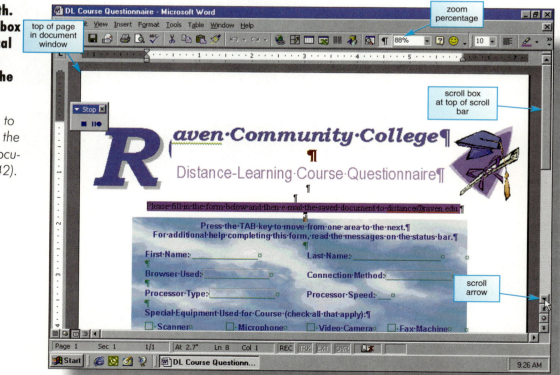

FIGURE 9-41

4 **Click Page Width. Drag the scroll box to the top of the vertical scroll bar. Point to the down scroll arrow on the vertical scroll bar.**

Word changes the zoom to page width and displays the top of the page in the document window (Figure 9-42).

FIGURE 9-42

5 **Click the down scroll arrow on the vertical scroll bar six times. Point to the Stop Recording button on the Stop Recording toolbar.**

The online form displays as shown in Figure 9-43.

6 **Click the Stop Recording button.**

Word stops recording the document activities, closes the Stop Recording toolbar, and dims the REC status indicator on the status bar.

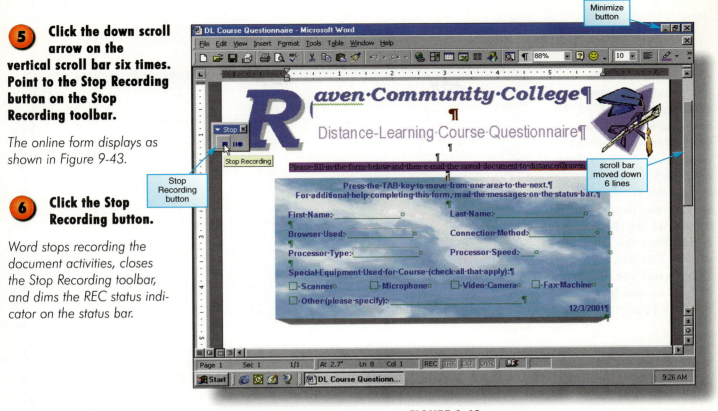

FIGURE 9-43

To test the automatic macro, you activate the event that causes the macro to execute. For example, the AutoNew macro runs whenever you create a new Word document that is based on the template. You learned in Project 8 that when you save a template to a disk in drive A, a user can create a Word document based on a template through the My Computer window or Windows Explorer.

Perform the steps on the next page to display a new Word document window that is based on the DL Course Questionnaire template.

Other Ways

1. On Tools menu point to Macro, click Record New Macro, enter macro name, click Keyboard button, press shortcut keys, click Assign button, click Close button, record macro, click Stop Recording button on Stop Recording toolbar

More About 2000

Recording and Running Macros

If Word does not allow you to record or run a macro in a document, the document probably is marked as read-only. To record or run a macro in this document, save it with a new name using the Save As dialog box and then record or run the macro in the newly named document.

Steps **To Test the AutoNew Macro**

1 Click the Save button on the Standard toolbar. Click the Minimize button in the Word window. When the Windows desktop displays, right-click the My Computer icon on the Windows desktop and then click Explore on the shortcut menu. When the Exploring window displays, click the Address text box to select it. Type **a:** and then press the ENTER key.

The Exploring - 3½ Floppy (A:) window displays (Figure 9-44). Word is still running.

2 Double-click the DL Course Questionnaire icon in the Contents pane.

Word displays a new document window that is based on the contents of the DL Course Questionnaire (Figure 9-45). The zoom is set to page width and the screen scrolls down six lines as instructed by the AutoNew macro.

3 Click the Close button at the right edge of the Word title bar. If necessary, click the DL Course Questionnaire - Microsoft Word program button on the taskbar.

The new document window closes. The DL Course Questionnaire template displays on the screen.

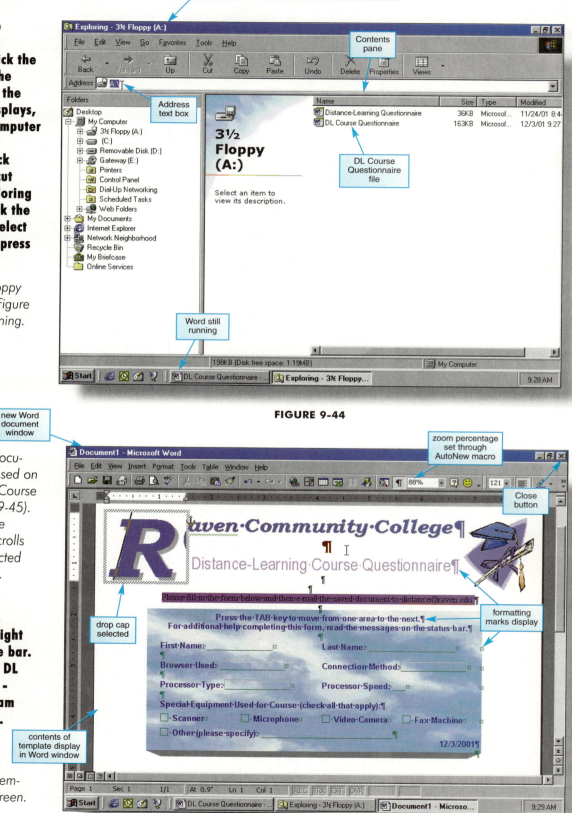

FIGURE 9-44

FIGURE 9-45

Notice in Figure 9-45 that the drop cap is selected. Recall that when you make a form available for users to access, you first protect the form. Protecting a form places the highlight in the first form field and allows users to access only the form fields. You did not protect the form yet because you are not finished modifying it. You simply tested the AutoNew macro to be sure it worked according to your plan.

When testing the AutoNew macro, you noticed that the formatting marks displayed on the screen (see Figure 9-45). You also noticed that the screen actually should scroll down one more line so it fits better in the Word window. Thus, you want to edit this macro. To edit a macro, you use VBA. The next section discusses VBA.

Editing a Recorded Macro

The next step in this project is to edit the AutoNew macro. Word uses VBA to store a macro's instructions. Thus, to edit a recorded macro, you use the Visual Basic Editor. All Office applications use the **Visual Basic Editor** to enter, modify, and view VBA code associated with a document. The following pages explain how to use the Visual Basic Editor to view, enter, and modify VBA code.

Viewing a Macro's VBA Code

As described earlier, a macro consists of VBA code, which the macro recorder automatically creates. You view the VBA code assigned to a macro through the Visual Basic Editor. Perform the following steps to view the VBA code associated AutoNew macro in the DL Course Questionnaire.

More About 2000

Using VBA

For more information about Using Visual Basic for Applications, visit the Word 2000 More About Web page (www.scsite.com/wd2000/more.htm) and then click Using VBA.

Steps **To View a Macro's VBA Code**

1 **Click Tools on the menu bar, point to Macro, and then point to Macros (Figure 9-46).**

FIGURE 9-46

2 **Click Macros. When the Macros dialog box displays, click the Macros in box arrow and then click DL Course Questionnaire (template). Click AutoNew in the Macro name list and then point to the Edit button.**

The Macros dialog box displays (Figure 9-47).

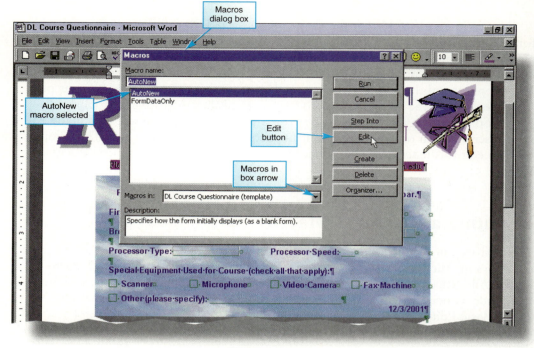

FIGURE 9-47

 3 **Click the Edit button. If the Code window does not display, click View on the menu bar and then click Code. If the Project Explorer displays, click its Close button. If the Properties window displays, click its Close button. If the Code window is not maximized, double-click its title bar.**

The Visual Basic Editor starts and displays the VBA code for the AutoNew macro in the Code window (Figure 9-48). Your screen may display differently depending on previous Visual Basic Editor settings.

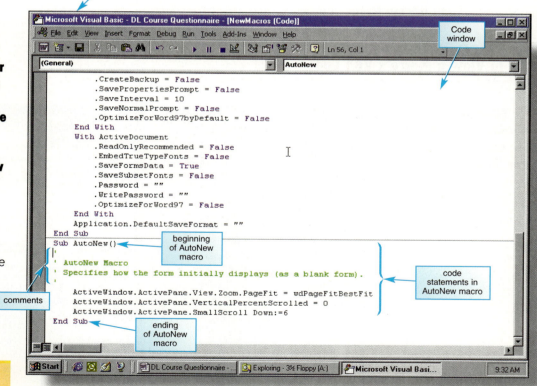

FIGURE 9-48

1. On Tools menu point to Macro, click Visual Basic Editor, scroll to desired procedure
2. Press ALT+F11, scroll to desired procedure

You have learned that the named set of instructions associated with a macro is called a procedure. It is this set of instructions, beginning with the words Sub AutoNew in Figure 9-48 and continuing sequentially to the line with the words End Sub, that is executed when you run the macro.

If you scroll up the Code window, you will see the code associated with the FormDataOnly macro. By scrolling through the two procedures of VBA code, you can see that the macro recorder generated many instructions.

The instructions within a procedure are called **code statements**. Each code statement can contain keywords, variables, constants, and operators. Table 9-3 explains the function of each of these elements of a code statement.

Table 9-3	Elements of a Code Statement	
CODE STATEMENT ELEMENT	DEFINITION	EXAMPLES
Keyword	Recognized by Visual Basic as part of its programming language. Keywords display in blue in the Code window.	Sub End Sub
Variable	An item whose value can be modified during program execution.	ActiveWindow.Active.Pane.SmallScroll TitleBar Text
Constant	An item whose value remains unchanged during program execution.	7
Operator	A symbol that indicates a specific action.	= +

A procedure begins with a **Sub statement** and ends with an **End Sub statement**. As shown in Figure 9-48, the Sub statement is followed by the name of the procedure, which is the macro name (AutoNew). The parentheses following the macro name in the Sub statement are required. They indicate that arguments can be passed from one procedure to another. Passing arguments is beyond the scope of this project, but the parentheses still are required. The End Sub statement signifies the end of the procedure and returns control to Word. For clarity, code statement lines between the Sub statement and End Sub statement are indented four spaces.

Adding Comments to a Macro

Adding comments before and within a procedure help you remember the purpose of the macro and its code statements at a later date. **Comments** begin with the word Rem or an apostrophe (') and display in green in the Code window. In Figure 9-48, for example, the macro recorder placed four comment lines below the Sub statement. These comments display the name of the macro and its description, as entered in the Record Macro dialog box. Comments have no effect on the execution of a procedure; they simply provide information about the procedure, such as its name and description.

The macro recorder, however, does not add comments to the executable code statements in the procedures. Any code statement that is not a comment is considered an **executable code statement**. The AutoNew procedure in Figure 9-48 contains three executable code statements. The first, ActiveWindow.ActivePane.View. Zoom.PageFit = wdPageFitBestFit, changes the zoom to page width. The macro recorder generated this code statement when you clicked the Zoom box arrow on the Standard toolbar and then clicked the Page Width command.

VBA Statements

Instead of a long VBA statement on a single line, you can continue a VBA statement on the next line by placing an underscore character (_) at the end of the line to be continued and then pressing the ENTER key. To place multiple VBA statements on the same line, place a colon (:) between each statement.

The next two code statements scroll the screen downward six lines from the top of the page. The macro recorder generated these code statements when you dragged the scroll box to the top of the vertical scroll bar and then clicked the down scroll arrow on the vertical scroll bar six times.

You would like to enter comments that explain the purpose of executable code statements in the AutoNew procedure. You make changes, such as these, using the Visual Basic Editor. The Visual Basic Editor is a full-screen editor, which allows you to enter a procedure by typing lines of VBA code as if you were using word processing software. At the end of a line, you press the ENTER key or use the DOWN ARROW key to move to the next line. If you make a mistake in a code statement, you can use the arrow keys and the DELETE or BACKSPACE keys to correct it. You also can move the insertion point to previous lines to make corrections.

Perform the following steps to add comments above the executable code statements in the AutoNew procedure.

Steps: To Add Comments to a Procedure

1 **Click to the left of the letter A in the first code statement beginning with the word ActiveWindow in the AutoNew procedure and then press the ENTER key to add a blank line before the code statement. Press the UP ARROW key. Type '** Sets screen to page width zoom **and then press the DOWN ARROW key. Make sure you enter the apostrophe at the beginning of the comment.**

The first comment is entered and displays in green (Figure 9-49).

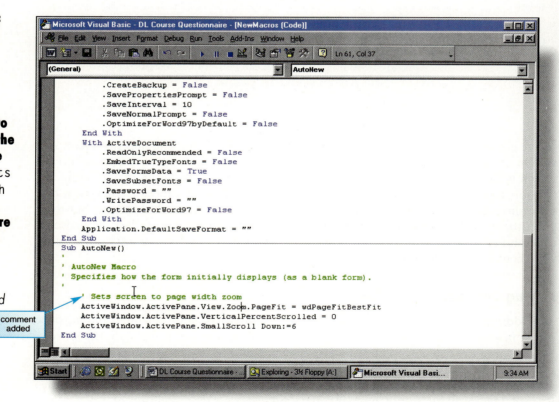

FIGURE 9-49

2 Click to the left of the letter A in the second code statement beginning with the word ActiveWindow and then press the ENTER key to add one blank line before the code statement. Press the UP ARROW key. Type

`' Scrolls down from top of page so entire form fits in window`

and then press the DOWN ARROW key. Make sure you enter the apostrophe at the beginning of the comment.

The second comment is entered and displays in green (Figure 9-50).

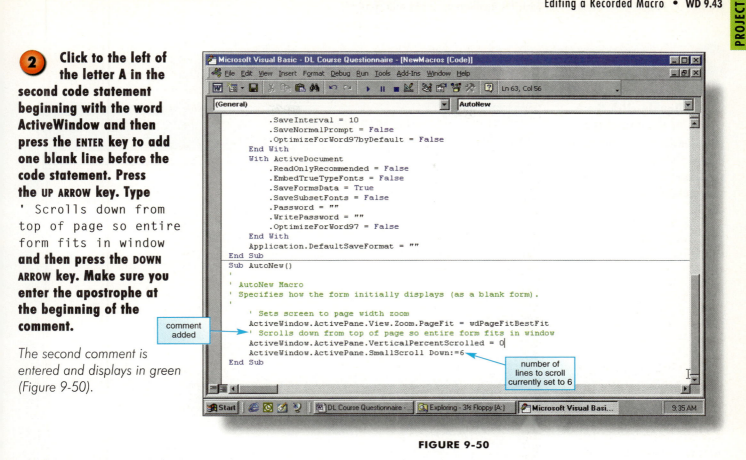

```
                   .SaveInterval = 10
                   .SaveNormalPrompt = False
                   .OptimizeForWord97byDefault = False
               End With
               With ActiveDocument
                   .ReadOnlyRecommended = False
                   .EmbedTrueTypeFonts = False
                   .SaveFormsData = True
                   .SaveSubsetFonts = False
                   .Password = ""
                   .WritePassword = ""
                   .OptimizeForWord97 = False
               End With
               Application.DefaultSaveFormat = ""
           End Sub
           Sub AutoNew()
           '
           ' AutoNew Macro
           ' Specifies how the form initially displays (as a blank form).
           '
               ' Sets screen to page width zoom
               ActiveWindow.ActivePane.View.Zoom.PageFit = wdPageFitBestFit
               ' Scrolls down from top of page so entire form fits in window
               ActiveWindow.ActivePane.VerticalPercentScrolled = 0
               ActiveWindow.ActivePane.SmallScroll Down:=6
           End Sub
```

comment added

number of lines to scroll currently set to 6

FIGURE 9-50

Modifying Existing Code in a Macro

The next step is to modify existing code in the AutoNew macro. Recall that when you tested the AutoNew macro, you noticed you should scroll down one more line so the college name displays closer to the top of the screen (see Figure 9-45 on page WD 9.38). Thus, you would like to change the 6 in the third executable code statement in the AutoNew procedure to a 7. Perform the step on the next page to change the constant in the executable code statement from a 6 to a 7.

Visual Basic for Applications

For more information about Visual Basic for Applications, visit the Word 2000 More About Web page (www.scsite.com/wd2000/more.htm) and then click Visual Basic for Applications.

Steps **To Modify Existing Code**

1 **Double-click the 6 at the end of the executable code statement above the End Sub statement. Type 7 as the new number of lines to scroll.**

The code statement is modified (Figure 9-51).

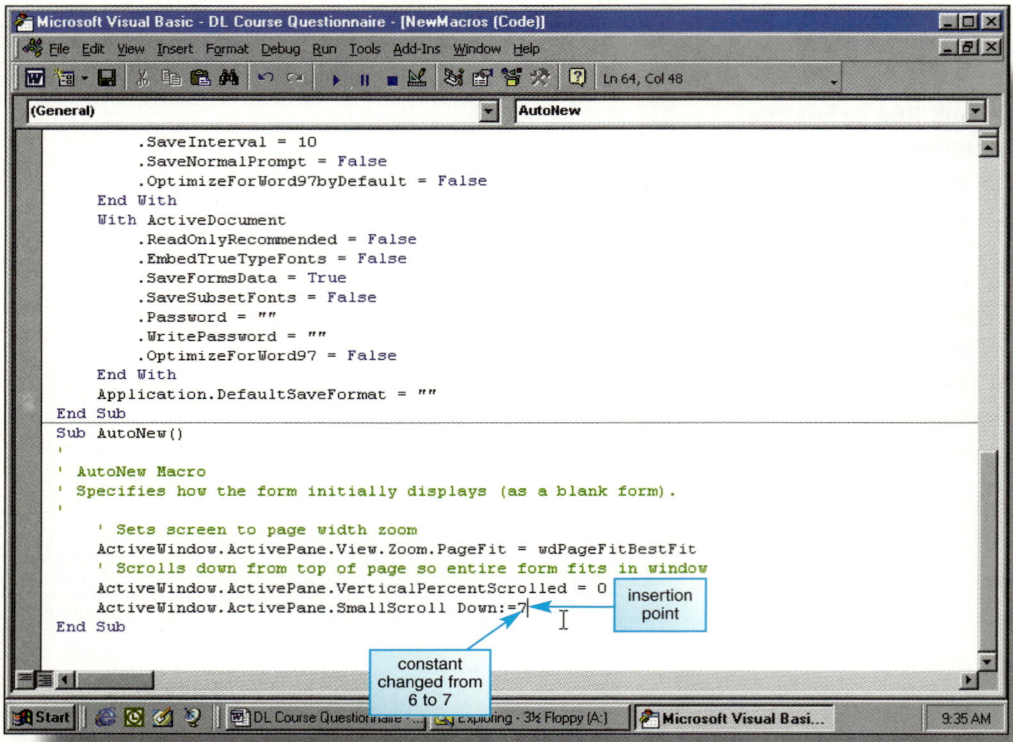

FIGURE 9-51

The next step is to add two more executable code statements to the AutoNew macro.

Entering Code Statements

In addition to changing the zoom to page width and scrolling down seven lines, you would like to hide formatting marks and gridlines when a user initially displays this form (as a blank form). Thus, you will add two executable code statements, each preceded by a comment. Table 9-4 shows the code statements to be entered.

Table 9-4 Code Statements Added to AutoNew Procedure	
First new code statement	' Turns off table gridlines
Second new code statement	ActiveDocument.ActiveWindow.View.TableGridlines = False
Third new code statement	' Turns off formatting marks
Fourth new code statement	ActiveDocument.ActiveWindow.View.ShowAll = False

Perform the following step to add these code statements to the procedure.

To Add Code Statements to a Procedure

1 With the insertion point following the 7 as shown in Figure 9-51, press the ENTER key. Type the first new code statement shown in Table 9-4. Press the ENTER key. Enter the remaining three code statements shown in Table 9-4. Make sure you enter an apostrophe at the beginning of each comment line.

The new code statements are entered into the AutoNew procedure (Figure 9-52).

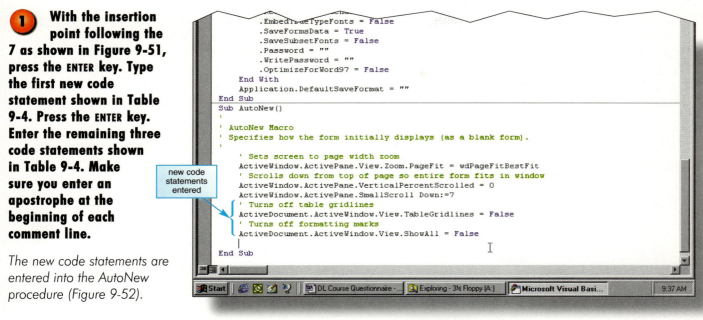

FIGURE 9-52

You now are finished modifying the AutoNew macro. Thus, perform the following steps to close the Visual Basic Editor and return control to Word.

 To Close the Visual Basic Editor

1 Point to the Close button on the right edge of the Microsoft Visual Basic title bar (Figure 9-53).

2 Click the Close button.

The Visual Basic Editor closes and control returns to Word.

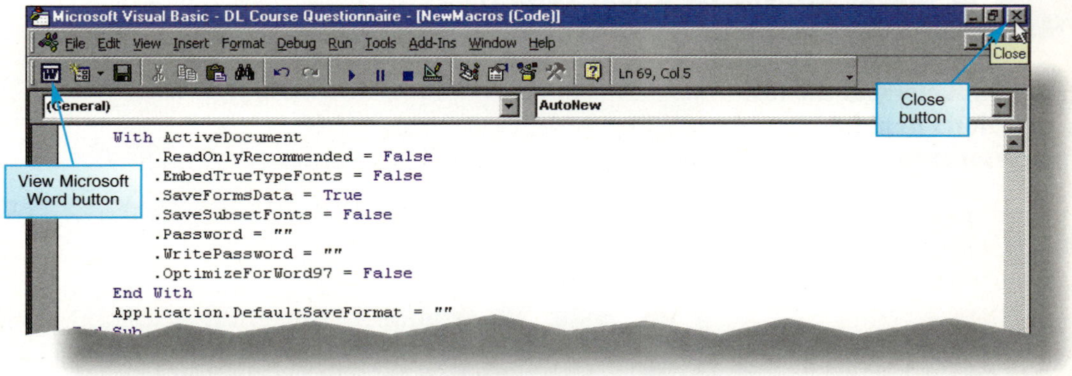

FIGURE 9-53

Instead of closing the Visual Basic Editor, you can click the **View Microsoft Word button** on the Visual Basic toolbar (Figure 9-53) to minimize the Visual Basic Editor and return control to Word. If you plan to switch between Word and the Visual Basic Editor, then use the View Microsoft Word button; otherwise use the Close button.

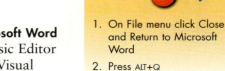

Other Ways

1. On File menu click Close and Return to Microsoft Word
2. Press ALT+Q

Creating a Macro from Scratch Using VBA

The next macro to be created in this project is the one that displays an error message if the user enters a nonnumeric value in the Processor Speed text box (see Figure 9-1b on page WD 9.5). The macro is to execute when the user presses the TAB key to advance out of the Processor Speed text box. The following pages explain how to create this macro and attach it to the text form field for the processor speed.

Modifying Form Field Options

The Processor Speed text box is a text form field. To modify a text form field, you double-click the text form field to display the Text Form Field Options dialog box. You have two changes to make in the dialog box: change the type and enter a bookmark.

In Project 8, you wanted only numbers to display in the text form field. Thus, you changed the text form field's type to Numeric. Doing so ensured that if a user entered a nonnumeric value in the text form field during data entry, the entry automatically was converted to a zero. In this project, you want to display an error message if the user enters a nonnumeric value. Thus, you must change the text form field's type back to Regular text so that you can display an error message if a user makes an incorrect entry.

Because you will be writing VBA code that references this text form field, you also want to change the bookmark for this text form field. You have learned that a **bookmark** is an item in a document that you name for future reference. Currently, the bookmark is Text3, which is not very descriptive. A more meaningful bookmark would be EnteredSpeed. Notice this new bookmark does not have a space between the words, Entered and Speed. This is because a bookmark cannot contain any spaces; a bookmark also must begin with a letter.

Perform the following steps to change the text form field type and change the bookmark.

Bookmark Names

Each time you create a form field, Word assigns it a sequential default bookmark name. For example, the first text form field has a bookmark name of Text1, the second text form field has a bookmark name of Text2, the third text form field has a bookmark name of Text3, and so on.

Steps ## To Change Options for a Text Form Field

1 **Double-click the text form field for processor speed.**

Word displays the Text Form Field Options dialog box (Figure 9-54).

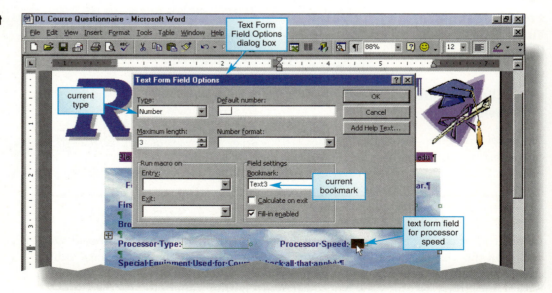

FIGURE 9-54

2 Click the Type box arrow and then click Regular text. Double-click the text in the Bookmark text box and then type `EnteredSpeed` as the new bookmark. Point to the OK button.

The form field options display as shown in figure 9-55.

3 Click the OK button.

Word changes the form field options as specified in the Text Form Field Options dialog box.

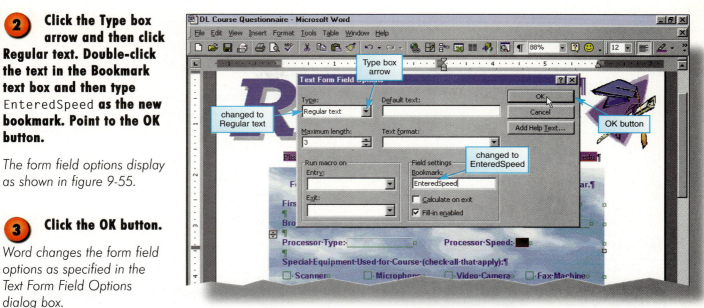

FIGURE 9-55

The next step is to change the bookmark for the drop-down list box for the processor type from Dropdown3 to a more meaningful name because this form field also will be referenced in the VBA code. Perform the following steps to change the bookmark for the drop-down form field.

TO CHANGE A BOOKMARK FOR A DROP-DOWN FORM FIELD

1 Double-click the drop-down form field for processor type.

2 When the Drop-Down Form Field Options dialog box displays, double-click the text in the Bookmark text box and then type `EnteredType` as the new bookmark. Point to the OK button (Figure 9-56).

3 Click the OK button.

Word changes the form field options as specified in the Drop-Down Form Field Options dialog box.

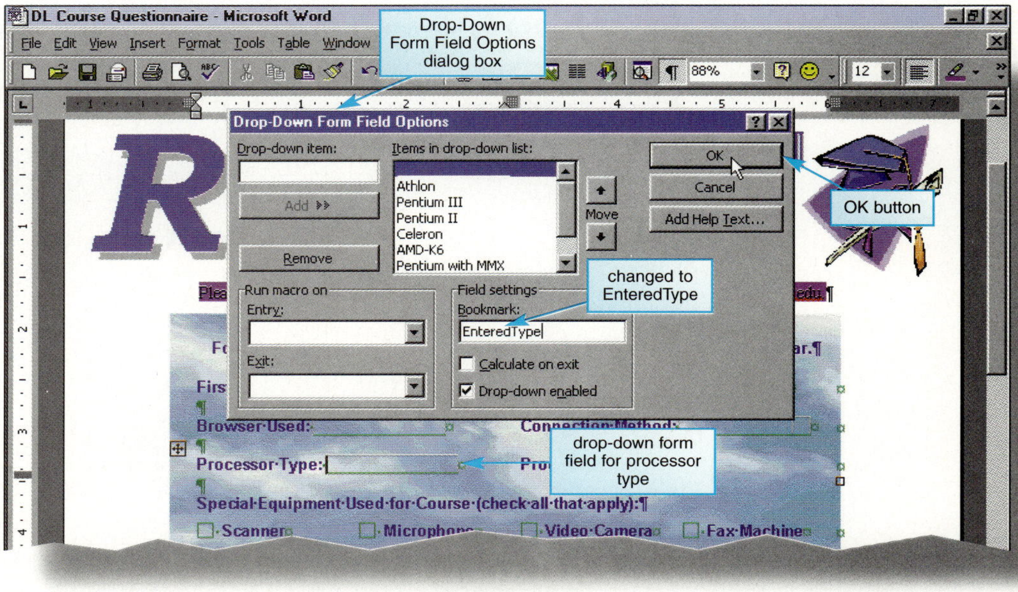

FIGURE 9-56

The next step is to insert a new procedure for the macro using the Visual Basic Editor.

Inserting a Procedure for the Macro

For the previous two macros, you used the macro recorder to create the macros, which generated corresponding VBA code from your actions. For this macro, you cannot record the displaying of the error message because an error message for this text form field does not exist. Thus, you must write the VBA code for this macro using the Visual Basic Editor.

You have learned that each macro is a procedure in Visual Basic. Perform the following steps to insert a new empty procedure named ProcessorSpeed.

Steps To Insert a Visual Basic Procedure

1 **Press the ALT+F11 keys to display the Visual Basic Editor in a new window. If the Project Explorer displays, click its Close button. If the Properties window displays, click its Close button. If the Code window does not display, click View on the menu bar and then click Code. If necessary, maximize the Code window. Click the Insert UserForm button arrow and then point to Procedure.**

The Visual Basic Editor displays as shown in Figure 9-57.

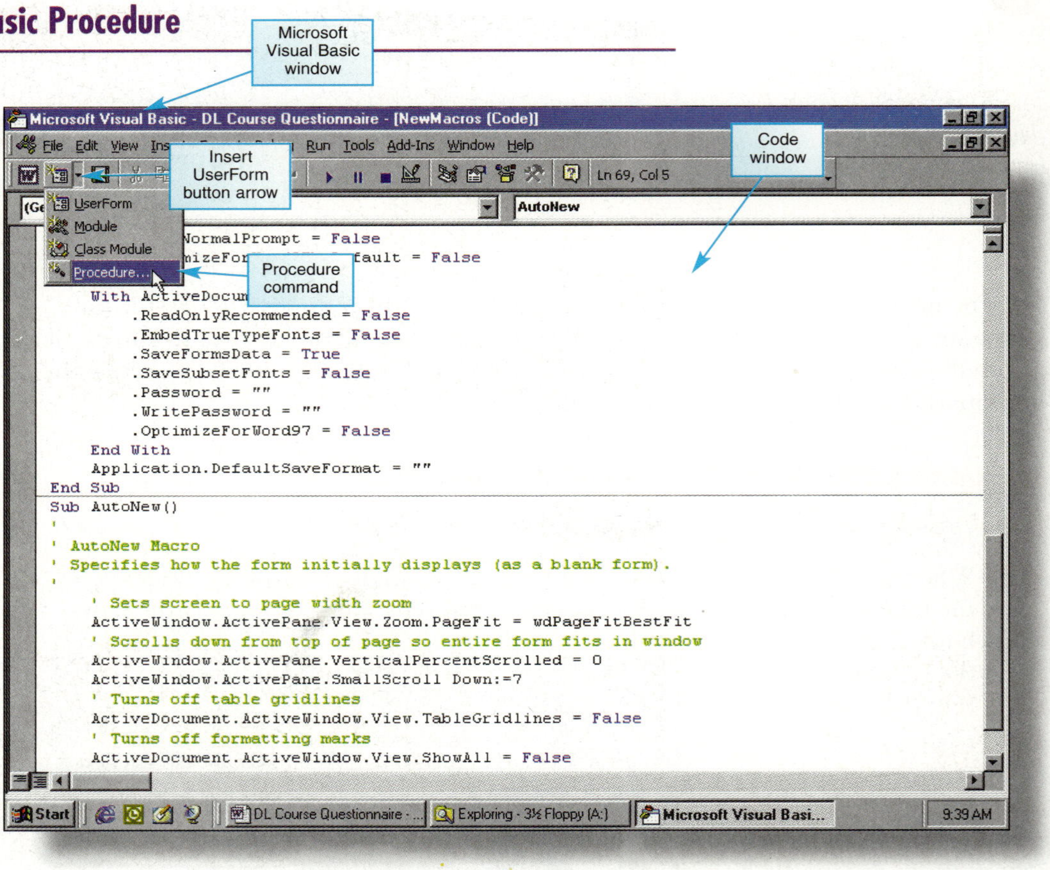

FIGURE 9-57

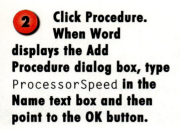

2 **Click Procedure. When Word displays the Add Procedure dialog box, type** ProcessorSpeed **in the Name text box and then point to the OK button.**

The Add Procedure dialog box displays (Figure 9-58).

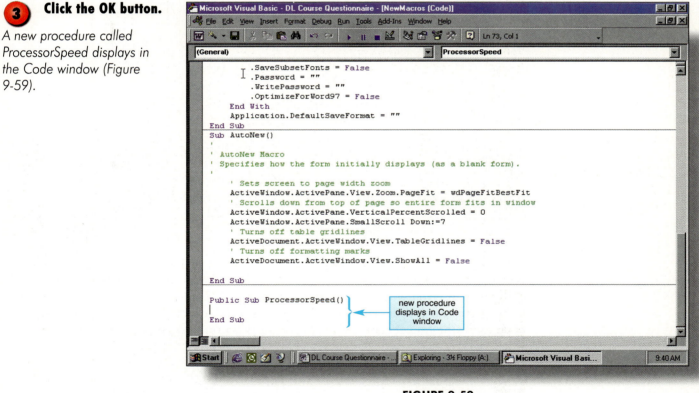

FIGURE 9-58

3 **Click the OK button.**

A new procedure called ProcessorSpeed displays in the Code window (Figure 9-59).

FIGURE 9-59

Notice in Figure 9-59 that Sub and End Sub statements automatically are inserted into the procedure. The Sub statement, however, begins with the keyword **public** which means that this procedure can be executed from other documents or programs. **Private**, by contrast, means that the procedure can be executed only from this document. If you wanted a procedure to be private, would click Private in the Scope area in the Add Procedure dialog box (see Figure 9-58).

Other Ways

1. On Insert menu click Procedure, enter procedure name, click OK button

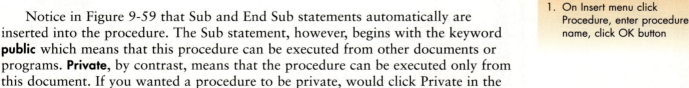

Planning and Writing a VBA Procedure

The next step is to write and then enter the code statements for the newly created ProcessorSpeed procedure. Before you write the statements, you should plan the procedure; that is, determine what tasks the procedure is to accomplish and the order in which the tasks should be executed. Planning the procedure is an extremely important activity because the order of statements determines the sequence of execution. If the order of statements is incorrect, the procedure will not execute properly.

Once you have planned the procedure thoroughly, the next step is to write the VBA code statements on paper similar to that shown in Table 9-5. Then, before entering the procedure into the computer, test it by putting yourself in the position of Word and stepping through the instructions one at a time. As you step through the procedure, think about how it affects the Word document. Testing a procedure before entering it is called **desk checking** and is an extremely important part of the development process.

Table 9-5	Code Statements for ProcessorSpeed Procedure
LINE	**VBA CODE STATEMENT**
1	`Public Sub ProcessorSpeed()`
2	`'`
3	`' ProcessorSpeed Macro`
4	`' Displays error message if entered processor speed is not numeric.`
5	`'`
6	`    ' Test if entry in EnteredSpeed text form field is numeric`
7	`    If IsNumeric(ActiveDocument.FormFields("EnteredSpeed").Result) = False Then`
8	`        ' Display error message`
9	`        MsgBox "Please enter processor speed in numbers", vbOKOnly + vbCritical`
10	`        ' Redisplay underscores in text form field`
11	`        ActiveDocument.FormFields("EnteredSpeed").Result = "___"`
12	`        ' Reposition highlight in text form field`
13	`        ActiveDocument.FormFields("EnteredType").Select`
14	`        SendKeys "{TAB}"`
15	`    End If`
16	`End Sub`

In the code statements shown in Table 9-5, lines 2, 3, 4, 5, 6, 8, 10, and 12 are comments. Lines 1 and 16 contain the Sub and End Sub statements that automatically were inserted when you created the procedure. Line 7 is the first executable code statement. It is called an **If...Then statement** because it executes the line(s) of code up to the End If statement if the result of a condition is true. The condition in line 7 is IsNumeric(ActiveDocument.FormFields("EnteredSpeed").Result) = False. In nonprogramming terms, this condition is testing whether the user entered a number in the EnteredSpeed form field. (Recall that earlier in this project, you changed the bookmark for this form field to EnteredSpeed.) If not, then the statements up to the End If statement will be executed. If the user did enter a number, then the statements up to the End If statement are not executed and control returns back to Word.

If the user entered a nonnumeric value in the EnteredSpeed form field, then the next executable code statement is in line 9, which uses the MsgBox keyword to display a message box on the screen. The text inside the quotation marks displays inside the message box; vbOKOnly places an OK button in the message box, and vbCritical places an icon of an X in the dialog box. Table 9-6 discusses other types of icons that can display in a message box.

Table 9-6	Types of Icons for a Message Box
ICON	**VISUAL BASIC CONSTANT**
Letter X	vbCritical
Question mark	vbQuestion
Exclamation point	vbExclamation
Information symbol	vbInformation

After a user reads the message in the message box and clicks the OK button, the next executable code statement is in line 11, which replaces the users invalid entry with underscores. Then, line 13 positions the highlight in the EnteredType drop-down form field and line 14 presses the TAB key so that the highlight is positioned in the EnteredSpeed text form field – ready for the user to make another entry in the Processor Speed text box.

Having desk checked the code statements on paper, you now are ready to enter them into the Visual Basic Editor. Perform the following steps to enter the code statements into the ProcessorSpeed procedure.

More About

InputBox

A MsgBox displays a message and one or more buttons that the user can click. If you would like the user to enter information that you can use in the VBA procedure, you should display an InputBox. An InputBox displays a message, a text box, and one or more buttons that the user can click. If the user clicks the OK button, the entered text is saved for use later in the procedure.

 To Enter the ProcessorSpeed Procedure

1 **With the insertion point on the blank line between the Sub and End Sub statements in the Code window, type the code statements shown in lines 2 through 15 in Table 9-5. Make sure you enter an apostrophe at the beginning of each comment line. For clarity, indent code statements as shown in Table 9-5**

The ProcessorSpeed procedure is entered (Figure 9-60).

2 **Verify your code statements by comparing them to Figure 9-60.**

3 **Click the Close button on the right edge of the Microsoft Visual Basic title bar to return to the template.**

The Microsoft Visual Basic window closes and control returns to Word.

Close button

```
Microsoft Visual Basic - DL Course Questionnaire - [NewMacros (Code)]
File  Edit  View  Insert  Format  Debug  Run  Tools  Add-Ins  Window  Help          Ln 87, Col 8

(General)                              ProcessorSpeed

        ' Sets screen to page width zoom
        ActiveWindow.ActivePane.View.Zoom.PageFit = wdPageFitBestFit
        ' Scrolls down from top of page so entire form fits in window
        ActiveWindow.ActivePane.VerticalPercentScrolled = 0
        ActiveWindow.ActivePane.SmallScroll Down:=7
        ' Turns off table gridlines
        ActiveDocument.ActiveWindow.View.TableGridlines = False
        ' Turns off formatting marks
        ActiveDocument.ActiveWindow.View.ShowAll = False

End Sub

Public Sub ProcessorSpeed()
'
'  ProcessorSpeed Macro
'  Displays error message if entered processor speed is not numeric.
'
        ' Test if entry in EnteredSpeed text form field is numeric
        If IsNumeric(ActiveDocument.FormFields("EnteredSpeed").Result) = False Then
            ' Display error message
            MsgBox "Please enter processor speed in numbers", vbOKOnly + vbCritical
            ' Redisplay underscores in text form field
            ActiveDocument.FormFields("EnteredSpeed").Result = "___"
            ' Reposition highlight in text form field
            ActiveDocument.FormFields("EnteredType").Select
            SendKeys "{TAB}"
        End If
End Sub
```

code statements entered into ProcessorSpeed procedure

Start | DL Course Questionnaire - | Exploring - 3½ Floppy (A:) | Microsoft Visual Basi...   9:44 AM

FIGURE 9-60

The next step is to attach this procedure for the macro to the text form field for the processor speed.

Running a Macro When a User Exits a Form Field

You want the ProcessorSpeed macro that you just created in the Visual Basic Editor to execute whenever a user presses the TAB key to move out of the Processor Speed text box. That is, pressing the TAB key out of the Processor Speed text box is the event that is to trigger execution of the procedure. With respect to form fields, Word allows you to execute a macro under these two circumstances: (1) when the user enters a form field and (2) when the user exits the form field. You specify when the macro should run through the Text Form Field Options dialog box. Perform the following steps to instruct Word to execute the ProcessorSpeed macro when a user exits the text form field for processor speed.

To Run a Macro When a User Exits a Form Field

1 **Double-click the text form field for the processor speed. When the Text Form Field Options dialog box displays, click the Exit box arrow, scroll to and then click ProcessorSpeed. Point to the OK button.**

Word displays the Text Form Field Options dialog box (Figure 9-61). The selected macro name displays in the Exit box.

2 **Click the OK button.**

The form field options are set as specified in the Text Form Field Options dialog box.

FIGURE 9-61

When you click the Entry or Exit box arrow in the Run macro on area of the Text Form Field Options dialog box, Word displays all available macros. You can select any one macro to run when the user enters or exits each form field in the form.

The ProcessorSpeed macro is complete. You will test this macro at the end of this project, after you create the next VBA procedure.

Adding an ActiveX Control to a Form

In addition to the form fields available on the Forms toolbar, you can insert an ActiveX control to a Word form. An **ActiveX control** is an object, such as a button or check box, that can be included in a form to be published on the World Wide Web. The major difference between a form field and an ActiveX control is that form fields require the use of Word, whereas ActiveX controls do not. Thus, if you intend to create a Web page form, you should place ActiveX controls on the form instead of form fields.

ActiveX controls have the appearance and functionality of Windows controls. For example, the check box ActiveX control displays like any check box in any Windows dialog box. A check box form field, by contrast, has an appearance unique to Word. That is, it displays an X (instead of a check mark). Users that are familiar with Windows applications will find it easier to work with ActiveX controls than working with form fields. With form fields, a user has to TAB from one form field to another to select it. With an ActiveX control, the user can click in the form field or TAB into it.

Adding an ActiveX control to a form involves four major activities: insert the ActiveX control, format the ActiveX control, set properties of the ActiveX control, and write the macro for the ActiveX control using VBA. Word refers to the time in which you perform these four activities as **design mode**. When you run the form (fill it in) as a user does, by contrast, you are in **run mode**. The following pages explain how to add an ActiveX control to an online form.

Inserting an ActiveX Control

For this form, you would like to insert a command button that the users click when they are finished filling in the form. When they click the button, you want three actions to occur:

1. If the user entered text in the Other text box, then Word places an X in the Other check box (in case the user forgot to place an X in the check box).
2. Word displays the Save As dialog box so the user can assign a file name to the filled-in form.
3. Word displays a thank-you message on the screen.

To insert an ActiveX control, such as a command button, you use the Control Toolbox toolbar. Perform the steps on the next page to insert a command button on the online form.

More About

ActiveX

For more information about ActiveX, visit the Word 2000 More About Web page (www.scsite.com/wd2000/more.htm) and then click ActiveX.

More About

Creating Documents for the Web

For more information about how to create documents to be published on the World Wide Web, visit the Word 2000 More About Web page (www.scsite.com/wd2000/more.htm) and then click Creating Documents for the Web.

To Insert an ActiveX Control

1 **If the Control Toolbox toolbar does not display on the screen already, click View on the menu bar, point to Toolbars, and then click Control Toolbox. Click the paragraph mark at the end of the data entry area and then press the ENTER key. Center the paragraph mark. Position the insertion point on the centered paragraph mark below the data entry area. Point to the Command Button button on the Control Toolbox toolbar (Figure 9-62).**

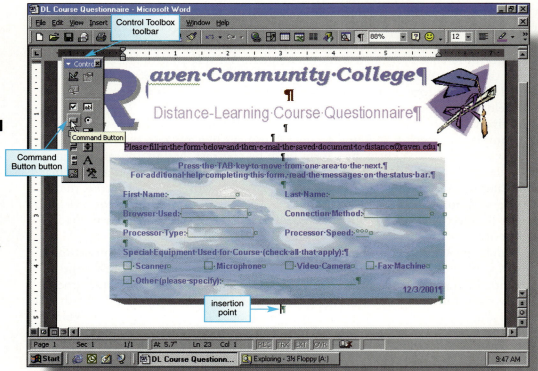

FIGURE 9-62

2 **Click the Command Button button.**

Word inserts a standard-sized command button at the location of the insertion point and switches to design mode (Figure 9-63). The text CommandButton1 partially displays on the face of the button. The button is selected and is surrounded by sizing handles.

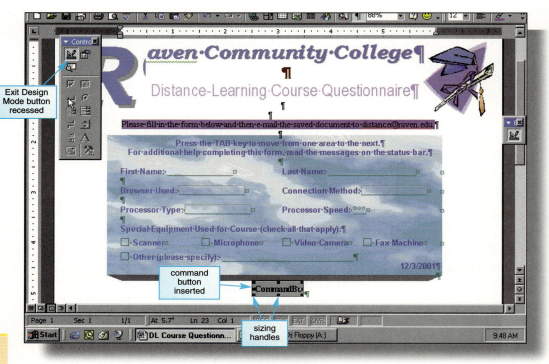

 Other Ways

1. Click Design Mode button on Visual Basic toolbar

FIGURE 9-63

When you click a button on the Control Toolbox toolbar, Word automatically switches to design mode, changes the Design Mode button on the Control Toolbox toolbar to an Exit Design Mode button, and recesses the Exit Design Mode button.

The Control Toolbox toolbar buttons are summarized in Table 9-7.

Table 9-7	Summary of Buttons on the Control Toolbox Toolbar					
BUTTON	**NAME**	**FUNCTION**	**BUTTON**	**NAME**	**FUNCTION**	
	Design Mode	Changes to design mode; Design Mode button changes to Exit Design Mode button when in design mode		Combo Box	Inserts a drop-down list box	
	Properties	Displays Properties window		Toggle Button	Inserts a toggle button	
	View Code	Displays Code window in Visual Basic Editor		Spin Button	Inserts a spin button	
	Check Box	Inserts a check box		Scroll Bar	Inserts a scroll bar	
	Text Box	Inserts a text box		Label	Inserts a label	
	Command Button	Inserts a command button		Image	Inserts an image	
	Option Button	Inserts an option button		More Controls	Displays a list of additional controls	
	List Box	Inserts a list box				

The next step is to format the ActiveX control.

Formatting the ActiveX Control

Word inserts the command button as an inline object; that is, part of the current paragraph. You want the command button to be a floating object so that you can position it anywhere on the form. Thus, perform the following steps to convert the command button from inline to floating.

Steps To Format the ActiveX Control

1 Right-click the command button just inserted and then point to Format Control on the shortcut menu (Figure 9-64).

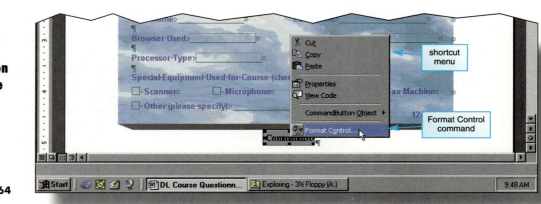

FIGURE 9-64

2 **Click Format Control. When the Format Object dialog box displays, if necessary, click the Layout tab. Click Square in the Wrapping style area. Click Center in the Horizontal alignment area. Point to the OK button.**

Word displays the Format Object dialog box (Figure 9-65). A square wrapping style changes an object to floating.

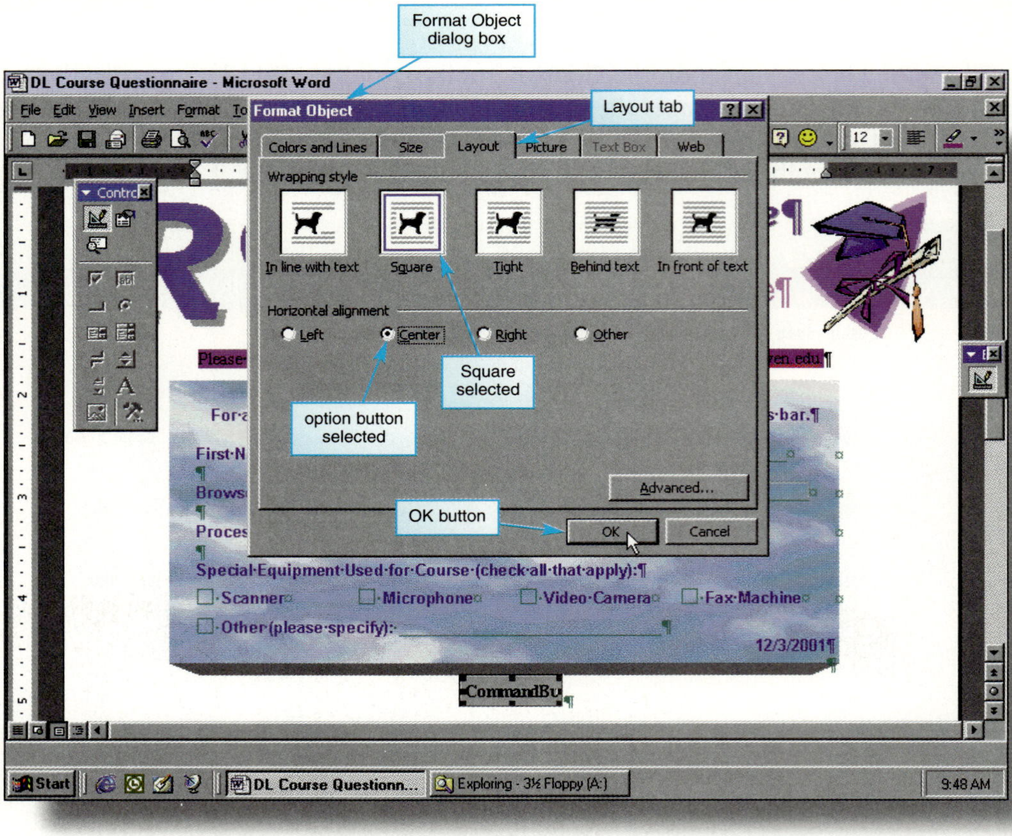

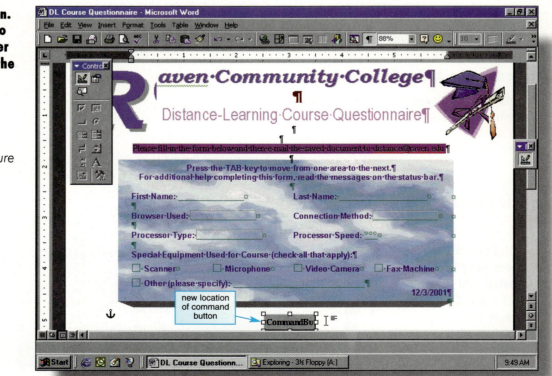

FIGURE 9-65

3 **Click the OK button. Drag the control so there is about one-quarter inch between the top of the command button and the bottom of the data entry area.**

The command button is positioned as shown in Figure 9-66.

FIGURE 9-66

The next step is to set the properties of the ActiveX control.

Setting Properties of an ActiveX Control

In Word, a command button ActiveX control has 20 different **properties** (see Figure 9-68 on the next page), such as caption (the words on the face of the button), background color, foreground color, height, width, font, and so on. After you insert a command button into a form, you can change any one of the 20 properties to improve its appearance and modify its function.

For this command button, you want to change its caption to the text, Click Here When Finished. Perform the following steps to change the Caption property of an ActiveX control.

More *About*

VBA Help

For help with VBA, code statements, and properties, display the Office Assistant and then type VBA help in the What would you like to do? text box. Click the Search button and then click Get Help for Visual Basic for Applications in Word.

 To Set Properties of an ActiveX Control

1 **With the command button selected and Word in design mode, point to the Properties button on the Control Toolbox toolbar (Figure 9-67).**

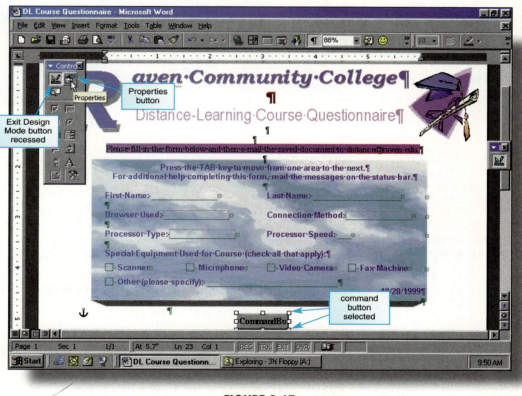

FIGURE 9-67

2 **Click the Properties button. When the Properties window displays, if necessary, click the Alphabetic tab. Click Caption in the list and then type** Click Here When Finished **as the new caption. Point to the Close button on the Properties window.**

Word displays the Properties window for the command button ActiveX control (Figure 9-68). The Caption property is changed.

3 **Click the Close button on the Properties window.**

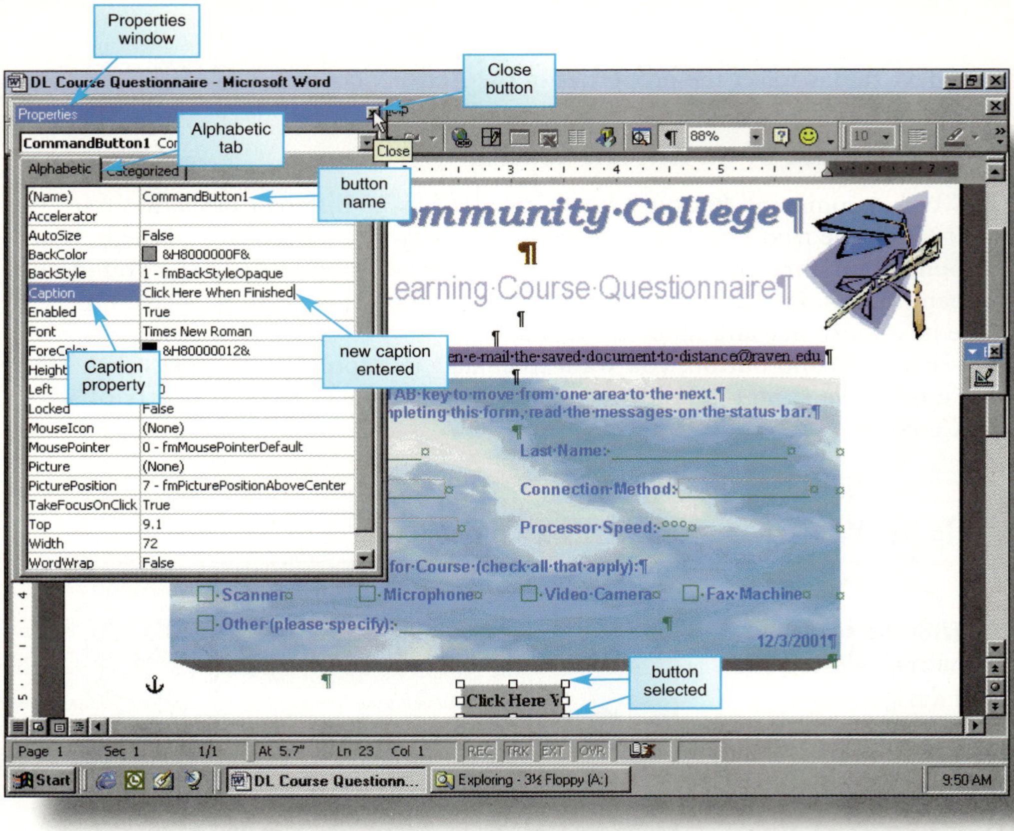

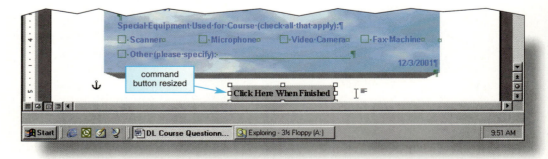

FIGURE 9-68

Other Ways

1. In design mode, right-click control, click Properties on shortcut menu
2. Click Properties Window button on toolbar when Visual Basic Editor is active

The Properties window in Figure 9-68 has two tabs, Alphabetic and Categorized. The Alphabetic sheet displays the properties in alphabetical order. The Categorized sheet displays the properties by subject, such as appearance, behavior, font, and miscellaneous.

The next step is to resize the command button so that the entire caption displays on the face of the button. You resize an ActiveX control the same way you resize any other object – by dragging its sizing handles as described in the following steps.

TO RESIZE AN ACTIVEX CONTROL

1 Drag the right middle sizing handle to the right until the entire caption displays on the face of the command button.

2 If necessary, drag the command button so it is centered on the form.

The command button displays as shown in Figure 9-69.

FIGURE 9-69

The next step is to enter the VBA code that will execute when a user clicks this command button.

Writing the Macro for the ActiveX Control

The next step is to write and then enter the procedure for the macro that will execute when a user clicks the Click Here When Finished button. Clicking the button is the event that triggers execution of the macro.

As mentioned earlier, you should plan a procedure by writing its VBA code on paper similar to that shown in Table 9-8. Then, before entering the procedure into the computer, you desk check it.

Table 9-8   Click Here When Finished Button Procedure

LINE	VBA CODE STATEMENT
1	`Private Sub CommandButton1_Click`
2	`'`
3	`' CommandButton1_Click Macro`
4	`' Executes when user clicks button called Click Here When Finished.`
5	`'`
6	`    ' If user entered text in Other text box, put X in Other check box`
7	`    If Left(ActiveDocument.FormFields("OtherText").Result, 1) <> "_" Then`
8	`        ActiveDocument.FormFields("OtherCheck").CheckBox.Value = True`
9	`    End If`
10	`    ' Display Save As dialog box`
11	`    Dialogs(wdDialogFileSaveAs).Show`
12	`    ' Display thank-you message`
13	`    TitleBarText = "Thank You For Your Time"`
14	`    MessageText = "Please e-mail " & ActiveDocument.FullName & " to distance@raven.edu."`
15	`    MsgBox MessageText, , TitleBarText`
16	`End Sub`

Notice in line 1 that the name of the procedure in the Sub statement is CommandButton1_Click, which Word determines from the name of the button (see Figure 9-68), and the event that causes the procedure to execute (Click).

The first executable code statement is an If…Then statement in line 7. This statement tests if the user entered text in the Other text box, which will have a bookmark of OtherText. If it does, then line 8 instructs Word to place an X in the Other check box, which will have a bookmark of OtherCheck; otherwise, Word skips line 8 and proceeds to line 10.

The next executable code statement is in line 11, which displays the Save As dialog box on the screen – allowing the user to save the form. Finally, line 15 displays a message box that contains two variables. The first is for the message text, which is defined in line 14; and the second is for the title bar text, which is defined in line 13. Because the text for the title bar and message is so long, variables are used to define these elements of the message box.

As illustrated earlier in this project, you use the Visual Basic Editor to enter code statements into a procedure. With Word in design mode and the ActiveX control selected, you can click the View Code button on the Control Toolbox toolbar to display the control's procedure in the Code window of the Visual Basic Editor.

The code statements in lines 7 and 8 use bookmarks that need to be defined. You have learned that you enter a bookmark in the Form Field Options dialog box. Perform the following steps to change the default bookmarks for the Other check box form field and the Other text form field.

TO CHANGE BOOKMARKS FOR FORM FIELDS

1. Double-click the check box form field for Other.

2. When the Check Box Form Field Options dialog box displays, double-click the text in the Bookmark text box and then type `OtherCheck` as the new bookmark. Click the OK button.

3. Double-click the text box form field for Other.

4. When the Text Form Field Options dialog box displays, double-click the text in the Bookmark text box and then type `OtherText` as the new bookmark. Click the OK button.

Word changes form field options as specified in the Form Field Options dialog boxes.

Perform the following steps to enter the code statements for the procedure for the macro that will execute when a user clicks the Click Here When Finished button.

Steps To Enter the Click Here When Finished Button Procedure

1. **With Word in design mode, click the Click Here When Finished button and then point to the View Code button on the Control Toolbox toolbar (Figure 9-70).**

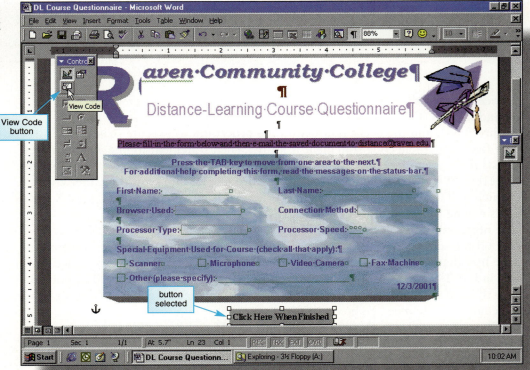

FIGURE 9-70

2 Click the View Code button. When the Visual Basic Editor displays, if the Project Explorer window displays, click its Close button. Double-click the Code window title bar to maximize the window.

Word starts the Visual Basic Editor and displays the Microsoft Visual Basic window (Figure 9-71). The Visual Basic Editor automatically inserts the Sub and End Sub statements and positions the insertion point between the two statements.

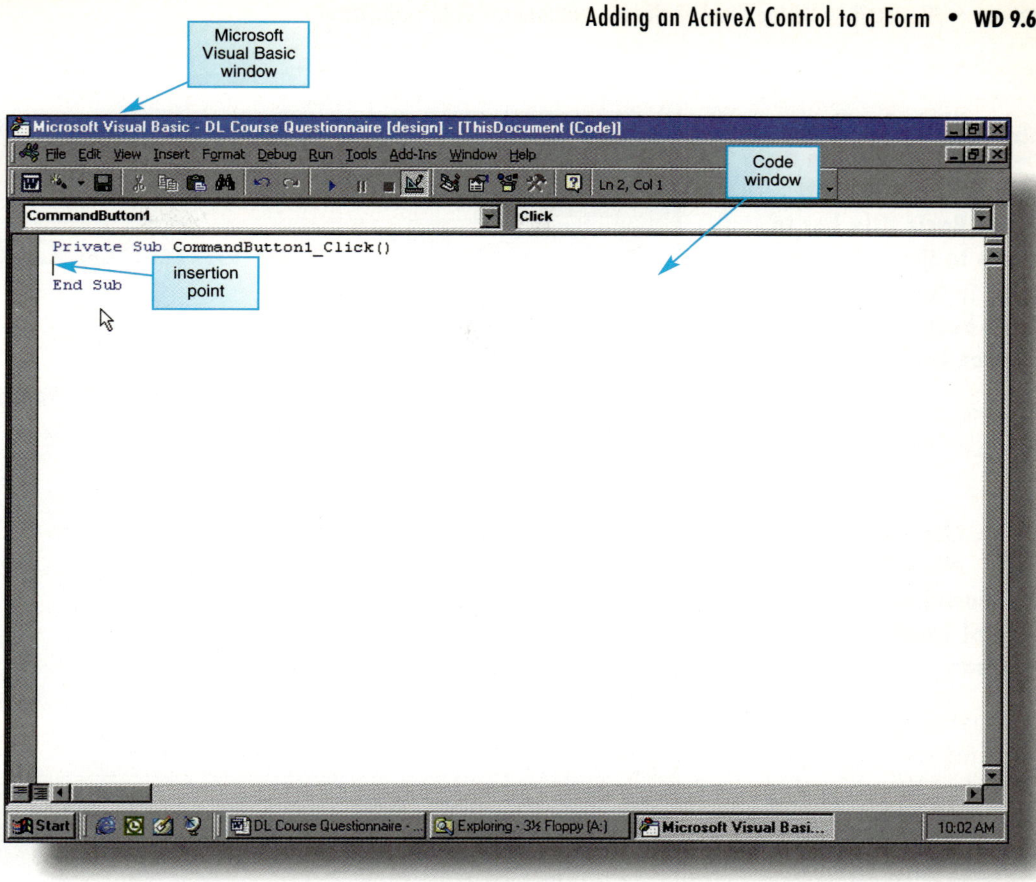
Microsoft Visual Basic window
Microsoft Visual Basic - DL Course Questionnaire [design] - [ThisDocument (Code)]
File Edit View Insert Format Debug Run Tools Add-Ins Window Help
Ln 2, Col 1
Code window
CommandButton1
Click
Private Sub CommandButton1_Click()
insertion point
End Sub
Start
DL Course Questionnaire -...
Exploring - 3½ Floppy (A:)
Microsoft Visual Basi...
10:02 AM

FIGURE 9-71

3 With the insertion point on the blank line between the Sub and End Sub statements in the Code window, type the code statements shown in lines 2 through 15 in Table 9-8 on page WD 9.59. Make sure you enter an apostrophe at the beginning of each comment line. For clarity, indent the code statements as shown in Table 9-8.

The command button procedure is complete (Figure 9-72).

4 Verify your code statements by comparing them to Figure 9-72.

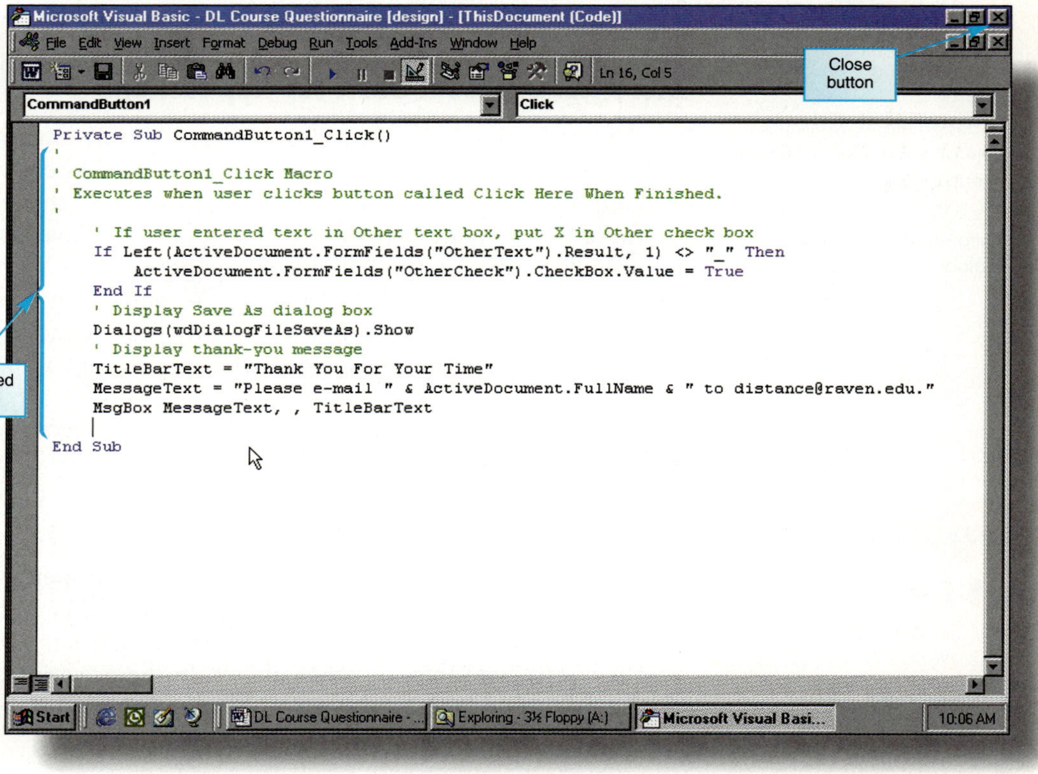
Microsoft Visual Basic - DL Course Questionnaire [design] - [ThisDocument (Code)]
File Edit View Insert Format Debug Run Tools Add-Ins Window Help
Ln 16, Col 5
Close button
CommandButton1
Click
Private Sub CommandButton1_Click()
'
' CommandButton1_Click Macro
' Executes when user clicks button called Click Here When Finished.
'
' If user entered text in Other text box, put X in Other check box
If Left(ActiveDocument.FormFields("OtherText").Result, 1) <> "_" Then
ActiveDocument.FormFields("OtherCheck").CheckBox.Value = True
End If
' Display Save As dialog box
Dialogs(wdDialogFileSaveAs).Show
' Display thank-you message
TitleBarText = "Thank You For Your Time"
MessageText = "Please e-mail " & ActiveDocument.FullName & " to distance@raven.edu."
MsgBox MessageText, , TitleBarText
End Sub
code entered for macro
Start
DL Course Questionnaire -...
Exploring - 3½ Floppy (A:)
Microsoft Visual Basi...
10:06 AM

FIGURE 9-72

5 Click the Close button on the right edge of the Microsoft Visual Basic title bar to return to the online form. Point to the Exit Design Mode button on the Control Toolbox toolbar.

The online form displays as shown in Figure 9-73.

6 Click the Exit Design Mode button. Click the Close button on the Control Toolbox toolbar title bar.

Word returns to run mode, which means if you click the Click Here When Finished button, Word will execute the associated macro.

FIGURE 9-73

Other Ways

1. In design mode, double-click control
2. In design mode, right-click control, click View Code on shortcut menu
3. Click Visual Basic Editor button on Visual Basic toolbar

Web Forms

If you intend to publish a form on the World Wide Web, you should limit ActiveX controls to the standard HTML controls, which include the following: checkbox, dropdown box, textbox, submit, reset, password, option button, list box, text area, submit with image, and hidden.

More About Visual Basic for Applications

Visual Basic for Applications uses many more statements than those presented in this project. These statements, however, should help you understand the basic makeup of a Visual Basic statement. For example, the code statement in line 11 of Table 9-8 on page WD 9.59 that displays the Save As dialog box includes a period. The entry on the left side of the period tells Word which object you want to affect (in this case, the dialog box). An **object** can be a document, a form field, a bookmark, a dialog box, a button, or any other control on a form. The entry on the right side of the period tells Word what you want to do to the object (in this case, display it).

Earlier you were shown how to change an object's properties using the Properties window (Figure 9-68 on page WD 9.58). This code statement from the ProcessorSpeed macro changed an object's property during execution of a procedure:

```
ActiveDocument.ActiveWindow.View.TableGridlines = False
```

This statement changes the TableGridlines property of the View object in the ActiveWindow object in the ActiveDocument object to false; that is, it hides table gridlines. An equal sign in a code statement instructs Word to make an assignment to a property, variable, or other object. In the previous code statement, the TableGridlines property was set to False.

Testing the Online Form

The macros for the DL Course Questionnaire file are complete. The next step is to protect the online form, save it, and then test it.

TO PROTECT THE FORM

 1 Click Tools on the menu bar and then click Protect Document.

2 When the Protect Document dialog box displays, click Forms in the Protect document for area, and then click the OK button.

Word protects the form.

TO SAVE A DOCUMENT

1 Click the Save button on the Standard toolbar.

Word saves the template with the same file name, DL Course Questionnaire.

TO TEST THE FORM

1 Click the Exploring – 3½ Floppy (A:) program button on the taskbar (see Figure 9-73) to display Windows Explorer.

2 Double-click the DL Course Questionnaire icon in the Contents pane to display a new Word document based on the contents of the DL Course Questionnaire. If Word displays a dialog box, click the Enable Macros button. As instructed by the AutoNew macro, the Word document should zoom page width, scroll down seven lines, hide table gridlines, and hide formatting marks (see Figure 9-1a on page WD 9.5).

3 With the highlight in the First Name text box, type LaShonda and then press the TAB key. Type Green in the Last Name text box. Press the TAB key to highlight the Browser Used drop-down list box and display its box arrow.

4 Click the Browser Used box arrow and then click Netscape. Press the TAB key.

5 Click the Connection Method box arrow and then click 33.6 Kbps Modem. Press the TAB key.

6 Click the Processor Type box arrow and then click Pentium III. Press the TAB key.

7 Type abc in the Processor Speed text box. Press the TAB key. As instructed by the ProcessorSpeed macro, an error message should display (see Figure 9-1b on page WD 9.5). Click the OK button in the message box. Type 400 in the Processor Speed text box. Press the TAB key.

8 Click the following check boxes: Microphone and Video Camera.

9 Press the TAB key three times to position the highlight in the Other text box. Type VCR and then click the Click Here When Finished button.

10 As defined by the CommandButton1_Click procedure, Word displays the Save As dialog box. Change the Save in location to drive A. Type Green Form in the File name text box and then click the Save button in the dialog box. When the save is finished, the CommandButton1_Click procedure then displays a thank-you message box that indicates the name and location of the file the user should e-mail back to the college (see Figure 9-1c on page WD 9.5). Click the OK button in the message box. Notice that Word placed an X in the Other check box.

Protecting Forms

If you want only authorized users to be able to unprotect a form, you should password-protect the form. To do this, click Tools on the menu bar, click Protect Document, click Forms in the Protect document for area, type the password in the Password (optional) text box, and then click the OK button. Then, reenter the password in the Confirm Password dialog box.

Printing

If you want to print a form and wish to save ink, print faster, or minimize printer overrun errors, lower the printer resolution. Click File on the menu bar, click Print, click the Properties button in the Print dialog box, click the Graphics tab, click the Resolution box arrow, click a lower resolution than that displayed currently, click the Apply button, click the OK button, and then click the Close button.

Assume you are the person tabulating the form results at the college and just received the Green Form. Click the Form Data Only button on the Standard toolbar, which instructs Word to place a check mark in the Save form data only check box in the Options dialog box. Click File on the menu bar and then click Save Copy As. Type Green Form in the File name text box and then click the Save button to save the document as a text file. Click the Yes button in the dialog box.

You have tested all aspects of the form. If a Word or Visual Basic error message displayed while you tested the form, you need to make necessary corrections and then retest the form. To do this, close the Word window displaying the blank form. Unprotect the template. Make the corrections. Protect the template again. Save the template again. Retest the form. Repeat this procedure until the form displays as intended.

You are finished with the form. Perform the following steps to quit Word and close Windows Explorer.

TO QUIT WORD

1 Click File on the menu bar and then click Exit.

The Word window closes.

TO CLOSE WINDOWS EXPLORER

1 Click the Close button on the Exploring - 3½ Floppy (A:) window's title bar.

Windows Explorer closes.

Copying, Renaming, and Deleting Macros

You may find it necessary to copy a macro, rename a macro, or delete a macro. Macros cannot be copied or renamed from Word; instead, you must use the Visual Basic Editor. You can, however, delete a macro from Word.

TO COPY A MACRO

1 Click Tools on the menu bar, point to Macro, and then click Macros. When the Macros dialog box displays, click the macro name to copy, and then click the Edit button to start the Visual Basic Editor and display the macro in the Code window.

2 Select all the text in the macro's VBA procedure; that is, drag from the Sub statement to the End Sub statement (including the Sub and End Sub statements).

3 Click Edit on the menu bar and then click Copy.

4 Click Edit on the menu bar and then click Paste.

You can paste a macro into the same document or a different document.

TO RENAME A MACRO

1 Click Tools on the menu bar, point to Macro, and then click Macros. When the Macros dialog box displays, click the macro name to rename, and then click the Edit button to start the Visual Basic Editor and display the macro in the Code window.

2 Select the macro name following the keyword Sub at the beginning of the macro's procedure and then type a new macro name.

The macro will be renamed in the Macros dialog box.

TO DELETE A MACRO

1 Click Tools on the menu bar, point to Macro, and then click Macros.

2 When the Macros dialog box displays, click the macro name to delete, and then click the Delete button.

3 Click the Yes button in the Microsoft Word dialog box.

CASE PERSPECTIVE SUMMARY

Before showing the modified DL Course Questionnaire to your supervisor, you decide to have two of your co-workers test it to be sure it works properly. They find one error. You unprotect the template, fix the error, protect the form again, and then test it one final time, just to be sure the error is fixed. Then, you e-mail the DL Course Questionnaire to your supervisor for her review. She is quite pleased with the results. Realizing the power of Visual Basic for Applications with Word, she asks you to train three members of her staff on how to create VBA procedures in Word.

Project Summary

Project 9 introduced you to working with macros and Visual Basic for Applications (VBA). You modified the template for the online form created in Project 8. To change its appearance, you formatted a letter as an in margin drop cap, changed the text by creating and applying a new style, filled the drawing object with a bitmap picture, and then added a 3-D effect to the drawing object. Then, you created a macro using the macro recorder and assigned the macro to a toolbar button. Next, you recorded an automatic macro. You viewed the macro's code using the Visual Basic Editor and added comments and code statements to the macro. You create another macro that executed when the user exits a form field. Finally, you inserted an ActiveX control, formatted it, set its properties, and wrote a VBA procedure for it.

Quick Reference

For a table that lists how to complete the tasks covered in this book using the mouse, menu, shortcut menu, and keyboard, see the Word Quick Reference Summary at the back of this book or visit the Shelly Cashman Series Office Web page (www.scsite.com/off2000/qr.htm) and then click Microsoft Word 2000.

What You Should Know

Having completed this project, you should now be able to perform the following tasks:

▶ Add a 3-D Effect *(WD 9.24)*

▶ Add Code Statements to a Procedure *(WD 9.45)*

▶ Add Comments to a Procedure *(WD 9.42)*

▶ Apply a Style Using a Shortcut Key *(WD 9.20)*

▶ Change a Bookmark for a Drop-Down Form Field *(WD 9.47)*

▶ Change a Highlight Color *(WD 9.15)*

▶ Change Bookmarks for Form Fields *(WD 9.60)*

▶ Change Graphics *(WD 9.12)*

▶ Change Options for a Text Form Field *(WD 9.46)*

▶ Close the Visual Basic Editor *(WD 9.45)*

▶ Close Windows Explorer *(WD 9.64)*

▶ Copy a Macro *(WD 9.64)*

▶ Create a Style that has a Shortcut Key *(WD 9.17)*

▶ Create an Automatic Macro *(WD 9.35)*

▶ Customize a Toolbar *(WD 9.30)*

▶ Delete a Macro *(WD 9.65)*

▶ Display Formatting Marks *(WD 9.9)*

▶ Enter the Click Here When Finished Button Procedure *(WD 9.60)*

▶ Enter the ProcessorSpeed Procedure *(WD 9.51)*

▶ Fill a Drawing Object with a Bitmap Picture *(WD 9.22)*

▶ Format a Character as an In Margin Drop Cap *(WD 9.14)*

▶ Format the ActiveX Control *(WD 9.55)*

▶ Insert a Visual Basic Procedure *(WD 9.48)*

▶ Insert an ActiveX Control *(WD 9.54)*

▶ Modify Existing Code *(WD 9.44)*

▶ Modify Text *(WD 9.12)*

▶ Protect the Form *(WD 9.63)*

▶ Quit Word *(WD 9.64)*

▶ Record a Macro *(WD 9.26)*

▶ Rename a Macro *(WD 9.65)*

▶ Reset Menus and Toolbars *(WD 9.8)*

▶ Resize an ActiveX Control *(WD 9.58)*

▶ Run a Macro *(WD 9.29)*

▶ Run a Macro When a User Exits a Form Field *(WD 9.52)*

▶ Save a Document *(WD 9.25, WD 9.63)*

▶ Save the Document with a New File Name *(WD 9.7)*

▶ Set a Security Level in Word *(WD 9.10)*

▶ Set Properties of an ActiveX Control *(WD 9.57)*

▶ Start Word and Open an Office Document *(WD 9.7)*

▶ Test the AutoNew Macro *(WD 9.38)*

▶ Test the Form *(WD 9.63)*

▶ Uncheck the Save Data Only for Forms Check Box *(WD 9.30, WD 9.34)*

▶ Unprotect a Document *(WD 9.8)*

▶ View a Macro's VBA Code *(WD 9.39)*

▶ Zoom Page Width *(WD 9.9)*

Apply Your Knowledge

Project Reinforcement at www.scsite.com/off2000/reinforce.htm

1 Debugging VBA Code

Instructions: In this assignment, you access a template through Windows Explorer. As shown in Figure 9-74, the template contains an online form. The form contains two macros: one that executes when you initially display the form on the screen and another that executes when you click the command button at the bottom of the screen. Each macro contains one coding error. You are to test the code by filling in the form. Then, correct the Visual Basic errors as they display on the screen.

The template is located on the Data Disk. If you did not download the Data Disk, see the inside back cover for instructions for downloading the Data Disk or see your instructor.

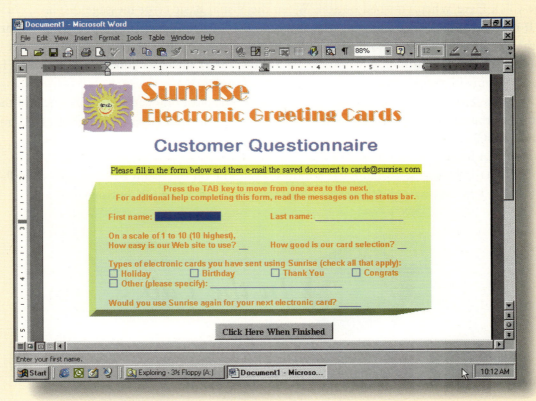

FIGURE 9-74

Perform the following tasks:

1. Right-click the My Computer icon on the Windows desktop and then click Explore on the shortcut menu. When the Exploring window displays, click the Address text box to select it. With the Data Disk in drive A, type a: and then press the ENTER key. Double-click the SG Questionnaire icon in the contents pane to display a new document based on the SG Questionnaire template.

2. When Word displays a dialog box about macros, click the Enable Macros button.

3. When a Visual Basic error message displays, click its OK button. If necessary, maximize the Visual Basic window. Notice the text, .TableGrdlines =, is highlighted because Visual Basic did not recognize it. The text should say, .TableGridlines = (it is missing the letter i). Click the selected text and insert the letter i between the letters r and d in Gridlines. Then, click the Continue button on the Visual Basic Standard toolbar. Close the Visual Basic window by clicking its Close button.

(continued)

Apply Your Knowledge

✚ **Project Reinforcement at www.scsite.com/off2000/reinforce.htm**

Debugging VBA Code *(continued)*

4. With the highlight in the First name text box, type `Mario` and then press the TAB key.
5. With the highlight in the Last name text box, type `Hernandez` and then press the TAB key.
6. Type 10 in response to How easy is our Web site to use? Press the TAB key.
7. Type 8 in response to How good is our card selection? Press the TAB key.
8. Place an X in the Holiday and Birthday check boxes by clicking them. Press the TAB key five times.
9. With the highlight on the drop-down list box at the bottom of the form, click the box arrow and then click Yes.
10. Click the Click Here When Finished button. When the Visual Basic error message displays, click the Debug button. If necessary, click the Microsoft Visual Basic - SG Questionnaire program button on the taskbar to display the Visual Basic Editor. Notice the code statement that displays the Save As dialog box is highlighted as an error. The word Show is misspelled as Shw. Insert the letter o between the letters h and w. Click the Continue button on the Visual Basic Standard toolbar.
11. Type `Hernandez Form` in the Save As dialog box, change the Save in location to drive A, and then click the Save button in the Save As dialog box. When Word asks if you want to save changes to the template, click the No button. Click the OK button in the Thank You message box.
12. Print the filled-in form.
13. Press the ALT+F11 keys. In the Visual Basic window, click File on the menu bar and then click Print. When the Print dialog box displays, click Current Project and then click the OK button.

In the Lab

1 Creating an Automatic Macro for an Online Form

Problem: You created the online form shown in Figure 8-69 on page WD 8.60 for The Web Grocer. Your supervisor has asked you to change its appearance and create a macro for the form so it displays properly on the screen when a user first displays it (as a blank form). You modify the form so it looks like the one shown in Figure 9-75.

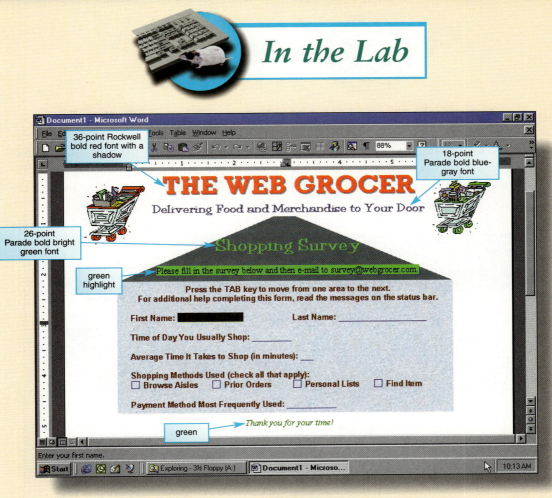

FIGURE 9-75

Instructions:

1. Open the template called Web Grocer Survey that you created in Lab 1 of Project 8 on page WD 8.60. Save the survey with a new file name of WG Survey.

2. Modify the formats of the company name, slogan, form title, form instructions, and thank-you message as shown in Figure 9-75. Remove the current clip art and insert the ones shown in Figure 9-75. Resize the clip art images to 60 percent of their original size.

3. Change the fill effect in the rectangle drawing object to the Blue tissue paper texture. Add the 3-D effect called 3-D Style 20.

4. Create a new character style called DataEntryArea that is formatted to an 11-point Arial bold brown font that has a shortcut key of ALT+D. Apply the style to all text in the data entry area.

5. Create an automatic macro called AutoNew using the macro recorder. The macro should change the zoom percentage to page width and scroll down so the entire form fits in the document window. Test the macro.

6. Modify the macro in the Visual Basic Editor so that it also hides formatting marks and table gridlines. Also, modify the number of lines it scrolls down, if necessary. Test the macro again.

7. Print the Visual Basic code for the macro (in the Visual Basic Editor, click File on the menu bar, click Print, click Current project, click the OK button).

8. Protect the form. Save the form. Print the blank form.

9. Access the template through Windows Explorer. Fill out the form. Save the filled-out form. Print the filled-out form.

In the Lab

2 Creating an Automatic Macro and ActiveX Control for an Online Form

Problem: You created the online form shown in Figure 8-70 on page WD 8.61 for Lincoln State Bank. Your supervisor has asked you to change its appearance, create a macro for the form so it displays properly on the screen when a user first displays it (as a blank form), and add a button that automatically displays the Save As dialog box for the user. You modify the form so it looks like the one shown in Figure 9-76.

FIGURE 9-76

Instructions:

1. Open the template called Lincoln Bank Survey that you created in Lab 2 of Project 8 on page WD 8.61. Save the survey with a new file name of LB Survey.

2. Modify the formats of the company name, form title, and form instructions as shown in Figure 9-76. Remove the current clip art and insert the one shown in Figure 9-76. Resize the clip art image to 30 percent of its original size. Left-align the company name and then format the first letter of the company name as an in margin drop cap. Change its font size to 94 and reposition it if necessary.

3. Change the fill effect in the rectangle drawing object to the bitmap file called Backgrnd. It is located with the Windows wallpaper bitmap files and also is on the Data Disk. Add the 3-D effect called 3-D Style 19.

4. Create a new character style called DataEntryArea that is formatted to an 11-point Arial bold indigo font that has a shortcut key of ALT+D. Apply the style to all text in the data entry area.

5. Create an automatic macro called AutoNew using the macro recorder. The macro should change the zoom percentage to page width and scroll down so the entire form fits in the document window. Test the macro.

In the Lab

6. Modify the macro in the Visual Basic Editor so that it also hides formatting marks and table gridlines. Also, modify the number of lines it scrolls down, if necessary. Test the macro again.

7. Remove the thank-you message line. Insert a command button ActiveX control. Format the command button as a floating object. Change its caption property to the text, Click Here When Finished. Change its Font property to 12-point Times New Roman bold font. Resize the button so the entire caption displays. Add code to the button so that when the user clicks the button it displays the Save As dialog box and displays a thank-you message.

8. Print the Visual Basic code for the macros (in the Visual Basic Editor, click File on the menu bar, click Print, click Current project, click the OK button).

9. Protect the form. Save the form. Print the blank form.

10. Access the template through Windows Explorer. Fill out the form. Save the filled-out form. Print the filled-out form.

3 Creating an Automatic Macro, Data Entry Macros, and ActiveX Control for an Online Form

Problem: You created the online form shown in Figure 8-71 on page WD 8.62 for World Cablevision. Your supervisor has asked you to change its appearance, create a macro for the form so it displays properly on the screen when a user first displays it (as a blank form), create a macro for each of the number of viewers text form fields, add a button that automatically displays the Save As dialog box for the user, and create a macro and corresponding button on the toolbar that places a check mark in the Save form data only check box. You modify the form so it looks like the one shown in Figure 9-77.

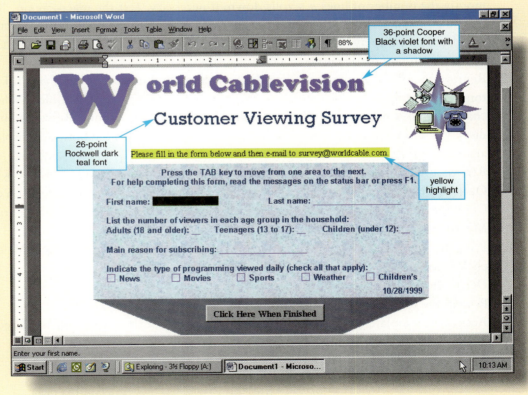

FIGURE 9-77

(continued)

In the Lab

Creating an Automatic Macro, Data Entry Macros, and ActiveX Control for an Online Form *(continued)*

Instructions:

1. Open the template called World Cablevision Survey that you created in Lab 3 of Project 8 on page WD 8.62. Save the survey with a new file name of WC Survey.

2. Modify the formats of the company name, form title, and form instructions as shown in Figure 9-77 on the previous page. Remove the current clip art and insert the one shown in Figure 9-77. Left-align the company name and then format the first letter of the company name as an in margin drop cap. Change its font size to 105 and reposition it if necessary.

3. Change the fill effect in the rectangle drawing object to the Bouquet texture. Add the 3-D effect called 3-D Style 15.

4. Create a new character style called DataEntryArea that is formatted to an 11-point Arial bold dark teal font that has a shortcut key of ALT+D. Apply the style to all text in the data entry area.

5. Create an automatic macro called AutoNew using the macro recorder. The macro should change the zoom percentage to page width and scroll down so the entire form fits in the document window. Test the macro.

6. Modify the macro in the Visual Basic Editor so that it also hides formatting marks and table gridlines. Also, modify the number of lines it scrolls down, if necessary. Test the macro again.

7. Create a macro for each of the three number of viewers text boxes on the screen (Adults, Teenagers, and Children) that displays an error message when the user exits each text box if the user leaves the entry blank or enters a nonnumeric entry.

8. Remove the thank-you message line. Insert a command button ActiveX control. Format the command button as a floating object. Change its caption property to the text, Click Here When Finished. If necessary, change its Font property to 12-point Times New Roman bold font. Resize the button so the entire caption displays. Add code to the button so that when the user clicks the button it displays the Save As dialog box and displays a thank-you message.

9. Record a macro that places a check mark in the Save data only for forms check box in the Save tab of the Options dialog box. Create a toolbar button for this macro; use the image of a coffee cup for the button.

10. Copy the AutoNew macro to a macro called TestMacro. Change the TestMacro name to the name MacroTest.

11. Print the Visual Basic code for the macros (in the Visual Basic Editor, click File on the menu bar, click Print, click Current project, click the OK button).

12. Delete the macro called MacroTest.

13. Protect the form. Save the form. Print the blank form.

14. Access the template through Windows Explorer. Fill out the form. Save the filled-out form. Print the filled-out form.

Cases and Places

The difficulty of these case studies varies:
▶ are the least difficult; ▶▶ are more difficult; and ▶▶▶ are the most difficult.

1 ▶ You created the online form for World Travel that was defined in Cases and Places Assignment 1 in Project 8 on page WD 8.63. Your supervisor has asked you to change its appearance; that is, change its fonts, font sizes, fill effects, colors, and clip art, and use a drop cap in the company name. He also asked that the form include the following:

1. When the form initially displays on the screen (as a blank document), Word zooms page width, scrolls down to display the entire form in the Word window, hides formatting marks, and hides gridlines.
2. If the user leaves the text boxes containing entries for the number of adult passengers or the number of child passengers blank or enters a nonnumeric entry, an error message should display.
3. The form should contain a Click Here When Finished button that when clicked does the following:
   a. If the user entered text in the Other text box, then Word places an X in the Other check box (just in case the user left it blank).
   b. The Save As dialog box displays so the user can assign a file name to the filled-in form.
   c. A thank-you message displays on the screen that informs the user what file should be e-mailed back to the school.

Use the concepts and techniques presented in this project to create and format this announcement.

2 ▶▶ You created the questionnaire for the Student Government Association at your school that was defined in Cases and Places Assignment 2 in Project 8 on page WD 8.63. The president of the Student Government Association has asked you to change the questionnaire's appearance (all fonts, font sizes, colors, graphics, and fill effects), create a macro for the form so it displays properly on the screen when a user first displays it (as a blank form), and add a button that when clicked automatically displays the Save As dialog box for the user and then displays a thank-you message. Use the concepts and techniques presented in this project to modify the online form. Be sure to use a different graphic from the Clip Gallery.

3 ▶▶ You created the questionnaire for your school's fitness center that was defined in Cases and Places Assignment 3 in Project 8 on page WD 8.63. The director of the fitness center has asked you to change the questionnaire's appearance (all fonts, font sizes, colors, graphics, and fill effects), create a macro for the form so it displays properly on the screen when a user first displays it (as a blank form), and add a button that when clicked automatically displays the Save As dialog box for the user and then displays a thank-you message. Use the concepts and techniques presented in this project to modify the online form. Be sure to use a different graphic from the Clip Gallery.

Cases and Places

4 ▶▶ You created the questionnaire for the computing center at your school that was defined in Cases and Places Assignment 4 in Project 8 on page WD 8.64. The director of the computing center has asked you to change the questionnaire's appearance (all fonts, font sizes, colors, graphics, and fill effects), create a macro for the form so it displays properly on the screen when a user first displays it (as a blank form), and add a button that when clicked automatically displays the Save As dialog box for the user and then displays a thank-you message. Use the concepts and techniques presented in this project to modify the online form. Be sure to use a different graphic from the Clip Gallery.

5 ▶▶▶ Your supervisor at Raven Community College would like to publish the Distance-Learning Course Questionnaire (Figure 9-1 on page WD 9.5) on the Web. Thus, all of the form fields must be changed to ActiveX controls; that is, you have to delete the Word form fields and insert similar ActiveX controls. Also, she would like every text box and drop-down list box to display an error message if the user leaves the entry blank, which means you will write a VBA procedure for each of the objects. Use the concepts and techniques presented in this project to modify the online form.

6 ▶▶▶ Your supervisor at Sunrise Electronic Greeting Cards would like to publish the Customer Questionnaire (Figure 9-74 on page WD 9.67) on the Web. Thus, all of the form fields must be changed to ActiveX controls; that is, you have to delete the Word form fields and insert similar ActiveX controls. Also, he would like every text box and drop-down list box to display an error message if the user leaves the entry blank, which means you will write a VBA procedure for each of the objects. Use the concepts and techniques presented in this project to modify the online form.

Microsoft Word 2000

Linking an Excel Worksheet and Charting Its Data in Word

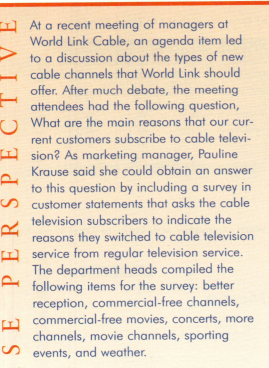

C A S E P E R S P E C T I V E

At a recent meeting of managers at World Link Cable, an agenda item led to a discussion about the types of new cable channels that World Link should offer. After much debate, the meeting attendees had the following question, What are the main reasons that our current customers subscribe to cable television? As marketing manager, Pauline Krause said she could obtain an answer to this question by including a survey in customer statements that asks the cable television subscribers to indicate the reasons they switched to cable television service from regular television service. The department heads compiled the following items for the survey: better reception, commercial-free channels, commercial-free movies, concerts, more channels, movie channels, sporting events, and weather.

One month later, Pauline received the completed surveys. Having tabulated the results in the form of an Excel worksheet, she would like to communicate these results to the department managers at World Link Cable. As her assistant, Pauline has asked you to create a memo that links the Excel worksheet to the memo. She also would like a chart of the Excel worksheet to portray the survey results graphically.

Introduction

With Microsoft Office 2000 products, you can insert part or all of a document, called an **object**, created in one application into a document created in another application. For example, you could insert an Excel worksheet into a Word document. In this case, the Excel worksheet (the object) is called the **source document** (inserted from) and the Word document is called the **destination document** (inserted into). You can use one of three techniques to insert objects from one application to another: copy and paste, embed, or link.

When you copy an object by clicking the Copy button on the Standard toolbar and then paste it by clicking the Paste button on the Standard toolbar, the source document becomes part of the destination document. You edit a pasted object using editing features of the destination application. For example, an Excel worksheet would become a Word table that you can edit in Word.

Similarly, an embedded object becomes part of a destination document. The difference between an embedded object and a pasted object is that you edit the contents of an embedded object using the editing features of the source application. For example, an embedded Excel worksheet remains as an Excel worksheet in the Word document. To edit the worksheet in the Word document, you double-click the worksheet to display Excel menus and toolbars in the Word window. If, however, you edit the Excel worksheet by opening the worksheet from within Excel, the embedded object will not be updated in the Word document.

A linked object, by contrast, does not become part of the destination document even though it appears to be part of it. Rather, a connection is established between the source and destination documents so that when you open the destination document, the linked object displays as part of it. When you edit a linked object, the source application starts and opens the source

Office 2000

For more information on the features of Microsoft Office 2000, visit the Word 2000 More About Web page (www.scsite.com/wd2000/more.htm) and then click Microsoft Office 2000 Features.

document that contains the linked object. For example, a linked Excel worksheet remains as an Excel worksheet. To edit the worksheet from the Word document, you double-click the worksheet to start Excel and display the worksheet in an Excel window. Unlike an embedded object, if you edit the Excel worksheet by opening it from Excel, the linked object will be updated in the Word document, too.

You would use the link method when the contents of an object are likely to change and you want to ensure that the most current version of the object displays in the source document. Another reason to link an object is if the object is large, such as a video clip or a sound clip.

As shown in Figure 1, this integration feature links an Excel worksheet to a Word document (a memo) and then links the Excel worksheet data to a Word chart. That is, the Excel worksheet is inserted into the Word document in the form of an Excel worksheet. Word also uses the data in the Excel worksheet to chart the worksheet data. Because the data is inserted into the Word document as a link, any time you open the memo in Word, the latest version of the Excel worksheet data displays in the memo. Figure 1a shows the memo draft (without any links to Excel); Figure 1b shows the Excel worksheet; and Figure 1c shows the final copy of the memo with links to the Excel worksheet and its data.

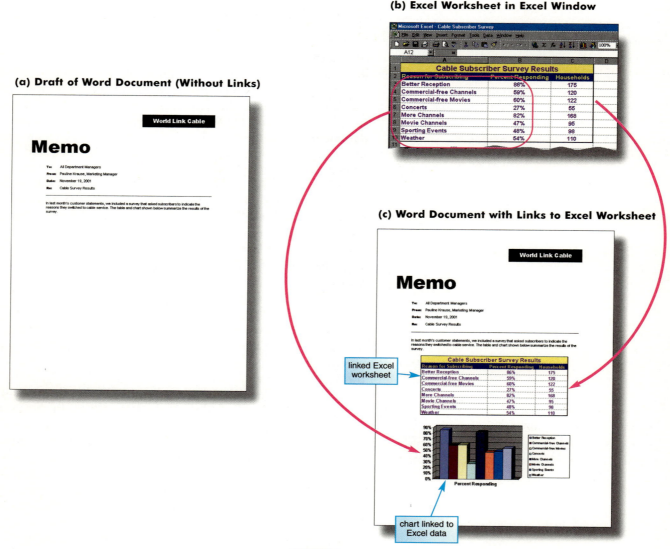

FIGURE 1

Starting Word and Opening a Document

The first step in this integration feature is to open the draft of the memo that is to include the linked worksheet data. The memo file named Cable Survey Memo Draft is located on the Data Disk. If you did not download the Data Disk, see the inside back cover for instructions for downloading the Data Disk or see your instructor. Perform the following steps to open the memo.

TO OPEN A DOCUMENT

1 If necessary, insert the Data Disk in drive A. Click the Start button on the taskbar and then click Open Office Document.

2 When the Open Office Document dialog box displays, if necessary, click the Look in box arrow and then click 3½ Floppy (A:). Double-click the file named Cable Survey Memo Draft.

3 When the Word window displays, if necessary, maximize it. Reset toolbars as described in Appendix C.

4 Click View on the menu bar and then click Print Layout. If the Show/Hide ¶ button on the Standard toolbar is not recessed, click it.

Word becomes active, opens the Cable Survey Memo Draft file, and displays it in the Word window.

Saving the Document with a New File Name

To preserve the contents of the original Cable Survey Memo Draft file, save a copy of it with a new file name as described in the following steps.

TO SAVE A DOCUMENT

1 With a floppy disk in drive A, click File on the menu bar and then click Save As.

2 Type `Cable Survey Memo` in the File name text box. Do not press the ENTER key.

3 If necessary, click the Save in box arrow and then click 3½ Floppy (A:).

4 Click the Save button in the Save As dialog box.

Word saves the document on a floppy disk in drive A with a new file name of Cable Survey Memo.

Linking an Excel Worksheet

The next step in this integration feature is to insert the Excel worksheet (source document) into the Cable Survey Memo (destination document) as a linked object. The Excel worksheet (Cable Subscriber Survey) is located on the Data Disk. Perform the steps on the next page to link the Excel worksheet to the Word document.

More About

Excel Worksheets

To insert a blank Excel worksheet into a Word document, click the Insert Microsoft Excel Worksheet button on the Standard toolbar and then click the grid at the location that represents the number of rows and columns to be in the worksheet. The menus and toolbars change to Excel menus and toolbars. To redisplay Word menus and toolbars, click outside the Excel worksheet in the Word document.

Steps **To Link an Excel Worksheet to a Word Document**

1 **Position the insertion point on the paragraph mark at the end of the memo (below the paragraph of text). Click Insert on the menu bar and then point to Object (Figure 2).**

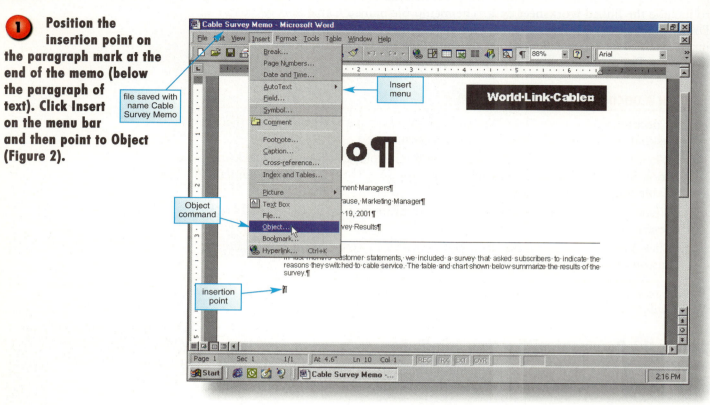

FIGURE 2

2 **Click Object. When the Object dialog box displays, if necessary, click the Create from File tab. With the Data Disk in drive A, click the Browse button. When the Browse dialog box displays, locate the Excel file called Cable Subscriber Survey on the Data Disk. Click Cable Subscriber Survey in the list and then point to the Insert button in the Browse dialog box.**

Word displays the Object dialog box and then the Browse dialog box (Figure 3).

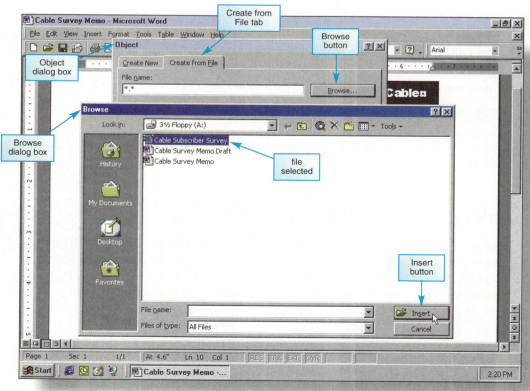

FIGURE 3

3 **Click the Insert button. When the Browse dialog box closes and the entire Object dialog box is visible again, place a check mark in the Link to file check box and then point to the OK button.**

The Object dialog box displays the name of the selected file in the File name text box (Figure 4). The .xls following the file name, Cable Subscriber Survey, identifies the file as an Excel worksheet.

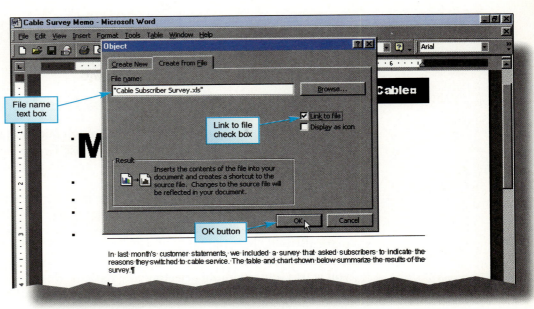

File name text box

Link to file check box

OK button

FIGURE 4

4 **Click the OK button. Double-click the move handle on the Formatting toolbar to display the entire toolbar. Click the Center button on the Formatting toolbar.**

Word inserts the Excel worksheet as a linked object at the location of the insertion point (Figure 5). The object is centered between the document margins.

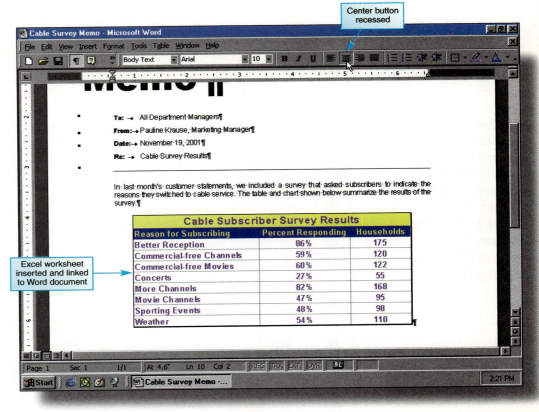

Center button recessed

Excel worksheet inserted and linked to Word document

FIGURE 5

The Excel worksheet now is linked to the Word document. If you save the Word document and reopen it, the worksheet will display just as it does in Figure 5. If you wanted to delete the worksheet, you would select it and then press the DELETE key.

Other Ways

1. Copy object in source application to Office Clipboard; in destination application, on Edit menu click Paste Special, click Paste link, click Microsoft Excel Worksheet Object, click OK button

If you wanted to embed an Excel worksheet instead of link it, you would not place a check mark in the Link to file check box in the Object dialog box (see Figure 4 on the previous page).

Creating a Chart from an Excel Worksheet

You easily can use Word to chart data through **Microsoft Graph 2000**, a charting application that is embedded in Word. Because Graph is an embedded application, it has its own menus and commands. With these commands, you can modify the appearance of the chart.

Graph can chart data in a Word table or it can chart data from another Office application, such as Excel. If you want Graph to chart data that is in a Word table, you should select the data to be charted prior to starting Graph, and Graph automatically will chart the selected data.

When you want Graph to chart data from another application, such as Excel, you start Graph without selecting any data. In this case, Graph creates a sample chart with sample data. Then, you either can copy and paste or link the data from another application to the sample chart.

In this integration feature, you want to link the Excel data to the chart in the Word document. Thus, you will start Graph and it will create a sample chart. Then, you will link the Excel data to the chart. Perform the following steps to start Graph.

Steps To Create a Chart

1 **Position the insertion point on the paragraph mark to the right of the Excel worksheet in the Word document and then press the ENTER key. Click Insert on the menu bar, point to Picture, and then point to Chart (Figure 6).**

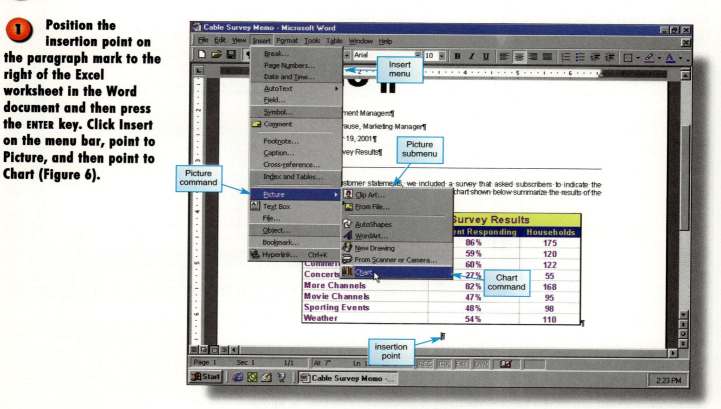

FIGURE 6

2 **Click Chart. If your screen does not display a Datasheet window, click the View Datasheet button on the Standard toolbar.**

Word starts the Microsoft Graph 2000 application (Figure 7). Graph creates a sample chart at the location of the insertion point and displays sample data in the Datasheet window.

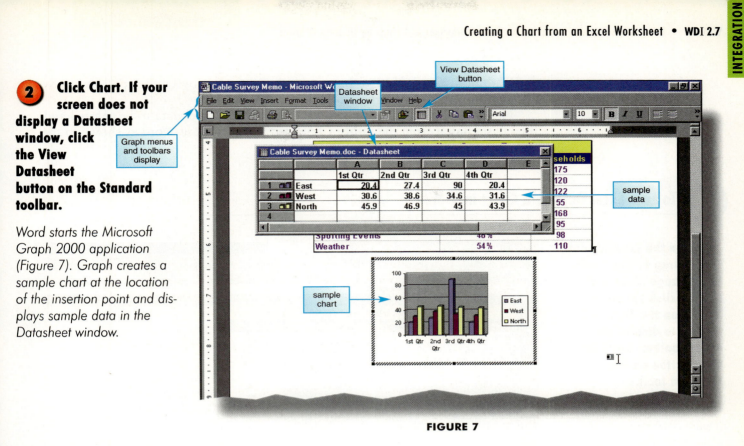

FIGURE 7

The menus on the menu bar and buttons on the toolbars change to Graph menus and toolbars. That is, the Graph program is running inside the Word program.

You can copy and paste data from an Excel worksheet into the sample chart or you can link the Excel data to the sample chart. In this integration feature, you will link the data to the chart. To link the data, you start Excel and display the workbook containing the worksheet data to be linked, copy the data in the worksheet to the Office Clipboard, and then use Word's Paste Link command to link the data on the Clipboard into the Word document.

Thus, the first step in linking the data from the Excel worksheet to the Word chart is to open the Excel workbook that contains the worksheet data to be charted. The Excel workbook that contains the data to be linked to the chart is the Cable Subscriber Survey, which is located on the Data Disk. Perform the following steps to start Excel and open this workbook.

TO START EXCEL AND OPEN AN EXCEL DOCUMENT

1 If necessary, insert the Data Disk into drive A. Click the Start button on the taskbar and then click Open Office Document.

2 When the Open Office Document dialog box displays, if necessary, click the Look in box arrow and then click 3½ Floppy (A:). Double-click the Excel file named Cable Subscriber Survey.

3 When the Excel window displays, if necessary, double-click its title bar to maximize the Excel window.

4 Reset Excel toolbars as described in Appendix C.

Excel starts and displays the Cable Subscriber Survey in the Excel window (see Figure 8 on the next page).

More About 2000

Starting Excel

If a Word document that displays on the screen contains a linked Excel worksheet, you also can start Excel by double-clicking the Excel worksheet in the Word document. For example, if you double-click the Cable Subscriber Survey worksheet in the Word document, Excel starts and then displays the Excel worksheet in an Excel window.

With both Word and Excel open, you can switch between the applications by clicking the appropriate program button on the taskbar.

Next, you will copy to the Office Clipboard the Excel data to be charted and then paste link it from the Office Clipboard to the chart in Word as shown in the following steps.

Steps: To Link Excel Data to a Chart in Word

1 **In the Excel window, drag through cells in the range of A3:B10. Double-click the move handle on the Standard toolbar to display the entire toolbar. Click the Copy button on the Standard toolbar.**

The Excel window is active (Figure 8). A marquee displays around the range A3:B10, which has been copied to the Office Clipboard.

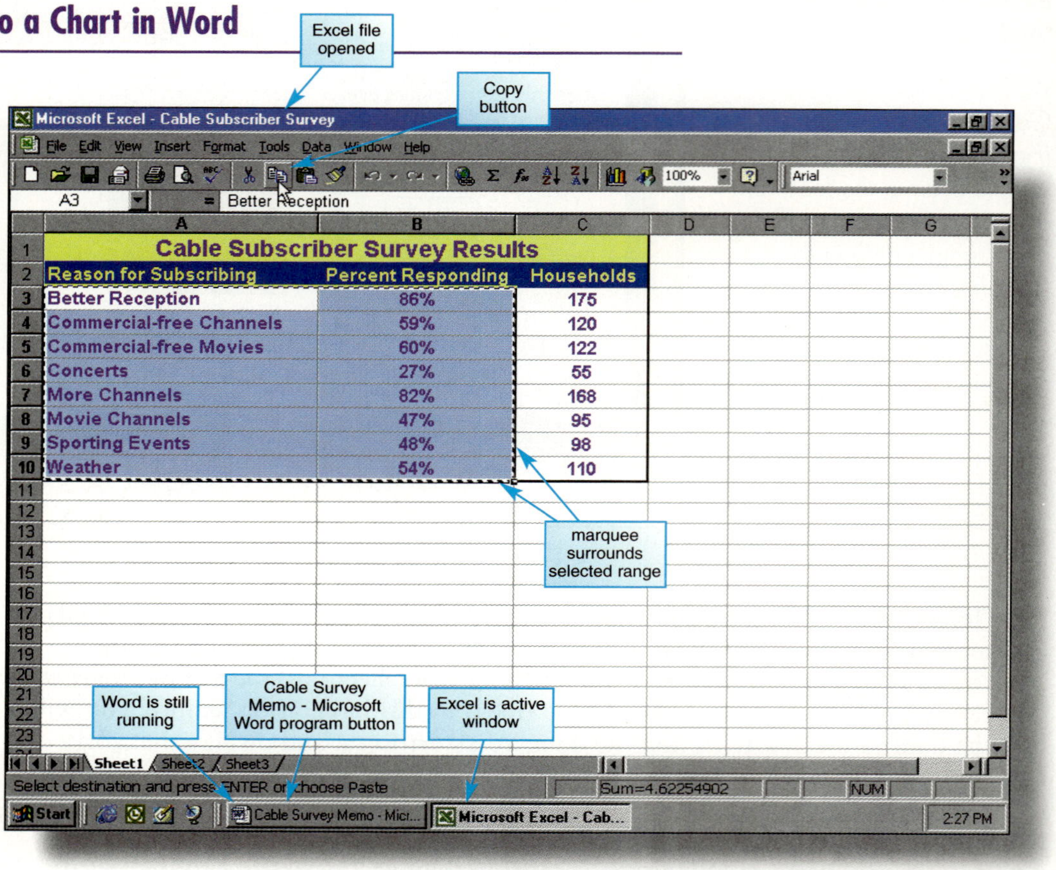

FIGURE 8

2 Click the Cable Survey Memo - Microsoft Word program button on the taskbar. Click anywhere in the Datasheet window. Click Edit on the menu bar and then point to Paste Link.

The Word window is active (Figure 9).

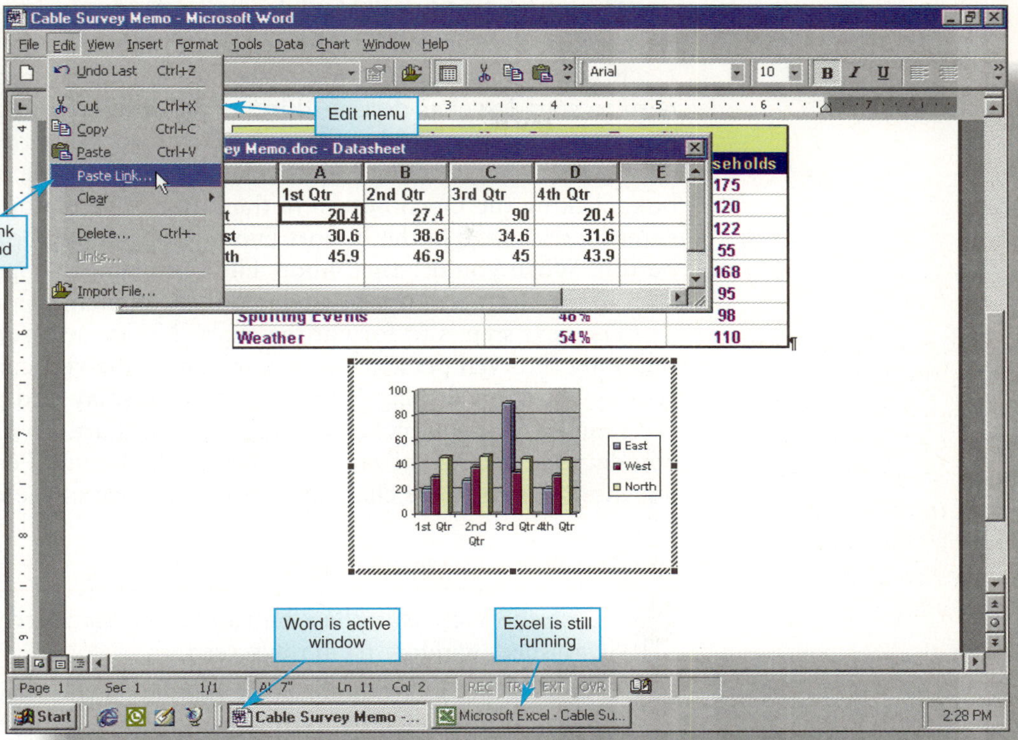

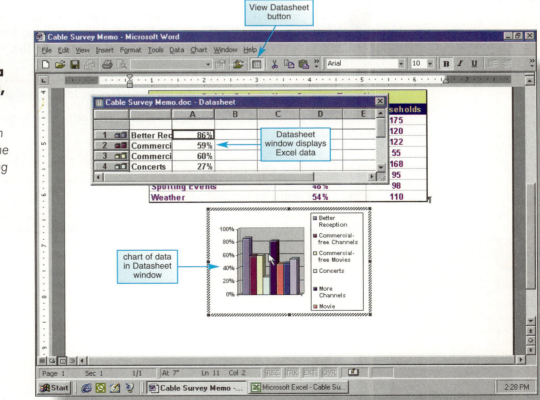

FIGURE 9

3 Click Paste Link. When Graph displays a dialog box indicating the linked data will replace existing data, click the OK button.

Graph copies the data from the Office Clipboard into the Datasheet window, replacing the sample data in the Datasheet window (Figure 10). Graph then charts the contents of the Datasheet window.

FIGURE 10

The Excel data is linked to the chart. Thus, if you change any of the data in the Excel worksheet, it will be reflected in the chart.

If you wanted to copy and paste the chart data, instead of link it, you would not need to start Excel as described in the previous steps. After starting Graph, you simply would instruct Word to copy the Excel worksheet data by clicking Edit on the Graph menu bar, clicking Import File, locating the file name in the Import File dialog box, clicking the Open button in the Import File dialog box, clicking Entire sheet or entering the range in the Import File Options dialog box, and then clicking the OK button. When you use the Import File command to copy Excel worksheet data, the data in the chart will not be updated if the contents of the Excel worksheet change.

The next step is to format the chart. Notice in Figure 10 on the previous page that only the even percentages display along the vertical axis on the chart and only six of eight items display in the legend. To display odd percentage values (such as 70% and 90%), you increase the size of the chart. To display all the legend items, you decrease the size of the characters in the legend. Perform the following steps to increase the size of the chart and reduce the size of the characters in the legend.

TO FORMAT THE CHART IN GRAPH

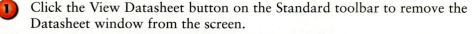

1 Click the View Datasheet button on the Standard toolbar to remove the Datasheet window from the screen.

2 Point to the right-middle sizing handle on the selection rectangle that surrounds the chart and legend and drag it rightward until the chart and legend are as wide as the table.

3 Point to the bottom-middle sizing handle on the selection rectangle and drag it downward approximately one inch.

4 Point to the legend in the chart and then right-click. Click Format Legend on the shortcut menu. When the Format Legend dialog box displays, if necessary, click the Font tab. Click Regular in the Font style list. Click 8 in the Size list. Click the OK button.

Graph reduces the font size of the characters in the legend and resizes the chart.

You are finished modifying the chart. The next step is to exit Graph and return to Word.

TO EXIT GRAPH AND RETURN TO WORD

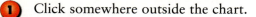

1 Click somewhere outside the chart.

Word closes the Graph application (Figure 11). Word's menus and toolbars redisplay below the title bar.

Linking Excel Data

If you want to display a linked worksheet as an icon, instead of as the worksheet itself, do the following: copy the data to be linked in Excel, switch to Word, click Edit on the menu bar, click Paste Special, click Paste link, click the desired option in the As list, place a check mark in the Display as icon check box, and then click the OK button.

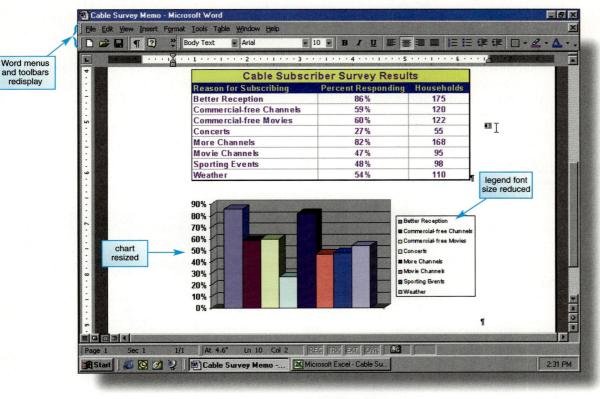

FIGURE 11

If, for some reason, you wanted to modify an existing chart in a document, you would double-click the chart to reopen the Microsoft Graph 2000 application. Then, you can make any necessary changes to the chart. When you are finished making changes to the chart, click anywhere outside the chart to return to Word.

You are finished with the memo. Save the document again, print it, and then quit Word as described in the following steps.

TO SAVE A DOCUMENT

1 Double-click the move handle on the Standard toolbar to display the entire toolbar. Click the Save button on the Standard toolbar.

Word saves the document on a floppy disk in drive A.

TO PRINT A DOCUMENT

1 Click the Print button on the Standard toolbar.

Word prints the memo as shown in Figure 1c on page WDI 2.2.

TO QUIT WORD

1 Click the Close button on Word's title bar.

The Word window closes.

Editing a Linked Worksheet

At a later time, you may find it necessary to change the data in the Excel worksheet. Any changes you make to the Excel worksheet while in Excel will be reflected in the Word document. Perform the following steps to change the number of households preferring cable because of its concerts from the number 55 to the number 65.

To Edit a Linked Object

1 **With the Excel worksheet displaying on the screen, click cell C6 to select it. Type** 65 **and then press the ENTER key.**

The number in cell C6 changes from 55 to 65 (Figure 12). Excel recalculates all formulas in the workbook.

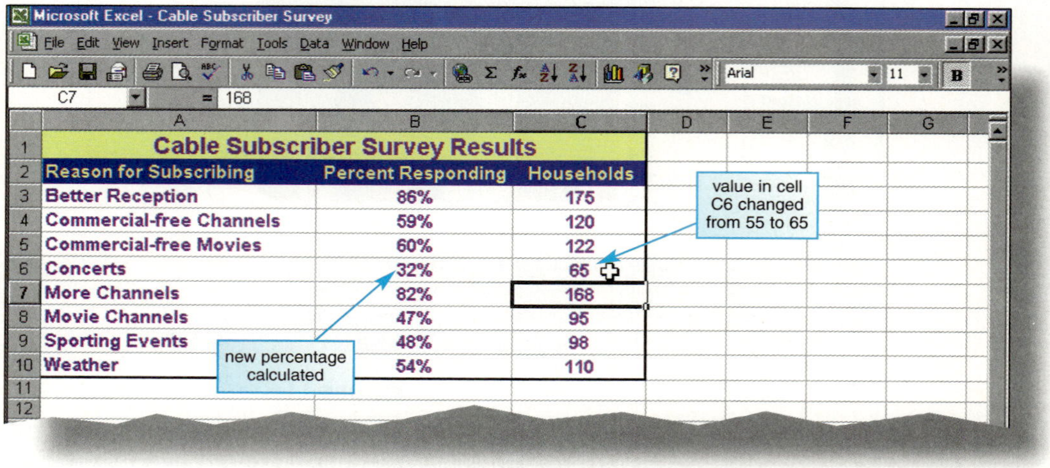

FIGURE 12

2 **Click the Save button on the Standard toolbar. Click the Close button at the right edge of Excel's title bar.**

Excel saves the changes to the worksheet. The Excel window closes.

3 **Start Word and then open the Cable Survey Memo document on your disk. If the chart does not display updated data, double-click the chart and then click outside the chart to exit Graph.**

The Word document displays the updates to the Excel worksheet object and chart object (Figure 13).

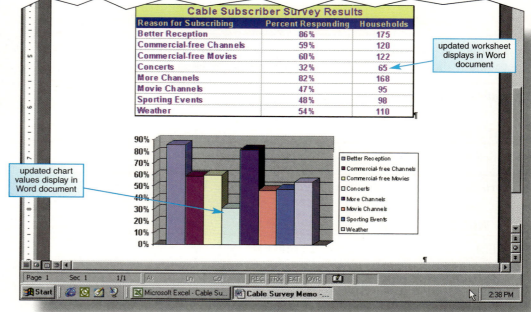

FIGURE 13

You also can edit any of the cells in the Excel worksheet (the object) while it displays as part of the Word document. To edit the worksheet, you double-click it. If Excel is running already, the system will switch to it and display the linked workbook in Excel. If Excel is not running, the system will start Excel automatically and then display the linked workbook in Excel.

Perform the following series of steps to save the Word document and then quit Word.

TO SAVE THE WORD DOCUMENT AGAIN

1 Click the Save button on the Standard toolbar.

Word saves the revised Cable Survey Memo on a floppy disk in drive A.

TO QUIT WORD

1 Click the Close button at the right edge of Word's title bar.

The Word window closes.

C A S E   P E R S P E C T I V E   S U M M A R Y

Pauline distributes the memo to the department managers so they can review it prior to the next weekly meeting. At the meeting, they quickly conclude from the memo that the majority of current customers subscribe to their cable service for two major reasons: better reception and more channels. Thus, they decide to offer seven additional cable channels beginning in two months.

After the meeting, Jerry Cromwell asks Pauline how she included the table and chart in the memo. Pauline confesses that she actually did not compose the memo and directs Jerry to you so that you can show him how to link documents between applications.

Integration Feature Summary

This Integration Feature introduced you to linking an Excel worksheet into a Word document. You also linked Excel data to a chart using Word's embedded Microsoft Graph charting application. Then, you modified the linked worksheet to see the changes reflected in the Word document.

Quick Reference

For a table that lists how to complete the tasks covered in this book using the mouse, menu, shortcut menu, and keyboard, see the Word Quick Reference Summary at the back of this book or visit the Shelly Cashman Series Office Web page (www.scsite.com/off2000/qr.htm) and then click Microsoft Word 2000.

Microsoft Certification

The Microsoft Office User Specialist (MOUS) Certification program provides an opportunity for you to obtain a valuable industry credential - proof that you have the Word 2000 skills required by employers. For more information, see Appendix D or visit the Shelly Cashman Series MOUS Web page at www.scsite.com/off2000/cert.htm.

In the Lab

1 Linking an Excel Table to a Word Document

Problem: Cecilia Doranski, director of admissions at Eastern University, has created an Excel worksheet that lists the number of full-time and part-time students majoring in each department on campus. She would like you to prepare a memo that includes the Excel worksheet.

Instructions:

1. Create a memo using a memo template. Save the memo using the name Department Major Memo. The memo is to all department heads, from Cecilia Doranski, and should have a subject of Full-Time and Part-Time Student Distribution by Department. In the memo, type the following paragraph: The table shown below lists the total number of full-time and part-time students in each department on campus. Please call me if you have any questions.
2. Link the Excel worksheet to the Word memo file.
3. Save the Word memo file again.
4. Print the Word memo file.

2 Linking Data from an Excel Worksheet to a Word Document

Problem: Cecilia Doranski, director of admissions at Eastern University, has created an Excel worksheet that lists the number of full-time and part-time students majoring in each department on campus. She would like you to prepare a memo that includes a chart of the Excel worksheet data.

Instructions:

1. Create a memo using a memo template. Save the memo using the name Department Major Memo With Chart. The memo is to all department heads, from Cecilia Doranski, and should have a subject of Full-Time and Part-Time Student Distribution by Department. In the memo, type the following paragraph: The chart shown below shows the total number of full-time and part-time students in each department on campus. Please call me if you have any questions.
2. In the memo, create a chart and then link the Excel worksheet data to the Word chart.
3. Save the Word memo file again.
4. Print the Word memo file.

3 Creating an Excel Worksheet and Linking It to a Word Document

Problem: Your science instructor, Ms. Yolatnik, has requested that you collect the daily high and low temperatures for a ten-day period and create an Excel worksheet that lists the data. Then, you are to prepare a memo that links the Excel worksheet into the memo and includes a chart that links to the Excel worksheet data.

Instructions:

Create a memo to Ms. Yolatnik using a memo template. Explain the contents of the worksheet and chart in the memo. Link the Excel worksheet to the Word memo file. In the memo, create a chart and then link the Excel worksheet data to the Word chart. Save the Word memo file again. Print the Word memo file.

Microsoft **Word 2000**

APPENDIX A
Microsoft Word 2000 Help System

Using the Word Help System

This appendix demonstrates how you can use the Word 2000 Help system to answer your questions. At any time while you are using Word, you can interact with the Help system to display information on any Word topic. It is a complete reference manual at your fingertips.

The two primary forms of Help are the Office Assistant and the Microsoft Word Help window. The one you use will depend on your preference. As shown in Figure A-1, you access either form of Help in Microsoft Word by pressing the F1 key, clicking Microsoft Word Help on the Help menu, or clicking the Microsoft Word Help button on the Standard toolbar. Word responds in one of two ways:

1. If the Office Assistant is turned on, then the Office Assistant displays with a balloon (lower-right side of Figure A-1).
2. If the Office Assistant is turned off, then the Microsoft Word Help window displays (lower-left side of Figure A-1).

Table A-1 on the next page summarizes the nine categories of Help available to you. Because of the way the Word Help system works, please review the rightmost column of Table A-1 if you have difficulties activating the desired category of Help.

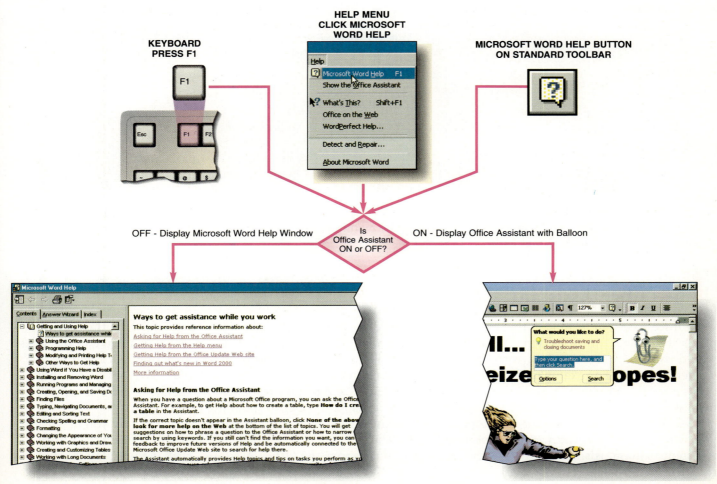

FIGURE A-1

Table A-1   Word Help System

TYPE	DESCRIPTION	HOW TO ACTIVATE	TURNING THE OFFICE ASSISTANT ON AND OFF
Answer Wizard	Similar to the Office Assistant in that it answers questions that you type in your own words.	Click the Microsoft Word Help button on the Standard toolbar. If necessary, maximize the Help window by double-clicking its title bar. Click the Answer Wizard tab.	If the Office Assistant displays, right-click it, click Options on the shortcut menu, click Use the Office Assistant to remove the check mark, click the OK button.
Contents sheet	Groups Help topics by general categories. Use when you know only the general category of the topic in question.	Click the Microsoft Word Help button on the Standard toolbar. If necessary, maximize the Help window by double-clicking its title bar. Click the Contents tab.	If the Office Assistant displays, right-click it, click Options, click Use the Office Assistant to remove the check mark, click the OK button.
Detect and Repair	Automatically finds and fixes errors in the application.	Click Detect and Repair on the Help menu.	
Hardware and Software Information	Shows Product ID and allows access to system information and technical support information.	Click About Microsoft Word on the Help menu and then click the appropriate button.	
Help for WordPerfect Users	Used to assist WordPerfect users who are learning Microsoft Word.	Click WordPerfect Help on the Help menu.	
Index sheet	Similar to an index in a book. Use when you know exactly what you want.	Click the Microsoft Word Help button on the Standard toolbar. If necessary, maximize the Help window by double-clicking its title bar. Click the Index tab.	If the Office Assistant displays, right-click it, click Options, click Use the Office Assistant to remove the check mark, click the OK button.
Office Assistant	Answers questions that you type in your own words, offers tips, and provides Help for a variety of Word features.	Click the Microsoft Word Help button on the Standard toolbar or double-click the Office Assistant icon. Some dialog boxes also include the Microsoft Word Help button.	If the Office Assistant does not display, click Show the Office Assistant on the Help menu.
Office on the Web	Used to access technical resources and download free product enhancements on the Web.	Click Office on the Web on the Help menu.	
Question Mark button and \What's This? command	Used to identify unfamiliar items on the screen.	In a dialog box, click the Question Mark button and then click an item in the dialog box. Click What's This? on the Help menu, and then click an item on the screen.	

The best way to familiarize yourself with the Word Help system is to use it. The next several pages show examples of how to use the Help system. Following the examples is a set of exercises titled Use Help that will sharpen your Word Help system skills.

The Office Assistant

The **Office Assistant** is an icon that displays in the Word window (lower-right side of Figure A-1 on the previous page). It has dual functions. First, it will respond with a list of topics that relate to the entry you make in the What would you like to do? text box at the bottom of the balloon. This entry can be in the form of a word, phrase, or written question. For example, if you want to learn more about saving a file, you can type, save, save a file, how do I save a file, or anything similar in the text box. The Office Assistant responds by displaying a list of topics from which you can choose. Once you choose a topic, it displays the corresponding information.

Second, the Office Assistant monitors your work and accumulates tips during a session on how you might do your work better. You can view the tips at any time. The accumulated tips display when you activate the Office Assistant balloon. Also, if at any time you see a light bulb above the Office Assistant, click it to display the most recent tip.

You may or may not want the Office Assistant to display on the screen at all times. You can hide it, and then show it at a later time. You may prefer not to use the Office Assistant at all. In this case, you use the Microsoft Word Help window (lower-left side of Figure A-1 on page WD A.1). Thus, not only do you need to know how to show and hide the Office Assistant, but you also need to know how to turn the Office Assistant on and off.

Showing and Hiding the Office Assistant

When Word is first installed, the Office Assistant displays in the Word window. You can move it to any location on the screen. You can click it to display the Office Assistant balloon, which allows you to request Help. If the Office Assistant is on the screen and you want to hide it, you click the **Hide the Office Assistant command** on the Help menu. You also can right-click the Office Assistant to display its shortcut menu and then click the **Hide command** to hide it. When the Office Assistant is hidden, then the **Show the Office Assistant command** replaces the Hide the Office Assistant command on the Help menu. Thus, you can show or hide the Office Assistant at any time.

Turning the Office Assistant On and Off

The fact that the Office Assistant is hidden, does not mean it is turned off. To turn the Office Assistant off, it must be displayed in the Word window. You right-click it to display its shortcut menu (right side of Figure A-2). Next, click Options on the shortcut menu. Invoking the **Options command** causes the Office Assistant dialog box to display (left side of Figure A-2).

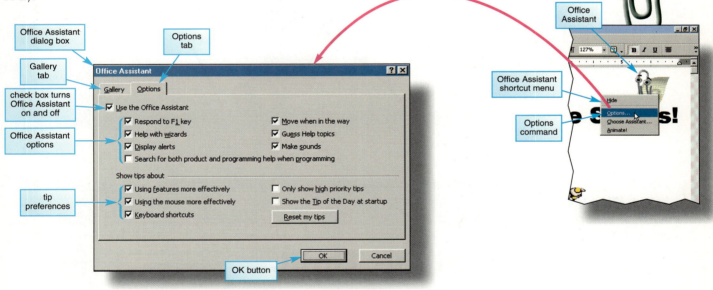

FIGURE A-2

The top check box in the Options sheet determines whether the Office Assistant is on or off. To turn the Office Assistant off, remove the check mark from the **Use the Office Assistant check box** and then click the OK button. As shown in Figure A-1 on page WD A.1, if the Office Assistant is off when you invoke Help, then the Microsoft Word Help window displays instead of the Office Assistant. To turn the Office Assistant on at a later time, click the Show the Office Assistant command on the Help menu.

Through the Options command on the Office Assistant shortcut menu, you can change the look and feel of the Office Assistant. For example, you can hide the Office Assistant, turn the Office Assistant off, change the way it works, choose a different Office Assistant icon, or view an animation of the current one. These options also are available by clicking the Options button that displays in the Office Assistant balloon (Figure A-3 on the next page).

The **Gallery sheet** (Figure A-2) in the Office Assistant dialog box allows you to change the appearance of the Office Assistant. The default is the paper clip (Clippit). You can change it to a bouncing red happy face (The Dot), a robot (F1), a professor (The Genius), the Microsoft Office logo (Office Logo), the earth (Mother Nature), a cat (Links), or a dog (Rocky).

Using the Office Assistant

As indicated earlier, the Office Assistant allows you to enter a word, phrase, or question and then responds by displaying a list of topics from which you can choose to display Help. The following steps show how to use the Office Assistant to obtain Help about online meetings.

To Use the Office Assistant

1 If the Office Assistant is not turned on, click Help on the menu bar and then click Show the Office Assistant. Click the Office Assistant. When the Office Assistant balloon displays, **type** what are online meetings **in the text box. Point to the Search button.**

The Office Assistant balloon displays as shown in Figure A-3.

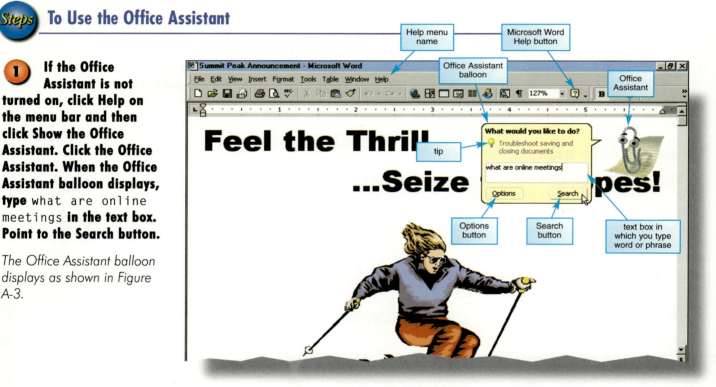

FIGURE A-3

2 Click the Search button. When the Office Assistant balloon redisplays, point to the topic, About online meetings (Figure A-4).

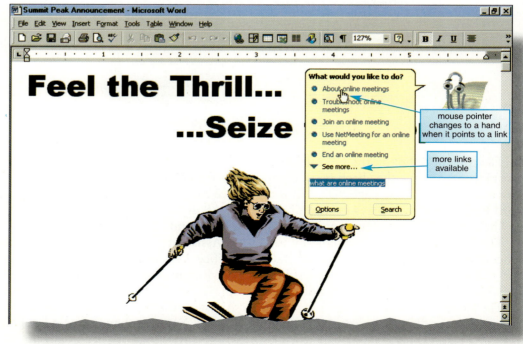

FIGURE A-4

3 **Click the topic, About online meetings. Double-click the Microsoft Word Help window title bar to maximize it. If necessary, move or hide the Office Assistant so you can view all of the text in the Microsoft Word Help window.**

The Microsoft Word Help window displays the information about online meetings (Figure A-5).

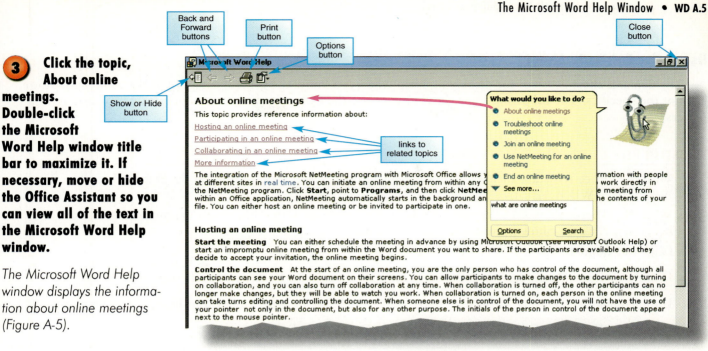

FIGURE A-5

When the Microsoft Word Help window displays, you can choose to read it or print it. To print the information, click the Print button on the Microsoft Word Help toolbar. Table A-2 lists the function of each button on the Microsoft Word Help toolbar. To close the Microsoft Word Help window shown in Figure A-5, click the Close button on the title bar.

Table A-2	Microsoft Word Help Toolbar Buttons	
BUTTON	**NAME**	**FUNCTION**
or	Show or Hide	Displays or hides the Contents, Answer Wizard, and Index tabs
	Back	Displays the previous Help topic
	Forward	Displays the next Help topic
	Print	Prints the current Help topic
	Options	Displays a list of commands

Other Ways

1. If Office Assistant is turned on, on Help menu click Microsoft Word Help, or click Microsoft Word Help button on Standard toolbar to display Office Assistant balloon

The Microsoft Word Help Window

If the Office Assistant is turned off and you click the Microsoft Word Help button on the Standard toolbar, the **Microsoft Word Help window** displays (Figure A-6 on the next page). This window contains three tabs on the left side: Contents, Answer Wizard, and Index. Each tab displays a sheet with powerful look-up capabilities. Use the Contents sheet as you would a table of contents at the front of a book to look up Help. The Answer Wizard sheet answers your queries in the same manner as the Office Assistant. You use the Index sheet in the same manner as an index in a book.

Click the tabs to move from sheet to sheet. The five buttons on the toolbar, Show or Hide, Back, Forward, Print, and Options also are described in Table A-2.

Besides clicking the Microsoft Word Help button on the Standard toolbar, you also can click the Microsoft Word Help command on the Help menu or press the F1 key to display the Microsoft Word Help window to gain access to the three sheets. To close the Microsoft Word Help window, click the Close button in the upper-right corner on the title bar.

Using the Contents Sheet

The **Contents sheet** is useful for displaying Help when you know the general category of the topic in question, but not the specifics. The following steps show how to use the Contents sheet to obtain information about Web folders.

TO OBTAIN HELP USING THE CONTENTS SHEET

1 With the Office Assistant turned off, click the Microsoft Word Help button on the Standard toolbar (Figure A-3 on page WD A.4).

2 When the Microsoft Word Help window displays, double-click the title bar to maximize the window. If necessary, click the Show button to display the tabs.

3 Click the Contents tab.

4 Double-click the Working with Online and Internet Documents book on the left side of the window.

5 Double-click the Creating Web Pages book below the Working with Online and Internet Documents book.

6 Click the About Web Folders subtopic below the Creating Web Pages book.

Word displays Help on the subtopic, About Web Folders (Figure A-6).

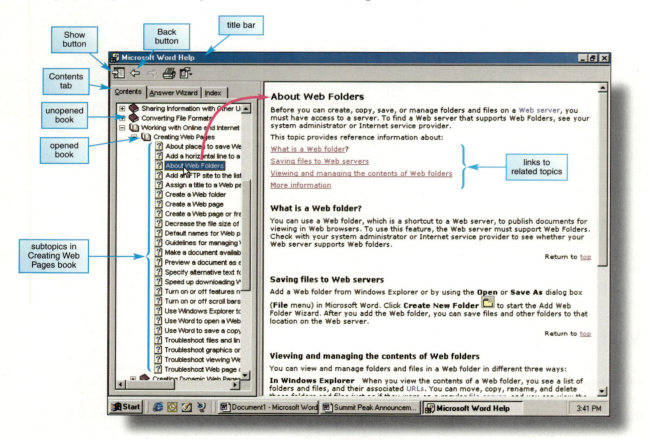

FIGURE A-6

Once the information on the subtopic displays, you can scroll through the window and read it or you can click the Print button to obtain a hard copy. If you decide to click another subtopic on the left or a link on the right, you can get back to the Help page shown in Figure A-6 by clicking the Back button as many times as necessary.

Each topic in the Contents list is preceded by a book icon or question mark icon. A **book icon** indicates subtopics are available. A **question mark icon** means information on the topic will display if you double-click the title. The book icon opens when you double-click the book (or its title) or click the plus sign (+) to the left of the book icon.

Using the Answer Wizard Sheet

The **Answer Wizard sheet** works like the Office Assistant in that you enter a word, phrase, or question and it responds with topics from which you can choose to display Help. The following steps show how to use the Answer Wizard sheet to obtain Help about discussions in a Word document.

TO OBTAIN HELP USING THE ANSWER WIZARD SHEET

1 With the Office Assistant turned off, click the Microsoft Word Help button on the Standard toolbar (Figure A-3 on page WD A.4).

2 When the Microsoft Word Help window displays, double-click the title bar to maximize the window. If necessary, click the Show button to display the tabs.

3 Click the Answer Wizard tab. Type what are discussions in the What would you like to do? text box on the left side of the window. Click the Search button.

4 When a list of topics displays in the Select topic to display list box, click About discussions in Word.

Word displays Help about discussions (Figure A-7).

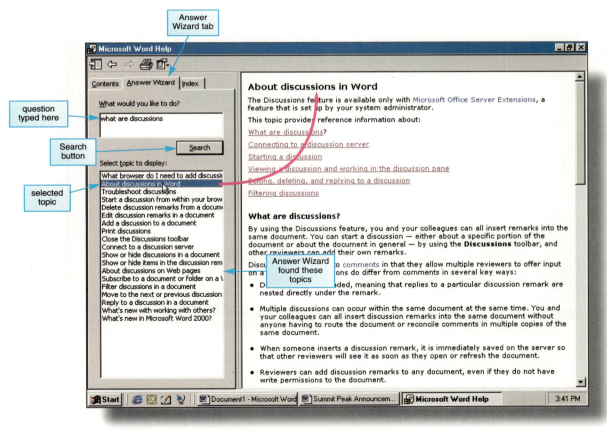

FIGURE A-7

If the topic, About discussions in Word, does not include the information you are searching for, click another topic in the list. Continue to click topics until you find the desired information.

Using the Index Sheet

The third sheet in the Microsoft Word Help window is the Index sheet. Use the **Index sheet** to display Help when you know the keyword or the first few letters of the keyword you want to look up. The following steps show how to use the Index sheet to obtain Help on understanding the readability statistics available to evaluate the reading level of a document.

TO OBTAIN HELP USING THE INDEX SHEET

1 With the Office Assistant turned off, click the Microsoft Word Help button on the Standard toolbar (Figure A-3 on page WD A.4).

2 When the Microsoft Word Help window displays, double-click the title bar to maximize the window. If necessary, click the Show button to display the tabs.

3 Click the Index tab. Type readability in the Type keywords text box on the left side of the window. Click the Search button.

Word highlights the first topic (Readability scores) on the left side of the window and displays information about two readability scores on the right side of the window (Figure A-8).

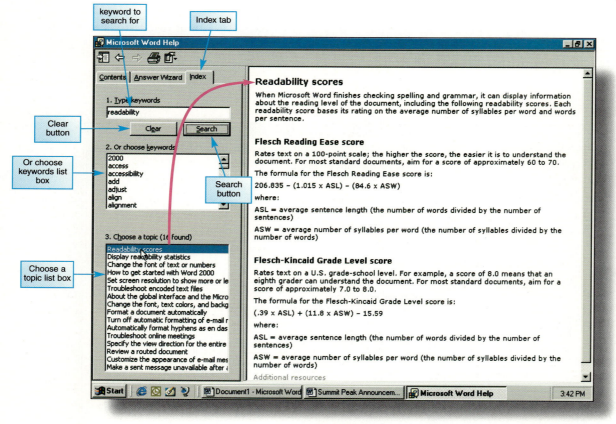

FIGURE A-8

In the Choose a topic list box on the left side of the window, you can click another topic to display additional Help.

An alternative to typing a keyword in the Type keywords text box is to scroll through the Or choose keywords list box (the middle list box on the left side of the window). When you locate the keyword you are searching for, double-click it to display Help on the topic. Also in the Or choose keywords list box, the Word Help system displays other topics that relate to the new keyword. As you begin typing a new keyword in the Type keywords text box, Word jumps to that point in the middle list box. To begin a new search, click the Clear button.

What's This? Command and Question Mark Button • **WD A.9**

APPENDIX A

What's This? Command and Question Mark Button

Use the What's This command on the Help menu or the Question Mark button in a dialog box when you are not sure what an object on the screen is or what it does.

What's This? Command

You use the **What's This? command** on the Help menu to display a detailed ScreenTip. When you invoke this command, the mouse pointer changes to an arrow with a question mark. You then click any object on the screen, such as a button, to display the ScreenTip. For example, after you click the What's This? command on the Help menu and then click the Zoom box on the Standard toolbar, a description of the Zoom box displays (Figure A-9). You can print the Screen-Tip by right-clicking it and then clicking Print Topic on the shortcut menu.

FIGURE A-9

Question Mark Button

In a response similar to the What's This? command, the **Question Mark button** displays a ScreenTip. You use the Question Mark button with dialog boxes. It is located in the upper-right corner on the title bar of dialog boxes, next to the Close button. For example, in Figure A-10, the Print dialog box displays on the screen. If you click the Question Mark button, and then click the Print to file check box, an explanation of the Print to file check box displays in a ScreenTip. You can print the ScreenTip by right-clicking it and then clicking Print Topic on the shortcut menu.

If a dialog box does not include a Question Mark button, press the SHIFT+F1 keys. This combination of keys will change the mouse pointer to an arrow with a question mark. You then can click any object in the dialog box to display the ScreenTip.

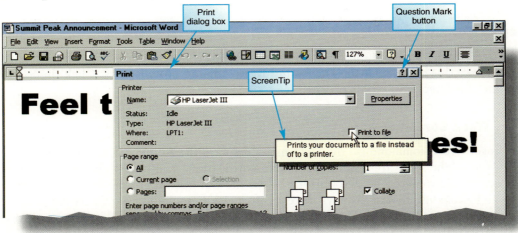

FIGURE A-10

Office on the Web Command

The **Office on the Web command** on the Help menu displays a Microsoft Web page containing up-to-date information on a variety of Office-related topics. To use this command, you must be connected to the Internet. Once the page displays, you can click the Word link on the left side of the window and then click the Assistance link (Figure A-11). The Word Assistance Web page contains several links such as Knowledge Base Articles about Word and Frequently Asked Questions about Word.

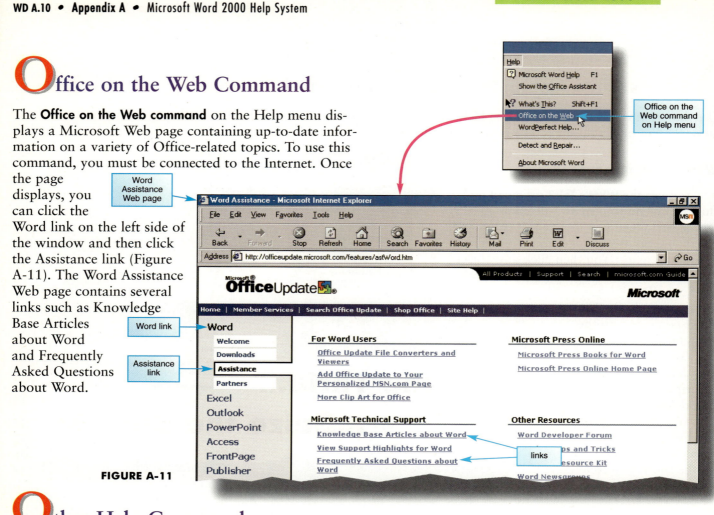

FIGURE A-11

Other Help Commands

Three additional commands available on the Help menu are WordPerfect Help, Detect and Repair, and About Microsoft Word. The WordPerfect Help command is available only if it was included as part of a Custom install of Word 2000.

WordPerfect Help Command

The **WordPerfect Help command** on the Help menu offers assistance to WordPerfect users switching to Word. When you choose this command, Word displays the Help for WordPerfect Users dialog box. The instructions in the dialog box step the user through the appropriate selections.

Detect and Repair Command

Use the **Detect and Repair command** on the Help menu if Word is not running properly or if it is generating errors. When you invoke this command, the Detect and Repair dialog box displays. Click the Start button in the dialog box to initiate the detect and repair process.

About Microsoft Word Command

The **About Microsoft Word command** on the Help menu displays the About Microsoft Word dialog box. The dialog box lists the owner of the software and the product identification. You need to know the product identification if you call Microsoft for assistance. The two buttons below the OK button are the System Info button and the Tech Support button. The **System Info button** displays system information, including hardware resources, components, software environment, and applications. The **Tech Support button** displays technical assistance information.

Use Help

1 Using the Office Assistant

Instructions: Perform the following tasks using the Word Help system.

1. If the Office Assistant is turned on, click it to display the Office Assistant balloon. If the Office Assistant is not turned on, click Help on the menu bar, and click Show the Office Assistant.
2. Right-click the Office Assistant and then click Options on the shortcut menu. Click the Gallery tab in the Office Assistant dialog box and then click the Next button to view all of the Office Assistants. Click the Options tab in the Office Assistant dialog box and review the different options for the Office Assistant. Click the Question Mark button and then display ScreenTips for the first two check boxes (Use the Office Assistant and Respond to F1 key). Right-click the ScreenTips to print them. Hand them in to your instructor. Close the Office Assistant dialog box.
3. Click the Office Assistant and then type show me the keyboard shortcuts in the What would you like to do? text box at the bottom of the balloon. Click the Search button.
4. Click Keyboard shortcuts in the Office Assistant balloon. If necessary, double-click the title bar to maximize the Microsoft Word Help window. Click the Function keys link and then click the SHIFT+Function key link to view the set of shortcut keys using the SHIFT key and function keys. Click the Print button on the Microsoft Word Help toolbar to print the list of shortcut keys. Hand in the printouts to your instructor.
5. Close all open Help windows.
6. Click the Office Assistant. If it is not turned on, click Show the Office Assistant on the Help menu. Search for the topic, what is a netmeeting. Click the Use NetMeeting for an online meeting link. When the Microsoft Word Help window displays, maximize the window and then click the the Start an impromptu online meeting with Microsoft Word link. Read and print the information. Close the Microsoft Word Help window.

2 Expanding on the Word Help System Basics

Instructions: Use the Word Help system to understand the topics better and answer the questions listed below. Answer the questions on your own paper, or hand in the printed Help information to your instructor.

1. Right-click the Office Assistant. If it is not turned on, click Show the Office Assistant on the Help menu. When the shortcut menu displays, click Options. Click Use the Office Assistant to remove the check mark, and then click the OK button.
2. Click the Microsoft Word Help button on the Standard toolbar. Maximize the Microsoft Word Help window. If the tabs are hidden on the left side, click the Show button. Click the Index tab. Type undo in the Type keywords text box. Click the Search button. Click Reset built-in menus and toolbars. Print the information. Click the Hide button and then the Show button. Click the four links below What do you want to do? Read and print the information for each link. Close the Microsoft Word Help window. Hand in the printouts to your instructor.
3. Press the F1 key. Maximize the Microsoft Word Help window. Click the Answer Wizard tab. Type help in the What would you like to do? text box, and then click the Search button. Click Ways to get assistance while you work. Read through the information that displays. Print the information. Click the first two links. Read and print the information for both.
4. Click the Contents tab. Click the plus sign (+) to the left of the Typing, Navigating Documents, and Selecting Text book. Click the plus sign (+) to the left of the Selecting Text book. One at a time, click the three topics below the Selecting Text book. Read and print each one. Close the Microsoft Word Help window. Hand in the printouts to your instructor.
5. Click Help on the menu bar and then click What's This? Click the E-mail button on the Standard toolbar. Right-click the ScreenTip to print the ScreenTip. Click Format on the menu bar and then click Paragraph. When the Paragraph dialog box displays, click the Question Mark button on the title bar. Click the Special box. Right-click the ScreenTip to print the ScreenTip. Hand in the printouts to your instructor. Close the Paragraph dialog box and the Microsoft Word window.

APPENDIX B
Publishing Office Web Pages to a Web Server

With a Microsoft Office 2000 program, such as Word, Excel, Access, or PowerPoint, you use the **Save as Web Page command** on the File menu to save the Web page to a Web server using one of two techniques: Web folders or File Transfer Protocol. A **Web folder** is an Office 2000 shortcut to a Web server. **File Transfer Protocol (FTP)** is an Internet standard that allows computers to exchange files with other computers on the Internet.

You should contact your network system administrator or technical support staff at your ISP to determine if their Web server supports Web folders, FTP, or both, and to obtain necessary permissions to access the Web server. If you decide to publish Web pages using a Web folder, you must have the Office Server Extensions (OSE) installed on your computer. OSE comes with the Standard, Professional, and Premium editions of Office 2000.

Using Web Folders to Publish Office Web Pages

If you are granted permission to create a Web folder (shortcut) on your computer, you must obtain the URL of the Web server, and a user name and possibly a password that allows you to access the Web server. You also must decide on a name for the Web folder. Table B-1 explains how to create a Web folder.

Office adds the name of the Web folder to the list of current Web folders. You can save to this folder, open files in the folder, rename the folder, or perform any operations you would to a folder on your hard disk. You can use your Office program or Windows Explorer to access this folder. Table B-2 explains how to save to a Web folder.

Using FTP to Publish Office Web Pages

When publishing a Web page using FTP, you first add the FTP location to your computer and then you can save to it. An **FTP location**, also called an **FTP site**, is a collection of files that resides on an FTP server. In this case, the FTP server is the Web server.

To add an FTP location, you must obtain the name of the FTP site, which usually is the address (URL) of the FTP server, and a user name and a password that allows you to access the FTP server. You save and open the Web pages on the Web server using the name of the FTP site. Table B-3 explains how to add an FTP site.

Office adds the name of the FTP site to the FTP locations in the Save As and Open dialog boxes. You can open and save files on this FTP location. Table B-4 explains how to save using an FTP location.

Table B-1 Creating a Web Folder

1. Click File on the menu bar and then click Save As; or click File on the menu bar and then click Open.
2. When the Save As dialog box or the Open dialog box displays, click the Web Folders shortcut on the Places Bar along the left side of the dialog box.
3. Click the Create New Folder button.
4. When the first dialog box of the Add Web Folder wizard displays, type the URL of the Web server and then click the Next button.
5. When the Enter Network Password dialog box displays, type the user name and, if necessary, the password in the respective text boxes and then click the OK button.
6. When the last dialog box of the Add Web Folder wizard displays, type the name you would like to use for the Web folder. Click the Finish button.
7. Close the Save As or the Open dialog box.

Table B-2 Saving to a Web Folder

1. Click File on the menu bar and then click Save As.
2. When the Save As dialog box displays, type the Web page file name in the File name text box. Do not press the ENTER key.
3. Click Web Folders shortcut on the Places Bar along the left side of the dialog box.
4. Double-click the Web folder name in the Save in list.
5. When the Enter Network Password dialog box displays, type the user name and password in the respective text boxes and then click the OK button.
6. Click the Save button in the Save As dialog box.

Table B-3 Adding an FTP Location

1. Click File on the menu bar and then click Save As; or click File on the menu bar and then click Open.
2. In the Save As dialog box, click the Save in box arrow and then click Add/Modify FTP Locations in the Save in list; or in the Open dialog box, click the Look in box arrow and then click Add/Modify FTP Locations in the Look in list.
3. When the Add/Modify FTP Locations dialog box displays, type the name of the FTP site in the Name of FTP site text box. If the site allows anonymous logon, click Anonymous in the Log on as area; if you have a user name for the site, click User in the Log on as area and then type the user name. Type the password in the Password text box. Click the OK button.
4. Close the Save As or the Open dialog box.

Table B-4 Saving to an FTP Location

1. Click File on the menu bar and then click Save As.
2. When the Save As dialog box displays, type the Web page file name in the File name text box. Do not press the ENTER key.
3. Click the Save in box arrow and then click FTP Locations.
4. Double-click the name of the FTP site you want to save to.
5. When the FTP Log On dialog box displays, type your user name and password and then click the OK button.
6. Click the Save button in the Save As dialog box.

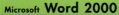
Microsoft **Word 2000**

APPENDIX C
Resetting the Word Menus and Toolbars

When you first install Microsoft Word 2000, the Standard and Formatting toolbars display on one row. As you use the buttons on the toolbars and commands on the menus, Word personalizes the toolbars and the menus based on their usage. Each time you start Word, the toolbars and menus display in the same settings as the last time you used the application. The following steps show how to reset the menus and toolbars to their installation settings.

Steps **To Reset My Usage Data and Toolbar Buttons**

1 **Click View on the menu bar and then point to Toolbars. Point to Customize on the Toolbars submenu.**

The View menu and Toolbars submenu display (Figure C-1).

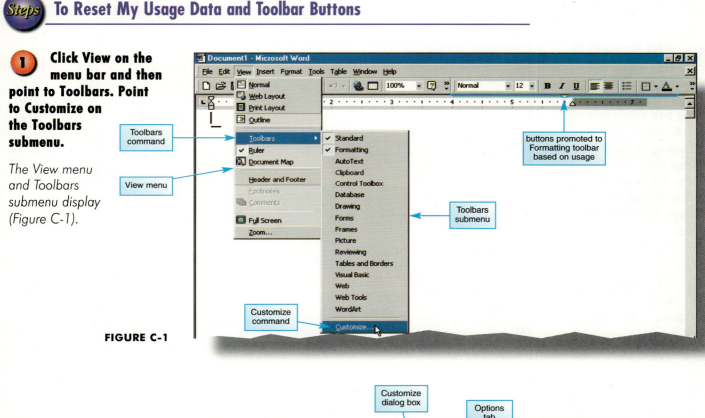

FIGURE C-1

2 **Click Customize. When the Customize dialog box displays, click the Options tab. Make sure the three check boxes in the Personalized Menus and Toolbars area have check marks and then point to the Reset my usage data button.**

The Customize dialog box displays as shown in Figure C-2.

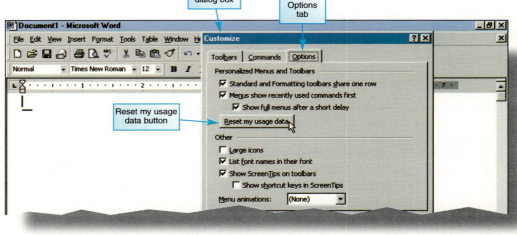

FIGURE C-2

3 **Click the Reset my usage data button.** When the Microsoft Word dialog box displays explaining the function of the Reset my usage data button, click the Yes button. In the Customize dialog box, click the Toolbars tab.

The Toolbars sheet displays (Figure C-3).

4 **Click Standard in the Toolbars list and** then click the Reset button. When the Reset Toolbar dialog box displays, click the OK button. Click Formatting in the Toolbars list and then click the Reset button. When the Reset Toolbar dialog box displays, click the OK button.

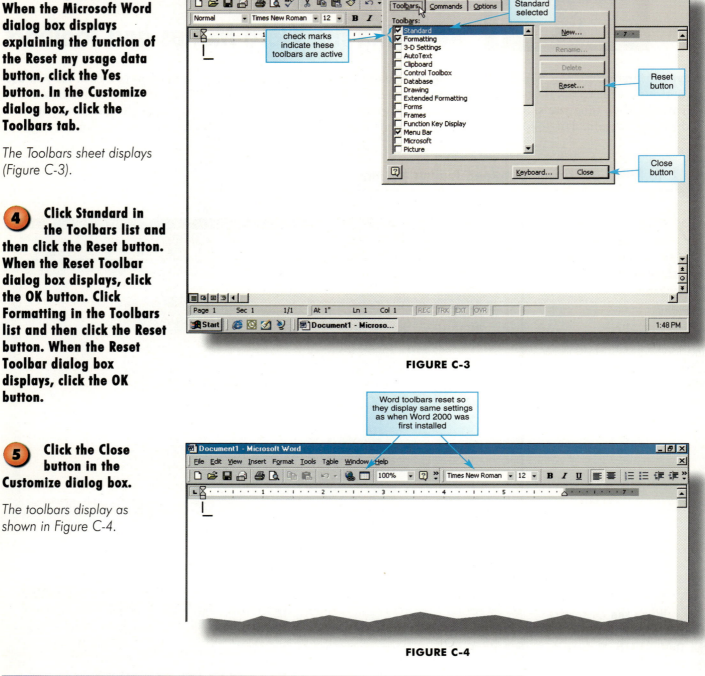

FIGURE C-3

5 **Click the Close button in the** Customize dialog box.

The toolbars display as shown in Figure C-4.

FIGURE C-4

Steps 3 and 4 display or remove any buttons that were added or deleted through the use of the Add or Remove Buttons button on the More Buttons menu.

You can turn off both the toolbars sharing a single row and the short menus by removing the check marks from the two top check boxes in the Options sheet in the Customize dialog box (Figure C-2 on the previous page). If you remove these check marks, Word will display the toolbars on two separate rows below the menu bar and will show only full menus.

Microsoft **Word 2000**

APPENDIX D

Microsoft Office User Specialist Certification Program

The Microsoft Office User Specialist (MOUS) Certification Program provides a framework for measuring your proficiency with the Microsoft Office 2000 applications, such as Word 2000, Excel 2000, Access 2000, and PowerPoint 2000. Three levels of certification are available — Master, Expert, and Core. The three levels of certification are described in Table D-1.

Table D-1	Three Levels of MOUS Certification		
LEVEL	**DESCRIPTION**	**REQUIREMENTS**	**CREDENTIAL AWARDED**
Master	Indicates that you have a comprehensive understanding of Microsoft Office 2000	Pass all FIVE of the required exams: Microsoft Word 2000 Expert Microsoft Excel 2000 Expert Microsoft PowerPoint 2000 Core Microsoft Access 2000 Core Microsoft Outlook 2000 Core	Candidates will be awarded one certificate for passing all five of the required Microsoft Office 2000 exams: Microsoft Office User Specialist: Microsoft Office 2000 Master
Expert	Indicates that you have a comprehensive understanding of the advanced features in a specific Microsoft Office 2000 application	Pass any ONE of the Expert exams: Microsoft Word 2000 Expert Microsoft Excel 2000 Expert	Candidates will be awarded one certificate for each of the Expert exams they have passed: Microsoft Office User Specialist: Microsoft Word 2000 Expert Microsoft Office User Specialist: Microsoft Excel 2000 Expert
Core	Indicates that you have a comprehensive understanding of the core features in a specific Microsoft Office 2000 application	Pass any ONE of the Core exams: Microsoft Word 2000 Core Microsoft Excel 2000 Core Microsoft PowerPoint 2000 Core Microsoft Access 2000 Core Microsoft Outlook 2000 Core	Candidates will be awarded one certificate for each of the Core exams they have passed: Microsoft Office User Specialist: Microsoft Word 2000 Microsoft Office User Specialist: Microsoft Excel 2000 Microsoft Office User Specialist: Microsoft PowerPoint 2000 Microsoft Office User Specialist: Microsoft Access 2000 Microsoft Office User Specialist: Microsoft Outlook 2000

Why Should You Get Certified?

Being a Microsoft Office User Specialist provides a valuable industry credential — proof that you have the Office 2000 applications skills required by employers. By passing one or more MOUS certification exams, you demonstrate your proficiency in a given Office application to employers. With nearly 80 million copies of Office in use around the world, Microsoft is targeting Office certification to a wide variety of companies. These companies include temporary employment agencies that want to prove the expertise of their workers, large corporations looking for a way to measure the skill set of employees, and training companies and educational institutions seeking Microsoft Office teachers with appropriate credentials.

The MOUS Exams

You pay $50 to $100 each time you take an exam, whether you pass or fail. The fee varies among testing centers. The Expert exams, which you can take up to 60 minutes to complete, consist of between 40 and 60 tasks that you perform online. The tasks require you to use the application just as you would in doing your job. The Core exams contain fewer tasks, and you will have slightly less time to complete them. The tasks you will perform differ on the two types of exams.

How Can You Prepare for the MOUS Exams?

The Shelly Cashman Series® offers several Microsoft-approved textbooks that cover the required objectives on the MOUS exams. For a listing of the textbooks, visit the Shelly Cashman Series MOUS Web page at www.scsite.com/off2000/cert.htm and then click the Shelly Cashman Series Office 2000 Microsoft-Approved MOUS Textbooks link (Figure D-1). After using any of the books listed in an instructor-led course, you will be prepared to take the MOUS exam indicated.

How to Find an Authorized Testing Center

You can locate a testing center by calling 1-800-933-4493 in North America or visiting the Shelly Cashman Series MOUS Web page at www.scsite.com/off2000/cert.htm and then clicking the Locate an Authorized Testing Center Near You link (Figure D-1). At this Web page, you can look for testing centers around the world.

Shelly Cashman Series MOUS Web Page

The Shelly Cashman Series MOUS Web page (Figure D-1) has more than fifteen Web pages you can visit to obtain additional information on the MOUS Certification Program. The Web page (www.scsite.com/off2000/cert.htm) includes links to general information on certification, choosing an application for certification, preparing for the certification exam, and taking and passing the certification exam.

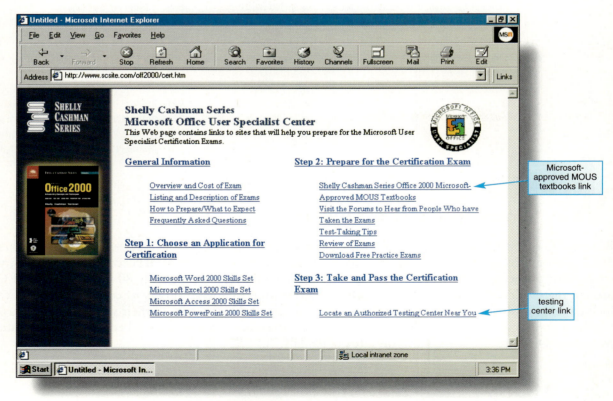

FIGURE D-1

Microsoft Word 2000 User Specialist Certification Map

This book has been approved by Microsoft as courseware for the Microsoft Office User Specialist (MOUS) program. After completing the projects and exercises in this book, students will be prepared to take the Core level Microsoft Office User Specialist Exam for Microsoft Word 2000. Table D-2 lists the skill sets, activities, and page number where the activity is discussed in the book for the Core level Microsoft Office User Specialist Exam for Microsoft Word 2000. You should be familiar with each of the activities if you plan to take the Microsoft Word 2000 Core examination. Table D-3 on the next page lists the skill sets, activities, and page number where the activity is discussed in the book for the Expert level Microsoft Office User Specialist Exam for Microsoft Word 2000.

Table D-2   Microsoft Word 2000 MOUS Core Skill Sets, Activities, and Map

SKILL SETS	ACTIVITIES	PAGE NUMBERS
Working with text	Use the Undo, Redo, and Repeat command	WD 1.35, WD 1.36
	Apply font formats (Bold, Italic and Underline)	WD 1.33, WD 1.39, WD 1.42
	Use the SPELLING feature	WD 1.22, WD 1.59, WD 2.50
	Use the THESAURUS feature	WD 2.48, WD 2.61
	Use the GRAMMAR feature	WD 1.22, WD 1.59, WD 2.50
	Insert page breaks	WD 2.31, WD 2.35, WD 4.21
	Highlight text in document	WDW 1.9, WD 6.61
	Insert and move text	WD 1.54, WD 2.46, WD 2.56
	Cut, Copy, Paste, and Paste Special using the Office Clipboard	WD 1.54, WD 2.45, WD 3.33, WD 3.35, WD 6.35
	Copy formats using the Format Painter	WD 6.57
	Select and change font and font size	WD 1.17, WD 1.31, WD 1.32
	Find and replace text	WD 2.43, WD 2.56
	Apply character effects (superscript, subscript, strikethrough, small caps and outline)	WD 2.18, WD 4.16, WD 4.17
	Insert date and time	WD 6.17
	Insert symbols	WD 2.33, WD 3.37, WD 3.46
	Create and apply frequently used text with AutoCorrect	WD 2.20, WD 2.21
Working with paragraphs	Align text in paragraphs (Center, Left, Right and Justified)	WD 1.33, WD 1.35, WD 2.17, WD 2.18, WD 6.26
	Add bullets and numbering	WD 3.50, WD 3.51, WD 4.40, WD 5.30, WD 6.63
	Set character, line, and paragraph spacing options	WD 2.9, WD 2.11, WD 2.18, WD 4.38, WD 6.42
	Apply borders and shading to paragraphs	WD 3.39, WD 4.8, WD 6.37, WD 6.45
	Use indentation options (Left, Right, First Line, and Hanging Indent)	WD 2.18, WD 2.19, WD 2.37, WD 6.43
	Use TABS command (Center, Decimal, Left, and Right)	WD 3.31, WD 3.32, WD 3.43, WD 6.49
	Create an outline style numbered list	WD 3.51, WD 5.30
	Set tabs with leaders	WD 3.31
Working with documents	Print a document	WD 1.50, WD 5.40, WD 6.47
	Use print preview	WD 3.24, WD 4.57
	Use Web Page Preview	WDW 1.11, WDW 1.14
	Navigate through a document	WD 1.25, WD 1.26, WD 1.40, WD 4.25
	Insert page numbers	WD 2.14

Table D-2   Microsoft Word 2000 MOUS Core Skill Sets, Activities, and Map

SKILL SETS	ACTIVITIES	PAGE NUMBERS
Working with documents (con't)	Set page orientation	WD 5.24
	Set margins	WD 2.8, WD 6.7
	Use GoTo to locate specific elements in a document	WD 2.42, WD 2.43
	Create and modify page numbers	WD 2.14, WD 4.29
	Create and modify headers and footers	WD 2.12, WD 2.15, WD 4.28
	Align text vertically	WD 3.35, WD 3.36, WD 4.42
	Create and use newspaper columns	WD 6.23, WD 6.25
	Revise column structure	WD 6.30, WD 6.48, WD 6.51
	Prepare and print envelopes and labels	WD 3.58, WD 5.48, WD 5.54
	Apply styles	WD 2.26, WD 4.19, WD 6.33
	Create sections with formatting that differs from other sections	WD 4.21, WD 4.29, WD 6.24
	Use click & type	WD 2.13
Managing files	Use save	WD 1.26, WD 1.49
	Locate and open an existing document	WD 1.52, WD 4.23
	Use Save As (different name, location, or format)	WD 1.49, WD 3.42, WDW 1.11
	Create a folder	WD 1.49
	Create a new document using a Wizard	WD 3.7, WDW 1.5
	Save as Web Page	WDW 1.3
	Use templates to create a new document	WD 3.18, WD 5.6, WD 5.9
	Create Hyperlinks	WD 2.39, WD 2.53, WDW 1.10
	Use the Office Assistant	WD 1.55
	Send a Word document via e-mail	WD 2.54, WDI 1.7
Using tables	Create and format tables	WD 3.52, WD 3.55, WD 4.42, WD 4.49
	Add borders and shading to tables	WD 3.55, WD 4.59, WD 4.61
	Revise tables (insert and delete rows and columns, change cell formats)	WD 3.15, WD 3.62, WD 4.46, WD 4.53
	Modify table structure (merge cells, change height and width)	WD 4.47, WD 4.48, WD 4.53, WD 4.59
	Rotate text in a table	WD 4.50, WD 4.59
Working with pictures and charts	Use the Drawing toolbar	WD 4.15, WD 6.9, WD 6.40
	Insert graphics into a document (WordArt, ClipArt, Images)	WD 1.43, WD 4.12, WD 4.33, WD 4.54, WD 6.9

Table D-3 Microsoft Word 2000 MOUS Expert Skill Sets, Activities, and Map

SKILL SETS	ACTIVITIES	PAGE NUMBERS
Working with paragraphs	Apply paragraph and section shading	WD 4.10, WD 4.51, WD 6.45
	Use text flow options (Widows/Orphans options and keeping lines together)	WD 2.32, WD 7.33
	Sort lists, paragraphs, tables	WD 2.40, WD 5.45, WD 5.59
Working with documents	Create and modify page borders	WD 6.59, WD 8.48
	Format first page differently than subsequent pages	WD 4.7, WD 4.21, WD 4.28, WD 7.60
	Use bookmarks	WD 7.59, WD 9.47
	Create and edit styles	WD 2.26, WD 9.17
	Create watermarks	WD 4.54, WD 6.44
	Use find and replace with formats, special characters, and non-printing elements	WD 2.45
	Balance column length (using column breaks appropriately)	WD 6.25, WD 6.51
	Create or revise footnotes and endnotes	WD 2.23, WD 2.30, WD 2.61
	Work with master documents and subdocuments	WD 7.36, WD 7.65
	Create and modify a table of contents	WD 7.57, WD 7.63, WD 7.67
	Create cross-reference	WD 7.29
	Create and modify an index	WD 7.31, WD 7.56, WD 7.63, WD 7.67
Using tables	Embed worksheets in a table	WD 7.23, WDI 2.6
	Perform calculations in a table	WD 3.62, WD 4.59
	Link Excel data as a table	WD 7.24, WDI 2.4, WDI 2.12
	Modify worksheets in a table	WD 7.22, WDI 2.12
Working with pictures and charts	Add bitmapped graphics	WD 6.53, WD 6.54, WD 9.22
	Delete and position graphics	WD 1.46, WD 5.12, WD 6.20, WD 6.46, WD 6.54
	Create and modify charts	WD 4.33, WD 4.35, WD 4.36, WD 4.37, WDI 2.6
	Import data into charts	WDI 2.8
Using mail merge	Create main document	WD 5.14, WD 5.25, WD 5.27, WD 5.29
	Create data source	WD 5.17
	Sort records to be merged	WD 5.45, WD 5.59
	Merge main document and data source	WD 5.41, WD 5.43, WD 5.59
	Generate labels	WD 5.48
	Merge a document using alternate data sources	WDI 1.4
Using advanced features	Insert a field	WD 5.34, WD 5.37, WD 8.17, WD 8.20, WD 8.28
	Create, apply, and edit macros	WD 9.26, WD 9.29, WD 9.39
	Copy, rename, and delete macros	WD 9.28, WD 9.64
	Create and modify form	WD 8.8, WD 8.15, WD 9.8
	Create and modify a form control (e.g., add an item to a drop-down list)	WD 8.17, WD 8.20, WD 8.28, WD 9.54, WD 9.57, WD 9.59
	Use advanced text alignment features with graphics	WD 5.13, WD 6.20, WD 6.28, WD 6.40, WD 6.54, WD 7.25
	Customize toolbars	WD 1.14, WD 9.30
Collaborating with workgroups	Insert comments	WD 7.10, WD 7.17
	Protect documents	WD 7.34, WD 7.42, WD 8.8, WD 8.47, WD 9.8
	Create multiple versions of a document	WD 7.15
	Track changes to a document	WD 7.13, WD 7.19
	Set default file location for workgroup templates	WD 8.56
	Round Trip documents from HTML	WDW 1.12

Index

Microsoft **Word 2000**

Microsoft Word 2000 Quick Reference Summary

In Microsoft Word 2000, you can accomplish a task in a number of ways. The following table provides a quick reference to each task presented in this textbook. You can invoke the commands listed in the MENU BAR and SHORTCUT MENU columns using either the mouse or keyboard.

Microsoft Word 2000 Quick Reference Summary

TASK	PAGE NUMBER	MOUSE	MENU BAR	SHORTCUT MENU	KEYBOARD SHORTCUT
1.5 Line Spacing	WD 2.18		Format | Paragraph | Indents and Spacing tab	Paragraph | Indents and Spacing tab	CTRL+5
ActiveX Control, Format	WD 9.55		Format | Control	Format Control	
ActiveX Control, Insert	WD 9.54	Desired button on Control Toolbox toolbar			
ActiveX Control, Set Properties	WD 9.57	Properties button on Control Toolbox toolbar		Properties	
ActiveX Control, Write Code	WD 9.60	View Code button on Control Toolbox toolbar		View Code	
Animate Text	WD 8.45		Format | Font | Text Effects tab	Font | Text Effects tab	
AutoCorrect Entry, Create	WD 2.21		Tools | AutoCorrect | AutoCorrect tab		
AutoShape, Add	WD 7.49	AutoShapes button on Drawing toolbar			
AutoText Entry, Create	WD 3.45		Insert | AutoText | New		ALT+F3
AutoText Entry, Insert	WD 3.47		Insert | AutoText		Type entry, then F3
Blank Line Above Paragraph	WD 2.18		Format | Paragraph | Indents and Spacing tab	Paragraph | Indents and Spacing tab	CTRL+0
Bold	WD 1.33	Bold button on Formatting toolbar	Format | Font | Font tab	Font | Font tab	CTRL+B
Bookmark, Add	WD 7.59		Insert | Bookmark		
Bookmark, Go To	WD 7.60	Select Browse Object button on vertical scroll bar	Edit | Go To		CTRL+G
Border, Bottom	WD 3.39	Border button arrow on Formatting toolbar	Format | Borders and Shading | Borders tab		
Border, Outside	WD 4.8	Border button arrow on Tables and Borders toolbar	Format | Borders and Shading | Borders tab		
Border, Page	WD 6.59		Format | Borders and Shading | Page Border tab	Borders and Shading | Page Border tab	

(continued)

Microsoft Word 2000 Quick Reference Summary *(continued)*

TASK	PAGE NUMBER	MOUSE	MENU BAR	SHORTCUT MENU	KEYBOARD SHORTCUT
Bulleted List	WD 3.50	Bullets button on Formatting toolbar	Format	Bullets and Numbering	Bulleted tab	Bullets and Numbering	Bulleted tab	* and then space followed by text, then ENTER
Capitalize Letters	WD 2.18		Format	Font	Font tab	Font	Font tab	CTRL+SHIFT+A
Caption, Add	WD 7.26		Insert	Caption		
Caption, Update Caption Number	WD 7.27			Update Field	F9
Case of Letters	WD 2.18				SHIFT+F3
Center	WD 1.35	Center button on Formatting toolbar	Format	Paragraph	Indents and Spacing tab	Paragraph	Indents and Spacing tab	CTRL+E
Center Vertically	WD 4.17		File	Page Setup	Layout tab		
Character Formatting, Remove	WD 2.18		Format	Font	Font	CTRL+Q
Character Spacing	WD 6.42		Format	Font	Character Spacing tab	Font	Character Spacing tab	
Chart, Format Axis Numbers	WD 4.35	Click axis, Increase or **Decrease** Decimals button on Formatting toolbar	Click axis, Format	Format Axis	Right-click axis, click Format Axis on shortcut menu	
Chart, Move Legend	WD 4.36		Click legend, Format	Format Legend	Right-click legend, click Format Legend on shortcut menu	
Chart Table	WD 4.33		Insert	Picture	Chart		
Clip Art, Insert	WD 1.43		Insert	Picture	Clip Art		
Clip Gallery Live	WD 4.12		Insert	Picture	Clip Art		
Close All Documents	WD 3.60		SHIFT+File	Close All		
Close Document	WD 1.54	Close button on menu bar	File	Close		CTRL+W
Color Characters	WD 3.28	Font Color button arrow on Formatting toolbar	Format	Font	Font tab	Font	Font tab	
Column Break	WD 6.31		Insert	Break		CTRL+SHIFT+ENTER
Columns	WD 6.25	Columns button on Standard toolbar	Format	Columns		
Columns, Balance	WD 6.51		Insert	Break		
Columns, Format	WD 6.25		Format	Columns		
Comment, Delete	WD 7.18	Delete Comment button on Reviewing toolbar		Right-click comment reference mark in document window, click Delete Comment	
Comment, Insert	WD 7.10	Insert Comment button on Reviewing toolbar	Insert	Comment		
Comment, Modify	WD 7.12	Double-click comment reference mark in document window	View	Comments	Right-click comment reference mark in document window, click Edit Comment	
Comment, Review	WD 7.17	Next Comment button on Reviewing toolbar			

Microsoft Word 2000 Quick Reference Summary *(continued)*

TASK	PAGE NUMBER	MOUSE	MENU BAR	SHORTCUT MENU	KEYBOARD SHORTCUT
Comment, Print	WD 7.12		File | Print | Options button		
Copy	WD 3.33	Copy button on Standard toolbar or Clipboard toolbar	Edit | Copy	Copy	CTRL+C
Count Words	WD 2.49		Tools | Word Count		
Cross-Reference, Create	WD 7.29		Insert | Cross-reference		
Current Date, Insert	WD 6.17		Insert | Date and Time		
Data Source, Add Field	WD 5.23	Manage Fields button on Database toolbar			
Data Source, Add Record	WD 5.24	Add New Record button on Database toolbar			
Data Source, Change Designation	WDI 1.4	Mail Merge Helper button **on** Mail Merge toolbar	Tools | Mail Merge		
Data Source, Create	WD 5.17	Mail Merge Helper button on Mail Merge toolbar	Tools | Mail Merge		
Data Source, Delete Record	WD 5.24	Delete Record button on Database toolbar			
Delete Text	WD 1.54	Cut button on Standard toolbar	Edit | Cut	Cut	DELETE or BACKSPACE
Demote List Item	WD 3.51	Decrease Indent button on Formatting toolbar			
Distribute Columns Evenly	WD 4.48	Distribute Columns Evenly button on Tables and Borders toolbar	Table | AutoFit | Distribute Columns Evenly		
Document Map	WD 7.66	Document Map button on Standard toolbar			
Distribute Rows Evenly	WD 4.47	Distribute Rows Evenly button on Tables and Borders toolbar	Table | AutoFit | Distribute Rows Evenly		
Document Window, Open New	WD 3.27	New Blank Document button on Standard toolbar	File | New | General tab		
Double Strikethrough, Characters	WD 4.17		Format | Font | Font tab	Font | Font tab	
Double-Space Text	WD 2.9		Format | Paragraph | Indents and Spacing tab	Paragraph | Indents and Spacing tab	CTRL+2
Double-Underline	WD 2.18		Format | Font | Font tab	Font | Font tab	CTRL+SHIFT+D
Drawing Object, 3-D Effect	WD 9.24	3-D button on Drawing toolbar			
Drawing Object, Fill	WD 8.43	Fill Color button on Drawing toolbar	Format | AutoShape | Colors and Lines tab	Format AutoShape | Colors and Lines tab	

(continued)

Microsoft Word 2000 Quick Reference Summary *(continued)*

TASK	PAGE NUMBER	MOUSE	MENU BAR	SHORTCUT MENU	KEYBOARD SHORTCUT
Drawing Object, Order	WD 8.42	Draw button on Drawing Order toolbar, Order			
Drawing Object, Rotate	WD 7.51	Draw button on Drawing toolbar, Rotate or Flip			
Drawing Object, Shadow	WD 9.24	Shadow button on Drawing toolbar			
Drawing Objects, Group	WD 7.52	Select objects, Draw button on Drawing toolbar, Group		Right-click selected object, click Grouping	
Drop Cap	WD 6.28		Format | Drop Cap		
E-mail Document	WD 2.54	E-mail button on Standard toolbar	File | Send To | Mail Recipient		
Embed Excel Worksheet	WD 7.23		Insert | Object | Create from File tab		
Embedded Object, Convert to Word Graphic	WD 7.24				CTRL+SHIFT+F9
Emboss, Characters	WD 4.17		Format | Font | Font tab	Font | Font tab	
Engrave, Characters	WD 4.17		Format | Font | Font tab	Font | Font tab	
Envelope	WD 3.58		Tools | Envelopes and Labels		
Envelopes Using Data Source	WD 5.54	Mail Merge Helper button on Mail Merge toolbar	Tools | Mail Merge		
Erase Table Lines	WD 4.45	Eraser button on Tables and Borders toolbar			
Field Codes, Display	WD 5.39		Tools | Options | View tab		ALT+F9
Field Codes, Print	WD 5.40		Tools | Options | Print tab		
Fill-in Field	WD 5.37	Insert Word Field button on Mail Merge toolbar	Insert | Field		
Find	WD 2.45	Select Browse Object button on vertical scroll bar	Edit | Find		CTRL+F
Find and Replace	WD 2.43	Select Browse Object on vertical scroll bar	Edit | Replace		CTRL+H
First-Line Indent	WD 2.19	Drag First Line Indent marker on ruler	Format | Paragraph | Indents and Spacing tab	Paragraph | Indents and Spacing tab	
Floating Graphic	WD 6.20	Text Wrapping button on Picture toolbar	Format | Picture | Layout tab	Format Picture | Layout tab	
Folder, Create	WD 1.49		File | Save As		
Font	WD 1.31	Font button on Formatting toolbar	Format | Font | Font tab	Font | Font tab	CTRL+SHIFT+F
Font Size	WD 1.17	Font Size box arrow on Formatting toolbar	Format | Font | Font tab	Font | Font tab	CTRL+SHIFT+P
Footnote, Create	WD 2.23		Insert | Footnote		

Microsoft Word 2000 Quick Reference Summary *(continued)*

TASK	PAGE NUMBER	MOUSE	MENU BAR	SHORTCUT MENU	KEYBOARD SHORTCUT
Footnote, Delete	WD 2.30	Delete note reference mark in document window			
Footnote, Edit	WD 2.30	Double-click note reference mark in document window	View | Footnotes		
Footnotes to Endnotes, Convert	WD 2.30		Insert | Footnote		
Form, Add Help Text	WD 8.36	Double-click form field		Right-click form field, click Properties	
Form, Change Bookmark	WD 9.47	Double-click form field		Right-click form field, click Properties	
Form, Check Box Options	WD 8.29	Double-click check box form field		Right-click form field, click Properties	
Form, Drop-Down Form Field Options	WD 8.21	Double-click drop-down form field		Right-click form field, click Properties	
Form, Insert Check Box	WD 8.28	Check Box Form Field on Forms toolbar			
Form, Insert Drop-Down Form Field	WD 8.20	Drop-Down Form Field button on Forms toolbar			
Form, Insert Table	WD 8.15	Insert Table button on Forms toolbar	Table | Insert | Table		
Form, Insert Text Form Field	WD 8.17	Text Form Field button on Forms toolbar			
Form, Protect	WD 8.47	Protect Form button on Forms toolbar	Tools | Protect Document		
Form, Remove Field Shading	WD 8.39	Form Field Shading button on Forms toolbar			
Form, Save Data Only	WD 8.52		File | Save As | Tools | General Options		
Form, Text Form Field Options	WD 8.18	Double-click text form field		Right-click form field, click Properties	
Format Painter	WD 6.57	Format Painter button on Standard toolbar			
Formatting Marks	WD 1.20	Show/Hide ¶ button on Standard toolbar	Tools | Options | View tab		CTRL+SHIFT+*
Formatting Toolbar, Display Entire	WD 1.13	Double-click move handle on Formatting toolbar			
Full Menu	WD 1.12	Double-click menu name	Click menu name, wait few seconds		
Go To	WD 2.42	Select Browse Object button on vertical scroll bar	Edit | Go To		CTRL+G
Gridlines, Show	WD 8.16		Table | Show Gridlines		
Gutter Margin	WD 7.62		File | Page Setup | Margins tab		

(continued)

MICROSOFT WORD 2000 QUICK REFERENCE SUMMARY

Microsoft Word 2000 Quick Reference Summary *(continued)*

TASK	PAGE NUMBER	MOUSE	MENU BAR	SHORTCUT MENU	KEYBOARD SHORTCUT
Hanging Indent, Create	WD 2.37	Drag Hanging Indent marker on ruler	Format | Paragraph | Indents and Spacing tab	Paragraph | Indents and Spacing tab	CTRL+T
Hanging Indent, Remove	WD 2.18	Drag Hanging Indent marker on ruler	Format | Paragraph | Indents and Spacing tab	Paragraph | Indents and Spacing tab	CTRL+SHIFT+T
Header, Different from Previous	WD 4.28	In print layout view, double-click header area	View | Header and Footer		
Header, Display	WD 2.12	In print layout view, double-click header area	View | Header and Footer		
Headers, Alternating	WD 7.60	Page Setup button on Header and Footer toolbar	File | Page Setup | Layout tab		
Help	WD 1.55	Microsoft Word Help button on Standard toolbar	Help | Microsoft Word Help		F1
Hidden Characters	WD 4.17		Format | Font | Font tab	Font | Font tab	
Highlight Text	WD 6.61	Highlight button on Formatting toolbar			
HTML Source	WDW 1.11		View | HTML Source		
Hyperlink, Add	WDW 1.10	Insert Hyperlink button on Standard toolbar		Hyperlink	
Hyperlink, Create	WD 2.39	Insert Hyperlink button on Standard toolbar		Hyperlink	Web address then ENTER or SPACEBAR
Hyperlink, Edit	WDW 1.10	Insert Hyperlink button on Standard toolbar		Hyperlink	
IF Field	WD 5.34	Insert Word Field button on Mail Merge toolbar	Insert | Field		
Index Entry, Mark	WD 7.31		Insert | Index and Tables | Index tab		ALT+SHIFT+X
Index, Build	WD 7.56		Insert | Index and Tables | Index tab		
Index, Update	WD 7.67			Right-click selected table of contents, click Update Field	Select table of contents, F9
Insert File	WD 4.23		Insert | File		
Insert Merge Fields	WD 5.27	Insert Merge Field button on Mail Merge toolbar			
Italicize	WD 1.39	Italic button on Formatting toolbar	Format | Font | Font tab	Font | Font tab	CTRL+I
Justify	WD 6.26	Justify button on Formatting toolbar	Format | Paragraph | Indents and Spacing tab	Paragraph | Indents and Spacing tab	CTRL+J
Landscape Orientation	WD 5.24		File | Page Setup | Paper Size tab		
Last Editing Location	WD 4.25				SHIFT+F5
Leader Characters	WD 3.31		Format | Tabs		
Left-Align	WD 2.17	Align Left button on Formatting toolbar	Format | Paragraph | Indents and Spacing tab	Paragraph | Indents and Spacing tab	CTRL+L

Microsoft Word 2000 Quick Reference Summary *(continued)*

TASK	PAGE NUMBER	MOUSE	MENU BAR	SHORTCUT MENU	KEYBOARD SHORTCUT
Line Break, Enter	WD 3.22				SHIFT+ENTER
Link	WD 6.34		Edit | Paste Special		
Link Excel Data to Word Chart	WDI 2.8		Edit | Paste Link		
Link Excel Worksheet	WDI 2.4		Insert | Object | Create from File		
List Item, Demote	WD 5.32	Increase Indent button on Formatting toolbar			SHIFT+TAB
List Item, Promote	WD 5.32	Decrease Indent button on Formatting toolbar			TAB
Macro, Copy	WD 9.64	In Visual Basic Editor, Copy button on Standard toolbar, then Paste button on Standard toolbar	In Visual Basic Editor, Edit | Copy; then Edit | Paste	In Visual Basic Editor, Copy then Paste	In Visual Basic Editor, CTRL+C then CTRL+V
Macro, Delete	WD 9.65		Tools | Macro | Macros		
Macro, Record	WD 9.26	Double-click REC status indicator on status bar	Tools | Macro | Record New Macro		
Macro, Run	WD 9.29	Run Macro button on Standard toolbar in Visual Basic Editor	Tools | Macro | Macros		ALT+F8
Macro, Run on Exit	WD 9.52	Double-click form field		Right-click form field, click Properties	
Macro, View VBA Code	WD 9.39		Tools | Macro | Macros		ALT+F11
Mailing Label	WD 3.58		Tools | Envelopes and Labels		
Mailing Labels Using Data Source	WD 5.48	Mail Merge Helper button on Mail Merge toolbar	Tools | Mail Merge		
Main Document, Identify	WD 5.14	Mail Merge Helper button on Mail Merge toolbar	Tools | Mail Merge		
Margins	WD 2.8	In print layout view, drag margin boundary	File | Page Setup | Margins tab		
Master Document, Open	WD 7.65	Open button on Standard toolbar, then Expand Subdocuments button on Outlining toolbar			
Menus and Toolbars, Reset	WD 2.7		View | Toolbars | Customize | Options tab		
Merge Certain Records	WD 5.43	Merge button on Mail Merge toolbar			
Merge to E-mail Addresses	WDI 1.4	Merge button on Mail Merge toolbar			
Merge to Printer	WD 5.40	Merge to Printer button on Mail Merge toolbar			

(continued)

Microsoft Word 2000 Quick Reference Summary *(continued)*

TASK	PAGE NUMBER	MOUSE	MENU BAR	SHORTCUT MENU	KEYBOARD SHORTCUT
Merged Data, View	WD 5.47	View Merged Data button on Mail Merge toolbar			
Move Selected Text	WD 2.46	Drag and drop	Edit | Cut; Edit | Paste		CTRL+X; CTRL+V
Nonbreaking Hyphen	WD 3.46		Insert | Symbol | Special Characters tab		CTRL+SHIFT+HYPHEN
Nonbreaking Space	WD 3.46		Insert | Symbol | Special Characters tab		CTRL+SHIFT+SPACEBAR
Normal Style, Apply	WD 4.19	Style box arrow on Formatting toolbar	Format | Style		CTRL+SHIFT+N
Note Pane, Close	WD 2.29	Close button in note pane			
Numbered List	WD 3.51	Numbering button on Formatting toolbar	Format | Bullets and Numbering | Numbered tab	Bullets and Numbering | Numbered tab	1. and then space followed by text, then ENTER
Open Document	WD 1.52	Open button on Standard toolbar	File | Open		CTRL+O
Orphan	WD 2.32		Format | Paragraph | Line and Page Breaks tab	Paragraph | Line and Page Breaks tab	
Outline Numbered List	WD 5.30		Format | Bullets and Numbering | Outline Numbered tab		
Outline, Characters	WD 4.17		Format | Font | Font tab	Font | Font tab	
Outline, Create	WD 7.37	Outline View button on horizontal scroll bar	View | Outline		
Outline, Demote Heading	WD 7.45	Demote button on Outlining toolbar			TAB
Outline, Demote Heading to Body Text	WD 7.47	Demote to Body Text button on Outlining toolbar			TAB until style is body text
Outline, Promote Heading	WD 7.45	Promote button on Outlining toolbar			SHIFT+TAB
Outline, Show First Line of Paragraphs	WD 7.46	Show First Line Only button on Outlining toolbar			
Page Break	WD 2.35		Insert | Break		CTRL+ENTER
Page Numbers, Insert	WD 2.14	Insert Page Number button on Header and Footer toolbar	Insert | Page Numbers		
Page Numbers, Modify	WD 4.29		Insert | Page Numbers		
Paragraph Formatting, Remove	WD 2.18		Format | Paragraph	Paragraph	CTRL+SPACEBAR
Paragraphs, Keep Together	WD 7.33		Format | Paragraph	Paragraph	
Password-Protect File	WD 7.34		File | Save As | Tools | General Options		

Microsoft Word 2000 Quick Reference Summary *(continued)*

TASK	PAGE NUMBER	MOUSE	MENU BAR	SHORTCUT MENU	KEYBOARD SHORTCUT
Paste	WD 3.35	Paste button on Standard toolbar or click icon on Clipboard toolbar	Edit	Paste	Paste	CTRL+V
Picture Bullets	WD 4.40		Format	Bullets and Numbering	Bulleted tab	Bullets and Numbering	Bulleted tab	
Picture, Insert	WD 6.53		Insert	Picture	From File		
Print Document	WD 1.50	Print button on Standard toolbar	File	Print		CTRL+P
Print Preview	WD 3.24	Print Preview button on Standard toolbar	File	Print Preview		CTRL+F2
Promote List Item	WD 3.51	Increase Indent button on Formatting toolbar			
Quit Word	WD 1.51	Close button on title bar	File	Exit		ALT+F4
Rectangle, Draw	WD 8.40	Rectangle button on Drawing toolbar			
Redo Action	WD 1.35	Redo button on Standard toolbar	Edit	Redo		
Repeat Command	WD 1.36		Edit	Repeat		
Resize Graphic	WD 1.47	Drag sizing handle	Format	Picture	Size tab		
Restore Graphic	WD 1.48	Format Picture button on Picture toolbar	Format	Picture	Size tab		
Reviewer Initials, Change	WD 7.12		Tools	Options	User Information tab		
Right-Align	WD 1.33	Align Right button on Formatting toolbar	Format	Paragraph	Indents and Spacing tab	Paragraph	Indents and Spacing tab	CTRL+R
Rotate Text in Table	WD 4.50	Change Text Direction button on Tables and Borders toolbar	Format	Text Direction	Text Direction	
Ruler, Show or Hide	WD 1.11		View	Ruler		
Save as Web Page	WDW 1.3		File	Save as Web Page		
Save Document – New Name	WD 1.49		File	Save As		F12
Save Document – Same Name	WD 1.49	Save button on Standard toolbar	File	Save		CTRL+S
Save New Document	WD 1.26	Save button on Standard toolbar	File	Save		CTRL+S
Save Version	WD 7.15	Save Version button on Reviewing toolbar	File	Versions		
Section Break, Continuous	WD 6.24		Insert	Break		
Section Break, Next Page	WD 4.21		Insert	Break		

(continued)

Microsoft Word 2000 Quick Reference Summary (continued)

TASK	PAGE NUMBER	MOUSE	MENU BAR	SHORTCUT MENU	KEYBOARD SHORTCUT
Security Level	WD 9.10		Tools	Macro	Security	Security Level tab		
Select Document	WD 2.46	Point to left and triple-click	Edit	Select All		CTRL+A
Select Graphic	WD 1.46	Click graphic			CTRL+SHIFT+RIGHT ARROW
Select Group of Words	WD 1.41	Drag through words			CTRL+SHIFT+RIGHT ARROW
Select Line	WD 1.37	Point to left of line and click			SHIFT+DOWN ARROW
Select Multiple Paragraphs	WD 1.30	Point to left of paragraph and drag down			CTRL+SHIFT+ DOWN ARROW
Select Paragraph	WD 2.46	Triple-click paragraph			
Select Sentence	WD 2.45	CTRL+click in sentence			CTRL+SHIFT+RIGHT ARROW
Select Table	WD 3.56	Drag through table	Table	Select	Table		ALT+5 (on numeric keypad)
Select Word	WD 1.38	Double-click word			CTRL+SHIFT+ RIGHT ARROW
Shade Graphic	WD 6.21	Format Picture button on Picture toolbar	Format	Picture	Colors and Lines tab	Format Picture	Colors and Lines tab	
Shade Paragraph	WD 6.45	Shading Color button on Tables and Borders toolbar	Format	Borders and Shading	Shading tab	Borders and Shading	Shading tab	
Shadow, on Characters	WD 4.17		Format	Font	Font tab	Font	Font tab	
Single-Space Paragraph	WD 4.31		Format	Paragraph	Indents and Spacing tab	Paragraph	Indents and Spacing tab	CTRL+1
Small Uppercase Letters	WD 2.18		Format	Font	Font tab	Font	Font tab	CTRL+SHIFT+K
Sort Data Records	WD 5.45	Merge button on Mail Merge Merge toolbar			
Sort Paragraphs	WD 2.40		Table	Sort		
Spelling Check as You Type	WD 1.22	Double-click Spelling and Grammar Status icon on status bar		Right-click flagged word, click correct word on shortcut menu	
Spelling Check At Once	WD 2.50	Spelling and Grammar button on Standard toolbar	Tools	Spelling and Grammar	Spelling	F7
Standard Toolbar, Display Entire	WD 1.15	Double-click move handle on Standard toolbar			
Strikethrough, Characters	WD 4.17		Format	Font	Font tab	Font	Font tab	

Microsoft Word 2000 Quick Reference Summary *(continued)*

TASK	PAGE NUMBER	MOUSE	MENU BAR	SHORTCUT MENU	KEYBOARD SHORTCUT
Style, Apply	WD 6.33	Style box arrow on Formatting toolbar	Format | Style		
Style, Create	WD 9.17		Format | Style		
Style, Modify	WD 2.26		Format | Style		
Subdocument, Break Connection	WD 7.46	Remove Subdocument icon on Outlining toolbar			
Subdocument, Create	WD 7.43	Create Subdocument button on Outlining toolbar			
Subdocument, Delete	WD 7.46	Click subdocument icon, press DELETE			
Subdocument, Insert	WD 7.40	Insert Subdocument button on Outlining toolbar			
Subdocuments, Collapse	WD 7.41	Collapse Subdocuments button on Outlining toolbar			
Subdocuments, Expand	WD 7.41	Expand Subdocuments button on Outlining toolbar			
Subscript	WD 2.18		Format | Font | Font tab	Font | Font tab	CTRL+=
Superscript	WD 2.18		Format | Font | Font tab	Font | Font tab	CTRL+SHIFT+PLUS SIGN
Switch from Data Source to Main Document	WD 5.25	Mail Merge Main Document button on Database toolbar			
Switch to Open Document	WD 3.33	Program button on taskbar	Window | document name		
Symbol, Insert	WD 3.37		Insert | Symbol		ALT+0 (on numeric keypad)
Synonym	WD 2.48		Tools | Language | Thesaurus	Synonyms | desired word	SHIFT+F7
Tab Stops, Insert	WD 3.31	Click location on ruler	Format | Tabs		
Table AutoFormat	WD 3.55	AutoFormat button on Tables and Borders toolbar	Table | Table AutoFormat		
Table of Contents, Create	WD 7.57		Insert | Index and Tables | Table of Contents tab		
Table of Contents, Update	WD 7.67			Right-click selected table of contents, click Update Field	Select table of contents, F9
Table of Figures, Create	WD 7.54		Insert | Index and Tables | Table of Figures tab		
Table, Create	WD 3.52	Insert Table button on Standard toolbar	Table | Insert | Table		
Table, Draw	WD 4.42	Tables and Borders button on Standard toolbar	Table | Draw Table		

(continued)

MICROSOFT WORD 2000 QUICK REFERENCE SUMMARY

Microsoft Word 2000 Quick Reference Summary *(continued)*

TASK	PAGE NUMBER	MOUSE	MENU BAR	SHORTCUT MENU	KEYBOARD SHORTCUT
Template	WD 5.6		File | New		
Template, Create	WD 8.9		File | New		
Text Box, Convert to a Frame	WD 7.28	Double-click text box	Format | Text Box	Format Text Box	
Text Box, Format	WD 6.41	Double-click text box	Format | Text Box	Format Text Box	
Text Box, Insert	WD 6.40	Text Box button on Drawing toolbar	Insert | Text Box		
Toolbar, Customize	WD 9.30		Tools | Customize	Customize	
Top Alignment	WD 4.22		File | Page Setup | Layout tab		
Track Changes	WD 7.13	Double-click TRK status indicator on status bar	Tools | Track Changes | Highlight Changes		
Track Changes, Stop	WD 7.14	Double-click TRK status indicator on status bar	Tools | Track Changes | Highlight Changes		
Tracked Changes, Display	WD 7.14		Tools | Track Changes | Highlight Changes	Right-click TRK status indicator on status bar, click Highlight Changes	
Tracked Changes, Print	WD 7.21		Tools | Track Changes | Highlight Changes	Right-click TRK status indicator on status bar, click Highlight Changes	
Tracked Changes, Review	WD 7.29	Click Next Change button on Reviewing toolbar		Right-click TRK status indicator on status bar, click Accept or Reject Changes	
Underline	WD 1.42	Underline button on Formatting toolbar	Format | Font | Font tab	Font | Font tab	CTRL+U
Underline Words, not Spaces	WD 2.18		Format | Font | Font tab	Font | Font tab	CTRL+SHIFT+W
Undo Command or Action	WD 1.36	Undo button on Standard toolbar	Edit | Undo		CTRL+Z
Unlink a Field	WD 5.28				CTRL+SHIFT+F9
Unprotect Document	WD 9.8	Protect Form button on Forms toolbar	Tools | Unprotect Document		
Visual Basic Editor, Close	WD 9.45	Close button on title bar	File | Close and Return to Microsoft Word		ALT+Q
Visual Basic Editor, Insert Procedure	WD 9.48	Insert UserForm button arrow on Standard toolbar	Insert | Procedure		
Vertical Rule	WD 6.37		Format | Borders and Shading | Borders tab		
Watermark	WD 4.54	In print layout view, double-click header area	View | Header and Footer		

Microsoft Word 2000 Quick Reference Summary *(continued)*

TASK	PAGE NUMBER	MOUSE	MENU BAR	SHORTCUT MENU	KEYBOARD SHORTCUT
Web Page Frame, Resize	WDW 1.9	Drag frame border	Format | Frames | Frame Properties | Frame tab		
Web Page, View	WDW 1.11		File | Web Page Preview		
Web Page Wizard	WDW 1.5		File | New | Web Pages tab		
Widow	WD 2.32		Format | Paragraph | Line and Page Breaks tab	Paragraph | Line and Page Breaks tab	
Wizard, Resume	WD 3.7		File | New | Other Documents tab		
WordArt Drawing Object, Format	WD 6.12	Format WordArt button on WordArt toolbar	Format | WordArt	Format WordArt	
WordArt Drawing Object, Insert	WD 6.9	Insert WordArt button on Drawing toolbar	Insert | Picture | WordArt		
WordArt Drawing Object, Shape	WD 6.14	WordArt Shape button on WordArt toolbar			
Wrap Text Around Graphic	WD 6.54	Text Wrapping button on Picture toolbar	Format | Picture | Layout tab	Format Picture | Layout tab	
Zoom Page Width	WD 1.15	Zoom box arrow on Formatting toolbar	View | Zoom		
Zoom Text Width	WD 3.17	Zoom box arrow on Formatting toolbar	View | Zoom		
Zoom Whole Page	WD 6.32	Zoom box arrow on Formatting toolbar	View | Zoom		